THE GREAT AMERICAN
1879-1945
ANTIQUE TOY BAZAAR

5,000 old engravings from original trade catalogs

Edited by Ronald S. Barlow

Printed in the United States of America
International Standard Book Number:
0-933846-06-1

Additional copies of this book may be
ordered through your local museum shop,
independent bookstore, or directly from:

Windmill Publishing Company
2147 Windmill View Road
El Cajon, California 92020

Send check or money order for $19.95 plus $3.00 postage.
(Please allow 2 to 4 weeks for delivery by Post Office.)

Summary of Contents.

INTRODUCTION

Trade catalogs are perhaps one of the best sources of business history available today. Manuscripts and printed reports are valuable, but the illustrated catalogs, that actually sold the goods, have no equal—a picture is indeed worth a thousand words.

In studying these early catalogs bear in mind that some are retail order-books, while others may be "wholesale to the trade". When prices are quoted by-the-dozen, you are probably looking at a distributor's or a manufacturer's catalog.

Also keep in mind the price difference that inflation has made over the years. The prevailing wage for an average worker during the Victorian period was about a dollar a day. In the early 1930s a hired farm hand was lucky to receive $200 a year. Lawyers made about $4,200, doctors took home $3,382, nurses made $936 and there were more than seven million families living in cities whose income was less than $1,500 a year. The purchase of a two dollar toy was not likely done on impulse.

My father was a factory worker in the 1940s and our big toys—bicycles, scooters and wagons—were repainted, secondhand, purchases. One new doll or windup toy might appear under the Christmas tree, along with the usual outdoor sports equipment. I vividly remember one classmate in grammar school who owned a brand new Schwinn bicycle, and he guarded it with his life.

Expensive mechanical toys and electric train sets were found only in upper class homes. Dolls, on the other hand, were quite affordable and most every little girl owned a family of dolls and Teddy bears and a tea set for entertaining them.

In Victorian America most rural children had no need for factory-made toys. Farm animals, favorite pets and the great outdoors offered more than enough recreational outlets for country youngsters. Christmas presents often consisted of candy, fruit, caps, mittens, shoes and handmade wooden toys.

Appalachian favorites were wooden horses, wagons, oxen, bull-roarers, cigar box violins, whistles, dolls and jig dancers. Grandma could also make a very lovable doll out of an apple, cornstalk, or potato, and a scrap of cloth. Her rag dolls were stuffed with bran or sawdust from the mill. Country boys fashioned bows and arrows, kites, peashooters, popguns, stilts and slingshots out of tree limbs or scrap lumber. Their only investment was labor.

Urban children made sidewalk scooters from apple boxes, 2 x 4's and roller skates. A sturdy go-cart could be constructed from baby buggy wheels and a soap box. Steering was accomplished by a rope, or by one's feet, firmly planted on the front axle.

At the turn-of-the-century nearly every red-blooded American boy carried a jack-knife, a wooden top and a pocketful of marbles to school. Mumblety-peg was a favorite lunch hour game, but marbles were eventually outlawed because winners often left losers empty-handed. The tradition of marble playing in America dates back to the Civil War when many young recruits carried a marble bag in one pocket and a bullet pouch in the other.

School girls spent their recess time playing jacks, jump-rope and hop-scotch. The opposite sexes rarely met in play except, perhaps for a Sunday afternoon of polite croquet or badminton. Hide-and-seek could also be played in mixed company, but coeducational hayloft frolic was strictly verboten.

In Colonial times gloomy Calvinism forbade fun on the Sabbath day and in many households the only "Sunday toy" permitted was a miniature Noah's Ark. The demand for this popular parlor toy—which consisted of Mr. and Mrs. Noah, their sons, a tub-shaped ark with a hinged roof, and from 100 to 400 hand carved animals—continued well into the 19th century.

Toy shops evolved rapidly in cities near seaports and along river fronts. Ship captains found a ready market among merchants for novelties, trinkets and dolls from Europe and the Orient. Tobacco, potash, and beaver pelts had made some colonies cash rich. One tobacco farmer could earn 200 pounds sterling a year by his own labor, and another 200 for every man he could buy or hire. All that money trickled down and by 1713 a seven year old Benjamin Franklin had no trouble finding a toy store to take his first pocket-money for a penny whistle. Even red Indians were often seen carrying cheap copies of French fashion dolls.

At the end of the Civil War American munitions factories began to manufacture everything from washing machine wringers to cast-iron toys and the rest is history.

The catalog collection contained in this book took several years of flea market foraging to assemble and another 12 months of careful retouching and restoring to make "camera ready". As an illustrator and graphic designer I deeply respect the fact that perhaps a million man-hours were required to prepare the finely detailed woodcuts and ink drawings contained in these vintage volumes. The muddy photographs found in most postwar "wish books" pale by comparison and fine engraving is now a lost art.

Thanks to Messrs. Marshall Field, E. C. Simmons, Richard W. Sears, Aaron Montgomery Ward, the Butler Brothers, and all the other mail-order pioneers who made this Antique Toy Bazaar possible. Those readers who desire more information about their childhood playthings need go only as far as the nearest library or bookstore. Hundreds of price guides to dolls and toys have been published during the current collectibles boom.

Ronald S. Barlow

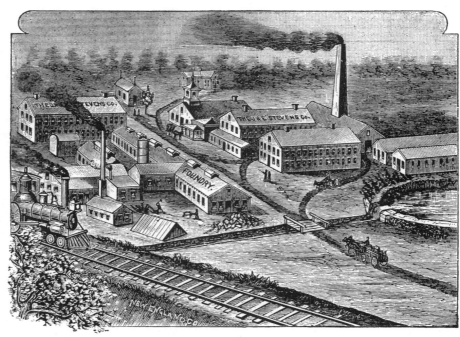

Merten de vos jnuentor. *Nic de Bruyn fecit.* *Joannes a Londerseel exeudebat*

A 16th century engraving of children at play.

THE EVOLUTION OF TOYS

There is nothing new under the sun and it naturally follows that as long as there have been children there have been dolls and toys. Ancient Egyptian tykes played with dolls, dishes, boats, carts and horses made of clay, cloth and wood. Early Greek and Roman youngsters had access to these toys and many others. Among their possessions were miniature instruments of war, including bows and arrows, javelins and chariots. More peaceful playthings ran the gamut from board games to spinning tops, rolling hoops and broom-stick hobby horses.

Chinese children of the 9th century were treated to a delightful array of wind toys and colorful paper kites in addition to the usual assortment of dolls and miniature animals. They were also the first kids on earth to play with fireworks (their parents invented gunpowder using an explosive mixture of charcoal, sulfur and saltpeter.)

The concept of mechanical toys dates from the age of Plato (427 - 347 B.C.) when flying-wooden birds were the latest rage. It has been recorded that nearly every household in ancient Greece owned a favorite self-propelled novelty. By the second century B.C. Hero, of Alexandria, was building air, water and gravity powered automata, which to the masses seemed almost god-like. These performing figures walked, talked, wrote and growled. One of Hero's simpler inventions, the singing-bird water pipe, remains a best-seller to this very day.

Greek and Roman inventors soon came out with additional mechanical marvels including tiny toy bowmen who repeatedly shot arrows at a hissing, thrashing, dragon; and a miniature blacksmith's shop complete with anvil, forge and three hammer-wielding workmen.

When French clock makers began to replace drive weights with coiled steel springs in the early 1700s, a new toy industry was born. Just about any sound effect or motion could be imitated by the new spring-driven motors, including bleating sheep, barking dogs, singing birds, racing horses and revolving planets.

These expensive first-generation windup toys were made for adults, and called "automata", after the Greek word "automatos", meaning mechanical toy.

The French were the first mass-marketers of rubber-band-powered toys. By the mid 1880s they were also exporting an impressive array of animated bears, birds, bugs, butterflies, motorboats and tricycles.

France is also famous for her early exploitation of doll lovers. The Queen of England ordered a batch of expensive French fashion dolls in 1391, followed by the Queen of Spain in 1466, and a third shipment to the Duchess of Bavaria in 1577. Henry IV wrote to his fiancée, Maria de Medicis, in 1660: "I understand that you desire patterns of our fashion of dress. I will send you,

therefore, some model dolls (from France)." During the French Revolution little guillotines were manufactured which were quite capable of beheading mice, rats or aristocratic dolls.

Dolls were supposedly used in religious rites and in burial chambers long before they became the favorite companions of little girls. Paper dolls were employed in Japanese religious festivals as early as 1,000 A.D. French children of the 1700s played with puppet paper dolls called pantins. The first American-made paper dolls were patterned after the famous singer, Jenny Lind, circa 1835.

From 1825 to 1850 wax-coated papier-mâché dolls supplanted the crude "Dutch babies" made, in the Netherlands, of wood, with plaster of Paris faces. The very name "doll" is said to have come from the Dutch "dol", meaning stupid or senseless. Other authorities say the word derived from the French "dot": trumpery, a trick, or that it may be an abbreviation of the word idol.

Victor Hugo wrote this insightful appraisal of idol worship more than a hundred years ago. "A doll is one of the most imperious wants, and at the same time one of the most delicious instincts, of feminine childhood. To clean, clothe, adorn, dress, undress, dress again, teach, scold a little, nurse, lull, send to sleep, and imagine that something is somebody — the whole future of a woman is contained in this. While dreaming and prattling, making little trousseaux and cradles, while sewing little frocks and aprons, the child becomes a girl, the girl becomes a maiden, and the maiden a woman. The first child is a continuation of the last doll."

"Mama and papa" talking dolls were first exhibited in Paris in 1823. They were invented by a London workman who devoted nine years of his life to the task of making them utter these simple words.

China-head dolls, with pegged wooden arms and legs, appeared in 1750 but were not mass-produced until the 1850s, at which time porcelain-head dolls from Paris made their first appearance at the London Exhibition.

A manufacturer's survey, published in 1884, claimed that an average American girl would wear out 50 dolls in her lifetime. The fragile nature of these substitute babies had not been lost on earlier entrepreneurs. B. F. Lee bought out the all-rubber "Goodyear" doll in 1851; and Ludwig Greiner's, U. S. patented, papier-mâché dolls were big sellers from 1858 to 1878.

As early as 1866 the New Brunswick Rubber Company of New York published a 4-page price list offering rubber footballs, roly-poly dolls, toy monkeys, dogs, cats, eagles, soldiers and elephants. Boston based A. F. Farrar issued a 96 page catalog the same year, offering "Indian rubber and gutta percha goods including painted dolls, animals, firemen and other human figures."

MAGNIFICENTLY DRESSED IN SILK AND LACE

FULL JOINTED BODY

WATCH AND CHAIN

EXACTLY 24 INCHES TALL

THE NEW MECHANICAL
BIG BEAUTY
FRENCH BISQUE

DOLL

"The Girl from Paris"
FULLY TWO FEET TALL

Latest Doll Wonder of the Century. Dolly can be dressed and undressed, also sleep and call for its little mother as naturally as any real live baby. A magnificent imported doll, beautifully and elaborately dressed in silk, lace and satin. Easily earned by disposing of only THIRTY articles at ten cents each.

This new premium production, "The Girl from Paris," is an **extra large size**, **imported French Doll**, with latest improved patent mechanical talking attachment, and is without doubt, the largest and most elegantly dressed doll that was **ever given** away by any concern as a premium.

"The Girl from Paris" is a beauty and will be highly appreciated by every girl who receives her.

Dolly's pretty head is made of bisque, with long, natural curls. Her handsome costume is made of silk and lace, fancy trimmed picture hat, lace trimmed underwear, open-work stockings, pretty satin sash with silver finished buckle, dainty patent leather shoes, watch and chain, etc., complete, neatly and beautifully dressed in the latest French doll fashion. The picture of dolly does not do her justice, as it is not possible to show up her beatuy and elegance in this illustration. However, to see her is to love her, as she is a big beauty.

We desire to call your attention to the fact that "The Girl from Paris" is not a cheap, stuffed rag affair, so extensively advertised, but **a full-jointed bisque doll**, elegantly dressed from top to toe. **Exactly twenty-four inches tall.** The only real talking doll in existence that can say papa and mamma perfectly, and not easily gotten out of order. No unsightly strings to pull or break, no squeaking sound, and no disappointment. Simply press the button under dolly's arm and she will speak as plainly as any living child. This new talking attachment is patented and controlled by us, therefore **"The Girl from Paris"** is the only talking doll that operates perfectly and gives satisfaction, all others are cheap imitations.

Girls, write us at once for outfit, and we will promptly mail to your address, thirty useful, handy and fancy articles, to dispose of at ten cents each; when sold, remit us the money **(three dollars)** and we will promptly forward to you, carefully packed, one of our lovely Talking French Dolls, "The Girl from Paris," **fully two feet tall,** as illustrated and described in this advertisement.

We are a reliable concern and do exactly as **we advertise**. Order the thirty articles at once, and receive this Big Beauty Doll in time for Christmas. Address at once

MECHANICAL DOLL WORKS
4 BANK BUILDING, NEW MILFORD, CONN.

An 1895 magazine advertisement.

In 1875 a pair of Kentucky inventors, W. Fletcher and P. Goldsmith, brought to market a successful line of "Patent Head Dolls" made of flour, glue and wood pulp. Other composition dolls soon followed.

"Can't Break'em Dolls" were introduced to the trade by a Brooklyn firm in 1892. Enthusiastic salesman would astonish shop owners by throwing these hard-headed babies against a concrete floor, with no apparent damage.

Anyone who has ever broken open a doll's head knows that its eyes are simply hollow glass balls made of white enamel. The introduction of "sleepy-eye" dolls, with a weighted wire opening and closing mechanism, in the 1880s was a boon to the trade.

The first "wet-your-diaper" doll was patented in the U.S. by Rudolph Steiner, of Germany, circa 1900. Mr. Steiner came here because we were the world's biggest market. Germany, however, was the undisputed doll and toy capital of the world. A single German factory of the period ran 30 ovens around the clock. Each firing produced 5,000 china head dolls, all bound for American wholesale houses and department stores. At one point, Butler Brothers (the largest U.S. toy and doll distributor) contracted for the entire yearly production of 15 German doll factories.

Before 1860 German engineers had developed machines which could roll, cut, stamp and fold brass or tinplate parts, faster than the eye could see. These first sheet metal toys were hand-soldered and hand-painted. Within two decades even faster steam-driven presses were introduced which could turn out die-cut sheets of colored tin toys at the rate of a mile a minute.

In 1852, Nuremburg-based George H. Bestelmeir published a wholesale catalog listing 12,000 varieties of toys and dolls. No other country could compete with the long established multitude of German toy makers and doll artists, who worked for peasant wages from the crowded comfort of their own tiny cottages. Today, in China, toy factory workers occupy a similar niche in this labor-intensive industry with an average wage of only 25 cents an hour.

Twice a year European exporters, such as Bestelmeir, would scour the hinterlands buying home-made wooden and ceramic toys, for pennies on the dollar, and transport them to the Nuremburg market for foreign buyers to view.

By the year 1900 more than 400 German toy factories had sprung up to serve a booming U. S. market, which was then absorbing one third of all Teutonic doll and toy production. In 1902 we imported $4,023,670 worth of playthings from abroad and it was not until the end of World War I that American toy makers could match the Kaiser's output. Finally, in 1917, the United States actually exported more toys and dolls than they imported.

As popular as dolls were at the turn-of-the century, it seems astonishing that by 1906 these long-cherished idols were replaced in children's' hearts by a new toy.....Teddy Bear. Yes, Teddy was outselling Miss Dolly by at least 10 to 1 in November of 1906. A leading importer of the day stated to the news media, "It is impossible to get enough bears now. Originally the creature was made in Germany, but within the past few months they are being manufactured here. We could sell a thousand dozen bears a day if we had them, but we haven't."

In 1903 Rose and Morris Michtom, recent Russian immigrants, created a stuffed bear based on a *Washington Post* cartoon which portrayed Teddy Roosevelt refusing to shoot a bear cub which was tied to a tree. The Michtom's displayed a few of the movable-jointed bears in their Brooklyn, N.Y., shop window and the rest is history. Children just couldn't resist these soft little furry coated creatures "who loved them back".

About this time, in Germany, Margarete Steiff — who had been making stuffed animal toys for 12 years — began production of her own version of the Teddy Bear. Steiff, already being an established manufacturer, beat the Michtom couple to the market, but the pent up demand soon outpaced her factory's round-the-clock output. Mr. and Mrs. Michtom closed their novelty store and devoted all their resources to the production of Teddy Bears at their newly established Ideal Novelty & Toy Company. Steiff won the contest, turning out nearly a million bruins for the U. S. Market in 1907. But the several hundred thousand bears sold by the Michtoms enabled their Ideal Toy Company to eventually become the nation's largest producer of dolls and stuffed toys.

America's toy-making industry had its roots in Vermont where skilled Yankee craftsmen began commercial production of wooden sleds, carts and wagons around 1810. The first domestic doll carriages were made in Waterbury, Vermont, in 1857 by the Colby Brothers. Within a decade production had risen to more than 600 doll-sized baby buggies a week.

China-head dolls were mass-produced in Philadelphia as early as 1830. The Pennsylvania Dutch had also been busy in their country workshops turning out gaily decorated miniature kitchen sets, wooden whistles and Dutch windmills. Many of these products made their way to merchants in Philadelphia and New York City.

No record of wooden toy makers would be complete without mentioning Albert Schoenhut, a third generation craftsman who emigrated to the United States from Germany in 1865. In 1873 he patented, and began producing, toy pianos, using sturdy iron sounding plates instead of traditional fragile glass rods. The pint-sized pianos were an instant hit and production continued into the 1930s. Schoenhut's 1903 patented "Humpty-Dumpty Circus" was the firm's biggest success. A Lathe-carved, jointed wooden clown, donkey and elephant were soon joined by 29 figures, 37 animals, several parade wagons, a tent and 40 other colorful pieces. By Christmas of 1909 more than 50,000 sets had been sold. In later years Schoenhut's life-like wooden dolls, doll houses and furniture also became big sellers. Albert died in 1912 and his six sons faithfully continued the business until 1935.

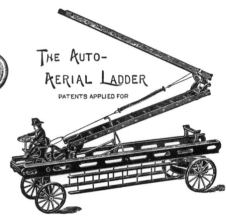

From Playthings Magazine, January, 1914.

Victorian hobby horses evolved from the common stick-bodied cockhorse that all Roman boys rode nearly 2,000 years ago. The first equestrian evolution, from crude clay effigies to toy horses mounted on wheels, probably took at least ten or twelve centuries.

Conversely, only a few years were required for the early 17th century wheeled-hobby-horse to evolve into the legless English rocking horse of the late 1600s. In a short time galloping legs appeared, fastened to bow-shaped rockers. Hand painted dappling, leather harness, and a hair mane and tail, had become the standard of excellence by 1870.

Various "improvements" followed including platform bases, spoke wheels, metal bodies and coil springs. Rocking horses were a staple item in mail-order catalogs from 1880 to 1940, and as of late have begun another round of popularity as home-craftsman-produced playthings.

Well known for its wooden toys was the W. S. Reed Toy Company, established in Leonminster, Mass, in 1875. Reed often decorated his clipper ships and circus wagons with colorful lithographs glued to their wooden sides. His huge Hippodrome circus set of 1880 came complete with a ringmaster, acrobats, clowns and horses. A hand-crank propelled the entire menagerie into vibrant action. Reed also patented several other toys including the "U.S. Capital", a construction set, and a cast iron bank, entitled "Old Lady in the Shoe". Mr. Reed retired in 1897.

Connecticut was also an important toy making center. Local tinsmiths had been soldering together sheetmetal horns, whistles, bubble-pipes and other small novelties in this Yankee stronghold since the early 1820s.

J. & E. Stevens established an iron foundry in Cromwell, Connecticut, in 1843 and began casting cap pistols and toy cannons in addition to their regular utilitarian fare. By 1870 the toy line had grown to include hundreds of items, including toy furniture, stoves, tiny tools, and mechanical banks with moving parts. Stevens also made cast-iron wheels for the nearby Gong Bell Manufacturing Company of East Hampton, established in 1866. Its rolling, ringing, action toys were big sellers for more than half a century.

Another Connecticut businessman/inventor, Edward Ives, put together a number of small firms in 1868 and began production of a new line of wind-up tin toys that were powered with motors made by local clock factories. The Ives Company produced higher quality toys than most manufacturers of the day. Some of their automobiles and trains could run up to 30 minutes on a single winding! After 60 years of operation E. R. Ives succumbed to the Depression of 1929 and was sold to the Lionel Corporation.

Two distant relatives, Jesse and Charles Crandall, separately excelled in the manufacture of two unique types of wooden building blocks.

Charles' Pennsylvania based company became famous for its 1867 introduction of tongue-and-groove style interlocking architectural building blocks. Jesse's father started his toy business in New York City in 1841. Jesse worked for his father until 1860 when he received his own patents for a new shoo-fly rocker and a spring mounted rocking horse. Later Jesse developed many other toys including velocipedes, wheelbarrows, carts and carriages. However, he is best remembered for his much-imitated hollow wooden nursery school blocks with their colorful lithographed letters and images, introduced in 1875. These thin-walled blocks nested inside one another for compact storage.

After the Civil War dozens of American iron foundries turned their munitions-making skills toward peacetime production. Cast-iron toys soon became a large segment of their profit picture. These almost indestructible playthings were instant favorites with all the big mail order houses because few were ever returned as defective. Tin toys, on the other hand, sometimes ceased to function after only an hour or two of Christmas morning torture trials.

John Hubley's Lancaster County, Pennsylvania, firm was founded in 1894 and over the next 50 years became the world's largest manufacturer of cast-iron toys. Hubley made everything from steam-powered trains, and trolleys, to doll house stoves. Anything on wheels was worth reproducing. Automobiles, trucks, fire engines, circus wagons and motorcycles were perennial favorites. Eventually, the company discontinued cast-iron in favor of cheaper, lighter, zinc, or lead alloys, which could be die-cast in metal molds with cookie-cutter precision. Hubley was also well known for its cap guns and became a bomb fuse manufacturer during World War II.

Another great American cast-iron toy-making firm, the Arcade Manufacturing Company, began business as the Novelty Iron Works of Freeport, Illinois, in 1866. The Hazen family made everything from cast-iron store fronts to windmills until new owners took over in 1885. Their first products were cork extractors, screen door hinges and table-top coffee mills. In 1897 yet another group of new owners added miniature coffee mills to the line, and the company gradually evolved into a premium producer of cast-iron toys; including airplanes, automobiles, banks, trains, fire engines, boats, circus wagons, doll house furniture and facsimile editions of farm machinery with dozens of moving parts. Their cars were exact copies of the Fords, Chevrolets, Buicks and square Yellow Cabs of the 1920s and were manufactured under the "They Look Real" trademark. World War II defense production brought an abrupt end to their toy business and in 1945 the company was sold to Rockwell Standard Corporation.

Keene, New Hampshire, was the home of two famous toy makers. James Wilkins converted his 1880s washing machine wringer factory to a high grade tinplate toy vehicle operation in 1890. Harry Kingsbury bought Wilkins out in 1895 and continued making deluxe quality reproductions of automobiles, trucks and fire engines under the Wilkins banner until 1919 when he began using his own name. Kingsbury toys were top-of-the-line wind-up motor models made of electrically-welded heavy gauge steel. Production ceased in the 1940s.

Steam powered toys were first produced in this country by Eugene Beggs, of Patterson, New Jersey, in 1871. However, a pocket watch company employee, named William Weeden, hit a vein of gold when he sent *The Youth's Companion* a model of his flame-powered toy steam engine in 1876. The magazine publisher ran a test advertisement and quickly ordered 10,000 of Weeden's one dollar kerosene-burning toys to give away as premiums to boys who signed up one new subscriber and sent in 25 cents to cover the postage. Weeden's Manufacturing Company went on to build a wide variety of popular steam toys, including locomotives, steamboats and fire engines. In the 1930s Weeden converted most of their engines to electric heating elements and, with the novelty of an open flame gone, sales eventually evaporated.

Bicycles, tricycles, boneshakers and velocipedes arrived here from Europe in the 1860s. They were made for adults, who generally went to a "bicycle academy" to learn to mount and ride these new high-wheeled steeds. Within a few years smaller, safer versions for children, came on the market. By 1890 a million bicycles a year were being made in the United States and modern balloon-tired "safety bikes" had made high-wheelers obsolete.

Sewing machine factories and firearms makers were the first to mass-produce bicycles. Among them were Singer, Remington, Pope, Weed and White. By 1898 there were a hundred other manufacturers including Sears, Roebuck and Company and the once-expensive playthings became affordable to all classes.

Bicycles had a huge impact on the Victorian economy. Cigar makers and saloon operators folded like dominoes. Livery stables and piano teachers bit the dust and church attendance dropped greatly. Able-bodied city dwellers relished their Sunday outings in the countryside with friends or fellow bicycle club members. One hundred mile "Century" runs were the rage of the day. Many young people spent their afternoons in Central Park cruising the newly-paved bike paths, hoping to meet an attractive cyclist of the opposite gender.

Photographers were among the best customers of bicycle dealers. Children no longer wanted to be pictured astride a wooden hobby horse. From 1880 onward bicycles and tricycles outnumbered other indoor studio props by three to one. Pony and goat carts became the favored vehicles for outdoor photos.

Toy pedal-cars appeared on the scene soon after their Detroit counterparts, in about 1905. Ohio was the home of the wire wheel making industry and naturally evolved as a pedal-car manufacturing center.

New models came out every season and many were almost carbon copies of popular automobiles of the period. The most expensive models sported nickel-plated trim, detailed dashboards, glass windshields, brass headlamps, horns, gear- shift levers and real brakes!

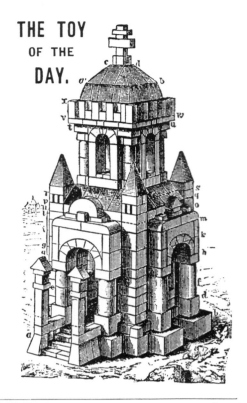

Construction toys were made strictly for boys. The aim was to develop mechanical aptitude and dexterity at an early age; perhaps even leading to an engineering career for those who could master the subtle geometry and physics lessons offered in the most advanced kits.

Who knows how the first construction toys evolved? Perhaps a workman at the pyramids fashioned a set of tiny mud or stone bricks for his first-born son? A more likely scenario is a carpenter or cabinet maker bringing home a tool box full of scrap lumber cut-offs to keep his kids amused over the weekend.

We hate to keep giving the Teutonic race credit for inventing most of the toys in this book, but facts are facts. The Richter company (Anchor Blocks) was supposedly founded in Rudolstadt, Germany, in about 1508. The company obtained a U.S. patent for its composition, ground-stone building blocks in 1880. They were sold through a New York distributor and also by direct mail advertisements in upscale magazines like *Harper's Monthly*. Miniature blocks, columns, arches and steeples could be purchased in various sized sets, furnishing enough stones to build impressive castles, towers, bridges, forts, or temples. Thousands of sets were sold every year for several decades. A. C. Gilbert (Erector Sets) bought out the sole North American rights in 1913.

Other smaller, one or two-project building kits had arrived at toy shops in New York and London in the 1850s. These German and Russian imports were more brightly colored than Anchor Blocks and could form simple churches, bridges, palaces and villages. Most all of these blocks were held together solely by the weight of individual pieces stacked one upon another. A considerable accomplishment when you consider that some of Richter's buildings were four or five feet tall.

Milton Bradley, the kindergarten toy producer, came out with wooden building blocks with numeral and animal images on each side in the 1860s. He was the biggest maker of alphabet blocks, in the U.S., from 1880 onward.

The R. Bliss Mfg. Co. Of Pawtucket, Rhode Island (established in 1832) jumped on the band wagon in 1871 with a set of "Improved Architectural Building Blocks" which was also a big seller for a decade or two.

We've previously mentioned Charles Crandall, who introduced interlocking-type architectural blocks in 1867, and his cousin Jesse Crandall, who began manufacturing hollow, lithographed, nesting-style nursery school blocks in 1875. (Several other Crandalls were toy makers too.)

Lincoln Logs, "America's National Toy", evolved from Joel Ellis' 1860s introduction of packaged, pre-cut wooden logs for building toy cabins. Twentieth century Lincoln Logs were the brainstorm of John Wright, a son of Frank Lloyd Wright, the famous architect. Mr. Wright was inspired while watching a Japanese construction project, using nail-less, interlocking members, in 1916. His first marketing efforts failed, but in 1924 Wright hooked up with a Chicago firm that successfully promoted Lincoln Logs as a patriotic toy for America's children. They are still being made today by the Little Jimmy Company.

Metal girder-style construction kits were a turn-of-the century invention that appeared almost simultaneously on both sides of the Atlantic.

Frank Hornby, of Liverpool, England, quit school in 1879 at the age of 16, and went to work in a local meat packing plant. Hornby's inventive talent came to light when, at the age of 35, he developed a siphon system for his employer's flooded bacon brine pit. Subsequent professional journeys exposed him to various construction sites where he became fascinated by the huge steam-driven cranes that could lift anything from bridge girders to locomotive engines.

Hornby's evening hours were spent in his home workshop in a futile attempt to develop a perpetual motion machine—which was the goal of many inventors of that period. With some of his leftover parts Frank began building simple model bridges and cranes for the amusement of his two young sons.

By 1901, starting with easily formed and drilled copper strips, Hornby developed and patented the first articulated girder-style construction kit. It consisted of 1/2 inch wide strips cut into various lengths, up to a foot long, and fastened together with L-shaped brackets, using simple screws and nuts.

Hornby's first sets were sold only to friends and relatives, with a few going to local toy stores for a trial run. Kids were delighted with the new toy and parents spread the word. During the 1902 Christmas season Frank sold all the sets he had on hand and quit his day job to become a full-time toy salesman. In 1903 he coined the "Meccano" trademark (meaning "Mechanics made easy") and hired his first employee, a young girl who served as both secretary and chief kit assembler.

For the next five years more orders came in than Frank could fill from his tiny two-room factory. Quick expansion followed and in 1909 Meccano sets were in world wide distribution. By 1914 Meccano kits were so popular that they were given full-page treatment in Montgomery Ward's big catalog. In 1916 an optional electric motor replaced the hand-crank for power. You will find Meccano's model autos, trucks, ships, planes, cranes, bridges, steam shovels, windmills and merry-go-rounds illustrated on pages 148-150.

America's answer to Meccano's invasion was A. C. Gilbert's famous Erector set which was first mass-marketed in 1913.

Alfred Carlton Gilbert was born in Oregon in 1884 and by the age of 24 had won an Olympic gold medal in the pole vault and a medical degree from Yale—quite a contrast to Frank Hornby's humble beginnings in a Liverpool meat packing plant.

While still in college, Gilbert (also an amateur magician) developed a box of magic tricks which he and a partner sold under the "Mysto" trade name. Alfred was a natural born merchandiser and self-promoter and he

This circa 1880 pen and ink drawing reveals much about giftware merchandising 120 years ago. An artistically designed show window attracts a huge crowd to view the sleeping Gulliver mannequin. The entire store is apparently devoted to the sale of toys and fancy goods, with an emphasis on holiday gifts. Dolls and other expensive toys are hanging from the ceiling, or on tall shelves behind the counter, as was the custom of the day.

quickly grasped the fact that New York toy merchants were always on the lookout for the next hot new toy or novelty item.

Gilbert undoubtedly knew of Meccano's overseas popularity but he claimed that his inspiration for the Erector set was his daily commuter's view of a New Haven construction site. Anyhow, the major difference between the two girder-based sets was the superior strength of Gilbert's box-shaped steel members (Hornby's girders were cheaper, flat strips of metal). From 1913 to 1923, Erector set girders were a full 1 1/8 inch wide by 12 inches long and a correctly assembled model bridge could support the weight of a 200 lb. man.

By 1921 Gilbert's line of educational toys had expanded to include an experimental sound set, an electric science kit, a hydraulic engineering outfit, a miniature weather station, a chemistry outfit, an aircraft set, a toy machine gun, and a full-sized go-cart kit.

The "Golden age" of Erector toys was probably the late 1920s. Prior to the stockmarket crash of 1929, Gilbert introduced a metal zeppelin set, an airplane kit, a giant steam shovel, an ocean liner and a Ferris wheel. During this period Gilbert acquired the North American rights to Meccano and combined Hornby's set with his own to create "The New American Meccano".

In 1938 Gilbert bought W. O. Coleman's American Flyer line of model trains and began production of "O" gauge electric locomotives. World War II spelled the end of giant metal toys and more or less disrupted the toy business everywhere—since Japan and Germany had been major suppliers. After the war Erector sets were again produced, from 1950 into the 1980s, under a series of new owners which included Meccano of France, Gabriel Industries, CBS Toys, and the Ideal Mfg. Co.

Alfred Carlton Gilbert died in 1961 at the age of 77; an icon among three generations of American boys. Millions of Erector sets were sold over a 75 year period and Tinkertoy was the only other real competitor for the title of "America's Greatest Toy".

I suspect that nearly every child of my generation owned, or at one time played with a set of Tinkertoys. You didn't need pliers or a screwdriver to assemble this simple spool-and-stick jointed toy. It's no wonder that Tinkertoy's "Wonder Builder" became the world's all-time best-selling construction set.

However, unless you hale from Evanston, Illinois, you have probably never heard of the Toy Tinker's founding partners, Charles H. Pajeau and Robert Pettit. The two met on the Chicago-to-Evanston commuter train in 1911. Charles was a 36 year old tombstone company executive and Robert, six years younger, was a trucking company operator and commodity trader.

Both gentlemen were extremely bored with their present occupations and looking for new business opportunities closer to Evanston.. Charles Pajeau was already an accomplished inventor of toys, having filed a

sidewalk scooter patent in 1897, and a children's sulky design in 1905. Robert Pettit was the bean counter and behind-the-scene manager who enabled the pair to survive and prosper through two world wars and several recessions.

Charles had conceived the stick-and-spool idea for Tinkertoys after observing some children playing with pencils and sewing thread spools. Soon the pair rented a 15 by 20 foot factory space in Evanston and set to work.

The Tinkertoy's trademark canister was designed to also serve as a mailing tube. No other carton was necessary. Their first "Wonder Builder" kit contained 73 spools and sticks in varying lengths that would automatically enable children to construct a series of connecting triangles. Theoretically, one could produce a thousand different toys from the first 73 piece kit.

1914 was a terrible year in which to launch a toy business. World War I had just begun and German toy shipments were in a flux. Department store toy buyers were leery about placing any new orders, so the partners turned to cigar stores, news stands and drugstores as an alternative marketing ploy.

Display windows at key corners in Chicago and New York City were secured, and a Ferris wheel Tinkertoy was assembled at each location during the week of the annual toy show. The whirling stick-and-spool displays attracted large crowds and the Toy Tinkers were overwhelmed with wholesale orders. Some jobbers ordered 720 sets at a time and more than 900,000 sets were shipped in the 1915 season. Luckily, the partners had found a Swedish machinery designer who jury-rigged an automated drill press that bored all eight spool holes in a single stroke. Henry Svebilius became an indispensable employee.

By 1920 over six million sets had been sold and 30 competitors had bit the dust. During the next nine years there were moves to larger quarters and many new toy designs came off Charles Pajeau's drawing board. Prior to the crash of 1929 more than 65,000 square feet were devoted to Wonder Builder Tinkertoy kits. Boxcars arrived weekly, filled with 100 lb. burlap sacks full of spools and three foot long bundles of white birch dowels. Production grew to 1,750,000 sets a year.

Between the economic depression of the 1930s and the end of World War II production ebbed and flowed. At one point the Toy Tinkers had to lay off everyone but the night watchman. But the baby boom following the war revived the business and by 1947 factory output reached a record level of 2,500,000 sets a year. (That's 100 million sticks and 40 million spools....count'em.)

The Toy Tinkers sold out to A. G. Spalding Brothers in 1952 and Charles Pajeau passed away, at the age of 72. In 1969 Spalding was acquired by Questor Corp. who continued the line and introduced a giant sized version in 1971. Today's Tinkertoy construction set is made of colorful plastic by the Playskool Division of Hasboro, in Central Falls, Rhode Island.

Children's books are probably the most popular form of collectible illustrator art. Their history dates back to the 17th century juvenile title, *Orbis Pictus*, which was filled with woodcuts of people at play and other interesting objects to encourage reading. By the middle 1700s a few London printing houses had begun to specialize in juvenile literature, but the emphasis was on highly moralistic tales. Gradually, however, the works of Puritan authors were superseded by more exciting classics such as *Gulliver's Travels* and *Robinson Crusoe*.

The trend continued in 1807 when a banker named William Roscoe wrote a best-seller entitled *The Butterfly's Ball and the Grasshopper's Feast*. In the same year Mrs. Catherine Dorset penned *The Peacock at Home*, which sold more than four million copies in 12 months. By the 1820s *Old Mother Hubbard* and *The Tale of Cock Robin* had both been mass-produced in hand colored editions—by child labor.

In America the most widely read children's book was *The New England Primer*. This popular educational tool remained in print for 150 years. Between 1690 and 1830 several million copies were sold. *The Primer* was not recreational reading material. It contained the religious instruction, several pages of hymns and prayers, and multiple forms of an illustrated alphabet. Every child of the period was required to memorize this dull tome from cover to cover; often under threat of corporal punishment.

A 1776 edition in very good condition recently sold at auction for $2,000. Most editions printed from 1800 to 1826 are currently worth about $150 to $175. No example of the 1690 first edition has survived.

In the mid 1800s color lithography gradually began to replace earlier watercolor-tinted woodcuts and steel engravings in some children's books. The Germans excelled in chromolithography and most fine color printing was done in Germany and then bound up with the text after being shipped back to England or America for distribution.

Also of Germanic origin were the brothers Grimm and their "shocking" 1812 to 1815 series of fairy tales which were later illustrated in English language versions by such notables as George Cruikshank (1792-1878), Arthur Rackham (1867-1939), John R. Neill (1878-1943), Johnny Gruelle (1880-1938) and Jesse Wilcox Smith (1863-1935).

Three of the most prominent artists of the 1860-1880 period were Randolph Caldicott (1846-1886), Kate Greenaway (1846-1901) and Walter Crane (1845-1915).

America was not without its share of children's book publishers during the 19th century. In the early 1800s it was a common practice for book shop owners to print original (or pirated) editions for their own inventory and then sell the surplus to the trade at large. Many small sized "toy books", with hand colored plates, were issued by Yankee merchants and printers in the 1850s.

The Night Before Christmas— a poem penned in 1822 by a New York doctor named Clement. C. Moore—

was later made famous by the McLoughlin Brothers and their chief illustrator, Thomas Nast, the Santa Claus artist.

An already ancient collection of nursery rhymes, *Mother Goose's Melodies*, was issued in a color-litho edition by Porter & Coates, of Philadelphia, in the 1870s. Subsequent editions illustrated by Kate Greenaway, Maud Humphrey and Maxfield Parrish have appeared onward to this day.

To make a long story short; it is estimated that more than a hundred children's book publishers were thriving in the United States by the year 1870.

Chief among these firms was a giant book, board game, paperdoll and postcard publishing house named after its founder, John McLoughlin, a Scottish immigrant.

Starting in 1828 with a used handpress, John McLoughlin wrote and printed his own small instructional pamphlets of conduct and morals for children. Later editions were bound into larger books and within 20 years McLoughlin was able to retire, leaving the business to his two sons—Edmund and John, Jr.

The McLoughlin Brothers continued to expand their father's successful operation and by the late 1880s were the world's largest publisher of children's books. They employed the cream of America's illustrators, including Thomas Nast (1840-1902), Palmer Cox (1840-1924) and Howard Pyle (1853-1911). At their peak of production in the 1890s, the McLoughlins employed a staff of 75 artists.

In 1920 a third generation of McLoughlins sold out to Milton Bradley, a leading manufacturer of toys, games, crayons and other grammar school supplies. Bradley used the McLoughlin label for three more decades and then the once-famous name passed quietly into history.

The children's book business was, however, not without controversy. Take, for instance, the story of *Little Black Sambo* which was first published in England in 1899. This book's setting was laid in an imaginary land, a mixture of India and Africa. Author-illustrator Helen Bannerman's hero, Sambo, was hardly controversial. He had pleasing features, dressed well, was intelligent and had loving parents. Because a friend's mistake weakened the book's copyright, more than 50 editions have been published with which Mrs. Bannerman had no connection.

In the United States the term "Sambo" as used in *Uncle Tom's Cabin* had become a derogatory term, a fact unknown to Mrs. Bannerman. American illustrators drew Sambo and his family as plantation-slave stereotypes. The book was extremely popular, but charges that it was racist did not appear until the 1940s. Today, though generally relegated to a special section in libraries, the classic story of *Little Black Sambo* is still being published.

Perhaps critic Selma Lanes hit the mark when she pointed out that the book introduced blacks to American children as human beings. They were human beings, not racist stereo-types, in Helen Bannerman's original version. The villains may well have been those American illustrators, who exaggerated Sambo's features.

DAVIS BROTHERS' BUILDING

1879 SAN FRANCISCO, CALIFORNIA 1880

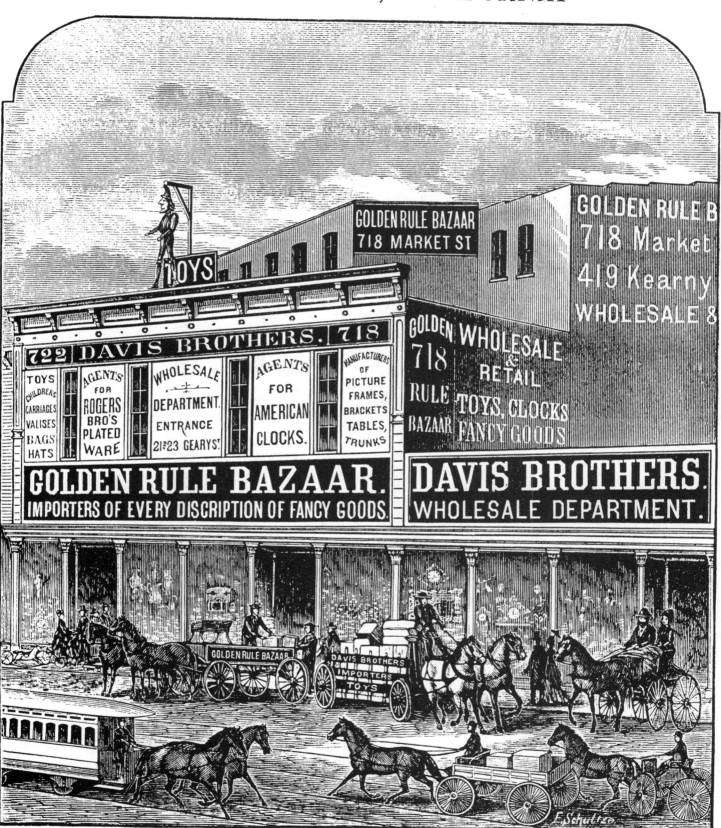

The Davis Brothers erected this five story building in 1877. It covered an entire block from Market to Geary streets. Steam powered machinery in the basement was used to manufacture toys and picture frames.

Tops.

THE TIP TOP.

A wonderful toy. A top that tips, or turns over. This little novelty fascinates both old and young. Any child can spin it.

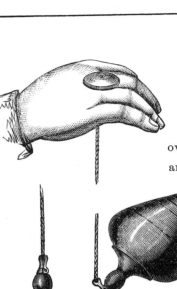

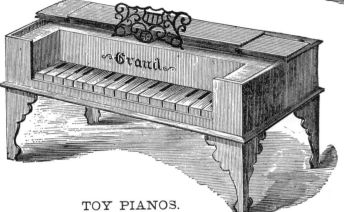

TOY PIANOS.

The Grand, imitation walnut, see cut, has 15 metallic keys, hinged folding top, adjustable music rack, moulded body, legs unscrew, sole agents, size 18½x9½x9 in..............

No. 3007.
REVERSIBLE DRAWING SLATE
Size 6½x10.
Has three separate parts—for ciphering, drawing and writing.
$2 50 doz.

METAL DRUMS.

The following Horses Hitch and Unhitch.

Plain wood dump cart, with platform horse ....
Gaily painted dump cart, with platform horse, see cut.........

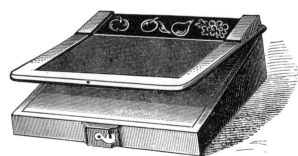

Is a Writing and Slate Desk combined, 8x11½. $11 00 doz.

CHILDREN'S ROLLING HOOPS.

Oak, 12 sizes, smallest 22, largest 30 in., with sticks......
Oak, 12 sizes, smallest 23, largest 34 in., with sticks......
Oak, 12 sizes, smallest 33, largest 44 in., round edges.

The metropolitan buggy, see cut, horses trot when propelled.

Davis Brothers' Catalogue.

Crandall's Blocks.

HEAVY ARTILLERY.
No. 2432—$30 00 doz.

TWO JOLLY BLACKS.
No. 2423—$4 50 doz.

VELOCIPEDE RIDER.
No. 3421—$4 50 doz.

THE LIVELY HORSEMAN.
No. 3424—$4 50 doz.

HILL'S KINDERGARTEN BLOCKS.

TEA SET.
No. 3434—$1 75 doz.

WIDE AWAKE.
No. 3427—$9 00 doz.

Architectural Blocks

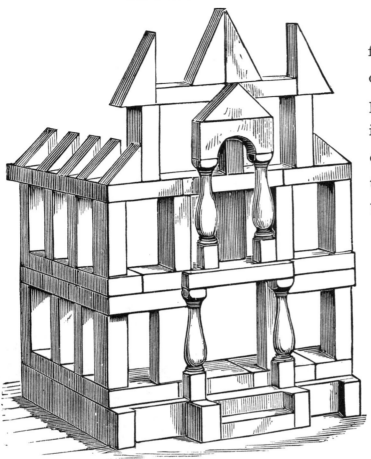

Made from hard wood, neatly finished, free from paint or other poisons, safe for a child's play room, simple and attractive, a daily delight. Every child should have a box of them. Directions with each box.

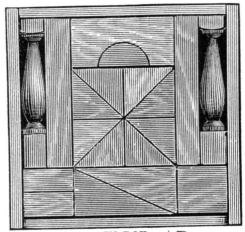

No.	SET UP.	IN BOX.	Dozen.
3399	Box 6 x 6 x 2¼, contains 34 blocks........................		5 50
3400	Box 7⅜ x 7⅜ x 2⅞, contains 34 blocks, of a larger size.........		8 00
3401	Box 9 x 6 x 3, contains 60 blocks...........................		9 00
3402	Box 10¾ x 7¼ x 3¼, contains 60 blocks, of a larger size.........		12 00
3403	Box 9 x 9 x 3, contains 90 blocks..........................		13 50
3404	Box 12 x 12 x 4, contains 90 blocks, of a larger size...........		17 00
3405	Box 17½ x 11 x 5½, contains 115 blocks, wagon shape, with wheels		48 00

Hill's Alphabet Blocks.

No. 3414.

3406	18 flat blocks, not painted, paper box	1 00
3407	18 flat blocks, not painted, paper box	80
3408	18 flat blocks, not painted, paper box	1 10
3409	18 flat blocks, painted, album box....	2 25
3410	16 cube blocks, not painted, wood box	4 50
3411	6 cube blocks, not painted, paper box	2 25
3412	20 cube blocks, not painted, wood box	6 50
3413	6 cube blocks, painted, wood box...	2 75
3414	16 cube blocks, painted, wood box...	5 50
3415	20 cube blocks, painted, wood box...	8 00
3416	20 cube blocks, painted, wood box ..	8 75
3417	18 Kindergarten painted blocks, wd bx	2 50
3418	58 Kindergarten painted blocks, wd bx	8 00
3419	51 building blocks, painted, wood box	11 00

Closer Prices may be Relied on.

Wooden Toys—Continued.

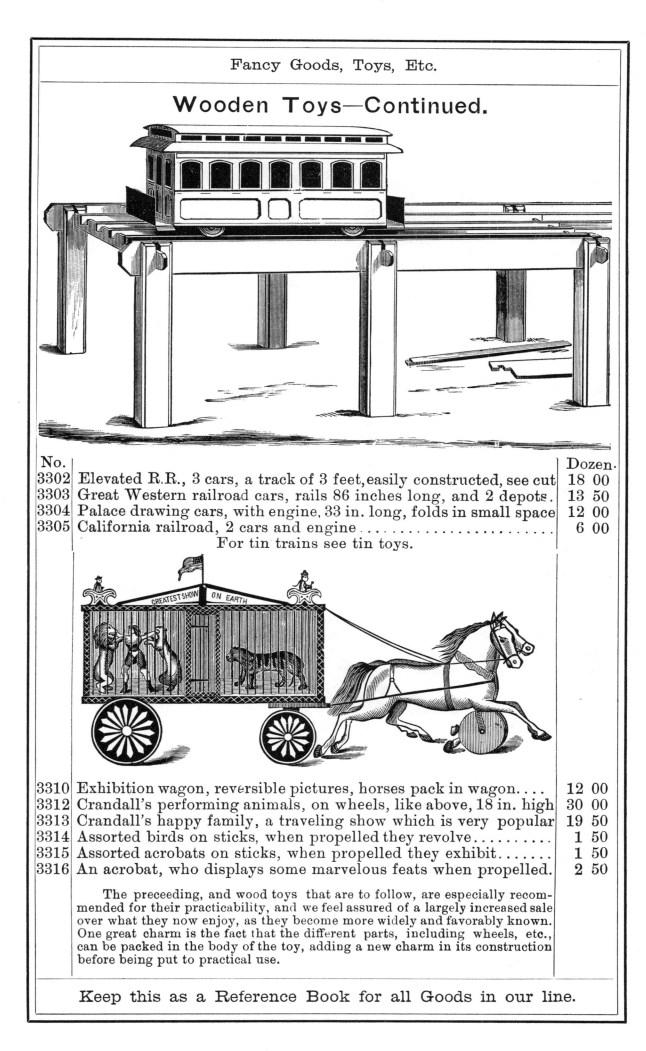

No.		Dozen.
3302	Elevated R.R., 3 cars, a track of 3 feet, easily constructed, see cut	18 00
3303	Great Western railroad cars, rails 86 inches long, and 2 depots	13 50
3304	Palace drawing cars, with engine, 33 in. long, folds in small space	12 00
3305	California railroad, 2 cars and engine	6 00

For tin trains see tin toys.

3310	Exhibition wagon, reversible pictures, horses pack in wagon....	12 00
3312	Crandall's performing animals, on wheels, like above, 18 in. high	30 00
3313	Crandall's happy family, a traveling show which is very popular	19 50
3314	Assorted birds on sticks, when propelled they revolve..........	1 50
3315	Assorted acrobats on sticks, when propelled they exhibit.......	1 50
3316	An acrobat, who displays some marvelous feats when propelled.	2 50

The preceeding, and wood toys that are to follow, are especially recommended for their practicability, and we feel assured of a largely increased sale over what they now enjoy, as they become more widely and favorably known. One great charm is the fact that the different parts, including wheels, etc., can be packed in the body of the toy, adding a new charm in its construction before being put to practical use.

Keep this as a Reference Book for all Goods in our line.

CHAIR ROCKERS.

No.		Each.
3204	Double horse heads, handsomely ornamented, see cut.........	2 00
3205	Single horse head, handsomely ornamented, style of cut.......	1 25
3206	Propeller, 3 wheels, head to turn, iron axles...............	4 25

3207	Stick horse, skin stuffed head, 40 inches long, see cut.........	1 00
3208	Stick horse, wood head, 36 inches long, like cut.............	50
3209	Stick horse, wood head, 36 inches long, solid block wheels.....	20

SHOO-FLY ROCKERS.

No.	Gaily Painted.	
3210	Upholstered, enameled cloth........	2 00
3211	Upholstered, enameled cloth, larger.	2 50
3212	Upholstered, wool reps, large.	3 00
3213	Small two-horse Dexter..............	1 50

TOY PLATFORM HORSES.—Substantially Made.

No.		Dozen.
3214	Finely painted, height 6 inches	1 50
3215	Finely painted, height 7¼ "	2 25
3216	Finely painted, height 8½ "	4 50
3217	Finely painted, height 9¼ "	5 50
3218	Finely painted, height 12½ "	8 50

Real Skin Covered.
Leather Saddles and Stirrups, Mane and Tail.

No.		
3220	Height 8½ inches	9 00
3221	Height 9 "	13 50
3222	Height 10½ "	16 50
3223	Height 12½ "	21 00
3224	Height 14 "	24 00
3225	Height 18 "	42 00

Closer Prices may be Relied on.

Davis Brothers' Catalogue.

Wooden Toys—Continued.

TOY WOODEN WARE.

No. 3440a WASH SET (5 pieces).
$4 50 dozen sets.

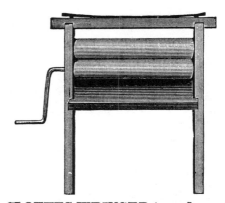

XX CLOTHES BAR.
No. 3458—$1 75 doz.

WASH BOARD.
No. 3454—50c doz.

CLOTHES WRINGER (wood crank)
No. 3465—$1 75 doz.

ORNAMENTED CEDAR PAILS.

X CLOTHES BAR.
No. 3457—$1 00 doz.

No. 3451   No. 3449   No. 3450
$1 00 doz. 75c doz. $1 00 doz.

Address all Orders Davis Bros., 718 Market St.

Mechanical Toys.

CHAMPION DANCERS.
No. 5328—$27.00 per dozen.

CHALLENGE DANCER.
No. 5327—$21.00 per dozen.

JUBILEE DOUBLE GYMNASTS.
No. 5329—$48.00 per dozen.

SMOKING GRANT.
No. 5333—$60.00 per dozen.

Davis Brothers' Catalogue.

Mechanical Toys—Continued.

No. 5348—Mechanical Locomotive, $36.00 per dozen.

No. 5357—Buggy with Galloping Horse, $25.00 per dozen.

No. 5346—Mechanical Locomotive, $13.50 per dozen.

Catalogue Prices subject to Market Changes.

—1881—

House Furnishing Catalogue.

DEPARTMENT No. 9.

SIMMONS HARDWARE COMPANY,

Bicycles, Velocipedes, Baby Carriages

ST. LOUIS.

BICYCLES.

Steel Wheel.

Otto.

Otto Bicycles, Wood Spokes, and Flat Steel Tires.

NO.	Diameter of Front Wheel.	Diameter of Hind Wheel.	Length of Leg, Inside Measure to Sole of Foot.	PRICE.
1	28 inches,	14 inches,	23 inches,	$6.50
2	32 inches,	14 inches,	25 inches,	8.00
3	36 inches,	18 inches,	28 inches,	15.00
4	42 inches,	18 inches,	30 inches,	20.00
5	46 inches,	18 inches,	32 inches,	25.00
6	48 inches,	18 inches,	33 inches,	27 50
7	50 inches,	18 inches,	34 inches,	30.00

Steel Spokes and Round Rubber Tires.

NO.	Diameter of Front Wheel.	Diameter of Hind Wheel.	Length of Leg, Inside of Measurement to Sole of Foot.	PRICE.
13	28 inches,	14 inches,	23 inches,	$12.50
14	32 inches,	14 inches,	25 inches,	18.00
15	36 inches,	18 inches,	28 inches,	25.00
16	42 inches,	18 inches,	30 inches,	35.00

IRON FRAME VELOCIPEDES.

No. 1—Velocipedes, Wheels, 16 and 12 inches, Welded Tires, Upholstered Seats, for Boys 3 to 5
  years old, ...   each, $4.00
No. 2—Velocipedes, Wheels, 20 and 16 inches, Welded Tires, Upholstered Seats, for Boys 6 to 8
  years old, ...   "   5 00
No. 3—Velocipedes, Wheels, 24 and 20 inches, Welded Tires, Upholstered Seats, for Boys 9 to 12
  years old, ...   "   6.00
No. 4—Velocipedes, Wheels, 28 and 24 inches, Welded Tires, Upholstered Seats, for Boys 12 to 15
  years old,   .   .   , ...   "   7.00

Wood Frame Velocipedes.

No. 5—Velocipedes, Wheels 16 and 12 inches, Spring Saddles, for Boys 5 to 7 years old,   .   each, $5 00
No. 6—Velocipedes, Wheels 20 and 16 inches, Spring Saddles, for Boys 6 to 8 years old,   .   "   6.00
No. 7—Velocipedes, Wheels 24 and 20 inches, Spring Saddles, for Boys 9 to 12 years old,   .   "   7.00
No. 8—Velocipedes, Wheels 28 and 24 inches, Spring Saddles, for Boys 12 to 15 years old,   .   "   8.00

GIRLS' PROPELLERS.

No. 1—Propellers, Wheels 20 inches, for children 5 to 8 years, ...   each, $8 00
No. 2—Propellers, Wheels 24 inches, for children 9 to 10 years, ...   "   9.00

Invalid Chairs.

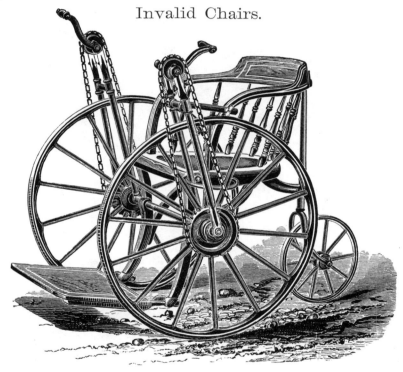

Invalid Chairs, ... each, $25.00

Persons with weak or paralyzed lower limbs will find this machine the most convenient and practical one of any yet introduced. It is perfectly safe and easily propelled by means of cranks and endless chains running over the sprocket wheels, as shown in above cut. Each wheel moves independently of the other, thereby enabling the occupant to turn on the spot, as well as move in any direction. This chair will prove a most valuable companion to invalids, not only on the streets, but far more so in the house. To extend its usefulness in this respect, the propelling apparatus is adjusted, by means of thumb screws at the side of the arm-rails, so as to loosen the crank bearing standards and drop them back of the seat entirely out of the way. The foot rest is so arranged, by means of set screws, that it can be raised or lowered according to the length of the Legs. The seat is that of a so-called "office-chair." The front wheels, 28 inches in diameter, and the hind wheels, 12 inches in diameter, are made of the very best material; all connections are of iron tubing, and the axles of steel, totally strong enough to carry a weight of 500 pounds. The motion of the cranks being transmitted by its sprocket wheels of but three inches diameter, to those on the front wheels of six inches diameter, the working power is doubled, so that even weak persons are able to propel it with ease. This machine will work comparatively well on a rough or sandy road, even when ascending a moderate inclination; its speed is that of an ordinary walk.

PORTLAND CUTTERS.

No. 10—Portland Cutters, Beautifully Shaped, has Three Bent Knees, Shod with Half Round Iron, Finished in High Colors, Richly Ornamented, and has a Seat Upholstered with Fancy Plush, each, $15.00

Boys' and Girls' Sleighs.

No. 7.   No. 8.

No. 7—Boys' Sleighs, Size 35 inches long by 13 inches wide, has Three Bent Knees, Square Tenoned, Strongly Made, with Six Plated Braces; Painted in High Colors, Neatly Scrolled and Ornamented, ... each, $2.50

WHITNEY'S BABY CARRIAGES.

Nos. 76½ and 675.

No. 76½—In the Carriage represented in the cut we present a new design, having the body made of Rattan, upholstered with fine fancy goods. It is hung upon nice Steel Springs, and it is supplied with a fine Parasol Top, which folds up and is attached to our improved Adjustable Rod. It has our Patent Reversible Handle, and the wheels have round tires and tapered spokes, ... each, $24.25

No. 675—Same as No. 76½, without the Reversible Handle, ... " 23.00

Light Perambulators.

No. 131—Substantial willow body unlined, plain cushion seat without top, resting on wooden bars with elastic springs, iron axles, wheels with welded oval tires. Each, . $5.50

No. 132 — Willow Body, style as above cut, body lined with enameled cloth, without top, iron axles, wheels with welded oval tires. Each, . $6 25

WHITNEY'S BABY CARRIAGES.

Nos. 185 and 956.   Reversible Handles.

No. 185—Finished on the Exterior with Woven Cane Panels, Upholstered throughout in fine all-wool Terry, with Rolls in Back, Standards, Side Rails, Handle Tips and Hub Caps full Silver Plated, each, $24.00

No. 956—Same as No. 185, excepting it is Upholstered with Coteline or Nice Broadcloth, in Rolls both Front and Back, and the Wheels have Flat Spokes, ...   each,   29.00

No. 356

No. 356—Light and Durable, with White or Black Rattan Body, Upholstered in Terry, Steel Springs and Canopy Top.   The Wheels and Gearing are Finished in the Natural Color of the Wood, each, $14.00

TOY BANKS.

No. 3244.

No. 3244—Toy Banks, Dark Antique, Bronzed, ... each, $ .35

No. 3234.

No. 3234—Toy Banks, Dark Antique, ... each, $1.00

SUMMER SPORTS AND PASTIMES.

Archery.

All Archery and Lawn Tennis goods should be sent by express only.

1. Polished Lancewood Bows, 2¾ feet, 12c; 3 feet, 15c; 5¼ feet, 20c; 3½ feet, 25c; 4 feet, 30c; 4½ feet, 40c; 4¾ feet, 50c; 5 feet, 75c; 5½ feet, $1.25; 6 feet............ ....$1.50

2. Polished Lancewood Bows, horn tipped, with velvet handles, 3½ feet, 75c; 4 feet, $1.00; 4½ feet, $1.25; 5 feet, $1.35; 5½ feet, $1.85; 6 feet.. 2.25

3. Fine quality Lancewood Bows, stained and polished, horn tipped, with plush handles

Base Balls and Bats.

15. Spalding's Official League Ball, as adopted by the National League. Each ball wrapped in tinfoil, and put up in separate box and sealed, in accordance with the latest League regulations..$1.00

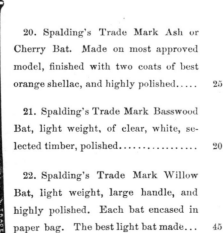

20. Spalding's Trade Mark Ash or Cherry Bat. Made on most approved model, finished with two coats of best orange shellac, and highly polished..... 25

21. Spalding's Trade Mark Basswood Bat, light weight, of clear, white, selected timber, polished................. 20

22. Spalding's Trade Mark Willow Bat, light weight, large handle, and highly polished. Each bat encased in paper bag. The best light bat made... 45

23. Base Ball Belts, of cotton webbing 25

24. The same, of worsted webbing... 50

25. Caps, second quality flannel...... 45

26. The same, first quality flannel.... 65

Gents' best Back Bows, 2 pieces, with best Flemish strings, 60 to 50 lbs.

Pistols and Revolvers.

16. The CLIMAX, single barrel Pistol, for Fourth of July use; for No. 22 blank cartridges only. A safe pistol for a boy, which will make as much noise as he desires without any risk of injury....$0.35

17. The short cylinder RANGER. A very efficient little 7 chamber Revolver, of 22 calibre. Nickel-plated, with walnut stock.... .... 1.15

18. The long cylinder RANGER. Same as above in every respect, but with longer cylinder....... 1.25

19. The same as No. 18, engraved and enameled 1.60

20. The same as No. 19, with gold-plated cylinder, engraved and enameled.................... 1.85

21. The RANGER No. 2, 32 calibre. A strong and useful 6-chambered Revolver. Rosewood stock, with nickel-plated cylinder and barrel........... 2.45

22. The same, engraved and enameled....... 2.85

23. The CZAR, 22 calibre, 7 chambers, with 4-inch long octagon barrel. Nickel-plated, with vulcanized handle............................ 2.35

24. The same, engraved and enameled....... 2.75

25. The same, with gold-plated cylinder and pin; engraved and enameled.................... 3.00

26. The Gem Solitaire. A delightful and ingenious pastime for a single player. Complete with pins and board, packed in neat box........ 25

27. The Spectrograph. A useful invention, by means of which the most finished drawings can be easily and accurately copied. Full directions for use are enclosed in each box, together with a set of choice drawings for copying. Price...... 10

36. Best Green Baize Bow Covers..........$
37. Canton Flannel,   "   "   ....

38. Club Score Books, 600 to 1,200 rounds, blank page for observations, summary, etc., $1.00, $1.50 and......................

39. How to Train in Archery; a complete study of the York round. By Maurice Thompson, President of the Grand National Archery Association of the United States............................

40. Book of Instruction in Archery, with Constitution and Rules of the National Association....

41. Quiver Belts and Quivers, japanned, for Ladies or Gents, each, 75c and.................$

42. Finer quality, leather covered, $1.75 and...

43. Score Cards, per 100......................

44. Pocket Score Cards, in colors, per dozen..

45. Pocket Score Book, bound in red leather, each.......................................

Targets.

46. English Straw Targets, with canvas facings, without stands, 12 in., 95c; 15 in., $1.10; 18 in., $1.60; 21 in., $1.75; 24 in., $2.25; 27 in., $2.60; 30 in., $3.60; 36 in., $3.20; 42 in., $4.50; 48 in..................................$

Target Facings, one-quarter of above prices.

47. Wood Target Stands, 5 feet 75c; 6 feet....

48. Iron Target Stands, small, $1.25; medium, $1.50; large...................................

49. Patent Rubber Target Gun. Shoots arrows or bullets. Length, 39 inches. Loads from muzzle. Will shoot about 600 feet, with surprising power and accuracy. With every gun are included five metal pointed arrows, two targets, and one globe sight...............................

CROQUET

Croquet sets cannot be sent by mail.

1. Eight-ball Set, full sized, varnished balls, [turn]ed mallets and handles; packed in strong [d]ove-tailed box, with hinged cover..............$1.00
2. Same, finer quality. Mallets and balls [w]ell painted, and varnished all over............ 1.45
3. Professional eight-handed Set, with 6-inch [m]allet heads................................. 2.85

4. Patent Socket Index Croquet. Eight-ball [se]t, varnished, with patent socket and index [pi]ns 1.35
5. Same, with ornamental painted mallets, [ba]lls and handles; two large fancy painted [st]akes, heavy enameled arches, and patent [so]cket and index pins...................... 2.50
6. Full Eight-ball Extra Set. Made in first-[c]lass style in every respect. Selected rock maple [b]alls and mallets, soaked in oil, with handles of [se]cond growth ash, finished with seven stripes; [fa]ncy turned and elegantly painted mallets and [st]akes; extra heavy enameled arches, with pa-[te]nt socket and index pins. A really magnificent [se]t. Price.................................... 3.25

Swings.

7. A neat Swing, with covered seat, and stout [ro]pes. Fitted with two screw bolts for adjust-[m]ent to any beam, limb or door frame. Price....$0.50
8. Same style as above, with wicker back and [si]des to seat, and front guard; for smaller chil-[dr]en's use.................................... 1.00
(By express only.)

Foot Balls.

9. 20 inches circumference, each............$1.15
10. 22 " " " 1.35
11. 24 " " " 1.75
12. 26 " " " 2.00
13. 28 " " " 2.50
14. 30 " " " 2.50
(By mail, 25c extra.)
15. Rubber Parlor Balls (plain) 2¼ inches [di]ameter.................................... 08
16. Rubber Parlor Balls (painted) 2¼ inches [di]ameter................................... 10
17. Quoits, japanned, per pound............ 08
18. Dumb Bells, polished maple, per pair, [1] lb., 65c; 2 lbs., 85c; 3 lbs., $1.10; 4 lbs........1.25
19. Iron Dumb Bells, nicely japanned, per lb. 08

20. Indian Clubs. The most healthful exercising implements ever invented, better than dumb bells, and fully equal to rowing. The best physicians recommend them as the most effectual means for expanding the chest, and improving the figure and carriage. The lighter sizes are intended for ladies' and children's use.

Weights,	1,	2,	3,	4 pounds,
Prices,	75c,	75c,	85c,	$1.00,
Weights,	5,	6,	7,	8 pounds.
Prices,	$1.00,	$1.00,	$1.50,	$1.50 per pair.

21. Kehoe's model Indian Clubs, first quality, per pair, 1 lb., $1.00; 2 lbs., $1.25; 3 lbs., $1.50; 4, 5 and 6 lbs., $2.00; 7 and 8 lbs., $2.50; 10 lbs.$3.00
22. Same, second quality, 5, 6 and 7 lbs., per pair... 1.00

Bat and Trap.

23. The Game of the Season. As here represented, the articles necessary to play this game, are *one bat, one ball,* and *the trap.* Any number of persons can engage in the game, from one to five on a side, and it can be played by ladies and gentlemen, or girls and boys. It can be played on the lawn, meadow, or any place where base ball, lawn tennis, or croquet are played. The ground need not be smooth as for croquet. It is very fascinating, and has as much variety as any other popular game. Rules accompany each game, and they are easily learned.$1.35

Battledores and Shuttlecocks.

24. Best Parchment Battledores, bound in red and gilt, per pair, 50c, 60c and.................$0.75
(By mail, 30c extra.)
25. Shuttlecocks, white feathers, per pair, 20c, 25c, 30c, 35c, 45c and........................... 50
26. Shuttlecocks, colored feathers, per pair, 25c, 30c, 35c, 40c, 50c and..................... 55
(By mail, 8c extra.)

Grace Hoops.

An old and well-established favorite of the young people. For training the body to full and graceful movements, this pastime has absolutely no superior.
27. Polished sticks, covered hoops, per set...$0.35
28. " " " velvet hoops, " ... 50
29. " " " large sized hoops " ... 65
(By mail, 35c per set extra.)

Toy Reins.

30. Made of variegated rope, in assorted colors, bells on head-band................................$0.12
31. The same, finer.......................... 18
32. Made of webbing, similar to large reins, with leather breast-band, larger bells, etc...... 35
(By mail, 5c extra.)

Skipping Ropes.

33. Plain Rope, colored handles, 6 feet......$0.05
34. " " " 8 " 10
35. Fancy Colored Rope, colored handles, 8 feet... 15
(By mail, 7c extra.)

36. Try Your Luck. A most amusing game for any number of players. The apparatus consists of a spring humming top, a circular tray of tin, 10 inches in diameter, and eight marbles. Around the circumference of the tray are eight slight depressions or cups, numbered from 1 to 8. The humming top is spun in the centre of the tray, and knocks the marbles about in a very amusing manner; and the player counts according to the number of the cups which remain filled after the top has stopped spinning. Price................ 50

ODDS AND ENDS FOR THE LITTLE FOLKS.

We present below illustrations and descriptions of a small line of Holiday Goods, which we offer at specially reduced pri and which are eminently suited for Birthday Presents. As the quantity on hand is limited, we cannot absolutely guarantee to orders; but we have very little doubt that the stock will prove large enough to satisfy our readers' demands.

1. The world-famous play of Punch and Judy. A most amusing mechanical toy.................$0.75
(By mail, 40c extra.)

2. Old Mother Hubbard Cupboard. A novel arrangement, by which the box containing a set of tea things is made to serve as an old fashioned cupboard with shelves, on which various articles can be nicely arranged and displayed. The cover can be transformed into a folding-leaf table, with four legs, which can be detached and replaced. Contains a complete set of doll's ware in wood... 60
(By mail, 50c extra.)

3. Crandall's Menagerie. Contains 15 animals, with their keeper, all well made, strong and durable, and can be arranged in an endless variety of positions and combinations. The toy is so arranged that it can be used either as a wagon, a beautiful cage, or a completely equipped traveling show. A toy to delight the heart of any child.. 1.00
(Cannot be sent by mail.)

4. Doll with patent indestructible head, arms and legs, stuffed body, glass eyes, and flowing hair. Fitted with chemise and painted boots. Height, 21 inches.......... $0.75

5. The same. Height, 16 inches..................... 40

6. Patent indestructible head, wooden arms and legs, stuffed body, glass eyes and flowing hair. Fitted with chemise and painted boots. Height, 15 inches........... 20

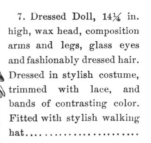

7. Dressed Doll, 14¼ in. high, wax head, composition arms and legs, glass eyes and fashionably dressed hair. Dressed in stylish costume, trimmed with lace, and bands of contrasting color. Fitted with stylish walking hat...................... 60

(By mail, 40c extra.)

8. Cow, on wheeled platform, 10 inches long by 6½ high. Covered with real hide. The cow can be made to low by turning her head to one side..... 65
(By mail, 25c extra.)

9. The Patent Bean Pistol. A popgun, operated by means of strong rubber springs. Shoots a bean, or paper wad, to considerable distance, and with very accurate aim..................... 25
(By mail, 8c extra.)

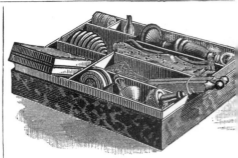

10. The Conjuror's Cabinet. Containing apparatus and instructions for performing nine of the most interesting tricks in the magician's repertoire.. $
(By mail, 30c extra.)
11. The same, smaller, containing six tricks...
(By mail, 18c extra.)

12. Elephant, with howdah, excursionists and mahout driving. Length, 9 inches..............
(By mail, 25c extra.)
13. The same, without howdah..............
(By mail, 18c extra.)

14. Trotting Horse, 9 inches long.............
(By mail, 25c extra.)

15. Locomotive Engine, 8 inches long.........
(By mail, 25c extra.)

1883

S. A. SMITH AND CO'S

Seventeenth Semi-Annual Catalogue and Price-List

—OF—

CHILDREN'S SLEIGHS,

DOLL CARRIAGES, EXPRESS WAGONS,

VELOCIPEDES, ROCKING HORSES,

CARTS, WHEELBARROWS, &c., &c.,

219 NORTH THIRD STREET,

PHILADELPHIA.

TALLY HO SULKY.

Each

No. 111.   Tally Ho Sulky, the leverage is so great that a small Boy can
drive it.   It is capable of greater speed than any other kind of
Propeller or Velocipede in the market.   It is suitable for Boys
only, of any age from 3 to 8 years.   It affords the finest exercise
for the arms and body, ... $ 9.00

No. 112.   Tally Ho sulky, larger size, suitable for boys from 8 to 15
years, ...   11.00

No. 1.

ROCKING HORSES.

													Each
No. 0.	Full Thug Trimmed, 4½x4½ block,						.	.	.	.	.	.	$1.00
No. 1.	"	"	"	5x5	"	hair tail,		.	.	.	.	.	1.25
No. 2.	"	"	"	5x5	"	tail, mane and stirrups,			.			.	1.45
No. 3.	"	"	"	6x6	"	"	"	"	"			.	1.95
No. 3½.	"	"	"	7x7	"	"	"	"	"	"		.	3.15

No. 4.	Full trimmed, 6x6 block,		.	.	.	.	.	$2.75
No. 5.	Carved legs and body, 6x6 block, tail, mane and stirrups,						.	4.00
No. 6,	"	"	"	7x7	"	"	"	"	.	5.00
No. 7.	"	"	"	8x8	"	"	"	"	.	6.50

No. 5.

PATENT LEAPING HORSES.

			Each
No. 125.	6 inch block, painted	. . . .	$10.00
No. 126.	7 inch " "	. . . .	12.00
No. 127.	8 inch " "	. . . .	14.00
No. 128.	9 inch " "	large double springs, ...	20.00

SPRING HORSES.

Each

No. 132.   7x7 inch body, full shape and trim, highly ornamented, and
           leather saddle, ... $ 9.50

No. 133.   8x8 inch body, full shape and trim, highly ornamented, and
           leather saddle, ...   11.50

No. 134.   10x10 inch body, full shape and trim, highly ornamented,
           and leather saddle, ...   15.00

GALLOPING SHOO FLY HORSE.

Something entirely new in the hobby-horse line; has given great satisfaction. Is so constructed that the motion imparted in rocking is precisely similar to the movement of a galloping horse, but is smooth and even.

					Each.
No. 21.	Small.	Upholstered with Oil Cloth,	. . . . . .	$2.25
No. 22	Medium.	" " "	. . . . .	2.95
No. 23.	" "	" Fancy Goods,	. . . .	3.40
No. 24.	Large.	" " Oil Cloth,	. . . .	3.40
No. 25.	" "	" Fancy Goods,	. . . .	3.95

GALLOPING HORSE.

The motion of this horse is the same as described on Page 11. The horses are well-made, mounted on substantial platforms, and finished in bright colors in a superior manner.

			Each
No. 13.	5x5 block, Thug Trimmed, with hair mane and tail and stirrups,		$2.75
No. 14.	6x6 " " " " " " "	.	4.20
No. 15.	6x6 " " " full saddle, mane, tail "	.	4.75
No. 16.	6x6 " Carved legs. " " " " " "	.	5.50
No. 17.	7x7 " " " " " " " " "	.	7.75
No. 18.	8x8 " " " " " " ' " "	.	9.25

QUADRICYCLES.

The **QUADRICYCLE** will be furnished in four sizes, viz :

									Each
No. 208.	Driving wheels 24 inches diam., for child of 3 to 5 years,							.	$ 7.50
No. 209.	"	"	28	"	"	"	5 to 8	"	.	10 00
No. 210.	"	"	32	"	"	"	7 to 10	"	.	12.00
No. 211.	"	"	36	"	"	"	9 to 14	"	.	15.00

HAND PROPELLERS.

		Price.
No. 14.	Patent Four-wheeled Velocipede, very strongly made, suitable for boys or girls from 3 to 5 years............	$4 38
No. 15.	Same style, suitable for boys or girls from 5 to 10 years..................	4 95
No. 16.	Same, larger, suitable for young ladies................................	5 38

BOYS' THREE-WHEELED VELOCIPEDES.

		Price.
No. 17.	13-inch Front Wheel, suitable for a child from 3 to 4 years...........	$2 85
No. 18.	16-inch Front Wheel, suitable for a child from 4 to 6 years...........	3 15
No. 19.	18-inch Front Wheel, suitable for boys from 6 to 8 years...........	3 45
No. 20.	21-inch Front Wheel, suitable for boys from 8 to 10 years...........	3 75
No. 21.	24-inch Front Wheel, suitable for boys from 10 to 14 years...........	4 20

(By Express or Freight only.)

GIRLS' TOY SAD IRONS.

PERFORATED IRON HANDLE.

WALNUT HANDLE.

Handle not Detachable.

No. 105, Plain, Polished, with Stand
for Each Iron, - - per dozen, $7 50

Handle Detachable.

No. 90, Nickel Plated, Complete with
Handle and Stand for Each
Iron, Weight 2 lbs., - per dozen, $7 50

TOY SAD IRON AND STAND.

TOY DUCK AND STAND.

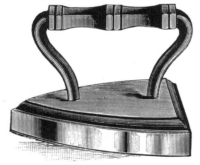

Plain Polished with Coppered Stand.

No. 75, Weight ½ lb. Each, - per dozen sets, $1 50

D, 2¾-inch Long, Fancy Painted, per dozen sets, $1 25
E, 3¼ " " " " " 1 50

2 1-2 LB. SAD IRON.

"GEM" WOOD HANDLE AND STAND.

Nickel per dozen, $5 50

No. 1, Size 2½ inches high 4 long, 2½ wide.

Polished, Japanned, Bronzed Stand, per doz. sets, $3 00

❀ Milwaukee, Wisconsin. ❀

TOY BANKS.

PUNCH & JUDY.

TRICK PONY.

Punch & Judy, all Iron, Highly Finished in Fancy Colors, 7½ inches High, 6¼ inches Wide, per dozen, $12 00
Judy receives the coin in the plate. The Thumb Piece at the side is pressed upon, when Judy turns and deposits the coin in the Bank.

Trick Pony, all Iron, Highly Finished in Fancy Colors, 8 inches High, 7¼ inches Long,   per dozen, $12 00
The Pony receives the coin in the mouth, and deposits it in the manger; a trap door at the bottom of the latter opens at same time, and then closes over the coin.

HUMPTY DUMPTY.

AMERICAN EAGLE.

Humpty Dumpty, all Iron, Highly Finished in Fancy Colors, 7½ inches High, 6 inches Wide, per dozen, $15 00
The coin is placed in the hand, the arm is then raised by a small projecting thumb piece behind the left shoulder, the coin being deposited in the mouth, the tongue falling back and the eyes rolling upwards at the same time.

American Eagle, all Iron, Highly Finished in Fancy Colors, 8 inches Long, 6 inches High, 4 inches
Wide,   -   -   -   -   -   -   -   -   -   -   -   -   per dozen, $15 00
Place a coin in the Eagle's Beak, press the lever and the Eaglets rise from the nest actually crying for food. As the Eagle bends forward to feed the Eaglets the coin falls into the nest and disappears.

MINIATURE STEAM LOCOMOTIVE AND RAILWAY.

ONE OF THE LATEST AND BEST NOVELTIES.

A practical toy, and perfectly safe. Can not explode. So simple that a child 10 years of age can run one and keep it in working order by following the printed directions. Amusing and instructive to the whole family. Made in the most careful manner. Every Engine thoroughly tested with steam, and in good running order before leaving the Factory. A great attraction for store windows. Will run from twenty to thirty minutes, the driving wheels making from ten to fifteen revolutions per second, the exhaust steam escaping from the smoke-stack. Will draw a train of cars, giving it the exact appearance of a train on a large road. Engine and track may be packed in a space 5x7 inches, and 25 inches long.

4 wheel Locomotive with Circular Track...Price complete, $6 00
Full Nickel-plated 4 wheel Locomotive with Circular Track.................... "   "   9 00
Tracks 4 feet 4 inches in diameter.
Express Car.........................each, $1 00 | Passenger Car ....each, $1 25
Palace Car.......................... "   1 50 | Extra Tracks for Steam Locomotives.. "   1 50

No. 19-0.—FINE MECHANICAL LOCOMOTIVES.

Length, 8¼ inches; height, 5¼ inches. The above cut of our Mechanical Locomotive, which the trade will pronounce to be the most perfect toy of the kind ever offered at so low a price. It is neatly and strongly made, and works perfectly well. Each one in a neat box.................Price, $1 00.

No. 19-1.—Length, 9½ inches; height, 7 inches. Each one in a neat box.
Price, $1 75

No. 19-3.—Large Fine Locomotive, length, 11¼ inches; height, 8¼ inches. Each one in a neat box...................Price, $3 00

19-2—WHISTLING LOCOMOTIVES.

These locomotives are the same sizes as those mentioned above and are provided with our *patent whistling arrangement*, so that when running they give forth a sharp, shrill, rapid whistle, making them among the most attractive and salable toys ever put upon the market. (See cut.)......Price, each, $3 00

No. 19-4—Whistler, length, 11¼ inches; height, 8¼ inches. Each one in a neat box.
Price, $3 50

IRON FREIGHT TRAIN, "BIG 6," (24 inches long.)

This train is strongly made and neatly painted, and consists of a locomotive, tender, and two cars. Made entirely of iron. A very salable toy. Each train in a strong wood box.   Price, each, $1 00
N. B.—We carry a full stock of Imported Model Steam Locomotives. Price, $5 00 to $75 00 each.

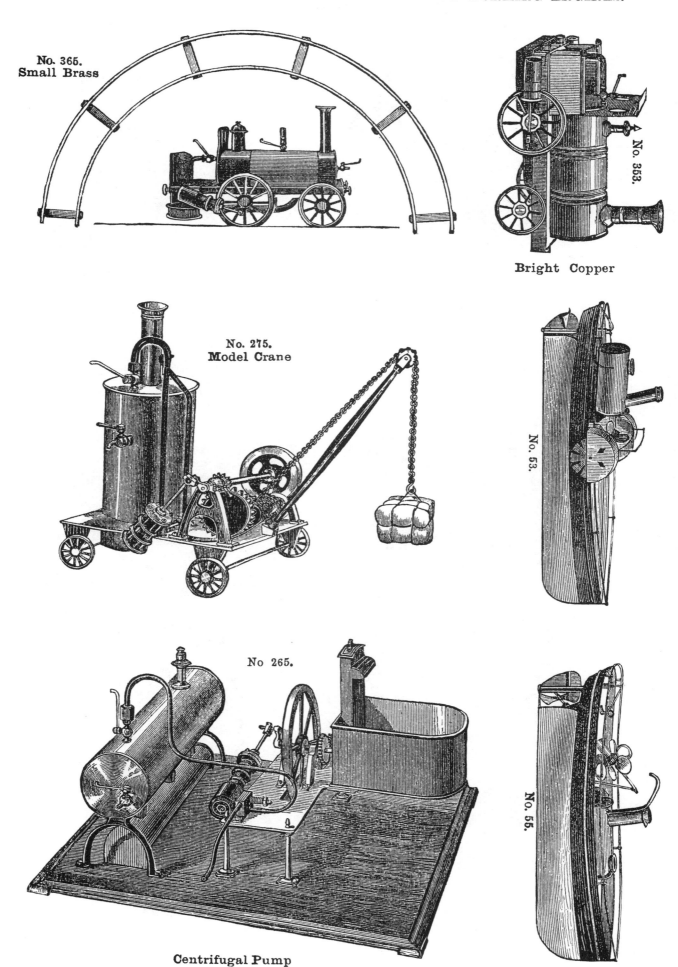

No. 365.
Small Brass

No. 353.

Bright Copper

No. 275.
Model Crane

No. 53.

No 265.

No. 55.

Centrifugal Pump

STRONG IRON SAVINGS BANKS FOR CHILDREN.

No. 200. Height, 8 in. Length, 7½ in. Width, 3 in.
Price,..................................$1 00

No. 265. Height, 8¼ in, Length, 7¾ in. Width, 3½.
Price,..................................$1 00

No. 285. Height, 6½ in. Width, 5¼ in. Depth, 5¼ in.
Price,..................................$1 00

No. 275. Length, 4¼ in. Height, 3⅝ in. Width, 3 in.
Price,..................................50 cts.

No. 120. Height, 6¾ in. Width, 4⅔ in. Depth, 4⅔ in.
Price,..................................$1 00

No. 111. Height, 3 in. Diameter. 4 in
Price,..........................50 cts.

(1889)

WALBRIDGE & CO., BUFFALO, N. Y.

TOY SAVINGS BANKS.
MADE WHOLLY OF IRON, HIGHLY FINISHED IN BRILLIANT COLORS.

"Jolly Nigger," .... $ 5.45 dozen.
"Humpty Dumpty," .... 7.15 "
"Uncle Sam," .... 8.00 "
"Stump Speaker," .... 8.00 "

"TRICK DOG"
TOY SAVINGS BANK.

Size 7½ inches high, 8¾ inches long.

(EXCELSIOR SERIES.)

Made wholly of iron. Highly finished in brilliant colors. Coin is placed in the dog's mouth. When the thumb piece is pressed upon, the dog jumps through hoop held by clown and deposits the coin in top of barrel. Trap door in barrel prevents coin from being shaken out.

"Santa Claus," .... $ 3.75 dozen.
"Trick Dog," .... 8.00 "
"Mason," .... 8.00 "
"Speaking Dog," .... 8.00 "
"Trick Pony," .... 7.45 "
"Punch and Judy," .... 7.45 "

Net.

51

WALBRIDGE & CO., BUFFALO, N. Y.

INDESTRUCTIBLE MALLEABLE IRON AND STEEL

• TOYS •

NEW DESIGNS.   BEAUTIFULLY FINISHED.

No. A. SULKY.

Horse, Black ; Harness, Gilt Trimmed ; Sulky, Black, Gilt Striped ; Driver in Jockey Costume, $ 4.00 dozen.

No. B. DRAY.

Horse, Black ; Harness, Gilt Trimmed ; Dray, Wheels Red, Sides and Front Green, Gilt Striped ;

Load, one box . . . . $ 4.00 dozen.

Net.

INDESTRUCTIBLE MALLEABLE IRON AND STEEL TOYS.

No. 1. SINGLE TRUCK.

Horse, Black ; Harness, Silver Trimmed ; Collar and Housings, Red. Truck—Gear, Red, Black Striped ; Side Stakes, Green ; Panels and Foot Board, Red, Gilt Striped. Load— One Box, One Barrel, One Sack.. $ 8.50 dozen.

No. J. DOUBLE TRUCK.

Horses, Black ; Harness, Gilt Trimmed ; Hames and Collar, Red. Truck—Gear Red, Black Striped ; Side Stakes Green, Gilt Striped ; Panels, Seat and Foot Board, Red. Load—Two Boxes, Two Barrels, One Sack................................. $18.75 dozen.

No. G. RAILROAD TRAIN.

Locomotive—Boiler Black, Gilt Bands ; Wheels, Red ; Stack Red and Black. Brass Bell. Cab, Maroon, Gilt Striped ; Tender, Black, Red Wheels, Gold Number. Cars, Red, Black Lettered. Wheels, Black. Total Length of Train, 34 inches.................. $ 8.50 dozen.

Net.

HAND SLEIGHS.

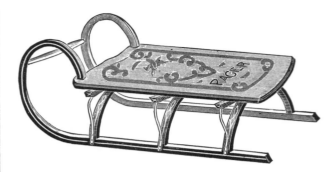

No. 26.   Has two knees bent in form of one-half circle, strongly made and braced, handsomely painted and ornamented, half-oval shoes. Size, 12 x 32 inches.............. $ 8.05 dozen.

No. 28.   Has three knees bent in form of one-half circle, strongly made and braced, handsomely painted and ornamented, with half oval shoes. Size, 12½ x 34 inches......... $ 9.10 dozen.

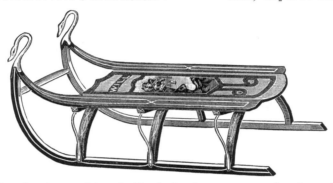

No. 30.   Three knees bent in the form of one-half circle, has swan necks, braced down to the runner, neatly painted and ornamented ; half-oval shoes.   Size 13 x 32 inches..... $ 8.40 dozen.

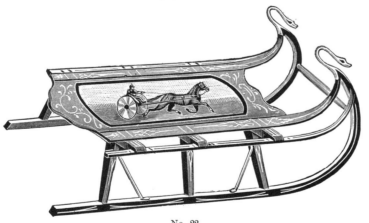

No. 22.

CHAMFERED KNEE SLEIGHS.

No. 22.   Strong, and a very neatly painted and ornamented Sleigh, with chamfered knees, fenders, and swan necks, with heavy half-oval shoes and tinned wrought iron braces.

Size, 16 x 36 inches............$ 17.50 dozen.

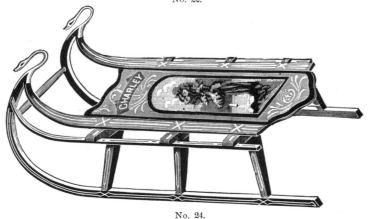

No. 24.

No. 24.   Neatly painted and ornamented Sleigh, with fenders, swan necks, chamfered knees, half-oval shoes.

Size, 16 x 36 inches............$ 16.10 dozen.

Net.

WALBRIDGE & CO., BUFFALO, N. Y.

No. 20. A very strong and beautiful Oak Sleigh. The knees made in the form of a half circle. Thoroughly strengthened by tinned braces brought down to the runners, and neatly ornamented ; half oval shoes. Size, 12 x 32 inches............................ $ 12.60 dozen.

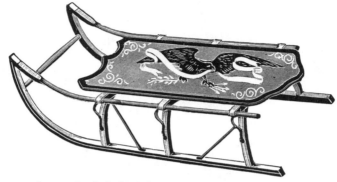

No. 21. A strong and very neatly made Oak Sleigh ; the knees bent in form of a half circle. Thoroughly strengthened by tinned braces brought down to the runners, and neatly ornamented ; half oval shoes. Size, 13 x 34 inches........................... $ 14.70 dozen.

NEW PATTERN SLEIGHS.

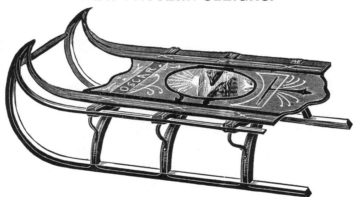

No. 17. Has three knees, made in a form of a half circle, braced and made very neatly, strong, with square fender, handsomely decorated, shod with half-oval iron. Size 15x35 inches $ 11.20 dozen.

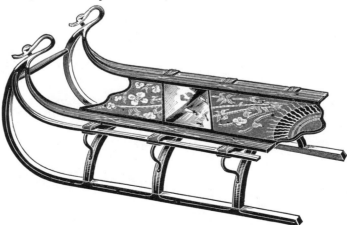

No. 19. A similar sleigh to No. 17, has swan necks, is braced and highly ornamented. Size, 15 x 35 inches... $ 13.30 dozen.

Net.

Our New Dressed Doll, Paulina.

Concerning Paulina.

BOSTON, MASS., MARCH 3, 1889.

MESSRS. ————,

DEAR SIRS : This season we wish to arrange with you to manufacture for us jointed Dolls, the same model as you made for us last year. We wish, *in addition*, that each Doll shall be furnished with a complete Wardrobe, including a trimmed hat.

Please make samples for us and dress with a variety of suits, and forward to us for examination by first steamer.

Yours very truly, PERRY MASON & COMPANY.

In response to the above letter we received the samples in due time, made our selection, and then gave the manufacturers a contract to make for us a large number of Dressed Dolls.

The Doll is made after the celebrated Jumeau model, having the ball and socket joints at the elbows, shoulders, knees and hips, also joint at the neck, so that the head can be turned naturally. It has a beautiful Bisque head, with " natural " eyes and flowing hair.

The Kitchen Set and Dishes.

All given for one new name.

This Set consists of a nice Stove and Furniture, and about 50 useful Tin Dishes, Tea Kettle, etc., etc. The cut gives you a little idea of the variety. No Rolling Pin goes with this Set. This premium is about double the value of the one given last year for one new name.

We give the Set entire for one new name. For sale by us for 90 cts. **Postage and packing, 40 cts.**, when sent as a premium or purchased ; or sent by express, and charges paid by receiver.

Doll's Metal Bedstead, with Mattress and Pillows.

Given for one new name.

This beautiful Bedstead will be a delight to a "little mother" for all the year round. It is made of solid metal, bright finish. It is very durable, and can be folded flat. Size, 11 x 18 inches. The handsomely striped Mattress and Pillows are all made up ready for use.

Premium offer above. Price, complete, $1. **They must be sent by express, and charges paid by receiver**, when sent as a premium or purchased.

Doll's Dressmaking Establishment.

Given for one new name.

What little girl does not find her greatest delight in making and dressing paper Dolls ? This is a large and complete Outfit of bodies, heads, legs, arms, fancy paper and colored tissue for dresses, lace paper, silver paper, etc., in great variety. Also, complete directions. We never saw a collection so complete, and so well adapted to its purpose. It's a regular Doll's Bazaar. All enclosed in a handsome box, and will furnish hours of profitable amusement.

Given for one new name. Price, $1. **Postage and packing, 35 cts.**, when sent as a premium or purchased.

Doll's Saratoga Trunk, for " Paulina."

Given for one new name, and 25 cts. additional.

This handsome and well-made Doll's Trunk should belong to every child who possesses one of our Dolls. It is made with a real "Saratoga" shape. It has partitions for bonnets, dresses, and other portions of a Doll's wardrobe.

The Trunk is 16 inches long, 10 inches wide and 12 inches high, and is fastened by lock and key. It also has leather straps and handles, and metal guards. The Trunk is sufficiently large for an extensive Doll's wardrobe.

Given for one new name, and 25 cts. additional.

The Village Church.

Given for one new name, and 10 cts. additional.

Of the Toys introduced into our the first place. It is composed of packed in a convenient wood Case, forms a beautiful Gothic Church, as inches, and 18 inches to the top of are handsomely painted in colors, in

own family, this one takes only thirty parts, all and when put together, seen in a cut, 10 x 14 the steeple. The windows imitation of stained glass.

Scripture Texts. On the inside of the blocks, composing the different parts of the Church, Scripture Texts from the Bible are printed.

Any child can easily put it together. It is durable, and will last for years. It is certainly one of the very best, as well as most useful of Toys. Last year the demand for this Toy was greater than the supply.

Given for one new name, and 10 cts. additional. Price, $1. **It must be sent by express, and charges paid by receiver**, when sent as a premium or purchased.

The Youth's Companion (1886-1889)

During the Summer

the manufacturers have been busy with our large order for Dolls. Nimble fingers and skilled hands have cut the little dresses and underclothing, fashioned and trimmed the pretty hats, knit the tiny stockings, and made the dainty shoes. Other hands have dressed the Dolls, and arranged their toilet for the long ocean voyage.

The Voyage Ended.

Think of it ! Thousands of beautiful Dolls, all dressed just alike. How in the world they are able to make and dress them at the price, we do not understand. We have heard mothers say that it is easier to dress little girls than Dolls.

The Dolls are beauties, and we are very sure the little girls will love Paulina better than they have loved Cousins Reta, Adele, or Elena.

Given for one new name, and 25 cts. additional. Price, only $1.25. **Postage and packing, 40 cts.**, when sent as a premium or purchased.

Child's Decorated China Tea Set, No. 72½.

23 Pieces. Given for one new name, and 10 cts. additional.

This is the largest and prettiest Child's imported Tea Set we ever used. Each piece is beautifully hand-painted in colors, with gold lines. The Set consists of 23 pieces,—Tea Pot, Sugar Bowl, Cream Pitcher, 6 Plates, and 6 Cups and Saucers. The Tea Pot is 5 inches high, other pieces in proportion.

Given for one new name, and 10 cts. additional. Price, $1. **It must be sent by express, and charges paid by receiver**, when sent as a premium or purchased.

Gilt Edge Building Blocks, No. 4.

Given for one new name, and 10 cts. additional.

Well-made Building Blocks are a source of delight to a child. The Blocks which we offer are made of fine-grained hard wood, and fit each other with great accuracy.

The variety and quantity of Blocks are sufficient to build the most elaborate models, while the number of combinations that can be made is almost unlimited. They stand firmly, are indestructible, and will afford a profitable and fascinating pastime. A sheet of building designs is given with each box. The engraving shows a few of the Blocks only. The Set complete contains 162 Blocks.

Given for one new name, and 10 cts. additional. Price, $1. **It must be sent by express, and charges paid by receiver**, when sent as a premium or purchased.

Child's Toy Parlor Set, No. 7,124, and Three French

Paper Dolls, with Wardrobe. Given for one new name.

This Set comprises nine pieces, including a real Marble-Top Table, Sofa, six Chairs and a Bureau. It is imitation ebony and gold upholstered in figured cretonne. We have no room for cut. We also give three beautiful Paper Dolls, with Wardrobe of thirty-two pieces—two girls and a boy ; the faces and suits are lithographed in beautiful colors. Full directions.

All given for one new name. Price, 90 cts **Postage and packing, 35 cts.**, when sent as a premium or purchased.

Doll's Carriage, with Canopy.

This Carriage will delight the heart of every child who loves a Doll. It is just the right size for the beautiful Doll we offer.

The basket is made of woven willow, lined with light blue silesia and lace edging. The blue Canopy has a frame of wire ribs, allowing it to be either opened or closed, or taken off, if you wish. The Perambulator stands about 22 in. high.

Given for one new name,

56

Battledoor and Shuttlecock.

Given for one new name, and 10 cts. additional.

This is always an interesting as well as healthful sport for both in and out of doors. Price, $1. Given for one new name, and 10 cts. additional. **Postage and packing, 20 cts.**, when sent as a premium or purchased.

Gold-Plated Thimble and Scissors.

Given for one new name.

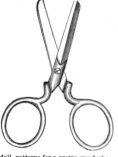

This premium has been selected with special reference to the many young girls who may obtain one of the Bisque Dolls. You will see that we give with each doll, patterns for a pretty wardrobe.

Now every little girl ought to have a pair of Scissors of *her own* with which to cut out the garments.

We here offer a *fine* pair with *blunt* points, just suited for the girls. We give with the Scissors a beautiful gold-plated Thimble.

These goods are useful for the mother's work-basket also.

Both given for one new name. Price, 90 cts. **Postage and packing, 10 cts.**, when sent as a premium or purchased.

Jack and Jill Marble Toy.

This pretty Toy is made for the little folks. It will amuse the children for hours. By pressing a lever, "Jack" tips the marble into the race-way. The marble rolls along down. Jack bends over, holds the bucket in position and catches the ball as it rolls off. He then stands up and rolls the ball again into the race-way, and so on. We will send one of these pretty games to any address for 25 cts. **Postage and packing, 25 cts.** additional.

Improved American Panorama. Given for one new name.

This Panorama consists of thirty-five colored pictures of scenes in American history arranged on rolls. By turning the crank they are presented to view. We include 42 Tickets, Lectures, etc.

Given for one new name. Price, 90 cts. **Postage and packing, 25 cts.**, when sent as a premium or purchased.

Beautiful Bisque Doll,

AND PAPER PATTERNS FOR DOLL'S WARDROBE.

Given for only one new name, and 15 cts. additional.

All Bisque Dolls are very durable and not easily broken. They are also handsomer and far superior to any Wax Doll made. Our new Bisque Doll is exceedingly beautiful, and far ahead of even the one offered last year.

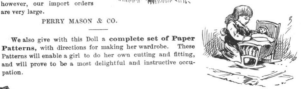

TO MY FRIENDS:

My name is Adèle, and I've just come from France. My sister Reta, who came to visit you last year, had such a good time that I've come too. I am nearly 16 in. tall—three more than Reta—and have light blue eyes and long golden hair. I have come with a whole set of Paper Patterns for my wardrobe, and I know that you will enjoy making my trousseau. I will stand very still when you fit my clothes, and won't make the least trouble.

ADÈLE.

ADÈLE is the finest and most beautiful Doll we have ever offered. Last year the demand for little "RETA" was so great that our supply was exhausted long before the holidays were over. This year, however, our import orders are very large.

PERRY MASON & CO.

We also give with this Doll a **complete set of Paper Patterns**, with directions for making her wardrobe. These Patterns will enable a girl to do her own cutting and fitting, and will prove to be a most delightful and instructive occupation.

The head, neck and hands are made from real French Bisque. It has a **jointed kid body**, and is well stuffed. The **head is movable**, and can be turned in natural positions. The long flaxen hair, the "human" eyes, the rosy cheeks and beautiful expression of this pretty Doll will captivate any little girl's heart. It has lace stockings and slippers with bright buckles. Height 15½ inches.

Given for only one new name, and 15 cts. additional. Price, $1.15. **Postage and packing, 35 cts.**, when sent as a premium or purchased.

Tivoli Board, No. 2058-44, and 2,000 Riddles.

All given for one new name.

The pretty game of Tivoli is always fascinating to the children. The Board we offer is 9 x 17¼ in. The game can be played by any number of persons, and is quite amusing for the social or family circle. We have also added **Two Books of Riddles**, 1,000 Riddles in each book—over 100 pages in each book. No two Riddles alike.

The Tivoli Board, and two Riddle Books, all given for one new name. Price of all, $1. **Postage and packing, 50 cts.**, when sent as a premium or purchased. Price of Tivoli Board, only $1, postpaid. Price of one Riddle Book, 18 cts., postpaid. Price of both Riddle Books, 30 cts., postpaid.

Folding-Chair for Adèle.

We place this Chair on the list for the special use of little Adèle, the pretty miss who has just come over from Paris, and for little Reta, who came over last year.

The Chair is neatly made from birch, has a pretty cloth seat, and fancy-sawed back. It is 11 inches high. Every little girl who has a doll will be delighted with this Folding-Chair.

We will send one of these Chairs to any address for 25 cts. **Postage and packing, 15 cts.** additional.

Package of Toys for Little Ones.

Given for one new name.

This consists of—1st, A Choral Top, in which are placed organ reeds tuned in harmony. When this Top spins the reeds give forth a sweet harmony, which constantly changes, according to the speed of the Top. 2d, A beautiful Rubber Ball. 3d, A very pretty Rubber Doll, ready dressed.

All given for one new name. Price, 75 cts. **Postage and packing, 25 cts.**, when sent as a premium or purchased.

Numerical Frame. Given for one new name.

This Frame is 9x12 in. in size. On this Frame are strung on pins 144 wooden balls in green, red and black colors.

With this Frame teachers and parents can illustrate principles in arithmetic much quicker than by other methods.

As a mere toy it is attractive to the children. A child will spend hours in arranging various combinations of shapes and colors. Given for one new name. Price, 75c. **Postage and packing, 25 cts.**, when sent as a premium or purchased.

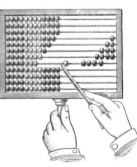

Tin Kitchen Set and Dishes.

All given for one new name.

This Set consists of a nice Stove and Furniture, and about 50 useful Tin Dishes, Tea Kettle, &c., &c. The cut gives you a little idea of the variety. No Rolling Pin goes with this set. This premium is about double the value of the one given last year for one new name. We give the entire Set for one new name. For sale by us for 90 cts.

Doll's Toy Parlor Set, No. 7124, and Three

French Paper Dolls with Wardrobe. Given for one name.

This Set comprises nine pieces, including a real Marble-Top Table, Sofa, six Chairs and a Bureau. It is imitation ebony and gold upholstered in figured cretonne, and is much handsomer than cut shows. We also give three beautiful Paper Dolls with Wardrobe of thirty-two pieces—two girls and a boy; the faces and suits are lithographed in beautiful colors.

Child's Decorated China Tea Set, No. 72 1-2.

23 Pieces. Given for one new name, and 10 cts. additional.

This is the largest and prettiest Child's imported Tea Set we ever used. Each piece is beautifully hand-painted in colors with gold lines. The Set consists of 23 pieces—**Tea Pot, Sugar Bowl, Cream Pitcher, 6 Plates and 6 Cups and Saucers.** The Tea Pot is 5 in. high, and other pieces in proportion. All packed in moss in a wooden box. Given for one new name,

The Young Storekeeper's Outfit, with Cash Carrier.

Our Latest for Young People.

This is one of our most attractive premiums for the young people. It consists of: 1st, A Box containing an assortment of Toy Money, representing gold and silver coin to the amount of $100 ; 2d, Four sheets of Labels, 140 in all, to be cut up and attached separately to packages of bran or sawdust, supposed to contain whatever is printed on the Label ; 3d, A form for making Paper Bags, with an assortment of bag paper ; 4th, A printed price list of general merchandise, groceries, dry goods, fancy goods, hardware, etc., etc. ; 5th, One Rapid Transit Cash Carrier. The Cash Carrier is complete, ready to set up, as seen in the cut. A bright boy and girl will need no instruction as to the proper way to "run a store."

Not only will this novel premium serve to amuse and entertain, but it will teach the children in a very practical way the use of money, how to make change rapidly, how to buy and sell, and to transact business.

Given for one new name, and 10 cts. additional. Price, $1.25. Postage and packing, 25 cts., when sent as a premium or purchased. This will prove a popular game.

Ten Social Games for the Home. Given for one new name.

Nickel Bracket Saw Outfit.

Given for one new name.

This Outfit now consists of 1 Nickel-Plated Bracket Saw Frame, 5 x 12 inches, 24 Saw Blades; 1 sheet Impression Paper ; 1 Manual of Sawing and Wood-Carving ; Designs for Brackets, etc., full size ; 1 Drill Point.

Below is a list of some of the useful articles which any boy or girl can easily make. We give over 70 original and choice designs with the Saw, but as our space is limited, we number but twenty-four: **Match Safes, Toilet Racks, Card Receivers, Picture Rests, Photograph Frames** (Cabinet Size), **Wall Brackets, Paper Knives, Hanging Baskets, Stereoscopic View Holders, Pen Racks, Watch Stands, Glove Boxes, Beautiful Work Boxes, Handkerchief Boxes, Pretty Easels, Wall Pockets, Fancy Ornamental Designs, Letter Boxes, Book Covers, Table Mats, Yarn Winders, Flower Stands, Mirror Frames.**

Given for one new name. Price, $1 Postage and packing, 25 cts., when sent as a premium or purchased.

Outfit for Tapping Boots and Shoes.

Given for one new name, and 60 cts. additional.

Most people look upon the work of tapping boots or shoes as a very difficult thing to do. With proper appliances, however, a person soon discovers that it is really a very simple matter. He also discovers that he can save a large per cent. of his expenses for repairs by doing his own work.

Our Outfit is very complete. It not only contains a large assortment of appliances for tapping boots or shoes, but also for sewing leather, harnesses, etc. A pair of Taps and Heel-lifts, all cut and shaped, ready for nailing to the shoe, and full directions, are also given with each Outfit.

With this Outfit even a boy can soon learn to do the repairing in his own home, at a large saving to the family pocket-book. He can also earn considerable sums of money by receiving orders from friends and neighbors.

Price of complete Outfit, $2. Given for one new name, and 60 cts. additional. Sent by express, and charges paid by receiver, when sent as a premium or purchased.

This novel idea of setting up the "family cobbler" in business with a full kit of tools has met with a successful response from our subscribers. We now offer it the second season, and feel more confident than ever that this combination of tools will find a place in many homes.

Improved Foot-Power Scroll Saw and Lathe.

Description of the New Rogers Scroll Saw.

The entire frame-work is made from iron, painted and japanned black, and ornamented with red and gilt stripes.

The arbors, etc., are made of steel, and are all carefully gauged and fitted to their bearings. The Arms and Pitman are of the best selected ash.

We provide each machine with a Dust Blower, which is a very great advantage.

The Balance Wheel is 4¼ inches in diameter, and has a rim of solid Emery for grinding and polishing.

The attachment for Drilling is on the right-hand side of the machine. Each machine is set up, run and carefully inspected before leaving the factory ; it is then taken down and shipped in a box.

The machine is provided with a Tilting-Table for inlaying. With each machine we give **24 Saw Blades, Screwdriver, Belt Hooks, Direction Sheet, Wrench, 71 Designs, and 6 Drill Points.** The Saw alone weighs 25 lbs.; Saw and Box together, 45 lbs. Price of this fine machine, with extras, $3.50.

This machine is the strongest and in every respect the most satisfactory working amateur Scroll Saw that has yet been made.

Given for three new names, and 35 cts. additional ; or two new names, and 85 cts. additional; or one new name, and $1 35 additional.

The Companion Lathe and Saw is the best combination Lathe and Jig Saw now made. It combines the most valuable qualities and improvements of all our former styles. The superior points of this machine are found in the following reasons : 1, Strong and heavy castings and extra finish. 2, Large Treadle. 3, Automatic Dust Blower. 4, Anti-friction Dust Wheel. 5, Large Emery Wheel 6, Rigid Head and Tail Stocks. 7, Improved Saw Clamps. 8, New Straining Rod. 9, High Speed. The Lathe will turn a piece of wood 16 in. in length. Swing of Lathe, 3½ inches. We send with each machine **3 Turning Tools, Screwdriver, Belt Hooks, Direction Sheet, Wrench, 24 Saw Blades, 6 Drill Points, 71 Designs.**

Weight of machine, 50 lbs. Boxed, all ready for shipping, about 75 lbs.

Given for nine new names ; or for six new names, and $1.50 additional; or three new names, and $3 additional. Price of machine, $8.50 complete.

New Rogers Scroll Saw.

Companion Lathe and Scroll Saw.

Nickel Bracket Saw Outfit.

WITH OUR BRACKET SAW OUTFIT

tens of thousands of homes have been made more beautiful, young people have been made happy, money has been earned, and time (often spent in the streets) has been usefully and profitably employed.

Below is a list of some of the useful articles which any boy or girl can easily make. We give over 70 original and choice designs with the Saw, but as our space is limited, we number but twenty-four: **Match Safes, Toilet Racks, Card Receivers, Picture Rests, Photograph Frames** (Cabinet Size), **Wall Brackets, Paper Knives, Hanging Baskets, Stereoscopic View Holders, Pen Racks, Watch Stands, Glove Boxes, Beautiful Work Boxes, Handkerchief Boxes, Pretty Easels, Wall Pockets, Fancy Ornamental Designs, Letter Boxes, Book Covers, Table Mats, Yarn Winders, Flower Stands, Mirror Frames, Photograph Frames** (Card Size).

Given for one new name. Price, $1. **Postage and packing, 30 cts.**, when sent as a premium or purchased.

Improved Companion Tool Chest.

CONTENTS OF CHEST.

The Chest contains the following Tools: — 12-inch Hand-Saw, Block Plane, Bit Brace, 3 Bits, Screw-Driver, Draw Knife, Hammer, Compasses, Chisel (¼-inch), Chisel (½-inch), Scratch Awl, Pliers, Two-Foot Rule, Try Square, Gauge, 2 Gimlets, Awl, Mallet, File, Plumb Bob, Chalk Line, Nail Set, Monkey Wrench, Bench Vise, Spirit Level, Screw-Driver for Bit Brace, Hand Clamp, Bottle Le Page's Glue, making thirty-one different Tools in all.

We have published a special edition of the valuable book, "How to Use Wood-Working Tools." This book contains about ninety cuts, many of them full-page in size, showing how to use the Tools. This book we give free with each Chest. Price of book alone, 50 cts., postage paid by us.

The Chest of Tools, with Book, given for three new names, and $2 additional. Price, $5. **It must be sent by express**, and charges paid by receiver, when sent as a premium or purchased.

Nickel-Plated Bit-Brace and Five Auger Bits.

Bit Brace given for one new name. Five Auger Bits for one new name, and 10 cts. additional.

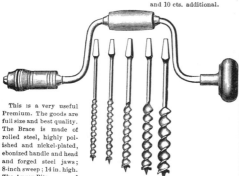

This is a very useful Premium. The goods are full size and best quality. The Brace is made of rolled steel, highly polished and nickel-plated, ebonized handle and head and forged steel jaws; 8-inch sweep; 14 in. high. The Auger Bits are good quality, and the sizes most used, viz., ¼, ⅜, ½, ⅝, ¾.

We give the Brace for one new name. Price, $1. **Postage and packing, 40 cts.**, when sent as a premium or purchased. We also give the set of five Bits for one new name, and 10 cts. additional. Price, $1.10 for the set. **Postage and packing, 20 cts.**, when sent as a premium or purchased.

The Whitney Breast Drill, with Six Twist Drills.

All given for one new name.

This is a first-class tool. It is the latest improved and best Hand Drill that has ever been made. It is the largest Drill we have ever offered—10½ inches long, wheel 3½ inches diameter. It is nicely japanned and striped in red and gold. It has Wrench and six improved twist Drills of different sizes, made of best tempered steel, also an improved Chuck for holding the drill points firmly. All enclosed in a hinged wooden box, with upright rack for holding drills.

All given for only one new name. For sale by us for $1. **Postage and packing, 25 cts.**, when sent as a premium or purchased.

Six Carving Tools and Instruction Book

In a Black Walnut Case. Given for one new name.

Wood Carving is growing in favor each year. Girls as well as boys engage in this delightful employment.

The Carving Tools we here offer are manufactured expressly for the COMPANION readers. With the Book of Instruction you can learn this pleasant and profitable art. The cut shows the different shapes of the tools. There

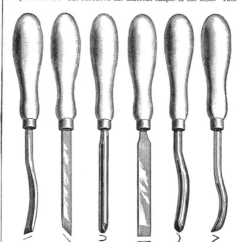

are six tools in the set, and they all have Rosewood handles, and are sharpened ready for use. The process of carving is very simple. It is now eight years since we first made this set of tools for our subscribers. The demand for them now is as great as ever.

We give with each set of tools twelve designs; among these designs there is a pattern for a Bread Board with oak leaf border. This elegant Bread Board is not only useful but very pretty.

All given for one new name. Price, $1. **Postage and packing, 10 cts.**, when sent as a premium or purchased.

Set of Tools, No. 60. Given for one new name.

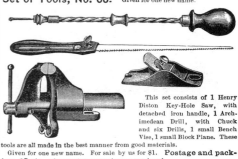

This set consists of 1 Henry Diston Key-Hole Saw, with detached iron handle, 1 Archimedean Drill, with Chuck and six Drills, 1 small Bench Vise, 1 small Block Plane. These tools are all made in the best manner from good materials.

Given for one new name. For sale by us for $1. **Postage and packing, 25 cts.**, when sent as a premium or purchased.

Soldering Casket, Glass Cutter, and Crispin's

Pocket Companion. Given for one new name.

We recommend the use of a Soldering Set in every home. It will pay for itself many times over every year, beside saving the trouble of sending to the tin-shop whenever the tin dish leaks. The set consists of a fine Soldering

Iron, with solid copper end, one Bar of Solder, one Scraper and a box of powdered Resin, and Directions. We also give a reliable Glass Cutter and a Crispin's Pocket Companion. The cut shows a sectional view of the Companion and tools, etc., enclosed. All given for one new name. Price, 80 cts. **Postage and packing, 20 cts.**, when sent as a premium or purchased.

Improved Patent Pocket Tool-Holder and Ten Large Tools.

THE TOOLS.

We call your attention to the quality of the Tools we give with this Holder.

These tools are all made from the best quality of steel, and are well sharpened and tempered, ready for use.

The cut shows this Tool-Holder at about two-thirds its full size, and a sectional view of the hollow handle, where the tools are kept when not in use. The handle is made from rosewood,

highly polished, and has a Lignum Vitæ screw cap. The chuck is polished steel, nickeled, and will hold any tool, from a pin to a large millfile. This tool is so very useful and convenient that it ought to be in every family in the country. It will earn its price for you many times over in a year.

Given for one new name and 10 cents additional. For sale by us for $1. **Postage and packing 15 cts.**, when sent as a premium or purchased.

American Side-Wheel Steamer "Acushnet."

Given for one new name, and 85 cts. additional.

A Beauty.

This beautiful Side-wheel Steamer, built expressly for our use, is modelled after the famous steamers that once sailed between New Bedford and Martha's Vineyard.

Before the manufacturer was able to offer these boats for sale it necessitated the employment of expert machinists for nearly a year, and the expenditure of a large amount of money.

Description.

We now offer them to our subscribers for the first time. The Steamers are twelve inches in length, are painted with a bronze bottom, white side and yellow top, with stripings of red and gilt, have a rocking-beam motion, and a tight fuel compartment, which leads from the bow to the reservoir.

Not Explosive.

It cannot explode, is perfectly safe, and will steam on a smooth body of water for over half an hour with only one filling of the boiler.

The boiler is capable of developing a large steam-power reserve.

Scientific Toys.

This Steamboat adds one more to the list of Scientific Toys brought out by THE YOUTH'S COMPANION. We believe, as far as it is possible, that it is wise to combine instruction with amusement.

Given for only one new name, and 85 cts. additional. Price, $2.50. Postage and packing, 30 cts. additional, when sent as a premium or purchased.

Royal Game Parcheesi, Complete.

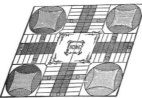

This is a very entertaining Game for the family circle. It can be played by either two, three or four persons at a time, besides greatly interesting the lookers-on. It is a Game of which people seldom tire. Full instructions accompany each Game.

Given for one new name. Price, $1. Postage and packing, 35 cts. additional, when sent as a premium or purchased.

Table Croquet, 8 Balls and Mallets.

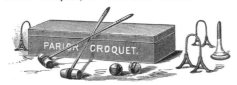

Table Croquet is a pleasing Game for winter evenings. This Set consists of eight Balls, eight Mallets, Bridges, Stakes, Copper Wire Standards and Webbing. Stretch the Webbing around the edge of an ordinary dining-table by means of the Standards, and you have a good croquet table. The Set is beautifully polished and striped.

Given for one new name. Price, $1 Postage and packing, 35 cts., when sent as a premium or purchased.

Two Sun Kites and a Montgolfier Balloon.

All given for one new name.

This Kite is the invention of Mr. Crandall, and will delight the boys. It is **self-poising**, is waterproof, and is absolutely perfect.

It can be flown in the lightest summer breeze, or in a strong wind. Ordinary No. 8 white cotton spool thread is strong enough for a very high wind.

By reason of the elastic cord attachment, the Kite poises itself, and thus equalizes the pressure of the wind.

Each Kite is furnished **complete** with tail, etc., all ready for flying, as shown in the cut. The **Montgolfier Balloon** is six feet in circumference, and is made of bright paper.

The Two Kites and Balloon given for one new name. Price of all, 75 cts. Postage and packing, 25 cts., when sent as a premium or purchased.

Home Entertainment Combination.

Given for one new name, and 10 cts. additional.

Checkers and Chess will entertain, but you will want a change in the programme during the evening. The

Vacuum-Tipped Arrow Pistol is safe, convenient, and especially adapted for parlor practice. The Arrow Tip is made from rubber. It is concave in shape. When it hits the Target it will adhere to its surface, on the same principle that a fly's feet stick to the wall. It is one of the best and most popular target toys yet made.

The set of Checkers, the Board, a set of Chess, the Pistol and Target, given for one new name, and 10 cts. additional. Price, $1.15. Postage and packing, 45 cts., when sent as a premium or purchased.

Please observe all that goes in this combination, as it is not shown complete in the cut. 1st—A set of wood Chessmen, not quite like the cut. 2d—A set of Checkers, Dice and Cups. 3d—A Chess, Checker and Backgammon Board, so these three games can be played. 4th—A Vacuum Air Pistol, with Arrow and Target complete.

We will sell the Pistol separate for 50 cts., and 20 cts. additional for postage and packing. Price of all the Games separate from the Pistol, 65 cts.

Steam Locomotive and Circular Track.

Given for one new name, and $1 additional.

The King of Toys.

Three years ago we began a series of experiments and investigations. **A Steam Locomotive** was what we were after. We first imported models of the English, of the French, and of the German Toy Steam Locomotive, all of which were very costly and very clumsy-looking, about as much like our new Locomotive as a dump-cart resembles a fine coach.

As the foreign engines were of no use to us, and the only American Locomotives then made cost from $6 to $10 each, we decided to have a Locomotive designed for us, and made after our superb American models. By means of special tools and large orders, we hoped to be able to offer our subscribers this king of toys at a low price.

Our Success.

The Steam Locomotive illustrated in the cut is the result of our efforts. It is a great success in every way. The Engine is a beauty.

Fill the boiler about two-thirds full of water, light the wicks under the boiler, and in a few minutes "steam is up," and the Locomotive is ready for a spin on the Track — for a Track about 12 feet in circumference is included with each Engine.

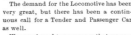

A Safe Locomotive.

It has a safety-valve, which ensures perfect safety. By means of a new invention the steam is superheated at a point just before it enters the steam-chest. This adds greater power to the Locomotive.

A Railroad President.

America is the home of the great railroad kings and managers. Now, every boy who obtains one of these Locomotives can, no doubt, work up from engineer to president of his own road, providing, of course, that he owns the controlling interest.

The Engine.

The Engine is 8 inches in length, from tip of cowcatcher to end of the cab, and is 4¾ inches in height to the tip of the smoke-stack. It is beautifully painted.

We give the Locomotive, including a Track 12 feet in circumference, for only one new name, and $1 additional. Price, including the Track, only $2.50. Postage and packing, 45 cts., when sent as a premium or purchased. Or it can be sent by express, not paid.

A New Offer.

This cut illustrates the Locomotive attached to the Tender and Passenger Car. It is making its trip around the Circular Track. This train is always on time.

The demand for the Locomotive has been very great, but there has been a continuous call for a Tender and Passenger Car as well.

We are pleased to announce that we can now offer the Engine, with Track, Tender and Passenger Car, all complete, as seen in the cut. This makes a perfect combination. Read the description and offer.

charges paid by receiver. Be particular, in ordering, to say whether you wish Engine with Track alone, or Engine, Track, Tender and Passenger Car, **and send money accordingly.**

Description.

The Tender and Car are made in imitation of the handsome cars of the Pullman lines. They are beautifully decorated in every particular.

We give the Locomotive, with Track, Tender and Car, for one new name, and $1.50 additional. Price, complete, $3. It must be sent by express, and

Weeden's New Upright Steam Engine, Nickel-Plated.

An Interesting Statement. Three years ago Mr. Weeden made for us, from plans suggested by ourselves, the Upright Steam Engine here illustrated.

Its success has been wonderful. Already more than **50,000** have been ordered from the manufacturer. It is the most perfect Toy Steam Engine made in the world.

Our New Nickel-plated Engine. From time to time improvements have been made on the Engine, but we now offer it beautifully *Nickel-plated* and as bright as a new silver dollar.

Description of Engine. Its size is 8½ x 4¼ inches.

Safety-Valve. The Engine has a perfect-working Safety-Valve, which makes it impossible for the boiler to explode.

Steam-Whistle. By referring to the cut, you will notice the location of the Steam-Whistle. You will also see the valve by which the whistle is operated.

The Throttle-Valve. One important feature of this Engine is its Throttle-Valve. No other amateur Engine has this feature.

The Power of the Engine. The Engine has sufficient power for running toy machinery. So perfectly and so accurately is this Engine made that the **screw-nuts** on the cylinder-head and the **rivet-heads** on the boiler and fire-box are imitated (see cut).

A Mechanical Curiosity. This Engine is not only interesting to boys, but as an object of mechanical beauty and perfection, it has great interest to engineers and practical machinists.

We offer the Engine for only **one new name.** Price, $1.25. Postage and packing, 40 cts., when sent as a premium or purchased.

Fishing Outfit Complete. Given for one new name.

This is a complete Outfit for general brook and lake fishing, and consists of the following pieces: 1 10½ ft. Jointed Rod, polished ash, 3 double Brass Joints, and ringed throughout; 1 Belt Bait Box; 1 Furnished Line, with Pfleuger's Luminous Bob; 1 Trout Line; 1 Coachman's Fly; 1 Polka Fly; 2 Trout Hooks, mounted with gut; 10 assorted Limerick Hooks; 2 Lead Sinkers; 1 Pfleuger's Adjustable Luminous Bob; 1 Trolling Line, 50 ft.; 1 Keystone Spoon Bait for same, with nickel Spoon and 3 Fly Hooks.

Parlor Target Air-Gun.

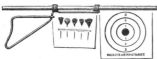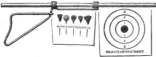

This is one of the most beautiful and interesting toys on the market, and can be used by man, woman or child. It is very beneficial to the health, strengthens the lungs, develops the chest, and makes the sight accurate. For Parlor Target parties it has no equal. It is 15 in. in length. The Barrel is Nickel-plated; Target and Darts go with the gun.

We will give this gun, together with any three of the 25-cent card games named below, for one new name. Price of the Gun and three 25-cent Games, $1. Postage and packing, 30 cts., when sent as a premium or purchased.

Size, 8½ inches high and 4½ inches in diameter.

The Merry-Go-'Round. Given for one new name.

This attractive Toy has been made to be run by the Weeden Steam Engine. Description of the "Merry-Go-'Round:" It is 13½ inches high and 10 inches diameter. The top of the Toy is covered with colored striped cloth. The Horses and Riders are made from tin, and are painted in different colors.

By attaching the belt from the driving wheel of the Steam Engine to the large pulley-wheel of the Toy, the Horses and Riders go round and round as natural as life.

Given for one new name. Price, $1. Postage and packing, 35 cts., when sent as a premium or purchased.

Football, No. 5, and Manual.

Both given for one new name, and 30 cts. additional.

Size, 27 inches in circumference. We give with each Football an Official Manual, giving Referee's Duties, Score Sheet, Field Chart, and Football Rules, as authorized and adopted by the American Inter-collegiate Association.

The Football and Manual given for one new name, and 30 cts. additional. The regular price of the Ball and Manual is $2.35.

Social Games for the Home Circle.

Any of the following Card Games to the value of $1.00 will be sent for ONE NEW NAME. Postage and packing, 15 cts., when sent as a premium. Postage paid by us on all Card Games when purchased.

Fortunatus, or Wishes and Consequences. This is a very amusing game. The changing of the cards makes the wishes and consequences so funny at times that it is impossible to play it without roars of laughter. Price, 25 cts.

Polo. This is a new game. It will prove very popular wherever it is played. Price, 25 cts.

The Evening Party. As the name implies, this is for the entertainment of an evening party. The box contains Puzzles, illustrated Rebus Cards, Acting Charades, Games and Tricks, Conundrums, Solutions to Illustrated Rebuses, &c. Price, 25 cts.

Picture Dominoes. A pleasing game for the little people. It is easy to learn, and easy to play. Price, 25c.

Spelling-School. An intensely interesting and social Game. It will afford hours of rare sport for young or old. This cut is omitted for want of room.

FORTUNATUS. PRICE, 25 CTS. POLO. PRICE, 25 CTS. EVENING PARTY. PRICE, 25 CTS. AUTHORS. PRICE, 25 CTS. PICTURE DOMINOES. PRICE, 25 CTS.

AUCTION. PRICE, 25 CTS. JACKSTRAWS. PRICE, 25 CTS. CROQUET. PRICE, 25 CTS. CORN AND BEANS. PRICE, 25 CTS. TRIPS. PRICE, 25 CTS.

Game of Authors. It contains a sketch of the Authors used in the Game and the names of the principal characters in their books. Price, 25 cts.

The Game of Auction. A popular game for all ages. Price, 25c.

American Jackstraws. It contains more than 70 pieces of assorted wood, many made into various shapes. Price, 25 cts.

The Social Game Croquet is always a popular game. This can be played around the fireside. Price, 25c.

Corn and Beans. "The funniest Game out," and all who buy it, play it, laugh over it, and get fat. Price, 25 cts.

Trips. Japhet Jenkins and Sally Jones' visit "tu Bosting with the old mare and a load of produce." Also the travels of Sam Slick from Weathersfield to Paris, and the great Exposition. These two games in one. Price, 25 cts.

Wilcox Breech-Loading Target Gun.

Given for one new name.

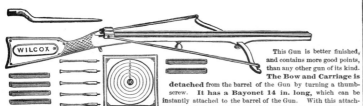

This Gun is better finished, and contains more good points, than any other gun of its kind.

The Bow and Carriage is detached from the barrel of the Gun by turning a thumb-screw. **It has a Bayonet 14 in. long,** which can be instantly attached to the barrel of the Gun. With this attachment you have a regular gun for drilling purposes. This Gun shoots with great accuracy and force. For target practice is better than Archery.

The Companion Union Web Hammock.

Given for one new name, and 10 cts. additional.

The demand for Hammocks increases each year, especially the demand for the Union Web. We have arranged with the makers for a **Special** Hammock made from extra heavy cord, the same cord from which the $3 Hammocks are made. It also has the safety lacing cords and patent rings.

The Companion Union Web Hammock is ten feet in length and has a six-foot bed.

ASSORTED CASES OF TOYS.

The articles selected for these cases are all new and saleable goods direct from the manufacturers. Novelties an staples that sell every day of the year. Prices as itemized are as low in these quantities as from open stock. We giv the approximate retail prices each article will actually bring and be a ready seller. Each assortment contains a particula good line of toys for boys. We would suggest to make a selection of dolls in about the same amount as of toys.

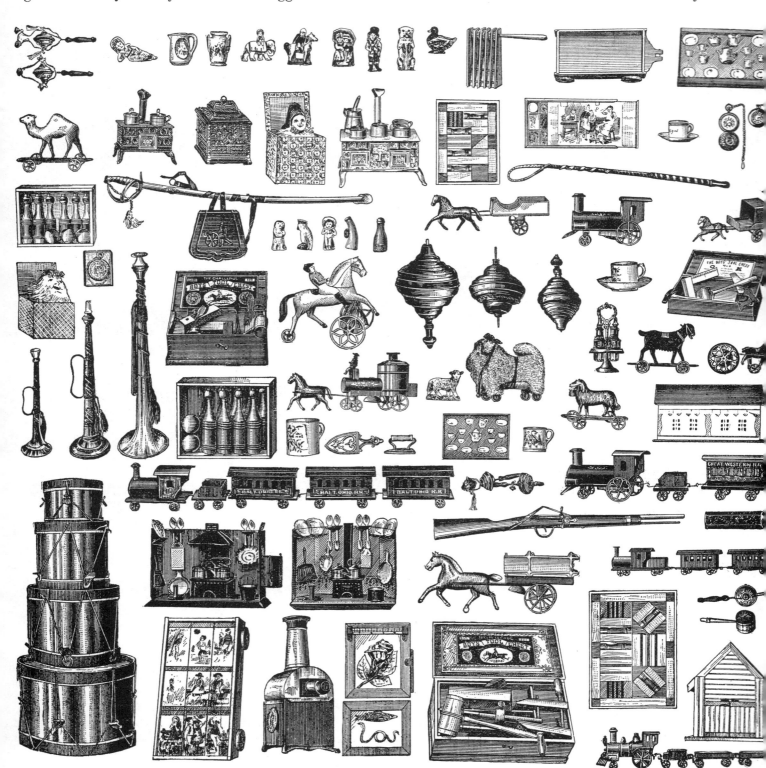

The above cut represents a few of the toys in Case L, and also shows the class of goods in all the assortments.

Marshall Field & Co.

Illustrated Catalogue of

HOLIDAY GOODS,
TOYS, DOLLS,
STATIONERY,
SMALL WARES, ETC.

Adams, Quincy, Franklin, Fifth Avenue.
CHICAGO.

FINE FRENCH DRESSED DOLLS.

No. 2908-1.

No. 3058BH-45.

No. 2698K–1. Boy, full satin costume, satin lace trimmed hat, 16 inches long...	per doz.,	$36
" 3058BH-45. Velvet hat, velvet cape, 20 inches long...	"	36
" 3061BH-50. Matelasse satin dress, gold lace trimmed, satin bonnet, moving eyes, 22 inches long...........................	"	48
" 2908-1. Gold trimmed satin dress, satin bonnet, 16 inches long..	"	48
" 2698M-10 Girl, full satin and velvet costume, fluted satin, lace trimmed hat, 16 inches long.......................	"	54
" 348. Velvet and satin dress, fluted puff front, ostrich tip. 26 inches long......................................	"	60

No. 361BH–45.

No. 2698-10.

No. 348.

DOLLS.

BISQUE DRESSED DOLLS.

No. 2956-32.

No. 1998-1.

No. 71.

No. 70.	Fancy striped dresses, blue and white flannel, 1 boy and girl in package. 13½ inches. 1-6, doz. in package							per doz.	$	9.00
" 71.	" " satin, fancy bonnet, 13½ inches. 1-6 doz, in package,							"		10.50
" 356.	Schoolgirl, fancy checked dresses, 14 " " " "							"		9.00
" 3014c-36.	" " striped " 15 " " " "							"		12.00
" 2889-32.	Boy, velvet costume, hat, 14 " " " "							"		12.00
" 2956-32.	Schoolgirl, fancy dress, 13 " " " "							"		9.00
" 3019-832.	Girl, lace trimmed dress, fancy bonnet, shoes and stockings 14 inches							"		9.00
" 2821b 32.	" fancy pleated dress, " " " " 14 "							"		9.00
" 2976-32.	" assorted satin dresses, " " 14 "							"		13.50

INFANTS IN INFANTS' DRESSES.

No. 1996	Moving eyes, lace cap, white flannel dress, ribbon trimmed, shoes and stockings, 16 inches			per doz.	$13.50
" 1998-1.	" " cape dress, lace edges, with baby rattle, " " 15 "			"	16.00
" 1998-2.	" " " " fancy striped " " " " " 20 "			"	24.00

No. 2821b 32.

No. 2976-32.

DOLLS.

PATENT DRESSED DOLLS.

No. 64.   No. 56.   No. 54.   No. 4007B-27.

No. 54.   Patent heads, assorted Greenaway dresses, 13 inches long, ⅓ dozen in box...................................... per dozen, $2
" 55.   Assorted sailors, 10½ inches long, ½ dozen in box.. " " 2
" 56.   Sateen dresses, poke bonnets, 16 inches long, ⅓ dozen in box....................................... " " 4
" 57.   Girls in assorted fancy dresses, shoes and stockings, 18 inches long, ⅓ dozen in box....................... " " 5
" 58.   Sateen dresses, one boy and two girls in each package, 16 inches long....................... " " 8

BISQUE DRESSED DOLLS.

No 57.   No. 58.   No. 66.   No. 65.

No. 60.   Fancy assorted dresses, 8½ inches long, ⅓ dozen in package... per dozen, $2
" 62.   Boys and girls, satin waists sailor costumes, 9 inches long, ⅓ dozen in package.......................... " " 2
" 64.   Jointed body, satin fronts, lace hoods, shoes and stockings, 13 inches long, ½ dozen in package........................... " " 4
" 65.   Jointed body, lace trimmed, fancy dresses and bonnets, shoes and stockings, 12 inches long, ⅓ dozen in package........... " " 4
" 66.   Jointed body, cloth dresses, lace trimming, 12 inches long, ⅓ dozen in package.......................... " " 5
" 4007B-27.   Boys assorted dresses, ½ dozen in package..................................... " " 5

RUBBER DOLLS.

Cut No. 424—4.

Cut No. 48.

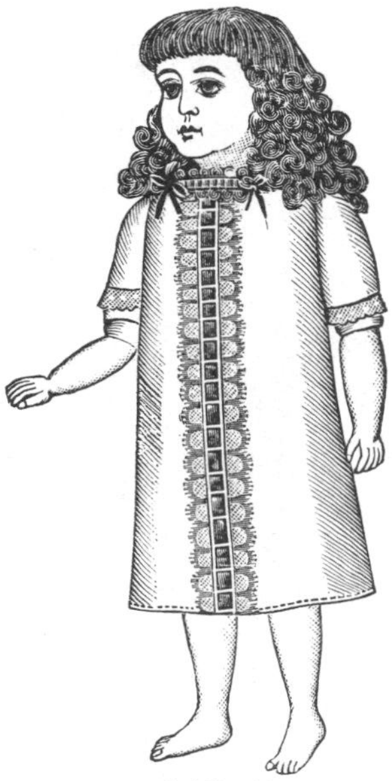

Cut No. 52.

No 900.	Assorted figures, 5½ inches long, 1 doz. in package	per doz.,	$1 75
" 901.	Assorted, boys and girls, 6 inches long, 1 doz. in package	"	2 00
" 904.	Assorted, with fancy shirts and hats, 7 inches long, 1 doz. in package	"	2 00
" 913.	Girls, fancy dresses, with sash, 7 inches long, 1 doz. in package	"	2 00
" 914.	Assorted, boys and girls, lace shirt, 9 inches long, ½ doz. in package	"	3 75
" 901.	Girls, fancy shirt and hat, 11 inches long, ½ doz. in package	"	5 50
" 909.	Sailors, extra quality open front jackets, pants and sailor's caps, 9 inches long, ½ doz. in package	"	4 50
" 910.	" " " " " " " " " " 10½ " " ½ " "	"	8 50
" 911.	" " " " " " " " " " 11½ " " ½ " "	"	10 50
" 915.	Extra quality heavy bodies, fine knit dresses, with sashes, large hats; 10 inches long, ⅓ doz. in a package	"	6 50
" 916.	" " " " " " " " " " " 12 " " ⅓ " " "	"	9 00
" 917.	" " " " " " " " " " " 13 " " ⅓ " " "	"	13 50

JOINTED DOLLS, WITH BISQUE HEADS.

No. 47.	Stationary eyes, shirt, 12 inches long, 1 doz. in package	per doz.,	$2 00
" 48.	Moving eyes, shirt, 12 inches long, ½ doz. in package	"	2 75
" 49.	Teeth, stationary eyes, fancy shirt; 13½ inches long, ⅓ doz. in package	"	4 00
" 50.	" " " " " 15 " " ⅓ " "	"	4 50

FINE QUALITY.

No. 52.	Fancy shirts, stationary eyes, teeth, 10½ inches long	per doz.,	$10 50
" 53.	" " " " " 12 " "	"	12 00
" 424-4.	" " " " " 17 " "	"	18 00

No. 50.

WOOL DOLLS.

No. 566.	Length, 9½ inches;	Clowns and jockeys;	1 doz. in a package	..	per doz.,	$1 90
" 572.	" 9 "	Sailors;	1 " " "	..	"	3 50
" 577.	" 10½ "	Laplanders;	½ " " "	..	"	4 00
" 576.	" 10½ "	Milkmaids;	½ " " "	..	"	4 50
" 582.	" 13 "	Russians;	½ " " "	..	"	6 00

No. 904.

ALPHABET BLOCKS.

No. 5. Twenty-five pieces. natural wood in paper boxes with fine labels. ½ doz. in package.....................per doz., $1 65

No. 0. Eighteen pieces, embossed hard wood, in glazed paper boxes with label in three colors, glossed. Bear the alphabet and numerals, ⅛ doz. in package.........................per doz., $0 8

No. 6. Twelve pieces, natural wood, printed in colors, packed in paper boxes with fine label.
No. 8. Twenty pieces, in wood frame boxes with entirely new label, thirty-six illustrations of animals, all the letters and numerals, ½ doz. in package.................................per doz., $2 00

No. 88a. Eighteen pieces, printed in colors, ornamented letters and with embossed silver ends, thirty-six illustrations, several impressions of each letter and figure, painted in oils and varnished, packed in wood frame boxes with varnished covering, made specially for them, ¼ doz. in package..........per doz., $6

No. 25. Sixteen pieces, natural wood, in paper boxes with fine labels, an excellent block, ½ doz. in package.........per doz., $1 85

No. 4. Twenty half-cubes, of the beautiful cameo desigh, containing all the pleasant features of the best half-cube varieties, in wood frame boxes, ¼ doz in packege.................per doz., $4

No. 60. Twelve pieces, natural wood, in wood frame boxes with fine labels, illustrations embossed in cameo upon the wood. This effect in relief is entirely new in blocks and is not only beautiful but presents illustrations more realistic to the child's eye than engravings do. ¼ doz. in package ....per doz., $5 35

No. 24. Twelve pieces, natural wood, embossed ends, twenty-five illustrations of the alphabet. specially designed, printed in two colors, chromatic letters, packed in wood frame boxes, handsomely covered and labeled, ¼ doz. in package........per doz., $5 8

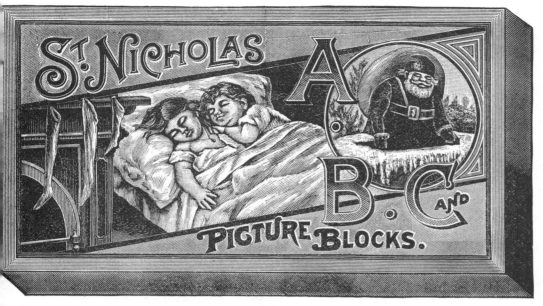

No. 664. 24 Oblong blocks very handsomely covered with the alphabet, and a bright Christmas scene as a picture puzzle, ½ doz. in package...per doz. $2 00

No. 674. Tommy Snooks' A B C. The picture upon the handsome label of this set of blocks shows "Tommy Snooks and Bessie Brooks" walking merrily along a flowry path. Well may they be merry, as Master Tommy carries under his arm a set of these blocks labeled "Tommy Snooks, his blocks." Tommy had excellent taste. The set consists of 24 large, handsome blocks with the alphabet beautifully illustrated upon one side while the reverse is covered by combination circus pictures in fine gold colors, ½ doz. in package....... per doz., $2 00

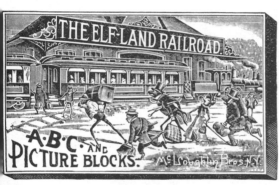

No. 669. Elf-land railroad. Nine flat blocks, each 2¼x4 and 1 in. thick, make up this set, the blocks are covered on one side with picture of an immense train of cars upon the "Elf-land railroad," the reverse being covered with a very funny set of pictures illustrating the familiar story of "the frog who would a wooing go." The edges of blocks bear the entire alphabet in fine colors.....................per doz., $4 00

No. 516. The banner A B C, contains 12 oblong blocks. 6¼ inches square, the sides covered with elegantly colored pictures of bright children, in different fancy dresses, each bearing a banner, upon which is a large illuminated letter, and upon the ends of the blocks are also handsomely colored letters, box is large and handsome, with label in fine colors and gold, ½ doz. in package....................per doz., $4 00

No. 670 Tommy Toddyhigh's A B C. This set contains 9 flat blocks, each 2¼x4 in. and 1 in. thick, upon one side of the blocks is a beautifully illustrated story of "two little birdies that sat on a tree," while the reverse side has a very funny story about the summer vacation of a grasshopper, an ant a bumble bee and a beetle, a most beautiful and desirable set of blocks, ½ doz. in package per doz.................................. $2 00

No. 502. The Fairy land railroad A B C, new and largely improved this season. On one side is shown the train to Fairy land, on the opposite Punch and Judy and letters, on the edges, soldiers, ½ doz. in package...........per doz., $1 85

No. 501. Every baby's A B C. This is a very handsome set of 12 blocks 2¼ x3½ inches and ¼ inch thick On these 12 blocks the entire alphabet is illustrated in a very pretty and instructive manner, ½ doz. in package, per doz.................. $1 85

ALPHABET BLOCKS.

No. 669. Christmas blocks. These blocks, new this season, we recommend to the trade with full assurance that they will find a ready sale. In appearance they are entirely unequaled, and the plan upon which the blocks are illustrated enables us to give, upon the 9 blocks in a set, 3 complete stories, each beautifully illustrated, besides a fine train of cars, always a popular and desirable feature in blocks....................per doz., $4 00

The star of Bethlehem A B C and bible picture blocks. A very attractive scriptural block. Lithographed in rich colors, with fine alphabet and several elegant puzzle pictures representing bible scenes. Put up in handsome wood and paper boxes with showy labels. Brick-shape blocks of ⅞-inch stock with yellow edges.

No. 53 12 blocks; size, 8½x11½x2 in.......................per doz., $4 00
"   54   24   "   "   17½x12x2 in.......................   "   8 00

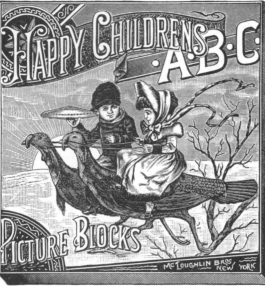

No. 510. Treasures of Mother Goose contains 12 flat blocks, 2½x3½ inches, 1 inch thick On one side of the 12 blocks is given, complete, with bright illustrations, the story which is indicated by the title; while the reverse has miscellaneous pictures illustrative of "Mother Goose," and the edges the alphabet. 'The House that Jack built," ¼ doz. in package..per doz., $3 75

Golden letter blocks; size 3, 24 cubes—new. These are large 2⅜ inch cubes covered with beautiful golden letters and pictures illustrating each letter of the alphabet The gold letters are on a bright crimson background, which produces a most brilliant effect. The pictures are from fine etched plates, and in combination with the bright letters form a most elegant line of cubes.

No. 482. Golden letter blocks, 18 cubes. All the above are in handsome wood boxes, with very showy labels..per doz., $8 00

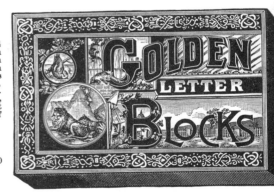

No. 514. Happy children's A B C. These beautiful blocks cannot fail to make happy children in all the homes where they are introduced. There are 12 large blocks 4x6 inches and ½ inch thick, covered with very beautiful and unique pictures in bright colors and also giving the letters of the alphabet. Nothing will better please a boy or girl than these blocks ....per doz., $6 00

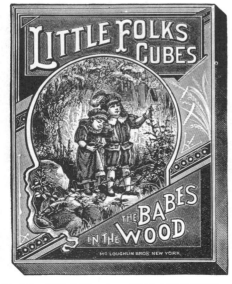

No. 520. Little folk's cubes. The great popularity our Little Folk's Cubes has induced us to bring out an entirely new and elegant series which, from their increased size, the attractive and beautiful pictures used, with the fine wood boxes and most striking and attractive labels, together make the handsomest series of blocks we have ever offered.......................... per doz., $5 35

No. 665. Our little one's A B C. This set contains 12 blocks, and they are the largest and handsomest upon the market at the price at which they are offered. Covered edges and thoroughly well made; ½ doz. in package ....per doz., $2 00

No. 488. Little word A B C block. This set is one of the best made. It is in itself a little primer, giving all the large and small letters in connection with a large number of simple words, and forms an excellent means for instructing children. The blocks are bright and attractive in design, and their size is the favorite one with the general public. Put up in a wood box, expressly designed for the blocks per doz

MAMMOTH ALPHABET BLOCKS.

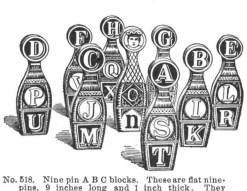

No. 518. Nine pin A B C blocks. These are flat ninepins, 9 inches long and 1 inch thick. They contain all the letters of the alphabet, and are designed for a game of nine pins, for which purpose the box contains three balls........per doz., $6 00

No. 100. Noah's ark, improved, Consists of a strongly made ark on wheels, covered with a rich lithograph and filled with blocks, having animals, birds and full alphabet upon them; size, 16x8½ inches; contains 15 blocks .... per doz., $4 00

No. 110. Shadow blocks. Contains 14 lithographed alphabet blocks of ⅝-inch stock, with frogs and mosquitoes in uniform upon the sides; size of box, 11x8 inches, with bright label; ½ doz. in package.................................per doz., $2 00

No. 578½. The pictures upon the "Red Riding Hood" nest are all from original designs, made for the purpose by a very distinguished artist, and we have spared no pains to reproduce these designs in the finest colors and most artistic manner; this nest of blocks has only to be seen to be appreciated ....per doz., $6 75

No. 578. Mother Hubbard blocks—nested. This beautiful set of nested blocks is entirely new this season, and consists of ten boxes. The pictures are all original designs from a distinguished artist, and we have spared neither expense or exertion to reproduce these designs with the finest colors, and in the most artistic manner. The pictures are all illustrative of various Mother Gooserhymes, each picture having in connection with itself the rhyme or story illustrated. The letters of the alphabet are given on top of boxes, in bright colors, and the entire general appearance of this unequaled nest of blocks is, beyond question, the finest ever produced in this class of goods ....per doz., $9 00

No. 512. Lightning express and menagerie blocks. This set of blocks is, without exception, the most elegant in appearance: makes the largest display when set up in order, and the most compact when returned to its box, that we have ever offered There are 12 oblong blocks, each 6¼ inches long by 3¾ inches wide and 1¼ inches thick. When properly matched they make an elegant train of cars over six feet long, and on being reversed they show a handsome picture, 78 inches long, of the great parade of "Barnum's greatest show on earth" through the streets of New York, the drawings being made from "life." The edges bear a brigade of boys and girls in fancy dress, each carrying the A B C banner, while the ends of the blocks combined make a full series of pictures from the circus, each picture 3x3¾ inches..per doz., $8 00

No. 1S. Champion A B C and picture blocks. The Champion A B C still holds the market, being the finest nested blocks ever offered to the trade at the price. It consists of ten boxes, the largest of which is about 7¼ inches square. Into this large box all the others are nested, forming a compact package for shipment and handling. When the boxes are taken from the nest and piled one upon the other, as shown in cut, they form an immense tower of bright and beautiful pictures over 63 inches high. On the ends of the boxes are given in finely colored letters, the entire alphabet. There are descriptive lines upon each picture which enables the child to understand the meaning of the pictures set before him Each nest in separate wrapper...per doz., $9 00

MAGIC LANTERNS.

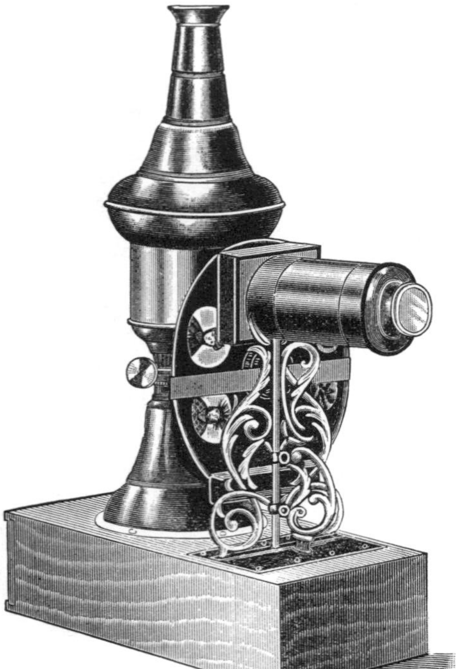

No 306. **Magic lantern with magascope;** with this lantern you can reflect transparent slides as well as photographs and pictures upon the screen. A full description with each lantern; black lacquered body and brass trimmings, 15 inches high, 1¾-inch lenses, round burner, and glass chimney. With each apparatus we give 12 long slides, 3 moving, and 2 chromotrope slides, some photographs and pictures; packed in strong wood box..........each, $7 50

No 307. Black lacquered body, brass trimmings, 14½ inches high, 2⅝-inch lenses; improved sliding lamps with duplex burner and glass protections; each lantern with 12 long, 2 moving, and 1 chromotrope slide; packed in strong wood box with metal handle, each..................................$10 50

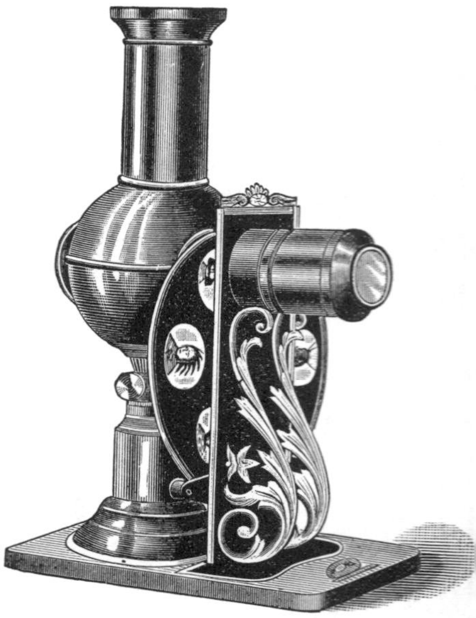

No. 302. Latest design, all brass body and trimmings; each lantern contains 4 long, 6 rotating and 2 moving slides, also a full lecture outfit, such as show bill, tickets of admission, etc.; packed in paper covered wood boxes, 9½ in. high, 1⅝ in. lenses. per doz., $27 00

No. 301. New design, all nickel plated body with brass trimmings; 10½ inches high, $1\frac{3}{16}$-inch lenses; each apparatus fastened on a flat wood box which contains 5 long, and 3 rotating slides; a book with each lantern, packed in paper box ....per doz., $12

TOY CHINA TEA SETS.

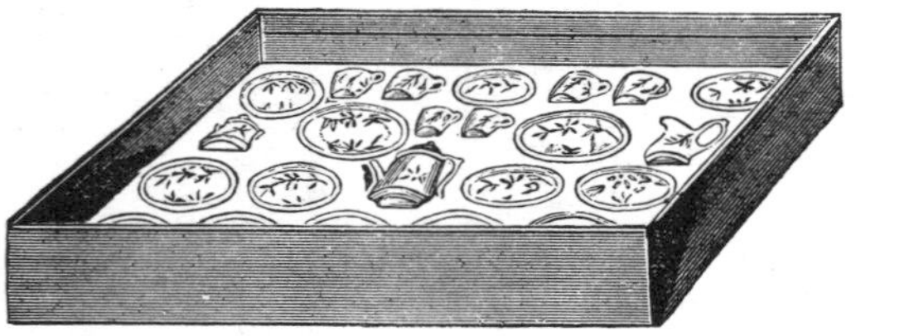

No 46¾

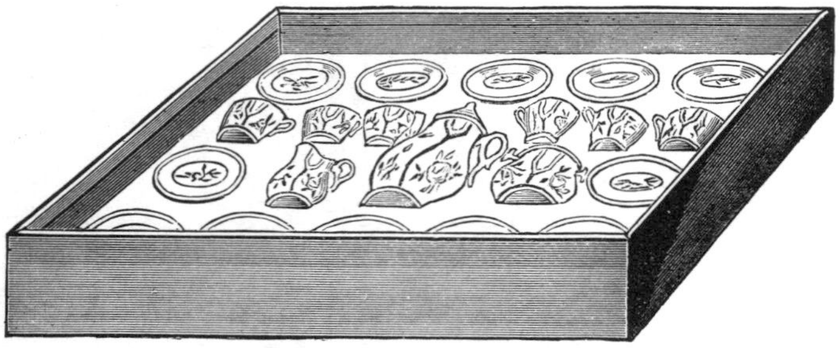

No. 71½

The line comprises the newest shapes and decorations and the largest pieces possible in this staple article which to dolls, holds the next place as a toy for girls.

ASSORTED DECORATIONS.

No. 492.	Tea set	....per gro.,	$10 75
" 100½	Dinner and tea set	.... "	24 00
" 30	" "	.... "	33 00
" 40.	" "	.... "	42 00
" 46¾.	" "	............................per doz.,	4 50
" 36.	" "	.... "	6 00
" 71½.	" "	.... "	8 50
" 150-1	" "	.... "	12 00
" 141½.	" "	.... "	30 00
" 948.	" "	.... "	36 00

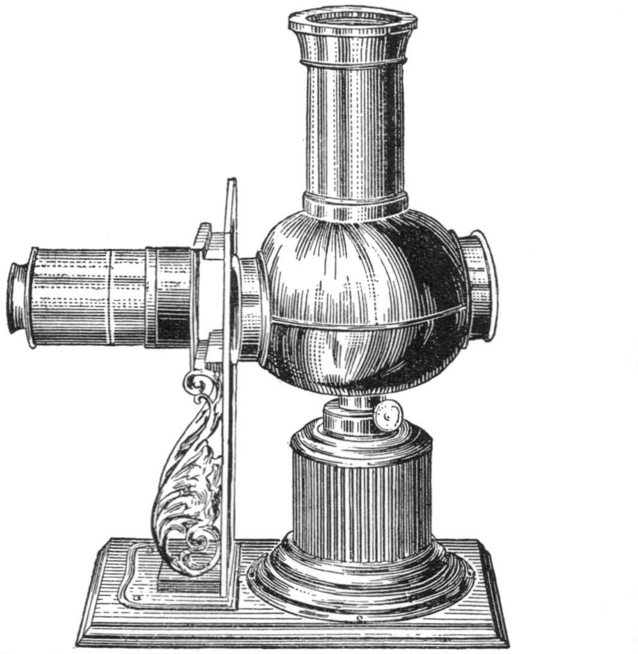

The above is the latest design as to beauty and power in the line of lanterns, the most entertaining of all the novelties in toys. As a boy's article it has no peer; bodies painted red, 12 assorted slides with each.

No. 300.	9 inches high	1 inch slides	....................per doz.,	$ 9
" 201.	9½ " "	1⅛ "	.... "	21
" 303.	9¾ " "	1½ "	.... "	39
" 204.	10 " "	3⅛ "	.... "	48
" 304.	11¾ " "	1¾ "	.... "	72
" 305.	14½ " "	2⅛ "	.... "	96

GAMES.

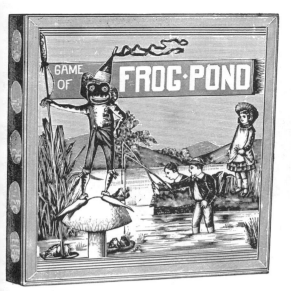

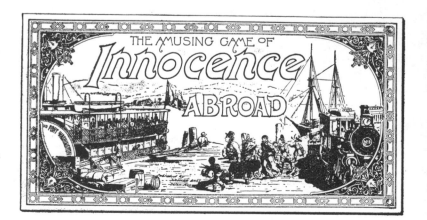

GAMES.

No 535. Improved game of fish pond. We have at last succeeded in getting a new and novel style of the ever popular game of fish pond. It is gotten up in the most handsome and durable manner, and its sales have been simply enormous. No other game of fish pond approaches ours, either in appearance or real merit, all distinctive features are patented, and we caution the trade agaist selling any fish pond games having our patented features except such as bear our imprint........ per doz., $8 00

No. 441. District messenger boy game. This new folding game is showy in design and especially pleasing in construction, it is based upon the events of every day life. The players start as messenger boys, and during the game meet with all kinds of vicissitudes of a business career, with the corresponding excitements, the successful player attains the presidency, the highest office in the telegraphic service, having passed through all the subordinate positions. Put up in showy box designed expressly for the game, and equipped with our new metalic men ....per doz., $10 00

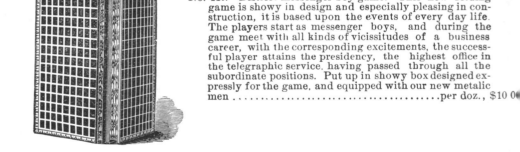

No. 424. Go-bang, Russian Tivoli, fox and geese, solitaire and the German siege game, five games in one board..per doz., $8 00

No. 452. The Giant Killer. Is there a boy or a girl who is not familiar with the story of "Jack the Giant Killer," and his valorous career? This story is here made into a delightful game, for both young and old, which shows the trials gallant Jack endured before he received the king's beautiful daughter as his bride..........................per doz., $4 00

No. 536. Fish pond game. This new and improved edition of the ever popular game of fish pond, has already become deservedly popular in the trade. We have spared no pains or expense in getting the game up in a handsome and durable style, with the best of implements and with our improvements over the regular game, this stands at the head. ....per doz., $4 00

No. 536¼. Fish pond game, ½ doz. in package................. " 2 00

GAMES.

No. 552. Reversi (fine edition) was first introduced by us in the season of 1888, and in a very inexpensive style; but it has so grown upon the public that we are now forced to issue this fine, new edition. Reversi is played upon a board arranged specially for the game, and with checkers for men or implements. These checkers are of different color upon each side, and at certain points of the game the player has the right to *reverse* one or more of his men, giving them increased power. This game, first introduced in London, was the reigning sensation for months, meeting with a most unprecedented sale. ½ doz. in package..per doz., $5 35

No. 562. Game of Migration is entirely new and original and is attracting much more than ordinary attention, from the fact that it is one of the very few games now published which at once awakens great interest among the players, and also holds them fascinated until the game is closed. One game only leads to another, and no two games are alike. Migration is pronounced by many to be far superior to Halma and other games of a similar character, and it already commands a large and constantly increasing sale ....per doz., $5 35

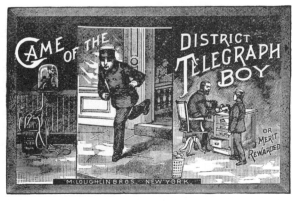

No. 441½. "The Telegraph Boy or Merit Rewarded," as a title, fully indicates the character of this new game. It shows the advantages gained by a boy by activity, promptness, carefulness, honesty and courtesy; and also the darker picture drawn by habitual slothfulness, unfaithfulness, carelessness, dishonesty and lack of courtesy. All this is shown without making the game a bit dry or uninteresting. Such a game in the household is of inestimable value, and can not fail of popularity. It is handsomely put up, and presents a very attractive appearance, per doz...$8 00

No. 499. Improved Scripture Cards. These cards are arranged similar to the two games following, but cover only Scriptural facts. They are very accurate in all the information which they impart, and they never fail to interest all who once use them...per doz., $6 75

No. 497. Improved Historical Cards. In this most excellent and desirable game are 200 large and finely printed cards. These cards represent an original method of acquiring rapidly and permanently the prominent facts in American history, and at the same time present an amusing and instructive game. They are very desirable for use both in public and private schools for teaching young children, who, while being pleasantly engaged, unconsciously acquire a great deal of permanent information, while for the family circle they are unexcelled, per doz., $6 75

No. 498. Improved Geographical Cards. The description of improved historical cards given above may well apply to these, except that geography here takes the place of history. They are desirable for use in schools and parties, and especially designed for the home circle. It is an acknowledged fact that no means of education are so successful as those which interest and please the pupil, while imparting at the same time the knowledge which is desired to teach, and in this particular feature these cards are unexcelled...............................per doz., $6 75

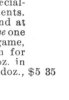

BELL TOYS.

No. 7.   Half size cut,.....................per doz., $3 75

No. 38.   Half size cut, Dog and Cat fight............................per doz.

No. 39.   Half size cut; horse swings on pedestal and rings the
bell...per doz., $4 00

No. 15.   Half size cut; ⅓ dozen in package............per doz.

No. 37.   Half size cut; girl with doll on sled, with chimes, per
dozen $4 00

No. 23.   Half size cut; jumping horse and monkey rider, per doz., $3 7

MALLEABLE IRON TOYS.

No. 92. Donkey wheel toy; length, 9 in., height, 5½ in., width, 3¼ in.; handsomely painted in fancy colors. As the toy is drawn, each revolution of the wheels causes the driver to strike the donkey with the whip. ⅙ doz. in package......per doz., net, $4 25

No. 23. Belfry, with jumping horse and monkey, half size cut; per doz., net.. $4 25

No. 24. The bell ringers; half size cut.............per doz., net, $4 00

No. 35. Bell toy; pig and cart, with clown driver; half size cut; ⅓ doz. in package...............................per doz., net. $2 00

Half size cut of No. 2.

Three-eighth size cut of No. 6.

Revolving chimes, malleable iron wheels; patented.

No. 00.	1 doz. in package	....	per doz., net,	$0 75
" 0.	1 "	"	"	"	1 15
" 1½.	½ "	"	"	"	2 00
" 2.	⅓ "	"	"	"	3 75
" 3.	1/12 "	"	"	"	6 00

Revolving chimes, with horses; patented.

No. 4.	½ doz. in package	....	per doz., net,	$1 75
" 5½.	⅓ "	"	"	"	2 25
" 6.	⅓ "	"	"	"	4 25

MALLEABLE IRON TOYS.

No. J.   Double truck; horses black, harness gilt trimmed; harness and collar red; truck gear red, black striped, side stakes green, gilt striped, panels, seat and foot-board red; load, two boys, two barrels, one sack; length, 17½ inches; per doz., net $21 00

No. I.   Single truck; horse black, harness silver trimmed, collar and housings red; truck gear red, black striped, side stakes green, panels and foot board red, gilt striped; load, one box, barrel and sack; length, 14 inches..........per doz., net, $9 00

No. E.   Surrey; Horse brown, harness black, gilt trimmed; hip blanket buff; surrey body black, seats buff; gear black, red striped; driver in livery; length 15 inches........per doz., net, $9 00

No. L.   Express wagon; two horses, driver and wagon; length, 17½ inches......................................per doz., net, $21 00

No. K.   Barouche; horses cream, harness black, silver trimmed; hip blanket gold; barouche gear maroon, gold striped; body black, panels red, gold striped, inside gold; driver in coachman's livery; length, 18 inches ...per doz., net, $21 00

No. W.   Artillery; horses mismatched in color; gun carriage and limber dark green, red striped; gun dead black, brass mounted, men in uniform; length of toy, 36 inches................. per doz., net, $48 00

Tally-Ho.   Galloping horses, harness, metal figures; length, 18 inches; per doz., net $54 00

No. D.   Hansom; horse black, harness silver trimmed, hip blanket maroon, hansom black, panels yellow, with red stripes; driver in coachman's livery....................per doz., net, $9 00

Bell toy No. 36. Wild mule Jack, half size cut.....................per doz, net, $4 50

No. 29. Ding Dong Bell, half size cut.......per doz, net, $4 50

No. 27. Cinderella's chariot and chime, half size cut...................per doz, net, $4 50

Dray No. B. Horse black, harness gilt trimmed, dray wheels red, sides and front green, gilt stripes, load one box; length 11½ in..per doz, net, $4 50

Sulkey No. A. Horse black, harness gilt trimmed, sulky black, gilt striped, driver in jockey costume, length 9½ inches, per doz, net $4 50

No. 8. Pony cart, galloping pony, 9½ in. long, per doz. net............,...................$4 50

Dog Cart No. C. Horse black, harness gilt trimmed, hip blanket blue, cart black, gilt stripes with buff panels, inside blue, driver in coachman's livery, length 14 inches, per doz, net................................ $9 00

MALLEABLE IRON TOYS.

Engine house V; size 26½x10x18.......................per doz., net,, $39 00

No. 35. Hose cart, with galloping horse, rubber hose;
15 inches long....................per doz , net, $15

No. 55.

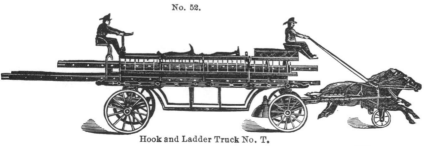

No. 52.

Hose cart S S. Horse white, harness black, hames and
housings red, cart body green, gilt striped, gear red,
black striped, panels, seat, footboard and inside of
reel red; length 15¾ inches........... per doz., net, $1

No. 55. Fire patrol, galloping horses, metal firemen, 18
inches long.........................per doz., net,, $

No. 52. Hook and ladder truck, with buckets, galloping
horses, 28 inches long.................per doz,. net,, $

Hook and Ladder Truck No. T.

No. 53—3.

Hook and Ladder No. T. Horses white, harness black,
hames and housings red, gear red, black striped,
body black and green, with gilt stripes and orna-
mentations, four red extension ladders, which can be
united, making a ladder 51 inches long, 2 axes with
red handles, men in uniform; length of toy, 29 inches,
per doz., net,,...................................... $

Fire Engine No. R. Horses black, harness gilt trimmed,
harness and housings red; engine gear red, black
striped, nickel plated boiler and valves, body green
and black, gilt striped, brass bell, gauge and whistle,
engineer and driver in uniform; length 18½ inches,
per doz., net .... $

No. 53—3. Fire engine, galloping horses, rubber
hose, bright colors; 18 inches long.....per doz., net, $

MALLEABLE IRON TOYS.

No. H. Railroad train; locomotive, boiler black, gilt bands, wheels red, stack red; tender black, red wheels; car red, black striped, wheels black; total length of train, 20 inches...per doz., net, $4 50

No. 441. Carpenters' iron train; best maleable iron train made...per doz., net, $4 50

No. F. Passenger train, locomotive, boiler black, gilt bands, wheels red, stack red and black, brass bell, cab maroon, gilt striped, tender black, red wheels, gold number, car maroon, gilt striped, gilt ornaments; length of toy, 30 inches.........................per doz. net, $9 00

No. G. Railroad train, locomotive, boiler black, gilt bands, wheels red, stack red and black, brass bell, cab maroon, gilt striped, tender black, red wheels, gold number; cars red, black lettered, wheels black; total length of train, 34 inches ....per doz., net, $9 00

No. 60. Iron train, painted in bright colors; 24 inches long..per doz., net, $8 50

No. 70. Iron train, painted in bright colors; 36 inches long..per doz., net, $13 50

No. 200. Carpenters' iron freight train, with removable figures....................................... per doz., net, $9 00

MECHANICAL BANKS

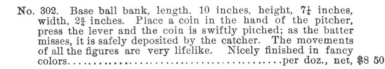

No. 302. Base ball bank, length, 10 inches, height, 7¼ inches, width, 2¾ inches. Place a coin in the hand of the pitcher, press the lever and the coin is swiftly pitched; as the batter misses, it is safely deposited by the catcher. The movements of all the figures are very lifelike. Nicely finished in fancy colors....................................per doz., net, $8 50

No. 321 Bad accident bank, length, 10 inches. height, 6¼ inches, width, 3½ inches Place a coin under the feet of the driver, and press the lever. The boy jumps into the road, frightening the donkey, and as he rears, the cart and driver are thrown backward, when the coin falls into the body of the cart and disappears. Nicely finished in bright colors.........per doz., net, $8

JUMPING ROPE BANK.

No. 322. The most ingenious and complete mechanical iron toy ever offered to the trade. A new and patented mechanical movement, combined with an artistically constructed and handsomely finished design, with novel performing parts adapted thereto, also patented. In manufacturing this toy the aim has been to produce a prolonged or continuous performance of its amusing features without the aid of an expensive and delicate clock-work mechanism.

This has been accomplished by inventing a simple, strong and durable motor, by means of which all the results of clock-work are obtained at much less cost and greater durability. The simulation of "skipping the rope" is perfect—the body, head, feet and rope all moving in unison, but each part performing independently in its own peculiar and appropriate manner. In addition to the essential requirements of entire novelty in a new toy, which this bank possesses to the fullest extent, it is further claimed that it is throughout, of such merit as to classify it with toys of double its cost, and render it a matter of surprise that such a handsome and effective toy can be sold at a price comparatively so low..................per doz., net, $18

SELF-INKING PRINTING PRESSES.

Practical perfect working, self-inking model presses—very instructive—no boy should be without one. Learn the art of printing. These perfect working model presses, on which a good job can be turned out.

No. 9. With complete outfit, 1 roller, will print a form 2⅛x3¼ inches...each, net, $3
" 10.   "   "   "   1   "   "   "   "   2⅛x4   "   .... "   "   6
" 11.   "   "   "   2   "   "   "   "   2½x4   "   .... "   "   8

TOY BANKS AND WHEELTOY.

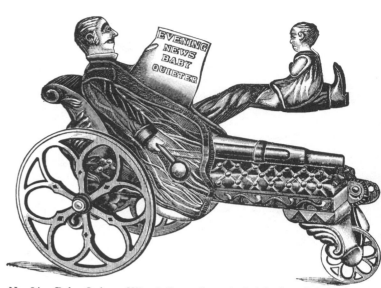

No. 300. Eagle Bank. Length, 8 inches; height, 6 inches; width, 4 inches. Place a coin in the Eagle's beak, press the lever, and the Eaglets rise from the nest crying for food. As the Eagle bends forward to feed them, the coin falls into the nest, and disappears in the receptacle below..per doz., $8 50

No. 94. Baby Quieter Wheel Toy. Length, 7½ inches; height, 6 inches; width, 3¾ inches. As the toy is drawn, each revolution of the wheels rings the bell and jumps the baby. Handsomely finished in fancy colors, ⅙ doz. in package...per doz., $4 25

No. 119. Organ Bank, with new dancing figures, complete with lock and key; size, 8½ inches high, 5½ wide, 3¾ deep. This handsomely finished bank has proven the most satisfactory article of the kind ever put on the market. It has very sweet chimes of bells, which sound when the handle is turned, and the monkey deposits all coin in the bank, and politely raises his cap, while the figures at his side revolve, producing a pleasing effect. Packed one in a wooden box........................per doz., $8 00

No. 324. Cat and Mouse Bank. Height, 11½ inches; width, 5½ inches; depth, 4 inches. Place a coin in front of the mouse over the cat, press the lever, and as the coin disappears into the bank, the kitten, in fancy dress, appears, turning a somersault, holding the mouse and ball. Handsomely ornamented in fancy colors................................per doz., $8 50

TOY BANKS.

No. 323.   Bicycle Bank.   Length, 11 in., height, 8 in., width 3½ in.   As the crank is turned and the lever pressed, Prof. Pug Frog performs his great bicycle feat, and the coin placed on the bicycle is deposited in the bank.   During the performance, Mother Goose gives attention to her melodies.. per doz., $8 5

No. 225.   Organ Bank, with revolving figure.   Size, 4 in. high, 3½ wide, 2½ deep.   Place the coin in the recess before the figure, and when the handle is turned a chime of bells will ring and the monkey will revolve and deposit the money in the bank. Appropriately decorated in colors, and packed one half dozen in a box...................... per doz., $2 00

No. 116.   Size, 6½ in. high, 4 wide, 3 deep.   This bank is calculated to highly amuse children, as it is a musical toy as well as a savings bank.   When the handle is turned a chime of bells will ring continuously, while at the same time the monkey will deposit in the bank any coins which may be placed on his tambourine, expressing his thanks by lifting his cap.   Highly decorated, and packed one in a box.. per doz., $4 00

No. 127.   Size, 5½ inches high, 6 long, 3 deep.   This article is a combination of a mechanical and registering bank.   It is a very attractive novelty and cannot fail to please.   The bucket is designed for dimes, in ordinary use only, and not for mutilated or old-fashioned coin of approximately the same size.   Put a dime in the slot and push the pump handle up and down, when the amount will be correctly registered.   When $5 have been deposited the lid of the bucket can be taken off; when replaced it is ready for business.   If the directions pasted on the bottom of each bank are complied with, it cannot fail to work properly.   Handsomely finished in nickel and wood colors, and packed one in a wooden box..................... per doz.,

MECHANICAL TOYS.

49—0. Mechanical performing bear with staff. A perfect model of a bear, full of life and motion. Very natural in all its movements Opens and closes its mouth, pounds the staff on the floor vigorously, snaps its jaws, growls and moves its head from side to side: size, 9½ inches high, per doz., net...................... $32 00

No. 49—6. The old colored fiddler. The face and expression is natural and so funny, that they provoke laughter wherever shown. There is a "point" to each, fun for old and young alike; size, 9½ inches high ....per doz., net, $24 00

No. 30—3. Mechanical Santa Claus, very attractive toy, appropriately dressed, walks quite naturally when wound up; size. 10 inches high..............per doz., net, $36 00

49—1. Mechanical performing bear. This toy is covered with fur, and is made in perfect imitation of a "live bear." When wound, it will go through all the motions of a bear about to pounce upon its prey. Lifelike and natural in all its movements, it opens and closes its mouth, gets down on its fore paws, rises again, snaps its jaws and growls and moves its head from side to side, white; size, 9½ inches high, per doz., net, $32 00

No. 49—9. The mechanical stump speaker This colored orator when wound up will go through all the motions of a stump speaker perfectly. The figure moves his head from side to side constantly and "pounds" the table with his umbrella vigorously. This toy is full of life and motion; size, 11 inches high, each one in wood box...................per doz., net, $28 00

No. 190. Model Landau; length 16½ inches, finest iron horse toy ever made......................................per doz., $13 50

No. KK. Pony Phaeton; horse, white; harness, gilt trimmed; hip blanket, maroon; phaeton—body, black; seat, maroon; mat, orange; gear, red, black striped; wheels, red, black striped; lady driver.................................per doz., $10 50

GATHMANN TORPEDO GUN.

A neat model of the most powerful weapon of war of the day. It is entirely harmless, no explosives or powder being used; rubber bands are used to furnish the propelling power. Torpedo is upheld in its flight by wings which guide and balance it, keeping it straight. It will hit the mark.

No. 1. Cannon 11 inches, nicely mounted..............................per doz., $ 8 00
"   2. "   15 "   U. S. Navy pattern........................... "   16 50
Two torpedos, four bullets and a ship target are with each cannon.

Home Savings bank. Height, 6 in.; width, 4½ depth, 3½ in. ¼ doz. in package, per doz...$2 00

No. W. Extra large, heavy Artillery; horses mismatched in color, gun carriage and limber dark green, red striped, gun dead black, brass mounted, men in uniform, length of toy 34 inches...per doz., $48 00

No. 409. Flying Artillery; brass cannon, 2 running horses, driver and odd rider; size 24x6½.................................per doz., $27 00

MECHANICAL LOCOMOTIVES.

No. 19—9.   Iron locomotive, runs by clock work. 7 in. long, per doz, net, $ 8 50
"   19—11   "   "   "   "   9½   "   "   "   "   16 00

No. 19—10.   Iron locomotive with tender, run by clock work, 10½ in. long,
per doz, net..$11 25

No. 19—12.   Iron locomotive, with tender, run by clock work, 13¾ inches long...per doz, net, $20 00

MALLEABLE IRON LOCOMOTIVES.

No. 1   Passenger locomotive, in full pattern, 14 inches long,
per doz, net $16 50

No. 500.   Extra large locomotive, in bright colors, 18 inches long .... per doz, net, $27 00

TOY STOVES.

The Pet.   A perfect working toy range;
length, 11½ in.; height, 7 in.; width,
7 in.; has 4 boiling holes, reservoir,
dumping grate, reservoir damper, large
fire box with door, oven with door, front
door with draft damper, etc.   Large and
small kettle, spider, baking pan, length
of pipe and lifter included.

Each range is packed in a box.
Per doz, net........................$18 00

The I X L.   A perfect working toy
range, length, 8¼ in.; height, 5¼ in.;
width, 5⅛ in.; has 4 boiling holes, reservoir, dumping grate, large fire box, oven
with door, front door, damper openings.
Kettle, spider, baking pan, griddle,
length of pipe, and lifter included.

Each range is packed in a paper box.
Per doz, net $9 00

Cut of The Pet.

Cut of the I. X. L.

MECHANICAL TOYS.

No. 49-14, the mechanical boxers, size 8½x11, a new and very life-like toy, the figures go through all the motions of two men boxing, excellent motion, comical, life-like action, finely made and finished, not liable to get out of order.................... per doz, net, $32.00

No. 1. Mechanical assorted velocipede riders, 10 inches high, a new comical toy, a dressed figure seated on a velocipede which when wound up will run around rapidly in a large or small circle.............................per doz. net, $24.

No. 22-2. Double dancers full of motion, very comical and life-like, 10 inches high per doz., net.......... $24.00

No. 49-7. The old nurse, handsomely and strongly made, appropriately dressed, excellent motion, comical, life-like action, finely made and finished, not liable to get out of order.......................per doz. net, $24.00

No. 49-2. The mechanical walking bear, covered with fine fur, made in good imitation of a bear, when wound up it will walk in exact imitation of a bear, and will open and close its mouth and growl, size 8 inches long......................per doz. net, $48.

MECHANICAL TOYS.

No. 11–2. Mechanical Monkey, by clockwork, per doz...................................$33 00

Mechanical Cake Walk..per doz.,$33 00

No. 32–9. Mechanical Clown Rider.......per doz., $33 00

No. 49–16. Mechanical Acrobats, performing on bar.........per doz., $36 00

IRON TOYS.

No. 170.   Fire captain's wagon, 12½ inches long,
5½ inches high....................per doz., $7 50

No. 135.   Model Hose Cart, length 15 inches...........................per doz., $ 8
" 135½.   Same as No. 135, with rubber hose, length 15 inches...........   "   10

No. 0.   Fire Chief's Wagon.   Horse white, harness black, hames
and housings red; body of wagon red, gear red, wheels red,
black striped; driver in uniform ....per doz., $13 50

No. B.   Dray; horse black, harness gilt trimmed, dray wheels
red, sides and front green, gilt stripes, load one box; length,
11½ inches.......................................per doz., $

MODEL FIRE ENGINE No. 125.

Length 19 inches..per doz., $18

No. 40-5.   Mechanical Fire Engine, extra large, 2 running horses, driver, fireman and sectional hose; when wound 2 small wheels and the
pump work rapidly imitating an engine at work at a fire; size, 19x7x5..per doz., $33

CARL P. STIRN,

(FORMERLY OF STIRN & LYON,)

597 BROADWAY, NEW YORK,

OPPOSITE THE METROPOLITAN HOTEL.

✦ 1894 ✦

TRADE PRICE LIST

—OF—

TOYS,

SPORTING GOODS, GAMES, NOVELTIES, SCHOOL SUPPLIES,

FIVE AND TEN CENT SPECIALTIES,

FLAGS, PISTOLS, LANTERNS, ETC.

NEW STOCK. LOW PRICES. LIBERAL TERMS.

CARL P. STIRN,

(For Eighteen Years a member of the firm of STIRN & LYON,)

597 BROADWAY, NEW YORK.

All Prices in this Catalogue are subject to change without notice.

TERMS: NET 60 DAYS, OR 2 PER CENT. DISCOUNT FOR CASH WITHIN 10 DAYS.

TRICK ELEPHANT BELL RINGER.

Half size cut.

Elephant swings on the tub and rings the bell.

No. 40 . . . . per dozen, $4.00

THE PIG AND COLUMBUS EGG BELL TOY.

Half size cut.

The action of the pig in trying to set the egg on end, and at the same time ring the bell, very attractive feature.

No. 41 . . . . per dozen, $4.00

MONKEY VELOCIPEDE AND CHIMES.

Painted in fancy colors. As the toy is drawn the monkey rider appears to be propelling velocipede, each revolution of the wheels causing the bell to ring. Height, 8 in.; length, 8 in.

No. 90 . . . . per dozen, $4.00

COLUMBIAN WHEEL.

Diameter of wheel . . . . 14 inches
Extreme height . . . . 17 "

This is a well constructed toy throughout—strong and durable. The wheel is stamped from steel, the design of the centre being a six point star, all lines of which are heavily embossed. The axle is of steel. The columns, base, toy men and crank are of malleable iron. Price, per dozen $12.00

Fire Cracker Cannons.

No.		Per Doz
1. Artillery, 6½ inches long, for No. 1 Cannon Crackers		$2 00
20-1. Artillery, 9 inches long, for No 1 Cannon Crackers		4 00
30-2. Artillery, 16 inches long, for No. 2 Cannon Crackers		9 00

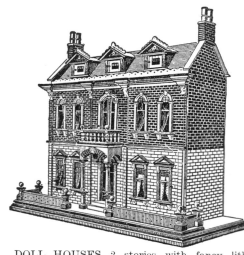

DOLL HOUSES, 2 stories, with fancy lithographed front; two larger sizes with glass windows, with gable roof and 2 chimneys.

No. 308.	25	50	100
	$2.00	4.00	9.00 per doz.

(1893-1894)

CARL P. STIRN, Formerly of Stirn & Lyon, No. 597 BROADWAY, N. Y.

FINE MECHANICAL TIN TOYS.

432. Patent Galloping Mary and her little Lamb, with chime bells, 9½ inches. One in a box..per dozen, $3.87

433. Patent Galloping Horse, Jockey and Bell Tree, with chime bells, 9½ inches. One in a box........ per dozen, $3.87

No. 534. Santa Claus in Sleigh, drawn by two goats, 21 inches. One in a box........per dozen, $30.00

No. 530. Patent Mechanical Blondin Velocipede rider, dressed figure, diameter 19 inches. One in a box..............per dozen, 39.00

No. 531. Patent Mechanical Carousel, 14 figures, diameter 16¼ inches. One in a box..............per dozen, 39.00

404. Hurdle Race, Cantering Horse No. 2, Monkey rider and gong, movable, 12 inches. One-half dozen in a box..............per dozen, $6.00

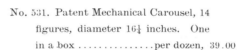

No. 532. Patent Mechanical Elevated Rail Road, consisting of dummy engine and three cars; diameter 19 inches. One in a box, per dozen, 39.00

No. 423. Patent Picnic Party, movable, striking two gongs, 12 inches. One in a box.........per dozen, $6.75

No. 533. Patent Mechanical Merry-Go-Round; dressed figure turning crank; 19 inches. One in a box..............per dozen, 45.00

ORGAN BANK.

		Per Dozen.
No. 235.	Organ Banks..	$1.85
No. 116.	" " monkey, with music........................	4.00
No. 119.	Large Organ Bank, monkey, with music................	8.00

DANCING BEAR BANK.
With Clock-work Mechanism and Chimes.
JUST OUT.

In this bank we have introduced some ingenious mechanism which produces very attractive results. It represents the front of a country house, with an Italian organ grinder and a bear on the lawn. After winding up the mechanism, place a coin in the slot and push the knob in front of the organ grinder, he will then deposit the coin and play the organ, while the bear performs his part. Handsomely painted. Packed one in a wooden box.

No. 132. Size, 6⅞ inches long, 4¾ wide, 5¼ high.....per dozen, $9.00

KICKING MULE BANK.

The mule and rider being brought into position, a slight touch on a knob at the base causes the mule to kick and throw the rider over his head, when the coin is thrown from the rider's mouth into the receptacle below. One in a box.

No. 190...................................per dozen, $8.00

COLUMBUS BANK.—New.

Place a coin in the slot at the feet of Columbus. Press the lever, and the coin disappears an Indian chief suddenly leaps from his place of concealment in the log, extending the pipe of peace as Columbus salutes him.

The design is of historic interest. On one side, in bold relief, is the s of Columbus, and on the other a mounted Indian hunter in full chase buffalo. The bank is entirely and richly finished in bronze of gold, silver a other shades. One in a box.

No. 326...per dozen, $8.00

PAVILION BANK.

No. 45.   Newest 5c Bank ....per dozen $. 37

SECURITY BANK.

CUT HALF SIZE.

No. 120.   New, finished with handsome gold top.....................per dozen, $1.75

CARL P. STIRN, Formerly of Stirn & Lyon, No. 597 BROADWAY, N. Y.

IRON TOY PISTOLS.

Hammerless.
. X. A new fast seller, very popular
the boys. 8 inches long Per
................................70c

Dead Shot.—Japanned.
No. 35. The largest best selling 10c. Pistol,
japanned, 9½ inches long.........per doz. 63c.

Cut is half size of original.
Volunteer.
No. 50. Japanned,
long............per doz., 30c.

. 125. Japanned Revolver Shape, 5½ ins.
...................per doz., 33c.
. 76N. Fine polished, full nickel, revolver
, 5½ ins. long...........per doz., 70c.

No. 25. Bronzed, 4 inches long...................per doz., 20c.

. 2. Penny Pistols, 3½
long..... per gross, 75c

Comet.
No. V. Fine Japanned, Revolver shape, 6
inches long...................per doz., 37c.

Lionhead.
. 205. The finest finished, highly polished nickel,
shape, 5¾ ins. long...................per doz., 80c.

Columbia.
No. C. Best japanned 10c. Pistol out
this season, 9¼ ins. long....per doz., 75c

No. XX. The same as No. C. finest
polished nickel, 9¼ ins. long, $1.65 per doz

. 86J. Japanned, 4 inches
................per doz. 25c.

White Cap.
No. 201. The leading 15c. pistol this season, polished.
nickel, 7½ ins. long...................per doz., $1.25

SPRING TOYS
AND
NOVELTIES.

Return Balls.

No. 2.
Polished and
Gilded
Return Ball.

No. 4.
Painted
Return Ball.

No. 5.
Polished, Striped
and Gilded
Return Ball.

WITH RUBBER ELASTIC AND RINGS.

No.				Per gross.
2.	Painted, ½ gross in Box	.	.	$0 60
4.	" " ½ " "	.	.	70
2.	Mottled, ½ gross	.	.	85
4.	" " ½ " "	.	.	I 55

Jumping Ropes.

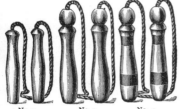

No. 1.
Jute Jumping
Rope.

No. 3.
Jute Jumping
Rope.

No. 4.
Colored
Jumping Rope.

Jute Ropes.

No.					Per doz.
1.	Stained handles, 6 ft. long	.		.	$0 20
2.	" " 6½ "				30
3.	" " 7 "				40
4.	" " 7 "				63
5.	" " 8 "			.	70

Stained Ropes.

No.					
10.	Colored handles, 6 ft. long,				25
30.	" " 6½ "				37
40.	Fancy " 7 "		.		70

Wire Chain Jumping Ropes (New).

		Per doz.
W 50, With Colored handles,	- -	$0 72

HOOPS.

Packed 1 Gross of 12 different sizes.

No.				Per doz.
36.	Ash, 22 to 32 inches,	.		$0 35
37.	" 36 to 44 "	.		67
38.	" 36 to 48 "	.		I 25
20.	Painted, with Bells, 28 to 36 in.	.		I 75

STAR HOOPS.

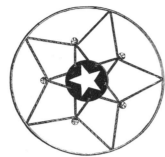

Star Hoop, stained, Red Star on stained wood centre, Small Bells.

No.		Per doz.
2.	Sizes 26 to 30 inches, - -	$2 00

Princess Hoops.

Hoop is made entirely of wood, painted red, 20 inches in diameter. Two tuned gongs ring constantly as Hoop is pushed.

No.							Per doz.
3.	.	.	.	.	.	.	$2 00
4.	.	.	.	.	.	.	4 00

Fancy Rolling Hoops.

No.		Per doz.
5.	Small, 15 inches in diameter, with 24 inch handles, . . .	$1 88

New Patent Pushing Hoop,
WITH CHIME.

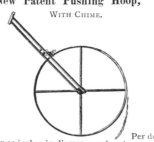

No.		Per doz.
6.	Hoop 13 inches in diameter, painted red, 24 inch Ash handle, . .	$1 88

Barnum's Calliope Cart.

A handsome 2-wheel Cart, with a set of chimes, which make a pleasant musical sound when the cart is set in motion.

No.		Per doz.
1.		$2 00

Patent Roller Chime.

This is a set of chimes arranged in a finely decorated barrel with a handle, which when drawn strikes several notes, making a very good imitation of a set of chimes.

26 inches long, per dozen, $4 00

Rattler Chimes (New).

Per doz.
An entirely new musical toy with chimes and colored pictures, - - - $2 00

Boys' Horse Reins.

No.		Per doz.
A	Red, white and blue web with leather belt, 1 bell, - -	$0 37
47	Red, white and blue web, 2 large bells and leather belt, - - -	70
I U	Red, white and blue web, with 1 large chime bell, - - -	75
2 D	Fancy striped web, with 2 heavy bells, - - -	2 00
35	Fancy striped web, with 2 heavy bells, - - -	2 00

Boys' Horse Reins—Contin

No.		
25	Fine, heavy web, with leather and three large bells,	
31	Fine, heavy web, fancy leat belt, with 6 large bells, -	
80	Fine, heavy all red web, with large chime bells, - -	
I F	Fine, heavy fancy web, with leather straps and 10 large b (packed each in a box), - -	

Whips and Switches.

No.		
29	Switch, Loop on handle, - per do	
33.	" with whistle,- -	
6.	" Jockey head,	
9.	" Ring lash,	
40.	" with handle, ring lash,	
21.	Whip, leather lash, - -	
22	" Straight, fine quality,	
48.	" Riding, fancy, - -	
790/15 "	Assorted, 12 on a card, inches long, - -	
790/25 "	Assorted, 12 kinds on a ca 56 inches long, - -	

Kites.

No.		
1.	Paper, assorted colors, -	
2.	" " "	
3.	" " "	
4.	" " " -	
5.	" " " -	

Japanese Bird Kites.

Small, - - - - - - per
Medium, - - - - - -
Large, - - - - - -

Columbia Parachute.

This toy can be carried in the pock ready to fly at any moment.

A toy that will have an enormous sal the coming spring and summer season.

Packed three dozen in a box, with she Price, per dozen, 75 cents.

Bean Shooter.

No.		
2.	Wood handles, - - - per do	
1.	Metal "	

RUBBER BALLS AND TOYS.

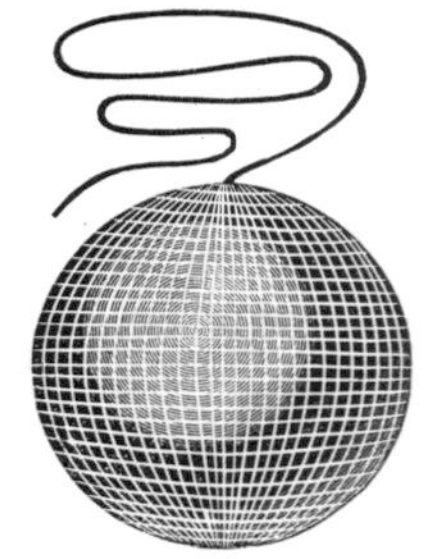

Knit Worsted Return Balls.

Per Doz.

Very showy toy, to each ball is attached an elastic cord. Assorted colors. 1 dozen in box. $ 35

, Knit worsted balls in fancy colors. 4 inches in diameter. 1 dozen in box. 75

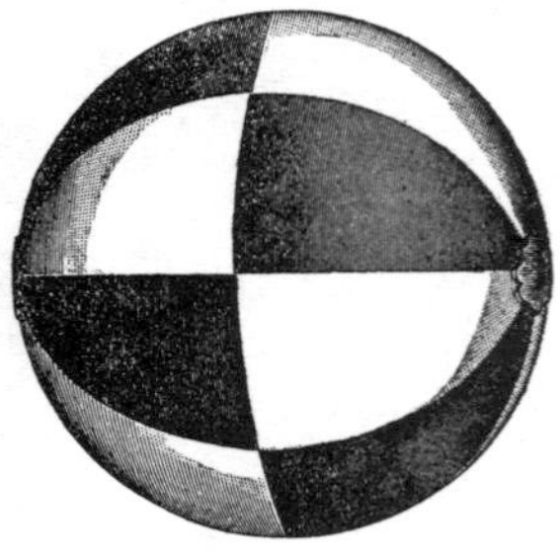

Kid Parlor Balls.

Per Doz.

The balls are covered with fine colored kid leather, stuffed with cotton, 2¼ inches in diameter. One dozen in box. 65

Same as before, 4 inches in diameter. Half dozen in a box. 1 75

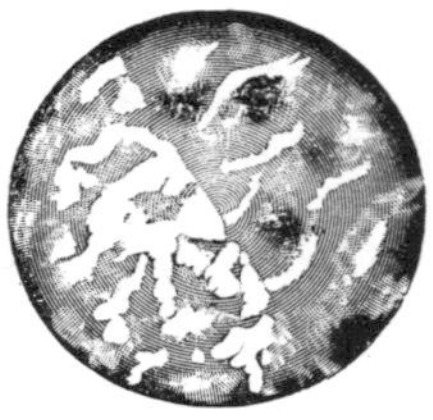

Celluloid Balls.

Variegated Colors.

	Per Doz.
½	$ 30
	37
½	67
	1 50

Celluloid Columbus Balls, (new).

y handsome balls in assorted colors, with pictures of the World's fair buildings and Columbus' portrait.

	Per Doz.
	75
	1 75

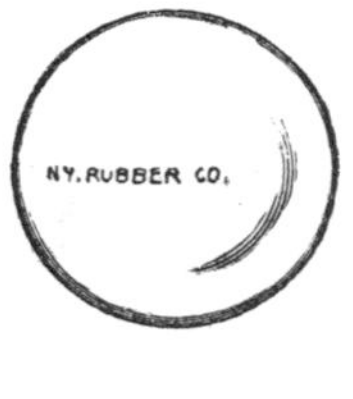

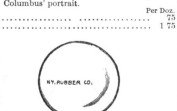

White Bat Balls.

	Diameter.	Per Doz
	1½ inch,	$0 20
	1⅝ "	24
	1¾ "	30
	1⅞ "	36
	2 "	42
	2¼ "	60
	2½ "	75
	2¾ "	1 00
n bulk	per gross,	2 00

White Inflated Balls.

No.	Diameter.	Doz.
105	1⅝ inch	$ 33
110	1¾ "	38
115	2 "	40
130	2½ "	75
155	3 "	1 50
175	4½ "	2 00

Red Inflated Balls.

No.	Diameter.	Doz.
132	2½ inch	$0 75

Solid Rubber Balls.

No.	Diameter.	Doz.
5	1½ inch	$0 25
10	1⅝ "	30
15	1¾ "	36
20	1⅞ "	40
25	2 "	45
30	2¼ "	70
35	2⅜ "	80
40	2½ "	1 00
45	2¾ "	1 25
Jack Stone Ball	per gross	75

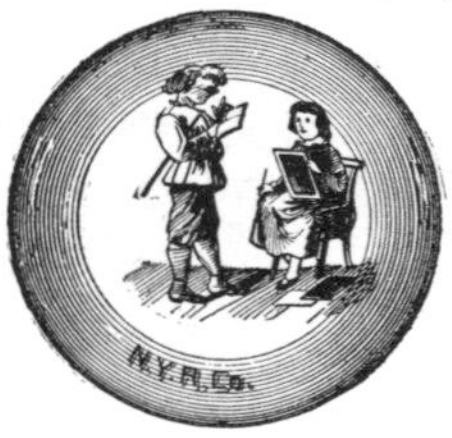

Fancy Colored Inflated Balls.

No.	Diametet.	Per Doz.
113	1¾ inch	$0 40
133	2¼ "	75
149	3 "	1 25
163	4 "	2 00
193	5½ "	4 00

Columbia Inflated Rubber Balls.

WITH VIEWS OF WORLD'S FAIR BUILDINGS.

No.		Per Doz.
1	3½ inches,	$1 88
2	5 "	3 75
3	7 "	8 50

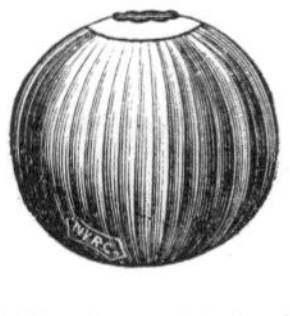

Colored Musical Fluted Balls.

No.	Diameter.	Per Doz.
15	1¾ inch	$ 38
25	2 "	50
35	2½ "	75
45	3 "	1 25
55	3½ "	2 00

Red Balloon Balls.

	Per Doz.
3½ inch diameter	$1 88
5 " "	3 50

Rubber Balloon Whistles.

No.		Per Gross.
1	Assorted colors, small penny size	$0 85
45	" " medium	2 50
50	" " large	3 75
60	" " extra large	4 25

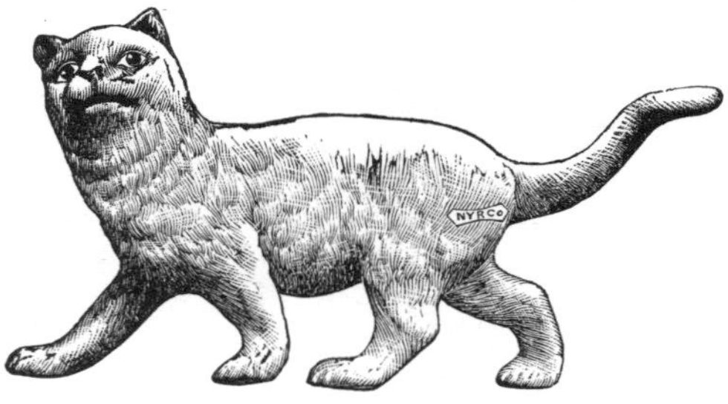

No.		Per
96.	Newfoundland Dog, 8 inches long. Each one in a box	
97.	Pug Dog, 7 inches long. Each one in a box	
98.	Cat, 8 inches long. 1 in a box	$

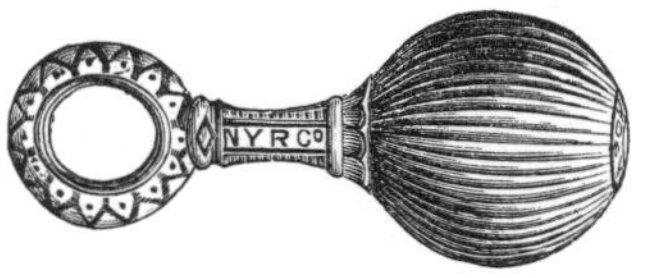

India Rubber Rattles.

No.		Per Doz.
63.	Globe shape, short ringed handle	$0 75
94.	Fancy shape, with long handle	1 00
11.	Dumb-bell shape	1 13
1 to 6.	Assorted long barrell, fancy heads, and other fancy shapes, with long ringed handles	1 12

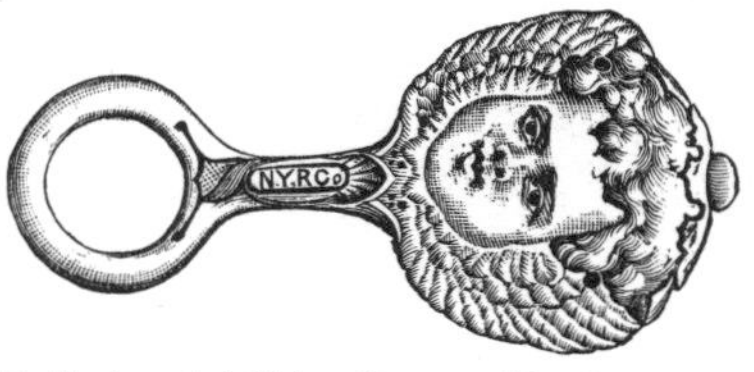

7 to 9. Assorted Baby Faces, with short ringed handles $1 25

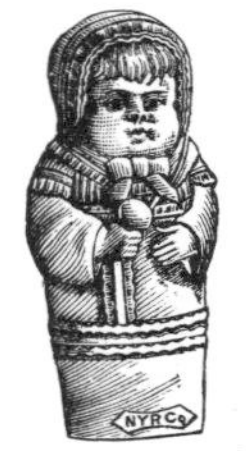

India Rubber Toys with Voices.

No.		Doz.
00.	Assorted Boys and Girls, 3 inches long.	$0 70
8.	Assorted Animals	75
7.	" Boys and Girls, 5 inches long.	1 25
6.	Assorted Figures, 5 inches long	1 75

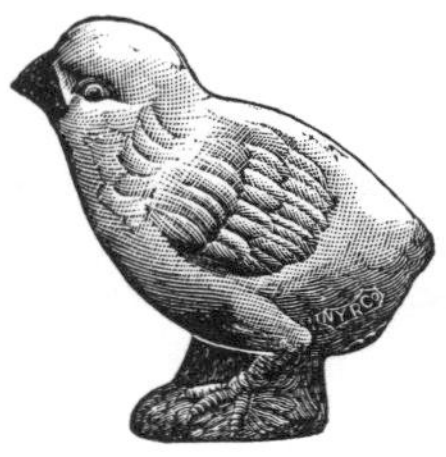

No.		Per Doz.
99.	Chickens	$0 75
54.	Assorted Soldiers, 4½ inches long	1 25
9.	Zuaves and Chinese	2 00
86.	Roly Poly Babies	1 88
10.	Assorted Animals	2 00
11.	" Cats and Dogs	2 00
106.	Cat in Boot	2 00
107.	Dog in Boot	2 00
109.	Cat in Basket	2 00
112.	Doll in Slipper	2 00
121.	Dogs, Lions, Goats, etc. ½ doz. in box	3 75

Rubber Teething Rings.

No.		Per
1.	White	$

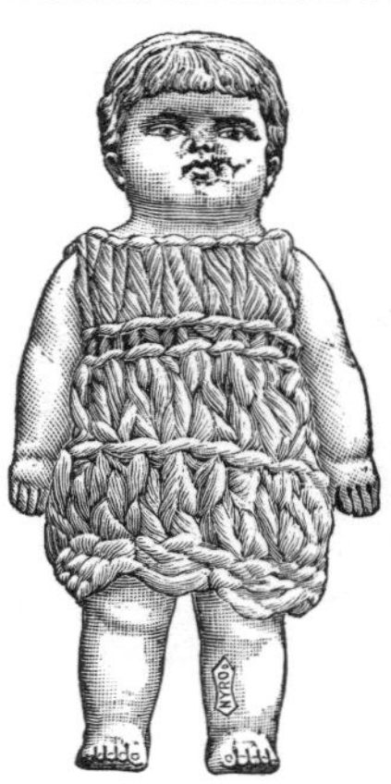

India Rubber Dolls.

No.		Per
83.	Babies, 3 inches long	$
4.	" 4½ "	
76.	" 5 "	

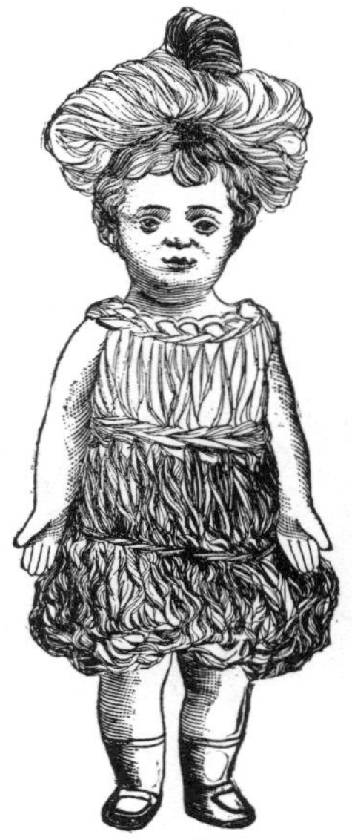

Rubber Dolls with Knit Worsted Dres

No.		Per
74D.	Fat Babies, 5½ inches long	$
65D.	" 7½ "	
85D.	" 10½ "	
113D.	Girls, 7 inches long	
117D.	" 9 "	
118D.	" 13 "	

GARDEN TOOLS, SEA SIDE AND SUMMER TOYS.

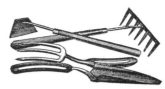

Floral Set.

No.		Per Doz
1.	3 Piece Set, all iron, consisting of trowel, weeder and fork, in a box	$ 75
8.	3 Piece Set, larger size, all iron	1 25
600.	4 Pieces, steel, with wooden handles	1 75

Extra Parts of Floral Tools.

No.		Per Doz
15.	Forks, iron	$ 35
20.	Trowels, iron	35
11.	Shovels, "	35
500.	Weeders, "	35

Garden Sets, Iron, with Long Wooden Handles.

No.		Per Doz
0.	3 Piece Sets	$0 75
1.	3 " larger	1 25
3.	3 " better quality	1 75
100.	3 Piece Steel Sets	1 88
30.	4 " " " fine, with varnished handles	4 00
7.	3 " Fine Polished Steel, black enamel finish, extra long handles	8 00

Tin Watering Pot, or Sprinkler.

No.		Per Doz
1.	Painted red or green	$0 38
3.	" " "	70
6.	Silverine	70

Sea Side Pails and Shovels.

No.		Per Doz
3.	Tin painted pails and shovels with wood handles	$0 38
5.	Same as before, large size	65
16.	Tin painted pail with japanned wood handle, and wood handle shovel	75
OO-13.	Silverine Pails with shovels	38
O-2.	Same as before, larger	65
O-5.	Extra large size with wooden handle and stamped Jumbo in the bottom	75

Sea Side Shovels.

No.		Per Doz
6.	Black japanned, with wooden handle, 16 inches long	$0 33
7.	Same as above, galvanized shovel	37

Wooden Sea Side Sand Pails,

No.		Per Doz
	Infant, small	$0 40
	" medium	72
	Wooden Sea Side Sand Shovels	35

Sea Side Sand Mill.

No		Per Doz
25	A new toy made of white wood, with figure turning the mill	$2 00

Children's Swings.

For Out and In-door use.

No.		Per Doz.
1.	Globe Swing, plain	$2 00
2.	Swing, upholstered with creton	3 60
3.	Swing, cushioned seat and back	4 00

Camp Stools.

No.		Per Doz
A.	Hard Wood, 12x12 inch, duck seat. 1 dozen in a bundle	$2 00

Buck and Saw.

Made to take apart. Put up in a neat [

No.		
1.	15 inches long	
2.	23 " "	

Roaming Parrot, 7½ inches l[

The Walking Parrot.

Similar to the Walking Alligator and Walking Turtle, which has had so great a sale...

Roaming Alligator, Painted, 10 inches long.

The Roaming Alligator.

No.		
660.	Tin, painted in bright colors. Operates similar to the Roaming Turtle. Size, inches long. Packed one dozen in package	

The Roaming Hippopotamus.

The Roaming Hippopota[

A new toy similar to the a[painted in natural colors, [moving jaw

The Roaming Turtle.

No.	
661.	Made of Tin, Beautifully colored—gold, green and blue. Always on the go. Acts like a live Turtle. Led by a string. No hunting the Turtle; no winding up; no stopping. With a little practice any one can learn to guide the turtle by the string, like a pet animal. 7 inches long. Packed 1 dozen in a package

Roaming Turtle, 7 inches

98

CARL P. STIRN, Formerly of Stirn & Lyon, No. 597 BROADWAY, N. Y.

IRON, TIN AND PEWTER TOYS.

Jack Stones.

No.				Per Gross
0.	Jack Stones, 2 gross in box			$0 09
1.	"	2	"	12
1½.	"	2	"	14
2.	"	1	"	18

Toy Hammers.

	Per Doz
Copper	$0 20
"	30
"	65
Tack, polished	67

Toy Hatchets.

	Per Doz
	$0 30
	33
	37
	63
	75

Iron Penny Toys.

Pick, Shovel, Hatchet, Rake and Hoe.

	Per Gross
, (assorted, ⅓ gross in box)	$0 80
, (with wooden handles)	85

Toy Sad Irons.

	Per Doz
ith Stands	$0 33
"	40
"	67
ith wooden handles and stands	37
" "	70
olishing Iron, 1 in a box	2 00

Iron Safes.

	Per Doz
Daisy, with lock and key	$0 40
Special Safe, with lock and key, 3 ins. high	70
Fancy Safe, with lock and key, bronzed, and ornamented with gold	75
Security Safe, with combination lock	2 00
Same style as No. 100, extra size	4 00

Pocket Banks, (Nickel Plated).

	Per Doz
Dime Bank	$0 65
Magic Bank for dimes	75

No. 13B Rattle. (New).

No.		Per Doz
13B.	Rattle with 4 bells. One dozen in a package	$0 38
14B.	Same style, larger	67

Best 5c rattle made. Nickel bell. Japanned handle. Packed 1 dozen in a package... 35

Double Rattles.

	Per Doz
panned handle. 1 dozen in package	$0 38
ame style as No. 6, with extra large bells	75

No.		Per Doz
8.	Double rattle, double ends. Four separate rattles. Packed one dozen in a package	$0 80

Tea Bells.

	Per Doz
White metal, black handle. 1 dozen in a box	$0 30
Same style, larger	37
Japanned handle. Packed 1 dozen in a package	40

New Tea Bell.

No.		Per Doz
93.	Bell Metal, Japanned handle. Height, 5½ inches. The best 10c bell ever offered. Packed one dozen in a package	$0 75
40.	Special Nickel Bell, with japanned handle, extra size	1 65

Call Bells.

No.		Per Doz
201.	New style. Nickel plated. The best 10c call bell ever offered. Packed 1 dozen in a package	$0 67

No.		Per Doz
75.	New style. Nickel Plated Metal base. The best 25c call bell on the market. Packed 6 in a package	$2 00

Bicycle Bells.

No.		Per Doz
10.	All nickel, special size for 10c	$0 75
25.	Bicycle Bells, best bell metal. All nickel. Large size	2 00

No.		Per Doz
126.	Double Chime Bells, with tin horse, (new)	$0 75
129.	Same style, extra large	2 00

No.		Per Doz
00½	Chimes on Wheels	$0 70
1½	"	1 75
2½	"	
	very large	4 00

Pewter Toys.

No.		Per Gross
3.	Nightingale Whistles, small	$2 00
5.	" " large	3 00
30.	Cockoo Whistles, small	2 00
40.	" " large	3 00

No.		Per Gro
40.	Rooster Whistles, small	$2
60.	" " large	3

Metal Whistles and Dog Calls.

No.		Per Doz
3.	Metal Dog Calls	$0 25
5.	" " " nickel	33
10.	" " " "	63
25.	Duplex Bicycle, with chain	1 25

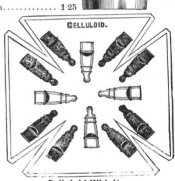

CELLULOID.

Celluloid Whistles.

One Dozen on a Card.

	Per I
Celluloid, small, very salable	$0
Same style, medium	1
Same style, large	1

Tin Flutes.

					Per Gr
7 inches, plain, 1 gross in a box					$0
10	"	"	¼	"	2
12	"	"	1-6	"	2
14	"	"	1-6	"	3
10	"	colored, ¼ gross in a box			2
12	"	"	1-6	"	3
14	"	"	1-6	"	3

Fine Tin Flageolets.

	Per
Flageolets with brass tips, finely tuned, 1 dozen in a box	$0

Tin Fish Horns.

Best quality.

			Per
10 inches, with flange			$0
12	"	"	
14	"	"	
16	"	"	
18	"	"	
22	"	"	
25	"	"	1
			Per Gr
6	"	colored, penny	
			Per
10	"	" with flange	
12	"	"	
14	"	"	
16	"	"	
18	"	"	
22	"	"	1
25	"	"	1

Tin Jubilee Horns

	Per
38. 3 Horns connected	$2
58. 5 " "	4

GUNS, AIR RIFLES, FISHING TACKLE AND SPORTSMEN'S OUTFITS.

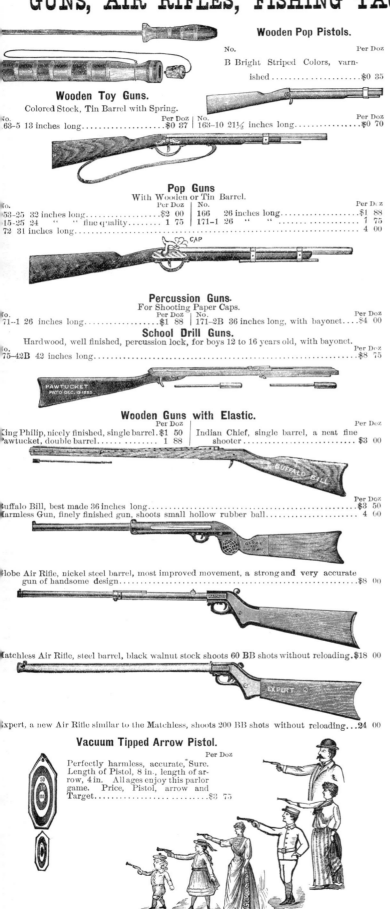

Wooden Pop Pistols.

No.	Per Doz
B Bright Striped Colors, varnished	$0 35

Wooden Toy Guns.
Colored Stock, Tin Barrel with Spring.

No.	Per Doz	No.	Per Doz
163-5 13 inches long	$0 37	163-10 21½ inches long	$0 70

Pop Guns
With Wooden or Tin Barrel.

No.	Per Doz	No.	Per Doz
153-25 32 inches long	$2 00	166 26 inches long	$1 88
15-25 24 " " fine quality	1 75	171-1 26 " "	1 75
72 31 inches long	4 00		

Percussion Guns.
For Shooting Paper Caps.

No.	Per Doz	No.	Per Doz
71-1 26 inches long	$1 88	171-2B 36 inches long, with bayonet	$4 00

School Drill Guns.
Hardwood, well finished, percussion lock, for boys 12 to 16 years old, with bayonet.

No.	Per Doz
75-42B 42 inches long	$8 75

Wooden Guns with Elastic.

	Per Doz		Per Doz
King Philip, nicely finished, single barrel	$1 50	Indian Chief, single barrel, a neat fine shooter	$3 00
Pawtucket, double barrel	1 88		

	Per Doz
Buffalo Bill, best made 36 inches long	$3 50
Harmless Gun, finely finished gun, shoots small hollow rubber ball	4 00

Globe Air Rifle, nickel steel barrel, most improved movement, a strong and very accurate gun of handsome design ... $8 00

Matchless Air Rifle, steel barrel, black walnut stock shoots 60 BB shots without reloading . $18 00

Expert, a new Air Rifle similar to the Matchless, shoots 200 BB shots without reloading ... 24 00

Vacuum Tipped Arrow Pistol.

	Per Doz
Perfectly harmless, accurate, sure. Length of Pistol, 8 in., length of arrow, 4 in. All ages enjoy this parlor game. Price, Pistol, arrow and Target	$3 75

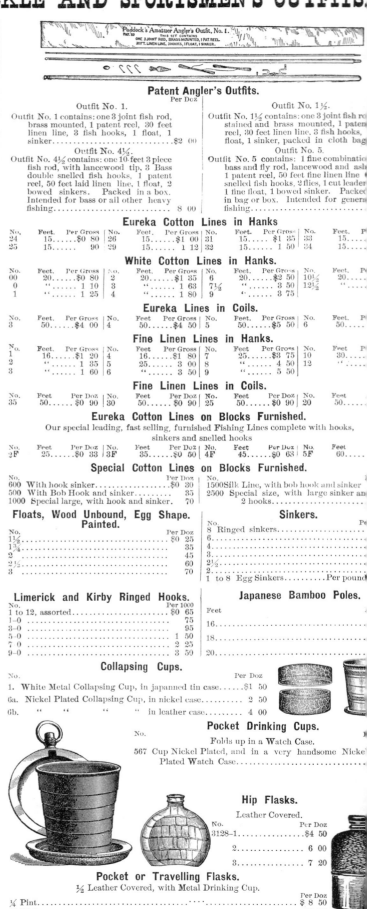

Patent Angler's Outfits.

Per Doz

Outfit No. 1.
Outfit No. 1 contains: one 3 joint fish rod, brass mounted, 1 patent reel, 30 feet linen line, 3 fish hooks, 1 float, 1 sinker ... $2 00

Outfit No. 1½.
Outfit No. 1½ contains: one 3 joint fish rod, stained and brass mounted, 1 patent reel, 30 feet linen line, 3 fish hooks, 1 float, 1 sinker, packed in cloth bag

Outfit No. 4½.
Outfit No. 4½ contains: one 10-feet 3 piece fish rod, with lancewood tip, 3 Bass double snelled fish hooks, 1 patent reel, 50 feet laid linen line, 1 float, 2 bowed sinkers. Packed in a box. Intended for bass or all other heavy fishing ... 8 00

Outfit No. 5.
Outfit No. 5 contains: 1 fine combination bass and fly rod, lancewood and ash, 1 patent reel, 50 feet fine linen line, 3 snelled fish hooks, 2 flies, 1 cut leader, 1 fine float, 1 bowed sinker. Packed in bag or box. Intended for general fishing.

Eureka Cotton Lines in Hanks

No.	Feet.	Per Gross	No.	Feet.	Per Gross	No.	Feet.	Per Gross	No.	Feet.
24	15	$0 80	26	15	$1 00	31	15	$1 35	33	15
25	15	90	29	15	1 12	32	15	1 50	34	15

White Cotton Lines in Hanks.

No.	Feet.	Per Gross	No.	Feet.	Per Gross	No.	Feet.	Per Gross	No.	Feet.
00	20	$0 80	2	20	$1 35	6	20	$2 50	10½	20
0	"	1 10	3	"	1 63	7½	"	3 50	12½	"
1	"	1 25	4	"	1 80	9	"	3 75		

Eureka Lines in Coils.

No.	Feet.	Per Gross	No.	Feet.	Per Gross	No.	Feet.	Per Gross	No.	Feet.
3	50	$4 00	4	50	$4 50	5	50	$5 50	6	50

Fine Linen Lines in Hanks.

No.	Feet.	Per Gross	No.	Feet.	Per Gross	No.	Feet.	Per Gross	No.	Feet.
1	16	$1 20	4	16	$1 80	7	25	$3 75	10	30
2	"	1 35	5	25	3 00	8	"	4 50	12	"
3	"	1 60	6	"	3 50	9	"	5 50		

Fine Linen Lines in Coils.

No.	Feet	Per Doz	No.	Feet	Per Doz	No.	Feet	Per Doz	No.	Feet
35	50	$0 90	30	50	$0 90	25	50	$0 90	20	50

Eureka Cotton Lines on Blocks Furnished.
Our special leading, fast selling, furnished Fishing Lines complete with hooks, sinkers and snelled hooks

No.	Feet	Per Doz	No.	Feet	Per Doz	No.	Feet	Per Doz	No.	Feet
2F	25	$0 33	3F	35	$0 50	4F	45	$0 63	5F	60

Special Cotton Lines on Blocks Furnished.

No.		Per Doz	No.	
600	With hook sinker	$0 30	1500	Silk Line, with bob hook and sinker
500	With Bob Hook and sinker	35	2500	Special size, with large sinker and 2 hooks
1000	Special large, with hook and sinker	70		

Floats, Wood Unbound, Egg Shape. Painted.

No.	Per Doz
1½	$0 25
1¾	35
2	45
2½	60
3	70

Sinkers.

No.	Per
8 Ringed sinkers	
6	
4	
3	
2½	
2	
1 to 8 Egg Sinkers	Per pound

Limerick and Kirby Ringed Hooks.

No.	Per 1000
1 to 12, assorted	$0 65
1-0	75
3-0	95
5-0	1 50
7 0	2 25
9-0	3 50

Japanese Bamboo Poles.

Feet
16
18
20

Collapsing Cups.

No.		Per Doz
1.	White Metal Collapsing Cup, in japanned tin case	$1 50
6a.	Nickel Plated Collapsing Cup, in nickel case	2 50
6b.	" " " " in leather case	4 00

Pocket Drinking Cups.
Folds up in a Watch Case.

No.	
567	Cup Nickel Plated, and in a very handsome Nickel Plated Watch Case

Hip Flasks.
Leather Covered.

No.	Per Doz
3128-1	$4 50
2	6 00
3	7 20

Pocket or Travelling Flasks.
½ Leather Covered, with Metal Drinking Cup.

	Per Doz
¼ Pint	$8 50
½ Pint	12 00

CARL P. STIRN, Formerly of Stirn & Lyon, No. 597 BROADWAY, N. Y.

✠ BASE BALLS AND BASE BALL GOODS ✠

Carr's Base Balls.

BEST QUALITY BALLS, WARRANTED PERFECT.

	Per Doz.
, Boys' size, 2 piece ball...$ 35
Favorite, 2 " " 75
Regulation, 2 " " 1 25
Club, full regulation size.............................. 1 75
Prof. Dead, Horsehide cover........................ 1 75
League, " " extra fine............................ 3 75
Junior, regulation size.............................. 2 75
Club, selected Horsehide.......................... 3 75
yn Club, selected Horsehide...................... 3 75
sional Dead, finest quality, double cover...... 5 50
Club, extra fine Horsehide, " " 8 00

Base Ball Belts.

	Per Doz.
ys' size, sliding buckle, solid or striped colors................$ 35
ys' extra size, anchor buckle, solid or striped colors........... 79
n's special extra wide, silk finish, snake buckle.............. 80
n's all silk, assorted colors.......................... 1 75
n's fine satin, new patent buckle.................... 1 75
n's fine grained leather belts........................ 2 00
n's extra fine, calf skin belts, extra lengths............ 4 00

Base Ball Caps.

Assorted Colors.

	Per Doz.
ey Shape, muslin...................................$ 25
nd " " with star.......................... 33
" Flannel, with Braid........................ 70
" striped muslin.......................... 70
Top, white duck, with B. B. Bats and Ball design on top...... 75
e as before, with the design in front.................. 75
Top, white duck, with diamond design.................. 75
nd Shape, striped flannel, lined...................... 1 38
ked, flannel, Tennis.............................. 1 35

Catchers' Masks.

No.		Per Doz.
1	Boys'..$ 2 00
D	Spalding's Boys' Mask......................... 4 00
C	Youths' Mask................................. 8 00
B	Boys' Amateur................................ 13 50
A	Amateur...................................... 16 00
0	Regulation League............................ 27 00
00	Special League............................... 30 00
000	Patent Neck Protecting Mask................. 36 00
0000	Sun Protecting Mask......................... 45 00

Spalding's Base Balls.

BOYS' SIZE, EACH BALL IN A BOX.

No.		Per Doz.
13	Rocket,.......................................$ 45
9B	Boys' Lively.................................. 75
7B	Boys' League Junior, Horsehide............... 2 00
11	Boys' Bouncer, all rubber inside.............. 2 00

REGULATION SIZES, EACH BALL IN A BOX.

No.		Per Doz.
8	Eureka.......................................$ 75
6	Victor....................................... 1 50

FOLLOWING ALL HORSEHIDE.

7	Boys' Favorite............................... 2 00
5	King of the Diamond......................... 3 75
3	Amateur..................................... 6 00
2	Professional................................. 8 00
0	Double Seam................................. 12 00
1	Official League.............................. 12 00

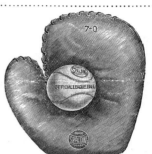

Base Ball Catchers Mitts.

No.		Per Doz. Pair
5	Boys' Canvas, leather back....................$ 2 00
4	Boys' Canvas, Tan, all leather, with fingers...... 4 00
3	Men's leather, large size...................... 8 00
2	Boys' leather laced back...................... 18 00
A	Amateur, extra large......................... 21 00
0X	Men's Decker's Patent back................... 30 00
5-0	Men's Precaria Hog Mitts.................... 45 00
6-0	Men's Buck, calf back........................ 51 00
7-0	Men's All Buck, best quality.................. 66 00

BASEMEN'S MITTS.

No.		Per Doz
4X	Buck...$18 00
3X	" fine quality.............................. 21 00

	Per Doz.
Base Ball Guides.............................$ 8

B. B. Body Protectors.

No.		Each
A	Chamois Canvas..............................$2 50
1	Amateur...................................... 4 50
0	League....................................... 7 50
00	Umpire....................................... 8 00

Base Ball Bats.

SPALDING'S TRADE MARKED BATS.

No.		Per Doz
54	Maple, 26 to 28 inches.......................$ 3
53	" polished, 28 to 32 inches................. 7
56	" stained and polished, with gold stripes, 28 to 32 in... 7
2X	Antique Ash................................. 2 0
0XB	Boys' Axle Tree............................. 2 0
0X	Men's Axle Tree............................. 3 7
000	Wagon Tongue Ash League Bats.............. 8 0

101

C. F. RICE, 204-208 S. GREEN ST., CHICAGO.

IRON VELOCIPEDE.

Well made and finished.

STEEL TIRES.

No. 1. 16 inch front wheel, each.....$1 55
No. 2. 20 " " " 1 85
No. 3. 22 " " " 2 20

RUBBER TIRES.

No. 4. 16 inch front wheel, each.....$2 75
No. 5. 20 " " " 3 25
No. 6. 22 " " " 3 70

TRICYCLES.

Very easy running and handsomely finished. Have an improved spring seat, which takes all vibration and makes riding easy and comfortable. Can be shipped K. D. when desired.

BLACK FRAME, C PLATE OVAL IRON TIRE WHEELS, UPHOLSTERED IN CRIMSON PLUSH.

No. 18. Rear wheels 18 in. for girls 2 to 4 years (without fenders), each, $4 00
No. 20. " " 20 " " 3 " 5 " " 5 35
No. 22. " " 22 " " 4 " 7 " " 6 65
No. 26. " " 26 " " 7 "10 " " 8 00
No. 30. " " 30 " " 10 "15 " " 9 35

BLACK FRAME, C PLATE RUBBER TIRE WHEELS, UPHOLSTERED IN PLUSH.

No. 18X. Same as No. 18, but with rubber-tired wheels, each.....$ 6 65
No. 20X. " No. 20, " " 8 00
No. 22X. " No. 22, " " 11 50
No. 26X. " No. 26, " " 12 75
No. 30X. " No. 30, " " 14 00

Send for my large 1895 Catalogue if you have not got it.

THE BEST STEEL WAGON.

Patented 1888—1891

Size of body.		Size of wheels.	
No. 00.	11x22	8 and 11 inch, each	$1 20
No. 0.	12x24	8 and 12 " "	1 30
No. 2.	14x28	12 and 16 " "	1 60

The box is constructed of the best quality of sheet steel, bent over a steel rod, and is nailed firmly to the bottom board. The bodies are handsomely painted, striped and nicely lettered. Malleable iron gear, japanned. Packed four in a crate. I do not break crates.

No. 49. WAGON.

Four wheels, tin tire; has 6 and 8-inch wheels. Body, 8x16 inches; stenciled and varnished on wood. Front wheels turn under body. Six in crate. I do not break crates. Order by crates.

Price, per doz.....$3 15

No. 15. CAB WAGON.

Body 15x30 inches, with rail and dash, painted and scrolled. Wheels 12 and 16 inches, with hub caps. Has iron axles, tinned malleable iron draw and circle plates. One-third dozen in crate.

Each.............................$1 25

WILLOW DOLL CABS ON WOOD SPRINGS.

No. 210.

Body 24 inches long, set on wood springs, 8 and 10 inch wood wheels, bent handles, 6 in a crate.   Per dozen, $7.00.

No. 212.

Same carriage as No 210, with silesia lining and lace on edge of same, with parasol and rod, 4 in a crate.   Per dozen, $12.00.

☞ **Do not forget my large Cash Discount of 10 per cent.**

No. 226. DOLL CARRIAGE.

Reed body 26 inches long, in fancy design, upholstered in velvet and plush, steel wheels, axles and springs brightly plated, 12 and 14 inch wheels, parasol and rod and long bent handles.   Each, $3.50.

No. 228. DOLL CARRIAGE.

Fancy body made of reed and turned wood with turned wood ball ornaments, upholstered in damask and plush, with oilcloth mat, steel wheels, axles and springs brightly plated, long bent handles, 12 and 14 inch wheels, parasol and rod.   Each, $3.75.

No. 230. DOLL CARRIAGE.

Fancy reed body, 27 inches long, upholstered in plush and damask, steel wheels, axles and springs brightly plated, long bent handles, 12 and 14 inch wheels, and oilcloth mat, parasol and rod.   Each, $4.00.

No. 232. DOLL CARRIAGE.

Reed body, 27 inches long, in beautiful, handsome design, upholstered in silk plush, with oilcloth mat, steel wheels, axles and springs brightly plated, long bent handles, 12 and 14 inch wheels, with parasol and rod, fine goods.   Each, $4.50.

HARDWOOD CLIPPERS.

No. 100. Same as cut: size. 11x37 inches; nicely varnished, with top board painted and ornamented, hand holes on sides, flat shoes, per dozen $4 80

No. 101. Same as cut, but half round shoes. per dozen............................. 6 00

No. 81. GIRLS' CUTTERS.

No. 81. Neatly varnished and ornamented; has seat and push handle, flat shoes. Cheapest cutter made, each $1 15

No. 43. GIRLS' CUTTERS.

No. 43. Nicely painted and ornamented throughout; has large, deep body and seat, not upholstered; push handle, round side fenders, brightly plated braces, half-round shoes, each...................... $2 25

No. 44. More expensively painted, and upholstered in plush... 3 90

C. F. Rice, The Leader (1895)

THE LEADER OF LOW PRICES.

No. 50. WAGON, WOOD AXLE.
Wood axles; body 12x24 inches; hardwood sides; wheels 10 and 14 inches. Front wheels turn under the body and tailboard takes out. Varnish, scrolled and lettered. Six in crate. I do not break crates. Order by crates.

    Price, per dozen...................$6.35

No. 51. WOOD AXLE.
Has 10 and 14 inch wheels. Front wheels turn under. Body 12x25 inches; varnished. Rail on top of body painted red. Edge at bottom painted red. A strong, serviceable wagon. Six in crate. I do not break crates. Order by crates.

    Price, per dozen...................$6.75

No. 52. WOOD AXLE.
Wheels 10½ and 16⅜ inches. Front wheels turn under. Curved front axles. Body 13x28 inches. Rail on top of body. Rail and wagon bottom painted red. This wagon has a malleable iron tongue holder. Half dozen in crate. I do not break crates. Order by crates.

    Price, per dozen...................$9.50

    Seats for any of above, 18 cents.

No. 53. WAGON, IRON AXLE.
Body, 13x26 inches, varnished on wood. Rail on body and edge of bottom painted red. Wheels 10 and 14 inches. Iron box in hub. Iron axles, right and left hand malleable nuts. Tinned malleable iron draw and circle plates. Half dozen in crates.

    Price, per dozen...............$8.25

No. 54. WAGON, IRON AXLE.
Body 13x28 inches, painted and scrolled. Rail on body and edge of bottom painted red. Wheels 10½ and 16 inches. Iron box in hub. Iron axles, with right and left hand malleable nuts. Tinned malleable iron draw and circle plates. Half dozen in crate.

    Price, each...............95 cents

No. 11. WAGON, IRON AXLE.
Iron axles. Body 14x28 inches; wheels 12 and 16 inches. Hardwood panel body, landscape painting, scrolled and varnished, hub caps, high seat and dashboard, iron braced; heavy iron axles in iron thimble skeins; oval tires, welded and shrunk on. Same as cut. Four in a crate. Order by crates as I do not break crates.

    Price, each...................$1.85

KID BODY DOLLS.

Best line of Kid Body Dolls in America. Quality right, price right, workmanship of the best. Please note that where sizes are given on kid dolls there is apt to be a difference, as for instance, a doll that is called 15¾ in. may measure even 16 in. and sometimes only 15½, for in stuffing dolls they may run a little stouter or thinner and this necessarily affects the length.

KID DOLLS WITH BISQUE HEADS & HANDS.

Popular dolls to retail at popular prices.

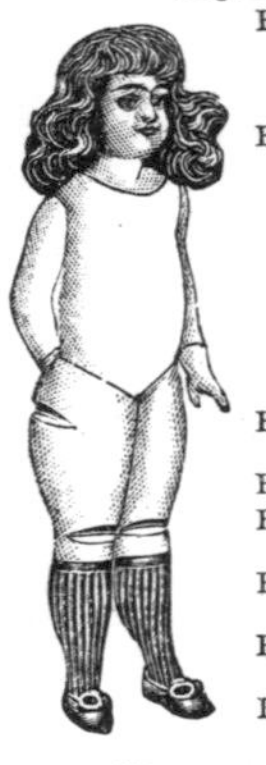

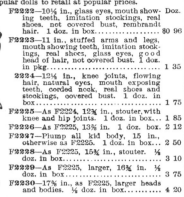

F2222—10½ in., glass eyes, mouth showing teeth, imitation stockings, real shoes, not covered bust, rembrandt hair. 1 doz. in box........ Doz. $0 96
F2223—11 in., stuffed arms and legs, mouth showing teeth, imitation stockings, real shoes, glass eyes, good head of hair, not covered bust. 1 doz. in pkg........ 1 35
2224—12½ in., knee joints, flowing hair, natural eyes, mouth exposing teeth, corded neck, real shoes and stockings, covered bust. 1 doz. in box........ 1 75
F2225—As F2224, 12¾ in., stouter, with knee and hip joints. 1 doz. in box... 1 85
F2226—As F2225, 13⅜ in. 1 doz. box. 2 12
F2227—Plump all kid body, 15 in., otherwise as F2225. 1 doz. in box... 2 50
F2228—As F2225, 15¾ in., stouter. ½ doz. in box........ 3 10
F2229—As F2225, larger, 16¾ in. ½ doz. in box........ 3 75
F2230—17⅜ in., as F2225, larger heads and bodies. ½ doz. in box........ 4 20

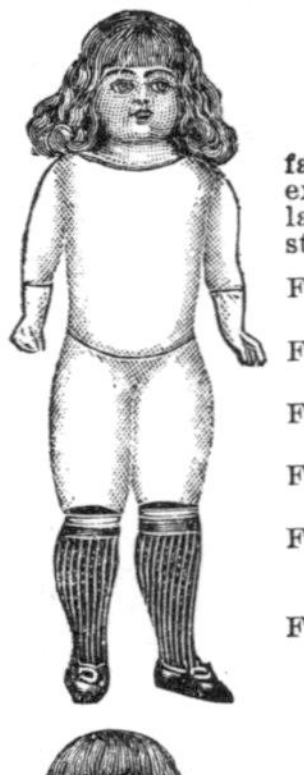

"SLEEPING" KID BODY DOLLS.

These have **moving eyes,** splendid faces, bisque heads, flowing hair, mouth exposing teeth, painted eyebrows and lashes, covered bust and real shoes and stockings.

F2234—12⅝ in., width hip and knee joints, flowing hair. 1 doz. in box. 2 15
F2235—As F2234, 13 in., with curls, openwork stockings. 1 doz. in box. 2 25
F2246—As F2235, 15 in. ½ doz. in box........ 3 00
F2237—As F2234, curly hair, 16½ in., natural eyes. ½ doz. in box....... 4 10
F2238—18½ in., hemstitched corded neck and wrists, asstd. stockings. ½ doz. in box........ 5 95
F2239—As F2238, 21 in., hip, knee and elbow joints. Each in box..... 8 50

"CURLY HAIR" KID BODY DOLLS.

A very good moderate priced line. Popular sellers.

F2231—18½ in., stout bodies, covered bust, real shoes, bisque hands, hip and knee joints, bisque head, natural eyes, lashes and eybrows, mouth showing teeth. Asstd. fancy and openwork stockings. ½ doz. in box. 5 50
F2232—As F2231, 21 in., with elbow, knee and hip joints. Each in box. 8 35
F2233—As F2232, 22½ in. Each in box........ 9 00

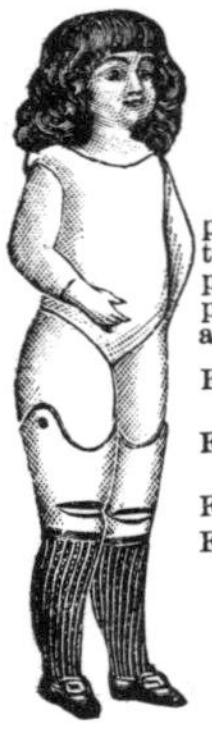

PATENT HIP-JOINTED KID BODY DOLLS.

Sample this line.

Good bisque heads and hands, curly hair, painted eyelids and lashes, mouth showing teeth, covered corded bust, joint at knee and patent riveted hip joints so dolls can be placed in any position, openwork stockings and slippers.

F2240—13¼ in., with flowing hair. 1 doz. in box........ 2 08
F2241—16¼ in., curly hair, larger in every way. ½ doz. in box........ 4 25
F2247—18½ in. As F2241. Each in box.. 6 15
F2242—22½ in., as above, only larger. Each in box........ 8 90

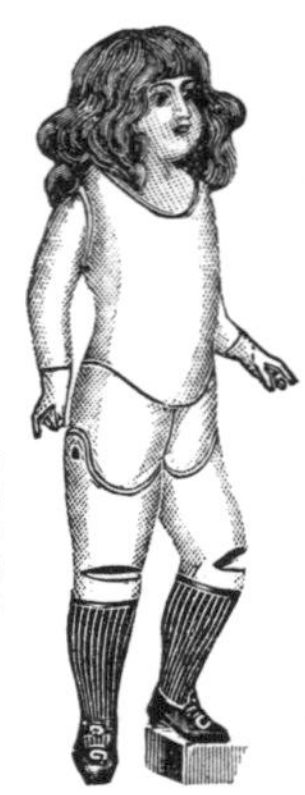

"SLEEPING" PATENT HIP-JOINTED KID BODY DOLLS.

As above with **moving eyes** and curly hair.

F2243—12½ in. *A value of exceptional merit.* 1 doz. in box...Doz. $2 25
F2248—13¾ in. 1 doz. in box...... 3 15
F2244—15⅝ in. ½ doz. in box...... 4 20
F2249—17¼ in. ½ doz. in box...... 6 00
F2245—21¼ in. Each in box....... 8 40

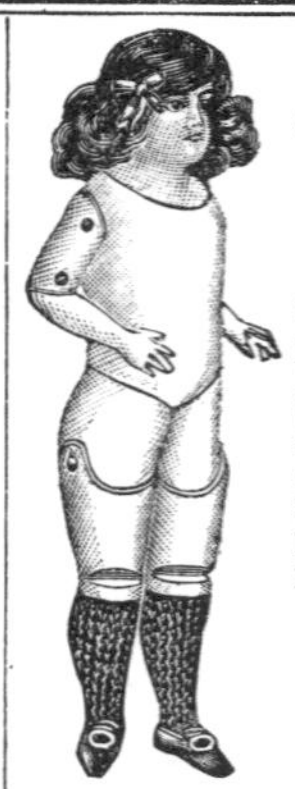

SLEEPING "PATENT RIVET JOINTED" KID BODY DOLLS.

High grade—not too high priced.

Bisque head, painted eyebrows and lashes, mouth exposing teeth, **moving eyes,** fine curly hair wig, part at side with ribbon bow, extra stout body, covered corded bust, bisque forearm and hand, patent riveted shoulder, elbow and hip joints, asstd. fancy stockings and real shoes. Each in box.

F2250—21¾ in........ Each $1 18
F2251—24½ "........ " 1 50
F2252—25⅝ "........ " 1 85

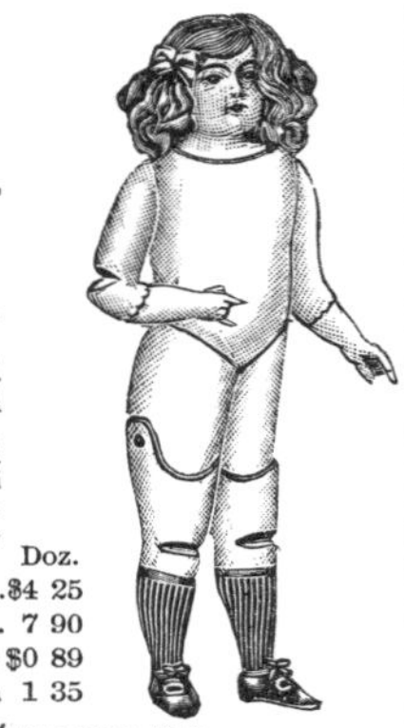

"MISS MILLIONAIRE" KID BODY DOLLS.

Sleeping Patent Hip-Jointed Kid Body Dolls With Real Eyelashes.

Fine bisque heads, curly hair, sewed wigs with side part and ribbon bow, painted eyebrows, real lashes, open mouth exposing teeth, **moving natural eyes,** covered busts, bisque hands, regular jointed knees, patent riveted hip joints. Can be placed in any position. Slippers and openwork stockings.

F2271—13½ in. ½ doz. in box....Doz. $4 25
F2272—17¾ " Each in box...... 7 90
F2273—20½ " " " " Each $0 89
F2274—24½ " " " " Each 1 35

KESTNER'S IMPROVED "MARVEL" KID BODY DOLLS.

The world's best.

MARVEL

The famous "Marvel" line comprises by far the best kid body dolls made. Made especially for us by Germany's best doll maker whose well known trademark (J. D. K.) is stamped on each, also our name "Marvel." Cork and saw dust stuffed, light and easy to handle. Each has hip and knee joints and **moving eyes** and, with the exception of the first 2 numbers, all have sewed wigs.

F2253—11 in., real shoes and attached stockings, asstd., bisque head and arms, **moving eyes,** curly hair, mouth exposing teeth, covered bust. 1 doz. in box......Doz. $2 25
F2254—13 in., good bisque head, mouth showing teeth, natural **sleeping eyes,** eye lashes, curly hair, covered bust, asstd. colored openwork stockings, real shoes to match. ½ doz. in box........ 4 20

The following have sewed **wigs,** in addition to all the other qualities of the "Marvel" line, and each one is built in proportion to its length.

F2255—15¾ in. Each in box........ 7 25
F2256—17 in., with elbow joints. Each in box........ 8 35
F2257—22¼ in. Each in box..Each $1 08
F2258—22⅜ in. Each in box.. " 1 50
F2259—24 in. Each in box..... " 1 85
F2260—28 in. Each in box.... " 3 00

"MARVEL" KID BODY DOLLS WITH BOY WIGS.

Staple sellers in every season.

F2261—10½ in. Bisque head and hands, natural eyes, eyelashes and mouth showing teeth, boy's curly wig, covered bust, hip and knee joints. 1 doz in box........ Doz. $2 18
F2262—As F2261. 13½ in., asstd. colored openwork stockings with real shoes to match, sewed wig........ 4 00
F2263—As F2262, 15½ in., sewed wig parted at side. Each in box........ 6 25
F2264—As F2262, 17¾ in, elbow joints. Each in box........ 8 95

"PAR EXCELLENCE" Full Jointed Patent Riveted KID BODY DOLLS.

All that we say in regard to our "Marvel" line can be said of this line, with additions. The extra cost arises from the fact that they are all kid from neck to soles of feet and that they are patent jointed at shoulder, elbow, hip and knee with nickeled rivets. Dolls can be placed in almost any position. Made by the celebrated J. D. Kestner. Each bears the famous crown trademark. Curly sewed wigs, **moving eyes,** mouth exposing teeth, covered bust with covered neck, well shaped bisque hands. Good kid stuffed with half cork and half saw dust. Asstd. colored openwork stockings with shoes to match.

F2265—15 in. Each in box........ Each $0 75
F2266—17 " " "........ 98
F2267—19¼ " " "........ 1 35
F2268—21 " " "........ 1 75
F2269—23½ " " "........ 2 50
F2270—26 " " "........ 3 30

IMITATION KID BODY DOLL.

Hard to tell from the genuine.

F2221—Bisque head, flesh tinted, glass eyes, mouth exposing teeth, painted eyebrows, flowing hair with side curls, imitation kid, stitched covered bust, bisque hands, imitation stockings with shoes. Size 10 in. 1 doz. in box. Per dozen, **92c**

"ABSOLUTELY UNBREAKABLE" AMERICAN DOLLS.

Patented. You can pound one against the counter, drop on the floor or throw across the room without breaking it.

F2281 — 13 in. handsome model face, natural eyes, flowing hair, patent washable head, arms and hands, cotton stuffed legs, real shoes and stockings, good bust, sitting body, fancy chemise with lace trimmed collar. Each doll with ribbon lettered "Patented, absolutely unbreakable." Each in box........ Doz. $4 50
F2282—As F2281, 14 in., with plaited chemise. Each in box........ 6 00
F2283—As F2281, 16 in., larger in proportion. Each in box........ Each $0 69
F2284—As F2251, 18 in., Each in box........ 89
F2285— As F2281, 19½ in. Each in box........ 95

"DOLLS OF THE FUTURE."

Unbreakable, very light composition linen covered hollow body and limbs, hip and knee jointed with nickel rivets, joined at shoulder, elbow and wrist, well formed hands, composition head, natural glass eyes, mouth exposing teeth, full head dress, flowing hair with 2 curls each side of head, openwork stockings with shoes, good lawn chemise with fancy trimmed revers, ribbon bow front, lace trimmed neck and sleeves. Each with butterfly shape tag. Each in box.

F2290—14 in........ Each. $0 33
F2291—16¾ in........ 69
F2292—18 in........ 75
F2293—21¾ in........ 98

KESTNER'S "EXCELSIOR" BISQUE HEAD SLEEPING DOLLS.

Perfect in model and finish. French jointed body and limbs made of layers of paper so hardened that they are next to impossible to break, although very light. Ball jointed at shoulder, elbow, wrist, hip and knee, open fingers. Turning heads of superior bisque, mouth showing teeth, life like **moving eyes,** elaborately sewed wigs with curls all over. Openwork fancy stockings, real patent leather slippers tied with fancy laces, fine chemise hemmed at bottom, yoke with lace insertion and shirred ribbon trimming, bow with streamers, lace trimmed sleeves. Each in box.

F2309 — 14¼ in. Small but very fine........ Each $0 72
F2310—17½ in........ 98
F2311—20 "........ 1 35
F2312—21½ "........ 1 80
F2313—24 "........ 2 25
F2314—27 "........ 3 00
F2315—31 "........ 3 75
F2316—33 in., wig with side part and bow........ Out

THE DOLL OF THE FUTURE.

Dressed unbreakable dolls, very light combination linen hollow body and limbs, hip and knee jointed with nickel rivets, jointed at shoulder, elbow and wrist, composition head, painted eyebrows and lashes, natural glass eyes, mouth exposing teeth, flowing hair with 2 curls each side.

F2294—15 in., satin dresses in 3 different models: (1) flowered dimity blouse front, satin shoulder revers, lace straps and satin belt, lace trimmed satin hat; (2) elaborate collar edged with lace, skirt, collar and yoke with fancy braid, lace brim hat with pink satin ruffle edge; (3) satin skirt, plaited white lawn blouse, box plaited lace edged satin collar, hat of satin and white lawn with artificial flowers, pinked edge. Trimmed underwear, openwork shoes and stockings. Each in box. Each, **69c**

WORLD'S FINEST DRESSED
BISQUE DOLLS—Continued.

F2431, $1.30 Each.　　　　F2432, $1.40 Each.

F2431—18¼ in., **moving eyes**, dainty baby dress of very fine white organdie over blue slip, 2 ruffle flounces on skirt each edged with lace, row of lace insertion, ribbon girdle and rosettes, blouse waist with large lace trimmed elbow sleeves, lace trimmed round collar with deep lace edge, white hat with elaborate lace edge and blue ribbon trimmings, 2 underskirts. Each in box....................Each, **$1.30**

F2432—18¼ in., **moving eyes**, light blue china silk **dress**, lace edge ruffled skirt with lace trimmed crinoline foundation, lace trimmed blouse waist, all over valenciennes lace yoke edged with swansdown, puffed sleeves of silk and lace with baby ribbon rosettes, silk **faced** poke hat, white swansdown around edge with 2 ribbon rosettes, and button ornaments. Each in box.............................Each, **$1.40**

F2433, $1.50 Each.　　　　F2434, $1.60 Each.

F2433—19 in., **moving eyes**, full jointed, red satin dress, white lace band on skirt, blouse waist with plaited solid lace jacket front and plaited shoulder revers edged with valenciennes lace, satin yoke trimmed with glass beads, lace trimmed puffed sleeves and neck, satin hat with lace edge and artificial flowers. Each in box.....Each, **$1.50**

F2434—19 in., **moving eyes**, full jointed, fine pink organdie with lace flounce skirt and ribbon run lace insertion heading and belt, blouse waist, plaited square yoke, extra deep collar with deep lace edge and ribbon threaded lace beading top and bottom, new style puff sleeves, fluted fluffy hat with deep lace ruching. Each in box..**$1.60**

F2435—19½ in., actress model costume of green velvet, full gathered skirt with white Mexican braid and button trimmings, blouse waist with pointed collar edged top and bottom with fancy braid, white "V" yoke and belt with button ornament, white cuffs on puffed sleeves, green velvet tam-o'-shanter with ribbon bow and 6 quills. Each in box..............Each, **$1.75**

F2435, $1.75 Each.

F2436, $1.90 Each.　　　　F2437, $2.15 Each.

F2436—19 in., **moving eyes**, sage green Panama cloth with fancy black and white figures, very full skirt with 2 rows of white satin ribbon, blouse waist, "V" front filled in with dotted chiffon, wide allover lace revers with deep lace edge, puffed sleeves, ribbon rosette in front, black inserted hat with pink maline, buckle ornament and pink ostrich feather. Each in box...............................Each, **$1.90**

F2437—21 in., **moving eyes**, pink satin, extra long full skirt with 2 lace trimmed flounces and lace heading, lace covered yoke, pointed collar edged with deep ruffle of satin and lace, braid trimming all around, pink and white ribbon bow with tabs and buckle in front, lace brim hat with ruffle of satin and lace, ribbon and feather trimming. Each in box..Each, **$2.15**

F2438, $2.50 Each.　　　　F2439, $2.75 Each.

F2438—22 in., **moving eyes**, full jointed shoulder, elbow, wrist, hip and knee, fine white mull dress, extra full gathered skirt with 3 plaited flounces each with black and white ribbon, yoke to match with lace ruffle revers and chiffon rosette with tab ends, full sleeves with plaiting in oversleeve effect edged with black and white baby ribbon, mull drop skirt, fine fluffy mull hat with plaitings and shirrings of same and chiffon ribbon trimming, 2 underskirts.................Each, **$2.50**

F2439—23 in., full jointed, **moving eyes**, flowered dimity blouse waist and sleeves with fancy red satin collar in revers and tab design, satin skirt and belt, collar and skirt with white braid, combination hat of flowered dimity with straw edge trimmed with coque feathers and quills....Each, **$2.75**

F2440, $3.00 Each.　　　　F2441,

F2440—22 in., full jointed, **moving eyes**, not large but exceptionally fine. White silk chiffon, full skirt with 5 rows of shirring, 2 dainty ruffles around bottom, shirred yoke and sleeves, extra large puff at wrist with ribbon ruchings, ribbon trimmed waist, lace neck, allover plain light pink slip, shirred silk faced hat with ribbon ruffle around edge, ribbon rosettes and many quills, white swansdown boa with tabs and ruffle of chiffon and ribbon.................Each, **$3.00**

F2441—27 in., full jointed, **sleeping eyes**, full gathered costume of blue satinette, 2 lace edged ruffle flounces on skirt with lace heading, extra deep double collar edged with lace and fancy blue and white braid trimming, lace covered yoke, lace neck, puffed sleeves, ribbon bow with buckle in front, flowered tulle hat with lace edge, ribbon and artificial flowers. Lace trimmed underwear with box plaited lace flounces and blue, white openwork stockings, white shoes....Each, **3.25**

F2442, $4.00 Each.　　　　F2443, $5.00 Each

F2442—25 in., **moving eyes**, full jointed, old rose satin costume with long shirred blouse, tinseled lace covered square yoke in Mexican design, band of lace on skirt and around sleeves, yellow and white fancy ribbon sash, flowing sleeves with 2 rows of stitched braid, lace ruffle inside, puffed tops, lace trimmed neck, flaring straw hat with pink ribbon and elaborately faced with puffed satin. ....Each, **$4.00**

F2443—27 in., **moving eyes**, full jointed, elaborate costume of yellow and white novelty stripe grenadine, extra fine skirt with 2 rows of lace and yellow silk braid, full blouse front, square yoke, full sleeves with 4 rows of white chiffon across yoke and on top of sleeves, ruffle full of extra deep ecru lace in front, fancy yellow straw hat draped with yellow chiffon, artificial flowers, 2 underskirts. Each in box........................Each, **$5.00**

NOVELTY JAPANESE
LADY DOLL.

F2447—16 in., full jointed, natural glass eyes, bisque head, mouth exposing teeth, box plaited dress with kimona in Persian effect figures, figured band trimming and lined with plain color cambric, plain knickerbockers, colored Japanese shoes and stockings, hair with metal ornament and 2 floral rosettes, tinseled necklace with locket. Each in box. Each, **68c**

F2444, $6.00 Each.　　　　F2445, $7.50 Each.

F2444—26 in., **moving eyes**, full jointed, white accordion plaited chiffon flounced skirt with 2 rows of red chiffon trimming, accordion plaited chiffon overskirt in point design edged with red ribbon and with 5 rows of silk braid on each side, deep white lace yoke, lace trimmed puff sleeves, flowing oversleeves of white chiffon edged with 2 rows of ribbon, deep lace caps, lace trimmed neck, rosette of red and white ribbon, brilliant set stick pin, black lace hat with red crepon rosettes and 2 red and black ostrich tips, ribbon bow on hair, 2 underskirts. ....Each, **$6.00**

F2445—Lady doll, 29 in., handsome costume of rose pink ladies' cloth, circular skirt, deep gathered flounce with 3 rows of gathered chiffon ribbon at bottom and 4 rows at top, full blouse front, square yoke with deep white lace and 4 rows of chiffon ribbon, gray eiderdown evening coat lined and faced with green satinette, 2 lace medallions on satinette collar, lace medallion on bell shape sleeves faced with green satinette, braid trimmed front, pink tulle hat with yellow straw edge and elaborately trimmed with shaded chiffon, drooping pink and black ostrich plumes with long silk ribbon bow, 2 underskirts. Each in box. Each, **$7.50**

F2446—29 in., full jointed, **moving eyes**, blue costume elaborately trimmed with white lace, 2 flounces on extra full skirt with chiffon ribbon trimming, long blouse waist, plaited "V" yoke, elaborate pointed collar of extra wide lace, 3 rows of gathered chiffon ribbon and lace insertion, lace trimmed neck and shirred puffed sleeves with lace edging and deep lace ruffle, lace straw hat draped with tulle and trimmed with bunches of artificial flowers and draped chiffon ribbon with rosettes. Very striking. Underwear trimmed with embroidery, 2 underskirts. Each in box.............................Each, **$8.50**

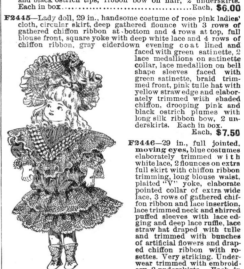

F2446, $8.50 Each.

"PAPA AND MAMMA" TALKING DOLLS.

With **moving eyes**, bisque heads, painted eyebrows and lashes, mouth exposing teeth, flowing hair, sitting bodies with soft limbs. Hats trimmed to match suit. Lace trimmed underwear, shoes and stockings. Each has 2 cords attached to bellows, when pulled will say "Mamma" or "Papa." Mysterious and lifelike.

F2406, $4.25 Doz.

F2406—14¼ in. 3 styles, (1) flowered dimity baby dress, lace edged and headed plaited ruffle, satin lace trimmed collar; (2) satin dress, flowered dimity blouse and revers, jacket lace edged; (3) figured cord stripe dimity with ribbon trimmed plaiting around skirt and satin yoke. Asstd. colors. Each in box.¼ doz. in pkg. Doz. **$4.25**

F2407—16¾ in. As F2406, 3 styles and colors: (1) figured and striped dimity, blouse waist with large revers collar lace and braid trimmed, satin yoke; (2) figured corded organdie with ribbon trimmed plaiting on skirt and around satin yoke; (3) satin revers costume with flowered dimity blouse and lace trimmed revers, ribbon rosettes. Each in box. ¼ doz. in pkg. Doz. **$7.80**

SKIN AND HAIR DOGS.

F3416, 42c Doz.    F3409, 85c Doz.

Standing Positions—Each on 4 wheel wood platform, Doz.
long black hair.
F3416—*Special 5 center.* Painted face, ht. 4½ in.,
length 5 in. 1 doz. in box.........................$0 42
F3405—About 6½x5½. *Biggest 10 center on the market.* 1
doz. in box.. 73
F3406—7½x7, metal wheels. 1 doz. in pkg.............. 89
F3407—On 9x8, metal wheels. 1 doz. in box..........
F3408—About 10½x9, iron wheels. ½ doz. in box...... 2 00
Sitting Positions—Natural glass eyes, 4 wheel platform.
F3409—Long black hair, ht.
about 6½ in., platform 6x
2½. 1 doz. in box 85
F3410—Wool and hair 8x
7½. ½ doz. in box...... 2 00
On Casters—Roller on each
leg, each with collar and
string.
F3413—About 8x7½. ⅙
doz. in box................ 2 15
F3414—10x9½. ⅙ doz. in
box........................... 4 25
F3415—13¼ x 13, ribbon
with bell, iron wheels
bound with wires. ⅛ doz.
in box..................... 8 10

F3413, $2.15 Doz.

DOMESTIC STUFFED FLANNEL DOGS ON WHEELS.

F823—Muslin well stuffed, fur Doz.
ears, black button eyes, ribbon
collar with bell, wire frame,
wooden wheels, 4½x5. 1 doz.
in box......................................$0 40
F824—As F823, fleecy flannel, 6¼
x6, asstd. white and spotted. 1
doz. in box.............................. 75
F825—As above, 7¼x7, asstd.,
spotted and white. 1 doz. in
box... 95

STUFFED HORSES ON WHEELS.

F826—Muslin, 9 in., ht. 8½
in., fur mane and tail, imit.
harness. 1 doz. in box. Doz. 89

GALLOPING DOGS.

On wire frames with long
stick handles.

F3449, 79c Doz.   F3450, $1.92 Doz.

F3449—Mechanically run on three wheels with long sticks
25 in. over all. Dog made of short curly wool, and
jumps when run over the floor. 1 doz. in box......... 79
F3450—As F3449, length about 23 in., 2 dogs, larger
wheels, wire frame 6½x4½. ¼ doz. in box........... 1 92

CLOTH COVERED DOGS.

F3411—7x7, asstd. kinds
and colors, wire frame
covered with astrakhan
and felt. Well made. ¼
doz. in box.................. 1 95
F3412—*Extra 50c value.*
All astrakhan in asstd.
colors, ht. 10 in., length
9. ¼ doz. in box........ 4 25

IMPORTED WHITE POODLE DOGS
—With Voice.

F3374—*50c leader.* Perfect
shape, part covered with canton flannel, which represents
body as shorn, head and
neck covered with real skin
and long hair, good features,
bell and ribbon around neck.
About 7 in. not large but
fine. ⅛ doz. in box......... 4 20
F3375—As F3374, larger,
large glass eyes. Length 12
in. ¼ doz. in box.......... 8 50

REAL WOOL COVERED SHEEP.

These lifelike woolly sheep are among the most popular
toys made. Splendid sellers as toys
proper, while the smaller sizes are
also largely used for tree ornaments.

F3361 and F3362.   F3363, 89c Doz.   F3364, $2.08 Doz.

F3361—Ram with golden tin horns, composition head, Doz.
painted wood feet, 2½ in. 1 doz. in flat box..........$0 33
F3362—As above, 4½ in., bell at neck.................... 75
F3363—Hollow compressed papier mache body, 5x4¾,
with rattle, good painted composition features painted
wood feet, ribbon collar and bow at tail. ½ doz. in box. 89
F3364—6x6¾, painted features, glass eyes, extra thick
wool, ribbon collar and bow at tail, painted wood feet.
6 in. varnished wood platform, 4 metal wheels, each
with voice. ½ doz. in box............................ 2 08
F3365—As F3364, polished platform, 4 iron wheels, 9x9½,
full ht. 9 in. A splendid 50 center. ¼ doz. in box.... 4 25
F3366—As F3364, thicker fleece, good collar, fancy ribbon
tied tail. 4 wheel platform, 12x4½, ht. of sheep 11.
about 12½ in. long. 1-6 doz. in box................. 8 35
F3367—As F3366, full ht. 14½ in., length 14½. Plat- Each
orm 15¼x15½. Each in box....................$1 15

IMPORTED FELT ANIMALS.

F3369, 84c Doz.

F3369—10c asst. Doz.
dogs, different spe-
cies stuffed cotton
cover in asstd. col-
ors, fluffy tails
and ears. Average
size 5½ in., free
legs. 1 doz. in box,
asstd.................$0 84
F3370—As F3369.
asstd. cats, dogs
rabbits, stout bod
ies, sitting posi
tions, painted and striped, ribbon neck band. About
6 in. 1 doz. in box....................................... 92
F3372—3 styles, rabbit, cat, dog, 8 in., painted and striped

F3371, $1.95 Doz.

backs, collars,
chenille balls,
each with voice.
¼ doz. in box,
asstd........... 1 85
F3371—Asstd.
25c animals,
glass eyes, cat,
dromedary,
donkey and
horse, 8¾ x 7.
½ doz. in box,
asstd........... 1 95
F3373—*Extra qual-
ity 50 centers,* asstd.
large elephant,
pig, etc., glass
eyes, natural
shapes and posi-
tions, free legs,
ribbon around neck
with bell and voice,
about 8x6¼. ½ doz.
in box, asstd....... 3 50

F3373, $3.50 Doz.

IMPORTED PLUSH ROCKING HORSES.

F3446—Fine
model, leather
bridle, plush
seat saddle,
fancy blanket,
good stirrups.
Each on plat-
form with 4
iron wheels
which can be
removed from
rocker. Plat-
form and rock-
ers red with
yellow stripes.
Ht. on plat-
form 22 in.,
length 21½,
platform 25½,
length of rockers 36 in.
Each, **$3.00**
F3447—As above, ht. on platform 23 in., length 23½,
platform 25½, length of rockers 36.............Each, **$3.50**
F3448—As above, ht. on platform 25½ in., length 25, platform
28, rockers 40.................................Each, **$4.25**

HARDENED PAPIER MACHE HORSES.

Made of layers of paper which have been
passed through a hardening process.

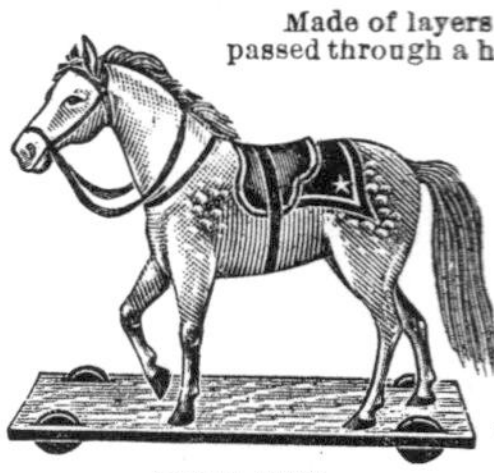

F3421 to F3424.    F3425 to F3427.

On 4 Wheel Platform—Wood legs, woolly mane and tail, Doz.
fancy colored paper saddle.
F3421—5½x5x5. 1 doz. in box.......................$0 37
F3422—7x6½. A splendid dime leader. 1 doz. in box. 79
F3423—About 10½x10½, easily worth a quarter. ½
doz. in box.. 2 15
F3424—About 13½x11½, platform 11¾x4. ⅓ doz. box. 3 97
On Rockers—Wood legs, woolly mane and tail, colored
paper.
F3425—6 in. long, ht. 5½. 1 doz. in box......... 42
F3426—7½ in. long,
ht. 6¾.............. 81
F3427—9¾ in. long,
ht. 10............... 1 98
F3428, Horse with
Cart—Horse with
wagon, hay and dump
carts, asstd., 2 wheels,
small wheel in cen-
ter, length 10½ in. ½
doz. in box.......... 95

F3428, 9½c Doz.

IMPORTED DAPPLE GRAY FELT HORSES.

F3444—Stylish model.
White and black spot-
ted, white fur mane
and hair tail, white
enameled martingale
with rosettes, leather
seat, saddle, felt blanket
and stirrups, striped
white enameled wood
platform, metal
wheels. ht. 12½ in.,
length 10¾. Each in
pkg.............Doz. **$4.00**
F3445—As F3444, ht.
16¾ in., length 15½
in. Each in pkg.
Each, **69c**

IMPORTED PLUSH HORSES.

Well made, natural appearance, mane and tail, saddle, harness,
blanket and bridle,
on iron wheel wood
platforms.
F3431—Ht. 8½ Doz.
in., length 7¾.
½ doz. in pkg....$2 18
F3432—Ht. 9¾
in., length 8¾.
½ doz. in pkg.... 3 25
F3433—Ht. 12 in.,
length 10¾. ⅓
doz. in pkg..... 4 00
F3434—With real
leather bridle, ht.
13¾ in., length
12, platform 12⅝.
1-6 doz. in pkg... 5 75
F3435—Ht. 16 in.,
length 15½, plat-
form 15. Each Each
in box...........$0 69
F3436—Ht. 18 in., length 16½, platform 16½. Each in pkg. 75
F3437—Ht. 18¾ in., length 17½, platform 18. Each in pkg. 89
F3438—Ht. 20½ in., length 18½, platform 19¾ in. Each
in pkg... 1 25
F3439—Extra stout, ht. 23½ in., length 21½, platform 22
in. Each in pkg...................................... 1 50

IMPORTED PLUSH HORSES—
With Adjustable Cooling Blankets
and Saddles.

F3440—All leath-
er bridle, saddle
with plush seat
fastened with
web belt and
buckle, fancy
checked cooling
blanket with red
binding, hitch-
ing chain. Ht.
14¾ in., length
13¼, platform
13¼. Each in
pkg............. 75
F3441—As F3440,
16¾ in., length
15½, platform 15.
Each in pkg..... 98
F3442—As F3441,
19½ in., length
18, platform 18.
Each in pkg..... 1 25

IMPORTED PAPIER MACHE HORSE WITH RIDER—
Mechanical Action.

F3430—Woolly mane and
tail, jockey in fancy costume, platform 11½x3,
when drawn across floor
horse's head bobs up and
down. Full ht. 11¼ in.
½ doz. in box.
Doz. **$4.25**

DOLL CARRIAGES.

Best make in America. Good style and thoroughly well made. Fancy woven reed body, turned wood posts and knobs, gimp trimmed, creton lining.

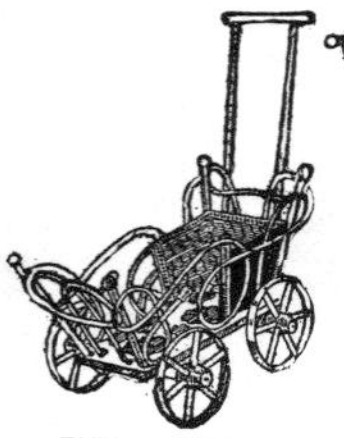

F1450 and F145.

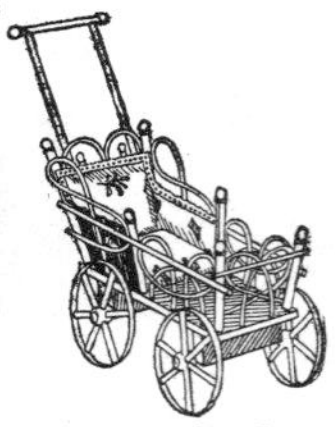

F1452, $3.75 Doz.

F1450—7½x15, 5 in. wheels, ht. 19 in. 1 doz. in crate, wt. 21 lbs Doz. **$1.90**

F1451—7½x15, 5 in. wheels with green metal tires. 1 doz. in crate. Doz. **$2.10**

F1452—9x19, covered removable seat, blocks between body and axles, 7 in. wheels ht. 21 in. ½ doz. in crate. 18 lbs. Doz. **$3.75**

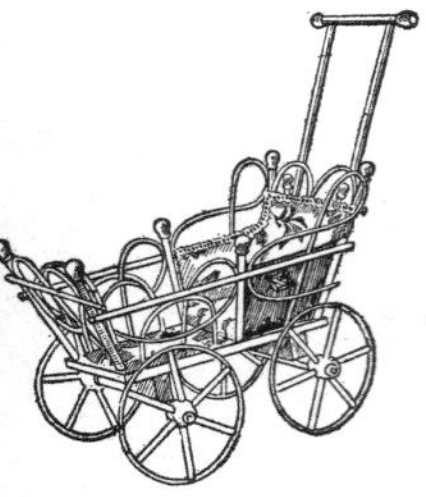

F1453, $4.10 Doz.

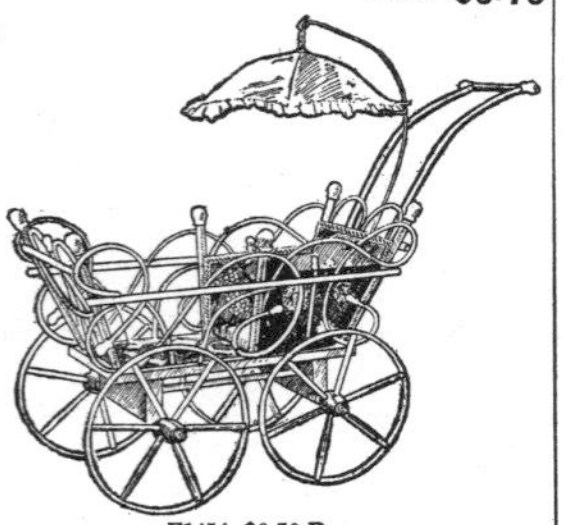

F1454, $6.50 Doz.

F1453—9x19, covered removable seat, blocks betwen body and axles, 7 in. block wheels, metal tires, ht. 21 in. ½ doz. in crate, wt. 18 lbs..............................Doz. **$4.10**

F1454—10x20, removable covered seat, blocks between body and axles, with strengthening rod, 8 in. wheels, heavy green enameled metal tires, metal rod with folding parasol, ht. 26 in. ½ doz. in crate. 25 lbs. Doz. **$6.50**

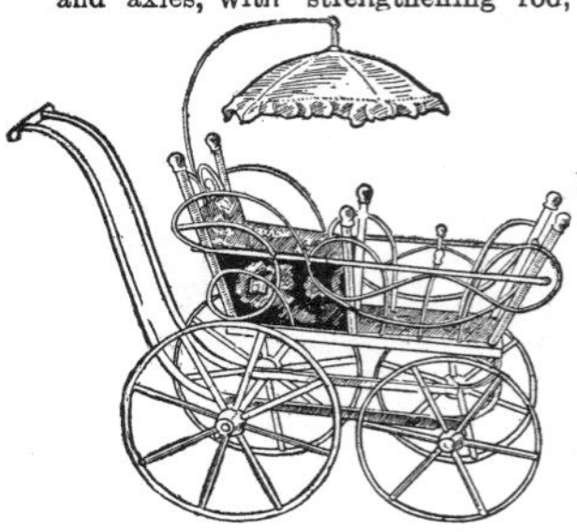

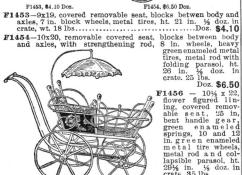

F1456, $8.75 Doz.

F1456 — 10¼ x 22, flower figured lining, covered removable seat, 25 in, bent handle gear, green enameled springs, 10 and 12 in. green enameled metal tire wheels, metal rod and collapsible parasol, ht. 29½ in. ½ doz. in crate, 35 lbs. Doz. **$8.75**

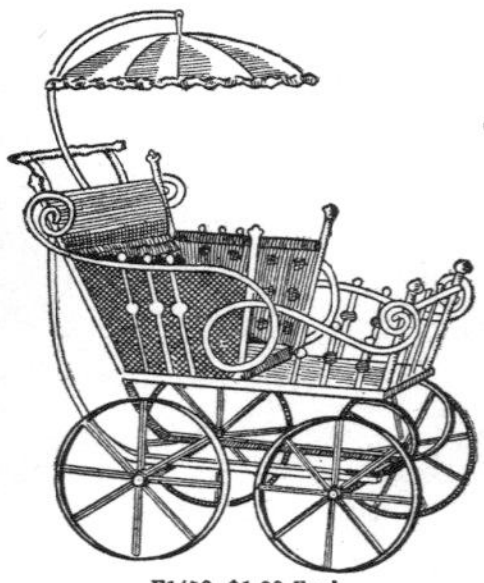

F1459, $1.30 Each.

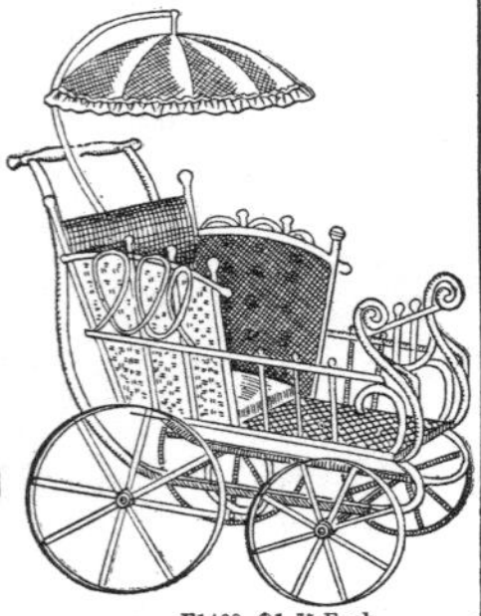

F1460, $1.75 Each.

F1459 – Spiral reed trimmed, varnished body, turned wood knobs, figured upholstery, gimp trimmings, green enamel double spoke 10 in. wheels, metal tires, scroll design springs, metal handle, folding parasol. 3 in crate. 35 lbs... Each, **$1.30**

F1460÷As F1459, more scroll and reed work, plush roll in back and fancy ruffle trimmed parasol. 2 in crate. 35 lbs. Each, **$1.75**

DOLL FOLDING GO-CARTS.

Exact models of the large size. Each folds neatly and compactly.

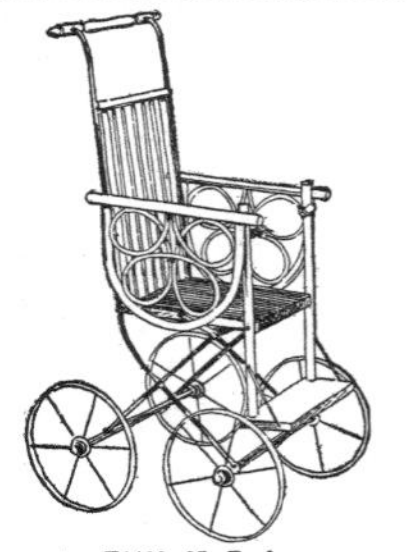

F1488, 87c Each.

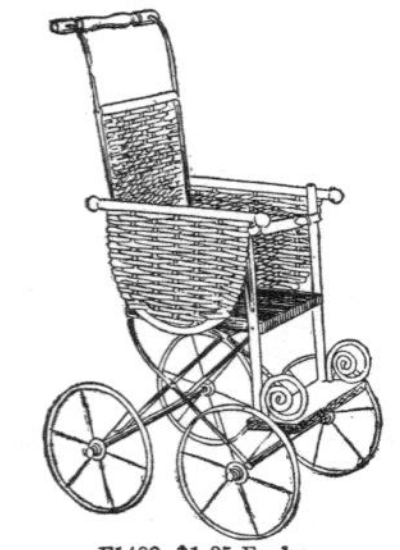

F1489, $1.35 Each.

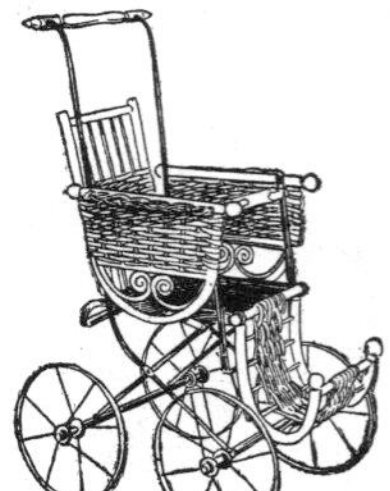

F1488 – Varnished body, reed scroll sides, spindle back, creton covered seat, 7½x8, green enameled, English metal gear, handle to match, guard strap, 4 in crate, 35 lbs. Each, **87c**

F1489 – Wood frame, turned knobs, scroll ornamented foot rest, solid reed woven sides, half woven back, varnished, 7½x8½, cloth covered seat, metal English gear, green enameled, metal wheels and handle, guard strap. 3 in crate. 30 lbs... Each, **$1.35**

F1490 – As F1489, adjustable woven dasher and back, woven reed arm rests, double spoke wheels. 2 in crate, 20 lbs..............Each, **1.75**

GO-CARTS.

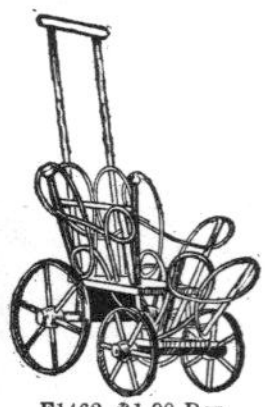

F1462, $1.90 Doz.

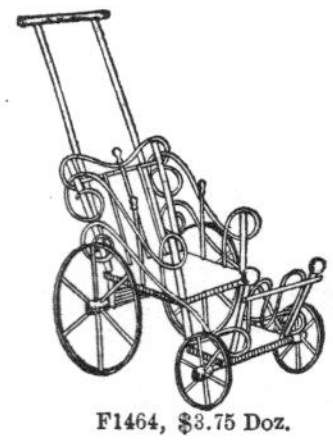

F1464, $3.75 Doz.

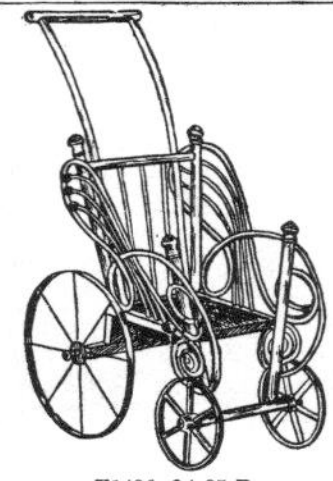

F1466, $4.25 Doz.

F1462—Large body, high dasher, straight handle, 7 in. rear and 5 in. front wheels. 1 doz. in crate. 21 lbs..Doz. **$1.90**

F1464 – Style as F1462, but with more woven rattan scroll work, seat 7½x7, wheels 5 and 8 in., green metal springs, ht. 23 in. ½ doz. in crate. 18 lbs..........Doz. **$3.75**

F1466 – Reed, covered 7x7½ seat, colored web guard, 19½ in. handle, 5 in. wood spoke front and 10 in. tinned metal rear wheels. ½ doz. in crate, 25 lbs.....Doz. **$4.25**

F1467—Reed body dasher front, varnished, 7½x8 seat creton covered, 6 and 10 in. green metal tire wheels, handle, ht. 24 in. ½ doz. in crate, 25 lbs. Doz. **$6.50**

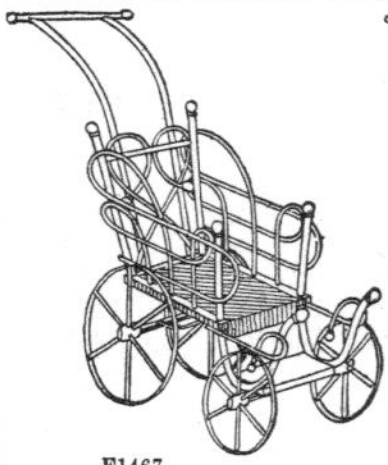

F1467,

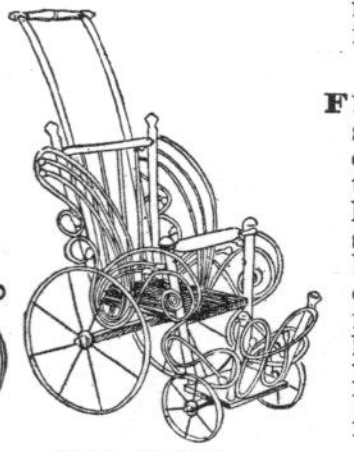

F1468, $8.50 Doz.

F1468÷ Reed, shellaced colored knobs, turned posts, leather guard strap, nickel buckles, 8x8½ covered seat, foot rest, 22 in. handle. 5 and 11 in. bright metal wheels, 4 in crate, 40 lbs. Doz. **$8.50**

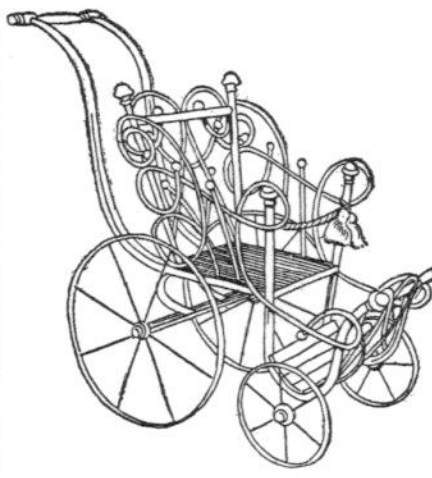

F1469, $8.90 Doz.

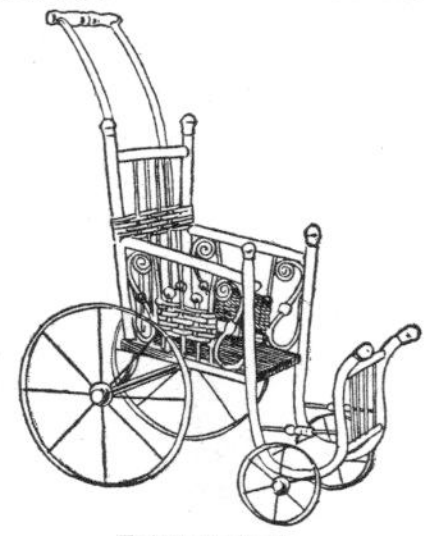

F1470, 85c Each.

F1469÷Varnished woven body, bent dasher, turned posts with knobs, oil cloth covered seat, 8x 8½, bent wood handle, metal springs, 6 and 12 in. green enamel solid tire metal wheels, ht. 22 in. ½ doz. in crate.......Doz. **$8.90**

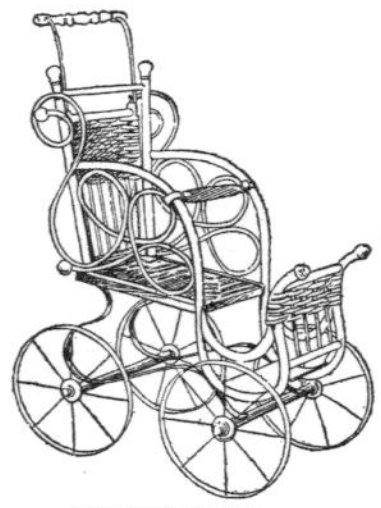

F1471, $1.00 Each.

F1470 – Turned wood frame, shellacked woven reed sides and back, leather guard strap, 8x7½ in. seat, 5 and 11 in. green enamel metal spoke wheels, iron axles and springs, 4 in. crate. 35 lbs. Each, **85c**

F1471 ÷ Adjustable back, wood frame, turned knobs, woven reed back and dasher, cloverleaf rattan sides, varnished, covered seat, English metal gear, enameled green, 8 in. wheels, guard strap. 3 in crate. 25 lbs. Each, **$1.00**

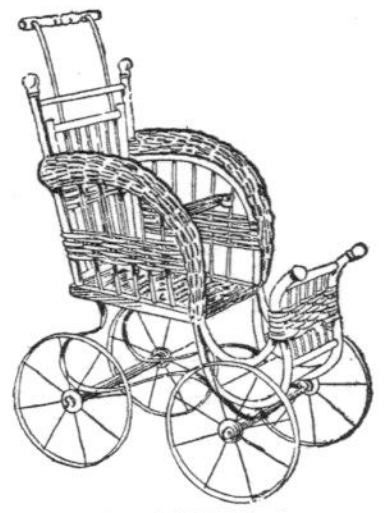

F1474, $1.50 Each.

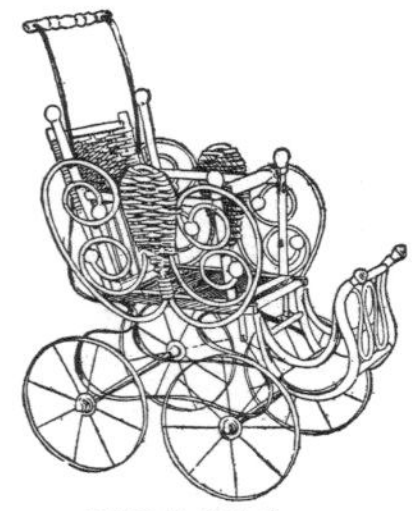

F1475, $1.75 Each.

F1474—Varnished wood, turned knobs, adjustable back, woven back, sides, dasher and roll arm rest, covered seat, English metal gear, green enamel, 8 in. double spoke wheels, iron handle, guard strap. 2 in crate, 25 lbs..........Each, **$1.50**

F1475—Varnished reed, fleur de lis scroll sides, woven reed back, patent adjustable dasher and back, English metal gear, green enamel, 8 in. double spoke wheels, metal handle, covered seat, guard strap. 2 in crate, 25 lbs..................Each, **$1.75**

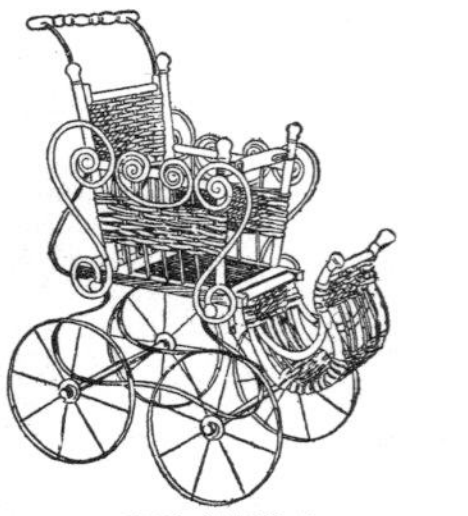

F1476, $2.10 Each.

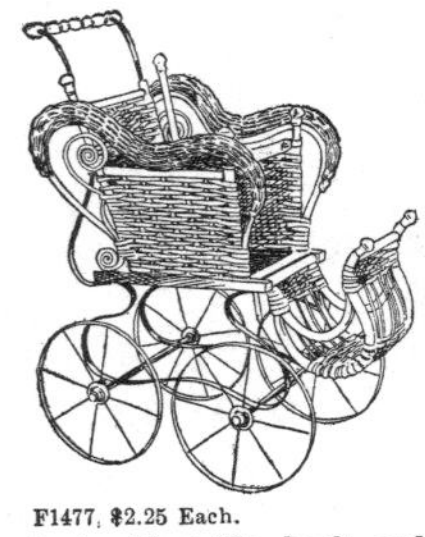

F1477, $2.25 Each.

F1476—Woven reed, varnished, patent adjustable back and dasher, scroll sides, imit. plush covered seat, metal English gear, enameled green, iron handle, 8 in. double spoke wheels, guard strap. 2 in crate, 25 lbs........................Each, **$2.10**

F1477—Wood frame, turned knobs, solid reed sides, roll arm rests, woven dasher front and back, both adjustable, imit. plush covered seat, English metal gear enameled green, 8 in. spoke wheels, metal handle. 2 in crate, 25 lbs..Each, **$2.25**

JUVENILE STEEL AUTOMOBILES.

1905 Improved models, auto steering gear, steel bodies, open bottom, workmanship and finish A1. Each in crate knocked down.

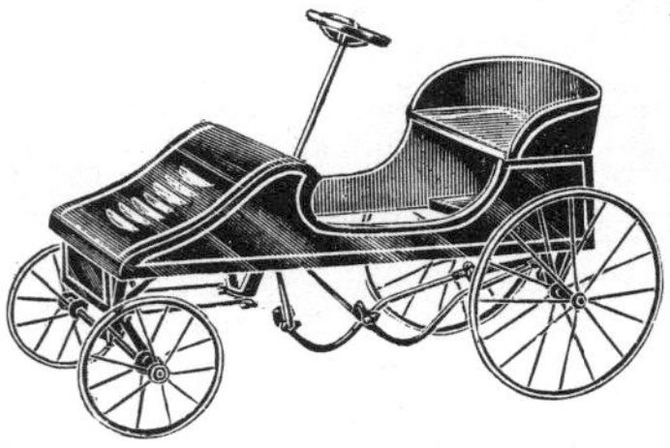

F1994—"American Boy," red painted, beaded and striped body, 15x36, green inside, green enameled 12 and 18 in. pressed steel hub, wire spoke wheels, welded tires, adjustable top seat, 50 lbs. *An excellent value at $5.00.* Each, **$3.50**

F1995—"Whirlwind," as F1994, ⅝ in. rubber tires, body blue enameled, beaded and striped, 50 lbs............Each, **$4.25**

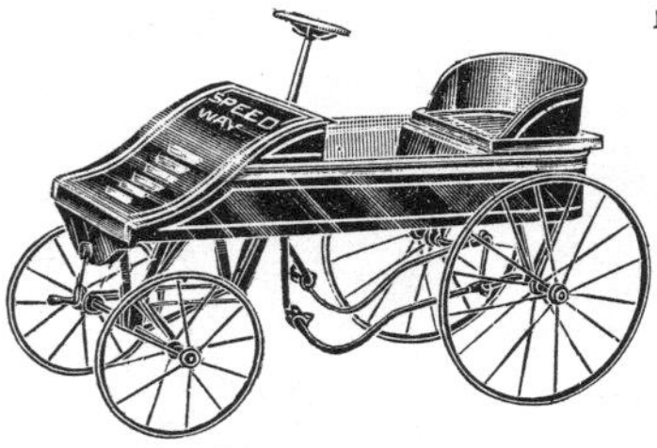

F1996—"Speedway," red enameled, beaded and striped, 15x36. painted inside, green enameled 12 and 18 in, pressed steel hub, wire spoke wheels, ½ in. rubber tires, lever starting crank at front, license tag, high flaring back seat, 50 lbs Each, **$5.00**

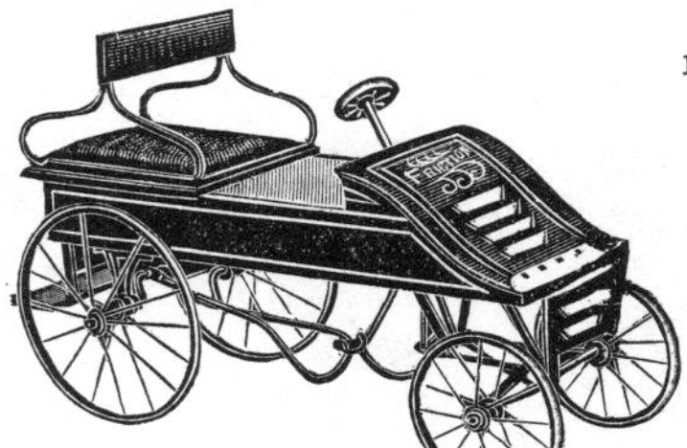

F1997 — "Victor," upholstered double seat, maroon painted and varnished. 44x 15, striped and brass trimmings, dash front, step at back, tool box, 12 and 18 in. green enameled wheels, rubber tires, 65 lbs. Each, **$6.25**

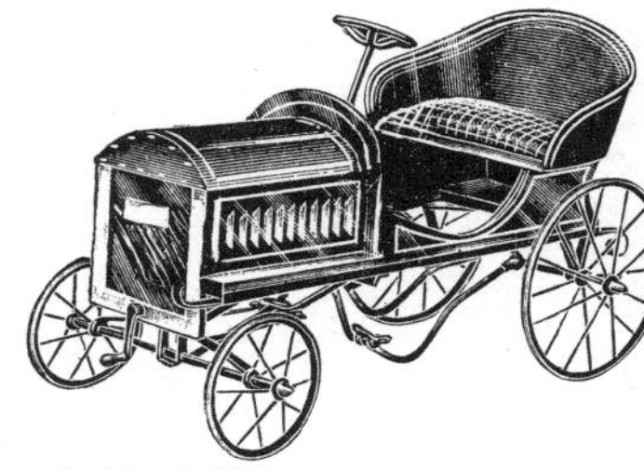

F1998:—"Daredevil" racer type, painted in bright red, striped, brass trimmed front and sides, steel riveted frame, practically indestructible, upholstered high back seat, body 19x45, green enameled 10 and 16 in. wheels, large brass extension hub nuts, ½ in. rubber tires, lever starting crank at front, 65 lbs..............................Each, **$7.75**

The following shipped from factory in Central Ohio.

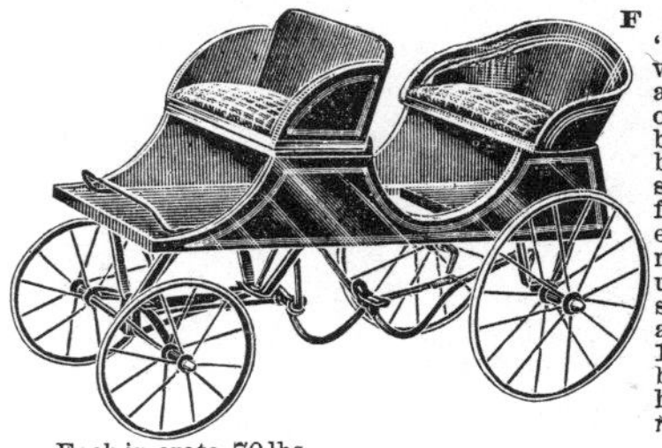

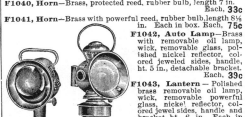

F1999:—"Boulevard," wood body enameled in orange, striped, body 15 x 45, brass finish steering gear, front hood raises (as in cut) making 2 seats, upholstered seats, green enameled 12 and 18 in. wheels, brass extension hub nuts, ½ in. rubber tires. Each in crate, 70 lbs..............................Each, **$9.50**

Sundries for the above—*Shipped from our house.*

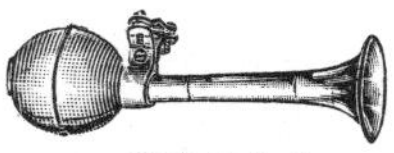

F1040, 33c Each.

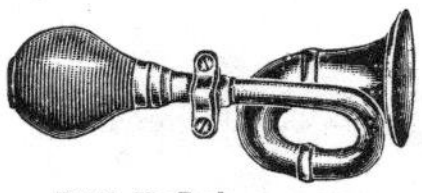

F1041, 75c Each.

F1040, Horn—Brass, protected reed, rubber bulb, length 7 in. Each, **33c**

F1041, Horn—Brass with powerful reed, rubber bulb, length 8½ in. Each in box. Each, **75c**

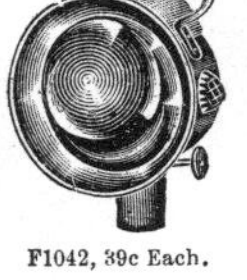

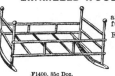

F1042, 39c Each.

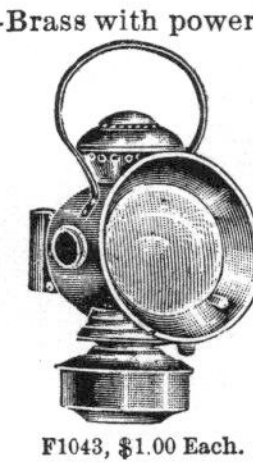

F1043, $1.00 Each.

F1042, Auto Lamp—Brass with removable oil lamp, wick, removable glass, polished nickel reflector, colored jeweled sides, handle, ht. 5 in., detachable bracket. Each, **39c**

F1043, Lantern — Polished brass removable oil lamp, wick, removable powerful glass, nickel reflector, colored jewel sides, handle and bracket, ht. 6 in. Each in box..............Each. **$1.00**

ENAMELED WOOD TOY CRADLES.

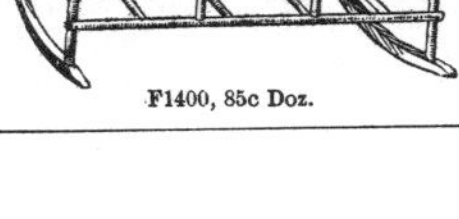

F1400, 85c Doz.

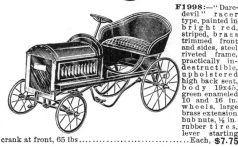

First class goods, well made, attractively painted with beautiful finish.

F1400—14 in. long, 7 wide, selected stock, enameled pink, blue and white. 1 doz. asstd. (6 only white, 3 only each of pink and blue) in pkg.

IMPORTED PLUSH HORSE WITH CART.

Big seller in any locality.

F3429—Good model, fur mane and tail, leatherette harness, metal wheel platform, 6¾ in. long, full ht. 6½ in.; 2 styles, 2 wheel neatly painted hay and sand carts, 3½ in. open spoke wheels, horse can be unhitched, extreme length about 13½ in. Asstd. ½ doz. in box. Per dozen, **$2.25**

IMPORTED PLUSH COVERED HORSES WITH WAGONS.

F3536—Asstd. 3 styles wagons — express, contractor's and hay, each with 4 wheels and hinged shaft, painted and striped, harnessed horse on 4 wheel platform, can be unhitched, length 18½ in., 3 in box ass.d. Each $0 35

F3536, 35c Each.

F3537—4 wheel truck with seat, as F3536, 24x9½. Each in box...Each 75

F3537, 75c Each.

F3538—4 wheel truck with 3 asstd. cases which can be filled and 1 barrel, hinged unloading slide and tie chain, as F3536, length 22½ in. Each in box.. Each 75

F3538, 75c Each.

IMPORTED NODDING HEAD ANIMALS.

Asstd. styles, each on 4 wheel platform.

F3386—Doz. Asstd. horses and donkeys. about 4⅝x4⅝ in. 1 doz. in box...$0 39

F3386, F3387, F3388. F3393, $2.00 Doz.

F3387—Natural finish, each with saddle, about 5¼x6. Asstd. horses, donkeys and cows in box of 1 doz... 75

F3388 "Leader" Dime Assortment—Extra size and finish, length 6¼ in., asstd. as above, platform 6⅛ in. 1 doz. in box... 89

F3393—Pig, very naural. stout fancy blanket on back, 7½ in. ½ doz. in box... 2 00

F3389, $2.08 Doz. F3390, $3.90 Doz.

F3389—Cows, donkeys and horses with bridles, 8¼x8 in. Papier mache. covered with a preparation like cloth. ½ doz. in box... 2 08

F3390—About 11x11, donkey, platform 10¼ x 3½, wood feeding trough on front, well made in every way, imitation cloth covering, painted eyes and features, with saddle. ½ doz. box. 3 90

SHAKING. HEAD DONKEYS. WITH RIDERS.

Each on 4 wheel platform.

F3391 — Fancy dressed riders, monk, clown, jockey, etc. About 8x9½ in., platform 7½x2¾. ½ doz. in box, asstd... 2 20

F3392—As F3391, about 9x12. platform 8¾x3. ¼ doz. in box, asstd... 3 98

WADDLING DUCKS.

F3451—Flock of 3. Cotton stuffed, fur backs, painted eyes and beak, with bell and bellow voice. On wire frame, 5 metal wheels, long handle, when drawn across floor moves life-like. Length 30 in. ½ doz. in box...Doz. **$1.98**

FLOATING DUCKS.

A novelty that will prove a ready seller.

F829 — Composition wax painted in different colors, tested to 100 degrees of heat. Each set of 1 large duck and 4 ducklings in box. 1 doz. sets in pkg. Doz. sets, **89c**

GENUINE LEATHER COVERED ANIMALS.

F3398 Asst.—Small but fine, wood bodies, leather in natural colors, lifelike appearance, bead eyes. Asstd. horses, cows, donkeys, etc. in box of 1 doz... Doz. $0 84

F3399, On Wood Platform — Fine models, well made, in natural colors, 4 iron wheels, donkey and horse with saddle and bridle, and cow ½ doz. in box... 2 24

F3404, Elephant with Trumpet Voice—Natural gray color, well modeled. When ring is pulled elephant roars and moves trunk at same time, about 10 in., on 11½x5½ platform, red iron wheels. Each in box....Each $0 79

LEATHER COVERED COWS—With Voice.

Mounted on 4 iron wheel platform.

F3400—Modeled shape, free legs, natural eyes, with voice, made by pushing head to one side, collar with bell, outside wheels. Length about 8 in. ½ doz. in box...Doz. 4 25

F3401 — Fine model in every way. loud natural voice. Length about 11 in., wheels inside. Each in box. Each $0 73

F3402—As F3401, very much larger, 14 in. long, powerful voice, platform 14¼x4½. Each in box... 1 15

F3403—As F3402, 16 in. long, platform 15⅝x5¼. A $2 value to sell at $1.75. Each in box... 1 35

NODDING HEAD ELEPHANTS.

F3394 — 5x3½, natural finish and color, well proportioned. 1 doz. in box... Doz. $0 89

F3395—8x5. ½ doz. in box... 2 00

F3396 — About 10½x6, run away elephant, head and tail move at same time. ½ doz. in box... 4 00

F3397—Extra size, good show piece as well as toy, 14½x8¾. gilt lace trimmed flannel blanket, mounted on wheels. Each in box... Each $0 72

FELT ELEPHANTS.

F3366½ — Natural gray color, stuffed felt, good model, free legs. trunk and tail, glass eyes, tusks, red flannel blanket, length 7½ in., ½ doz. in box. Doz. $2 25

F3367½—Well made, about 9½x7, and in good proportions, free legs, long trunk, tusks, natural glass eyes, large free ears, embroidered blanket. ¼ doz. in box... 3 98

F3368—As F3366¼, embroidered head piece. About 13x11, circum. of body 18 in. A good showy piece. Each in pkg...Each $0 79

FUR SKIN SITTING ANIMALS.

F3357—10c asst. cats, rabbits and dogs, natural eyes, long fur, with voice, made by pressing sides. 1 doz. in box... Doz. $0 85

F3358—As above, 8 in. long. ½ doz. in box... 1 95

F3359—Rabbit with carrot, long fur, natural eyes, upright position, when tail is pressed raises carrot to mouth and voice squeaks, ht. 6¼. ½ doz. in box. 2 25

F3360—As above, 8 in. high. ½ doz. in box... 3 75

IMPORTED PAPIER MACHE ANIMALS.

The genuine goods. Almost unbreakable. Can be dropped or thrown around with impunity.

F3380 — *To retail for 3c each or '2 for 5."* Felt covered, well modeled, asstd. horses, donkeys, cows, sheep, etc., about 2¾ in. 1 doz. in flat box, asstd... 22

3381 — As F3380, average about 3¾. ½ doz. in flat box, asstd... 39

F3382—As F3380, 5 in., *fine 10 centers.* ½ doz. in box... 79

Asstd. Animals--Glazed Finish.

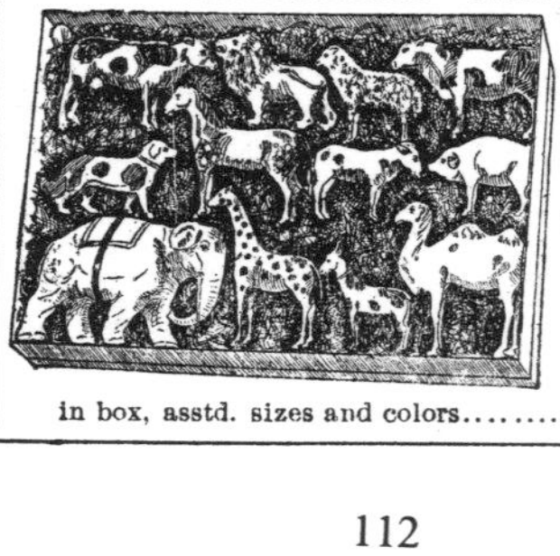

F3383—6 styles, horses, sheep, pigs, elephants, etc., painted in colors. Average size 4½ in. 1 doz. in box, asstd... 39

F3384—Wild and domestic animals in flat display box, 17¼x11¼, green packing to represent grass. 1 doz. in box, asstd. sizes and colors... 72

SHEEP FOLD.

F3452—Wood, stained in bright colors, 2¾ x 7 platform, 4 wool covered sheep, colored bands, small tree. ½ doz. in box... Do $0 7

FLANNEL FELT CATS.

F3376 — *Our 25 cent cat.* 9½x4¼, cat at play with celluloid ball between fore paws, tail extended, glass eyes, ribbon around neck with bell, painted natural color. ½ doz. in box... 2

F3377—As F3376, 12x6. ½ doz. in box... 4

IMPORTED FELT AND VELVET ANIMALS ON WHEELS.

F3378—Asstd. 6 styles felt animals—dogs, cats, horses, elephants, donkeys, etc., bell shaped, with free legs, axles with iron wheels, some with neck ribbons and bells or medallions, horses and donkeys with saddle covers and bridles. Average size 6¼x5½ in. ½ doz. in box... 2.

F3379—50c asst. About 8¼x6¼ in., covered with velvet in asstd. colors, camels, cows, elephants. etc., tinsel trimmed blankets, ribbon neck bands and bells, horses, donkeys and camels with bridles, iron axles with iron wheels. ½ doz. in box... 4

GERMAN TOY ASSORTMENTS.

F2880, 35c Doz.

F2880—5 cent asst. 9½ in. dressed clapping figure, 9 in. litho-wood jumping jack, horse, sheep, shaking head donkey on 4 wheel platform, 2 sheep drawing hat cart, 5 tongue cricket rattle, 7 in. wood trumpet, 8 in. sail boat, dressed figure on stick with voice, surprise box and trumpet. 1 doz. in box...

F2881, 75c Doz.

F2881 — Special 10 cent asst. 14½ in. litho wood jumping jack, 6 in. Punch and Judy show, 12 in. dressed clapping figure, 10 in. sail boat, horse with mane & tail and shaking head donkey on 4 wheel platforms, wool sheep and horse with hay carts, 3¾x3¾ surprise box, dressed acrobat with chair, soldier boy in chair with clappers, litho performing horse and jockey. 1 doz. in box...

PERFORMING FIGURES ON 4 WHEEL PLATFORMS.

Perform when drawn across the floor. Asstd. colored costumes, painted features.

F2903, 89c Doz. F2904, $1.85 Doz. F2905, $4.00 Doz.

F2903 — Lace collars, gilt trimmings, shake bells, play fiddle or cymbals, ht. 8¼ in., platform 5¼ in. long. 1 doz. in box, asstd...

F2904—Clowns, bisque heads, colored costumes, lace trimmings, flannel caps, shake bells, play fiddle or cymbals, ht. 12 in. ¼ doz. in box, asstd... 1

F2905—4 styles, bisque heads, glass eyes curly wigs, part with caps, standing positions, playing bells, cymbals, etc., ht. about 12 in. Action as F2903. ⅛ doz. in box, asstd... 4

COMICAL SHAKING HEAD FIGURES.

Heads "wig-wag," giving them a most droll appearance.

Two Styles F2934. Two Styles F2933. Two Styles F2935.

F2934—Boy, girl and heathen Chinee, papier mache, about 5½ in. 1 doz. in box, asstd...

F2933—Asstd. 6 styles. Extra size heads, Foxy Grandpa, Happy Hooligan, etc., attractive colors, wood base, ht. about 6½. 1 doz. in box...

F2935—Asstd. comical figures, as F2933, painted eye, features and clothes. 8¼ in. 1 doz. box.

Two Styles F2936. Two Styles F2937, $2.25 Doz.

F2936 — As F2933, 6 nations, 11½ in. ½ doz. in box, asstd. 1

F2937—Asstd. 4 styles, extra large heads, short bodies, comical combination. Ht. 11½ in. ½ doz. in box .. 2

IMPORTED MECHANICAL TOYS.

All wound by attached keys, unless specified, good springs.

F2660,

F2671,

F2673,

F2660, Automobile Touring Car—5¼ in., paint and gilt finish, modern model, imit. rubber tires, runs ahead or in circle. Each in box, ½ doz. in pkg............Doz. **1.35**

F2671, Automobile—A big seller painted, motorman. Each in box, ½ doz. in pkg.....Doz. **$1.55**

F2672,

F2673, Naughty Boy Interfering with Chauffeur—Automobile body lithographed in white, blue striping, double spoke red wheels, imit. rubber tires, runs every way, length 4½ in. Each in box. ½ doz. pkg. Doz. **$1.57**

F2672, Century Cycle—Gentleman salutes and umbrella revolves. 5x5½, painted, imit. rubber tires. Each in box, ½ doz. in pkg. Doz. **$1.59**

F2670, $1.75 Doz.

F2674, $1.75 Doz.

F2675, $1.90 Doz.

F2670, Clown Swinging Ball—Painted bright color costume, painted features and cap, walks and swings balls. Each in box, ½ doz. in pkg..........Doz. **$1.75**

F2674, Beetle—6 legs, moving wings, all in motion at once, bright colors. Each in box, ½ doz. in pkg..........................Doz. **$1.75**

F2675, Trolley Car—Coil spring, 4 wheels, decorated, 6 in. long, ½ doz. in box..Doz. **$1.90**

F2681,

F2676, $1.95 Doz.

F2677, $1.98 Doz.

F2681, Windmill Toy—Decorated bottom, 13 in. tube, miller's house and 9 in. windmill miller climbs windmill and descends, with bag on his head. Operated by weights. Each in box, ½ doz. in pkg........................Doz. **$1.65**

F2676, Asst. Waddling Duck and Hopping Canary—Painted in natural life like colors, length 6¾ in. Each in box, ½ doz. in pkg...................................Doz. **$1.95**

F2677, Asstd. Walking Indian and Frog—Painted in colors, Indian 8 in., bow, arrow and hatchet, swaying movement; 6¾ in., frog with red painted coat, white shirt, hat and cane. Each in box, ½ doz. in pkg..............................Doz. **$1.98**

F2680, $2.00 Doz.

F2678,

F2679, $2.10 Doz.

F2680, Goose—2 wheels, flaps wings, painted in colors. 6 in. long, 8¾ wide. Each in box, ½ doz. in pkg......Doz. **$2.00**

F2678, Hansom Cab with Walking Horse—Painted in colors, driver, imit. rubber tire metal wheels, dapple gray horse, length 7½ in. Each in box, ½ doz. in pkg. Doz. **$1.90**

F2679, Drummer Boy—Painted in bright colors, ht. 7¼ in., drum and sticks, moves arms and body and drum. Each in box, ½ doz. in pkg.................................Doz. **$2.10**

F2661, $2.15 Doz.

F2662, $2.75 Doz.

F2661, Performing Twin Clowns—Painted in bright colors, on wheels, asstd. 3 acts, average 5½ in., ht. 6. Each in box, ½ doz. in pkg..................................Doz. **$2.15**

F 2 6 6 2, Boy Athlete—2 styles, swinging dumb bells and Indian clubs, painted, ht. 7½ in. Each in box, ½ doz. in pkg..Doz. **$2.75**

MECHANICAL TOURING AUTOMOBILE.

Exceptional value to retail at 25 cents.

F2682—2 seat touring car, painted and striped in black, blue and white, red seats, hood front and mud side guards, gilt finished imit. rubber tire open spoke metal wheels, chauffeur and passenger, wound by attached key, good spring, runs straight or in a circle, 6¼ in., ht. 4¾. Each in box, ½ doz. in pkg. Per dozen, **$2.18**

IMPORTED MECHANICAL JUGGLING CLOWNS.

So good it seldom retails on the bargain counter at less than 50c.

F2684—Painted features and uniforms in bright colors, on metal base, ht. 9¼ in. Wound by attached key, when in action one swings arms juggling balls, other turns pin wheel with 8 bells. Good action, full of life. Each in box, ½ doz. in pkg., asstd. 2 styles. Per dozen, **$3.35**

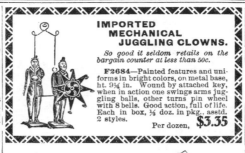

F2663, $3.25 Doz.

F2690, $3.25 Doz.

F2663, Boy with Cart—Painted and lithographed colors. Boy runs draws cart with little girl. 7¼ in., ht. 5¾ in. Each in box. ½ doz. in pkg...................................Doz. **$3.25**

F2690, Darky Cake Walkers—Painted features and fancy costumes, man with cane and handkerchief, girl holding skirt, characteristic actions, ht. 8 in. Each in box. ½ doz. in pkg. Doz. **$3.25**

F2683,

F2664, $3.30 Doz.

F2683, Asstd. Foxy Grandpa and Old Sport on Roller Skates—Painted costumes in asstd. bright colors—Foxy Grandpa with spectacles, Old Sport with hat and cigar, skate sideways moving arms as if balancing, ht. 8 in. Each in box, ½ doz. in pkg. asstd Doz. **$3.00**

F2685,

F2664, Rocking Clowns Juggling Ball—Painted and gilded, rocks continually, ball rolls in tray, 9 in. long. Each in box, ½ doz. in pkg..........Doz. **$3.30**

F2685, Clown Stubborn Donkey and Cart—Patented, donkey goes forward, backs, kicks. About 7½ in. long, cart decorated with circus figures. Each in box, ½ doz. in pkg.........................Doz. **$2.80**

F2665, $3.50 Doz.

F2666, $3.60 Doz.

F2665, Comical Negro Drummer—Painted in colors, plays cymbals and beats drum, ht. 8½ in. Each in box, ½ doz in pkg...Doz. **$3.50**

F2666, Touring Automobile—Lithographed in royal blue, gilt and white stripes, imit. rubber tires, 2 passengers, runs straight ahead or in circle 7½ in long. Each in box, ½ doz. in pkg...Doz. **$3.60**

F2686, $3.70 Doz.

F2667, $3.80 Doz.

F2687, $4.00 Doz.

F2686, Auto Sisters—Automobile hansom cab painted in bright colors, erratic movement, imit. rubber tire, open spoke wheels, 2 lady passengers try to drive dog from step, sway bodies to and fro, signal through trap to chauffeur. Each in box. ½ doz. in pkg..................................Doz. **$3.70**

F2667, Clown Slack Wire Performer—Painted features, colored cloth costume, ht. 8½ in., on suspended cord will go hand over hand from end to end. Each in box, ½ doz. in pkg...........................Doz. **$3.80**

F2687, Automobile Coach—Lithographed in red, green and white, oak finished top, baggage rack, gilt finished metal mud guard, rubber tire open spoke wheels, hood front and 2 lamps, lamp on roof, chauffeur in uniform, extra seat in back, 5 open windows, runs straight or in circle, 8 in., ht. 5½. Each in box. ½ doz. in pkg. Doz. **$4.00**

F2691—Tent shape on tin base, wire frame, flag staff and black canvas tent, 6 attached horses or baskets with riders, painted in bright colors. Measure 13x9 in. Each in box, ½ doz. in pkg. Doz. **$4.00**

F2689,

F2639, $4.25 Doz

F2689, Automobile—Lithographed in white, red trimmings, open double spoke imit. rubber tire wheels, 2 gilt metal dashboard lanterns, chauffeur blows gilt horn, steers and changes course, 6¾x6¾. Each in box, ¼ doz. pkg. Doz. **$3.75**

F2639, Walking Doll—Bisque head, natural glass eyes, rembrandt hair, fancy dress, lace trimming, ruffle trimmed hood, flowers in each hand. Runs across floor, hands move alternately, ht. 9 in. Each in box, ¼ doz. in pkg....Doz. **$4.25**

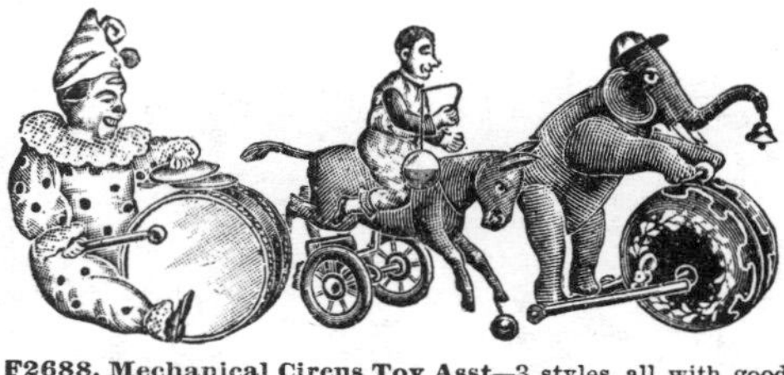

F2688, Mechanical Circus Toy Asst—3 styles, all with good springs, wound by attached keys: (1) clown with painted uniform and ball on end of stick, riding felt covered trick mule, mounted on two iron wheels, length 7½ in., performs all manner of tricks, shaking head and bobbing tail; (2) composition felt covered and attractively lithographed elephant rolling globe, also rings bell, length 8 in.; (3) clown beating bass drum and playing cymbals, fancy lace trimmed cloth costume with fool's cap, painted features, length 8¾ in., bobs head while playing. Each in box, ¼ doz. in pkg., asstd. Doz. **$4.20**

F2693, 72c Each.

F2765, 75c Each.

F2693, Waltzing Doll—Pyroxyline head (practically unbreakable), painted features, hair and eyebrows, indestructible metal arms and painted hands, figured sateen dress, lace trimmed neck, sleeves and ruffled bottom, ribbon sash, gilt necklace with charm. Invisible platform with wheels, waltz motion. Each in box.............................Each, **72c**

F2765, Bicycle Game—8 in., circular race course with raised open work enclosure. Pole and flag at starting point, 3 riders in fancy costumes. Wound with key. Each in box. Each, **75c**

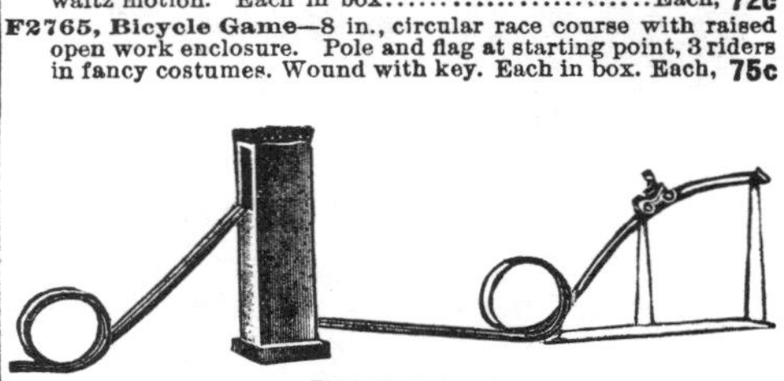

F2669, 75c Each.

F2669, Loop the Loop—Double loop with elevator tower, all metal, adjustable car with passengers, 4 sections, after taking 1 loop car passages into tower on elevator which automatically hoists it and then goes to second loop. Length 44 in., ht. of tower 11½ in. In box, knocked down. Each, **75c**

F2709, $1.50 Each.

F2709, Merry-go-Round—*A good show piece as well as a toy.* Velveteen canopy top in colors, chenille ball fringe, U. S. banner and flags on top, wire frame with 8 hanging double horses and baskets, rider on each horse and 2 figures in each basket, runs about 40 minutes, center tin pole with socket, fancy scroll on tin platform, 14x17. Each in box. Each, **$1.50**

MECHANICAL HORSE RACE GAMES.

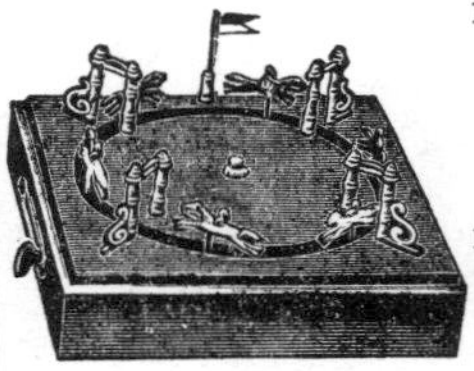

F2757—Square cabinet, 7½x7½, track 6 in. diam., green baize covering, 4 asstd. color bronze horses with jockeys, by pressing lever horses pass through 4 gates, winning post with American flag. Each in box. Each, **38c**

F2758—As F2757, 9½x9½, 6 horses with jockeys, painted in colors, fancy design metal gates, diam. of track 7½. Each in box...................Each, **72c**

MECHANICAL LAUNCH.

F2715½—Entirely of metal, will sail in water, each tested before leaving factory, body painted red with white and black stripes, open window cabin, cockpit with seat, captain at wheel, smokestack and attached key for winding, single screw propeller, adjustable rudder, length 8½ in. Each in box, ¼ doz. in pkg. Doz. **$2.15**

MECHANICAL OCEAN STEAMERS.

F2716, Steamer:—7⅝ in., painted and striped in red and white, funnel with imit. smoke serves as key for winding, minute gun, gilt rail, single screw, rudder. Each in box. ⅓ doz. in pkg.............Each, **35c**

F2717, Steamer:—10 in., white and red painted body, black and gilt stripes, buff top, gilt rails, cabin with open windows and rail, 2 smoke stacks with imit. smoke, one serves as key, 2 funnels, 2 sailors, single screw rudder, 2 American flags. Each in box. Each, **72c**

F2718:—As F2717, 11¼ in. has 2 masts and steering wheel. Each in box..............................Each, **95c**

F2719, Gun Boat:—17¾ in., red painted body, black and gilt striping, raised gilt ornamented front, drab decks, pilot house, etc., 8 gilt cannons, smokestack and flag, single screw propeller, detachable rudder, attached key. Each in box...............................Each, **79c**

IMPORTED MECHANICAL LOCOMOTIVES.

All with attached key and good spring.

F2710—8 in. body and wheels lithographed in red with silver stripings, cab, smokestack and cowcatcher, 6 wheels, bell rings. Each in box, ⅙ doz. in pkg. Doz. **$1.90**

F2711—14⅛ in. with detachable 4 wheel tender, American pattern. Lithographed in red, black and gilt stripes, side foot rails, gong, double truck, 8 gilt metal wheels, clock spring motor, cog wheel. 3 in box..Each, **35c**

F2712—Latest American model, length 17½ in., lithographed in red with black and red stripes, 2 gilt domes, striped wheels, driving rod, gilt dome gong, cog wheel, 6 wheel tender. Each in box.................Each, **68c**

F2713—As F2712, length 19 in...................Each, **75c**

F2714—Length 26 in., striped and lithographed to represent gauges, etc., 2 gilt domes, bell and headlight, striped wheels with driving rod and gong, cog wheel, 8 wheel tender. Each in box...............................Each, **$1.50**

F2715—As F2714, 29 in. long piston rod in addition to driving rod...............................Each, **$2.95**

MECHANICAL MUSICAL TOYS.

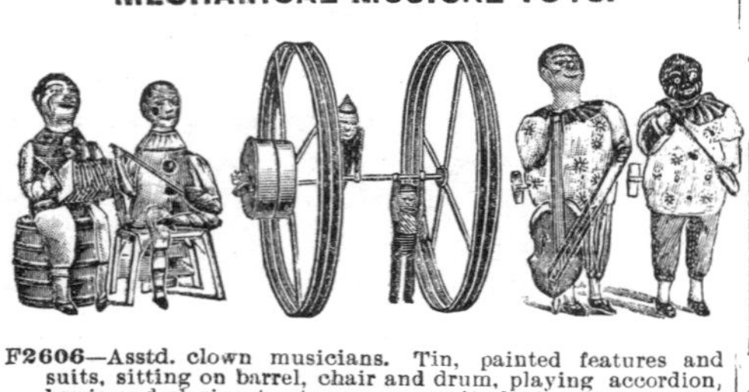

F2606—Asstd. clown musicians. Tin, painted features and suits, sitting on barrel, chair and drum, playing accordion, banjo and clarionet. Arms move as if playing instruments, heads bob back and forth, invisible music. Ht. about 7 in. Each in box. ¼ doz. in pkg.......................Doz. **$3.50**

F2610—Acrobatic clowns on revolving double wheel, 9 in., painted in bright colors, clowns perform acrobatic feats while wheels revolve. Music box plays continuously. Full of life. Each in box. ¼ doz. in pkg.......Doz. **$3.95**

F2607—Asstd. white and negro clowns. Playing banjo and fiddle, painted features, figured cotton shirts, painted trousers. Arms and hands move. Ht. 8 in. Each in box. 1-6 doz. in pkg...............................Doz. **$4.25**

F2611—Performing musical clowns. 2 styles—(1) clown playing banjo and mate juggling barrel, (2) clown playing banjo and dog dancing. Painted features bright costumes. Painted beveled platform, 9x4¾, good spring, music plays continuously. Each in box. 1-6 doz. in pkg. asstd... Each, **55**

F2608—Pianist. Upright piano 5x5, black, regulation keyboard, music box inside, tin painted base 4⅝x5¼. Artist has painted features, long locks, flannel suit. Moves body and runs hands along keyboard. Each in box...........Each, **67c**

Two Styles F2609.

F2609—Asstd. 4 styles musical performing clowns with dogs. Painted in colors, part with fancy cloth blouses, 4½x8½, painted platform, invisible musical reeds. Ht. 9½ in. Each in box. Asstd. 4 in pkg...............................Each, **75c**

F2612—Jockey on painted horse with wheel, runs around in circle, jockey bobs up and down and catches rings from rack on post with sword, painted and striped in bright colors, figured flannel blouse, painted trousers, cap and features. Music plays. Ht. 7¼ in. Each in box......Each, **75c**

F2613—Performing trained horses. Metal circus ring with fancy fence, diam. 9¼ in., painted in bright colors, 3 trick horses with trainer and clown holding hoop through which horses pass, moving forelegs, good spring, music plays, extreme ht. 9½ in. Each in box...............................Each, **75c**

F2614—Revolving carousal. Made of metal, painted in white, gilt decorated with canopy top and flag, 4 horses with riders, painted in attractive colors, revolving platform, music plays. 8¼ in. diam., ht. 15½ in. Each in box. Each, **79c**

MECHANICAL TROLLEY CAR WITH TRACK.

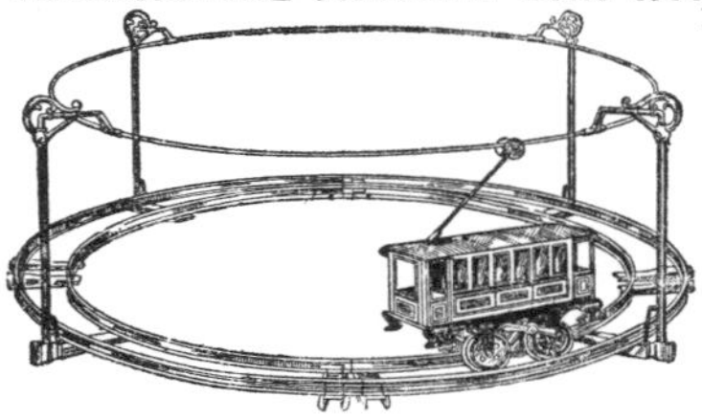

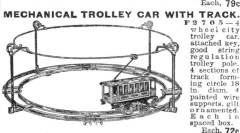

F2705—4 wheel city trolley car, attached key, good string regulation trolley pole, 4 sections of track forming circle 18 in. diam. 4 painted wire supports, gilt ornamented. Each in spaced box. Each, **72c**

PEWTER TOYS.

Particularly popular with the children for furnishing doll houses. We list only the best sellers and best goods.

PEWTER TOY TEA SETS.

F830—Bright embossed pattern, 5x7 spaced box, 23 pieces—6 cups, 6 saucers, 6 spoons, 1 cake dish, 1 teapot, 1 creamer. 1 doz. in pkg. Doz. $0 73

F831—As F830, 8x10, more elaborate. 24 pieces. ⅓ doz. in pkg.. 1 78

F832—As F831, 14x9½, larger pieces and finer design. ⅙ doz. in pkg...... 3 70

F833—As F831—large enough for child's use, fluted pattern, 25 pieces in 12½x19 box..................... 8 65

PEWTER TOY FURNITURE SETS.

F834—Parlor set, table, sofa, 2 chairs, 1 rocker, scroll design frames. 1 doz. in pkg..................... 36

F835—Sofa, rocker and chair, plush bottoms and fancy scroll frames. 1 doz. in pkg.. 75

F836—Dining room set—4 chairs with plush bottoms and 1 table. 1 doz. in pkg... 79

F837—Similar to F835, but larger and heavier, consists of 1 sofa, 2 chairs and 1 rocker. ⅙ doz. in pkg.......... 1 85

PEWTER DOLL CARRIAGES.

F838—Openwork filigree body and parasol, upholstered, moving wheels, 3⅛x4. Each in box, 1 doz. in pkg.......... 80

F839—Similar to F838, larger and more fancy, 5¼x6. Each in box. 1 doz. in pkg.......... 75

PAPER CAP EXPLODING CANE.

N2089÷About 34 in. long, flag pattern stick, red ball handle, strong cast iron exploder riveted to stick...Doz.$0 3

THE POPULAR AUTO PAPER CAP REPEATER.

N650—Two 3½ in. steel saw tooth edge rotary discs, rough surface axle and roller, between which is placed strip of caps. Pushing along makes 21 explosions without reloading. Length with wood handle 33 in. 1 doz. in box.......... Doz. 7

N. B.—With every order for 1 doz. Auto Repeaters at least 3 doz. boxes of caps must be ordered.

N651, Paper Cap Ammunition÷For N650 Auto Repeater, 21 caps on paper strip. 12 strips (252 caps) in box, 3 doz. boxes in carton..........Doz. 2

CARNIVAL CANE.

N52—Hickory—*not pine as offered by many.* Flexible hardwood, regulation length, ball top, red, white and blue striped stick. 100 in pkg..........Per 100 1 2

NICKELED PAPER CAP PISTOLS.

N2090, 22c Doz. N2091, 24c Doz. N2092, 32c Doz.

N2090, "Pluck"—3⅛ in., bright finish, fancy handle. 3 doz. in box, no less sold..........Doz. 2

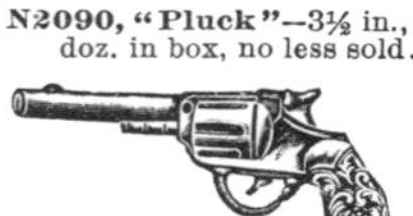

N2091, "Fido"—4 in., revolver pattern, bright finish, grip pattern handle. 3 doz. in box. no less sold. Doz. 2

N2092, Revolver Model—6 in., smooth parts bright finished, finger guard. 1 doz. in box..........Doz. 3

N2096, 72c Doz.

N2096, "Eagle"—8 in., revolver model, nickel finish, checkered handle, finger guard. 1 doz. in box...Doz. 72

N2097, S. & W. Model—7¼ in., bright finish, rim sight, diamond pattern handle, finger guard. 1 doz. in box. Doz. 75

N2097, 75c Doz.

"YOUNG AMERICA" CANNON.

N1608÷3½ in., aluminum finish, wood base, breech loader, exploded by string. Simple and harmless. 1 doz. in box...Doz. 72

N. B. With every dozen cannons at least 2 doz. boxes caps (*see below*) must be ordered.

Caps for N1608 Cannon.

N1609—Caps for N1608 cannon, extra loud. 100 in box. 1 doz. boxes in carton..........Doz. 27

BLANK CARTRIDGE PISTOLS, ETC.

Four big leaders. 22 caliber. Perfectly reliable.

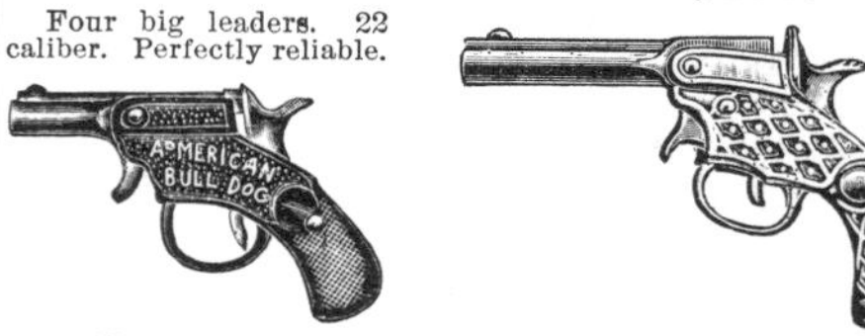

N3021, 68c Doz. N3022 and N3023.

N3021, "American Bulldog"—5 in., japanned stock, white nickeled trigger, hammer and spring tilting barrel (shell easily extracted), diamond pattern handle, finger guard. ⅙ doz. in box..........Doz. 68

N3022, "Rival"—6¼ in., all nickel finish, ornamental stock, spring tilting barrel, finger-guard, flared safety hammer. Each in box..........Doz. 1 35

N3023, "Rival"—Solid nickel plated and highly polished, otherwise as N3022. Each in box..........Doz. 1 80

NOVELTY PAPER CAP EXPLODERS.

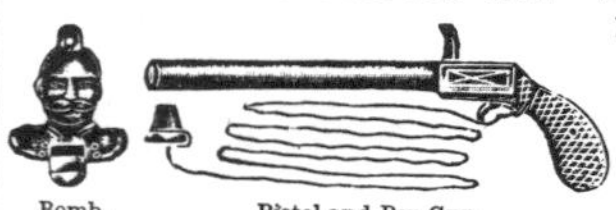

Bomb. Pistol and Pop Gun.

N1942, Bomb Cap Exploder÷Cast nickel bust, tumble nickel finish exploding attachment with string hole. 1 doz. in box..........Doz. 25

N1947, Cap Pistol and Pop Gun—8½ in., heavy metal barrel, cap placed in muzzle, plug inserted, pull the trigger and "she's off." 1 doz. in box..........Doz. 42

WOOD TEN PINS.

F885—Stained turned hardwood, beaded center 7 in. pins, 3 balls. Each set in wood box. Per dozen sets, **89c**

F886—Varnished hardwood, painted top and beaded center, 8 in. pins, 3 balls. Each set in sliding cover wood box..........Doz. sets 2 10

F887—Extra large set, varnished hardwood with painted and striped center, 11 in. pins, 3 balls, each set in sliding cover wood box.....Doz. sets 3 87

IRON TOYS TO RETAIL AT 75c AND UP.

F1318—Cannon with 2 horses and driver, length 18 in., cannon in bright colors. Each in box.................Doz. **$4.75**

F1319—Iron wagon with team of oxen, iron log painted in natural color, darkey driver, wagon and oxen painted bright colors, length 16 in. Doz. **$7.80**

F1320—Carriage with 2 horses in tandem style, driver and footman, all painted in bright colors, length 22 in., ht. 6¾ in. Each in box.....................................Doz. **$8.75**

F1321—Dray with team of horses, driver and 7 barrels, length 21 in., wagon painted bright red, gold trimmings, yellow wheels. Regular $1.25 toy.........................Doz. **$8.75**

STEEL TOYS.

Strong and durable, attractive designs, neatly painted and finished. Well packed.

F1135, 85c Doz.

F1135, "Daisy" Cart—5½x3¼, enameled in bright colors, name on sides, iron axles and wheels, aluminum finish, steel sides, 24 in. twisted wire handle. 1 doz. in box.....Doz. **85c**

F1130—Steel box wagon with seat, dapple horse, wheels turn under body, length 15½ in. ⅙ doz. in box. Doz. **$1.90**

F1136, "Express" Wagon — 9½x4¼, enameled red and yellow, black decoration, iron running gear, aluminum finish, 24 in. twisted wire handle, front wheels turn under. ⅙ doz. in box..Doz. **$1.95**

F1131 — Asstd. "Ice," "Delivery" and "Express" wagons. Steel throughout, painted and striped in attractive colors, removable top, transforming wagon into express, dapple gray horse with movable legs. Full length 14¼, ht. 6½. ½ doz. in box, asstd. Doz. **$1.98**

F1132, "Boy Blue" Automobile — 12½x6x6, wood platform, blue steel body, gilt trimmed, red painted iron wheels, large chauffeur. ⅙ doz. box..Doz. **$4.15**

F1133—As F1131, 2 horses Length 20, ht. 8½. Each in box. ¼ doz. in pkg., asstd. Doz. **$4.25**

F1134—Milk wagon with 3 horses, full length 31¼ in., removable folding top wagon, making an express wagon. Attractively lithographed in colors, made entirely of steel, horses painted, moving legs. Each wagon has 8 aluminum finished imitaion milk cans. Each in box.................Each, **72c**

IMPROVED ORIGINAL HILL CLIMBING FRICTION TOYS.

Wood and steel, iron wheels, painted and striped in colors. Simple in construction, nothing to get out of order. Set in motion by running forward a few times over the floor. Will climb an inclin or steeep grade, return and travel many feet on the level.

F1230, $4.00 Doz.

F1231, $4.00 Doz.

F1230, Racer—9x6 in., painted in orange and red enamel, gold striping, chauffeur and two passengers. Each in box. Doz. **$4.00**

F1231, Patrol — 10x7¼, in blue enamel, gold wheels, rail and striping, chauffeur and passenger. Each in box, Doz. **$4.00**

F1232, Hose Cart — 11x7½, maroon enamel, gilt striping, reel with imit. fire hose, which revolves chauffeur and passenger. Each in box. Doz. **$4.00**

F1233, Day Coach —*Extra large 50c toy*, 13x6 orange and maroon enamel, gilt striping. Each in box......Doz. **$4.00**

F1234, Locomotive and Tender—20x7, black and maroon en. amel, gilt striping, with gong. Each in box. Doz. **$8.50**

F1236, $8.50 Doz.

F1235, Auto—10½x8, olive enamel with red wheels, gilt striping, chauffeur and two lady passengers. Each in box. Doz. **$8.50**

F1237, $8.50 Doz.

F1236, Fire Engine — 11¾ x8, maroon enamel, gilt and bronze decoration, chauffeur and gong. Each in box. Doz. **$8.50**

F1237, Hook and Ladder Truck – 19x 8, maroon and orange enamel, gilt striping, double automatic extension 29 in. ladder, gong, driver and steersman. Each in box......Doz. **$8.50**

F1238, Menagerie Wagon — 14¾x9½, white and blue enamel, bronze striping 4 animals in each, which move to and fro, with chauffeur. Each in box. Doz. **$8.50**

F1239, White Flyer Automobile—12½x 5½, ht. 7½, white enamel, maroon inside with gold and bronze striping, 3 search lights, chauffeur and two lady passengers. Each in box. Each, **$1.25**

AMERICAN MADE MECHANICAL TOYS.

These toys have extra strong springs that will last for years with ordinary use.

F1240, Express Wagon — Enameled in bright colors. length 7 in., front wheels turn under. Each with driver. Each in box...Doz. **$4.00**

F1241, Automobile — Painted in bright yellow, red stripes, double seat with driver, full length 7½ in. ¼ doz. in box. Doz. **$4.00**

F1772, $8.90 Doz.

F1772, Automobile —Heavy tin, japanned black plush seat, gold tracings, bronze wheels with rubber tires, 11x7x7½, extra strong spring with stop handle. Each in box......Doz. **$8.90**

F1773, F1242.

F1773, Auto Truck—11x 6¾x10, with top cover, all made of tin and enameled, metal wheels finished in bronze, rubber tires, extra strong spring. Each in box.........Doz. **$8.90**

F1243.

F1242, Mechanical Racer — Steel, painted in bright colors, gold tracings, yellow seat and driver, heavy rubber tire wheels, width 4 in., length 10. Each in box. Doz. **$8.65**

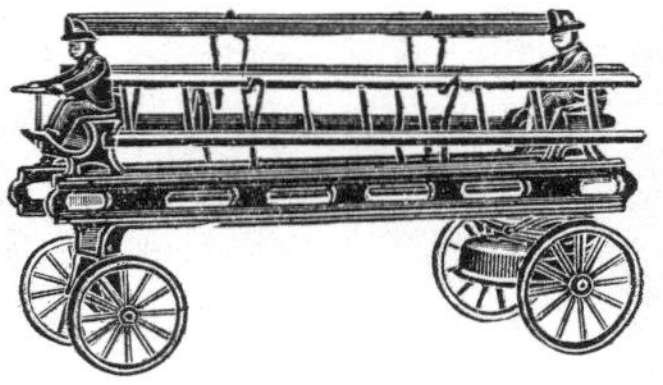

F1243, Automobile Dray — Steel, blue enameled with gold striping, 15x4, front wheels turn under, rubber tires, driver and 6 barrels. Each in box. Doz. **$8.65**

F1244, Hook and Ladder — Enameled in bright colors, striped. length 13½ in., driver and steersman, 3 ladders, front wheels turn under. Each in box. Doz. **$8.65**

F1245, 75c Ea h.

F1245, Fire Engine —10x6½, in., enameled in bright colors, gold and silver striping, rubber tire wheels, front wheels turn under, driver. Each in box....Each **75c**

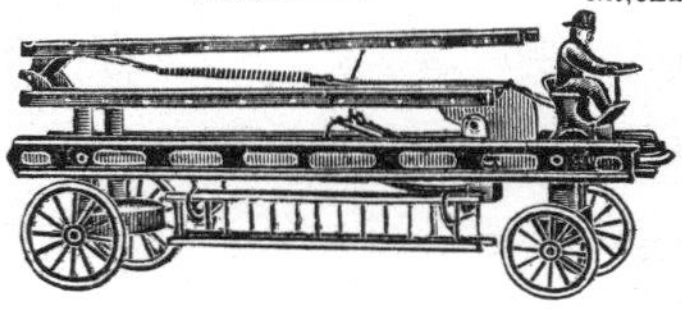

F1246, Hook and Ladder Truck — Length 18 in., enameled in bright colors, gold striping, rubber tire wheels, 2 ladders, 1 jointed automatic extension ladder, ladder raises and extends automatically, driver. Each in box. Each **$1.15**

Mechanical See-Saw with Dolls.

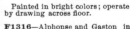

F1247 — Ebonized wood frame, 4 supports, 28 in. see-saw, 2 dressed bisque head detachable dolls, pendulum spring movement, aluminum finish. Each in box. Each, **72c**

COMICAL MECHANICAL IRON TOYS.

Painted in bright colors; operate by drawing across floor.

F1316—Alphonse and Gaston in automobile, bowing to each other, 7 in long, gold and silver striped, with driver. Each in box........Doz. **$4.00**

F1317 — Donkey cart with sailor driver and Mrs. Katzenjammer spanking bad boy, length 11½ in. Each in box.......Doz. **$4.25**

"NEVER-STOP" SEW SAW.

F1128 — Made of steel, enameled and striped in bright colors, ht. 14 in., reversible boy and girl figures at ends of 12 in. cross piece, figures, see saw from end to end by inverting. Each in carton, ⅙ doz. in pkg........Doz. **$4.00**

TOY COFFEE MILLS.

F1722, 36c Doz. F867, 75c Doz.

F1722 — 1⅝x1⅝x1⅝ cherry finish, lacquered. 1 doz. in box............ 36

F867—One that will grind coffee, 2½x2½x2. The metal parts are finished in gilt bronze, all wood work with three coats of varnish. One of the best 10c toys on the market. 1 doz. in box............ 75

DECEPTION WINE AND WHISKY GLASSES.

F3505—Regular blown wine glass filled with red liquor, thin glass top. One naturally starts to drink before he finds that he is "sold." H. 3 in. Each in box. 1 doz. in pkg. .... Doz. $0 30

F3508—Whisky glass, 2¼ in. high, top 2 in., filled with amber colored fluid. Each in box. 1 doz. in pkg. 40

F3506—As F3505, 4 in. Each in box. 1 doz. in pkg.... 42

F3507—As F3505, each in wood box. Ht. 4½ in., width 2¼. 82

SOAP BUBBLE OUTFITS.

F687, 87c Gro.

F687 — Penny toy, 6½ in., reed stem and tin cone shape bowl, containing pure soap, which can be renewed. Show card and directions in each box. ½ gro. in box............Gro. $0 87

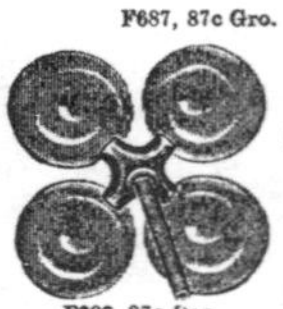

F688, 37c Doz.

F688—5c outfit, quadruple clay pipe with bamboo stem. 1 pkg. of prepared soap, one with wire ring with stem with which tricks can be made, in illustrated envelope, with directions. 1 doz. in box with show card.............Doz. 37

PNUEMATIC TOYS.

Each with rubber bulb on rubber tube. Pressure on bulb causes toy to perform.

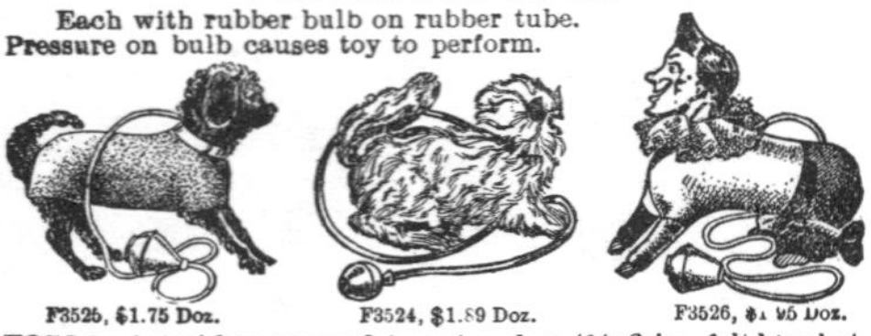

F3525, $1.75 Doz. F3524, $1.89 Doz. F3526, $1.95 Doz.

F3525—Astrakhan covered jumping dog, 4½x6 in., felt blanket, with voice which squeaks. ½ doz. in box.........Doz. $1.75

F3524—Jumping fur kitten, 4x5½ in., glass eyes, ribbon neck band. ½ doz. in box.............Doz. $1.89

F3526—Jumping clown, 4¾x4. composition head, painted features, flannel prints, lace collar. ½ doz. box...Doz. $1.95

F3527, $2.10 Doz. F3528, $3.25 Doz. F3529, 37c Each.

F3527—25c asst. of dancing toys. Animals on wire, platform, 3½x3¼, 6 styles asstd., monkeys, cows, dogs, etc. Doz. $2.10

F3528—Dancing clown and pig, ht. 8 in., clown in lace trimmed flannel suit in colors, painted face, has hold of pig. Each in box.............Doz. $3.25

F3529—Fur bear drummer., ht. 8 in., beats drum and plays cymbols, 4½x3½ wood base. Each in box.........Each, 37c

F3530, 67c Each.

F3531, 68c Each.

F3530.—Circus boy with trained dog. Ht. of boy 9½ in. bisque head, glass eyes, painted features, fancy colored cloth costume, lace trimming, holds whip. Fur dog, ht. 6 in., dog jumps around in circle, boy going same way. Polished wood platform. Each in box.............Each, 67c

F3531—Performing clown on wood rockers. Ht. 10 in., length 11½. Fancy colored cloth costumes, lace trimming, composition head, painted features, holds balancing rod with bell at each end. Each in box.............Each, 68c

F3532, 69c Each.

F3532—Wrestling clown and bear. Ht. 11 in., clown in colored fancy cloth costumes with pompons, composition head, painted features, black fur bear. Each in box. Each, 69c

F3533, 72c Each.

F3534, 75c Each.

F3533—Fur rabbits. Glass eyes, cloth costumes, gilt and lace trimmings. Small one dances with flowers, large one plays guitar. Wood platform, 6¾ in. long, ht. 11. Each in box.............Each. 72c

F3535, 98c Each.

F3534:—"Buster Brown and his dog "Tige." Ht. 9 in., regulation suit, composition head, painted features, fur dog 6½ in., Buster lashes whip and Tige runs and barks. Each in box....Each, 75c

F3535—Policeman and tramp, cloth costumes, composition heads, painted features. Tramp punches policeman and policeman clubs tramp. Each in box.............Each, 98c

NOVELTY TRICK FANS.

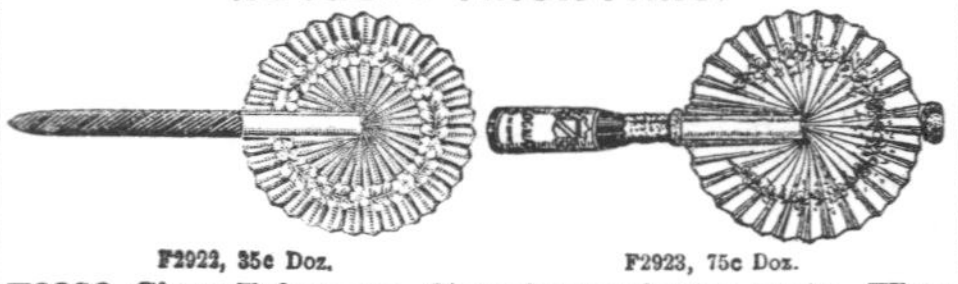

F2922, 35c Doz. F2923, 75c Doz.

F2922, Cigar Telescope—Cigar shape and color, 5¼ in. When top of cigar is pulled, 6½ in. fan appears. Full length 12. 1 doz. in pkg.............Doz. 35c

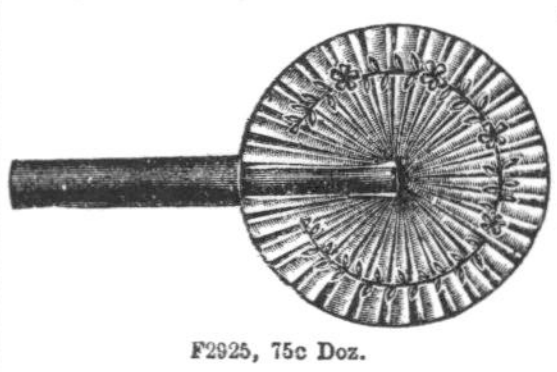

F2925, 75c Doz.

F2923, Bottle Telescope—Variegated tinfoil in imit. of glass, colored label with word "Champagne," length 5¼ in., fan appears when cork is pulled. 1 doz. in box....Doz. 75c

F2925, Cannon Fire Cracker — 5½ in., floral decorated muslin telescope fan appears when fuse is pulled, diam. 7 in. 1 doz. in box. Doz. 75c

MAGIC LANTERNS.

Our line is selected from the few good lines which have given *satisfaction* over the counter and in use. Our prices must be *right* or we could not get the business.

GENUINE BRASS GLOBE MAGIC LANTERNS.

F2730—Nickeled base attached to wood stand 4½x2⅝, gilt smokestack, brass burner with wick, 2 extension lenses, ht. 7½ in. Each in box with three 1 in. slides. ½ doz. in pkg. Doz. $2.25

F2731—Globe shape, polished brass, nickel base, removable smokestack, japanned support for telescope lens, wood base 3x 4⅝. ht. 7½ in. reflector lamp, burner, and six 1¼ in. slides. Each in neat box...Doz. $4.25

F2732—As F2731, base 6½x3½, total ht. 10 in., chimney, twelve 1⅜ in. slides. Each in box. Each, 75c

SQUARE SHAPE.

F2725—Painted red, bronze trimmings, gilt and russia tin smokestack, perforated firebox, telescope lens, lamp with chimney, ht. 10¼ in., platform 5½x4¼, six 1¼ in. slides. Each in box....Each, 30c

F2726—*Special value.* As F2725, lamp with reflector, ht. 11½ in., platform 6½x4½, six 1¼ in. slides. Each in box.............Each, 39c

F2727—As F2726, ht. 12¾ in., platform 7½x5½, twelve 1½ in. slides. Each, 65c

F2728—*Mammoth dollar leader.* As F2726, ht. 13½ in., platform 8x5¾. twelve 1⅜ in. slides. Each in box.............Each, 75c

F2729—As F2726, ht. 15 in., extra size body, platform 8¾x6. twelve 1¾ in. slides. Each in box.............Each, 95

"EUREKA" MAGIC LANTERNS.

F2747—Russia steel, square shape, gilt metal feet, nickel plated brass telescope lens with three glasses, patent regulating thumb screw, round corrugated elbow smokestack, extension collar, lamp with brass burner and chimney, door at side, six 1⅜ in. slides, body 4x 4½, ht. about 9½ in. Each in box.............Each, 36c

F2748 — As F2747, twelve 1⅜ in. slides, body 4½ x 5½, ht. 12½ in. Each in partition box...Each, 72c

F2749 — As F2748, twelve 1¼ in. slides, body 4¾ x 5⅝, ht. 12¾ in. Each in partition box...Each, 95c

NEW ARCHED TOP BODY MAGIC LANTERNS.

In hinged wood cabinet with handle.

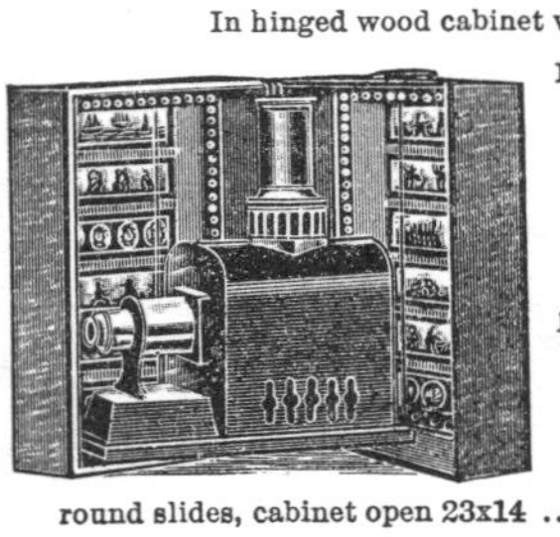

F2744—Red painted perforated fire box, gilt and russia tin smokestack, reflector lamp with chimney, telescope lens, ht. 10½ in. platform 9¾x 4¼, twelve 1⅜ in. slides in holders, cabinet open 21¼x11⅝.....Each, 75c

F2745—Nickel finish, red and black decorations, ht. 12¼ in., 3 glass telescope lenses, brass burner lamp, nickel smokestack, six 1⅜ in. oblong slides and three 4⅜ in. round slides, cabinet open 23x14 ....Each, $1.20

BRASS UPRIGHT MAGIC LANTERNS.

F2733—Polished brass lantern and lamp, good reflector and lens, removable smokestack, gilt striped green enamel rod support for lens, ht. 13 in., platform 5⅝x3¾, twelve 1⅜ in. slides. Each in box. Each, 78c

F2733½—As F2733, ht. 13¼ in. platform 6x3¾, six 1⅜ in. oblong slides and three 4¼ in. round slides. Each in box. Each, 95c

F2734—As F2733, ht. 14¾ in., platform 6¾x4½, six 1⅜ in. oblong slides and three 4¼ in. round slides. Each in box. Each, $1.40

TRICK NOVELTIES.

People will look, laugh and buy.

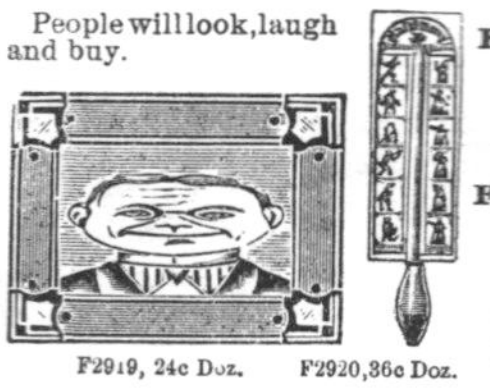

F2919, 24c Doz. F2920, 36c Doz.

F2919, Trick Mirror—"Long and Short" trick mirror with fancy pasteboard frame, 3½x 2⅞. The only sure cure for leanness and fatness. Doz. 24c

F2920, Matrimonial Thermometer — 7 in. blown glass filled with red fluid, on lithographed card indicating fury, anger, jealousy, etc. When held in hand fluid rises. Each in box. 1 doz. pkg. Doz. 36c

TOY BEADS IN WOOD BOXES.

Very popular with children for making necklaces for dolls and fancy work. Asstd. shapes, sizes and colors in each box. Ours are full depth boxes and full measure.

F672—About 200 in round wood box, diam. 1⅜ in., ht. ¾. ½ gro. boxes in carton... Gro. 85c

F673—Neat turned wood box, 2¾x1¼. 1 doz. boxes in pkg.............Doz. 39c

F674—About 400 in round wood box, 2½x1½. 1 doz. boxes in carton.............Doz. 75c

"IMPERIAL" MAGIC LANTERNS.

Made by the world's leading manufacturer. Absolutely guaranteed in every respect. Each bearing the well known "E. P." trademark, which in lanterns is what Kestner is in dolls. In wood frame boxes with hinged covers and cabinet spaces for 12 slides.

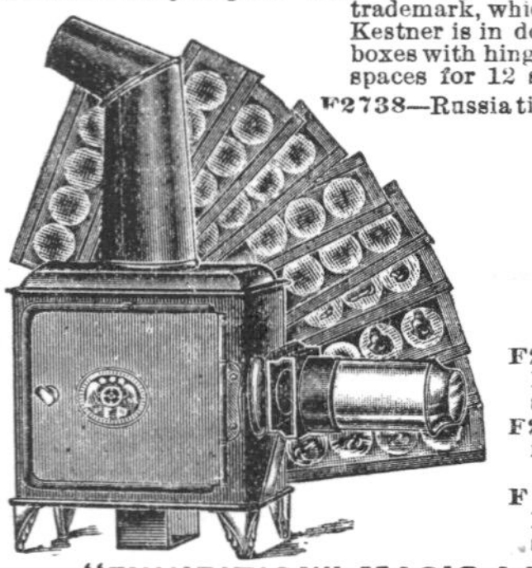

F2738—Russia tin, brass feet and elbow funnel, hinged door. set in lamp, burner and chimney, large regulator telescope and lens, extreme ht. 10 in. Not large but highest quality. twelve 1⅜ in. slides. Each in wood case. Each, 75c

F2739 — Extreme ht. 11 in., twelve 1⅜ in. slides...Each, $1.15

F2740—Ht. 11¾ in. 12 in. slides. Each, $1.50

F 2741—Family size, 13 in., takes 2⅜ in. slides...Each, $2.50

"EXHIBITION" MAGIC LANTERNS.

F2735—Round body, red painted, black and gilt striped, gilt trimmings, russia tin smokestack, brass collar, lamp and burner with reflector, brass trimmed telescope lens. iron holder, ht. 11½ in., varnished platform, six 1⅝ in. double glass and three 4¼ in. round slides, one moving glass slide and one chromotrope slide with crank. Slides fastened in folding wood case, nickel handle, open 22¾x13¾. Each, $1.59

F2736—13½ in. high, six 2x7 double glass and three 6 in. round slides, chromotrope with crank, 1 turning slide in wood frame, show bills, etc. Each in box, open 25½x15.....Each, $2.35

F2737—Large enough for smallhall, ht. 14½ in., reflector lamp, six 2⅜x8 double glass and three 6 in. round slides, one chromotrope and one moving glass slide in wood frame. Each in box, open, 29x16¾. Each, $2.87

KINETOSCOPE MAGIC LANTERN.

F2746—Russia iron body and elbow smokestack, brass burner. lamp and chimney, nickel reflector, hinged door, 3 powerful lenses, nickel extension telescope. metal reel with spring, 2 revolving lenses for removing picture films, varnished wood platform, 8½x4, ht. 14 in., 6 asstd. pictures, moving gelatine films, length 35 in., and six 1⅝ in. oblong glass slides. Each in hinged cover case. Each, $3.75

THE "KODAK" MAGIC LANTERN.

Made by the famous "E. P." maker. *A splendid article.*

F 2742—Known as the photographer's lantern, as the slides are 3½ in., regulation width of a kodak picture. Photographers can reproduce their pictures on glass instead of paper, and exhibit pictures taken by themselves. Oval shape, 4 brass feet, turned funnel, painted green all over, gold edges, complete lamp on inside, large reflector, opening in back, brass bound telescope lens. Set of 3 lenses. Total ht. 17 in. full width with lens about 12 in. Twelve 3½x11 slides, 2 round slides and 1 chromotrope with each. Each in box. Each, $4.75

MAGIC LANTERN SLIDES.

A well selected line. The first size is the width, so you can easily tell which of the above lanterns each number fits. Each number 1 doz. in box (except F3085, which is ½ doz.), 12 subjects.

F3077—1x4	Doz.	12c	F3081—1¾x6⅝	Doz.	35c
F3078—1¼x4¾	"	15c	F3082—2x7	"	45c
F3079—1⅜x5	"	25c	F3083—2⅜x8	"	55c
F3080—1½x6	"	30c	F3084—2⅞x8¾	"	65c
			F3085—3½x11	"	$1.50

TOY STEEL RANGES.

Made exactly as "full grown" ranges. Doors swing, covers are removable, grates turn, and best of all *a fire can be made in them*. All complete with kitchen utensils.

F1248, F1249, $1.85 Doz. F1250, $2.25 Doz.

F1248—3x2¼, ht. 4 in., oxidized plate. 1 doz. box.....Doz. 71c

F1249—5x4¾x3½, full nickeled, burnished edges and legs. Complete with skillet, square pan and length of pipe. ⅓ doz. in box................Doz. $1.85

F1250—6⅛x3⅝x4⅝ in., oxidized finish, extension front, fry pan, kettle and lifter. ¼ doz. in box. Doz. $2.25

F1251—8¼x5¼x4⅝, asstd. oxidized and black, large kettle, fry pan, lifter, towel rack. Each in box. Each in pkg. Doz. $3.90

F1251, $3.90 Doz.

F1252, $4.40 Doz. F1253, $ 7.90 Doz.

F1252 — Nickel plated stove, polished rims, 7¾x4½ in., ht. 4¾ in., extreme ht. with shelf 8½ in., fittings, towel rod and water back. Complete with kitchen utensils. Each in box ....Doz. $4.40

F1253—11x6⅝, ht. 7 in., burnished oxidized finish, water tank, tea kettle, skillet, sauce pan, length of pipe, lifter and towel rod. Complete in box. Doz. $7.90

F1254 — Extra large "Dollar" stove. 13¼x6⅝x6¼, black finish, nickel plated trimmings, water tank, kettle, fry pan, skillet, coal hod, shovel and towel rack. Each complete in box...Doz. $8.75

F1254, $8.75 Doz.

F1255, $1.00 Each. F1256, $1.25 Each.

F1255. "Peerless"—10¼x7, ht. 10 in., highly polished nickel plate with top shelf and water back, kettle, fry pan, coal hod, shovel, lifter, griddle iron and towel rod..Each, $1.00

F1256—13½x7, ht 12½ in., oxidized finish, top shelf and extension back. Complete as F1255. Each in box. Each, $1.25

F1257, $1.75 Each. F1258, $2.00 Each.

F1257—Large oxidized, 13¼x7, ht. 9¼ in., 6 holes, water back, fry pan, skillet, pot, coal hod and towel rod. Each in box. Each, $1.75

F1258 — Black steel range, white metal door and top, burnished edge and ornament with large shelf, 6 holes, fittings as F1257. 15x7. ht. 9¼ in. extreme ht. 15 in. Each in box.Each, $2.00

F1260 — Extra large nickel plated stove, fine finish. 15x7, ht. 9¼ in., 3½ in. extension back, 8x7½ in. back shelf, full ht. 16 in., 6 holes and water back. Complete as F1258......Each. $2.50

F1260, $2.50 Each.

"WEEDEN" AMERICAN STEAM TOYS.

Exact imitations of the big engines All fitted with genuine brass boilers and Russian steel fire boxes each tested before leaving factory and guaranteed perfect. Full directions with each.

F1155, F1158, 75c Each.

F1155, Upright Engine—Ht. 9 in., 1⅞ in. balance wheel, 2 color painted molded edge, wood base 3½x3¼, perfect in every detail. Each in box, ½ doz. in pkg.............Doz. $1.85

F1156—As 1155, ht. 11 in. 2¼ in. bal. whl., base 4½ x4⅛, whistle, each in box, ¼ doz.in pkg. Doz. $3.95

F1157—As 1155, ht. 12 in. 3¼in.balance wheel, base 5¼x5¼, glass gauge and whistle. Each in box. Doz. $8.10

F1158 — Locomobile — Heavy tin, steel running gear and wheels, rubber tires, painted red, black trim, boiler under seat, run straight or curved, 9x3x5¼. Each in wood box. Each, 75c

F1159—Beam Engine—Sheet steel, 10¼ in. ht. 9¾, boiler polished brass, hardwood base, safety valve, whistle and walking beam, iron supports, balance wheel is turned finished faced, shaft has belt pulley. Each in box. Each, 72c

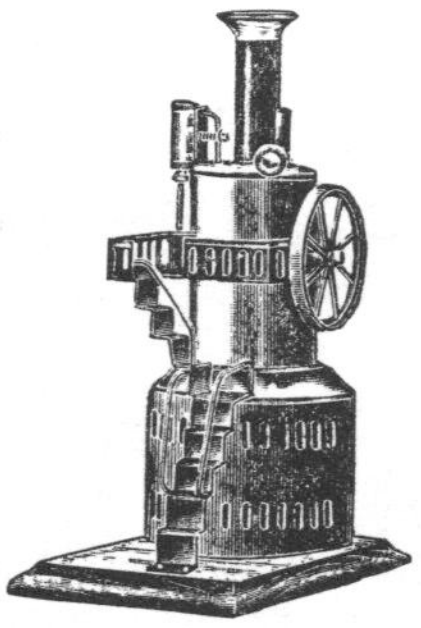

F1159,

F1160, Upright Engine—Ht. 12 in., base 5x8 stairway and railing, brass boiler, water glass register watcr in boiler, sheet iron fire box, whistle. Perfect in every detail. Each in box....Each, 77c

F1161, Rotary Engine—8⅞ x 6 x 7¾, decorated in colors, kaleidoscope attachment, boilers and steam pipes of polished brass, brass smoke stack top. Base fire box and engine box of cold, rolled steel tinned on inner sides. Has belt pulleys. Each in box........Each, 79c

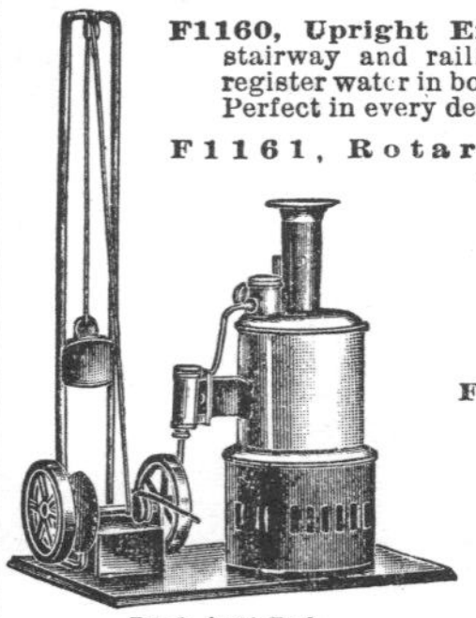

F1162—Steam Pile Driver—Ht. 13 in., base 6x8½, polished brass boiler, safety valve, filler whistle and water glass, engine with double balance wheel and winding drum, shipper lever, gallows frame or hammer guides and hammer, working parts all polished nickel plate. Each in box......Each, $1.00

F1162, $1.00 Each.

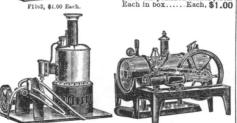

F1163, F1165,

F1163, Steam Engine and Force Pump—Ht. 8¾ in., base 6 x8½, engine and pump on strong base, boiler of brass, safety valves, whistle and water glass, suction hose, leading hose and nozzle, with each pump, pump finished in polished nickel plate and colors. Each in box..................Each, 89c

F1165, Horizontal Engine—Frame of cast malleable iron, cylinder, steam chest and slide rest cast in 1 piece, eccentric slide valve, nickel trim, boiler 6 in., base 6x6. Each in wood box. Each, $1.95

F1166, Locomotive, Tender and Car—Length 24 in., diam. of track, 3½ ft. All parts properly fitted and tested, runs 30 minutes. Each in box. Each, $2.50

F1167, Double Mill Engine—2 complete engines, boilers polished brass, boiler frame, engine frame and base of Russia iron, painted in bright colors. Fire from 2 alcohol lamps with double wicks, size 7x10. Each in box.......Each, $2.55

F1167, $2 55 Each.

F1168, Walking Beam Engine

—Iron base 6x10 in., enameled top and nickeled edge, gun metal finish brass boiler, upright iron frame, nickel walking beam and trimmings. ht. 8½ in., eccentric movement. Each in box. Each, $2.

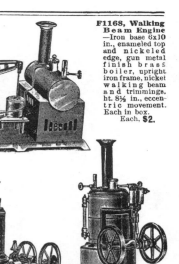

F1169, $3.30 Each. F1170, $4.10 Each.

F1169, Double Upright Engine—Frame of cast malleable iron, large steel blue brass boiler, whistle, safety valve, polished nickel trim, base 7x11, ht. 12 in., eccentric movement. Each in wood box........Each, $3.30

F1170, Upright Engine—Ht. 13½, polished brass boiler 3½ in. diam. base 6 in., fire box blued steel, base of iron. Engine frame and double balance wheel of iron, polished nickel boiler fittings, steam pipes, unions and valves, turned polished nickel balance wheel faces, parts interchangeable. Each in box........ ......Each, $4.10

F1171, $4.00 Each. F1172, $5.50 Each.

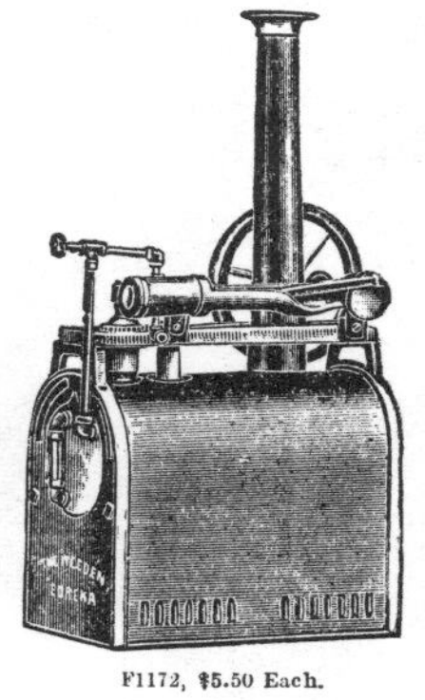

F1171, Horizontal Engine—10x8x3 balance wheel 4¼ in., boiler of brass enclosed in blued steel jacket, safety valve, whistle and water glass, steam and water pipes are brass, elbows, unions, pipes and valves of polished nickel, engine frame and balance wheel iron nickel plated, cylinder of iron, all fittings brass, double slide valve eccentric movement. Each in box.................................Each, $4.00

F1172, "Eureka" Engine—15⅛x8x4¼, balance wheel 4¼ in., diam. of boiler 3 in., brass boiler, in blued steel jacket, boiler frame iron with edges and all letters polished nickel, swing door, safety valve, whistle and water glass, steam and water pipes of brass, elbows, unions, pipes and valves, polished nickel, engine frame and balance wheel iron nickel plated. Cylinder of iron, all fittings brass, double slide valve, eccentric movement. Each in box........ .....Each, $5.50

IMPORTED STEAM ENGINES
With Separate Mechanical Devices.

F2835, 35c Each. F2836, 72c Each.

F2835—Upright engine, brass whistle, cylinder and fly wheel with attaching groove, perforated Russian tin firebox with lamp, imit. brick metal base. Ht. 9¼ in. Separate circular metal saw on bench with attaching wheel, also grindstone. In spaced box.........................Each, 35c

F2836—Engine as F2835, ht. 11 in. 3 mechanical pieces. Circular saw on bench, double steel hammers on wood base, and separate attaching wheel by which both devices can be operated at same time. Each in spaced box......Each, 72c

Assorted Separate Mechanical Devices.

Can be attached to any toy steam engine.

F2837—Asstd. 3 styles. Lithographed in colors, mechanics at drill, grindstone, etc., on painted metal base. When attached to engine and set in motion machinery revolves and men work in life like manner. 3 in box ....Each 18c

SIMMONS HARDWARE COMPANY, ST. LOUIS, MO.

BOYS' BUCKBOARD WAGONS.

PER DOZEN.

No. 76—Boys' Buckboard Coasters, Length, 42 in., Wheels, 12 and 17 in......................$50.00
Weight, per Dozen, 300 lbs.

PER DOZEN.

No. 91—Boys' Buckboard Coasters, Length, 42 in., Wheels, 12 and 18 in., Half Oval Tires, Seat and Dasher Painted, other Parts Striped and Varnished on the Wood, Wagon is Guided by the Shafts and Speed Regulated by the Brake Attachment.....$72.00
Weight, per Dozen, Crated, 560 lbs.

PER DOZE

No. 88—Boys' Buckboard Coasters, Length, 50 in., Wheels, 15 and 21 in., Two Seats $100
Weight, per Dozen, 600 lbs.

Goat Sulkies.

PER DOZEN

No. 1—Goat Sulkies, without Harness, Hickory Shafts, Painted Red, Steel Springs, Steel Wheels, 22 in. Diameter; Whip Socket, Foot Rest, Springs, Axle and Wheels are Tinned $48.00
Weight, per Dozen, 360 lbs.

PER DOZEN SETS.
Harness for Goat Sulkies, as shown in illustration..$30.00

Toy Carts.

PER DOZEN.

No. 11—Body, 5½ x 11 in., Wheels, 6 in., Tin Tires, Painted in Bright Colors................. $3.00

PER DOZE

No. 12—Body, 7 x 14 in., Wheels, 8 in., Tin Tires, Painted and Striped...................... $4

One Dozen in a Crate.

VELOCIPEDES AND TRICYCLES.

VELOCIPEDES WITH REGULAR SEAT.

With Oval Steel Tire Wheels.				With Rubber Tires.			
	Front Wheel.	Rear Wheels.	Weight, each, lbs.	EACH.		Front Wheel.	Rear Wheels.	EACH
No. 1......16 in.	12 in.	10½	$2.50	No. 6 ....16 in.	12 in.	$5.00
No. 2......20 in.	14 in.	12	3.00	No. 7 ....20 in.	14 in.	6.00
No. 3......24 in.	16 in.	15	3.50	No. 8 ....24 in.	16 in.	7.00
No. 4......26 in.	18 in.	18	4.00	No. 9 ....26 in.	18 in.	8.00
No. 5......28 in.	18 in.	20	4.50	No. 10 ....28 in.	18 in.	9.00

ADJUSTABLE SEAT VELOCIPEDES.

With Oval Steel Tire Wheels.				With Rubber Tires.			
	Front Wheel.	Rear Wheels.	Weight, each. lbs.	EACH.		Front Wheel.	Rear Wheels.	EACH.
No. 101 ....16 in.	12 in.	10½	$3.00	No. 106 ....16 in.	12 in.	$5.50
No. 102 ....20 in.	14 in.	12	3.50	No. 107 ....20 in.	14 in.	6.50
No. 103 ....24 in.	16 in.	15	4.00	No. 108 ....24 in.	16 in.	7.50
No. 104 ....26 in.	18 in.	18	4.50	No. 109 ....26 in.	18 in.	8.50
No. 105 ....28 in.	18 in.	20	5.00	No. 110 ....28 in.	18 in.	9.50

Saddle can be raised or lowered as desired, making it possible for a boy to use for several years.

TRICYCLES.

With Oval Steel Tires.		With Rubber Tires.	
	EACH.		EACH.
No. 32—18 in. Wheels, Weight, each, 20 lbs.....................$ 6.00		No. 37—20 in. Wheels, Weight, each, 21 lbs.......$10.00
No. 33—20 in. Wheels, Weight, each, 25 lbs..................... 8.00		No. 38—22 in. Wheels, Weight, each, 26 lbs....... 17.00
No. 34—22 in. Wheels, Weight, each, 29 lbs..................... 10.00		No. 39—26 in. Wheels, Weight, each, 31 lbs....... 19.00
No. 35—26 in. Wheels, Weight, each, 34 lbs..................... 12.00		No. 40—30 in. Wheels, Weight, each, 36 lbs....... 21.00
No. 36—30 in. Wheels, Weight, each, 37 lbs..................... 14.00		

REED SEAT TRICYCLES.

With Oval Steel Tires.		With Rubber Tires.	
	EACH.		EACH.
No. 133—20 in. Wheels, Weight. each, 25 lbs....................$ 8.50		No. 137—20 in. Wheels, Weight, each, 21 lbs......$10.50
No. 134—22 in. Wheels, Weight, each, 29 lbs................. 10.50		No. 138—22 in. Wheels, Weight, each, 26 lbs...... 17.50
No. 135—26 in. Wheels, Weight, each, 34 lbs................. 12.50		No. 139—26 in. Wheels, Weight, each, 31 lbs...... 19.50
No. 136—30 in. Wheels, Weight, each, 37 lbs................. 14.50		No. 140—30 in. Wheels, Weight, each, 36 lbs...... 21.50

The handsomest and lightest Tricycle made.

Saddle Horses, $2.50, $3.00, $3.75, $4.50.

Yrs.	S.T.	⅜ R.T.	⅝ R.T.
3- 5	$1.50	$3.75	$4.75
4- 6	2.00	4.50	6.00
5- 8	2.50	5.25	7.50
7-12	3.00	6.00	9.00

Yrs.	S.T.	⅜ R.T.	⅝ R.T.
3- 5	$3.50	$5.50	$8.00
4- 6	4.50	6.50	9.00
5- 8	5.50	7.50	10.50
7-12	6.75	10.00	13.50

Wood Swing Horses,
$2.75, $3.25, $4.25, $5.25, $6.75, $8.25, $9.50
Hair Swing Horses.
$8.50, $10.50, $13.50, $15.00.

Wheelbarrows.
No. 0—24-in. Shafts, 25c.
No. 1—28-in. Shafts, 50c.
No. 2—34-in. Shafts, 75c.
No. 4—38-in. Shafts, $1.00
No. 5—43-in. Shafts, $1.50

Express Wagons, 9x18 body, 50c.
13x26 body, $1.00.

Farm Wagon, 18x36 body, $7.00.

Automobile Horn, 50c.

Carts, 25c., 50c., 90c.

Automobile Caps,
50c., 75c., $1.00.

Coasting Wagon, 11x30 in. body, $1.50.

Express Wagons,
13x28 body, with seat, $1.75
14x30 body, with seat, $2.50
16x32 body, with seat, $2.75

Coasting Wagon, 14x36 body, $3.00.
Larger sizes, $4.00, $6.50.

Goggles, 25c.

Patrol Wagons,
32x16 body, $5.00; 36x16 body, $8.00;
40x18 body, $10.00.

Automobile
Horn $1.00.

Spring Wagon, 21x44 body, $7.00.

Iron Patrol Wagons, 50c., $1.00, $1.75.

Iron Fire Engines, 25c., 50c., $1.00, $1.75, $2.25.

Steel Trolley Car, 15 ins. long, $1.00; with Clock work, $2.00.

Self Inking Printing Press, $1. Larger sizes, $1.25, $2, $4, $6.75.

Iron Hook and Ladders, 50c, $1.00, $1.75.

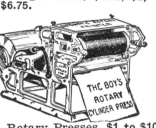

Rotary Presses, $1 to $10 Ask for Booklet.

Hot Air Engine, 10 ins. high, $2.50. Larger sizes, $4.50, $6.50, $8.00.

Mechanical Carousel, 8 in. high, 50c., 12 in, $1.

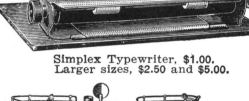

Simplex Typewriter, $1.00. Larger sizes, $2.50 and $5.00.

Mechanical Boat, 9 ins. long, $1.00. Larger sizes, $1.50, $2, $3.

Mechanical Auto, 7 ins. long, 50c.

Mechanical Ferris Wheel, 13½ ins. high, $1. Smaller size, 50c.

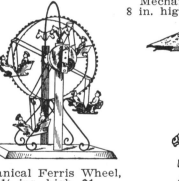

Mechanical Foxy Grandpa 7½ ins. high, 50c.

Steel Bank with Key, 4x3x2 ins., 75c.

110.—Mechanical Engine, $1.25.

Mechanical Horse, 4 ins. high, 50c.

Iron Ranges, 25c., 50c., $1, $2, $2.50, $3, $5.

Steel Passenger Trains, 30 ins. long, 50c. 42 ins., $1.00.

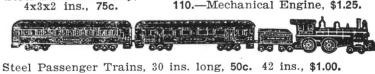

53.—Steel Freight Trains, 37½ ins. long, 50c.

Collapsible Doll House, 10x14 in., 2 Rooms, $1.00.

Grocery Stores, $1.50 to $3.50.

205.—Parlor set, $1.00.

Collapsible Doll House, 14x18 in., 4 Rooms, $2.00.

Pastry set, $1.00
Smaller size, 50c

Doll Houses, $1.00 to $3.00.

Doll Houses, $3.25 to $8.00

206.—Bedroom set, $1.00.

Comical Ladder, 25c. Doll Trunks, 50c. to $5.00.

Theatre, 12¾x15¾, $1.00.

Theatres, $1.00 to $5.50.

Stables, $2.00 to $4.50.

Butcher Shops, 25c. to $1.00.

Stables, 50c. to $1.75.

Kitchens, $3.25 to $6.75.

Kitchens, 50c. to $2.50.

Toy Carpet Sweepers, 25, 50, $1.

2278.—Child's Reed Rocker, $2.00.

2280.—Child's Reed Rocker, $3.25.

6300.—Child's Reed Chair, $6.00.

6301.—Child's Reed Rocker, $6.00.

633.—Weathered Oak Rocker, $2.50.

313.—Mission Morris Chair, $2.75.

103.—Golden or Weathered Oak Rocker, $1.50.

100.—Golden or Weathered Oak Chair, $1.50.

306.—Mission Chair, $1.00.

305.—Mission Rocker, $1.25.

796.—White Enameled Doll High Chair, 75c.

798.—White Enameled Doll Rocker, 75c.

799.—Doll Chair, White Enameled, 65c.

733.—Golden or Weathered Oak Rocker, $1.75.

99.—Golden or Weathered Oak Chair, $1.75.

919.—Mission Chair $1.25.

920.—Mission Rocker, $1.50.

903.—Mission Doll Bed, $2.50.

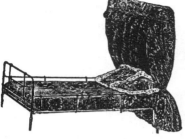

Furnished Brass Doll Beds.
18 in. long,   75c.
24 in. long, $1.00
30 in. long, $1.25

Coasters, 50c. to $2.50.

Sleds, $1.75 to $2.50.

Sleds, 50c. to $1.50.

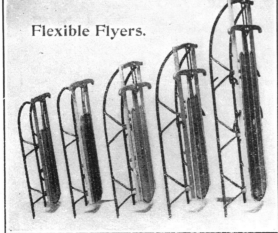

Flexible Flyers.

Flexible Flyers.
30 in. long, $2.50   40 in. long, $3.00
44 in. long, $3.75   50 in. long, $4.50
62 in. long, $6.00   101 in. long, $10.00

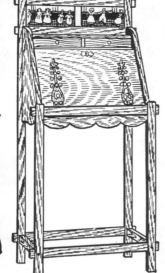

909.—Mission Desk, $6.75.

Shoofly Rockers, $1.00,
$1.25, $1.50.

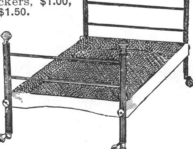

1422.—Brass Doll Bed, $1.00.

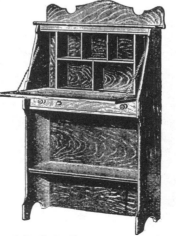

2/0 Oak Secretary Desk,
$2.75.

316.—Mission Book Case,
$1.50.

915.—Mission Sideboard, $7.50

Blackboard Desks, $1.00,
$1.50, $1.75, $2.25.

White Enameled Chiffoniers,
$1.25, $1.75, $2.25, $3.50, $5.25.

White Enameled Wash
Stands, $1.25, $2.50.
White Enameled Bureaus.
$1.00, $1.25, $1.75, $2.50, $3.00,
$3.50, $4.00.

1701.—Brass Doll Bed, $2.75.

Horse and Cart, 50c.
Larger sizes, $1.00 to $6.00.

Saddle Horse.
8 in. high, $1.00.
Smaller sizes,
25c. and 50c.

"Biaphone"
Telephone.
$5.00 pair.

Toy Telephone, $1.00.

Horse and Truck, $1.00.
Larger sizes, $1.50 to $6.00.

Pig Banks, 5c. and 10c.

The Newest Top.
Set of 3, 50c.
Set of 2, 30c.

The Wizard
Trick Top.
25c.

The "Never Stop"
Top, 10c.

Cow. 7 in. high, $1.00.
Other sizes,
50c. and $1.50.

Hand
Sewing Machine. $4.00.

3000.—Tool Chest, $2.50.
Other sizes,
50c., $1.00, $1.50, $2.00.

Leather
Horse Reins,
10c., 15c., 25c., 50c

Woolly Sheep. 7 in. high. $1.00.
Other sizes, 50c., $1.50, $2.00.

Gem Toy Freezers.
$1.25.

Electric Motor.
$1.00.
Larger sizes,
$3.00, $5.00, $10.00

American made Pewter Soldiers,
$1.00. Other sizes, 25c. to $2.25.

Magic Lanterns.
$1.00 to $10.00.

Wooden Cannons.
50c and $1.00.

Pewter Tea Set. $1.00. Smaller sizes, 25c. and 50c.

China Tea Set. $1.00. Other styles, 25c. to $6.00.

Continental, Model 20, **$9.00.**
Body 42x22, Wheels 10x16, ½ in. Rubber Tires, Horn and Lamps extra.

Irish Mail,
1 passenger, **$5.75**
2 passengers, **$7.50**

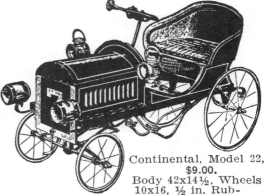

Continental, Model 22,
$9.00.
Body 42x14½, Wheels
10x16, ½ in. Rubber Tires, Horn and Lamps extra.

Continental, Model 30, **$18.50.**
Body 50x24, Wheels 12x16, ⅝ in. Rubber Tires, Horn and Lamps extra.

100. — Keystone Automobile,
$6.00.
Body 15x36½, Wheels 12x18,
⅜-in. Rubber Tires.
Smaller sizes **$5.** and **$4.50.**

Continental, Model 15, **$7.50.**
Body 46x15, Wheels 12x18, ½ in.
Rubber Tires.

Continental, Model 10,
$5.50.
Body 35x15. Wheels 12x18, ⅜ in.
Rubber Tires.
A size for smaller children, **$4.50.**

200.—Keystone Automobile,
$10.50.
Body 15x60 in,, Wheels 12x18
⅜ in. Rubber Tires.

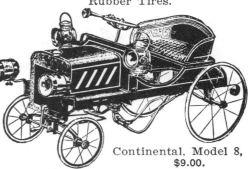

Continental. Model 8,
$9.00.
Body 30x14, Wheels 10x16, ½ in. Rubber Tires. Horn and Lamps extra.

Continental, Model 24
$8.50.
Body 42x14½, Wheels 10x16, ½ in. Rubber Tires, Lamps and Horn extra.

020.—English Doll Perambulator,
$12.00.
Other styles, **$4.50, $7.50, $8.00,
$9.00, $10.00, $13.50.**

Fairy Velocipedes,
3-5 years. **$10.50.** 4-6 years, **$13.50.**
5-8 years, **$15.00**

Continental, Model 32, **$22.50.**
Body 54x15. Wheels 16x16, ⅝ in. Rubber Tires, Horn and Lamps extra.

Automobile Lamp. **50c.**
Larger style, **$1.00.**

20th Century Locomotive,
$20.00.
Engine length. 52 in.: Tender length, **24 in.**
½ in. Rubber Tires.

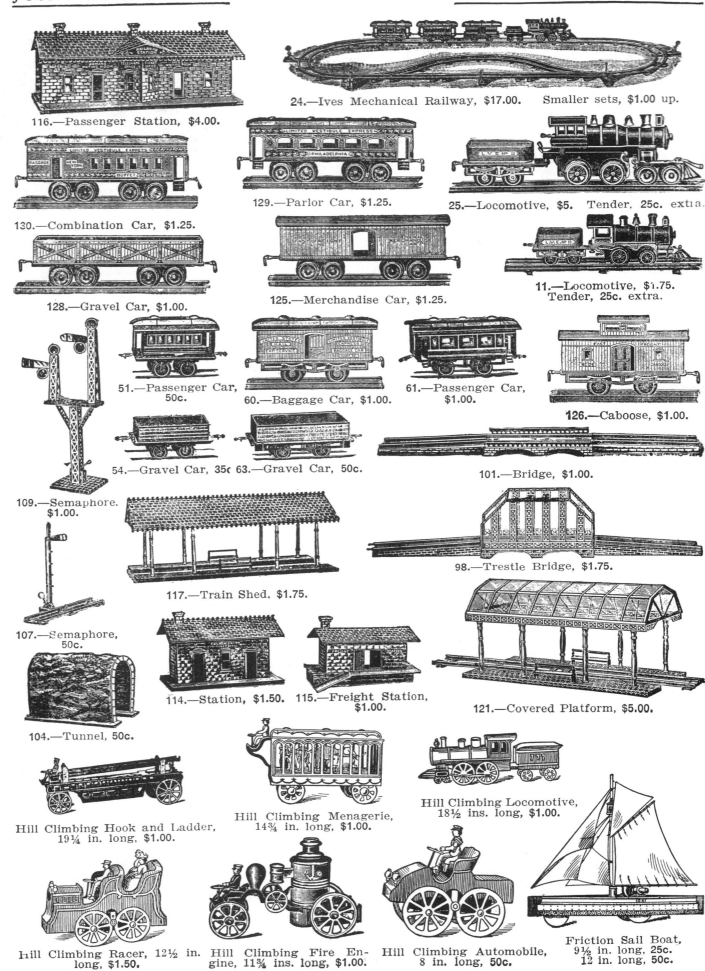

116.—Passenger Station, $4.00.

24.—Ives Mechanical Railway, $17.00.   Smaller sets, $1.00 up.

130.—Combination Car, $1.25.

129.—Parlor Car, $1.25.

25.—Locomotive, $5.   Tender, 25c. extra.

128.—Gravel Car, $1.00.

125.—Merchandise Car, $1.25.

11.—Locomotive, $1.75.
Tender, 25c. extra.

109.—Semaphore. $1.00.

51.—Passenger Car, 50c.

60.—Baggage Car, $1.00.

61.—Passenger Car, $1.00.

126.—Caboose, $1.00.

54.—Gravel Car, 35c 63.—Gravel Car, 50c.

101.—Bridge, $1.00.

107.—Semaphore, 50c.

117.—Train Shed, $1.75.

98.—Trestle Bridge, $1.75.

104.—Tunnel, 50c.

114.—Station, $1.50. 115.—Freight Station, $1.00.

121.—Covered Platform, $5.00.

Hill Climbing Hook and Ladder, 19¼ in. long, $1.00.

Hill Climbing Menagerie, 14¾ in. long, $1.00.

Hill Climbing Locomotive, 18½ ins. long, $1.00.

Hill Climbing Racer, 12½ in. long, $1.50.

Hill Climbing Fire Engine, 11¾ ins. long, $1.00.

Hill Climbing Automobile, 8 in. long, 50c.

Friction Sail Boat, 9½ in. long, 25c. 12 in. long, 50c.

25c.

$1.25.

12 and 15c.

50c.

Trick Box, 25c.
Larger sizes, 50c, $1, $1.50.

38, 50 and 75c.

25c.

50c.

25c.

PRETTY VILLAGE

20, 40 and 75c.

TIDDLEDY WINKS

20 and 40c.

Parchessi.
75c. and $1.50.

GAME OF AUTHORS

M^cLOUGHLIN BROS.

15c.

50c.

40c.

Parlor Bowling, 50c., $1, $2.

50c.

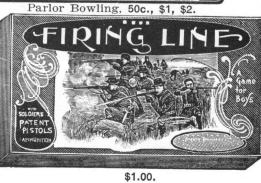

$1.00.

THE COMICAL GAME
SIR HINKLE
FUNNYDUSTER

25c.

Color Kit, 50c. and $1.

25c.

Muslin Parties — Donkey, Elephant, Dude, Chinamen, 20c.

Muslin Party, 25c.

50c. and $1.

50c.

Muslin Party, 25c.

TOOT
The AUTOMOBILE GAME
A BRIGHT. NOVEL CARD GAME

50c.

40c.

Spelling Board, 75c.

75c.

50c.

Picture Sewing Cards, 20c.

50c.

Sliced Animals, Birds, Objects and Nations, 20c.

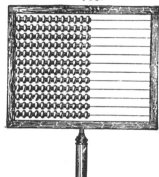

Numeral Frames, 20c.

Nested Blocks, 25c., 50c., 75c., $1.00.

50c.

BUSTER BROWN RUBBER STAMPS

RESOLVED THAT I WILL LEAVE MY STAMP IN EVERY HOME BUSTER

25 and 50c.

Progressive Anagrams

MILTON BRADLEY CO SPRINGFIELD, MASS

25 and 50c.

50 SOLDIERS ON PARADE

20 and 40c.

Somersault Game, 50c.

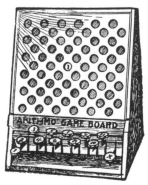

ARITHMO GAME BOARD

$1.00.

FOXY GRANDPA RUBBER STAMPS

25 and 50c.

African Dodger, 50c.

Fascination, 25c.

A Toy Piano That Plays

Even the cheapest of the

"Schoenhut"

Toy Pianos makes real music, cultivates the child musician's ear and fingers.

This picture shows one of the

"Schoenhut"

Fine Upright Pianos

beautiful in finish and workmanship. On it many a good musician has, as a child, taken his first lesson.

Here is an illustration of the

"Schoenhut"

Extra Fine Upright Piano

All of these larger sizes have stools to suit, sold separately. They are the finest toy pianos made anywhere in the world.

Schoenhut's Toy Wooden Boats

Over forty different styles
and sizes

Schoenhut Toy Guns

For shooting rubber balls, paper and percussion caps.
Harmless and practical for the purpose.

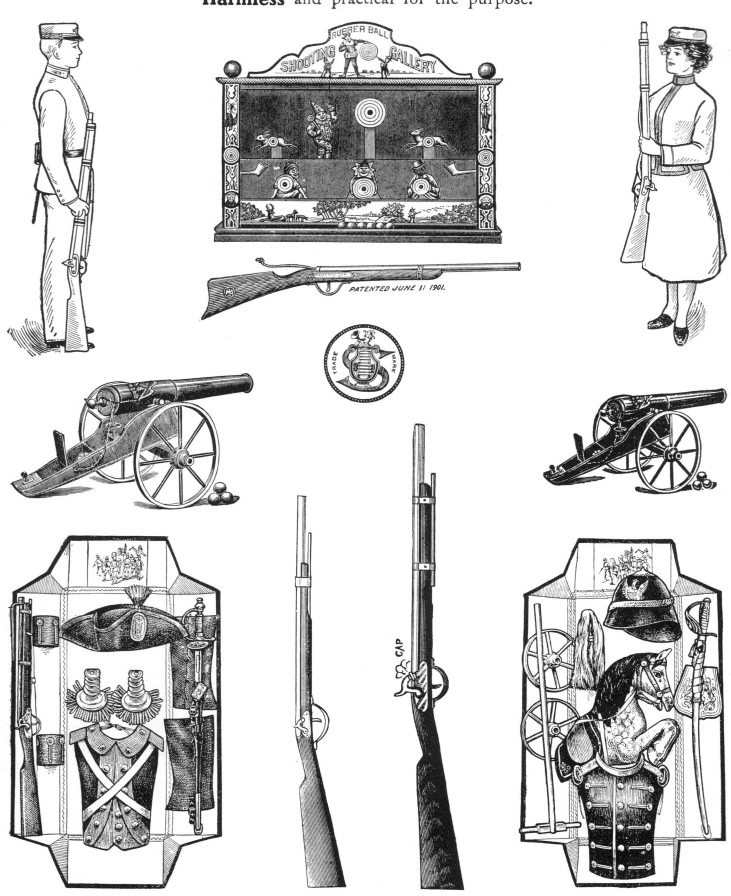

Illustrations and Retail Prices of the different sets of Schoenhut's Humpty Dumpty Circus

Set No. 15/1, 4 pieces, 50 cents
Weight 15 ozs

Set No. 20/22, 10 pieces, $3.00
Weight 3 lbs. 3 ozs.

Set No. 20/3, 7 pieces, $1.25
Weight 2 lbs.

Set No. 20/7, 5 pieces, $1.50
Weight 2 lbs. 11 ozs.

Set No. 20/16, 7 pieces, $2.25
Weight 3 lbs. 14 ozs.

EXTRA FINE
Set No. 20/26, 15 pieces, $4.00
Weight 6 lbs. 12 ozs.

FAVORITE STUFFED ANIMALS AND PETS

Papier mache lion in genuine calfskin cover, glass eyes, bushy mane and tail, resembling a real lion in every respect. Growling voice produced by pulling metal ring. Feet firmly attached to wooden base on wheels. Length, 11½ inches. Shipping weight, 1½ pounds.
No. 49G813 Price..................**97c**

Plush Covered Horse, fitted with leather harness and velvet top saddle and fancy blanket. Mounted on heavy wooden base with wheels. Height, 17½ inches, length, 17½ inches. Shipping weight, 3½ pounds.
No. 49G800 Price.. **98c**

Plush Covered Horse, made same as above but without plush saddle and measures only 11 inches in height and 9¼ inches in length. Shipping weight, 1¼ pounds.
No. 49G801 Price..................**47c**

Jumping Fur Dog in Hut.

Contains a small natural faced dog, made of high grade soft black fur, securely fastened in small dog house. Has mechanical spring in back and by pressing down makes the dog jump and bark in a most natural manner. Size, 9x4x5 inches. Each carefully packed in box. Shipping weight, 16 ounces.
No. 49G400 Price..................**47c**

The Bear Family Only 19c.

This Bear Family is one of the most popular toys ever produced. Consists of one bear, 7¾ inches high and two bears 4½ inches high. Bears are made of prepared cotton on strong wire; arms and legs are movable. Each set in neat box. Shipping weight, 6 ounces.
No. 49G830 Price.......... **19c**

Silk Mohair Dogs With Voices.

This dog is exceptionally well made; has voice attachment, flexible frame, covered with beautiful white and brown mohair cloth. Brown ears, natural face and glass eyes, with ½-inch fine blue silk baby ribbon collar with bow around neck. Length over all, 12½ inches. Height, 10½ inches. Shipping weight, 2½ pounds.
No. 49G806 Price..........**$1.00**

Same high grade and beautiful finished Dog as above, but of smaller size. Size of dog, 10 inches long by 8½ inches high. Carefully packed in box. Shipping weight, 1½ pounds.
No. 49G807 Price................**79c**

Plush Dog.

Well proportioned and lifelike. Leather collar. Each with voice. White plush with black ears and tail. Length, 10 inches. Shipping weight, 8 ounces.
No. 49G832 Price.......... **45c**

Fine White Plush Cat.

Very beautiful glass eyes, ribbon collar and brass bell. Each has natural voice. Entire length, 12 inches. Shipping weight, 8 oz.
No. 49G831 Price................**45c**

CELEBRATED BLACK FUR CASPER DOGS.

These are the genuine Casper dogs of Europe, and are not to be confused with the cheap imitations of these exceptionally high class toys. These are the finest manufactured, well made in every detail, beautiful fur, black, heavy and soft. The frame is of wood, extra strong. The general appearance of the dogs is most natural, the bodies being of the best shape, natural faces, eyes, mouth and nose in proper proportion. They have metal rollers on feet and pull string. Can be used either in the house or on sidewalks.

OUR BEST DOG.	A BIG SELLER.	ONLY 21 CENTS.	OUR 10-CENT WONDER.
10½ inches long by 11½ inches high, metal feet on rollers. Shipping weight, 3 pounds.	**10 inches high, 9½ inches long,** without metal feet, with rollers. Shipping weight, 2½ pounds.	**8 inches high, 7 inches long,** without metal feet, with rollers. Shipping weight, 2 pounds.	**6½ inches high, 6 inches long,** on wooden platform, with wheels. Shipping wt., 1½ lbs.
No. 49G802 Price **93c**	**No. 49G803** Price **43c**	**No. 49G804** Price **21c**	**No. 49G805** Price **10c**

BUY THIS BEAUTIFUL HORSE FOR YOUR BOY.

Ride and Steer It Like a Velocipede, Horse's Head Turns While Steering.

Imported by us direct and introduced in this country for the first time. Order one of these horses early, for when our supply is exhausted we will be unable to secure more of them this year. The highest quality toy possible to produce. Real skin covered, long mane and tail, fine genuine leather, double strap bridle, curb bit, genuine leather padded top saddle, with strong cinch straps. Handsome decorated blanket and collar. Bridle and saddle removable. Platform of heavy wood, nicely painted. Wheels are gilt decorated, strongly made, with heavy solid rubber tires. Steering handle of ⅜ inch metal, with wooden turned hand grips. Rod passes through horse's head and body, and is fastened to front wheels with bolt. Slight pressure on handle will turn horse's head and neck, giving the animal a strikingly lifelike appearance. Horse itself is 2 feet 3 inches high, 2 feet 2 inches long. Platform is 2 feet 6 inches long, 10 inches wide, 6¾ inches high. Sufficient room on rear for little child to stand while his playmate rides the horse. Propelling device is of lever principle, best made, simple, strong metal, almost impossible to break it. This toy is absolutely safe, easy to guide, easy to propel, and far better than any velocipede. Very healthy exercise. Brings muscles of back and limbs into play. Teaches boy to love and care for a horse. Understand, while we have purchased a big supply yet it is the first time they were ever sold in this country and the demand will be enormous, therefore, order early to avoid a chance of disappointment. Actual weight, about 30 pounds. Shipping wt., carefully boxed for shipment, 40 lbs. Regular price $20 to $25.
No. 49G3064¼ Price..............................**$13.85**

SNOW WHITE FRENCH POODLE DOGS.

Exceptionally handsome, finely made, practical. Nothing about the dogs to get broken or injured in any way. Excellent stuffed flannel covered hand sewed very natural shape bodies and limbs, lifelike faces, with brown glass eyes, pretty ribbons around the neck, and the two largest dogs have also fancy blankets, with pinked edges. Long silk angora hair on heads, shoulders and tails. Easily cleaned when soiled.

Height, 6 inches; length, 7 inches. Shipping weight, 7 ounces.	**Height, 8 inches; length, 8 inches.** Shipping weight, 12 oz.	**Height, 10 inches; length, 12½ inches.** Shipping wt., 1½ lbs.	**Height, 13½ inches; length, 15 inches.** Shipping wt., 2½ lbs.
No. 49G835 Price **21c**	**No. 49G834** Price **42c**	**No. 49G833** Price **95c**	**No. 49G836** Price **$1.95**

Our Prize Winner Angora Cat.

Highest class toy cat made. Fur covered, snow white, large green glass eyes, and natural voice. By moving side to side produces a most natural "meow." Most natural lifelike appearance. Height, 8½ inches; length, not counting tail, about 8½ inches. $2.50 value. Shipping wt., 1 lb.
No. 49G840 Price..........**$1.85**

Real Wool Natural Voice Sheep.

One of the most beautiful toy sheep ever manufactured. Very large glass eyes. Has a most natural bleat, produced by moving sheep from side to side. Mounted on metal wheels. Has wide ribbon around neck, and gilt metal bell. Stands 13½ inches high, 15 inches in length. An animal that always appeals to the children. Shipping wt., packed, 2½ pounds.
No. 49G842 Price..................**$1.95**

Our Natural Voice Goat.

Entirely fur covered, mounted on wheels, extra well made in every way, and most lifelike. Fancy velvet collar, gilt trimmed, and gilt bell, horns and glass eyes. Has the most natural bleat possible to produce by artificial means. Voice produced by moving animal from side to side. An exceptionally fine quality toy. Total height, 9¼ inches; length, 9 inches. Shipping wt., packed, 1 lb.
No. 49G841 Price..................**95c**

Red Rubber Animals.

Made entirely of red rubber. Very practical and harmless toys for small children. Shipping weight, each, 5 ounces.

No. 49G839 Cat. Length, 5 inches. Price..............................**29c**
No. 49G821 Dog. Length, 5 inches. Price..............................**29c**
No. 49G838 Horse. Length, 5½ inches. Price..............................**29c**
No. 49G837 Sheep. Length, 4¾ inches. Price..............................**29c**

Real Wool Covered Sheep on Platform.

Toys that never fail to delight a child. Very natural appearance, well proportioned, heavy white wool, glass eyes, pretty blue and gilt decorated collar, with gilt bell ribbon on back, and feet firmly set on wooden wheel platform. Moving the head causes the sheep to bleat. All made the same, only difference is size. Fine quality. Very attractive appearance. Can be used in house or on sidewalk.
No. 49G814 Height, 11 inches; length, 13 inches. Shipping weight, 3½ pounds. Price..............................**95c**
No. 49G815 Height, 8½ inches; length, 8½ inches. Shipping wt., 1½ lbs. Price.**43c**
No. 49G816 Height, 6½ inches; length, 6¼ inches. Shipping wt., 1 lb. Price...**21c**

Teddy Bear On Wheels.

A very lifelike imitation. A cinnamon plush covered bear, with metal wheels on feet. Has well made leather muzzle and halter, with buckle, and drawing chain. Height, 7½ inches; length, 10 inches. Very natural face, with glass eyes. A big favorite everywhere. Shipping weight, 1 pound.
No. 49G817 Price..................**$1.25**

Velvet Bunny.

Made of soft white velvet with brown trimmings and fur tail. Has blue baby ribbon collar, brass bell and voice attachment. A fine toy for the baby. Length, 8 inches. Shipping weight, 8 ounces.
No. 49G808 Price..................**33c**

Velvet Bunny With Voice.

Very nicely finished, natural color, with fancy colored felt vest and brass buttons. Has voice attachment. Very attractive present for child. Well sewed and will keep its shape. Height, 8 inches. Shipping weight, 10 ounces.
No. 49G810 Price... **19c**

Fur Cat With "Meow."

A very pretty kitty, fur covered, natural appearance, good face, glass eyes and well made. The fur is white, with Maltese spots. Pressing hips causes it to open its mouth and "meow." Red strip of felt in mouth to resemble tongue, and red gums with little white pieces to imitate teeth. (Not sharp.) Tail is 5 inches in length. Length over all, 12 inches; height, 5½ inches. Shipping weight, 11 ounces.
No. 49G818 Price..................**63c**

Six Cut-Out Animals.

Printed on very heavy muslin, the piece measuring nearly 3 feet square. Animals average in height from 7 to over 9 inches. All printed in natural colors, very lifelike, with plain dotted lines for cutting and simple complete directions. When made up they are practical, nothing to break, no way for child to get injured. Shipping weight, 5 ounces.
No. 49G812 Price for the big sheet with **6** animals..................**21c**

A Very Pretty Toy.

Cloth Covered Horse, white with dark rings, with mane, long tail, glass eyes, leather reins, imitation leather bridle, gilt trimmed blanket and mounted on wheels. Boy doll has painted face, glass eyes, curls, fancy cap, and very fancy cloth suit, all in colors, and lace trimmings, with lace collar and cuffs. Size over all, 14 inches high; 10 inches long. Shipping weight, 1½ pounds.
No. 49G819 Price.......... **$1.19**

RELIABLE TOY AUTOMOBILES

$5.00 Auto for $2.98

An exact reproduction of the very finest type of touring car. Made of heavy sheet metal, handsomely painted and trimmed, opening doors on each side with handles. Seven beveled glass windows, four nickel plated lamps, strong wheels and axles, heavy ½-inch cushion rubber tires, Runs forward, backward and in circle. Heavy key springs in well protected sheet metal case, real brakes on rear wheels. Total height, 8⅞ inches; length, 15⅛ inches; width, 6⅞ inches. The largest, most handsome and very best toy auto we have ever offered. Shipping weight, 5 pounds.
No. 49G471 Price............ **$2.98**

A Very Fine Automobile.

Made in best manner, of sheet metal, nicely finished in gray enamel, with red, white and blue striped decorations. Glass front, beveled glass side and back windows, nickel plated lamps and cooler. Metal driver, one passenger. White enamel finish wheels, with heavy rubber tires. Winds with key, and has brake and lever. Will run forward, backward, or in circle and can be stopped. Size, 12½x5¼x7½ inches. Shipping weight, 3 pounds.
No. 49G418 Price............ **$1.89**

Our Big $1.25 Leader.

A reproduction of big red touring car, with glass front, but without glass windows in sides or ends. Opening doors. Tires of metal, painted to imitate rubber. Will run forward, backward or in a circle. A very nice, well made automobile for this money. Shipping weight, 2½ pounds.
No. 49G419 Price............ **$1.25**

Our Wonder 79-Cent Value.

A Handsome White Enameled Gilt Finished Toy Automobile. Made of highest grade sheet metal, nicely finished in white enamel, with dark blue and gilt trimming and red wheels. Has glass front and lamps. Wound up by key and has brake and lever so automobile will stop or run forward or backward as desired. Wheels are fitted with rubber tires. Size, 8½x4x5½ inches. Shipping weight, 24 ounces.
No. 49G420 Price............ **79c**

This Fine Auto for 43 Cents.

Similar to the above, but smaller in size and cheaper finish. Extraordinary value however, for the price. Size, 7½x3½x5 inches. Shipping weight, 10 ounces.
No. 49G421 Price...... **43c**

Auto Garage and Cars.

Heavy cardboard garage with words "Auto Garage" painted across the two opening doors. Size, 8½x4½x6½ inches. One stall for the touring car, which will run straight ahead, or circles to right or left, and the other stall for racing auto. Both autos made entirely of metal, have drivers, and are nicely painted. Both about 5½ inches long, 3½ inches high, and 3¼ inches wide, and operate by winding spring. Shipping weight, 20 oz.
No. 49G467 Price...... **47c**

AIRSHIPS AND FLYING MACHINES.

A Real Airship for $1.65.

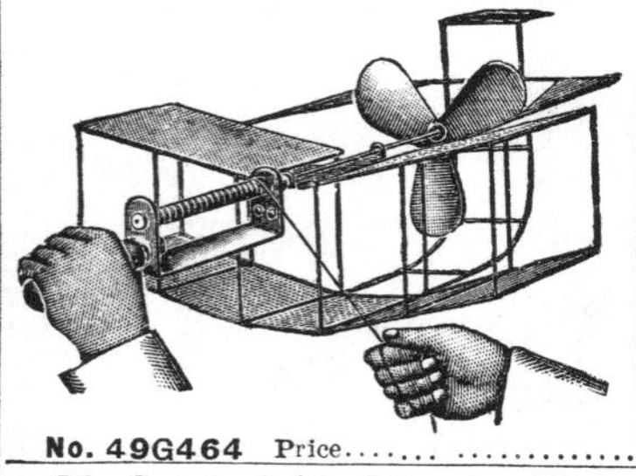

It actually flies through the air. A good reproduction of the famous new model Biplane, and will fly about 15 yards high, and for a distance of 50 yards. Made of the best steel spring wire and therefore very substantial and unlikely to get out of order. Practically no danger to the framework if machine should fall in a tree or strike a wire. The planes are covered with light silk material, so if through an accident they should get torn, they can easily be replaced. The mechanism is very simple, and can be operated by a child. Entire length, 12 inches; height, 7 inches. The momentum is produced by pulling a cord wound around patented starting handle. A most delightfully interesting and instructive toy for boy or girl. Complete with starting handle and cord. Shipping weight, 2 pounds.
No. 49G464 Price........................ **$1.65**

Mechanical Airship.

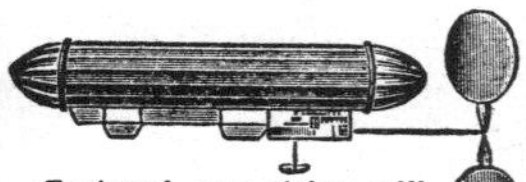

Fastened on a string will fly around the room in a most natural manner. Same construction as regular airships. 15-inch boat. Length over all, 18 inches. Good spring and very high class airship. An educating, strong and nicely finished metal toy. Shipping weight, 10 oz.
No. 49G409 Price... **39c**

Flying Airship.

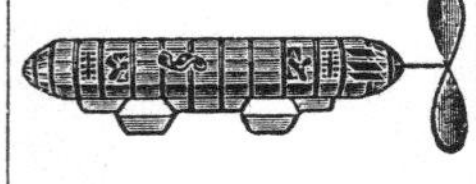

Mechanical Flying Airship, with attachments. Nicely finished. Length, 8 inches. When suspended on a string it will fly around the room like a real airship. Shipping weight, 8 ounces.
No. 49G451 Price **17c**

Flying Machine.

Another model of the well known airships. Very well made and finely finished in four colors of enamel. Fastens on string and will fly around room in most natural manner. Good spring and a fine toy. Size, 6x10 inches. Each in box. Shipping weight, 10 oz.
No. 49G408 Price **39c**

FAMOUS HESS TOYS OF GERMANY.

Hess-Mobile.

THE PATENT FRICTION MOTOR. **39c**

A very popular mechanical auto. Has crank attachment, which when wound up starts machine. By turning lever same can be made to go forward or stop at will. Nicely finished, very practical. Made by one of the best makers in Europe. Can be relied upon. Size, 7½x2¾x4½ inches. Full instructions for running with car. Shipping weight, 1 pound.
No. 49G412 Price............ **39c**

Dynomobile.

89c

Most simple and interesting. Obtains its power through friction by simply turning the crank. Attached to this motor by means of pulley cords is a stamp mill and a grind mill. These three pieces are mounted on a wooden base, measuring 14x4½ inches. This toy is strongly made. All parts enameled in high colors. Shipping weight, 3 pounds.
No. 49G410 Price............ **89c**

The Famous Hess Roller No Key Toys.

These three mechanical rolling toys are late inventions of a reliable German manufacturer, and while suitable for larger children, are especially made for little tots, who would have difficulty in winding up a spring. No keys are required. No winding. Simply take the toy in the hand and rub wheels over the floor and the friction will cause the patent device to revolve the wheels rapidly. The toys will run backward or forward. Can be operated equally well on boards, carpets or rugs. Can be used outdoors or in the home. Made entirely of metal, nicely painted in colors, difficult to get out of order, and are extra good value.

Boy on Sled. Size, 6½x1½x3¼ inches. Shipping weight, 8 ounces.
No. 49G469 Price. **19c**

Moving Duck. Size, 4x2x3 inches. Shipping weight, 8 ounces.

No. 49G468 Price.. **17c**

Eight-Wheel Engine. Size, 6x1½x2½ inches. Shipping weight, 9 ounces.
No. 49G470 Price.. **18c**

BING QUALITY TOYS OF GERMANY.

The Walking Dog.

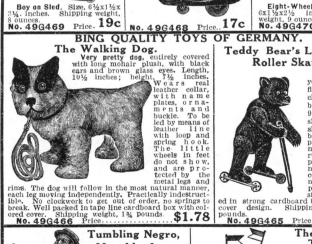

Very pretty dog, entirely covered with long mohair plush, with black ears and brown glass eyes. Length, 10½ inches; height, 7½ inches. Wears real leather collar, with name plates, ornaments and buckle. To be led by means of leather line with loop and spring hook. The little wheels in feet do not show, and are protected by the metal legs and rims. The dog will follow in the most natural manner, each leg moving independently. Practically indestructible. No clockwork to get out of order, no springs to break. Well packed in tape line cardboard box with colored cover. Shipping weight, 1¾ pounds.
No. 49G466 Price............ **$1.78**

Teddy Bear's Lessons in Roller Skating.

Mohair plush, yellow gold color, fitted with strong clockwork inside body. Bear about 9 inches high, on skates, and will skate forward or backward, propelling itself with nicely finished rubber tipped pole. Very original and extremely comical. Furnished with complete simple instructions. Packed in strong cardboard box, with catchy cover design. Shipping weight, 1¼ pounds.
No. 49G465 Price............ **$1.15**

Tumbling Negro, Movable Jaw.

Winds up by arms and tumbles around floor turning somersaults. Has movable jaw. Assumes varied positions. Comically dressed. Shipping weight, 6 ounces.
No. 49G442 Price, **39c**

Mechanical Rocking Negro in Chair.

Laughable toy. Merely wind up the spring and the negro rocks back and forth in chair. Has movable jaw and is very comically dressed. Finely finished. Size, 6½x3½x7 inches. Shipping weight, 8 ounces.
No. 49G403 Price, **35c**

The Teeter-Totter.

Two clowns with flags. Size over all, 5½x3x6½ inches. Painted in colors. Clowns "Teeter-Totter" by winding spring. Very comical. Shipping weight, 12 ounces.
No. 49G449 Price........ **19c**

'Punch" Tumbling Clown.

All metal, painted in different colors to resemble "Punch." Good spring. When wound, goes through antics like a clown. Shipping weight, 12 ounces.
No. 49G450 Price.............. **18c**

MECHANICAL ENGINES.

Our Best Value.

$2.35

A handsome engine and will please any boy. A beam engine has always been very popular and is the style that will attract attention. Size base, 6x18 inches. Height over all, 12 inches. Finished in seven-color enamel securely baked on and handsomely bronze decorated. Has easel clock spring and is the very best mechanical engine made, and one that will keep the boy amused for hours. Shipping weight, 6 pounds.
No. 49G436 Price.......... **$2.35**

Our Little Hustler.

This Handsome Horizontal Engine is one of the very best made in Europe. Has an exceptionally strong heavy clock spring and is one that is built for wear instead of show. All parts of heavy sheet metal, beautifully enameled in seven colors, with imitation bronze trimming. Size, 4¼x13x5½ inches. Perfect and easy movement, strongly and well built and an engine that sells on sight. Shipping weight, 3 pounds.
No. 49G433 Price............ **$1.59**

Our Big 93-Cent Value.

A very well constructed Mechanical Engine. A high class reliable medium priced engine. Has heavy clock spring which will run the fly wheel and piston rod in a most natural manner. Has pulley attachments for operating various small implements. Made of very heavy sheet metal, enameled in bright colors and imitation bronze fittings and trimmings. Size, 9¼x5x5 inches. Shipping weight, 3¼ pounds.
No. 49G434 Price............ **93c**

This Engine for 42 Cents.

Same style engine as above, but of smaller size. Measures 3¾x6½x4¼ inches. Beautiful enamel finish. A very good value at the price. Shipping weight, 1¼ pounds.
No. 49G435 Price.. **42c**

Flying Acrobat.

This toy is fastened to the ceiling by means of a cord, and when wound up flies around the room in the same manner as an aerial performer in a circus or show. Strongly made and finished in bright colors. Length, 7 inches. Shipping weight, 8 ounces.
No. 49G455 Price............ **23c**

Mechanical Dove.

Movable head and wings. Natural color finished. A good spring, and when wound up moves along in most natural manner, flapping its wings and moving its head at the same time. A big seller. Length, 8 inches. Shipping wt., 10 oz.
No. 49G406 Price............ **39c**

Pig in Sulky.

Mechanical Clown Driving Movable Pig and Sulky. Finely finished and when spring is wound up goes through all the motions of driving. Runs around in a circle in a most comical manner. Made of metal and finished in bright colors. Size, 7½x3x6 inches. Shipping weight, 6 ounces.
No. 49G404 Price............ **39c**

Rocking Horse.

Made entirely of metal, nicely painted in colors to resemble real horse and boy rider. Rider has movable arms. The horse's movable legs are securely fastened to metal rocker, and when spring is wound, the metal frame rocks back and forth and movable legs on horse give it a galloping motion. Shipping weight, 14 ounces.
No. 49G473 Price............ **37c**

Popular Novelty Dressed Dolls With Unbreakable Character Heads

THE "ATHLETIC" BABY 48c and 89c

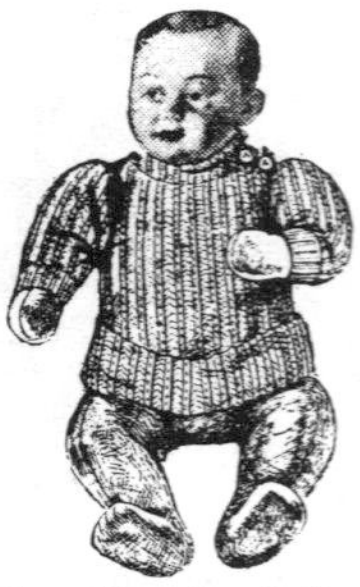

Fine Character Doll with unbreakable composition head, painted hair. Modeled from life. Durable cotton flannel, well stuffed body, riveted hips and shoulders. Dressed in knitted sweater, buttoned at shoulder. Large size illustrated, 13½ inches high, comes also in a smaller proportioned body with small head and thinner body, 9½ inches high.

No. 18G23280 Large size. Price............**89c**
Shipping weight, 1½ pounds.

No. 18G23275 Small size. Price............**48c**

"SWAT MULLIGAN" No. 18G23267 98c

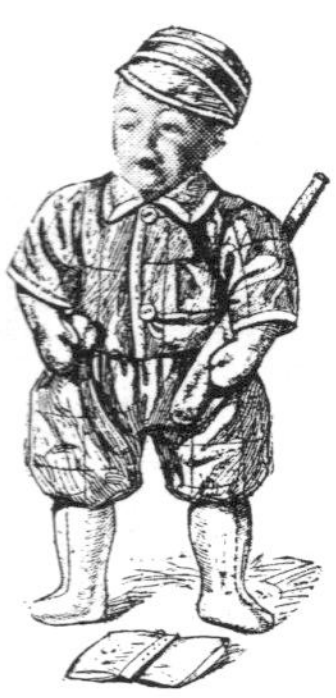

One of the cleverest Character Dolls ever produced. A great favorite with young America. Genuine unbreakable composition head in most lifelike finish. Heavy sateen body, riveted hips and shoulders. Neat baseball uniform and cap, which can be removed. A toy wooden baseball and bat with each doll. Height, 12½ inches.

"DOLLY DRAKE" AND "BOBBY BLAKE." 48c and 98c

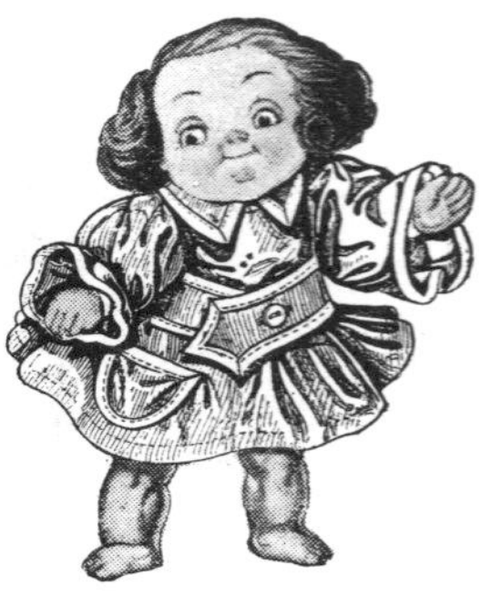

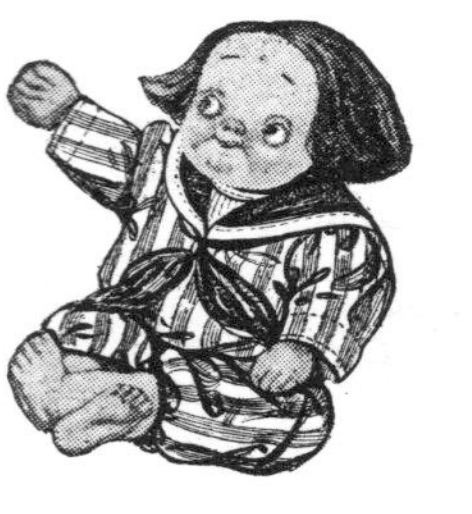

These original characters are well known to children. Genuine unbreakable composition heads, painted in fast colors. Safe in hands of smallest child. Stuffed silesia body, riveted hips and shoulders. Neatly made removable clothes in light colors. Large size dolls illustrated, 11½ inches high, with large heads and full bodies. Smaller dolls are of same type, but of smaller proportions and not so elaborately dressed.

No. 18G23271 "Dolly Drake," large size. Price......**98c**
No. 18G23272 "Bobby Blake," large size. Price......**98c**
Shipping weight, 1 pound.
No. 18G23273 "Dolly Drake," small size. Price.....**48c**
No. 18G23274 "Bobby Blake," small size. Price.....**48c**

"BONNIE BRIGHT." No. 18G23282 89c

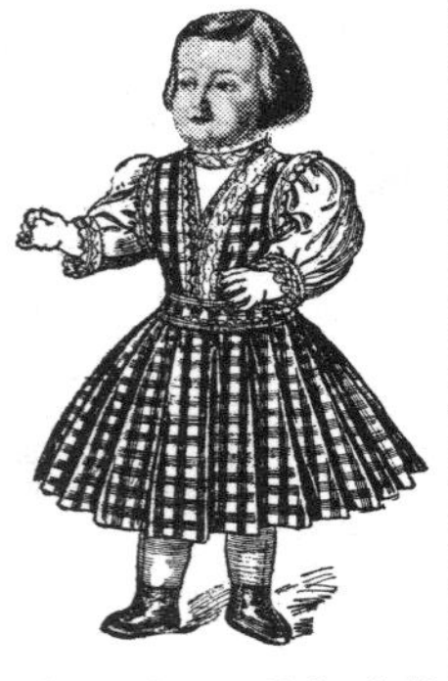

Genuine Unbreakable Dressed Character Doll with patented composition head. Modeled from real life. Beautiful painted face in lifelike colors. Neat lace trimmed dress over white guimpe. White muslin underwear. Body is of pink silesia, cotton stuffed. Cloth hands and feet. Full height, 13 inches.

GENUINE "BABY BUMPS" 47c and 95c

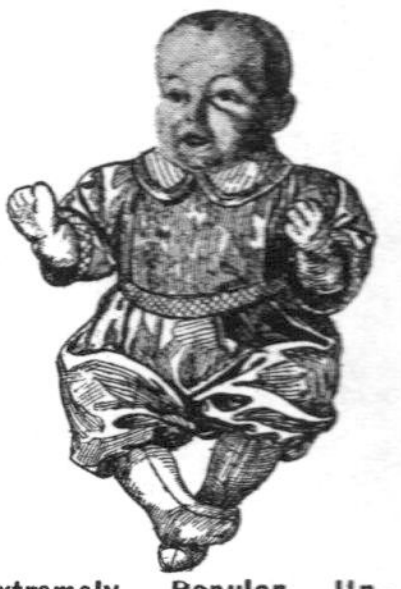

Extremely Popular Unbreakable Doll, with comical lifelike unbreakable head, painted in absolutely fast colors. Safe in hands of smallest child. Body of good sateen, cotton stuffed; riveted hips and shoulders. Rompers of good light color material, neatly trimmed. Large size has full stout body and is 11½ inches high. Small size has same features, but of smaller sizes and proportions.

No. 18G23283 Large size. Price............**95c**
Shipping weight, 1¼ pounds.

No. 18G23284 Small size. Price............**47c**

THE "KIMONO" BABY. No. 18G23281 48c

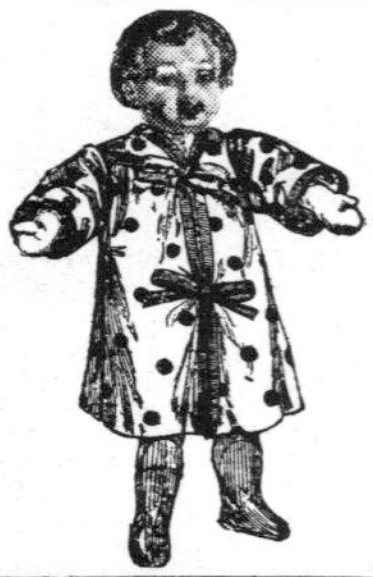

Great Value Doll for the very young child. Simply dressed and absolutely unbreakable. Pretty character head of patented composition, painted in truly lifelike fast colors. Removable kimono allows of different style home dressing, if desired. Good pink silesia body. Height 11 inches.

IMPORTED NOVELTY MECHANICAL DOLLS.

23c and 48c

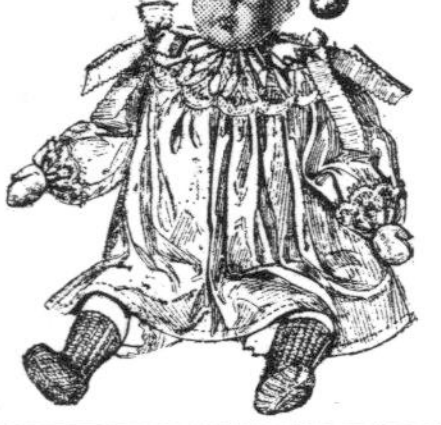

Pretty character head of bisque, curved baby legs in papier mache, jointed hips. Pressing of mechanical arrangement in body, waves arms back and forth, also produces a comical sound. Neat baby dress with cap and socks. Large doll is 9¼ inches high. Small size has same mechanical feature, but of smaller sizes and proportions.

No. 18G23290 Large size. Price..**48c**
Shipping wt., 17 oz.

No. 18G23285 Small size. Price..**23c**

No. 18G23270 25c

Imported Character Doll with lifelike unbreakable head. Durable stuffed body containing mechanical voice. Movable arms and legs. Neat romper dress. Greatest value ever offered for so low a price. Height, 8½ inches.

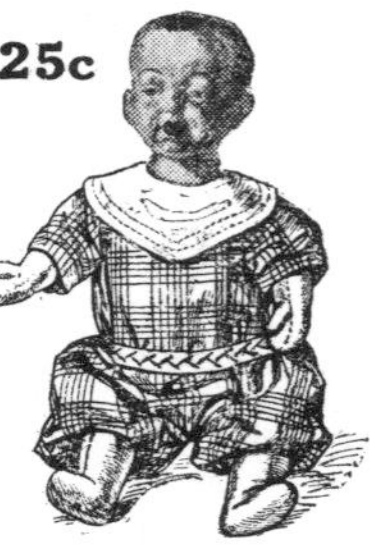

"JACK FROST."

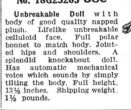

The North Pole Baby.

No. 18G23265 38c

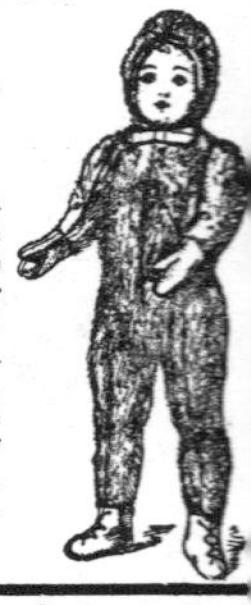

Unbreakable Doll with body of good quality napped plush. Lifelike unbreakable celluloid face. Full polar bonnet to match body. Jointed hips and shoulders. A splendid knockabout doll. Has automatic mechanical voice which sounds by simply tilting the body. Full height, 13½ inches. Shipping weight, 1½ pounds.

HIGH GRADE IMPORTED HEADS AND BODIES, 8 CENTS TO $1.98

In ordering a Doll Head to fit a body be sure to measure the body from shoulder to shoulder across the top, as the sizes of our doll heads are measured across the shoulders in this manner. It is necessary for us to have this measurement so that we can fill your order correctly.

Genuine Minerva Metal Doll Heads at Reduced Prices.

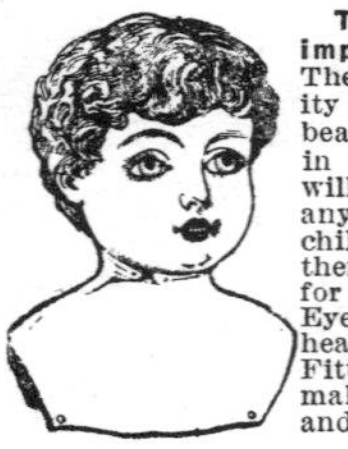

These Doll Heads are imported from Germany. They combine the durability of sheet metal and the beauty of bisque, are light in weight, washable, and will not chip; will stand any reasonable wear. Small children cannot injure them; larger ones love them for their unequaled beauty. Eyes are clear and tender, head flexible at the bust. Fitted with sewing holes, making it easy to adjust and fasten it to body.

Catalog No.	Height, Inches	Inches Across Shoulders	Shipping Weight, Ounces	Price
18G23432	3¼	2¾	3	12c
18G23434	3¾	3	3	17c
18G23436	4⅛	3⅜	8	22c
18G23438	4½	3⅝	8	29c
18G23440	5¼	4	9	33c
18G23442	6¼	4¾	14	49c
18G23444	6¾	5½	17	65c

Nos. 18G23442 and 18G23444 have glass eyes and open mouth, showing teeth.

Very Finest Quality Kid Doll Bodies.

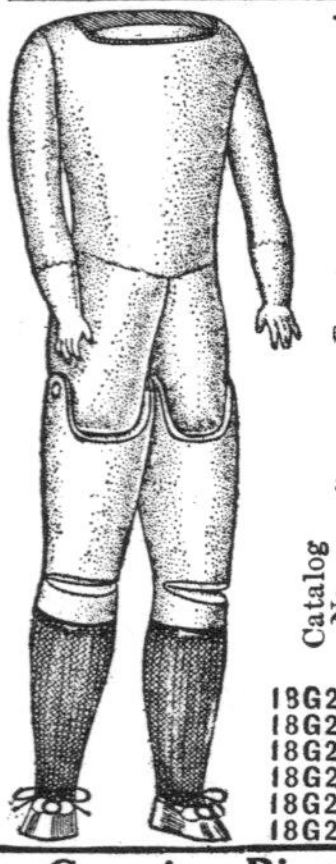

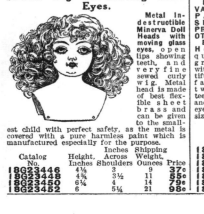

We sell only the very best make of Kid Doll Bodies. Very full size, extra quality half cork stuffed, strictly high grade. Riveted hip joints, and bisque arms, shoes and stockings. These doll bodies are sure to please, for they are the best obtainable.

Catalog No.	Length, Inches	Inches Across Shoulders	Shipping Weight, Ounces	Price
18G23402	12½	3½	16	$0.45
18G23404	16	4	25	.65
18G23406	19	4½	35	.88
18G23408	21½	5½	45	1.25
18G23412	23¾	6	60	1.48
18G23416	25½	6½	75	1.98

Silesia Doll Bodies.

Hair Stuffed Pink Silesia Doll Bodies. Very high grade silesia bodies that will give best of wear and satisfaction. Bisque arms, and removable shoes and stockings.

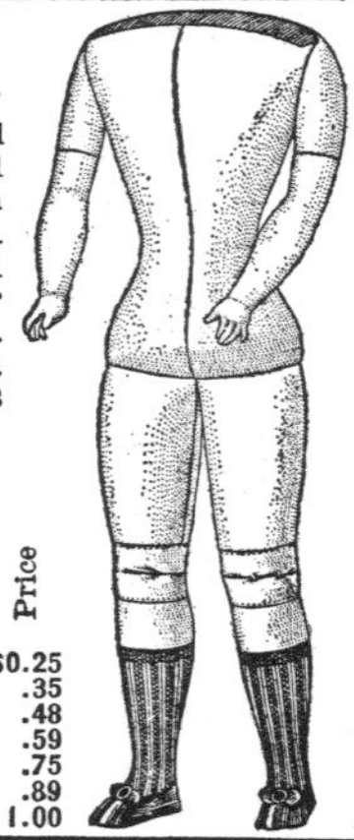

Catalog No.	Length, Inches	Inches Across Shoulders	Weight, Ounces	Price
18G23418	12	3¼	10	$0.25
18G23420	15½	4	11	.35
18G23422	16½	4½	11	.48
18G23424	21	5½	25	.59
18G23426	23½	6½	30	.75
18G23428	25½	7	35	.89
18G23430	26¾	8½	40	1.00

Celluloid Doll Heads.

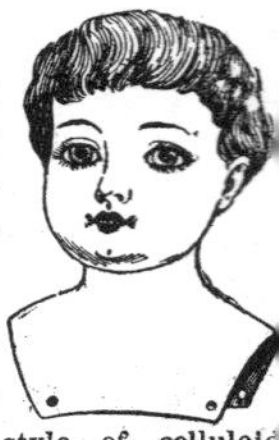

Celluloid Doll Heads, until recently, have been extremely high priced. We have succeeded in making arrangements so that we can offer them at exceptionally low prices, considering the distinct advantage this head has over the ordinary doll head. Faces are beautifully molded. Made of best celluloid, absolutely unbreakable, light as a feather, and at the price we quote will surely make them exceedingly popular. This style of celluloid doll head has painted hair and eyes, with open mouth showing teeth.

Catalog No.	Height, Inches	Inches Across Shoulders	Shipping Weight, Ounces	Pric
18G23500	3½	2¾	4	8
18G23502	3¾	3	6	13
18G23504	4¼	3½	6	21
18G23506	5	4¼	8	29
18G23508	6½	5¼	11	42

Sewed Wig and Moving Glass Eyes.

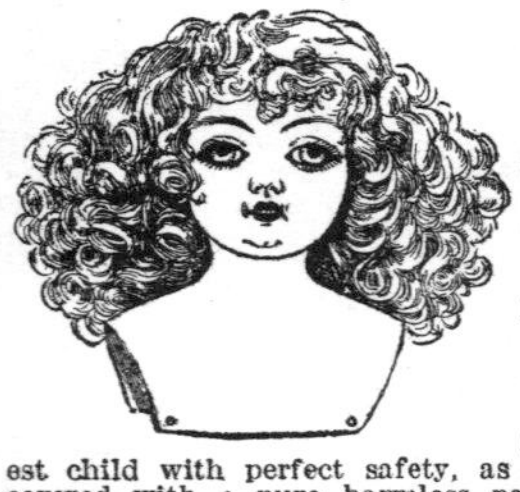

Metal Indestructible Minerva Doll Heads with moving glass eyes, open lips showing teeth, and very fine sewed curly wig. Metal head is made of best flexible sheet brass and can be given to the smallest child with perfect safety, as the metal is covered with a pure harmless paint which is manufactured especially for the purpose.

Catalog No.	Height, Inches	Inches Across Shoulders	Shipping Weight, Ounces	Price
18G23446	4⅛	3	9	37c
18G23448	4¾	3½	11	55c
18G23450	6¼	4	14	79c
18G23452	6	5¼	21	98c

Genuine Bisque Doll Heads.

IMMENSE VALUES. COMPARE OUR SIZES AND PRICES WITH OTHERS.

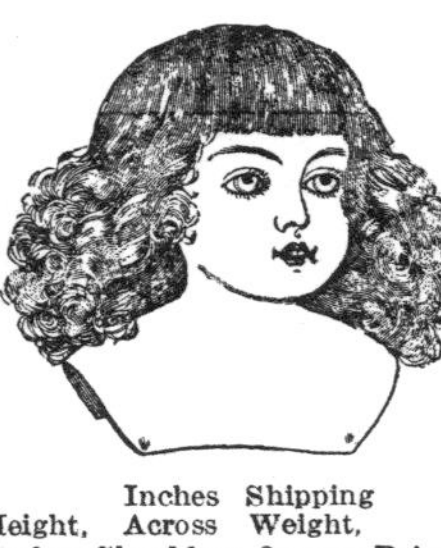

Bisque Doll Heads. Good quality, high grade bisque, with very beautiful molded faces, showing two rows of teeth. Sewed wig and movable eyes. Come in sizes as follows:

Catalog No.	Height, Inches	Inches Across Shoulders	Shipping Weight, Ounces	Price
18G23454	3⅞	3¼	9	$0.21
18G23456	4½	3½	13	.30
18G23458	5¼	4¼	15	.38
18G23460	6	5	17	.59
18G23462	7	5½	24	.88
18G23464	8¼	6¼	39	1.25
18G23466	8½	7½	42	1.65

Finest Bisque Doll Heads.

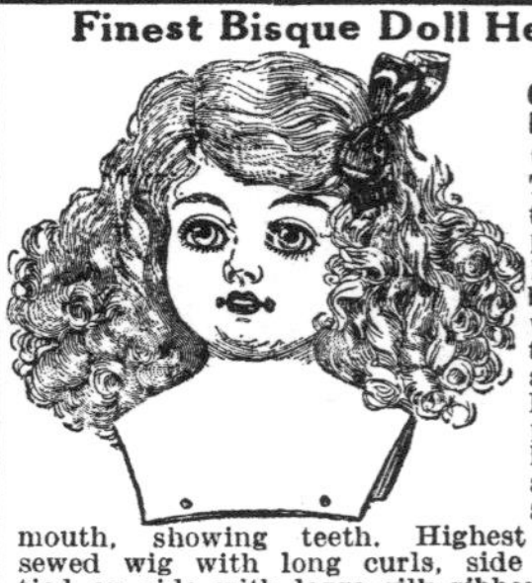

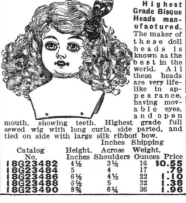

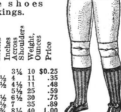

Highest Grade Bisque Heads manufactured. The maker of these doll heads is known as the best in the world. All these heads are very lifelike in appearance, having movable eyes, and open mouth, showing teeth. Highest grade full sewed wig with long curls, side parted, and tied on side with large silk ribbon bow.

Catalog No.	Height, Inches	Inches Across Shoulders	Shipping Weight, Ounces	Price
18G23482	4½	3½	16	$0.55
18G23484	5	4	17	.79
18G23486	6½	4½	22	1.10
18G23488	6½	5	32	1.38
18G23490	8¾	6¼	36	1.96

Bisque Finish Patented Celluloid Doll Heads.

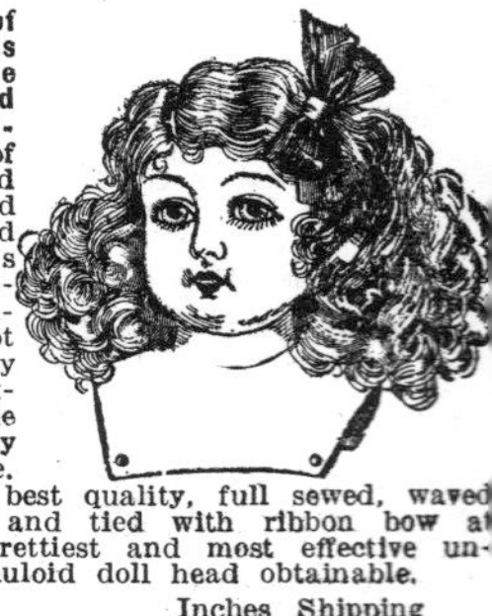

This line of Doll Heads is by far the prettiest and most serviceable. Made of heavy celluloid and fitted with patented moving eyes that we absolutely guarantee will not fall out. They are unbreakable, bisque finish, pretty and lifelike. Wigs are of best quality, full sewed, waved and parted, and tied with ribbon bow at side. The prettiest and most effective unbreakable celluloid doll head obtainable.

Catalog No.	Height, Inches	Inches Across Shoulders	Shipping Weight, Ounces	Pric
18G23511	3¾	3	4	35
18G23513	4¼	3¼	7	48
18G23515	4¾	4	8	63
18G23517	5½	4¾	13	85
18G23519	6¼	5½	15	98

HIGH GRADE TOY DISHES

Big Value China Tea Sets.

Very Large and Beautifully Decorated.

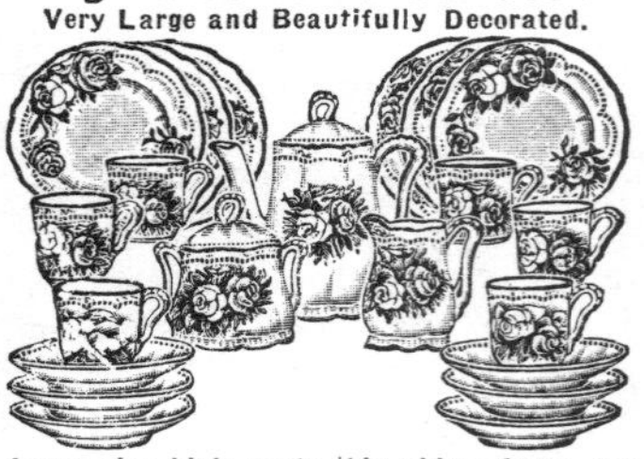

Large size high grade thin china fancy rose decorated Toy Tea Set. Consists of twenty-three extra large size pieces of the best grade imported china, hand decorated in natural color rose pattern with fancy gilt trimming. Consists of six cups and saucers, teapot and sugar bowl with covers, creamer and six 5-inch diameter fancy plates. A set that is practical and sure to please any child. Shipping weight, 8 pounds.

No. 49G700 Price............**$1.39**

Toy Tea Set, same style as above, but with fancy bowl and without the six large size plates (eighteen pieces in all). A beautiful set. Shipping weight, 6 pounds.

No. 49G701 Price............**$1.00**

Same as No. 49G701, but not decorated. Shipping weight, 6 pounds.

Price................**75c**

Our Big 49-Cent Value.

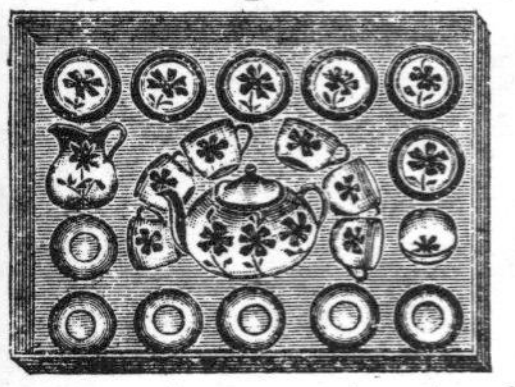

China Tea Set. Beautifully color decorated flower design, and finished in gilt. Consists of twenty-three pieces, including good size cups, saucers, plates, teapot, sugar and creamer. A very pretty set and good value. Size, 11x14 inches. Shipping weight, 2½ pounds.

Price..............**49c**

Our 23-Cent China Tea Set.

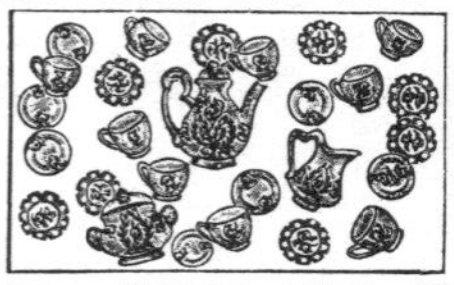

China Tea Set. Similar to above and consists of twenty-three pieces, including cups, saucers, sugar, creamer and six plates, all decorated in fancy colors. An exceptional value. Size, 9x12½ inches. Shipping weight, 20 ounces.

Price..............**23c**

Decorated Tin Tea Sets.

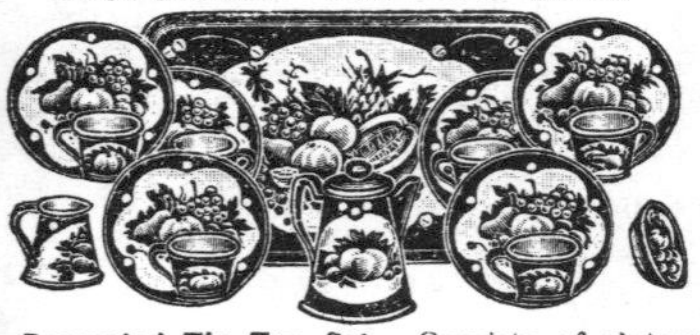

Decorated Tin Tea Set. Consists of sixteen pieces, six large size cups and saucers, cream pitcher and teapot with cover, saucepan, and tray measuring 9x13 inches. All decorated in high colors on heavy metal, pictures being of assorted fruits, flowers, etc. These are very attractive sets for the younger children. Put up in heavy cardboard box. Shipping weight, 24 oz.

No. 49G710 Price..............**47c**

Same style as above, but smaller, consists of fourteen pieces, including five cups and saucers, creamer, sugar bowl, teapot and cover and tray 6x9 inches, enameled in high colors. Put up in heavy cardboard box. Size 9½x11½ inches. Shipping weight, 16 ounces.

No. 49G711 Price..............**23c**

Britannia Tea Sets.

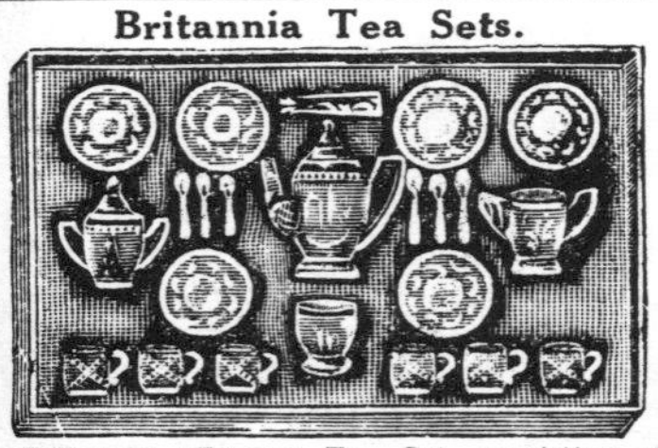

Britannia (Pewter) Tea Set, consisting of about twenty-three pieces, silver finished. Consists of cups, saucers, teapot, sugar bowl and creamer and other articles. Large size, beautifully finished and a ready seller. Size of box, 10½x16½ inches. Shipping wt., 40 oz.

No. 49G722 Price, per set......**89c**

Britannia Tea Set, silver finished, about twenty-four pieces, similar to above, but smaller in size. Size of box, 9½x14 inches. Shipping weight, 28 ounces.

No. 49G721 Price, per set.......**47c**

Britannia (Pewter) Tea Set. Silver finished, with very handsome filigree design. Small cups, saucers and other pieces. Set consists of about twenty-three pieces. Size of box, 8x10 inches. Shipping weight, 17 ounces.

No. 49G720 Price, per set.......**19c**

FINEST ENAMELED TOY TEA SETS

Our Finest Tea Set.

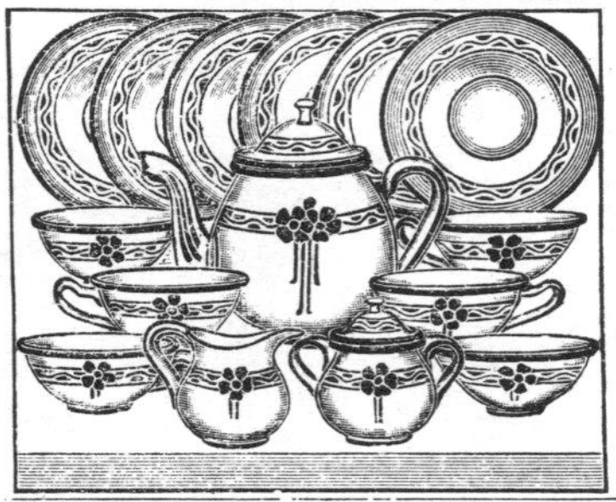

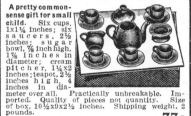

Quality Not Quantity.

Toy Tea Set. Beautifully decorated, heavy white enameled, gold trimmed. Six 4-inch saucers; six cups, 2⅝ inches in diameter, 1¾ inches high, with small raised flower design in colors; cream pitcher, 2¼ inches high; sugar bowl, 2¾ inches high; teapot, 4¾ inches high and 6 inches wide over all. Resembles china, but far more durable. A very handsome yet practical present. Will last for years. On account of having four coats of enamel it has no rough edges and is smooth as glass. All decorations in fine light artistic lines. Not gaudy but rich. A present that will be appreciated all the time, as no child will grow weary of it, or of showing it to her playmates. New and original design, imported by us direct from one of the best German manufacturers, and offered this season for the first time. A little more expensive than other tea sets, but well worth the difference. Size box, 12x13½x4 inches. Shipping weight, 4 pounds.

No. 49G705 Price...........**$2.98**

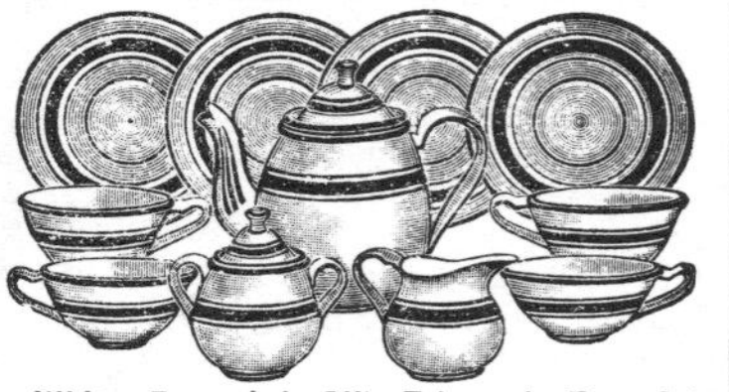

White Enameled Gilt Trimmed Tea Set. Exceptionally fine. Four plates, 4¼ inches in diameter, with light and heavy rich gilt lines; four cups, 1¼ inches high, 2⅝ inches in diameter; cream pitcher, 2 inches high, 3 inches in diameter; sugar bowl, 2½ inches high; teapot 2⅝ inches high, 5 inches in diameter. Each piece with regular accurately drawn gilt lines, very smoothest finish, made from best ware. Size box, 11x11x3½ in. Shipping wt., 3½ lbs.

No. 49G706 Price...........**$1.95**

Our Best Blue Enameled Tea Set.

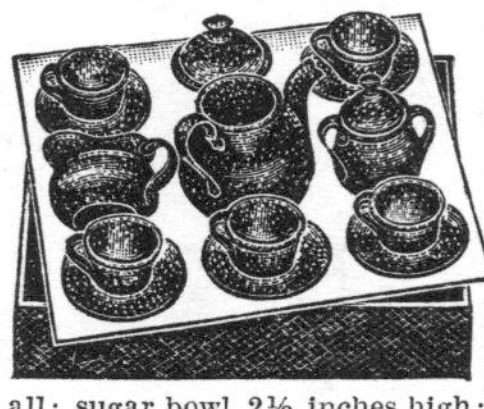

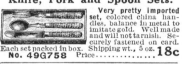

Light mottled blue, excellent grade, practically unbreakable, pretty design. Six cups, 1½ inches high, 2 inches in diameter; saucers, 3 inches in diameter; cream pitcher, 2 inches high, 2⅞ inches in diameter over all; sugar bowl, 2½ inches high; teapot, 4 inches high, 5 inches over all. A sensible, practical and acceptable gift. New design. Imported by us from Germany. Size of box, 12½x11x3 inches. Shipping weight, 3 pounds.

No. 49G707 Price...........**$1.45**

Child's Oatmeal Set.

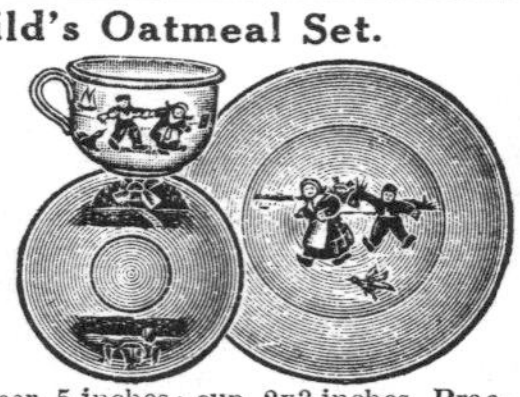

Extra high grade, white enameled, hand decorated, gold trimmed. Figures and pictures as shown in illustration, are raised in colors. Plate, 8 inches in diameter; saucer, 5 inches; cup, 2x3 inches. Practically unbreakable. No peeling or chipping and better than china. Our own German importation. Original design. Size of box, 13½x8x3 inches. Shipping weight, 2½ pounds.

Price..............**95c**

Plain Blue Enameled Tea Set.

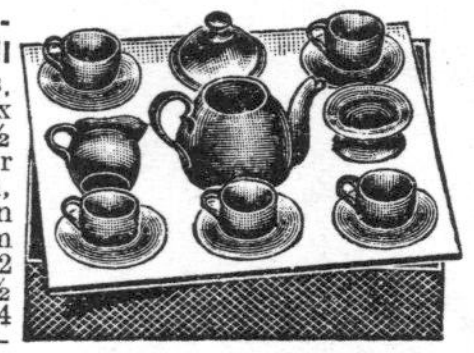

A pretty common-sense gift for small child. Six cups, 1x1¼ inches; six saucers, 2½ inches; sugar bowl, ⅞ inch high, 1⅞ inches in diameter; cream pitcher, 1¼x2 inches; teapot, 2½ inches high, 4 inches in diameter over all. Practically unbreakable. Imported. Quality of pieces not quantity. Size of box, 10½x9x2½ inches. Shipping weight, 2 pounds.

No. 49G708 Price...................**77c**

Dolly's Knife and Fork Set.

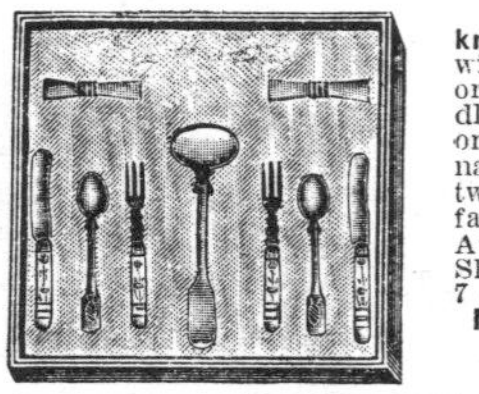

Comprises two knives and forks with fancy decorated china handles, two spoons, one ladle, two napkin rings and two napkins; all fastened in box. A very popular toy. Shipping weight, 7 ounces.

No. 49G749

Price....**29c**

Knife, Fork and Spoon Sets.

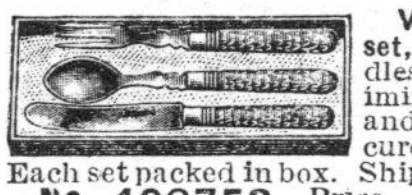

Very pretty imported set, colored china handles, balance in metal to imitate gold. Well made and will not tarnish. Securely fastened on card. Each set packed in box. Shipping wt., 5 oz.

No. 49G758 Price..........**18c**

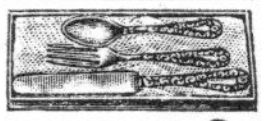

Good value set, bright metal finish. Will not tarnish. Nice little gift for small child. Packed in tufted lined box. Shipping weight, 5 ounces.

Price..................**8c**

Child's Table Set.

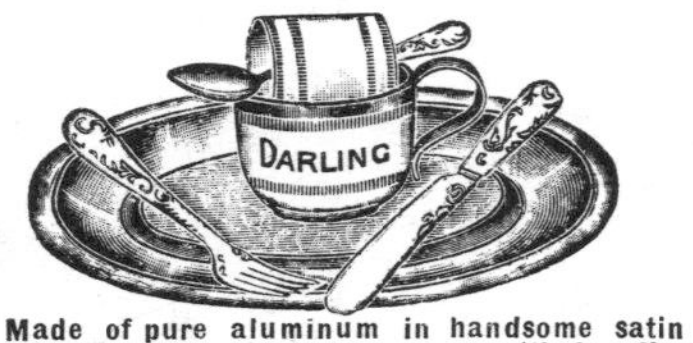

Made of pure aluminum in handsome satin finish. Consists of good size cup with handle, saucer, 7-inch plate, knife, fork, spoon and napkin ring. All parts are well made and of sufficient size for regular use. Cup has name "Darling" hand engraved upon it. Can be used without danger of breakage. A very attractive set and excellent value at the price. Shipping weight, 9 ounces.

Price................**95c**

Satin Aluminum Kitchen Sets.

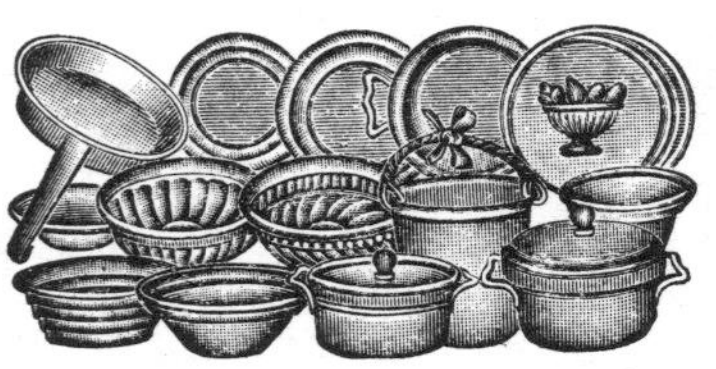

Aluminum kitchen sets have of late become very popular. Light in weight, handsome in appearance, non-rusting. The various utensils have turned edges and is a set always remaining the same. Comprises fourteen medium size pieces, including pans, pail, cake dishes, covered and uncovered saucepans, frying pans and all necessary kitchen utensils. All in beautiful and popular satin finish aluminum. Packed in lace trimmed box. Size, 12½x13½ inches. Shipping weight, 20 ounces.

No. 49G715 Price.... ....**89c**

Fancy Aluminum Kitchen Set, similar to the above, but containing only twelve pieces. Utensils are smaller, but all have turned edges and are in fine satin aluminum finish. Packed in lace trimmed box. Size, 12x12 inches. Shipping weight, 1 pound.

No. 49G716 Price..................**47c**

Set similar to the above, but containing only ten pieces, four of which have turned edges. Size of box, 10x12 inches. Shipping weight, 14 ounces.

No. 49G717 Price..................**29c**

Set of eight pieces, nicely finished aluminum, similar to above. Box, 8x11¾ inches. Shipping weight, 8 ounces.

No. 49G718 Price..................**19c**

Fancy Tin Dishes.

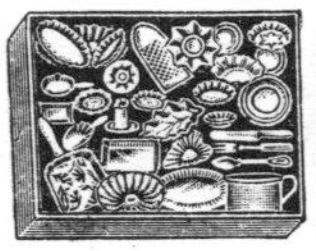

Big value in a toy tin dish set. Imported. About fifty-five pieces, including enameled cups and saucers, two 4-inch enameled plates, and other assorted plain and decorated pieces. Big favorite with children. Shipping weight, 16 ounces.

No. 49G709 Price..............**21c**

Tin Dish Set.

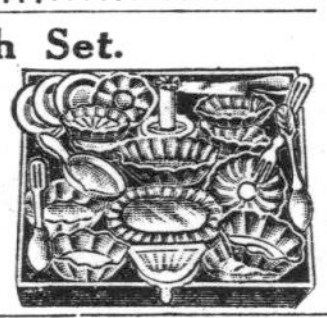

Similar to above, but having about thirty pieces, somewhat smaller, and two cups and saucers. Good bargain. Shipping weight, 8 ounces.

No. 49G769

Price..........**10c**

Imitation Cut Glass Water Set.

38c

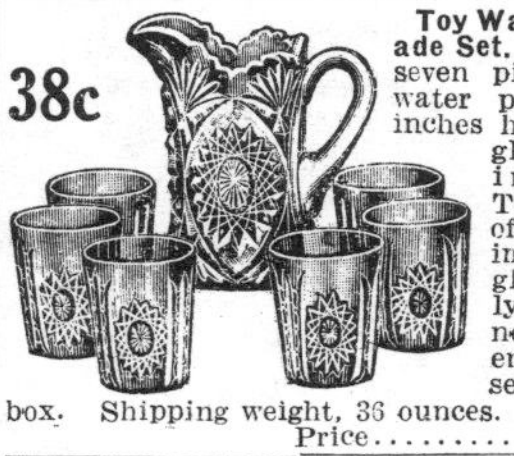

Toy Water or Lemonade Set. Consists of seven pieces: Glass water pitcher, 4½ inches high, and six glasses, each 2¼ inches high. These are made of extra heavy imitation cut glass, very nicely finished and not easily broken. Packed one set complete in box. Shipping weight, 36 ounces.

Price...............**38c**

Imitation Cut Glass Tea Set.

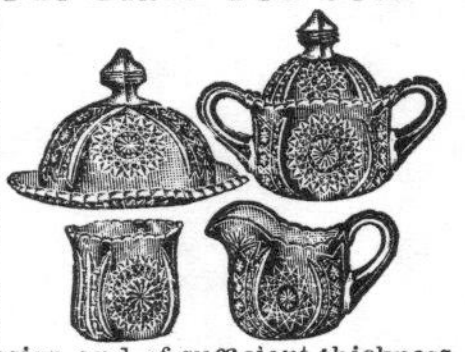

Handsome in appearance and of beautiful design. Consists of a 5-inch diameter fancy edge covered butter dish, a 5-inch covered sugar bowl, a fancy creamer and a 2½-inch high spoonholder. Very useful items of heavy beautiful design and of sufficient thickness so as not to be easily broken. One of the best selling sets ever manufactured. Shipping weight, 36 ounces.

Price..............**33c**

Imitation Cut Glass Set.

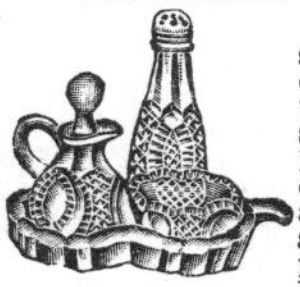

A very pretty and popular set. A good addition to every tea set. Consists of vinegar bottle, pepper shaker, salt dish and fancy leaf tray. Beautiful design. No children's tea set or playthings are complete without this set. Carefully packed. Shipping weight, 3 pounds.

Price..............**25c**

Doke's Tea Party.

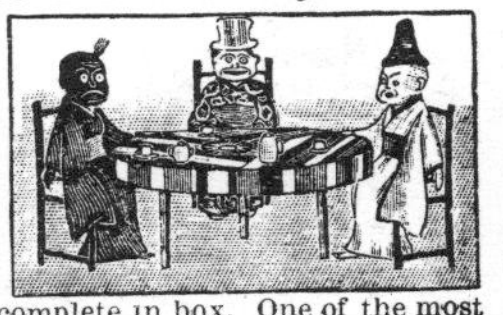

A really wonderful little set at the price. Comprises three Japanese wicker chairs, circular 4½-inch table and set china decorated dishes and three 4½-inch Japanese dolls, all complete in box. One of the most popular and best sellers

No. 49G728 Price...(Postage 11c)..**29c**

Child's Aluminum Cup and Saucer.

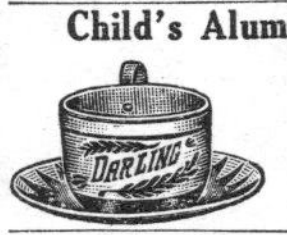

Nicely polished aluminum with word "Darling" carved on side. Big favorite. Unbreakable. Practical. Shipping weight, 5 ounces.

No. 49G724

Price..............**19c**

Aluminum Salt and Pepper.

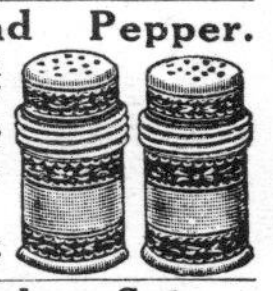

Fancy decorated. Easily filled and cleaned. Aluminum toy sets are now most popular. Fine finish. No danger of breaking. Shipping weight, 4 ounces.

No. 49G753

Price..................**8c**

Blue Enameled Kitchen Sets.

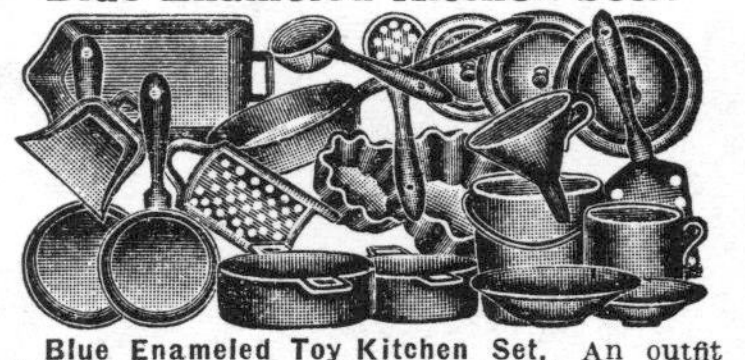

Blue Enameled Toy Kitchen Set. An outfit that will afford no end of pleasure to any girl. Consists of twenty-one pieces, including all the various kitchen utensils, such as pots, pans, spoons, ladles, covers, grater, cups, pails, etc. Absolutely unbreakable and made the same as the large best quality enameled kitchen ware. Size of box, 12½x16 inches. Shipping weight, 3¼ pounds.

No. 49G725 Price...............**97c**

Blue Enameled Toy Kitchen Set, similar to the above, but consisting of fourteen pieces. Made of very high grade blue enameled ware, but the fittings are smaller in size. A big value for our price. Size of box, 9½x13½ inches. Shipping weight, 2½ pounds.

No. 49G727 Price...............**55c**

Blue Enameled Toy Kitchen Set, same make and style as above, but consisting of only nine pieces. A very attractive set at the price. Size of box, 8x11 inches. Shipping wt., 20 oz.

No. 49G726 Price...............**35c**

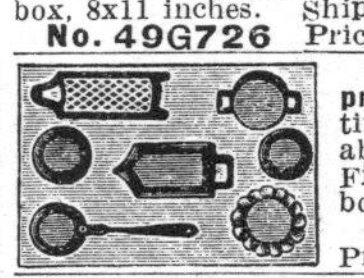

An excellent set for the price. Dark blue enameled tin. Well made. Unbreakable. Polished surface. Fine for small child. In box. Shipping wt., 5 oz.

No. 49G747

Price..............**19c**

A Ten-Piece Blue Enameled Finish Tin Set. Smaller pieces. Smooth surfaces. Good bargain. Sensible gift for little child. Shipping weight, 5 ounces.

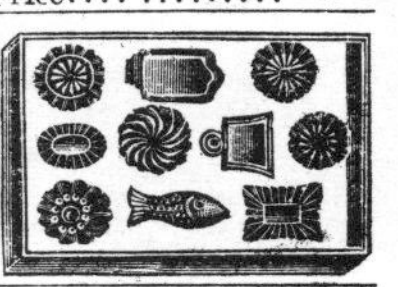

No. 49G771

Price..............**8c**

POPULAR MUSICAL TOYS

Hand Music Boxes.

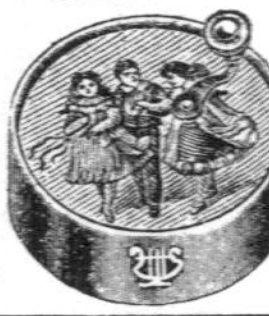

Fine Imported Genuine Swiss Music Box, playing popular and pleasing tune. Finely nickel plated edge, and embossed instruments on edge. Diameter 2¾ inches. Shipping weight, 6 ounces.
No. 49G327 Price 49c

Two-Air Music Box.

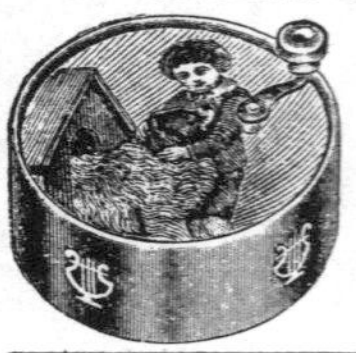

Larger instrument than above, and plays two popular tunes. Beautifully nickel plated edge, fancy picture on top. High class and very popular instrument. Shipping weight, 8 ounces. Each in box.
No. 49G326 Price 98c

Three-Air Music Box.

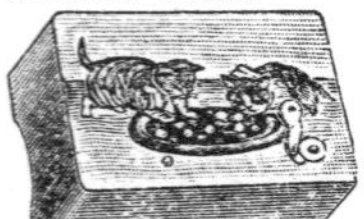

Beautifully polished square hardwood box. Very pretty picture on top. Crank attachment. Handsome finish throughout. Size, 4¾x3½x2¾ inches. Shipping weight, 1 pound.
No. 49G325 Price $1.85

Open Lid Music Box.

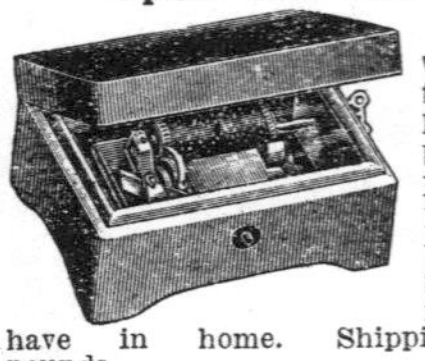

Genuine Swiss, with patent spring for winding. Fancy holly hinged cover box, under glass. Picture on top. Music can be turned on or off. Size, 4¾x3½x2¼ inches. Nice to have in home. Shipping weight, 1½ pounds.
No. 49G324 Price $1.65

Our Finest Music Box.

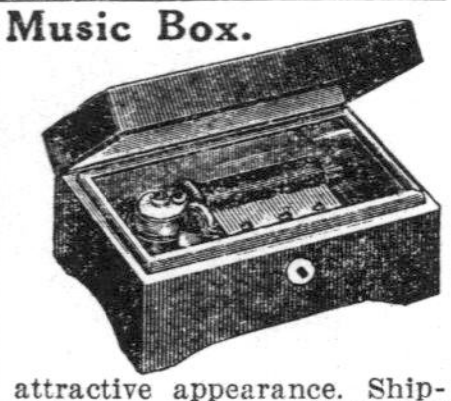

Genuine mahogany box, three tunes, patent spring for winding. Music can be turned on or off. Hinge cover case under glass. Extra handsome finish. Size, 5¼x3½x2¾ inches. Makes unusually attractive appearance. Shipping weight, 2 pounds.
No. 49G323 Price $2.95

Cheap Music Boxes.

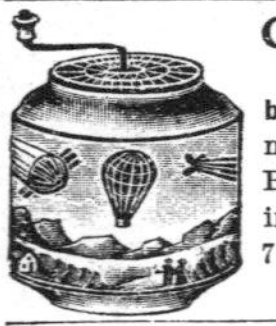

Very pretty metal music box, decorated, crank attachment. Nice toy for child. Box, 3¼ inches high, 3 inches in diameter. Shipping weight, 7 ounces.
No. 49G330 Price 19c

Big Selling Toy Music Box.

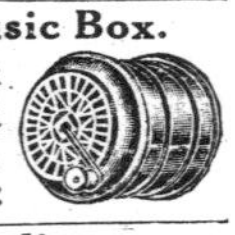

Made of metal, with crank handle. Size, about 2¼x2¼ inches. Very good present for small child. Shipping weight, 4 ounces.
No. 49G331 Price 8c

Fine Toy Accordion.

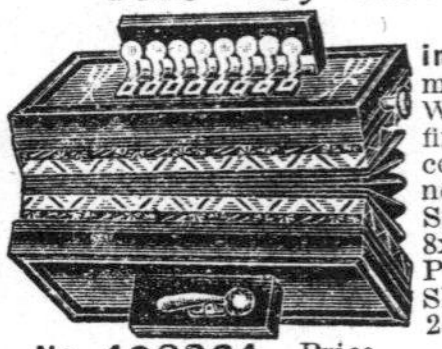

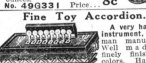

A very handsome instrument, German manufacture. Well made and finely finished in colors. Has eight notes and bass key. Size, not extended, 8x6½ inches. Packed in box. Shipping weight, 24 ounces.
No. 49G364 Price 47c

Four-Key Accordion.

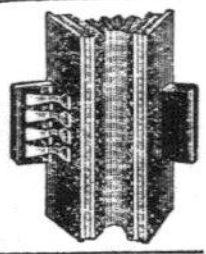

Same style as above, but not so finely finished, with four notes. Size, not extended, about 6½x4½ inches. Shipping weight, 12 ounces
No. 49G343 Price 18c

Bird Whistles.

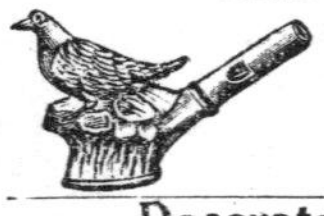

Colored Metal Bird Whistles. Can be made to resemble canary bird notes. Shipping weight, 4 ounces.
No. 49G329 Price, 3 for 10c

Decorated Tin Horn.

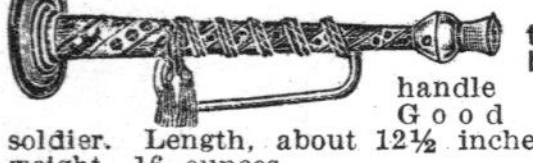

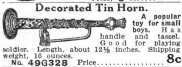

A popular toy for small boys. Has handle and tassel. Good for playing soldier. Length, about 12½ inches. Shipping weight, 16 ounces.
No. 49G328 Price 8c

Toy Cornets.

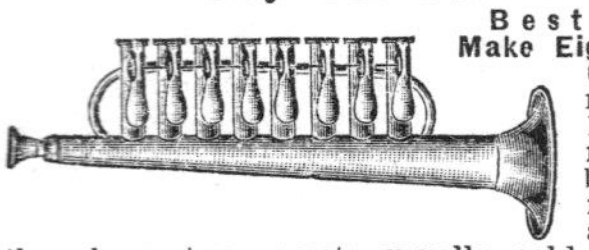

Best German Make Eight-Note Cornet, made of heavy metal in brass finish and not the cheap toy cornets usually sold at this price. Has full octave of eight notes. Many popular airs can be played, for with each cornet we furnish printed music. A sensible toy and a decided contrast to the noisy horns so often given to children. Length, 12½ inches. Shipping weight, 6 ounces.
No. 49G300 Price 89c

Four-Note Cornet. Same style as above, but with only four notes. Military airs and calls can easily be produced on this cornet. We furnish music sheet with each instrument. Length, 12 inches. Shipping weight, 6 ounces.
No. 49G301 Price 47c

Toy Trombones.

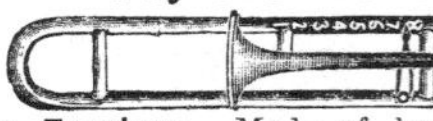

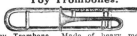

Toy Trombone. Made of heavy metal in brass finish. Has eight notes, marked by means of sliding scale, so that most any popular air can be played. We furnish numbered music sheet with each instrument, so that any beginner can play with ease. Entire length, 20 inches. Shipping weight, 15 ounces.
No. 49G302 Price 89c

Toy Trombone. Same style as above, but smaller and with four notes. We furnish numbered music sheet with each instrument. Size, 13 inches. Shipping weight, 10 ounces.
No. 49G303 Price 47c

Tin Violins and Bows.

Our Best Toy Violin in Case.

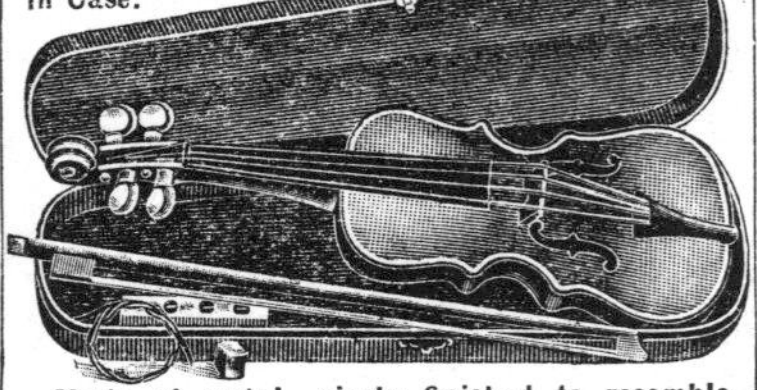

Made of metal, nicely finished to resemble a real violin. Four genuine violin strings, tightening pegs, extra strings, rosin and tuning instrument, enabling proper tuning. Total length, 19 inches; width, 6 inches; bow, 17½ inches. The case is made to resemble metal, painted inside and outside, and 19½x6½ inches in size. One of the very best and most popular musical instruments. Shipping weight, 3½ pounds.
No. 49G304 Price 89c

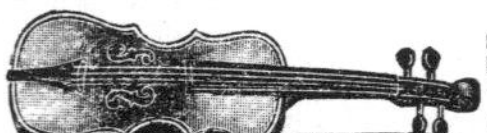

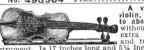

A very nice violin, similar to above, but without case, extra strings and tuning instrument. Is 17 inches long and 5¼ inches wide. Four genuine bow strings and tightening pegs. Bow, 15¾ inches long. Very large selling toy and one that is sure to please. Shipping weight, 1½ pounds.
No. 49G305 Price 45c

A good value violin, similar to above, but not so nicely finished. Without case. Length, 12½ inches; width, 4 inches. Four violin strings and tightening rods. Fine for small children. Shipping weight, 1 pound.
No. 49G365 Price 21c

Fancy Nickeled Tin Trumpet.

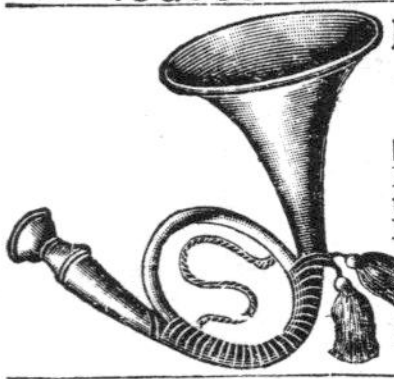

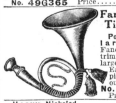

Popular design, large mouthpiece. Fancy gilt and green trimming, with two large fancy tassels. Each in box. Shipping weight, 12 ounces.
No. 49G306 Price 19c

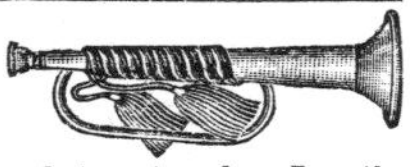

Heavy Nickeled Trumpet, correct pattern, strongly made. Has clear note and recall. Ornamented with red and gilt cord and two tassels. Length, 13 inches. Shipping weight, 10 ounces.
No. 49G308 Price 21c

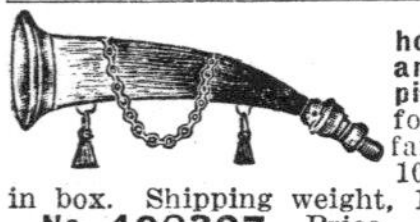

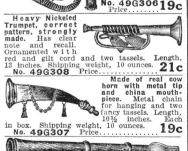

Made of real cow horn with metal tip and china mouthpiece. Metal chain for hanging and two fancy tassels. Length, 10½ inches. Each in box. Shipping weight, 10 ounces.
No. 49G307 Price 19c

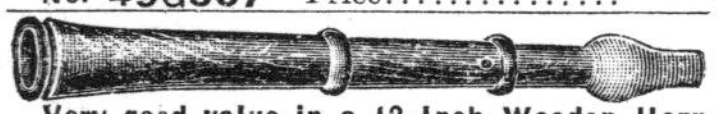

Very good value in a 12-Inch Wooden Horn, painted red and white. Favorite toy for small boys. Shipping weight, 12 ounces.
No. 49G347 Price 8c

Fancy Celluloid Trumpet.

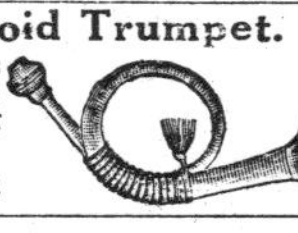

Two notes. With fancy cord and tassel. 25-cent value. Shipping weight, 8 ounces.
No. 49G344 Price 15c

Eight-Key Clarinet.

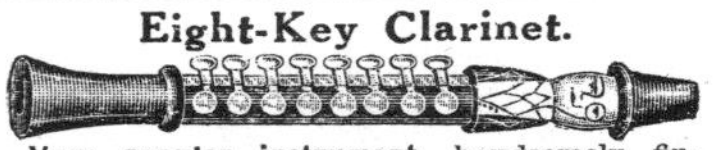

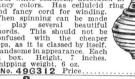

Very popular instrument, handsomely finished, three colors. Natural color hand painted face on top. Length, 14 inches. Large selling toy. Shipping weight, 5 ounces.
No. 49G311 Price 21c

A Very Good Flute.

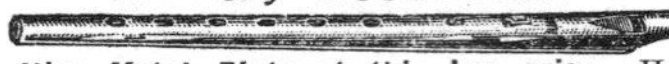

Nice Metal Flute at this low price. Has six notes; 14 inches long. Shipping weight, 5 ounces.
No. 49G346 Price 9c

Twenty-Key Metalaphone.

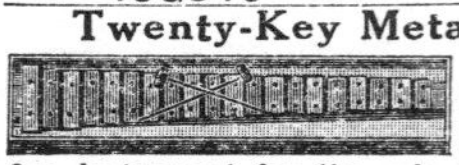

Two hammers, large size metal plates, beautifully finished and a fine instrument for the price. Packed in red box. Size instrument, 4x17½ inches. Shipping weight, 2 pounds.
No. 49G309 Price 19c

Our 8-Cent Value.

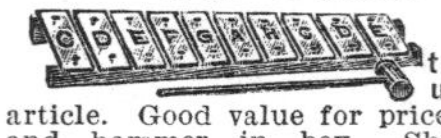

A number of tunes can be played upon it. Imported article. Good value for price. The instrument and hammer in box. Shipping weight, 1 pound.
No. 49G310 Price 8c

Our Best Musical Top.

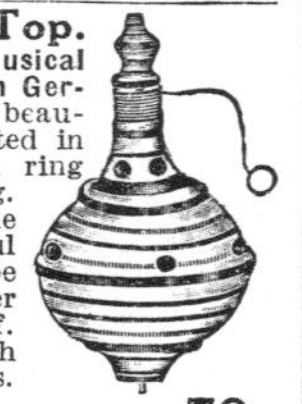

This is one of the finest musical tops that can be purchased in Germany. Made throughout of beautiful white celluloid, decorated in fancy colors. Has celluloid ring and fancy cord for winding. When spinning can be made to play several beautiful chords. This should not be confused with the cheaper tops, as it is classed by itself. Packed in fine box. Handsome in appearance. Each in box. Height, 7 inches. Shipping weight, 6 oz.
No. 49G312 Price 79c

Nickel Plated Musical Top.

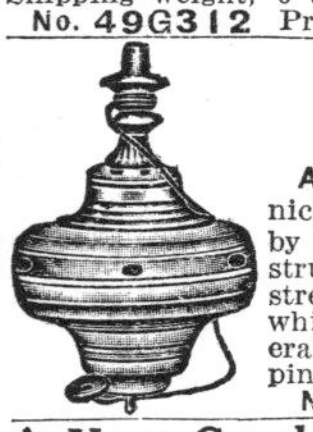

A very handsome top, nickel plated, and preferred by many boys, as its construction makes it a better street top. By tapping the top while spinning it gives several distinct chords. Shipping weight, 8 ounces.
No. 49G337 Price 41c

A Very Good Singing Top.

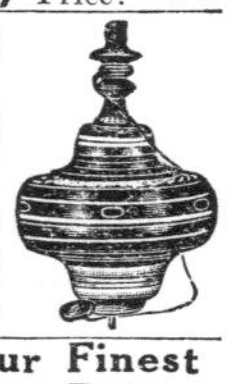

Beautifully Lithographed Metal Choral Top, 7 inches high, and cord for spinning. By gently tapping top while top is in motion several distinct chords are produced. A big seller and wonderful value. Shipping weight, 6 ounces.
No. 49G313 Price 21c

Our Finest Toy Reins.

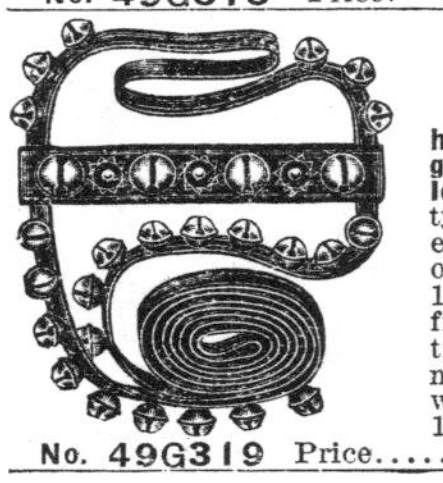

Exceptionally heavy soft fine grade orange color leather, with twenty-four nickel plated bells of steel on reins, and four 1¼-inch bells on front. Not cheap tin, but finest reins made. Shipping weight, in box, 1½ pounds.
No. 49G319 Price 89c

Our Twenty-Five Bell Toy Reins.

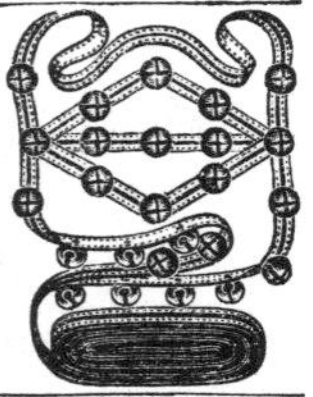

White oilcloth, securely sewed, with fancy front piece. Sixteen bells on reins and nine 1¼-inch bells on front. Bells of genuine steel, not tin. Shipping weight, 1 pound.
No. 49G320 Price 42c

Eleven-Bell Toy Reins.

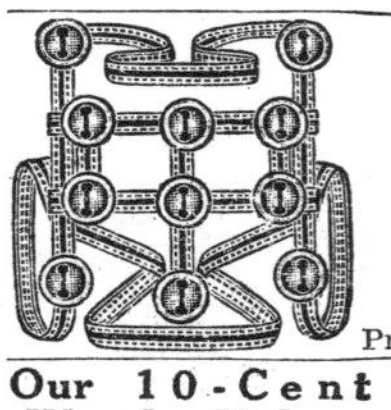

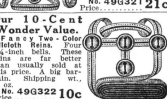

Fancy Two-Color Oilcloth Reins, nicely sewed, eleven nickel plated good sounding bells. Big value at this price. Shipping weight, 8 ounces.
No. 49G321 Price 21c

Our 10-Cent Wonder Value.

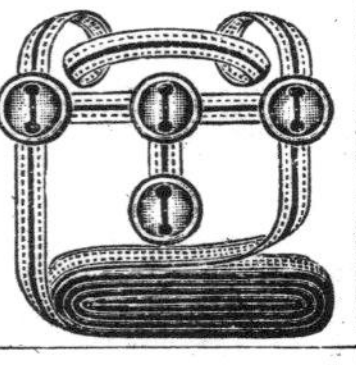

Fancy Two-Color Oilcloth Reins. Four 1¼-inch bells. These reins are far better than usually sold at this price. A big bargain. Shipping wt., 5 oz.
No. 49G322 Price 10c

Musical Floor Chimes.

Our Finest Value.

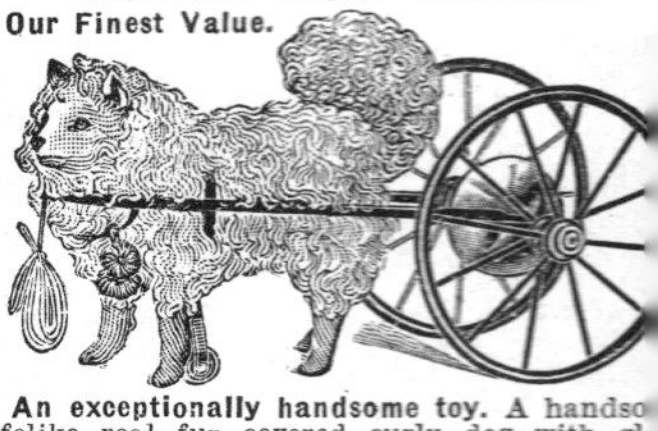

An exceptionally handsome toy. A handso lifelike real fur covered curly dog with gl eyes and large bushy tail. Dog, 8½x10 inch Fancy tassels and drawing cord. The la wheels are painted red, 8½ inches in dia eter, strong metal, securely fastened me spokes and brass finished hubs. Axle, ⅜ in in diameter. Wheels have oval rims to p vent marring floor. The bell is 3½ inches diameter, heavy steel, good sounding chim Harness of metal, gilt bronze finish. To length, 19 inches. Shipping weight, packed pounds.
No. 49G340 Price $1.8

Horse and Bell Chimes.

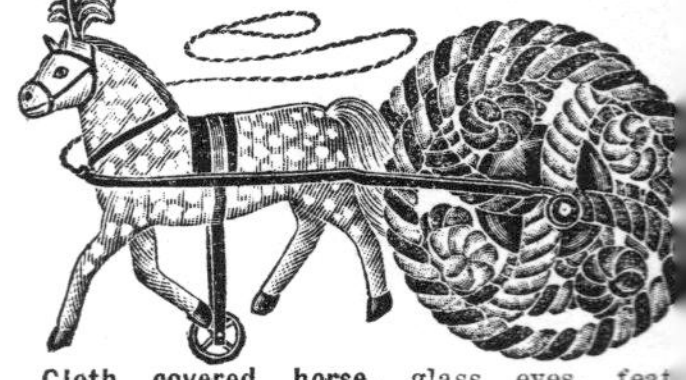

Cloth covered horse, glass eyes, feat plume on head. Steel chime bell, 2½ inc in diameter, with heavy drawing cord. I tation leather harness, shafting nicely finish Large wheels, 7 inches in diameter, and tirely covered with colored wool, to prot floor and give wheels parade appearance. addition to metal axle, wheels are connec with four metal strips, giving additio strength. Total length, 15¾ inches. Sh ping weight, packed, 3 pounds.
No. 49G339 Price $1.4

Horse and Bell Chimes.

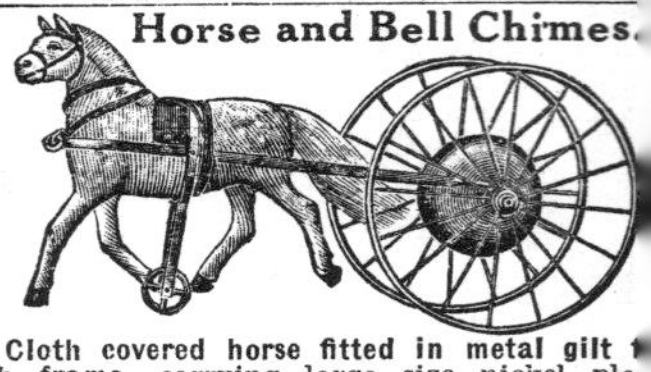

Cloth covered horse fitted in metal gilt ish frame, carrying large size nickel pla bell of very sweet tone. Large 7-inch blue enamel finish gilt trimmed metal whe wooden horse finely finished with fine ma and tail. Has glass eyes and very natural every respect. Size horse, 7½x7 inches. G uine leather draw string with clasp. Size o all, 15x7½ inches. A toy that sells on sig Shipping weight, 2 pounds. (Unmailable.)
No. 49G314 Price 9

Only 47 Cents for This Chim

Same as above, but smaller size. 4½-i wheel, and horse in proportion. Each ca fully packed in box. Shipping weight, pound.
No. 49G315 Price 4

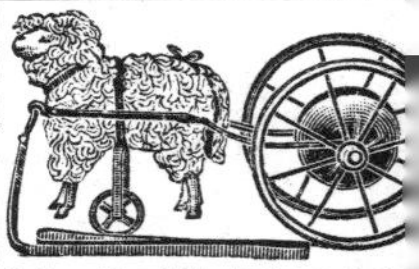

Natural wool covered sheep, nice enameled drawing cord. All other parts painted metal. Wheels, 4⅜ inches in diameter. Steel bell chime, 2⅜ inches in diameter; total length, 9½ inches; heig 5 inches. Wheels have oval rims. Shipp weight, 1½ pounds. Very good value.
No. 49G338 Price 4

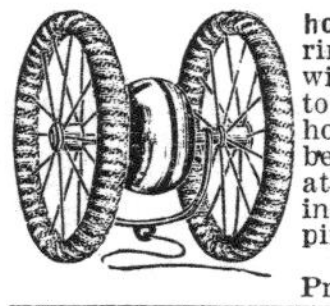

Very popular toy house use. Metal whe rims of which are cove with soft woolen mate to make it noiseless in house. Large nickel pla bell in center, with pull attachment. Wheels inches in diameter. Sh ping weight, 1 pound.
No. 49G318 Price 3

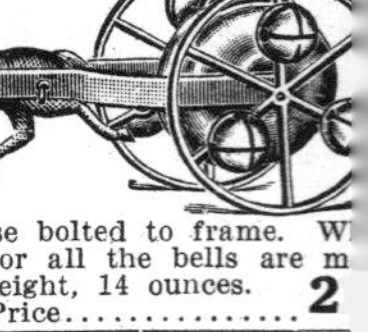

Steel frame, cast iron horse and red enameled wheels with large gong between wheels and three 1¼-inch nickel plated bells on each. Horse bolted to frame. W drawn along the floor all the bells are m to ring. Shipping weight, 14 ounces.
No. 49G316 Price 2

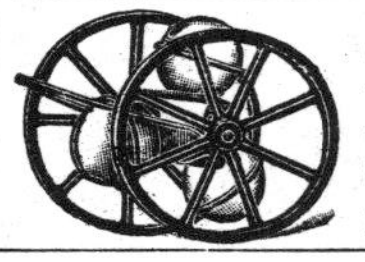

Red metal whe Three 1¼-inch nic bells and drawing tachment. Big va Shipping weight, 8
No. 49G370 Price

RELIABLE MECHANICAL TOYS

Ideal Shooting Gallery.

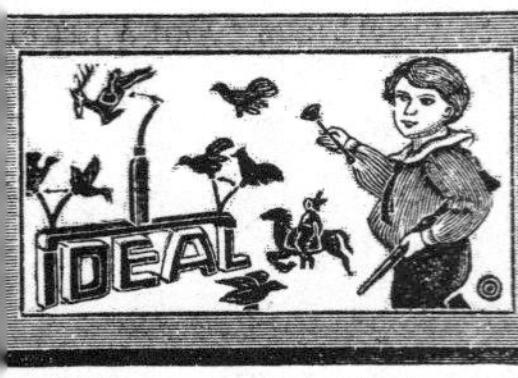

Has wooden base, with three movable springs, upon which are placed eight moving birds, animals, Indians, ., which move back and forth at a distance of 4 8 inches. Has 18-inch metal barrel gun, wood eech fitted with strong metal spring and trig- which shoots rubber tipped arrows. Carelly packed. Size of box, 11x19 inches. Shipg weight, 3 pounds.
No. 49G424 Price............. $1.00

Ideal Gun and Pistol Set.

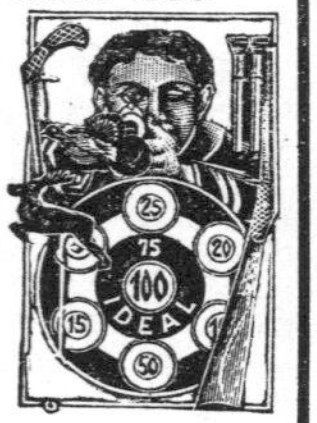

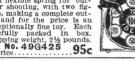

Comprises 18-inch metal rrel gun and 8-inch metal rrel pistol with two rubber oped arrows. Also large, utifully colored decorated rget, size 13x20 inches. as screw table attachment th flexible spring for outor shooting, with two fig- es, making a complete out- and for the price is an ceptionally fine toy. Each refully packed in box. ipping weight, 2½ pounds.
No. 49G425 Price............... 95c

Ideal Patent Machine Rifle.

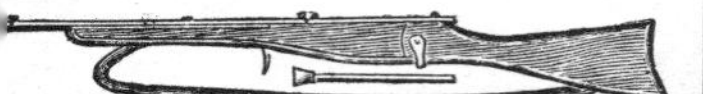

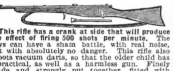

This rifle has a crank at side that will produce e effect of firing 500 shots per minute. The ys can have a sham battle, with real noise, t with absolutely no danger. This rifle also oots vacuum darts, so that the older child has practical, as well as a harmless gun. Finely ade and strongly put together, fitted with curate sight. Correct shape. Has heavy band carrying the gun across the shoulder. Length, inches. Shipping weight, 32 ounces.
No. 49G430 Price........................67c

Ideal Machine Fire Gun.

Same style gun as above with rapid firing and rt shooting attachments, but of smaller size d not quite as nicely finished. Has cloth in- ad of leather shoulder attachment. Has long utifully colored target on cover of each x. Length, 22 inches. Shipping weight, 24 nces.
No. 49G431 Price........................45c

Ideal Safety Target Pistols.

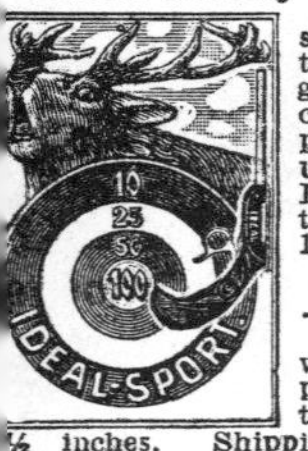

This set consists of 9-inch spring pistol, two rubber tipped suction darts, target lithographed in high colors and box of colored paper stickers which are used to mark the shots. Every boy will want to own this set. Shipping weight, 1¼ pounds.
No. 49G426 Price, complete ... 41c

Same style as above, but with only one rubber tipped arrow and smaller target. Size of target, 7½x ½ inches. Shipping weight, 1 und.
No. 49G427 Price...... 19c

Ideal Safety Gun Sets.

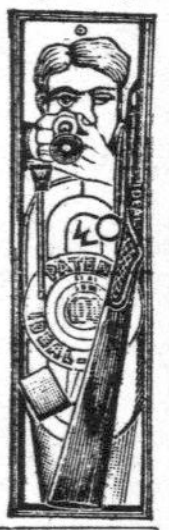

Ideal Safety Gun Set. Same prin- le as No. 49G426. Consists of ring gun 24 inches in length, two bber tipped darts and set of mark- s, also target, 5½x20 inches. Ship- g weight, 1¾ pounds.
No. 49G428 Price...... 41c

Same as above, with only one bber tipped arrow and smaller e target. Size of target, 5x19 ches. Shipping weight, 1 pound.
No. 49G429 Price....... 19c

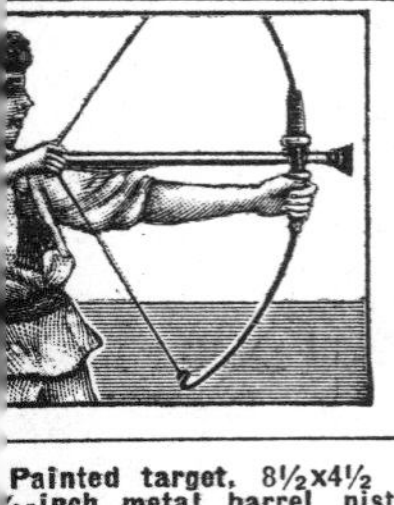

Folding Metal Steel Bow and long soft suction Rubber Tipped Arrow. With beautifully colored target on outside of cover. Size of bow, 20 in. Size of box, 3¼x14 inches. Shipping weight, 1½ pounds. Regular price, 25c.
No. 49G432 Price... 19c

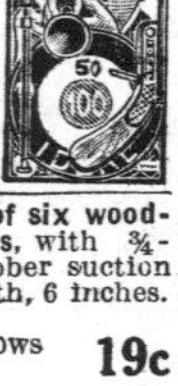

Painted target, 8½x4½ inches; ¼-inch metal barrel pistol and bber tipped wooden arrow. Good ring. A fine set for this low price. ipping weight, 10 ounces.
No. 49G472 Price.................... 10c

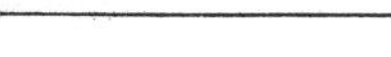

A set of six wooden arrows, with ¾-inch rubber suction os. For use with above sets. Length, 6 inches. ipping weight, 5 ounces.
Price for 6 arrows 19c

HIGH GRADE POPGUNS FOR BOYS.

The Celebrated King Popguns.

The "Three-In-One."

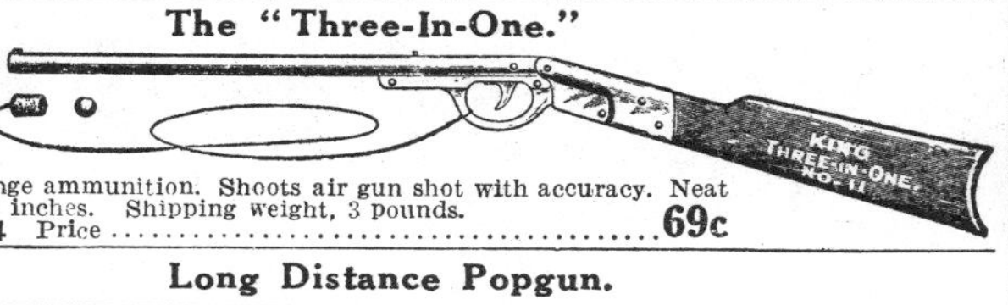

One of the finest combination air rifles, popguns and small rubber ball shooters made. No changing of parts. Simply change ammunition. Shoots air gun shot with accuracy. Neat sights. Length, 29 inches. Shipping weight, 3 pounds.
No. 49G474 Price.................................... 69c

Long Distance Popgun.

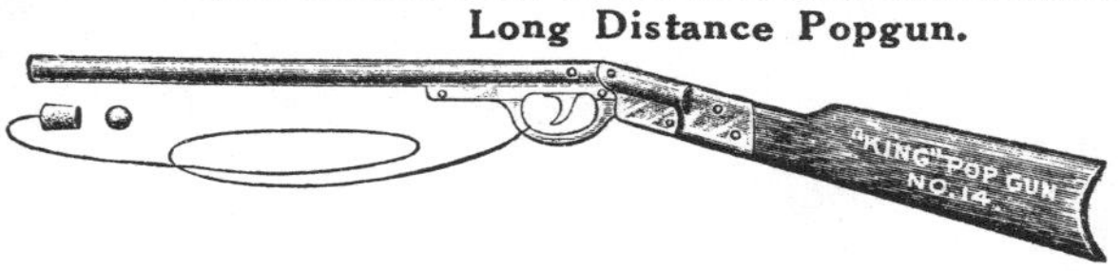

Shoots large cork and rubber ball. No danger. Use cork for noise and rubber ball for sport. Length, 21 inches. Shipping weight, 1½ pounds.
No. 49G422 Price.................................... 39c

King Popgun.

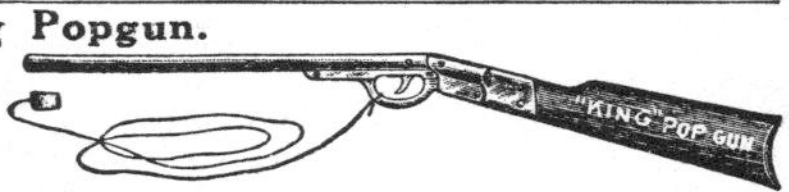

Made on same principle as above, but without ball. Length, 15½ inches. Shipping weight, 10 ounces.
No. 49G423 Price.......... 21c

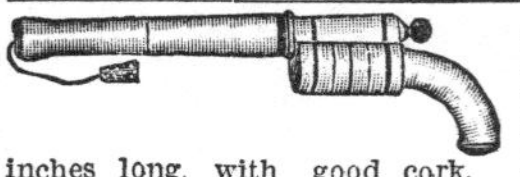

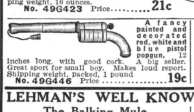

A fancy painted and decorated red, white and blue pistol popgun, 12 inches long, with good cork. A big seller. Great sport for small boy. Makes loud report. Shipping weight, packed, 1 pound
No. 49G446 Price............... 19c

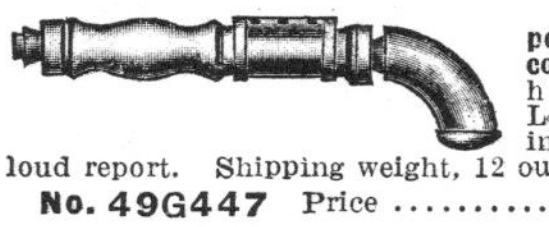

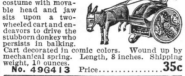

Big value popgun with cork, wooden handle. Length, 10½ inches. Makes loud report. Shipping weight, 12 ounces.
No. 49G447 Price.................. 10c

LEHMAN'S WELL KNOWN MECHANICAL TOYS.

The Balking Mule.

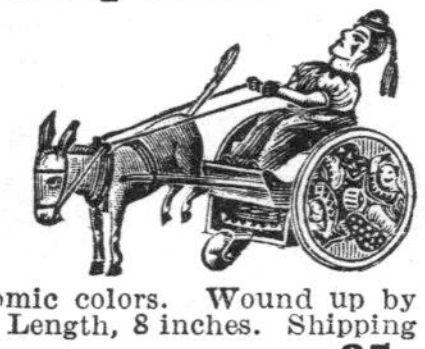

A really comical mechanical action toy. Clown in funny costume with movable head and jaw sits upon a two-wheeled cart and endeavors to drive the stubborn donkey who persists in balking. Cart decorated in comic colors. Wound up by mechanical spring. Length, 8 inches. Shipping weight, 10 ounces.
No. 49G413 Price.................. 35c

The Climbing Monkey.

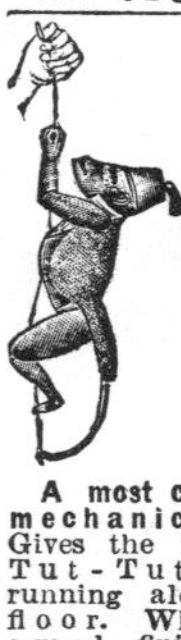

Distinctly a boy's toy. Mechanical monkey which moves at will up and down heavy cord. Movable arms and legs and can be made to stop in any position. Natural color finished. Cap with tassel, and felt covered coat. Full instructions with package. Size of monkey, 8 inches. Shipping weight, 10 ounces.
No. 49G414 Price..... 21c

The Tut-Tut Automobile.

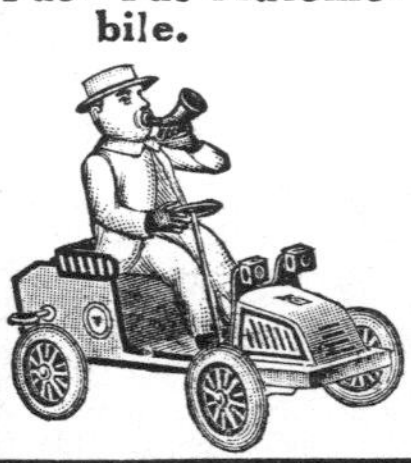

A most clever mechanical toy. Gives the familiar Tut-Tut when running along the floor. White enamel finish, red decorated, with imitation rubber tires. Size, 7x3½x6½ inches. Shipping weight, 10 ounces.
No. 49G415 Price.... 47c

The Popular Autobus.

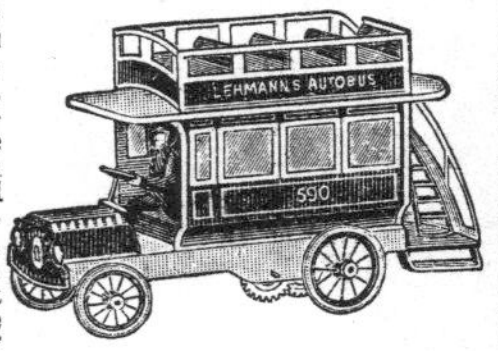

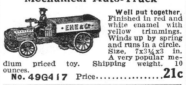

Made by the best German manufacturer. All sheet metal, attractively finished in white enamel, with yellow and brown decoration. Size, 8x3x5 inches. Platform at rear seats inside and on top of bus reached by spiral stairway. Strong spring motor. Winds with key. Driver in front. Shipping weight, 13 ounces.
No. 49G416 Price................ 38c

Mechanical Auto-Truck.

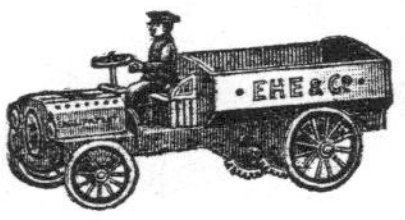

Well put together. Finished in red and white enamel with yellow trimmings. Winds up by spring and runs in a circle. Size, 7x3¼x3 in. A very popular medium priced toy. Shipping weight, 10 ounces.
No. 49G417 Price.................. 21c

Mechanical Alligator.

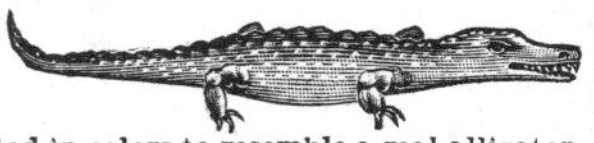

Made entirely of metal, with ridges, and painted in colors to resemble a real alligator. No wheels. Feet rest on floor, and it runs along in its natural manner, opening and closing its jaws and moving its tail. Length, 9¼ inches. Shipping weight, packed, 10 ounces.
No. 49G452 Price.................... 19c

VERY GOOD TOY SEWING MACHINES.

ALL THESE MACHINES ARE FURNISHED COMPLETE WITH NEEDLE AND THREAD.

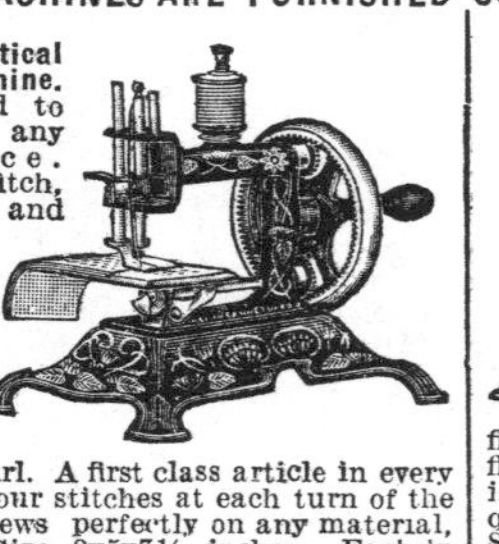

A small but practical Toy Sewing Machine. Can be attached to table, chair or any convenient place. Makes a good stitch, sews perfectly and runs smoothly. Fancy gilt decoration on black enamel, nickel plated wheel and trimmings. Uses regular sewing machine needles. A very nice toy for any girl. A first class article in every respect. Makes four stitches at each turn of the driving wheel. Sews perfectly on any material, thick or thin. Size, 8x5x7½ inches. Each in box. Shipping weight, 6 pounds.
No. 49G437 Price.............. $2.98

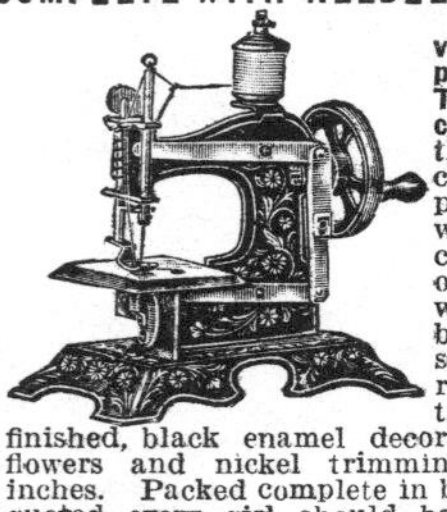

A medium priced very simple and perfectly working Toy Sewing Machine. Construction very simple, contains no complicated parts whatever and cannot get out of order. Can be worked easily even by a child. Sews seam very rapid, regular, neat and tight. Beautifully finished, black enamel decorated with colored flowers and nickel trimming. Size, 7½x4x7 inches. Packed complete in box. At the price quoted every girl should be able to have one. Shipping weight, 3 pounds.
No. 49G438 Price................ $1.47

Our Little Gem.

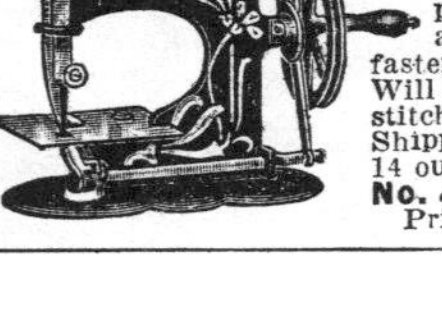

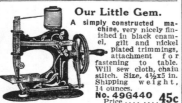

A simply constructed machine, very nicely finished in black enamel, gilt and nickel plated trimmings, attachment for fastening to table. Will sew cloth, chain stitch. Size, 4½x5 in. Shipping weight, 14 ounces.
No. 49G440 Price............ 45c

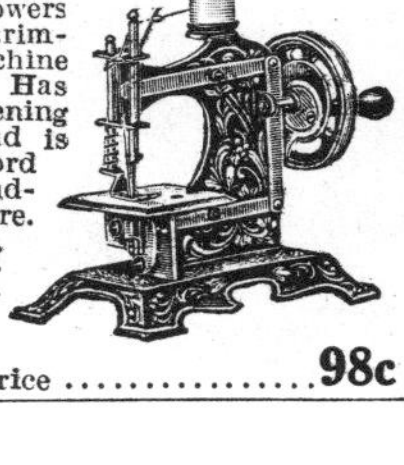

Very practical, beautifully trimmed in black enamel, colored decorated flowers and nickel plated trimmings and a little machine that sews perfectly. Has attachment for fastening on table or chair and is a toy that will afford any little girl an endless amount of pleasure. Size, 6x3¾x6½ inches. Each packed complete in box. Shipping weight, 2½ lbs.
No. 49G439 Price................. 98c

Squirrel in Cage.

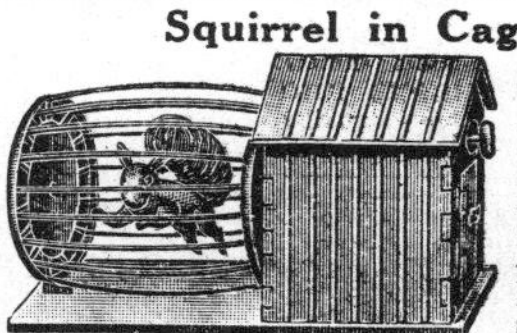

One of our very best children's toys. Runs for about ten minutes. Made entirely of metal, painted to resemble squirrel house and has whirling wire cage, with covered mechanical squirrel with real bushy tail. Has movable legs and rests on a metal bar. While the cage revolves the squirrel moves body and legs, its feet striking the wires in a very natural manner. All mechanism protected in the squirrel house. Total length, 8½ inches; width, 3⅞ inches. Shipping wt., packed, 1½ lbs.
No. 49G458 Price.................. 73c

The Jolly Dancers.

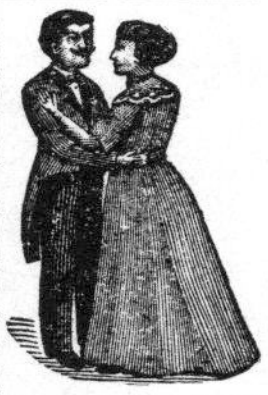

One of the most amusing toys ever invented. Figures of lady and gentleman, painted faces, cloth dressed, ball costume. Mechanism protected by metal case and invisible. When wound, the figures waltz over the floor, turning and waltzing in the most lifelike manner. Arms can be placed in any position. Length about 7 inches. Shipping weight, packed, 14 ounces.
No. 49G460 Price, 69c

The Fisherman.

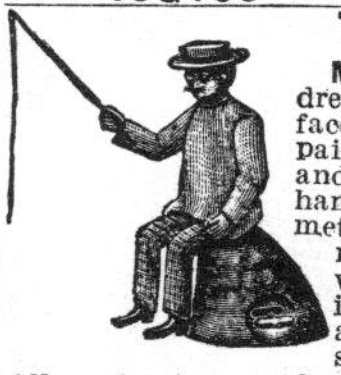

Made of metal, figure cloth dressed, metal hat, painted face. Fisherman sits on painted metal imitation log, and holds rod and line in hand, to which is attached metal fish. Imitates fisherman drawing fish through water and then "landing" it. Angler moves body and head from side to side and up and down. All mechanism inside the log. Length, 8 inches. Shipping weight, 1 pound.
No. 49G461 Price................. 47c

Moving Apple Man.

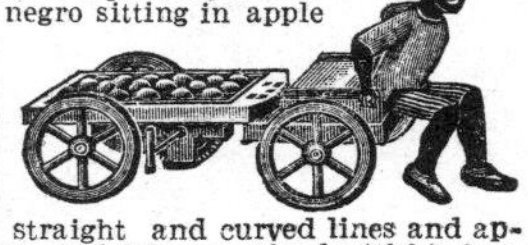

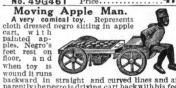

A very comical toy. Represents cloth dressed negro sitting in apple cart, with painted apples. Negro's feet rest on floor, and when toy is wound it runs backward in straight and curved lines and apparently the negro is driving cart back with his feet, as they beat on the floor. Made of metal in colors. Length, 7 inches. Shipping weight, 14 oz.
No. 49G462 Price................... 45c

Monkey on the Bar.

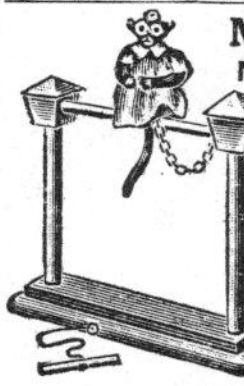

Metal stands and posts with performing bar and cloth dressed monkey tied to chain. No springs to wind. Pull string and monkey performs on bar, back and forth, moving body and arms. Very comical toy and very difficult to get out of order. Made of metal, painted in colors. Height, 9 inches; width, 6¼ inches. Shipping weight, 14 ounces.
No. 49G463 Price................... 45c

A Real Mechanical Steamboat.

$1.45

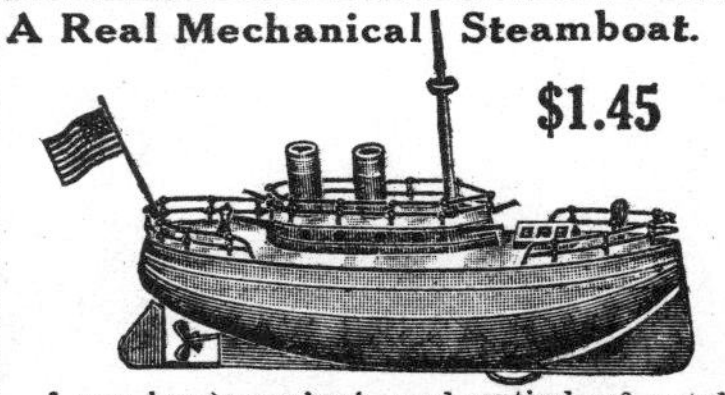

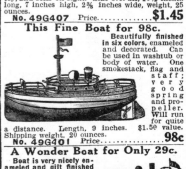

A very handsome boat, made entirely of metal to resemble a real steamboat. Heavily enameled and decorated in colors, all railings and imitation gun barrels in gilt. Two painted smokestacks, and flag. Floats in water, and when wound the mechanical propeller will run the boat for considerable distance in whatever direction rudder is placed. This is an exceptionally well made toy, and sells on sight. Size over all, 10½ inches long, 7 inches high, 2⅜ inches wide, weight, 25 ounces.
No. 49G407 Price.............. $1.45

This Fine Boat for 98c.

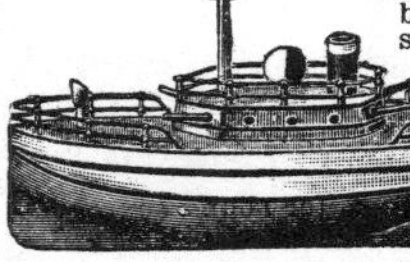

Beautifully finished in six colors, enameled and decorated. Can be used in washtub or body of water. One smokestack, flag and staff; very good spring and propeller. Will run for quite a distance. Length, 9 inches. $1.50 value. Shipping weight, 20 ounces.
No. 49G401 Price........... 98c

A Wonder Boat for Only 29c.

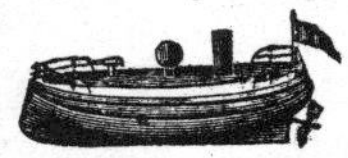

Boat is very nicely enameled and gilt finished throughout. The spring and propeller are well made, and boat is nicely constructed. Length, 6 inches. Shipping weight, 15 ounces.
No. 49G402 Price................ 29c

RELIABLE AUTOMOBILES AND BOATS

Bing's Auto Garage and Car.

Heavy cardboard garage with high grade beautifully finished mechanical automobile of finest quality. Runs straight or in circle. With driver. Size garage, 6x4x4 inches.

Price..**21c**

Mechanical Auto-Truck, 19c.

Finished in red and white enamel with yellow trimmings. Winds up by spring and runs in a circle. Size, 6¾x3½x3 inches.

Price **19c**

Hess Friction Auto.

Runs with good speed. Naturally shaped and strongly made. By rubbing on floor will run. No spring to break. Nicely painted. Strongly made. Size, 5½x3 inches.

Price **19c**

Bing's Touring Car.

An exceptionally well made, nicely decorated, lifelike chauffeur figure. Strong superforce clockwork. Starting and stopping device. Adjustable steering gear. Size, 8 inches.

Price. **23c**

Hess-Mobile.

Has crank attachment, which starts machine. By adjusting lever can be made to go forward or stop at will. Size, 8x3x3½ in. Shipping wt., 1 lb.

Price.**37c**

Auto Garage With Two Automobiles.

Heavy cardboard garage with double doors, one touring and one racing car with extra strong clockwork. Run straight or in circle. Size, each, 5½x3½x3¼ in.

Price....**39c**

Motor Car.

Very strong superforce clockwork. Beautifully enameled in bright colors. Doors that open. With driver. Flexible front wheels. Car runs straight or in circle. Size, 7x4½x3½ inches.

Price........**47c**

Real Cranking Touring Car.

Merely turn the crank and the car starts. Has starting and stopping device. Nicely decorated in bright colors. No springs to get out of order. Runs straight only. Very substantially made. Size, 9x3¾x3 inches.

Price....**39c**

Hess Friction Auto, 57c.

Cranks like real car. Racer type with driver. Nicely painted. Has starting and stopping device. No spring to break. Size, 9x4½ inches.

.**57c**

Touring Car.

Strong superforce clockwork. Sheet metal, beautifully finished in bright colors. Runs straight or in circle. Brake on rear wheel. Size, 8x4½x 3½ inches.

Price..........**67c**

Friction Delivery Wagon.

No springs to get out of order. One or two cranks of starter and car runs across the room. Starting and stopping device. Size, 10½x6x 3¼ in.

Price.....**89c**

Very Fine Touring Car.

Strong spring, metal tires, steering gear, brake. Can run straight or in circle. Beautifully finished in bright colors. Size, 10x5¾x4½ inches.

Price.........**98c**

Bing's Auto Garage.

Stiff cardboard. Contains runabout, 6½ inches long; touring car 7 inches long. Garage, 9x7x5½ in.

Price..........**89c**

Touring Car.

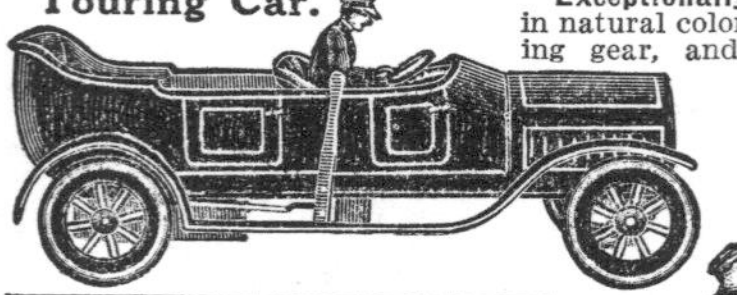

Exceptionally well made. Enameled in natural colors. Has adjustable steering gear, and starting and stopping device. Lifelike chauffeur. Size, about 12 in. Shipping wt., 2 lbs.

Price..........**87c**

Friction Touring Car With Chauffeur.

Cranks like a real car, deriving thereby great power from friction motor contained therein. Touring car type with driver. Nicely painted. Has starting and stopping device. No spring to break. Size, 10x5 inches.

Price.....**89c**

Real Cranking Friction Auto.

Merely crank the car and watch it go. Glass windows, movable doors. Handsomely decorated. Chauffeur. Starting and stopping device. Size 10½x6x3¼ inches.

Price...**$1.37**

Touring Car With Wind Shield.

Nicely enameled in colors. Two lamps, strong clockwork, starting and stopping device. Biggest value ever offered for the money. Length, 12½ inches.

Price..........**$1.67**

Auto Coal Car.

Exceptionally well made, very realistic. Two lamps and chauffeur. Starting and stopping device, rubber tires. Strong superforce spring. Size, 11x4¾x3⅛ inches. Shipping

Price...........**$2.67**

Auto Dump Cart.

Good imitation of the real article. Handsomely painted and decorated. Canvas canopy. Chauffeur. Dumping device. By turning brake load can be dumped off wagon. Two lamps, rubber tired wheels. Length, 11½ inches. Shipping wt., 2 lbs.

Price..........**$2.89**

Touring Car.

Enameled in dark blue, red and gilt trimmings. Four lights. Reversing gear, movable doors. Rubber tires. Good spring. Can be made to run straight or in a circle. Size 12½x6 inches.

Price..........**$4.65**

Length, 16½ inches.

Torpedo Boat, $2.47.

Strong superforce clockwork. Very fast. Made of extra heavy metal, painted in gray and black. Has four smokestacks, flag mast with lookout basket, removable turrets and cannon. Finish of boat and quality of springs the finest.

Price..........**$2.47**

Bing's Famous Model of Battleship

Made of metal painted the famous fighting gray. Equipped with extraordinary strong superforce clockwork. Regulated to run very long time. Has two masts, each having armored lookout baskets. Eight revolving gun towers with cannon. Large size screw, two anchors with chains and all details pertaining to a warship. Will propel itself through the water at good speed. Strong and well made. Will last for years. Length, 18 inches. Shipping wt., 4 lbs.

$4.87

Toy Steamboat.

An exceptionally well made boat. Nicely decorated in colors. Good imitation of an ocean steamer. Has extra strong superforce clockwork spring, not easily broken. Four smoke stacks, adjustable rudder, two flag poles. Length of boat 13 inches. Shipping wt., 2¾ pounds.

Price..........**$2.35**

Bing's Toy Torpedo Boat.

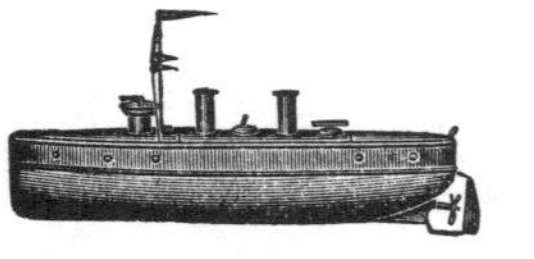

Exceptionally well made, all metal. Has extra strong superforce clockwork spring. Painted in natural colors.

Price.....**98c**

War Boat.

All metal. Nicely decorated in gray. Two guns, three smokestacks. Strong spring, movable rudder. Good value. Size, 10x 6½ inches. Shipping weight, 1½

$1.35

Bing's Famous Model of U. S. Gunboat, $1.47.

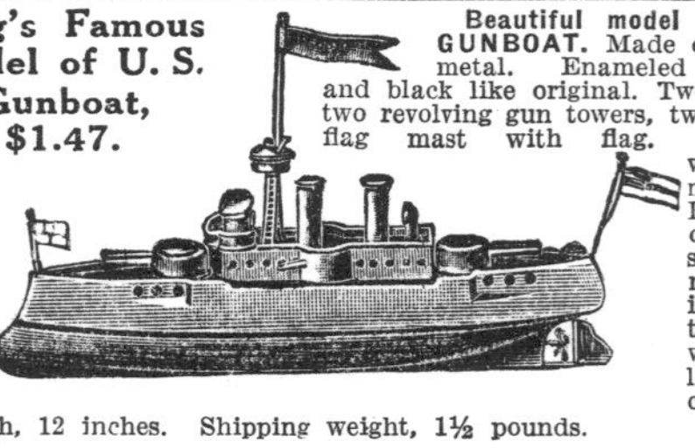

Length, 12 inches. Shipping weight, 1½ pounds.

Beautiful model of U. S. GUNBOAT. Made entirely of metal. Enameled in gray and black like original. Two funnels, two revolving gun towers, two cannon, flag mast with flag. Equipped with famous Bing's clockwork spring mechanism. A toy that will delight any child.

$1.47

Toy Steamboat.

An exceptionally well made boat. Nicely decorated. Has four smokestacks, mast and flags. Adjustable steering gear, and superforce clockwork, which propels boat through water very fast. Length of boat, 10 inches.

Price..........**98c**

Strong superforce clockwork, adjustable steering gear, two smokestacks and one mast. Will travel very fast through the water. Length, 7½ in.

49c

Fire Boat.

Good imitation. All metal with strong clockwork spring. Nicely decorated. When wound boat propels self through water, throwing stream of water through hose. Size, 7¾ inches.

98c

Gunboat.

All metal. High grade clockwork spring. Three smokestacks. Imitation guns. Decorated in gray. Size, 8½ inches long. Shipping wt. 1 pound.

89c

Gunboat.

Painted gray. Two guns, two smokestacks. Strong superforce clockwork. Size, 7½ inches long. Shipping wt., 10 ounces.

47c

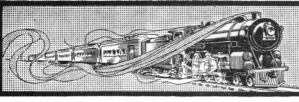

BING'S MECHANICAL TOY RAILWAY TRAINS

Our Finest Passenger Train.

Absolutely the best we have to offer. A very large train, fully 46 inches long. Has 12-inch, large, high grade cast iron engine, very heavily made, solid and substantial, nicely enameled in black with nickel plated trimmings. Front truck of engine is movable, assisting in rounding curves. Has outside movable piston rods, bell and starting and stopping device, one tender and two unusually large modern type Pullman and baggage coaches with double trucks. Included with each train is 14 feet of track, large 2-inch gauge, including stop rail which stops or reverses train at will after engine passes over the section. Very strong spring clockwork, winds with key. Shipping weight, carefully packed, 16 pounds.
Price..........................**$11.95**

This large passenger express train comes complete with track and stop rail. When train runs around track you may stop it within half its own length by simply pressing the lever on the stop rail section.

ALL TRAINS ON THIS PAGE FURNISHED WITH OVAL SECTIONAL TRACK

No. 49N5108 Price.........**$4.65**
This Fine Train, $4.65. Extraordinary superforce brass clockwork with speed regulator and brake. Includes tender with imitation coal and two Pullman and baggage cars, four wheels. 28-inch train and 12 feet of track, including stop rail.

Passenger train with heavy cast iron engine, strong superforce brass clockwork and starting and stopping device. Two four-wheel coaches. Train, 31 inches long, with 12-foot track in sections, including one stop rail. Shipping weight, 6 pounds.
No. 49N5106 Price.........**$2.89**

Has good grade cast iron locomotive with nickel plated piston rod, starting and stopping device. Good strong superforce clockwork spring. Engine is 7 inches long; has four wheels; 3½-inch tender; baggage car and passenger coach. Size of cars, 5½ inches long. Enameled in natural colors. Comes complete with 12 feet of track, with automatic stopping device. Shipping weight, 5 pounds.
No. 49N5116 Price.........**$2.89**

Large 9-inch cast iron engine enameled in black, with nickel plated trimmings. Has large tender filled with imitation coal, movable front truck and outside moving piston rods and starting and stopping device. Three large coaches with eight-wheel trucks, nicely japanned and colored after the genuine Pullman and baggage car models. Train measures 42 inches long and is packed complete with 14 feet of track, including stop rail section. Very strong spring clockwork. Train runs a long while. Size of box, 17x17 inches. Shipping weight, 10 pounds.
No. 49N5110 Price.....................**$8.65**

Our Medium Priced Train.

Has large 8½-inch cast iron locomotive with eight steel rim wheels. Has movable truck cowcatcher, nickel plated piston rods, starting and stopping device as well as reversing. This locomotive has specially strong superforce clockwork spring and speed governor. A very realistic and good imitation of a modern engine. Size, 9 inches long. Has six-wheel tender, 4½ inches long. Comes complete with very realistic vestibule passenger car and one combination passenger and baggage car, each 8 inches long with eight wheels and movable trucks. Comes complete with 12 feet of track with automatic stop whereby engine can be stopped by throwing switch which automatically sets the device on the locomotive. Comes packed in handsome box, size 16½x17 inches. Shipping weight, 8 pounds.
No. 49N5118 Price.....................**$7.95**

Large cast iron locomotive, nickel plated piston rod. Has both starting and stopping device, exceptionally strong superforce clockwork spring. Steel rim wheels. Size of engine, 7½ inches long by 3½ inches high. Size of tender, 4 inches long. Comes complete with one baggage car and two Pullman vestibule cars, 6½ inches long. Each passenger car has eight wheels and movable trucks. Has 12 feet of track, with automatic stop whereby engine can be stopped by throwing the switch which automatically sets a device on the locomotive. One of the best values ever offered. Comes packed in a box, size 14½x16 inches. Shipping weight, 7 pounds.
No. 49N5117 Price...................**$5.45**

Freight Train. Cast iron engine with unusually strong brass clockwork, starting and stopping device, outside piston rods and brake, tender and three long double truck freight cars. 34 inches long; has 14 feet of track, including stop rail. Box, 15x16½ inches. Shipping weight, 7 pounds.
No. 49N5109 Price...................**$5.67**

Four-Car Freight Train. Superforce brass clockwork in engine. Starting and stopping device and brake, one tender and three nicely enameled freight cars and caboose. 38-inch train with 12 feet of track, including stop rail. Shpg. wt., 9 lbs.
No. 49N5107 Price...........**$3.27**

Freight Train. Cast iron engine with superforce brass clockwork, starting and stopping device and brake. Includes one tender and three freight cars. 31-inch train with 12 feet of track, including stop rail. $3.50 value. Shpg. wt., 6 lbs.
No. 49N5104 Price...........**$2.95**

Examine This 47-Cent Value.

All Metal Train, consisting of engine with extra strong superforce clockwork, starting and stopping device and brake, one tender and two finely japanned Pullman cars. Train measures 21½ inches long and comes with 5 feet of track to form circle. **47c**

This Fine Train For Only $1.38.

All Metal Train, consisting of engine with extra strong clockwork, speed governor and brake, one tender and three Pullman cars. Train 28 inches long and comes with 10 feet of track, including stop rail. Shipping weight, 3½ pounds. **$1.38**

A Wonder Value at 95 Cents.

All Metal Train, has cast iron nicely finished engine with extra strong clockwork, speed governor and brake, one tender and two finely japanned Pullman cars. Train 26 inches long and comes with 8 feet of track, including a stop rail. Shipping weight, 3½ pounds. **95c**

STEAM AND HOT AIR ENGINES THAT RUN

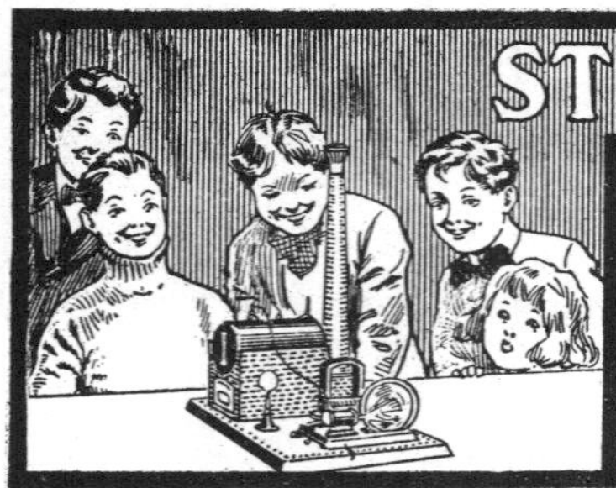

The Best Medium Priced Engines You Can Buy.

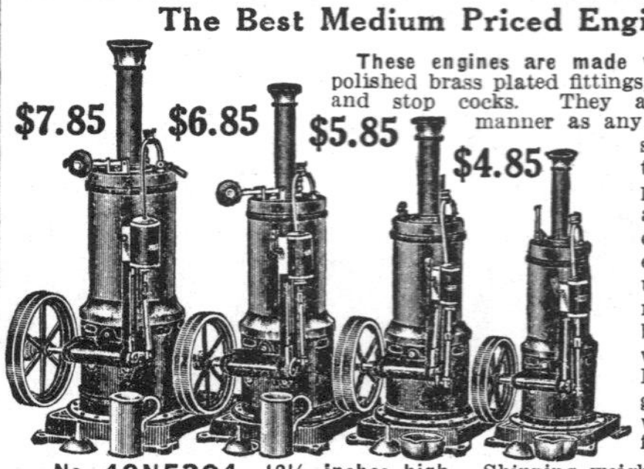

$7.85 $6.85 $5.85 $4.85

These engines are made with seamless brass boilers, beautifully polished brass plated fittings, with ebony stained steam valve handles and stop cocks. They are constructed in exactly the same manner as any large steam engine built, with tubular slide valves, jointed crank shaft and tight fitting bearings. It is almost impossible to give you any idea of the accuracy with which the parts for these engines are cut. You must see the engines to understand them. Alcohol is used for fuel—the engine beginning to run a few minutes after heat is applied beneath the boiler. Prices include small vapor lamp and complete equipment. Base and chimney are of metal. Regular glass water gauge on boiler. You will never regret buying any one of the following sizes:

No. 49N5304	12¼ inches high.	Shipping weight, 4¾ pounds.	Price..........$4.85
No. 49N5305	13½ inches high.	Shipping weight, 5 pounds.	Price............ 5.85
No. 49N5306	14¾ inches high.	Shipping weight, 6 pounds.	Price............ 6.85
No. 49N5307	16½ inches high.	Shipping weight, 8 pounds.	Price............ 7.85

Horizontal Stationary Steam Engines.

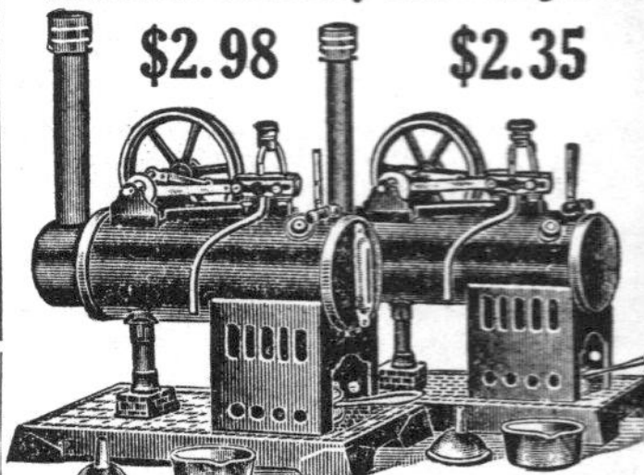

$2.98 $2.35

Blue oxidized brass boiler, double actic valve engine, large wheel, chimney, beautiful polished nickel plated trimmings. **Made i two sizes.**

No.	Height	Length	Shpg. Wt.	Pric
49N5329	8½ in.	7½ in.	2¼ lbs.	$2.3
49N5328	9½ in.	8¼ in.	2¾ lbs.	2.9

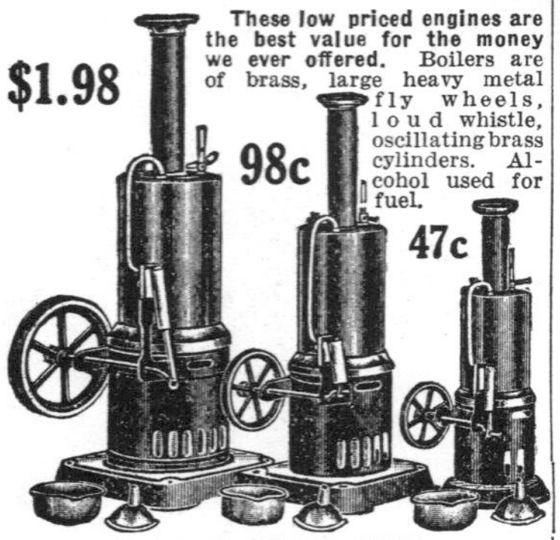

$1.98 98c 47c

These low priced engines are the best value for the money we ever offered. Boilers are of brass, large heavy metal fly wheels, loud whistle, oscillating brass cylinders. Alcohol used for fuel.

MADE IN THREE SIZES.

No.	Height	Shipping Wt.	Price
49N5300	8 in.	1¼ lbs.	$0.47
49N5301	10½ in.	1½ lbs.	.98
49N5302	12½ in.	2½ lbs.	1.98

Two Very Powerful Toy Steam Engines.

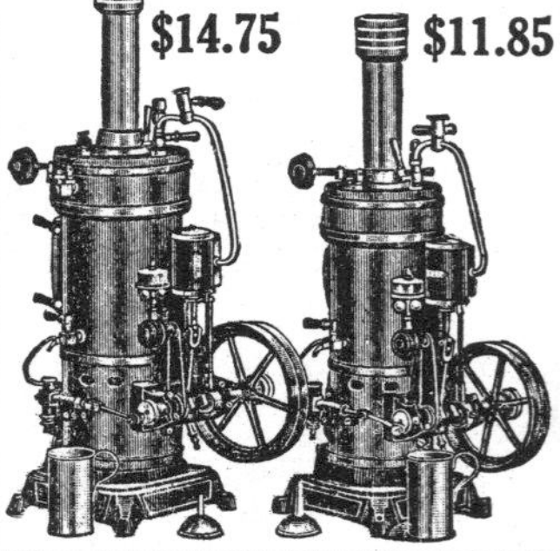

$14.75 $11.85

These vertical model steam engines are the most powerful toys we have ever offered. They run noiselessly and steadily and use very little alcohol as fuel. Boilers are seamless brass, oxidized, with nickel plated bands and fittings. The pistons are cut as neatly and perfectly as on a large automobile engine. The bearings are smooth and tight. Belt that runs the governor is of a patent spring construction. The fly wheel may be used for running small attachments, see page 939. Engine is equipped with shrill whistle, governor, water gauge, safety valve, automatic air pump for boiler, small alcohol lamp and complete equipment ready to run. We import these engines from Germany and know there is nothing better on the market. The engine is quality through and through. While sold as a toy, it will be very instructive to older boys and men. It is built and runs on the same principle as a large engine. Made in two sizes.

No. 49N5309¼ 17 inches high. Shipping weight, 8 pounds. Price..............................$14.75

No. 49N5308¼ 15 inches high. Shipping weight, 6 pounds. Price..............................$11.85

This big engine and boiler looks and runs just like any big engine. One of our finest values.

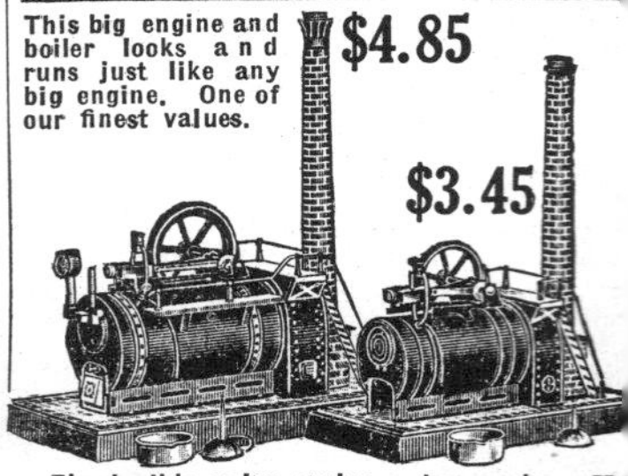

$4.85 $3.45

Fixed slide valve engine. Large size. Ha whistle and gauges. Both have imitation bric chimney and alcohol vapor stove for makin steam. **Made in two sizes.**

No.	Height	Length	Shpg. Wt.	Pric
49N5331	12½ in.	10½ in.	3¼ lbs.	$3.4
49N5330	13¾ in.	13 in.	4½ lbs.	4.8

Our Big $2.89 Value.

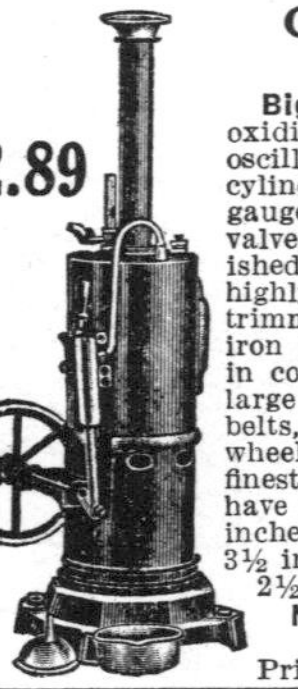

$2.89

Big seamless brass boiler, oxidized blue finish, finest oscillating nickel plated cylinders, steam whistle, gauges, bearings, safety valve, etc. All parts finished in best style, with highly polished nickel plated trimmings. Mounted on cast iron base, neatly japanned in colors. Engine has extra large fly wheel grooved for belts, and has small pulley wheel at side. One of the finest imported engines we have ever sold. Height, 12½ inches; length of boiler, 3½ inches. Shipping weight, 2½ pounds.

No. 49N5303
Price..........$2.89

This Is Our Best Offer.

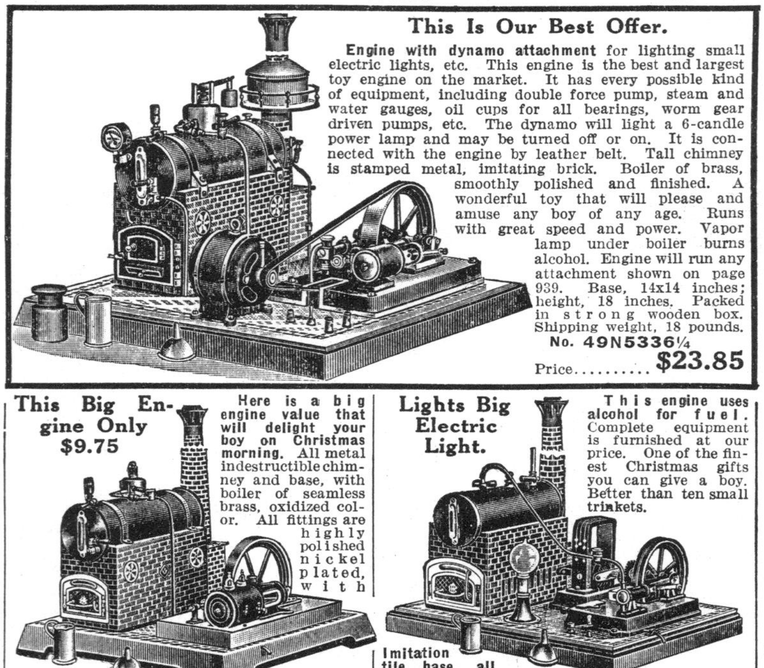

Engine with dynamo attachment for lighting small electric lights, etc. This engine is the best and largest toy engine on the market. It has every possible kind of equipment, including double force pump, steam and water gauges, oil cups for all bearings, worm gear driven pumps, etc. The dynamo will light a 6-candle power lamp and may be turned off or on. It is connected with the engine by leather belt. Tall chimney is stamped metal, imitating brick. Boiler of brass, smoothly polished and finished. A wonderful toy that will please and amuse any boy of any age. Runs with great speed and power. Vapor lamp under boiler burns alcohol. Engine will run any attachment shown on page 939. Base, 14x14 inches; height, 18 inches. Packed in strong wooden box. Shipping weight, 18 pounds.

No. 49N5336¼
Price..........$23.85

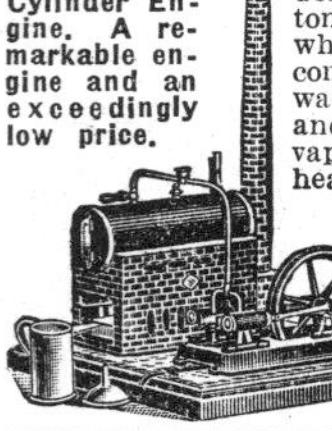

Big Twin Cylinder Engine. A remarkable engine and an exceedingly low price.

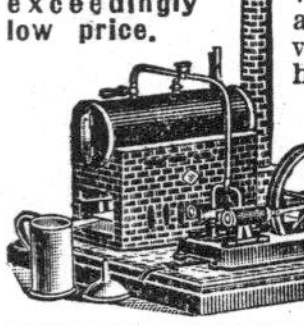

Two sliding valve cylin ders, with tight fitting pis tons, large nickel plated f wheel, and double actic connecting rods. Fitted wi water gauge, safety valv and shrill whistle. Alcoh vapor lamp furnishes stead heat and engine ha great power an speed. Imitatio tile base, 9½x1 inches. Height chimney, 14 i Shpg. wt., 6 lb

No. 49N533
Price $6.6

Horizontal Steam Engine.

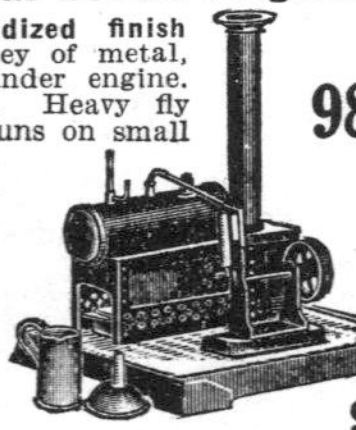

98c

Big brass oxidized finish boiler, tall chimney of metal, with upright cylinder engine. Nicely enameled. Heavy fly wheel. Engine runs on small amount of alcohol as fuel in vapor lamp. Loud whistle. Big value. Height, 7½ inches; base, 6½x6½ inches. Shipping weight, 1¾ pounds.

No. 49N5325
Price..............................98c

Big Steam Roller.

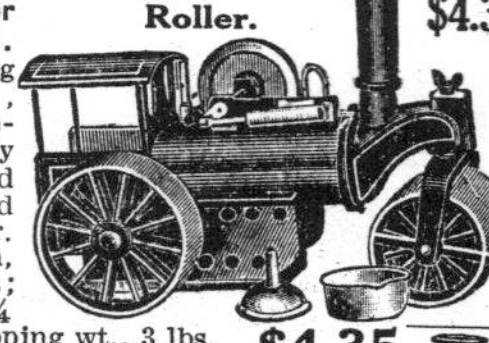

$4.3

Runs either forward or backward. Has big boiler, whistle, reverse safety valve and oxidized brass roller. Total length, 9½ inches; height, 6¼ inches. Shipping wt., 3 lbs.

No. 49N5350 Price..$4.35

This Big Engine Only $9.75

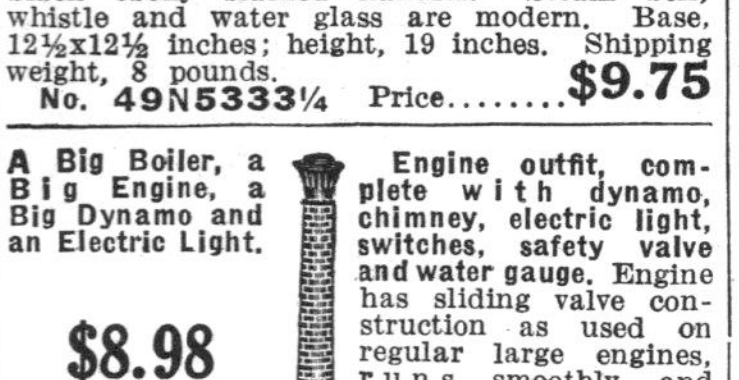

Here is a big engine value that will delight your boy on Christmas morning. All metal indestructible chimney and base, with boiler of seamless brass, oxidized color. All fittings are highly polished nickel plated, with black ebony stained handles. Steam bell, whistle and water glass are modern. Base, 12½x12½ inches; height, 19 inches. Shipping weight, 8 pounds.

No. 49N5333¼ Price........$9.75

Lights Big Electric Light.

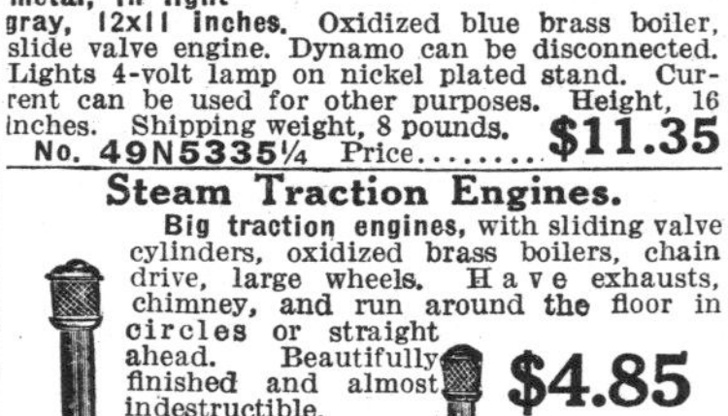

This engine uses alcohol for fuel. Complete equipment is furnished at our price. One of the finest Christmas gifts you can give a boy. Better than ten small trinkets.

Imitation tile base, all metal, in light gray, 12x11 inches. Oxidized blue brass boiler, slide valve engine. Dynamo can be disconnected. Lights 4-volt lamp on nickel plated stand. Current can be used for other purposes. Height, 16 inches. Shipping weight, 8 pounds.

No. 49N5335¼ Price........$11.35

Twin Cylinder Hot Air Engine.

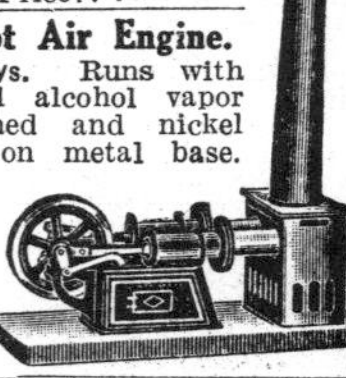

Best for small boys. Runs with hot air, using small alcohol vapor lamp. Nicely finished and nickel trimmed. Mounted on metal base. Tall chimney. Air cooled. Height, 13 inches; size of base, 5x10 inches. Shipping wt., 4½ lbs.

No. 49N5377
Price........$4.35

This Big Steam Engine will delight any boy as a Christmas gift.

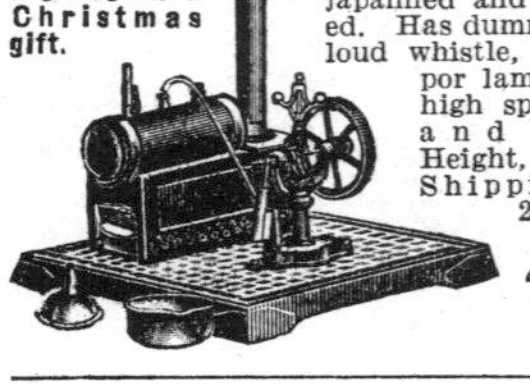

A big metal base, 7 inches square, with large engine and boiler. Engine is all metal, heavily japanned and nickel plated. Has dummy governor, loud whistle, alcohol vapor lamp. Runs at high speed, quietly and powerfully. Height, 8 inches. Shipping weight, 2¼ pounds.

No. 49N5326
Price, $1.45

One-Cylinder Engine.

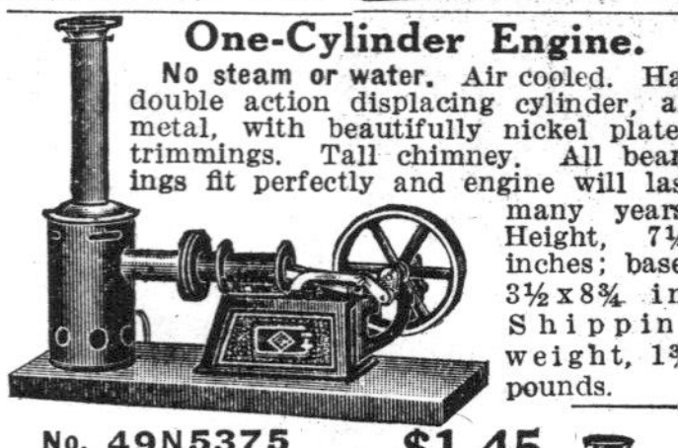

No steam or water. Air cooled. Ha double action displacing cylinder, a metal, with beautifully nickel plate trimmings. Tall chimney. All bear ings fit perfectly and engine will las many years. Height, 7½ inches; base 3½x8¾ in Shipping weight, 1½ pounds.

No. 49N5375
Price..........$1.45

Reversible Engine.

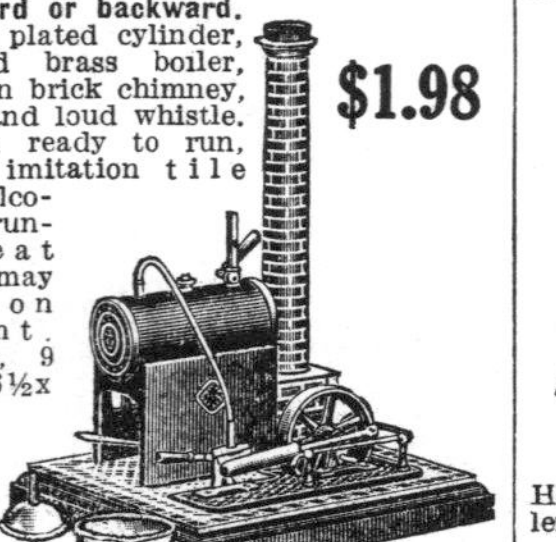

$1.98

Runs forward or backward. Single nickel plated cylinder, blue oxidized brass boiler, large imitation brick chimney, safety valve and loud whistle. All complete, ready to run, mounted on imitation tile base. Uses alcohol for fuel, running at great speed, and may be reversed on the instant. Height, 9 inches; base, 6½x 6½ inches.

A Big Boiler, a Big Engine, a Big Dynamo and an Electric Light.

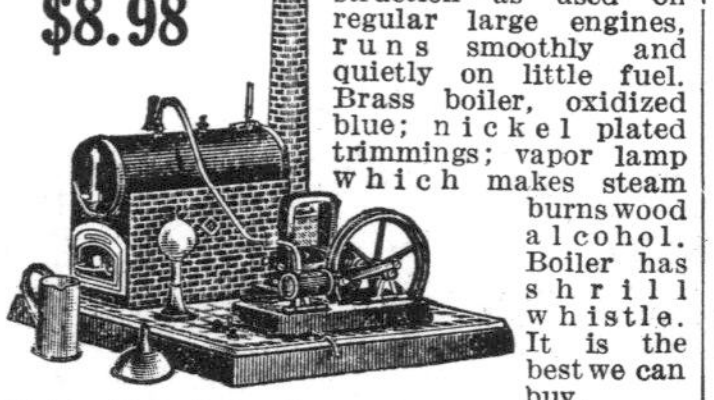

$8.98

Engine outfit, complete with dynamo, chimney, electric light, switches, safety valve and water gauge. Engine has sliding valve construction as used on regular large engines, runs smoothly and quietly on little fuel. Brass boiler, oxidized blue; nickel plated trimmings; vapor lamp which makes steam burns wood alcohol. Boiler has shrill whistle. It is the best we can buy.

Height, 14 inches; size of base, 9½x11 inches; length of boiler, 6 inches.

Steam Traction Engines.

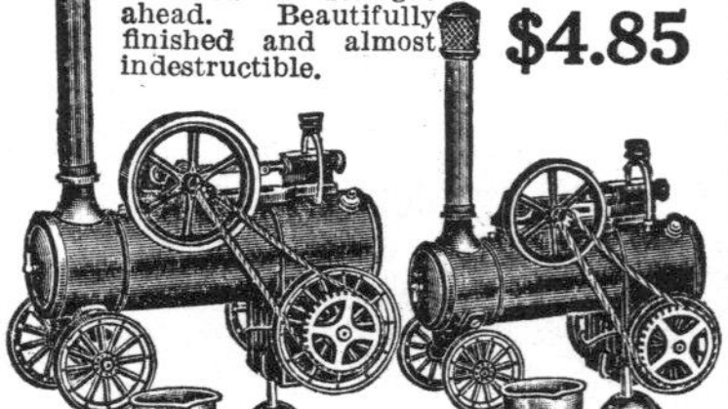

$4.85

Big traction engines, with sliding valve cylinders, oxidized brass boilers, chain drive, large wheels. Have exhausts, chimney, and run around the floor in circles or straight ahead. Beautifully finished and almost indestructible.

Height	Length	Shpg. Wt.
10 in.	7 in.	3 lbs.

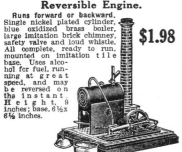

A Speedy Running Engine

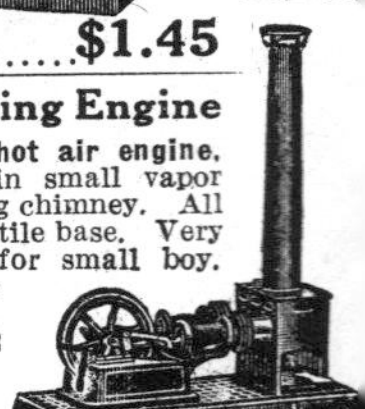

Big twin cylinder hot air engine, burns wood alcohol in small vapor stove. All metal. Big chimney. All complete on imitation tile base. Very highest grade. Fine for small boy. Height, 10 inches; base, 3½x9 inches. Shipping weight, 2 pounds.

STEAM ENGINE ATTACHMENTS

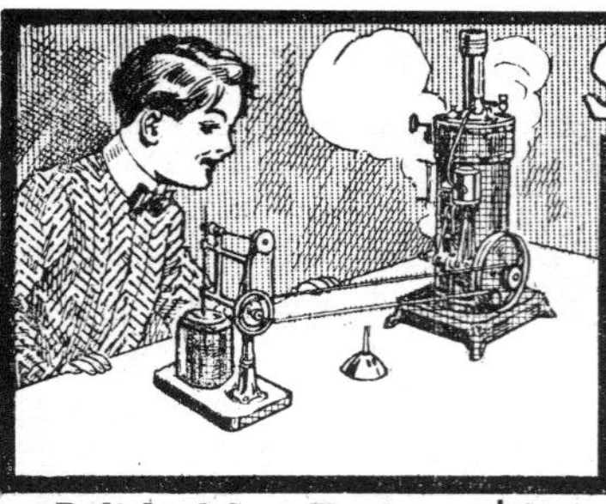

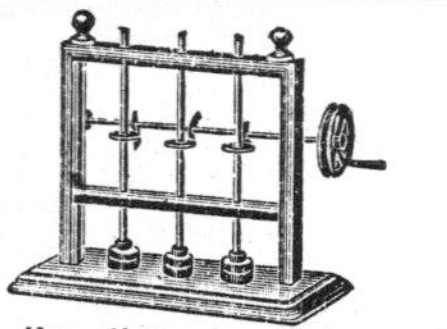

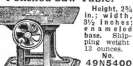

Has three heavy hammers which raise, one at a time, dropping with great force. Well made, lots of action. Will please every boy who has a steam engine. Height, 4¾ inches; width, 5¼ in. Shipping wt., 12 oz.
No. 49N5403 Price......39c

Water Wheel.

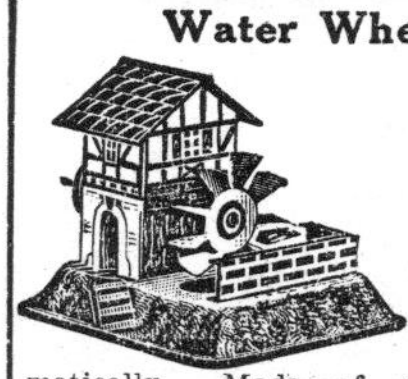

Boys' favorite attachment. Big mill, with wheel which illustrates principle of water wheel. Trip hammer on side pounds automatically. Made of metal nicely enameled in bright colors. Height, 4 inches. Shipping wt., 12 oz.
No. 49N5402 Price.... 25c

Large Metal Pile Driver.

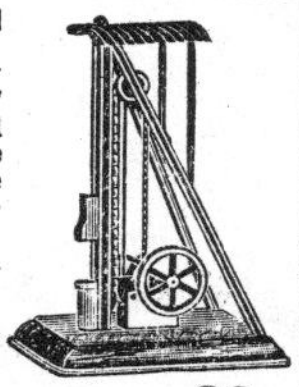

Can be attached to any engine. Raises heavy weight to top of standard and drops it just like the big pile drivers. Made entirely of metal, nicely enameled and japanned in assorted colors. Height, 10 inches. Shipping weight, 1½ pounds.
No. 49N5410 Price....98c

Blacksmiths at Anvil.

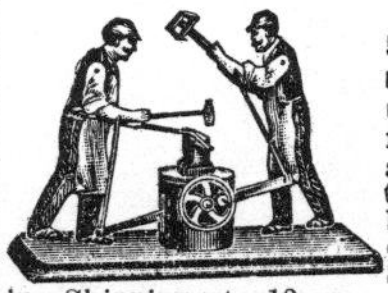

Two large 5-inch metal figures. Each man hits anvil in turn. Runs by hand or power. Size, 8x6 in. Shipping wt., 12 oz.
No. 49N5412 Price....57c

Polished Saw Table.

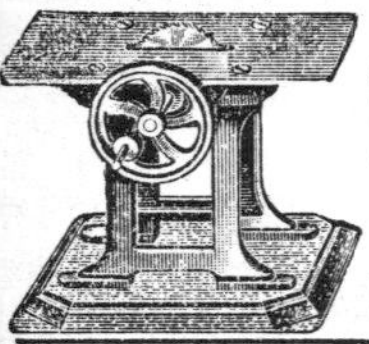

Height, 2¾ in.; width, 3½ inches; enameled base. Shipping weight 13 ounces.
No. 49N5400
Price. 25c

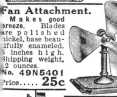

Fan Attachment.

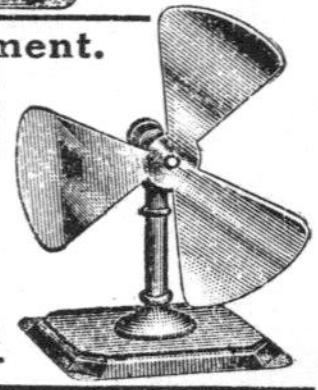

Makes good breeze. Blades are polished nickel, base beautifully enameled. 5 inches high. Shipping weight, 12 ounces.
No. 49N5401
Price..... 25c

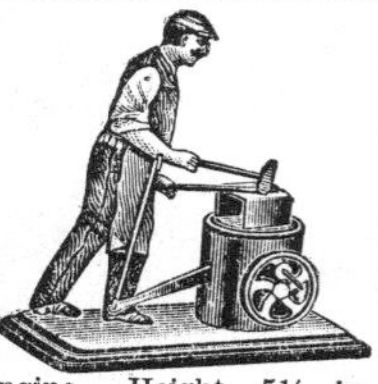

Metal blacksmith, naturally colored, who pounds rapidly on piece of what appears to be red hot iron. All parts are of metal and should last long time. Connects to any steam engine. Height, 5¼ in. Shipping weight, 12 oz.
No. 49N5404 Price......39c

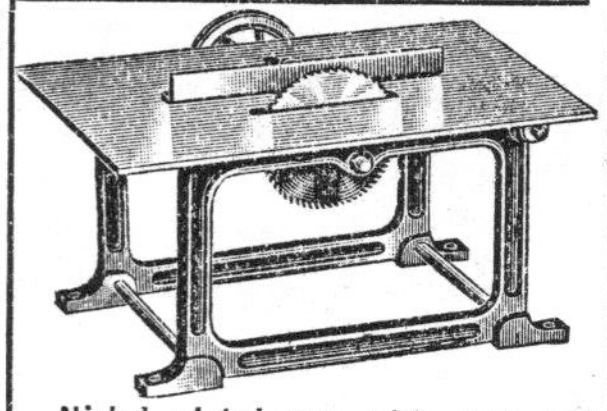

Nickel plated saw with gray cast iron base. Steel circular saw, movable saw gauge, all of metal. Table top tilts up. Height, 4¼ inches; width, 4⅜ inches; length, 6½ inches. Shipping weight, 2 pounds.
No. 49N5414 Price.. $1.45

Man at Pile Driver.

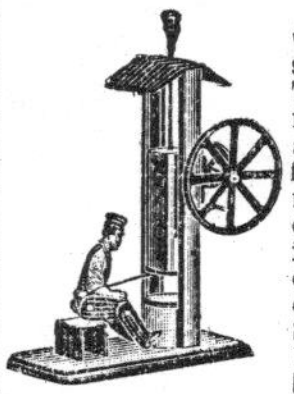

Runs by power when attached to steam engine. Trip hammer raises and falls and man leans forward and back, running machinery. Height, 8½ inches. Nicely enameled and colored. All metal. Shipping weight, 1 pound.
No. 49N5409
Price.......................79c

Emery Stone.

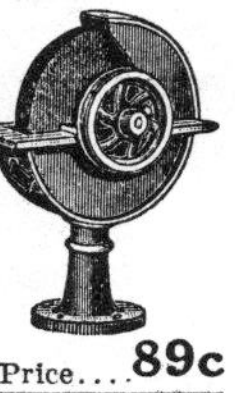

Made with cast metal base, nicely enameled in gray and red. Has genuine carborundum stone, fine bearings. One of our best attachments. Height, 5 inches. Shipping wt., 1¼ lbs.
No. 49N5413 Price....89c

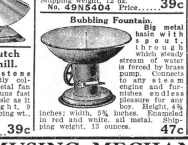

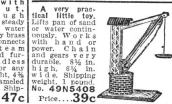

Old Dutch Windmill.

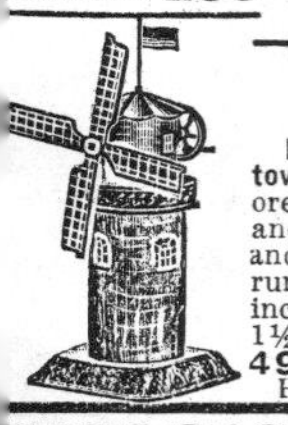

Imitation stone tower, brightly colored, with metal fan and base. Runs fast and plays music as it runs. Height, 9 inches. Shipping wt., 1½ pounds.
49N5406
Price........39c

Bubbling Fountain.

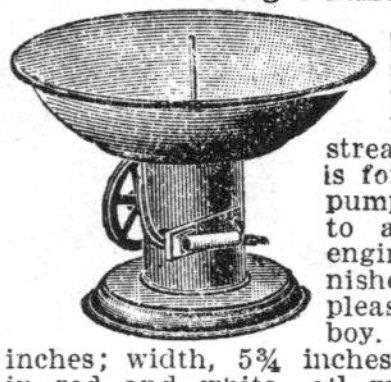

Big metal basin with spout, through which steady stream of water is forced by brass pump. Connects to any steam engine and furnishes endless pleasure for any boy. Height, 4⅜ inches; width, 5¾ inches. Enameled in red and white. all metal. Shipping weight, 13 ounces.
47c

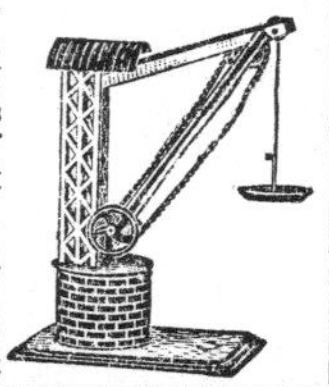

A very practical little toy. Lifts pan of sand or water continuously. Works with hand or power. Chain and gears very durable. 8½ in. high, 6¼ in. wide. Shipping weight, 1 pound.
No. 49N5408
Price....39c

A Real Butter Churn.

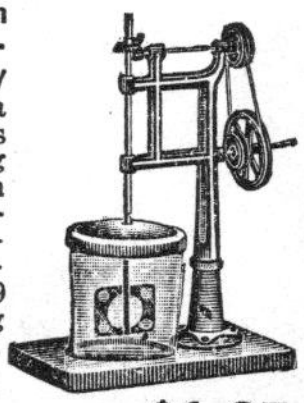

Runs at high speed when attached to any engine. Has a large size glass and churning knife. Will churn cream into butter. Shown attached in illustration. Height, 9 inches. Shipping weight, 1¾ lbs.
No. 49N5411
Price.................$1.27

Sand or Water Dredge.

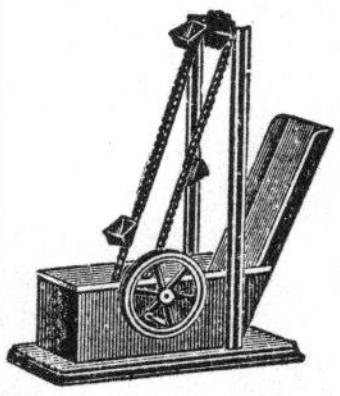

Bright red and yellow enameled. Turns by hand or power. Container watertight. Size, 6¼x8 inches. Shipping wt. 1 lb. 3 oz.
No. 49N5407
Price. 39c

These attachments can be used with any engine shown on opposite page.

BING'S AMUSING MECHANICAL TOYS AND WALKING ANIMALS

One of Bing's Best Toys.

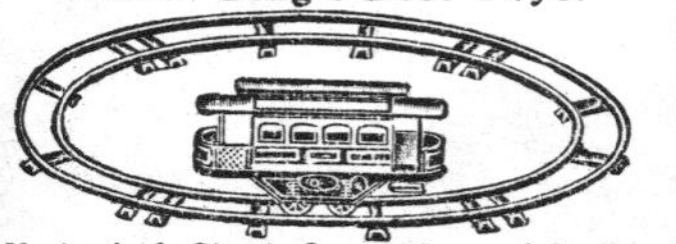

Mechanical Street Car with special strong clockwork and brake. Car, 6½ inches long and 3¼ inches high, with 5 feet of track. Great value at the price. Shipping weight, ¼ pounds.
43c

Our Special Value, 43c.

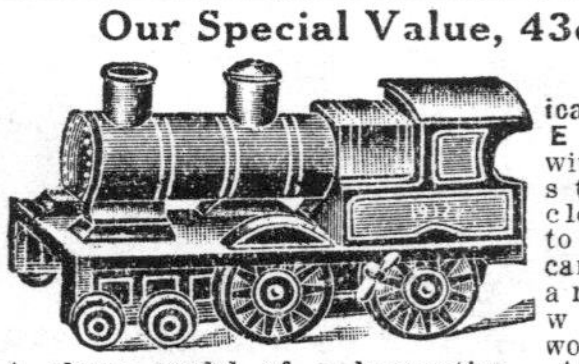

Mechanical Floor Engine with extra strong clockwork, to run on carpet or any floor when wound up. A clever model of a locomotive. All metal with eight wheels. Beautifully japanned and decorated. Size, 8x3½ inches. Shipping wt., 12 ounces.
No. 49N5380 Price............43c

Our Latest Novelty, 89c

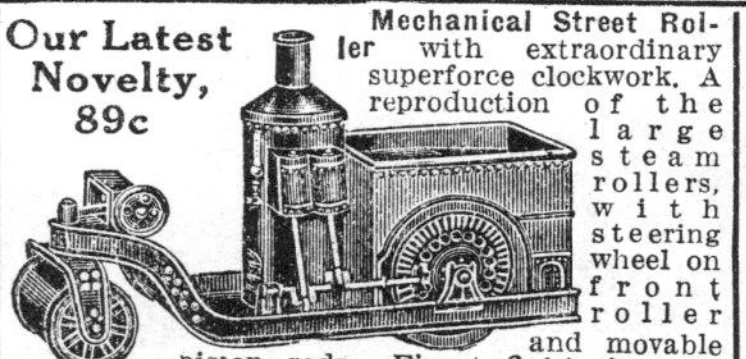

Mechanical Street Roller with extraordinary superforce clockwork. A reproduction of the large steam rollers, with steering wheel on front roller and movable piston rods. Finest finish in steel gray. Measures 8x5½x3 inches. Shipping weight, 1½ pounds.
No. 49N5763 Price.................89c

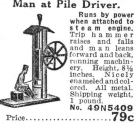

"Pay as You Enter" Car.

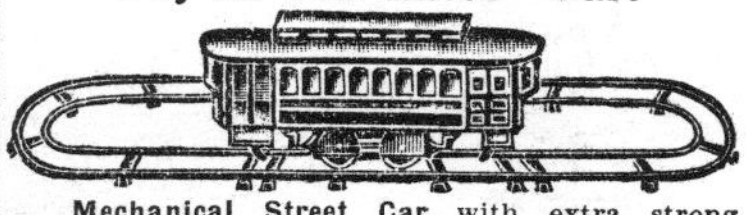

Mechanical Street Car with extra strong clockwork and brake. A copy of the modern "Pay as you enter" car. Size of car, 8 inches long and 3¼ inches high, with 8 feet of track. Shipping wt., 2¾ lbs.
No. 49N5101 Price............89c

Very Enjoyable Outdoor Toy.

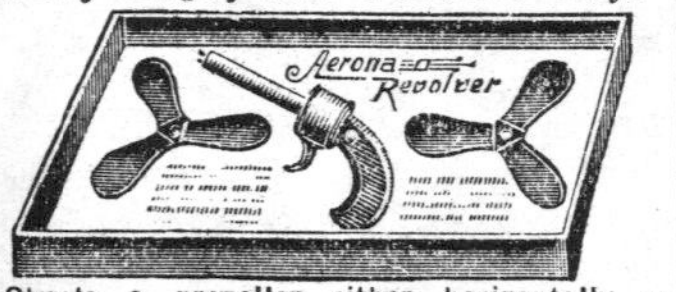

Shoots a propeller either horizontally or vertically. Two celluloid propellers. Box, 3x7 inches. Shipping wt., 12 oz.
No. 49N5715 Price............79c
Extra Propellers (celluloid) for Aerona Revolver. Shipping weight, 2 ounces.
No. 49N5716 Price, per box of 3 propellers..............21c

Our 47-Cent Steam Roller.

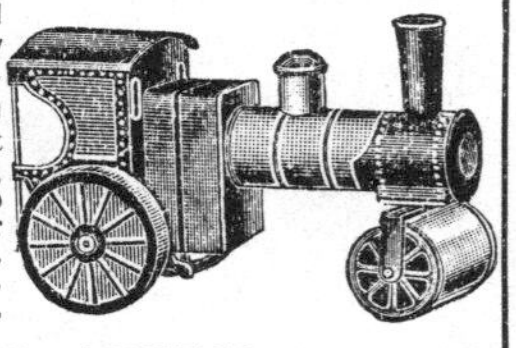

A Very Well Made Nicely Enameled Mechanical Steam Roller. Front roller turns, enabling it to go in circle or straight. Size, 7x3½x4 inches. Shipping wt., 2 pounds.
No. 49N5764
Price...... 47c

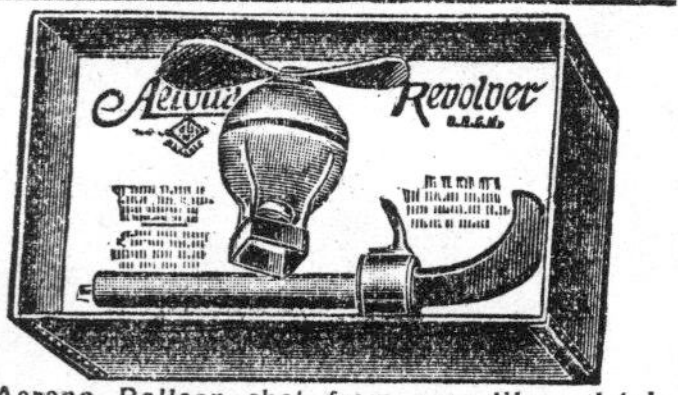

Aerona Balloon shot from propelling pistol. Celluloid balloon in bright colors, equipped with celluloid basket. Balloon soars high in the air. Shipping wt., 1 lb.
No. 49N5729 Price............89c

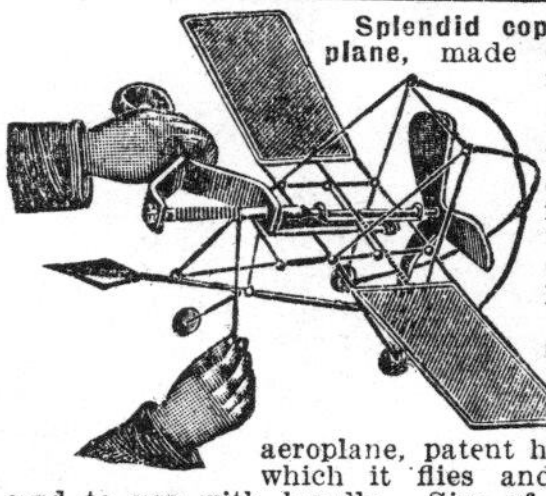

Splendid copy of aeroplane, made of flexible wire and silk. Can be handled by any child. Full instructions with each aeroplane. Complete set in box, consisting of aeroplane, patent handle from which it flies and prepared cord to use with handle. Size of aeroplane, 10x15x6 inches. Shipping wt., 1 lb.
No. 49N5722 Price............98c

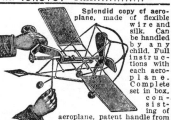

Our Bull Puppy, 89c.

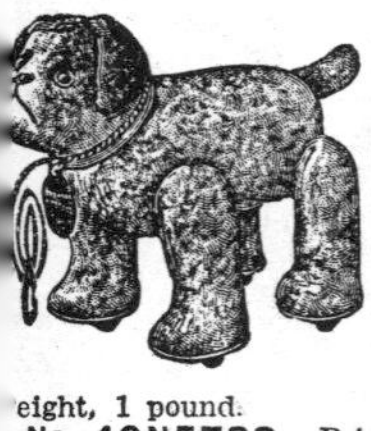

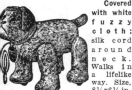

Covered with white fuzzy cloth; silk cord around neck. Walks in a lifelike way. Size, 8½x6½ in. Shipping weight, 1 pound.
No. 49N5733 Price...89c

The Funny Dachshund, 89c.

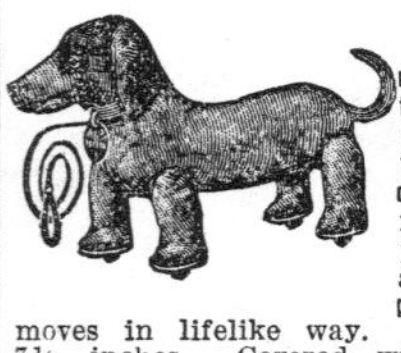

Comical reproduction of Germany's funniest dog. Most natural expression and when pulled moves in lifelike way. Size, 14x7½ inches. Covered with brown felt. Cord on collar, imitation eyes. Shipping weight, 1¾ lbs.
No. 49N5731 Price...89c

Fine Bulldog, $1.25.

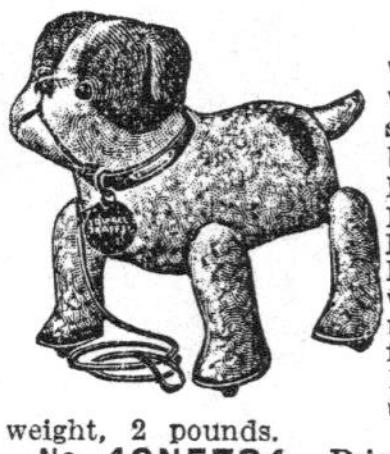

Covered with soft white felt, spotted black, with leather collar band and leather leash. Will walk in most lifelike fashion. Size, 10½x8 in. Shipping weight, 2 pounds.
No. 49N5734 Price...$1.25

Walking Pussy Cat, $1.48.

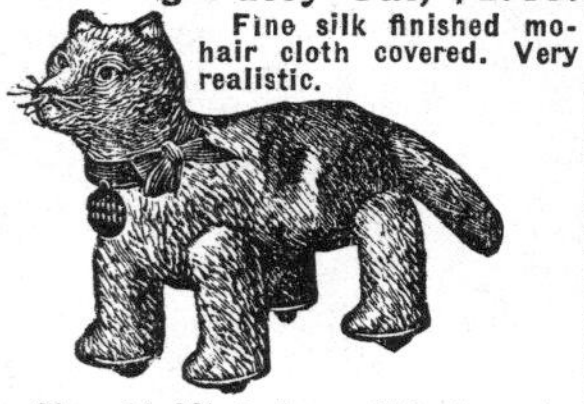

Fine silk finished mohair cloth covered. Very realistic. Size, 14x8¾ inches. Shipping wt., 1½ pounds.
No. 49N5735 Price..$1.48

Beautiful Spaniel $2.25.

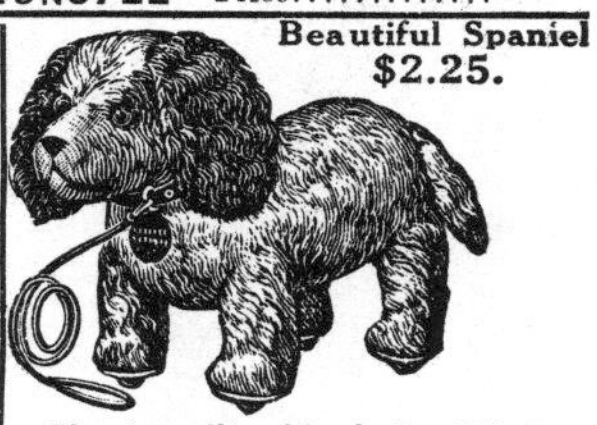

Finest quality silk plush. Coloring white and tan. Leather collar and leash. Size, 15x8½ inches. Shipping weight, 1½ pounds.
No. 49N5736 Price..$2.25

Walking Duck, 89c.

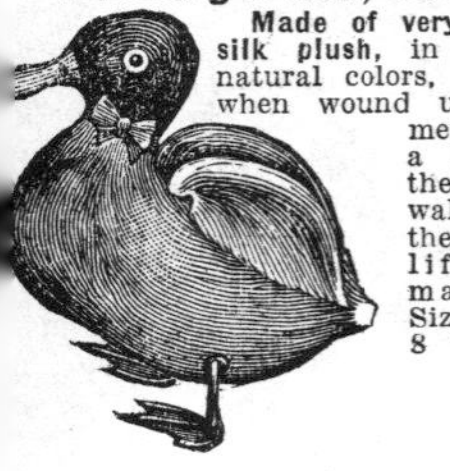

Made of very fine silk plush, in most natural colors, and when wound up by means of a key, the duck walks in the most lifelike manner. Size, 6x8 in.

Puss on Skates, $1.27.

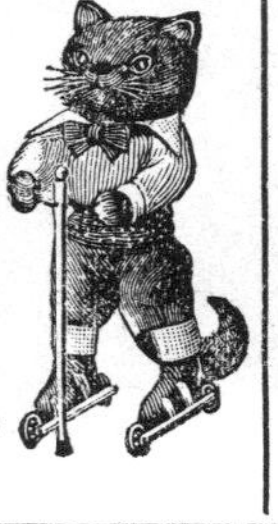

Made of finest quality silk plush. Fitted with a pair of roller skates. Winds with a key; moves forward and backward in the most lifelike manner. Size, 9¼ inches

This Fine Boat for 89c.

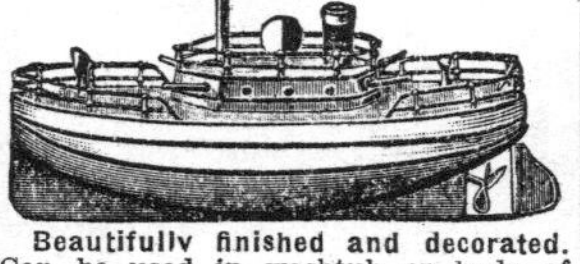

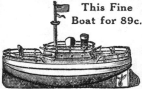

Beautifully finished and decorated. Can be used in washtub or body of water. Very good spring and propeller. Length, 9 inches.

Mechanical Dog and Ball. 49c

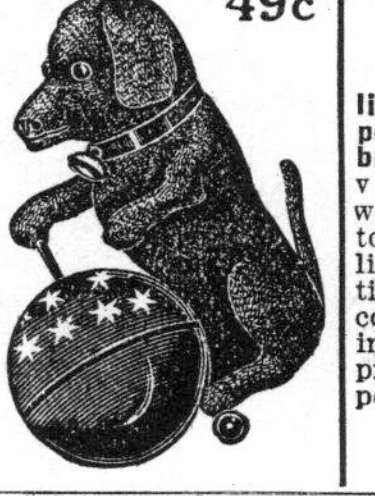

Cloth covered dog on wheels rolling a bright red and white enameled 2¼-inch diameter ball. 5½ in. high. Each in box. Shipping weight. 1 lb.

Famous Luck Bird, 89c.

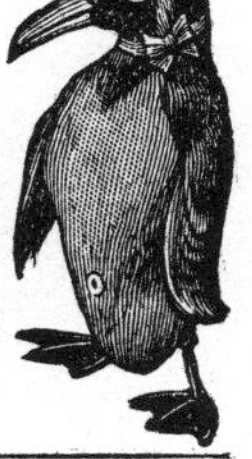

Sailors have believed the sight or possession of such a bird brings luck. A very strong clockwork enables the bird to walk in most lifelike manner. Beautifully colored. Very comical. Size, 8¾ inches high. Shipping weight, 1¼ pounds.

TEDDY BEARS AND COMICAL MONKEYS

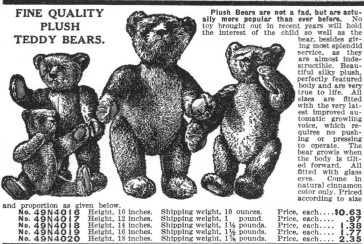

FINE QUALITY PLUSH TEDDY BEARS.

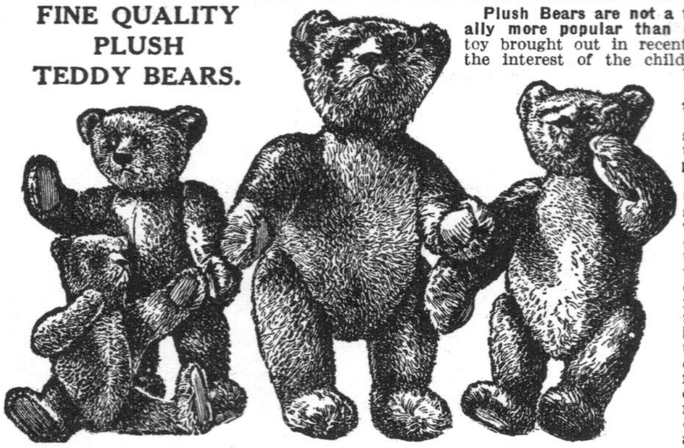

Plush Bears are not a fad, but are actually more popular than ever before. No toy brought out in recent years will hold the interest of the child so well as the bear, besides giving most splendid service, as they are almost indestructible. Beautiful silky plush, perfectly featured body and are very true to life. All sizes are fitted with the very latest improved automatic growling voice, which requires no pushing or pressing to operate. The bear growls when the body is tilted forward. All fitted with glass eyes. Come in natural cinnamon color only. Priced according to size and proportion as given below.

No. 49N4016	Height, 10 inches.	Shipping weight, 10 ounces.	Price, each....$0.63
No. 49N4017	Height, 12 inches.	Shipping weight, 1 pound.	Price, each.... .97
No. 49N4018	Height, 14 inches.	Shipping weight, 1⅛ pounds.	Price, each.... 1.38
No. 49N4019	Height, 16 inches.	Shipping weight, 1½ pounds.	Price, each.... 1.77
No. 49N4020	Height, 18 inches.	Shipping weight, 1⅞ pounds.	Price, each.... 2.35

Comical and Lifelike Monkeys of Exceptional Quality.

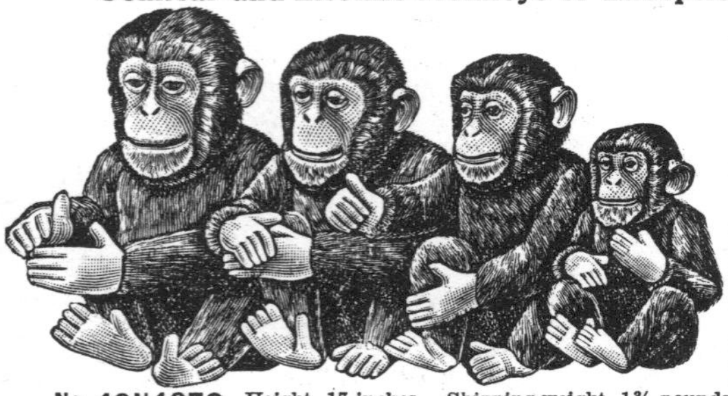

Made of extra fine soft and long cinnamon brown plush, neatly sewed. Jointed arms and feet and perfectly formed body. Hands, feet and face are made of fine grade flesh colored felt, presenting a very natural appearance. Very natural glass eyes. Do not compare these with the cheap monkeys sold on the market. Ours are far superior. Made in four sizes as listed below.

No. 49N4069 Height, 19 inches. Shipping wt., 2 lbs. Price, each $2.45

No. 49N4070	Height, 17 inches.	Shipping weight, 1¾ pounds.	Price, each.... 1.98
No. 49N4071	Height, 15 inches.	Shipping weight, 1¼ pounds.	Price, each.... 1.45
No. 49N4072	Height, 12 inches.	Shipping weight, 10 ounces.	Price, each.... .98

OUR FINEST GRADE LONG SILKY PLUSH TEDDY BEAR

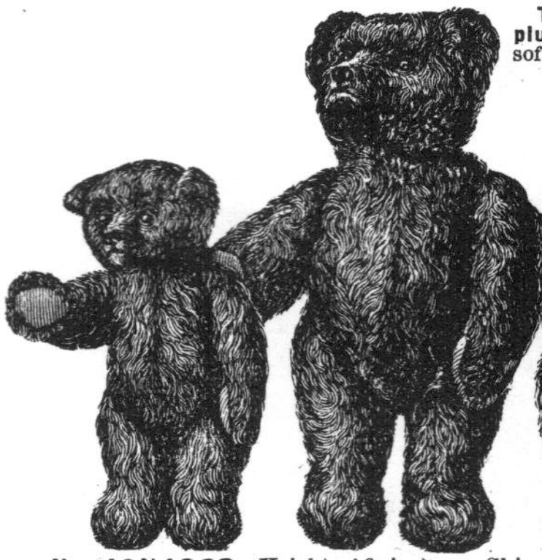

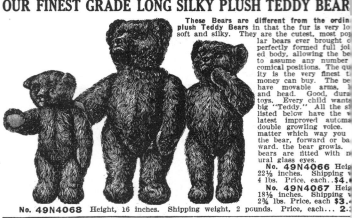

These Bears are different from the ordin[ary] plush Teddy Bears in that the fur is very lo[ng,] soft and silky. They are the cutest, most pop[u]lar bears ever brought o[ut,] perfectly formed full joi[nt]ed body, allowing the be[ar] to assume any number [of] comical positions. The qu[al]ity is the very finest t[hat] money can buy. The be[ars] have movable arms, l[egs] and head. Good, dura[ble] toys. Every child wants [a] big "Teddy." All the si[zes] listed below have the v[ery] latest improved automa[tic] double growling voice. [No] matter which way you [tip] the bear, forward or ba[ck]ward. the bear growls. [All] bears are fitted with n[at]ural glass eyes.

No. 49N4066 Heig[ht,] 22½ inches. Shipping w[eight,] 4 lbs. Price, each..$4.[…]

No. 49N4067 Heig[ht,] 18½ inches. Shipping w[eight,] 2¾ lbs. Price, each $3.[…]

No. 49N4068 Height, 16 inches. Shipping weight, 2 pounds. Price, each... 2.[…]

Fine Grade Bears on Whee[ls]

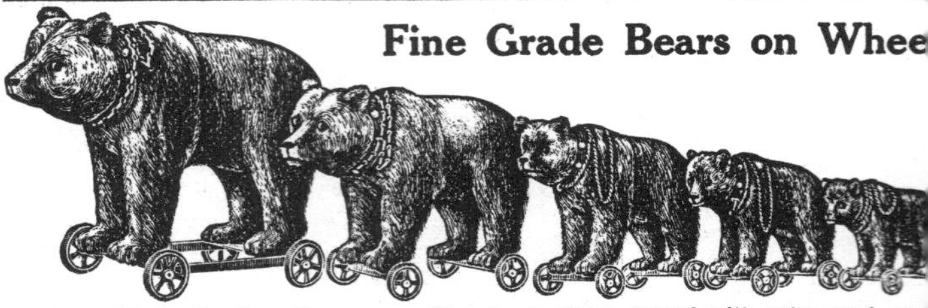

A novelty in the Bear line. Large Fine Grade Bears covered with extra good qua[lity] cinnamon brown plush. Bears have leather collar, long chains. Can be drawn around the floor. Fitted with fine natural glass eyes and squeaking voice. The largest size bear [is] large and strong enough to bear the weight of a child. Everything the very finest gra[de.] Wheels and all equipment strong, solid and substantial.

49N4073¼	Lgth., 24 in.;	ht., 18 in.	Shpg. wt., 20 lbs.	Regular price, $7.50.	Each..$5.[…]
49N4074	Lgth., 19 in.;	ht., 13½ in.	Shpg. wt., 6 lbs.	Regular price, $5.00.	Each.. 3.[…]
49N4075	Lgth., 14¼ in.;	ht., 11½ in.	Shpg. wt., 3 lbs.	Regular price, $3.50.	Each.. 2.[…]
49N4076	Lgth., 11 in.;	ht., 9 in.	Shpg. wt., 2½ lbs.	Regular price, $2.00.	Each. 1.[…]
49N4077	Lgth., 9 in.;	ht., 7 in.	Shpg. wt., 1¾ lbs.		Each..........................

Roller Skating Bear, 97c.

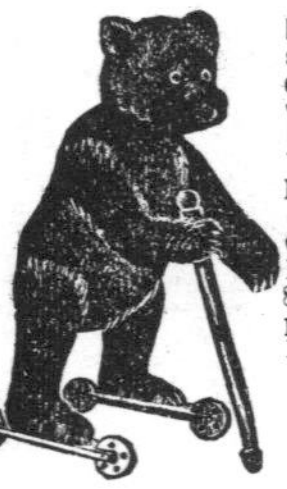

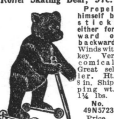

Propels himself by stick, either forward or backward. Winds with key. Very comical. Great seller. Ht., 8 in. Shipping wt., 1¼ lbs.

No. 49N5723 Price, **97c**

Teddy Bear, 89c.

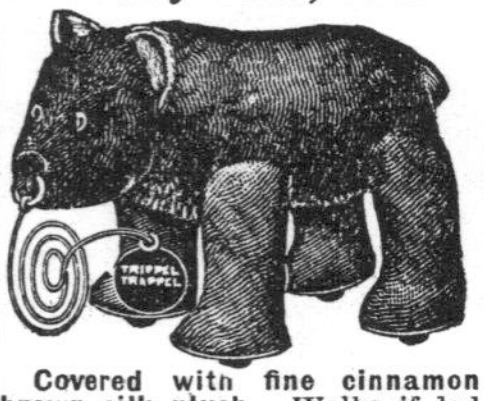

Covered with fine cinnamon brown silk plush. Walks if led by silk cord. Size, 5 inches. Shipping wt., 1½ lbs.

No. 49N5732 Price.................. **89c**

Dressed Tumbling Monkey.

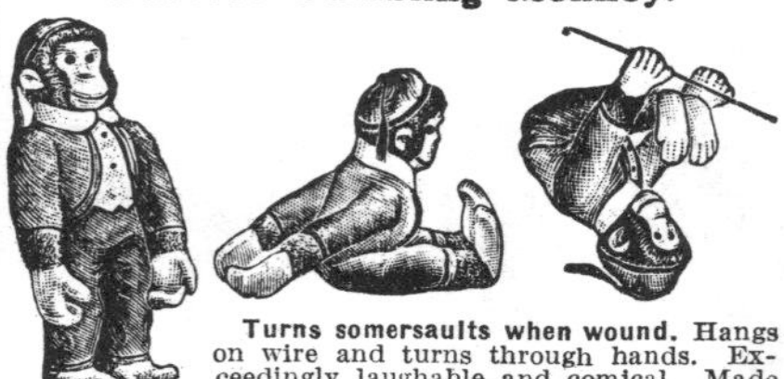

Turns somersaults when wound. Hangs on wire and turns through hands. Exceedingly laughable and comical. Made of brown plush, with red felt jacket and blue pants trimmed with gilt braid. Natural glass eyes. Height, 7 in. Shipping wt., 1 pound.

No. 49N5755 Price.................. **89c**

Amusing Tumbling Bear.

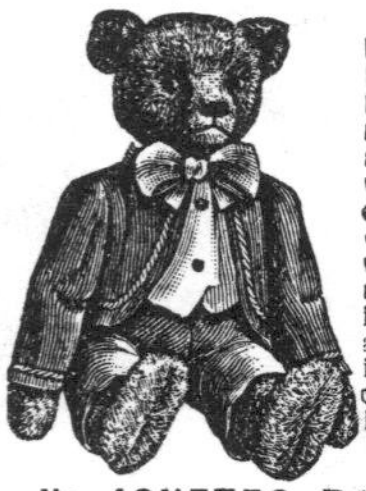

Large Size Mechanical Bear made of fine grade plush. When arms are wound according to directions will perform many amusing tumbling acts. Dressed in fancy colored suit. Height, 11 in. Shipping wt. 12 oz.

No. 49N5756 Price.... **89c**

Roller Skating Monkey.

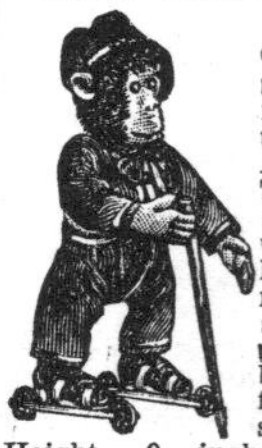

Plush C[ov]ered Monk[ey] nicely dres[sed] in gold br[aid] trimmed s[uit.] A very favor[ite] Toy. Has com[ic]al red t[…] with tass[el.] Monkey [is] mounted [on] skates and p[ro]pels itse[lf] backward a[nd] forward. V[ery] strong spri[ng.] Height, 9 inches. Shipp[ing] weight, 14 ounces.

No. 49N5757 Price **8[…]**

Comical Monkey on Wheels.

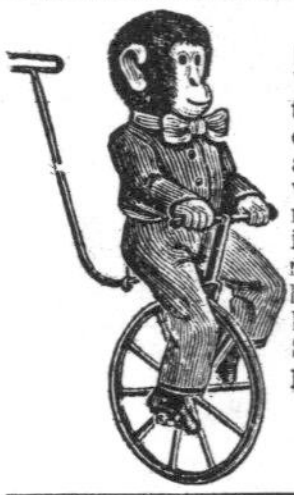

Brightly Colored Dressed Monkey on Wheels. A very fine toy for small children. When pushed along on the floor, wheel revolves and monkey's legs work in a very realistic manner. Length, with handle, 27 inches; height, 11½ inches. Shipping weight, 1¼ pounds.

No. 49N5758 Price........ **89c**

Our 25c Teddy Bear.

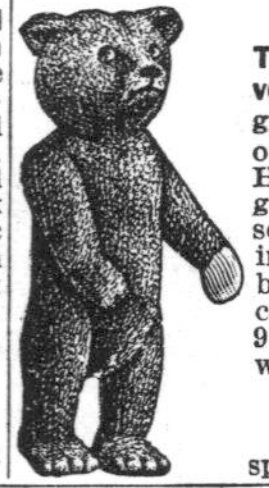

A Good Grade Teddy Bear with voice. Made of good grade cinnamon colored brown plush. Has black natural glass eyes and squeaker voice. Equal in quality to many bears sold at 50 cents. Total height, 9½ inches. Shipping weight, 10 ounces.

No. 49N4096 Price, special at..... **25c**

Jumping Monkey.

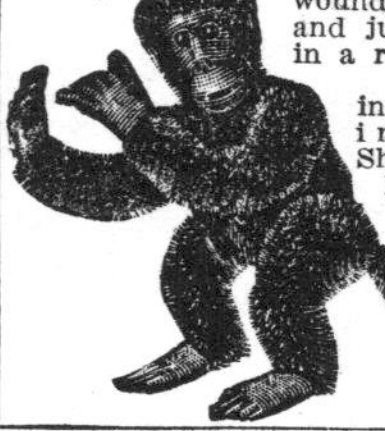

Made of fine silk plush. Most lifelike motion when wound up by key and jumps forward in a realistic manner. Very amusing. Size, 6½ inches high. Shipping wt., 1½ pounds.

No. 49N5739 Price **89c**

Mechanical Bear.

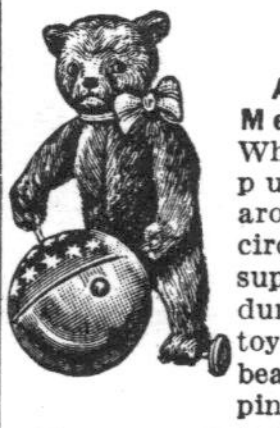

A Very Amusing Mechanical Bear. When wound up bear pushes red ball around on floor in circle. Very strong superforce spring. A durable and lasting toy. Total height of bear, 8 inches. Shipping weight, 1¼ lbs.

No. 49N5759 Price.................. **$1.47**

Teddy Bea[r]

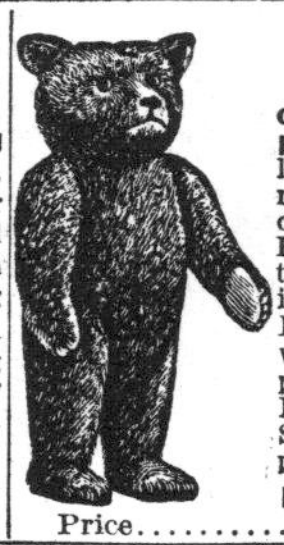

Made of light c[ol]ored cinnamon bro[wn] plush. One of [the] largest and most [re]markable values e[ver] offered in a Te[ddy] Bear. Consider[ing] the quality the pr[ice] is extremely l[ow.] Bear has automa[tic] voice and when t[ip]ped forward grow[ls.] Height, 12 inch[es.] Shipping weight, […] pounds.

No. 49N4097 Price.......................... 4[…]

Remarkable Values in Low Priced Teddy Bears.

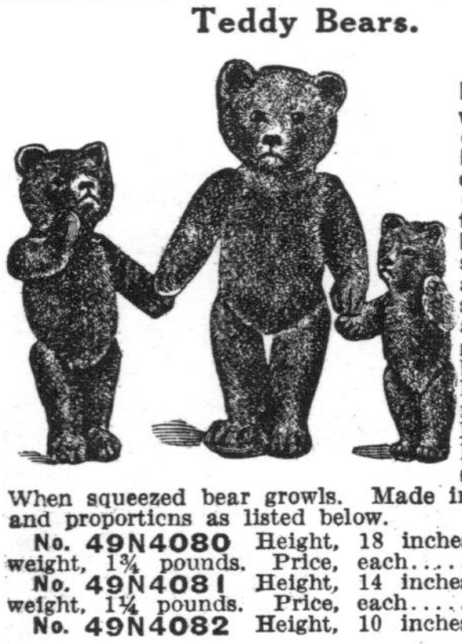

At the very low price for which we are offering these Bears we consider the quality above the average bear usually sold. Bears are well stuffed and are made of good grade brown plush, light cinnamon color. Each bear has fine pressure voice. When squeezed bear growls. Made in three sizes and proportions as listed below.

No. 49N4080 Height, 18 inches. Shipping weight, 1¾ pounds. Price, each.............89c

No. 49N4081 Height, 14 inches. Shipping weight, 1¼ pounds. Price, each.............69c

No. 49N4082 Height, 10 inches. 39c

Teddy Bear on Wheels, 98c.

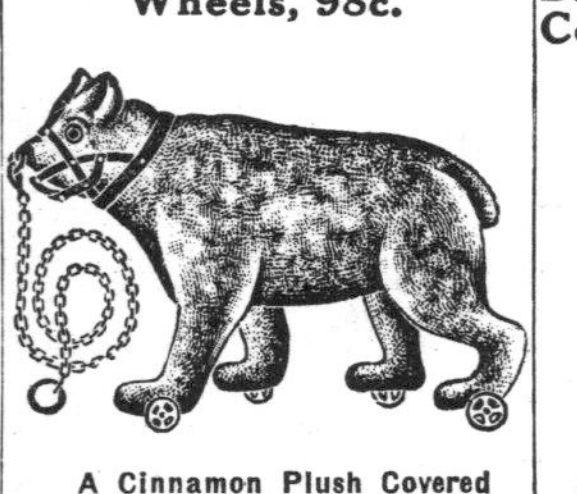

A Cinnamon Plush Covered Bear with metal wheels on feet. Has leather muzzle and halter with buckle, and drawing chain. Glass eyes. Height, 7¼ inches; length, 10 inches. Shipping weight, 1 pound.

No. 49N4050 Price.................. **98c**

Teddy Bear on Cord.

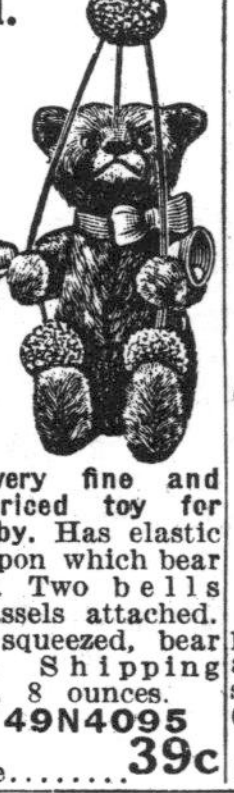

A very fine and low priced toy for the baby. Has elastic cord upon which bear dances. Two bells and tassels attached. When squeezed, bear growls. Shipping weight, 8 ounces.

No. 49N4095 Price........ **39c**

The Bear Family, Only 19c.

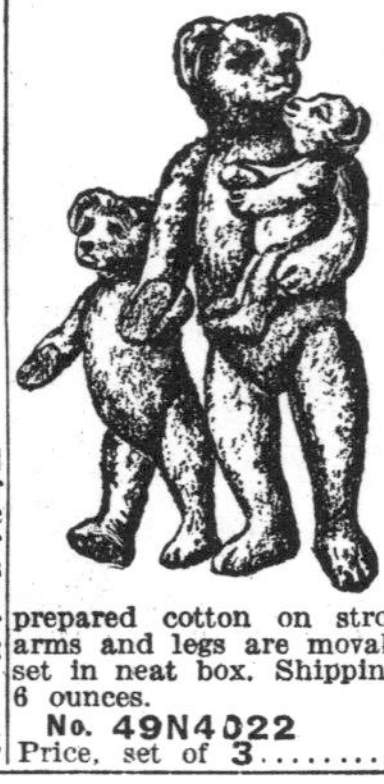

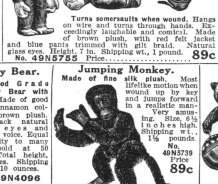

This Bear Family is one of the most popular toys ever produced. Consists of one bear, 7¾ in. high and two bears 4½ in. high. Bears are made of prepared cotton on strong wire; arms and legs are movable. Each set in neat box. Shipping weight, 6 ounces.

No. 49N4022 Price, set of 3.............. **19c**

Fine Grade Dressed Teddy Bear[s]

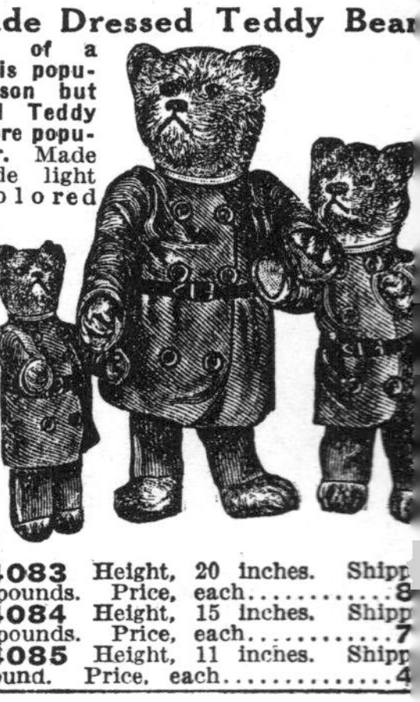

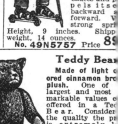

Any kind of a Teddy Bear is popular this season but these dressed Teddy Bears are more popular than ever. Made of fine grade light cinnamon colored heavy plush with natural glass eyes. Dressed in regular military khaki cloth, trimmed with brass buttons with "bear" stamped on each. Leather belt. Made in three sizes and proportions as listed below.

No. 49N4083 Height, 20 inches. Shipp[ing] weight, 2¼ pounds. Price, each...............8[…]

No. 49N4084 Height, 15 inches. Shipp[ing] weight, 1½ pounds. Price, each...............7[…]

No. 49N4085 Height, 11 inches. Shipp[ing] weight, 1 pound. Price, each...............4[…]

DOLL SUPPLIES · NOVELTY DOLLS

Finest Grade Doll Hats.

Made of good quality lace braid. Genuine ostrich feather, chiffon trimmed. Size of hat from brim to brim, 7 inches. Will fit average doll head from 10 to 12 inches in circumference. Good $1.00 value. Comes in assorted colors. Shipping weight, 6 ounces.

Price is for hat only.

No. 49N7125 Assorted colors. Price..69c

Delicately trimmed with pink ribbon and roses. Made for Dolly's wardrobe. Will fit 10 to 12-inch circumference doll head. Size of brim, 8x9 inches. Shipping wt. 6 ounces.

Price is for hat only

No. 49N7127 Price....................49c

With beautiful pink ribbon bands and rosettes. Six artistic silk tassels. Adapted for doll head from 9 to 12-inch circumference. Comes in pink only. Shpg. wt., 6 oz.

No. 49N7128 Price. 39c

Draped with blue tinted bird of Paradise spray, mull and rosette. Will fit 9 to 12-inch circumference doll head. Shipping wt. 6 oz.

No. 49N7129 Price, 29c

White straw. Trimmed with bows of blue ribbon. Will fit average doll head 9 to 12 inches in circumference. Blue only. Shpg. wt., 6 oz.

No. 49N7130 Price, 19c

Price is for hat only.

Genuine white straw. Edged with lace effect plaited pink ribbon. Will fit average doll head from 9 to 12 inches in circumference. Pink only. 10c

Price is for hat only

FAMOUS DORST ROLY POLY DOLLS FROM NURNBERG, GERMANY.

Clown figure, red felt cap, cloth collar, turning head painted in bright colors. Height, 17 inches. Shpg. wt., 3¾ lbs. 49N7015 Price........69c

Foxy Grandpa. Turning head. Nicely painted, with natural face. Height, 12½ inches. Shpg. wt., 3 lbs. No. 49N7006 Price........49c

Clown Roly Poly, decorated in colors, turning head. Height, 11½ inches. 50-cent value. Shpg. wt., 2½ lbs. No. 49N7009 Price.......37c

Comical Roly Poly. Movable head. Height, 7½ inches. Assorted designs. Shpg. wt., 1 lb. No. 49N7007 Price, each 25c

Comical Roly Poly Doll. Height, 4½ inches. Assorted subjects. Painted in colors. Shpg. wt., 10 oz. No. 49N7010 Price, each......10c

Painted in natural colors. Height, 3½ inches. Shpg. wt., 6 oz. No. 49N7014 Price 13c

Cat Roly Poly. Made of celluloid in natural colors. Glass eyes. 5½ inches high. Shpg. wt., 9 oz. No. 49N7011 Price, each.......29c

Musical Roly Poly. Handsome celluloid face doll, with colored net worsted cape and hood. Two musical voices. Height, 8½ in. Shpg. wt., 1 lb. No. 49N7003 Price..........39c

The Rolling Roly Poly. Can be drawn along floor and globe revolves. Height, 8½ in. Shpg. wt., 1¾ lbs. No. 49N7019 Price..........43c

Funny and amusing Dog Roly Poly. Height, 5½ in. Shipping wt., 9 oz. No. 49N7012 Price...29c

Very pretty celluloid dog. 3½ inches high. Shpg. wt., 6 oz. No. 49N7028 Price. 13c

Golden Locks Dolly and Family, 19 Cents.

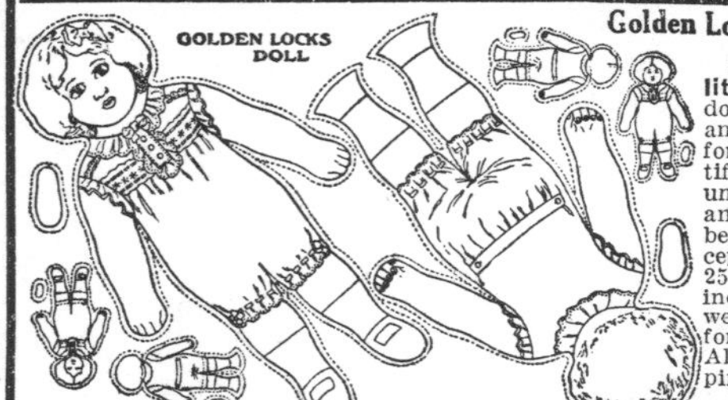

Large size cut out doll with two little dolls. Heavy grade of cloth. A doll that can be cut out and stuffed and you will have an ideal toy doll for the children. Printed in five beautiful colors to represent a child in underclothes. Large enough to dress and wear baby clothes. Prettiest and best selling rag doll ever sold. Exceptionally large size. Height of doll, 25 inches. Height of little dolls, 7 inches. The all around dolly for wear. Cannot break. Just the thing for baby. Size of sheet, 23x36 inches. All ready to cut out and stuff. Shipping weight, 4 ounces.

No. 49N7202 Price...... 19c

Little Red Riding Hood Muslin Doll, 9c.

A very pretty rag doll, height 17 inches, printed in five colors, showing Red Riding Hood with basket. Just the thing for baby. Full directions with each doll how to cut out and stuff. If you want a non-breakable doll, one that baby cannot hurt itself on, then buy one of our cut out rag dolls. Shipping weight, 4 oz.

No. 49N7206 Price......................9c

Dolly's Comb Set, 33 Cents.

A Complete Doll Set, including back and two side combs, barrette and two large hairpins, all made of celluloid in imitation tortoise shell effect. Shipping weight, 8 oz.

No. 49N7100 Price............. 33c

White Rubber Dolls.

Exceptional quality white rubber dolls, natural shape. Hollow and cannot hurt baby's teeth or mouth. German silver whistle. Three kinds as follows. Shpg. wt., each, 4 oz.

No. 49N7025 **Sailor Boy, with whistle.** Height, 5⅛ in. Price 10c

No. 49N7026 **Fat Boy, with whistle.** Height, 4¾ inches. Price.................10c

No. 49N7027 **Dressed Girl, with tambourine.** Has whistle. Height, 5¼ inches. Price....................................10c

Cut Out Boy and Girl, 8 Cents.

Shown in fashionable summer costumes, printed on strong muslin, in five indelible colors. Simple outlines, easy to cut out and when stuffed makes a very beautiful doll. Size of sheet, 12x15 inches. Shipping wt., 3 oz.

No. 49N7203 **Baby Boy Doll.** Price..8c

No. 49N7204 **Baby Girl Doll.** Price..8c

Made of the best quality red rubber, and each one fitted with a German silver whistle. Light in weight, washable and difficult to destroy. Shipping weight, 5 oz.

49N7016 **Indian Girl,** Height, 6¼ inches. Price..........................25c

No. 49N7017 **Boy Doll.** Height, 6¼ Price..................................25c

White Rubber Dolls, 39 Cents.

Made of best quality rubber with German silver whistle in back. Squeezing makes it whistle amusingly. Easily cleaned with soap and water. Painted cheeks and eyes. Cannot injure baby. Shpg. wt., 7 oz. each.

No. 49N7022 **Boy, Colonial dress.** Height, 9¼ inches. Price................39c

No. 49N7020 **Girl, in bathing suit.** Height, 8½ inches. Price.................39c

Doll Fur Set, 57 Cents.

Doll Fur Set. Imitation ermine fur set in white with black spots. Consists of boa, 24 inches long, and muff, 3½x3½ inches. Muff has cord, by means of which it can be fastened around the neck of doll. Will very much improve the appearance of any doll. Exceptional value. Each set complete, packed in lace trimmed box. Size, 19x5¾ inches. Shipping weight, 8 ounces.

No. 49N7102 Price..........................57c

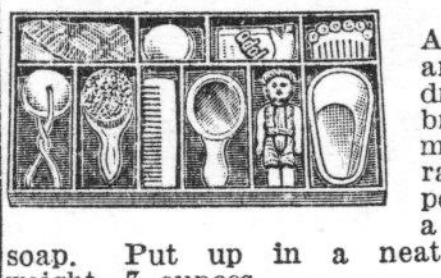

Doll Toilet Set. A popular new article. Consists of dressing comb, hair brush, back comb, mirror, powder box, rattle and tooth powder bottle, also a small cake of soap. Put up in a neat box. Shipping weight, 7 ounces.

No. 49N7103 Price..............39c

A very nice assortment of doll jewelry including blue and white glass bead necklace, earrings, butterfly pin, watch, real eiderdown powder puff; hairpins and band mirror. Size of box, 7½x11 inches. Shipping weight, 8 oz.

No. 49N7101 Price........39c

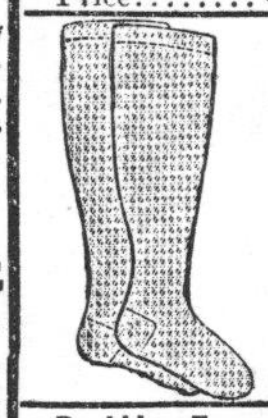

Come in all sizes. No dolly's wardrobe complete without an assortment of different color stockings. Well made. **In ordering give size of foot in inches from heel to toe.** Shpg. wt., 1 oz.

No. 49N7135 **White.** Price, per pair.............10c

No. 49N7136 **Pink.** Price, per pair.............10c

No. 49N7137 **Blue.** Price, per pair.............10c

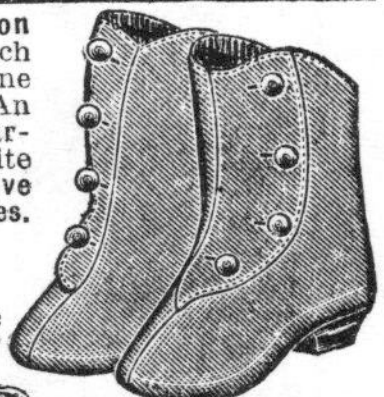

Doll's Four-Button Shoes with heel. French toe. Made of genuine kid. Well shaped. An exceptionally nice article. Come in white only. **In ordering give length of foot in inches.** Shpg. wt., 3 oz.

No. 49N7140 Price, per pair..........47c

Made of white kid. Has two ribbon bows and buckles. French toe. **In ordering give size of foot in inches.** Shpg. wt., 3 oz.

No. 49N7141 Price, pair..25c

Kid rosette. One kid strap with cord. French toes. **In ordering give size of doll's foot in inches.** Shpg. wt., 2 oz.

No. 49N7142 Price, per pair..........10c

Made from extra fine quality human hair, carefully selected and sterilized. Ribbon bows on side, and extra long large curls. Come in four sizes to fit heads 10 to 13 inches in circumference. **In ordering be sure to specify circumference around doll's head.** Come in two colors as follows. Shpg. wt., 6 oz.

No. 49N7147 **Brown.** Price..$1.89

Hair carefully selected and sterilized. Two ribbon bows. Exceptionally well made and attractive wigs. Ten 5½-inch curls. Come in four sizes to fit heads 10 to 13 inches in circumference. **In ordering give circumference of head in inches.** Come in two colors. Shpg. wt., 8 oz.

No. 49N7145 **Blond.** Price....79c

No. 18N23196   **$1.45**

Beautiful 19-Inch Doll.

Fine quality lifelike bisque head, bright sleeping eyes with eyelashes. Open mouth showing teeth. Charming dress of fine materials in light colors, beautifully trimmed with lace, soft net and satin baby ribbon. Close fitting straw bonnet with ribbon trimming and ties to match dress. Good quality underwear. Doll can be undressed.

Average height, with hats, about 15 inches. Pretty, large size bisque heads with bright lifelike eyes, automatic closing lids. Full curly wigs. All with removable shoes and stockings. Medium quality underwear.

Choice 48c

Choice 48c

No. 18N23171 Dress of narrow striped material. Imitation patent leather belt. Braid trimmed collar with bow. Large straw hat with ostrich feather.

No. 18N23172 Dainty flowered organdy dress, trimmed with ribbon drawn lace insertion and yoke. Pretty lace trimmed ruffle around collar and skirt. White hat with rosette and flowers.

No. 18N23173 Very pretty long waisted French blouse. Dainty braid trimming on plaited skirt. Real Swiss embroidery and silk braid collar. Pretty bonnet with Valenciennes trimming.

No. 18N23174 Exceptionally well made stylish dress of pin striped gingham. Wide sailor collar and flouncing in contrasting shade. Pretty bonnet to match dress.

Only 75 Cents for Choice

Have dainty babylike bisque heads, moving eyes, very curly wigs, shoes and stockings, all on jointed bodies. Neat underwear. Height, including hats, about 16 inches.

Choice 75c

Two Wonderful Value Dolls.

No. 18N23177 Pretty dress of allover dotted Swiss. Panel of lace insertion down front. Wide flounce, lace trimmed. Silk ribbon bows at waist. Bonnet of straw and mull to match.

No. 18N23180 Light colored box plaited dress with wide sash. Fancy braid decorations and buttons on collar. Close fitting Tam o' Shanter hat of same material.

Fine large bisque heads with bright lifelike eyes, automatic closing lids with eyelashes. Good jointed bodies. Full curly wigs. Good quality underwear, lace stockings and tied shoes. All clothes come off. Average height, without hats, 17 to 18 inches.

Choice 98c

Choice 98c

No. 18N23182 Full box plaited dress of pincheck gingham, ribbon trimming and sash. Shirred mushroom brim hat of same material, ostrich feathers and ribbon trimming.

No. 18N23185 Very latest French style in light colored lawn with pannier of flowered organdy, all lace edged, all folded revers of same material. Yoke of allover lace, with colored buttons. Silk ribbon sash. Bonnet to match.

No. 18N23189 Dress is made of crossbar lawn. Skirt accordion plaited with rows of ribbon and flouncings of lace. Belt is caught with a baby ribbon rosette. Collar and cuffs also trimmed with this ribbon. Dainty hat of dotted lawn, trimmed with lace and flowers. Has ribbon ties.

No. 18N23190 Our Party Baby has a pretty long waisted lawn dress with skirt of real Swiss embroidery with beading. Trimming of dainty beading drawn with silk baby ribbon and large bows. Embroidery and ribbon trimming at shoulders. Silk ribbon hairband with two large bows.

Dressed Dolls 23c Take Your Choice

All with good quality pretty bisque heads, sleeping eyes, curled mohair wigs, and shoes and stockings. Average height, 13 inches with hats. The best values ever offered for such a low price. Shipping weight, 1⅜ lbs.

No. 18N23156 Dress of white crossbar material, neat jacket with wide collar and gilt buttons. Straw hat with rosettes.

No. 18N23158 Dress of mercerized satin, trimmed with fancy braid, lace and gilt buttons. Plaited hat to harmonize.

No. 18N23160 Blouse style with revers collar and flouncing, button trimming. Straw hat with bow. Neat dress.

No. 18N23162 Flannelette dress in sailor style with dark colored sailor collar and flouncing. Sailor cap to match.

No. 18N23166 White lawn dress, elaborate cut embroidery trimming with lace and ribbon bows. Bonnet to match.

$1.45

A beautiful dress on a large size doll. Large childlike bisque head with bright eyes and automatic closing lids with eyelashes. Full curly wig and medium quality jointed body. Fine French gingham dress combined with fine white lawn, heavily trimmed with silk embroidered trimming braid, real Swiss embroidery and all silk ribbon. Good underwear. Clothes will come off. Close fitting bonnet to match. Height, including hat, 19 inches.

Make the Little Girl Happy with a New Doll

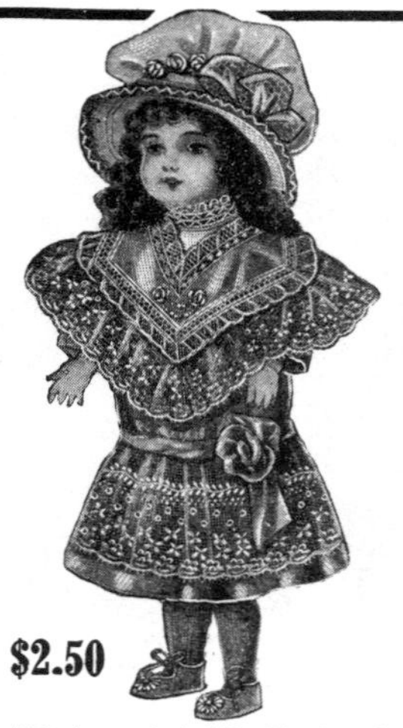

$2.50

This is our best doll. Finest quality full jointed body. Beautiful large bisque head. Long curly lifelike hair. Self-closing eyes, with **lashes** and **eyebrows** of natural hair. Stands about 22 inches high, including hat. Fine quality, lace trimmed underwear. White lawn underskirt, with 3-inch silk bottom. Silk trimmed sleeves, with fancy girdle to match. Overskirt and waist of fancy figured white lawn. Lace collar. Yoke of silk in the latest design, trimmed with wide shadow lace. Rosettes and jeweled bead ornament. White lawn hat on wire frame: edged with lace and silk fringe; trimmed with white net and artificial roses. Colored stockings. Shoes, with silk laces and real eyelets.

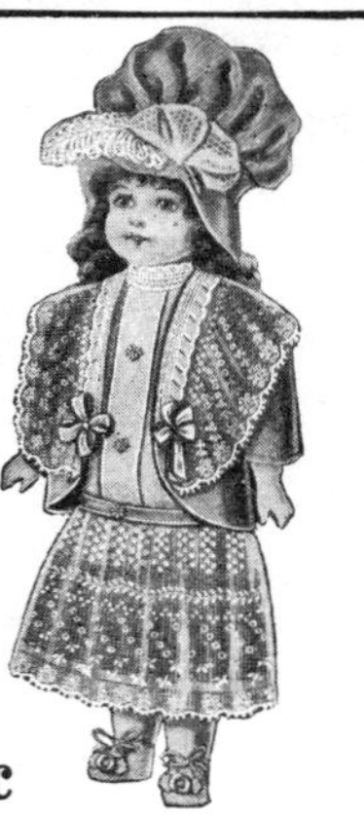

98c

American Princess. A dainty doll. Bisque head. Perfect features. Long curly lifelike hair. White teeth. Closing eyes. Full jointed arms and legs. Stands about 20 inches high, with hat. Lace trimmed underwear. White lawn underskirt, trimmed with colored material. Pretty net overskirt. Plaited lawn waist, with jeweled buttons and ribbon belt. Stylish coat of cerise serge, trimmed with figured chiffon, silk braid, cerise, and white ribbon rosettes. Lace collar. Bonnet of cerise serge, trimmed with chiffon and large white plume. White stockings. Tied shoes.

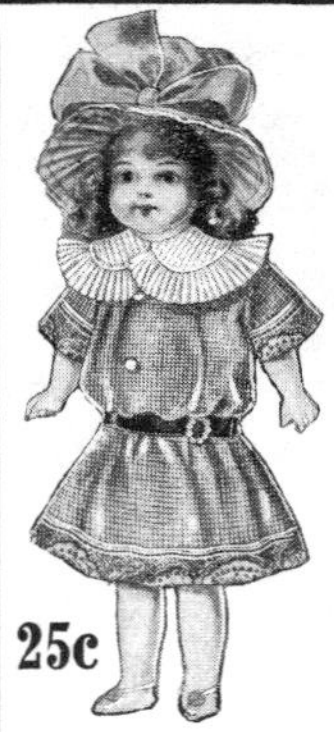

25c

"Little Fairy" dressed doll, of excellent quality. Very attractive face. Closing eyes. Stylish dress of good material. Cloth hat. Shoes and stockings. Hip joints. Well made. Stands 11 inches high. Others ask 40c to 50c. Neat black enameled belt with gilt buckles. Large white lawn collar. Two gilt buttons on front of waist.

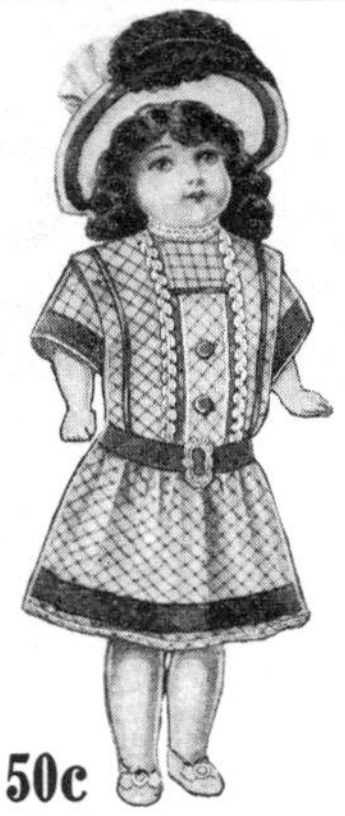

50c

Dressed Doll. Has lifelike hair. Closing eyes. Perfect features. Pretty teeth. Movable arms and legs. Dress of fine material, neatly trimmed. Fancy braid-trimmed waist. Belt with nickeled buckle. Hat of white lawn, with large colored plume, trimmed to match dress. White stockings. Buckle slippers. Stand 16 inches

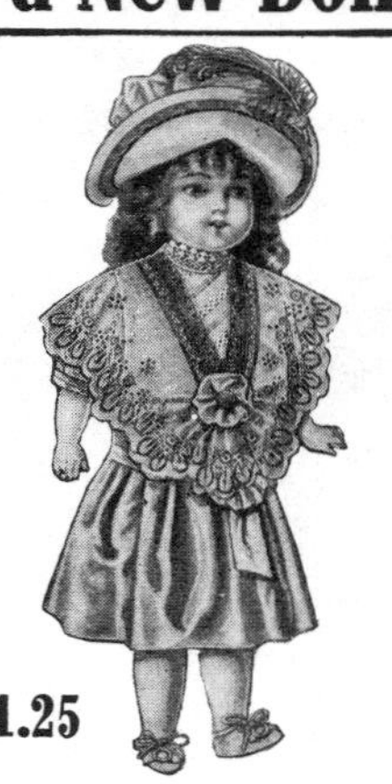

$1.25

Baby Queen. Extra fine, full ball jointed, well shaped body. Bisque head. Life-like, self-closing eyes. Perfect teeth. Curly lifelike hair. Lace trimmed underwear. Satin gown, with full lining; trimmed with fancy figured chiffon and silk braid. Ribbon girdle, with silk-covered button. Gimp of fancy lawn, with sleeves of same material edged with velvet. Lace collar. Bonnet of white lawn, well stiffened; fancy edge. Large colored plume to match. A dainty lady. 18 inches high.

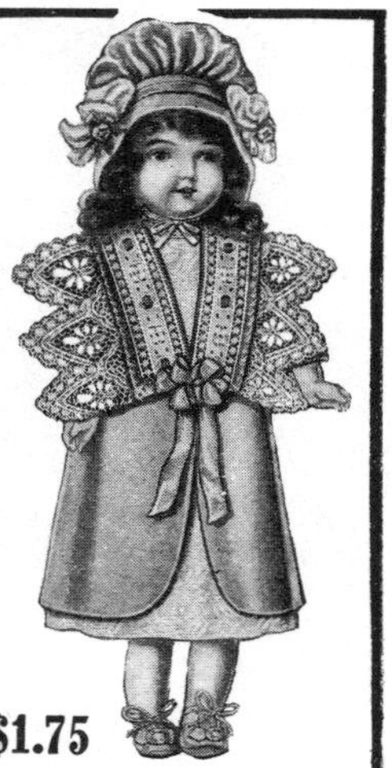

$1.75

Miss Columbia. Height, with bonnet, 21 inches. Fancy lace-trimmed underwear. White stockings. Tied shoes. Full length dress of fancy figured voile. Lace collar. Long, full-lined coat of colored cassimere, trimmed with wide cluny lace, silk fringe, insertion with drawn ribbon, rosettes, and ribbon streamers. Stylish bonnet trimmed with white net and ribbon, and two artificial roses. Bisque head. Perfect features. Self-closing eyes, with real lashes. Long, curly lifelike hair. Full jointed body of good quality.

Rag Dolls

Just the thing for young children. Unbreakable, and soft to handle. New process moulded faces. Will hold their shape. Well stuffed bodies. Stylishly dressed.

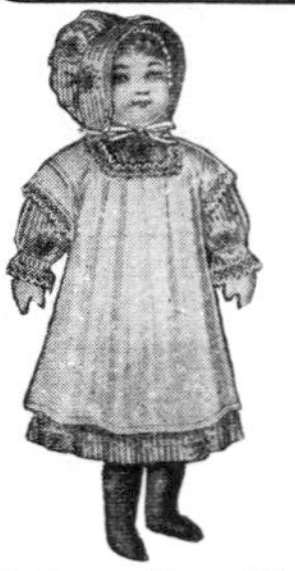

Shipping wt., 11 oz. **25c**
4L5871—Price .
Rag Doll. Excellent quality. Length, 13 in. Face made from a new moulded process, and will hold its shape. Painted hair. Cotton-stuffed body. Colored wrapper, neatly finished. Shaker style bonnet.

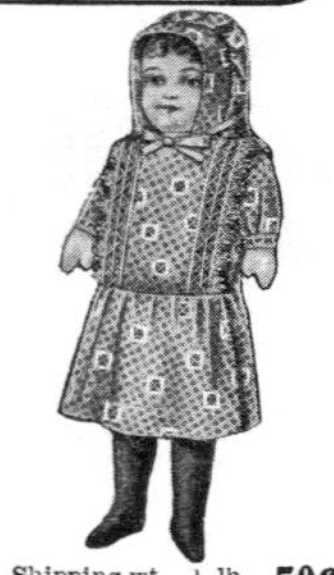

Shipping wt., 1 lb. **50c**
4L5873—Each .
Rag Doll, of much better quality. Length, 14½ in. Cotton-stuffed body and legs. Painted hair. Underclothing of good quality. Stylish dress of fine material, trimmed with lace and satin ribbon. Is sold by others at 75c and more.

Indestructible Dolls

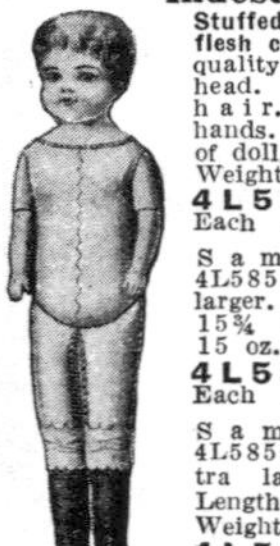

Stuffed body, flesh color. Best quality metal head. Painted hair. Wood hands. Length of doll, 11¼ in. Weight, 12 oz.
4L5855—Each **25c**

Same as 4L5855, only larger. Length, 15¾ in. Wt., 15 oz.
4L5856—Each **50c**

Same as 4L5855, but extra large size. Length, 21 in. Weight, 36 oz.
4L5857—Each **98c**

Same as 4L5855, with kid body. Minerva metal head. Painted hair. Length, 14 in. long. Weight, 15 oz.
4L5858—Each **45c**
Same is 4L5858. Length, 18 in. long. Weight. 22 oz. **80c**

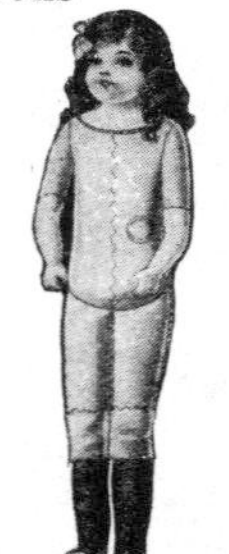

Same as 4L5855, but with real hair on head. Length, 15½ in. Wt., 15 oz.
4L5861—Ea. **50c**
Same as 4L5855. L'gth, 19 in. Natural hair. Wt., 24 oz. **85c**

Fine Quality Kid Body Dolls

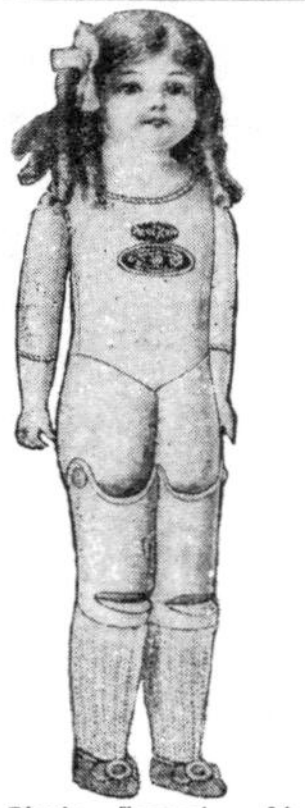

Finely Formed. Attractive and Durable Doll for Young Children. The dressing of this doll will afford much pleasure to the grown ups as well as the children. It makes a pretty gift at any time. The bodies are covered with fine white kid to below the knees. Shoes and knee length stockings. Riveted hip joint. The finest Minerva metal head. Has teeth, closing eyes. Sewed wig with long, fine hair, side part and ribbon. Very lifelike in appearance and well worth the low price.

4L5835—Minerva Kid Doll, 17 in. long. Wt., 2 lbs. Each....**$1.00**
4L5837—Length, 20½ inches. Wt. 2½ lbs. Each **$1.50**
4L5839—Length, 22½ inches. Wt. 3 lbs. Each **$1.75**
4L5841—Length, 26¼ inches. Wt., 3½ lbs. **$2.25**

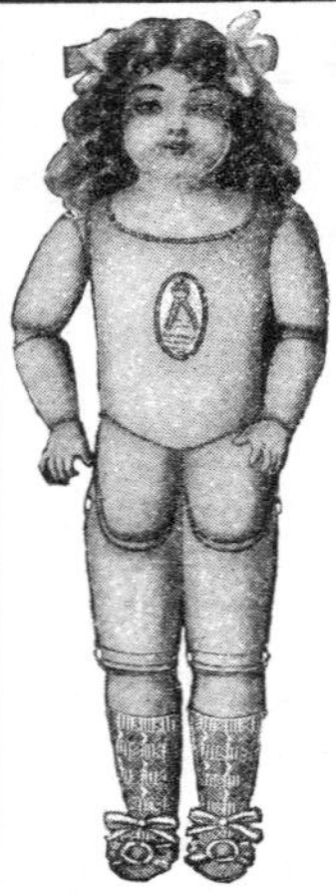

The Kestner Dolls are recognized the world over as positively the best made. The heads and faces are perfectly moulded, eyes are expressive, and the bodies are large and finely proportioned. Extra fine quality kid. Full formed, stout bodies, half cork stuffed. Riveted hip and knee joints. Composition arms, with ball jointed shoulder, elbow and wrist. Large, fine quality bisque head, with teeth, moving eyes, eyelashes and fine sewed wigs. Fitted with shoes and stockings.

4L5842—Length, 20 in. Shipping wt., 4½ lbs. Each **$3.25**
4L5850 — Length, 23 in. Shipping wt., 5 lbs. Each **$4.25**
4L5860 — Length 24½ in. Shipping wt., 6 lbs. **$5.95**

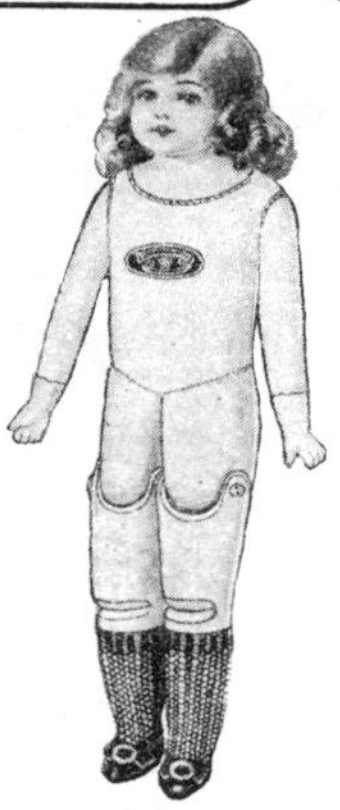

Real Human Hair

Fine Quality, White Kid Body Doll. Plump and well stuffed. Swivel jointed hips. Shoes and stockings can be taken off. Large bisque head. Sewed wig, of long, curly natural hair. Self-closing eyes, with **eyelashes of natural hair.** Large bright eyes, and pearly teeth. Bisque forearms. An exceptional value in a kid body doll.

4L5843—Kid Doll, as described. Height, 17 inches. Shipping wt., 3¼ lbs. Each ..**$1.05**
4L5844—Kid Doll, as described. Height, 20 inches. Shipping wt., 4 lbs. Each ...**$1.70**
4L5845—Kid Doll, as described. Height, 26½ inches. Shipping wt., 4½ lbs. Each..**$3.25**

Character Dolls

Fitted with unbreakable heads and hands. Firmly stuffed bodies. Movable arms and legs. Dressed in dainty frocks and clothing that will surely appeal to the little ones. The pretty life-like character face will prove a source of constant pleasure and enjoyment.

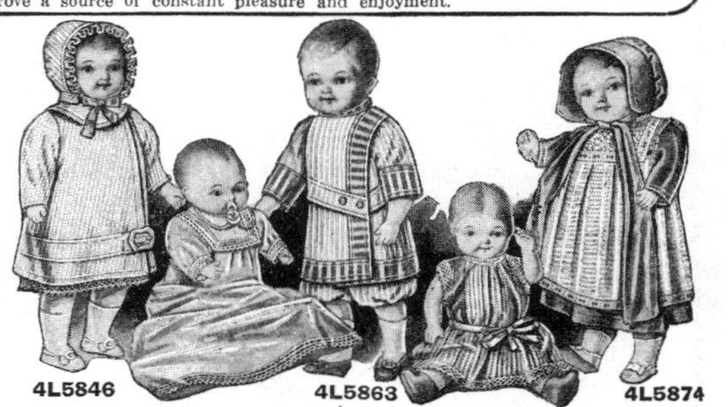

4L5846 4L5863 4L5874

Little Sunshine. Height, 14 in. White stockings and shoes. Pretty auto coat. Belt and gilt buckle. Lace trimmed hood.
4L5846—Price **98c**

Little Baby Blossom. Height, 10½ inches. White lawn dress, trimmed with lace, and lace yoke. Miniature baby pacifier.
4L5854—Price **49c**

Billy Boy. Height, 15 inches. Pretty Norfolk suit. White stockings. Black shoes.
4L5863—Price **98c**

"SUNSHINE BABY"
Dressed in pretty striped frock edged with lace. Ribbon belt and bow. Black feet. Flesh colored body. Height, 11 in. Shipping wt., ¾ lbs.
4L5887—Price **48c**

Sunbonnet Sue. Lace trimmed under wear. White shoes and stockings. Fancy lawn apron, lace trimmed. Blue lawn dress. Sunbonnet with big streamers. Height, 15 in. **4L5874**—Price, **98c**

"OUR BABY"

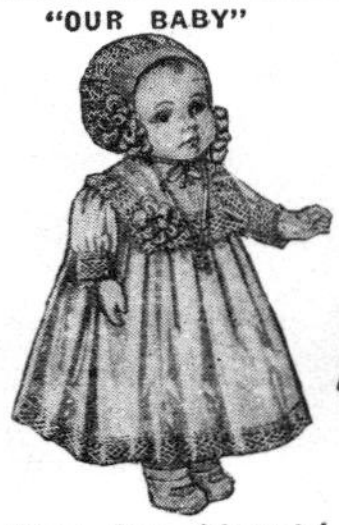

Pretty lace trimmed white lawn dress, with fancy yoke, floss rosette. Lace trimmed cap, with two pink rosettes. Ribbon around neck with small bell. White shoes and stockings. Height, 13½ in. Shipping wt. 1 lb.
4L5878—Price ..**98c**

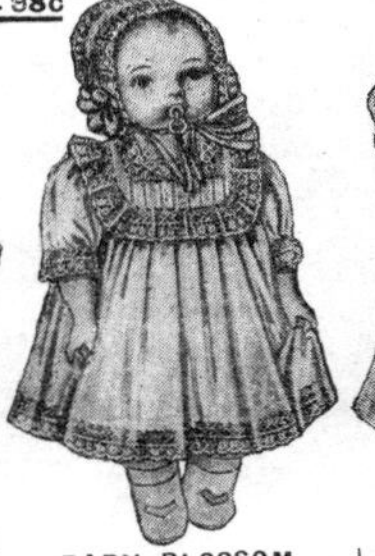

BABY BLOSSOM
Lace trimmed white lawn dress and underwear. White stockings. Felt moccasins. Lace trimmed lawn cap. Little rubber baby pacifier. Height, about 17 in. Shipping weight, 2 lbs.
4L5883—Price **$1.95**

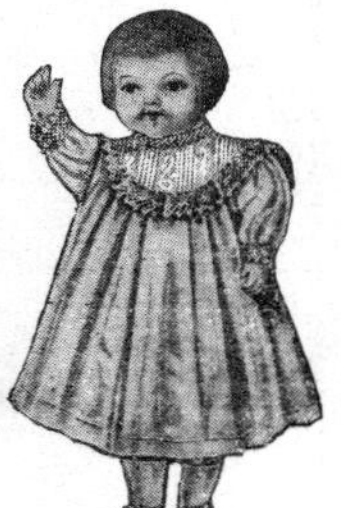

Tootsie. Height, 14 in. White shoes and stockings. Pretty lawn dress; lace edged sleeves and yoke. Shipping weight, 1 lb.
4L5869—Price .**98c**

Moving Eye, Kidlyne Body Doll

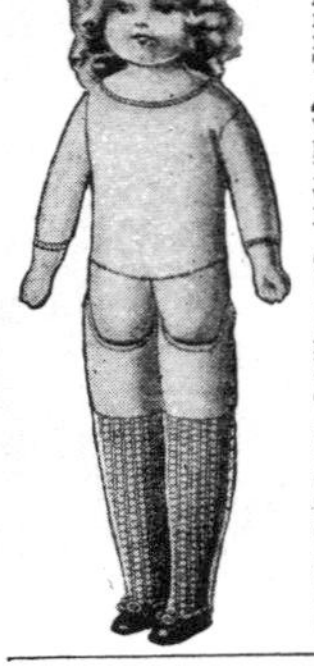

With Wavy Hair Wig long enough to comb. Head is made of bisque. Has pretty face. Has shoes and stockings. Hip swivel joints. They will all sit up straight.

4L5847—Kid Body Dolls. With bisque heads, flowing hair, teeth and hip joints. Length, 12 in. Shipping weight, 1 lb. Each **28c**

4L5848—Kid Body Dolls. With bisque heads, woven wig, flowing hair, teeth and moving eyes. Length, 14 inches. Shipping weight, 1½ lbs. **Each** **50c**

4L5849—Kid Body Dolls. Bisque heads, woven wigs, flowing hair and with teeth. Length, 20 in. Shipping weight, 2 lbs. **Each** **$1.00**

4L5852—Kid Body Dolls. Bisque heads, woven wigs, flowing hair, and pearly teeth. Length, 23 in. Shipping wt., 4 lbs. **$1.50**

Our "Baby Bright" Talking Doll

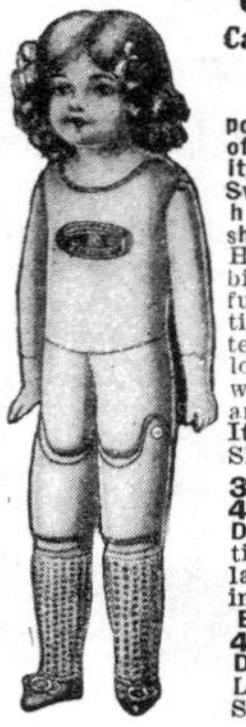

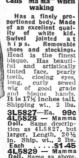

Opens its eyes and Calls "Ma Ma" when waking

Has a finely proportioned body. Made of an excellent quality of white kid. Swivel jointed at hips. Removable shoes and stockings. Head is the finest bisque. Has beautiful and artistically tinted face, pearly teeth, closing eyes, long, curly sewed wig of good grade and bisque hands. **It is 17½ inches tall.** Shipping wt., 2 lbs.

3L5827—Ea. **99c**
4L5828 — Mamma Doll. Same description as 4L5827, but larger. Length, 20½ in. Ship. wt., 3 lbs. **Each** **$1.45**
4L5829 — Mamma Doll. Same as above. Length, 22½ inches. Shipping weight, 3½ **$1.95**

JOINTED PAPIER MACHE DOLLS

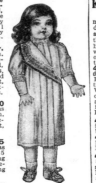

The faces are not only beautifully moulded, but the hair, the heavy, carefully moulded ball joints and every detail are perfect.

Flesh color. Length, 20 in. With fine bisque-turning head, moving eyes, long, curly sewed wig, muslin shirt, shoes and stockings. Wt., 2½ lbs.
4L5865—Each ...**$1.00**
Same as 4L5865, 24 in. long, with eyelashes. Weight, 5 lbs.
4L5866—Each ..**$1.75**
Same as 4L5865, but 25 in. long. Moving eyes, with eyelashes. Shipping weight, 5 lbs.
4L5867—**$2.25**

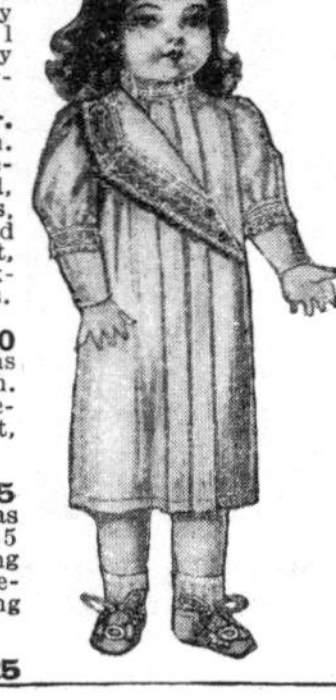

Kewpie Dolls

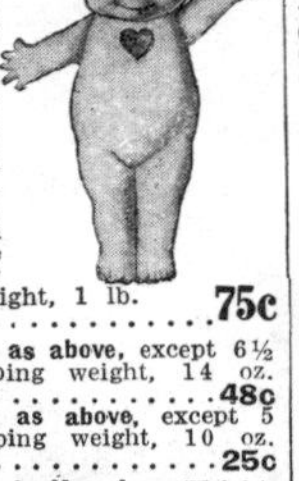

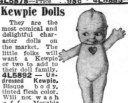

They are the most comical and delightful character dolls on the market. The little folks will want a Kewpie or two to add to their doll family.

4L5892 — Undressed Kewpie. Bisque body, tinted flesh color. Will not wash off. Movable arms. Height, 9 in. Shipping weight, 1 lb. Price **75c**
4L5891—Same as above, except 6½ in. long. Shipping weight, 14 oz. Price **48c**
4L5890—Same as above, except 5 in. long. Shipping weight, 10 oz. Price **25c**
4L5893—Dressed Kewpie. Height, 5 in. Bisque body. Painted shoes and stockings. Colored dress, net drop, lace trimmed. Ribbon belt. Movable arms. Shipping weight, 6 oz. **50c**

$4.98 Life Size Babies

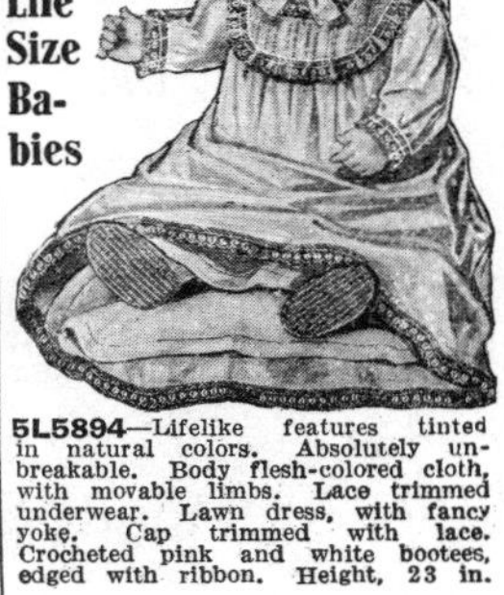

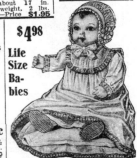

5L5894—Lifelike features tinted in natural colors. Absolutely unbreakable. Body flesh-colored cloth, with movable limbs. Lace trimmed underwear. Lawn dress, with fancy yoke. Cap trimmed with lace. Crocheted pink and white bootees, edged with ribbon. Height, 23 in.

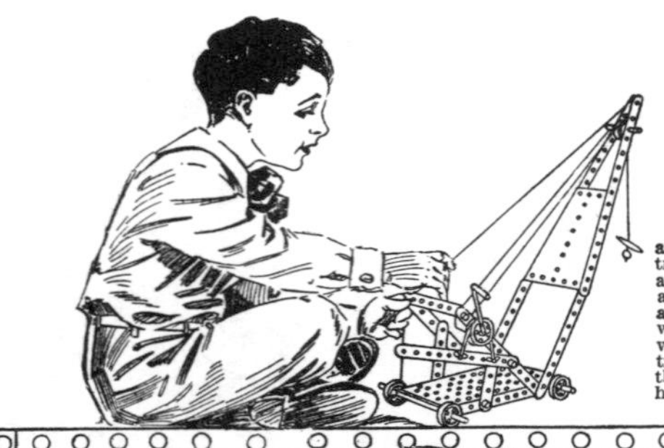

MECCANO

Instructive, Entertaining, Educational

With Meccano any boy can build hundreds of working models on correct engineering principles. The outfits contain nicely plated metal strips accurate gear wheels, pulleys, rods, nuts and bolts, etc. Everything necessary is provided in each outfit, including tools and our 100 page illustrated manual giving complete instructions how to build the different models. There is nothing further to buy. The parts are all standardized and interchangeable, and new parts and new outfits may be added at any time. The parts "go together," without straining or forcing. They are indestructible, and may be used over and over again. When you are tired of one model, you just take it to pieces and use the same parts again to construct another quite different type of model. This is one of the best features of Meccano. You can make hundreds of toys with it, all working, each one different and capable of giving hours of play and fun. All the time you are playing you are learning something which may prove very useful. You are learning how to build bridges, Cranes, Monoplanes, derricks, signals, wagons, cars, towers, swings, windmills, motor busses, trucks of different kinds, lighthouses and machinery of all kinds. Meccano teaches a boy to think. It teaches him patience. It teaches him thoroughness, because every model must be thoroughly and properly constructed, and fixed up good and firm before it will work properly. It teaches him to invent, because after he has made all the models shown in the book of instructions he can go on designing other models from his own ideas.

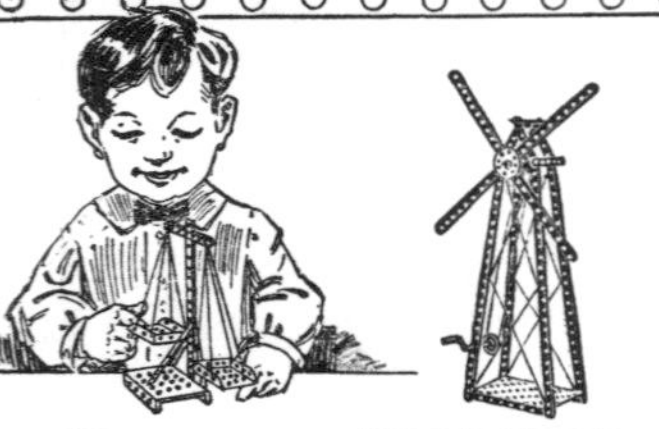

The Models are Fully Explained

Meccano is easy to understand, only you should build the smaller and simpler models first, building better and bigger designs each time. Building the models is only half the game. The other half is playing with them when they are finished.

It is unnecessary to puzzle over the instructions because there are only a few. You simply use your eyes and work straight from the "Manual of Instructions" given with each outfit. Thousands of boys are doing this and so can you.

The Meccano book of instructions, which is included with each outfit, is a splendid production, consisting of 140 pages, and containing a full, detailed description of over 100 models, each illustrated big and clear.

The whole of the outfits are connected by means of accessory outfits, so that no matter where you begin, you can build up. For instance, if you buy a No. 1 Outfit, you can at any future time convert it into a No. 2 by purchasing a No. 1A. The next purchase will be a No. 2A, converting the No. 2 into a No. 3, and so on.

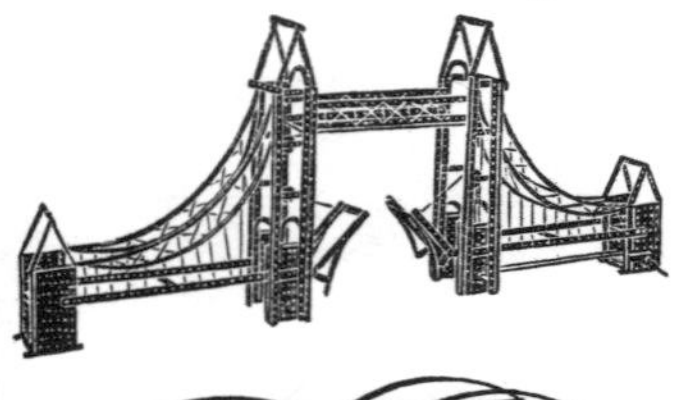

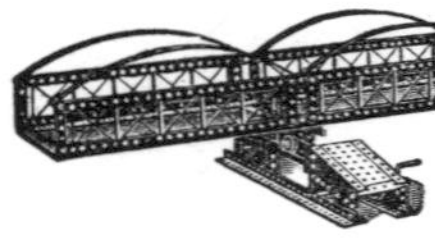

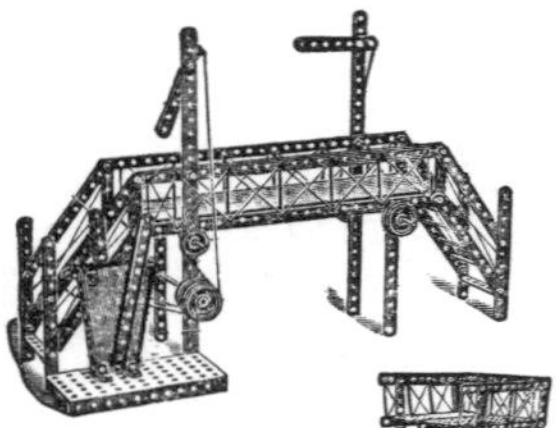

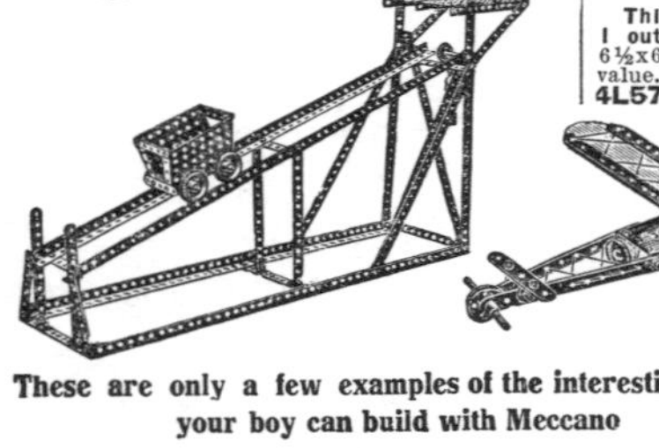

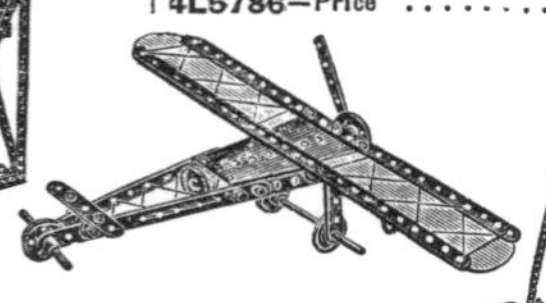

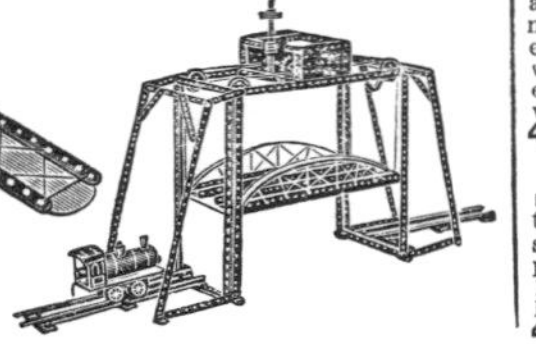

These are only a few examples of the interesting things your boy can build with Meccano

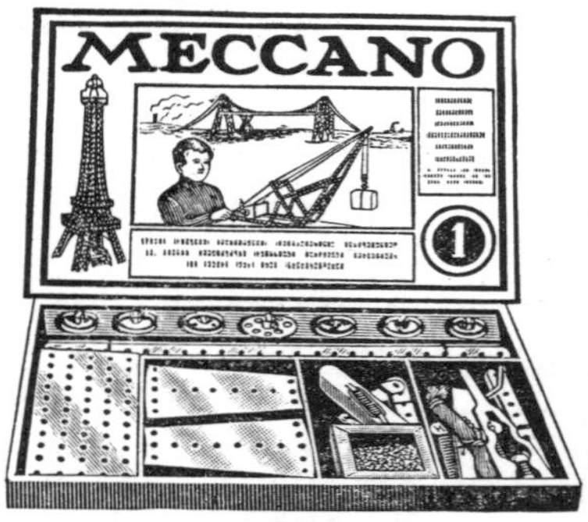

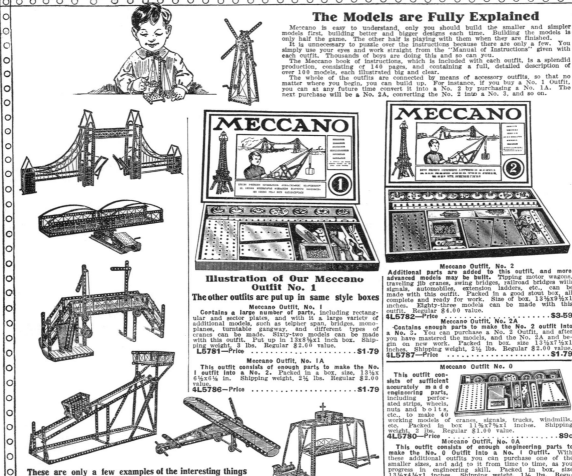

Illustration of Our Meccano Outfit No. 1

The other outfits are put up in same style boxes

Meccano Outfit, No. 1

Contains a large number of parts, including rectangular and sector plates, and with it a large variety of additional models, such as telpher span, bridges, monoplanes, turntable gangway, and different types of cranes can be made. Sixty-two models can be made with this outfit. Put up in 13x8½x1 inch box. Shipping weight, 3 lbs. Regular $2.00 value.
L5781—Price **$1.79**

Meccano Outfit, No. 1A

This outfit consists of enough parts to make the No. 1 outfit into a No. 2. Packed in a box, size, 13½x 6½x6½ in. Shipping weight, 2½ lbs. Regular $2.00 value.
4L5786—Price **$1.79**

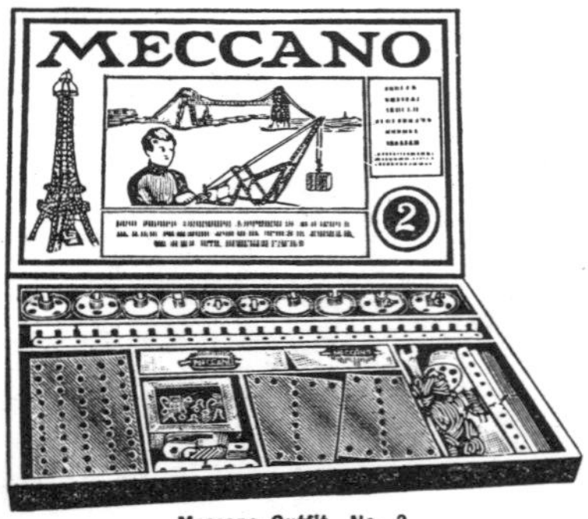

Meccano Outfit, No. 2

Additional parts are added to this outfit, and more advanced models may be built. Tipping motor wagons, traveling jib cranes, swing bridges, railroad bridges with signals, automobiles, extension ladders, etc., can be made with this outfit. Packed in a good stout box, all complete and ready for work. Size of box, 13½x9½x1 inches. Eighty-three models can be made with this outfit. Regular $4.00 value.
4L5782—Price **$3.59**

Meccano Outfit, No. 2A

Contains enough parts to make the No. 2 outfit into a No. 3. You can purchase a No. 2 Outfit, and after you have mastered the models, and the No. 2A and begin on new work. Packed in box, size 13½x7½x1 inches. Shipping weight, 2½ lbs. Regular $2.00 value.
4L5787—Price **$1.79**

Meccano Outfit No. 0

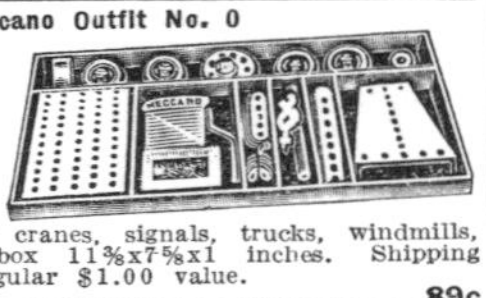

This outfit consists of sufficient accurately made engineering parts, including perforated strips, wheels, nuts and bolts, etc., to make 40 working models of cranes, signals, trucks, windmills, etc. Packed in box 11⅜x7⅝x1 inches. Shipping weight, 2 lbs. Regular $1.00 value.
4L5780—Price **89c**

Meccano Outfit, No. 0A

This outfit consists of enough engineering parts to make the No. 0 Outfit into a No. 1 Outfit. With these additional outfits you can purchase one of the smaller sizes, and add to it from time to time, as you progress in engineering skill. Packed in box, size 13½x4½x1 inches. Shipping weight, 1½ lbs. Regular $1.00 value.
4L5785—Price **89c**

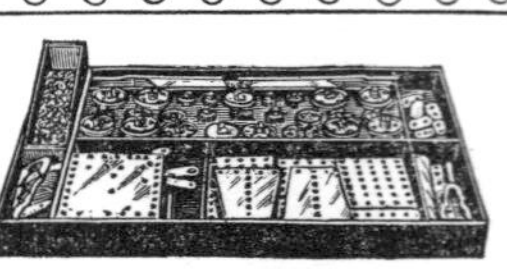

Meccano Outfit, No. 4

This is a complete outfit and makes a valuable present. A large number of additional parts are included. Makes large models of traveling cranes, elevated jib cranes, warehouse with elevators, viaduct bridges, suspension bridges, cable railways, motor buses, coal tips, drilling machines, flying machines, girder cranes, etc. In addition, this outfit contains a fine spring motor, which can be attached to most of the models to operate them. It is built into and becomes a part of each model. One hundred and thirteen other models can be made with this outfit. Put up in box, size 17x12½x2 inches. Shipping weight, 10 lbs. Regular $10.00 value.
4L5794—Price **$8.99**

Meccano will not be delivered to purchasers in our city retail department.

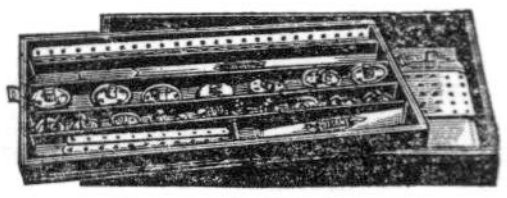

Meccano Outfit, No. 3

This is a more advanced outfit, containing many extra plated strips, and other parts. It includes cut gear and worm wheels, etc., enabling gears of various descriptions to be constructed on correct engineering lines. Among the models you can make with this outfit are rotating cranes, pit headgear, tower wagons, fire-escapes, inclined delivery chutes, etc. Ninety-seven models can easily be constructed with this outfit. Packed in a neat box, size 14½x8¾ x2 inches. Shipping weight, 7 lbs. Regular $6.00 value.
4L5786—Price **$5.39**

Meccano Outfit, No. 3A

Enough extra mechanical parts to make the No. 3 outfit into a No. 4. Packed in box, size 13½x9¼x2 in. Shipping weight, 4 lbs. Regular $4.00 value.
4L5788—Price **$3.59**

Sleds and Self-Steering or Flexible Coasters

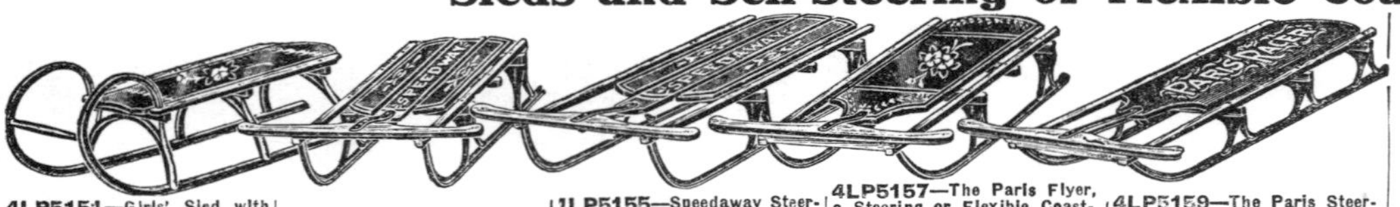

4LP5151—Girls' Sled with Three Bent Knee Bow Runner, 33x12 in. Gear varnished on the wood, top painted and decorated. Has six tinned braces and oval shoes. Others ask $1.50. Weight, 6 lbs. Each **$1.00**

4LP5153—Steering or Flexible Coaster, 33 in. long, 6 in high, with full steel runners and braces, enameled in light color, light in weight but strongly built, solid board top finished in natural color, neatly decorated, fitted with steering attachment. Shipping weight, 10 lbs. Each .. **98c**

1LP5155—Speedaway Steering Flexible Coaster, 36 in. long, 13 in. wide. Made of best materials, spring steel runners, hardwood rails and ash tops. Has 2 knees, is well braced. Gear is enameled in red; woodwork in natural color, with neat decorations and name "Speedaway" on top. Weight, 8 lbs. Others ask $1.75.
Our price **$1.25**

4LP5157—The Paris Flyer, a Steering or Flexible Coaster. Can be steered by the slightest touch of the handle bar. It has full steel runners maroon color, hardwood cross pieces, white oak hand rails and steering bar finished in natural color; seat is enameled in bright red with black stripes and decorations. Length, 42 in. Weight, 10 lbs. Worth $3.00.
Each **$2.25**

4LP5159—The Paris Steering Racer. Something entirely new. The general description is same as the **Paris Flyer only it is a little lower and longer** (length, 48 in.), **and built more for speed; full steer gear, all brightly enameled, fitted with steering gear.** Shipping wt., 12 lbs. Worth $3.00.
Each **$2.50**

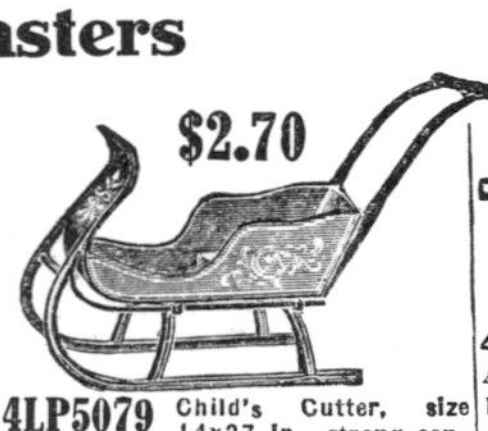

$2.70

4LP5079 Child's Cutter, size 14x27 in., strong construction, large deep body and seat, round side fenders, 2 knees, push handle, brightly plated braces, half oval runners, **all enameled in pure white striped with gold,** neat decorations on front and sides. Shipping weight, 25 lbs.
Each **$2.70**

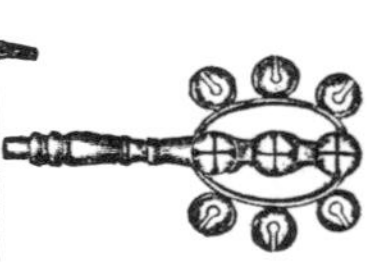

4L5461—The Bell Rattle. A neat little toy for the baby. Made with white enameled **frame** and handle, 6½ in. long with straps and bells attached. Each bell is ⅞ inches in diameter. Shipping wt., 7 oz. Each **19c**

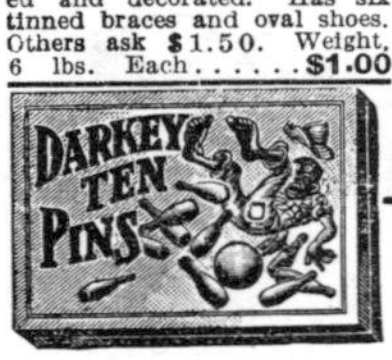

4L5337 —Price

10c

Darkey Ten Pins. Consists of a set of 10 colored pasteboard figures of comical old plantation darkies. Height, 6½ in. Cut out and mounted on wooden bases. Present an amusing appearance, and provide an interesting ten pin game. The figures are knocked down by wooden balls, 1¼ inches in diameter. Two wooden balls packed with each set.

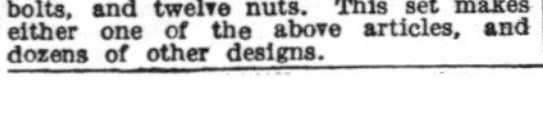

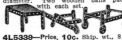

4L5339—Price, 10c. Ship. wt., 8 oz. **Toy Building Outfit for the small boy.** Made of metal. Include 46 pieces, consisting of twelve assorted size steel strips, six corner pieces, four wheels, twelve bolts, and twelve nuts. This set makes either one of the above articles, and dozens of other designs.

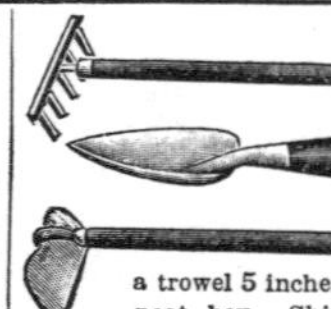

4L5631— Toy Garden Set, consisting of hoe and rake with 10 in. wood handles, and a trowel 5 inches long, put up in neat box. Shipping weight, 11 oz. Price, complete...... **15c**

Rubber Dog

25c

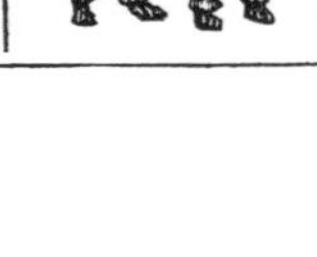

4L5639 — Fine Red Rubber Dog, 4½x3 in. fitted with whistle. Shipping wt. 4 oz.

4L5647— Baby Rattle. Made of six fancy colored celluloid balls 1½ in. in diameter with small bells inside. Weight, 6 oz. Each .. **50c**

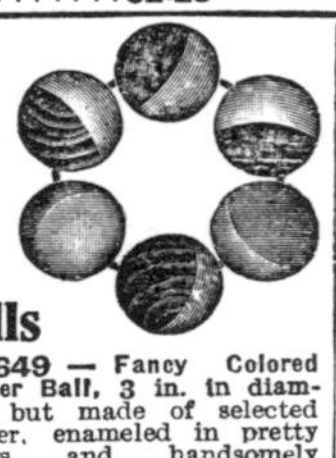

Rubber Balls

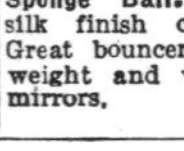

4L5649 — Fancy Colored Rubber Ball, 3 in. in diameter but made of selected rubber, enameled in pretty colors and handsomely decorated. Shipping weight, 5 oz. Each **20c**

4L5650 — Net Covered Sponge Ball. Covered with silk finish colored netting. Great bouncer, very light in weight and will not injure mirrors.

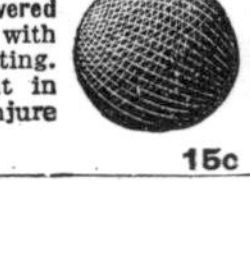

15c

Rattles

4L5643— Musical Rubber Rattle with teething ring.
Each **10c**
Per doz. **$1.00**
Shipping weight, 3 oz.

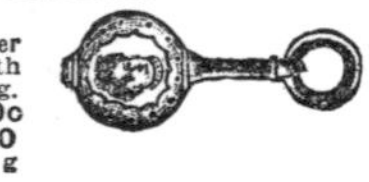

Celluloid Rattles

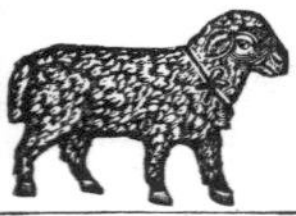

4L5645 — Combination Rattle and Teething Ring. Made of "Pyralin" (same composition as celluloid), in four colors. Length, 4½ in. Shipping wt., 4 oz.
Each **19c**

4L5641 — Red Rubber Sheep, 4¼ in. long, 3 in. high, with whistle. Shipping wt., 4 oz. **25c**

Rolly Dolly Toys

You Can't Keep Him Down

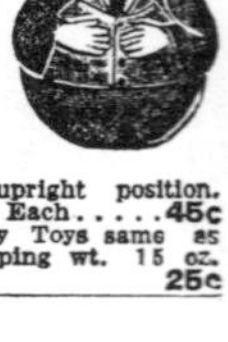

4L5275—Rolly Dolly is one of the best playthings in the market, particularly for the little ones as they are almost indestructible. They are made of papier mache. Size 9x5 inches, in imitation of popular comic figures, like "Foxy Grandpa," clown, etc., enameled in colors. They are made with round, heavy base and unless held down will always return to an upright position. Shipping weight, 20 oz. Each...... **45c**
4L5276—Rolly Dolly Toys same as 4L5275, 6 in. high, shipping wt. 15 oz. **25c**

ERECTOR

This Big Outfit Has 775 Steel Parts and Motor

This Motor FREE with Outfits No. 4, 5 or 6

The new Erector Motor which is very practical, is constructed from flat steel pieces bolted to each other with an armature made in the same fashion, will run on one or two dry batteries and will propel your cars, elevators, machine shops, etc.

Each set packed in a handsomely labeled box, with 64 page book of instructions and diagrams and working drawings of over 300 models which can be made from ERECTOR Sets.

ERECTOR OUTFIT No. 6. This outfit consists of 775 Polished Parts, including motor, patented girders, complete assortment of screws, wheels, angle connections, shells for building wheels, pulleys, gears and flange wheels. The patent girders are exactly like those used in modern steel construction work, the patent feature being the turned over edge which makes it neater and stronger in every way. Every piece in this outfit is made of steel and all parts fit together perfectly. Over 250 different models can be made with this outfit, such as dredges flying boats, swings, battleships, band saws. trestles, sewing machines, turn-table cranes, machine shops, locomotives, motor boats, etc. Packed in hardwood hinged cover box. Sizes, 15x10x4 inches. Complete outfit, motor and instruction book. Our price, including motor. **$8.75**

This Outfit has 537 Steel Parts and Motor

ERECTOR OUTFIT No. 5. We offer the only construction sets in which you receive a motor **free.** This outfit contains 537 polished steel parts from which can be built over 225 large and interesting models, monoplanes, sand shovels, girder bridges, lamps, cranes, water motors, auto trucks, double windmills, towers and many models used in connection with motor. These outfits will give any boy a splendid mechanical knowledge. Packed in hardwood hinged box 15x9x3 inches, contains 537 parts complete outfit, motor and instruction book. **$6.95**

Outfit No. 4 has 325 Steel Parts and Motor

ACCESSORY OUTFIT

ERECTOR ACCESSORY SET No. 6A. OF 356 PARTS. This will build the No. 6 set into the No. 7, as illustrated in instruction book. Packed in wooden box 13½x 9⅜x3⅛ in. Any boy who owns the No. 6 outfit will look forward with eagerness to the No. 6A which will allow him to build 278 models. He will then have nearly 1,300 parts. Shpg. wt., 6 lbs. **$4.25**

ERECTOR OUTFIT No. 4. Motor for furnishing power, free with this construction outfit of 325 extra strong parts made of beautiful polished hard steel that can be made into 207 different models by following book of instructions. Among the models possible to build are Torpedo Boats, Revolving Draw Bridges. Four-Arm Semaphore, Telegraphic Sending and Receiving Instrument, Police Patrol, Drill Press, Barber's Chair, Gear Boxes, etc., all carefully packed in hardwood box. Size 13x9x3 inches. Complete outfit, motor and instruction book. Shipping weight, 8 lbs. Our price................................ **$4.49**

Outfit No. 3—229 Steel Parts

ERECTOR ACCESSORY SET No. 3A. 121 PARTS AND ONE ERECTOR MOTOR. This set builds the No. 3 set into a No. 4. Packed in a strong box, a valuable set for enlarging any set on this page. Buy this accessory outfit and build some of the larger and more interesting models. Complete Instruction Book and Diagrams with each set. Shpg. wt., 4 lbs. Price.................... **$1.75**

box, size 12½x9¾x2½ inches. Our price.

ERECTOR OUTFIT No. 3. The only actual structural steel construction toy on the market. **All steel,** real girders, 229 parts that can be formed into 176 models. Steam Shovels, Hay Wagon, Telegraph Conveyor, Pile Driver, Portable Crane, Girder Bridge, Boom Crane, Gear Boxes, Ice Boats, Lawn Swing, Dump Wagon, etc., etc. Packed in strong box and instruction book. Complete outfit and instruction book. **$2.75**

Outfit No. 2—173 Parts

Car, Railway, Aeroplane, Road Scraper, etc., etc. Packed in neat box, size 12½x9½x1 inches. Complete outfit and instruction book. Shpg. wt., 3 lbs. Our price.................... **$1.75**

ERECTOR ACCESSORY SET No. 2A. 64 parts. This set builds our No. 2 set into a No. 3. Packed in a strong box. Any set may be enlarged with this accessory outfit. Price.. **90c**

ERECTOR OUTFIT No. 2. All Erector sets are made of the same material, polished steel and perfect fitting parts. The most popular toy on the market today. Outfit consists of 173 parts and makes 120 models, Bicycle, Irish Mail, Lawn Swing, Jib Crane, Hand

Outfit No. 1—93 Parts

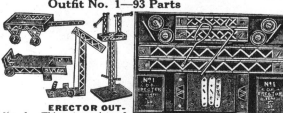

ERECTOR OUTFIT No. 1. This set consists of 93 parts made of highly polished steel. Instructions for making over 85 models. Windmills, Derricks, Cannon, Counter Shafting, Truck, Double Arm Semaphore, Grindstone, etc.; box 12½x9½x1 in. Outfit and instruction book. Price.................... **85c**

Mechanical Friction Automobiles, Trains and Toys

Friction Mechanical Auto Truck

37T6700 Friction mechanical auto truck 10x4x3½ in. Made of sheet steel, lithographed in red, gold striping, gold-bronzed wheels, seat and fenders operates automatically by pressing friction motor. No springs. Shpg. wt., 1½ lbs. **39c**

Mechanical Automobile

37T6702 Made of sheet steel, lithographed in up-to-date colors. Operates automatically by pressing friction motor. No springs to get out of order. Two passengers. Size, 14x6½x5½ in. Shpg. wt., 3½ lbs. **$1.25**

Mechanical Roadster

37T6704 Made of sheet steel enameled in attractive colors. Size, 9x3½x5 in. Driver at wheel. Spare wheel in back of car. Operates by winding spring. Shpg. wt., 1 lb. **65c**

Mechanical Hook and Ladder

37T6706 Size 11½x6x3½ in. Made of sheet steel lithographed in attractive colors, driver and two ladders each 8½ in. long. Operates by pressing friction motor. Shpg. wt. **63c**

Mechanical Clown Jiggers

37T6718 Made of sheet steel lithographed with a circus design, fitted with a clock spring and two metal clowns each 7 in. high lithographed in natural and life-like colors. By winding spring the clowns dance. Size of frame 8½x8x1¼ **48c**

Friction Mechanical Fire Engine

37T6710 Made of sheet steel enameled in bright colors, wheels, engine and ornaments finished in gold. Driver at wheel, Size, 11½x7½x4 in. Operates automatically by pressing motor. No springs. Shpg. wt., 2 lbs. **63c**

Friction Mechanical Locomotives

37T6712 Mechanical locomotive and tender, 12½x3½x3 inches. Made of red enameled sheet steel, decorated with gold bronze. Operates by pressing friction motor, no springs. **29c**

37T6714 Mechanical locomotive and tender, 17x4¼x2½ inches. Red enameled sheet steel, decorated with gold bronze. Operates by pressing friction motor, no springs. **59c**

Extra Large Steel Train

37T6716 Made of sheet steel lithographed in bright colors. Length over all 23 in. Consists of locomotive 12x4x2 in. Pullman car 10½x4x2½ in. Will please any child and is one of the largest trains made. Retails at $1.25. Shpg. wt., 2 lbs. **63c**

Mechanical War Boat, 63c

37T6708 Mechanical war boat on wheels, operates by pressing friction motor. Made of sheet metal, enameled in marine colors. 13½ inches long, 8 inches high. **63c**

Friction Mechanical Automobiles

37T6720 Mechanical automobile, 7½x3½x2½ inches, made of red enameled sheet steel, gold enameled wheels, operates by pressing friction motor, no springs. **48c**

37T6722 Mechanical automobile 13x5x5 inches. Made of red enameled sheet steel, gold striping and gold enameled wheels. Operates by pressing friction motor, no springs. **63c**

Merry-Go-Round

Made of sheet steel, lithographed in bright colors. Four metal cut-out horses and riders lithographed in life-like colors. By turning crank, canopy, horse and riders revolve in a circle. Size, 5½x4¾ in. Shpg. wt., 1 lb. **15c**

Friction

Performing Elephant

37T6726 Friction mechanical performing elephant. Made of sheet steel lithographed in bright colors. Driver mounted on box. Operates by pressing friction motor. Size, 10½x6½x3 in. Shpg. wt., 2 lbs. **63c**

Mechanical

Friction Mechanical Duck

37T6728 Friction mechanical duck operates by pressing friction motor. Made of sheet steel lithographed in bright colors. Size, 9x7½x5 in. Shpg. wt., 2 lbs. **63c**

Toys, 63c Each

Circus Mule

37T6730 Mechanical circus mule operates by pressing friction motor. Made of sheet steel enameled in bright colors. When in motion donkey moves head. Driver mounted on box. Size, 10¾x6½x3 in. Shpg. wt., 2 lbs. **63c**

Mechanical Toys for Boys and Girls

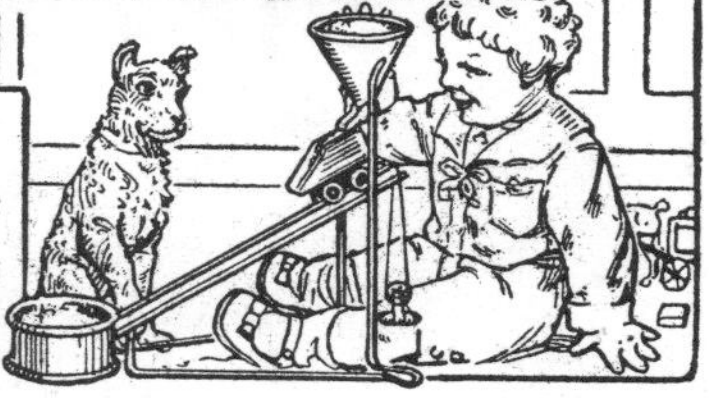

Little Hustler Motor

37T6600 3½-inch motor. Black enamel nickel-plated trimmings, 3-pole armature, drives a 4½-inch fan speed pulley for running mechanical toys, models, etc. Any dry cell will run the Little Hustler. Shpg. wt., 16 oz. Price **98c**

Leader Motor

37T6602 Drives from either pulley. Reducing gear easily thrown out of mesh with the pinion on shaft. Reversing switch is positive in action, operates either as a starting switch or to reverse the direction of motor. Made of heavy plate steel, enameled in black. Armature is laminated 1¼ in. diameter. Three poles, shaft 1.48 diameter, pulley 9/16 inches, base 5½x 3¼ inches, motor 4½x3x5 inches. **$2.48**

Electric Thriller

37T6604 By turning the crank slow or fast the current can be regulated so that a slight or severe shock can be produced. Furnished complete, mounted on a wood baseboard. **95c**

Boy Scout Telegraph Set

37T6606 Telegraph set, consists of sounder and receiver mounted on polished cherry board. Instructions for operating board, size 7x4½ in. Operates on dry cell. **$1.19**

Mechanical Pool Player

37T6608 Clock spring device operates balls into position for player to strike them with cue. These balls all deposit in one of the pockets at the other end. Made of sheet steel, enameled in attractive colors. Size, 6x4½x2½ inches. **25c**

Automatic Dumping Sandy 63c

37T6610 By pouring sand in the hopper it starts bucket dumping sand automatically in any direction desired. Made of heavy sheet steel 13 inches high, base 7½ inches wide. Furnished with paper tray, can of white sand and sand scoop. **63c**

Sandy Andy Sand Toy 98c and 60c

Sandy Andy sand toys are very popular and give an endless source of amusement to all children. The best and most practical sand toy made.

Sandy Andy, 98c

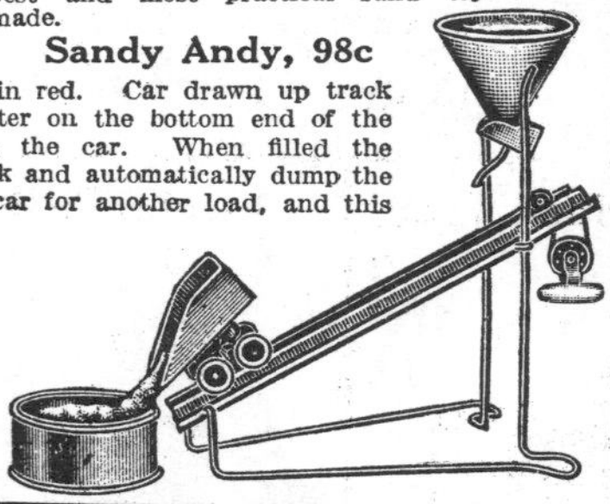

37T6612 Sheet steel, enameled in red. Car drawn up track by weight until it opens a swinging shutter on the bottom end of the hopper, allowing the sand to run into the car. When filled the sand causes the car to run down the track and automatically dump the sand. The weight then again pulls the car for another load, and this operation is automatically continued. Size, 21x18 inches. Furnished with a can of white sand. Price **98c**

37T6614 Constructed exactly as above, only smaller. Shpg. wt., 2½ lbs. Size, 11 x 11 **60c**

Automatic Sand Crane

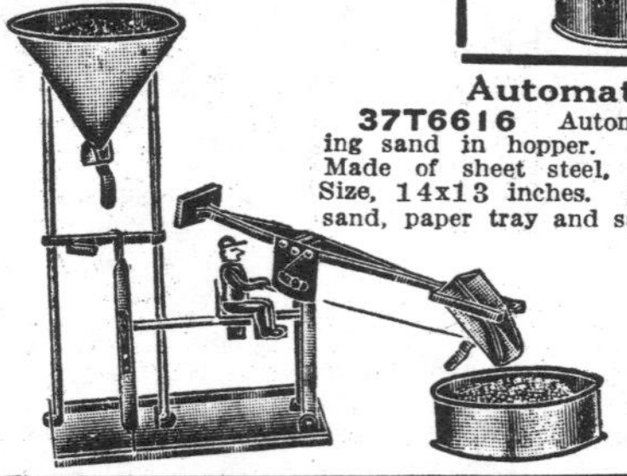

37T6616 Automatic sand crane operated by pouring sand in hopper. Fills and dumps sand automatically. Made of sheet steel, enameled base, nickel plated frame, Size, 14x13 inches. Furnished with a can of white sand, paper tray and sand scoop. Price **98c**

Panama Pile Driver

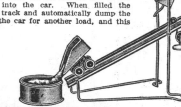

37T6618 Top member is a chute in which 12 marbles are placed. As long as one or more marbles are kept in this chute, the hammer keeps sliding up and down. There is a continuous "Tap, Tap, Tap" that makes this toy very amusing. Made of sheet steel, lithographed in bright colors, nickel plated and polished frame. Size 17x13x6½. Complete with 12 marbles Shipping weight, 2½ pounds. **95c**

Climbing Monkey

37T6620 Climbing monkey, made of sheet steel, enameled in bright colors. Mounted on strong cord with 2 metal rings at each end. By pulling on cord monkey automatically climbs up and down. Moving arms and legs. Cap trimmed with cord tassel, 8 inches high, 4 inches wide, **25c**

Mechanical Negro Jigger

37T6622 A lifelike reproduction of an Alabama coon jigger. Made of metal, enameled in bright, lifelike colors. Fitted with strong clock spring. By winding spring figure dances. The time of the dancer can be regulated by pressing levers. 11 inches high, base 4½x3. **48c**

37T6624 Motor cycle Charlie, made of sheet steel, lithographed in lifelike colors. Moving wheels, arms and legs. Size 11x8 inches. Price **23c**

37T6626 Uncle Sam mounted on bicycle, made of sheet steel lithographed in lifelike colors. Moving wheels, arms and legs. Size 11x8 in. Price **23c**

37T6628 Motorcycle Mike, made of sheet steel lithographed in lifelike colors. Moving wheels, arms and legs. Size 11x8 inches. Price **23c**

The above toys operate and race automatically when suspended on a heavy string.

37T6630 Sheet steel, enameled in bright colors. Clock spring trolley, eight wheels, open windows, 8½ inches long, 2 inches high. **65c**

Passenger Steamer

37T6632 7 inches long. 4½ in. high clock spring; when wound up floats in water. Made of metal enameled. Furnace, smokestacks and propeller **48c**

Mechanical Hook and Ladder

37T6634 Sheet steel, enameled. Size 9½x4. Clock spring, machine runs forward. Automatic extension ladder, 12 inches high. Operates by a lever device. Driver at wheel. **48c**

Mechanical Dump Cart

37T6636 Made of sheet steel, enameled. Size, 9½x3¾x4. Strong clock spring. Cart runs forward. Lever device for operating body of cart. Driver at wheel. **48c**

Torpedo Flying Machine

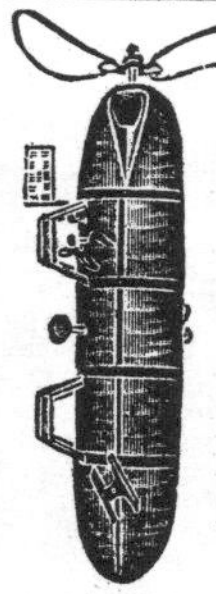

37T6638 Made of metal enameled. Strong clock spring, three revolving propellers. Regulator for starting and stopping, two passenger baskets and flag 11½ inches long. Weight, 10 oz. Price **25c**

Monoplane Flying Machine

37T6640 Clock spring, propeller operates machine, wings and aviator. Runs on the floor as well as in the air. 5 in. high, 7 in. wide. 8½ in. long. **25c**

BIKES FOR BOYS AND GIRLS

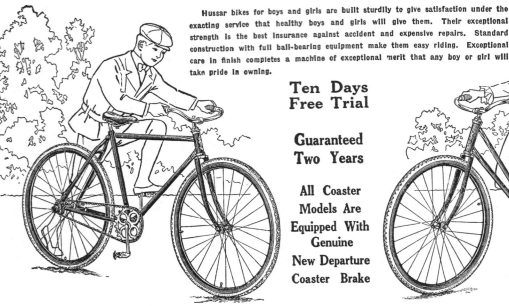

Hussar bikes for boys and girls are built sturdily to give satisfaction under the exacting service that healthy boys and girls will give them. Their exceptional strength is the best insurance against accident and expensive repairs. Standard construction with full ball-bearing equipment make them easy riding. Exceptional care in finish completes a machine of exceptional merit that any boy or girl will take pride in owning.

Ten Days Free Trial

Guaranteed Two Years

All Coaster Models Are Equipped With Genuine New Departure Coaster Brake

Specifications

Frame—One-inch, 19-gauge, seamless tubing, reinforced and brazed flush at all joints. **Equipment**—Full ball bearing; all moving parts specially tempered, rat trap pedals, one-piece removable hanger, adjustable handle bar ; full spring saddle with stretched leather top, guaranteed tires and complete tool kit in leather bag. **Finish**—Frame jet black, with red head rubbed and polished enamel. All exposed metal nickel plated. Name plate, gold with red lettering. Shipping weight each, 45 pounds.

Prices on Boys' Hussar 1916 Models		Prices on Girls' Hussar 1916 Models	
10M57 Roadster model, 16-inch frame, 24-inch wheels. Price . . $14.45		**10M65** Roadster model, 16-inch frame, 24-inch wheels. Price . . $14.65	
10M59 Coaster model, 16-inch frame, 24-inch wheels. Price . . 17.45		**10M67** Coaster model, 16-inch frame, 24-inch wheels. Price . . 17.65	
10M61 Roadster model, 18-inch frame, 26-inch wheels. Price . . 14.50		**10M69** Roadster model, 18-inch frame, 26-inch wheels. Price . . 14.75	
10M63 Coaster model, 18-inch frame, 26-inch wheels. Price . . 17.50		**10M71** Coaster model, 18-inch frame, 26-inch wheels. Price . . 17.75	

For Inseam Measurement up to 24 Inches Order 16 Inch Frame. For 24 to 28 Inch Inseam Order 18 Inch Frame.

---

10 Days Free Trial Guaranteed Two Years

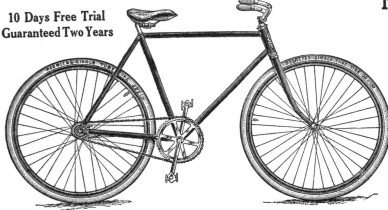

Men's Kingston Bicycle

The Kingston is our lowest priced bicycle. It is a good bicycle and exceptional value. It is covered by our liberal two-year guarantee. We are proud of it in that it shows at what a very low price we can sell a good bicycle. We think however, that you will be better pleased in purchasing one of our higher priced models, for with the few extra dollars of cost are added marked improvements in finish and equipment.

Specifications

FRAME—22 inches, made from 1-inch seamless steel tubing; all joints brazed and finished flush.

EQUIPMENT—One-piece drop forged, nickel plated, removable hanger, full ball bearing, rat trap pedals, adjustable handle bar, leather grips, padded leather saddle, Peerless tires.

FINISH—Jet black enamel.

Coaster model is equipped with genuine New Departure Coaster Brake. Shipping weight, 50 pounds.

10M1 Roadster model.
Price **$12.95**

10M3 Coaster model.
Price **15.95**

Tool bag with wrench, pump, oiler and tire repair outfit, extra **45c**

Ladies' Newport Bicycle

High-grade and dependable Ladies' Bicycle. Made of the very best materials, finished with exceptional care and carrying the latest 1916 equipment. It is sold under our liberal 10 days' free trial offer, which allows you to try it for ten days and return it if not satisfactory. We guarantee it for two years against defects of material or workmanship.

Specifications

FRAME—20 or 22-inch beautiful drop curved, made from 1-inch seamless steel tubing reinforced and brazed at joints and finished flush.

EQUIPMENT—One-piece drop forged removable hanger, rubber combination pedals, adjustable handle bar, truss coil spring easy riding saddle, genuine Peerless single tube tires, roller chain and mud guards, extra quality laced skirt guard. Full ball bearing in every detail. **Tool bag of selected leather and complete tools included.**

FINISH—Jet black, with handsome double gold stripe, rubbed and polished. Rims enameled to match. The many nickel-plated parts make a striking and beautiful contrast to this finish.

10M73 Ladies' Newport Bicycle, Roadster model, complete as described above. Price . . . **$17.95**

10M77 Ladies' Newport Bicycle, Coaster model, complete as described, and with New Departure Coaster brake. Price **$20.95**
Shipping weight, 50 pounds.

10 Days Free Trial Guaranteed Two Years

BOY SCOUT BICYCLE $9.75

Improved Model
Easy Running
Roller Bearing

Adjustable Handle Bars and Seat Post

Solid Rubber Tires

The best hard tire bicycle made for children from five to ten years

Frame — double ¾x¼ inch half oval steel, forks and rear stays are also ¾x¼ inch half oval steel. Arched fork crown, regular bicycle head. Rear fork ends equipped with chain adjusting plates. Top bar dropped at rear, motor bike style. Enameled carmine red, with gold striping. Handle bar, seat post springs, wheels and pedals bright tin plated, wheels 18 inches in diameter double spokes. Handle bars, adjustable Kelly pattern, Troxel leather saddle with double coil springs. Steel mud guards, ¾ inch cushion rubber tires, wired on, roller bearings in hanger bracket and both wheels, Diamond roller chain with 1 inch pitch. Height from floor to top of saddle 26 in. Length over all 50 inches. Shpg. wt., 35 lbs.

THE CONSTRUCTION IS MECHANICALLY PERFECT. A BICYCLE THAT WILL GIVE EXCELLENT SERVICE AND SATISFACTION.

Irish Mail Special Delivery Wagon

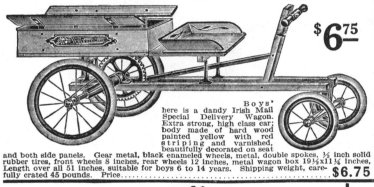

$6.75

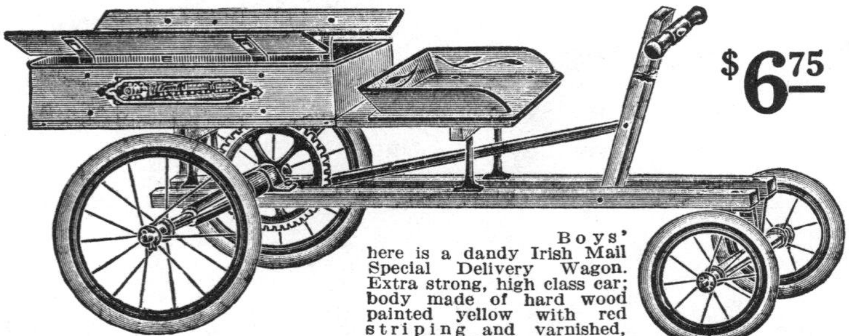

Boys' here is a dandy Irish Mail Special Delivery Wagon. Extra strong, high class car; body made of hard wood painted yellow with red striping and varnished, beautifully decorated on seat and both side panels. Gear metal, black enameled wheels, metal, double spokes, ½ inch solid rubber tires, front wheels 8 inches, rear wheels 12 inches, metal wagon box 19½x11¼ inches, Length over all 51 inches, suitable for boys 6 to 14 years. Shipping weight, carefully crated 45 pounds. Price.................................... **$6.75**

The Midget Racer

$4.75

Operates the same as a toy auto. Made of steel, green enameled. Gray dappled hardwood horse. 6-inch steel, ½-inch rubber tired front steering wheel. Head of horse and wheel turns in any direction desired. Red enameled hardwood shafts and seat, 12-inch steel ½-inch rubber tired rear wheels, steel railing. Size, 34 inches long, 19½ inches high, **$4.75**

Joy Rider Hand Car

Rubber Tire Wheels

$3.95

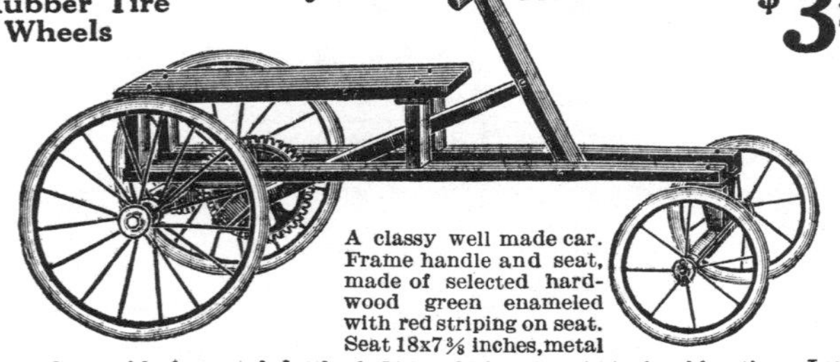

A classy well made car. Frame handle and seat, made of selected hardwood green enameled with red striping on seat. Seat 18x7¾ inches, metal wheels and gear black enameled, wheels 8½ and 12 inches, ½ inch rubber tires. Length over all 40 inches. Suitable for boys 6 to 14 years. Shpg. wt., 24 lbs. Price.. **$3.95**

The Monarch Racer

Rubber Tire Wheels

40 Inches Long

$3.45

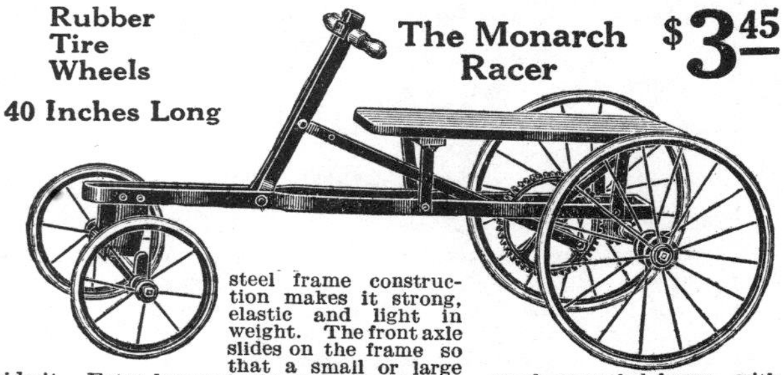

steel frame construction makes it strong, elastic and light in weight. The front axle slides on the frame so that a small or large child can ride it. Extra heavy double bar wrought iron, black enameled frame, with double pull, braced gear, ½-inch rubber tires, front wheel 8 inches high, ½-inch rubber tire, rear wheels 14 inches high. Wood seat painted and stenciled in gilt and colors; 40 inches long. Seat, 8x18 inches. Weight, packed, 28 pounds. **$3.45**

Genuine Kiddie Kars and Choo-Choo Horses

Choo-Choo Horse

	High in.	Floor to seat in. high	Wide in.	Long in.	Shipping weight	Price
437T7622	14	7	7¾	16½	5 lbs.	$0.98
437T7624	16½	8½	8¼	17½	6 lbs.	1.48
437T7626	18½	10	9½	19	7 lbs.	1.98
437T7628	21½	11¾	10¾	20½	8 lbs.	2.48

Hardwood varnished and polished turning handle and steering device. Hardwood wheels, inside bracket. Front wheel turns completely around, making a practical and safe steering device. Remember these are the genuine and original Kiddie Cars.

Choo-Choo Horses

	High in.	Floor to seat in. high	Wide in.	Long in.	Wheels in.	Plain wheels Price	Shpg. wt.		Rubber Tired wheels
437T7610	15½	8	8¼	22	4½	$1.50	6 lbs.	437T7616	$2.48
437T7612	17½	9¼	8¾	24½	5½	1.98	7 lbs.	437T7618	2.98
437T7614	20	12	9	26½	5¾	2.75	8 lbs.	437T7620	3.98

Choo-choo-horses, made for boys and girls too young for automobiles hand cars and velocipedes. Suitable for indoor and outside use. Made of hardwood, varnished and polished; shaped cut out and stenciled turning horse heads, leather ears, turned hardwood hand-grips. Four solid hardwood wheels, steel axles, hardwood inside bracket, head and front wheels turn completely around, which makes a practical steering device. Improved with a foot rest.

Kiddie Kar

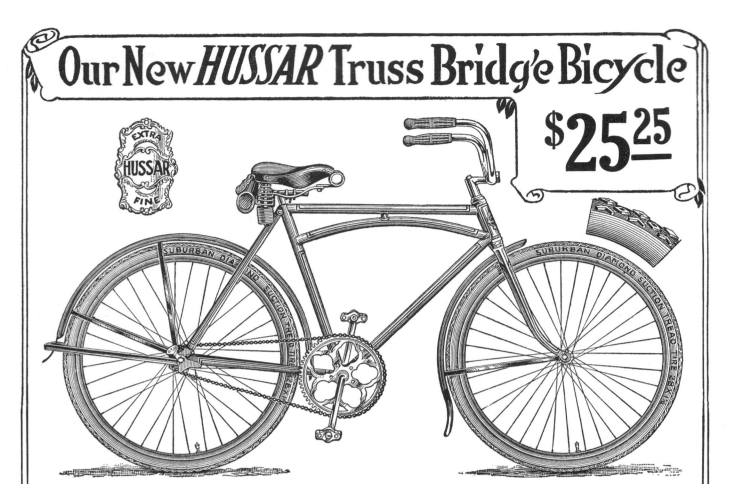

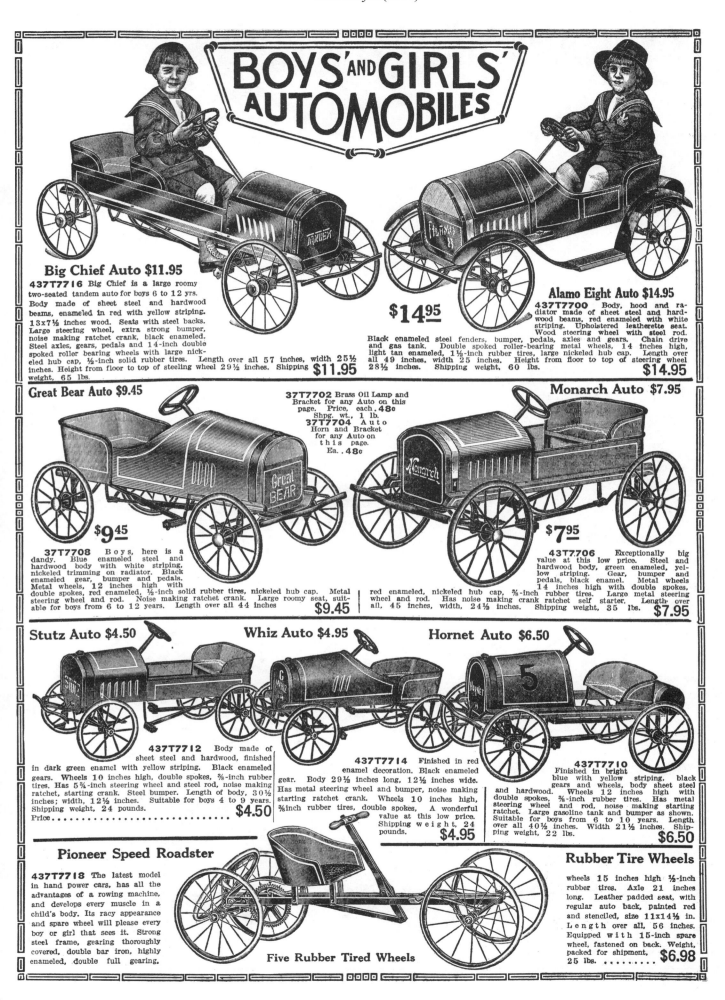

BOYS' AND GIRLS' AUTOMOBILES

Big Chief Auto $11.95

437T7716 Big Chief is a large roomy two-seated tandem auto for boys 6 to 12 yrs. Body made of sheet steel and hardwood beams, enameled in red with yellow striping. 13x7½ inches wood. Seats with steel backs. Large steering wheel, extra strong bumper, noise making ratchet crank, black enameled. Steel axles, gears, pedals and 14-inch double spoked roller bearing wheels with large nickeled hub cap, ½-inch solid rubber tires. Length over all 57 inches, width 25½ inches. Height from floor to top of steeling wheel 29½ inches. Shipping weight, 65 lbs.

$11.95

$14.95

Alamo Eight Auto $14.95

437T7700 Body, hood and radiator made of sheet steel and hardwood beams, red enameled with white striping. Upholstered leatherette seat. Wood steering wheel with steel rod. Black enameled steel fenders, bumper, pedals, axles and gears. Chain drive and gas tank. Double spoked roller-bearing metal wheels, 14 inches high, light tan enameled, 1½-inch rubber tires, large nickeled hub cap. Length over all 49 inches, width 25 inches. Height from floor to top of steering wheel 28½ inches. Shipping weight, 60 lbs.

$14.95

Great Bear Auto $9.45

37T7702 Brass Oil Lamp and Bracket for any Auto on this page. Price, each .48c Shpg. wt., 1 lb.
37T7704 Auto Horn and Bracket for any Auto on this page. Ea. .48c

37T7708 Boys, here is a dandy. Blue enameled steel and hardwood body with white striping, nickeled trimming on radiator. Black enameled gear, bumper and pedals. Metal wheels, 12 inches high with double spokes, red enameled, ½-inch solid rubber tires, nickeled hub cap. Metal steering wheel and rod. Noise making ratchet crank. Large roomy seat, suitable for boys from 6 to 12 years. Length over all 44 inches

$9.45

Monarch Auto $7.95

43T7.706 Exceptionally big value at this low price. Steel and hardwood body, green enameled, yellow striping. Gear, bumper and pedals, black enamel. Metal wheels 14 inches high with double spokes, red enameled, nickeled hub cap, ⅝-inch rubber tires. Large metal steering wheel and rod. Has noise making crank ratchet self starter. Length over all, 45 inches, width, 24½ inches. Shipping weight, 35 lbs.

$7.95

Stutz Auto $4.50

437T7712 Body made of sheet steel and hardwood, finished in dark green enamel with yellow striping. Black enameled gears. Wheels 10 inches high, double spokes, ⅝-inch rubber tires. Has 5¾-inch steering wheel and steel rod, noise making ratchet, starting crank. Steel bumper. Length of body, 30½ inches; width, 12½ inches. Suitable for boys 4 to 9 years. Price.................... **$4.50**

Whiz Auto $4.95

437T7714 Finished in red enamel decoration. Black enameled gear. Body 29½ inches long, 12½ inches wide. Has metal steering wheel and bumper, noise making starting ratchet crank. Wheels 10 inches high, ⅜-inch rubber tires, double spokes. A wonderful value at this low price. Shipping weight, 24 pounds.

$4.95

Hornet Auto $6.50

437T7710 Finished in bright blue with yellow striping, black gears and wheels, body sheet steel and hardwood. Wheels 12 inches high with double spokes, ⅝-inch rubber tires. Has metal steering wheel and rod, noise making starting ratchet. Large gasoline tank and bumper as shown. Suitable for boys from 6 to 10 years. Length over all 40½ inches. Width 21½ inches. Shipping weight, 22 lbs.

$6.50

Pioneer Speed Roadster

437T7718 The latest model in hand power cars, has all the advantages of a rowing machine, and develops every muscle in a child's body. Its racy appearance and spare wheel will please every boy or girl that sees it. Strong steel frame, gearing thoroughly covered, double bar iron, highly enameled, double full gearing.

Five Rubber Tired Wheels

Rubber Tire Wheels

wheels 15 inches high ½-inch rubber tires. Axle 21 inches long. Leather padded seat, with regular auto back, painted red and stenciled, size 11x14½ in. Length over all, 56 inches. Equipped with 15-inch spare wheel, fastened on back. Weight, packed for shipment, 25 lbs. **$6.98**

Boys'Air Rifles, Popguns & Water Pistols

THREE-IN-ONE AIR RIFLE

King Repeater—500 Shot Air Rifle

37T6500 Nickel-plated steel barrel and frame. Walnut stock, perfect sights, lever action, loads automatically, shoots five hundred shots into one loading. 31 inches $1.48

Three-in-One Air Rifle

37T6502 Shoots air gun shot. A large cork on string makes a strong noise and shoots a rubber ball. Change ammunition and you have whichever gun you want. Nickel steel barrel, black walnut stock, sights, 29 in. long. Furnished with ball and cork. 75c

Air Rifle—Lever Action

37T6504 Shoots B. B. shot or darts. Lever action. Made of nickel steel, highly polished stock of selected black walnut. Adjusted sights. Length, 2 feet 8 inches. Weight, packed for shipment, 2 lbs. $1.25

Magazine Water Pistol

37T6520 Made of steel, gunmetal finish. By pulling on the trigger when dipped in water gun is loaded ready for use. To fire pull trigger. Size, 5¼x3¼ inches. Price........ 29c

Toy Water Pistol

37T6522 Made of metal, highly nickel plated. Regular revolver style. By pulling on the trigger gun is loaded ready for use. To fire, all that is necessary is to pull on trigger, same action as a regular revolver. Price, each........ 25c

Gun Belt And Holster 33c

37T6534 Waterproof belt and holster, lever-action gun; shoots cork with a loud report; steel barrel, walnut handle. Gun 9½ inches long. 33c

Toy Magazine Pistol

37T6526 Self-repeating Toy Pistol; may be loaded with about 20 peas. By pulling on trigger gun shoots the peas one at a time without reloading. Made of cast iron, nickel plated, 7½ inches long. Furnished with a box of peas. 28c

Water Pistol

37T6528 Shoots and loads by pulling trigger. Made of nickeled metal. Shipping wt., 6 oz. Price...... 14c

37T6530 Sheet Steel Enameled Cannon, 8x4x3 in. Mounted on 3½-inch metal wheels. Spring lever action, automatic device for shooting wood ammunition furnished with four wood shells. Price........ 15c

Steamboat, $1.25

37T6532 Steamboat, length 15 in. A complete working steam launch, alcohol lamp, firmly connected in all its parts. Richly finished in brass and colors. Price......... $1.25

Soldiers and Gun, 15c

37T6524 Five Soldiers, 3 in. high, including captain on horse. Made of sheet steel, lithographed in lifelike colors. Popgun 9½ inches long. Shoots cork. Box 10x5 inches. Price.......... 15c

Shooting Gallery, 25c

37T6536 Toy town target or shooting gallery target 9½x4¼ in.; 3 revolving objects mounted on metal holder. Automatic gun 5½ in. long. Shoots wood pegs Price, including pegs.......... 25c

Soldier Game, 12c

37T5308 Eight soldiers, made of sheet steel, each 3 in. high, lithographed in lifelike colors. Packed in a box 8½x7½ in. 12c

---

Popular Priced Popguns, Pumpguns and Air Rifles

Junior Pumpgun— Shoots Wood Balls

37T6508 Automatic Repeater, shoots small half-inch harmless wood balls. Shoots ten times without reloading. Steel double barrel gunmetal finish, walnut stock; gun 24½ inches long. Price, including ten balls........... 75c

Sterling Break Action Air Rifle,

37T6506 Break action single shot steel, gunmetal finish frame and barrel, walnut finish stock 29 inches long. Price........ 48c

The Giant Lever Action Popgun

37T6510 The "Giant" Gun is built like an air rifle, made, entirely from steel, handsomely nickel plated and fitted with genuine black walnut stock. Length 21 inches. Shoots a cork and makes a loud noise, but with absolutely no danger; suitable for children too young to use air rifle. Safety lever action. Can't kick back. 33c

Chief Popgun

37T6512 Has a lever action, shoots a cork and make a loud noise. Steel barrel, walnut stock, 16½ inches long. Price, each...... 25c

Scout Popgun

37T6514 Steel barrel, walnut stock, lever action; shoots cork and makes a loud noise, no danger. 11 inches long. Shipping Price, each...... 15c

Shooting Galleries, War Games, Targets, Stock Farms

Rubber Ball Shooting Gallery, $1.48. A Great Favorite with The Boys.

37T5200 Size 13x13x4½. Complete with gun and rubber balls, perfectly harmless and can be used anywhere. Finished in fancy colors, cut out comical figures and animals which move and fall down when hit. Wt., 3 lbs. **$1.48**

Large Stock Farm For 49c

37T5202 Red painted stock farm barn, made of basswood, removable roof and chimney. Inside divided into three stalls and fitted with a large feed box. Building, 14 inches long, 15½ inches high; seven large cutout animals, mounted on wood stands. Weight, packed for shipment, 3½ **49c**

37T5204 Metal pistol, 9¼ inches long, wood, rubber tipped arrow, target 14½x9 in. Lithographed in bright colors. Price, complete **25c**

Six extra arrows for above outfit, wood, rubber tipped. **19c**

Extra Large Stock Farm Fourteen Animals

37T5208 An exact reproduction of a first-class stock farm, complete with fourteen large assorted cutout animals, mounted on wood stands. Largest animal, 5 inches high, 5¼ inches long. Barn made of extra strong wood painted in bright colors represents an up-to-date brick stock barn. Removable roof and chimney. Extra large sliding doors. Inside contains six stalls, fitted with six large feed boxes and windows. Building, 19¾ inches long, 18¾ inches high. **99c**

At The Front. Battle Game, 63c

37T5210 18 mounted soldiers, one captain, and one general, printed in colors, on wood stands, one rapid fire pistol, using small woodpins for ammunition, shoots 12 times with one loading. Box, 20½x14½ in. Shpg. wt., 2 lbs. **63c**

Battle Game Junior, 49c

37T5212 16 standing soldiers, six inches high, two captains on horses, seven inches high, two eight inch revolving wood cannons that shoot wood bullets. Complete with ammunition, box 17½x10 inches. Shpg. wt., 1½ lbs. **49c**

Battle Game of Siege, 39c

14 soldiers, 6 inches high, lithographed in lifelike colors, mounted on wood stands. Rapid fire repeating pistol, 5½ inches long, shoots 12 wood bullets with one loading. Furnished with wood ammunition, box 14x10½ inches lithographed in bright colors. **39c**

Coontown Shooting Gallery, 33c

37T5216 Six wood objects, painted in lifelike colors, mounted on wood frame and stand. Metal hinged holders. Each object has a different value. The one making the largest number of points in four shots wins the game. Gallery 16½x4 inches by 10½ inches. Gun metal gun, shoots wood bullets. **33c**

Battle Game Outpost, 48c

37T5218 Thirteen standing soldiers, 6 in. high. Captain on horse, 7 in. high. All printed in colors and mounted on wood stands. Revolving wood cannon, 6 in. long, shoots wood bullets. Packed in a strong lithographed box, 14x10½ in. Outfit including 25 wood bullets, price **48c**

33c each 2 for 59c

Lion Shooting Gallery

37T5220 Lion and hunter, lithographed in natural colors, size, 9x10 ins., mounted on wood base. When bullseye is hit hunter jumps up. 9½-inch gun metal gun, shoots wood bullets. Complete with wood ammunition. Shpg. wt., 1 lb. **33c**

Elephant Shooting Gallery,

37T5222 Elephant and hunter lithographed in lifelike colors, size 11x9 inches, mounted on wood base. When bullseye is hit hunter jumps up; 9½-inch gun metal gun, shoots wood bullets. Complete with wood ammunition. **33c**

Game of War, 24c
6 Soldiers

37T5224 Contains 6 soldiers, 4½ inches high, mounted on platforms, lithographed in appropriate colors. Metal pistol and wood pins or ammunition. Size of box, 10x7 inches. **24c**

33c each 2 for 59c

Tiger Shooting Gallery

37T5226 Tiger and hunter, lithographed in lifelike colors, size 9x10 ins., mounted on wood base. When bullseye is hit hunter jumps up. 9½-inch gun metal gun, shoots wood bullets. Complete with wood ammunition. Shipping wt., 1 lb. **33c**

Teddy Bears for Boys' and Girls'

Teddy Bear $3.75

These bears are made of the very best extra long silk plush, stout, well shaped bodies, double action, extra strong growling voices, growl almost like a life-like bear. Jointed front and back legs, jointed and movable heads glass eyes, long ears, are unbreakable and can be placed in any position desired. REMEMBER, these bears are fitted with voices.

37T6200 Height, 23 in. Shipping weight, 3½ lbs. Price $3.75

37T6202 Height, 18 in. Shipping weight, 2½ lbs. Price $2.45

37T6204 Height, 14 in.

Teddy Bear $1.75

37T6206 Teddy Bear with voice. Every child wants one. Made of extra fine bearskin plush. Stuffed body, front and back jointed legs, movable head and glass eyes. Can be placed in every possible position into which a live bear could get. Absolutely unbreakable which makes a teddy bear a very desirable plaything. No sharp corners to hurt the children. Furnished in brown plush only, 22 inches high. $1.75

Teddy Bear $1.45

37T6208 Every boy and girl is always pleased to receive a teddy bear. This is one of the best bears made, sold at retail from $2.00 and up, and which we offer at a low price of $1.45 each. Made of extra fine bearskin plush, stuffed shaped body, front and back jointed legs, movable head and glass eyes; can be placed in any position desired. Fitted with a strong voice making it very amusing for the little ones. No sharp corners to hurt the children, and absolutely unbreakable. Furnished in brown plush only. 18 inches high. $1.45 →

Teddy Bear 98c
With Voice

37T6210 Made of extra fine bearskin plush, stuffed body, front and back jointed legs, movable head and glass eyes. Can be placed in any position desired; no sharp corners to hurt the children. Fitted with a strong voice making it more amusing for the little ones. 18 in. high. Price.......... 98c ←

Teddy Bear 48c

37T6212 Made of extra fine bearskin plush, stuffed body, front and back jointed legs, movable head and glass eyes. Can be placed in any position desired. Furnished in brown plush only. 10 in. high. Price....... 48c

Teddy Bears 65c and 89c

Plush Teddy Bears with Voices. Made of fine bearskin plush, shaped, stuffed bodies, front and back jointed legs, movable head and glass eyes. Can be placed in any position desired. Fitted with strong voices thereby making them more amusing and interesting for the little ones; are unbreakable. Furnished in brown plush only. Please remember that these bears are fitted with strong voices.

37T6214 Teddy Bear, 14 inches high. Each 89c

37T6216 Teddy Bear, 12 inches high. Each 65c

Plush Animals on Platform and Wheels, 50c each

37T6100 Gray silk plush elephant, mounted on wood platform and wheels. Glass eyes, ribbon collar, size 6½x6¾ in. **50c**

37T6102 Gray silk plush cat, mounted on wood platform and wheels. Glass eyes, ribbon collar, size 6½x6¾ inches. **50c**

37T6104 Brown and tan silk plush dog, mounted on wood platform and wheels. Glass eyes, ribbon collar, size 6½x 6¾ inches. **50c**

37T6106 Brown silk plush bear, mounted on metal wheels, glass eyes, muzzle and metal chain, 8½x7½ inches. **50c**

37T6108 Brown silk plush horse, mounted on wood platform and wheels. Glass eyes, leatherette bridle, size 6½x6¾ inches. **50c**

Flannel Animals Squeeze Voices, 33c

37T6110 Flannel cat, 8 inches high, sitting position, fitted with squeeze voice, glass eyes. **33c**

37T6112 Flannel dog, fitted with squeeze voice, glass eyes, size 8½x7 in. **33c**

37T6114 Flannel rabbit, 10 inches high, sitting position, glass eyes, fitted with squeeze voice. **33c**

37T6116 Flannel cat, fitted with squeeze voice, glass eyes, size 9½x6 inches. **33c**

37T6118 Flannel dog, 8 inches high, sitting position, fitted with squeeze voice, glass eyes. **33c**

37T6120 Flannel rabbit, fitted with squeeze voice, glass eyes, size 7½ x6 inches. **33c**

Large Plush Animals, 50c each Large Flannel Animals, 25c each

37T6122 Tan and brown silk plush stuffed dog, glass eyes, leatherette collar, size 10x6½ in. **50c**

37T6124 Gray silk plush stuffed cat glass eyes, silk ribbon collar, size 10x 6½ in. **50c**

37T6126 Gray silk plush, stuffed elephant, glass eyes, silk ribbon collar, size 10 x6½ inches. **50c**

37T6128 Flannel stuffed dog, glass eyes, metal bell, size 9½x 8½ inches. **25c**

37T6130 Flannel stuffed rabbit, sitting position, glass eyes, ribbon collar, metal bell, size 8½x8 inches. **25c**

37T6132 Flannel stuffed cat, glass eyes, ribbon collar, metal bell, size 12x 8½ inches. **25c**

37T6134 Flannel stuffed cat, sitting position, glass eyes, ribbon collar, metal bell, size 11x 9½ inches. **25c**

PLUSH PETS WITH VOICES, 48c EACH   Flannel Dog and Pussy, 33c each

37T6136 Dog with voice, 7½x6½ inches. **48c**

37T6138 Duck with voice, 9x6½ inches. **48c**

37T6140 Rooster with voice, 9x 6½ inches. **48c**

37T6142 Rabbit with voice, 8x6 inches. **48c**

37T6144 Cat with voice, 9x6½ inches. **48c**

37T6146 Flannel stuffed cat, mounted on varnished wood platform containing metal wheels, glass eyes, ribbon collar, platform 9x3½ inches, cat 8½x4 in. **33c**

37T6148 Flannel stuffed dog, mounted on varnished wood platform containing metal wheels, glass eyes, ribbon collar, black cloth ears, size 9x3½ inches. **33c**

These pets are made of life-like colored silk plush mounted on metal wheels, glass eyes, fitted with voices.

Large Plush Animals on Platform and Wheels, 89c each

37T6150 Gray silk plush stuffed cat, mounted on wood platform and wheels. Glass eyes, ribbon collar. Platform 9x5 inches. Cat 13x9½ inches. **89c**

37T6152 Brown silk plush dog, mounted on wood platform and wheels. Glass eyes, leatherette collar. Platform 9x5 inches Dog 10x9½ inches. **89c**

37T6154 Gray silk plush stuffed elephant, mounted on wood platform and wheels. Glass eyes, ribbon collar. Platform 9x5 inches. Elephant 13x7½ in. **89c**

37T6156 Brown silk plush stuffed horse, mounted on wood platform and wheels. Glass eyes, leatherette bridle. Platform 9x5 inches. Horse 10x 9½ inches. **89c**

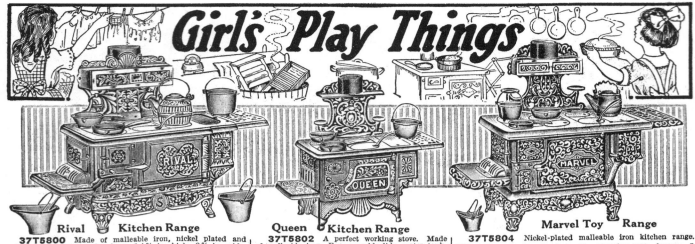

Girls' Play Things

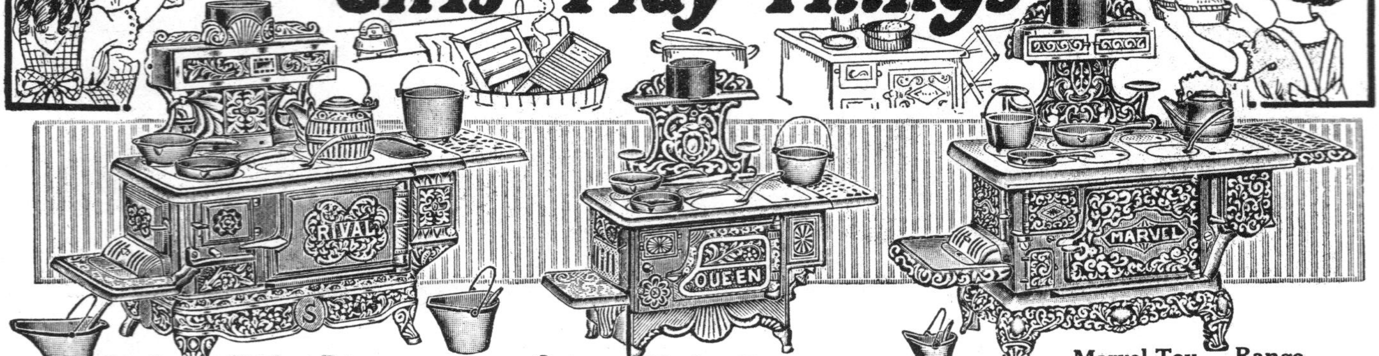

Rival Kitchen Range

37T5800 Made of malleable iron, nickel plated and polished. Size, 18 inches long, 14¾ in. high, 8¾ in. wide. Turning grate and damper, six removable lids and water tank. Nickel-plated cooking utensils, as follows: Water kettle, coal pail, cooking kettle, frying pan, boiling pot, shovel, stove lifter and stove pipe 7 inches long. Weight, packed for shipment, 23 lbs. **$3.25**

Queen Kitchen Range

37T5802 A perfect working stove. Made of malleable iron. Four movable lids, water tank, turning grate, front, side and rear detachable heating shelves. Four practical kitchen utensils and stove pipe. Size of stove, 12½ in. high, 14 in. long, 6 in. wide. Wt., packed for shipment, 12 lbs. **$1.98**

Marvel Toy Range

37T5804 Nickel-plated malleable iron kitchen range. Will really cook; has turning grate, warming oven, damper, 3 hinged doors, water compartment, front and back detachable shelves, 4 kitchen utensils and stove pipe; stove 16¼ inches high, 7½ inches wide, 16 inches long. Shpg. wt., 20 lbs. **$3.98**

Royal Kitchen Range

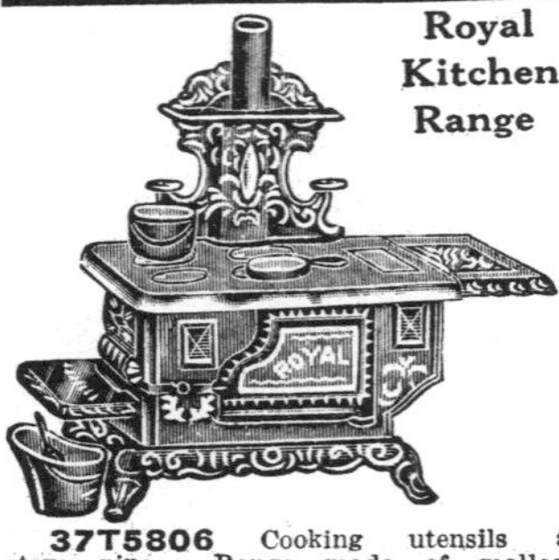

37T5806 Cooking utensils and stove pipe. Range made of malleable iron nickel plated, highly polished; hinged doors, front, side and rear; detachable heating shelves; four lids and water tank. Range 11 in. long, 9 in. high, 4¾ in. wide. Wt., packed for shipment, 6 lbs. **98c**

Royal Kitchen Range, 75c

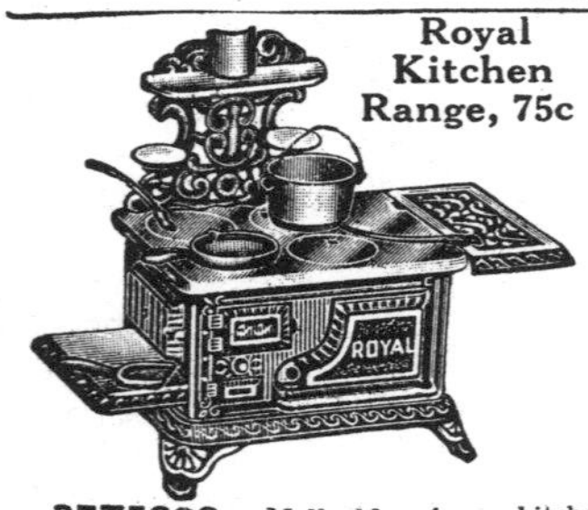

37T5808 Malleable iron kitchen range, nickel plated and polished. Hinge door, 4 lids, front shelf and water tank, set of cooking utensils. Range 7¼ in. high, 9 in. long, 4½ in. wide. **75c**

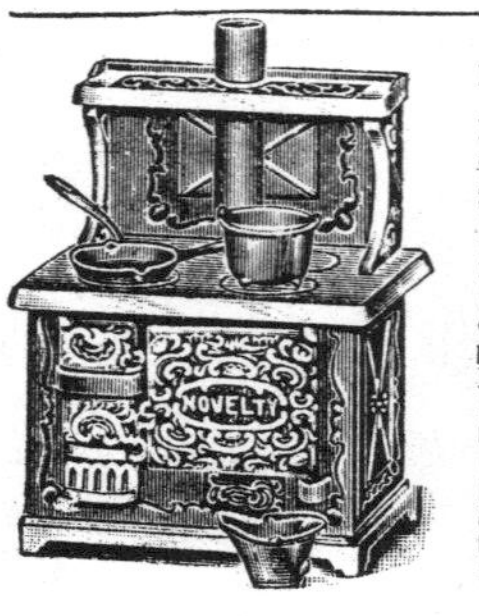

37T5810 Nickel plated, castiron base, heating shelf and doors, sheet steel body. Turning grate, 4 removablelids 3 hinged doors. Coal pail, stove lid lifter, water kettle and frying pan. 5⅛-in. stove pipe. Range 8x6x12 in. Shpg. wt., 9 lbs. **$1.45**

Dolly's Clothes Line Outfit 12c

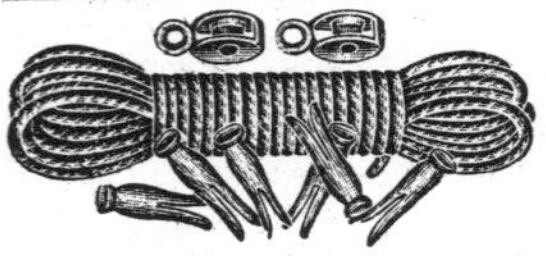

37T5846 20 feet of rope, 2 iron pulleys, 6 hardwood clothes pins. **12c**

TOY WASH SETS

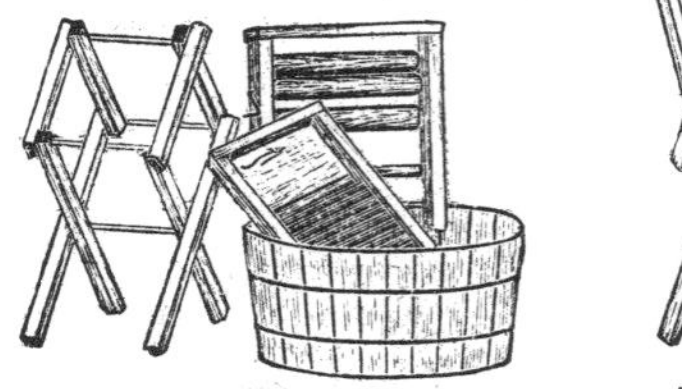

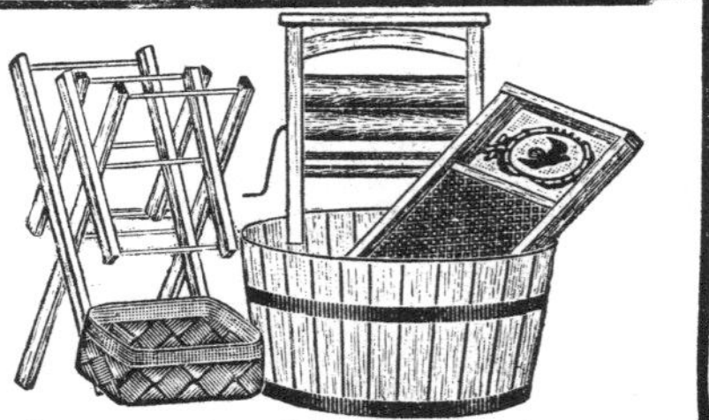

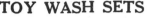

Our Baby Wash Set, 49c

37T5822 Four large pieces as follows: Hardwood tub, 9 in. wide, 4¼ in. high, protected with galvanized wire bands; wash board, wringer and clothes drier. Price for complete outfit packed **49c**

Star Wash Set, 98c

37T5826 Five practical pieces as follows: Hardwood tub, 11¼ inches wide, 5¾ inches high, protected with metal strips; clothes wringer, washboard, willow clothes basket, folding clothes drier. **98c**

TOY SAD IRONS — 3 PIECES 25c

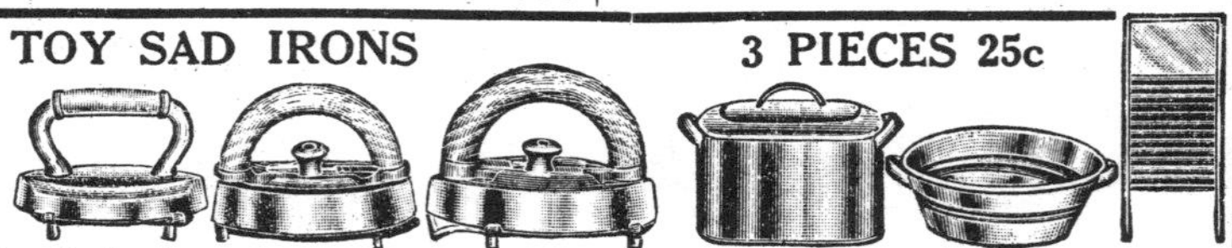

Toy Sad Iron, 10c

37T5840 Nickel plated. Gold painted top and handle; 3¾x1½. Including stand. Shpg. **10c**

Toy Sad Iron

37T5842 Nickel plated and polished. Detachable handle. Size, 3¾x 1¾ in. Including stand. **15c**

Perfection Toy Sad Iron, 25c

37T5844 Polished and nickel-plated. Detachable handle; 4 in. long, 2 in. wide, bronzed top. Including iron stand. . . . **25c**

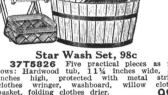

Toy Wash Set, 25c

37T5824 All metal; a very practical toy for any child; consists of wash tub, 7 in.; wash board, 7 in. high; wash boiler, 7¼x4½ in. Price **25c**

Six Piece Set Glassware

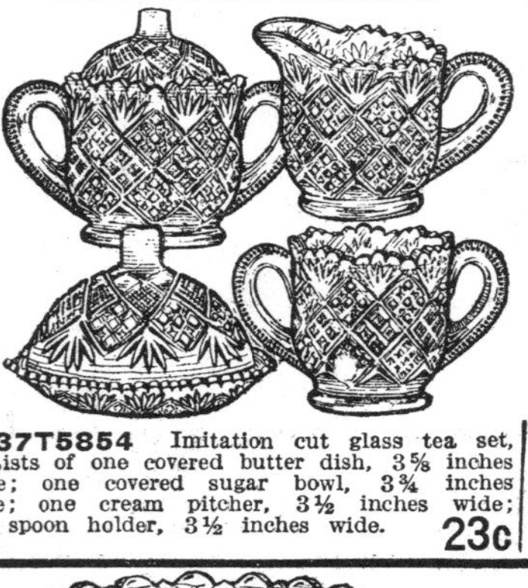

37T5854 Imitation cut glass tea set, consists of one covered butter dish, 3⅝ inches wide; one covered sugar bowl, 3¾ inches wide; one cream pitcher, 3½ inches wide; one spoon holder, 3½ inches wide. **23c**

Punch Bowl and Cups

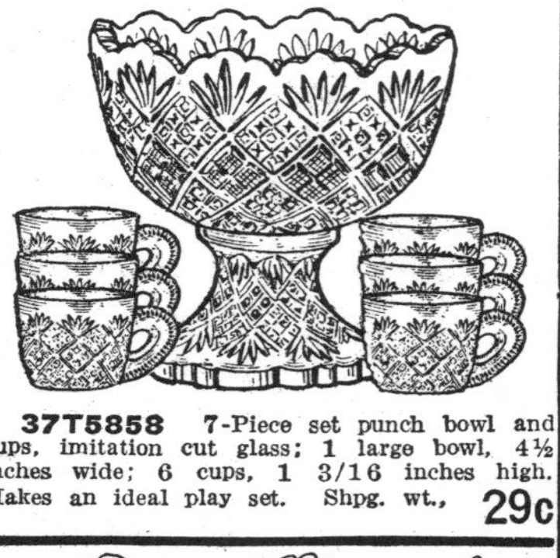

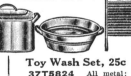

37T5858 7-Piece set punch bowl and cups, imitation cut glass; 1 large bowl, 4½ inches wide; 6 cups, 1 3/16 inches high. Makes an ideal play set. Shpg. wt., **29c**

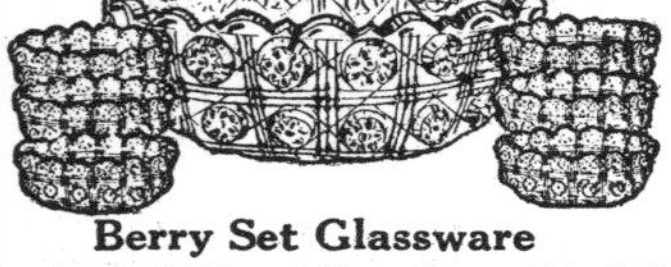

Berry Set Glassware

37T5856 7-Piece Berry Set, imitation cut glass, attractive design; 1 large berry bowl, 4⅜ inches wide; six saucers, 2⅜ inches wide. **25c**

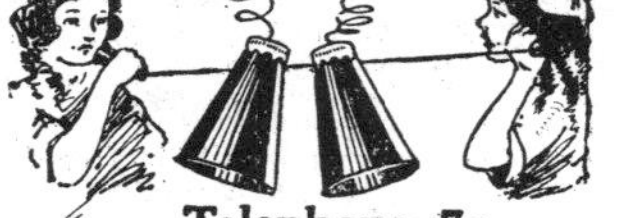

Telephone, 7c

37T5860 Telephone, metal mouth piece and receiver, 3 in. long, with 5 feet of cord. Children have lots of fun with this outfit. **7c**

Queen Kitchen Stove

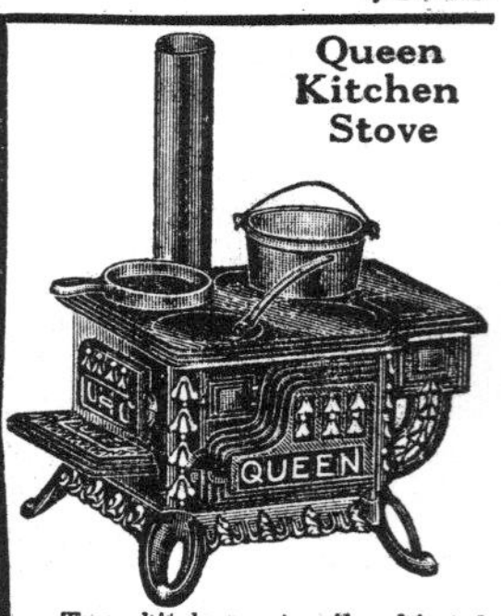

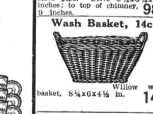

Two kitchen utensils, hinged door. Stove made of malleable iron. Size of stove, 5½x4½x3¾ inches. Shpg. wt., 3 lbs.

37T5812 **25c**

Alcohol Cooking Stove

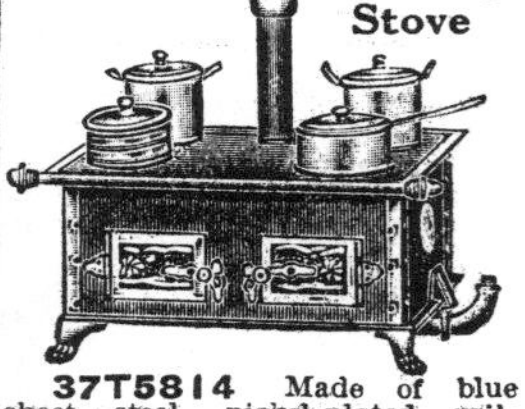

37T5814 Made of blue sheet steel, nickel-plated rail, seams and trimmings, two nickel-plated hinge doors, four heating openings, nickel-plated kitchen utensils, 2 burners with covers; stove pipe. Stove 9½x6½x4½ inches; to top of chimney, 9 inches. **98c**

Wash Basket, 14c

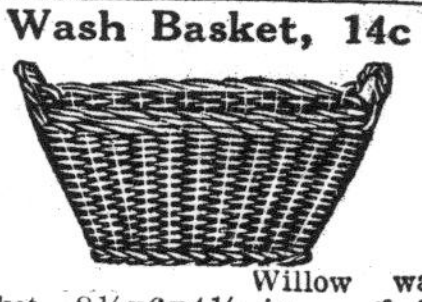

Willow wash basket, 8¼x6x4½ in. **14c**

Junior Washing Machine, 48c

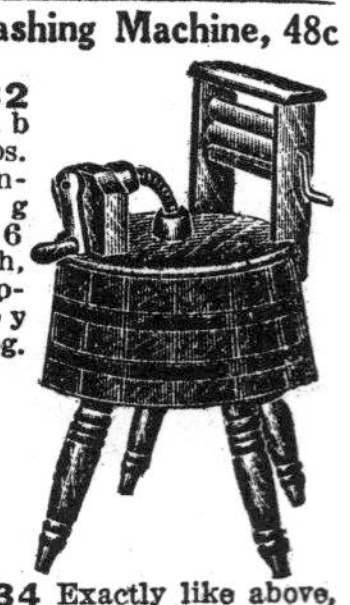

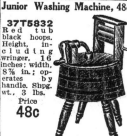

37T5832 Red tub black hoops. Height, including wringer, 16 inches; width, 8⅞ in.; operates by handle. Shpg. wt., 3 lbs. Price **48c**

37T5834 Exactly like above, only larger in every way. 21⅓ inches high over all, 11¼ inches wide; turned legs. **98c**

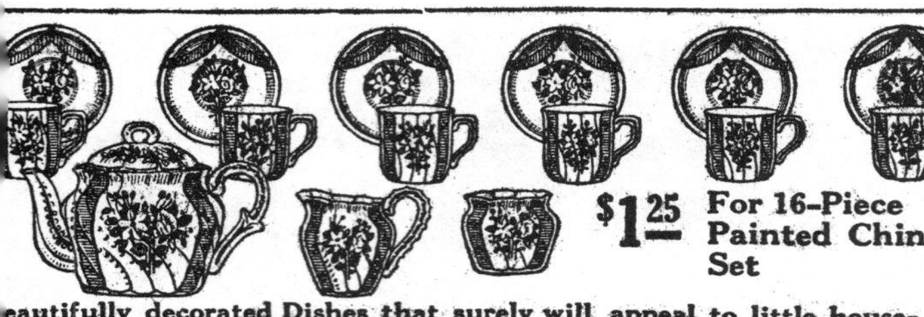

$1.25 For 16-Piece Painted China Set

eautifully decorated Dishes that surely will appeal to little house-eepers. This is an exceptionally big value at this Special $1.25 price.
37T5500 Hand painted china, 16 pieces; 6 saucers 2⅝ inches wide, 6 cups ½ inches high, 1 sugar bowl 1¾ inches high, 1 cream pitcher 1¾ inches high, arge tea pot with cover 3½ inches high. **$1.25**

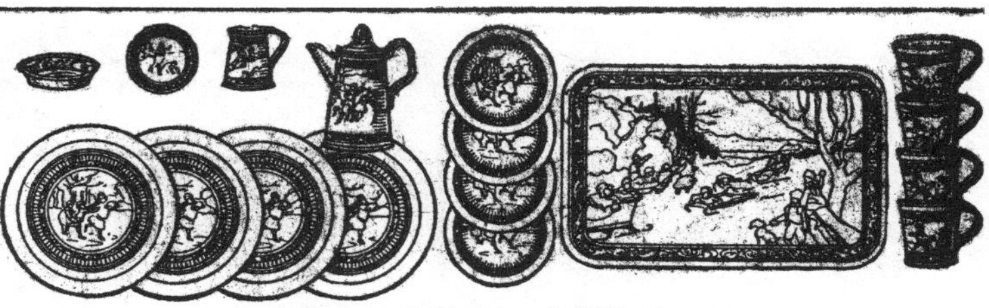

Decorated Unbreakable Set, 98c

37T5502 Beautiful colored decorated set. 1 large serving tray 13x9 inches. 4 large 6½ inch plates, four 4 inch saucers, 4 cups 2¼ inches high, 1 cream pitcher 2 inches high, 1 tea pot with cover 3½ inches high, 1 bowl 2⅜ inches in diameter. Set made of tin plate lithographed in bright colors with children's play scenes. **98c**

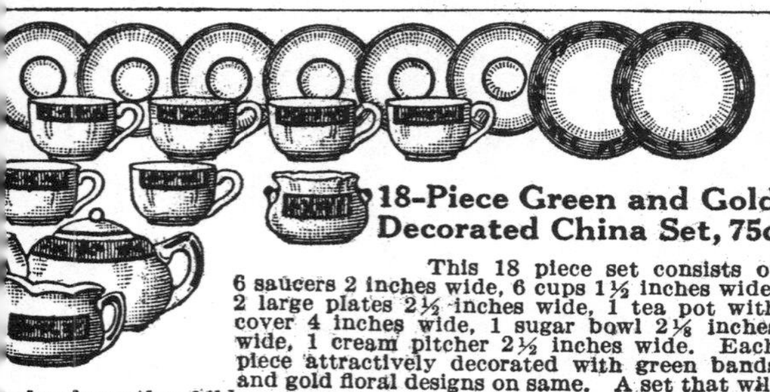

18-Piece Green and Gold Decorated China Set, 75c

This 18 piece set consists of 6 saucers 2 inches wide, 6 cups 1½ inches wide, 2 large plates 2½ inches wide, 1 tea pot with cover 4 inches wide, 1 sugar bowl 2⅛ inches wide, 1 cream pitcher 2½ inches wide. Each piece attractively decorated with green bands and gold floral designs on same. A set that will rely please the children. **75c**

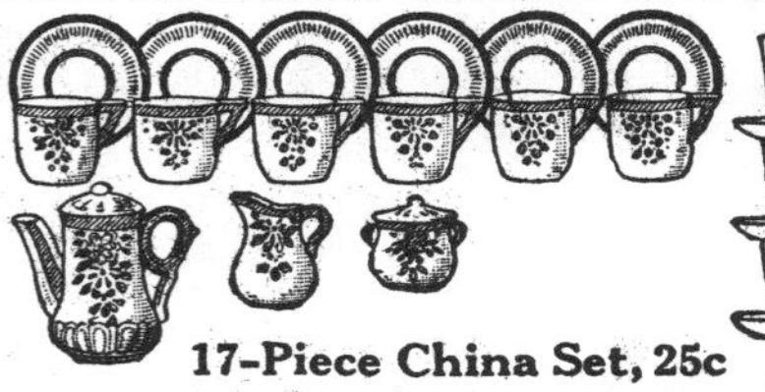

17-Piece China Set, 25c

37T5506 Set has blue band and colored floral decoration. Consists of the following pieces, 6 cups ⅞ inches high, 6 saucers 1¾ inches wide, 1 cream pitcher 1¼ inches high, 1 sugar bowl with cover 1¼ inches high, 1 tea pot with cover 2 inches high. Shipping weight, 1½ lbs. **25c**

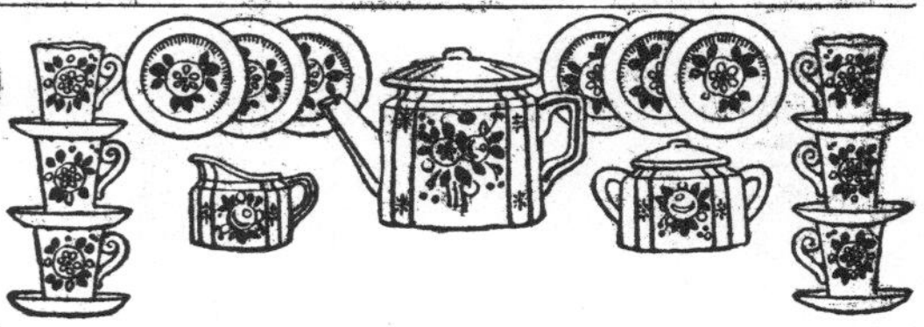

23-Piece Decorated China Set, 48c

37T5508 This handsomely decorated tea set consists of 6 tea cups 1¼ inches high, 6 saucers 1⅝ inches wide, 6 plates 1⅝ inches wide, 1 large tea pot with cover 3 inches high, 1 cream pitcher 2 inches wide, 1 sugar bowl 2¾ inches wide. Each piece is attractively decorated in colors, floral design. Shipping weight, 2¼ lbs. **48c**

16-Piece Blue Enameled Tea Set, $1.48

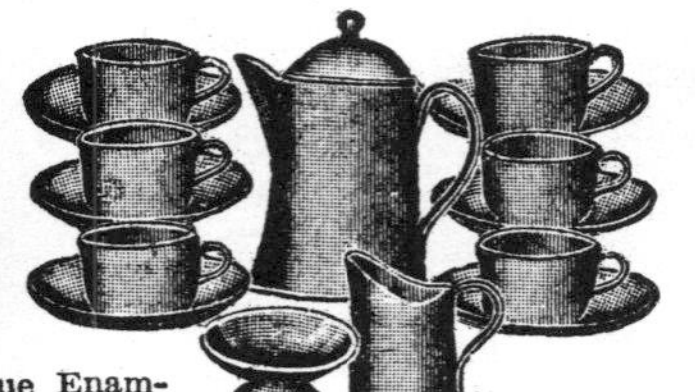

ue Enam-ed Tea t, 16 pieces, as follows: Tea or coffee pot d cover; six saucers, sugar bowl, six tea ps, creamer. Shipping weight, lbs. 8 oz. **$1.48**

TOYS THAT MAKE THE LITTLE GIRL HAPPY

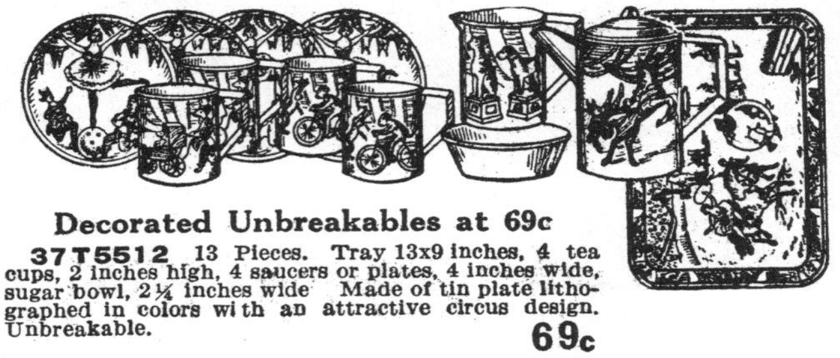

Decorated Unbreakables at 69c

37T5512 13 Pieces. Tray 13x9 inches, 4 tea cups, 2 inches high, 4 saucers or plates, 4 inches wide, sugar bowl, 2¼ inches wide Made of tin plate lithographed in colors with an attractive circus design. Unbreakable. **69c**

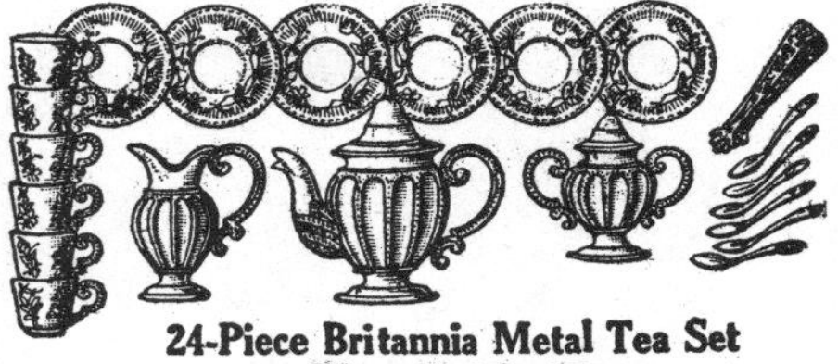

24-Piece Britannia Metal Tea Set Silver Finish, 69c

37T5514 This 24 piece set consists of 1 large tea pot with cover 3¾ inches high, 1 sugar bowl 2¾ inches wide, 1 cream pitcher 2½ inches high, 6 cups ⅞ inches high, 6 saucers 2 inches wide, 1 sugar tong 2⅝ inches long. **69c**

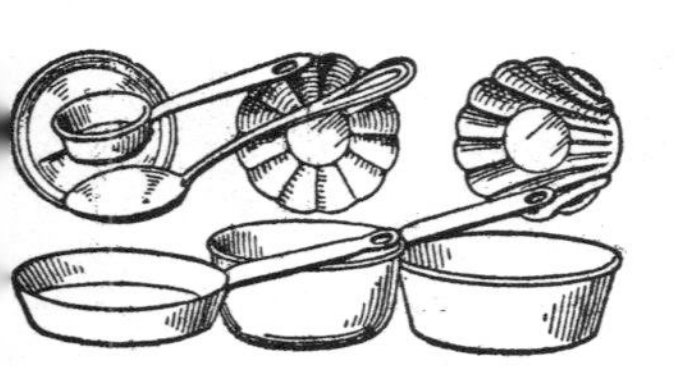

Kitchen Set, 29c

37T5516 Aluminum kitchen set, pieces—Bread mould, frying pan, pie ate, cooking pan, spoon, ladle, meat oiler and cake mould. **29c**

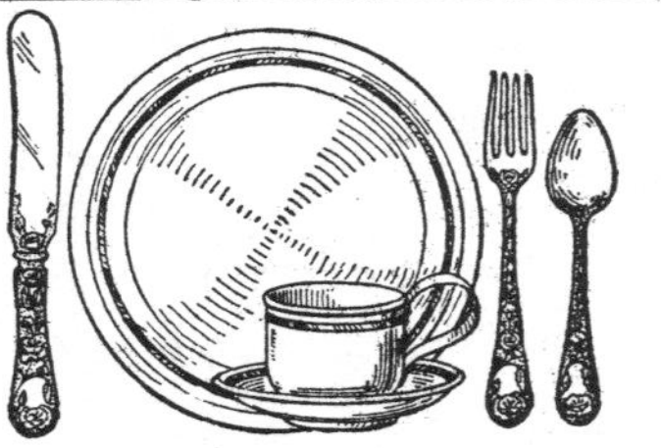

Child's Tea Set, 65c

37T5518 Child's aluminum tea set, can be used for baby's meals. Contains child's dinner plate, 7 inches wide. Tea cup 2½x3½ inches, 4 inch saucer, 4½ inch, spoon 6¾-inch knife, 5¼-inch fork. **65c**

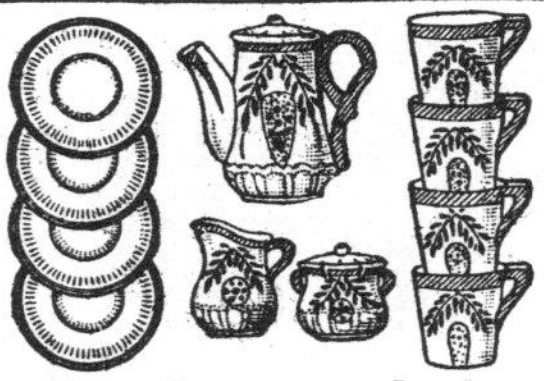

13-Piece Decorated China Tea Set, 19c

37T5520 Set consists of 1 large tea pot with cover 2 inches high. 1 cream pitches, 1⅛ inches high, 1 sugar bowl with cover 1⅜ inches high, 4 cups 1 inch high, 4 saucers 1¾ inches wide. Each piece has pink band and colored floral decoration. Packed in a neat box. **19c**

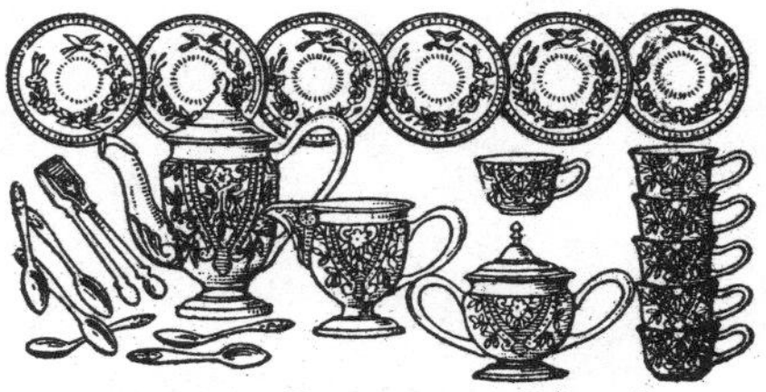

24-Piece Britannia Metal Tea Set, 39c

37T5522 Silver finished Britannia Metal Tea Set consists of 1 large tea pot with cover 2¾ inches high, 1 sugar bowl with cover 1¾ inches high, 1 cream pitcher 1⅜ inches high, 6 saucers 1½ inches wide, 6 cups 1⅛ inches wide, 6 tea spoons, 1 sugar tong. **39c**

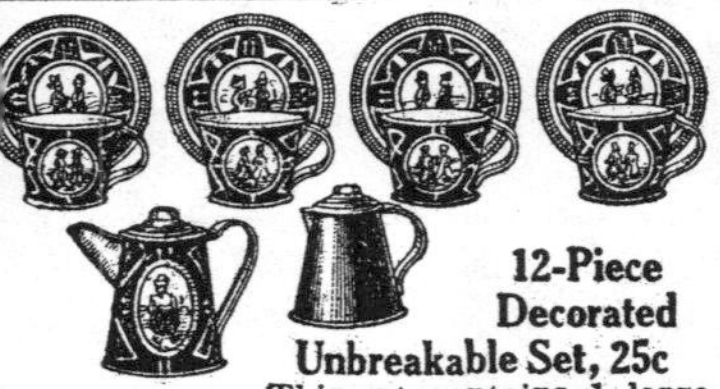

12-Piece Decorated Unbreakable Set, 25c

This set contains 1 large ea or coffee kettle with cover 2½ inches igh, 4 cups 2½ inches wide, 4 saucers 2¾ ches wide, 1 cream pitcher 1⅞ inches igh, 1 bowl 2⅜ inches wide. Made of tin ate and lithographed in contrasting colors. hildrens design Shpg. wt., 1 lb. **25c**

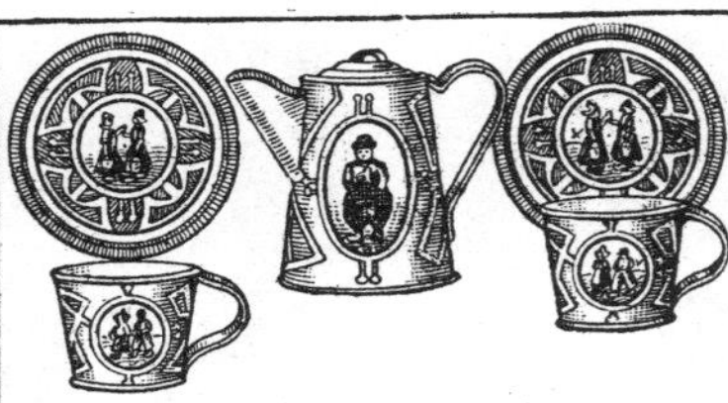

6-Piece Tea Set, 14c

37T5526 Unbreakable tea set, decorated tin plate, lithographed. Six pieces as illustrated. **14c**

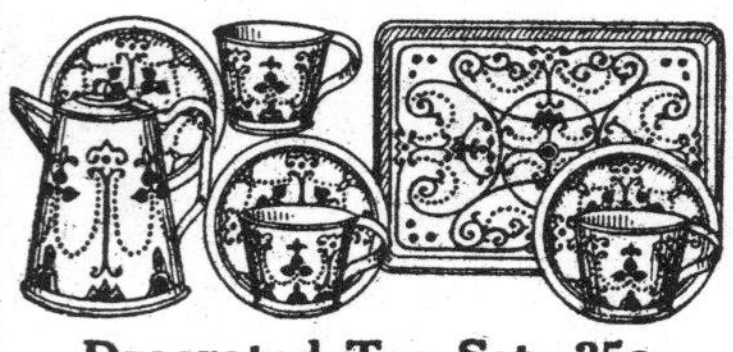

Decorated Tea Set, 25c

37T5528 Unbreakable decorated and embossed tea set, made of nickel tin plate, seven pieces—Tray 9x6¼ inches, 3 cups, 1¾ inches high, coffee pot and cover, 3 inches high, 3 saucers, 3½ inches wide. **25c**

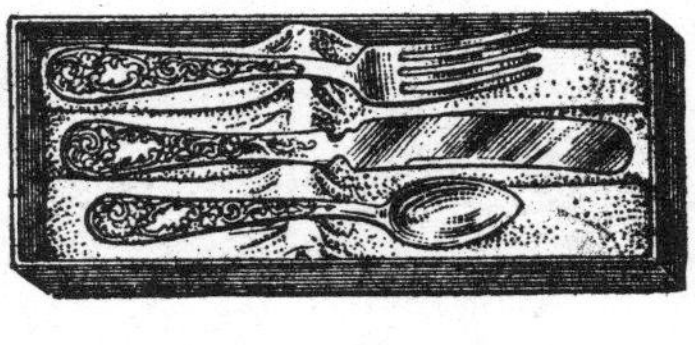

Child's Set, 12c

37T5530 Nickeloid plated child's set, stamped with a neat design. 7¼ inch knife, 6 inch fork, 5 inch spoon. **12c**

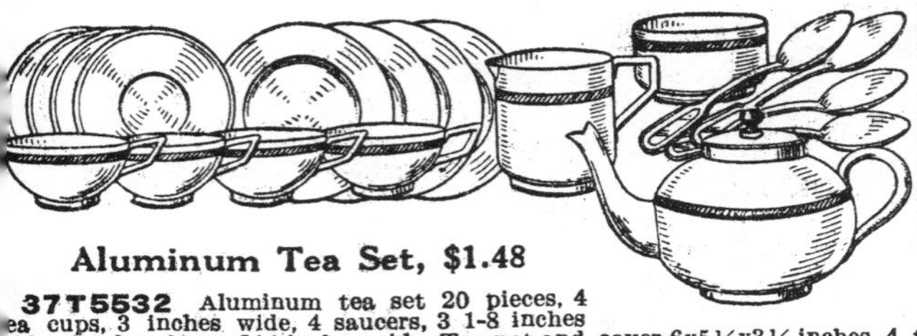

Aluminum Tea Set, $1.48

37T5532 Aluminum tea set 20 pieces, 4 ea cups, 3 inches wide, 4 saucers, 3 1-8 inches ide, 4 cake plates, 3½ inches wide. Tea pot and cover 6x5½x3½ inches, 4 teaspoons, ¼ inches wide, creamer 1¾ inches high, sugar bowl, 2 inches wide. rice.. **$1.48**

TOYS that produce many happy hours for the little girls.

MOTHERS will make no mistake in making their selections from this page.

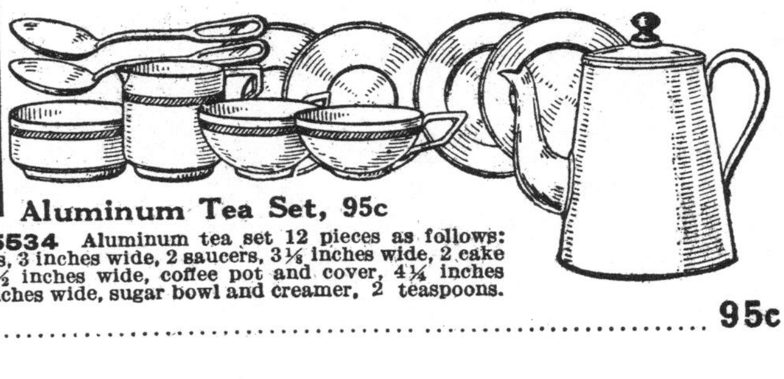

Aluminum Tea Set, 95c

37T5534 Aluminum tea set 12 pieces as follows: 2 tea cups, 3 inches wide, 2 saucers, 3⅛ inches wide, 2 cake plates 3½ inches wide, coffee pot and cover, 4¼ inches high, 5 inches wide, sugar bowl and creamer, 2 teaspoons.

Price.. **95c**

Toy Furniture and Children's Trunks at Low Prices

5-Piece Bed Room Set, 48c

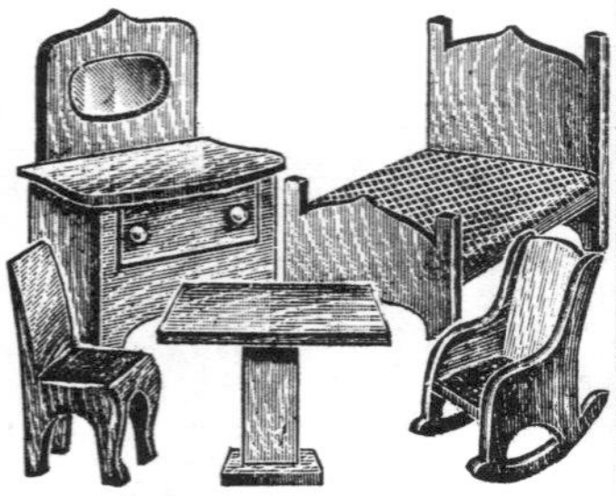

37M2000 Made of hardwood, polished in natural oak. Set consists of five pieces.
Dresser, containing mirror . . . 6½x4½ in.
Bed . . . . 5 x3¼ in.
Rocker . . . . 4 x4 in.
Chair . . . . 4¼x2 in.
Table . . . . 2¾x3½ in.
Per set (Shipping weight, 1¾ lbs.) . . **48c**

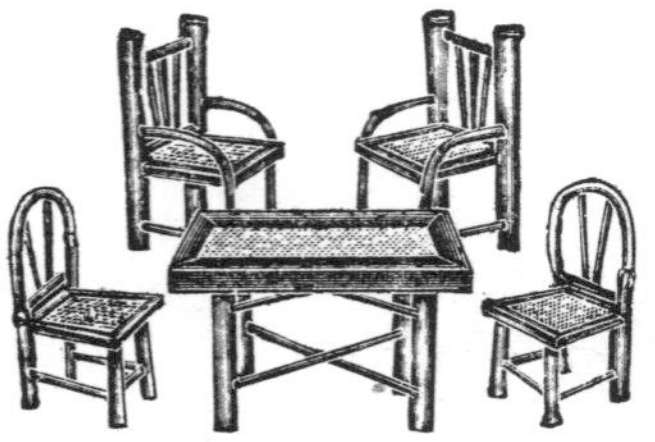

37M2002 Cane and reed dining room set, four chairs 4½x2½ inches, table 5x3⅛x3 inches. Shpg. wt., 1 lb.
Price, complete **29c**

5-Piece Dining Room Set, 29c

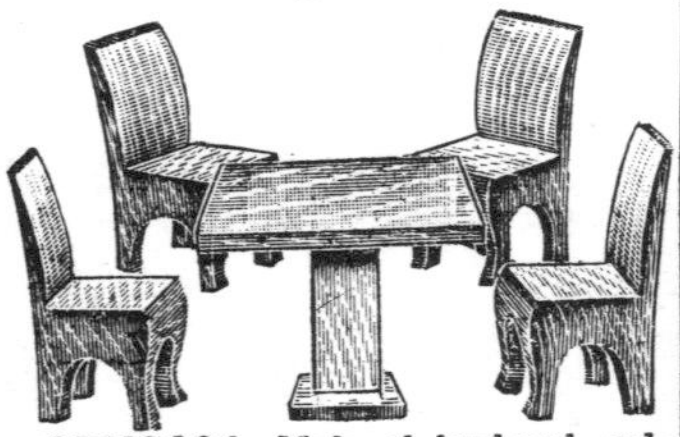

37M2004 Made of hardwood, polished in natural oak finish.
Four chairs . . . . 4 x1¾ in.
Table . . . . 2⅞x3½ in.

4-Piece Bed Room Set, 29c

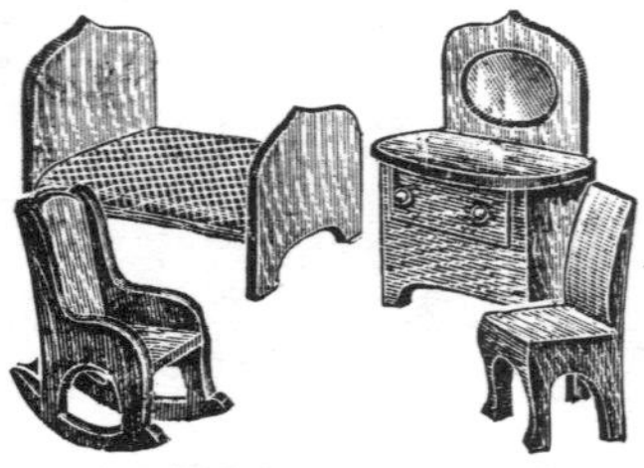

37M2006 Made of hardwood:
Dresser, containing mirror . . . 5 x4 in.
Rocker . . . . 4¼x3½ in.
Chair . . . . 4½x2 in.
Bed and mattress . . . . 4 x3 in.
Price, per set (Shpg. wt., 1½ lbs.) . . **29c**

Practical Refrigerator, $1.35

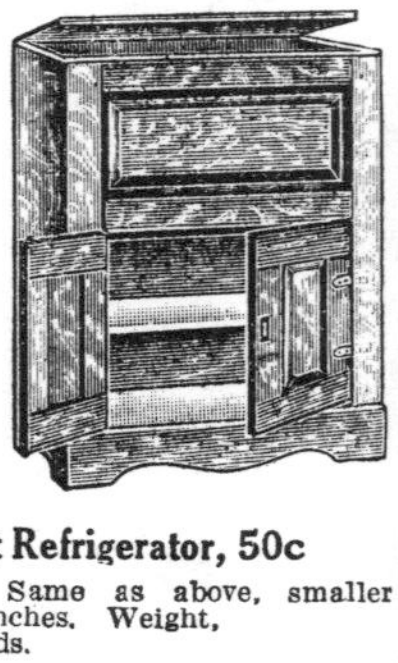

37M2018 White pine, golden oak finish, 16¼x11¾x7 inches, ice compartments, metal removable ice tray, metal covered shelves, water bucket, paneled metal hinged door, metal catch hinged cover. Shipping weight, 7 lbs. **$1.35**

Little Giant Refrigerator, 50c

37M2019 Same as above, smaller 9¾x6x3½ inches. Weight, 3 pounds.

Seven-Piece Set $1.25

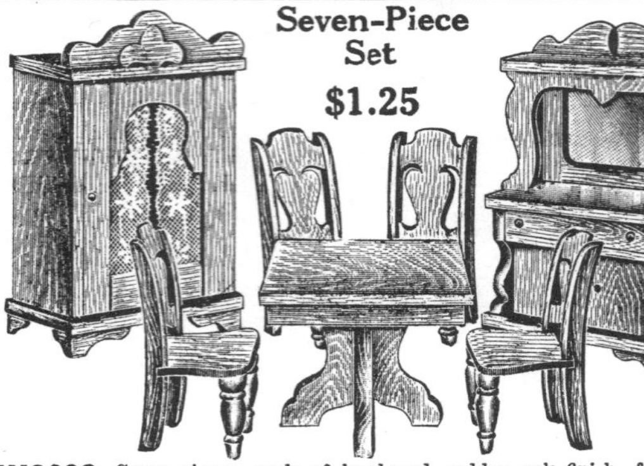

37M2008 Seven pieces, made of hardwood, golden oak finish, four chairs 5½x2¼ inches. Table 4x4x3 inches, sideboard 8½x5½x2¼ inches, with mirror; china closet 7½x4½x2½ inches, glass door.
Price, complete **$1.25**

Dining and Bed Room Set, 29c

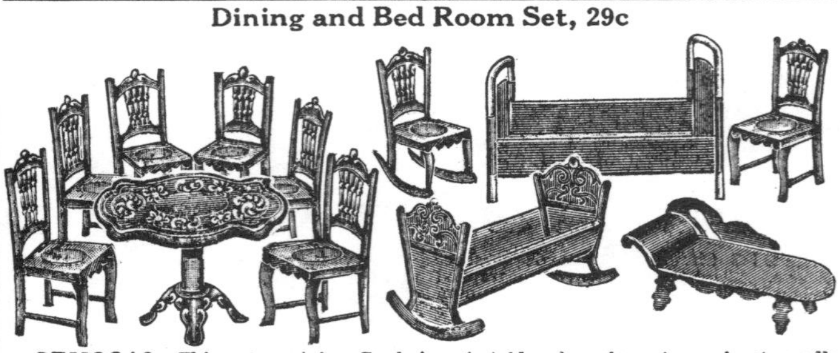

37M2012 This set contains 7 chairs, 1 table, 1 rocker, 1 couch, 1 cradle and 1 bed; made of tin; enameled in blue.
Bed . . . . 5½x3 in.
Table . . . . 3 x2 in.
Cradle . . . . 2½ in.
Couch . . . . 3¼ in.
Chairs, height . . . . 3 in.
Price for complete set **29c**

Children's Trunks 23c, 48c, $1.19

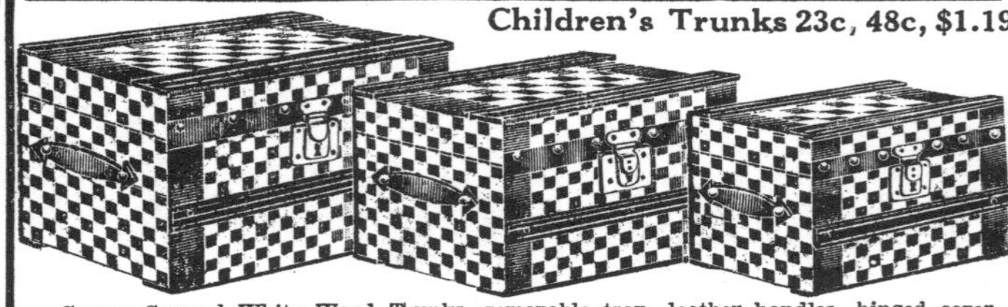

Canvas-Covered White Wood Trunks, removable tray, leather handles, hinged cover, hardwood slats, lock and key.

No.	Height	Length	Width	Shpg. Wt.	Price
37M2028	10½	18	10½	5¼ lbs.	**$0.23**
37M2030	5¾	12	6½	2½ lbs.	**.48**
37M2032	4¼	10	6	1½ lbs.	**1.19**

Extra Fine Children's Trunks $1.45 and $1.75

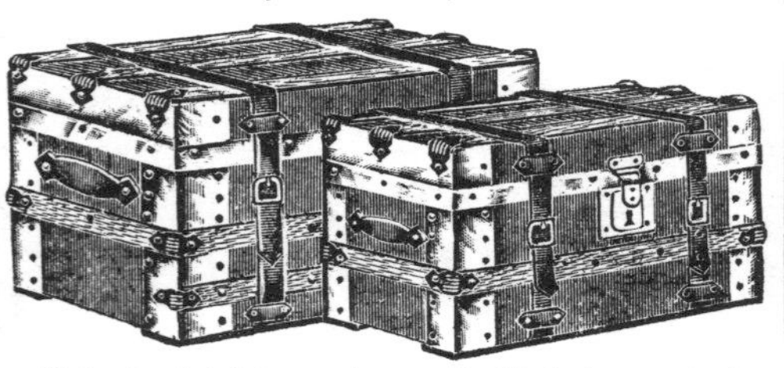

Made of selected basswood, covered with dark green leatherette, brass-plated edges, leather handles, hardwood slats, two leather straps, removable tray with hinged cover hat compartment, fitted with lock and key.

No.	Height	Length	Width	Shpg. Wt.	Price
37M2034	9¼	16	9¼	6 lbs.	**$1.75**
37M2036	7¾	14¼	8	4¾ lbs.	**1.45**

Chiffonier, 49c

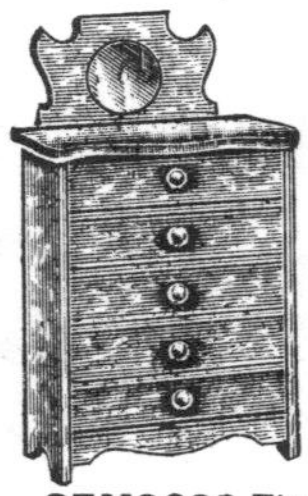

37M2022 Finished in golden oak, five drawers, mirror and frame, dresser 15 inches high, 8 inches wide, 5 inches deep. Shpg. wt., 3 lbs. **49c**

Dolly's Dresser

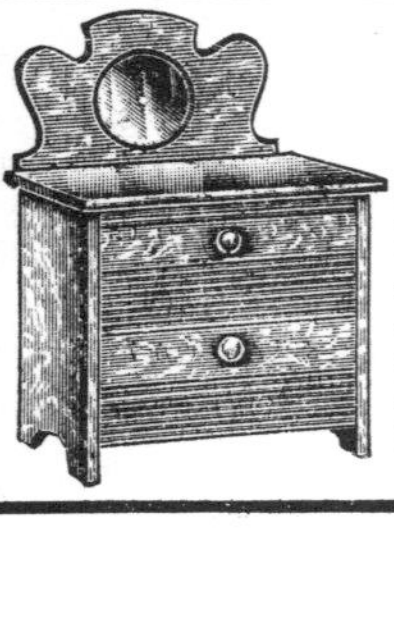

37M2020 Hardwood, golden oak finish, mirror and two pull-out drawers. Size, 13¼x10¼x4½ in.
Price. . . **48c**

Children's Toy Dresser

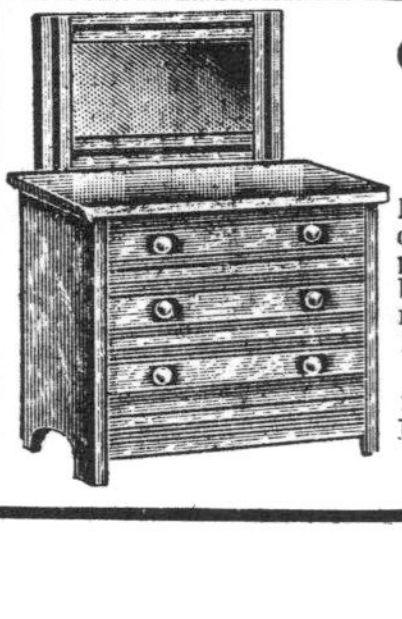

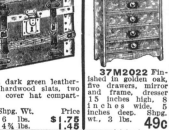

37M2024 Hardwood, golden oak finish, three pull-out drawers, brass knobs, mirror 3¾x7¾ in. Body of dresser 10¾x12½x5¾ inches.
Price. . **$1.25**

6-piece Dining Room Set 48c

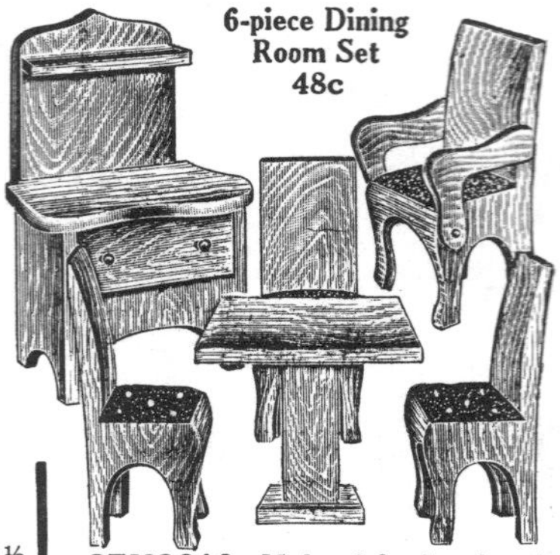

37M2010 Made of hardwood, polished in natural oak finish.
Three chairs, each . . . . 4 x1¾ in.
One side armchair . . . . 4⅛x2⅛ in.
Table . . . . 3¼x3¼ in.
Sideboard, containing drawer . 7½x4⅞ in.
Price, complete **48c**

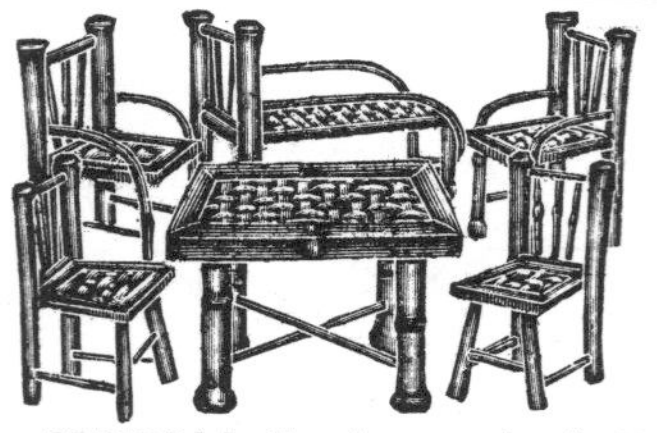

37M2014 Six pieces, made of cane and reed, finished in brown mahogany, two chairs 4¼ inches high, two armchairs 5 inches high, one porch chair 4½x4½x3 inches, table 4½x4½x3½ inches.
Price, complete **45c**

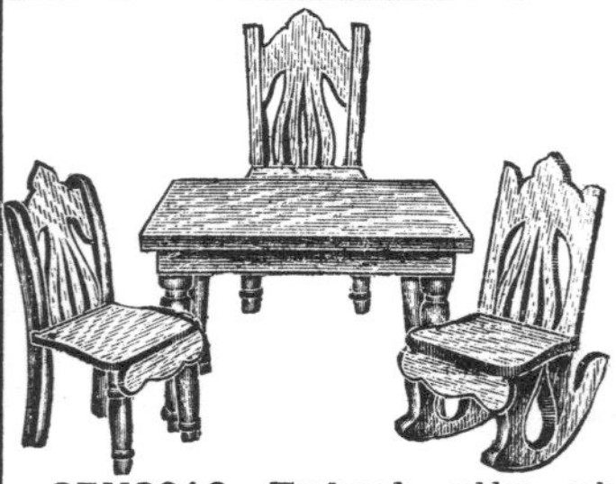

37M2016 Hardwood, golden oak finish, two chairs, 7x3½x3½ inches. Rocker 6½x5½x3 inches. Table 7x5x4 inches **25c**

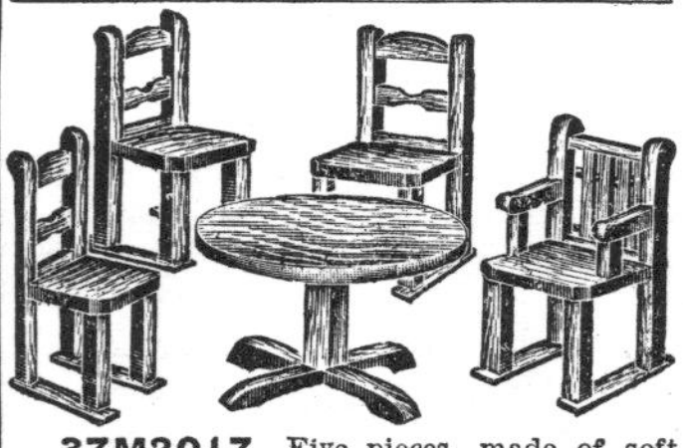

37M2017 Five pieces, made of soft wood round table 3¾x2½ inches, four chairs.
Price **9c**

Kitchen Cabinet $1.25

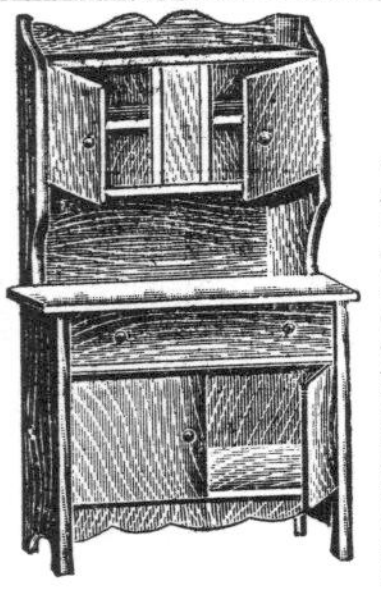

37M2026 White pine, golden oak finish, 21½x12½x6 in. high. Upper cabinet divided into four compartments. Glass compartment for flour, upper and lower swinging doors, brass knobs, large drawer and lower compartment. Shipping weight, 7 lbs.
Price. . **$1.25**

Kitchen Cabinet, 50c

37M2027 Same as above, only smaller. Size, 14 inches high, 8 inches wide, 4¼ inches deep. Weight, packed for shipment, 2½ pounds.

Registering Combination and Animal Banks

The Home Five-Coin Bank

37T5900 Save your pennies, nickels and dimes, quarters and halves. Registers and adds every coin deposited. Bell rings for each deposit. Opens automatically when it contains ten dollars, enameled in a beautiful shade of green, finished in gold. Size 7x7x4½ inches. **$1.98**

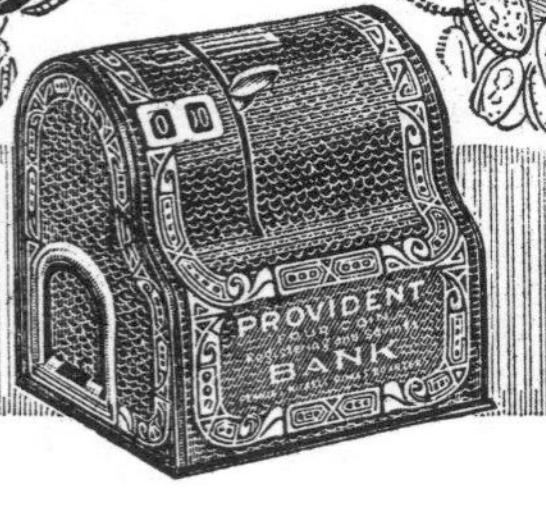

Four-Coin Provident Bank

37T5902 Registers and adds quarters, dimes, nickels and pennies. All coins are deposited through the same slot. Registers up to ten dollars and when ten dollars is deposited, opens automatically. Made of sheet steel, enameled in attractive colors. Size, 5x4½x4¼ inches. **$1.45**

Nickel, Dime and Quarter Register Bank

37T5904 Adds and registers nickels, dimes and quarters. All coins deposited through the same slot. When ten dollars is saved, opens automatically. Made of heavy sheet steel, enameled in attractive colors. Registers without errors; 5¾x 5¼x4½ in. Weight, packed for shipment, 2¼ lbs. **98c**

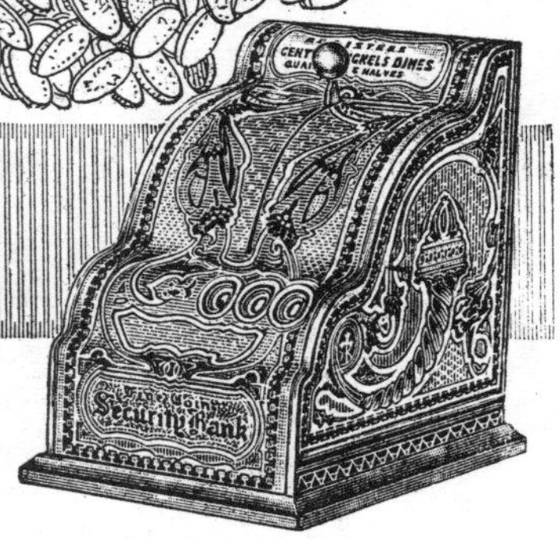

Five-Coin Security Bank

37T5906 Registers and adds every coin deposited, all coins inserted through the same slot. Holds half dollars, quarters, dimes, nickels and pennies. Opens automatically when it contains ten dollars. Made of sheet steel, ornamented in gold enameled effect and bright colors. Extension base. Size, 7½x7x5¼ inches. **$2.48**

Register Bank

37T5908 Cash register 3⅝x 3¼. Made of sheet steel, enameled in green gold lettering, registers and opens at the same time. contains five metal coins. **12c**

3 Coin Registering Bank

37T5910 Three coin bank. Registers and adds nickels, dimes and quarters. Lever action rings with every deposit. Registers up to ten dollars and then opens automatically, enameled in black, embossed gold ornamented plates. Bank 6x5 inches. Made of heavy sheet steel. **$1.75**

Dime Registering Bank

37T5912 Registers dimes; opens automatically when ten dollars is deposited. Made of sheet steel, enameled and gold ornamented. 3½x3x3 inches. **24c**

Uncle Sam Dime Registering Bank

Uncle Sam Dime registering bank. Registers and adds dimes, lever action. Rings with each deposit, registers up to ten dollars and then opens automatically. Made of heavy sheet steel, enameled in black, embossed gold ornamented, plates size 4¾x3½ inches. **$1.25**

Combination Bank

37T5916 Cast iron combination bank, 3¼x2½. Steel side slot for dropping coins. Price...... **10c** Shipping weight, 12 oz.

37T5918 Sheet steel combination bank, 3½x2¾ in. Enameled in black, fancy top and base, slot for dropping coins. **19c**

Balking Mule Trick Bank

37T5920 Balking Mule Trick Bank. Operates and deposits coins automatically. By pressing lever mule kicks darky backwards and deposits coin. Made of cast iron, enameled in attractive colors. Size 10½x6½ in. **$1.48**

Dime Savings Bank

Holds $5.00 Worth of Dimes

37T5922 The little Gem dime pocket savings bank; will open when five dollars has been saved; nickel plated. For saving dimes only. **10c**

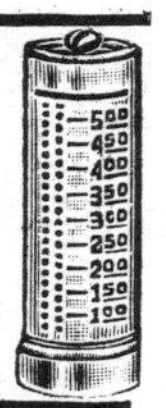

U. S. Mail Box Saving Bank

12c

Made of iron, silver finish, decorated with the words U.S. Mail in red. Slide opening on top for depositing money. Holds pennies, nickels, dimes and quarters. Money cannot be shaken out. Size 3¾x 2½ inches. **12c**

Security Combination Safe

iron, highly polished and nickel plated oven door, regular combination lock. Instructions on how to open, with each bank. Size, 4¾x3x 2½ inches. Shipping weight, 2 lbs. **35c**

Combination Bank

37T5926 Cast iron combination lock bank, sheet steel sides. Nickel plated and polished. Size, 5½x4½x 3½ in. **49c**

Combination Bank, 25c

37T5928 Cast iron combination lock bank, sheet steel sides nickelplated and polished. Size, 4½x3x2½ inches. **25c**

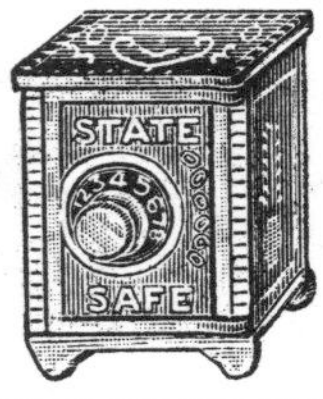

Cast Iron Animal Savings Banks at Low Prices

37T5934 Rabbit cast iron bank, enameled, slot for dropping coins, 4¾x4 inches. **17c**

37T5936 Cow cast iron bank, enameled in gold, slot for dropping coins, size 5½x 3 inches. **17c**

37T5938 Clown cast iron bank, enameled, slot for dropping coins, 6½ inches high. **19c**

37T5940 St. Bernard cast iron bank, enameled in black and gold, slot for dropping coins. **19c**

37T5942 Bear cast iron bank, gold decorated, slot for dropping coins, 5¾ inches high. **19c**

37T5944 Elephant Bank, made of cast iron, enameled, slot for dropping coins, size 5x3½ in. **19c**

37T5946 Rooster cast iron bank, decorated in gold and red, slot for dropping all coins, 5x4 inches. **15c**

DOLL BUGGIES AND GO-CARTS

Genuine Reed Doll's Buggy
37T4500 White enameled, steel gear, frame, handle and axles; black enameled wood hand grips, reclining back, upholstered seat, sides and hood, full roll body and full roll reversible hood; rubber tire steel wheels, 7¼ inches high. Buggy, 28 inches long, 24 inches high, 10½ inches wide. **$5.95**

Genuine Reed Doll's Buggy
37T4502 White enameled, full roll body, upholstered sides, seat and back; reversible, lined hood; reclining back; black enameled steel handle, gears, axles and springs; turned wood hand grips; steel rubber tire wheels, 9 inches high; hub caps. Buggy, 35½ inches long, 27 inches high, 13½ inches wide. **$7.95**

Genuine Reed Doll's Buggy
37T4504 Full roll genuine reed body, upholstered seat, sides and back, upholstered genuine reed full roll reversible hood; reclining back; black enameled steel handle, gears and axles; black enameled wood hand grips; steel rubber tire wheels 9 inches high; hub caps. Buggy 28 inches high, 30 inches long, 13 inches wide. **$8.95**

Genuine Reed Doll's Buggy
37T4506 White enameled, steel gear, frame, handle and axles, enameled in black, genuine reed hood, lined with Bedford cord, steel, 7-inch rubber tire wheels upholstered back, sides and seat, reclining back. Buggy, 28 inches long, 24 inches high, 8½ inches wide. **$4.75**

Go-Cart, 2.50
37T4508 Collapsible, all-steel black enameled doll's go-cart. Automobile hood, reclining back, foot rail, hood cross bar; 25 inches high from floor to handle; 25 inches long, 12½ inches wide; 7 in. rubber tire steel wheels. Reclining back. Boston leather collapsible hood, 17 in. long, 9 in. wide. Boston leather seat, side curtains and foot dash. Large enough for any doll. **$2.50**

Pullman Sleeper Doll Buggy
37T4510 Boston leather, folding hood, reclining back; black enameled steel frame, axle handle bar and wood cross piece; rubber tire wheels, 7 inches high; collapsible sides and front. 26 inches high from floor to top of handle, 22 inches long, 9½ inches wide. **$3.45**

English Doll Perambulator. $1.95
37T4512 Enameled wood body, reversible and collapsible jointed Boston leather hood; wood gear and axles. Steel spokes, ¼-in. rubber tire wheels, 6 in. high. Bent steel black enameled handle. Body, 16¾x8 in. Perambulator, 22 inches high from floor to top of hood. 21 in. long. **$1.95**

Doll Perambulator, Rubber Tire Wheels, $2.69
37T4514 Enameled and gold stripped wood body; folding and reversible Boston leather hood; steel gear and axle, rubber tire, steel wheels, 6½ in. high, steel handle with polished wood cross bar. 26½ inches long. 24 inches high, 7½ inches wide. **$2.69**

Full Folding Doll's Go-Cart, $1.48
37T4516 Steel one-motion folding go-cart, 24½ in. high from floor to top of handle, 20 in. long, 11 in. wide. Rubber tired wheels 7 in. high; black enameled steel frame and axles; Boston leather adjustable hood; 10¾ in. long, 8¾ in. wide. Boston leather seat, back and foot dash. Large enough for any doll up to 26 in. high. **$1.48**

Reed Doll's Buggy, $1.95
T4518 Natural finish, steel axles, handle and double steel wheels, enameled wood bar. Boston leather folding Buggy 22 inches long, 21½ high, 6 inches wide. **$1.95**

Doll's Folding Go-Cart, 48c
37T4520 Steel folding go-cart, black enameled, 20½ in. high from floor to top of handle, 13 inches long, 8¼ inches wide; steel tire wheels, 5 inches high; Boston leather seat and foot dash. **48c**

Doll's Go-Cart, 98c
Rubber Tire Wheels
37T4522 Collapsible all-steel black enameled doll's go-cart, 22 in. high from floor to top of handle; 15 inches long, 9¾ inches wide. Steel handle. Adjustable and folding Boston leather automobile hood, 9¾ inches long; rubber tire wheels, 5½ in. high; Boston leather back, seat and foot dash. Suitable for any doll. **98c**

Doll's Folding Go-Cart, 75c
37T4524 Made of steel; 20½ inches high from floor to top of handle; 12½ inches long, 8¼ inches wide; folding hood; steel tire, double spoke 5-inch wheels. Boston leather seat. **75c**

Genuine Reed Doll's Buggy
37T4526 Natural finish, enameled steel frame, axles and handle; enameled wood crass bar; steel rubber tire wheels, 6 inches high. Reversible, genuine reed hood. Buggy 27 inches long, 21 inches high, 9¼ inches wide. **$2.98**

In The Land Where the Child is King

2^{89}

An Excellently Constructed Shoofly
Pretty team of white horses with saddles and harness stenciled in colors. Upholstered seat with colored cretonne covering. Back of seat has conventional floral design. About 33½ in. long; 12 in. wide; height, 19 in. Well braced red enameled rockers. Shipping weight, about 12 pounds.
148C3578—Price................$2.89

Upholstered Seat and Back.

A sturdy shoofly. Horses have imitation black horsehair tails. Upholstered seat with cloth covering in floral design. Shelf between horses for baby's playthings and cookies. About 33 in. long, 12½ in. wide and 17½ in. high. Shipping weight, about 12 pounds.
148C3587—Price....$2.48

A rocking horse for the smaller child. Made entirely of wood, nicely varnished, natural color, with red striping. Tape reins. Length, over all, 37½ in.; width 14½ in.; height, 18¼ in. Ship. wt., about 11 lbs.
148C3589—Price... $4.98

Substantially built of wood, painted bright red. The two white horses have imitation horsehair tails. Seat and back upholstered in cretonne. Tape lines and toy tray in front. Length, over all, 30½ in. Width, 16 in. Height, 19½ in. Ship. wt., 18 lbs.
148C3565—Price.......$3.98

The two white horses have imitation horsehair tails. Rockers, toy tray and foot rest are painted red. Back and seat nicely upholstered with velvet corduroy. Tape reins. Length, over all, abt. 44 in.; width, 12½ inches; height, 20 in. Ship. wt., 15 lbs.
148C3588 Price $4.25

This is indeed a very handsome shoofly with long wood rockers. Painted red. Seat upholstered in corduroy. The roosters are very realistic, in white enamel and bright red combs. Length, over all, 36 in. Height of seat from floor, 9 in. Ship wt., 24 lbs.
148C3583—Price................$4.98

High-grade shoofly. Has comfortable swinging motion. Frame is well made of wood, enameled green and red, trimmed with gilt. Rabbits very substantially made of wood enameled white. Seat and back are upholstered in velvet corduroy. Hung on strong iron swings. Length, over all, 35 in. Height of seat from floor, 12 in. Ship. wt., 31 lbs.
148C3582—Price................$6.98

The Modern American Knight—Paul Revere

The Revere Swinging Horse

Like Paul Revere's Horse this one will stop for nothing until his full duty is done. Handsomely painted in dapple gray with long sweeping mane and tail. Leatherette saddle and bridle. Length, about 30 inches, height to top of head, 27 inches. Suitable for children from 2 to 7 years. Ship. weight, 20 lbs.
148C3557—Price.........$7.75

Jump on your horse like the Knights of Old and ride and ride. Horse painted dapple gray with imitation horsehair mane and tail. Glass eyes. Frame painted red. Length, 35 in. Height from floor, 22 in. Bent wood brace under horse. Ship. wt., 35 lbs.
148C3558—Price...............$10.95

Our large swinging horse, made of wood. Real mane and tail, pretty glass eyes. Length, over all, 41 in.; height of horse from floor, 36 in. Horse painted dapple gray, frame in red. Has bent iron brace under horse. Shipping weight, 60 pounds.
148C3559—Price $21.25

Outdoor Toys

Shooting Star Steering Sleds - Note Low Prices

Be in all the big races, and win them, too. Rely on the Shooting Star to keep you in the lead.

Zing!!! Like a flash it glides down hill and over the ice. A tug on the steering bar and she makes the curves as gracefully as a bird on the wing. Their light weight and fine construction are two good reasons why their owners are united in declaring that "They Can't Be Beat!"

Top is of best hardwood nicely varnished and decorated in colors. Runners are of hardened steel. We call your particular attention to the low prices we ask.

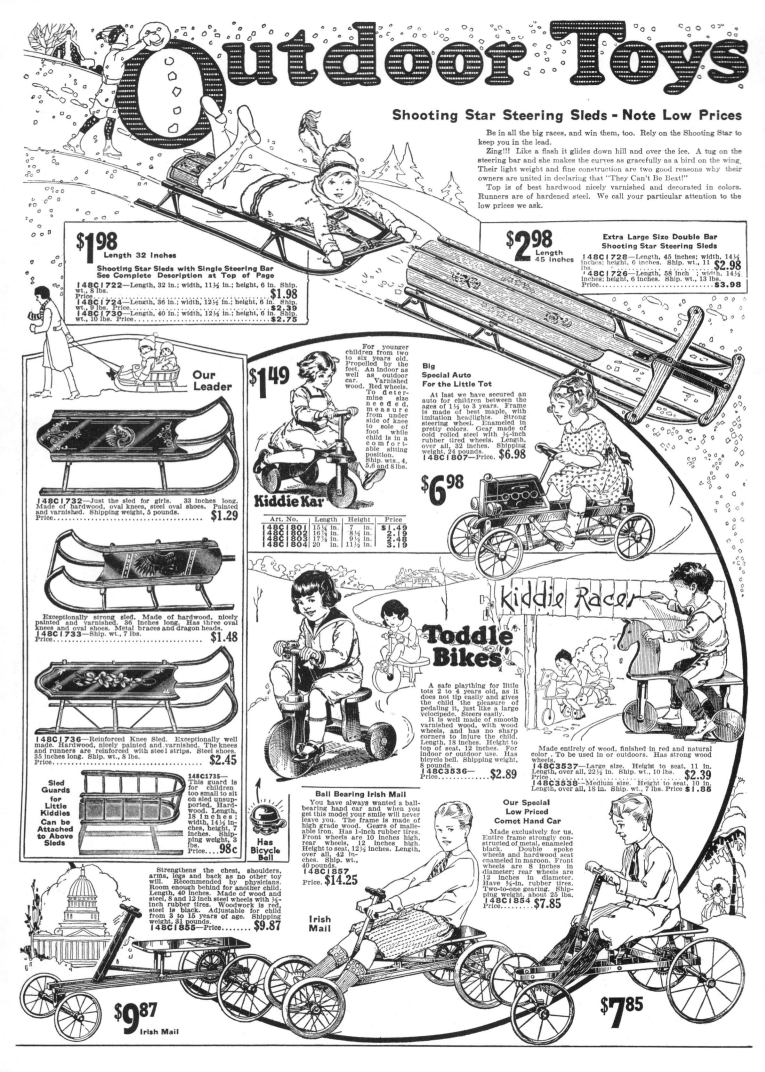

$1.98 Length 32 Inches

Shooting Star Sleds with Single Steering Bar
See Complete Description at Top of Page

148C1722—Length, 32 in.; width, 11½ in.; height, 6 in. Ship. wt., 8 lbs. Price...$1.98
148C1724—Length, 36 in.; width, 12½ in.; height, 6 in. Ship. wt., 9 lbs. Price...$2.39
148C1730—Length, 40 in.; width, 12½ in.; height, 6 in. Ship. wt., 10 lbs. Price...$2.75

$2.98 Length 45 inches

Extra Large Size Double Bar Shooting Star Steering Sleds

148C1728—Length, 45 inches; width, 14½ inches; height, 6 inches. Ship. wt., 11 lbs. **$2.98**
148C1726—Length, 58 inch; width, 14½ inches; height, 6 inches. Ship. wt., 13 lbs. Price.................................$3.98

Our Leader

148C1732—Just the sled for girls. 33 inches long. Made of hardwood, oval knees, steel oval shoes. Painted and varnished. Shipping weight, 5 pounds. Price..............................**$1.29**

Exceptionally strong sled. Made of hardwood, nicely painted and varnished. 36 inches long. Has three oval knees and oval shoes. Metal braces and dragon heads.
148C1733—Ship. wt., 7 lbs. Price.................................**$1.48**

148C1736—Reinforced Knee Sled. Exceptionally well made. Hardwood, nicely painted and varnished. The knees and runners are reinforced with steel strips. Steel shoes. 35 inches long. Ship. wt., 8 lbs. Price.................................**$2.45**

Sled Guards for Little Kiddies Can be Attached to Above Sleds

148C1735—This guard is for children too small to sit on sled unsupported. Hardwood, length, 18 inches; width, 14½ inches, height, 7 inches. Shipping weight, 3 lbs. Price...........**98c**

$1.49

Kiddie Kar

For younger children from two to six years old. Propelled by the feet. An indoor as well as outdoor car. Varnished wood. Red wheels. To determine size needed, measure from under side of knee to sole of foot while child is in a comfortable sitting position. Ship. wts. 4, 5, 6 and 8 lbs.

Art. No.	Length	Height	Price
148C801	15¼ in.	7 in.	$1.49
148C802	16⅞ in.	8½ in.	2.19
148C803	17⅞ in.	9½ in.	2.48
148C804	20 in.	11½ in.	3.19

Big Special Auto For the Little Tot

At last we have secured an auto for children between the ages of 1½ to 3 years. Frame is made of best maple, with imitation headlights. Strong steering wheel. Enameled in pretty colors. Gear made of cold rolled steel with ½-inch rubber tired wheels. Length, over all, 32 inches. Shipping weight, 24 pounds.
148C807—Price. **$6.98**

$6.98

Toddle Bikes

A safe plaything for little tots 2 to 4 years old, as it does not tip easily and gives the child the pleasure of pedaling it, just like a large velocipede. Steers easily. It is well made of smooth varnished wood, with wood wheels, and has no sharp corners to injure the child. Length, 18 inches. Height to top of seat, 12 inches. For indoor or outdoor use. Has bicycle bell. Shipping weight, 8 pounds.
148C3536—Price.............**$2.89**

Has Bicycle Bell

Kiddie Racer

Made entirely of wood, finished in red and natural color. To be used in or outdoors. Has strong wood wheels.
148C3537—Large size. Height to seat, 11 in. Length, over all, 22½ in. Ship. wt., 10 lbs. Price.................................**$2.39**
148C3538—Medium size. Height to seat, 10 in. Length, over all, 18 in. Ship. wt., 7 lbs. Price **$1.85**

Ball Bearing Irish Mail

You have always wanted a ball-bearing hand car and when you get this model your smile will never leave you. The frame is made of high grade wood. Gears of malleable iron. Has 1-inch rubber tires. Front wheels are 10 inches high, rear wheels, 12 inches high. Height to seat, 12½ inches. Length, over all, 42 inches. Ship. wt., 40 pounds.
148C857—Price. **$14.25**

Irish Mail

Strengthens the chest, shoulders, arms, legs and back as no other toy will. Recommended by physicians. Room enough behind for another child. Length, 40 inches. Made of wood and steel, 8 and 12 inch steel wheels with ½-inch rubber tires. Woodwork is red, steel is black. Adjustable for child from 3 to 15 years of age. Shipping weight, 31 pounds.
148C1855—Price.........**$9.87**

Our Special Low Priced Comet Hand Car

Made exclusively for us. Entire frame strongly constructed of metal, enameled black. Double spoke wheels and hardwood seat enameled in maroon. Front wheels are 8 inches in diameter; rear wheels are 12 inches in diameter. Have ¾-in. rubber tires. Two-to-one gearing. Shipping weight, about 25 lbs.
148C854—Price.........**$7.85**

$9.87 Irish Mail

$7.85

for Every Clime

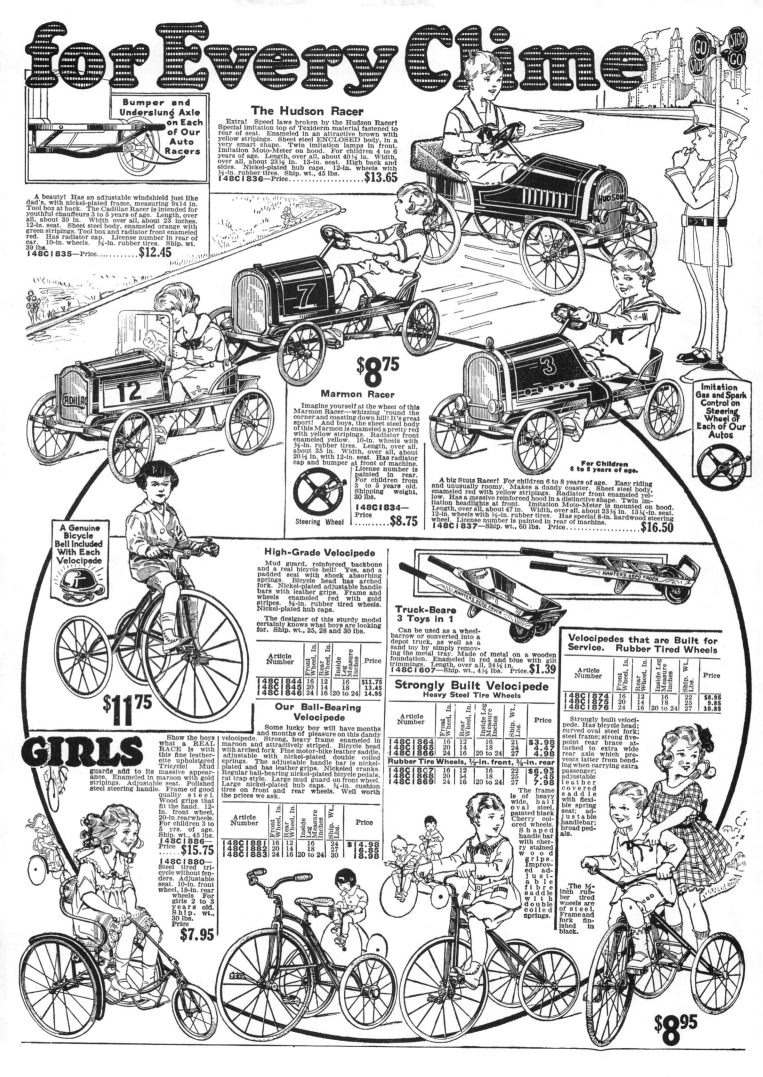

Bumper and Underslung Axle on Each of Our Auto Racers

The Hudson Racer

Extra! Speed laws broken by the Hudson Racer! Special imitation top of Texiderm material fastened to rear of seat. Enameled in an attractive brown, with yellow stripings. Sheet steel ENCLOSED body, in a very smart shape. Twin imitation lamps in front. Imitation Moto-Meter on hood. For children 4 to 6 years of age. Length, over all, about 40½ in. Width, over all, about 23½ in. 13-in. seat. High back and sides. Nickel-plated hub caps. 12-in. wheels with ½-in. rubber tires. Ship. wt., 45 lbs.
148C1836—Price.................$13.65

A beauty! Has an adjustable windshield just like dad's, with nickel-plated frame, measuring 9x14 in. Tool box at back. The Cadillac Racer is intended for youthful chauffeurs 3 to 5 years of age. Length, over all, about 39 in. Width over all, about 23 inches. 12-in. seat. Sheet steel body, enameled orange with green stripings. Tool box and radiator front enameled red. Has radiator cap. License number in rear of car. 10-in. wheels. ¾-in. rubber tires. Ship. wt. 39 lbs.
148C1835—Price...........$12.45

$8.75
Marmon Racer

Imagine yourself at the wheel of this Marmon Racer—whizzing 'round the corner and coasting down hill! It's great sport! And boys, the sheet steel body of this Marmon is enameled a pretty red with yellow stripings. Radiator front enameled yellow. 10-in. wheels with ¾-in. rubber tires. Length, over all, about 35 in. Width, over all, about 20½ in. with 12-in. seat. Has radiator cap and bumper at front of machine. License number is painted in rear. For children from 3 to 5 years old. Shipping weight, 30 lbs.
148C1834—Price $8.75

Steering Wheel

Imitation Gas and Spark Control on Steering Wheel of Each of Our Autos

For Children 6 to 8 years of age.

A big Stutz Racer! For children 6 to 8 years of age. Easy riding and unusually roomy. Makes a dandy coaster. Sheet steel body, enameled red with yellow stripings. Radiator front enameled yellow. Has a massive reinforced hood in a distinctive shape. Twin imitation headlights at front. Imitation Moto-Meter is mounted on hood. Length, over all, about 47 in. Width, over all, about 23½ in. 13¼-in. seat. 12-in. wheels with ½-in. rubber tires. Has special 8-in. hardwood steering wheel. License number is painted in rear of machine.
148C1837—Ship. wt., 60 lbs. Price...................$16.50

A Genuine Bicycle Bell Included With Each Velocipede

High-Grade Velocipede

Mud guard, reinforced backbone and a real bicycle bell! Yes, and a padded seat with shock absorbing springs. Bicycle head has arched fork. Nickel-plated adjustable handle bars with leather grips. Frame and wheels enameled red with gold stripes. ⅝-in. rubber tired wheels. Nickel-plated hub caps.

The designer of this sturdy model certainly knows what boys are looking for. Ship. wt., 25, 28 and 30 lbs.

Article Number	Front Wheel, In.	Rear Wheel, In.	Inside Leg Measure Inches	Price
148C1844	16	12	16	$11.75
148C1845	20	14	18	13.45
148C1846	24	16	20 to 24	14.95

Our Ball-Bearing Velocipede

Some lucky boy will have months and months of pleasure on this dandy velocipede. Strong, heavy frame enameled in maroon and attractively striped. Bicycle head with arched fork. Fine motor-bike leather saddle, adjustable with nickel-plated double springs. The adjustable handle bar is nickel-plated and has leather grips. Nickeled cranks. Regular ball-bearing nickel-plated bicycle pedals, rat trap style. Large mud guard on front wheel. Large nickel-plated hub caps. ¾-in. cushion tires on front and rear wheels. Well worth the prices we ask.

Article Number	Front Wheel, In.	Rear Wheel, In.	Inside Leg Measure Inches	Ship. Wt., Lbs.	Price
148C1881	16	12	16	24	$14.98
148C1882	20	14	18	27	16.85
148C1883	24	16	20 to 24	30	18.98

$11.75

GIRLS

Show the boys what a REAL RACE is with this fine leatherette upholstered Tricycle! Mud guards add to its massive appearance. Enameled in maroon with gold stripings. Adjustable seat. Polished steel steering handle. Frame of good quality steel. Wood grips that fit the hand. 12-in. front wheel, 20-in. rear wheels. For children 3 to 5 yrs. of age. Ship. wt., 45 lbs.
148C1886—Price $15.75

148C1880—Steel tired tricycle without fenders. Adjustable seat. 10-in. front wheel, 13-in. rear wheels For girls 2 to 3 years old. Ship. wt., 30 lbs. Price $7.95

Truck-Bearo 3 Toys in 1

Can be used as a wheelbarrow or converted into a depot truck, as well as a sand toy by simply removing the metal tray. Made of metal on a wooden foundation. Enameled in red and blue with gilt trimmings. Length, over all, 24½ in.
148C1607—Ship. wt., 4½ lbs. Price...$1.39

Strongly Built Velocipede
Heavy Steel Tire Wheels

Article Number	Front Wheel, In.	Rear Wheel, In.	Inside Leg Measure Inches	Ship. Wt., Lbs.	Price
148C1864	16	12	16	21	$3.98
148C1865	20	14	18	24	4.47
148C1866	24	16	20 to 24	27	4.98

Rubber Tire Wheels, ½-in. front, ⅜-in. rear

Article Number	Front Wheel, In.	Rear Wheel, In.	Inside Leg Measure Inches	Ship. Wt., Lbs.	Price
148C1867	16	12	16	22	$6.95
148C1868	20	14	18	25	7.47
148C1869	24	16	20 to 24	27	7.98

Velocipedes that are Built for Service. Rubber Tired Wheels

Article Number	Front Wheel, In.	Rear Wheel, In.	Inside Leg Measure Inches	Ship. Wt. Lbs.	Price
148C1874	16	12	16	22	$8.95
148C1875	20	14	18	25	9.85
148C1876	24	16	20 to 24	27	10.85

Strongly built velocipede. Has bicycle head; curved oval steel fork; steel frame; strong five-point rear brace attached to extra wide rear axle which prevents latter from bending when carrying extra passenger; adjustable leather covered saddle with flexible spring seat; adjustable handlebar; broad pedals.

The frame is of heavy wide, half oval steel, painted black. Cherry colored wheels. Shaped handle bar with cherry stained wood grips. Improved adjustable fibre saddle with double coiled springs.

The ⅝-inch rubber tired wheels are of steel. Frame and fork finished black.

$8.95

Comical Mechanical Toys

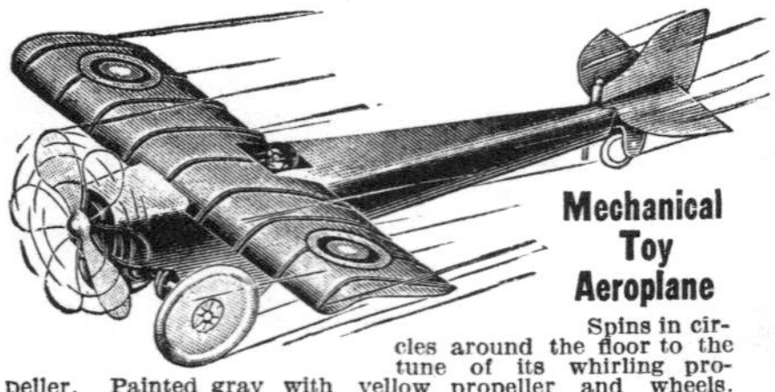

Mechanical Toy Aeroplane

Spins in circles around the floor to the tune of its whirling propeller. Painted gray with yellow propeller and wheels. Has strong spring. Length, 12¼ inches. Shipping weight, 1¼ pounds.
48C1062—Price..98c

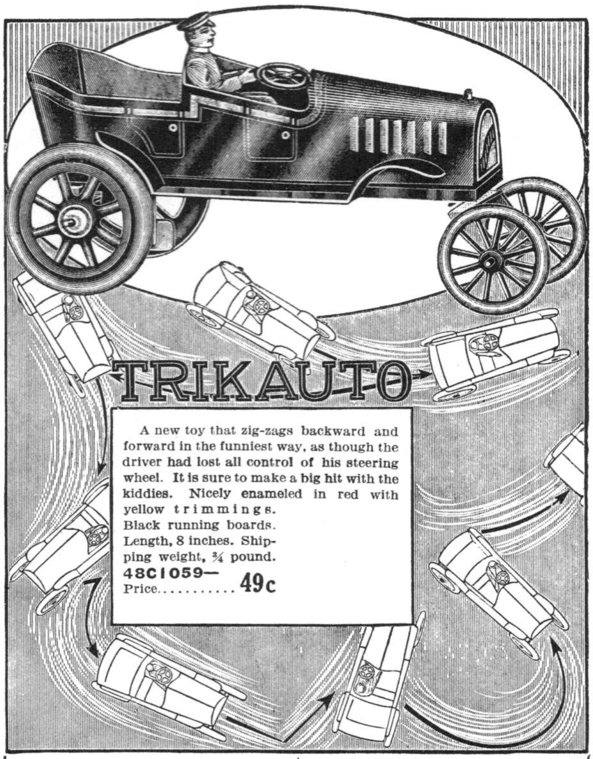

TRIKAUTO

A new toy that zig-zags backward and forward in the funniest way, as though the driver had lost all control of his steering wheel. It is sure to make a big hit with the kiddies. Nicely enameled in red with yellow trimmings. Black running boards. Length, 8 inches. Shipping weight, ¾ pound.
48C1059—
Price.......... 49c

Mechanical Jumping Rabbit

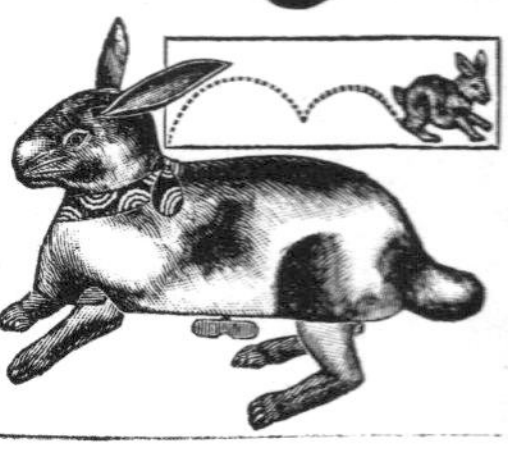

Made of brightly colored metal. Jumps and looks like a real rabbit. Length, over all, 6 in. Height, 3½ in. Ship. wt., 8 oz.
48C4002—
Price 84c

Mechanical Sand and Dumping Truck

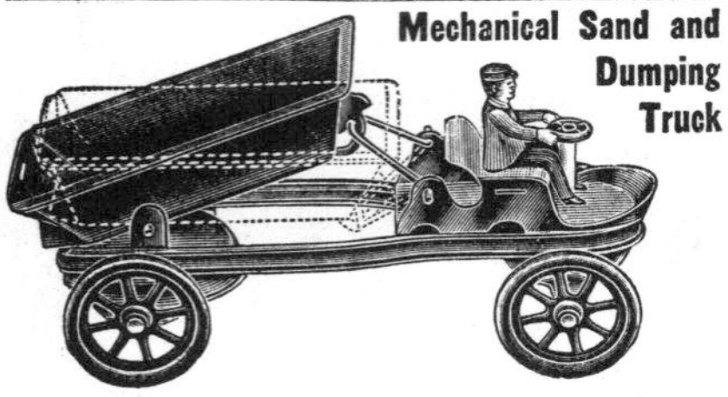

Like the real trucks as it has a Rear Drive; push a little lever and it spills the contents. Has strong, easy-to-wind spring. Painted blue with red wheels. Length, 9 inches. Shipping weight, 1¼ pounds.
48C1057—Price................................$1.15

Mechanical Toyland Auto Race

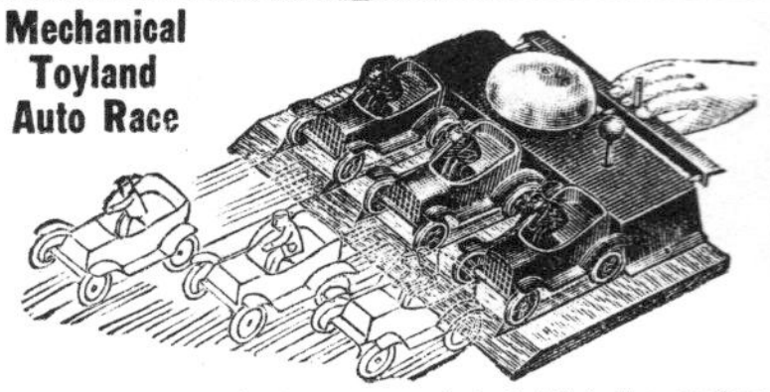

An exciting toyland auto race! Pull back the spring push the lever and the bell rings as the tiny autos spin away. Made of metal. Base, 5½x3¾ inches. Shipping weight 8 ounces.
48C4006—Price, complete with three autos...... 79c

Mechanical Destroyer Actually Runs in Water

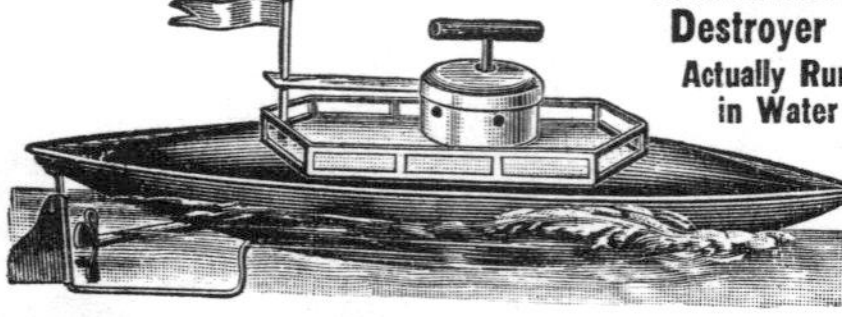

A little metal built destroyer that runs in the water. Painted battleship gray with white upper works. Red and white pennant. A strong clockwork spring accounts for its great speed. Has a rudder for steering. Length, 8¾ in.
48C4010—Shipping weight, 8 ounces. Price........85c

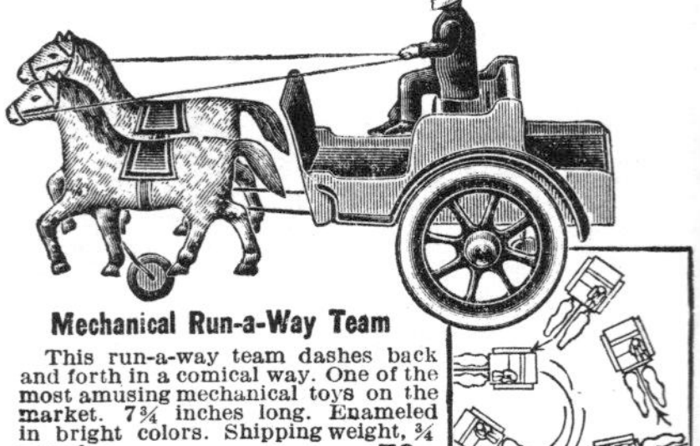

Mechanical Run-a-Way Team

This run-a-way team dashes back and forth in a comical way. One of the most amusing mechanical toys on the market. 7¾ inches long. Enameled in bright colors. Shipping weight, ¾ pound.
48C1061—Price...........72c

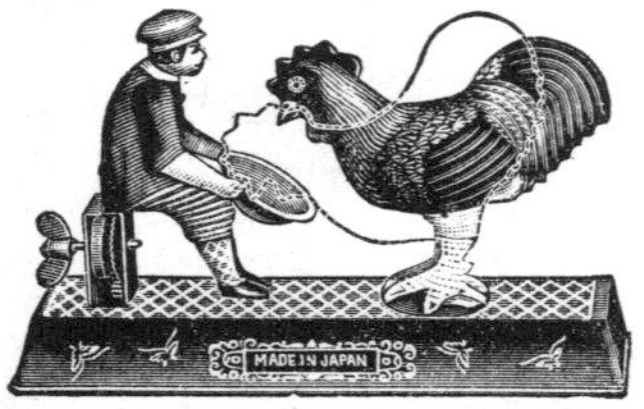

MADE IN JAPAN

Will He Ever Stop Eating?

This rooster keeps pecking at the imaginary corn in the basin. Long-running, strong clockwork spring. Size, over all 7¼x2½x4¾ inches. Shipping weight, about 12 ounces.
48C4004—Price......................................89c

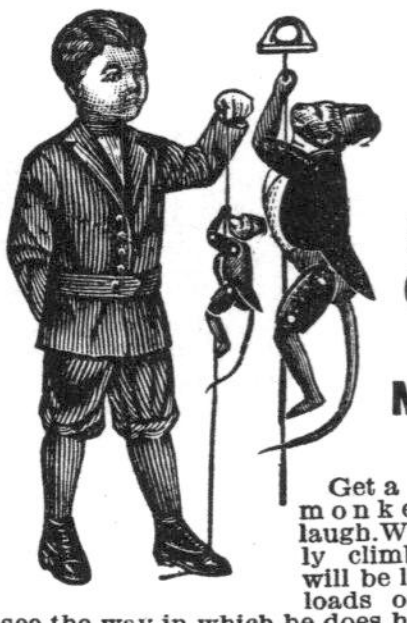

Our Funny Climbing Monkey

Get a climbing monkey and laugh. Will actually climb and it will be loads and loads of fun to see the way in which he does his tricks. He works his arms and feet like lightning. Made of metal, painted in bright colors. Length, 8 inches. Shipping weight, 6 ounces.
48C1064—Price 33c

The Jolly Negro Mechanical Clog Dancer

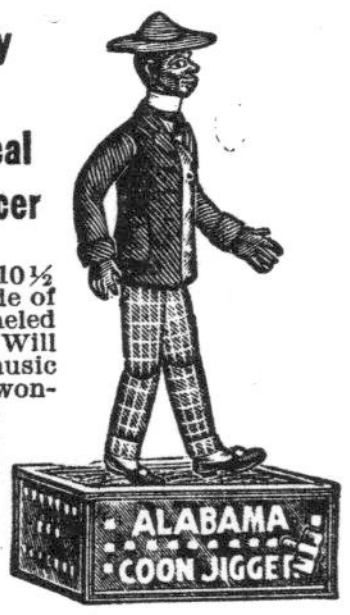

ALABAMA
COON JIGGER

Height, 10½ inches. Made of metal, enameled in colors. Will dance to music and make a wonderful racket with his feet. Arms and legs swing around in the most comical gestures.

Start him going with the piano and watch the fun. One of the most popular mechanical toys. Shipping weight, 1 pound.
48C3927—Price........... 62c

Mechanical Cat Wheeling Captive Mouse

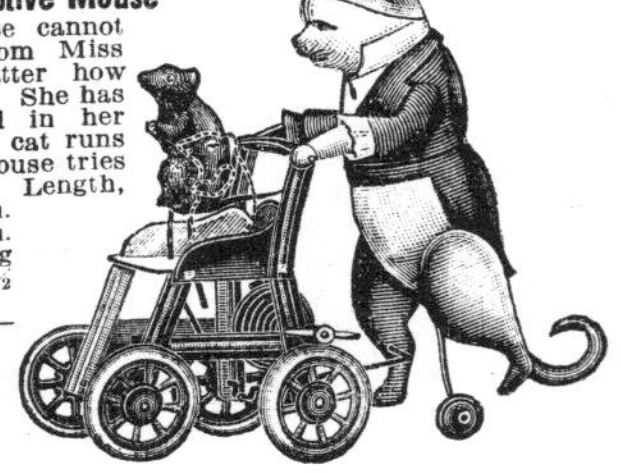

This mouse cannot get away from Miss Puss no matter how hard he tries. She has him fastened in her chair. When cat runs along Mr. Mouse tries to jump out. Length, over all, 7 in. Height, 6¼ in. Shipping weight, ½ pound.
48C4005—
Price.... 98

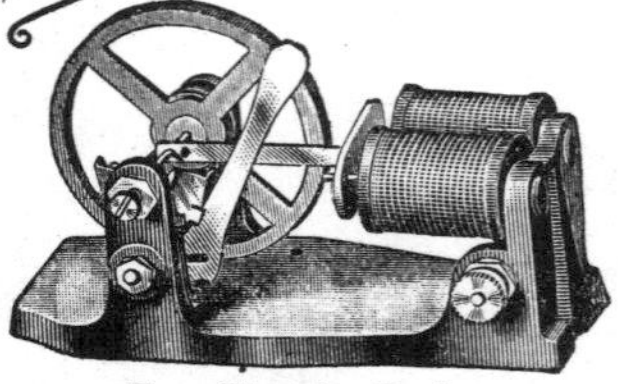

Toy Electric Engine

Operates on one dry cell battery. By shifting lever on side, action is reversed. Speed can be varied to suit the operator. Ideal for use in connection with Erector Outfits, etc., as well as experimental work. Well constructed and insulated. 4 inches long and 1¾ inches wide. Shipping weight, 1 pound.
48C1533—Price.................98c

Looks and Crawls Like a Live Baby Alligator

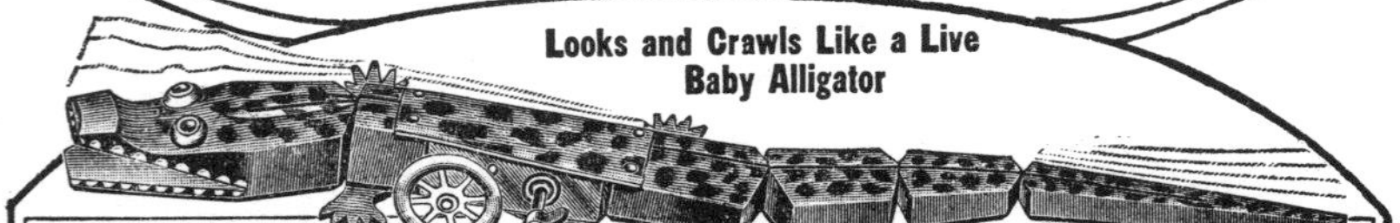

Strong clockwork spring. Body made of wood, jointed. Has leather feet. You should buy this toy to appreciate the amusement that you can give the children at this very low cost. Length of alligator, about 12½ inches. Shipping weight, 12 ounces.
48C4008—Price..72c

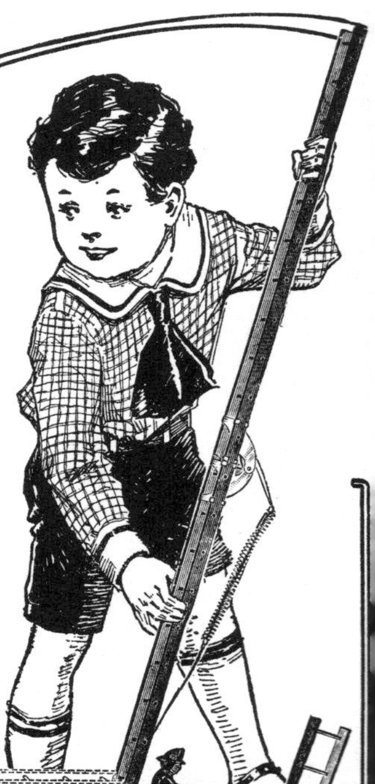

Mechanical Fire Department

Rubber Tired Mechanical Fire Engine

A fine big fire engine that can safely be trusted to guard your toyland treasures from all threatening fires. Has strong spring motor and runs in a circle. The gong rings a warning as it swiftly runs to the fire. Made of steel, enameled in red and yellow; gold bronze engine. Length, 11 in.
Ship. wt., 3½ lbs.
48C1072—
Price. $2.48

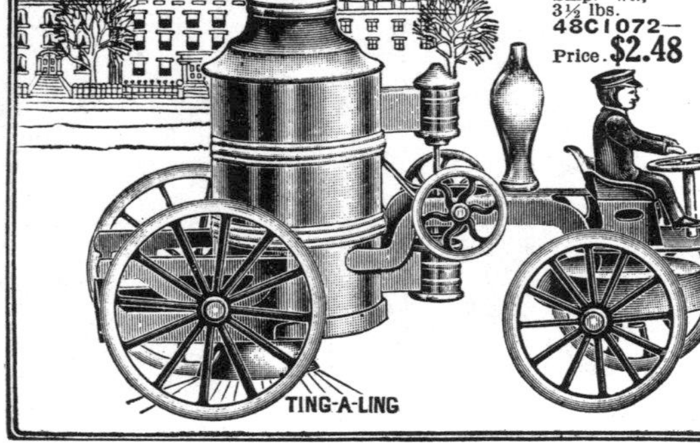

TING-A-LING

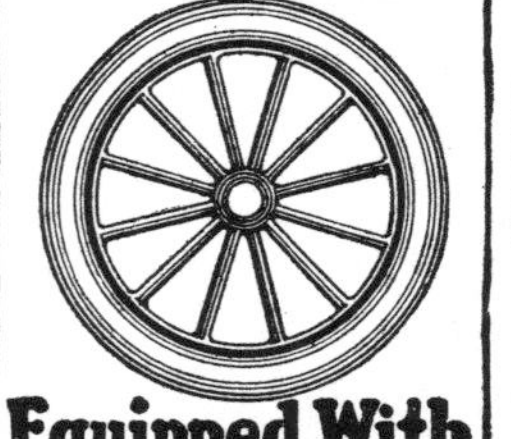

Equipped With Rubber Tired Wheels

Rubber Tired Hook and Ladder

The pride of every owner. When it collides with the wall, up shoots the extension ladder, ready to rescue some imaginary occupants of a burning building. Two 8½-inch ladders hooked on the sides make it resemble the real Hook and Ladders very closely. Height with ladder extended, 31 inches. Length of auto, 18 inches. Shipping weight, 3½ pounds.
48C1058—Price............ $2.48

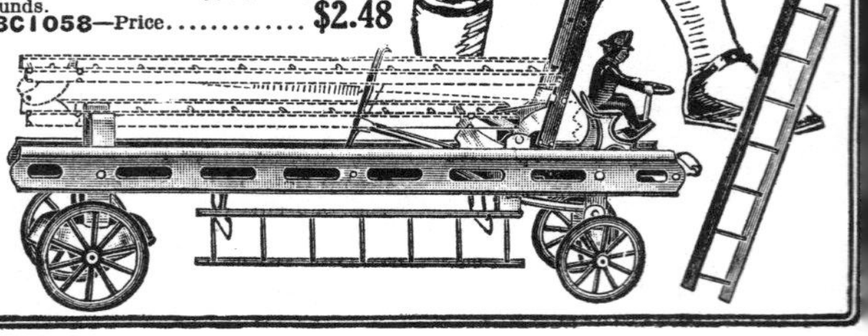

Hill Climbing Friction Toys
Will Climb a 20 Per Cent Incline

Large Friction Locomotive with Tender

Choo! Choo! Clear the track for the big flyer! It is 25 in. long. Runs all by itself, too. Just run the wheels over the floor to give it a start and away it goes. Finished in attractive colors. Shipping weight, 7 pounds. 48C1030—Price.................$1.98

$1.98

Friction Auto Racer

Every child expects the toy auto to climb hills the same as father's does. For that reason this model is exceedingly popular. Runs either backward or forward. Measures 7 in. in length. Enameled red, trimmed with gilt. Ship. wt., 1¾ lbs. 48C1027—Price...98c

Friction Mule with Driver

Whoa, Mule, Whoa! Length, 9¾ in.; strongly made of steel. Runs by friction motor. Brightly colored. Moves its head as it runs on floor. Ship. wt., 2 lbs. 48C1021—Price.......$1.27

Friction Duck

Made of sheet steel finely enameled in bright colors. Runs by friction motor, forward and backward or in circle. Length, about 7½ inches. Shipping weight, 4 pounds. 48C1033—Price.........$1.27

Large Size Friction Auto

When you send the big driver of this big automobile somewhere he is sure to get there. The large friction wheel never fails to work. About 12 inches long. Enameled maroon and green with gilt trimmings. Ship. wt., about 3½ lbs. 48C1029—Price...$1.98

This Aeroplane Will Not Get Out of Order

Oh! To be an aviator. How pleased you will be to get this strong aeroplane. Glides along the floor. As the wheels turn the propeller goes whirling around. Complete with aviator. Made of heavy sheet steel. 16¾ in. long; 10¾ in. wide; 6 in. high. Ship. wt., 5 lbs. 48C1102—Price.................$1.98

Bottom View Showing Simple Working Principle of Friction Toys

Spin the wheels on the floor a few times; by so doing a momentum is created on the large center drive giving the Friction Toys a pulling power of amazing proportions. Almost trouble-proof as there are no springs to get out of order.

Toys to be Pulled on the Floor

Unfasten lever on the side of this truck and contents is automatically dumped. To be pulled with a string. Enameled in red, gilt body. Ship. wt., 2½ lbs. 48C1106—59c

Large Fire Engine

Motor type fire engine with body enameled in red and gold. Length, 10½ inches; width, 3 inches; height, 6¾ inches. Made of iron. Ship. wt., 6 lbs. 48C1108—Price...72c

Large Iron Hook and Ladder

The horses on this hook and ladder are full of action. When pulled along the floor the gong under seat starts to ring, so everybody will jump out of its way. Body painted red, wheels and ladder in yellow. Length, over all, 25 inches; 9½ inches high, 4 inches wide. Ship-ping weight, 10 pounds. 48C1105—Price.................$2.65

Wooden Hook and Ladder

The horses' feet actually move as this toy is pulled along the floor. Has five wooden ladders, painted red. Driver made of metal. Length, over all 20½ inches. Height, 7¾ inches. Shipping weight, 4 pounds. 48C3949—Price.................$1.29

Set of three colored animals mounted on red platforms with yellow wheels. To be pulled by string, on floor. Length of platforms, 6¾ in. Ship. wt., about 1½ lbs. 48C3950— Price........62c

Galloping Horse with Wagon

Milk wagon with two tin milk cans. Horse's legs move automatically when wagon is pulled. Made of brightly colored wood. Metal wheels. Length, 15 in. 48C3955—Ship. wt. 2 lbs.$1.29

Fire Engine With Imitation Hose

Made of iron, complete with imitation hose, strong sash cord. Engine is enameled red and gold, wheels in yellow, and horses in black. Has driver and bell. A very attractive toy. Length, 19 inches; height, 7½ inches; width, 3½ inches. Shipping weight, 8 pounds. 48C1104—Price.................$2.65

Large Freight Train Set

Our five-piece train set. Made of iron, enameled in black. Tender made of sheet steel, also gondola car and dump car. The dump car has a regular dumping device, just like those on real railroad trains. Length, over all 37 inches. Shipping weight, 6 pounds. 48C1313— Price.................$2.25

Large Passenger Train Set

Locomotive and tender made of iron. Four coaches made of sheet steel enameled red, white, blue and yellow. Length over all, 37 inches. Ship. wt., 5 lbs. 48C1304—Price........$1.29

Railroad Train. Length, 27½ in. Locomotive and tender of iron, enameled in black. Four cars made of pressed steel, enameled in colors. Not mechanical. Ship. wt., 3 lbs. 48C1305—Price.................69c

Tiny Tots' Special Railroad Train. Length, 16 in. Locomotive and tender of iron, enameled in black. HAS TWO CARS. Made of pressed steel. Not mechanical. Ship. wt., 3 lbs. 48C1308—Price.................48c

The Caged Tiger

When Pulled on Floor He Nods His Head to Please the Kiddies

Look at the Tiger locked in his cage! Just like a real one. His head moves up and down as you drag him along the floor. Bright red cage on wheels. Length, 10¾ inches. Height, 8 inches. Shipping weight, 3 pounds. 48C3952.................98c

Baby's Most Welcome Entertainers
The Cinnamon Colored Bears With Voices

The Exciting End of Teddy's Search for Honey

Lucky Ted Hooks a Fish in the Cool Mountain Stream

IT takes more than talcum powder to keep baby smiling. That's why Santa is kept so very busy these days. He's packing his sled full with Teddy Bears. And they are such jolly looking companionable bears! Talkative and entertaining, too. Squeeze them and the chatter that follows is enough to enrapture any little child. Their cinnamon colored plush coats and glass eyes make them look just like their Big Brothers who roam the North Woods. Built to stand harder spankings than the "kiddies" will ever think of giving them.

* * *

The children, bless their hearts, deserve happiness! Arrange with Santa to surprise them with these splendid Teddy Bears Christmas Morn, and make the day One Long Remembered Success!

A Merry Walnut Hunt

Teddys Performing at the Circus

Teddy engages his biggest Brother in a wrestling match

They Borrow some Skis

24 INCH Cinnamon Colored **WITH VOICE** $3.98

20 INCH Cinnamon Colored
Has voice in both front paws instead of in back.
$2.98

18 INCH Cinnamon Colored **WITH VOICE** $2.79

12 INCH Cinnamon Colored **WITH VOICE** $1.19

10 INCHES Cinnamon Colored 98c **HAS NO VOICE**

16 INCH BEAR Cinnamon Colored **HAS VOICE** $2.24

Bunny, Has Voice
This rabbit is just like real—when you squeeze him he squeals. Made of white velvet. Glass eyes. Carries cane. Ribbon around neck. Height, over all about 13 in. Shipping weight, 1 pound.
48C3240—Price 89c

Plush Kitten with Voice
Like all real kittens it has hair on its upper lip. Of good quality gray and white plush. Has colored ribbon tied about neck. Length, about 5¾ inches. Shipping weight, 4 ounces.
48C3268—Price..........48c

Leaping Peter Rabbit
When pulled around he gets into lifelike action and leaps as gracefully as a real live rabbit. A durable and clever toy. Strongly made of compo-board, handsomely enameled in gay colors. Length, 18 inches. Shipping weight, ½ pound.
48C3010—Price $1.25

Quacky Duck with Voice
Has velvet coat as soft as down and fuzzy wings. Glass eyes. When wheeled along floor it gives one continuous flow of quacks. About 6½ in. long. Ship. wt., 5 oz.
48C3059—Price........$1.39

Airdale Dog with Voice
Made of good grade brown plush with glass eyes. Ribbon around neck. 7¼ inches high, over all. Shipping weight, ½ pound.
48C3244—Price.....$1.32

Jumbo The Bright-Eyed Elephant
Every child loves the elephant. This one is different from his wrinkled uncles, as his body is of fine smooth velvet. Has colored ribbon on neck. Glass eyes. About 8 in. long. Ship. wt., 7 oz.
48C3269—Price............79c

Cream Colored Velvet Dog
This cute little dog is made of cream color velvet with brown ears and tail and white under body. Glass eyes. Height, 5 in. Ship. wt. 6 oz.
48C3196—Price..........42c

Mrs. Peter Rabbit and Family on Cart
They are all here—Mrs. Peter Rabbit, Flopsy, Mopsy, Cotton Tail and Little Peter. A metal base holds them so that they can be moved into different positions. Made in bright colors. Length, 17½ in. Height, 10 in.
48C3015—Shipping weight, 1½ lbs. Price....78c

Gray and white composition cat with gay orange necktie and bell. Has a movable jaw and meows when you press down on her head. Stands 9½ in. high. Ship. wt., 1 lb. MEOW
48C3219—Price........98c

Plush Saddle Horses
Mounted on Platform with Metal Wheels
48C3223 — Length of platform, 11½ in. Height to top of head about 13½ in. Shipping weight, 1¼ lbs. Price...........$1.4
48C3222 — Length of platform, 15 in. Height to top of head, about 16½ in. Shipping weight, 2½ lbs. Price....$2.6

172

Toyland's Paradise

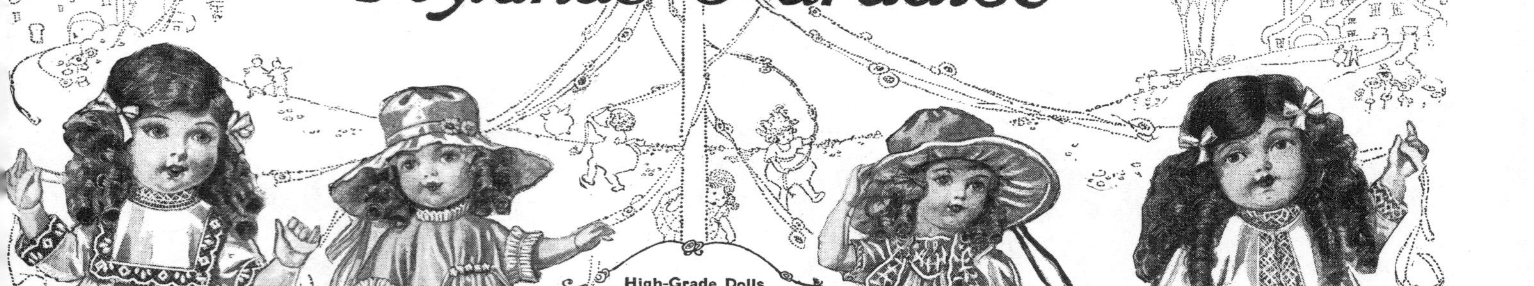

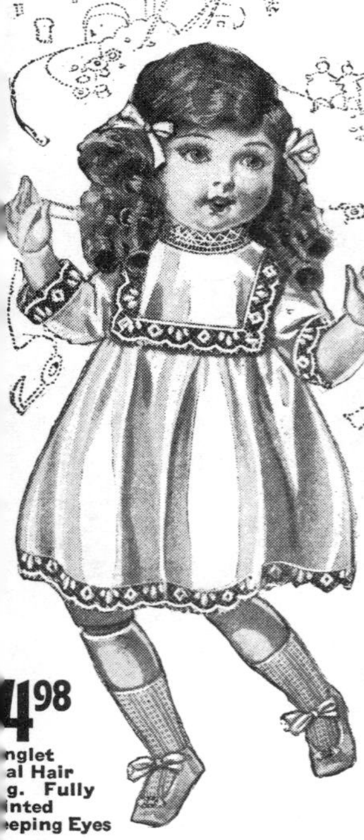

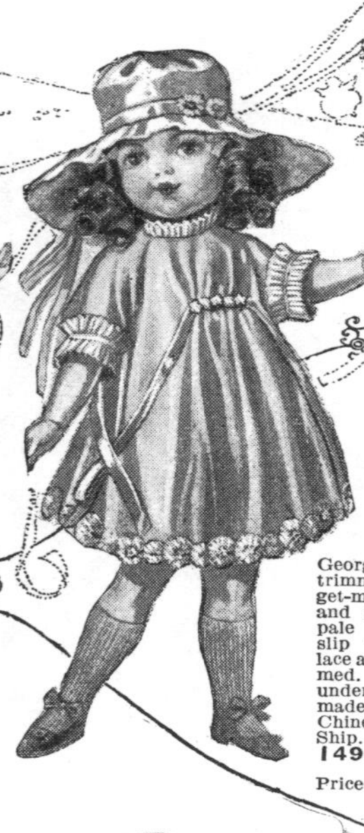

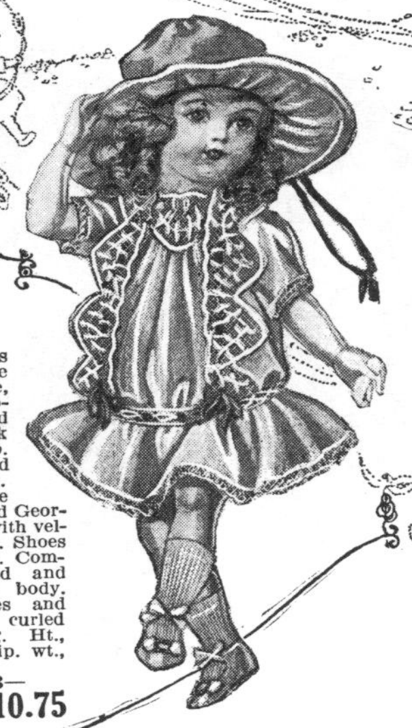

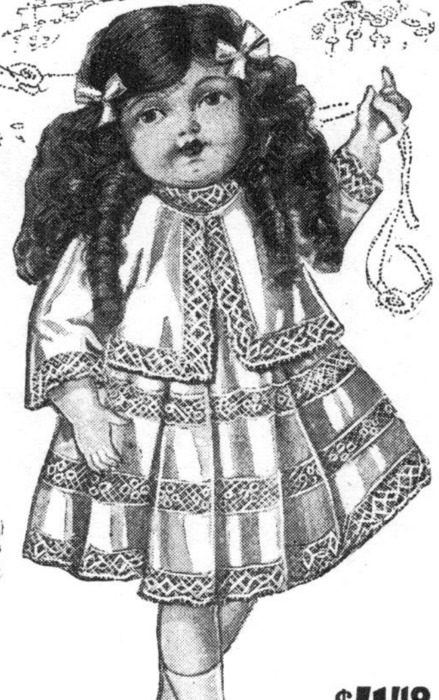

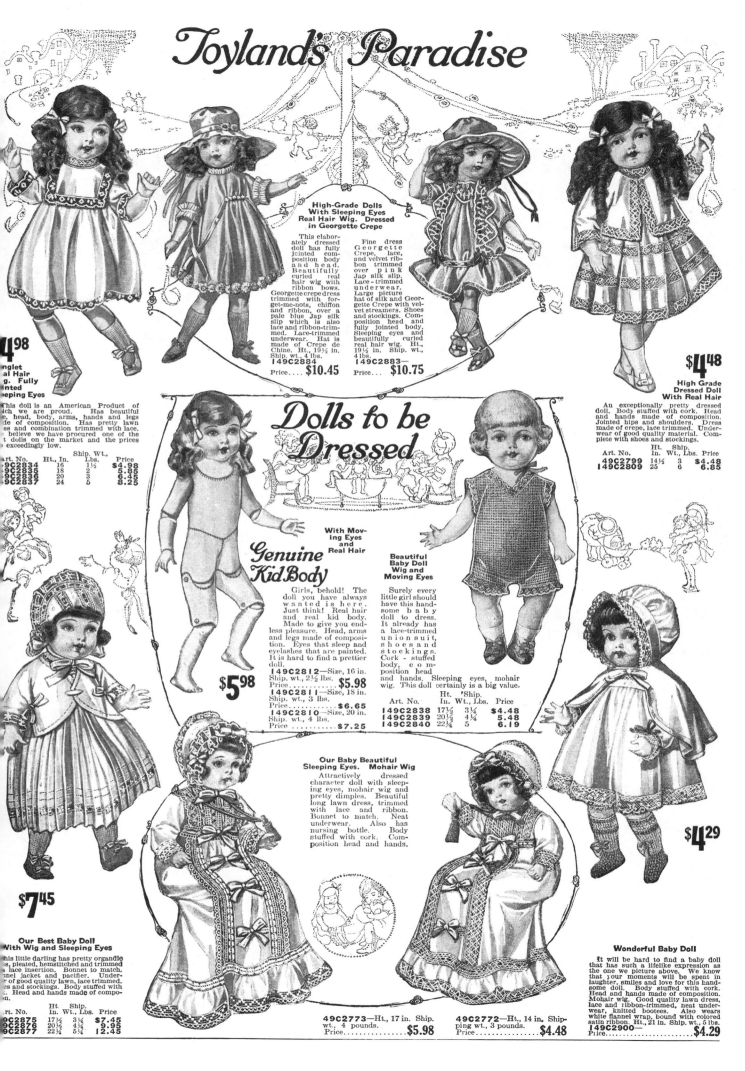

High-Grade Dolls With Sleeping Eyes Real Hair Wig. Dressed in Georgette Crepe

This elaborately dressed doll has fully jointed composition body and head. Beautifully curled real hair wig with ribbon bows. Georgette crepe dress trimmed with forget-me-nots, chiffon and ribbon, over a pale blue Jap silk slip which is also lace and ribbon-trimmed. Lace-trimmed underwear. Hat is made of Crepe de Chine. Ht., 19½ in. Ship. wt., 4 lbs.
149C2884
Price.... **$10.45**

Fine dress Georgette Crepe, lace, and velvet ribbon trimmed over pink Jap silk slip. Lace-trimmed underwear. Large picture hat of silk and Georgette Crepe with velvet streamers. Shoes and stockings. Composition head and fully jointed body. Sleeping eyes and beautifully curled real hair wig. Ht., 19½ in. Ship. wt., 4 lbs.
149C2883—
Price... **$10.75**

$4.98

nglet al Hair g. Fully inted eeping Eyes

This doll is an American Product of ich we are proud. Has beautiful e, head, body, arms, hands and legs de of composition. Has pretty lawn ss and combination trimmed with lace. believe we have procured one of the t dolls on the market and the prices exceedingly low.

rt. No.	Ht., In.	Ship. Wt., Lbs.	Price
9C2834	16	1½	$4.98
9C2835	18	2	5.85
9C2836	20	3	6.45
9C2837	24	5	8.25

$4.48

High Grade Dressed Doll With Real Hair

An exceptionally pretty dressed doll. Body stuffed with cork. Head and hands made of composition. Jointed hips and shoulders. Dress made of crepe, lace trimmed. Underwear of good quality material. Complete with shoes and stockings.

Art. No.	Ht. In.	Ship. Wt., Lbs.	Price
49C2799	14½	3	$4.48
149C2809	25	6	6.85

Dolls to be Dressed

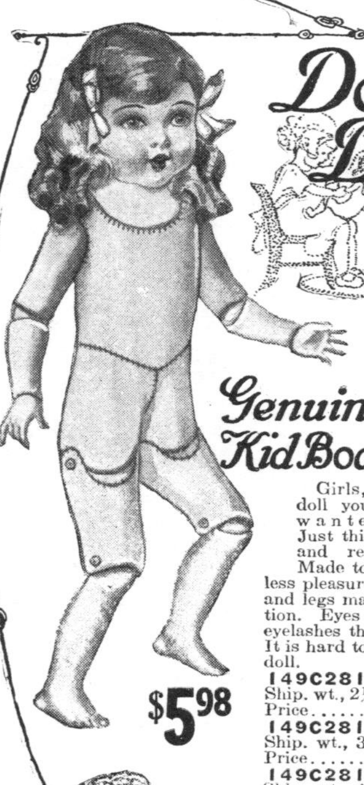

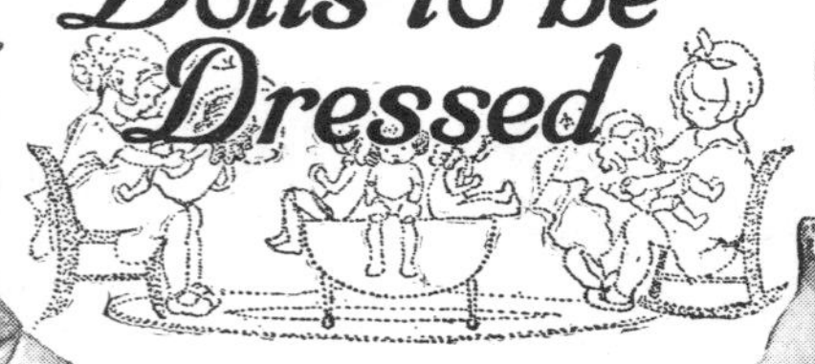

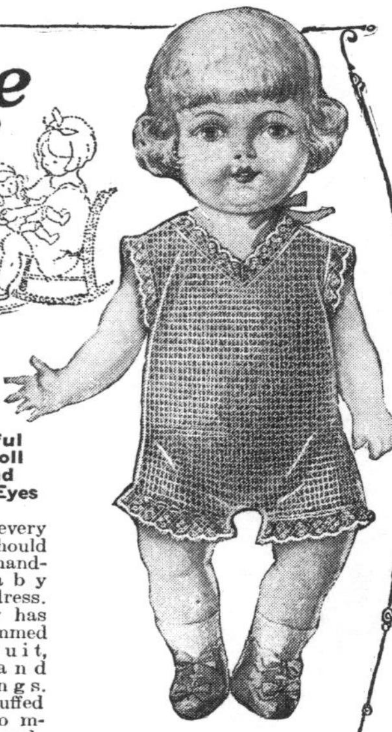

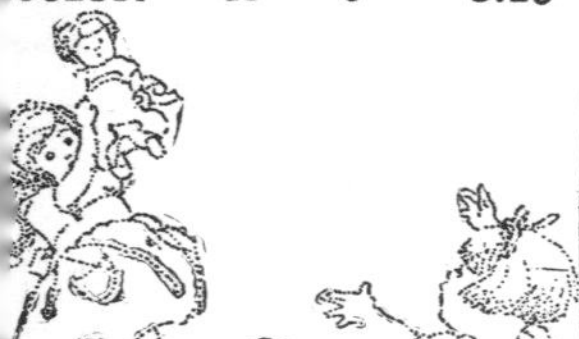

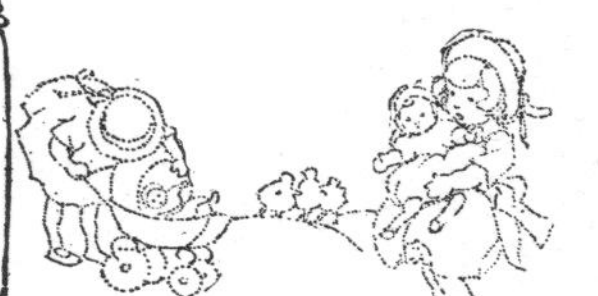

With Moving Eyes and Real Hair

Genuine Kid Body

Girls, behold! The doll you have always wanted is here. Just think! Real hair and real kid body. Made to give you endless pleasure. Head, arms and legs made of composition. Eyes that sleep and eyelashes that are painted. It is hard to find a prettier doll.

149C2812—Size, 16 in. Ship. wt., 2½ lbs. Price........... **$5.98**
149C2811—Size, 18 in. Ship. wt., 3 lbs. Price........... **$6.65**
149C2810—Size, 20 in. Ship. wt., 4 lbs. Price........... **$7.25**

$5.98

Beautiful Baby Doll Wig and Moving Eyes

Surely every little girl should have this handsome baby doll to dress. It already has a lace-trimmed union suit, shoes and stockings. Cork-stuffed body, composition head and hands. Sleeping eyes, mohair wig. This doll certainly is a big value.

Art. No.	Ht. In.	Ship. Wt., Lbs.	Price
149C2838	17½	3¼	$4.48
149C2839	20½	4¼	5.48
149C2840	22¼	5	6.19

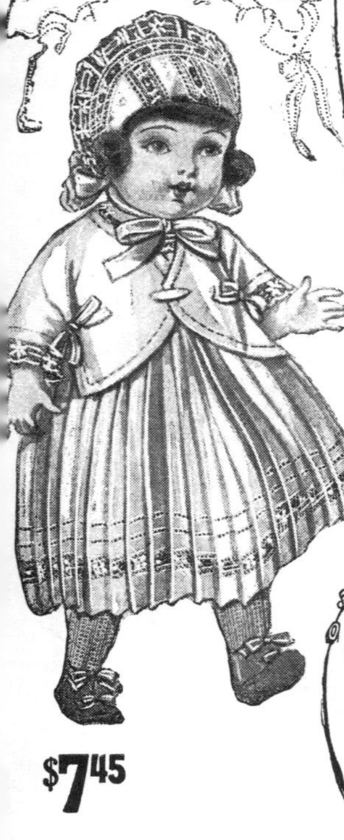

$7.45

Our Best Baby Doll With Wig and Sleeping Eyes

his little darling has pretty organdie s, pleated, hemstitched and trimmed lace insertion. Bonnet to match. nnel jacket and pacifier. Under- of good quality lawn, lace trimmed. es and stockings. Body stuffed with . Head and hands made of compo- n.

rt. No.	Ht. In.	Ship. Wt., Lbs.	Price
9C2875	17½	3¼	$7.45
9C2876	20½	4¼	9.95
9C2877	22¼	5¼	12.45

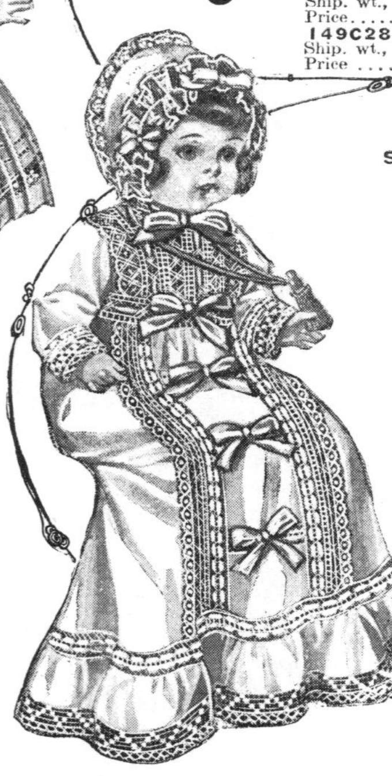

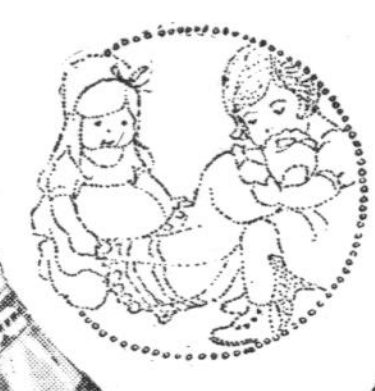

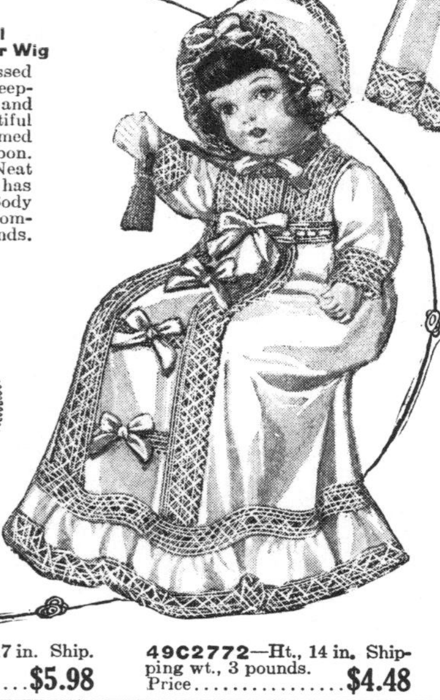

Our Baby Beautiful Sleeping Eyes. Mohair Wig

Attractively dressed character doll with sleeping eyes, mohair wig and pretty dimples. Beautiful long lawn dress, trimmed with lace and ribbon. Bonnet to match. Neat underwear. Also has nursing bottle. Body stuffed with cork. Composition head and hands.

49C2773—Ht., 17 in. Ship. wt., 4 pounds.
Price................ **$5.98**

49C2772—Ht., 14 in. Shipping wt., 3 pounds.
Price................ **$4.48**

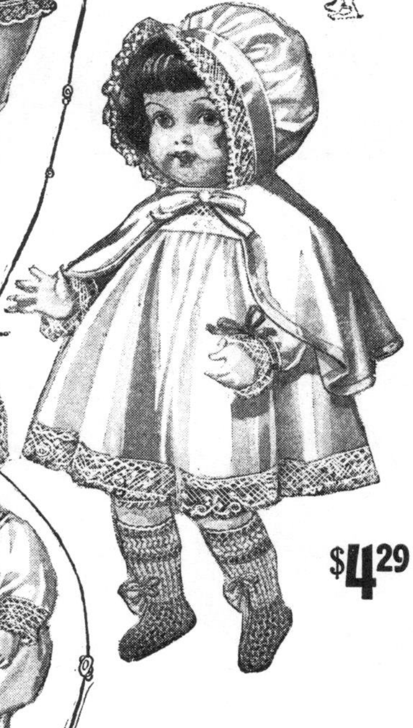

$4.29

Wonderful Baby Doll

It will be hard to find a baby doll that has such a lifelike expression as the one we picture above. We know that your moments will be spent in laughter, smiles and love for this handsome doll. Body stuffed with cork. Head and hands made of composition. Mohair wig. Good quality lawn dress, lace and ribbon-trimmed, neat underwear, knitted bootees. Also wears white flannel wrap, bound with colored satin ribbon. Ht., 21 in. Ship. wt., 5 lbs.
149C2900—
Price........................... **$4.29**

High Grade Full Jointed Doll, Moving Eyes, Real Hair

The cutest doll you ever saw. One day's play with her will convince you that there never was a better chum. She will move her head, arms, wrists, hips or knees in any life-like way you may want her to. Her dainty little mouth is open exposing a row of pearly white teeth. The nicely painted eyelashes and eyebrows provide an ideal setting for the realistic moving glass eyes. Her natural hair falls in graceful curls over her white lace-trimmed slip.
149C2911—Height, 19 in. Ship. wt., 2½ lbs. **$5.48**

Moving Eyes and Mohair Wig

This charming doll with its prettily designed dress and cap has captured the hearts of the little girls. Has special composition head and hands with well-formed cork stuffed body. Jointed at hips and shoulders. Blue linette suspender dress over white waist, with lace-trimmed hat to match. White underclothes, shoes and stockings. Height, 15½ in. Ship. wt., 1½ lbs.
49C2905—Price. **$1.98**

The Walking Doll

Where this doll goes, happiness follows. For whoever saw a walking doll in the possession of a little girl unless it was the attraction of the neighborhood. Santa tells us that it won't take a single step unless someone guides it by its arms. And when it is tired of walking you can put it to sleep. The moving eyes close every time you lay this dolly down. Has mohair wig. She wears a floral lawn dress, lace-trimmed, with hat to match. White buckled shoes and stockings and undergarments. Cork-stuffed body, arms and legs; composition head and hands. Jointed at shoulders and hips. Height, 20 in. Shipping weight, 2½ lbs.
149C2755—Price. **$4.98**

Walks in a Very Realistic Manner

Mohair Curls and Moving Eyes

Girls who have seen this doll claim that Santa never made one that was prettier. It's just the right size: measures 20½ inches in height, and the body is unusually well-formed. Cork-stuffed body, arms and legs. Jointed at hips and shoulders. Has composition head and hands, moving eyes and short curly mohair wig. The extra large pink satin bows on head and back of satin sash will delight the most particular little Miss. Figured and flowered lawn dress; lace-trimmed collar and cuffs. Lace-trimmed undergarments. White stockings and white metal buckled slippers. Ship. wt., about 3 lbs.
149C2890—Price. **$5.85**

Our Pretty Moving Eyed Hollander

Spreads smiles wherever she goes. Has mohair wig and moving eyes. Composition head and hands. Cork-stuffed body and legs. Jointed at hips and shoulders. She wears a pink pleated linette dress with white waist. The blue Eaton jacket matches her hat. Has white undergarments, shoes and stockings. Height, 17 in. Ship. wt., 1½ lbs.
49C2904—Price. **$3.19**

$1⁵⁹

A pleasant looking, plump little dolly, wearing a pretty lace trimmed dress in a floral design. Composition head and hands. Body stuffed with cork, making her very light in weight. Height, 15 inches. Shipping weight, 2¾ pounds.
49C2823—Price. **$1.59**

Has Mohair Wig

This pretty dolly has just bid her friend goodby. She knows that some lovely little girl will soon provide her with a cozy new home. Her lace-trimmed colored dress, with hat to match, is considered very stylish in Toyland. White undergarments, shoes and stockings. Composition head and hands, and well stuffed body, arms and legs. Jointed at hips and shoulders. Height, 18 in. Ship. wt., 1½ lbs.
49C2633—Price. **$2.45**

Sleeping-Eyed Doll With Wig, Silk Sweater and Cap

Girls, this dolly is just the cutest little playmate for you. She has a pretty white dress, lace trimmed. Cork-stuffed body. Her silk sweater and cap furnish her ample protection should she venture out with you on these cold wintry days. Composition head and hands. Moving eyes and good quality wig. Height, 13¾ inches. Shipping weight, 3 pounds.
49C2879—Price. **$2.75**

Children! I am very anxious to be with you and I must have someone to make dresses for me. My head, arms and hands are made of composition; my body is stuffed with cork, making me light in weight. I wear a good quality pinning slip, diaper and very pretty knitted mercerized bootees. Height, 18¼ in. Ship. wt., 4¼ lbs.
49C2624—Price. **$2.39**

This Dolly Can Say "Mamma"

This doll has a voice as true to nature as possible. Height, 12 inches. Dressed very becomingly in lawn, trimmed with lace. Face and hands made of composition which will not break easily. Body, arms and legs stuffed with material that makes doll exceedingly light. Shipping weight, 2½ pounds.
49C2820—Price. **$1.25**

$1²⁵

A Realistic Moving-Eyed Baby Doll

$5⁴⁵

The Golden Days of Childhood are all the sweeter when such a pretty baby doll becomes playmate to the child. Her loving disposition is strengthened when she has so life-like a doll to mother. It forms a valuable part of her childhood life. This doll has moving eyes, mohair wig and composition head and arms. Cork-stuffed body and legs; jointed at shoulders and hips. White lawn pleated dress, lace-trimmed, with pretty rosette-trimmed cap to match. Attractive figured blue mull jacket, lace edging. Wears knitted booties. Height, 18 in. Ship. wt., 3 lbs.

Baby Dolls To be Dressed

Notice the cute little smile on the doll illustrated here. She seems to hear you say, "Come, Baby, try on this new dress that I have made for you today," and she knows how pleased you will be planning new dresses for her. The body is stuffed with cork, covered with flesh-colored cloth. Composition head and hands. Good quality mohair wig. Jointed at shoulders and hips. Also has stockings.

$1⁸⁹

Art. No.	Height	Ship. Wt.	Price
49C2785	11½ in.	2 lbs.	$1.89
49C2786	14½ in.	2½ lbs.	2.48
49C2787	17 in.	3 lbs.	3.48

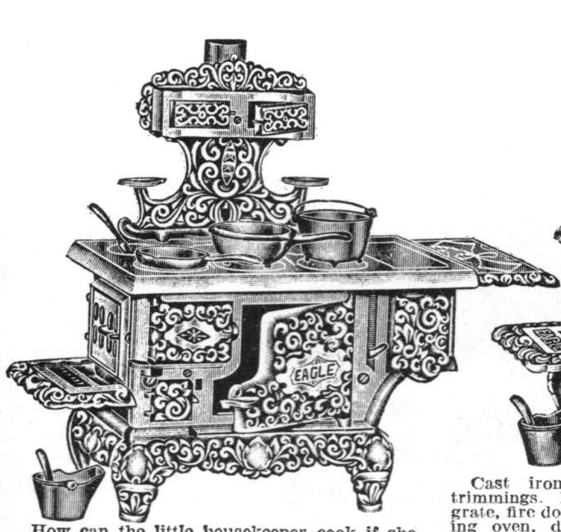

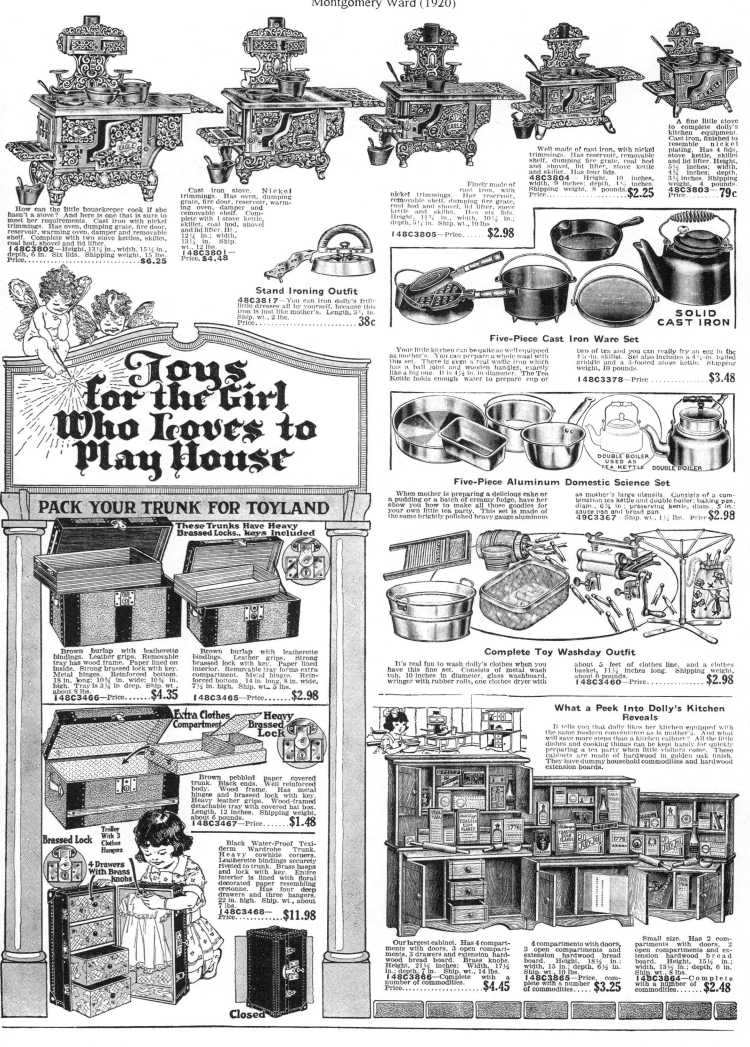

How can the little housekeeper cook if she hasn't a stove? And here is one that is sure to meet her requirements. Cast iron with nickel trimmings. Has oven, dumping grate, fire door, reservoir, warming oven, damper and removable shelf. Complete with two stove kettles, skillet, coal hod, shovel and lid lifter.
148C3802—Height, 13½ in., width, 15½ in., depth, 6 in. Six lids. Shipping weight, 15 lbs.
Price.............................. $6.25

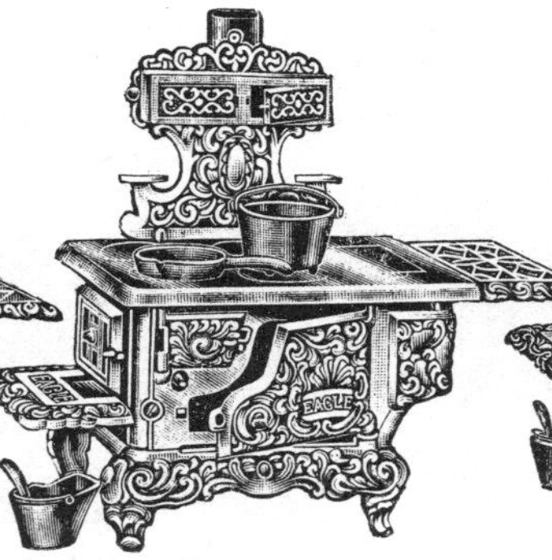

Cast iron stove. Nickel trimmings. Has oven, dumping grate, fire door, reservoir, warming oven, damper and removable shelf. Complete with 1 stove kettle, skillet, coal hod, shovel and lid lifter. Ht., 12¼ in.; width, 13½ in. Ship. wt., 12 lbs.
148C3801—
Price, $4.48

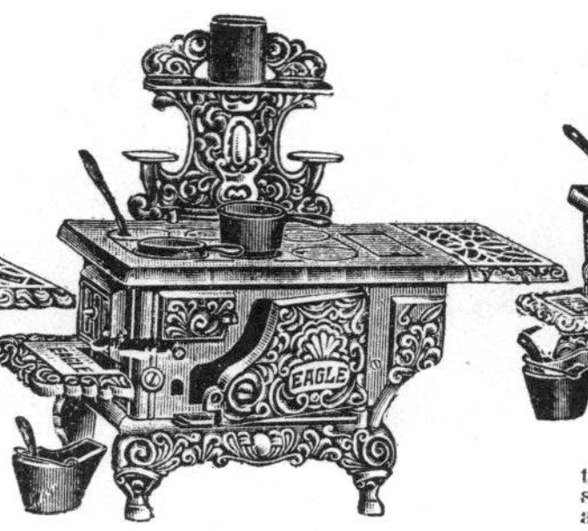

Finely made of cast iron, with nickel trimmings. Has reservoir, removable shelf, dumping fire grate, coal hod and shovel, lid lifter, stove kettle and skillet. Has six lids. Height, 11¾ in., width, 10½ in.; depth, 5¼ in. Ship. wt., 10 lbs
148C3805—Price...... $2.98

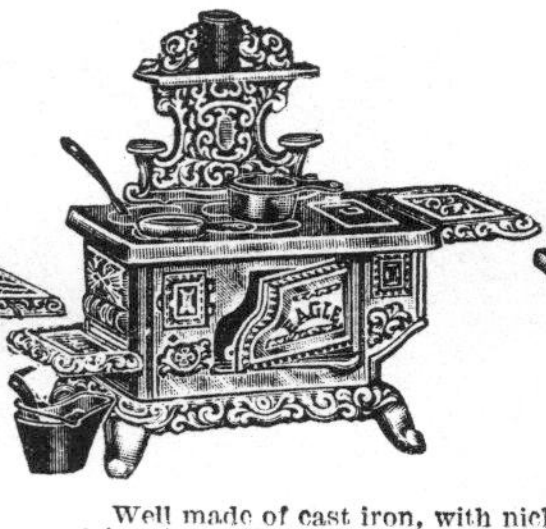

Well made of cast iron, with nickel trimmings. Has reservoir, removable shelf, dumping fire grate, coal hod and shovel, lid lifter, stove kettle and skillet. Has four lids.
48C3804 — Height, 10 inches, width, 9 inches; depth, 4½ inches. Shipping weight, 8 pounds.
Price.............................. $2.25

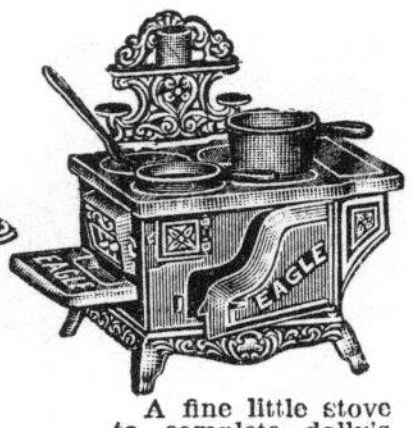

A fine little stove to complete dolly's kitchen equipment. Cast iron, finished to resemble nickel plating. Has 4 lids, stove kettle, skillet and lid lifter. Height, 5½ inches; width, 4¾ inches; depth, 3½ inches. Shipping weight, 4 pounds.
48C3803—79c
Price........

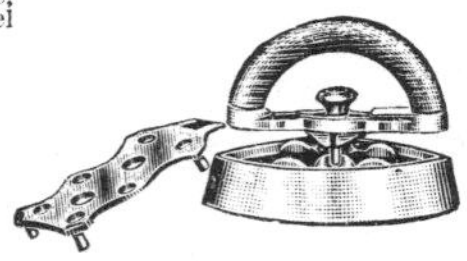

Stand Ironing Outfit

48C3817—You can iron dolly's frilly little dresses all by yourself, because this iron is just like mother's. Length, 3¾ in. Ship. wt., 2 lbs.
Price.............................. 38c

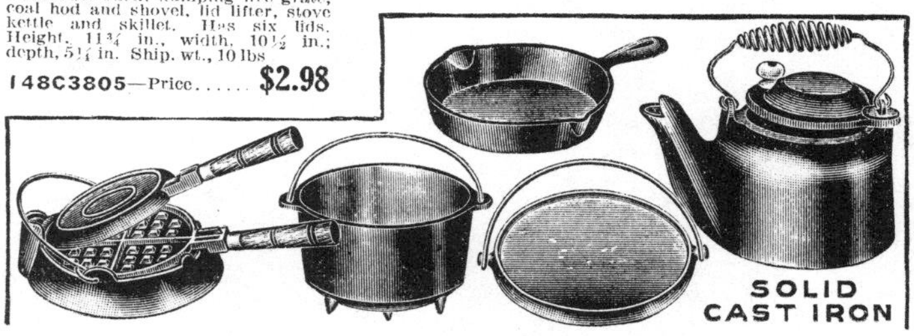
SOLID CAST IRON

Five-Piece Cast Iron Ware Set

Your little kitchen can be quite as well equipped as mother's. You can prepare a whole meal with this set. There is even a real waffle iron which has a ball joint and wooden handles, exactly like a big one. It is 4½ in. in diameter. The Tea Kettle holds enough water to prepare cup or two of tea and you can really fry an egg in the 4¾-in. skillet. Set also includes a 4¾-in. bailed griddle and a 3-footed stove kettle. Shipping weight, 10 pounds.
148C3378—Price.............. $3.48

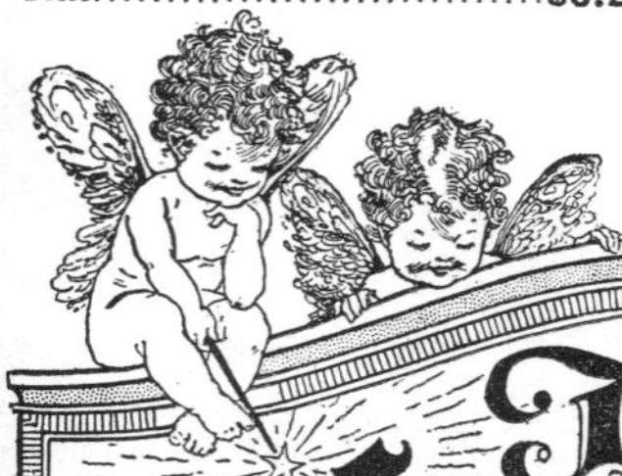

Toys for the Girl Who Loves to Play House

PACK YOUR TRUNK FOR TOYLAND

These Trunks Have Heavy Brassed Locks., keys Included

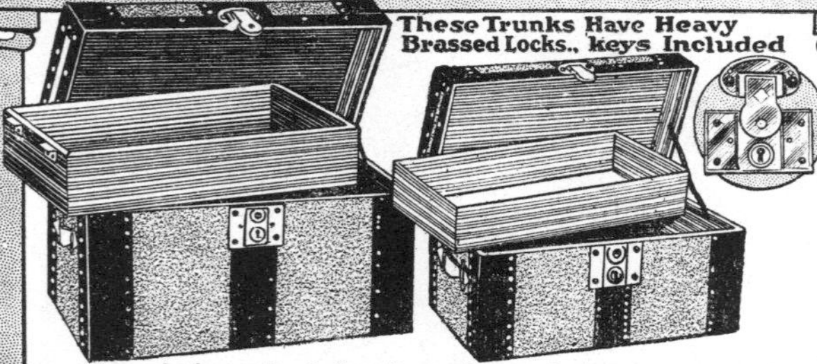

Brown burlap with leatherette bindings. Leather grips. Removable tray has wood frame. Paper lined on inside. Strong brassed lock with key. Metal hinges. Reinforced bottom. 18 in. long; 10¾ in. wide; 10¾ in. high. Tray is 3¼ in deep. Ship. wt., about 8 lbs.
148C3466—Price....... $4.35

Brown burlap with leatherette bindings. Leather grips. Strong brassed lock with key. Paper lined interior. Removable tray forms extra compartment. Metal hinges. Reinforced bottom. 14 in. long, 8 in. wide, 7½ in. high. Ship. wt., 5 lbs.
148C3465—Price...... $2.98

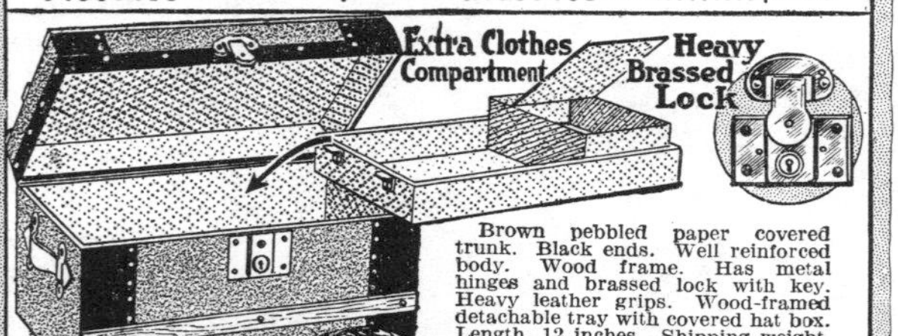
Extra Clothes Compartment
Heavy Brassed Lock

Brown pebbled paper covered trunk. Black ends. Well reinforced body. Wood frame. Has metal hinges and brassed lock with key. Heavy leather grips. Wood-framed detachable tray with covered hat box. Length, 12 inches. Shipping weight, about 6 pounds.
148C3467—Price....... $1.48

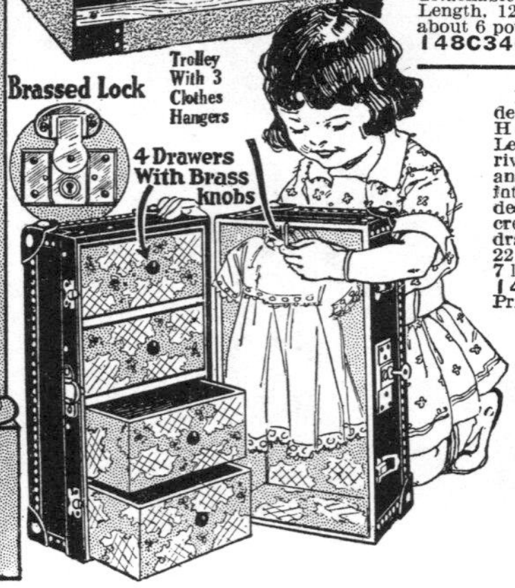
Brassed Lock
Trolley With 3 Clothes Hangers
4 Drawers With Brass knobs

Black Water-Proof Texiderm Wardrobe Trunk. Heavy cowhide corners. Leatherette bindings securely riveted to trunk. Brass hasps and lock with key. Entire interior is lined with floral decorated paper resembling cretonne. Has four deep drawers and three hangers. 22 in. high. Ship. wt., about 7 lbs.
148C3468—
Price........... $11.98

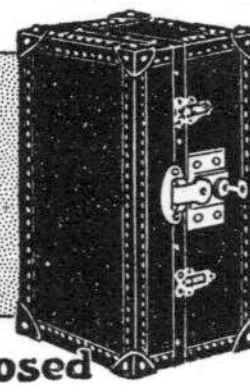
Closed

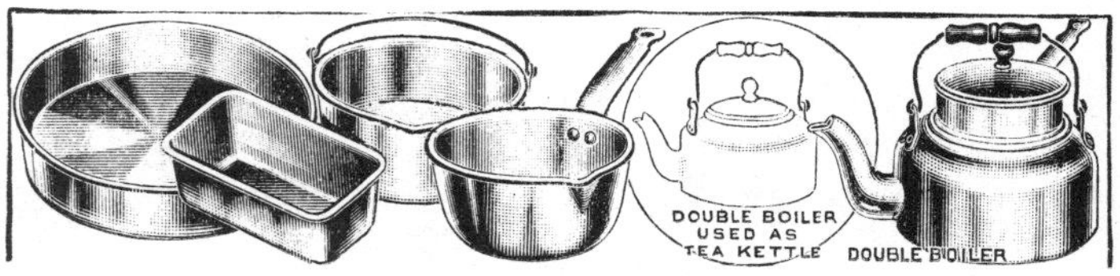
DOUBLE BOILER USED AS TEA KETTLE
DOUBLE BOILER

Five-Piece Aluminum Domestic Science Set

When mother is preparing a delicious cake or a pudding or a batch of creamy fudge, have her show you how to make all those goodies for your own little tea party. This set is made of the same brightly polished heavy gauge aluminum as mother's large utensils. Consists of a combination tea kettle and double boiler; baking pan, diam., 6⅞ in.; preserving kettle, diam., 5 in.; sauce pan and bread pan.
49C3367—Ship. wt., 1½ lbs. Price $2.98

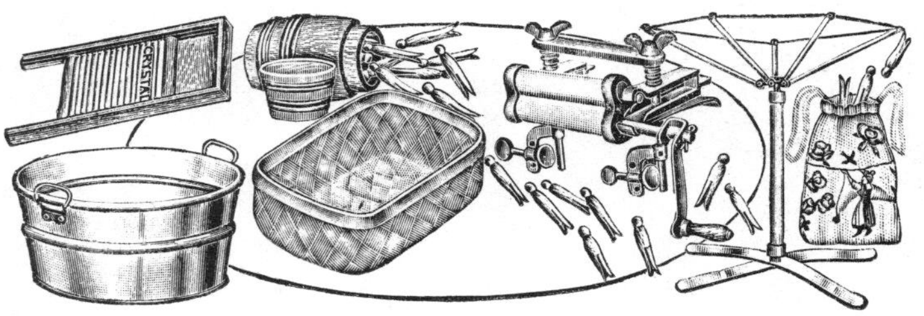

Complete Toy Washday Outfit

It's real fun to wash dolly's clothes when you have this fine set. Consists of metal wash tub, 10 inches in diameter, glass washboard, wringer with rubber rolls, one clothes dryer with about 5 feet of clothes line, and a clothes basket, 11½ inches long. Shipping weight, about 6 pounds.
148C3460—Price.............. $2.98

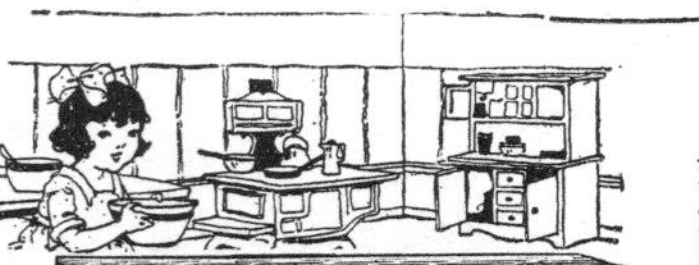

What a Peek Into Dolly's Kitchen Reveals

It tells you that dolly likes her kitchen equipped with the same modern convenience as is mother's. And what will save more steps than a kitchen cabinet? All the little dishes and cooking things can be kept handy for quickly preparing a tea party when little visitors come. These cabinets are made of hardwood in golden oak finish. They have dummy household commodities and hardwood extension boards.

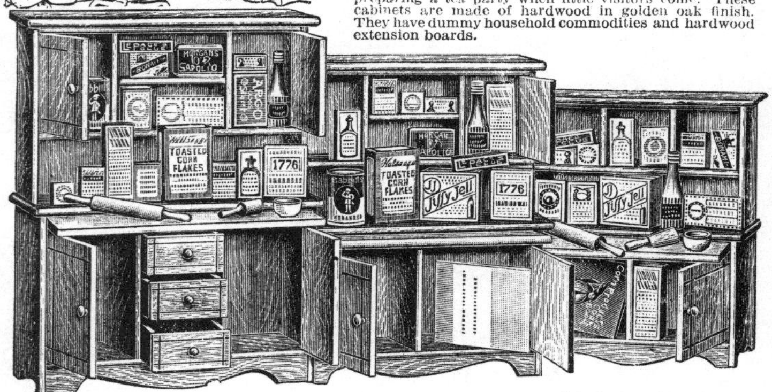

Our largest cabinet. Has 4 compartments with doors, 3 open compartments, 3 drawers and extension hardwood bread board. Brass knobs. Height, 21½ inches; Width, 17½ in.; depth, 7 in. Ship. wt., 14 lbs.
148C3866—Complete with a number of commodities.
Price.............. $4.45

4 compartments with doors, 3 open compartments and extension hardwood bread board. Height, 18½ in.; width, 15 in.; depth, 6½ in. Ship. wt., 10 lbs.
148C3865—Price, complete with a number of commodities..... $3.25

Small size. Has 2 compartments with doors, 2 open compartments and extension hardwood bread board. Height, 15½ in.; width, 13½ in.; depth, 6 in. Ship. wt., 8 lbs.
148C3864—Complete with a number of commodities....... $2.48

Modern Electric Trains

American Electric Flyer. Just as on the big electric trains that run so swiftly and silently, a third rail furnishes the power for operating this splendid little train. The power rail is laid between the other two and is well insulated. By means of the little controlling lever, you can operate the train at any speed you wish. The train runs on 3 dry cell batteries or regular electric light current, by using our transformer 48C1527.

Has the new electric type of engine. The headlight is so arranged that there is little danger of its being broken when train is derailed. 12 pieces of track, 120 in. in length. Length of train over all, 29 in. Has baggage car and two passenger coaches of light steel, with free-turning trucks. Ship. wt., complete (without batteries), 9 lbs.
48C1439—Price............$7.75

Big Value Electric Train with Headlight

Let her hum right through the tunnel. She's making up time—time that you have spent wishing for just such a toy as this. Run her fast or slow her down for the station, or stop her when you have the block signal set to show danger ahead. You can handle it with the little rheostat just as a dispatcher would in the big office that controls the trains on the railroad near your home. It operates on the third rail system and three dry cell batteries or by means of our transformer, 48C1527, attached to the electric light socket. Has a bright electric headlight. 14 pieces of track, 140 inches long, station, block signal and tunnel. Length of train over all 34 in. Iron engine, tender, baggage car and two passenger coaches of light sheet steel with free-turning trucks. Tunnel 14 in. long, 8½ in. high. Ship. wt., complete (without batteries) 12 lbs.
48C1436—Price......................$9.25

Mechanical Trains

Supplies

The Little Hummer
Locomotive with strong, clockwork steel spring, tender and a beautifully decorated passenger car. Four pieces of curved track, each fifteen inches long. Extra tracks and switches shown on right hand side of this page can be added to this set. Length, over all, 14½ in. Ship. wt., 2 lbs.
48C1421—Price....$1.10

$1.10

Oval Railway System
Here's a fine looking railway, boys. You'll have all kinds of fun with it. Iron locomotive has strong steel spring. The passenger coach, baggage car and tender are in bright colors. Complete as illustrated with ten pieces of track. Tracks and switches listed on right hand side of this page can be used to build this set into a much larger one. Length, over all 23 in. Shipping weight, 3½ pounds.
48C1415—Price.....$2.75

$2.75

Oval Track Railroad
Some train for speed. You'll think so when you see it tearing along the oval track and taking curves as fast as it can go. The engine is made of iron and is equipped with a brake. It has a very strong spring. Tender, box car and caboose are of light sheet steel, nicely enameled. Length of train, over all, about 25 in. Length of track, 120 in. Ship. wt., 5½ lbs.
48C1418—Price....$2.69

$2.69

The American Flyer
Engine, tender, passenger coach and 8 pieces of curved track. Runs around several times with one winding. Locomotive fitted with clockwork steel spring. Easy to wind. Any child can run this little train alone. Comes with 82 in. of track. You can add to the set by getting extra track and switches as shown on this page. Ship. wt. 3 lbs.
48C1420—Price..$1.98

$1.98

Transformer
48C1527—Practically fool-proof. To be used ONLY in homes where 100 to 120 volts alternating current is available. Capacity, 50 watts, 2 to 10 volts. 6-point switch regulates speed of trains. Does away with the need of batteries. Size, 3½x3½ in. Has 5½-foot electric cord. Ship. wt., 4 lbs.
Price............$4.75

Extra Third Rail Track
For electric trains. Ship wt., 8 oz.
48C1523—Third Rail Straight Track. Length, 10¼ inches.
Per section..........15c
48C1525—Third Rail Curve..........15c

Left Switch / Right Switch
48C1505—Switches O-Gauge. Ship. wt., 1 lb. Price, per set of two, one right and one left switch..........$1.25

48C1508—American Flyer O-Gauge Straight Track. The kind used on our trains. Lgth., 10¼ in. Ship. wt., 4 oz. Per section..........10c

48C1510—American Flyer O-Curved Track. The kind used on our trains. Length, 10¼ in. Shipping wt., 4 oz. Per section..........10c

Say, boys, couldn't you have loads of fun with this railway? Just look at that fine locomotive. Made of iron, too. And it has regular piston rods and an automatic brake on it to govern the speed. Strong steel spring. Attractively decorated coal tender, passenger car and express car with sliding side doors for loading baggage. Length, over all 24½ inches. Includes fourteen pieces of track that sets up in a figure eight with cross-over in center joining both loops. Shipping weight, 5 pounds.
48C1410—Price......................$3.48

$3.48

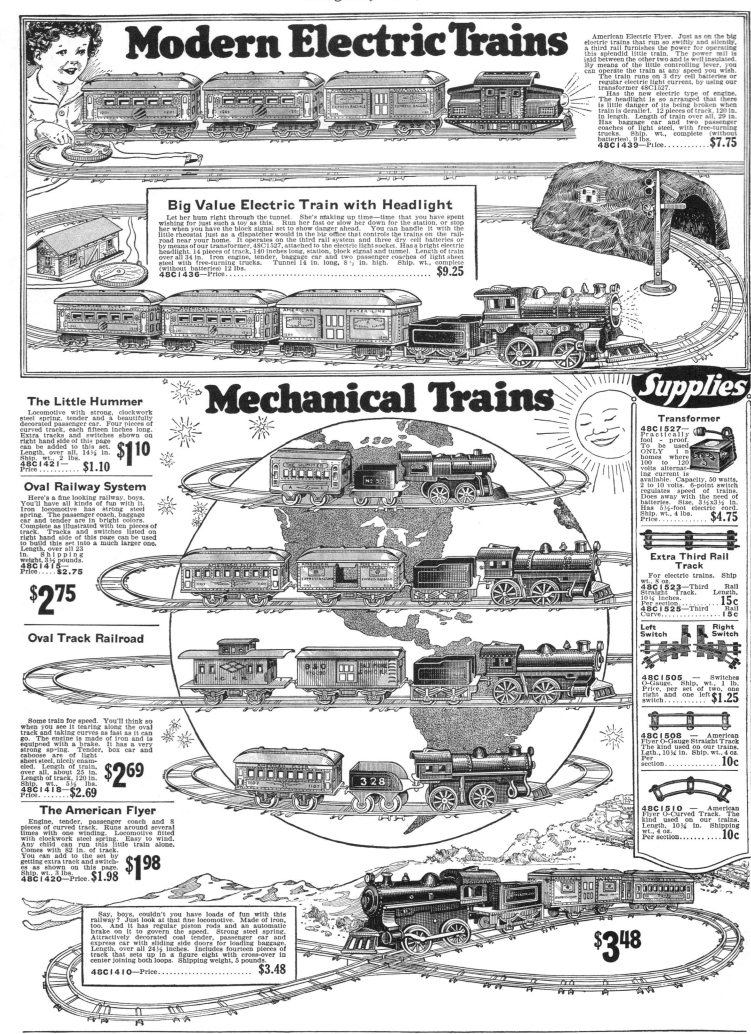

DAN PATCH AUTOS
All the Big Sellers From this Well Known and Widely Advertised Line

F271—37x19, blue enameled body, black wheels, orange trim, racer style, gasoline tank, steel steering wheel, starting crank, 8 and 10 in. wheels, ⅝ in. rubber tires. 1 in crate, 50 lbs. Each. **$5.75**

F253—40x18, red enameled body, black wheels and trim, large painted seat, gasoline tank, steel steering wheel, starting crank, auto steering knuckles, 8 and 10 in. double spoke wheels, ⅝ in. rubber tires. 1 in crate, 35 lbs. Each, **$6.25**

F272—46x19, orange enameled body, black trim, large tool box at rear, complete with adjustable metal windshield, starting crank, 10x12 in. double spoke wheels, ⅝ in. rubber tires. 1 in crate, 48 lbs. Each, **$7.25**

F255—44x20, yellow enameled body, black wheels and trim, windshield, gasoline tank, mahogany finish wood rim steering wheel. 10 and 12 in. double spoke wheels, ⅝ in. rubber tires. 1 in crate. Each, **$8.25**

F370—48x12½ in., bright red enameled body and wheels, black trim, 2 coats varnish, 19x12½ in. wagon box, back with raised side rails and hinged tarboard, knuckle joint auto steering gear, 8 in. mahogany finish steering wheel, heavy steel fender, extra heavy 10 in. auto style wheels with iron hub and roller bearings. 1 in crate, 95 lbs. Each, **$12.00**

F256—44x20, yellow enameled body, black wheels and trim, gasoline tank, steel steering wheel, electrically equipped, electric lights operated by switch on dash board, buzzer by push button at seat. 10 and 12 in. double spoke wheels, ⅝ in. rubber tires. 1 in crate, 50 lbs. Each, **$12.25**

F262—64x24, yellow enameled body, red wheels, black trim, gasoline tank, mahogany finish dash and 15x11 adjustable Pyroline windshield, mud guards, high backed seat, black steel gearings, 14 in. double spoke wheels, ⅝ in. rubber tires. 1 in crate. 96 lbs. Each, **$17.00**

F260—48x22, sky blue enameled body, red wheels, yellow stripes and trim, mahogany finish dashboard and steering wheel, electrically equipped, electric lights operated by switch on dashboard, has horn, windshield, headlights and gasoline tank, 10 and 12 in. heavy ball bearing wheels, ¾ in. oversize rubber tires, large brass hub caps. 1 in crate, 55 lbs. Each, **$21.00**

BUTLER BROTHERS—TOY HEADQUARTERS OF AMERICA

ROCKING HORSES AND SHOOFLIES

One Solid Page of money makers and profit payers for you. Every item here has been selected as the very best that can be manufactured for the money and every reliable maker's choice values are represented. We challenge you to equal this showing. Order your needs here.

SHOOFLY ROCKING HORSES

F401—17x32 in., cretonne upholstered seat and back, white enamel horses, printed mane saddle, etc. outside only, natural finish rockers. ½ doz. in crate, 46 lbs. Doz. **$20.00**

F381—17x32 in., cretonne upholstered seat and back, white enameled horses, printed manes, saddle, etc., on outside only, play box, natural finish rockers. ½ doz. in crate 50 lbs............ Doz. **$22.50**

F403—21x38 in., cretonne upholstered seat and back, extra large white enameled horses, printed mane, saddle, collar, etc., on both sides, hair tails, play box, red painted rockers. ½ doz. in crate, 60 lbs. Doz. **$28.00**

F386—21x38 in., cretonne upholstered seat, natural willow back, dappled white enameled horses, printed mane, saddle and collar, etc., play box, tape reins. 4 in crate, 4 lbs...................... Each, **$3.00**

F404—21x38 in., fancy pattern velour upholstered seat, white enameled horses, red stenciled harness, high grade green enameled fancy fiber reed back, tape reins, play box, stenciled foot rest. 2 in crate, 30 lbs. Each, **$3.90**

SHOOFLY SWINGING HORSES

White painted and dappled horses, red rockers.

F383—22x32 in., cretonne upholstered seat and back, play box, hair tail, striped red rockets. 2 in crate, 37 lbs...... Each, **$3.25**
(Total **$6.50**

F385—22x36 in., velour upholstered seat, closely woven rattan back, varnished play box, red rockers. 2 in crate, 50 lbs. Each, **$5.75**

F383   F385

"SPECIAL" SHOOFLY ROCKING HORSE ASSORTMENT

F405—Asst. comprises: 2 only 17x32 natural finished and varnished, 2 only 17x32 white painted, 1 only 17x32 white painted, cretonne upholstered seat and back, 1 only 17x32 white painted, cretonne upholstered seat and back with play box. Asstd. 6 in case, 50 lbs.................................ASST. (6 pcs.), **$10.25**

ROCKING HORSES

F416—Ht. 24 in., dapple white, enameled, leatherette bridles, gimp trim, English saddles, stirrups, hair manes and tails, turned legs, bright red stenciled hardwood rockers. 4 in crate, 56 lbs...Each, **$3.25**

F417—Ht. 27 in., dapple white, leatherette saddle and bridle, curved legs, hair manes and tail, red hardwood rocker. 2 in crate, 26 lbs........(Total $10.00) Each, **$5.00**

IMPROVED SWINGING AND GALLOPING HORSES

Well painted, carved legs, long hair manes and tails, swing on iron rods, red painted and striped stands.

F419—Ht. 26½ in., 5 in. block, leatherette bridle. 1 in crate, 15 lbs..... Each, **$4.75**
F421—Ht. 28 in., 5½ in. block, **leather bridle** and martingale, corduroy saddle............... Each, **$5.25**

F433—Ht. 27 in., 5 in. block, leatherette saddle and bridle, stirrups, varnish finish, natural oak base. 1 in crate, 21 lbs..Each, **$6.00**

OUR SHOWING OF WHEEL GOODS IS THE FINEST IN THE COUNTRY

"PONY EXPRESS"—On rockers

F206—Ht. 19½ in., length 18 in., dapple gray enamel body with red rockers and saddle. ½ doz. in pkg....... Doz. **$12.00**

"READSBORO" ROCKING HORSES AND SHOOFLIES

The well known "Readsboro" line of high class shooflies, etc., made of the best quality hardwood, highly enameled with the greatest care. All rockers and braces steam bent, making them durable and strong enough to stand the roughest use.

Rocking Horse—40 in. long, 20 in. high, heavy white wood, white ash rockers, painted bridle, mane, saddle, stirrup and reins.
F434—2 in crate, 32 lbs..... Each, **$2.50**

Duck Shoofly—28 in. long, 20 in. high, heavy white wood, white enamel finish, decorated in blue, yellow and black, with tray.
F395—2 in case, 45 lbs...... Each, **$3.95**

Sir Chanticleer Shoofly—40 in. long, 23½ in. high, made of heavy white wood, white enamel finish, red painted comb, heavy reinforced rocker.
F396—2 in crate, 51 lbs..... Each, **$4.50**

ROCKING, SWINGING AND GALLOPING HORSE ASSORTMENT

F430—Comprising 4 of our best selling numbers, a good asst. for a small investment. For full description see regular line. 1 only F416, 1 only F417, 1 only F421, 1 only F433. Asstd. 4 in case..ASST. (4 pcs.), **$17.50**

178

WOOD CARTS—Long Wood Handles

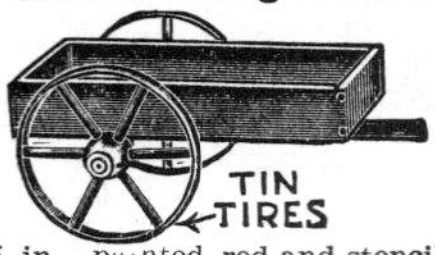
TIN
TIRES

F40—9x5 in., painted red and stenciled cart, wood body, 6 in. wood wheels, tin tires. 2 doz. in crate, 25 lbs ....Doz. **$1.90** (Total $3.80)

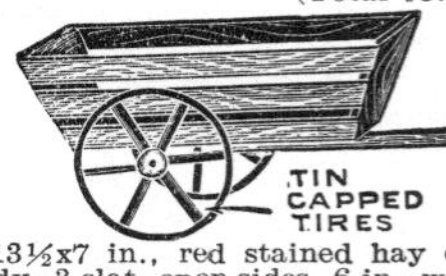
TIN
CAPPED
TIRES

F39—13½x7 in., red stained hay cart wood body, 3 slat, open sides, 6 in. wood spoke wheels, tin tires. 2 doz. in crate, 26 lbs (Total $4.40) Doz. **$2.20**

"VICTORY" STEEL COASTER WAGON

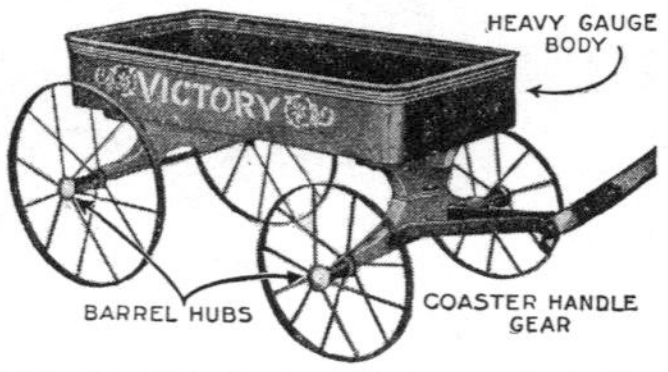
HEAVY GAUGE
BODY
VICTORY
BARREL HUBS
COASTER HANDLE
GEAR

F125—13x26 in. body with heavy steel sides and wood bottom, green enameled outside, red inside, 10 and 13 in. double spoke wheels with barrel hubs and nickeled caps, heavy steel axles, strong bolstered body, wood braced hounds, strong wood "D" grip set-in extension coaster handle. 1 in crate, 20 lbs..................Each, **$2.50**

JUNIOR SIZE WOOD WAGONS

Hardwood body and gearing, natural varnish finish with red trim, fancy solid turned wood wheels with red centers.

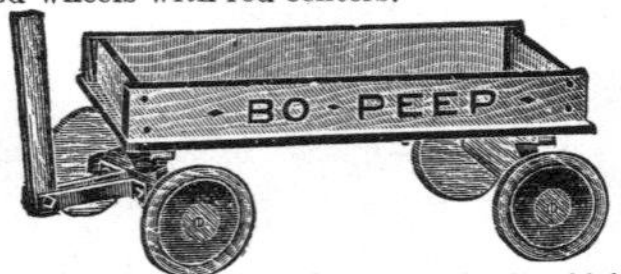
BO PEEP

"Bo-Peep"—Body 18x9½ in., wheels 4½ in.
F72—4 in carton............Each, **$1.35** (Total $5.40)

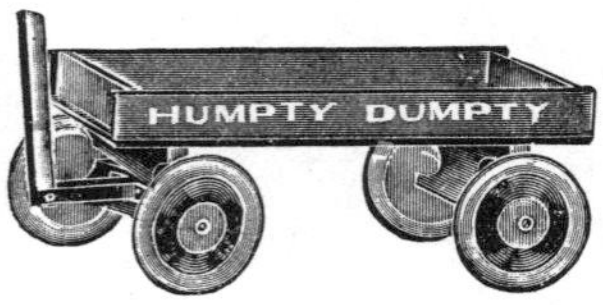
HUMPTY DUMPTY

"Humpty Dumpty"—Body 21x11 in., wheels 6 in.
F77—4 in crate.............Each, **$1.65** (Total $6.60)

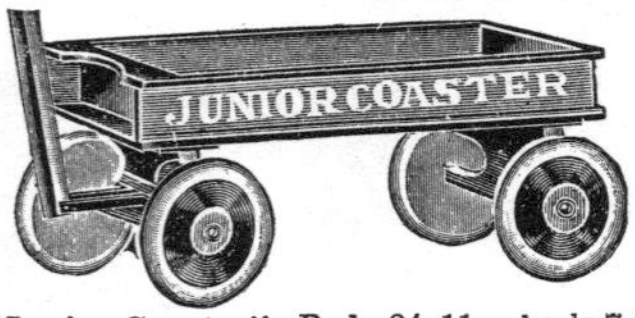
JUNIOR COASTER

"Junior Coaster"—Body 24x11, wheels 7 in.
F78—2 in crate.............Each, **$1.90** (Total $3.80)

WOOD BODY EXPRESS WAGON

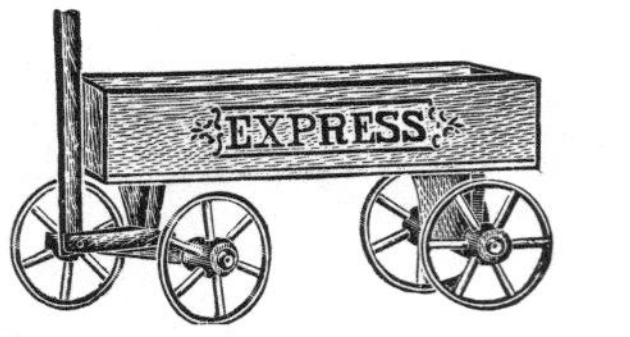
EXPRESS

F47—12x7 in., varnished wood body, 20 in. handle, black stenciled "Express" on each side, 4½ in. wood spoke wheels, steel tires. 1 doz. in crate, 30 lbs.........Doz. **$4.50**

"BULL DOG" STEEL BODY EXPRESS WAGON

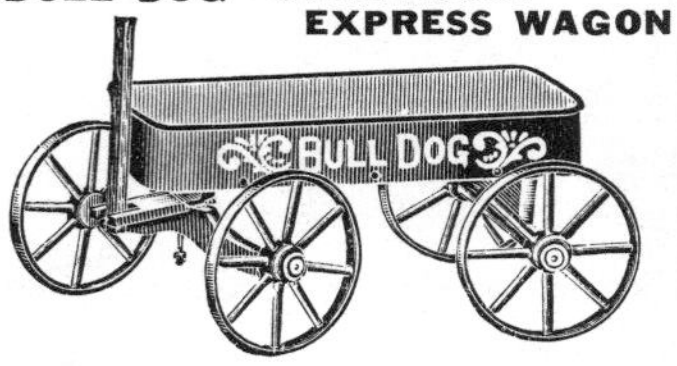
BULL DOG

F52—10x20 in steel body, bright red, gold stripe, wood axle, hardwood gear, 8 and 10 in. wood wheels, steel tires, 19 in. wood handle. ½ doz. in crate, 44 lbs. Doz. **$10.50**

"HORSCYCLE"

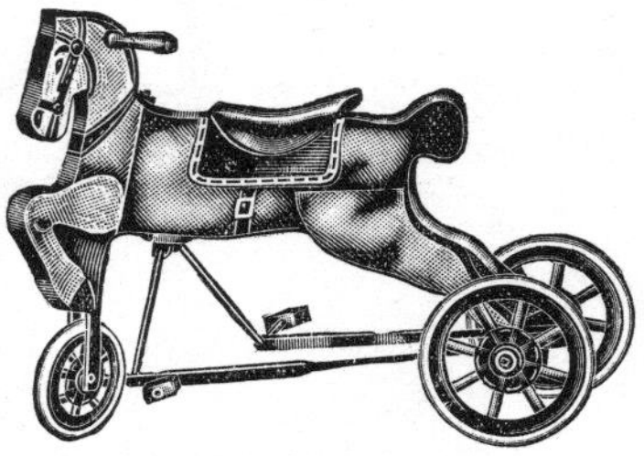

F869—28 in. high, 39 in. long, 17 in. wide, for children 3 to 8 years of age, rear wheels 1 in. thick, 11 in. diameter, front wheel 1 in. thick, 8 in. diameter, rubber tires, chrome steel bearings, over tested steel axle, harness, collar and saddle blanket red and yellow, wheels red and saddle brown, self propelling action, pedals 2¾x2 in. 2 in crate, about 40 lbs. (Total $10.00) Each, **$5.00**

"IRISH MAIL" HAND CARS

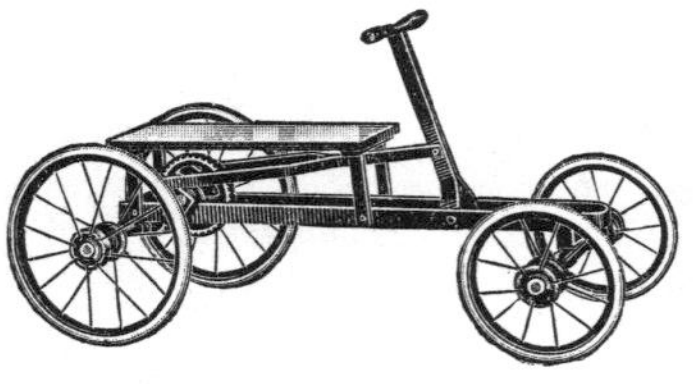

Junior—Length 27 in., seat 7x14 in., wheels 6 & 8 in., ⅜ in. rubber tires, black enameled steel frame and gear, gold bronze decorated seat, red wheels, heavy axles, cog drive.
F199—2 in crate, 45 lbs......Each, **$3.75** (Total $7.50)

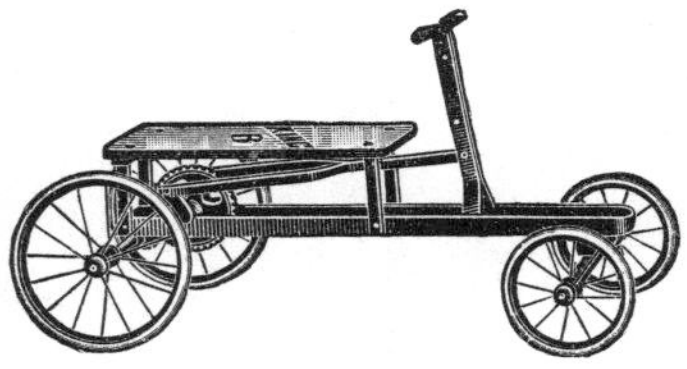

Traveler—Length 31 in., seat 7¾x16 in., wheels 12 and 8 in., ⅜ in. rubber tires, black enameled steel frame and gear, red wheels and seat, gold bronze decorations heavy axles and cog drive.
F200—1 in crate, 30 lbs......Each, **$5.25**

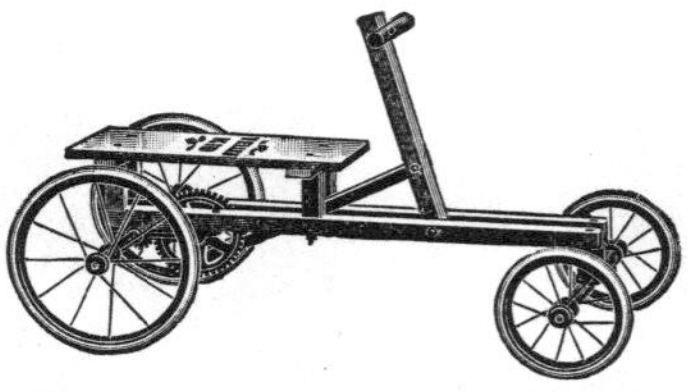

"Yellow Kid"—Length 39 in., seat 7½x15 in., 8 & 12 in. steel wheels with heavy spokes, ½ in. rubber tires, bright yellow finish, black striped.
F203—1 in crate, 48 lbs.....Each, **$4.50**

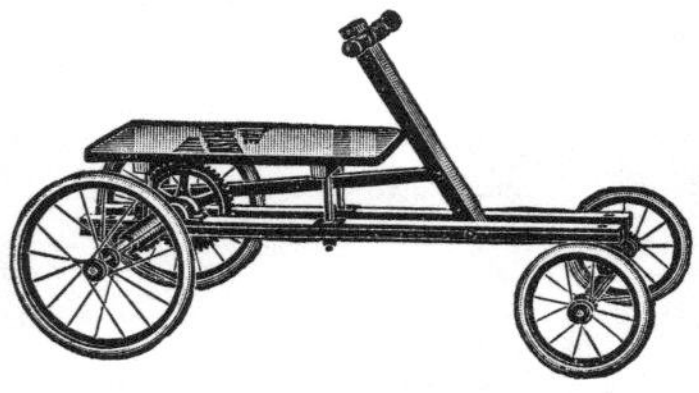

Irish Mail—Length 40 in., seat 20x9 in., wheels 8 and 12 in., ½ in. rubber tires, sanded natural finish, red with narrow green striping, seat and wheels in dark green, gears and axles black, hickory frame which stands greater tension than steel.
F204—1 in crate, 32 lbs......Each, **$6.00**

BALL-BEARING "SCUDDER CAR"

Operates entirely by the weight of the rider—safe and noiseless.

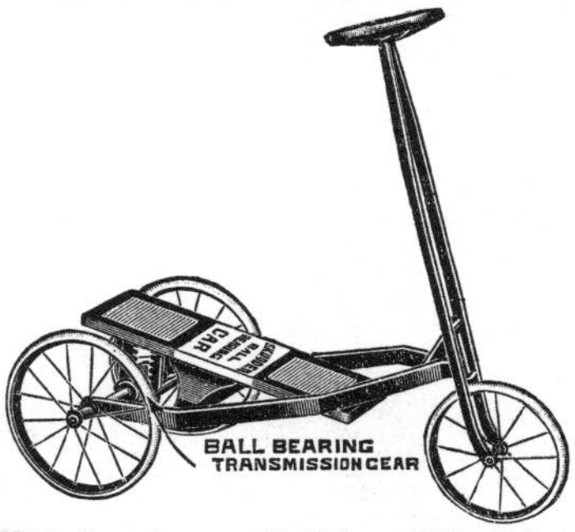
BALL BEARING
TRANSMISSION GEAR

F211—Length over all 40 in., width 18 in., ball-bearing axle and transmission gear, red enameled steel frame and steering posts, 8 in. nickel plated auto steering wheel black enameled axle and wheels, ⅝ in. rubber tires. Propelled by rider standing on tilting board and throwing weight of body first on one foot then on the other. Has no dead centers, coasts without movement of tilting board. 2 in crate....Each, **$5.25** (Total $10.50)

"DAN PATCH" SELF-PROPELLING SULKIES

For children from 3 to 6 years of age

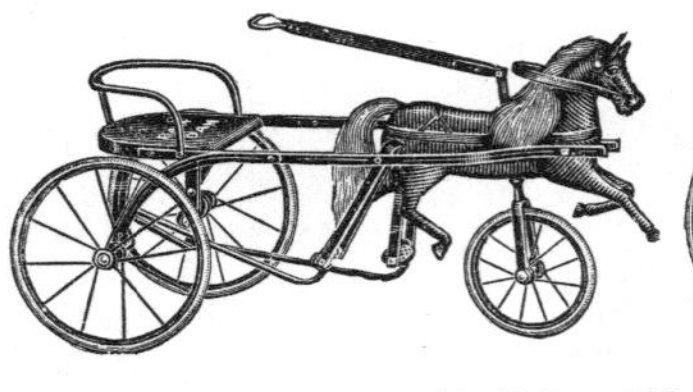

"Baby Dan"—Length 36 in., ht. 19 in., width 22 in., ht. of seat rail 5 in., 8 and 12 in. wheels, ⅜ in. rubber tires, brown painted solid wood horse with metal legs, real hair mane and tail, reversible handle for pulling.
F817—1 in crate..........Each, **$6.50**

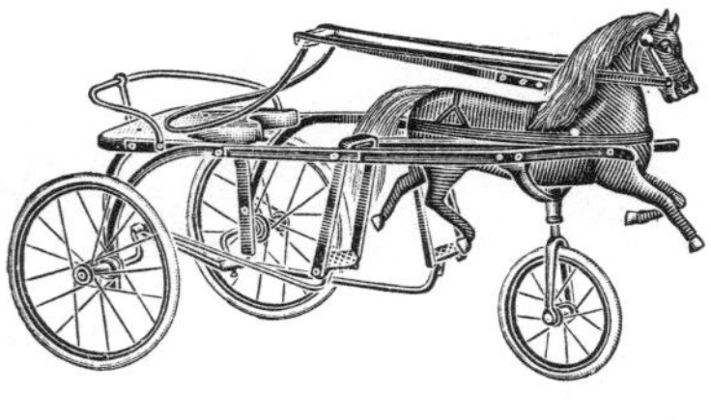

"Dan Patch"—Length 43 in., extreme ht. 21 in., red enameled, black striped, 12 in. double spoke wheels, ½ in. rubber tire, 8 in. rubber tire guide wheel, heavy steel gear, shafts and bent riveted braces, wood seat, tubular steel back, solid wool, model bay horse, mohair mane and tail, leather reins, steering handle.
F248—1 in crate..........Each, **$8.00**

BALL-BEARING SCOOTER

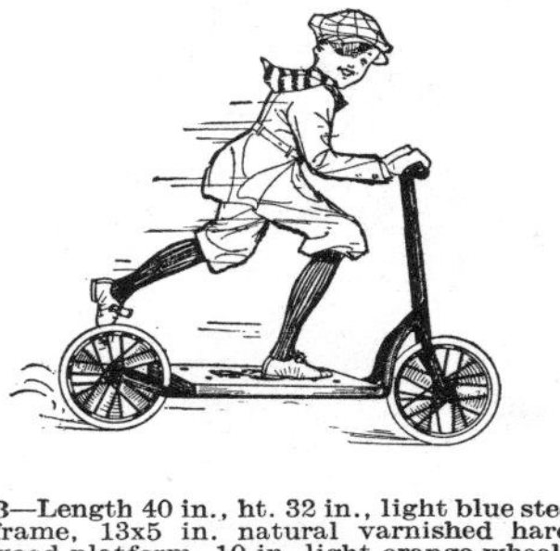

F223—Length 40 in., ht. 32 in., light blue steel frame, 13x5 in. natural varnished hardwood platform, 10 in. light orange wheels, **barrel hubs with ball-bearings,** ⅞ in. rubber tires, black enameled wood cross handle. 2 in crate, 35 lbs...Each, **$3.75** (Total $7.50)

Miniature Wood Farm Wagons

Always meets with great popularity wherever shown. Our low price allows you a good profit.

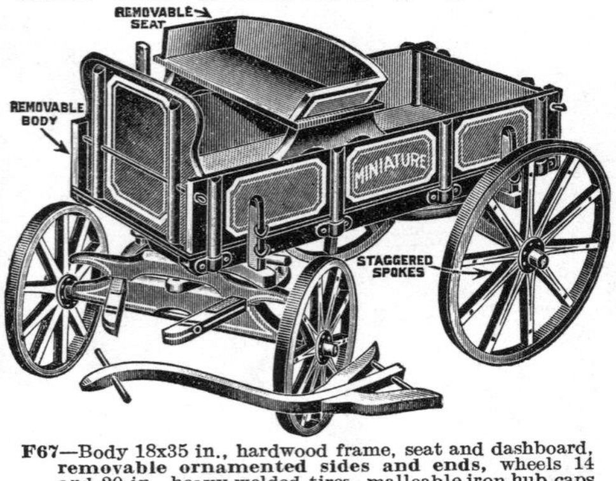
REMOVABLE
SEAT
REMOVABLE
BODY
MINIATURE
STAGGERED
SPOKES

F67—Body 18x35 in., hardwood frame, seat and dashboard, **removable ornamented sides and ends,** wheels 14 and 20 in., heavy welded tires, malleable iron hub caps and bands, strongly ironed and braced, $\frac{5}{16}$ in., round steel axles, heavy handle. 1 in crate, 57 lbs. Each, **$8.25**

Goat Or Dog Shaft

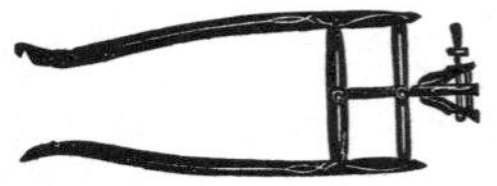

F70—For F67 farm wagon length 42 in., width 17, painted red, black striped. 1 in pkg., 5 lbs. Each, **75c**

TOY TRAILER CAR

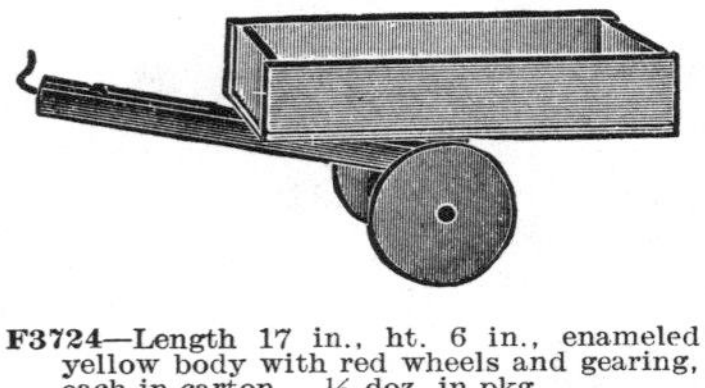

F3724—Length 17 in., ht. 6 in., enameled yellow body with red wheels and gearing, each in carton. ½ doz. in pkg. Doz. **$2.25**

SLED RUNNERS FOR WAGONS

Transforms a wagon into an easy running "Bob," for pulling loads or coasting. Doubles the pleasure and use of the wagon.

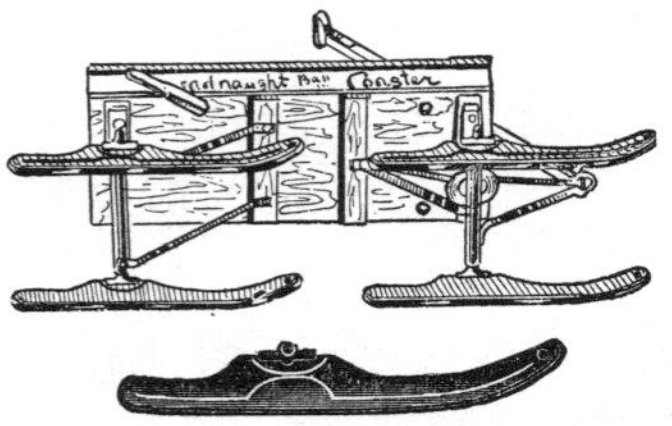

F1496—Length 23 in., made from tough stock red with black striping, front runners bored for use with rope if desired, full round, spring steel shoes, fits any wagon with axles not over $\frac{9}{16}$ in. diam. and hub width not less than 2⅝ in., larger hub widths adjustable with washers. 1 set of 4 in pkg. Set, **$1.90**

"Cash And Carry" Wood Express Wagon

A proven seller—you will always find a ready sale for this item.

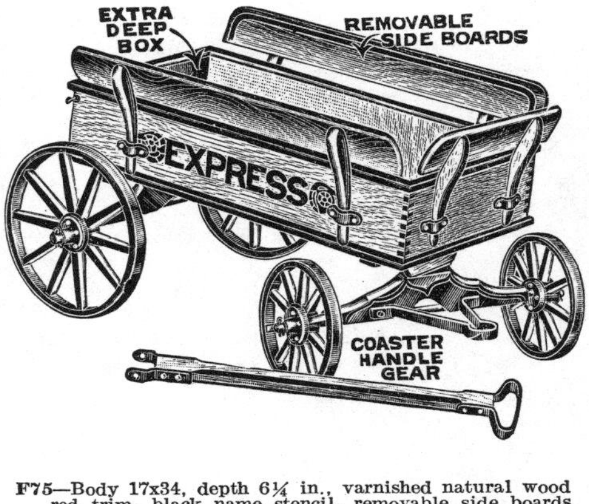
EXTRA
DEEP
BOX
REMOVABLE
SIDE BOARDS
EXPRESS
COASTER
HANDLE
GEAR

F75—Body 17x34, depth 6¼ in., varnished natural wood red trim, black name stencil, removable side boards and dash, wheels 10 and 14 in., shaved spokes, ¾x⅛ flat welded tire shrunk on, $\frac{7}{16}$ round steel axles, coaster handle gear, body and wheels painted bright red with black striping, 1 in crate, 50 lbs. Each, **$6.00**

DOLL CABS

ETC., FIBER AND REED

Choice selections from manufacturers of dependable products who build these numbers exactly like the full size ones. Our lower prices make it possible for you to interest a wider range of people than heretofore, and get more business, too. The fiber strollers shown here are exceedingly popular sellers.

FIBER DOLL CABS

Reclining back, adjustable hoods, shellacked steel springs and gears, enameled black for natural bodies and gray for gray bodies.

Ht. 23 In—Loom woven fiber, body 19x8 in., body upholstered with Printzess corduroy. 7 in. double spoke wheels, rubber tires. 1 in carton, 11 lbs.
F318—Natural .... { Each
F319—Gray .... { **$3.25**

Ht. 27 In—Body 23x10, hand woven fiber, body upholstered with Printzess corduroy, 7 in. double spoke wheels, rubber tires. 1 in carton, 12 lbs.
F331—Natural .... { Each
F332—Gray .... { **$6.00**

Ht. 26 In—Body 23½x11 in., hand woven fiber, body and hood upholstered with Printzess corduroy, 7 in. double spoke wheels, rubber tires. 1 in carton, 13 lbs.
F333—Natural .... { Each
F334—Gray .... { **$7.25**

Ht. 32 In—Body 26x14 in., hand woven fiber, body and hood upholstered with Printzess corduroy, 9 in. double spoke wheels, rubber tires, wheel brake. 1 in carton, 25 lbs.
F335—Natural ...... Each, **$9.75**

REED DOLL CABS

Attractive shell and fancy patterns, all beautifully enameled in the staple colors.

Ht. 29 In—Body 19½x8½ in., half round reed body and hood, Printzess corduroy upholstered sides and hood, 8 in. double spoke wire wheels, rubber tires, hub caps, reclining back, round steel pushers, polished wood handle. 1 in carton, 10 lbs.
F359—Natural .... { Each
F360—Gray .... { **$4.75**

Ht. 29 In—Body 21½x10 in., half round reed body and hood, full round reed rolls, Printzess corduroy upholstered sides and hood, reclining back, 8 in. double spoke wire wheels, rubber tires, hub caps, round steel pushers, polished wood handle. 1 in carton, 12 lbs.
F361—Natural .... { Each
F362—Gray .... { **$6.50**

Ht. 29 In—Body 20½x9 in., narrow half round reed body, full round reed roll on hood, Printzess corduroy upholstered hood and body, 8 in. double spoke wire wheels, rubber tires, hub caps, reclining back, round steel pusher, polished wood handle. 1 in carton, 15 lbs.
F363—Natural ...... Each, **$8.00**

Ht. 32 In—Body 24x 9½ in., narrow half round reed body and hood, upholstered in corduroy, reclining back, 9 in. double spoke wire wheels, rubber tires, hub caps, wheel brake, round steel pushers, polished wood handle. 1 in carton, 18 lbs. Each
F365—Royal blue .. { **$10.00**
F366—Natural ..... {

Ht. 33 In—Body 25x12 in., narrow half round reed body and hood with rolls, upholstered in Printzess corduroy, 9 in. double spoke wire wheels, rubber tires, hub caps, wheel brakes, reclining back, round steel pushers, polished wood handle. 1 in carton, 20 lbs.
F367—Natural ...... Each, **$12.00**

Ht. 37½ In—Body 27x13½, flat reed body and hood, full round reed rolls on hood and body, corduroy upholstered, 10 in. wheels, rubber tires, hub caps, wheel brake, reversible gear, footwell, with flap, reclining back, round steel pushers, polished wood handle. 1 in crate, 39 lbs.
F372—Natural .... { Each
F373—White .... { **$17.00**

Ht. 40 In—Body 28x14½ in., narrow half round reed hood and body, sloping round reed roll on hood, upholstered in corduroy, 12 in. double spoke wire wheels, rubber tires, hub caps, wheel brake, reversible gears, footwell with flap, reclining back, round steel pushers, polished wood handle. 1 in crate, 41 lbs.
F374—Royal blue.... Each, **$19.00**

Ht. 40 In—Body 30x15½ in., very attractive pattern, full round reed throughout, upholstered in corduroy, **reversible gear**, 12 in. double spoke wire wheels, rubber tires, wheel brake, footwell, reclining back, round steel pushers, polished wood handle. 1 in crate, 41 lbs.
F375—Frosted blue ..Each, **$21.00**

COMBINATION WOOD AND FIBER DOLL CAB

F336—Body 21x10 in., ht. 27 in., combination 3 ply veneer and loom woven gray fiber with white roll, reclining back, Printzess corduroy upholstered reversible steel gears, 8 in. wheels, ⅝ in. rubber tires, nickel hub caps, wheel brake. 1 in crate, 22 lbs...... Each, **$6.00**

FIBER DOLL STROLLERS

There is an increasing demand every season for this style doll vehicle. You will sell them readily if shown.

Ht. 24 In—Body 18x11 in., narrow flat fiber, black enamel steel gears, wheels 8 and 6 in., rubber tires, leatherette upholstered seat. 1 in carton, 10 lbs.
F310—Natural ...... Each, **$3.50**

Ht. 25 In—Body 19x12½ in., narrow flat fiber, half round rolls, body and footwell, wheels 8 and 6 in., rubber tires, leatherette upholstered seat. 1 in carton, 11 lbs.
F311—Natural ...... Each, **$4.75**

Ht. 25 In—Body 22x12½ in., narrow flat fiber with half round fiber roll, reclining back, body upholstered in Printzess corduroy, adjustable footwell, wheels 8 and 6 in., rubber tires. 1 in carton, 17 lbs.
F312—Natural ...... Each, **$7.50**

Ht. 26 In—Body 24x12½ in., body and hood, narrow flat and round fiber, full round roll, reclining back, adjustable footwell, wheels 8 and 6 in., rubber tires, body upholstered in Printzess corduroy, leatherette seat. 1 in crate, 18 lbs.
F313—Natural ...... Each, **$9.00**

"Unusual Value" Fiber Reed Doll Cabs

Loom woven, popular priced numbers. Better values than offered anywhere else today.

Loom woven, fiber body and hood, reclining back, adjustable hood, shellacked steel springs and gears, enameled in black for natural bodies and gray for gray bodies, rubber tires, double spoke wheels.

Ht. 23 In—Body 18x8 in., 6 in. wheels, 2 in carton, 20 lbs.
F317—Natural. **$3.00**
(Total $6.00)

Ht. 24 In—Body 21½x9 in., 7 in. wheels, hub caps, Printzess corduroy upholstered. 1 in carton, 13 lbs.
F320—Natural. } Each
F321—Gray.... } **$5.00**

F317

F320-21

"IDEAL" SLEEPING DOLLS

With perfect moving eyes. These "Ideal" sleeping dolls are quick selling and pay good profits. People like them because they are made so well and finished so nicely. Our stock comprises nothing but new and clean goods. Buy here for better values, so that you can get your share of the business during the Holiday season.

NOTE: Flesh finish composition heads and hands, painted features and hair, also mohair wigs, stuffed bodies, hip and shoulder joints, underwear. Each in box.

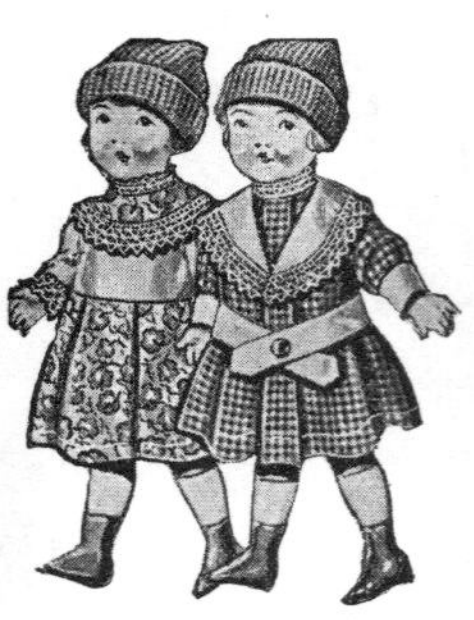

F7301—2 styles, 13 in., Russian and white guimpe models, figured percale and flowered lawn, lace trim collars, white knit toques, composition shoes. Asstd. 1/6 dz. in pkg..........Doz. **$9.00**

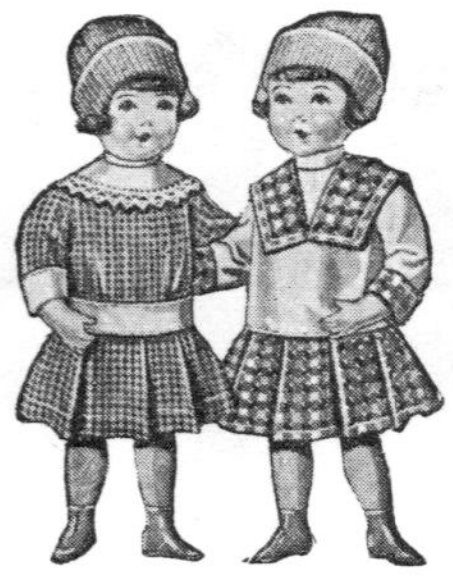

F7305—2 styles, 12 in., **mohair wigs,** middy and Russian models of fine checked gingham, novelty braid trim collars, white knit toques, composition shoes. Asstd. 1/6 doz. in pkg...Doz. **$9.00**

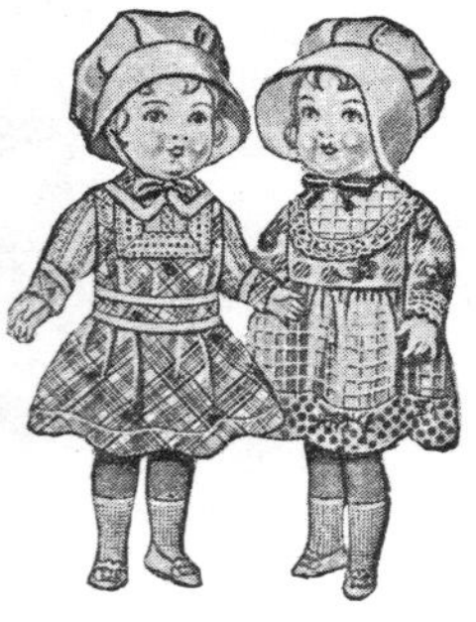

F7302—2 styles, 14 in., "baby" dress of dimity check and dotted lawn; gingham plaid, white collar, braid trim, both with white puff crown bonnets, white socks, buckled slippers. Asstd. 1/6 doz. in pkg...........Doz. **$12.00**

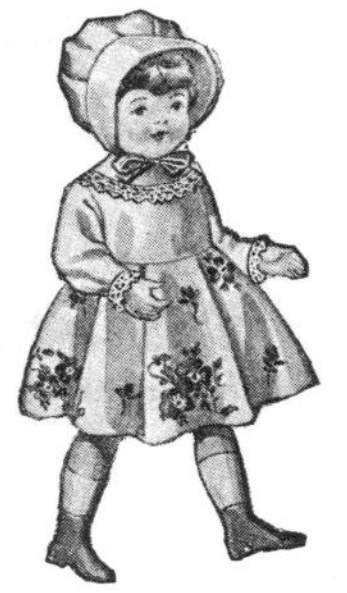

F7306—13 in., mohair wig, white lawn guimpe, figured lawn plaited skirt, lace edge collar and sleeves, white puff crown bonnet, composition shoes. 1 in box...Each, **98c**

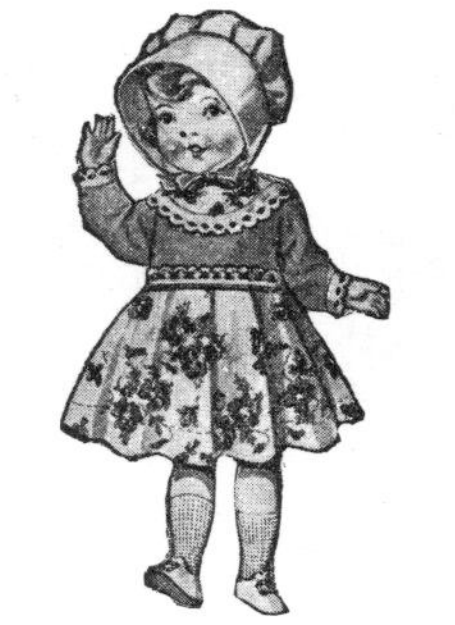

F7303—15 in., solid color lawn blouse, flowered lawn skirt, braid trim figured collar, cuffs and belt, white puff crown bonnet, lace trim envelope, white socks, buckled slippers. 1 in box. Each, **$1.25**

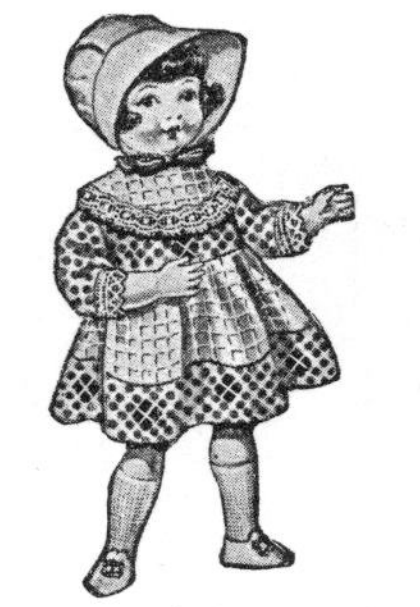

F7307—14 in., mohair wig, white dimity check dress, colored figured lawn waist and deep fold on skirt, lace trim white collar and cuffs, white puff crown bonnet, white socks, buckled slippers. 1 in box Each, **$1.25**

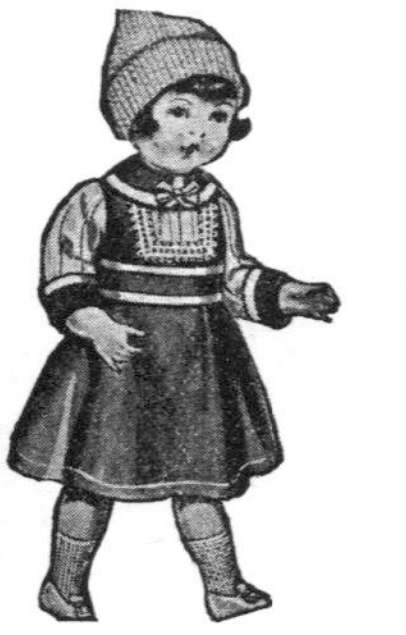

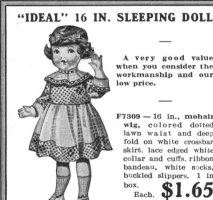

F7304—16 in., white figured madras guimpe with solid color linene dress, lace trim collar, 2 color cap to match, lace trim underwear, white socks, buckled slippers. 1 in box...........Each, **$1.50**

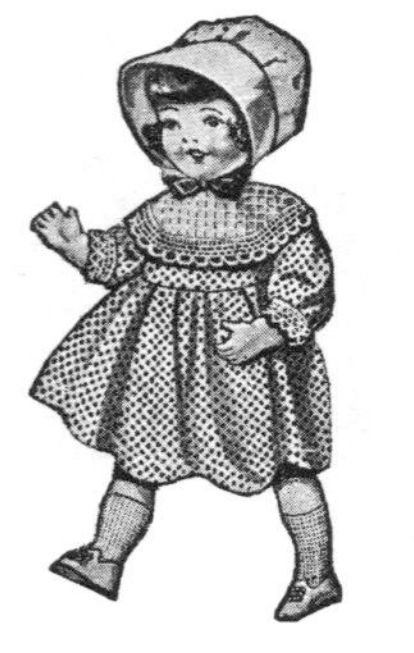

F7308—15 in., mohair wig, fine dotted lawn "baby" dress, lace edged white crossbar collar and cuffs, white puff crown bonnet, white socks, buckled slippers. 1 in box...........Each, **$1.50**

"IDEAL" 16 IN. SLEEPING DOLL

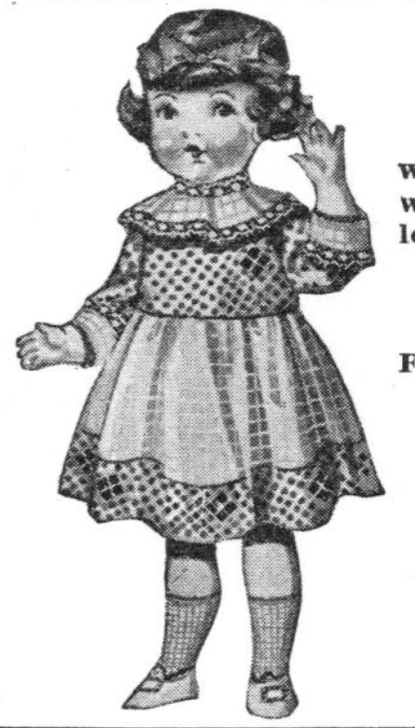

A very good value when you consider the workmanship and our low price.

F7309 — 16 in., mohair wig, colored dotted lawn waist and deep fold on white crossbar skirt, lace edged white collar and cuffs, ribbon bandeau, white socks, buckled slippers. 1 in box. Each, **$1.65**

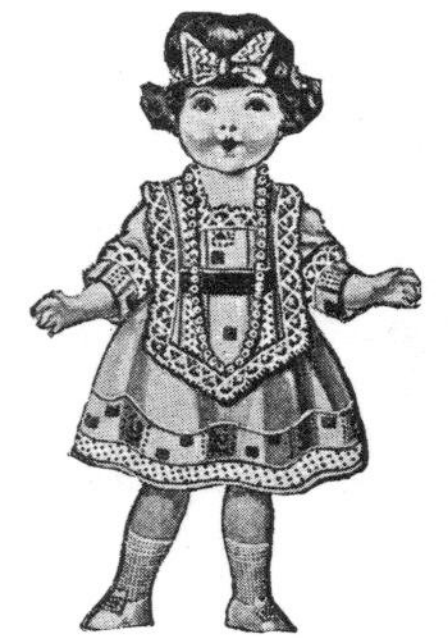

F7310—16 in., mohair wig, "party" dress, white lawn lace trim peplum, cuffs and fold on skirt, black velvet girdle, ribbon bandeau, lace trim underwear, white socks, buckled slippers, gold bead necklace. 1 in box. Each, **$1.90**

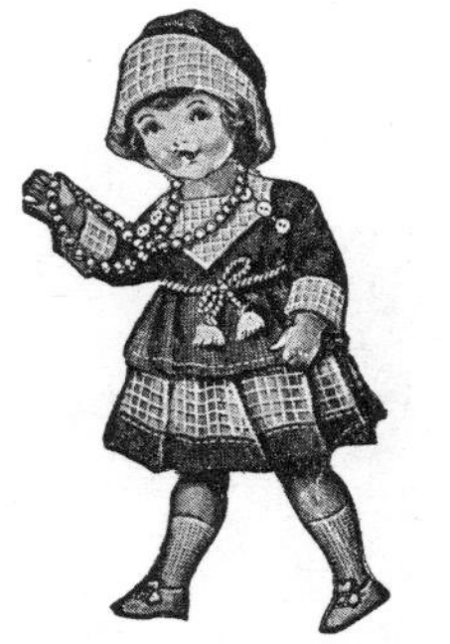

F7311—16 in., mohair wig, green mercerized smock, deep fold on white crossbar skirt, button trim white collar and cuffs, gold bead necklace, cord girdle, 2 color hat to match, lace trim underwear, white socks, buckled slippers. 1 in box.......Each, **$2.10**

KEWPIE & NOVELTY DOLLS

The biggest selling novelty dolls on the market today. No others can compare with them for originality and big selling features. All genuine Kewpies here, so attractively modeled and dressed that people instantly buy them when on display. Your doll stock is not complete without a representative showing of these popular dolls.

KEWPIE DOLLS

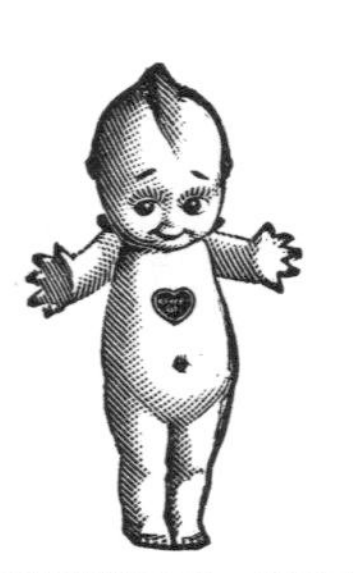

Imported Bisque — Genuine imported bisque, known the world over, jointed arms, tinted features and hair, large roguish eyes. 1 doz. in box.
F7164—4½ in...Doz. **$1.75**

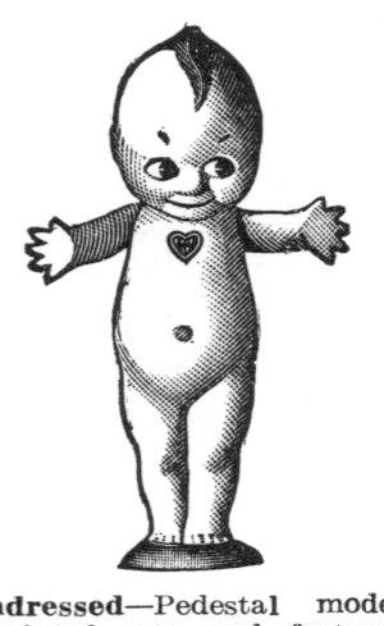

Undressed—Pedestal model, painted eyes and features, tinted body, jointed arms on pedestal. ½ doz. in box.
F7920—9½ in...Doz. **$4.00**

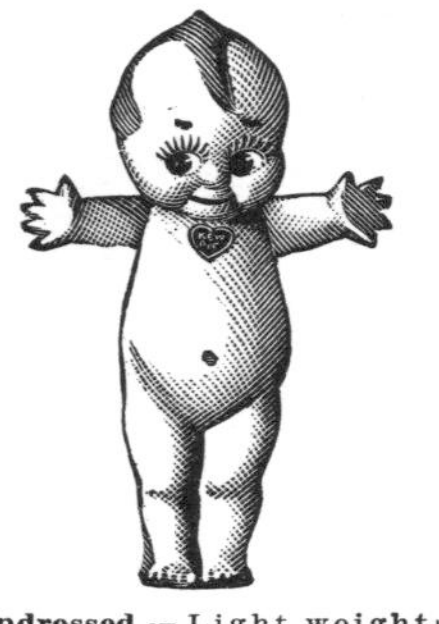

Undressed — Light weight compositon body, flesh tinted air brush finish, droll painted features, jointed arms. 1/12 doz. in box.
F7922— 9 in..Doz. **$4.50**
F7923—10½ " . " **6.50**
F7924—12½ " . " **8.00**

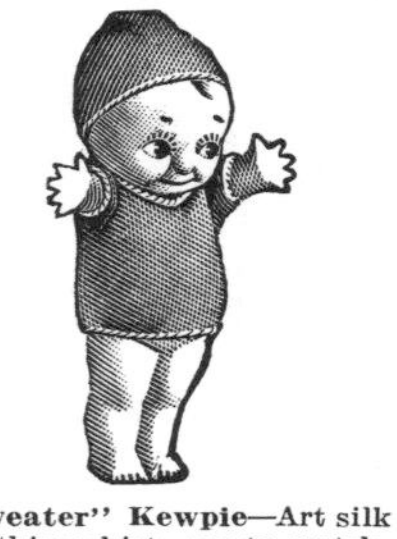

"Sweater" Kewpie—Art silk bathing shirt, cap to match. 1/12 doz. in box.
F7928— 9 in..Doz. **$6.50**
F7929—10½ " . " **9.00**

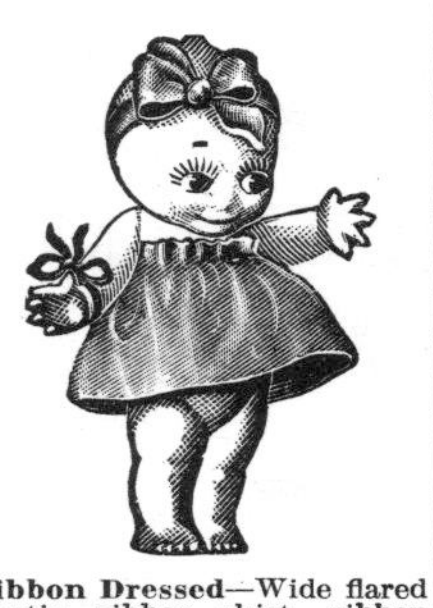

Ribbon Dressed—Wide flared satin ribbon skirt, ribbon hair band with bow.
F7925—9 in. ½ doz. in box..........Doz. **$8.00**
F7926—10½ in. 1 in box. Each, **90c**
F7927—12½ in. 1 in box. Each, **$1.10**

"TISS ME" DOLLS

An appealing little novelty figure, creation of Hy. Mayer. Modeled composition bodies, flesh tinted bisque finish, painted features, coaxing expressions, dimpled shoulders, tinted negligee.

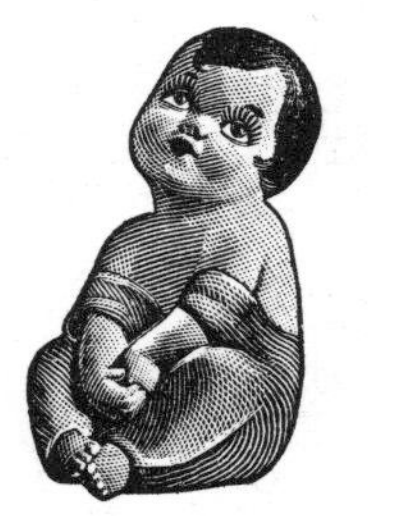

Painted Hair—½ doz. in box.
F7948—5 in......Doz. **$2.25**
F7945—7 " .... " **4.50**

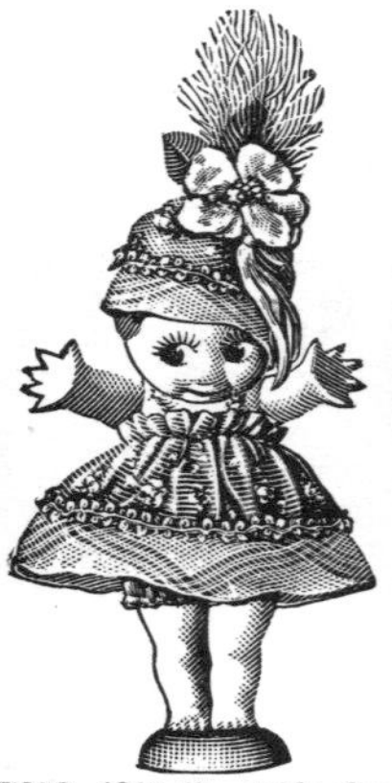

F7958—12½ in., wide flared silk ribbon skirt, pantalettes, silk braid trim, braid shoulder straps, cap to match. 1 in box. Each, **$1.50**

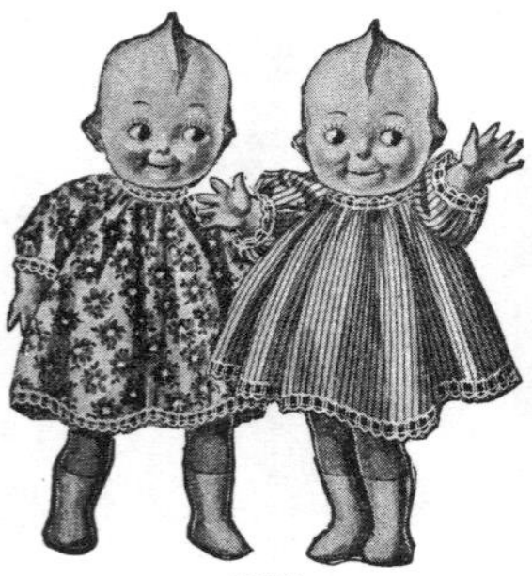

F7545

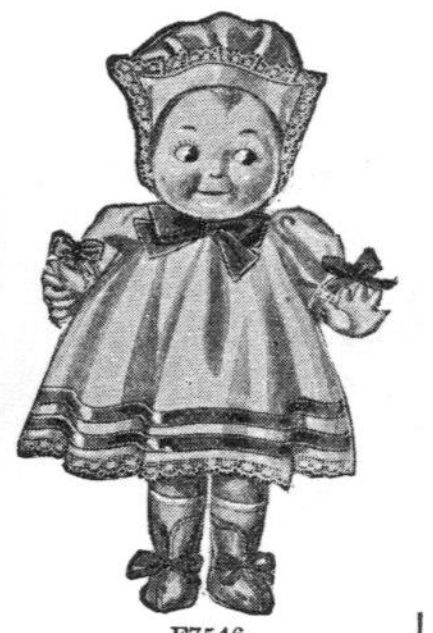

F7546

Cork Stuffed Kewpies — Composition head and hands, painted features, concealed hip and shoulder joints, cork stuffed, well shaped bodies. Each in box.

F7545 — 2 styles, 12½ in., lace and ribbon trim lawn dresses, underwear and stockings. Asstd. 1/6 doz. in pkg.........Doz. **$7.80**

F7546—12½ in., fine white lawn dress, lace and ribbon trim cap to match, lawn underwear, stockings and stitched lawn bootees. 1/6 doz. in box.........Doz. **$9.00**

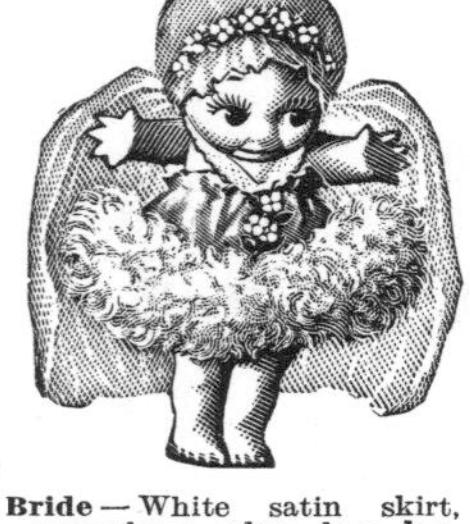

Bride — White satin skirt, swansdown edge, lace bretelles, long net veil with wreath, corsage bouquet. 1 in box.
F7954—9 in. ½ doz in box.........Doz. **$10.25**
F7955—10½ in. 1 in box. Each, **$1.25**
F7956—12½ in. 1 in box. Each, **$1.50**

"SPLASH ME" DOLLS

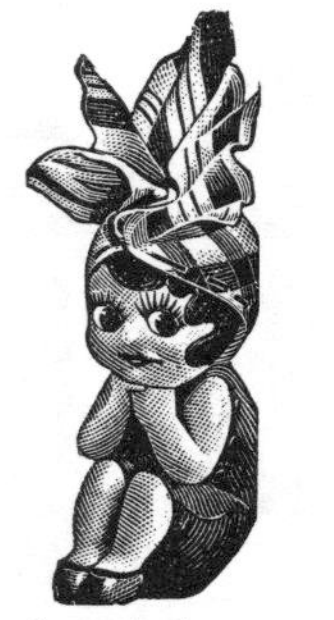

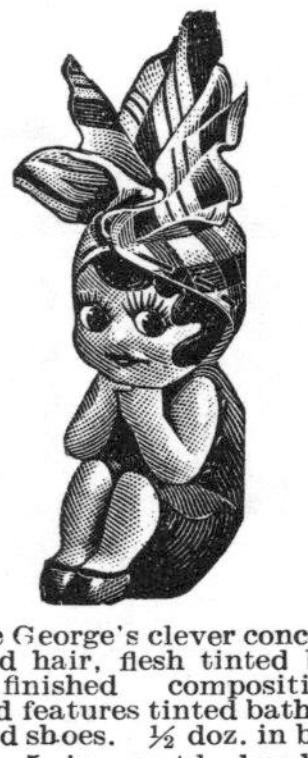

Gene George's clever conceit. Painted hair, flesh tinted bisque finished composition, painted features tinted bathing suit and shoes. ½ doz. in box.
F7944—5 in. asstd. kerchief caps..............Doz. **$2.25**
F7941—7 in. plaid taffeta kerchief caps....Doz. **$4.50**

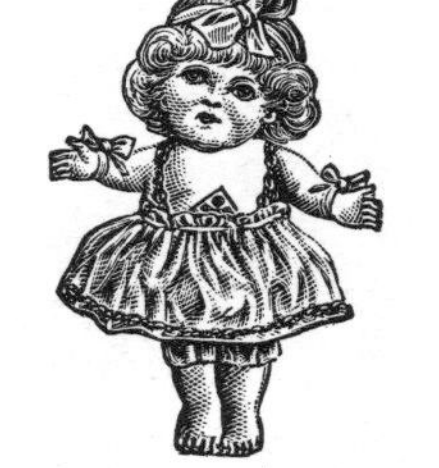

Mohair Wig—Asstd. color braid trim skirt and pantalettes, silk braid shoulder straps, silk band on hair, ribbon wristbands. 1/12 doz. in box.
F7981—9 in.... Doz.**$10.75**

CELLULOID DOLLS

Small size dolls in large demand for dressing, carriage trim and babies' baths. These are the kind you can sell all year round and during the Holiday season realize extra good profits.

Heavy celluloid bodies, painted features and hair unless stated, hollow feather weight bodies

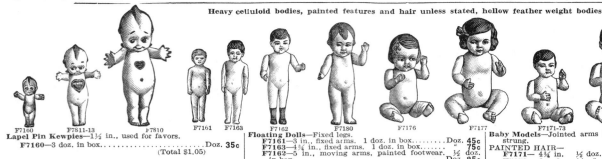

F7160   F7811-13   F7810   F7161   F7163   F7162   F7180   F7176   F7177   F7171-73    F7175-79   F 185-87

Lapel Pin Kewpies—1½ in., used for favors.
F7160—3 doz. in box.............Doz. **35c**
(Total $1.05)

Kewpies — Too well known to need description.

F7811—2¼ in., jointed arms. 1 doz. in box Doz. **$0.45**
F7812—4⅛ "   "   ½ " " "   .89
F7813—5 "   "   1/12 " " "   2.00
F7810—7¼ "   "   1/12 " " "   3.75

Floating Dolls—Fixed legs.
F7161—3 in., fixed arms. 1 doz. in box........Doz. **45c**
F7163—4¾ in., fixed arms. 1 doz. in box. "   75c
F7162—5 in., moving arms, painted footwear. ½ doz. in box..Doz. 95c
Character Doll Assts—Asstd. boy and girl embossed character heads.
F7180—Aver. 5½ in., boy with jointed arms, girl with jointed arms and position limbs. Asstd. ½ doz. in pkg. ....Doz. **$1.75**
F7176—6¾ in., jointed arms and limbs. Asstd. ½ doz. in pkg...Doz. $2.25
F7177—8¾ in., jointed arms and limbs. Asstd. ⅙ doz. in box..Doz. $4.25

Baby Models—Jointed arms and legs, stout bodies, elastic strung.
PAINTED HAIR—
F7171— 4¾ in.	½ doz. in box			Doz. $0.95
F7172— 6 "	¼ " "			2.25
F7173— 8 "	1/12 " "			4.00
F7175— 9 "	1/12 " "			4.50
F7178—10 "	1/12 " "			7.80
F7179—12 "	1/12 " "			8.00

MOHAIR WIGS—
F7185—5¼ in.   ¼ doz. in box............Doz. **$2.25**
F7187—8 "   1/12 " "   4.50

IMPORTED DOLLS

A large variety of popular imported dolls, including celluloid, bisque and china models. With a small investment you can carry a good showing and do a profitable business—the turn is unusually fast.

IMPORTED CELLULOID DOLLS

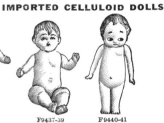

F9445   F9436-49   F9437-39   F9440-41

F9445—12 styles, 2½ in., fixed arms and legs, painted features. Asstd. 2 doz. in box. (Total 48c) Doz. **24c**

Red Band Baby Dolls— Featherweight body, standing position, jointed arms, lifelike expression, painted features and hair, red band around head. In box Doz.
F9430—3½ in.   2 doz. $0.36
F9431—4 "   1 "   .45
F9432—4½ "   1 "   .65
F9433—5 "   1 "   .89
F9434—6 "   ½ "   1.65
F9435—7 "   ½ "   2.00
F9436—8 "   ½ "   2.25
F9449—12 "   1/12 "   8.50

F9444—6 styles, 3¾ in., heavy celluloid, decorated in bright and fancy costumes, painted features, juvenile characters with painted jump ropes, toy gun and holster, toy cannon, etc. in hands. Asstd. bright colored costumes, with hats, black painted shoes. Asstd. 1 doz. in box...........Doz. **38c**

F9972—3¾ in., painted features, painted orange, red and green dresses, pink socks, black shoes, jointed arms. Asstd. 2 doz. in box. (Total $78c) Doz. **39c**

F9300   F9442

F9300—6 styles, 3½ in., painted features, hair, dress and head. Asstd. 6 doz. in box. (Total $2.52) Doz. **42c**

F9442—3 styles, 4 in., 1 plain, 2 asstd. bright colors, jointed painted features and hair, standing position. Asstd. 1 doz. in box. Doz. **45c**

Jointed Arms and Legs — Painted features and hair. 1 doz. in box.
F9437—3¾ in....Doz. $0.45
F9438—4½ " ... "   .65
F9439—5½ " ... "   .92

Jointed Arms—Standing position, painted features and hair.
F9440—4 in. 1 doz. in box. Doz. **45c**
F9441—5½ in. 1 doz. in box. Doz. **87c**

F9976   F9977

F9976—5½ in., standing position, flesh color finish, painted features, hair, shoes and socks, jointed arms. 1 doz. in box..........................Doz. **65c**

F9977—5 in., painted features and 1 pc. bathing suit, asstd. colored socks, black shoes, jointed arms. Asstd. 1 doz. in box....................Doz. **75c**

F9446—3 styles, 4½ in., celluloid head, asstd. dresses. 1 doz. in box......Doz. **78c**

F9981   F9980

F9981—6¾ in., 1 style, red painted coat, green bloomers, gilt buttons, lavender hat, black shoes, jointed arms. 1 doz. in box........Doz. **84c**

F9980—5½ in., featherweight body, standing position, jointed arms, lifelike expression, painted features and hair, red band around head. 1 doz. in box......Doz. **92c**

F9448 — 6½ in., jointed arms and legs, gold band around head and body with rosette, painted features and hair, asstd. colors, red, blue and green. ½ doz. in box. Doz. **$1.75**

F9447—6¼ in., flesh color, painted features and hair, red band around head, painted arms and legs. ½ doz. in box. Doz. **$1.75**

"UNIQUE" CRYING DOLL

F9650 — 6 in., composition head, red and blue striped gingham dress with lace collar, 2 rosettes, cries when body is pressed. 1 doz. in box..................Doz. **$1.68**

IMPORTED BABY DOLLS IN BATH TUBS

1¾ in., sitting detachable baby, painted hair and features, white china 2¾ in. tub, heavy rim. 1 doz. in box.
F9786—Bisque doll.........Doz. **75c**
F9787—China " .... "   **84c**

IMPORTED JOINTED BISQUE DOLLS

F9648   F8176   F9646

F9648—4¼ in., flesh tinted body, painted hair and ribbon, features, shoes and stockings. 1 doz. in box................Doz. **36c**

F8176—4½ in., flesh tinted body, painted features, shoes and stockings. 1 doz. in box...............Doz. 39c

Head Dress—Standing position, flesh tinted body, painted features and hair, blue band around head, jointed arms. 1 doz. in box.
F9809—4½ in....Doz. 68c
F9646—4¾ " ..... "   78c

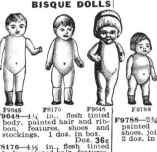

F9647   F9653-57

F9647—5½ in., fine flesh tinted body, painted features, roguish eyes, jointed position arms. Will stand. 1 doz. in box.........................Doz. **89c**

Stout Bodies—Flesh tinted, stout bodies, painted curly hair, features, shoes and stockings. ½ doz. in box.
F9653—6⅝ in....Doz. **$1.25**
F9657—7¼ "   1.35

IMPORTED SOLID CHINA DOLLS

White china body, painted features, blonde and brunette hair. 1 gro. in box.
F9780—1¾ in. Gro. 42c
F9781—2½ " "   65c

IMPORTED JOINTED CHINA DOLLS

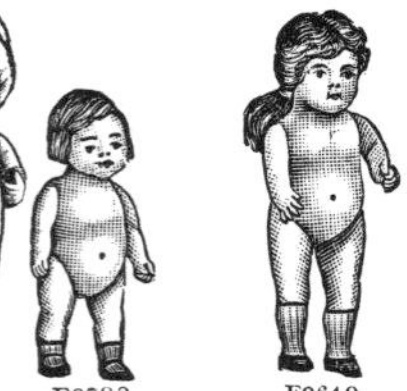

F9788   F9649

F9788—2¾ in., white china, painted features, hair and shoes, jointed arms and legs. 2 doz. in box........Doz. **24c**
(Total 48c)

F9649—4¼ in., flesh color china, mohair wig, painted features, shoes and stockings, jointed arms and legs. 1 doz. in box............Doz. 42c

IMPORTED BABY DOLLS

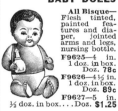

All Bisque— Flesh tinted, painted features and diaper, jointed arms and legs, nursing bottle.
F9625—4 in. 1 doz. in box. Doz. **78c**
F9626—4½ in. 1 doz. in box. Doz. **89c**
F9627—5 in. ½ doz. in box.... Doz. **$1.25**

Composition Body—6 in. composition body, bisque head, jointed arms and legs, socket head, painted hair and features, trimmed slip.
F9628—1 doz. in box. Doz. **96c**

IMPORTED "BALD HEAD NEXT-TO-NATURE" DOLLS

Excellent models, gen. bisque head, moving eyes, painted features, hair, hands jointed arms and legs, all with lawn slips. 1 in box.
F9475—11 in.   Each, **$0.89**
F9476—12 "   .98
F9477—13½ "   1.25

TURNING HEAD CHINA LIMB DOLLS

Turning china head and breast plate, china forearms and legs, sawdust stuffed strong red muslin body, painted features, hair and footwear. Sold exclusively by us.

F9658   F9664

Regulation Head—
	Size	In box	Doz.
F9658	5½ in.	2 doz.	$0.78
F9659	7½ "	1 "	.92
F9660	8½ "	1 "	1.25
F9661	10½ "	1 "	1.25
F9662	12½ "	½ "	2.50
F9663	13½ "	½ "	3.75

Character Head — Roguish expression.
	Size	In box	Doz.
F9664	5½ in.	1 doz.	$0.78
F9665	7½ "	1 "	.92
F9666	8½ "	1 "	1.25
F9667	10½ "	1 "	1.25
F9668	12½ "	½ "	2.50
F9669	13½ "	½ "	3.75

IMPORTED BABY DOLLS

Genuine bisque heads, asstd. blonde and brunette sewed mohair wigs, moving eyes, jointed arms and legs, painted features, hands and feet, flesh colored composition body, lawn slip. 1 in box.
F9480—12 in....Each, **$1.40**
F9481—13½ "   1.75

IMPORTED JOINTED BISQUE HEAD SLEEPING DOLLS

Bisque head, human hair wig, moving eyes, composition body, ball jointed shoulder, elbow, hip and knee. Lace trim slip. 1 in box.
F9483—14 in....Each, **$1.75**
F9484—16 " ..... "   2.00

IMPORTED "BABY BUD" BISQUE DOLLS

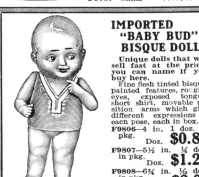

Unique dolls that will sell fast at the prices you can name if you buy here.

Fine flesh tinted bisque, painted features, roguish eyes, exposed tongue, short shirt, movable position arms which give different expressions at each pose, each in box.
F9806—4 in. 1 doz. in pkg.   Doz. **$0.89**
F9807—5½ in. ½ doz. in pkg.   Doz. **$1.25**
F9808—6¾ in. ½ doz. in pkg.   Doz. **$2.00**

182

PLUSH CATS, DOGS AND COWS

Fine quality plush, well stuffed bodies, excellent workmanship.

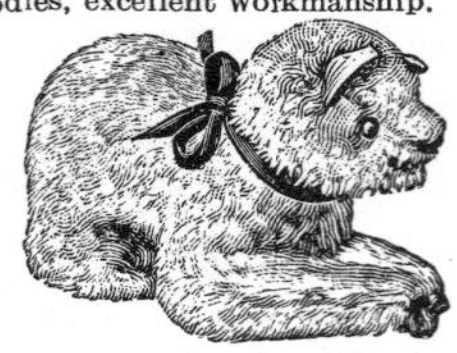

Sitting Cats—White mohair plush body, long tail, glass eyes, stitched nose and mouth, plush ball in fore-paws, ribbon collar. ½ doz. in pkg.
F5063—7½x5½ in.....Doz. **$ 8.00**
F5064—8x6 in........ " **12.00**

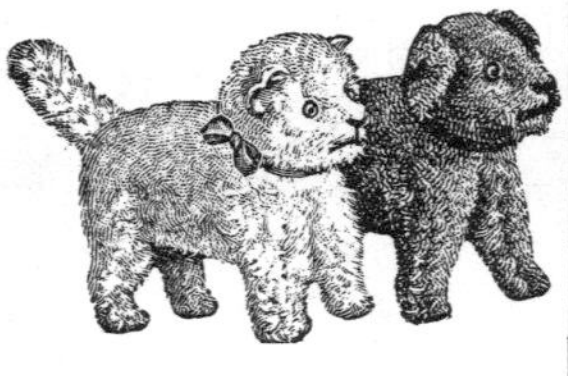

Cat and Dog Asst—Aver. 7x6½ in., plush gray cats & white dogs, glass eyes, stitched nose and mouth, ribbon and leatherette collars. Doz.
F5047—Asstd. ⅙ dz. in pkg. **$8.00**

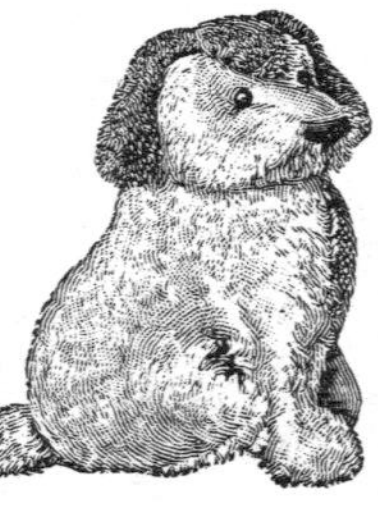

Grotesque Pups—Sitting position, white mohair plush body, cinnamon plush ears and glass eyes, sewed mouth and nose, turning heads.

Size	In box		
F5060—7 in.	⅙ doz..	Doz.	**$ 8.50**
F5061—8 "	1/12 " ..	"	**10.50**
F5062—9 "	½ " ..	"	**14.00**

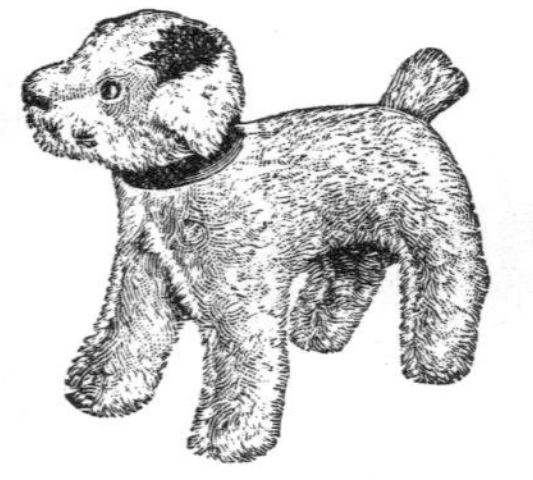

Standing Dogs—White plush bodies, cinnamon ears, glass eyes, stitched nose and mouth, imit. leather collars.

Size	In pkg.	Doz.
F5048—10x9½ in.	⅙ doz	**$ 9.00**
F5049—10½x10¼	½ "	**12.50**

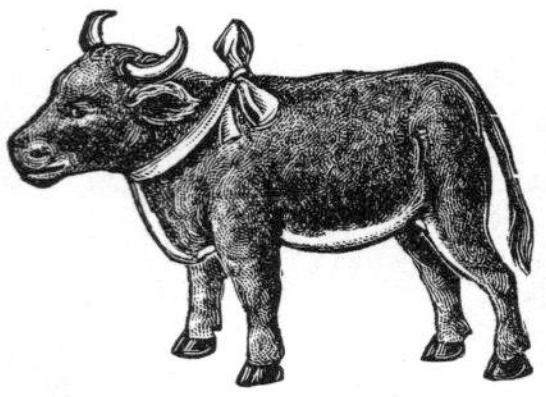

Cows with Voice—Cinnamon plush body and heavy tail, white plush underbody, felt ears, glass eyes, stitched nose and mouth, wire supported legs, ribbon collar.

	In box	Doz.
F5024—11x7 in.	½ doz..	**$12.50**
F5025—12x8½ in.	½ " ..	**15.00**
F5026—13½x9 in.	1 only Each,	**$1.50**

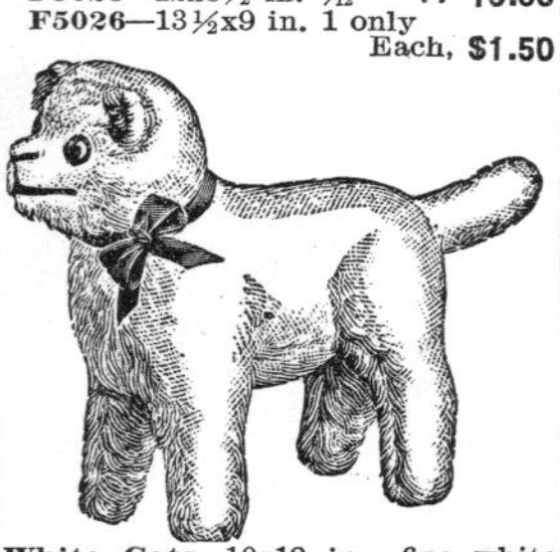

White Cats—10x12 in., fine white plush, long tail, glass eyes, stitched nose and mouth, wired leg supports, wide ribbon collar.
F5059—½ doz. in box. Doz. **$16.50**

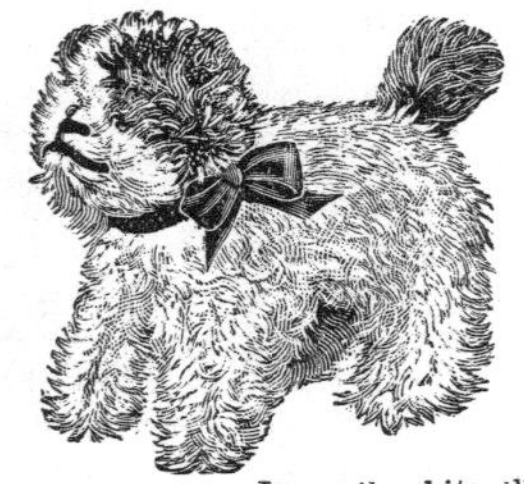

Long pile white silk plush body, black plush ears and tail, glass eyes, stitched nose, mouth and feet, ribbon collar. 1 in box.
F5083—9x8¼ in......Each, **$1.75**
F5084—10x9 in....... **2.00**

STANDING BROWN PLUSH POLAR BEARS

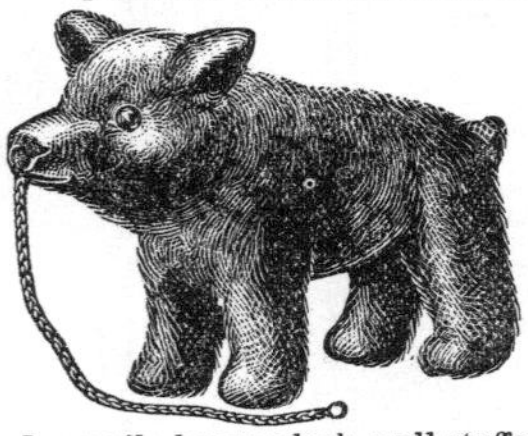

Long pile brown plush, well stuffed bodies, glass eyes, nickeled chain, ring in nose. 1/12 doz. in pkg.
F5067—10x7¼ in.......Doz. **8.00**
F5068—11x8¾ " ...... " **$12.00**
F5069—14x11 " ...... " **16.50**

PLUSH ANIMALS ON WHEELS

Best mohair plush, well stuffed bodies, glass eyes, all on open spoke metal wheels, strong axles. Will stand rough usage. Note dimensions given are extreme lengths and heights.

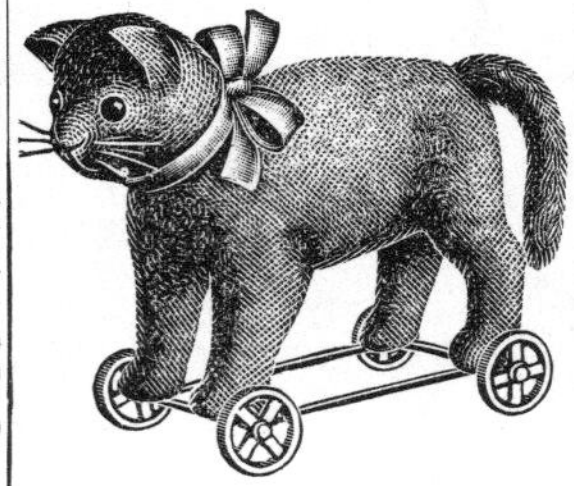

Cats—Fine dark gray plush, long tail, glass eyes, whiskers, ribbon collar.

Size in.	In box		
F5139—8x7	½ doz..	Doz.	**$15.00**
F5140—8¼x10	1 only..	Each,	**$1.75**
F5141—11x9¾	1 " ..	"	**2.10**

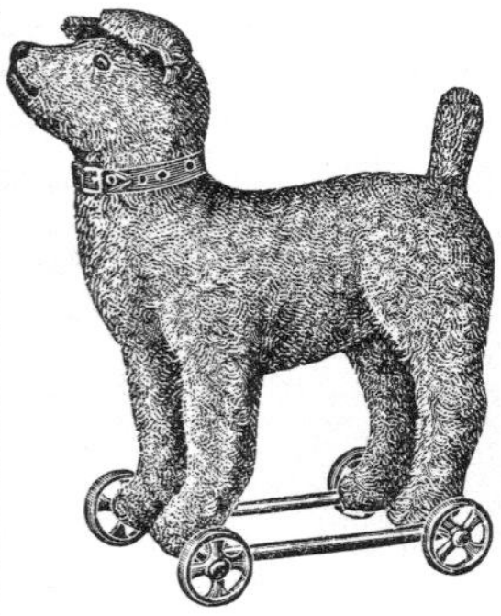

Irish Terriers—Short pile brown plush, glass eyes, stitched nose and mouth, studded leather collar with buckle. 1 in box.
F5136—10½x 9 in....Each, **$1.50**
F5137—13 x13 " .... " **2.10**
F5138—14 x13 " .... " **3.00**

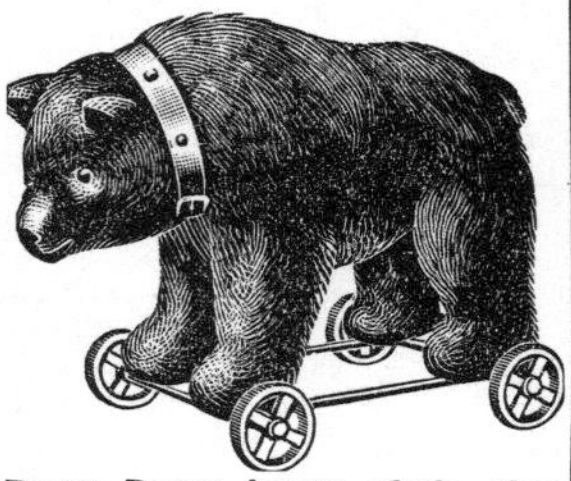

Bears—Brown beaver plush, glass eyes, studded leather collar with buckle. 1 in box.
F5130—10x 7 in......Each, **$1.50**
F5131—12x10 " ...... " **1.90**
F5132—16x11 " ...... " **3.25**

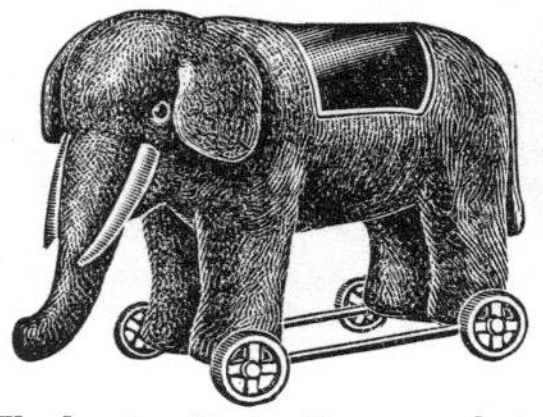

Elephants—Short pile gray plush, gold braid trim red flannel blanket, white felt tusks, button eyes. 1 in box.
F5133—10½x6½ in...Each, **$1.50**
F5134—14x9 in...... " **1.90**
F5135—15½x11 in.... " **3.00**

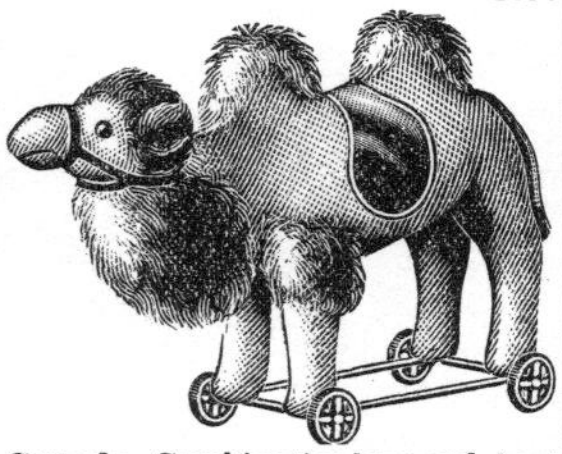

Camels—Combination long and short pile cinnamon plush, button eyes, stitched nose and mouth, studded leather harness with buckle, braid trimmed red felt blanket. 1 in box.
F5143—17x14 in......Each, **$3.25**

IMPORTED WOOLLY SHEEP

On 4-Wheel Platform

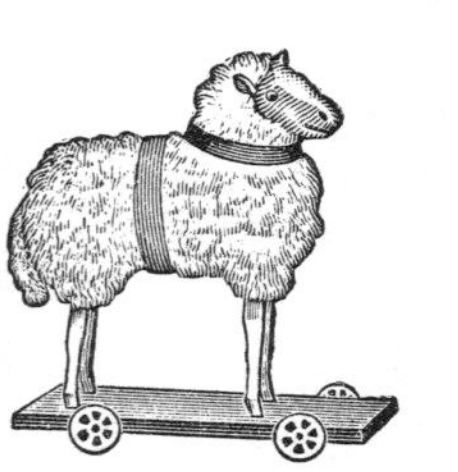

Woolly covered sheep, painted features, wood legs, colored bands and collars, on green stained wood platforms, metal wheels. Doz.
F6820—5x4½ in. 2 doz. in box.. **36c**
F6821—7x6½ " 1 " " **75c**

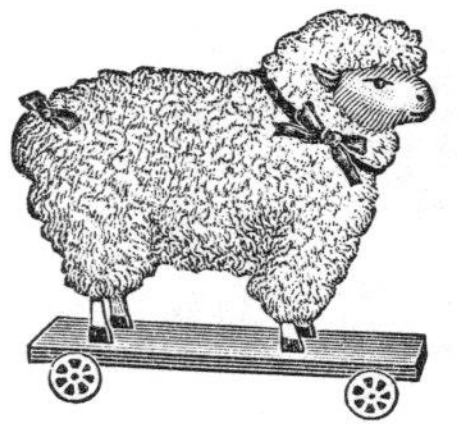

F6780—Thick wool covered, modeled face, glass eyes, colored collar, painted wood feet, on red stained wood platform with metal wheels, bleating voice when ring is pulled. ½ doz. in box..........Doz. **$4.50**

VELVET DOGS—On Metal Wheels

Well stuffed bodies, strongly sewed.

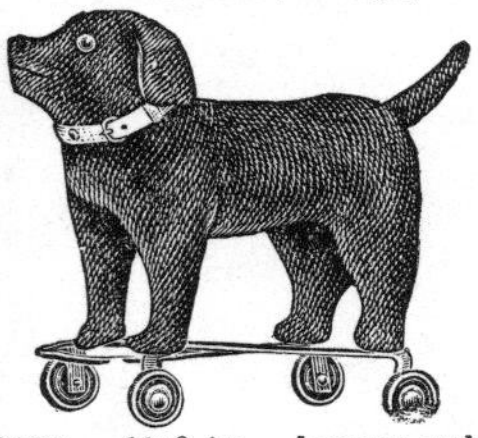

F9620 — 10x9 in., brown velvet mounted on nickel steel frame, glass eyes, sewed mouth, leather collar and buckle, 4 solid metal wheels. 1 in box......Each, **$1.10**

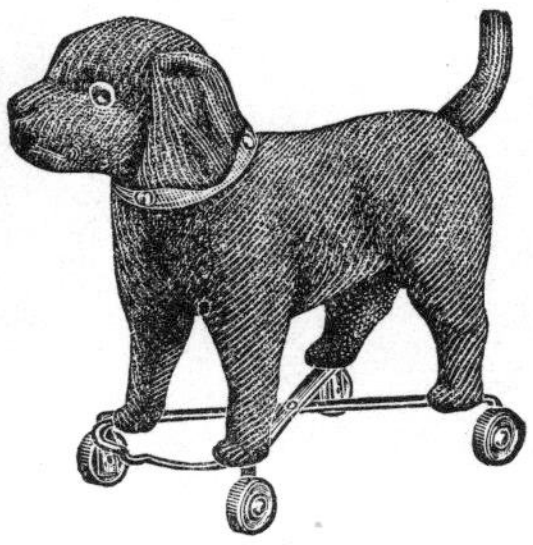

Brown velvet, glass eyes, real leather collar, metal buckle, mounted on steel frame, 4 solid metal wheels. 1 in pkg.
F9621—12½x10 in.....Each, **$1.50**
F9622—13½x12 " ..... " **1.75**

COMPOSITION ANIMALS On Wood Wheels

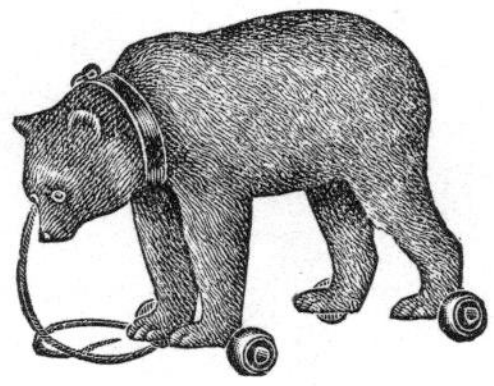

Bear—9x6 in., solid brown, glass eyes, painted features, leather collar with cord, on wood wheels.
F9606—1 in box......Each, **89c**

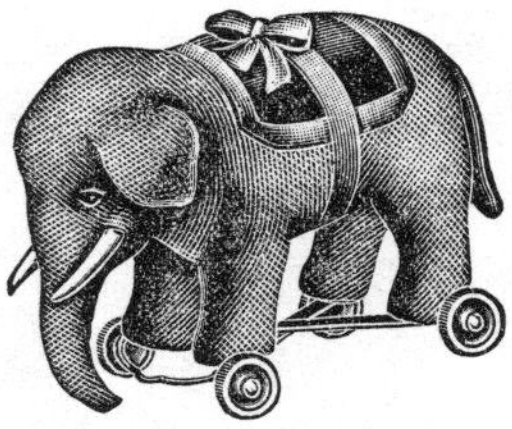

Elephant—9½x8 in. grayish blue velvet, glass eyes, wood tusks, red plush saddle, green trim, mounted on steel frame, 4 solid metal wheels.
F9629—1 in pkg..... Each, **$1.50**

CINNAMON PLUSH TEDDY BEARS

Exceedingly popular sellers at prices that will help you to do good business.

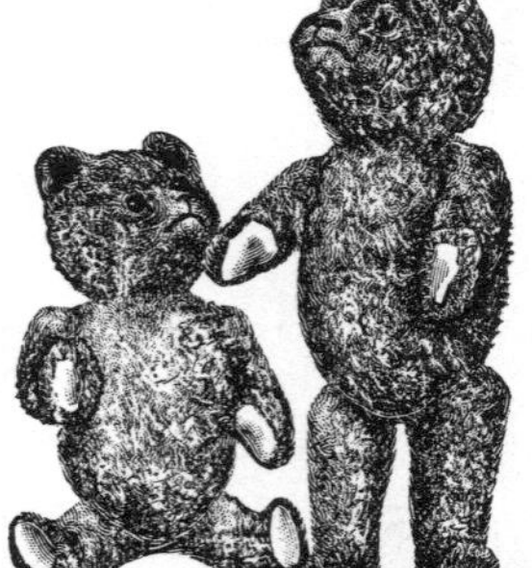

Well stuffed, good quality, brown plush, turning head, glass eyes, jointed limbs, felt soles, stitched mouth and nose, all with voices. ½ doz. in box.

F5070—12 in	Doz.	**$7.20**
F5071—14 "	"	**8.75**
F5072—16 "	"	**10.50**
F5073—18 "	"	**12.60**
F5074—20 "	"	**15.00**
F5075—22 "	"	**16.80**

"FLUFFY DUPLEX WHISTLER" BEAVER PLUSH BEARS

Very attractive and appealing. Your trade will quickly realize the real value embodied.

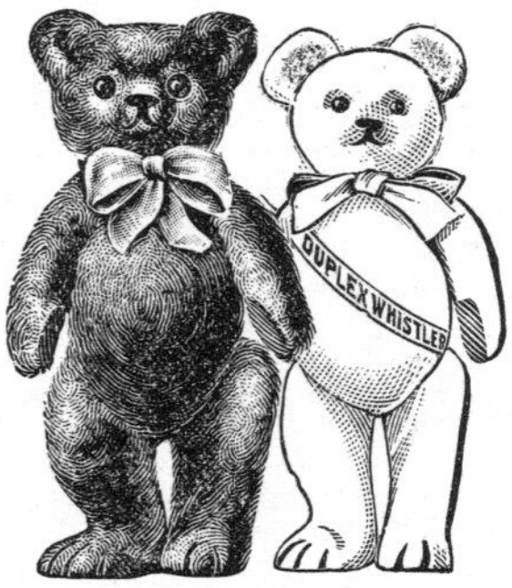

Beaver plush, cotton stuffed body, cork stuffed turning head, glass eyes, jointed limbs, felt soles, stitched mouth and nose, ribbon bow and band, when ears are pressed bear whistles. 1 in box.

F5096—12 in	Each,	**$1.75**
F5097—14 "	"	**2.10**
F5098—16 "	"	**2.50**

WHITE SILK PLUSH BEARS

Quality merchandise. All numbers are made with real sounding voices.

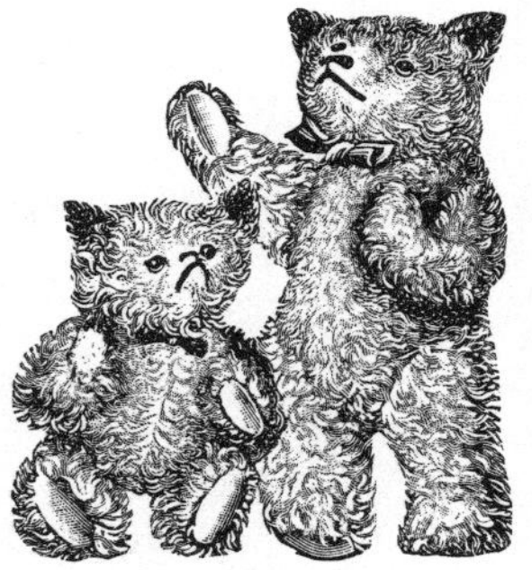

Fine quality, long pile silk plush, excellent models, turning head, glass eyes, felt soles, stitched nose, mouth and feet, jointed limbs, ribbon collars, well stuffed bodies, all with voice. 1 in box.

F5077—14 in	Each	**$1.90**
F5078—16 "	"	**2.50**
F5079—18 "	"	**3.25**

JUVENILE FURNITURE & NOVELTIES

Exact duplication of the full size kind. Big variety of chairs, dressers, cedar chests, etc. Made by manufacturers of high grade furniture specialties with materials, finish and construction equal to the best of full size furniture. The demand is always big—order sufficient to meet it.

RED PAINTED WOOD CHAIRS AND ROCKERS

Painted bright red, varnished and striped, well made and finished.
Packed in heavy shipping carton which prevents breakage and insures safe delivery.

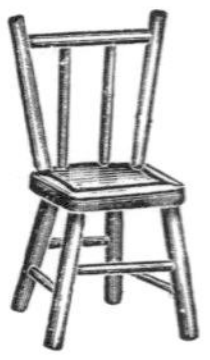
F640

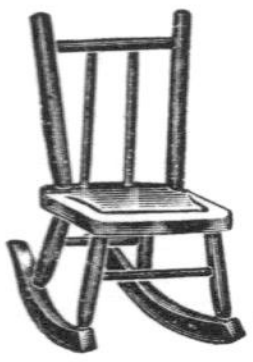
F641

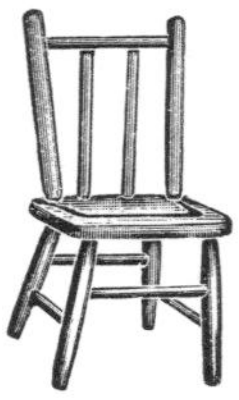
F644

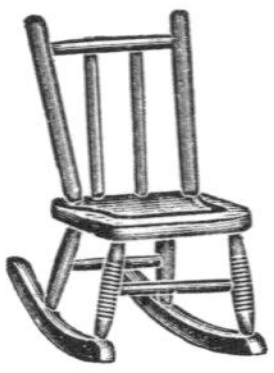
F645

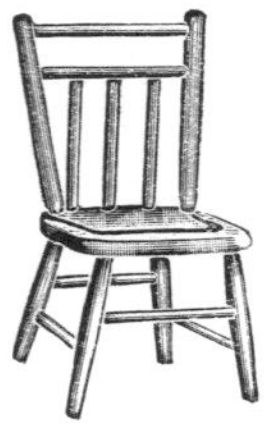
F646

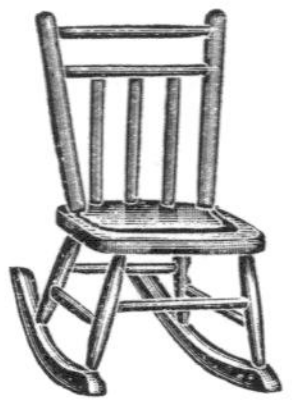
F647

Square Back—Ht. 15 in., seat 6½x6, ht. from floor 7½ in. ½ doz. in carton, 8 lbs.

F640—Chair .... Doz. **$2.75**
F641—Rocker .... " **5.25**

Square Back—Ht. 19 in., seat 9x9, ht. from floor 9 in. ½ doz. in carton, 13 lbs.

F644—Chair .... Doz. **$8.50**
F645—Rocker .... " **9.00**

Square Back—Ht. 22 in., seat 10x10, ht. from floor 9¾ in. ½ doz. in carton, 16 lbs.

F646—Chair .... Doz. **$ 9.50**
F647—Rocker .... " **10.50**

5 PIECE TABLE AND CHAIR SETS

White enamel finish, octagon shape table, 24x24 in. top, ht. 20 in., chair ht. 24 in., seat 10x10 in. 1 set in crate.

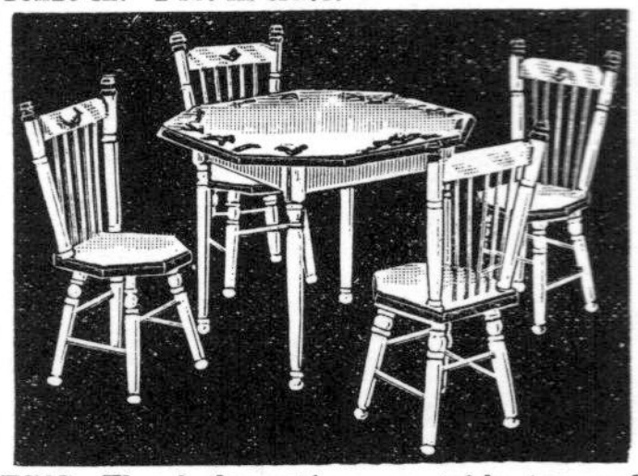

F707—Floral decorations on table top and chair back. SET (5 pcs.), **$12.00**

F708—Hand painted blue band around table edge and chair seats, animal designs on table top and chair backs. SET (5 pcs.), **$13.50**

WHITE ENAMELED FURNITURE NOVELTIES

White enameled novelty furniture. Hand painted floral and juvenile scenes and inlaid cretonne trimmings. Pieces to match.

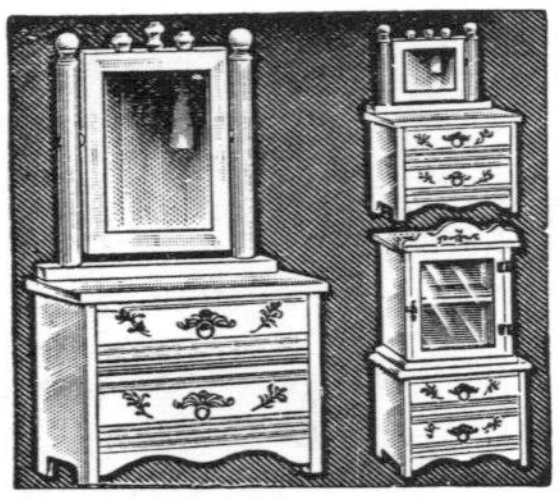

F715—4 styles, white enamel, **1 dresser** 18½x10½x6½ in. with 5x7 in. mirror, **1 china cabinet** 18x10x6½ in., 2 wash stands 15x10½x6½ in., **2 dressers** 15x10½x 6½ in. with 4x5 in. mirror, all with drawers, brass ring pulls, floral hand painted decorations. Asstd. 6 in crate, 35 lbs. (Total $9.00) Each, **$1.50**

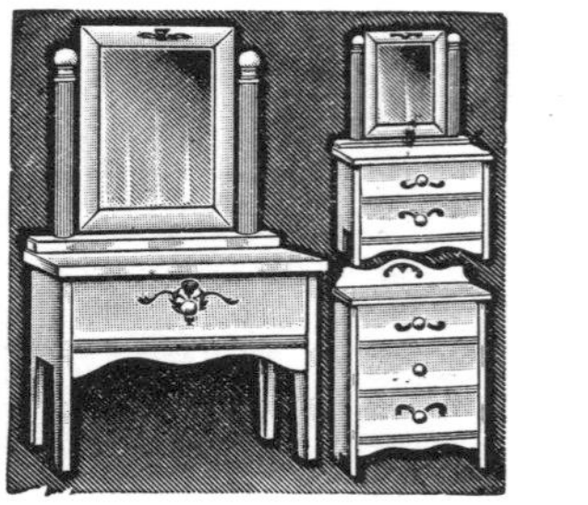

F716—4 styles, white enamel, 1 dressing table 17x10½x6½ in. with mirror 5x7 in., 1 china cabinet 18½x10½x6½ in., 1 chiffonier 15½x10½x6½ in., 1 dresser 17x10½x 6½ in. with mirror 5x7, drawers with wood knob pulls, hand painted floral decorations. 4 in crate, 40 lbs. (Total $8.00) Each, **$2.00**

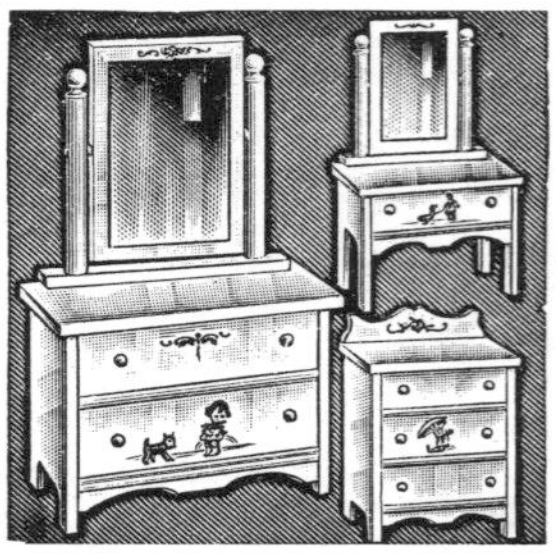

F717—3 styles, white enamel, **1 dressing table** 20x12½x7 in. with 6x9 in. mirror, **1 chiffonier** 15½x11½x7 in., **1 dresser** 20x12½x7 with 6x9 in. mirror, wood knob drawer pulls, hand decoration in nursery characters. 3 in crate, 30 lbs. Each, **$2.50** (Total $7.50)

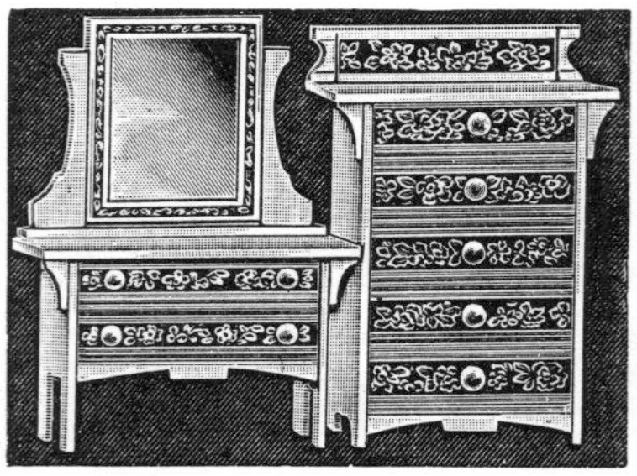

F726—2 styles, dresser 18x25x8 in. with 9½x 11½ in. mirror, 2 drawers; **chiffonier** 16¼x23x7 in., 5 drawers; drawer fronts cretonne trimmed, turned wood knob pulls. 2 in case, 30 lbs. .... Each, **$4.00** (Total $8.00)

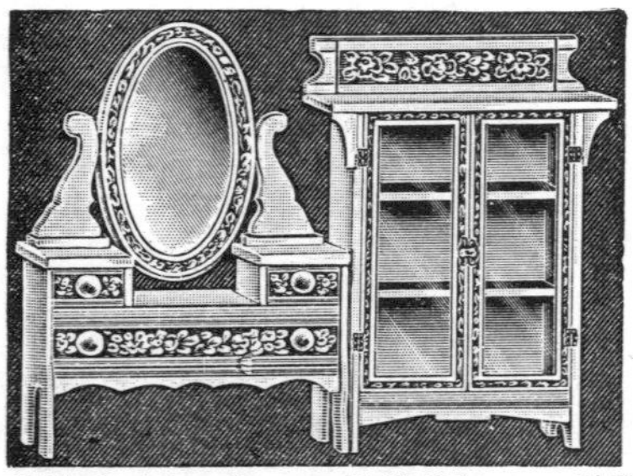

F727—2 styles, dresser 17x25x7½ in., oval mirror 8½x14½ in.; **china cabinet** 16¼x 23x7¼ in., two glass doors 5¼x16¼ in., nickel plated catch and hinges, doors with turned wood knob pulls, cretonne trimmed. 2 in case, 35 lbs. .... Each, **$4.50** (Total $9.00)

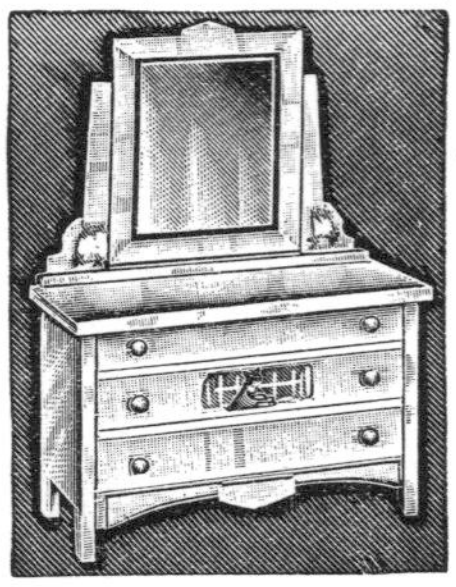

F720—White enamel dresser 30x22x11 in., 10x12 in. mirror, 3 full length drawers with wood knobs, attractive new design, hand painted decorations. 1 in crate, 27 lbs. .... Each, **$6.50**

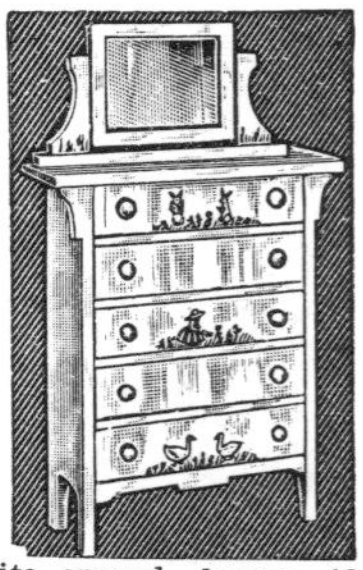

F722—White enamel dresser 40x23x10 in., mirror 8x10 in., 5 full length drawers with wood knobs, attractive new design, hand painted decors. 1 in crate. Each, **$12.00**

WHITE ENAMELED TEA WAGON

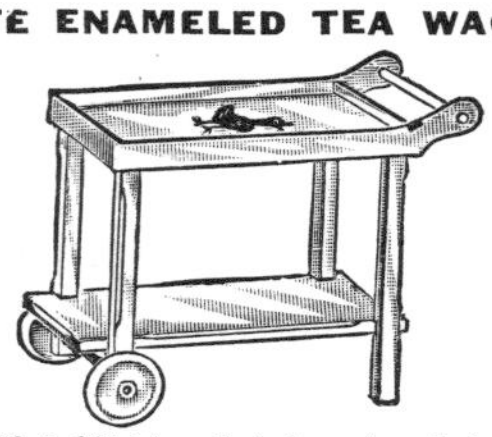

F743—16x9x12½ in., 2 shelves, beveled edges, wood handle, two 3 in. turned wood wheels, top shelf with litho bird and juvenile design, each in carton. 2 in pkg. Each, **$1.75** (Total $3.50)

FOLDING NURSERY CHAIR

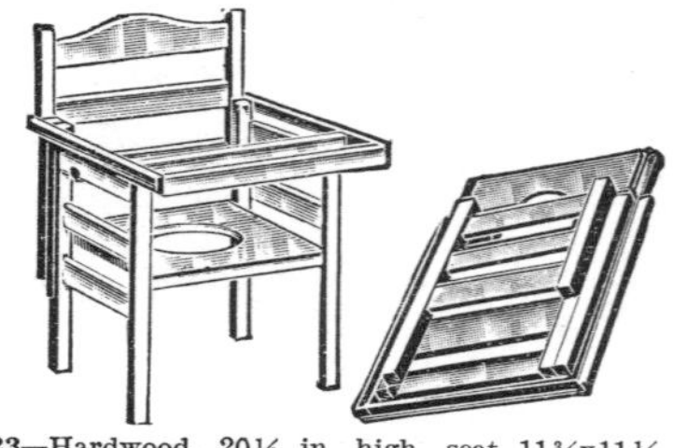

F623—Hardwood, 20½ in. high, seat 11¾x11¼ in., height of seat from floor 8¾ in., swinging tray, natural finish, when folded flat measures 21x14x3¼ in. 2 in crate, 10 lbs. .... Each, Out (Total

MINIATURE WARDROBE

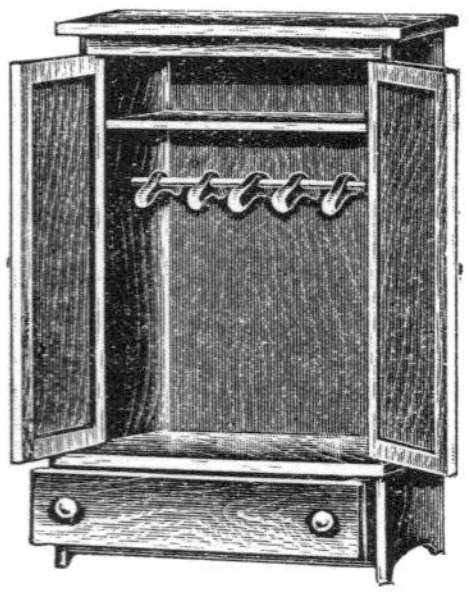

F729 — 16¼x10⅝x7 in., walnut finish, inside and out, hat shelf, steel rod through center with 6 coat hangers, large compartment for dolly's clothes, lower drawer for misc. articles, footed base, extra large panel swinging doors, counter-sunk dowels which prevent pulling out. 2 in carton. Each, **$1.50** (Total $3.00)

WIRE FURNITURE

Very strong and substantial—practically indestructible. Table tops and chair seats 5 ply veneer.

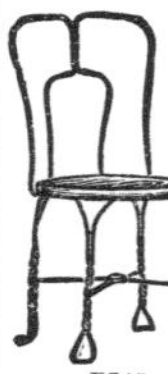
F745

Chair—Seat diam. 10 in., ht. 21 in., ht. seat from floor 10½ in., oxidized brass finish, steel wire base and back.

F745—2 in bdl., 11 lbs. Each, **$1.50** (Total $3.00)

Table—Top 9x16, ht. 17¾ in., oxidized brass finish, steel wire base, oak finish top.

F746—2 in bdl., 14 lbs. Each, **$2.50** (Total $5.00)

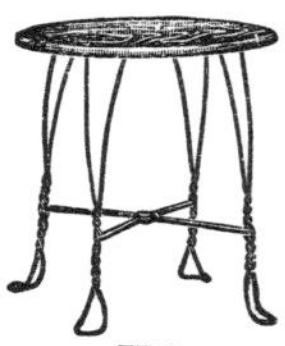
F746

MINIATURE CEDAR CHESTS

For dolly's clothes and fittings. A perfect duplicate of the large size chests. Genuine cedar, clean smooth finish, final coat of varnish brings out beautiful grains, wood lifting grips, brass hinges and adjustable catch for holding cover in upright position when open, fancy fluted edge and legs.

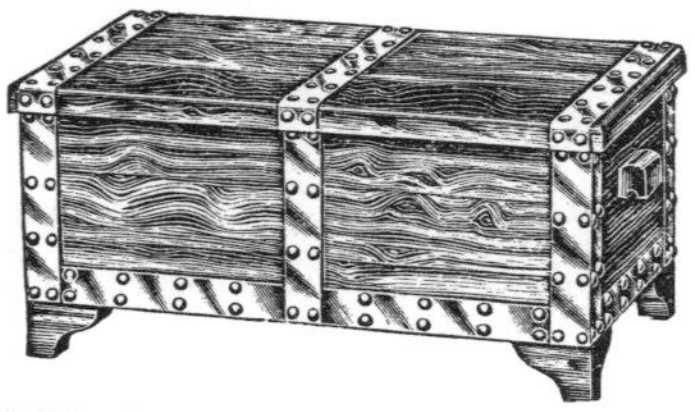

F754—18x9x9½ in., copper hand grip. 1 in carton. Each, **$3.25**

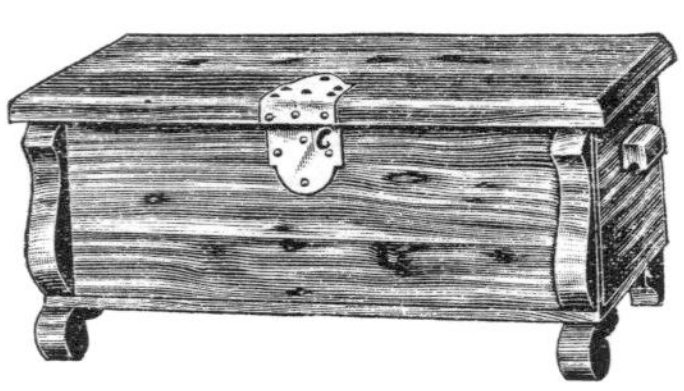

F751—18¼x9½x8¾ in., extension cover, copper straps and studding. 1 in carton .... Each, **$3.90**

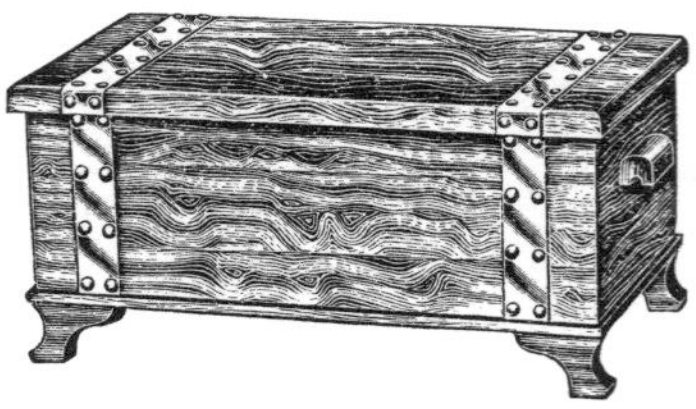

F752—18¼x9½x8⅞ in., extension cover, massive square corners, copper bands and studding. 1 in carton. Each, **$5.25**

TOY RANGES

A wide showing of popular sellers. It will pay you to offer a good selection of these numbers—your trade will appreciate the low prices you can name on items made as well as these are. The turnover is fast. Buying here enables you to undersell your competitor and still make good profits. Select your needs here and send us your order today.

LATEST TYPE BLACK STEEL TOY RANGES

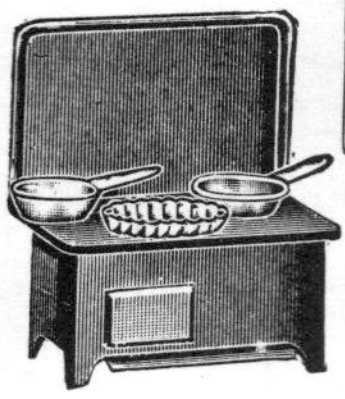
F2835

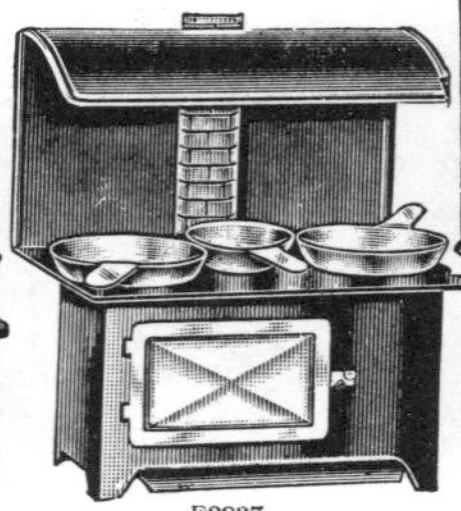
F2837

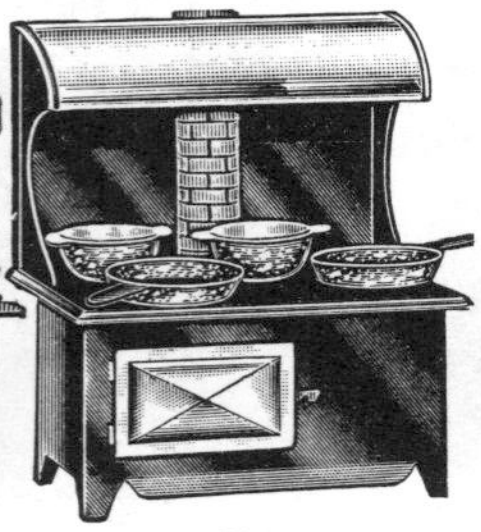
F2839

F2835—5¾x4⅞x2½, imit. red brick flue, 3 bright metal utensils. 1 doz. in box. 2 doz. in pkg.......Doz. **95c** (Total $1.90)

F2837 — 6¾x5⅞x3½, rounded hood, beveled edges, nickeled oven door, 2 small utensils, 1 large utensil with cover. ½ doz. in box.....Doz. **★1.89**

F2839—8x6½x4, nickel plated hood and oven door, sauce pot, large fry pan, 2 kettles with covers. ⅙ doz. in box..........................Doz. **$4.40**

EXTRA LARGE TOY RANGES

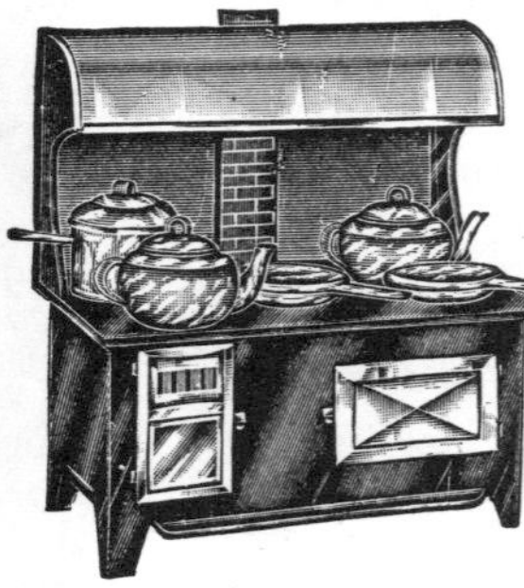

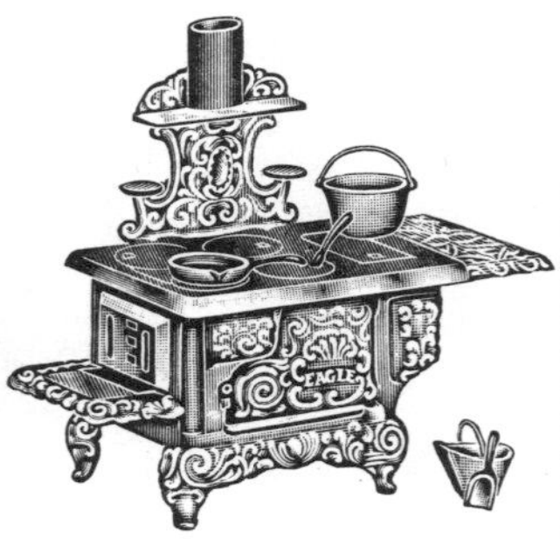

F2833—10¼x9x4⅛, black steel, nickeled hood, oven door and grate door, 2 extra large fry pans, stew pot and 2 large handled kettles. ½ doz. in box. Doz. **$9.75**

F3062—14x6½x12, polished steel high shelf back, stove pipe, water tank with cover, hinged oven with fire door, removable grates, hearth, 4 large lids, 5 large copper finish utensils. 1 in bx. Ea. **$2.75**

POLISHED STEEL TOY RANGES

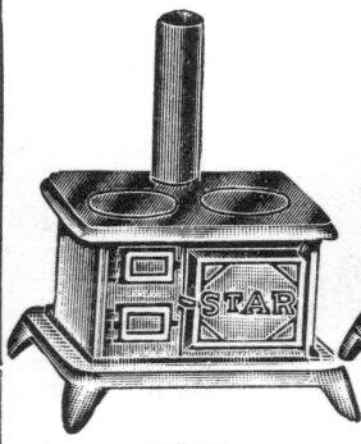
F3053

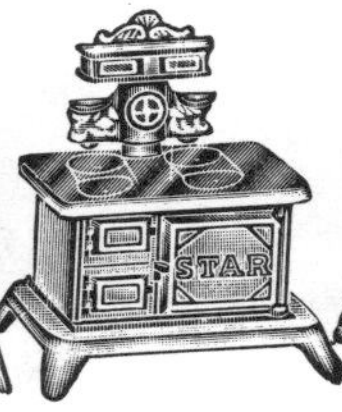
F3054

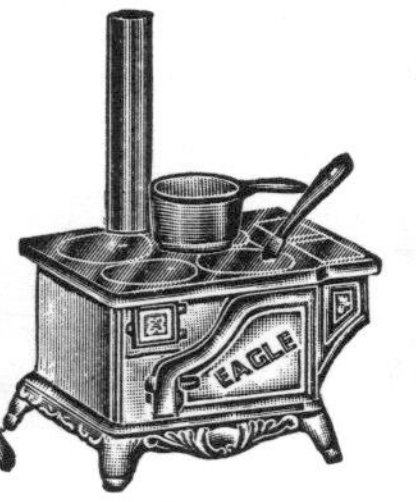
F3057

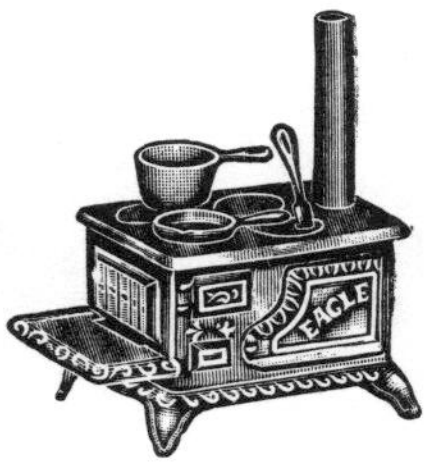

F3053 — 3¾x3x4½, polished steel body, stationary lids, black pipe. ½ doz. in box.

Doz. **$2.10**

F3054—3¾x4½x3, high shelf black, molded lids ½ doz. in box...............Doz. **$2.20**

F3057—5x4x6¾, polished steel body, black pipe, 4 loose lids, kettle, hinged door & lifter. ¼ doz. in box.....Doz. **$4.25**

F3059—7½x4¼x6¼ in., smoke stack, one loose side shelf, and one stationary side shelf, open side grate, hinged front door, nickel trimmed, copper finish pot, skillet and lifter. ½ doz. in box............Doz. **$8.75**

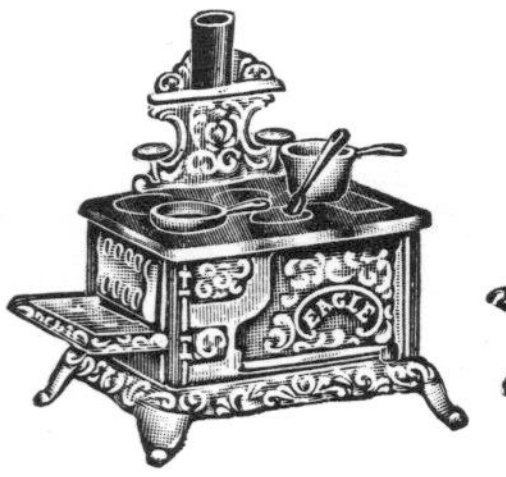

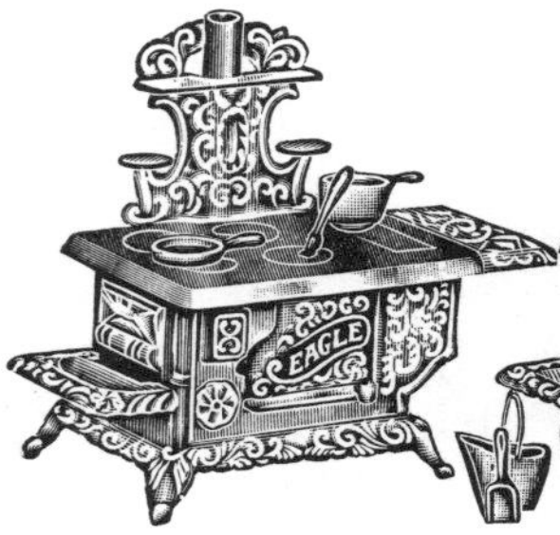

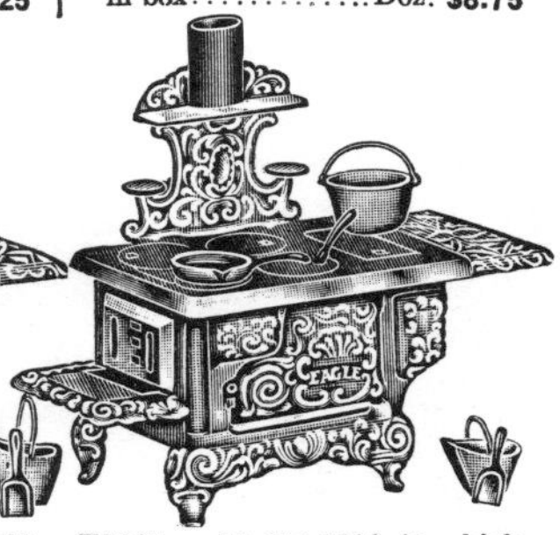

F3063—8x4¾x3¼, high shelf, nickel back, hearth, reservoir cover, 4 loose lids, copper finish lifters, skillet and kettle. 1/12 doz. in box......Doz. **$12.00**

F3064—11x5¼x9½ in. high shelf back with smoke stack, detachable extension sides, open grate on side, loose lids, copper finish skillet, pot, coal hod and shovel and lid lifter, hinged front door, nickel trimmed. 1 in box........Each, **$1.40**

F3065 — 12x5¼x11½ in. high shelf back with smoke stack, detachable extension sides, open grate on side, loose lids, copper finish utensils as above, hinged front door, fancy nickel trimmed. 1 each in box. Each, **$2.00**

"A B C" EDUCATIONAL TEA SETS

Beautifully lithographed—8 color juvenile design and A B C. These sets are exclusively ours. All cups with riveted handles. Each set in marbleized box with full double cover, very strong, special inside insert prevents pcs. working loose.

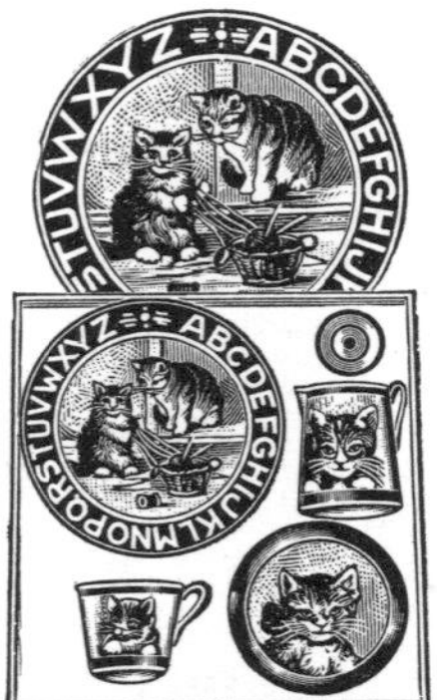

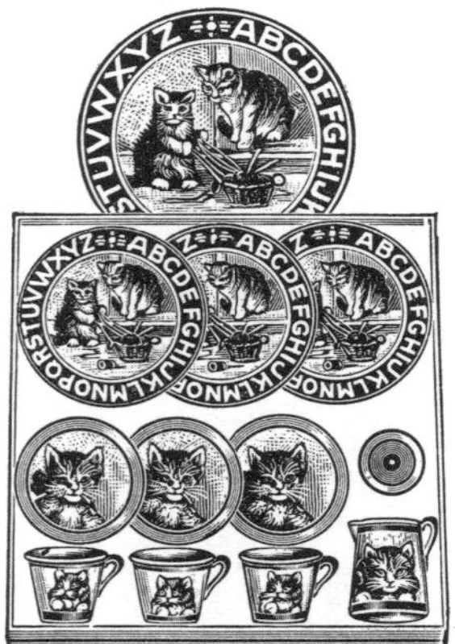

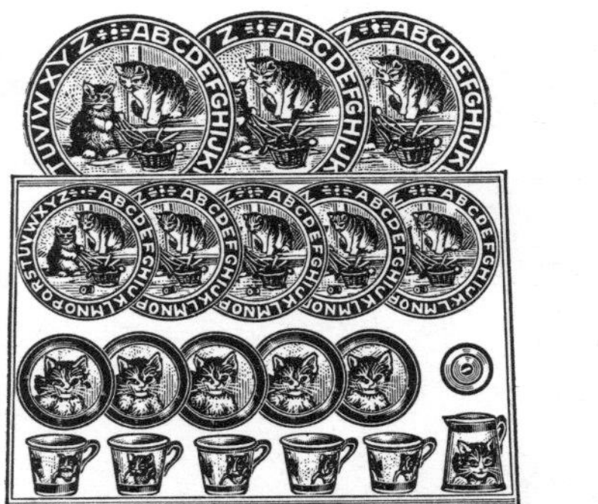

F2845 — 6 pieces, A B C design, cup 1¾x2¼ in., saucer 2⅞ in., bread & butter plate, 4½ in., dinner plate 6¼ in., pot 2¼x1⅞ in., with cover, box 8x8 in. 1 doz. sets in pkg.

Doz. sets, **$2.25**

F2846 — 12 pieces, A B C design, three 1¾x2⅞ in. cups, three 2⅞ in. saucers, three 4½ in. bread & butter plates, 6¼ in. dinner plates, 2¼x1⅞ in. pot with cover, box 10¼x10¼ in. ½ doz. sets in pkg.

Doz. sets, **$4.50**

F2847 — 20 pieces, A B C design, five 1¾x2⅞ in. cups, five 2⅞ in. saucers, five 4½ in. bread & butter plates, three 6¼ in. dinner plates, 2¼x1⅞ in. pot with cover, box 10¼x15¼ in. ¼ doz. sets in pkg.

Doz. sets, **$9.00**

TOY FLAT AND SAD IRONS

Smooth finish, polished nickeled irons, wood handles. Some large enough for light ironing

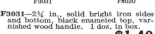

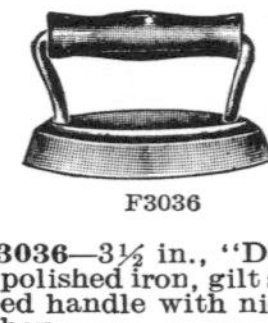

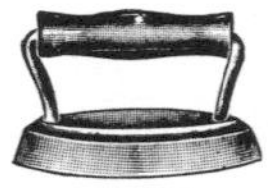
F3036

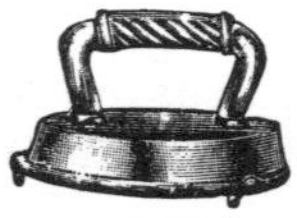
F3029

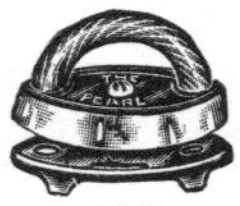
F3031

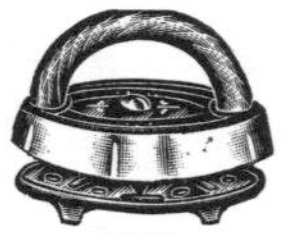
F3030

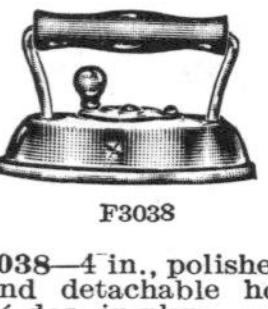

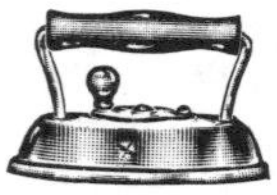
F3038

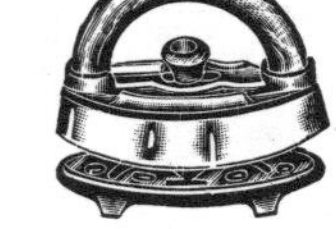
F3032

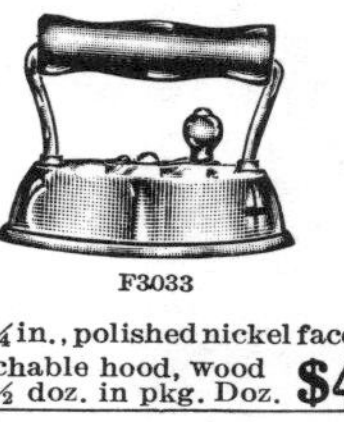

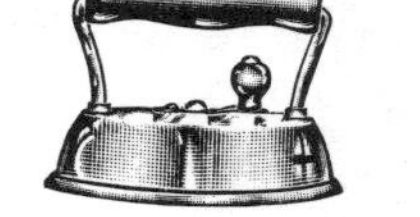
F3033

F3036—3½ in., "Dover" asbestos bright polished iron, gilt sides and black painted handle with nickel ends. 1 doz. in box. Doz. **85c**

F3029—3 in., solid, gilt top aluminum handle, polished bottom and sides. 1 doz. in box. Doz. **89c**

F3031—2¾ in., solid bright iron sides and bottom, black enameled top, varnished wood handle. 1 doz. in box. Doz. **$1.40**

F3030—3¾ in., black enameled top, varnished wood handle, heavy bright bottom and sides. 1 doz. in box. Doz. **$1.75**

F3038—4 in., polished nickel face, edges and detachable hood, black handle. ½ doz. in pkg. Doz. **$2.15**

F3032—3⅝ in., Potts pattern, extra heavy nickel plated iron, removable handle, varnished knob and grip. ½ doz. in box. Doz. **$2.25**

F3033—4¾ in., polished nickel face, edges and detachable hood, wood handle. ½ doz. in pkg. Doz. **$4.50**

TOY BANKS

Selected values that will draw business your way. Through very careful buying we have secured this line of live-wire sellers at bed-rock prices. A good display will produce quick turn at very good profits. Remember that the great thrift movement now in progress will greatly increase the demand over last year. Send us your order today.

NOVELTY IRON TOY BANKS

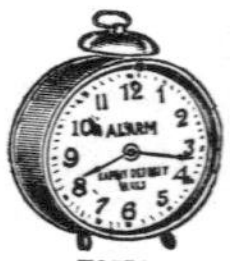

F2751

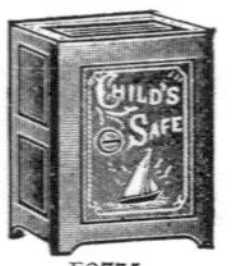

F2775

Steel Clock—4¼x3¼, bright metal sides and back, litho dial, alarm bell, ring grip, footed.
F2751—1 doz. in box.....Doz. **84c**

Safe—4x2¾x2½, heavy metal, painted red, decorated double strength door with lock and key.
F2775—1 doz. in box....Doz. **92c**

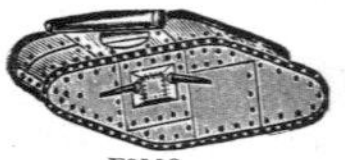
F2753

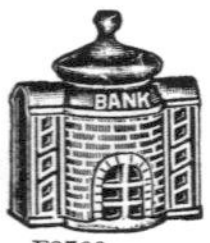

F2766

Tank—5½x1⅞x1⅞, steel body, litho battleship gray, black outline gun, brass finish cannon for coins up to 25c.
F2753—1 doz. in box....Doz. **89c**

Castle—3½x7⅞x2¾ in., gilt finish, perforated doors and windows.
F2766—1 doz. in box...Doz. **$1.25**

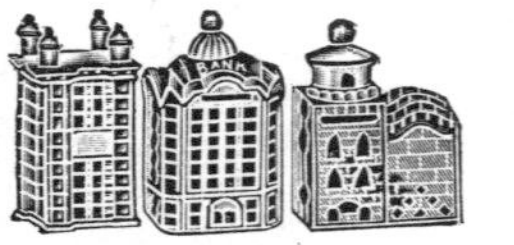

Building Asst—3 styles, aver. 3½ in., gilt and aluminum finish sky scrapers, gilt castle.
F2742—Asstd. 1 doz. in box.
Doz. **$1.40**

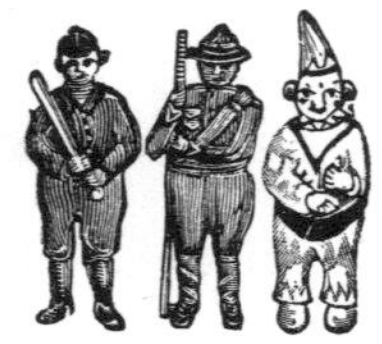

Character Asst—3 styles, aver. 6 in., brightly painted baseball player, gilt boy scout and clown, painted features and costumes.
F2758—Asstd. 1 doz. in box.
Doz. **$1.75**

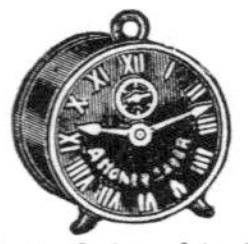

Clock—Diam. 3 in., ht. 3½, black enameled, gilt Roman numbers and hands, footed.
F2763—1 doz. in box...Doz. **$1.75**

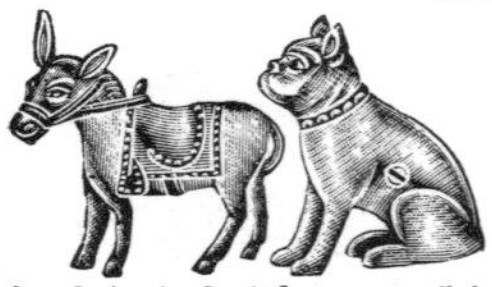

Animal Asst—6 styles, aver. 5 in., gilt camel with painted saddle, donkey, horse, cow, dog and rooster.
F2743—Asstd. ½ doz. in box.
Doz. **$1.90**

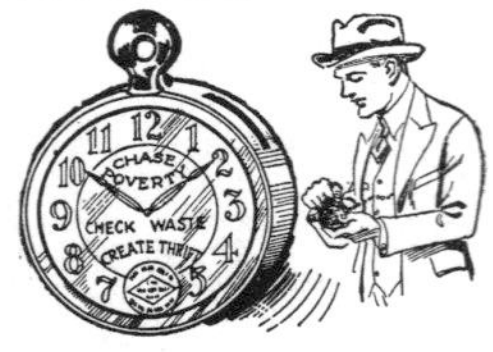

Watch Type—2⅛ in., for 25 dimes, highly nickel plated, stamped dial face, etched ring for chain, opens automatically. Especially designed to be carried in the pocket.
F2732—1 doz. in box...Doz. **89c**

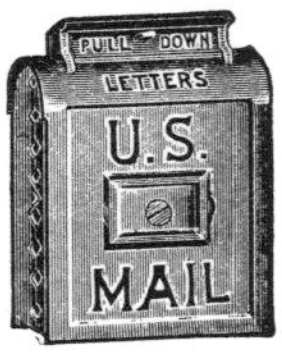

Mail Box—3½x2¼x1½ in., painted green, gold lettering.
F2740—1 doz. in box...Doz. **$2.00**

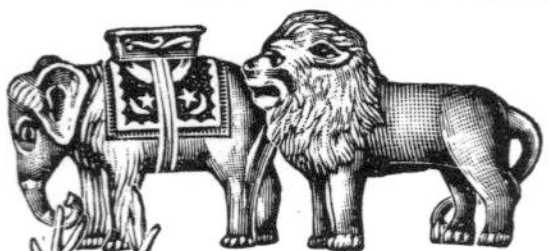

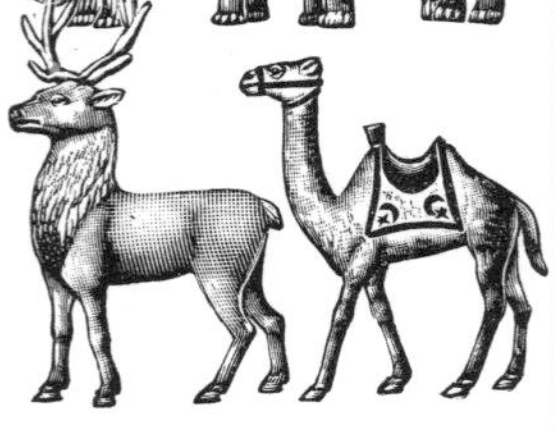

Animal Asst—4 styles, aver. ht. 6½ in., gilt lion, elephant, reindeer and camel, painted saddle and bridle.
F2746—Asstd. ⅓ doz. in box.
Doz. **$4.20**

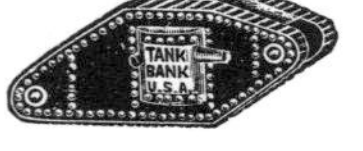

War Tank—Painted gold, model of famous war tanks, all details faithfully brought out—gun turrets, caterpillar tractor, etc.
F2779—5¾x3⅛x3⅛ in. ½ doz. in box...............Doz. **$3.25**

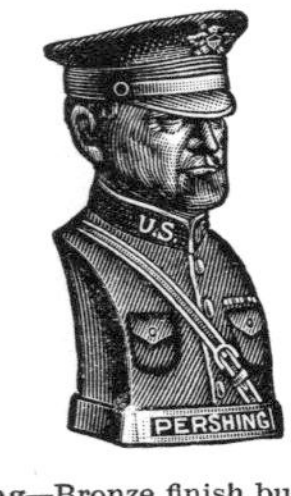

Pershing—Bronze finish bust of Gen. Pershing, reproducing features and uniform, slot in top for deposits, suitable for ornament.
F2781—½ doz. in box..Doz. **$8.00**

MECHANICAL ACTION BANKS

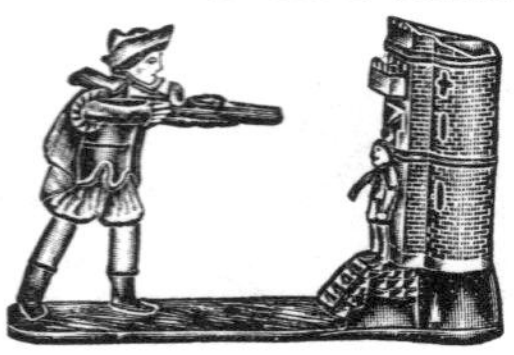

William Tell—10½x6¼ in., castle and figure in colors, place coin on gun, press lever, apple falls from child's head, depositing money.
F2770—1 in box.....Each, **$1.75**

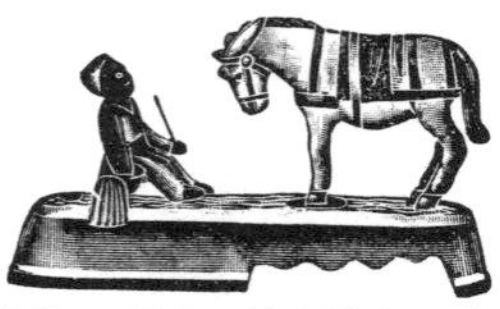

Kicking Mule—10x16½ in., place coin on bench, press lever, mule turns and upsets darkey, depositing coin.
F2767—1 in box......Each, **$1.75**

IRON COMBINATION TOY SAFES

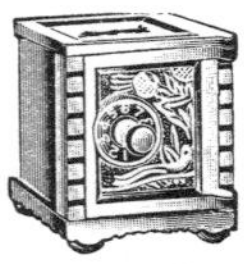

F2747—2¾x3x4 in., nickel plated embossed door, aluminum finish steel sides and back, dummy wheels. ½ doz. in pkg...........Doz. **$3.90**

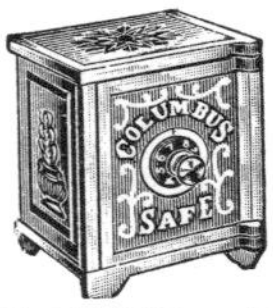

F2749—4⅛x3¾x5½ in., nickel plated embossed door and top, aluminum finish steel sides and back, dummy wheels. ¼ doz. in pkg. Doz. **$8.50**

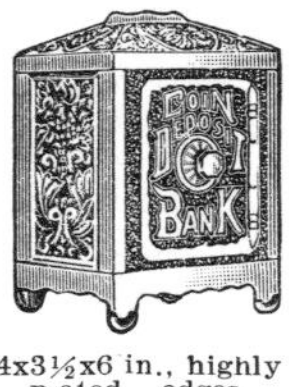

F2750—4x3½x6 in., highly polished, nickel plated edges, embossed design on door and top, aluminum finish steel sides and back, iron handle, each in box. 1 doz. in pkg.
Doz **$10.00**

GUARANTEED AUTOMATIC REGISTER BANKS

Cash register action.

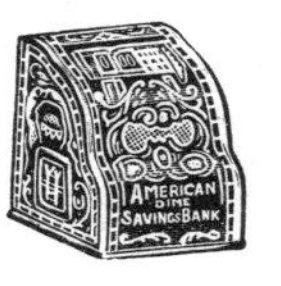

"American Dime"—3¾x3⅞x3¼, sheet steel, black enameled, gold ornamented, registers and takes dimes only, opens automatically when $10.00 has been registered, etched finish case, full directions on back.
F2790—1/12 doz. in box..Doz. **$9.50**

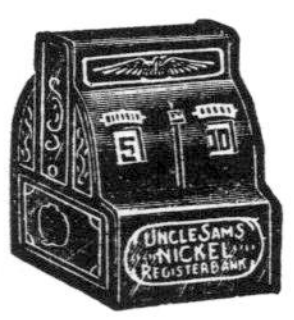

"Uncle Sam"—4½x3½ in., cold rolled steel, black enameled gun metal & brass plates, deposit rings bell. ½ doz. in box.

Register to
F2791—Nickel, $10.00.... } Doz.
F2792—Dime, $20.00.... } **$15.75**

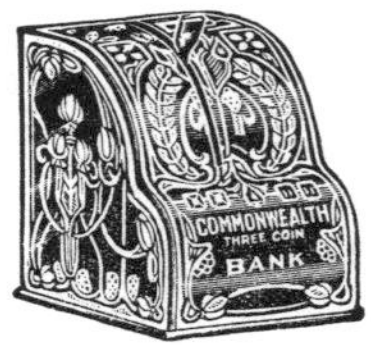

"Commonwealth" — 3 coin, nickels, dimes and quarters, 5x4x5½ in. heavy sheet steel, green enameled, fancy gold decorated. Registers up to $10.00.
F2797—½ doz. in box.Doz. **$18.00**

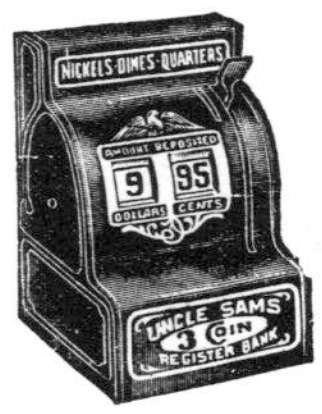

"Uncle Sam" — 6¼ x 5½ x 4 in., 3 coin, nickels, dimes and quarters, heavy cold rolled steel, black enameled, gold ornamented, locks and unlocks automatically, registers only the coins mentioned on bank, other coins deposited are returned through slot in back, guaranteed, full directions on cover of box, registers up to $10.00.
F2796—½ doz. in box.Doz. **$21.00**

POCKET COIN HOLDERS

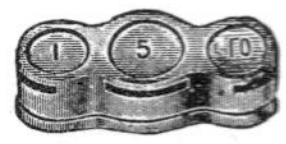

Tin Case—2½x1⅛ in., 3 spring compartment for pennies, nickles and dimes.
F2723—3 doz. in box....Doz. **45c**
(Total $1.35)

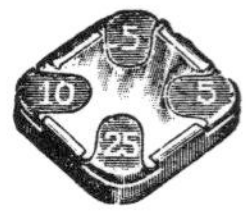

Nickel Case—1⅞x1⅞, 4 in., spring compartments for nickels, dimes and quarters.
F2731—1 doz. in box..Doz. **$1.25**

"GEM" POCKET SAVINGS BANKS

Polished nickeled, registers contents.

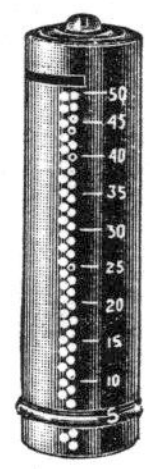

Spring Top—1 doz. in box.
F2726—For 20 nickels...Doz. **80c**
F2728—For 50 dimes.... " **80c**
Screw Top—1 doz. in box.
F2727—For 50 dimes..Doz. **$0.96**
F2725—For 50 pennies. " **.89**

W. S. S. THRIFT BANK

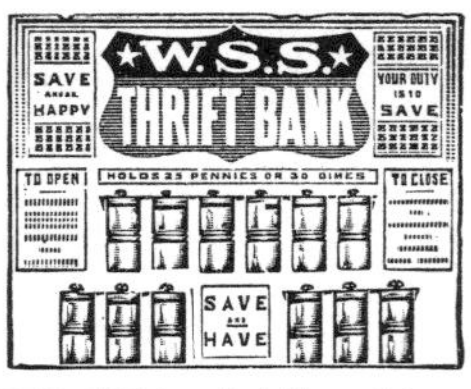

F2730—1¾ in., bright metal, screw adjustment, takes pennies and dimes. 1 doz. on display card.
Doz. **78c**

TIN BOOK BANK

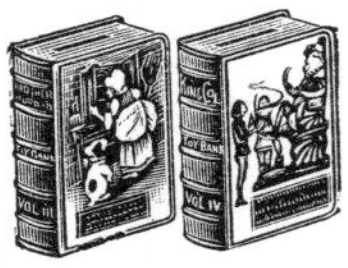

F2754—3x4x1⅜ in., 4 litho juvenile designs with verses. Asstd. 1 doz. in box..................Doz. **82c**

Wall Telephone Bank

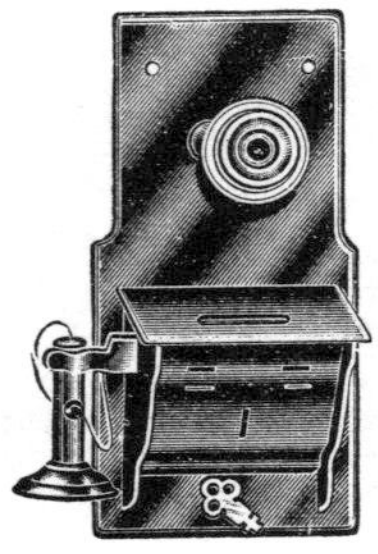

A big bargain item combining the features of a toy and bank.

F2562—7¼x3¾x2½ in., high luster bright metal, litho mouth piece, receiver with string, can be removed from hook, slot in top of box, opening in back for removing coins. 1 doz. in box, with keys.
Doz. **96c**

6 Style Animal Iron Bank Assortment

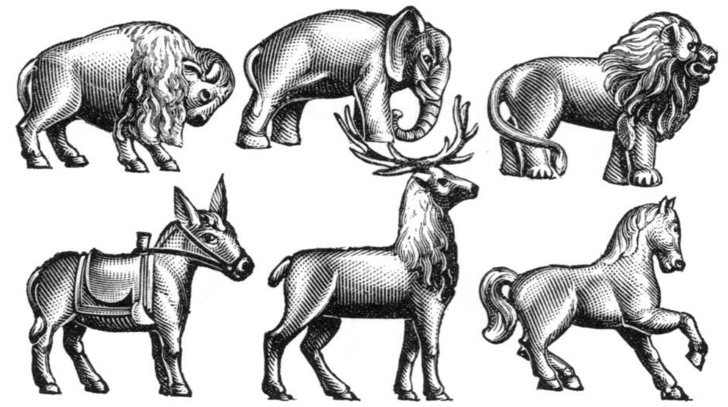

Up-to-the-minute sellers. Be sure to list this assortment in your line.

F2756—6 styles, aver. ht. 4 in., gilt lion, elephant, reindeer, buffalo, horse and donkey. Asstd. 1 doz. in box.
Doz. **$1.85**

FRICTION TOYS

"HIGH POWER" **Double friction power.** Guaranteed not to get out of order. All have heavy cast fly wheels, and are much faster and better than heretofore. The bright color, baked enamel finishes and new designs will make this line of Friction Toys a big business puller.

Battleship—10 in., gray enameled body, red stack, gilt wheels and stripings.
F3335—¼ doz. in pkg.......Doz. **$5.00**

Locomotive & Tender—12 in., red enameled body, gilt wheels and stripings.
F3337—¼ doz. in pkg.......Doz. **$5.00**

Auto Truck—10½ in., red enameled body, gilt wheels and stripings.
F3336—¼ doz. in pkg.......Doz. **$5.00**

Coaster Boy—9x2x4½ in., green enameled sled, gilt disc wheels, boy in bright colored costume.
F3300—½ doz. in box.......Doz. **$8.00**

Tricky Duck—7x9 in., yellow enameled body, orange wings, maroon head, gilt beak and wheels, runs straight or in circle.
F3305—½ doz. in box.......Doz. **$8.25**

Auto Truck—12¾ x 5 in., red enameled body and mud guard, gilt wheels and stripes.
F3310—½ doz. in box.......Doz. **$8.50**

U. S. Mail—11½x7½ in., blue enameled body, gilt wheels and stripes, painted driver.
F3313—½ doz. in box.......Doz. **$8.50**

Auto Gun Carrier—11x5½ in., orange enameled body and cannon, red turret, green mud guards and seat, gilt wheels, painted driver.
F3315—½ doz. in box.......Doz. **$8.25**

Battleship—15x5¼ in., white enameled body and hull, green water line, 4 orange cannons, 2 orange smoke stacks.
F3306—½ doz. in crate.......Doz. **$10.00**

Hook and Ladder—13x5½ in., orange enameled body, green running board and fender, three 7 in. red ladders, gilt wheels, chauffeur.
F3317—½ doz. in box.......Doz. **$10.00**

Delivery Van—12x4½x7 in., yellow enameled body, red fenders and running board, green stripings, gilt wheels, painted chauffeur.
F3304—½ doz. in box.......Doz. **$10.00**

Auto Truck—15x5½x4½ in., green enameled body, gilt striping and wheels, red fenders and running boards, painted chauffeur, loaded with packages.
F3307—½ doz. in box.......Doz. **$10.00**

Locomotive and Tender—18x5 in., bright red baked enameled body, green cab, gilt moving wheels and trim.
F3303—½ doz. in box.......Doz. **$10.00**

Armored Auto—11x6½ in., red enameled body, green mud guard, radiator and cannon, gilt wheels and stripes.
F3314—½ doz. in box.......Doz. **$10.00**

Hook and Ladder—11x5½ in., green body, 3 red 7 in. removable ladders, gilt wheels and stripes, painted chauffeur.
F3311—½ doz. in box.......Doz. **$10.00**

Aeroplane—17½x11x6 in., yellow enameled body and wings, red striping and propeller, gilt disc wheels, gilt propeller, 2 bulls eyes on wings, painted aviator.
F3370—½ doz. in box.......Doz. **$14.00**

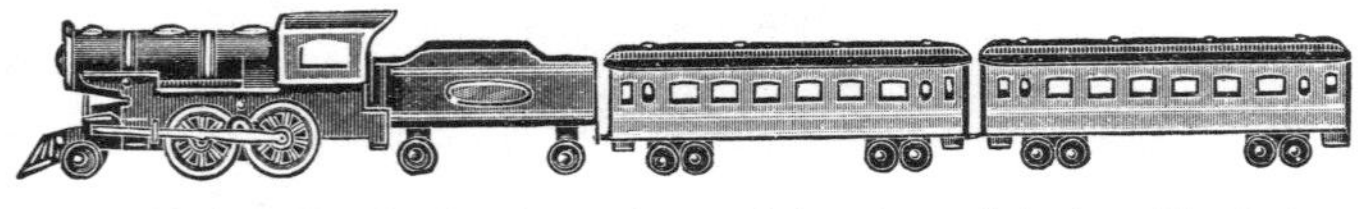

Passenger Train—38½x4½x3¼ in., red enameled engine and tender, gilt wheels and striping, 2 coaches, yellow body, red top, black wheels
F3342—¼ doz. in box.......Doz. **$14.50**

Touring Car—12¾x5 in., new 1920 model, red enameled body, gilt wheels and stripings, green fenders and running board, chauffeur, runs straight or in circle.
F3323—½ doz. in box.......Doz. **$14.00**

Auto Fire Engine—14x7x3½ in., yellow enameled body, gilt wheels, striping and bell, two 7 in. red ladders, red boiler, painted chauffeur and fireman.
F3322—½ doz. in box.......Doz. **$14.00**

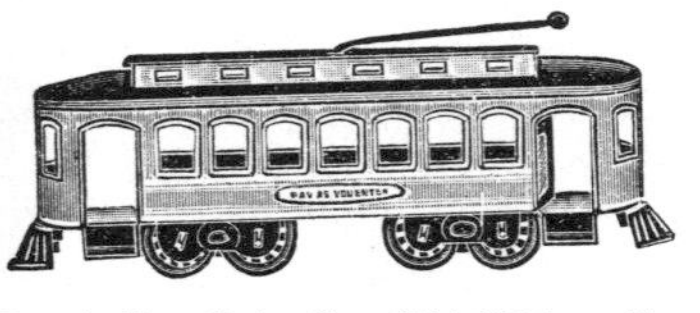

Pay-As-You-Enter Car—21½x8½ in., yellow enameled body, red roof, black fender and wheels, 8 in. metal trolley pole.
F3316—½ doz. in pkg.......Doz. **$14.50**

Trolley Car—13½x4¾x6½ in., open type, yellow enameled body, gilt wheels, red top and step, gold striping, painted motorman.
F3324—½ doz. in box.......Doz. **$14.00**

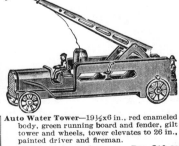

Auto Hook and Ladder—20x7½ in., yellow enameled body, gilt wheels, green running board and fenders, red striping, four 13 in. red ladders, adjustable to 20 in., painted driver and fireman.
F3320—½ doz. in pkg.......Doz. **$16.00**

Auto Water Tower—19½x6 in., red enameled body, green running board and fender, gilt tower and wheels, tower elevates to 26 in., painted driver and fireman.
F3318—½ doz. in box.......Doz. **$16.00**

Locomotive & Tender—24x6 in., red enameled green cab, gilt trim and stripes, moving piston rods, 12 gilt **movable open spokeless wheels.**
F3319—½ doz. in box.......Doz. **$16.00**

"Variety" Friction Toy Assortment
Best selling numbers—quantities chosen in proportion to their selling qualities

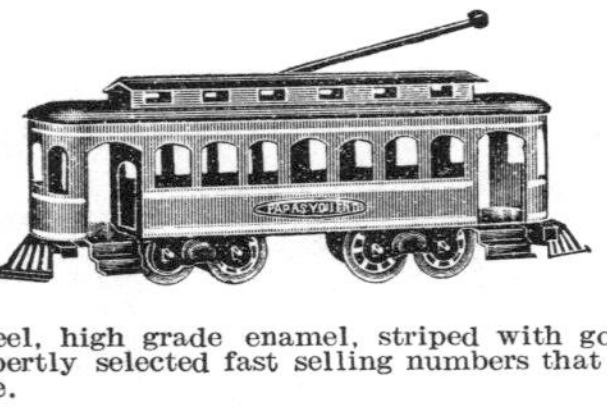

F3345 — Sheet steel, high grade enamel, striped with gold bronze. Asstd. 22 pieces comprising expertly selected fast selling numbers that will sell out evenly. Asstd. 22 pcs. in crate.
ASST. (22 pcs.), **$15.00**

187

MECHANICAL TOYS

A complete showing of real action, big value mechanical toys. A good display will attract attention and greatly increase your turn. You can depend upon every number to give absolute satisfaction. Note especially the new imported numbers. Comparison will prove that our prices are right. Goods in stock ready for shipment.

POPULAR SELLING MECHANICAL TOYS

Horse & Cart—(C. E. Carter), 8½ in. cart, blue outside and yellow inside, open spoke yellow wheels, dapple gray horse.
F3296—⅙ doz. in pkg. Doz. **$2.25**

Butterfly—8½x8½ in. natural colored wings, yellow body and wheels, wings flutter when drawn across the floor, strong spiral spring, each in box.
F3297—⅙ doz. in pkg. Doz. **$4.40**

Racing Auto—9¼x3½ in. red body, yellow wheels, gilt trim, concealed clock spring between rear wheels, each in box.
F3258—1/12 doz. in box. Doz. **$8.75**

Locomotive and Tender—17½x5x3½ in., heavy gauge steel, red body, gold trim, with running board, long action connecting rod, covered clock spring under cab.
F3290—1 in box. Each, **$1.80**

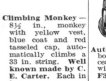

Climbing Monkey—8½ in., monkey with yellow vest, blue coat and red tasseled cap, automatically climbs a 33 in. string. **Well known made by C. E. Carter.** Each in box.
F3280—½ doz. in pkg.... Doz. **$2.25**

Auto Express—9⅜x3½ in. blue body, red wheels, gilt trim, concealed spring between rear wheels, with chauffeur, each in box.
F3259—1/12 doz. in pkg. Doz. **$8.50**

Auto Fire Engine—10x6½ in. yellow body, gilt boiler, silver trim, red wheels with imit. rubber tires, ringing gong, covered clock spring.
F3268—1 in box...... Each, **$1.30**

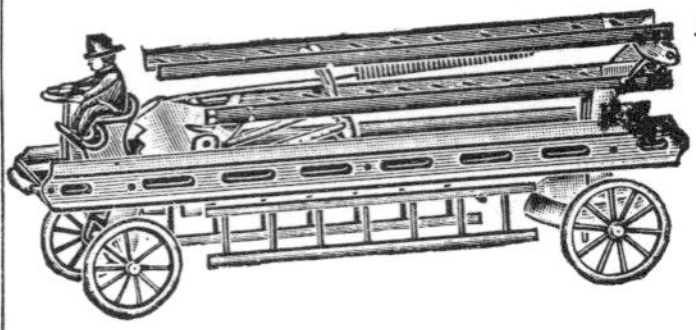

Auto Hook and Ladder—18x5 in., white body, red stripes and red wheels with **rubber tires**, rubber covered front bumper, two 9 in. ladders, one 27½ in. extension ladders which automatically raises when bumper strikes some object, covered clock spring.
F3263—1 in box. Each, **$1.85**

Train System—13½ in. over all, yellow and red engine, tender and car, 8 in. straight track, yellow and red stations at both ends, 1 with coil bumper spring, other with spring action pusher, red overhead type bridge, 9x6x7 in. paper machine tunnel painted to represent mountain scene.
F3293—1 in box...... Each, **$2.90**

STAR VALUE

Aeroplane — 13 in. long, 10 in. wing spread, all steel, monoplane type, gray metal finish, bullseye insignia, yellow painted wheels and propeller, adjustable tail, pilot, each in box.
F3288—⅙ doz. in pkg. Doz. **$8.75**

Auto Hook and Ladder—13½x4 in., red body, gilt trim, yellow wheels with imit. rubber tires, two 10½ in. and one 9 in. yellow ladders, blue painted driver and steersman, covered clock spring.
F3269—1 in box .... Each, **$1.35**

"Tip Top" Porter—6⅜ in., blue and yellow figure with red hat, walks in natural manner pushing 2½x3½ in. blue and yellow cart, yellow wheels. Can be filled with small toys, etc., each in box.
F3283—¼ doz. in pkg.. Doz. **4.00**

Limousine—11x3½x5 in. red and black body, hinged doors with locks, yellow open spokes, imit. rubber tire wheels. Can be set to run straight or in a circle. Each in box.
F3250—1/12 doz. in pkg. Doz. **$5.40**

Aeroplane—16x12x5½ in., runs on floor, red wings, yellow body, blue painted aviator, red, white and blue bullseye on wings and tail, propeller revolves, imit. rubber tire disc landing wheels.
F3289—1 in box...... Each, **$1.50**

Farmer Boy—6 in. red and yellow figure, 2½x3 in. gray wheelbarrow with yellow open spoke wheels and wood handled hoe and rake, figure walks in natural manner pushing barrow, long spring action., each in box.
F3286—¼ doz. in pkg. Doz. **$4.20**

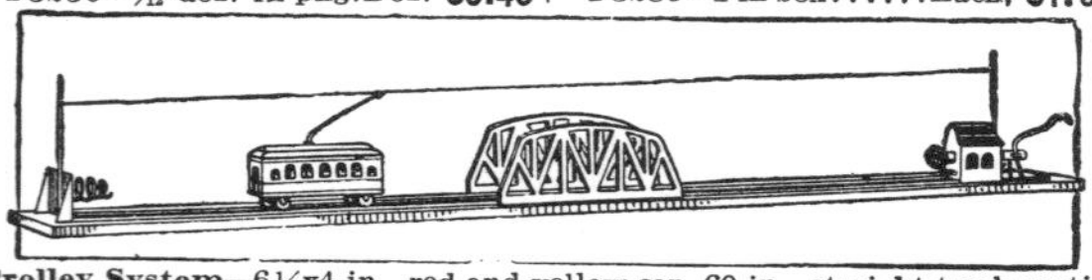

Trolley System—6¼x4 in., red and yellow car, 60 in., straight track on tin base, 12 in. red overhead type bridge, red station at one end, continuous action by holding crank spring bumper at other, spring pusher at station pushes car down track, overhead trolley.
F3291—1 in box...... Each, **$1.50**

Grinder—4¼ in. red and blue figure, 3 in. grindstone and stand, 2¾x4½ in. base, grinder makes sparks fly from wheel, each in box.
F3271—¼ doz. in pkg. Doz. **$4.20**

Trick Auto—6¾ in. latest type touring car, bright red and yellow imit. rubber tire wheels with chauffeur. Auto darts ahead or backs up with erratic change of direction, each in box.
F3287—½ doz. in pkg... Doz. **$4.25**

Auto Dump Cart—9¼x4 in. blue body, red wheels, lever dumps body, concealed springs between rear wheels, with driver. Each in box.
F3264—1/12 doz. in box. Doz. **$8.75**

Artillery Truck—11½ in. gray steel body, red cartridge carrier, 2¼ in. disc wheels, 8 in. adjustable black steel cannon, wood projectils, chauffeur, shoots long distance.
F3261—1 in box...... Each, **$1.35**

IMPORTED MECHANICAL TOYS

A selected line of the most reliable makes, good springs, wound by attached keys, unless stated.

Mechanical Snake—12 in., jointed wood body on wheels, bright green and yellow finish, crawls like wiggling snake.
F6550—½ doz. in box ...... Doz. **$2.20**

Dancing Figures—Average 6¾ in. 3 styles, bear, baby and dude negro, painted in bright colors, vibrating dancing motions.
F6552—Asstd. ½ doz. in box. Doz. **$4.20**

Touring Car—10x3½x3½ in., spiral spring red body, black striped mud guard, open spoke wheels, chauffeur runs straight or in circle.
F6559—⅓ doz. in box.. Doz. **$4.50**

Locomotive and Tender—12 in. overall, 8 wheel double truck, litho green and black yellow stripes, foot rail, hand bar, detachable tender.
F6557—⅓ doz. in box.. Doz. **$4.50**

Dancing Bear—8 in. brown enameled, vibrating dancing motion.
F6553—1/12 doz. in box.. Doz. **$6.75**

Bicycle Rider—8 in., brightly painted imitation rubber tires, rider, pedals, chain gear, strong spring, runs in circle.
F6556—1/12 doz. in box.. Doz. **$8.50**

Mechanical Beetle—6½ in. brightly painted, natural motion, crawls, stops, lifts wings and continues crawling, strong spring, key attached.
F6554—1/12 doz. in box.. Doz. **$9.50**

Mechanical Toy Autos

These values cannot be beaten. There is a tremenduous demand for mechanical toys.

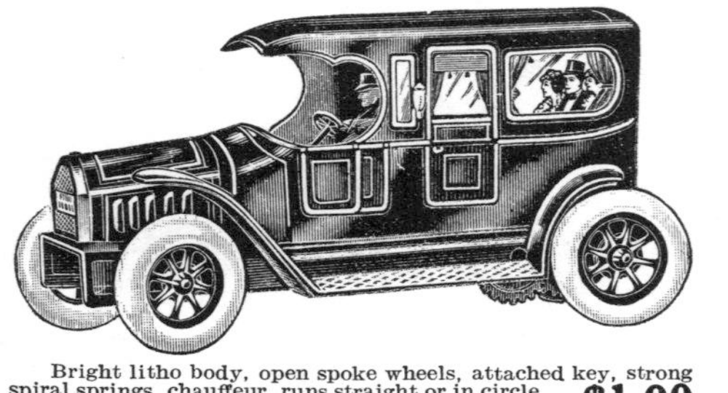

Bright litho body, open spoke wheels, attached key, strong spiral springs, chauffeur, runs straight or in circle.
F3248—6x2x3 in. 1 doz. in box............ Doz. **$1.90**
F3247—8x2⅞x3¾ in. ½ doz. in pkg....... **3.75**

Touring Car—Length 11⅜ in., heavy gauge steel, cream color body, gold trim, red rounded mud guards and running board, red open spoke wheels, imit. rubber tires, tank in rear, chauffeur and passenger.
F3251—1 in box...... Each, **$1.80**

Auto Fire Engine—11¾x7¼ in., yellow body, gilt boiler, aluminum trim, red wheels, imit. rubber tires, ringing gong, covered spring.
F3262—1 in box...... Each, **$1.75**

"Jazzbo" Jim Jigger Toy

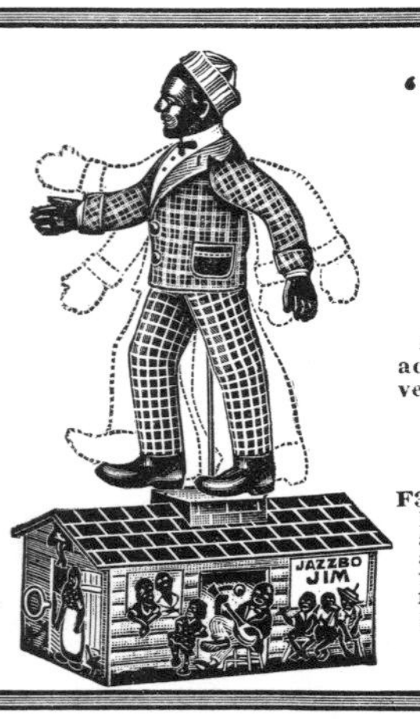

Attractively painted. Fine action mechanical toy at a very low price. Order now.

F3281—Ht. 10¼ in., bright litho figure, jointed legs and arms, 5¼x3½ in. platform, attractive litho log cabin with darky figures, speed regulates jigs, each in box. ½ doz. in pkg. Doz. **$4.75**

AIR RIFLES TOY PISTOLS AND GUNS

Well known makes. Our buyers have taken special care in picking out the most popular selling numbers from these reliable manufacturers.

All boys want an air rifle, toy pistol or gun, and an attractive display will draw the business to your store. Compare our prices with others.

THE FAMOUS "DAISY" AIR RIFLES

The following numbers represent the best sellers from the well known "Daisy" line. All models will shoot either air rifle shot or darts except F2631, which is for shot only. All with walnut stocks and accurately sighted.

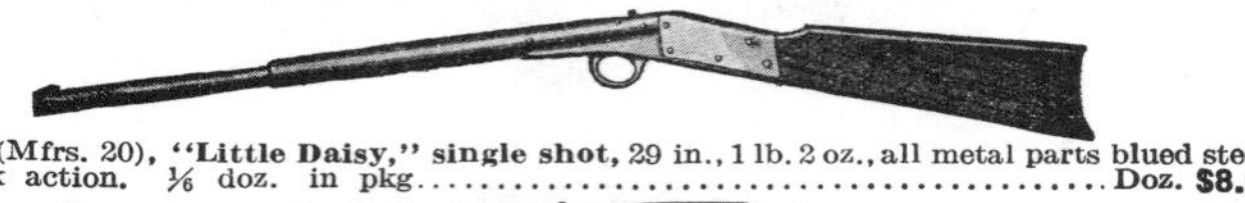

F2631—(Mfrs. 20), **"Little Daisy," single shot,** 29 in., 1 lb. 2 oz., all metal parts blued steel, break action. 1/6 doz. in pkg....Doz. **$8.50**

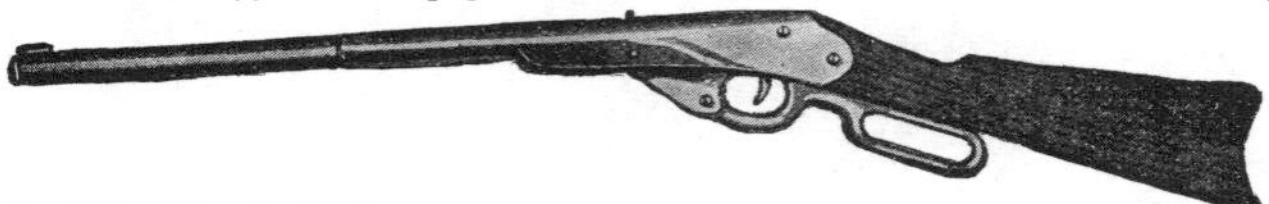

F2632—(Mfrs. 12), **single shot,** 31½ in., 1 lb. 8 oz., nickel plated barrel, blued steel lever action. 1/12 doz. in pkg....Doz. **$16.50**

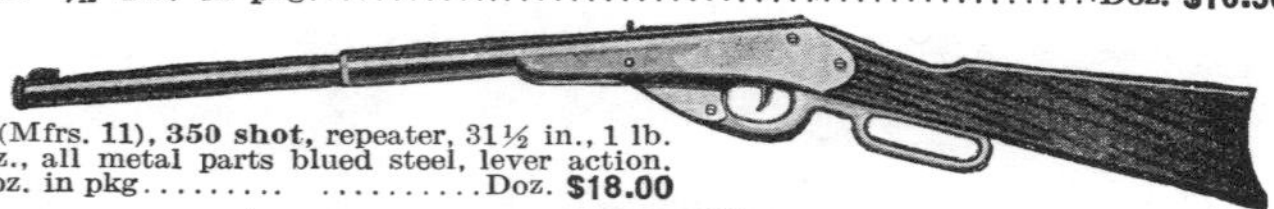

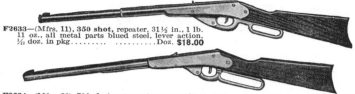

F2633—(Mfrs. 11), **350 shot,** repeater, 31½ in., 1 lb. 11 oz., all metal parts blued steel, lever action. 1/12 doz. in pkg....Doz. **$18.00**

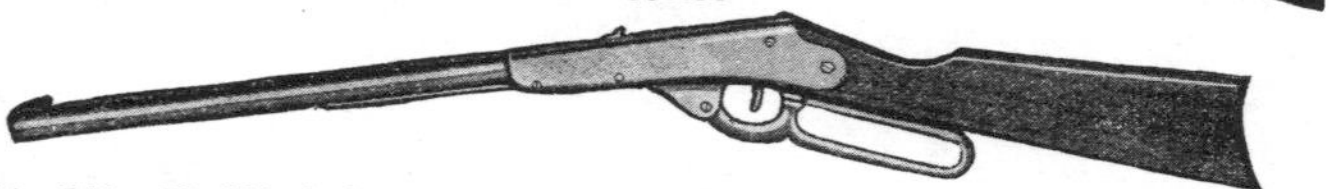

F2634—(Mfrs. 30), **500 shot,** automatic repeater 33 in., 2 lbs. 7 oz., all metal parts blued steel, lever action. 1/12 doz. in pkg....Doz. **$22.50**

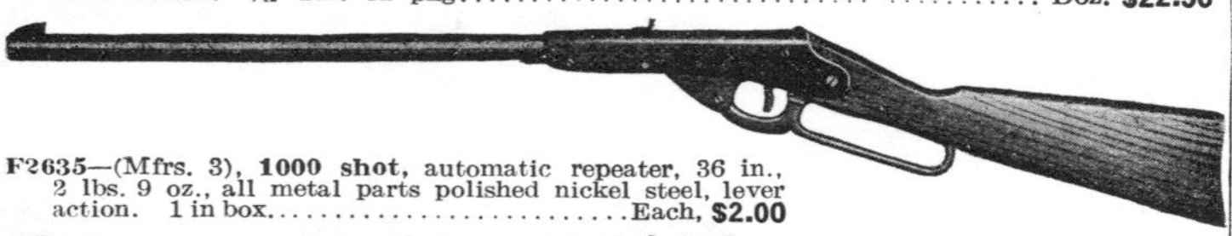

F2635—(Mfrs. 3), **1000 shot,** automatic repeater, 36 in., 2 lbs. 9 oz., all metal parts polished nickel steel, lever action. 1 in box....Each, **$2.00**

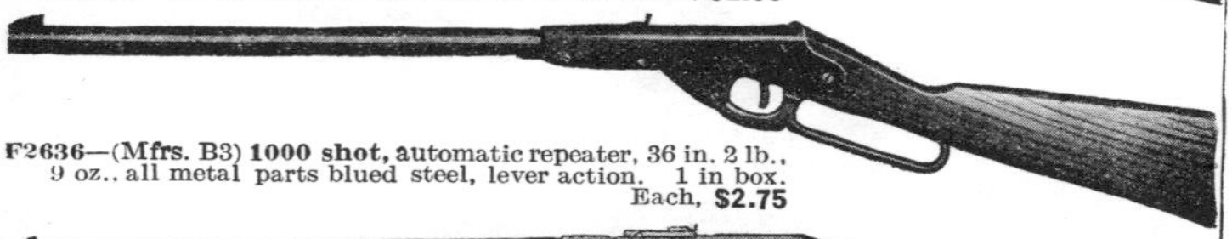

F2636—(Mfrs. B3) **1000 shot,** automatic repeater, 36 in. 2 lb., 9 oz., all metal parts blued steel, lever action. 1 in box. Each, **$2.75**

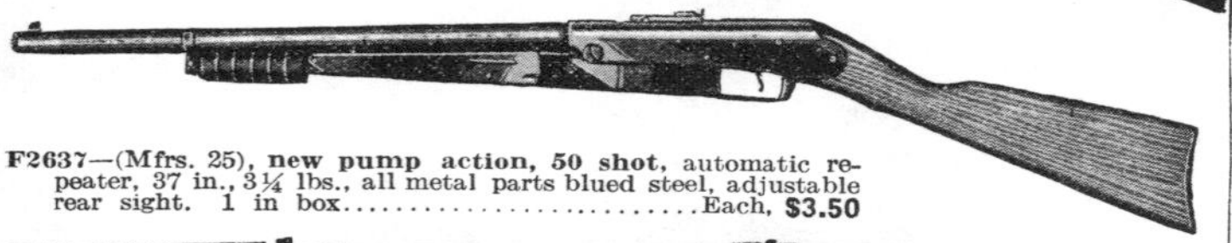

F2637—(Mfrs. 25), **new pump action, 50 shot,** automatic repeater, 37 in., 3¼ lbs., all metal parts blued steel, adjustable rear sight. 1 in box....Each, **$3.50**

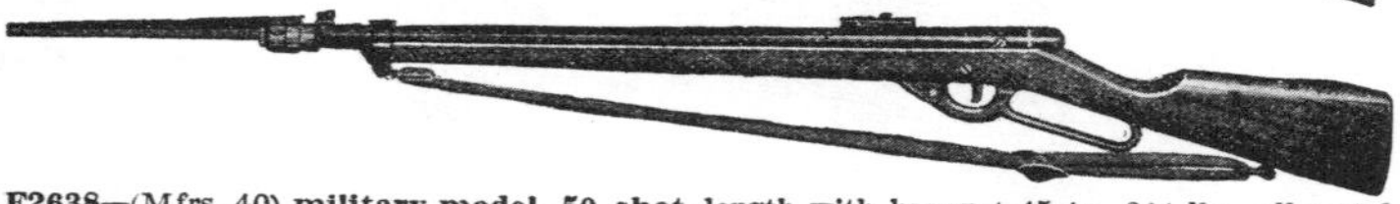

F2638—(Mfrs. 40), **military model, 50 shot,** length with bayonet 45 in., 3¾ lbs., all metal parts blued steel, lever action, rifle barrel with adjustable rear sight, removable bayonet with harmless rubber tip, heavy canvas shoulder strap with adjustable buckle and fasteners. 1 in box....Each, **$3.50**

AIR RIFLE SHOT

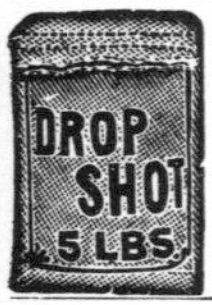

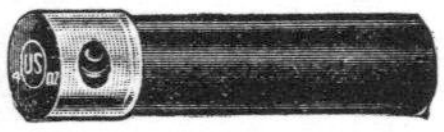

Drop Shot—

F2650—5 lbs. in canvas bag. BAG (5 lbs.), **$0.65**
F2651—25 " " " " (25 lbs.), **3.00**

Boy Scout "BB" Shot—2⅞x⅞ in. shell tube with perforated side sliding band to permit shot to be taken out, contains 4 ozs. of shot.

F2653—2 doz. shells in box....Doz. **65c**
Case of 100 shells, **$5.00** (Total $1.30)

"UPTON" AIR RIFLES—All Gun Metal Finished

Guaranteed against all defects of material and workmanship. Automatic safety device, prevents premature discharge and injury to fingers. Walnut stocks, gun metal finish barrels and metal parts, accurately sighted.

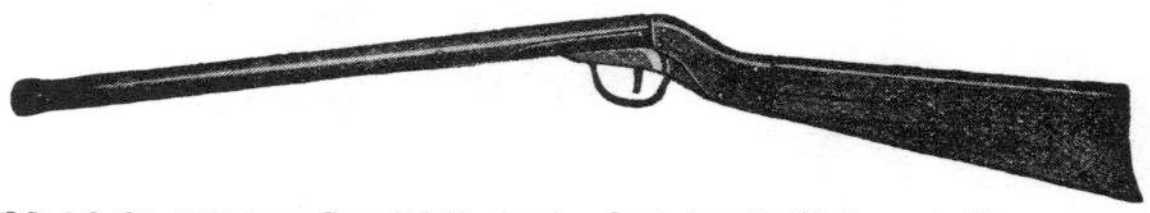

F2649—(Model C), **"Upton Special," single shot,** length 29 in., wt. 20 oz., round barre break action. 1/12 doz. in pkg....Doz. **$7.10**

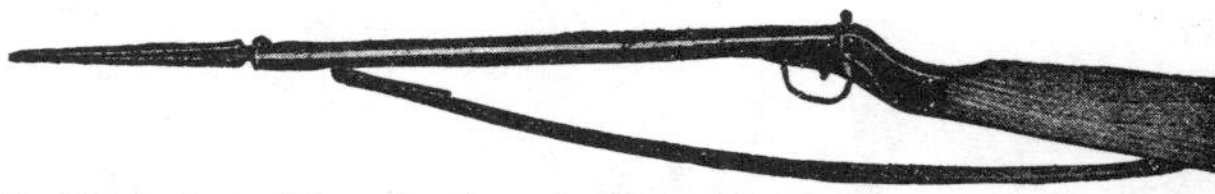

F2621—**Single shot** military air rifle, spring action, length 37 in., walnut finish stock, removable bayonet and adjustable sling, wt. 26 ounces, each in carton. 1/6 doz. in pkg..Doz. **8.00**

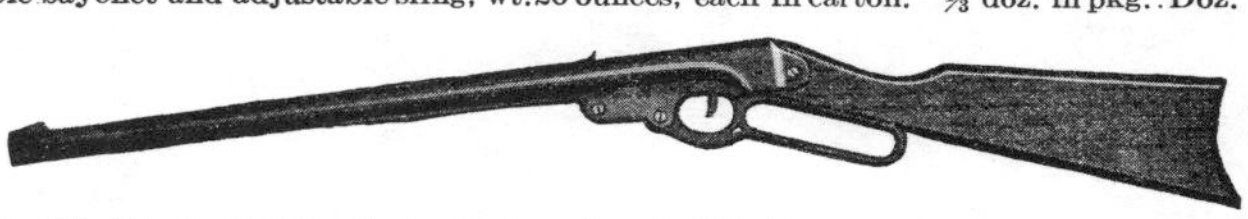

F2615—(Model D), **"Upton" single shot,** length 31½ in., wt. 34 oz., round tapering barrel, lever action. 1/12 doz. in pkg....Doz. **$12.00**

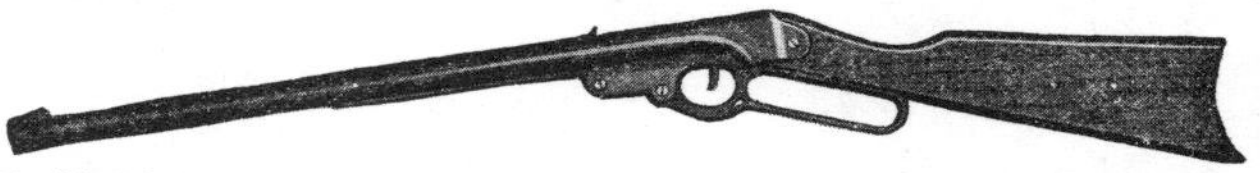

F2616—(Model E), **500 shot,** length 31½ in., wt. 34 oz., round tapering barrel, automatic shot retainer, lever action. 1/12 doz. in pkg....Doz. **$13.75**

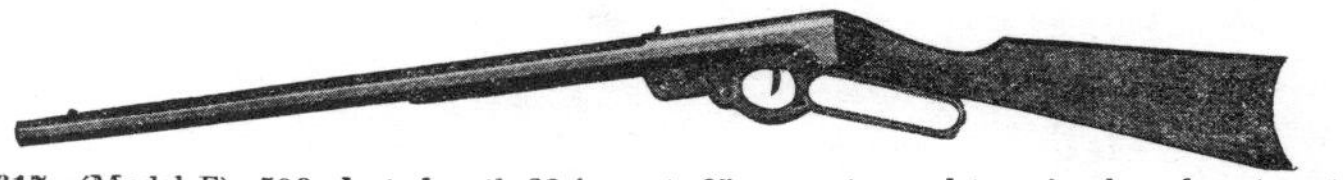

F2617—(Model F), **500 shot,** length 33 in., wt. 35 oz., octagonal tapering barrel, automatic shot retainer, lever action. 1 in pkg....Each, **$1.35**

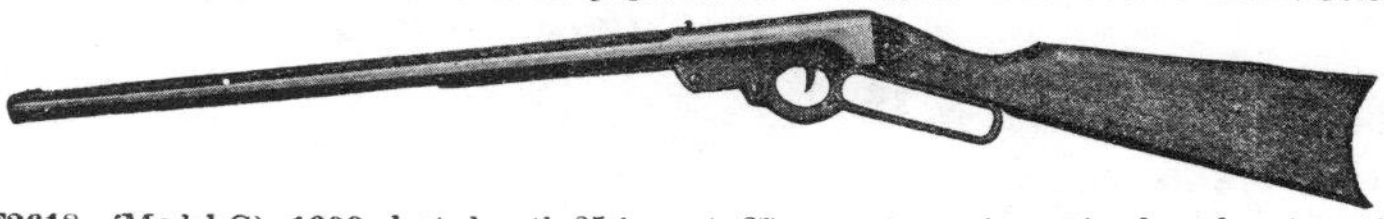

F2618—(Model G), **1000 shot,** length 35 in., wt. 37 oz., octagonal tapering barrel, automatic shot retainer, lever action. 1 in pkg....Each, **$1.50**

"LITTLE DAISY" RIFLE POP GUNS

Harmless, shoot corks, etc. single shot, break action, all metal parts blued steel, walnut stock, each with cork and string.

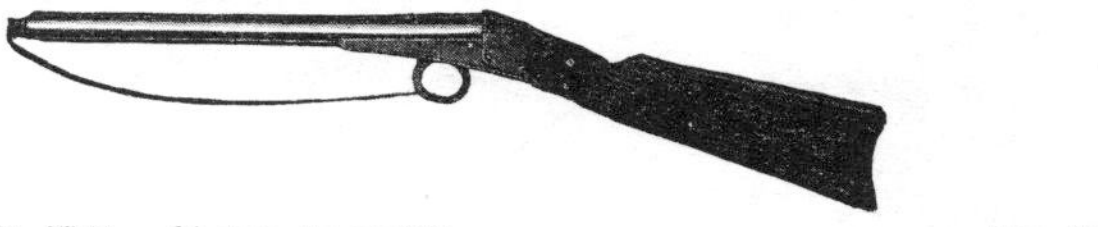

F2643—(Mfrs. 10), 17 in., ¼ doz. in carton....Doz. **$3.60**

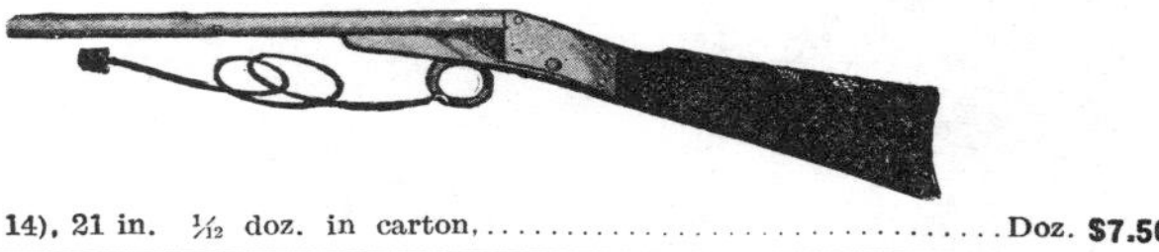

F2644—(Mfrs. 14), 21 in. 1/12 doz. in carton....Doz. **$7.50**

"SCOUT" AUTOMATIC TOY PISTOLS AND GUNS

Miniature automatic, shoots as fast as the trigger can be pulled, making a sharp cracking sound like a cap pistol without the use of caps

Note: As no caps are used, fireworks license is not necessary to sell this item.

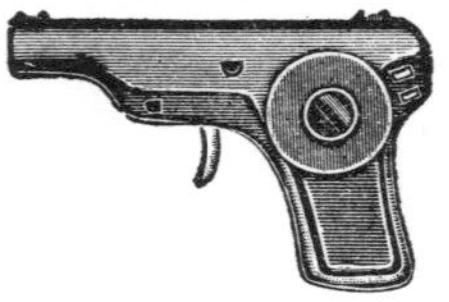

F2628—5½ in. long, heavy blued steel barrel and stock, shaped quick pull trigger, patent diaphragm action, makes a loud report. Each in box, 1 doz. in pkg....Doz. **96c**

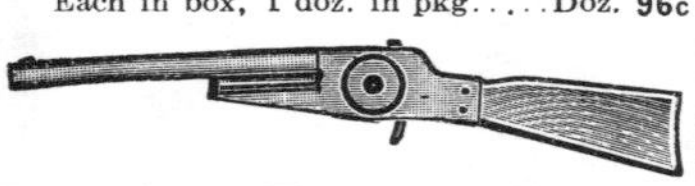

F2641—18½ in., Winchester rifle type, blued steel barrel and repeating chamber, rear and front sights, trigger, patented diaphragm action, makes loud report. Each in box, 1 doz. in pkg....Doz. **$2.15**

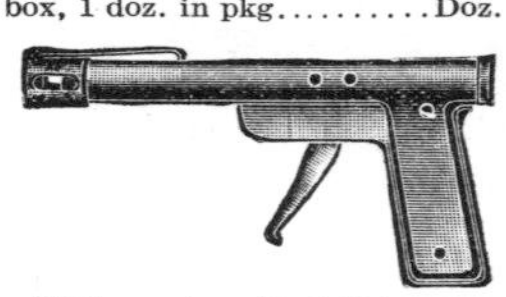

F2659—6¾ in., automatic Colt type, repeating pistol, blue steel, trigger action, cork is automatically inserted and exploded. Each in box, ½ doz. in pkg....Doz. **$2.25**

TARGET PISTOL AND AUTOMATIC POP GUN

All have stained wood stocks and gun metal finish barrels. Each in printed box with instructions.

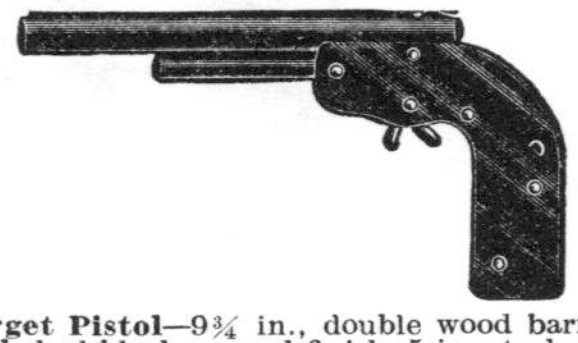

Target Pistol—9¾ in., double wood barrels, baked black enamel finish, 5 in. steel grip, makes loud repeating noise.
F2648—1 doz. in pkg....Doz. **95c**

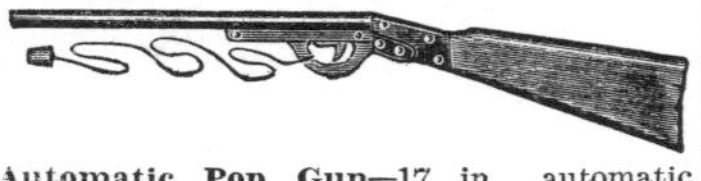

Automatic Pop Gun—17 in., automatic spring action, long string with cork.
F2639—1 doz. in pkg....Doz. **$2.25**

AUTOMATIC WATER PISTOLS

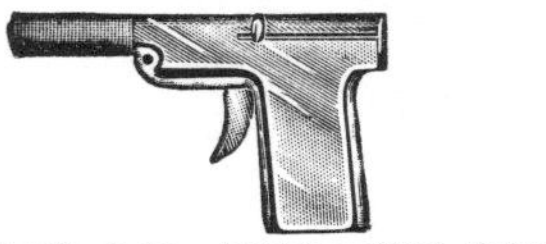

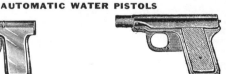

"Sure Shot"—5 in., bright natural finish metal body and grip, dummy trigger, brass barrel, lever action on side. Shoots 1 or several times.
F1666—1 doz. in box....Doz. **89c**

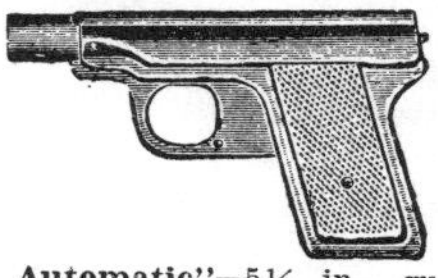

"Daisy Automatic"—5½ in., gun metal finish steel, double spring action barrel, corrugated pistol grip, trigger action, operates like genuine automatic pistol, shoots small repeating or large continuous stream. Each in carton with directions.
F1662—½ doz. in box....Doz. **$3.75**

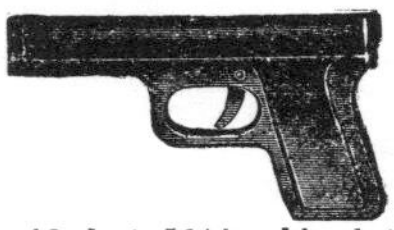

Repeater—10 shot, 5⅝ in., blued steel trigger action, automatic filler. Each in box with directions.
F1679—½ doz. in pkg....Doz. **$2.25**

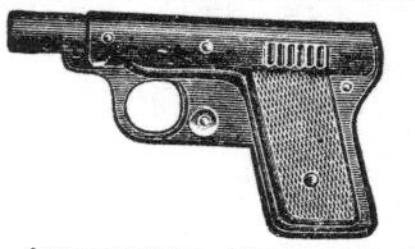

"Daisy" Automatic Repeater—5¾ in., blued steel, double spring barrel, guaranteed, shoots 5 streams of water in succession. Each in carton with directions.
F1615—1/6 doz. in pkg....Doz. **$4.50**

ARMY SIEGE GUN

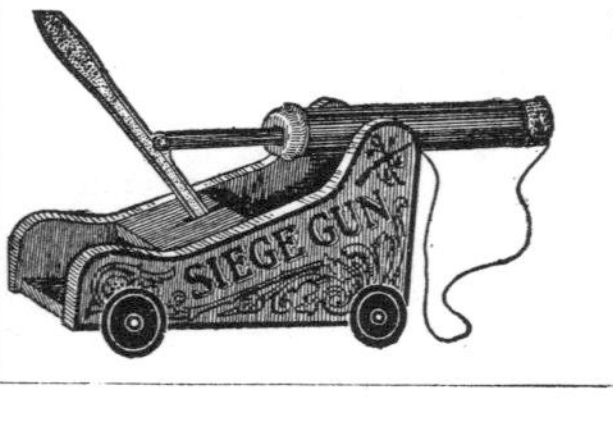

F2664—13 in. long, 6½ in. high, varnished and stenciled wood frame with solid metal wheels, 7 in. aluminum finish metal cannon with double spring, action and strong iron operating lever, cork string, each in box, 1/6 doz. in pkg. Doz. **$4.00**

NAVAL RAPID FIRE MACHINE GUN

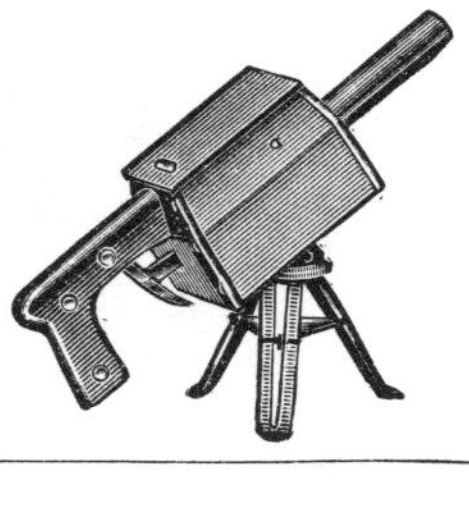

F2663—10 in. long, 6 in. high, all metal, shoots BB buckshot or any small round pellets, 1½x1x1 ammunition chamber, trigger action, rapid fire, set on tripod which revolves, can be raised or lowered for firing, with solder and tube of BB buckshot. 1/12 doz. in pkg. Doz. **$4.50**

BOYS' DRUMS

A complete line that covers every demand. Extra care has been given to the selection of these numbers as to quality of materials, workmanship and prices. These assortments give you the advantage of having a bigger variety of styles and sizes at the same prices you would pay for one style or size. Send us your order today.

METAL BODY DRUM ASST.

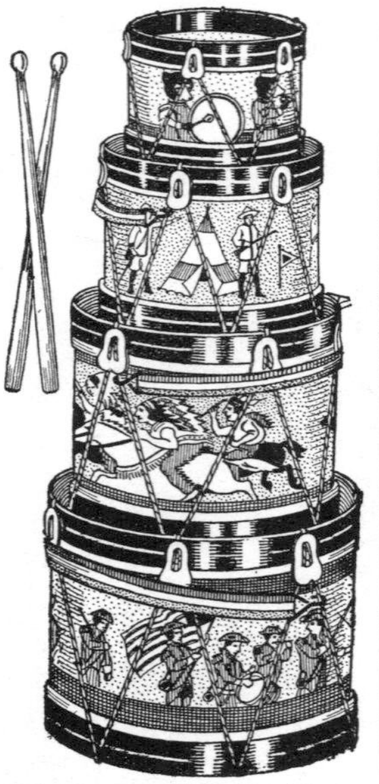

STAR VALUE F781—Metal bodies, bright colored National, Boy Scout, circus, Colonial soldier, Indian and Teddy Bear designs, silver gilt and colored bands, black hoops, with cord, web belts, sticks; all fiber heads and bottoms. Case contains:
6—7 in., retail for 50c
4—8 " " " 75c.
4—9 " " " $1.00.
2—10" " " $1.50.
1⅓ doz. in asst., 19 lbs. Asst. **$8.75**

FIBER HEAD WOOD SHELL DRUM ASST.

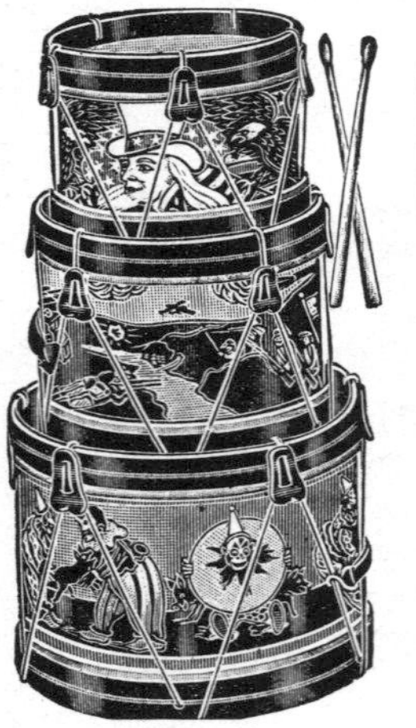

F782—Veneer wood shell, finished to represent oak and ash, high luster finish, fiber head, black painted wood hoops, gold stripe, cord adjustment, black leather ears, large sticks, with belt and hook. Case contains the following asst.:
½ doz. 7 in. to retail @ 50c.
⅓ " 8 " " @ $1.00.
⅙ " 10 " " @ $1.25.
1 doz. in case, 14 lbs..Case, **$6.25**

POPULAR PRICED METAL BODY DRUM ASSORTMENTS

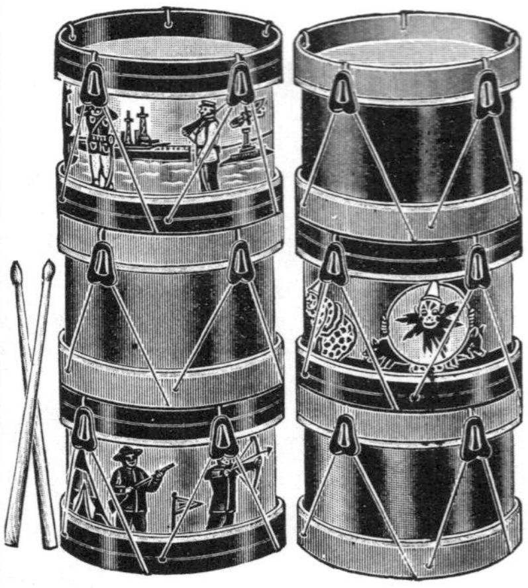

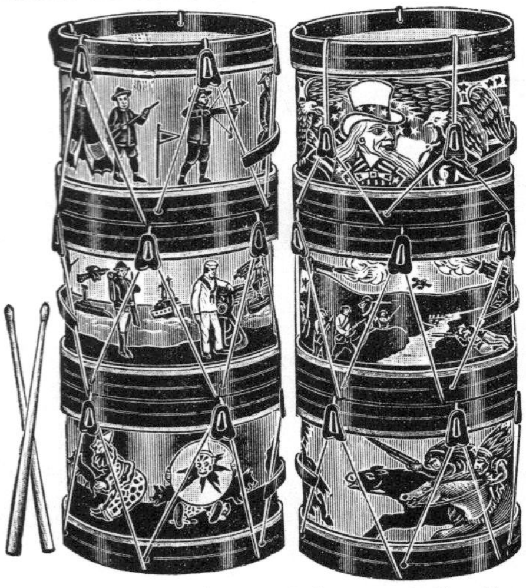

F774—6 styles, 7 in., metal body, fiber head and bottom. Boy Scout, U.S.A., clowns and plain, black painted hoops with gold stripes, cord and leather ears, shoulder straps, hook. ½ doz. in carton, 8 lbs.................................Doz. **$3.90**

F775—6 styles, 9 in., **war designs, metal sides,** fiber head and bottom, black painted hoops with gold stripes, cord adjustment with black leather ears, shoulder strap and hook. ½ doz. in carton, 14 lbs. Doz. **$8.50**

SHEEP HEAD METAL BODY DRUM

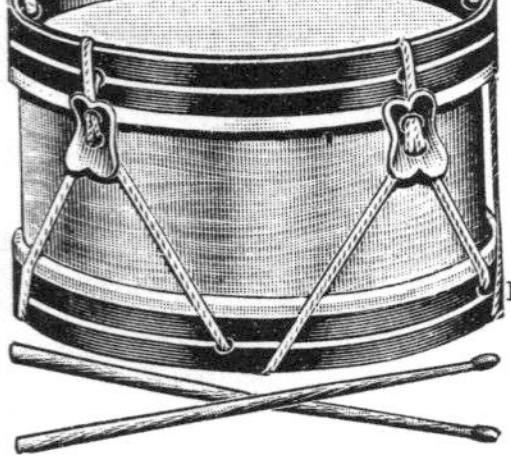

Asstd. 2 sizes

F776—2 sizes, 9 in., imitation ash, metal body, fiber head and bottom, 6 and 8½ in., gilt striped black wood hoops, cord leather ears, red, white and blue web belt. ½ doz. in crate, 15 lbs. Doz. **$8.50**

SHEEP HEAD NICKEL SHELL MILITARY DRUM ASST.

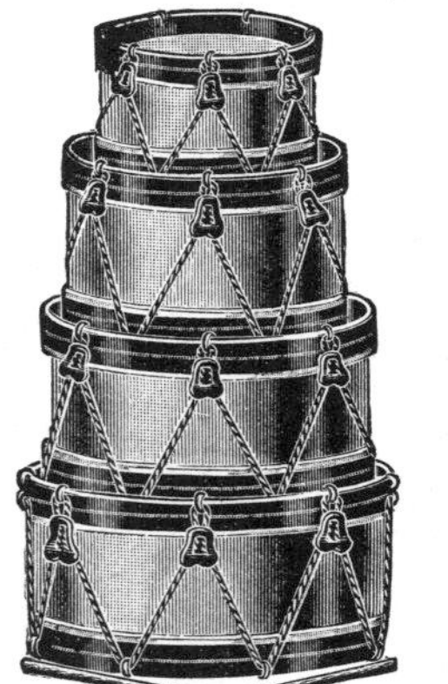

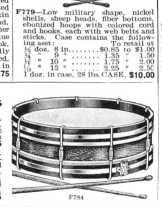

F779—Low military shape, nickel shells, sheep heads, fiber bottoms, ebonized hoops with colored cord and hooks, each with web belts and sticks. Case contains the following asst.: To retail at
½ doz. 8 in........$0.85 to $1.00
¼ " 9 " .... 1.35 " 1.50
⅙ " 10 " .... 1.75 " 2.00
1/12 " 12 " .... 2.25 " 2.5C
1 doz. in case, 28 lbs. CASE, **$10.00**

AUTOMATIC RATCHET DRUM

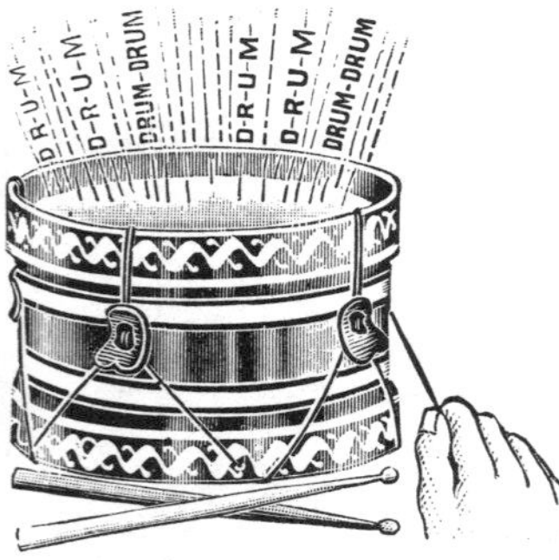

F789 — 7½ in., varnished oak finish body, black painted hoops, gold stripes, calfskin heads heavy cord bound, metal hooks, black leather ears, red, white & blue shoulder straps, with hook, sticks, drums automatically when knob at side is pulled, each in carton. ½ doz. in pkg., 10 lbs......Doz. **$8.75**

CALF HEAD WOOD SHELL MILITARY DRUM ASST.

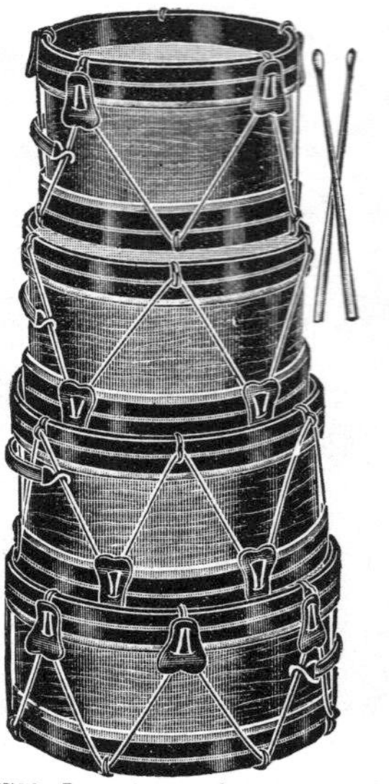

F780—Low shape, cherry and oak finish wood shells, ebonized hoops with hooks and colored cords, leather ears, fiber bottoms, web belts, sticks. Case contains the following asst:
¼ doz. 8 in.....To retail @ $1.50
1/12 " 9 " .... " @ 2.00
1/12 " 10 " .... " @ 2.50
1/12 " 11 " .... " @ 3.00
½ doz. in case, 18 lbs. Case, **$8.00**

"BOY SCOUT BAND" BASS DRUMS

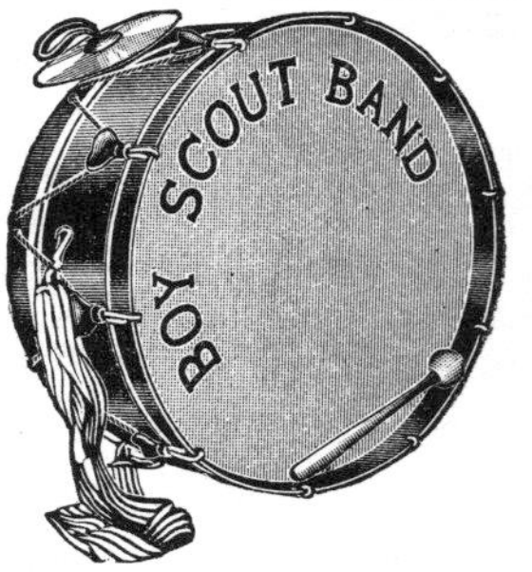

Nickel plated shells, black enameled wood hoops, heavy white cord with leather ears, for tightening, nickel ferrule sheep heads and bottomes, attached brass cymbals, solid rubber web shoulder straps, snap fasteners. 1 in carton, about 6 lbs.
F787—12 in...............Each, **$3.25**
F788—14 " .... " **4.00**

CALFSKIN HEAD DRUMS

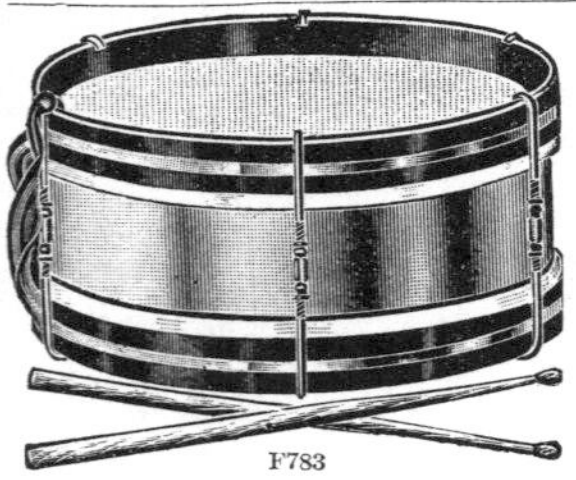

F783

F783 — 12 in., calfskin head, sheep bottom, 6 in. high stays, **solid nickel shell,** steel set bands, hardwood sticks. 1 in box, 7 lbs.........Each, **$3.75**

F784—Low orchestrain, 13 in. best calfskin head, sheep bottom, **varnished grained wood shell,** black enameled hoops, adjustable rod for tightening, heavy hook and sling, polished hardwood sticks. 1 in box. 8 lbs.............Each, **$5.25**

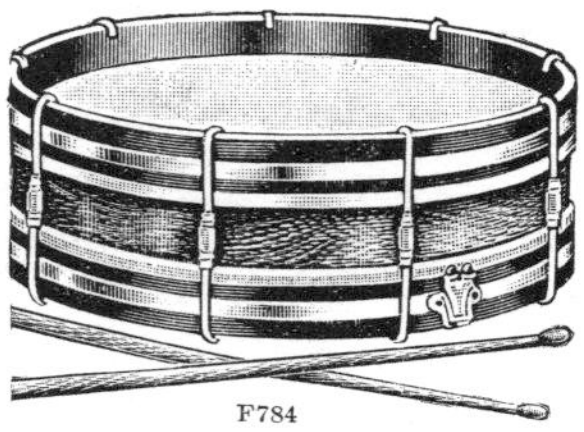

F784

A Big Advantage
Mail orders from this catalogue will enable you to have a variety of the kind of goods your customers ask for and keep your investment down to the minimum.

ALL METAL DRUMS

The cream sellers of the drum line. Our low prices give you the edge on competition

Exceptionally well made, all numbers except F798 lithographed in juvenile designs, white enameled heads, each with 2 smooth finish drum sticks. In corrugated shipping carton.

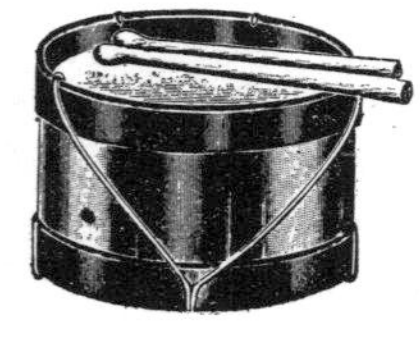

F798—5⅜ in., **red body,** wide black hoops. 6 doz. in carton. (Total $5.76) Doz. **96c**

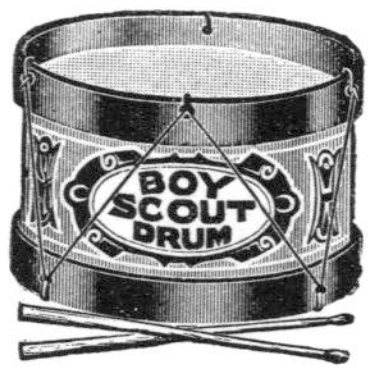

F797—7 in., **fancy litho sides,** Boy Scout and patriotic designs, black hoop. 2 doz. in carton. (Total $4.20) Doz. **$2.10**

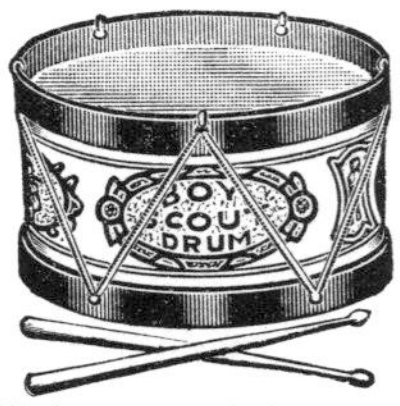

F795—8½ in., **fancy litho sides,** Boy Scout and patriotic designs, black hoops, heavy cord head adj. 1 doz. in carton. Doz. **$3.85**

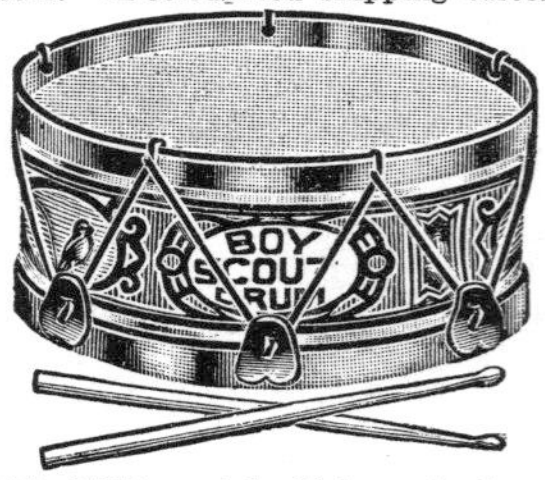

F796—Military style, 11 in., extra heavy cord, genuine leather ears large smooth finish mahogany stained drum sticks, red body, black hoops. ½ doz. in carton. Doz. **$7.50**

For Boys - Christmas Stockings - For Girls

This Solves the Problem—Armful of Toys for Each

We have had so many requests for an assortment for the boy and an assortment for the girl that we now offer two distinctive assortments. The boys' assortments contain distinctly boys' toys, such as guns, horns, automobiles, tops, musical toys, whistles, etc. Everything to please the boy. The girls' assortments are filled with pretty dollies, tea sets, story books, cut-out toys, kindergarten paper and many other articles to tickle the heart of the little girl. We make up two sizes for each. The smaller assortments are big value for 98 cents, but the larger contain much larger and better toys and a bigger variety. Some of the toys that we include retail elsewhere from 5 to 25 cents each. Each assortment is carefully selected and put up by us in our own store. Each one represents exceptional value for the money. Every toy in these assortments represents quality and a toy a child can play with and enjoy.

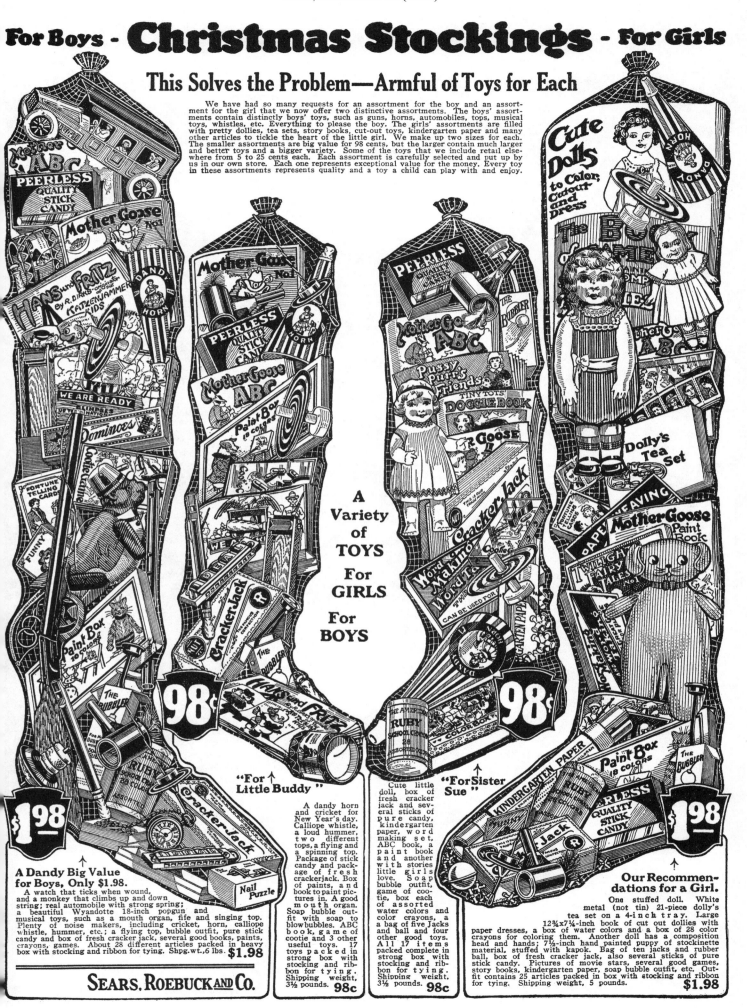

A Variety of TOYS For GIRLS For BOYS

"For Little Buddy"

"For Sister Sue"

A Dandy Big Value for Boys, Only $1.98.

A watch that ticks when wound, and a monkey that climbs up and down string; real automobile with strong spring; a beautiful Wyandotte 18-inch popgun and musical toys, such as a mouth organ, fife and singing top. Plenty of noise makers, including cricket, horn, calliope whistle, hummer, etc.; a flying top, bubble outfit, pure stick candy and box of fresh cracker jack, several good books, paints, crayons, games. About 28 different articles packed in heavy box with stocking and ribbon for tying. Shpg.wt. 6 lbs. **$1.98**

SEARS, ROEBUCK AND CO.

A dandy horn and cricket for New Year's day. Calliope whistle, a loud hummer, two different tops, a flying and a spinning top. Package of stick candy and package of fresh crackerjack. Box of paints, and book to paint pictures in. A good mouth organ. Soap bubble outfit with soap to blow bubbles. ABC book, game of cootie and 3 other useful toys. 17 toys packed in strong box with stocking and ribbon for tying. Shipping weight, 3½ pounds. **98c**

Cute little doll, box of fresh cracker jack and several sticks of pure candy, kindergarten paper, word making set, ABC book, a paint book and another with stories little girls love. Soap bubble outfit, game of cootie, box each of assorted water colors and color crayons, a bag of five Jacks and ball and four other good toys. All 17 items packed complete in strong box with stocking and ribbon for tying. Shipping weight, 3½ pounds. **98c**

Our Recommendations for a Girl.

One stuffed doll. White metal (not tin) 21-piece dolly's tea set on a 4-inch tray. Large 12¾x7¼-inch book of cut out dollies with paper dresses, a box of water colors and a box of 28 color crayons for coloring them. Another doll has a composition head and hands; 7½-inch hand painted puppy of stockinette material, stuffed with kapok. Bag of ten jacks and rubber ball, box of fresh cracker jack, also several sticks of pure stick candy. Pictures of movie stars, several good games, story books, kindergarten paper, soap bubble outfit, etc. Outfit contains 25 articles packed in box with stocking and ribbon for tying. Shipping weight, 5 pounds. **$1.98**

This "Ma~Ma" Doll Is Guaranteed Not to Break
Has Moving Eyes! Greatest Offer Ever Made!

TALKS   SLEEPS   WALKS

American Beauty.

WE GUARANTEE our AMERICAN BEAUTY DOLLS not to break under handling such as given by the average child. We do not claim that these dolls cannot be broken if deliberate attempt is made to break them. We set out to get real durable dolls for our customers, and we are sure our customers will appreciate our efforts.

Height, Abt., In.	Shpg. Wt., Lbs.	
19½	4½	$4.45
18	3¾	3.59
15	2¼	2.69
13	2	1.98

Here, at last, is the doll every little girl has wanted. Her mother will like it, too, for it is made so wonderfully strong that it will not break, even though it should accidentally fall out of its bed or carriage or get into any other such trouble. It is not delicate like the old fashioned china-bisque dolls yet it is just as pretty. In fact, it is prettier, as it looks like a sweet American child and is dressed like one. The beautiful head is of the strongest composition we could find, tinted in natural flesh color and crowned with a nice mohair wig. The eyes are most wonderful, set in very firmly and besides sleeping they will wink and blink as the child desires. Body is soft, stuffed plump, and designed so the doll can be made to toddle walk when guided by the arm, just like a real youngster learning its steps. Then there is the voice! When dolly is picked up she calls "Ma-Ma" just as plain and clear as can be. That pretty party style dress is of sheer white organdy, elaborately trimmed with lace. Bonnet to match has ribbon ties. Good white lawn, lace trimmed undergarments. The larger the size the better the proportions, and every doll is a great bargain value at our price!

Ma-Ma Doll With Moving Eyes.
Special $1.69

Well made character doll with hard to break composition head and soft mohair wig. Strongly set moving eyes that sleep, wink and blink. Cute romper suit of fancy printed cotton material, bonnet to match. Plump stuffed body fitted with a voice which calls "Ma-Ma" very plainly. Especially good doll for young children. Fancy socks and slippers. Height, about 13¼ inches. Shipping weight, 1½ pounds.

Beautiful Doll in Black Sateen Rompers.
Only $1.79

Just as pretty as her picture and a favorite with all children. Cute apron of orange colored cotton material having black and white squares and under this a nice quality black sateen romper with collar to match apron. Clever tam to match. Strong composition head with soft mohair wig and painted eyes. Stuffed body fitted with real plain "Ma-Ma" voice. Black sateen imitation socks and fancy imitation patent leather slippers. All composition arms and hands. Height, about 15 inches. Shipping wt., 2 lbs.

Big Baby Size
$2.39
Full 24½ Inches Tall

We believe this is the greatest value big baby size play doll to be found any place. Your child will have loads of fun and be kept real busy trotting this big doll around with her. The extra large size durable composition head is a lovely model with painted hair, eyes and features and has very lifelike flesh color tinting. The cloth covered body is well shaped and stuffed plump yet is light in weight, and doll will cry "Ma-Ma" most distinctly, as it is fitted with one of the best "Ma-Ma" voices on the market. Doll has neat checked cotton romper and hood to match. Has socks and baby size imitation black patent leather slippers.

Bargain Value Character Dolls.

$1.00

Good doll with a molded composition head fitted with bobbed style mohair wig. Painted eyes and features. Dress of good printed cotton material, neatly made; bonnet to match. Cloth covered stuffed body fitted with good "Ma-Ma" voice. Socks and slippers. Height, about 13½ inches.

79c

Neatly made doll with stuffed body fitted with good "Ma-Ma" voice. Rompers and bonnet of nice clean cotton materials. Composition head, painted hair, eyes and features. Socks and slippers. Height, about 13 in.

98c

Strong character doll with long, white, infant dress. Bonnet to match. Head and arms of strong composition. Painted hair, eyes and features. Stuffed body. Strong "Ma-Ma" voice. Height, about 13¼ inches.

SEARS, ROEBUCK AND CO.

Dishes and Girls Toys

Blue Enamel Sets for Your Party.
All metal, absolutely unbreakable toy dishes, rich turquoise blue enameled. The saucers are 2½ inches in diameter; cups, 1 inch high and 1⅓ inches in diameter; the teapot with cover is 3¼ inches high and 2½ inches in diameter; other pieces in proportion.

7-Piece Set. Two cups and saucers, creamer, sugar bowl, teapot and cover. Shpg.wt., 1 lb. **59c**

11-Piece Set. Four cups and saucers, creamer, sugar bowl, teapot and cover. Shipping weight, 1¼ lbs. **79c**

15-Piece Set. Six cups and saucers, creamer, sugar bowl, teapot and cover. Shipping weight, 1½ lbs. **98c**

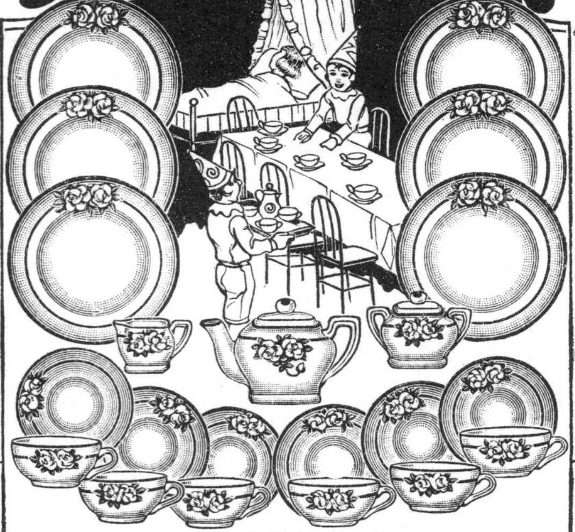

Decorated China Tea Sets.
Have your party in real style! Old time quality china, decorated in attractive colors. Teapot with cover, about 2½ inches; saucers, 2⅞ inches in diameter; cups, 2⅛ inches in diameter and about 1¼ inches high. Other pieces in proportion. Three different sets.

21-Piece Set. Six 4¼-in. plates, six cups and saucers as described above, sugar, creamer and teapot. Shipping weight 4½ pounds. **$1.48**

15-Piece Set. Six cups and saucers, sugar, creamer and teapot. Shpg. wt., 3 lbs. **98c**

9-Piece Set. Three cups and saucers, sugar, creamer and teapot with cover. Shipping weight, 2 pounds. **79c**

Beautiful Decorated White Enamel Sets.
White and blue enamel. Unbreakable. Look like china. Saucers, 2½ in. in diameter; cups, 1½ in. in diameter; teapot and cover, 3⅛ in. high; other pieces in proportion.

11 Pieces, $1.39. Four cups, four saucers, creamer, sugar, teapot and cover. Shpg. wt., 1¾ lbs. 49N1940 **$1.39**

7 Pieces, $1.00. Two cups, two saucers, sugar, creamer, teapot and cover. Shpg. wt., 2 lbs. 49N1941 **$1.00**

Dainty Japanese Ware.
This tiny set is the same beautiful solid green color of the famous Japanese Owaji ware used for fashionable tea parties. Two cups and saucers, creamer, and sugar bowl and teapot with covers. Strong green fiber tray. Diameter of teapot, 1 3/16 inches; other pieces in proportion. Shipping weight, 1 pound.
49N1604 .... **39c**

Baby Should Have This Set.
Absolutely unbreakable. Made of strong metal with an extra heavy coat of bird's egg blue enamel. Dainty and clean looking. The decorations are in white and colors. The little chicken group is in raised enamel. Plate, 8 inches in diameter; saucer, 5⅛ inches in diameter; cup, 2⅞ inches in diameter and 2 inches high. Shpg. wt., three pieces in box, 1½ lbs.
49N1939—Per Set........ **$1.19**

12-Piece Nickel Plated Etched Design, 98c.
Twelve pieces, nickel plated, highly polished etched scroll design. Three 6¼-inch plates, three 4¼-inch saucers, three cups 2⅜ inches high, 3¾-inch teapot, creamer and sugar bowl. Shipping weight, 2¾ pounds.
49N1820—Per set **98c**

These Sets Look Like Cut Glass.

Imitation Cut Glass Punch Set. Punch bowl, diameter, 4⅜ inches; six cups, size, 1¼ inches in diameter. Real heavy glass. **57c**

Imitation Cut Glass Table Set. 5¼-inch butter dish, 5-inch sugar bowl, creamer and 2½-inch spoon holder. **57c**

Remarkable Values in Enameled Tin Tea Sets.
Beautiful bluebird design enamel. 6¼-inch tray, 4¼-inch plates, 2¾-inch saucers, cups, 1⅞ inches in diameter, 2½-inch teapot.

20 Pieces, Six-Cup Set. Shipping weight, 2½ **59c**

14 Pieces, Four-Cup Set. Shipping weight, 1½ **39c**

8 Pieces, Two-Cup Set. Shipping weight, 1 pound. **25c**

Beautiful White Enamel Kitchen Furniture.

Just Like Mother's. A Quality Cabinet.
Plenty of dummy foods and pastry utensils. Two glass hinged doors at the top and two wooden hinged doors at the lower part of cabinet with a neat kiddie picture on each. Height, 16¾ inches; width, 10½ inches. This pretty white enameled cabinet makes a handsome gift for the girl. Shpg. wt., 6 lbs. **$2.39**

98c

Small Size Cabinet for the Little Cook.
Two open compartments and two lower compartments with doors. Dummy foods and small size pastry utensils included. Height, 12½ inches; width, 11¾ inches.

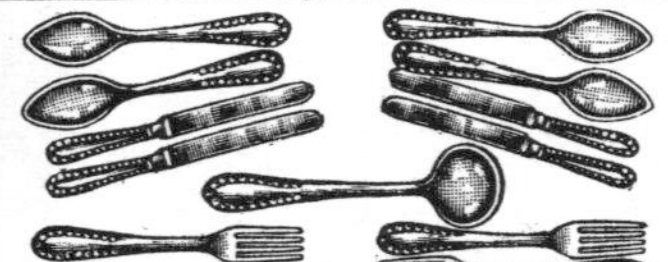

13 Pretty Toy Knives, Forks and Spoons.
Four knives, four forks, four spoons and one ladle. Heavy white metal. Length of knife, 4⅛ inches, other pieces in proportion. Shipping weight, 15 ounces. **47c**

Girls! Something New for You.
"Betty Taplin" real egg beater, aluminum grater, mixing bowl, 5 in. across, mixing spoon. Shpg. wt., 8 oz. **39c**

Your Party Not Complete Without This Pretty Sanitas Set.
Consists of a 10-inch centerpiece and four 4½-inch doilies. Mothers know how easy Sanitas is kept clean. Buff color decorated with blue Dutch kiddies design. **48c**

Toy Food to Complete Your Table.
Twelve stiff 2-inch cardboard plates, look like silver. On each plate is imitation food. Shpg. wt., per box, 12 pieces, 10 oz. **39c**

Girls! Make Your Own Pies and Cakes.
A dandy toy domestic science pastry set. Smooth bread board, 8x8 inches, masher, 6 inches high and rolling pin, about 10½ inches long and 1⅓ inches in diameter; aluminum measuring cup and brightly polished one-cup sifter with wire bottom. **59c**

Beautiful Enameled Tin 4-Pc. Dutch Kiddie Pantry Set.

A bread box, 4½x2⅜ inches; cake tin, 2⅝x1¾ in.; flour can, 2x2 inches; sugar can, 1½x1⅛ in. Trimmed in gilt. Packed in neat box. Shipping weight, 1 lb. **29c**

A 5-Piece Kitchen Set Like Mamma's.
Made of metal. Average length, 4¾ in. Shipping weight, 7 ounces.
49N1951.. **19c**

Art Linen Toy Luncheon Set.
Every little girl should have her own luncheon set. Very pretty, in ecru color with blue picot edging. Centerpiece has four nursery figures and each napkin one figure in very attractive colors. Centerpiece, 20x20 in.; napkins, 5x5 in. **69c**

SEARS, ROEBUCK AND CO.

Mechanical Toys

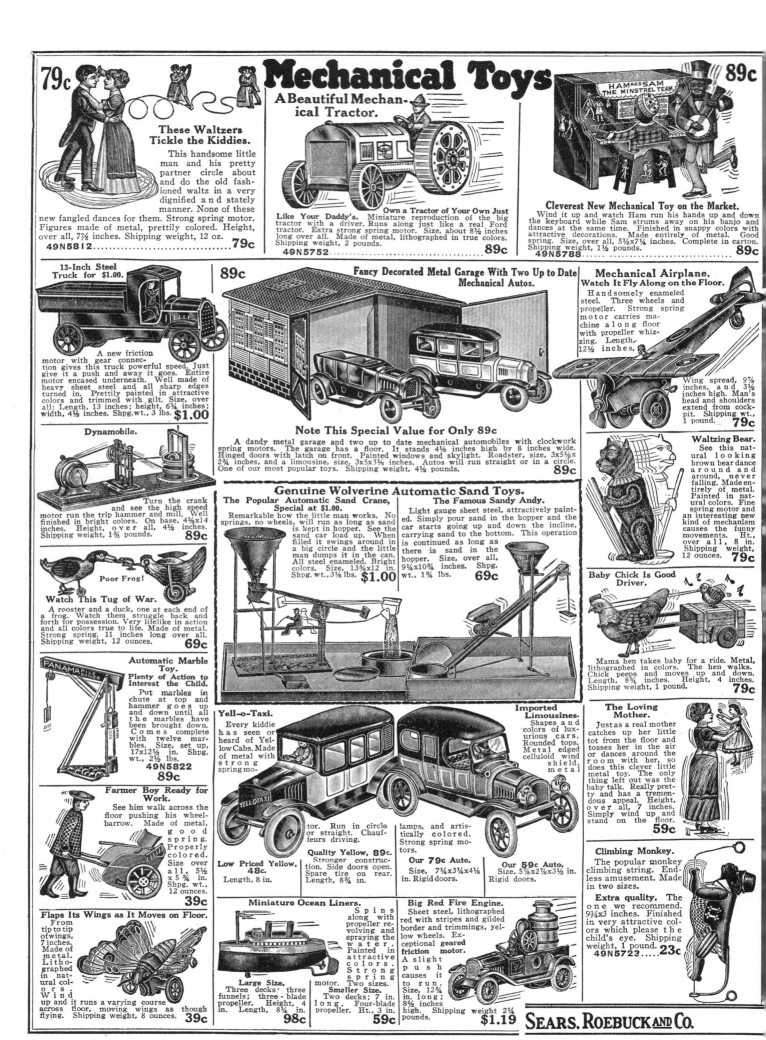

79c

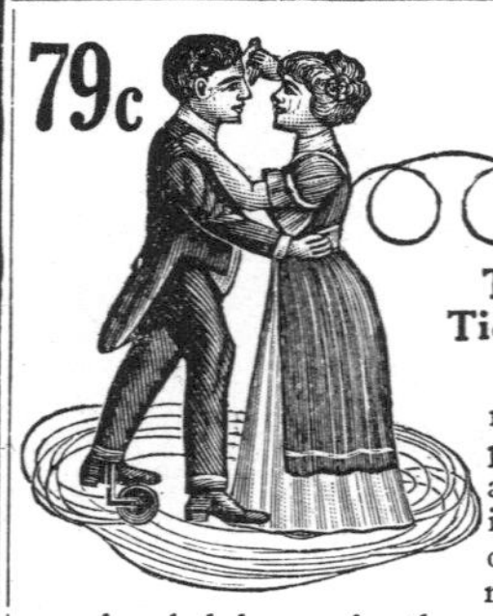
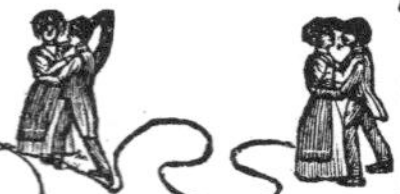

These Waltzers Tickle the Kiddies.

This handsome little man and his pretty partner circle about and do the old fashioned waltz in a very dignified and stately manner. None of these new fangled dances for them. Strong spring motor. Figures made of metal, prettily colored. Height, over all, 7⅞ inches. Shipping weight, 12 oz.

49N5812..**79c**

A Beautiful Mechanical Tractor.

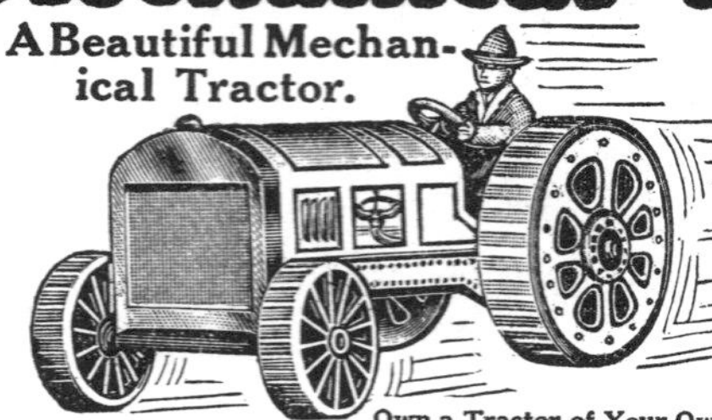

Own a Tractor of Your Own Just Like Your Daddy's. Miniature reproduction of the big tractor with a driver. Runs along just like a real Ford tractor. Extra strong spring motor. Size, about 8½ inches long over all. Made of metal, lithographed in true colors. Shipping weight, 2 pounds.

49N5752..**89c**

89c

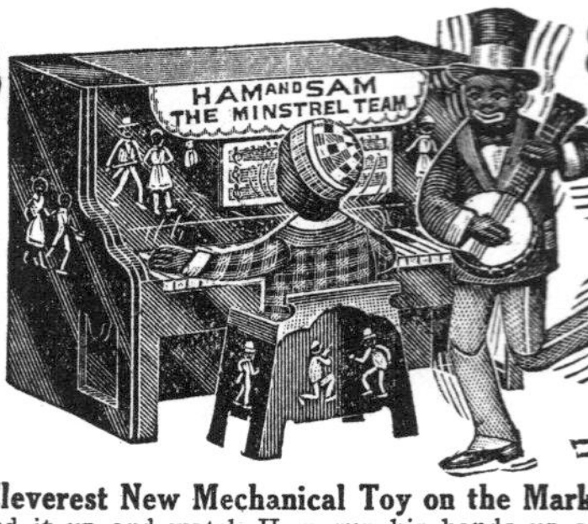

Cleverest New Mechanical Toy on the Market.

Wind it up and watch Ham run his hands up and down the keyboard while Sam strums away on his banjo and dances at the same time. Finished in snappy colors with attractive decorations. Made entirely of metal. Good spring. Size, over all, 5½x7¼ inches. Complete in carton. Shipping weight, 1½ pounds.

49N5788..**89c**

13-Inch Steel Truck for $1.00.

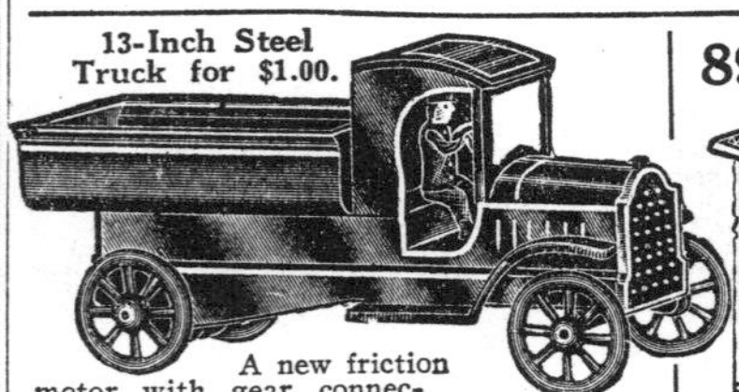

A new friction motor with gear connection gives this truck powerful speed. Just give it a push and away it goes. Entire motor encased underneath. Well made of heavy sheet steel and all sharp edges turned in. Prettily painted in attractive colors and trimmed with gilt. Size, over all: Length, 13 inches; height, 6¼ inches; width, 4½ inches. Shpg.wt., 3 lbs. **$1.00**

Dynamobile.

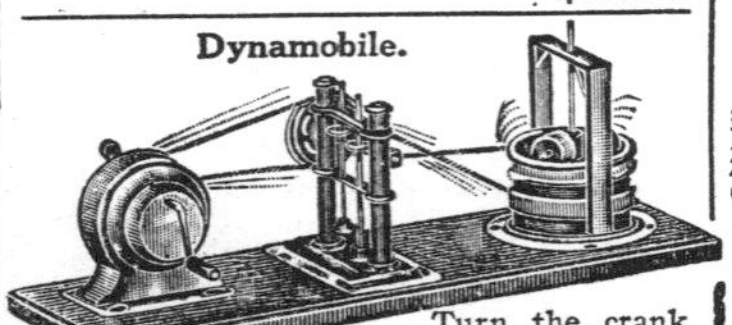

Turn the crank and see the high speed motor run the trip hammer and mill. Well finished in bright colors. On base, 4½x14 inches. Height, over all, 4½ inches. Shipping weight, 1¾ pounds. **89c**

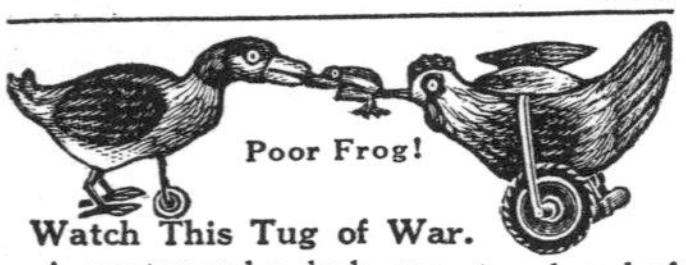

Poor Frog!

Watch This Tug of War.

A rooster and a duck, one at each end of a frog. Watch them struggle back and forth for possession. Very lifelike in action and all colors true to life. Made of metal. Strong spring. 11 inches long over all. Shipping weight, 12 ounces. **69c**

Automatic Marble Toy.

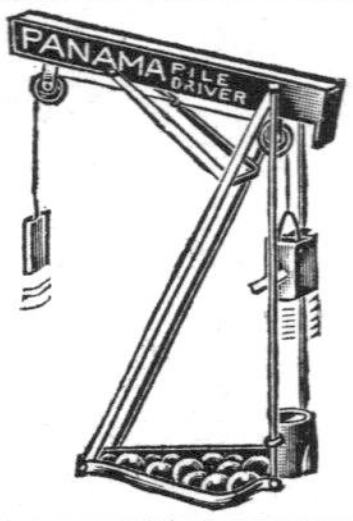

Plenty of Action to Interest the Child.

Put marbles in chute at top and hammer goes up and down until all the marbles have been brought down. Comes complete with twelve marbles. Size, set up, 17x12½ in. Shpg. wt., 2½ lbs.

49N5822

89c

Farmer Boy Ready for Work.

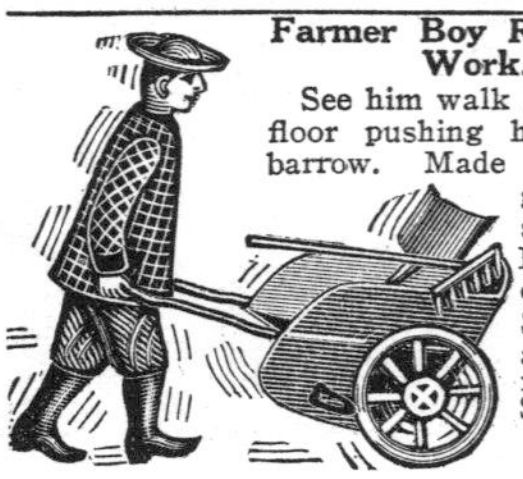

See him walk across the floor pushing his wheelbarrow. Made of metal, good spring. Properly colored. Size over all, 5½ x 5¾ in. Shpg. wt., 12 ounces.

39c

Flaps Its Wings as It Moves on Floor.

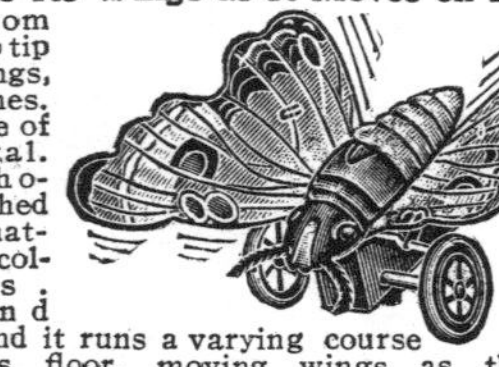

From tip to tip of wings, 7 inches. Made of metal. Lithographed in natural colors. Wind up and it runs a varying course across floor, moving wings as though flying. Shipping weight, 8 ounces. **39c**

89c

Fancy Decorated Metal Garage With Two Up to Date Mechanical Autos.

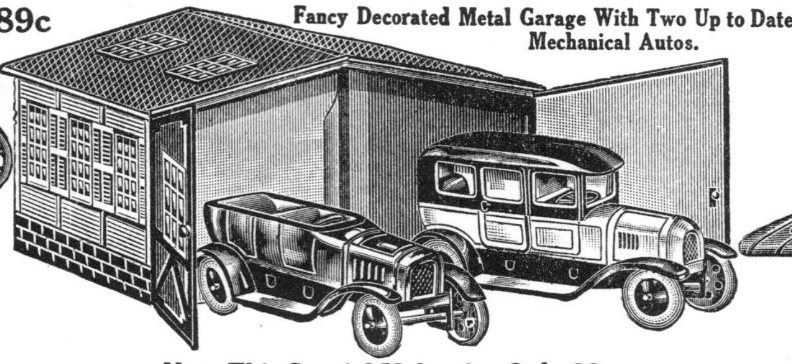

Note This Special Value for Only 89c

A dandy metal garage and two up to date mechanical automobiles with clockwork spring motors. The garage has a floor. It stands 4½ inches high by 8 inches wide. Hinged doors with latch on front. Painted windows and skylight. Roadster, size, 3x5½x2¾ inches, and a limousine, size, 3x5x3⅛ inches. Autos will run straight or in a circle. One of our most popular toys. Shipping weight, 4½ pounds. **89c**

Genuine Wolverine Automatic Sand Toys.

The Popular Automatic Sand Crane, Special at $1.00.

Remarkable how the little man works. No springs, no wheels, will run as long as sand is kept in hopper. See the sand car load up. When filled it swings around in a big circle and the little man dumps it in the can. All steel enameled. Bright colors. Size, 13⅜x12 in. Shpg. wt., 3⅛ lbs. **$1.00**

The Famous Sandy Andy.

Light gauge sheet steel, attractively painted. Simply pour sand in the hopper and the car starts going up and down the incline, carrying sand to the bottom. This operation is continued as long as there is sand in the hopper. Size, over all, 9¼x10¾ inches. Shpg. wt., 1¾ lbs. **69c**

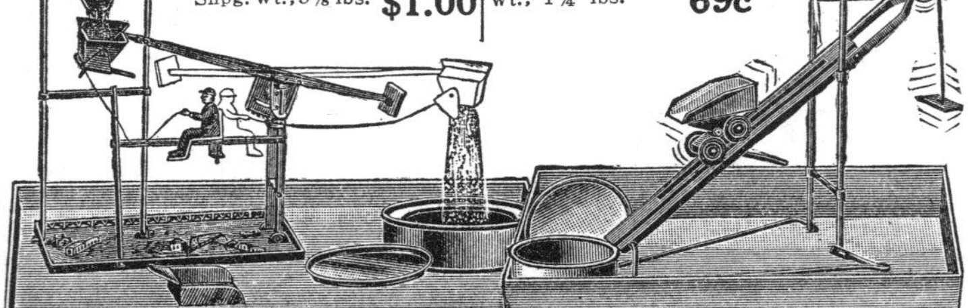

Yell-o-Taxi.

Every kiddie has seen or heard of Yellow Cabs. Made of metal with strong spring motor. Run in circle or straight. Chauffeurs driving.

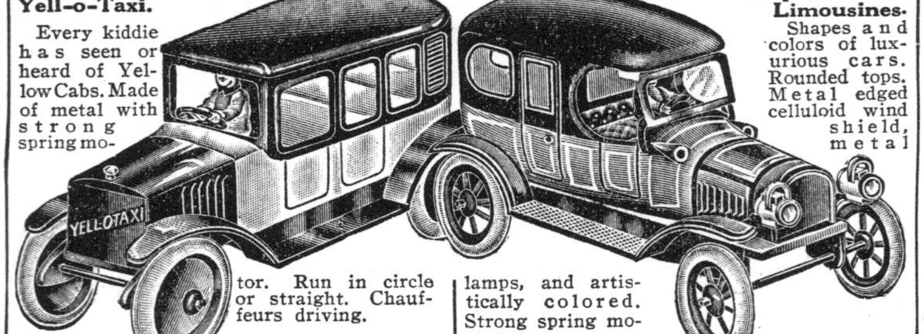

Imported Limousines. Shapes and colors of luxurious cars. Rounded tops. Metal edged celluloid wind shield, metal lamps, and artistically colored. Strong spring motors.

Low Priced Yellow, 48c. Length, 8 in.

Quality Yellow, 89c. Stronger construction. Side doors open. Spare tire on rear. Length, 8¾ in.

Our 79c Auto. Size, 7¼x3¼x4⅛ in. Rigid doors.

Our 59c Auto. Size, 5⅝x2⅞x3½ in. Rigid doors.

Miniature Ocean Liners.

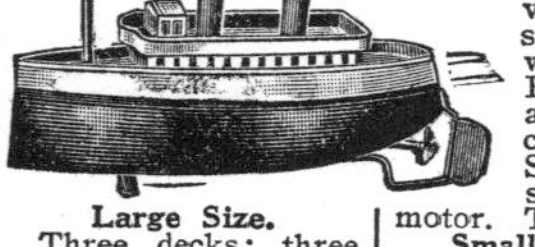

Spins along with propeller revolving and spraying the water. Painted in attractive colors. Strong spring motor. Two sizes.

Large Size. Three decks; three funnels; three-blade propeller. Height, 4 in. Length, 8¼ in. **98c**

Smaller Size. Two decks; 7 in. long. Four-blade propeller. Ht., 3 in. **59c**

Big Red Fire Engine.

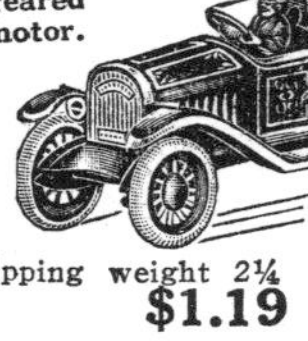

Sheet steel, lithographed red with stripes and gilded border and trimmings, yellow wheels. Exceptional **geared friction motor.** A slight push causes it to run. Size, 12¾ in. long; 8½ inches high. Shipping weight 2¼ pounds. **$1.19**

Mechanical Airplane.

Watch It Fly Along on the Floor.

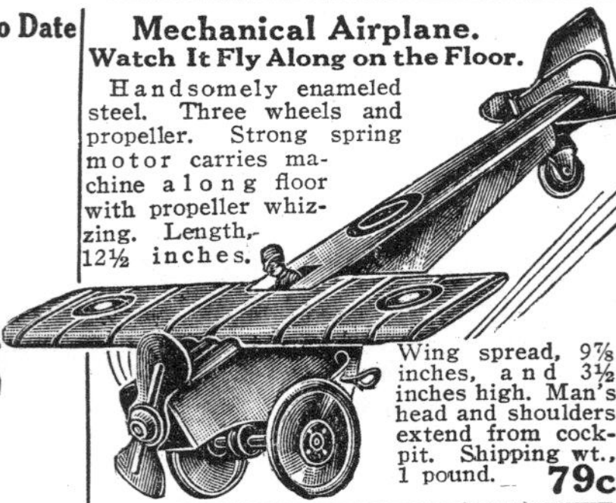

Handsomely enameled steel. Three wheels and propeller. Strong spring motor carries machine along floor with propeller whizzing. Length, 12½ inches. Wing spread, 9⅞ inches, and 3½ inches high. Man's head and shoulders extend from cockpit. Shipping wt., 1 pound. **79c**

Waltzing Bear.

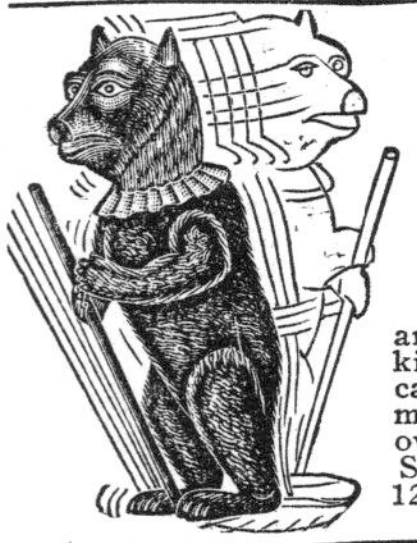

See this natural looking brown bear dance around and around, never falling. Made entirely of metal. Painted in natural colors. Fine spring motor and an interesting new kind of mechanism causes the funny movements. Ht., over all, 8 in. Shipping weight, 12 ounces. **79c**

Baby Chick Is Good Driver.

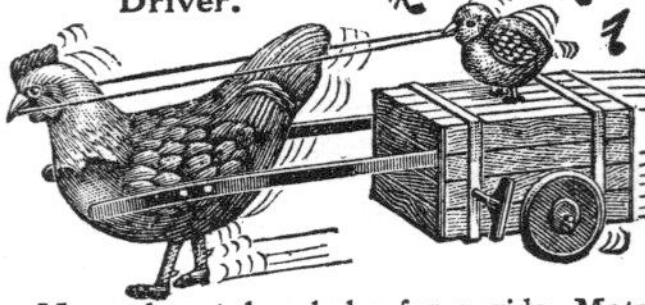

Mama hen takes baby for a ride. Metal, lithographed in colors. The hen walks. Chick peeps and moves up and down. Length, 8¾ inches. Height, 4 inches. Shipping weight, 1 pound. **79c**

The Loving Mother.

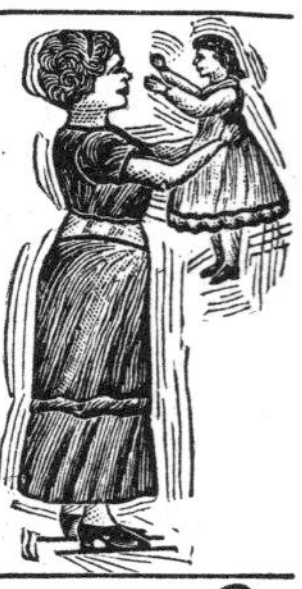

Just as a real mother catches up her little tot from the floor and tosses her in the air or dances around the room with her, so does this clever little metal toy. The only thing left out was the baby talk. Really pretty and has a tremendous appeal. Height, over all, 7 inches. Simply wind up and stand on the floor. **59c**

Climbing Monkey.

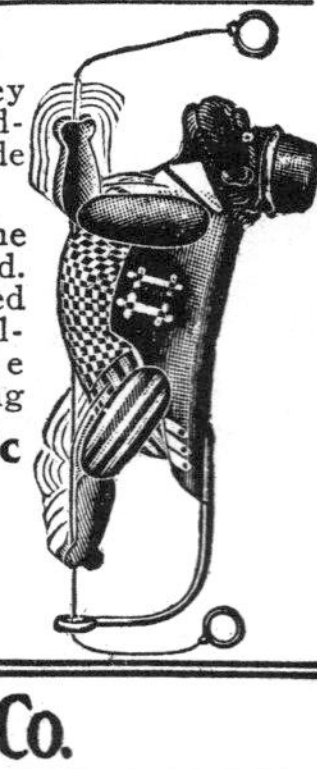

The popular monkey climbing string. Endless amusement. Made in two sizes.

Extra quality. The one we recommend. 9¾x3 inches. Finished in very attractive colors which please the child's eye. Shipping weight, 1 pound.

49N5723.....**23c**

SEARS, ROEBUCK AND CO.

Mechanical Toys

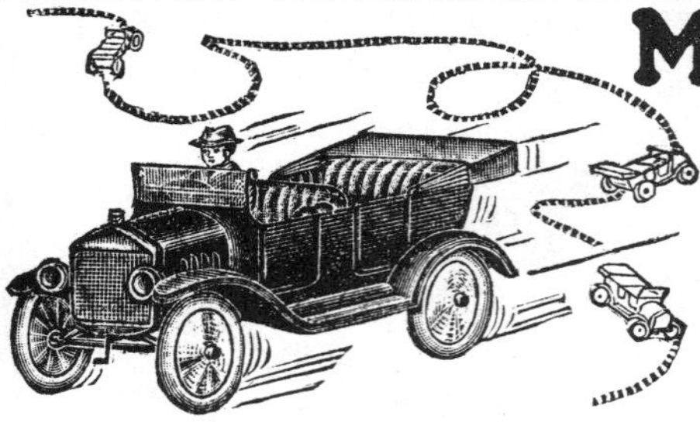

A Real Flivver for the Kiddies.

Something absolutely new. A duplicate of the Ford car, made of metal finished in appropriate colors and with a driver at the wheel. Front wheels so set that this flivver will zigzag around the floor, thus delighting the youngsters. Has strong spring motor. Size over all, 8½x4 inches. **68c**

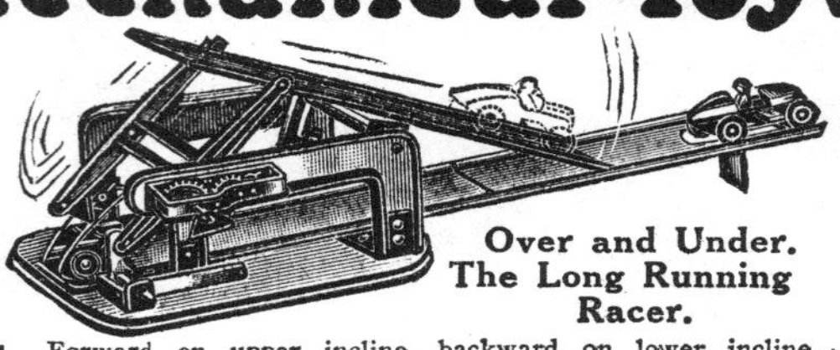

Over and Under. The Long Running Racer.

Forward on upper incline, backward on lower incline. Automatically lifts up and starts over again. Made of sheet steel, nicely decorated. Wind up spring, then place the 2½-inch racer on upper track and it will run down incline by its own weight. After it reaches lower end of bottom track the motor will automatically start and by means of the carrier will pick up the auto and carry it to the upper track. This will be repeated for two or three minutes until spring runs down. Size, over all, about 25x5 inches. Shipping weight, 2⅛ pounds. **89c**

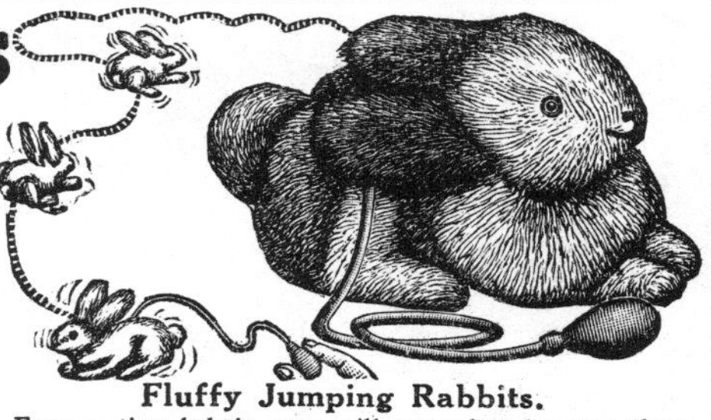

Fluffy Jumping Rabbits.

Even a tiny baby's eyes will pop when he sees them. About the size of a baby cottontail. Covered with real fur. Glass eyes. When bulb is pressed rabbit jumps and moves its ears. All children love bunnies. Two sizes and qualities.

Our Best, 98c. Large and fluffy. Size, over all, 7¼ inches. **98c**

Our Small One for 59c. Not so large or so fluffy. Size, over all, 6 inches. **59c**

The Marvelous Somersaulting Dog.

A Circus Dog. He Turns Somersaults Backward in the Air.

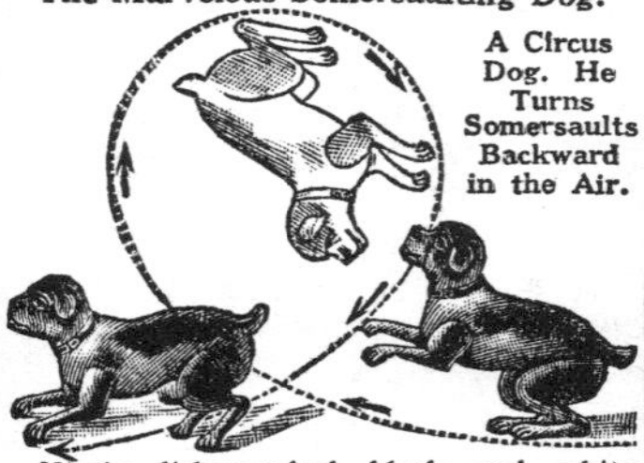

Nicely lithographed black and white metal dog. A wonderful toy. Wind him up and watch dog jump, turn a complete somersault in the air and light on his feet again. Exceptionally clever and well made. Size, 6x4 inches. Strong spring. **79c**

Attractive Durable Friction Locomotives and Tenders.

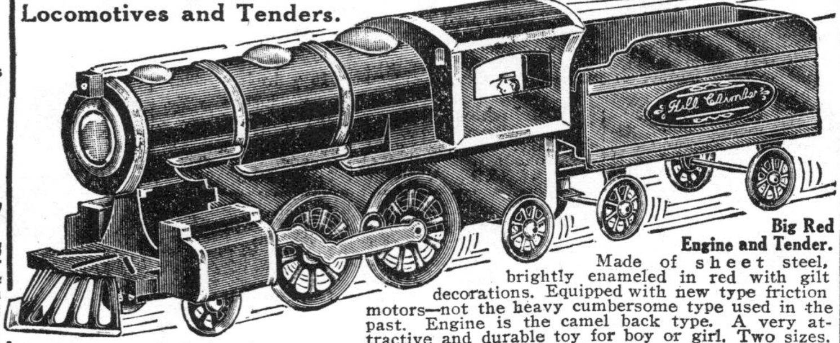

Big Red Engine and Tender. Made of sheet steel, brightly enameled in red with gilt decorations. Equipped with new type friction motors—not the heavy cumbersome type used in the past. Engine is the camel back type. A very attractive and durable toy for boy or girl. Two sizes.

21¼ Inches Long. 8-wheel locomotive, 7 inches high. **$1.39**

17¼ Inches Long. 6-wheel locomotive, 5¼ inches high. Ship- **98c**

Jenny, the Balking Mule.

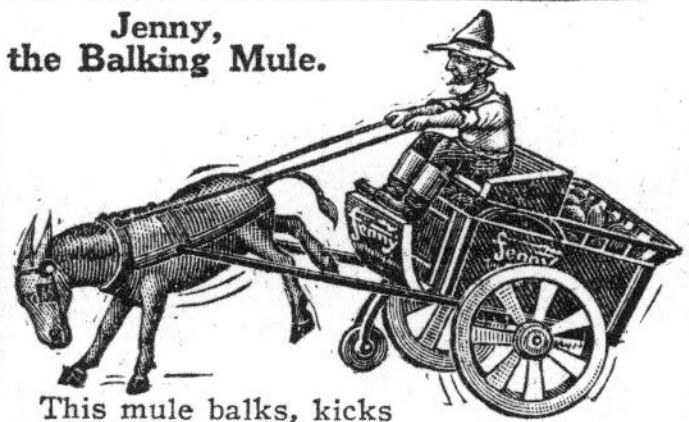

This mule balks, kicks up his heels, backs, whirls and the poor farmer is nearly thrown out at every jump. Lifelike gray mule. Metal cart decorated in colors, clown dressed in bright colored cloth. Length, 8¾ in. **42c**

This Is a Wise Old Beetle.

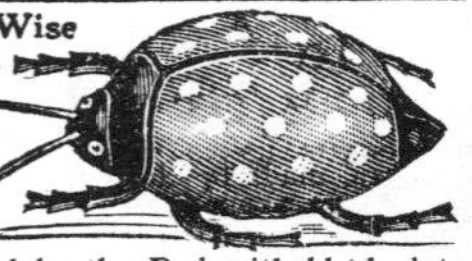

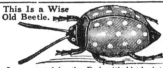

Large metal beetle. Red with black dots like a ladybug. Wind up the strong spring motor, put beetle on smooth table and he will crawl away in a hurry, but when he comes to the edge of the table he turns and follows around the edge. It will not fall off. Size, 7¾ inches long and 4¼ inches wide. Shpg. wt., 15 oz. **59c**

Have Your Own Little Fire Department.

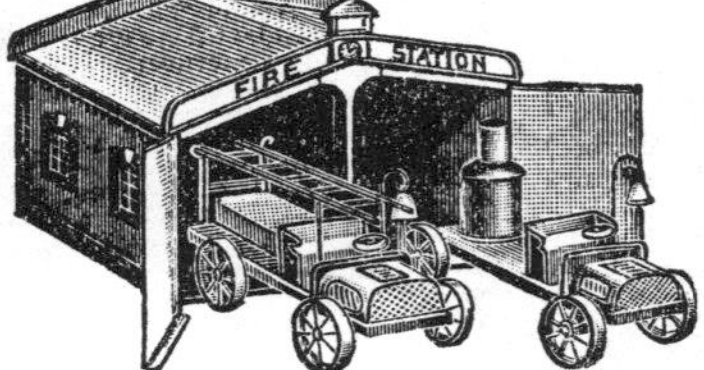

This little outfit is so very complete in every detail that even the grownups are interested. Metal garage with floor, 8x6⅝x6 inches, is lithographed in true colors. Metal doors lock together in center. The automobiles are 6⅛ inches long, 2¾ inches wide and 2⅜ inches to the top of bell hanger. One is built like a fire engine, the other resembles a chemical truck. Both equipped with strong spring motors, and will run quite a distance. **$1.25**

Famous Alabama Coon Jigger. 59c

A realistic dancing negro who goes through the movements of a lively jig. Natural colors. A good spring. A lever at side permits stopping and starting the movement at will. Height, 10½ inches. Shipping wt., 13 ounces.

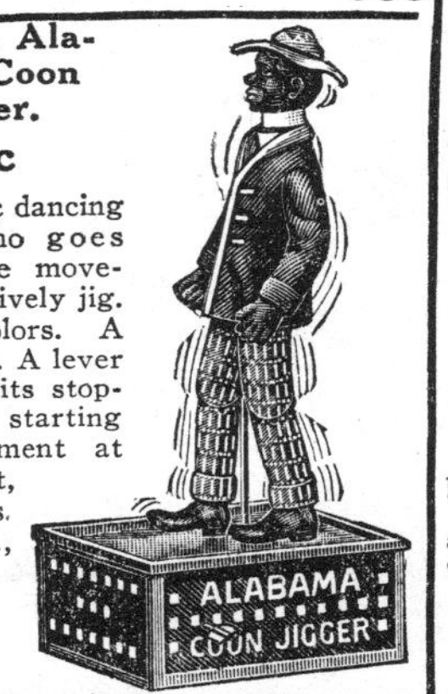

The Craziest Kind of an Automobile. The Krazy Kar.

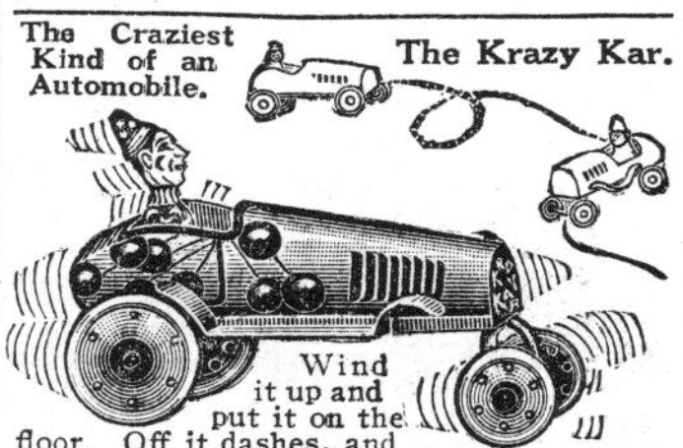

Wind it up and put it on the floor. Off it dashes, and does everything an auto shouldn't do. The clown can be so placed in car as to sway backward and forward with every action of car. Made of steel. Nicely lithographed in colors. 8 inches long. Shipping weight, 8 ounces **42c**

Playful Kitty.

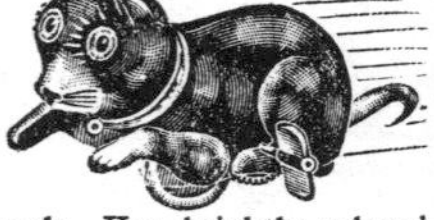

Runs around in real kitten-like manner. Realistically colored in black with decorative red ribbon around neck. Has brightly colored eyes. Made of durable metal and has a good mechanical motor. Size, 7¾ inches long by 3¾ inches high. Shipping weight, 8 ounces. **39c**

Balky Pony and Cart.

Watch clown's actions while driving pony. Made entirely of metal, nicely painted in attractive colors.

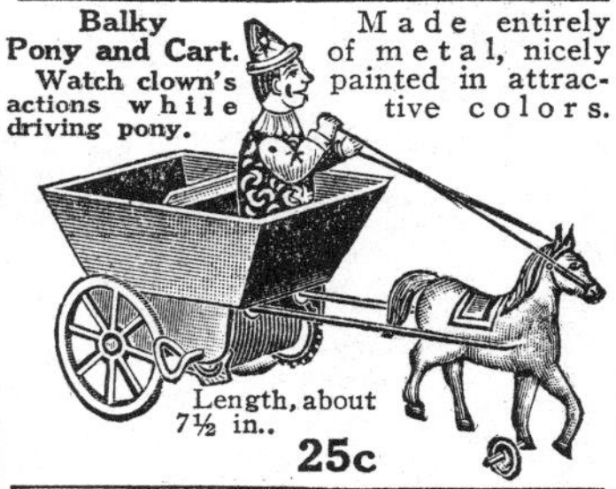

Length, about 7½ in. **25c**

Looks Like a Real Mouse.

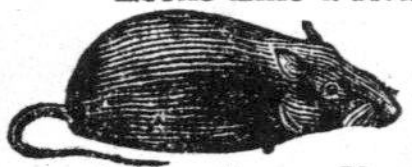

It's just the size and color of a mouse and when it runs along the floor the girls climb onto the furniture. If you want to have fun, get one. Made of metal, friction motor. Shipping wt., 3 oz. **19c**

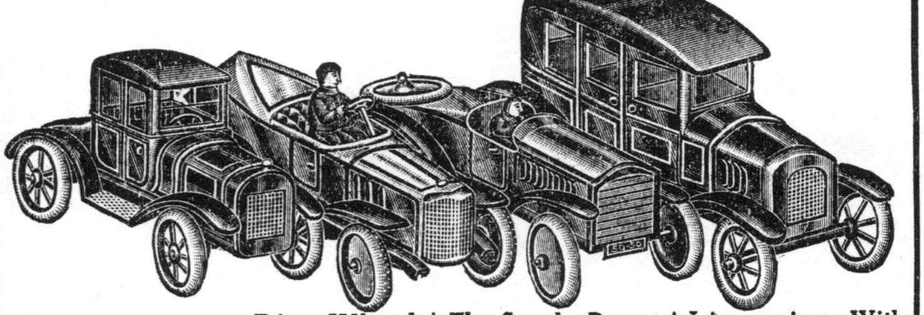

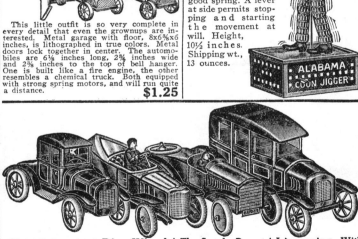

Closed Coupe.

Made of metal and finished in attractive colors with fancy striping. Strong spring motor. Driver at the wheel. Something new in toy autos. Very attractive. About 7 in. long. Shpg. wt. 14 ounces. **59c**

Disc Wheel Racer.

Bullet nose. Nicely finished in colors. Imitation springs. Size, 7¾x3¼ inches. Good spring motor. Shpg. wt., 8 oz. **39c**

The Speedy Racer.

A real classy racing car. Bright red with yellow wheels. Spare tire on back. Travels in circle or straight-away. Driver in the seat. All metal. Strong spring motor. 8 inches long, 3½ inches high. Shipping weight, 12 ounces. **25c**

Limousine With Doors That Open.

Our best limousine. Fashioned after up to date type, beautifully finished in attractive colors and striping. Has chauffeur in the seat. Made of durable metal and has strong spring. Length, 8 in. Shpg. wt., 1 lb. **59c**

Just Like a Real Street Roller.

Mechanical Street Roller with extra strong clockwork. Has device on front roller for controlling direction. Movable piston rods. Steam fittings lithographed on boiler. Steel gray. Measures 9x5x3 inches. Shipping wt., 1½ lbs **98c**

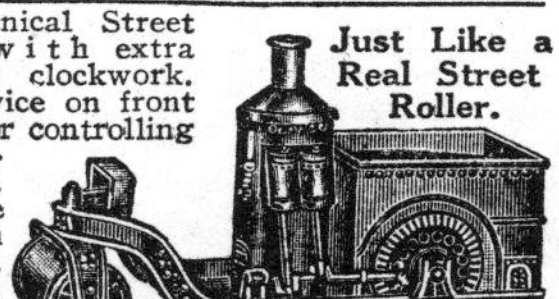

Mechanical Goose With Flapping Wings.

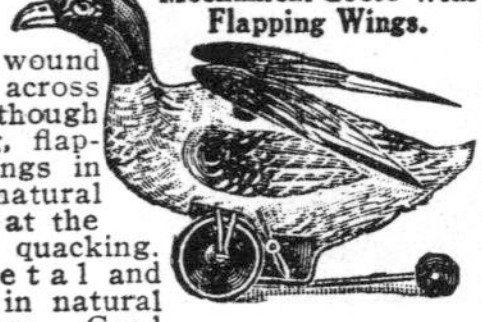

When wound goose darts across the floor as though after a frog, flapping its wings in a very natural manner and at the same time quacking. Made of metal and painted in natural looking colors. Good spring motor. Shpg. wt., 1 lb. **48c**

Really Rides His Kiddo Kar.

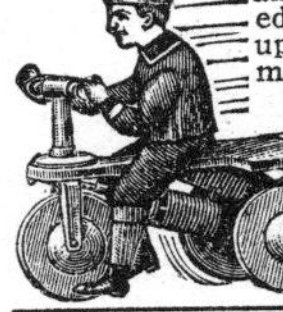

Little metal Kiddo Kar and boy rider. Lithographed in pretty colors. Wind up the strong spring motor and the little boy starts off just as in real life. Length, over all, 5½ in. 6 in. high. Shipping weight, 12 ounces. **39c**

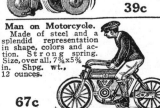

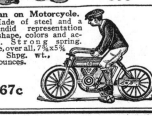

Watch Him Actually Play Pool.

Metal pool table. Spring motor. The man shoots the balls as fast as they are brought up. The holes are numbered. Guess which hole the ball will fall into or keep score. Size, over all, 7½x3⅛ inchees.

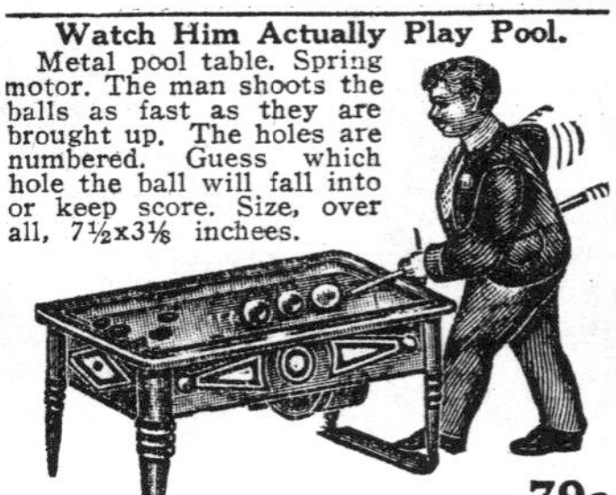

79c

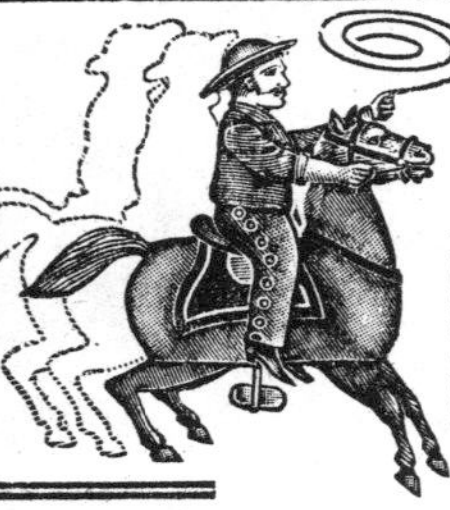

This Broncho Really Bucks.

A metal horse and cowboy rider, with lariat. Lithographed in colors. Horse gallops, rears and plunges along over the floor. Good strong spring. Size, over all, 6¼ inches long and 5½ inches high. **59c**

The Knockout Boxers. Real Action.

These little boxers battle like real professionals to the immense delight of the kiddies. The bout lasts over one minute for each winding. The mechanism is durably constructed. The toy is made of metal beautifully lithographed. A button on the side stops the bout when you wish. 6½ inches. **59c**

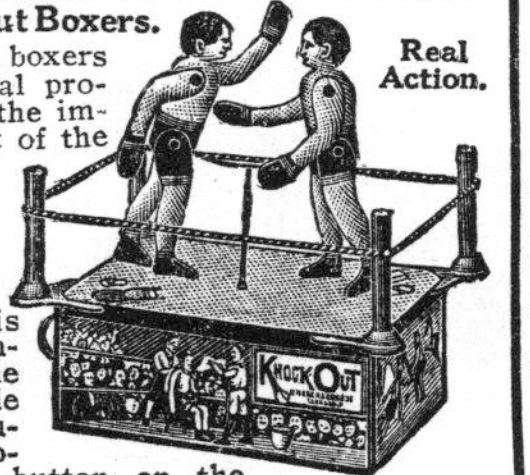

Man on Motorcycle.

Made of steel and a splendid representation in shape, colors and action. Strong spring. Size, over all, 7¾x5¾ in. Shpg. wt. 12 ounces. **67c**

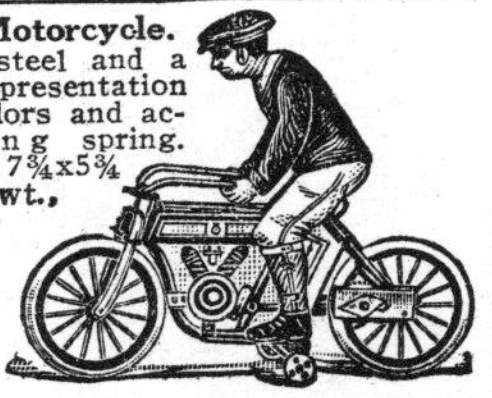

SEARS, ROEBUCK AND CO.

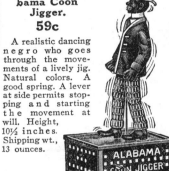

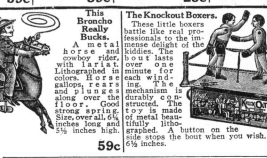

Tinker Toy

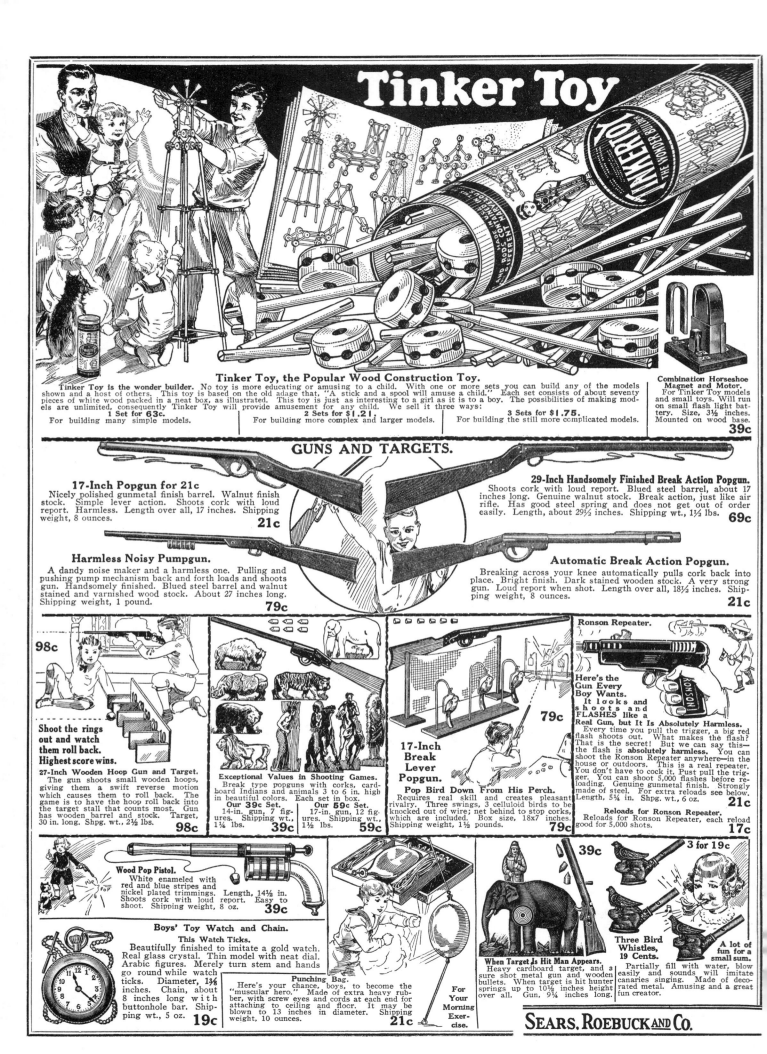

Tinker Toy, the Popular Wood Construction Toy.

Tinker Toy is the wonder builder. No toy is more educating or amusing to a child. With one or more sets you can build any of the models shown and a host of others. This toy is based on the old adage that, "A stick and a spool will amuse a child." Each set consists of about seventy pieces of white wood packed in a neat box, as illustrated. This toy is just as interesting to a girl as it is to a boy. The possibilities of making models are unlimited, consequently Tinker Toy will provide amusement for any child. We sell it three ways:

1 Set for 63c.
For building many simple models.

2 Sets for $1.21.
For building more complex and larger models.

3 Sets for $1.75.
For building the still more complicated models.

Combination Horseshoe Magnet and Motor.
For Tinker Toy models and small toys. Will run on small flash light battery. Size, 3½ inches. Mounted on wood base. **39c**

GUNS AND TARGETS.

17-Inch Popgun for 21c
Nicely polished gunmetal finish barrel. Walnut finish stock. Simple lever action. Shoots cork with loud report. Harmless. Length over all, 17 inches. Shipping weight, 8 ounces. **21c**

29-Inch Handsomely Finished Break Action Popgun.
Shoots cork with loud report. Blued steel barrel, about 17 inches long. Genuine walnut stock. Break action, just like air rifle. Has good steel spring and does not get out of order easily. Length, about 29½ inches. Shipping wt., 1½ lbs. **69c**

Harmless Noisy Pumpgun.
A dandy noise maker and a harmless one. Pulling and pushing pump mechanism back and forth loads and shoots gun. Handsomely finished. Blued steel barrel and walnut stained and varnished wood stock. About 27 inches long. Shipping weight, 1 pound. **79c**

Automatic Break Action Popgun.
Breaking across your knee automatically pulls cork back into place. Bright finish. Dark stained wooden stock. A very strong gun. Loud report when shot. Length over all, 18½ inches. Shipping weight, 8 ounces. **21c**

98c

Shoot the rings out and watch them roll back. Highest score wins.
27-Inch Wooden Hoop Gun and Target.
The gun shoots small wooden hoops, giving them a swift reverse motion which causes them to roll back. The game is to have the hoop roll back into the target stall that counts most. Gun has wooden barrel and stock. Target, 30 in. long. Shpg. wt., 2½ lbs. **98c**

Exceptional Values in Shooting Games.
Break type popguns with corks, cardboard Indians and animals 3 to 6 in. high in beautiful colors. Each set in box.

Our 39c Set.
14-in. gun, 7 figures. Shipping wt., 1¼ lbs. **39c**

Our 59c Set.
17-in. gun, 12 figures. Shipping wt., 1½ lbs. **59c**

17-Inch Break Lever Popgun.
79c

Pop Bird Down From His Perch.
Requires real skill and creates pleasant rivalry. Three swings, 3 celluloid birds to be knocked out of wire; net behind to stop corks, which are included. Box size, 18x7 inches. Shipping weight, 1½ pounds. **79c**

Ronson Repeater.
Here's the Gun Every Boy Wants.
It looks and shoots and FLASHES like a Real Gun, but It Is Absolutely Harmless.
Every time you pull the trigger, a big red flash shoots out. What makes the flash? That is the secret! But we can say this—the flash is **absolutely harmless.** You can shoot the Ronson Repeater anywhere—in the house or outdoors. This is a real repeater. You don't have to cock it. Pust pull the trigger. You can shoot 5,000 flashes before reloading. Genuine gunmetal finish. Strongly made of steel. For extra reloads see below. Length, 5¼ in. Shpg. wt., 6 oz. **21c**

Reloads for Ronson Repeater.
Reloads for Ronson Repeater, each reload good for 5,000 shots. **17c**

Wood Pop Pistol.
White enameled with red and blue stripes and nickel plated trimmings. Length, 14½ in. Shoots cork with loud report. Easy to shoot. Shipping weight, 8 oz. **39c**

Boys' Toy Watch and Chain.
This Watch Ticks.
Beautifully finished to imitate a gold watch. Real glass crystal. Thin model with neat dial. Arabic figures. Merely turn stem and hands go round while watch ticks. Diameter, 1⅜ inches. Chain, about 8 inches long with buttonhole bar. Shipping wt., 5 oz. **19c**

Punching Bag.
Here's your chance, boys, to become the "muscular hero." Made of extra heavy rubber, with screw eyes and cords at each end for attaching to ceiling and floor. It may be blown to 13 inches in diameter. Shipping weight, 10 ounces. **21c**

For Your Morning Exercise.

39c

3 for 19c

When Target Is Hit Man Appears.
Heavy cardboard target, and a sure shot metal gun and wooden bullets. When target is hit hunter springs up to 10½ inches height over all. Gun, 9¼ inches long. **39c**

Three Bird Whistles, 19 Cents.
A lot of fun for a small sum.
Partially fill with water, blow easily and sounds will imitate canaries singing. Made of decorated metal. Amusing and a great fun creator. **3 for 19c**

SEARS, ROEBUCK AND CO.

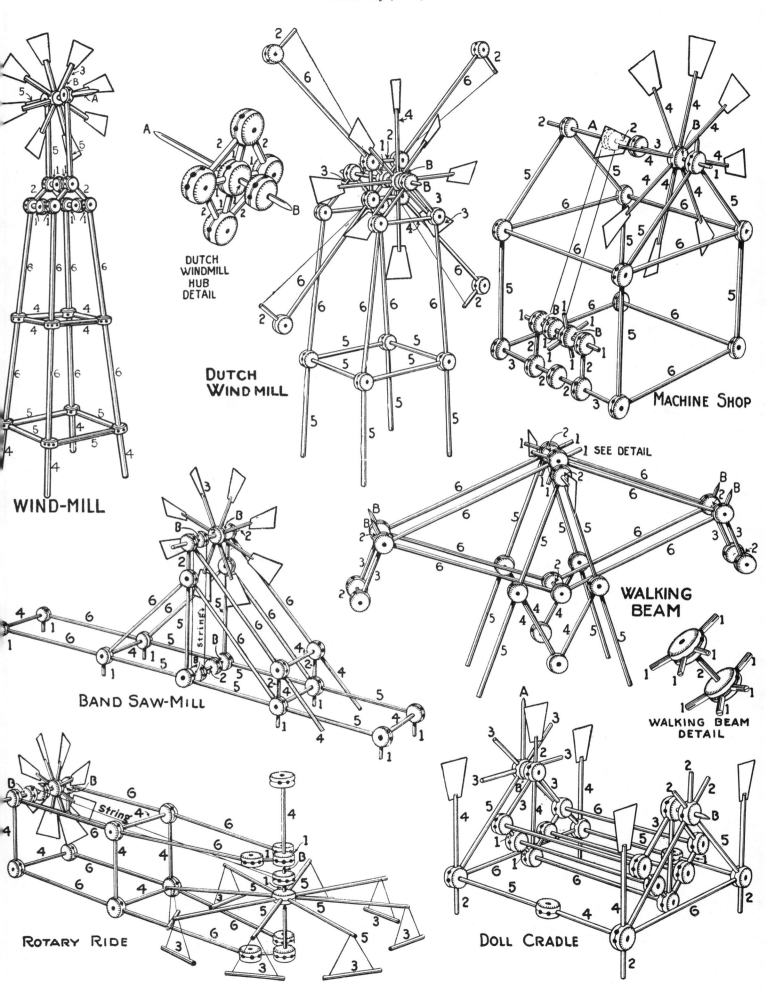

DUTCH WINDMILL HUB DETAIL

DUTCH WINDMILL

WIND-MILL

MACHINE SHOP

BAND SAW-MILL

WALKING BEAM

WALKING BEAM DETAIL

ROTARY RIDE

DOLL CRADLE

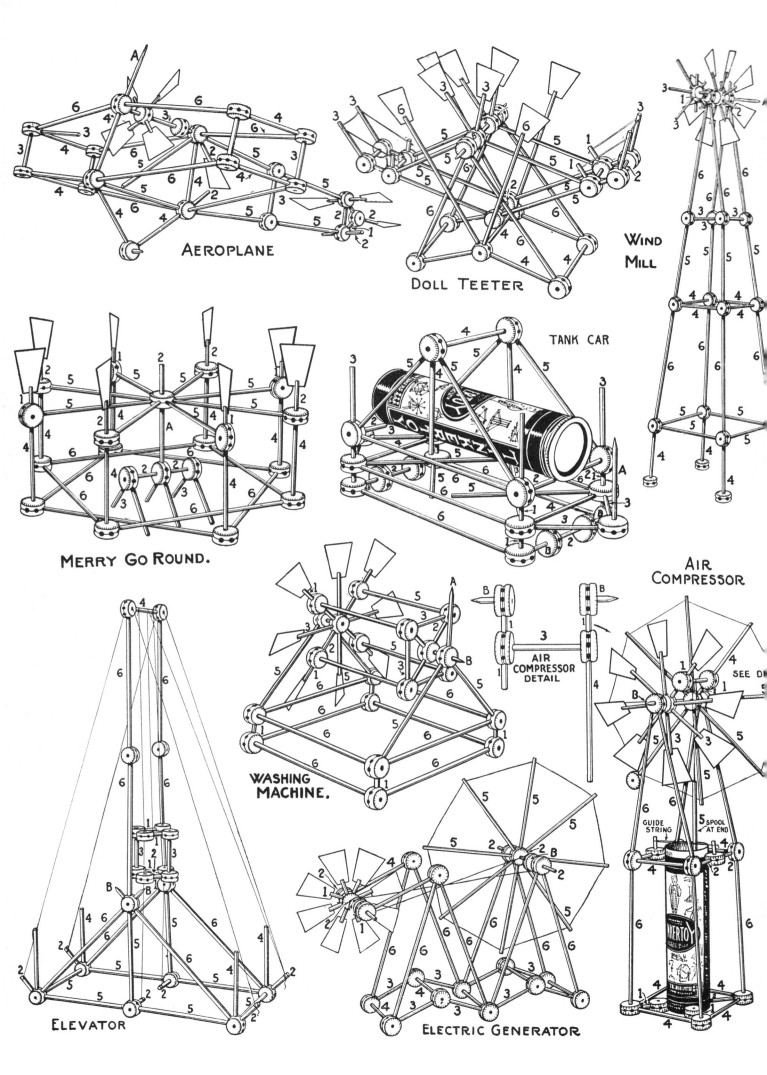

AEROPLANE

DOLL TEETER

WIND MILL

MERRY GO ROUND.

TANK CAR

AIR COMPRESSOR

AIR COMPRESSOR DETAIL

SEE D

WASHING MACHINE.

GUIDE STRING

SPOOL AT END

ELEVATOR

ELECTRIC GENERATOR

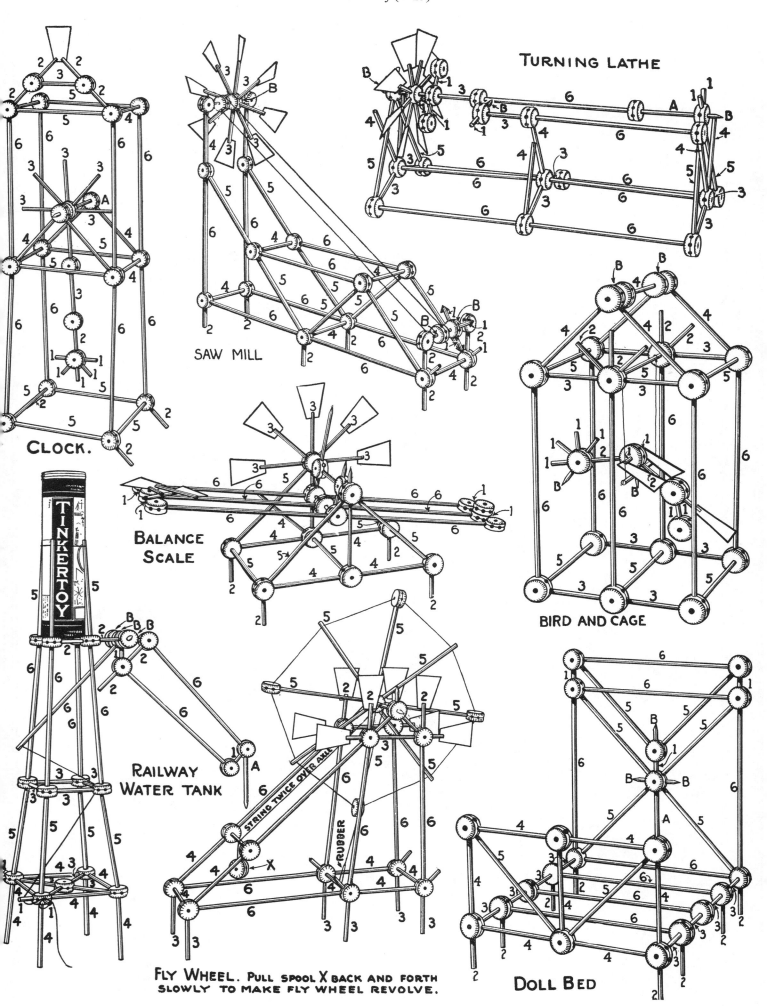

TURNING LATHE

SAW MILL

CLOCK.

BALANCE SCALE

BIRD AND CAGE

TINKERTOY

RAILWAY WATER TANK

STRING TWICE OVER AXLE

RUBBER

FLY WHEEL. PULL SPOOL X BACK AND FORTH SLOWLY TO MAKE FLY WHEEL REVOLVE.

DOLL BED

THE THREE WONDERS—Tremendous Sellers at These Prices!

"Spic and Span"

Action:— "Spic" plays drums and cymbals, "Span" fiddles and dances.

1F3258—10 in. high, red, blue, black and yellow uniforms, red drums with gold trim, elaborately decorated all over. With speed regulator. One figure plays both drums and cymbals—other plays violin and dances. Each in box. ¼ doz. in pkg. **Doz $7.75**

"Ring—A—Ling" Circus Toy

Action:— Animals move up and down in turn, when trainer snaps whip.

1F3184—7⅛ in. base, in bright colors with juvenile designs; 6½ in. trainer with whip in red, blue and yellow; elephant, monkey, lion, all in natural colors; 2¼ in. clown in yellow, black and white costume, speed regulator, long running spring. Figures move up and down in natural manner when trainer snaps whip. ¼ doz. in box. **Doz $8.00**

"Whee Whiz" Auto Race

Action:— Cars dash around speedway as runway oscillates. The first real action automobile race.

1F3180—Runway circle 11¾ in., 3½ in. high, 3 assorted color 2 in. automobiles, red, black and yellow finish. Runway moves with oscillating motion which causes cars to dash madly around at various speeds. ¼ doz. in box. **Doz $8.50**

On this page are the greatest toys of their kind—superior construction—Made in America

The Bulk of Your Mechanical Toy Sales Will Be Made With These Remarkable Numbers

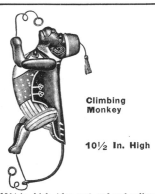

Climbing Monkey

10½ In. High

1F3282—10½ in. high, blue coat, red and yellow trousers, red and white vest, tassel cap. Finest on the market. ½ doz. in pkg. **Doz $1.88**

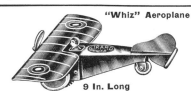

"Whiz" Aeroplane

9 In. Long

1F3176—9 in. long, 10 in. wing spread, blue body, red wings, yellow wheels and propeller, red tail, red, white and blue insignia. Each in box. ½ doz. in pkg. **Doz $3.95**

"Hee—Haw" Balky Mule

11 In. Long

1F3267—11 in. long, 7 bright colors. Dashes around in eccentric manner. Each in box. ¼ doz. in pkg. **Doz 3.75**

"Rex" Racer

8 In. Long

1F3279—8 in. long, red body, black trim, mud guards and running board, yellow disc wheels, spare wheel, blue chauffeur. Each in box. ½ doz. in pkg. **Doz $2.10**

"Jazzbo Jim" Dancer

11 In. High

1F3187—11 in. high, 7 colors, 4⅝ in. x 3½ in. platform representing log cabin, speed regulator. Small figure plays fiddle while large one jigs. Each in box. ½ doz. in pkg. **Doz $4.25**

Bronco Buster

8½ In. High

1F3290—8½ in. high, yellow platform with black and white horse and man. Runs along floor—horse backs up and down throwing rider from saddle. Each in box. ¼ doz. in pkg. **Doz $4.25**

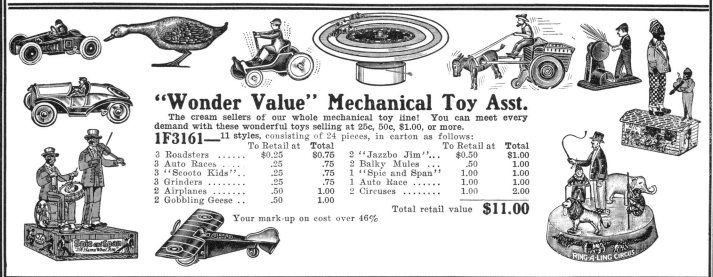

"Wonder Value" Mechanical Toy Asst.

The cream sellers of our whole mechanical toy line! You can meet every demand with these wonderful toys selling at 25c, 50c, $1.00, or more.

1F3161—11 styles, consisting of 24 pieces, in carton as follows:

	To Retail at	Total		To Retail at	Total
3 Roadsters	$0.25	$0.75	2 "Jazzbo Jim"	$0.50	$1.00
3 Auto Races	.25	.75	2 Balky Mules	.50	1.00
3 "Scooto Kids"	.25	.75	1 "Spic and Span"	1.00	1.00
3 Grinders	.25	.75	1 Auto Race	1.00	1.00
2 Airplanes	.50	1.00	2 Circuses	1.00	2.00
2 Gobbling Geese	.50	1.00			
			Total retail value		**$11.00**

Your mark-up on cost over 46%

200

AMERICAN MECHANICAL TOYS

You are looking at the best selection of "action" toys in the country! If you want ACTION in your toy department order from this page.

1F3294—Racer, 6¾ in. long, orange lithographed body, enameled red and black disc wheels, imitation rubber tires, gray chauffeur. 1 doz. in pkg. Doz **$1.25**

1F3250—Airplane, 6 in. long, 7 in. wing spread, gray enameled finish, red, white and blue insignia, yellow and black wheels, red propeller. 1 doz. in box. Doz **$1.35**

1F3262—Boat, 9 in. long, red enameled body, black trim. **Steersman** of metal. ½ doz. in box. Doz **$1.95**

1F3285 — "Speedo" auto racer, 8 in. long, red enameled body, yellow disc wheels. Doz **$2.00**

1F3271—Man, 4¼ in. high, red and blue. **Grindstone** 3 in. Sparks fly from wheel. ¼ doz. in pkg. Doz **$2.15**

1F3189—"Scooto," 3¼ in. long, yellow disc wheels, red body, colored figure with jointed arms and body. Figure moves backwards and forwards in life like manner. Doz **$2.15**

1F3263—Runaway team, 8½ in. long. **Wagon** red and black with yellow wheels. **Dapple horses** with red saddles and bridles. **Gray driver,** cord reins. Runs back and forth and whirls in circle, exceptional action. Doz **$3.75**

1F3269—"Indian motorcycle," 6½ in. long, red with black trimmings, equipped with headlight and windshield. Each in box. Doz **$3.90**

1F3272 — 3 styles, average 8½ in., **delivery van,** red and white, green disc wheels, driver; **truck,** red and yellow, green disc wheels, driver; **dump truck,** red and yellow, green disc wheels, chauffeur; long running springs. Asstd. Doz **$2.25**

1F3283—Porter, 6¾ in. high, blue and yellow with red hat. **Cart,** 2½x3½ in., blue with yellow wheels. Walks in natural manner pushing cart. ¼ doz. in pkg. Doz **$2.25**

1F3298—Hand-car, 6 in. long, gray with yellow wheels. **Two figures,** 4 in. high, with jointed arms, red and blue. Lifelike hand lever action. ¼ doz. in pkg. Doz **$3.25**

"Dapper Dan" Coon Jigger

An old favorite that's selling stronger than ever. The life-like action appeals to the children.

9½ in. high, finished in **7 colors,** with hotel and baggage labels. Has speed regulator and dances with perfect mechanical action. ¼ doz. in pkg. Doz **$3.65**

1F3263—Runaway team ... [see above]

Gobbling Goose
1F3289—9 in. long, white body with red and blue stenciled features and costume. Hops along and pecks at ground. Doz **$3.90**

1F3185 — Engine and tender, 10 in. long, black, yellow and red body and cab, black wheels. Doz **$2.25**

1F3248—Hobo train, 7½ in. long, freight car finished in 7 bright enameled colors, lithographed hobo figures, 3 in. hobo with dog on roof. When car moves dog chases tramp in highly amusing manner. ¼ doz. in pkg. Doz **$4.25**

1F3287—"Krazy Car," 7¼ in. long, circus type body, disc wheels, **clown chauffeur.** Auto darts ahead, backs up and circles. ½ doz. in pkg. Doz **$3.95**

1F3201—Golf Player, 6¼ in. high, 3 color platform with chute for golf balls, 5 in. 5 color figure with golf club, supply of balls. Figure hits balls in natural manner. Doz **$4.10**

1F3191—Prize fighter, 6½ in. high, finished in 6 bright enameled colors, lithographed juvenile designs, 3¾ in. figures with jointed arms and legs. Performs in a very realistic manner. Doz **$4.25**

1F3249 — "Buffalo Bill," 6¼ in. high, finished in red, blue, black, gray and brown. Horse bucks and trots in natural manner. Doz **$4.25**

"Spic" coon drummer, 7½ in. high, red coat and blue trousers with yellow trim, red platform with black and yellow figures, red drums with gold trim. With speed regulator. Plays both drums and cymbal at same time. Doz **$4.25**

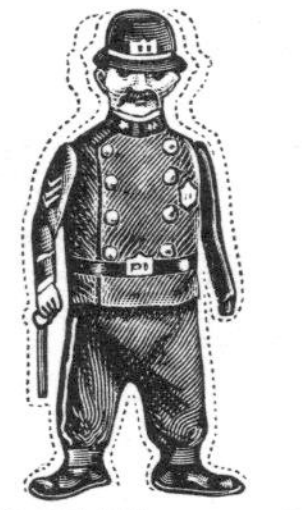

1F3162—Walking cop, 9 in. high, blue uniform, yellow trim, moving arms and club. Walks in comical manner. ¼ doz. in pkg. Doz **$4.25**

1F3291—"Cirko" clown cyclist, 8½ in. long, clown green on one side, other white enamel finish, red designs, red wheel with yellow circus characters. Runs along in amusing manner. Doz **$4.25**

1F3160—"Kid Samson," 4½ x3¼ in. platform, 6 in. figure with jointed arms and legs, hammer, 6 in. registering slide and bell, weight and lever, finished in 7 colors, speed stop and start. Figure hits lever with hammer and weight flies up and rings bell. Doz **$5.50**

"Ham and Sam," 8 in. high, finished in bright litho colors—red, yellow, blue, white and green—mahogany finish piano. With speed regulator. Piano player moves hands over keys and sways body to jazzy motion—banjo player dances and plays banjo. Doz **$7.75**

1F3181—"Stutz" racer, 16 in. long, red body, black trim, running boards and mud guards; red and black disc wheels with imitation rubber tires, motormeter, top with windshields, blue chauffeur, extra wheel, long running spring. ¼ doz. in pkg. Doz **$7.90**

1F3288 — Airplane, 13 in. long, 10 in. wing spread, all steel, gray metal finish, bulls eye insignia, yellow wheels and propeller. adjustable tail. ⅙ doz. in pkg. Doz **$8.00**

Wolverine "Over and Under"

A big seller—very well known. Lots of action with direct appeal to the children.

20 in. long, double incline railway, car with passengers, finished in red, yellow and green. Car runs down incline, drops to lower track and back to starting point, repeats many times without rewinding. ½ doz. in pkg. Doz **$8.25**

1F3199—Santa Claus and sleigh, 11 in. long, enameled in bright colors, juvenile designs, reindeer with brass bells. Santa Claus moves up and down, reindeer gallop and bell rings. Doz **$8.25**

1F3281 — Kentucky derby race, 13½x13½ in. platform representing race track, 7 bright enameled colors, juvenile racing designs, four 3 in. horses with jockeys. Natural oscillating motion furnished by revolving shaft causes horses to gallop in natural manner. 1 in box. Each **$1.10**

1F3155—Loop-the-Loop, 28 in. long, railway with loops, car with passengers and bodies, 5 bright enameled colors. Car races down incline and loops the loop, then returns to starting point, repeating many times without rewinding. 1 in box. Each **$1.10**

1F3195—The Speedway, 14 in. diameter, platform representing race track, four 2 in. racing autos with chauffeurs, 4½x3 in. center representing grandstand, 7 bright colors with lithographed figures. Platform has oscillating movement causing autos to dart ahead in rapid manner. Each **$1.50**

MENGEL'S MOTOR BOAT

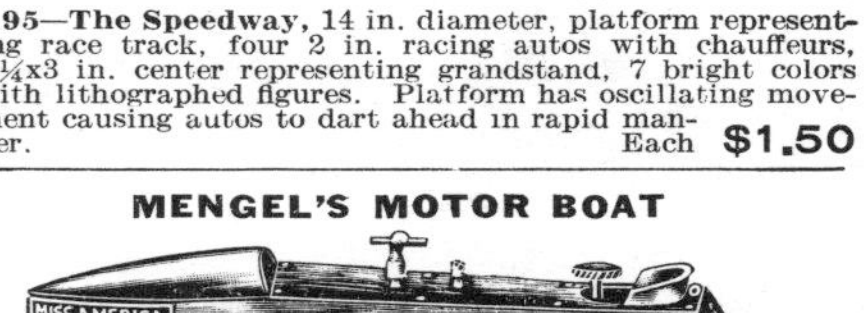

1F3260—Mengel's motor boat, 14½ in. long, 1 piece mahogany hull, brass spray hood, propeller, steering wheel and rudder, **non-sinkable.** Powerful spring motor drives boat 200 ft. 1 in carton with 2 wood racks. Each **$3.50**

IMPORTED MECHANICAL TOYS

Our resident European buyers gathered the cream of the new toys in this line—they're well made novelties that sell.

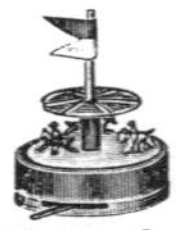

2F7113—Carousel, 2¾ in. base, 3 figures. Revolves. 1 doz. in box. Doz 68c

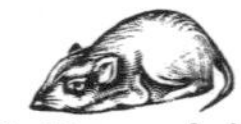

2F7050—Mouse, 3 in. gray enameled, wire tail. Runs along floor. **2 doz. in box**.........Doz 89c

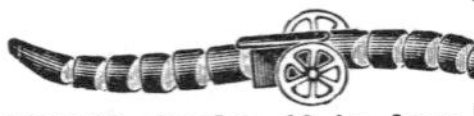

2F7068—Snake, 12 in. long, jointed wood body on wheels, bright green and yellow finish. Crawls like wiggling snake. Doz $1.75

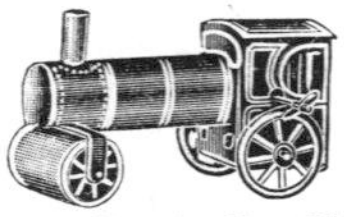

2F7117—Street roller, 5¼ in. bright colors. Runs straight and in circle. Doz $1.95

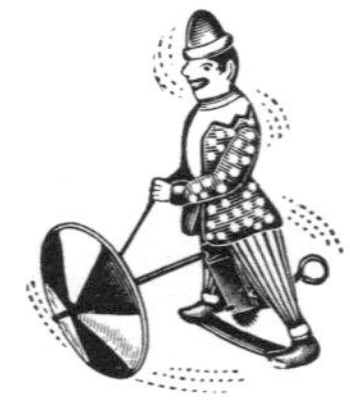

2F7071—Circus assortment, 3 styles, average 6¾ in. Monkey, clown, etc., bright colors. Asstd. ½ doz. in box. Doz $2.10

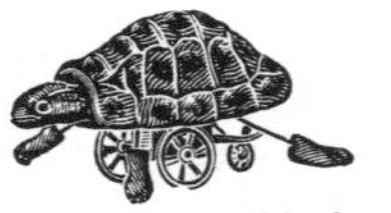

2F7069—Turtle, 6¼ in. long, bright colors. Moves legs and head in lifelike action. ½ doz. in box. Doz $2.10

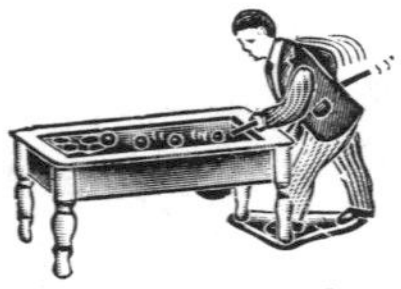

2F7098—Billiard player, 4¾ in. figure, 4½x2 in. table. Figure with cue shoots balls into numbered pockets. Each in box. pkg. Doz $2.75

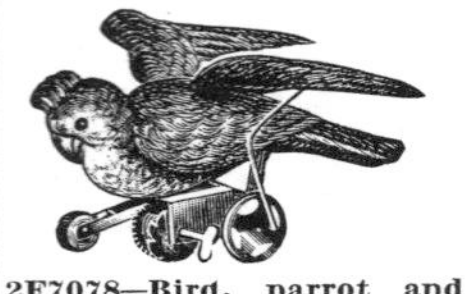

2F7078—Bird, parrot and duck, 7 in. high, bright colors. Runs and flaps wings up and down. Each in box. Doz $3.75

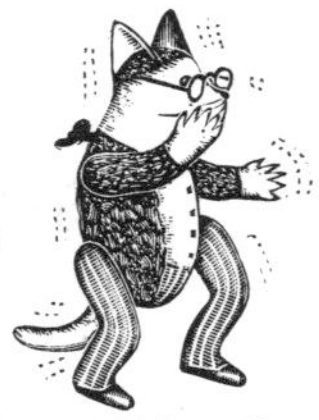

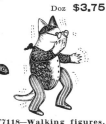

2F7118—Walking figures, 3 styles, 6¾ in., cat, negro and dog, bright colors, vibrating walking motion. Each in box. ½ doz. in pkg. Doz $3.90

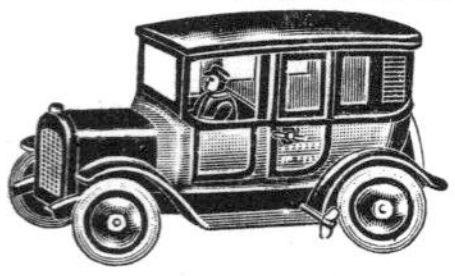

2F7111—Yellow taxi, 7¼ in. long, yellow and black colors, disc wheels, green chauffeur, extra wheel, doors open. Each in box. ¼ doz. in pkg. Doz $3.95

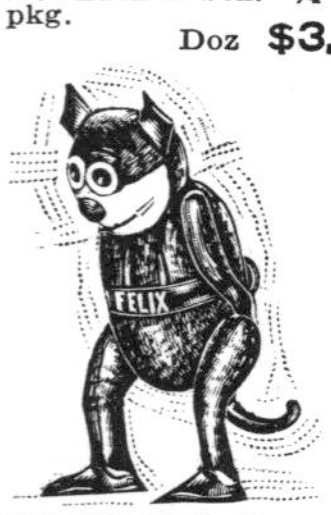
FELIX

2F7015—"Felix" the walking cat. Walks with swaying motion of body in characteristic position. Each in box. .Doz $4.00

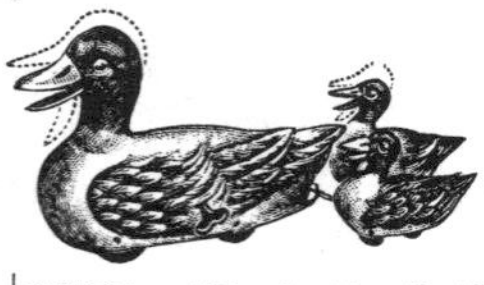

2F7000 — "Duck Family," 8 in., bright colors, mother duck and 2 ducklings. Heads move up and down, beaks open and close when running. Each in box. Doz $4.00

"Ford" Mechanical Autos

Exact reproduction of "Ford" cars, perfect in every detail. Will prove big sellers.

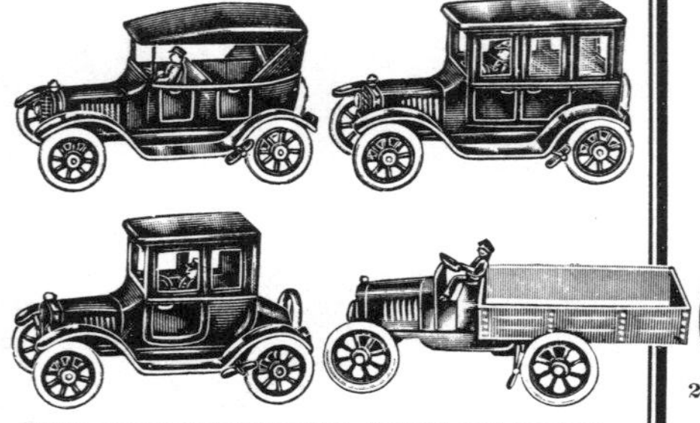

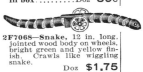

Black enameled finish bodies, "Ford" trademarked, imitation rubber tires, facsimile "Ford" radiator, each with driver, long running springs. Runs straight or in circle. Each in lithographed box.

6½ in. long. Imitation head lights, spare wheel.

2F7101—Touring car............
2F7102—Sedan..................
2F7103—Coupe.................. Doz ⋆3.75

8½ in. long—½ doz. in pkg.
2F7105—Truck.............Doz ⋆3.75

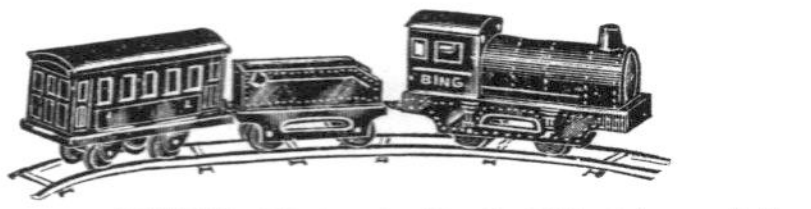

2F7060—12 in. train, bright colors, 5 in. locomotive, tender and passenger car, strong **long running clockwork spring,** 4 sections of circular track. Doz sets ⋆3.90

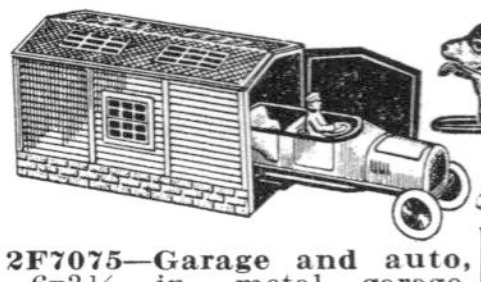

2F7075—Garage and auto, 6x3¼ in. metal garage, painted doors, windows and shutters, 6 in. red touring car and chauffeur. Doz sets $4.00

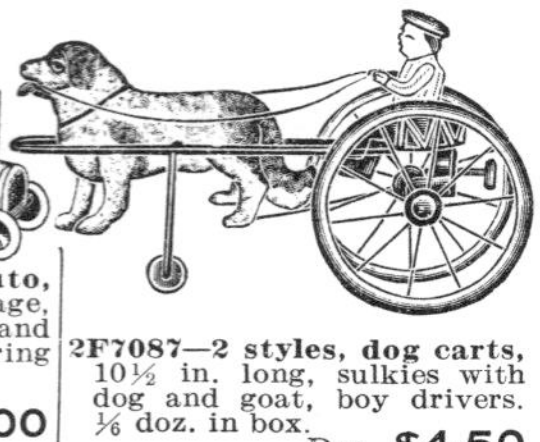

2F7087—2 styles, dog carts, 10½ in. long, sulkies with dog and goat, boy drivers. ⅙ doz. in box. Doz $4.50

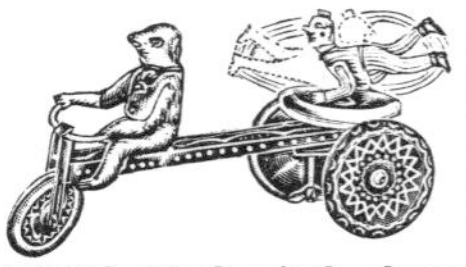

2F7086—Mechanical clown with bear driver, 8½ in. long, double action, 5 color trim. Runs in circle, clown on platform performs. Each in box. ½ doz. in pkg.......Doz $4.00

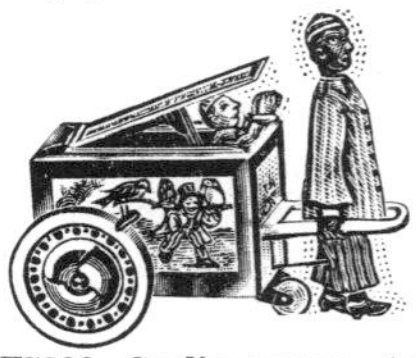

2F7089—Coolie wagon, triple action, 6½ in. long, 5 colors. Runs in circle, figure raises head out of wagon, coolie shakes head. Each in box. $4.25

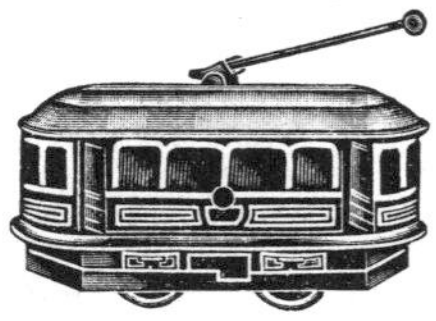

2F7093—Trolley car, 7 in., 4 colors. Bell rings when car is in motion. Each in box Doz $4.50

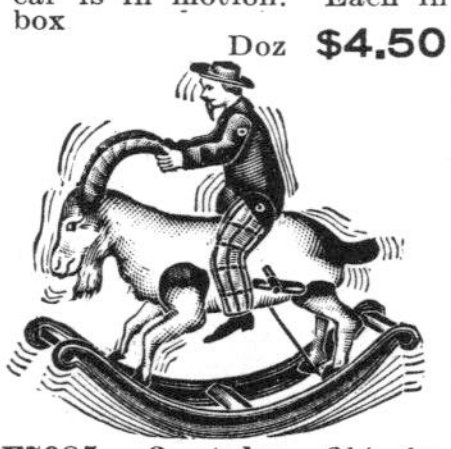

2F7085 — 3 styles, 6½ in. high, natural colors, soldier with dog, man on goat and Arab on elephant. All with rocking motion. ¼ doz. in box. Doz $4.50

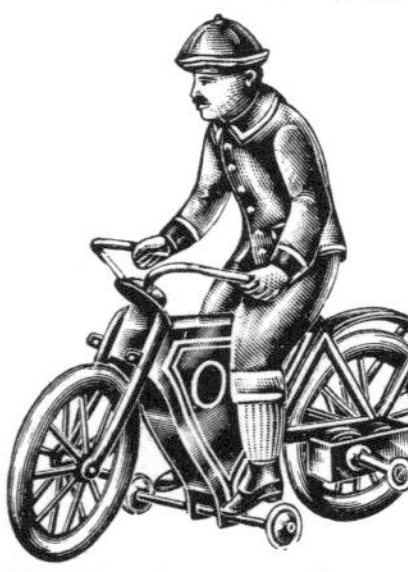

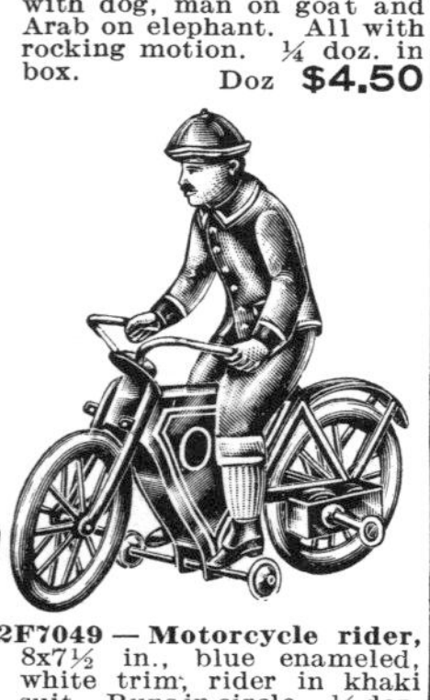

2F7049 — Motorcycle rider, 8x7½ in., blue enameled, white trim, rider in khaki suit. Runs in circle. ½ doz. in box. Doz $4.50

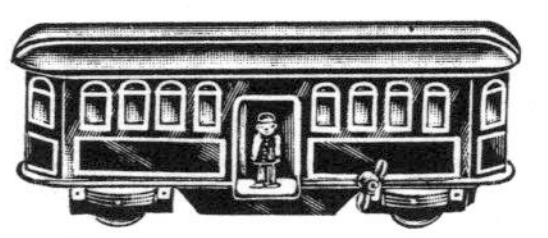

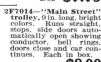

2F7014—"Main Street" trolley, 9 in. long, bright colors. Runs straight, stops, side doors automatically open showing conductor, bell rings, doors close and car continues. Each in box. Doz $8.00

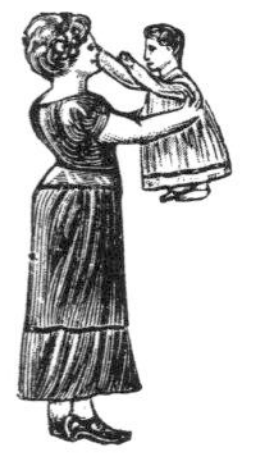

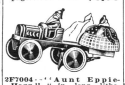

2F7063—Mother and baby, 8 in. high, brightly colored natural features. Toy revolves and mother lowers and raises baby in playful fashion. Each in box. Doz $5.50

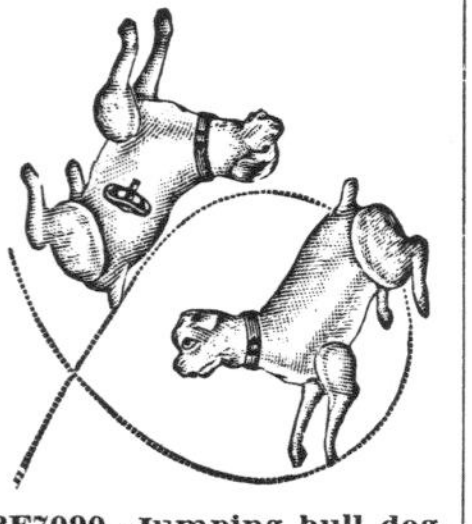

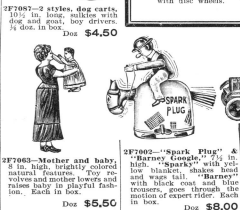

2F7090—Jumping bull dog, 6 in., natural finish, extra strong spring. Turns complete somersault. Each in box. ½ doz. in pkg..........Doz $6.00

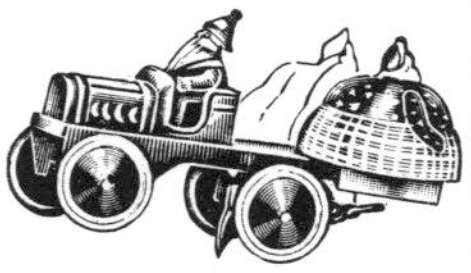

2F7004—"Aunt Eppie-Hogg," 8 in. long, lithographed in bright colors. Car runs a short distance, flies up in front almost shaking driver from seat, then moves on. Each in box. ¼ doz. in pkg. Doz $7.50

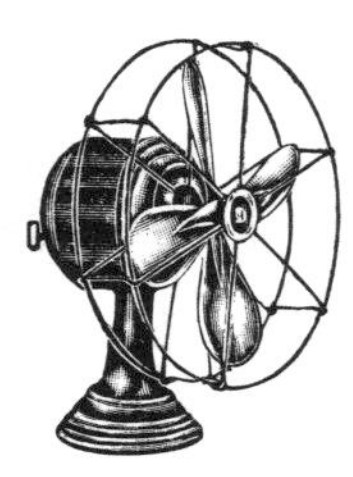

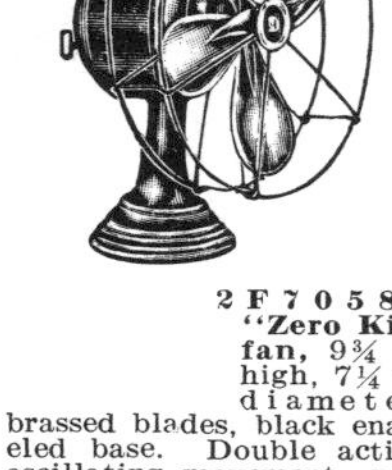

2F7058—"Zero Kid" fan, 9¾ in. high, 7¼ in. diameter, brassed blades, black enameled base. Double action, oscillating movement, extra long running spring. Runs 1 minute, 15 seconds with 1 winding. ⅒ doz. in box. Doz $7.75

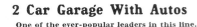

2 Car Garage With Autos

One of the ever-popular leaders in this line.

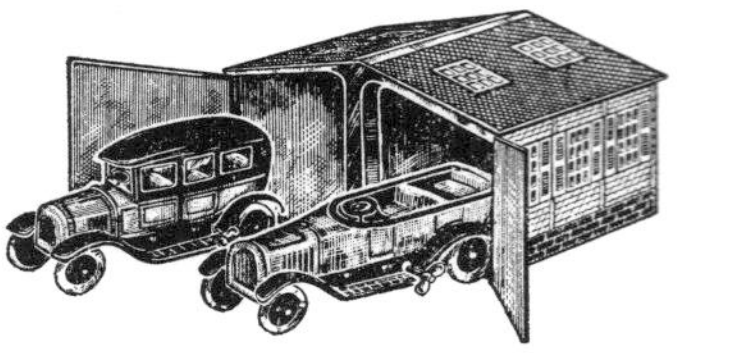

2F7110—2 car garage with autos, 8x6⅜ in. bright lithographed metal garage with painted doors, windows and shutters, one 6 in. red touring car, one 6 in. blue sedan, both with disc wheels. Doz sets $7.75

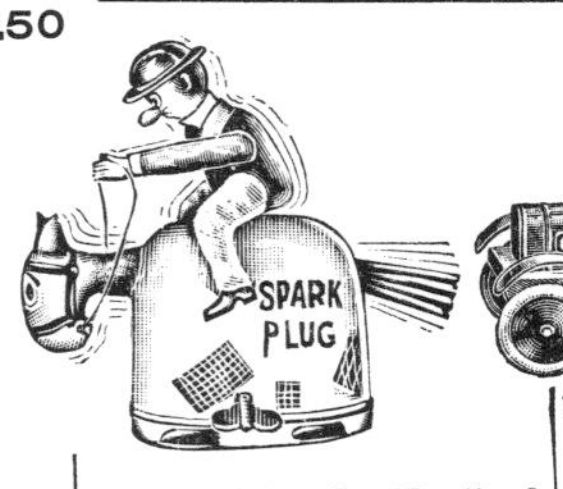
SPARK
PLUG

2F7002—"Spark Plug" & "Barney Google," 7½ in. high. **"Sparky"** with yellow blanket, shakes head and wags tail. **"Barney"** with black coat and blue trousers, goes through the motion of expert rider. Each in box. Doz $8.00

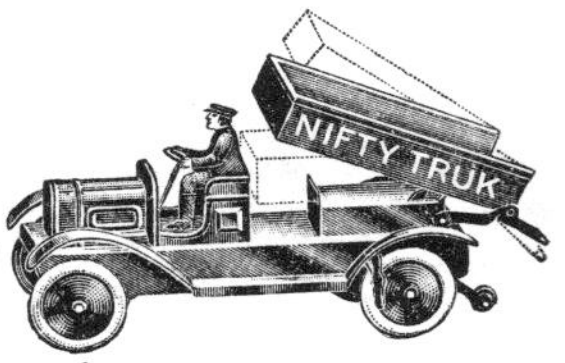
NIFTY TRUK

2F7003—Automatic dumping truck, 10 in. long, green painted body, red disc wheels, driver. Truck starts to move, stops and dumps contents. Each in box. Doz $8.00

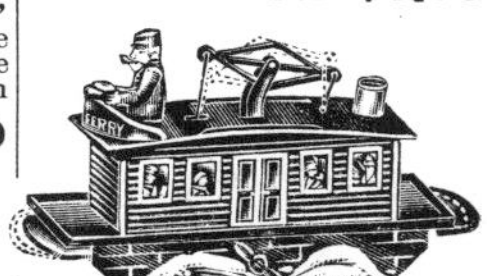

2F7016—"Nifty" ferry boat, 8 in. long, bright colors, nursery rhyme characters at windows. Walking beam moves up and down, runs straight but automatically reverses when bow or stern strikes obstructions. Each in box. ¼ doz. in pkg.........Doz $8.00

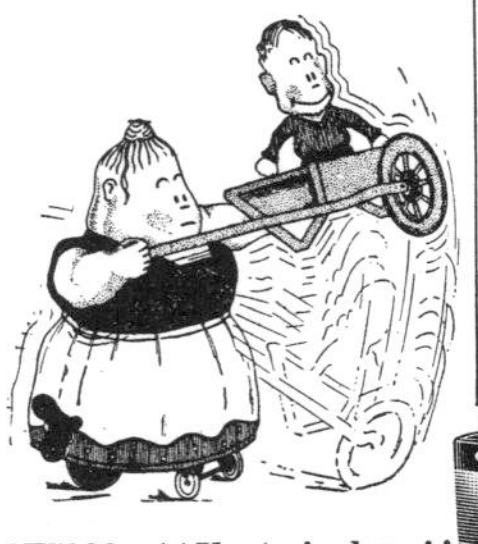

2F7009—"Katrinka," "Jimmy" and wheelbarrow, 6¾ in. high, red and blue lithographed, Katrinka raises and lowers Jimmy in wheelbarrow, then moves on. Doz $8.00

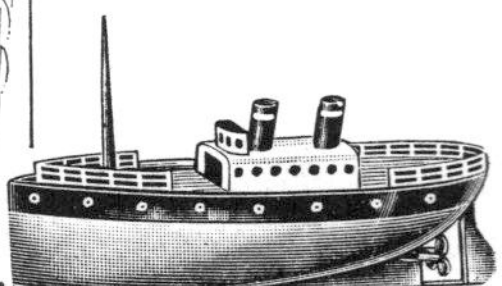

2F7107—Boat, 8½ in. long, red and blue enameled body, painted decks, smokestack, cabin, bridge, rail and mast. Doz $8.00

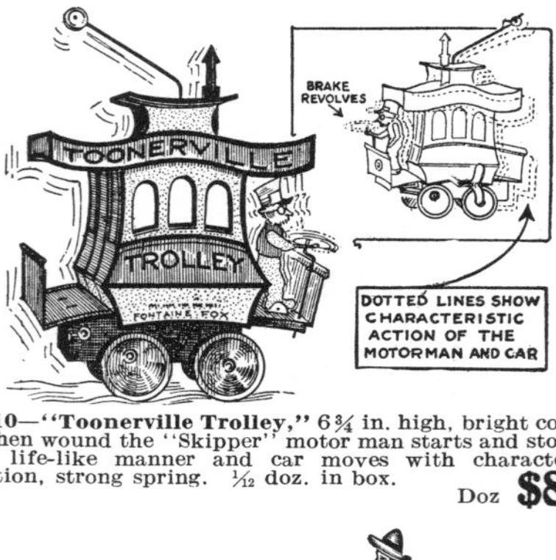

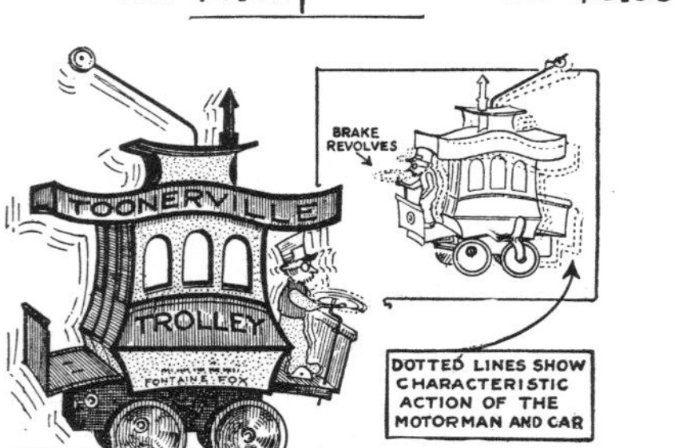
TOONERVILLE
TROLLEY
BRAKE REVOLVES
DOTTED LINES SHOW CHARACTERISTIC ACTION OF THE MOTORMAN AND CAR

2F7010—"Toonerville Trolley," 6¾ in. high, bright colored. When wound the "Skipper" motor man starts and stops car in life-like manner and car moves with characteristic action, strong spring. ½ doz. in box. Doz $8.00

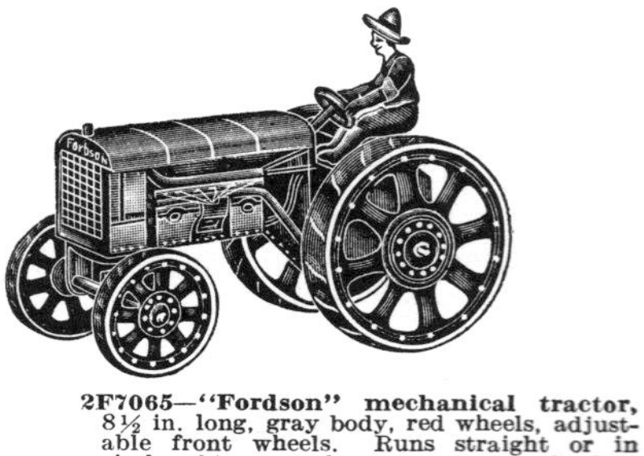

2F7065—"Fordson" mechanical tractor, 8½ in. long, gray body, red wheels, adjustable front wheels. Runs straight or in circle. Doz $8.00

IMPORTED MECHANICAL TOYS—Continued

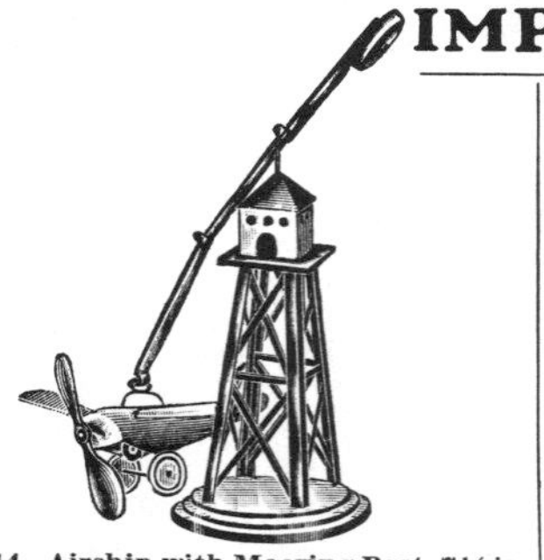

2F7114—Airship with Mooring Post, 7½ in. metal airship, 21½ in. metal balance rod moored to 8 in. post, 5 in. heavy base plate. Mechanical airship rises from ground and moves in circles. Each in display box. 1/12 doz. in pkg. Doz **$8.25**

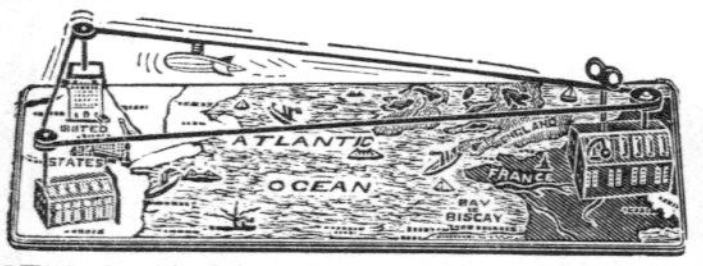

2F7028—Airship "Los Angeles." 14x6 in. metal base showing the countries sailed over on trip between Germany and U. S., with control stations, patrol boats and metal hanger concealing clock work spring. The "Los Angeles" makes the trip on a running string suspended about the control stations. Speed regulator. 1/12 doz. in box.................... Doz **$8.50**

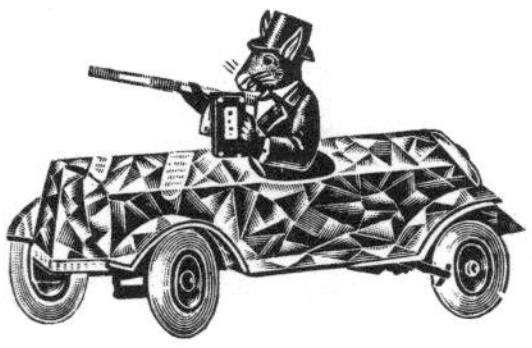

2F7012—"Uncle Wiggily's" crazy car, 10x7 in., "patchwork" painted body with characteristic "Uncle Wiggily" driver. Runs in zigzag motion. Each in box. ¼ doz. in pkg............. Doz **$8.75**

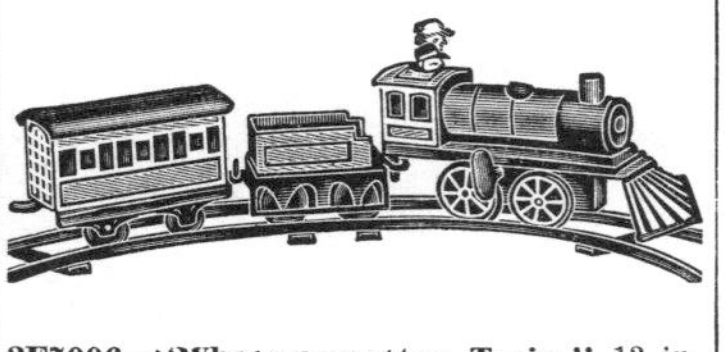

2F7006—"Whats-a-matter Train," 13 in. long, yellow painted 4 piece circular track. Train stops suddenly, engineer raises and turns head through top of cab, looks around and then goes back to former position. Each in box. 1/6 doz. in pkg.................. Doz **$8.75**

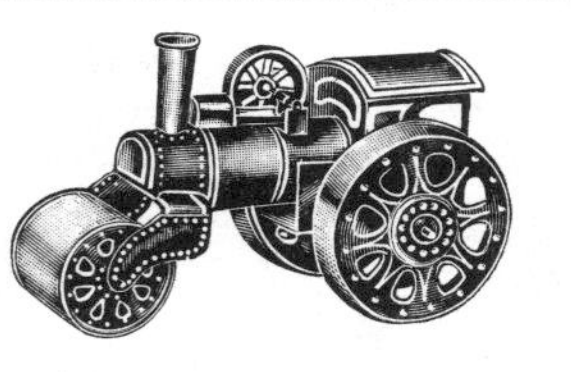

2F7051—Street roller, 9 in. long, black and green body, adjustable front wheels. Runs straight or in circle 1/12 doz. in box............ Doz **$9.50**

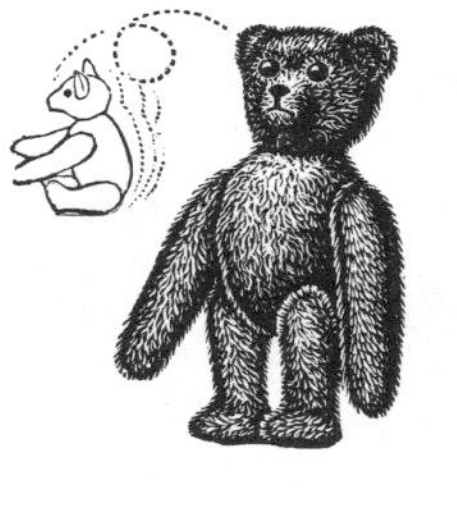

2F7210—Tumbling teddy bear, 8½ in. high, plush body, glass eyes, jointed arms and legs. Wound with arms, tumbling action. ½ doz. in box. Doz **$9.75**

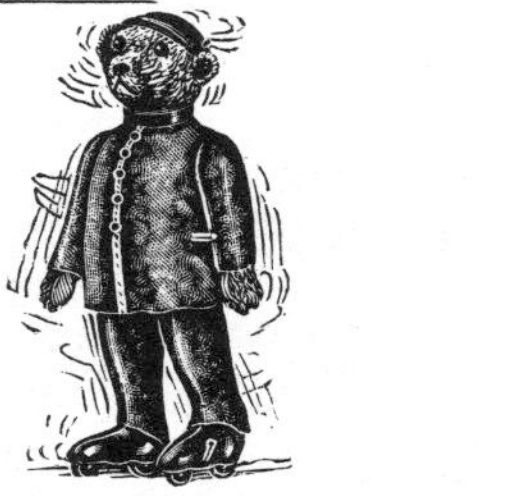

2F7272—Walking teddy bear, 9¾ in. high, plush head and hands, glass eyes, felt trousers, coat and hat, metal body. Walks forwards and backwards, turns in circle, moving head and arms, foot levers adjust action, automatic stop in back. 1/12 doz. in box........... Doz **$15.00**

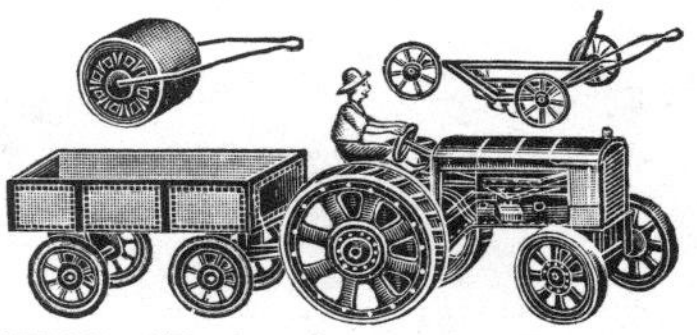

2F7146—"Fordson" mechanical tractor, with trailer, roller and plow, tractor 8½ in. long, gray body, red wheels, adjustable front wheels, 6¾ in. gray trailer, 2½ in. roller, 6 in. plow, 3 bright metal imitation plows. Runs straight or in circle. 1 in display box .. Each **$1.50**

MARKE
LEHMANN

"LEHMANN'S" IMPORTED MECHANICAL TOYS

Made by Europe's most dependable manufacturer. Each toy lithographed in bright colors. Strongly constructed with heavy springs.

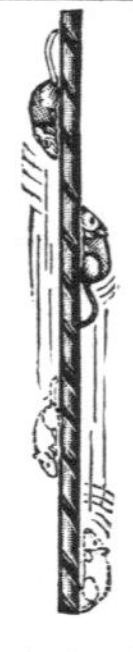

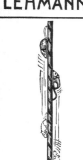

2F7120—Spiral mice, 15 in. red pole. Two white mice run up and down by reversing pole.
1 doz. in box.... Doz **72c**

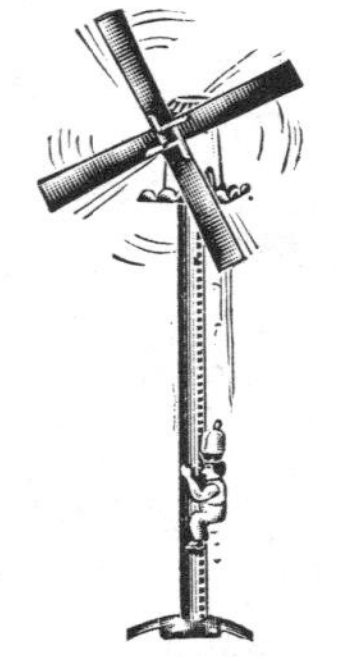

Climbing Miller

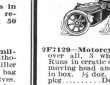

One of the best values in this well-known line to retail as a profit-paying 50 center.

2F7126—Climbing miller, 4 color lithographed, 17 in. ladder, miller climbs and descends with bag on head, wheel revolves. Each in box. ½ doz. in pkg.
Doz **$3.50**

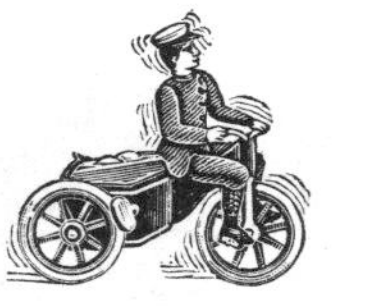

2F7129—Motorcycle, 5 in. over all, 3 wheeled cycle. Runs in erratic circle, driver moving head and legs. Each in box. ½ doz. in pkg.......... Doz **$3.75**

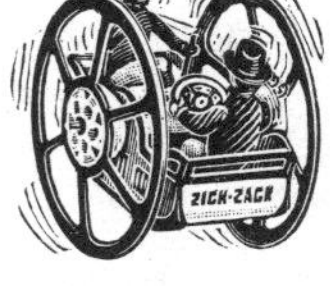

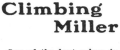

2F7138—"Zig-Zag," 5 in. cart. Travels in erratic fashion. Each in box. ¼ doz. in pkg. Doz **$7.20**

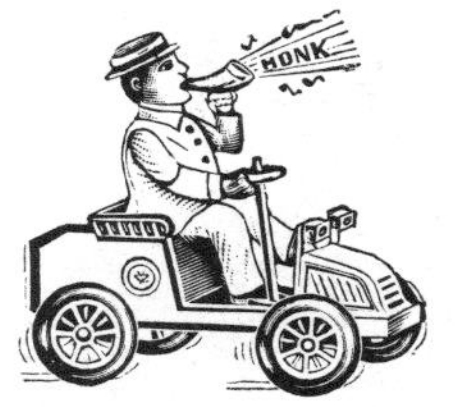

2F7143—7 in. long. Erratic action, man blows horn. 1/12 doz. in box. Doz **$7.50**

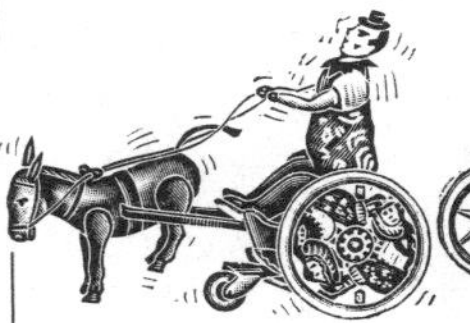

2F7133—Balky Mule, 7½ in. over all. Runs forward, backs and kicks, driver bounces up and down. Each in box. ½ doz. in pkg. Doz **$4.25**

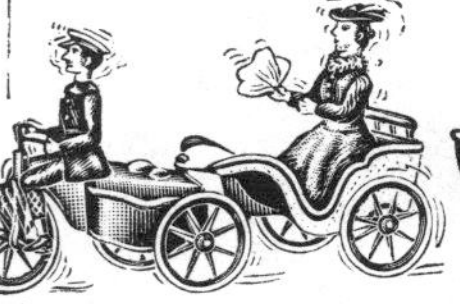

2F7141—"Nanni," 9 in. over all, motorcycle with trailer. Runs in circle, woman jumps up and down waving handkerchief. Each in box. ¼ doz. in pkg. Doz **$7.20**

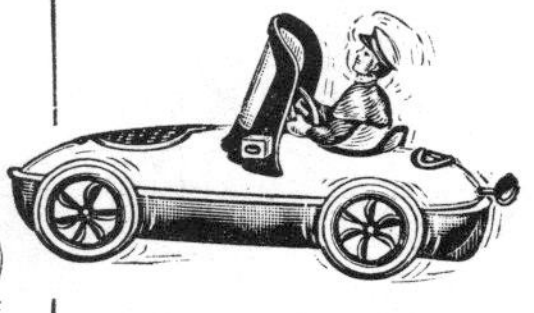

2F7144—9½ in. long, disc wheels, isinglass windshield. Runs in circle, figure turns head. ½ doz. in box.......... Doz **$7.50**

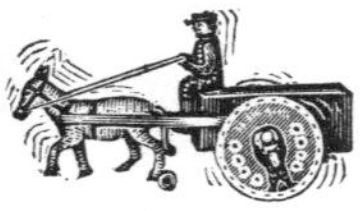

2F7121 — "Naob," 6 in. over all, donkey, cart and figure. Runs in circle in erratic fashion.
½ doz. in box. Doz **$1.85**

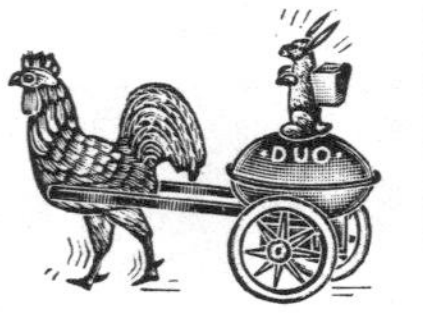

2F7132—"Duo," 7 in. over all. Runs straight, rabbit's ears move up and down. Each in box. ½ doz. in pkg. Doz **$3.75**

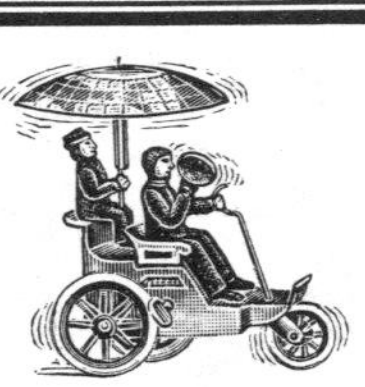

1F7128—"Ampol," 5¼ in. over all. Revolving parasol shows map of north pole, runs straight. Each in box. ½ doz. in pkg. Doz **$3.75**

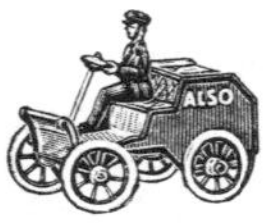

2F7122—"Also," 4 in. auto Runs in circle. ½ doz. in box. Doz **$1.85**

2F7124 — "Quack-Quack," 7½ in. over all. Runs straight, little ducks move up and down. Each in box. ½ doz. in pkg. Doz **$3.75**

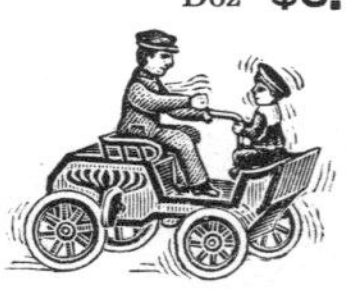

2F7130—"Naughty Boy", 6 in. car. Runs with zigzag motion. Each in box. ½ doz. in pkg. Doz **$3.75**

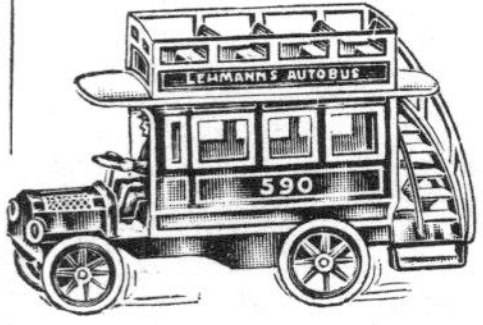

2F7139—Autobus, 8½ in. long. Runs in circle. Each in box. ¼ doz. in pkg.......... Doz **$7.20**

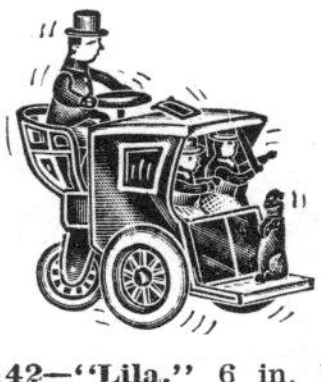

2F7142—"Lila," 6 in. bansom bus with driver, passengers and dog. Driver turns wheel, figures wave arms, dog shakes head. Each in box. ¼ doz. in pkg. Doz **$7.20**

You can Sell Now and Pay Dec. 31 by our special terms on Holiday Goods

"KINGSBURY" MECHANICAL TOYS—With Rubber Tires

Made of heavy gauge steel but light in weight—excellent designs and high grade workmanship throughout. Powerful and noted for long distance traveling. Note all numbers have steel disc wheels with rubber tires vulcanized on—they cannot come off.

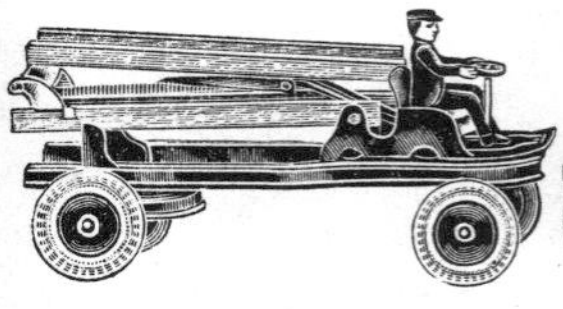

1F3125—Aerial ladder truck, 9½ in. long, disc wheels, rubber tires, fireman chauffeur, red, blue, gold and yellow finish. 13 in. extension ladder rises automatically when bumper strikes any object. ¼ doz. in pkg. Doz **$8.75**

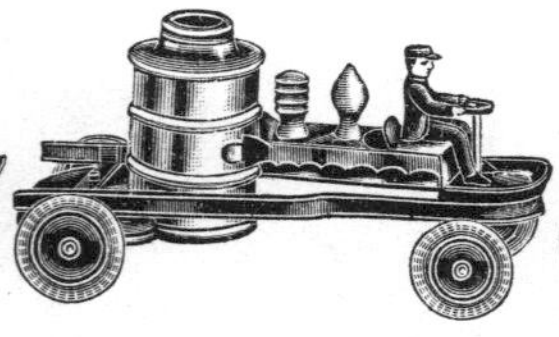

1F3119—Auto fire engine, 9½ in. long, disc wheels, rubber tires, fireman chauffeur, red, blue and gilt finish. 1/6 doz. in pkg............... Doz **$8.75**

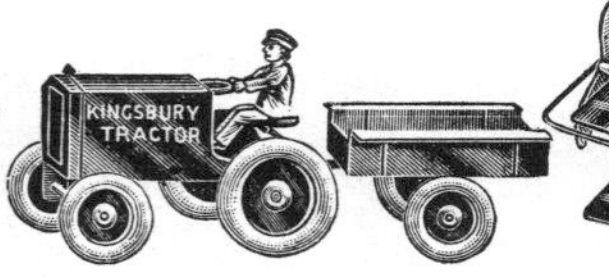

1F3270—Tractor and trailer, 12 in. long, red bodies, disc wheels, with **genuine rubber tires.** 3 color driver. 1 in box. Each **$1.05**

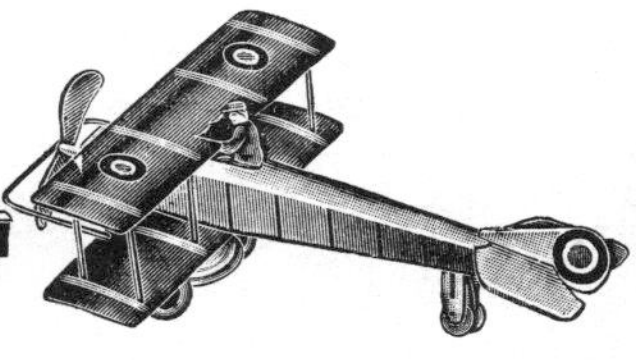

1F3200—Airplane, 15 in. long, 12 in. wing spread, red, yellow and blue with red, white and blue bullseyes, propeller revolves, rubber tire landing wheels. Runs on floor. 1 in box. Each **$1.25**

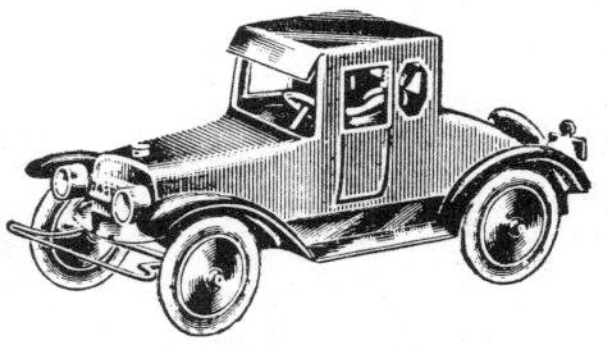

1F3275—Coupe, 11 in. long, finished in red, blue, black, green and gilt. disc wheels, rubber tires, extra wheel, headlights, license plates, "STOP" signal and chauffeur. 1 in box. Each **$1.75**

IRON TOYS

POPULAR PRICED ASSORTMENTS

Painted in bright colors. Note that we assort 3 or more styles.

1F3068—3 styles, average 4¾ in., locomotive and tender, car and chariot. Asstd. 1 doz. in box. **Doz 80c**

1F3070—6 styles, average 8 in., tractor, Ford coupe, car, sulky, sedan and buckboard. Asstd. ½ doz. in box. **Doz $2.10**

1F3074—6 styles, average 8 in., fire engine, hook and ladder, patrol, farm wagon, hansom and limousine. Asstd. ½ doz. in box. **Doz $2.25**

1F3075—6 styles, average 6½ in., fire engine, hook and ladder, dray, ice wagon, sulky and auto coal wagon. Asstd. ½ doz. in box. **Doz $2.25**

FAST SELLING NOVELTIES

1F3103—"Fordson" Tractor, 6 in. long, enamel body, red cleated rear wheels. ½ doz. in box. **Doz $4.00**

Safety coaches, exact models of auto coaches, red, white and blue enamel, balloon tires, disc wheels. Each in box. Length In pkg. Doz
1F3079—8 in. ½ doz. **$4.00**
1F3080—12 " ¼ " **11.00**

1F3085—3 styles, average 1½ in., dump wagon, coal wagon, loaded dray, drivers. Asstd. ¼ doz. in box. **Doz $4.25**

FORD CAR ASSORTMENT

1F3077—4 styles, 6½ in. long, touring car, coupe, coach and sedan, black enameled bodies, gilt trim, imitation tires, driver. Each in box. ¼ doz. in pkg. **Doz $4.00**

1F3098—Yellow taxi, 8 in. long, yellow enameled body, black trim, disc wheels, spare tire, driver. ½ doz. in box. **Doz $7.20**

1F3089—Milk wagon, 13½ in. long, white body, imitation bottles and milk cans, red driver. ½ doz. in box. **Doz $8.50**

1F3088—Santa Claus sleigh, 16½ in. long, red and gilt trim, Santa Claus, 2 white galloping reindeer on shaft with wheels. ½ doz. in box. **Doz $19.75**

FIRE ENGINES

1F3118—5 in. long, aluminum finish. 1 doz. in box. **Doz 84c**

1F3121—8 in. long, black enameled body, aluminum wheels. ½ doz. in box. **Doz $2.10**

1F3130—11 in. long, red and gold body, yellow wheels. ¼ doz. in box. **Doz $4.10**

1F3128—9¾ in. long, blue body, gilt trim, yellow wheels. ¼ doz. in box. **Doz $4.50**

1F3139—11¾ in. long, red and gold body, yellow wheels, imitation rubber tires, 3 horses. ½ doz in box. **Doz $8.00**

1F3178—11¼ in. long, yellow and gold body, red disc wheels, imitation rubber tires, gong. ½ doz. in box. **Doz $12.00**

1F3146—20 in. long, white and gold body, red wheels, imitation rubber tires, **hose, gong and extra fireman**, 2 galloping horses. ½ doz. in box. **Doz $21.00**

1F3148—21 in. long, **nickel plated body**, red wheels, imitation rubber tires, **3 galloping horses**, hose, gong and extra fireman. ½ doz. in box. **Doz $30.00**

HOOK AND LADDER TRUCKS

1F3117—5½ in. long, aluminum finish, movable wheels. 1 doz. in box. **Doz 84c**

1F3122—11 in. long, red body, 2 yellow steel ladders. ½ doz. in box. **Doz $2.10**

1F3135—11 in. long, red body, two 10 in. yellow wood ladders, imitation rubber tires, detachable uprights. ¼ doz. in box. **Doz $4.25**

1F3140—17½ in. long, blue and gold body, yellow wheels, driver and tillerman, two 10 in. wood ladders, imitation rubber tires, 3 horses. ½ doz. in box. **Doz $8.00**

1F3179—16 in. long, red and gold body, yellow disc wheels, imitation rubber tires, two 14 in. wood ladders, detachable uprights, gong, driver and tillerman. ½ doz. in box. **Doz $12.00**

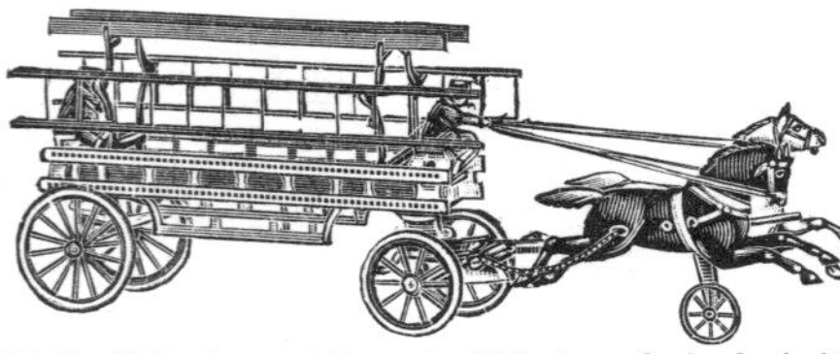

1F3147—24 in. long, white and gold body, red wheels, imitation rubber tires, 3 wooden ladders, gong, driver and tillerman, galloping horses. ½ doz. in box. **Doz $21.00**

1F3149—28 in. long, nickel plated body, red wheels, imitation rubber tires, 3 galloping horses, three wood ladders, detachable uprights, gong, driver, tillerman, steering wheel. ½ doz. in box. **Doz $30.00**

NOVELTY CIRCUS WAGONS

Bright colors, gilt trim, wagons with detachable doors

1F3086—3 styles, 8½ in., red, white and blue wagons, lion, tiger or bear, each in box. Asstd. ¼ doz. in pkg. **Doz $4.00**

1F3083—3 styles, 2 cage wagons and 1 van, average 12¼ in., blue, white and red bodies, tiger, lion or bear. Asstd. ¼ doz. in box. **Doz $8.00**

F3084—16¼ in. long, red wagon, 2 lions. ½ doz. in box. **$22.50**

1F3095—Clown van, 16½ in. long, 2 oval side mirrors, mechanical revolving clown on top, sliding doors. ½ doz. in box. **Doz $33.00**

GYRO TOYS

High Power—Large Size—Sturdy Construction

GYRO Toys are practical in every way. They will stand up under hard and continued use. These new models are improved and are better mechanically than ever before. Stronger, more powerful, smoother running! All have the famous GYRO High Power mechanism—no springs to wind or break.

1F3328—Aeroplane, 13½ in. long, 13 in. wing spread, brilliantly colored, with aviator. ½ doz. in box.
Doz **★8.50**

1F3346—Dump truck, 14 in. long, red body, yellow cab and chassis, lever for raising and lowering body, gold disc wheels, imitation rubber tires. ½ doz. in box..........Doz **$13.25**

1F3344—Racing car, 10 in. long, red body, yellow trim, chauffeur, each in box. 1 doz. in pkg.......Doz **$5.40**

1F3305—Tricky duck, 7¼ in. long, enameled in contrasting bright colors. Runs straight or in circle. ½ doz. in box............Doz **$7.60**

1F3329—Coupe, 13½ in. long, blue body, yellow wheels and trim. ½ doz. in box..........Doz **$11.35**

1F3348—Police patrol, 14½ in. long, blue body with "Police Patrol" lettering, gold disc wheels, **rubber tires.** ½ doz. in box..........Doz **$13.25**

1F3340—"Komical" elephant, 10 in. long, natural color body and tusks, bright trappings platform and wheels. Doz **$7.60**

1F3327—Touring car, 13 in. long, red body and top, chauffeur, gold disc wheels, imitation rubber tires.
Doz **$11.35**

1F3347—Chemical wagon, 14½ in. long, yellow body and trim, two 7 in. black ladders, gold disc wheels, **rubber tires,** firemen. ½ doz. in box..Doz **$13.25**

1F3363—Coupe, 13½ in. long, blue body, black top and trim, gold disc wheels, **rubber tires.** ½ doz. in box.
Doz **$13.25**

1F3362—Delivery van, 13 in. long, gray body, red trim, **rubber tires,** red chauffeur. ½ doz. in box. Doz **$13.25**

Long Distance Speed Toys

The Gyro high power motor has two sets of gears that develop double the power, speed and length of action over previous lines of friction toys.

1F3303—Locomotive and tender, 18 in. long, red enameled body, gilt wheels and trim.
Doz **$11.35**

1F3349—Express train, 30 in. long, red enameled body, gilt wheels and trim. ½ doz. in box...........Doz **$13.25**

GYRO BEST SELLERS

Sales last year marked these numbers as the biggest selling GYRO toys—the greatest profit makers for our customers. This year the improved models make them bigger values than ever.

1F3319—Dump truck, 14 in. long, red body, running board and trim, yellow cab and chassis, gold disc wheels, **rubber tires,** lever for raising and lowering body. ½ doz. in box. Doz **$15.00**

1F3323—Roadster, 19 in. long, yellow body, black trim, top lowered, spare wheel, gold disc wheels, imitation rubber tires. ½ doz. in box..................Doz **$15.00**

1F3358—Roadster, 19 in. long, red body, yellow and black trim, gold disc wheels, **rubber tires.** ½ doz. in box.............Doz **$18.75**

1F3359—Coupe, 19 in. long, blue body, black trim, gold disc wheels, **rubber tires.**
½ doz. in box....................Doz **$18.75**

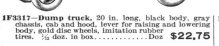

1F3317—Dump truck, 20 in. long, black body, gray chassis, cab and hood, lever for raising and lowering body, gold disc wheels, imitation rubber tires. ½ doz. in box............Doz **$22.75**

1F3310—Dump truck, 20 in. long, black body, running board and trim, gray chassis, cab and hood, gold disc wheels, **rubber tires,** lever for raising and lowering body. ½ doz. in box. ....Doz **$26.50**

BIG PROFIT PAYING ASST.

This assortment consists of sure selling Gyro toys. They are exceptionally well made and are big values.

21 Selected Gyro Toys

Your Mark-up on Cost Over

69%

1F3325—Assortment consists of the following:

	Retail each		Retail each
3 Komical Elephants	$1.00	1 Patrol	$1.75
2 Tricky Ducks	1.00	2 Coupes	1.75
1 Aeroplane	1.50	1 Chemical Wagon	1.75
2 Locomotives	1.50	1 Dump Truck	1.75
1 Coupe	1.50	1 Dump Truck	2.00
1 Touring Car	1.50	2 Roadsters	2.00
1 Truck	1.50	1 Coupe	2.50
1 Delivery Van	1.75		

Total Retail Value, $33.00.
Your Mark-up on Cost, $13.50.
ASST (21 pcs) **$19.50**

American-National-Automobiles

"STAR"—32½ in. long, 10½ in. wide. Cream body, blue and red striping, 8 in. spoke wheels, ⅜ in. rubber tires.
Equipment—Gas control lever, gas tank, motor meter. Bumpers, steel pedals, stationary frame. Steel seat and radiator front.
1F847—(Mfrs 5506) Each 1 in carton, 25lbs. **$4.65**

"ACE"—35 in. long, 12 in. wide. Red body, yellow and black stripes. 10 in. spoke wheels, ½ in. rubber tires.
Equipment—Gas and spark control, motor meter. Bumper, steel pedals, stationary frame. Steel seat and radiator front.
1F849—(Mfrs 5508) Each 1 in carton, 30 lbs. **$5.00**

"BUICK"—35 in. long, 12 in. wide. Royal blue with light blue and yellow trim panels. 10 in. double disc wheels, ½ in. rubber tires.
Equipment—Gas control lever, motor meter, bumper. Rubber pedals, road lamps, nickeled hub caps. All steel seat and radiator front, rear suspension spring.
1F850—(Mfrs 5511D) Each 1 in carton, 38 lbs. **$7.00**

"DURANT"—35 in. long, 12 in. wide. Red body, black and yellow striping. 10 in. disc wheels, ½ in. rubber tires.
Equipment—Gas control lever, motor meter, bumper. Steel pedals, stationary frame, nickeled hub caps. Steel seat and radiator
1F851—(Mfrs 5509D) 1 in carton, 35 lbs. Each **$6.00**

"HUDSON"

35 in. long, 12 in. wide. Red body, yellow stripes. 10 in. double disc wheels, ½ in. rubber tires.
Equipment—Gas control lever, rooter horn, adjustable tinned windshield. Motor meter, metal road lamps, license plate. Bumper, rubber pedals, oil can. Nickeled hub caps, steel seat and radiator front, rear suspension spring.
1F852—(Mfrs 5518D) 1 in carton, 48 lbs. Each **$8.75**

"PEERLESS"

40 in. long, 12 in. wide. Gray body, red trim and stripe. 10 in. double disc wheels, ⅝ in. rubber tires.
Equipment—Gas control lever, rooter horn, adjustable windshield. Gas tank, rubber pedals, gear shift. Metal road lamps with non-glare lenses, spot light, license plate. All steel seat and radiator front, rear suspension spring.
1F853—(Mfrs 5504D) Each in wire bound box, 48 lbs. ....Each **$10.25**

"FRANKLIN"

43 in. long, 12 in. wide. Dark blue with light blue trim. 10 in. double disc wheels, ½ in. rubber tires.
Equipment—Gas control lever, adjustable tinned windshield, motor meter. Fender, running board and bumper. License plate, rubber pedals, oil can. Metal road lamps, all steel upholstered seat and radiator front. Rear suspension spring.
1F854—(Mfrs 5526D) Each in wire bound box, 57 lbs ....Each **$11.00**

"NASH"

43 in. long, 13 in. wide. Red body, yellow and black trim. 10 in. double disc wheels, ⅝ in. rubber tires.

EQUIPMENT

Bumper	Instrument board.	Upholstered seat
Rooter horn	Metal road lamps	All steel nickel plated radiator
Motor Meter	License plate	Rear suspension springs
Gear shift	Oil can	Comp'n tilting wheel
Rear trunk	Rubber pedals	

1F855—(Mfrs 5524D) Each in wire bound box, 57 lbs. ....Each **$11.50**

"OVERLAND"

43 in. long, 12 in. wide. Maroon body, red panels, red and white stripings. 10 in. double disc wheels, ⅝ in. rubber tires.

EQUIPMENT

Oil can	Instrument board	Composition tilting wheel
Fenders	Motor buzzer	Steel radiator front
Gear shift	Metal road lamps	Upholstered seat
Rear trunk	Tool kit with tools	Rear suspension springs
Rooter horn	Rubber pedals	
Motor Meter	Running board	

1F856—(Mfrs 5528DM) Each in wire bound box, 60 lbs. ....Each **$13.25**

"OLDSMOBILE"

43 in. long, 13 in. wide. Fawn body with brown panels, red stripes. 10 in. double disc wheels, ⅝ in. rubber tires.

EQUIPMENT

Motor meter	Rooter horn	Rubber pedals
Oil can	Metal road lamps	All steel radiator, nickel plated band.
Gas tank	Instrument board	Composition tilting wheel
Spotlight	Adjustable windshield	Upholstered seat
Fenders	Motor buzzer	
Gear shift	Rear suspension spring	

1F857—(Mfrs 5535DM) 1 in wire bound box, 71 lbs. ....Each **$15.00**

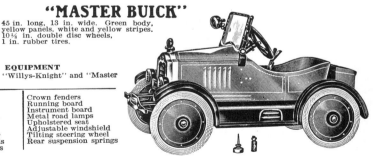

"WILLYS-KNIGHT"

51 in. long, 13 in. wide. Red body, black panels, yellow stripes. 12⅜ in. double disc wheels, 1 in. rubber tires.

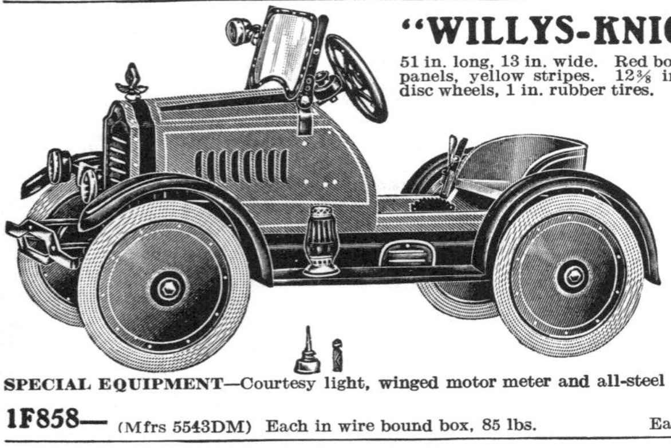

"MASTER BUICK"

45 in. long, 13 in. wide. Green body, yellow panels, white and yellow stripes. 10⅜ in. double disc wheels, 1 in. rubber tires.

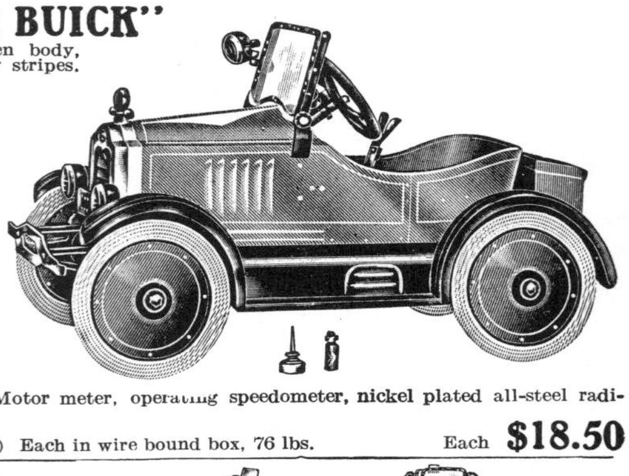

EQUIPMENT

Common to "Willys-Knight" and "Master Buick"

Bumper	Crown fenders
Oil can	Running board
Spotlight	Instrument board
Gear shift	Metal road lamps
Signal horn	Upholstered seat
Kick plates	Adjustable windshield
Motor buzzer	Tilting steering wheel
Rubber pedals	Rear suspension springs
License plates	

SPECIAL EQUIPMENT—Courtesy light, winged motor meter and all-steel radiator.
1F858—(Mfrs 5543DM) Each in wire bound box, 85 lbs. Each **$17.50**

SPECIAL EQUIPMENT—Motor meter, operating speedometer, nickel plated all-steel radiator and rear trunk.
1F859—(Mfrs 5540DM) Each in wire bound box, 76 lbs. Each **$18.50**

"STUDEBAKER"

51 in. long, 13 in. wide. Duco moon gray body, green panels, white and green stripings. 12⅜ in. double disc wheels, 1 in. rubber tires.

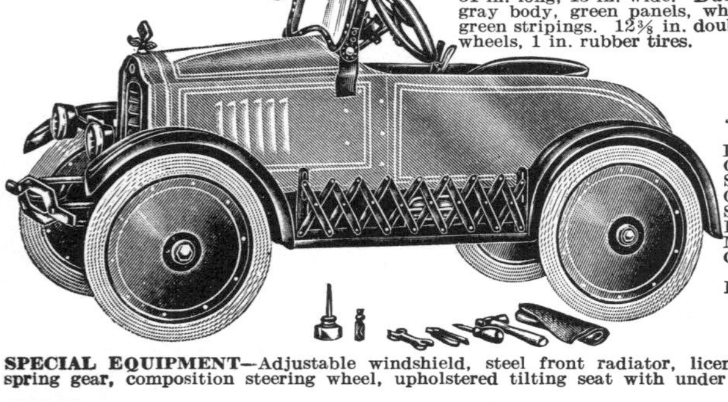

"PACKARD" SIX

51 in. long, 13 in. wide. Fawn body, with red panels, white and red stripes. 12⅜ in. double disc wheels, 1 in. rubber tires.

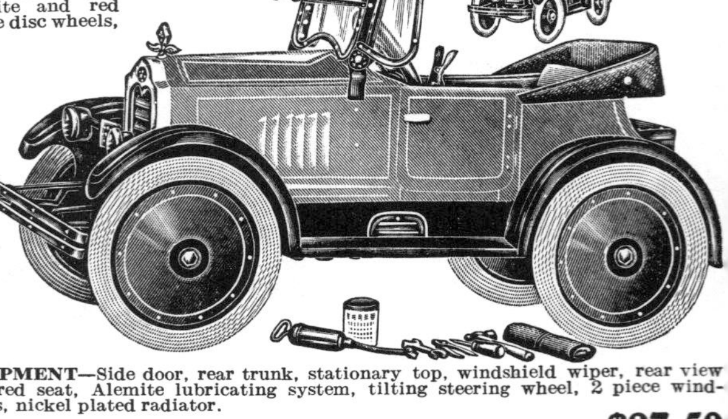

EQUIPMENT

Common to "Studebaker" and "Packard" Six.

Bumper	Luggage carrier
Oil can	Instrument board
Spotlight	Metal road lamps
Gear shift	Winged motor meter
Signal horn	Tool kit with tools
Kick plates	Adjustable pedals
Motor buzzer	Stop and Go signals.
Crown fenders	Operating speedometer.
Running board	

SPECIAL EQUIPMENT—Adjustable windshield, steel front radiator, license plate, full spring gear, composition steering wheel, upholstered tilting seat with under compartment.
1F860—(Mfrs 5546DM) 1 in crate, 125 lbs. Each **$23.00**

SPECIAL EQUIPMENT—Side door, rear trunk, stationary top, windshield wiper, rear view mirror, upholstered seat, Alemite lubricating system, tilting steering wheel, 2 piece windshield with wings, nickel plated radiator.
1F861—(Mfrs 5548 DM) 1 in crate, 125 lbs. Each **$27.50**

"AMERICAN-NATIONAL" AUTOMOBILES

HOSE AUTO
51 in. long, with ladders extending, 13 in. wide. Red body, yellow striping. 12 in. double disc wheels, 1 in. rubber tires.

EQUIPMENT

Fire bell.	2 ladders.	Upholstered seat.	Stationary frame.
Lantern.	Hose reel.	Oil can with holder.	Side rail supporting step and rear of auto.
Gear shift.	Rubber pedals.	Steel front radiator.	
Road lamps.	Instrument board.	"Jar Not" springs.	Composition tilting steering wheel.

1F865—(Mfrs 5578D) 1 in crate, 105 lbs.........................Each **$17.25**

HOOK AND LADDER AUTO
62 in. long, ladders extending, 13 in. wide. Red body with yellow striping. 12⅜ in. double disc wheels, 1 in. rubber tires.

EQUIPMENT

Bumper.	Gear Shift.	License plate.	Alemite lubricating system
Tool box.	Road lamps.	"Jar Not" springs.	Composition steering wheel.
Windshield.	2 lanterns.	Steel front radiator.	Extension ladders.
Spotlight.	Rubber pedals.	Stationary frame.	
Fire bell.	Instrument board.	Upholstered seat.	

1F866—(Mfrs 5584D) 1 in crate, 133 lbs.........................Each **$24.50**

FIRE ENGINE
52 in. long, ladders extending, 13 in. wide. Red body, yellow striping. 12⅜ in. double disc wheels, 1 in. rubber tires.

EQUIPMENT

Oil can.	Road lamps.	Nickel plated hub caps.	11x25 in. nickel plated boiler.
Bumper.	Spotlight.	Steam and water gauge.	Composition steering wheel with hand grips.
2 ladders.	Hinged fire door.	Fenders and running board.	
Gear shift.	"Jar Not" springs.	Upholstered seat.	
Fire bell.	Stationary frame.	Instrument board.	

1F867—(Mfrs 5586D) 1 in crate, 126 lbs.........................Each **$25.00**

"PAIGE"
65 in. long, 13 in. wide, maroon body, red panels, red and white stripings. 12¾ in. double disc wheels, 1¼ in. rubber balloon tires.

EQUIPMENT

Side door.	Instrument board.	Front and rear bumpers.	Upholstered all steel seat.
Gear shift.	Operating speedometer.	Nickeled rails.	2 piece adjustable windshield with side wings.
Spotlight.	Windshield wiper.	Rear compartment.	Side and rear parking lights.
Motor buzzer.	Rear vision mirror.	All steel chassis.	Crown fenders with running board.
Signal horn.	Winged motor meter.	Adjustable pedals.	Alemite lubricating system.
License plate.	Metal road lamps.	Stop and Go signal.	Flexible front and rear springs.
Kick plates.	Luggage carrier.	Tilting wheel.	Nickel plated mesh radiator.
	Tool kit with tools.		

1F863—(Mfrs 5551DM) 1 in crate, 160 lbs.........................Each **$35.00**

"Tornado"
Disc Wheel Scooter

Roller Brake Used on 1F15

"Tornado"—37 in. long, 34 in. high, black enameled steel frame, natural varnished wood platform, black stripes and word "Tornado," 9¾ in. red enameled double disc wheels, roller bearings, 1⁵⁄₁₆ in. corrugated rubber tires, varnished wood grip, with stand. 2 in carton, 35 lbs.

1F11—Without roller brake.
Each **$2.75**
6 or more, Each **2.65**

1F15—With roller brake.
Each **$3.10**
6 or more, Each **3.00**

"MARATHON" ALL STEEL SCOOTER

Red Enameled Frame, 7 In. Double Disc Wheels

1F249—30½ in. high, 30 in. over all, 12x4½ in. platform, red enameled all steel heavy frame throughout, red stained crosspiece handle, 7 in. double disc wheels, ⅝ in. rubber tires, parking stand, gilt stenciled "Marathon." 3 in crate, 23 lbs.................Each **$1.45**

"OVERLAND" SCOOTERS

Green Enameled Steel Frame 8 In. Double Spoke Wheels

34 in. long, 29 in. high, 4¾x12 in. natural varnished hardwood platform, green enameled steel frame, 8 in. double spoke wheels, red enameled cross handles, parking stand. 2 in carton, 15 lbs.
1F28—½ in. rubber tires..Each **$1.65**
1F29—¾ " " " .. " **1.95**

"VICTORY" DISC WHEEL SCOOTERS

Parking stand—with and without brakes.

37 in. long, 32½ in. high, red enameled steel frame, varnished wood platform, 10 in. red enameled double disc wheels, **roller bearing**, ¾ in. rubber tires, turned wood handle, stand. 2 in carton, 32 lbs.
1F9—Without brake......Each **✱2.40**
12 or more, Each **✱2.25**
1F10—With roller brake operated by pressing button on platform with heel..................Each **$2.75**
12 or more, Each **2.60**

"American Scooters"

Balloon Type Tires — Brakes—Parking Stands

Roller Bearing, Red Enameled Double Disc Wheels

1F25—(Mfrs 193) 39 in. long, 36 in. high, red enameled steel frame, 13 in. natural finished footboard, fancy striping, red stained crosspiece handle, 12 in. red enameled double disc wheels, roller bearing, 1 in. corrugated rubber tires. 2 in carton, 35 lbs.
Each **$3.50**

Corrugated Rubber Tires. Bicycle Bell

1F26—(Mfrs 199) 38 in. long, 35 in. high, red enameled steel frame, 13 in. footboard, rubber mat, red stained wood crosspiece handle, 10 in. double disc red enameled wheels, roller bearings, 1 in. corrugated rubber tires, bicycle bell. 2 in carton, 30 lbs..........Each **$3.65**

1¼ In. Tires Rubber Padded Foot Board

1F27—(Mfrs 198) 37 in. long, 36 in. high, red enameled steel frame, 13 in. footboard, rubber mat, red stained wood crosspiece handle, 10 in. double disc red enameled steel wheels, 1¼ in. corrugated tires, bicycle bell. 2 in carton, 30 lbs..........Each **$3.85**

POPULAR PRICED "DAYTON" ALL STEEL WAGONS

Beaded all steel bodies, black enameled steel bolsters and gearing, steel axle, double disc steel wheels

1F42—(Mfrs 7) 6x12 in., 4½ in. blue wheels, wire handle. 1 doz. in carton, 28 lbs. **Doz $4.75**

1F43—(Mfrs 8) 6x12 in. 4½ in. blue wheels, wood handle. 1 doz. in carton, 28 lbs. **Doz $5.75**

1F44—(Mfrs 9) 7½x15 in., 6 in. and 4½ in. blue wheels, wood handle. ½ doz. in carton, 25 lbs.....**Doz $8.00**

1F45—(Mfrs 10) 9x18 in., 7 in. 6 in. blue wheels, strong bolsters and bracing, wood handle. ½ doz. in carton, 35 lbs. **Doz $11.00**

1F46—(Mfrs 11) 9x18 in., double braces under bed, wood handle, 6 in. red wheels, ½ in. rubber tires. ¼ doz. in carton, 20 lbs. **Doz $15.50**

WOOD HAY CART

1F39—7x13½ in. red stained wood body, 3 slat open sides, 6 in. wood spoke wheels, tin tires, long wood handle. **Doz $1.75**

WOOD BODY EXPRESS WAGON

1F48—5½x12 in. yellow stained wood body, black stenciled "Express" on each side, 4½ in. wheels, steel tires, 16½ in. wood handle. 1 doz. in crate, 28 lbs. **Doz $2.25**

MENGEL WHEEL TOYS—Toys of Quality

"Trail-O-Wag"

Varnished natural finish hardwood body, embossed "Trail-O-Wag" and playtime scenes on each side, dovetailed corners, red painted 5 ply veneer wood wheels, red tongue.
1F30—6x12 in. body, 3 in. wheels. ½ doz. in carton, 15 lbs. **Doz $8.00**
1F31—7½x15 in. body, 3⅛ in. wheels. ½ doz. in carton, 20 lbs. **Doz $12.00**

Hay Wagon

1F37—11x19 in., 12½ in. high, red enameled bottom, axles and handle, 4 in. wheels, ivory stained removable slat sides. ½ doz. in carton, 20 lbs. **Doz $16.50**

JUVENILE HAND CARS

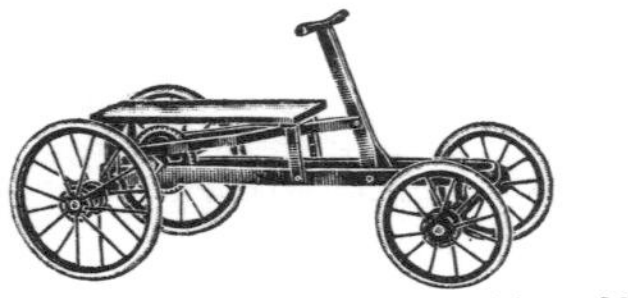

1F199—"Junior," 27 in. long, 7x14 in. gold bronze decorated seat, 10 in. and 6 in. red wheels, ⅜ in. rubber tires, black enameled steel frame and gear, heavy axles. 1 in crate, 25 lbs.........**Each $3.25**

1F204—"Irish Mail," 40 in. long, 9x20 in. green seat, 12 and 8 in. wheels, ½ in. rubber tires, hickory frame, sanded natural finish, red with narrow green striping. 1 in crate, 32 lbs. **Each $5.75**

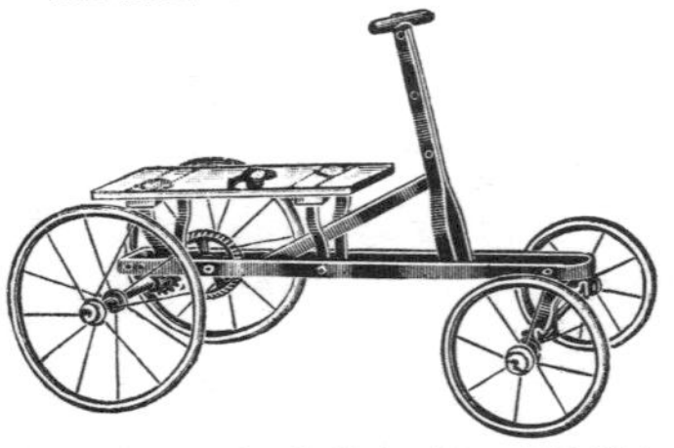

1F200—"Traveler," 31 in. long, 7¾x16 in. red seat, 12 and 8 in. red wheels, ⅜ in. rubber tires, black enameled steel frame and gear, gold bronze decorations, heavy axles and cog drive, nickel plated hub caps. 1 in crate, 30 lbs. **Each $4.50**

1F205—"Double Disc," 36 in. long, 7¾x16 in. natural hardwood seat, yellow striping, 12 and 8 in. double disc red enameled wheels, yellow striping, retained roller bearings, ⅜ in. rubber tires, nickel plated hub caps, black enameled steel frame. **Each $6.40**

TOY STEEL WHEELBARROWS

Sheet steel bodies, selected hardwood handles with round grips, heavy steel wheels.

1F16—Garden barrow, "Little Giant," 21 in. long, 6½x5x2 in. blue body, turned edges, stained handles, 4 in. blue stamped double steel wheel, steel supports. 1 doz. k.d in carton, 12 lbs. **Doz $2.10**

1F14—Garden barrow, 33 in. long, 10½x15 in. red enameled body, 7 in. blue enameled double disc wheels, green stained frame and handles. ½ doz. in carton, 23 lbs. **Doz $7.00**

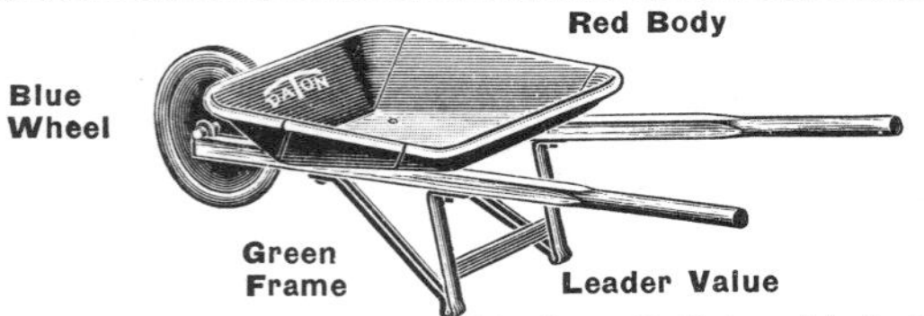

Blue Wheel — Red Body — Green Frame — Leader Value

1F12—(Mfrs 18) Dump barrow, 29 in. long, 11x13 in. red body, 6 in. double pressed blue enameled double disc wheels, green stained frame. 1 doz. in carton, 30 lbs.............**Doz $3.95**

1F21—Garden barrow, 29½ in. long, 9x12 in. body, striped and varnished, 8 in. double spoke wheel, black tipped handles. ½ doz. in crate, 25 lbs.....**Doz $8.50**

1F22—Garden barrow, 32 in. long, 11x15 in. body, striped and varnished, 10 in. double spoke wheel, black tipped handles. ⅓ doz. in crate, 22 lbs. **Doz $10.25**

CHILDREN'S "NEVER-TIP" SULKIES

Strongly Made—Will Carry 150 Lbs.

1F219—"Dandy," 11x14 in. seat, 56 in. long, 15 in. high, heavy 10 in. rubber tire wheels, assorted bright and red and green enameled wood pedal platforms 21½x5½ in., corrugated rubber pads, 8 in. red enameled double disc roller bearing wheels, rubber tires, starts instantly, easy to stop. 1 in carton, 22 lbs. **Doz $18.00**

Reinforced Brace for Reversing

1F220—10x14 in. heavy wood seat, 48 in. handle, 10 in. japanned double spoke wheels, ¾ in. rubber tires, red painted, reinforced brace for reversing, adjustable front and back foot rests. ⅙ doz. in crate, 24 lbs...**Doz $21.00**

"DUM-PED-KAR"

2 toys in one. The dumping action is a particularly good feature and makes easy sales.

1F234—30 in. long, 13½ in. high to seat, yellow enameled steel chassis, red enameled shaped seat, yellow enameled steel dump box which dumps automatically when lever is pulled, nickeled handle bars and steel front post, rubber grips, **bell**, 10 in. and 8 in. wheels, ½ in. rubber tires, red enameled steel pedals. **Each $4.00**

BALL-BEARING "SCUDDER CAR"

1F211—(Mfrs 1) 40 in. long, 18 in. wide, ball-bearing axle and transmission gear, red enameled steel frame and steering posts, 8 in. nickel plated auto steering wheel, black enameled axle and wheels, ⅝ in. rubber tires. 1 in crate, 27 lbs. **Each $5.75**

THE "GO-BOY" CAR

For Boys and Girls

1F206—32 in. long, 15 in. wide, 32¼ in. high, heavy red enameled steel frame, steel front post, turned wood cross handle, 2 yellow enameled wood pedal platforms 21½x5½ in., corrugated rubber pads, 8 in. red enameled double disc roller bearing wheels, rubber tires, starts instantly, easy to stop. 1 in carton, 22 lbs. **Each $7.00**

THE "GO-BIKE" CAR

Strong, safe and speedy—for girls and boys up to 12 years.

1F201—Red enameled all steel frame, 23 in. long, 11 in. wide, 13½x7 in. hardwood seat, chain driven, rubber tread ball-bearing pedals, guarded sprocket wheels, 8 in. red enameled disc wheels, solid rubber clincher tires. One revolution of the pedals drives the "Go-Bike" five feet. **Each $7.75**

"KEYSTONE" GIANT TOYS

Large sizes, made of heavy steel, enameled in bright colors, FULLY EQUIPPED. No other line has so many worth while features.

Exclusive talking points make "KEYSTONES" easy to sell. Extra strong—trucks will support 200 lbs. or more.

26 In. Long

1F2493—(Mfrs 42) **Packard truck**, 26 in. long, 9½ in. high, 8¼ in. wide, black enameled body, cab and running boards, red enameled steel chassis, red disc wheels, balloon type imitation rubber tires, **steering front wheels**, drop end, transparent celluloid windshield, imitation headlights, signal arm, nickel radiator and hub caps. 1 in carton..........Each **$4.00**

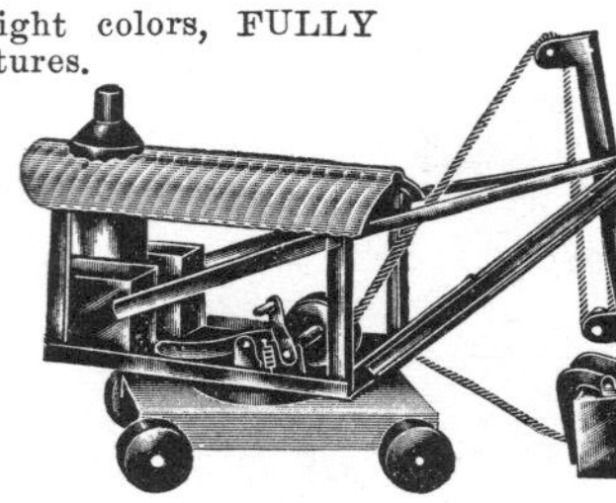

26 In. Long

1F2494—(Mfrs 47) **Steam shovel**, 12 in. high, 26 in. long, 6½ in. wide, black enameled frame, red enameled base and corrugated roof, heavy steel boiler, coal box, water tank, house and 16½ in. extension arm, 14 in. derrick on turntable, shovel **raised and extended** by turning crank, lowered by pressing lever, opened and closed by pulling string. 1 in carton..........Each **$4.00**

26 In. Long

1F2495—(Mfrs 43) **American Railway Express, Packard**, 26 in. long, 10½ in. high, 7½ in. wide, black enameled cab-radiator, running board, green body, red chassis and disc wheels with balloon type imitation rubber tires, **steering front wheels**, transparent celluloid windshield, imitation headlights, signal arm, separating doors on rear with lock and key, nickel radiator and hub caps. 1 in carton..........Each **$4.66**

27½ In. Long

1F2499—(Mfrs 51) **Police Patrol**, 27½ in. long, 11½ in. high, black and red enameled finish, 2 full length seats on inside of car, brass railing and foot step in rear, red enameled disc wheels, **steering front wheels**, imitation rubber tires, nickeled radiator and hub caps, protruding nickle lamps with celluloid lenses, transparent celluloid windshield, stop signal. 1 in carton. Each **$5.00**

1F2496—(Mfrs 41) **Dump truck, Packard**, 26 in. long, 9½ in. high, 8¼ in. wide, black enameled body, cab, radiator and running boards, red disc wheels, balloon type imitation rubber tires, **steering front wheels**, red enameled steel chassis, drop end with chute door, transparent celluloid windshield, signal arm, **crank and worm gear raises body** of truck into dumping position, will lift 200 lbs. 1 in carton.......Each **$5.00**

26 In. Long

26 In. Long

1F2491—(Mfrs 45) **U. S. Mail Truck, Packard**, 26 in. long, 10½ in. high, 7½ in. wide, black enameled cab, radiator, running board, green body, red chassis and disc wheels with balloon type imitation rubber tires, **steering front wheels**, transparent celluloid windshield, imitation headlights, signal arm, separating doors on rear with lock and key, nickel radiator and hub caps. 1 in carton. Each **$5.00**

25½ In. Long

1F2497—(Mfrs 53) **Sprinkling tank**, 25½ in. long, 10½ in. high, tank 12 in. long, 5¼ in. high, with inlet at top, will hold 4 qts. water, brass faucet with lock nut, red, green and black enameled finish, red disc wheels, imitation rubber tires, **steering front wheels**, nickel radiator and hub caps, transparent celluloid windshield, protruding nickeled lamps with celluloid lenses, stop signal, heavy perforated brass sprinkler tube with green enameled steel hangers, faucet of sprinkler connected with pure gum rubber hose. 1 in carton......Each **$5.66**

27½ In. Long

1F2498—(Mfrs 49) **Hook and Ladder Truck, Packard**, 27½ in. long, 11 in. high, 8½ in. wide, red enameled finish, disc wheels, balloon type imitation rubber tires, two 36 in. extension ladders, brass railing, bell, hose reel, imitation hose, heavy brass nozzle, imitation headlights, nickel hub caps, **steering front wheels**. 1 in carton. Each **$6.00**

STEEL TOYS

1F2574—**Taxicabs, 3 styles**, 6 in. long, 3 in. high, bluebird, checker and yellow cabs, disc wheels. Asstd. 1 doz. in box..........Doz **84c**

1F2547—**Autos, 2 styles**, average 7¼ in. long, dump cart and delivery wagon, disc wheels, yellow & green finishes. Asstd. 1 doz. in box..........Doz **84c**

1F2627—**Steel express wagon**, 4½x 1⅞ in., red and blue body, "Koaster Kids" lithographed in red and gold, yellow disc wheels turning front axle. 1 doz. in box. Doz **87c**

1F2490—**Covered wagon**, 11 in. long, 6 in. wide, wire frame top with heavy cloth covering, open spoke wheels, turning front axle, 19 in. heavy twisted wire handle. ½ doz. in box. Doz **$3.75**

Steel Toy Assortment

72 best selling items. Better values than ever in this new assortment.

1F2557— Assortment consists of—

1 doz. 5¾x4¼ in. Coal Hod and Shovel.
1 " 5¼x2¼ in. litho Tub and Board.
1 " 7¼ in. black & yellow enameled Telephone.
1 " 8 in. litho Trolley Car.
1 " 9 in. Parlor Car.
1 " 10 in. Locomotive and Tender.
Total 6 doz. in asst. Doz **89c**

(Total $5.34)

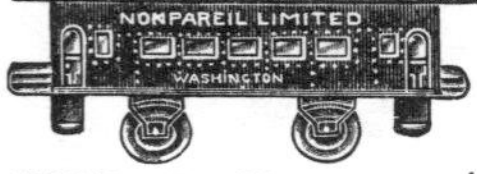

1F2543 — **Pullman and freight cars**, 8½ in. long, red & green bodies, blue & black roofs, juvenile designs. Asstd. 1 doz. in box. Doz **84c**

1F2535—**Red steel wagon**, 10x6 in. wagon box, heavy gauge steel. 1 doz. in box. Doz **$1.90**

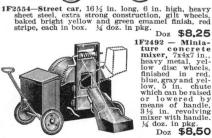

1F2529—**Steel train**, locomotive with 4 cars, length over all 19 in., cars in red, green and white enamel finishes, green disc wheels, locomotive in black and green enamel finish with green disc wheels, each in box. 1 doz. in pkg....Doz **$2.15**

1F2554—**Street car**, 16½ in. long, 6 in. high, heavy sheet steel, extra strong construction, gilt wheels, baked bright yellow and green enamel finish, red stripe, each in box. ¼ doz. in pkg. Doz **$8.25**

Grab Bucket Crane

A perfect miniature of large contractor's crane. Well made of heavy metal and with exceptionally good action. This toy is sold only by Butler Brothers.

1F2607— 3 x 2½ in. revolving engine house on 4½x3 in. platform, 1¼ in. disc wheels, 7 in. derrick, bucket with strong cord. Operated by crank handle with reversing wood pulleys which automatically opens and closes, bucket finished in red, green and black enamel. ½ doz. in box. Doz **$2.25**

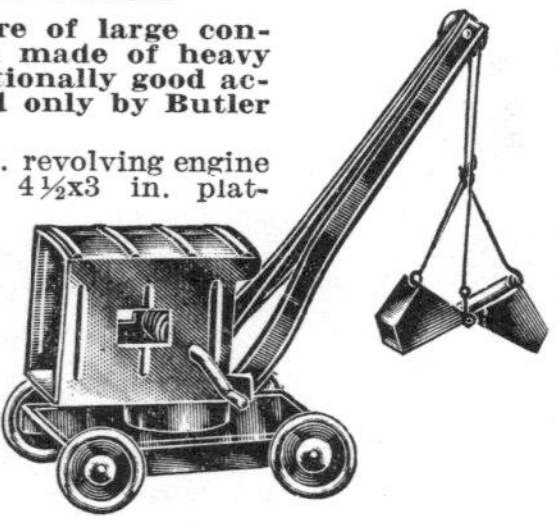

1F2492 — **Miniature concrete mixer**, 7x4x7 in., heavy metal, yellow disc wheels, finished in red, blue, gray and yellow, 5 in. chute which can be raised or lowered by means of handle, 3½ in. revolving mixer with handle. ¼ doz. in pkg. Doz **$8.50**

1F2553 — **Locomotive and tender**, 19½ in. long, 5½ in. high, heavy sheet steel, baked bright red enamel body, gilt and green stripes, gilt wheels, each in box. Each **88c**

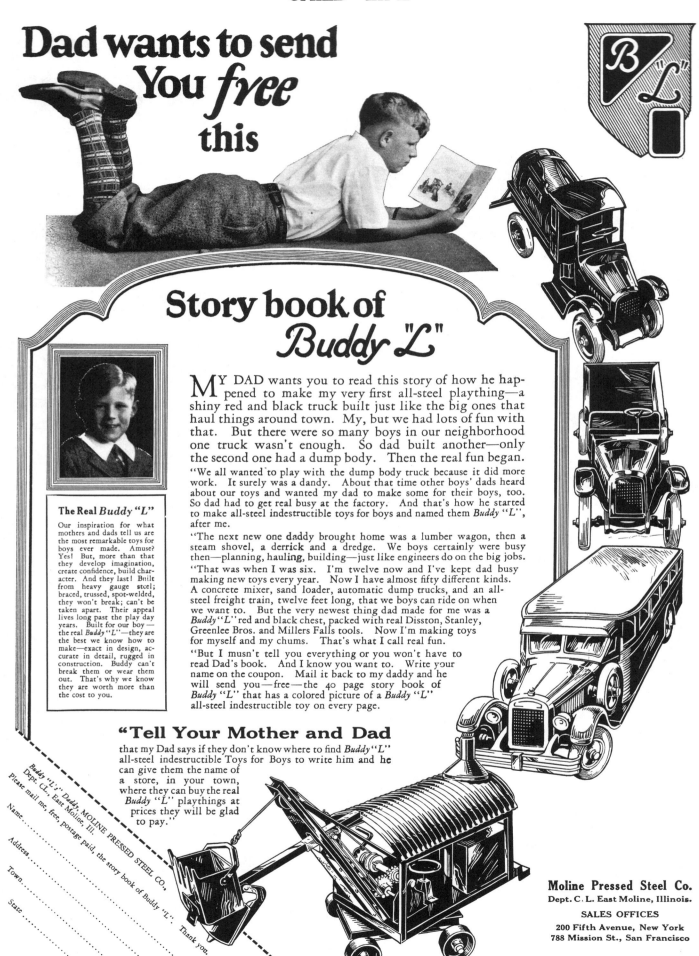

"BUDDY-L" FLIVVERS, TRUCKS, FIRE DEPT. AND CONTRACTORS' TOYS

These are the best known and biggest selling large size steel toys. The demand for this class of goods is tremendous. Fascinatingly real and practical in every respect. Built of heavy gauge steel and will stand the hardest kind of service. Constructed along the lines of the large machines. Do not pass up your share of this real profit-making business.

20 In. High

1F2580—(Mfrs 240) **Derrick,** 20 in. red enameled revolving derrick with pulleys on 10x11 in. black enameled platform, strong ropes for operating. 1 in carton.
Each **$4.00**

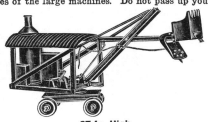

27 In. High

1F2560—(Mfrs 220) **Steam shovel,** 27 in. high, 11½x10½ in. black enameled frame, corrugated red steel roof, heavy steel boiler, coal box and water tank. House and 15 in. derrick with extension on turn table. Shovel raised and lowered by turning crank and opened and closed by pulling string attached.
1 in carton. Each **$4.00**

24 In. Long

1F2577—(Mfrs 200) **Truck,** 24 in. long, 8½ in. wide, 8 in. high, black enameled body, red open spoke wheels with imitation rubber tires, **steering front wheels.**
1 in carton. Each **$4.33**

All motor cars and trucks with moving steering gear which operates front wheels.

24 In. Long

1F2578—(Mfrs 201) **Dump truck,** 24 in. long, 9 in. wide, 7½ in. high, black enameled body with drop end, mudguards, running board, radiator and steering gear, red enameled steel frame, **steering front wheels.** 4½ in. red disc wheels, metal imitation rubber tires. Crank and chain gear raises body of truck into dumping position.
1 in carton. Each **$5.00**

1F2568—(Mfrs 204) **Moving van,** 24 in. long, 8 in. wide, green body, black radiator, running board and mud guards, red disc wheels, imitation rubber tires, **steering front wheels.** 1 in carton. Each **$5.00**

Exact duplicates of construction machinery. All models strongly built of steel.

18 In. High

1F2581—(Mfrs 110) **Conveyor,** 18 in. high, 7x4½ in. gray enameled body, 2 in. heavy black enameled iron wheels, gray enameled frame with chute and twelve 2x1½ in. black enameled sand buckets on heavy chain. Has controlling lever for raising or lowering frame, black enameled crank operates sand buckets. Each **$6.67**

"BUDDY-L" FIRE DEPT.

26 In. Long

1F2582— (Mfrs 205) **Hook and ladder truck,** red enameled, 26 in. long, 8½ in. wide, 10½ in. high, 4½ in. disc wheels, metal imitation rubber tires, **steering front wheels,** two 35 in. extension ladders, full length running board, brass railing and bell, hose reel with imitation hose and brass nozzle. Equipped with swinging crane, strong rope and pulley and operated by crank. 1 in carton.
Each **$8.00**

25 In. Long

1F2485— (Mfrs 205A) **Fire engine,** 25 in. long, 11 in. high, red enameled body and disc wheels, imitation rubber tires. Nickel plated boiler, brassed hand rails and bell, **steering front wheels.** 1 in carton. Each **$8.00**

24 In. Long

1F2569—(Mfrs 206) **Tank truck,** 24 in. long, 8 in. wide, green enameled tank, black enameled radiator, running board and mud guards, red enameled disc wheels, imitation rubber tires. Tank equipped with faucet and sprinkler attachment, **steering front wheels.** Each **$5.67**

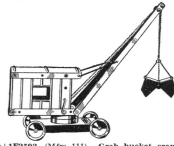

19½ In. Long

1F2483—(Mfrs 260) **Pile driver,** 19½ in. long, 12 in. high, black enameled frame, red enameled corrugated roof, donkey engine, coal box, water tank, 12x6¼ in. house, 21 in. shaft with pile driver on turn table. Pile driver raised and lowered by turning crank.
1 in carton. Each **$8.00**

"BUDDY-L" FLIVVERS

11 In. Long

1F2570—(Mfrs 210B) **Flivver coupe,** 11 in. long, 6¾ in. high, black enameled body, red open spoke wheels with imitation tires. **Steering front wheels.**
1 in carton. Ezch **$2.33**

12 In. Long

1F2572—(Mfrs 210) **Flivver truck,** 12 in. long, 7 in. high, black enameled body, red open spoke wheels with imitation tires. **Steering front wheels.** 1 in carton.
Each **$2.33**

RUBBER TIRES FOR "BUDDY L" TOYS

1F2487—Heavy duty tires, 4 in set. 1 set in pkg.
Set **45c**

"STRUCTO" TOYS

Miniature models of heavy duty contractors' machines. Built of heavy gauge steel to stand hard play, beautifully enameled. Large sizes that appeal to children. At these prices the "Structo" line has tremendous possibilities—order now and be sure of a complete showing.

1F2591—(Mfrs 112) **Steam shovel,** blue enameled platform, 5½x2½x4 in. red and blue enameled revolving engine house 10 in. high, black enameled derrick with steam shovel and chains. Has coppered crank handle with wood pulley by which steam shovel operates and automatically opens and closes. ½ doz. in box.
Doz **$8.75**

1F2593—(Mfrs 111) **Grab bucket crane,** 8x4x5½ in. green enameled platform, revolving red and green enameled engine house, 18½ in. black enameled derrick, bucket with chains, coppered crank handle with reversing wood pulleys by which bucket operates and automatically opens and closes. ½ doz. in carton.
Doz **$18.00**

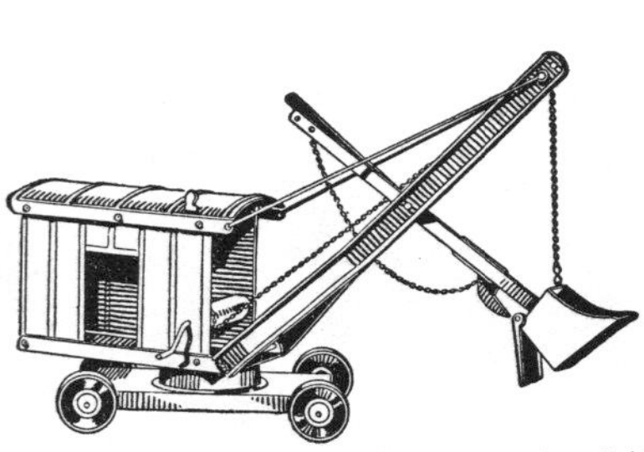

1F2594—(Mfrs 110) **Large steam shovel,** orange enameled platform, 8x4x5½ in. orange and blue enameled revolving engine house, 14½ in. black enameled derrick and sand shovel with chains. Has coppered crank handle with wood pulleys by which sand shovel operates and automatically opens and closes. ½ doz. in box.
Doz **$18.00**

1F2592—(Mfrs 44) **Tractor and trailer,** with strong spring motor, 7½x3¾x4 in. red and green enameled tractor, bright finish steel caterpillar tread, black enameled steering gear and seat, speed control lever, 5x4 in. green enameled trailer, black enameled disc wheels. 1 in box. Each **$2.00**

"SCHOENHUT" PIANOS CIRCUSES AND TOYS

''Schoenhut'' pianos are real musical instruments with each key an accurate note, the sound being produced by steel plates which never get out of tune. For fifty years ''Schoenhut'' pianos and toys have been leading lines in the Toy industry. Here are the best selling numbers.

UPRIGHT PIANOS

Varnished rosewood finish. Each key accurately tuned. Each with instruction book.

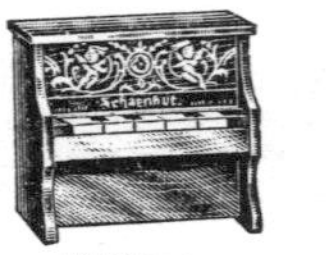

5 Keys

1F3501—6¼ in. front, 5¾ in. high. 1/12 doz. in box. Doz **$3.95**

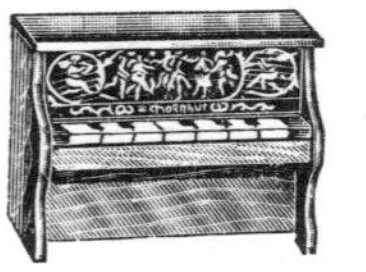

7 Keys

1F3503—8¼ in. front, 6¼ in. high. 1/12 doz. in box. Doz **$6.50**

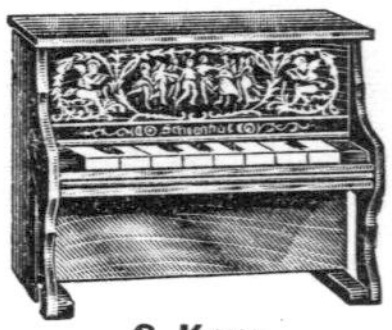

8 Keys

1F3502—9¼ in. front, 7 in. high. 1/12 doz. in box. Doz **$7.75**

9 Keys

1F3471—10¼ in. front, 7⅛ in. high. 1/12 doz. in box. Doz **$10.00**

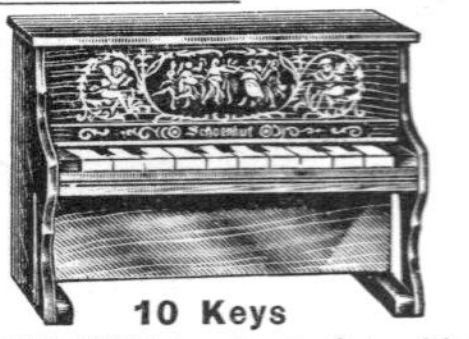

10 Keys

1F3492—11⅜ in. front, 8 in. high. 1/12 doz. in box. Doz **$11.25**

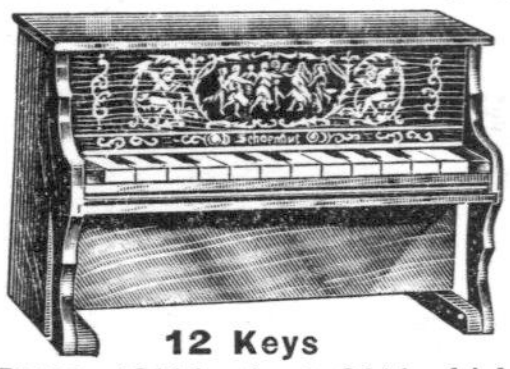

12 Keys

1F3493—13⅛ in. front, 8¾ in. high. 1/12 doz. in box. Doz **$17.50**

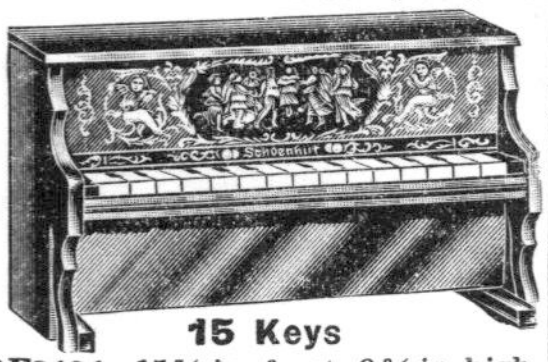

15 Keys

1F3494—15⅞ in. front, 9¾ in. high. 1 in box. Each **$1.95**

17 Keys

1F3495—17⅝ in. front, 11½ in. high. 1 in box. Each **$2.75**

BABY GRAND PIANOS

Varnished Rosewood Finish

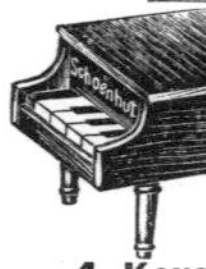

4 Keys

1F3476—5¾ in. front, 6¾ in. long. 1/12 doz. in box. Doz **$3.95**

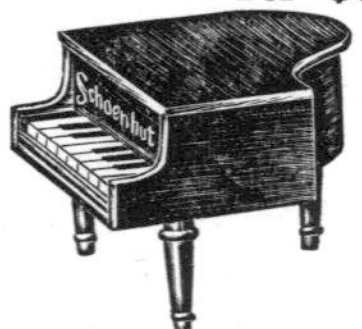

8 Keys

1F3477—9¼ in. front, 8 in. long. 1/12 doz. in box. Doz **$8.25**

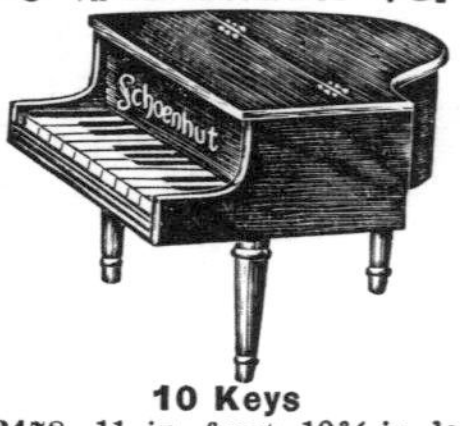

10 Keys

1F3478—11 in. front, 10¾ in. long, hinged back. 1/12 doz. in box. Doz **$13.50**

12 Keys

1F3525—12¾ in. front, 12¾ in. long. hinged front and back. 1/12 doz. in box....Doz **$18.50**

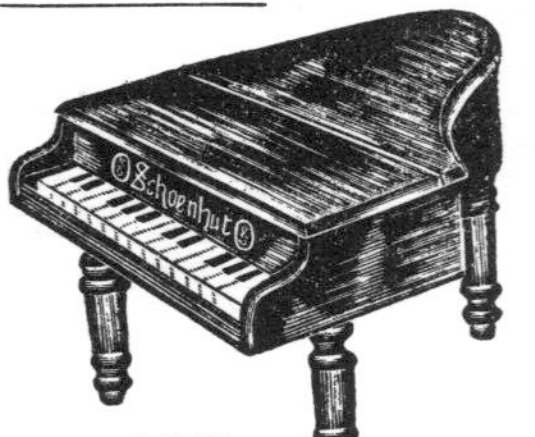

14 Keys

1F3508—15⅜ in. front, 14 in. long, hinged top. 1 in box. Each **$1.95**

16 Keys

1F3509—17⅜ in. front, 15½ in. long, hinged top. 1 in box. Each **$2.25**

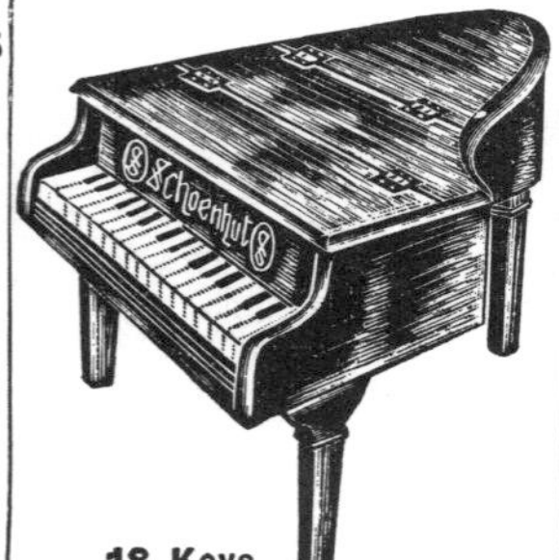

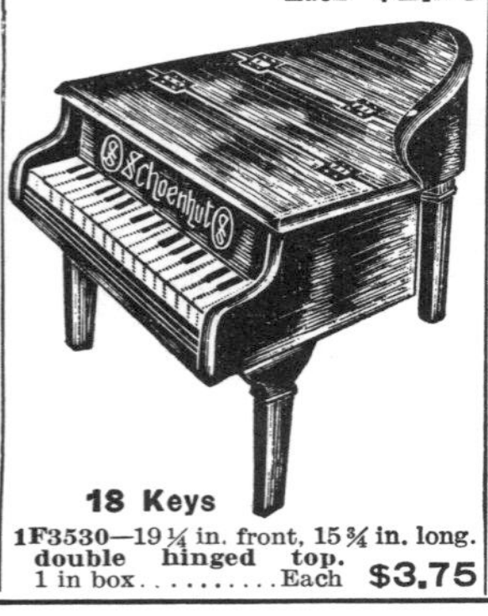

18 Keys

1F3530—19¼ in. front, 15¾ in. long. **double hinged top.** 1 in box..........Each **$3.75**

IMPROVED MODELS

Hinged top, paneled front, varnished rosewood finish, solid wood legs, music rest and pedals.

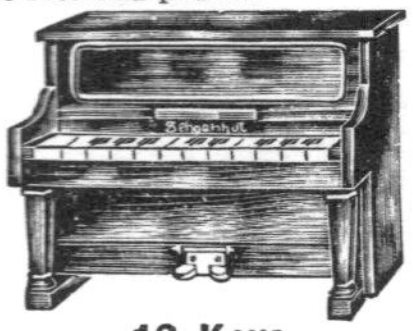

12 Keys

1F3507—13¼ in. front, 10¾ in. high. 1 in box. Each **$2.25**

14 Keys

1F3510—15 in. front, 12 in. high. 1 in box. Each **$2.75**

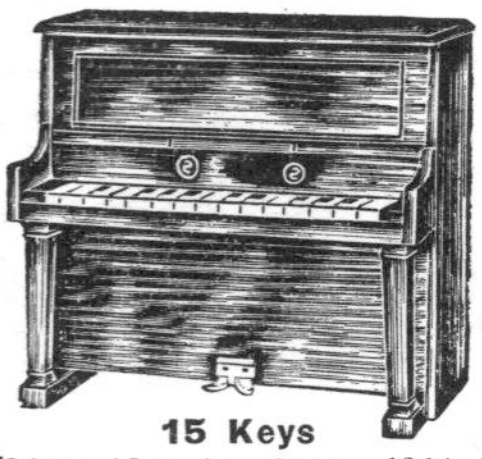

15 Keys

1F3496—16½ in. front, 13½ in. high. 1 in box. Each **$3.00**

18 Keys

1F3497—19⅜ in. front, 16½ in. high. 1 in box. Each **$4.00**

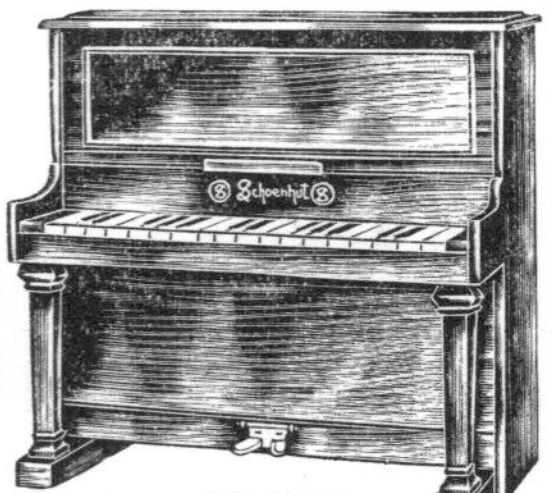

18 Keys

1F3514—19¼ in. front, 19⅝ in. high. 1 in case. Each **$6.50**

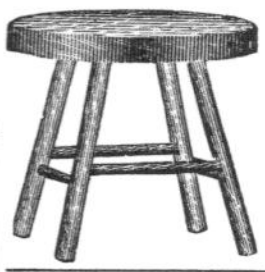

PIANO STOOL

1F3522 — 7 in. high, rosewood finish, each in box. ½ doz. in pkg. Doz **$4.00**

PLAYER PIANOS

Crank and Spring Action

Can be played by crank or spring action or on keyboard, same as regular pianos. Swiss works, mahogany finish, paneled fronts.

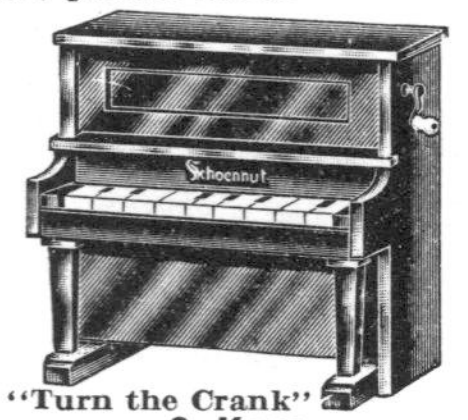

"Turn the Crank"

9 Keys

1F3505—10¼ in. front, 10¼ in. high, plays tune when crank is turned. 1 in box. Each **$2.75**

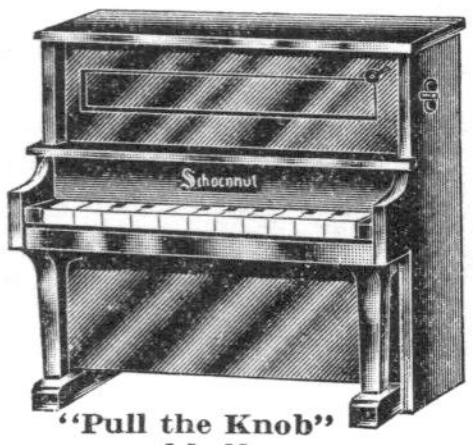

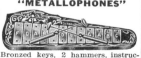

"Pull the Knob"

11 Keys

1F3506—12¼ in. front, 11¼ in. high, plays 2 tunes. Music started by pulling knob on front board which releases spring. Wound by key. 1 in box. Each **$3.75**

"METALLOPHONES"

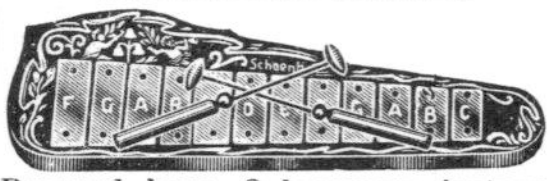

Bronzed keys, 2 hammers, instruction book. 1 in box.

1F3576—8 keys, 11¾ in. long. ¼ doz. in pkg. Doz **$4.20**

1F3578—12 keys, 16½ in. long. ⅙ doz. in pkg. Doz **$8.50**

1F3574—15 keys, 20 in. long. ½ doz. in pkg. Doz **$10.75**

"WALKING WALLAPUS"

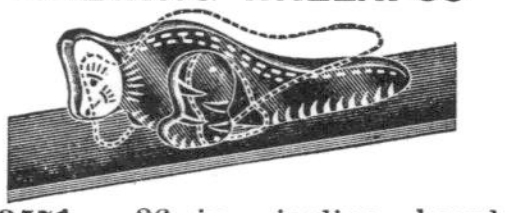

1F3571 — 26 in. incline board. ''Wallapus'' walks down the incline, tapping nose and tail with peculiar sound. 1/12 doz. in box. Doz **$8.25**

"BIG GAME" HUNTERS

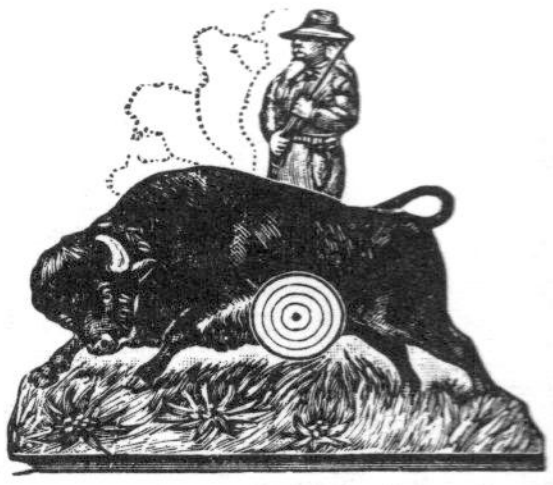

1F3572—6 styles, 12 in. long, large animals with concealed hunters which spring up when target center is hit. 13½ in. gun, belt with 8 wood cartridges, each set in box. Asstd. ½ doz. sets in pkg. Doz sets **$8.25**

SHOOTING GALLERIES

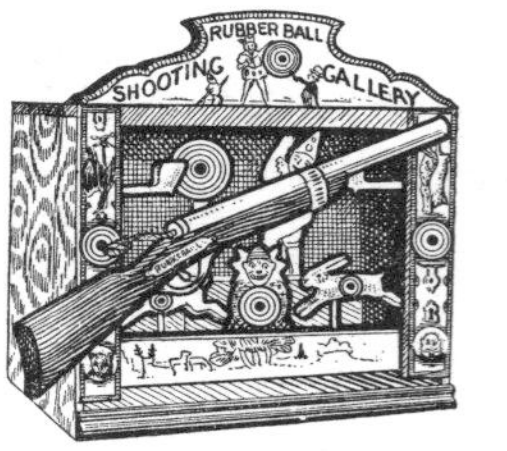

Patent gun shoots ⅝ in. rubber balls and cork. Rabbits, clown, negroes, brownies, pipes and bullseye figures that fall back when hit. When target is hit bell rings and clown appears.

1F3569—13x13x4¼ in., 7 figures, 15½ in. gun, 2 balls, 2 corks. ½ doz. sets in box. Doz sets **$17.50**

1F3570—16x14x4½ in., 9 figures 16¾ in. gun, 2 balls, 2 corks. 1 set in box. Set **$1.95**

PISTOL OUTFIT

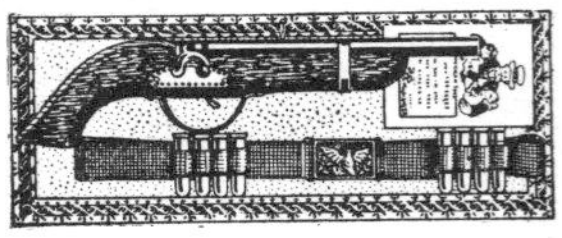

1F3568—10½ in. pistol, web belt containing 8 wood cartridges, each set on card. ½ doz. sets in pkg..........Doz sets **$4.50**

"ALPHIES" A B C BLOCKS

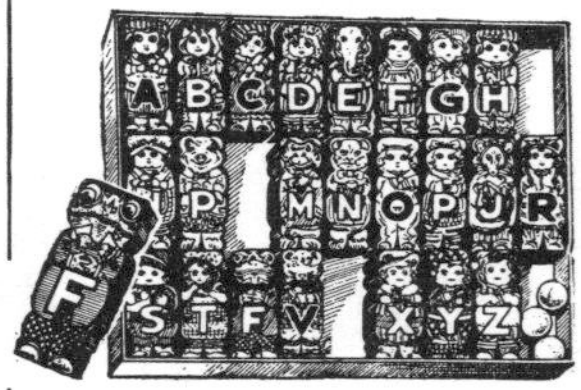

Hardwood blocks, 5 in. high, colored both sides, no two alike, letter on each side of block, with rubber balls to play ten pins. 1 set in carton.

HALF SETS—13 blocks.

1F2082—A to M juvenile side, N to Z animal side. SET (13 blocks) **$1.50**

1F2083—A to M animal side, N to Z juvenile side. SET (13 blocks) **$1.50**

FULL SET—26 blocks.

1F2084—A to Z both sides..SET (26 blocks) **$2.75**

"SCHOENHUT" FAMOUS CHARACTERS

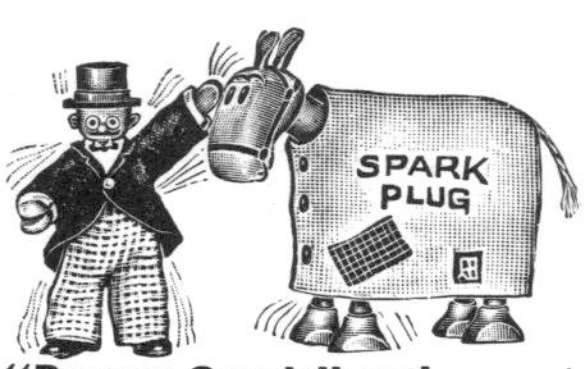

"Barney Google" and "Spark Plug"

1F3564—''**Spark Plug,**'' 9 in. long, wood body, movable parts, yellow felt blanket. ''**Barney Google**'' 7 in. wood figure, movable parts, checked trousers, black felt coat. 1/12 doz. sets in pkg. Doz sets **$19.00**

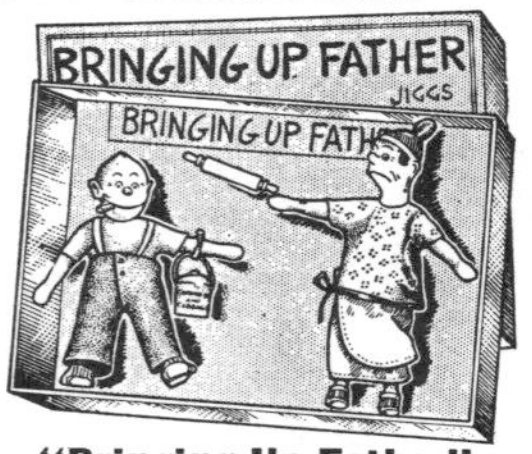

"Bringing Up Father"

1F3565—''**Jiggs,**'' 7¼ in. wood body, black trousers, red shirt, dinner pail. ''**Maggie,**'' 8½ in. wood body, blue skirt, flowered blouse, ribbon girdle, wood rolling pin. 1/12 doz. sets in pkg. Doz sets **$19.00**

"SCHOENHUT" HUMPTY DUMPTY CIRCUSES

Clowns 6½ in., elephants 6¼ in., donkey 8 in., barrel and stool 2¼ in., ladders 8½ in., chairs 4½ in.

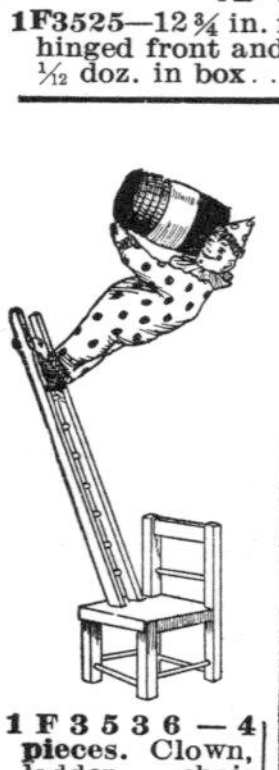

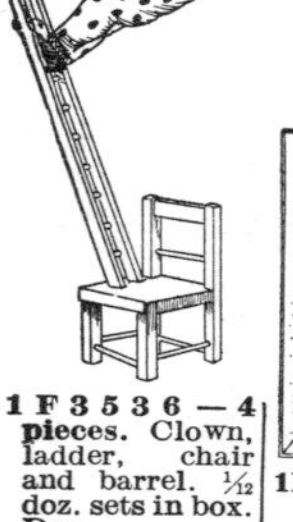

1F3536—4 pieces. Clown, ladder, chair and barrel. ½ doz. sets in box. Doz sets. **$6.00**

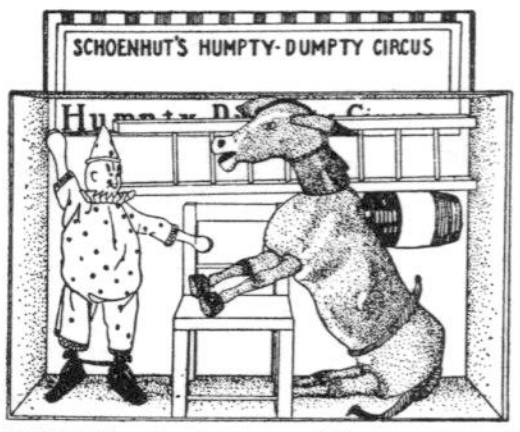

1F3537—5 pieces. Clown, donkey, ladder, chair and barrel. 1/12 doz. sets in box. Doz sets **$10.75**

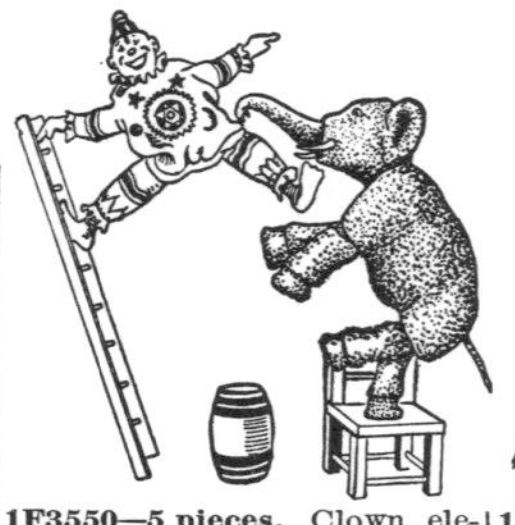

1F3550—5 pieces. Clown, elephant, ladder, chair and barrel. 1/12 doz. sets in box.....Doz sets **$13.25**

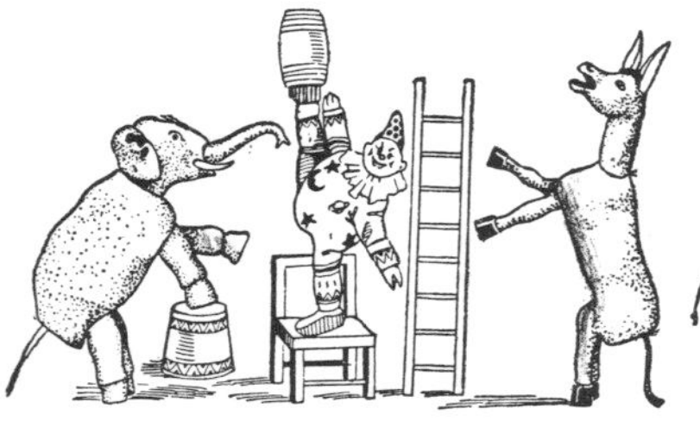

1F3551—7 pieces. Clown, elephant, donkey, ladder, chair, barrel and stool. 1/12 doz. sets in box..............Doz sets **$18.50**

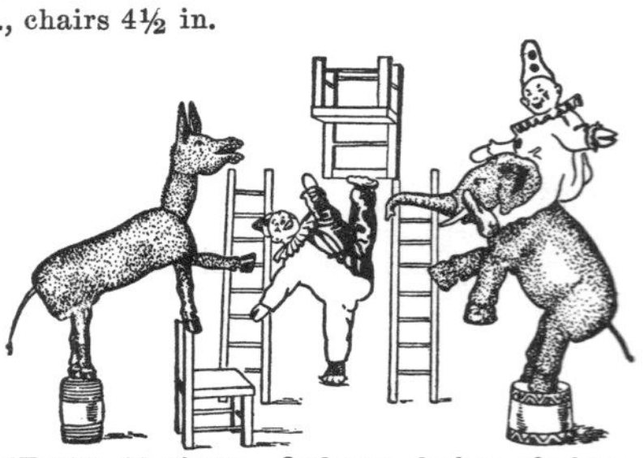

1F3552—10 pieces. 2 clowns, donkey, elephant, 2 chairs, 2 ladders, barrel and stool. 1 set in box.......................Set **$2.00**

ANIMAL TOYS

IMPORTED FLANNEL COVERED ANIMALS
Well stuffed bodies, strongly sewed.

2F7179—Dog, cat and rabbit, average 4¼ in., strongly sewed, stout flannel bodies, stitched nose and mouth, glass eyes, ribbonzene trim necks. **Asstd. 2 doz. in pkg.**..............Doz **80c**

2F9619 — Dog, 7 in. high, sitting position, white flannel covered composition body, black and brown spots, protruding glass eyes, black leatherette collar, opens mouth and barks. ½ doz. in box.
Doz **$1.95**

2F7205—Duck, 8 in. long, flannel covered, bright colored wings and tail, chenille top-knot, sewed mouth, glass eyes, on metal wheels. **Quacking voice** when drawn across floor. ½ doz. in box.
Doz **$2.00**

2F9618—Dog, 9 in. long, white flannel covered well stuffed body, brown spots, black leatherette collar with bell, glass eyes, **with voice.** ½ doz. in box. 1 doz. in pkg.......Doz **$2.15**

2F7202—Dog, 8 in. long, red, green and black, painted features, pressed paper body on metal wheels, large glass eyes, ribbon collar. ½ doz. in box......Doz **$2.25**

2F7257—4 styles, 9½ in. long, elephant, mule, camel, natural colors, pressed paper bodies, on metal wheels, glass eyes, imitation harness, muzzles and collars. **Asstd.** 1 doz. in box.
Doz **$2.25**

"ROLO TOY" ANIMALS
A new idea in stuffed animals. Friction principle produces action, animals can be made to run forward or backward, can also be used as pull toy. Substantially built—will stand rough usage.

Bulldog, terrier, cat and bear, fine quality long pile plush in white, tan and light and dark brown, white canton flannel under-bodies, stitched nose and mouth, glass eyes, imitation leather or ribbon collars. One wheel with friction principle — slight pressure will make animal run forward or backward considerable distance.

Each in box with printed label. **Asstd. ⅙ doz. in pkg.**
1F4968—Average 9x7½ in ....Doz **$19.50**
1F4969— " 11x9½ " **27.00**

1F4920—2 styles, average 5½x6¼ in., standing dog and cat, glass eyes, stitched nose and mouth, ribbon collars. **Asstd.** 1 doz. in box............Doz **$2.25**

Dog, cat and rabbit, strongly sewed, stout flannel bodies, glass eyes, stitched nose and mouth, ribbon trim neck. **Asstd.** ½ doz. in box.
2F7186—6 in. long..Doz **$2.25**
2F7185—8 " " **3.50**

2F7200—Cat, dog and rabbit, average 11 in. long, stout flannel covered bodies, painted and sewed features, glass eyes, extra well sewed. **Each with voice. Asstd.** ½ doz. in box.
Doz **$3.75**

2F7259—Dogs, 9½ in. assorted colors, painted features, glass eyes, imitation leather muzzle, bright colored flannel blankets, on metal wheels. ½ doz. in box.
Doz **$3.95**

1F4910—4 styles, 8 in. long, gray and white cat, brown and white dog, white dog and cat, flannel underlined, all with velvet ears and glass eyes. **Asstd.** ½ doz. in box............Doz **$4.25**

1F4921—4 styles, average 9½x10 in., dogs and cats, standing and sitting positions, glass eyes, stitched nose and mouth, black imitation leather collars. **Asstd.** ½ doz. in box......Doz **$4.25**

2F7178—3 styles, average 9 in., upright dogs, white flannel bodies with assorted color markings, glass eyes, stitched nose and mouth, strongly sewed. **Each with voice. Asstd.** ½ doz. in box.
Doz **$4.50**

2F7222—Bull dog and terrier, 9½ in. long, white flannel covered, natural spotting, painted features, glass eyes, each with muzzle, collar and leash. **Asstd.** ⅓ doz. in box............Doz **$4.75**

2F7228—Cow on roller platform, 11 in. cow, flannel covered on papier mache base, painted nose and mouth, glass eyes, imitation horns. **Voice when head is turned.** ⅙ doz. in box......Doz **$8.00**

2F7223—Bull dog and terrier, 13 in. long, white flannel covered, natural spotting, painted features, glass eyes, each with muzzle, collar and leash. **Asstd.** ⅙ doz. in box............Doz **10.80**

THE FAMOUS "GUND" WALKING ANIMALS
Legs move back and forth and tail wags when animal is drawn across floor by cord. Made of brown and gray duvetyne, stitched mouth and nose, glass eyes, ribbon collars, silk cord.

1F4942—3 styles, average 7½ in. high, 8 in. long, gray elephant, gray & white cat, brown & white dog. **Asstd.** ½ doz. in pkg..............Doz **$8.25**

1F4943—3 styles, average 9 in. high, 9½ in. long, gray elephant, gray & white cat, brown & white dog. **Asstd.** ¼ doz. in pkg.
Doz **$12.50**

IMPORTED FUR DOGS

2F7213—8 in. long, brown, black and gray with white markings, composition head, painted features, **with voice,** on platform. 1 doz. in box......Doz **$1.90**

2F7214—7 in. long, black, brown and gray, composition head, painted features, **with voice,** wood roller wheels, string. 1 doz. in box..............Doz **$3.75**

2F7218—10½ in. long, black and brown, white spotting, composition face, painted features, bead eyes, red linene collar and leash, wood rollers. ½ doz. in box..............Doz **$7.25**

2F7264—10 in. long, 10 in. high, white fur, glass eyes, composition nose and mouth. **Barks when string is pulled.** 1 in box..............Each **$2.00**

ALL VELVET ANIMALS
With Voices
Made of best quality velvet.

1F4913—4 styles, average 6½x7½ in., gray and white cat, brown dog, white dog and cat, well stuffed, cats with flannel ears, dogs with velvet ears, glass eyes, stitched nose and mouth, ribbon collars, **with voice. Asstd.** ½ doz. in box.
Doz **$4.25**

PLUSH ANIMALS
With Voices
Fine quality plush, well stuffed bodies, excellent workmanship.

1F4915—2 styles, average 7¾x8 in., white mohair plush cat with long tail, dog with brown plush tail and ears, glass eyes, stitched nose and mouth, ribbon or imitation leather collars, **with voice.** ⅓ doz. in box.
Doz **$8.25**

IMPORTED NOVELTY ANIMALS

Felt Covered Animals
2F7261—4 styles, average 10 in. long, horse, mule, camel and cow, natural colors, pressed paper bodies, glass eyes, imitation harness and collars. ⅓ doz. in box. Doz **$4.50**

Plush Animals
2F7270—3 styles, average 11 in., brown bear, brown and white dog with collar, gray elephant, all with glass eyes, stitched nose and mouth. **Asstd.** ¼ doz. in box......Doz **$9.00**

Fur Cat With Voice
2F7208—11½ in high, gray, brown and white fur, sitting position, glass eyes, composition mouth and nose. Mouth opens and meows when tail is pulled. 2 in box..........Each **$1.75**

Elephant on Wheels
2F7237—11 in., well stuffed gray plush body, red and gold blanket and body strip, white tusks, glass eyes, bell on end of long trunk, 4 gilt wheel stand, strong construction. 1 in box.
Each **$2.00**

NOVELTY DRESSED ANIMAL ASSORTMENT
With Squeak Voices
Plush and velvet heads, duvetyn bodies, stitched nose and mouth, squeak voices.

1F4922—2 styles, 14 in., teddy bear, green flannel coat, white bound edges, white vest and tie, 2 brass buttons, red sateen trousers; pup, brown & white plush head, red flannel shirt, khaki overalls, 2 brass buttons. **Asstd.** ⅙ doz. in box.
Doz **$8.00**

TOY TELEPHONES

1F2561—7 in. high, red, black, yellow and green enameled, adjustable mouthpiece, 2½ in. receiver, long string. 1 doz. in box. **Doz 79c**

2F7570—6 in. high, bright metal base and receiver hook, adjustable transmitter, black enameled wood receiver, green imitation wire, nickel gong bell, each in box. **Doz ★1.88**

1F2563—7 in. high, nickel plated base and receiver hook, black enameled mouthpiece and receiver, polished nickeled gong bell, imitation wire, each in box. 1 doz. in pkg. **Doz $3.85**

1F2559—"Silver Toyphone," 9¼ in. high, all parts nickel plated, glass mouthpiece, loud clear tone nickeled bell, felt base, nickel plated receiver, long strong string, conversation can actually be conveyed when string is held taut. ⅙ doz. in pkg. **Doz $7.50**

Both the transmitter and the receiver can be used for talking and for hearing so that two children can actually talk back and forth with one "Toyphone."

1F2565—8 in. high, all parts nickel plated, glass mouthpiece, adjustable transmitter, black enameled wood receiver, green imitation wire, green felt base, nickeled bell with loud clear tone, each in box. ⅙ doz. in pkg........**Doz ★7.20**

SUNDRY TOYS

JACK STONES

Always Front Rank Sellers

Complete Set
1F2949—5 nickeled jack stones and 1 solid rubber ball, each set in bag. 2 doz. sets in pkg. **Doz sets 39c**

JUMPING ROPE

1F2923 — 7 ft long, extra heavy twisted white cotton rope, 4 assorted color turned wood beads, red stained turned wood handles. **Doz 87c**

REVERSE ACTION PIN WHEEL

1F2624—Three 6¾ in. red, white & blue propeller shape blades, heavy stock, brass heads, 18 in. stick, blades revolve in opposite directions. 2 doz. in pkg.....**Doz 82c**

MINIATURE WINDMILL

1F2540—Miniature windmill, 15 in. high, galvanized metal, heavy frame, eight blades, ready to set up, each in box. **Doz 89c**

SOAP BUBBLE OUTFIT

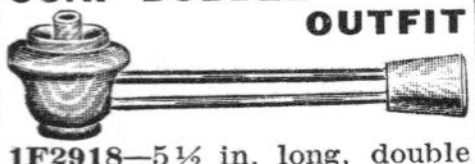

1F2918—5½ in. long, double turned wood bowl and mouthpiece, 2 brass tubes, blows double bubbles, each in box. 1 doz. in carton...**Doz 79c**

IMPORTED TOY TENNIS RACKET

2F7857—Wood frame racket, string lacing, red knitted return ball, white elastic string with bell. **Doz 80c**

IMPORTED HAND BALLS

Colored felt cover, elastic sponge filling. 1 doz. in box.
2F7324—8 in. circum. **Doz 39c**
2F7325—11 in. circum. **Doz 72c**

"ROLBAK" TOY

1F2976—2¼x2¼ in., tin ends, lithographed cardboard body, toy returns when rolled on floor. 1 doz. in box. **Doz 72c**

RIDING WHIPS

1F2951—36 in. long, thread covered rattan, enameled in bright colors, assorted color celluloid wound handles, wrist loop, tassel snap. 1 doz. in pkg. **Doz 42c**

MIDGET SPORT SET

1F2960—2 pairs heavy leather hair stuffed gloves, drill lining, well stitched. Heavy leather football, pure gum bladder. 1 set in hinged cover holly display box. **Set $2.50**

IMPORTED TOY HORSE SHOE MAGNETS

Red painted tops, polished ends, each with pin. 1 doz. in pkg.
Doz
2F7846—2 in. long...**15c**
2F7847—3 in. long...**33c**
2F7848—4½ in. long...**72c**

IMPORTED TOY SCALES

2F7925—2½ in. metal trays and balancer on metal base, each in box. 1 doz. in pkg......**Doz 69c**

2F7926—2½ in. metal trays and balancer on wood base with drawer, each in box. 1 doz. in pkg. **Doz $1.20**

2F7927—2½ in. brass finish metal trays and balancer on oval wood base, each in box. ½ doz. in pkg. **Doz $2.00**

IMPORTED BEAD NECKLACE

2F7424 — 12 in. long, bright colored composition beads alternating with bright colored glass beads, glass tassel, clasp. **Doz 42c**

GASOLINE TANKS

1F2585—Gasoline tank, 9 in. high, turning handle, red, green, black and white enameled finish, registering chart, imitation rubber hose. 1 doz. in box. **Doz 92c**

1F2584—Gasoline tank, 11 in. high, red and white enameled tank, handle, glass covered registering dial, imitation hose, price chart. 1 doz. in box. **Doz $1.90**

JUVENILE BOXING GLOVES

1F2803—Heavy glove leather throughout, hair stuffed, heavy drill lined, well stitched. Set of 4 in box. **SET of 4 $1.65**

IMPORTED TRANSFER PICTURES

Good colors, warranted to make clear transfers. Boy Scout, birds, animals, fruits, juvenile pictures.

2F7874—6 styles, 12 assorted sheets on 4x12 in. card. 1 doz. cards in pkg. **Doz cards 75c**

MINIATURE ENAMELED METAL AUTOMOBILES

Assorted color enameled bodies, blue, red, yellow, etc., bright disc wheels.

1F2446—Sedan. 3 in. long. Asstd. 1 doz. in box. **Doz 82c**

1F2448—6 style assortment, delivery autos — grocery, bakery, laundry, etc. 3¼ in. long. Asstd. **Doz 82c**

PEWTER RACING AUTO

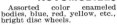

1F2440—3x1½ in., asstd. silver, red, green, blue body, disc wheels, driver. Asstd. **Doz 80c**

LITHOGRAPHED SNOW SHOVELS

1F2599—21 in. over all, blade 4¼x5¼ in., assorted 6 color designs, red stained waxed handle. **Doz 68c**

1F2967—27 in. over all, blade 6½x7½ in., assorted 6 color designs, red stained waxed handle. 1 doz. in box. **Doz $1.10**

SAND PAILS WITH SHOVELS

1F2854—4¼x4¼ in., assorted 7 color juvenile designs, riveted handle with turned edges. 8½ in. one-piece shovel. 1 doz. in box.........**Doz 84c**

1F2861—5x5¼ in., assorted 7 color juvenile designs, wide handle, 8½ in., one-piece shovel. 1 doz. in box.........**Doz $1.08**

Our "Leader"

1F2855—6½x6¾ in., 7 color juvenile design, riveted handle with turned edges, 11½ in. 1 pc. shovel. ½ doz. in box. **Doz $1.95**

LAUNDRY TOYS

TOY FLAT IRONS

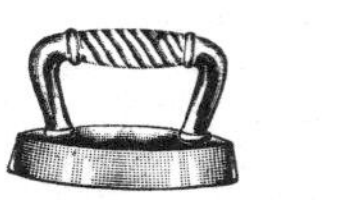

1F3040—3 in., gilt top, polished face and sides, aluminum handle. 1 doz. in box. Doz 82c

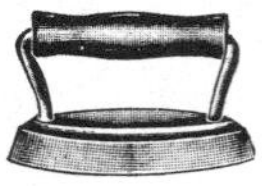

1F3041—3¾ in., gilt sides, polished face, black painted **wood handle,** with nickeled ends. 1 doz. in box. Doz 84c

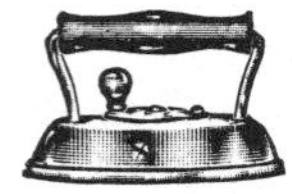

1F3042—3½ in., **polished nickeled** face, edges and removable hood, black enameled wood handle. 1 doz. in box. Doz $1.25

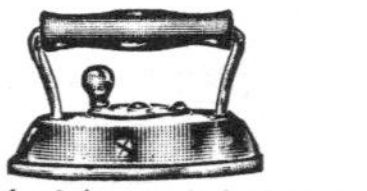

1F3044—4 in., polished nickeled face, edges and removable hood, black enameled handle. ½ doz. in pkg. Doz $1.95

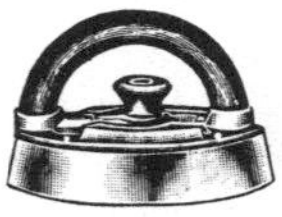

1F3039 — 3¾ in., polished nickeled face and edges, removable handle, varnished knob and grip. 1 doz. in box. Doz $1.95

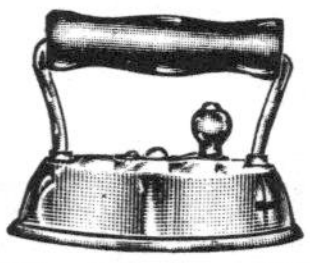

1F3045 — 4⅞ in., polished nickeled face, edges and removable hood, black enameled wood handle. ½ doz. in box. Doz $4.00

TOY ELECTRIC IRON

Somthing new that will be very popular with the little housekeeper.

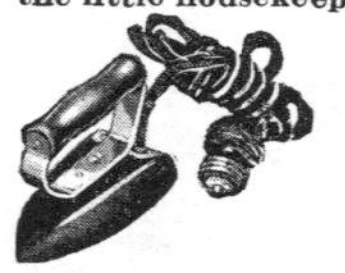

1F3024 — "Little Housekeeper," 1¼ lbs., 5¼ in. nickel plated ironing surface, Roman bronze finish top and handle, 34 watts, 110 volts, 6 ft. heavy electric cord, 2 piece attachment plug. 1 in box. Each **$1.50**

"WOLVERINE" LAUNDRY SETS

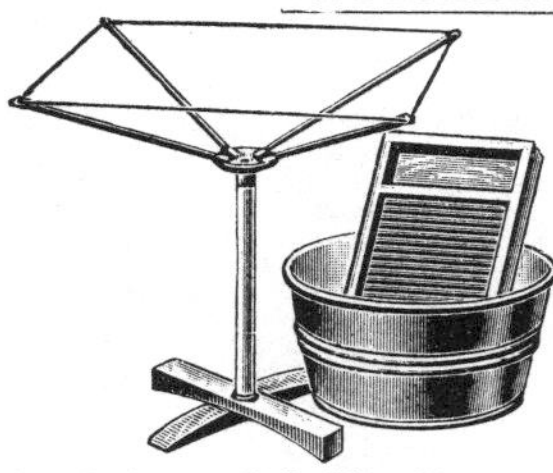

1F3680—3 pieces. Tub, 7 in., blue enameled outside, white inside. **Washboard,** 8 in., wood frame, metal rubbing surface. **Clothes rack,** folding type, 11 in. high, top spreads to 14 in., each set in box. ½ doz. sets in pkg. Doz sets $4.50

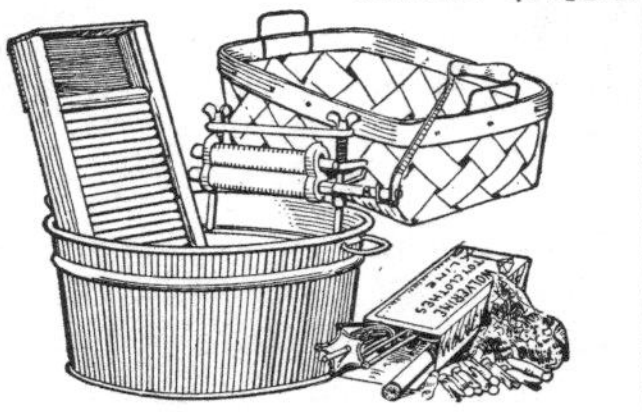

1F3676—17 pieces. Tub, 10 in., blue enameled outside, white inside. **Washboard,** 11 in. wood frame, glass rubbing surface. **Clothes rack,** folding type, 12 in. high, top spreads to 18½ in. **Wringer,** galvanized, adjustable, 2 rubber rolls. **Clothes basket,** 7½x11¾ in., wire handles. **Clothes pins,** 12 in bag. 1 set in box........SET (17 pcs) **$1.65**

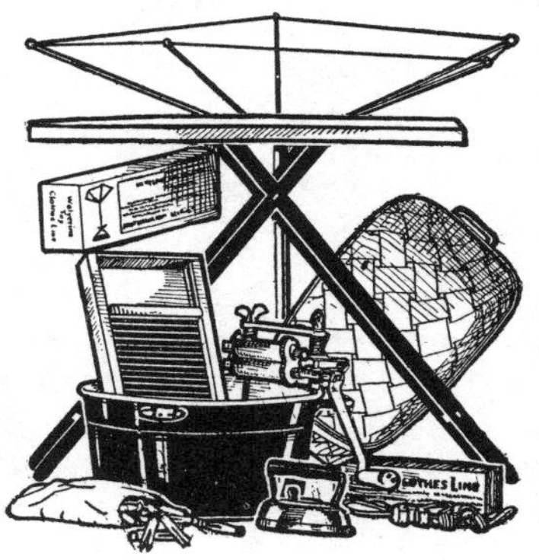

1F3674—30 pieces, Tub, 10 in., blue enameled outside, white inside. **Washboard,** 11 in., wood frame, glass rubbing surface. **Clothes rack,** folding type, 12 in. high, top spreads to 18½ in. **Wringer,** galvanized, adjustable, 2 rubber rolls **Clothes basket,** 7½x11¾ in., wire handles. **Clothes pins,** 12 in bag. Clothes line consisting of **2 pulleys, 2 rollers,** 9 ft. white cotton rope and **6 clothes pins. Ironing board,** 17 in.. collapsible, with blue enameled stand. **Sad iron,** 4 in., nickel plated, detachable hood, black wood handle. 1 set in box. SET (30 pcs) $2.25

WASHBOARD AND TUBS

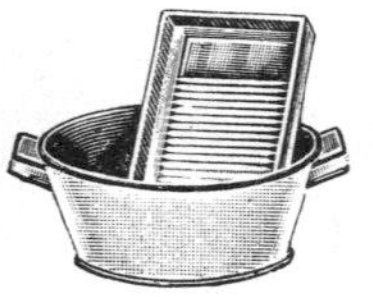

1F2814—Bright lithographed tub 2¼x5½ in., board 5¼x3½ in. Asstd. 1 doz. sets in pkg. Doz sets 89c

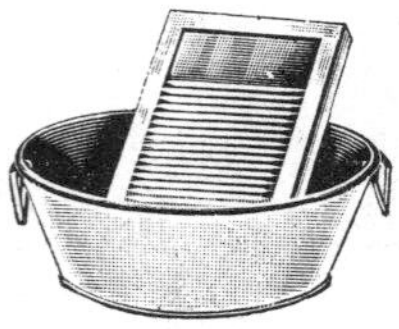

1F2813—Tub 3¼x8¾ in., assorted green, yellow, red and blue, board 4¾x7¾ in. ½ doz. sets in box. Doz sets $2.10

ASSORTED LAUNDRY PIECES

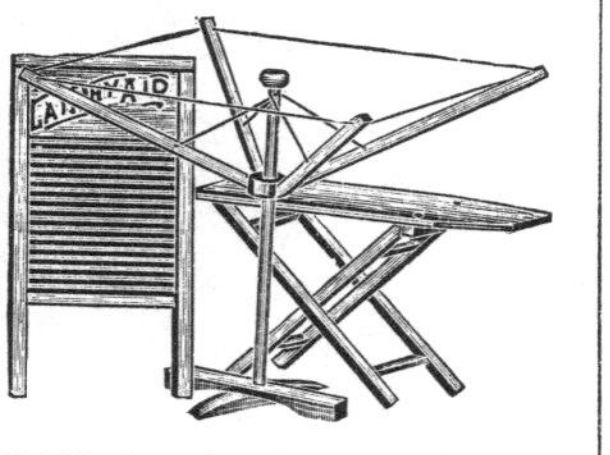

1F3668—3 styles, ironing board 14¼x 4x7⅝ in., washboard 13¾x6¼ in., clothes rack 14½ in., spreads to 19 in. **Asstd. 3 doz. pcs. in pkg.** Doz pcs 80c

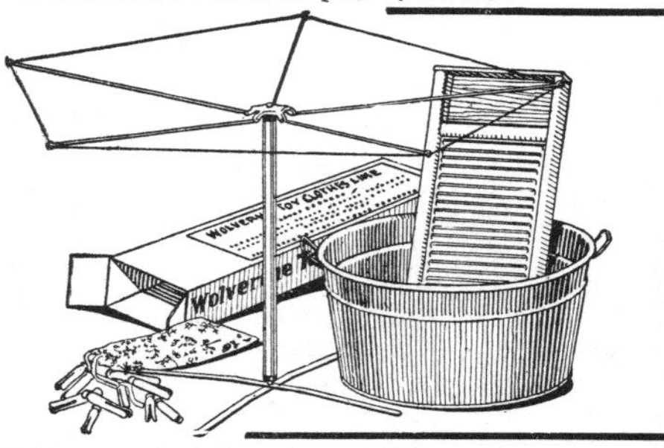

Dollar Leader

1F3675—16 pieces. Tub, 10 in., blue enameled outside, white inside. Washboard; 11 in. wood frame, glass rubbing surface. Clothes Rack, folding type, 12 in. high, top spreads to 18½ in. Clothes Pins, 12 in bag. ½ doz. sets in box. Doz sets $7.75

TOY IRON RANGES

All with high shelf back and hinged door.

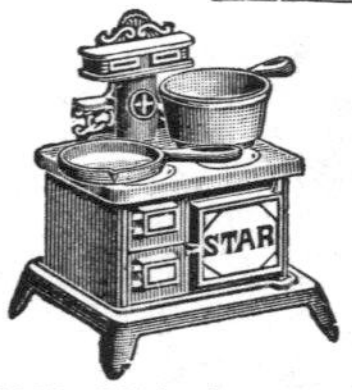

1F3050—3¾ in. long, moulded lids. With kettle and skillet. ½ doz. in box......Doz $2.10

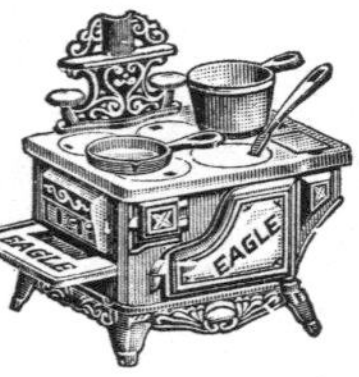

1F3051—5½ in. long, 4 loose lids, with kettle, skillet and lifter. ¼ doz. in box......Doz $4.25

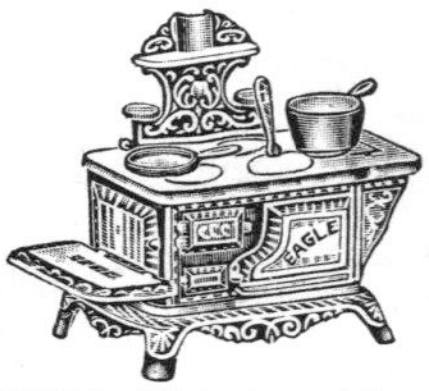

1F3059—6½ in. long, 4 loose lids. With kettle, skillet and lifter. ½ doz. in box. Doz $8.00

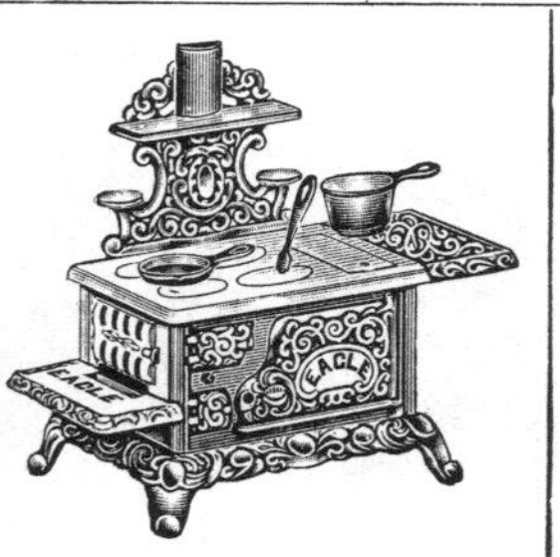

1F3056—9 in. long, extension side shelf, 4 loose lids, reservoir cover. With kettle, skillet and lifter. ½ doz. in box....Doz $12.00

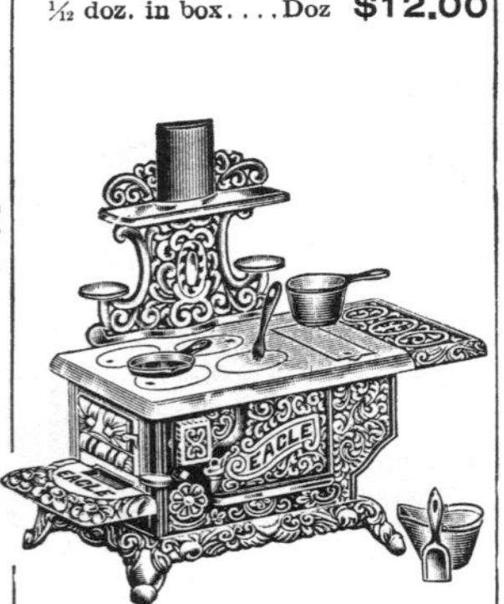

1F3058—10½ in. long, extension side shelf, 4 loose lids, reservoir cover. With kettle, skillet, lifter, coal scuttle and shovel. Doz $21.00

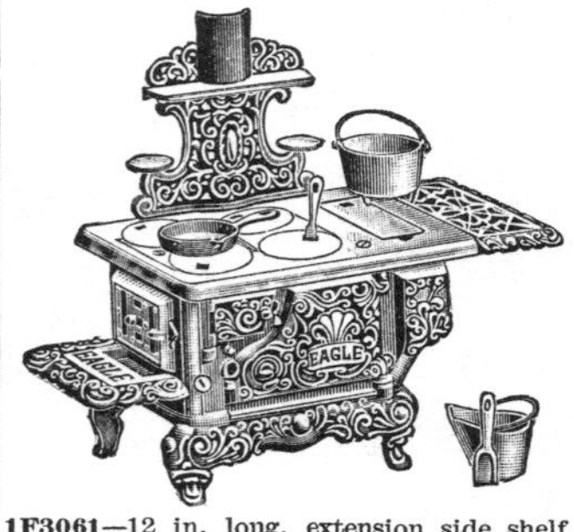

1F3061—12 in. long, extension side shelf, 4 loose lids reservoir. With kettle, skillet, lifter, coal scuttle and shovel. ½ doz. in box. Doz $30.00

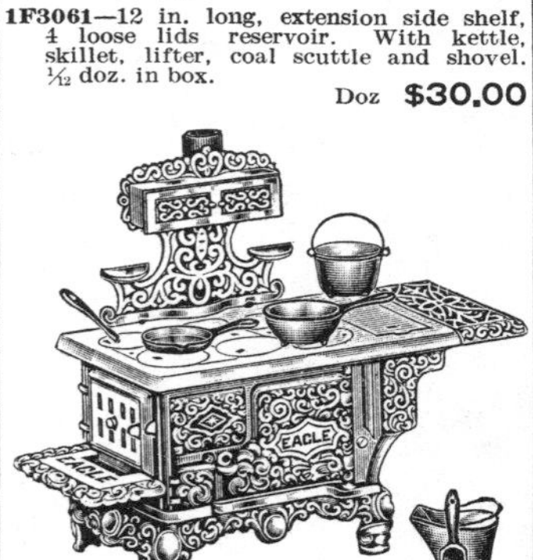

1F3066—13 in. long, extension side shelf, 6 loose lids, reservoir, removable grate, nickeled edges and doors. With large kettle, sauce pan, skillet, lifter, coal scuttle and shovel. ½ doz. in box. Doz $39.00

TOY GAS RANGES

A very attractive line of toy ranges in white enamel with light blue paneled doors. **All utensils nickel plated.**

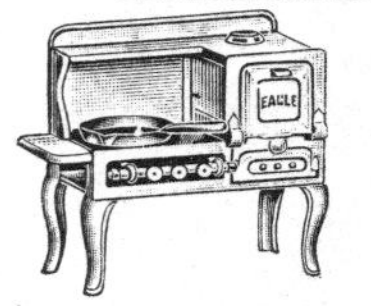

1F3030—5 in. long, utensil. ½ doz. in carton....Doz $3.90

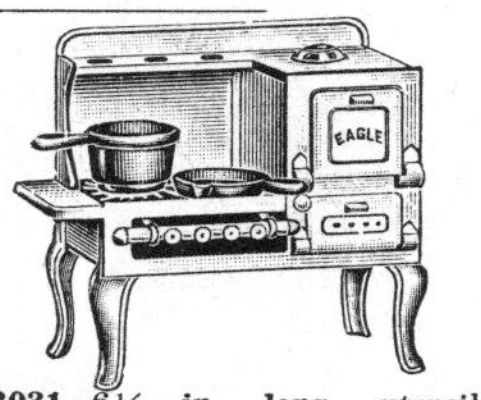

1F3031—6½ in. long, utensils. ½ doz. in box. Doz $8.00

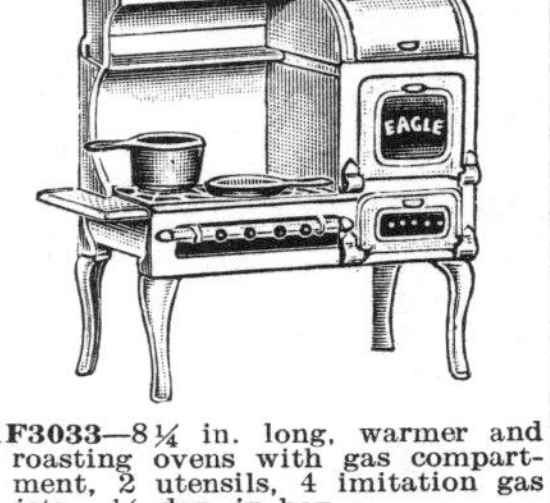

1F3033—8¼ in. long, warmer and roasting ovens with gas compartment, 2 utensils, 4 imitation gas jets. ½ doz. in box. Doz $16.50

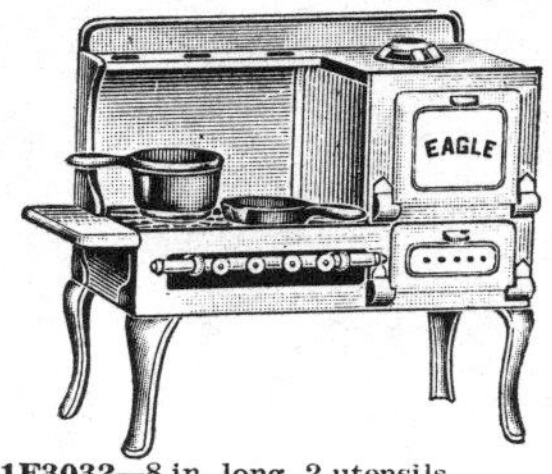

1F3032—8 in. long, 2 utensils. ½ doz. in box. Doz $12.00

ELECTRIC RANGE

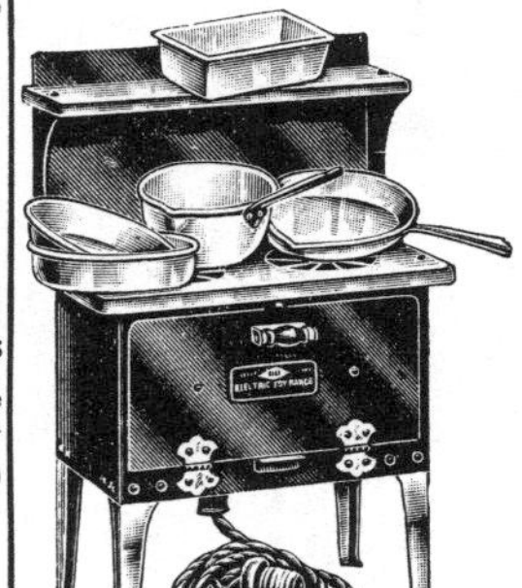

A practical electric range, will actually cook and bake, perfect in every detail.

1F2840—"Empire," 16¼ in. high, 10½ in. wide, heavy black japanned iron body, polished steel trimmings, large size oven with hinged door and enameled wood handle, 6 ft. cord and plug, 400 watts, 110 to 120 volts alternating or direct current, oven heats from both top and bottom, 5 piece aluminum cooking utensil set. Complete in strong carton. Each $6.00

Wonder Value Kilgore Pistols — Single Shot & Repeating

New Models, Smooth Castings, Bright Nickel Finish. NOTE—All Kilgore Pistols are sold on the 5-to-1 combination plan. With each dozen Kilgore Pistols, single shot or repeating, order must be accompanied with order for 5 doz. ammunition to each dozen pistols.

BIG BILL—SINGLE SHOT

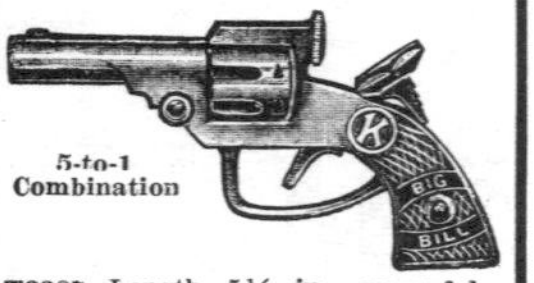

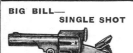

5-to-1 Combination

T3287—Length 5¼ in., powerful trigger, extra large explosion chamber.. Doz. **40c**
½ gro. or more..... Gro. **$4.50**

CAPS FOR ABOVE

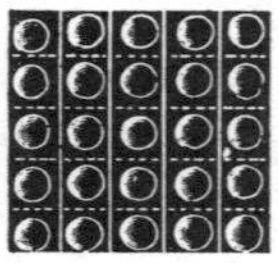

T3292—Super mammoth, perforated sheet of 60 caps in envelope. 5 doz. envelopes in box. Doz. envelopes, **37c**

DOUGHBOY—SINGLE SHOT

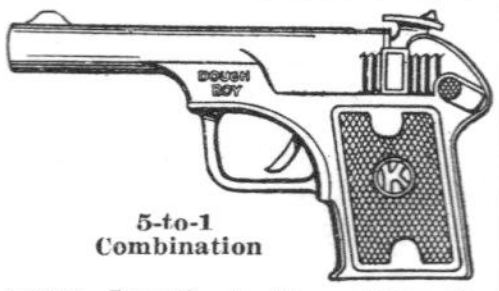

5-to-1 Combination

T3288—Length 5 in., automatic type. Doz. **40c**
½ gro. or more.....Gro. **$4.50**

CAPS FOR ABOVE

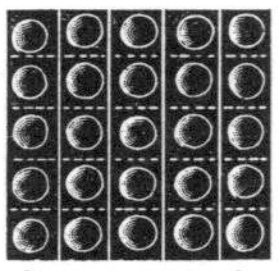

T3292 – Super mammoth, perforated sheet of 60 caps in envelope. 5 doz. envelopes in box. Doz. envelopes, **37c**

SPORT—SINGLE SHOT

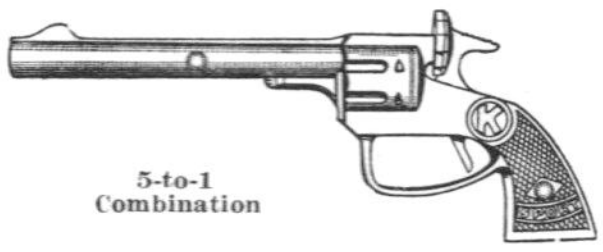

5-to-1 Combination

T3289 – Length 7½ in., extra size loud explosion chamber Doz. **65c**
½ gro. or more............Gro. **$7.20**

CAPS FOR ABOVE

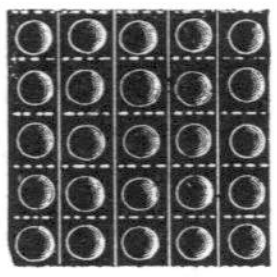

T3292—Super mammoth, perforated sheet of 60 caps in envelope. 5 doz. envelopes in box...........Doz. envelopes, **37c**

LONG BOY—SINGLE SHOT

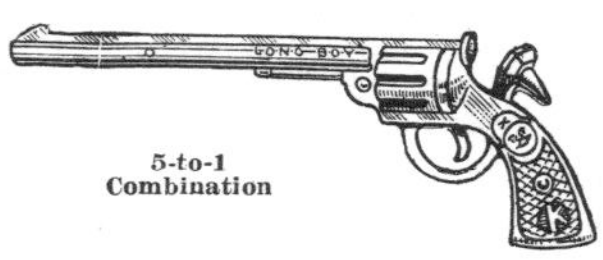

5-to-1 Combination

T3291 – Length 11 in., extra large, loud explosion chamber. Doz. **92c**
½ gro. or more...........Gro. **$10.80**

CAPS FOR ABOVE

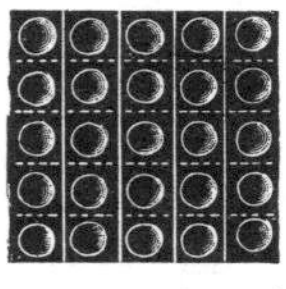

T3292 – Super mammoth, perforated sheet of 60 caps in envelope. 5 doz. envelopes in box.............Doz. envelopes, **37c**

CAPS FOR KILGORE PISTOLS

Sold Separately Without Pistols

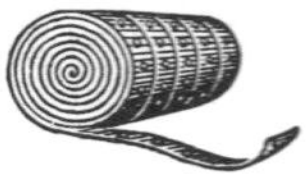

T3290—50 shots on roll, 5 rolls in box (250 shots) 5 doz. boxes in carton; no less sold. Doz. boxes, **15c**

SINGLE-SHOT MAMMOTH SIZE

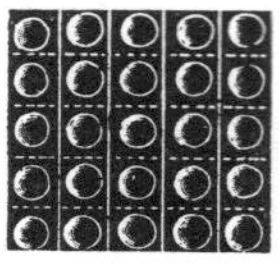

T3284—Perforated sheet of 60 caps in envelope, 5 doz. envelopes in box, no less sold. Doz. envelopes, **15c**

BORDER PATROL—50-SHOT REPEATER

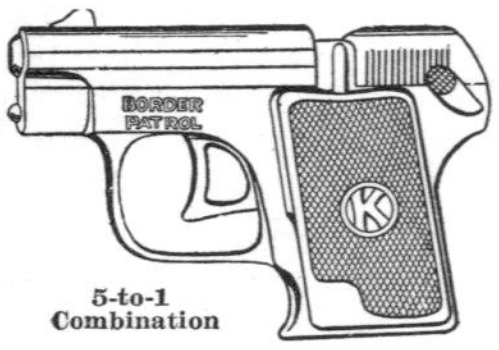

5-to-1 Combination

T3280—Automatic style, 4½x3 in. Doz. **70c**
½ gro. or more.....Gro. **$7.80**

CAPS FOR ABOVE

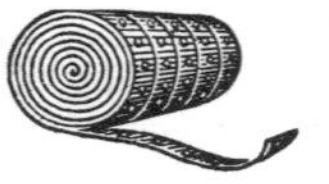

T3282—50 shots on roll, 5 rolls in box (250 shots to box) 5 doz. boxes in carton..Doz. boxes, **40c**

INVINCIBLE—50-SHOT REPEATER

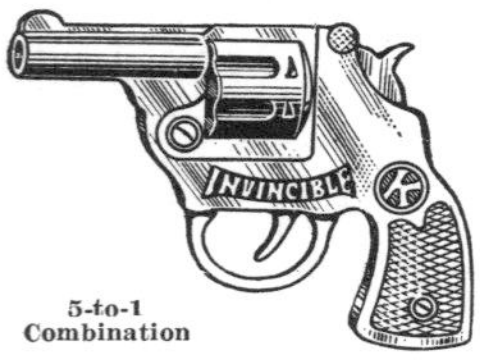

5-to-1 Combination

T3285—Length 5¼ in. Doz. **92c**
½ gro. or more....Gro. **$10.80**

CAPS FOR ABOVE

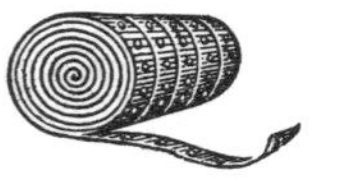

T3286—50 shots on roll, 5 rolls in box (250 shots to box) 5 doz. boxes in carton..Doz. boxes, **40c**

TROOPER—50-SHOT REPEATER

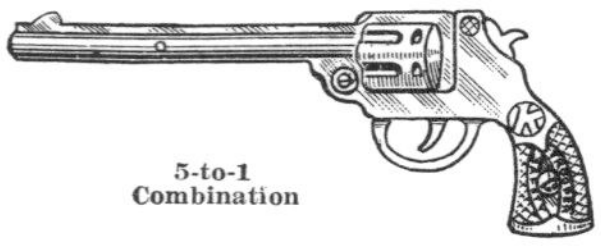

5-to-1 Combination

T3281—Length 10 in.. Doz. **$1.85**
½ gro. or more..........Gro. **$21.00**

CAPS FOR ABOVE

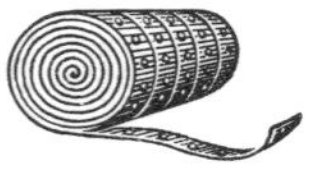

T3282 – 50 shots on roll, 5 rolls in box (250 shots to box) 5 doz. boxes in carton................Doz. boxes, **40c**

Single Shot Pistols

Sold Separately, With or Without Caps

Smooth castings, bright nickel finish, inproved models.

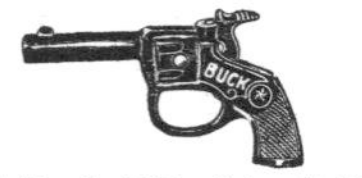

T1014—Buck, 3¼ in. 2 doz in box. Doz. **42c**
½ Gro. or more.....Gro. **$4.80**

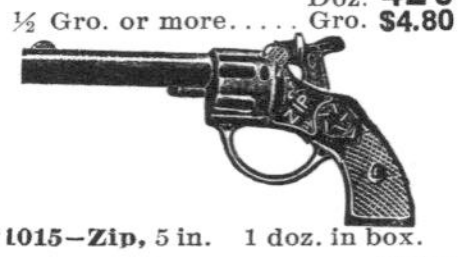

T1015—Zip, 5 in. 1 doz. in box. Doz. **77c**
½ Gro. or more.....Gro. **$9.00**

"STAR" BRAND PAPER CAPS

T95—50 caps in brown pasteboard box. 1 gro. boxes in wood case.................Gro. **58c**
T96—Mammoth. 15 large caps in brown pasteboard box. 1 gro. boxes in wood case....Gro. **67c**

Following with New Large Explosion Chambers.

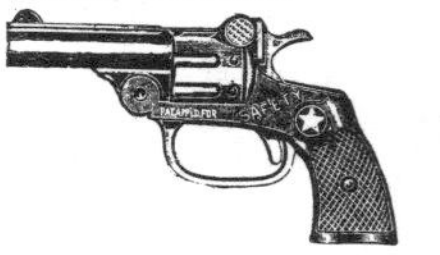

T1016—Safety, 5 in., shoots any size cap. 1 doz. in box Doz. **$1.25**

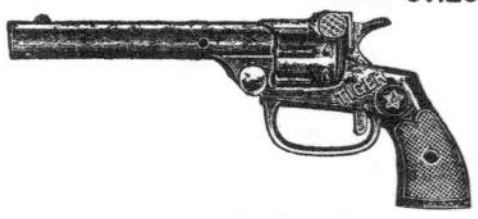

T1017—Tiger, 6¾ in., shoots any size cap. 1 doz. in box. Doz. **$1.65**

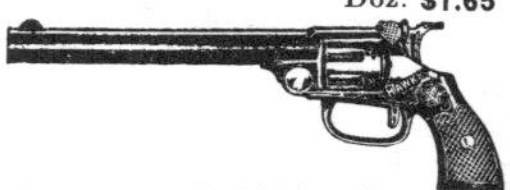

T1018—Hawk, 8¾ in., shoots any size cap. ½ doz. in box. Doz. **$1.87**

Archery Sets And Target Games

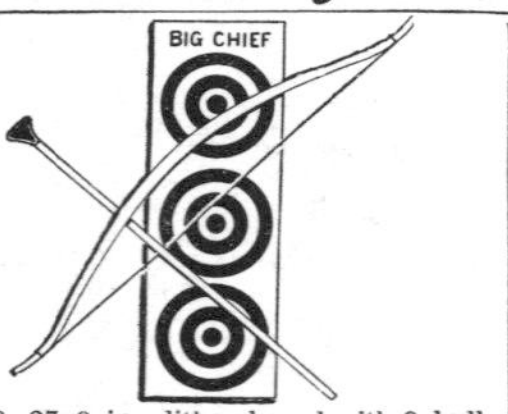

T1618—27x9 in., litho. board with 3 bulls eyes, 27½ in. bow, and arrow with felt head. ½ doz. in box....Doz. **$1.87**

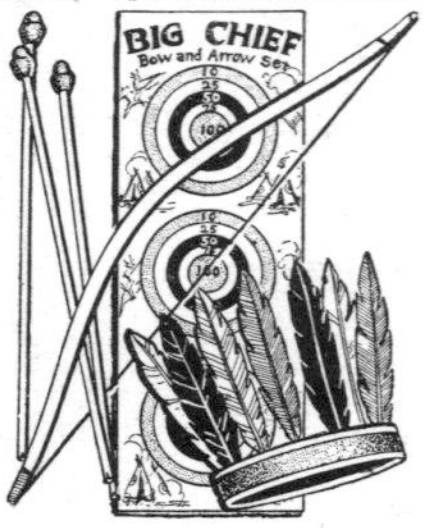

T1619—27x9 in., litho. board with 3 bulls eyes, 27 in. bow, 3 rubber tipped arrows Indian headgear. ½ doz. in box. Doz. **$3.95**

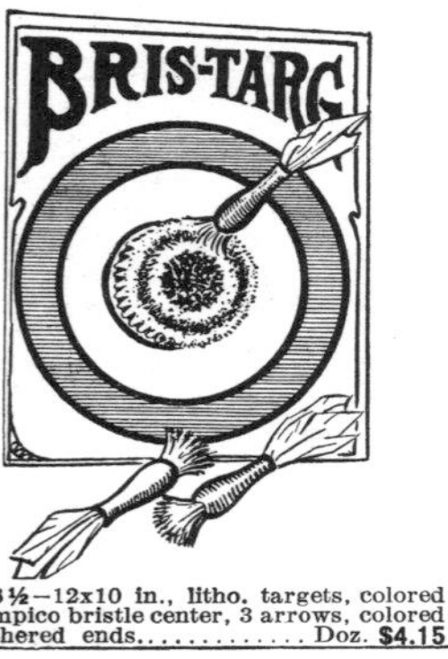

1358½—12x10 in., litho. targets, colored Tampico bristle center, 3 arrows, colored feathered ends............ Doz. **$4.15**

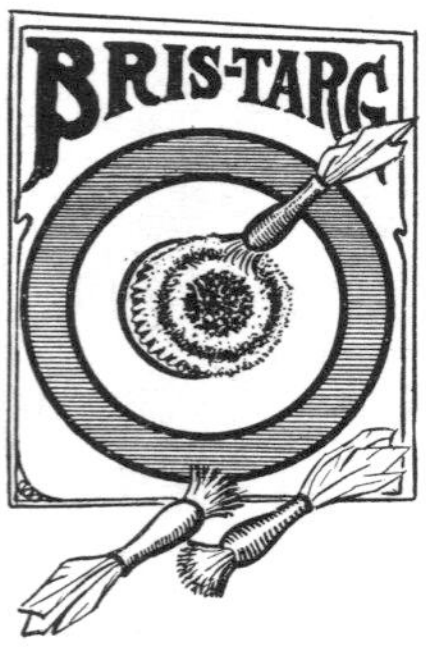

T1359 – 13¾x12 in., large center, extra size arrows ...Doz. **$8.50**

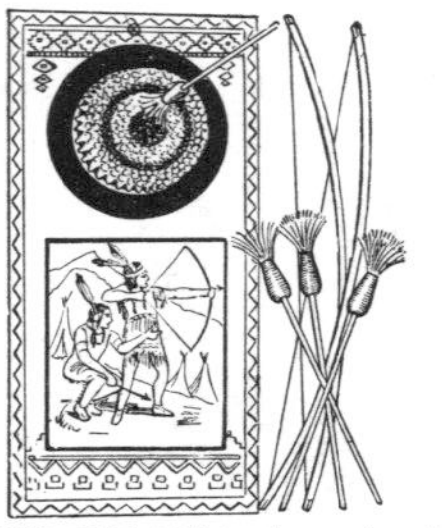

T1360—21½x10½ in., h eavy board litho. target with stand, 6 in. Tampico bristle bulls eye, complete with 2 bows and arrows. Set, **95c**

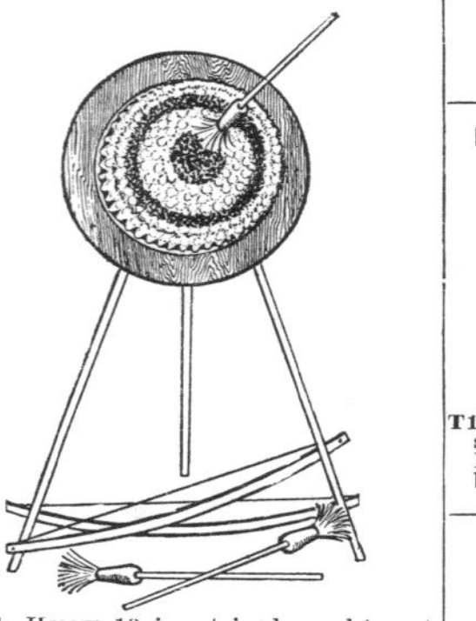

T1361—Heavy 10 in. stained wood target on tripod, Tampico bristle center, complete with 2 bows and 4 arrows Each. **$1.25**

SOLDIER GAME

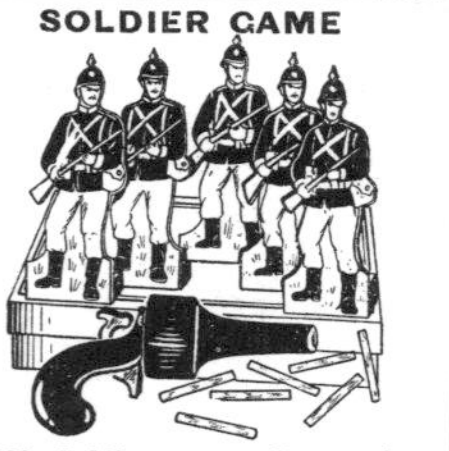

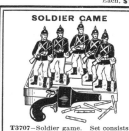

T3707—Soldier game. Set consists of 5 litho. cardboard soldiers each on wood base, ht. 5½ in. spring revolver, wood ammunition. ½ doz. in package.......Doz. **$2.05**

Increase Your Sales
Use Holiday Gift Boxes

Rodeo Cap Pistol

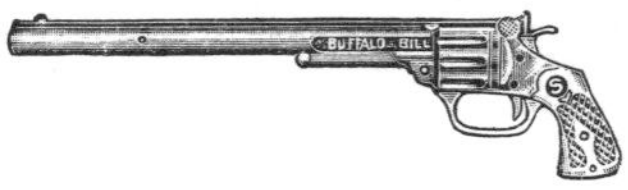

T1019—Rodeo, 11 in., Buffalo Bill type shoots any size cap, Japan finish. ½ doz. in box Doz. **$1.92**

POP PISTOL and HOLSTER

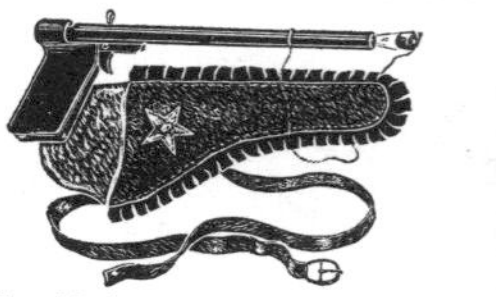

T1225 – 12 in., patent leather holster, slashed edge, cloth belt, 10 in. Buffalo Bill style pop-pistol. 1 doz. in box..................Doz. **$2.05**

Wolverine Sand Pails

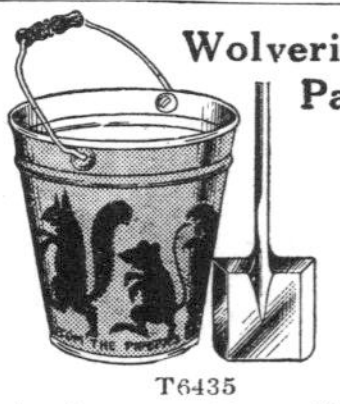

T6435

Extra heavy metal, asstd. Blue, Red, Pink. Asstd. nursery rhymes and juvenile designs. 1 piece steel shovel.
T6435–4⅝x4½ in. 8¼-in. shovel, wire handle. 1 doz. in pkg. Doz. **82c**
½ gro. or more............Gro. **$9.50**
T6436–6½x6½ in. 9¼-in. shovel, wire handle, black enameled grip. 1 doz. in pkg............Doz. **$2.15**

CAPTAIN KID SAND BOAT

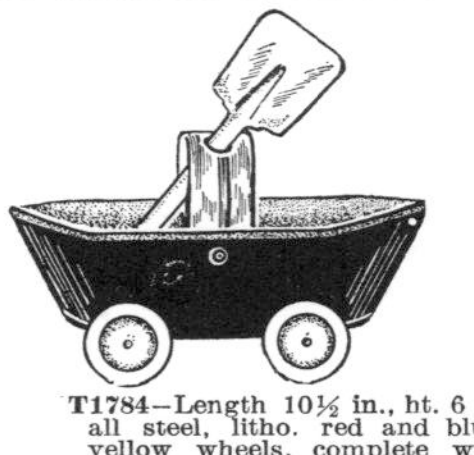

T1784—Length 10½ in., ht. 6 in. all steel, litho. red and blue, yellow wheels, complete with strap handle and shovel. Each in box.....................Doz. **$2.15**

SAND PAILS WITH SHOVELS

Made of heavy block tin. Lithographed in 4 colors. Reinforced strap handles. Galvanized shovels.

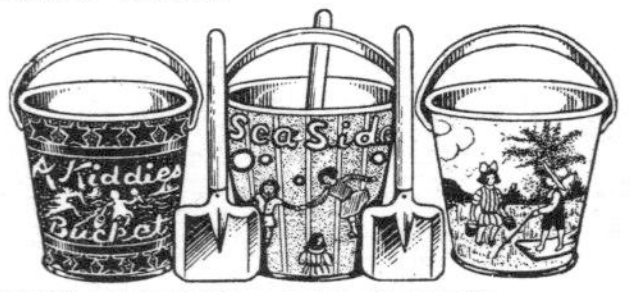

T1797–4½x4¼ in. 1 doz. in bundle. Doz. **78c**

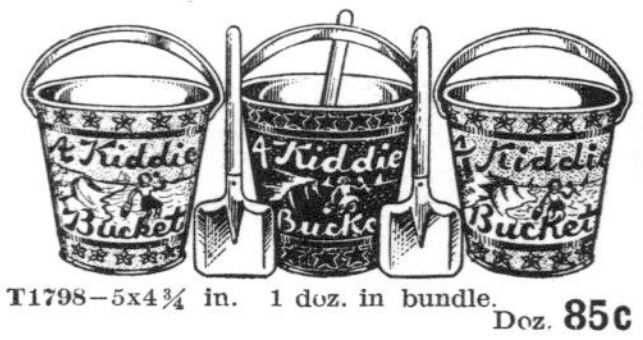

T1798–5x4¾ in. 1 doz. in bundle. Doz. **85c**

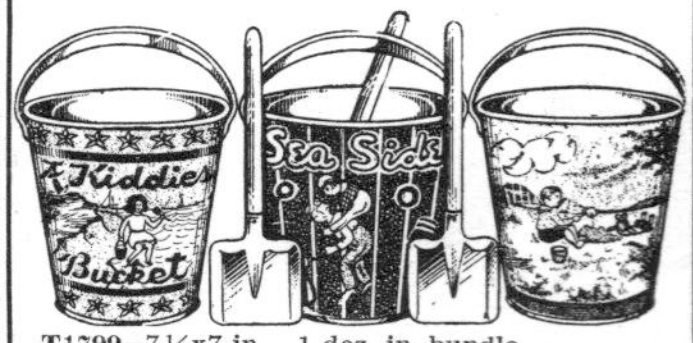

T1799–7½x7 in. 1 doz. in bundle. Doz. **$1.95**

"SANDY ANDY" SAND SET

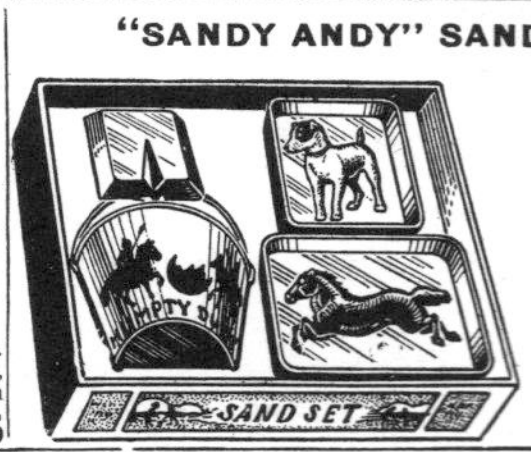

T6437-Display box, 13x11½ x5 in. Set consists of 4⅝x 4½ in. pail with shovel, asstd. designs Animal Molds all in bright colors. Doz. Sets, **$4.25**

Marx Guaranteed Mechanical Toys

Springs that are specially constructed, cannot be wound too tight, practically unbreakable. In size, attractiveness and durability Marx mechanical toys outsell all other makes.

Climbing Monkey

T1901—Ht. 10 in., blue coat, red and yellow jacket, monkey cap, climbs up and down.
Doz. $1.85

THE BIG PARADE

This Year's Big Hit

Band, Artillery, Troops and Ambulance pass through arches at either end and in review of grandstand, miniature buildings, street arches and revolving airplane complete in detail, finished in brilliant colors.
T7450—Length 24 in.............. $9.00 Doz.

Big Value Mack Dump Truck

T1742—Length 13½ in., mammoth size, yellow body, red trimmed, black wheels, side lever dump device...........Doz. $4.25

Rex Racer

605—Length 9 in., bright enameled yellow and red body, disc wheels and spare black fenders.
doz. or more............Doz. $1.80

Collegiate Ford

T7512—Length 7 in., black enameled body and wheels, imitation rubber tires, body covered with numerous comic phrases...............Doz. $2.05

New! Hy-Lo Railway

T7518—Length 12¾ in., complete with 2 cars, car leaves upper incline descends to end of track, is automatically picked up and repeats operation, both cars operate at same time.........Doz. $3.95

New! Stunt Flyer

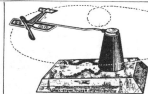

T7513—6¾x4x1½ in. litho. base, a 2¼-in. tower, airship attached, fast revolving airship makes complete somersault. ½ doz. in box.....Doz. $2.15

Star Value King Racer

06—Length 9 in., green and yellow body with cab, nickel finish bumper, headlights and motometer, blue enameled disc wheels and spare; red fenders.
doz. or more...........Doz. $2.00

Stutz Flyer

T1740—Length 16¼ in., yellow body, green trimmed, large red dics wheels, imitation rubber tires, nickel finished front and rear bumpers, headlights, spare tire.
Doz. $3.95

Honeymoon Express

T7522—9½-in. base, litho in 5 colors, farm scenes, express train, etc., 3-car train 4½ in. long, fancy litho. station, 3 tunnels, flagman with jointed arm and signal flag, as train runs flagman signals in natural manner.
Doz. $4.25

Mack Dump Truck

07—Length 9 in., green body and disc wheels, red cab, Mack type, hand lever dump device.
Doz. $2.05

Stutz Flyer—With Driver's Cab

T7516—Length 16¼ in., yellow body, green trimmed, large red disc wheels, imitation rubber tires, nickel finished front and rear bumpers, headlights, spare tire.
Doz. $4.25

Main Street

T7448—Houses, arc lights, park scenes, etc., 6 asstd. autos and trolleys moving back and forth along street, center arches and traffic cop, enameled bright colors, length 24 in., width 3¾ in.............Doz. $8.25

Mack Tanker

08—Length 9 in., green body, disc wheels and tank, red cab.
Doz. $2.05

New!! Sparks Racer

T7514—Length 8¼ in., yellow and red body, yellow wheels, emory wheel in rear emits sparks as car speeds along.
$2.15 Doz.

Pinched

T1746—10x10-in. base, bright colors, enameled cop on motorcycle, auto with chauffeur, tunnels, station, bridges, etc., auto runs in circle, cop hides behind station, shoots out and pinches auto driver.
Doz. $8.67

Mack Wrecker

09—Length 8 in., green, blue and red, sliding lift operated by side crank...............Doz. $2.05

Balky Mule

T7519—Length 10¼ in., finished bright colors, cart with miniature milk cans, comic action, mule balks, runs forward or backward and leaps in air.
Doz. $3.95

Walking Darkey

T7520—Ht. 9 in., figure walks in very amusing manner, dog hanging on seat of trousers, darkey with chicken in hand, bright colors throughout.
Doz. $4.20

New York

One of This Year's Big Hits

T7451—9½-in. base, bright litho., harbor and skyline scene, 5-in. train speeds past numerous streets with their tall buildings, etc., accompanied by airplane.
$4.40 Doz.

Star Value Royal Van

10—Length 9¾ in., yellow and red body, disc wheels, bumper and fenders, rear doors.......Doz. $2.05

Sky Bird Flyer

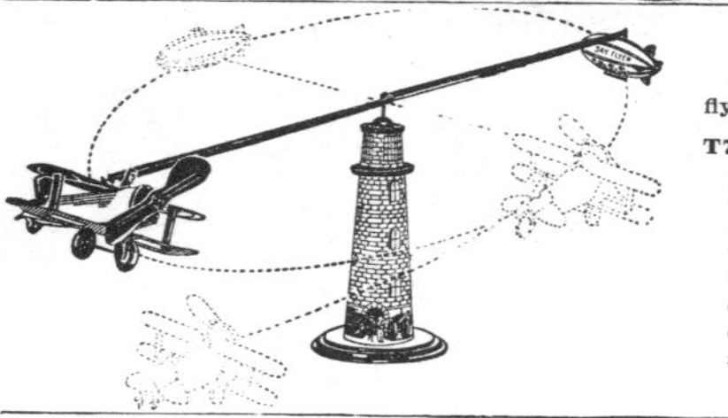

Airplane and Dirigible fly in circle around tower.

T7523—10-in. tower representing light house, red, white and blue enameled 24-in. metal cross beam with 6-in. red, yellow and blue enameled airplane on one end, and 4½-in. dirigible in gilt, yellow and red on other.
Doz. $8.25

Big Value Mack Tank Truck

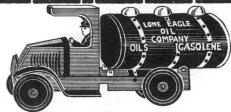

T1743—Length 12 in. mammoth size, yellow body, red trimmed, black wheels, large tank...........Doz. $4.25

Royal Bus

11—Length 10¼-in., low built type, yellow body, red striping, blue wheels, nickel finish bumper.
Doz. $2.05

American Tractor

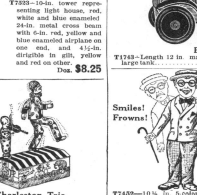

T7515—Length 8 in., width 4¼ in., litho. engine, rear wheels with wide tires.........Doz. $3.95

Charleston Trio

T7521—5x3½x2¼-in. base, decorated circus designs, 7 and 4-in. figures, one plays violin, other dances.
Doz. $3.95

Smiles! Frowns!   **Walks & Sways Body**

Funny Face

T7452—10½ in. 5-color litho. features sectional face, changing expression. Body sways side to side, arms swinging. ¼ doz. in package.
Doz. $4.50

Funny Flivver

T1736—Length 7 in., black enameled body with stenciled comics, "So's Your Old Man," "My Lizzie Of The Valley," etc., blue and white wheels, comic chauffeur with turning head, dog and suit case on running board. Flivvers dart ahead, backs up and circles about in amusing manner, chauffeur's head turns at the same time..........Doz. $3.95

217

Guaranteed American Mechanical Toys

SPIRIT OF ST. LOUIS SHOW PIECE

110 Volts, A. C. or D. C. Current.
Operated By Universal Motor Concealed In Plane Can Be Run 10 Hours Without Attention

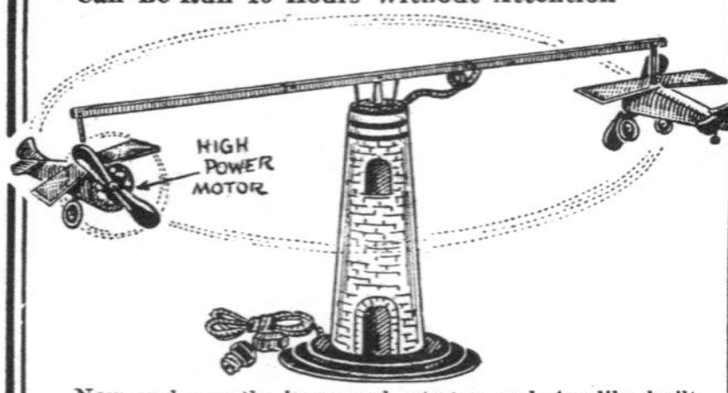

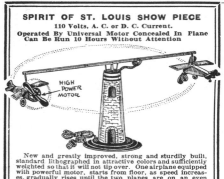

New and greatly improved, strong and sturdily built, standard lithographed in attractive colors and sufficiently weighted so that it will not tip over. One airplane equipped with powerful motor, starts from floor, as speed increases, gradually rises until the two planes are on an even keel when it starts to dip as they both whirl around the standard. When circuit is broken plane glides gracefully to the floor.
T6450—Ht. of standard, 20 in., length of plane, 12 in., cross arm, 28 in. .... Each, **$7.50**

GARAGE WITH ONE CAR

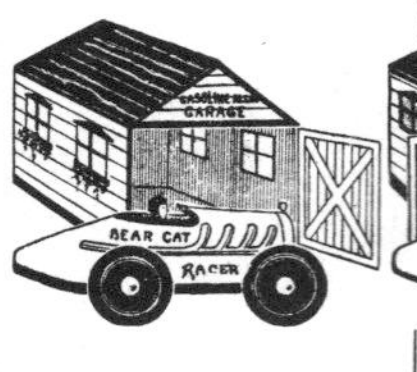

T1782—6¾x3½x3¼ in., all-steel garage, red roof, litho. design frame, side open windows, hinge door, 6¾ in. bear-cat racer. 1 doz. in carton .... Doz. **$2.10**

GARAGE AND TWO CARS

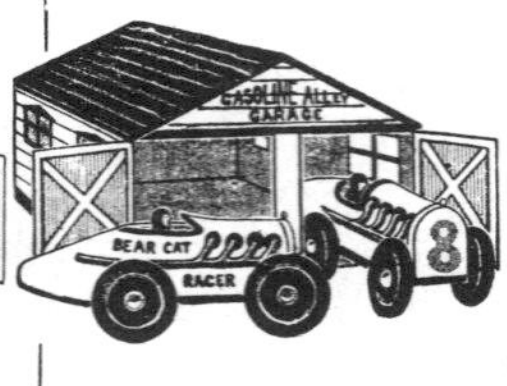

T1785 — 6¾x3¼x3¼ in Steel garage, litho. framework, open windows, hinge door. Complete with two bear cat racers. Length 6½ in .... Doz. **$3.95**

Chrysler Roadster

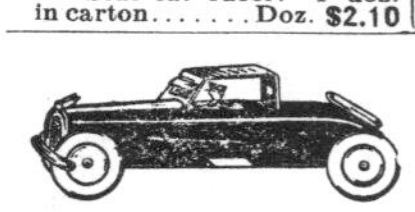

T1781—8½ in. Blue body, yellow cab and striping. Red disc wheels and spare. Nickel radiator and bumper.... Doz. **$2.10**

DANCING BETTY MECHANICAL TOY

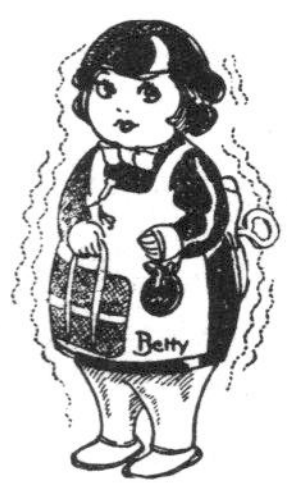

T1802—8 in. extra large body, litho. bright costume and features, dances and shimmies in comical manner.
Doz. **$2.05**

NEW!! DARE-DEVIL FLYER

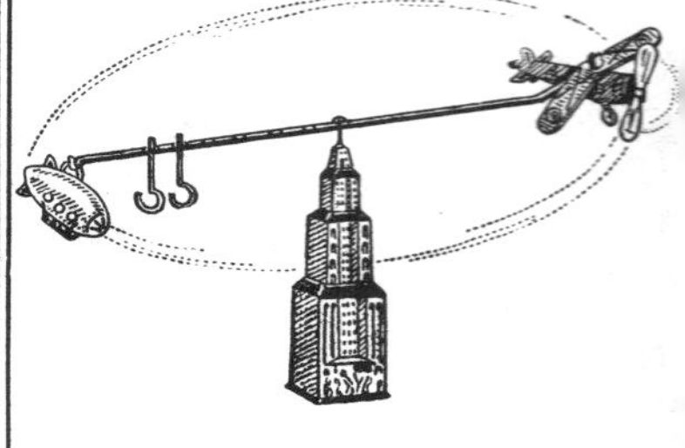

T7449—Bright litho. skyscraper tower, 26 in. arm with dirigible and airplane, as arm revolves airplane performs many stunts .... Doz. **$9.00**

Mack Hauler and Trailer

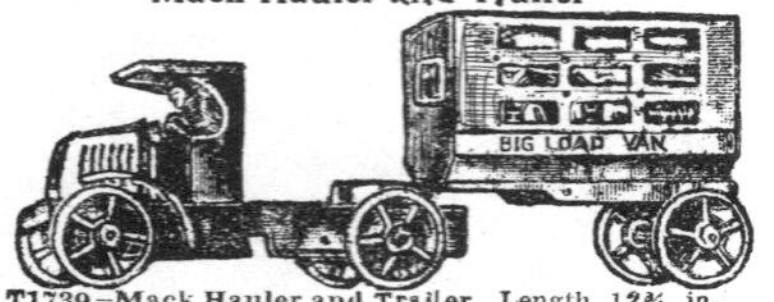

T1739—Mack Hauler and Trailer. Length 12¾ in., width 3¾ in., ht. 5¼ in. Something new in the Mack vehicle line, consisting of sturdy heavy-duty Mack truck with large size trailer attached, loaded with little cartons of nationally known products.
Doz. **$3.75**

American Express With Trailer

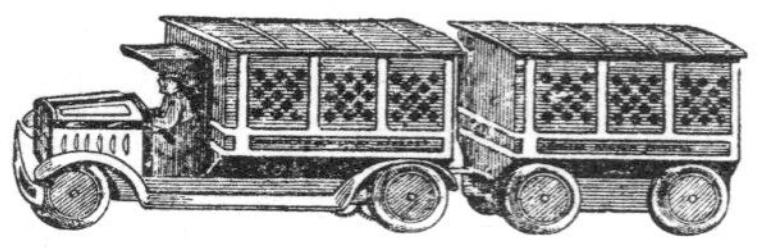

T1909—Length 16½ in., blue body, white striping, disc wheels, fenders and bumper. Each in box.
Doz. **$4.20**

Soldier's Parade

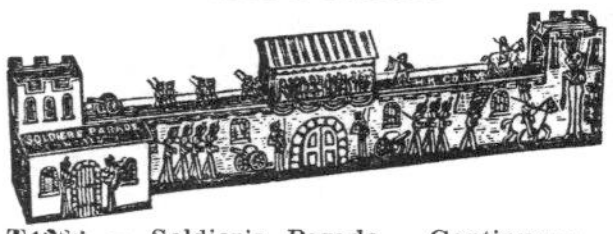

T4286 — Soldier's Parade. Continuous parade of soldiers, leaves armory passes reviewing stand and disappears into fortress, bright litho. colors, length 16 in. Each in box.
.... Doz. **$4.10**

Grand Central

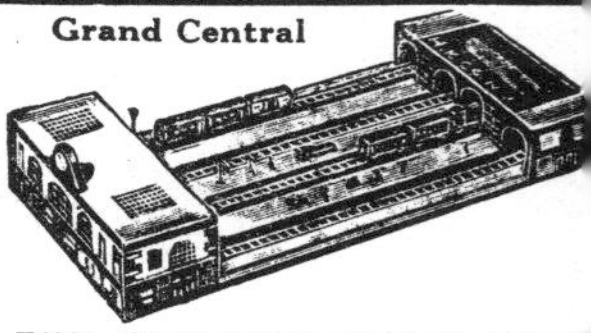

T4287—Grand Central, miniature railroad terminal, consists of 4 tracks with double operating train system, trains move in and out of tunnels, semaphore at side, litho. in bright colors, length 16 in., width 8 in.
.... Doz. **$9.00**

Motor Boats

Run in water long time, heavy steel litho. in bright colors, powerful spring attached key.

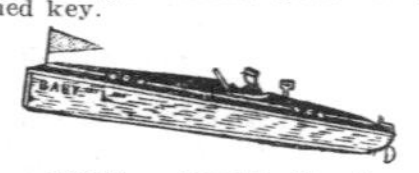

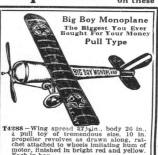

T1908 — Length 11 in., racer model. Doz. **$2.25**

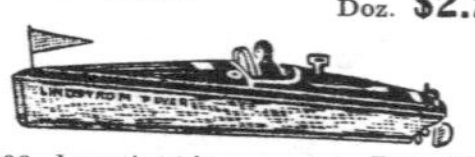

T1906—Length 14 in .... Doz. **$3.95**

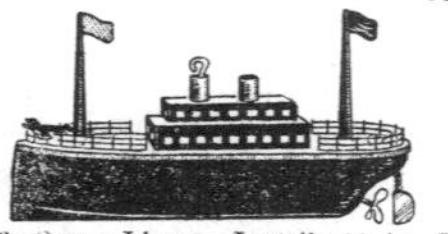

T1786—Ocean Liner. Length 11 in. Red, yellow. Yellow deck. Nickel deck rails. Masts, smoke stacks and staterooms. Runs. long time in water.
Doz. **$3.95**

Seesaw Coaster

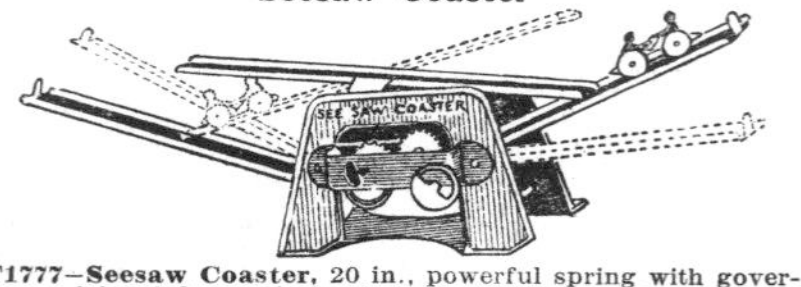

T1777—Seesaw Coaster, 20 in., powerful spring with governor, jointed figures in hand car speed to top and descend to coaster, 40 trips with one winding .... Doz. **$7.95**

Loop-The-Loop

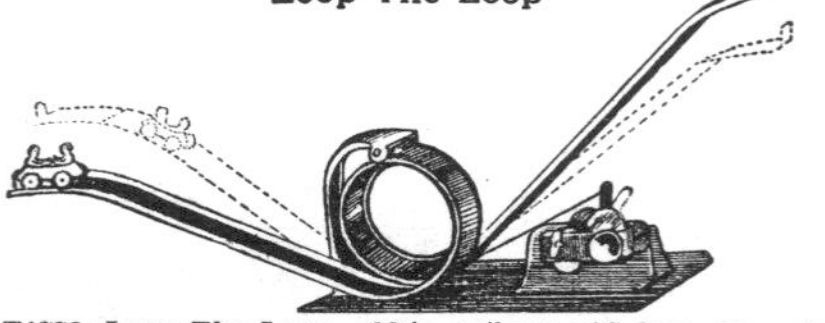

T1776—Loop-The-Loop. 28-in. railway with loop, car and passengers with jointed arms and bodies, races down, incline, loops the loop and returns to starting point, repeats many times without rewinding .... Doz. **$8.25**

PILE DRIVER

Full of Action

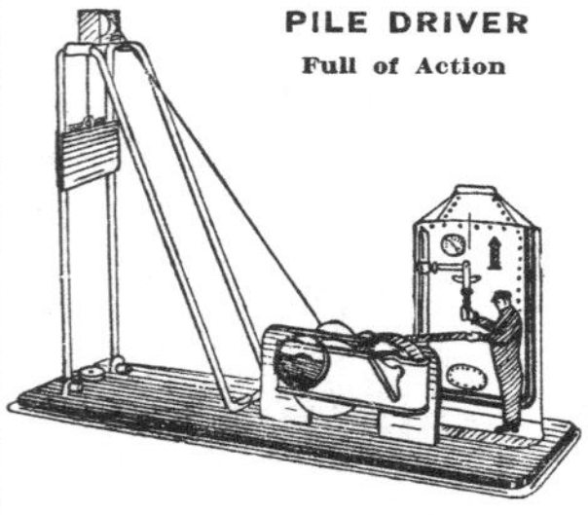

T1775—Clever Fascinating. Green enameled base 12x4 in., ht. of driver 10 in., litho. metal boiler and engineer, powerful spring motor with governor, engineer operates with lever, very realistic. Each in box .... Doz. **$7.95**

Performing Toys

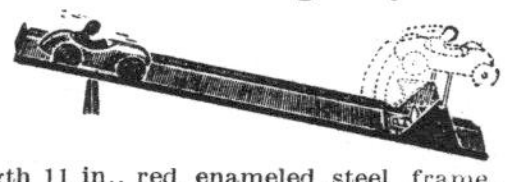

T7503—Length 11 in., red enameled steel frame, auto speeds to bottom, strikes lever, leaps in air. 1 doz. in box .... Doz. **85c**

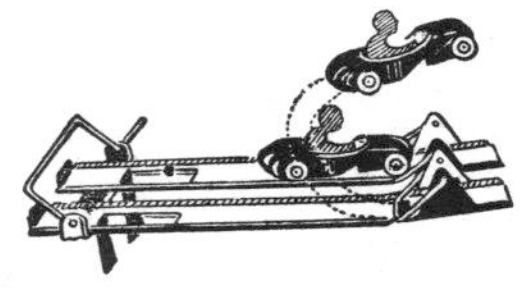

T7527—Length 11 in., width 3¼ in., double incline with 2 autos, hand lever releases cars which speed to bottom, strike spring release and leap in air .... Doz. **$1.95**

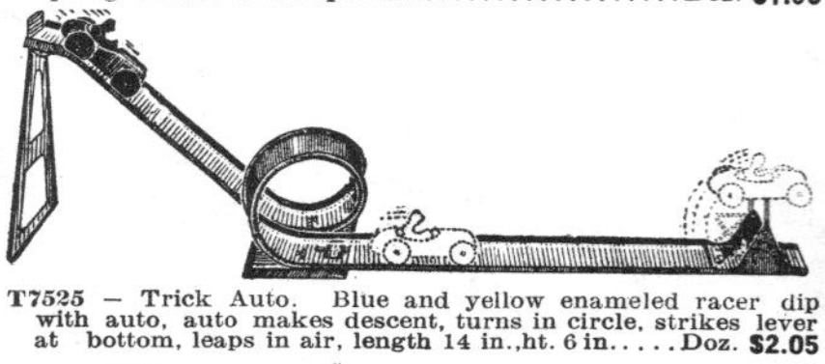

T7525 — Trick Auto. Blue and yellow enameled racer dip with auto, auto makes descent, turns in circle, strikes lever at bottom, leaps in air, length 14 in., ht. 6 in. .... Doz. **$2.05**

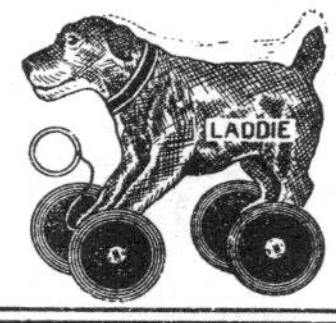

T1907 — Jumping Dog. Length 5½ in., ht. 4¾ in., 4 red enameled disc wheels, as drawn along dog jumps up and down. 1 doz. in box .... Doz. **82c**

Airplanes—

Right now at the very height of their popularity, the boys are going wild over airplane toys, you cannot afford to miss sales on these items.

Mechanical and Pull Type

Big Boy Monoplane

The Biggest You Ever Bought For Your Money

Pull Type

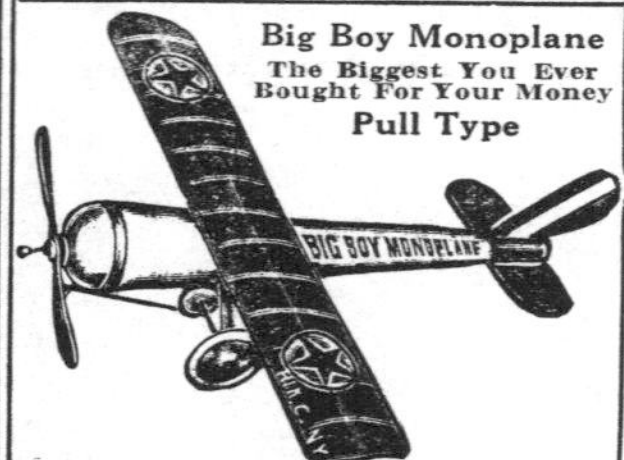

T4288—Wing spread 27½in., body 26 in., a pull toy of tremendous size, 10 in. propeller revolves as drawn along, ratchet attached to wheels imitating hum of motor, finished in bright red and yellow. Each in box.
Doz. **$9.00**

Pull Type

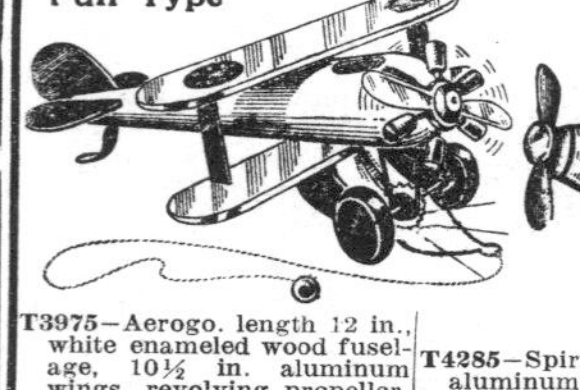

T3975—Aerogo. length 12 in., white enameled wood fuselage, 10½ in. aluminum wings, revolving propeller, enameled ball end rotor attached to pulley, as drawn along makes sound like motor, forms rainbow colors.
Doz. **$7.95**

Mechanical

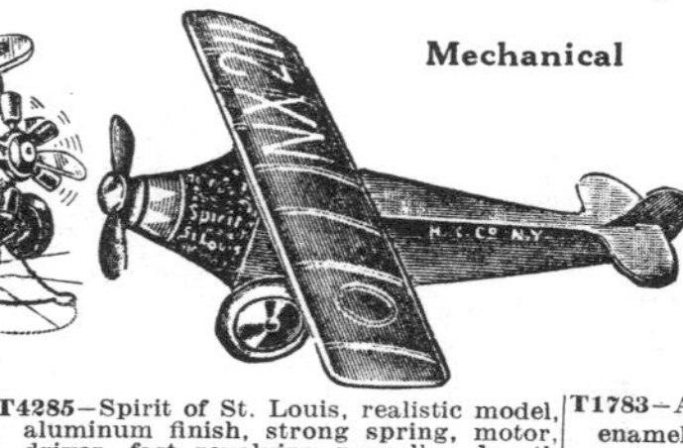

T4285—Spirit of St. Louis, realistic model, aluminum finish, strong spring, motor, driver, fast revolving propeller, length 12½ in. 12¼ in. wing. Each in box.
.... Doz. **$4.10**

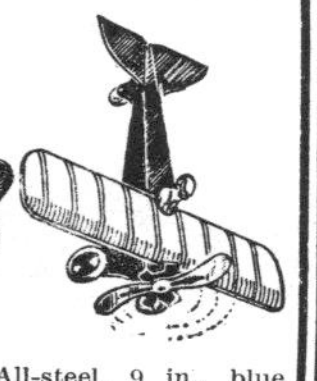

T1783—All-steel, 9 in., blue enameled fuselage, 7 in. red enameled wing, fast revolving propellor, disc wheels. 1 doz. in box.
Doz. **$2.10**

Pull Type

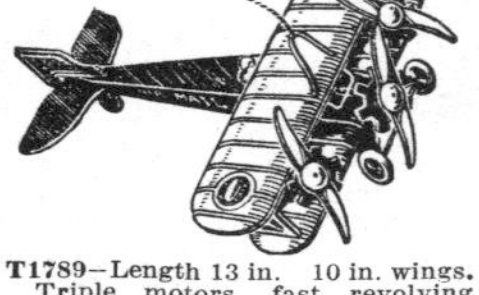

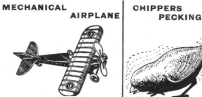

T1789—Length 13 in. 10 in. wings. Triple motors, fast revolving propellors, as pulled along makes noise like roar of motor. Lithographed in blue and red. Long pull cord. Each in box.
Doz. **$8.10**

Pull Type

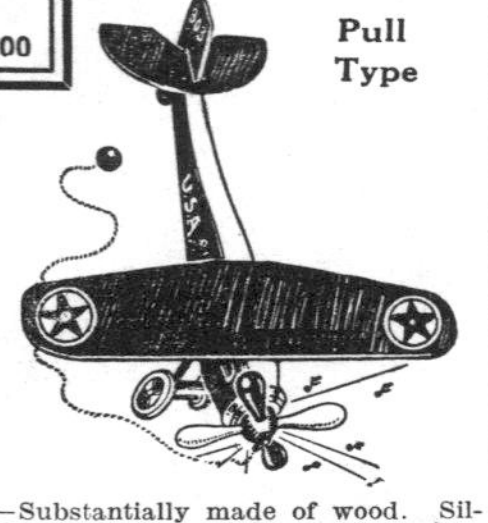

T3410—Substantially made of wood. Silver finish fuselage and blue enamel wing. Nickel motor head and vari-colored propellor. Wing spread 18 in. As drawn along propellor revolves and gong strikes. Length 21 in ...... Each, **$2.25**

MECHANICAL AIRPLANE

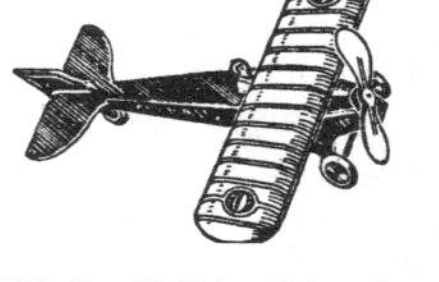

T1787—Length 13 in. 10 in. wings. Blue fuselage. Fast revolving propeller. Pilot.
Doz. **$4.25**

CHIPPERS PECKING BIRD

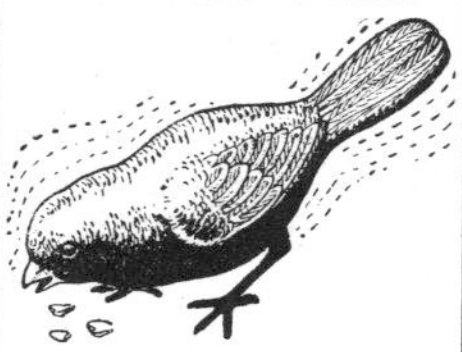

T1915 — 5 in. long, heavy gauge metal, litho, natural colors, long running concealed spring, when wound hops and pecks in realistic manner. Each in box.
Doz. **$2.10**

Lindy Pull Planes

Cast iron fuselage and wing, enameled gray, Lindy in red enamel letters, nickel plated motor head and propeller, 9 gray enameled cylinders, nickel wheels.

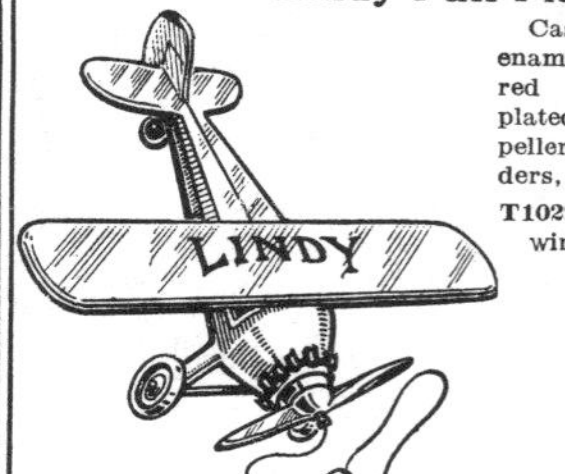

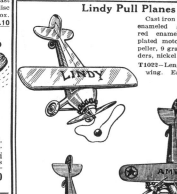

T1022—Length 9 in., 10 in. wing. Each in box.
Doz. **$8.50**

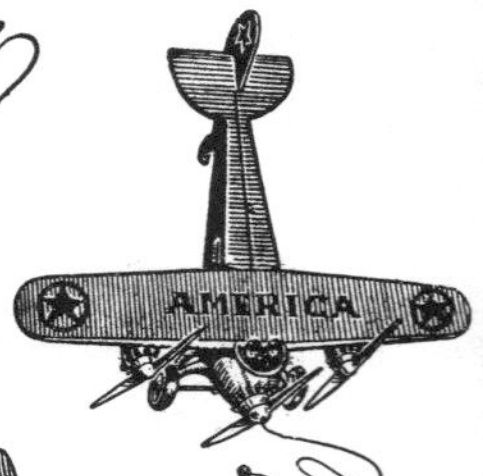

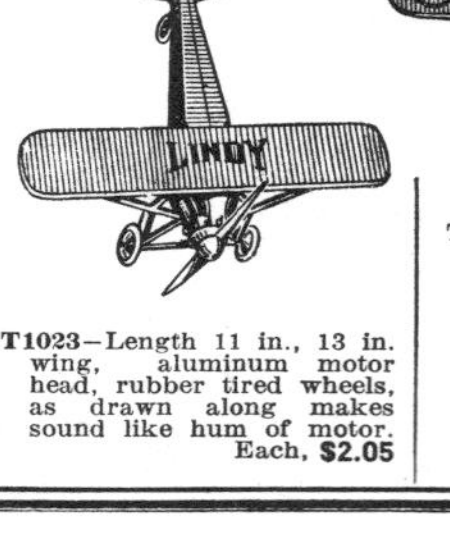

T1023—Length 11 in., 13 in. wing, aluminum motor head, rubber tired wheels, as drawn along makes sound like hum of motor.
Each, **$2.05**

T1024—Length 14 in., 17 in. wing, America and insignia in red, triple aluminum motors, each with 9 cylinders, pilot and mechanician, 2½ in. double disc nickel wheels, ballon rubber tires, as drawn along 3 propellers revolve, makes sound like hum of motor.
Each, **$3.45**

Pull Type

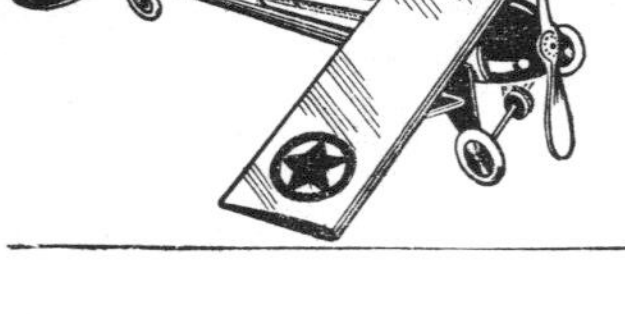

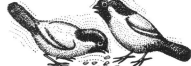

LINDYPLANE

T1887—Gracefully built. Very substantial. When pulled across floor imitation motor roars as auminum propellor revolves. Decorated in 5 bright colors. Length 11 in., width 10 in., ht. 5½ in. Each in box.
Doz. **$8.50**

Imported Mechanical Pecking Bird

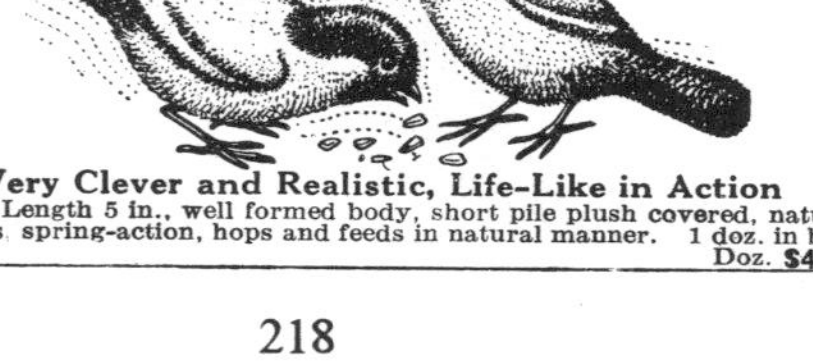

Very Clever and Realistic, Life-Like in Action

T8697—Length 5 in., well formed body, short pile plush covered, natural colors. spring-action, hops and feeds in natural manner. 1 doz. in box.
Doz. **$4.25**

Juvenile Automobiles—

New snappy models, heavy gauge steel bodies enameled in new prevailing colors. Latest Equipment & accessories.

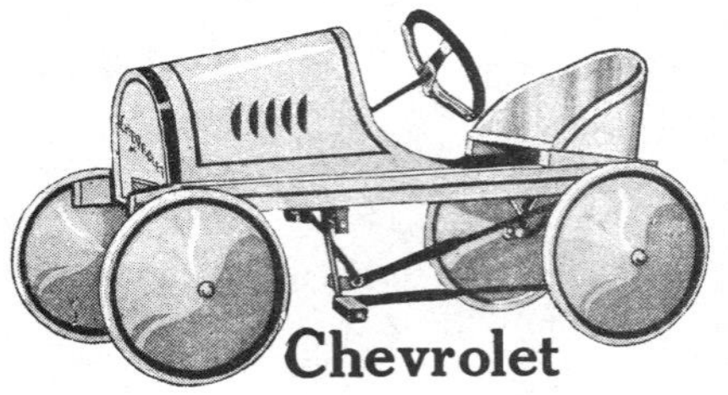

Chevrolet

TO4883—Body 30 in., wood frame, steel hood and back of seat, brilliant red, yellow striping, black enameled gear, rubber pedals, strong steering wheel, 8-in. red enameled double disc wheels, ½-in. rubber tires.

$4.15

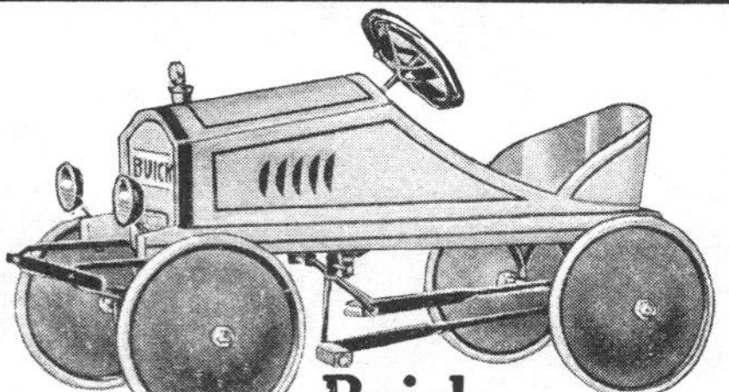

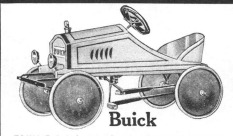

Buick

TO4884—Body 30 in., wood frame, steel hood and back of seat, yellow, red striping, black enameled gear, rubber pedals, steering wheel with gas lever, 10-in. red enameled double disc wheels, ½-in. rubber tires, equipment includes instrument board, motometer, headlights, bumper.

$4.85

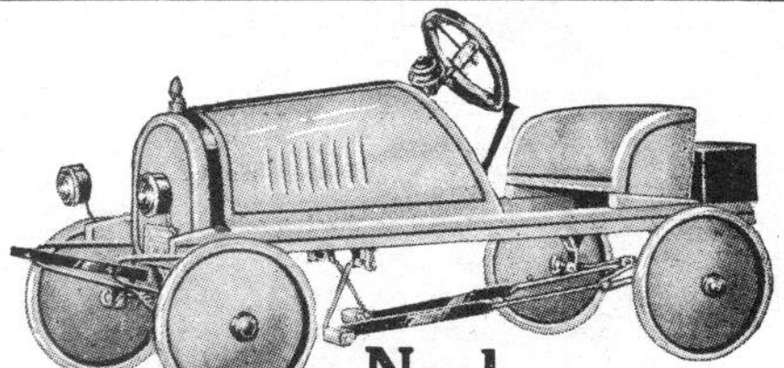

Nash

TO4885—Body 40½ in., red enameled, black and yellow striping, black enameled gear, rubber pedals, 10-in. red enameled double disc wheels, ½-in. rubber tires, equipment includes trunk on rear, bumper, headlights, motometer, steering wheel with gas cortrol, instrument board and gear shift.

$7.85

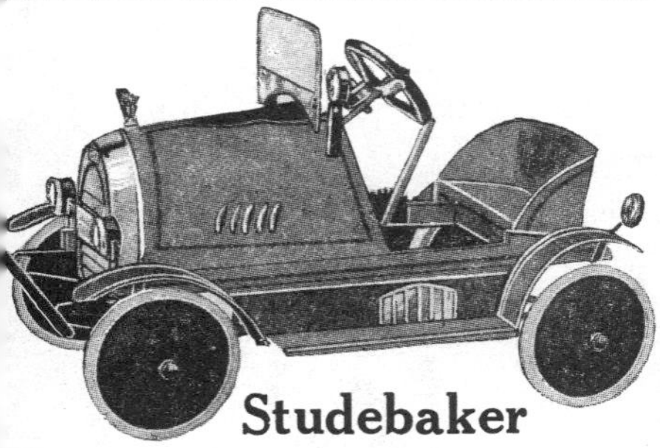

Studebaker

TO4886—Body 41 in., enameled buff, green and red striping, nickel radiator, 10-in. red enameled double disc wheels, ½-in. rubber tires, black enameled gear, rubber pedals, cantilever springs, equipment includes bumper, headlights, motometer, adjustable windshield with spotlight, horn and gear shift.

$10.50

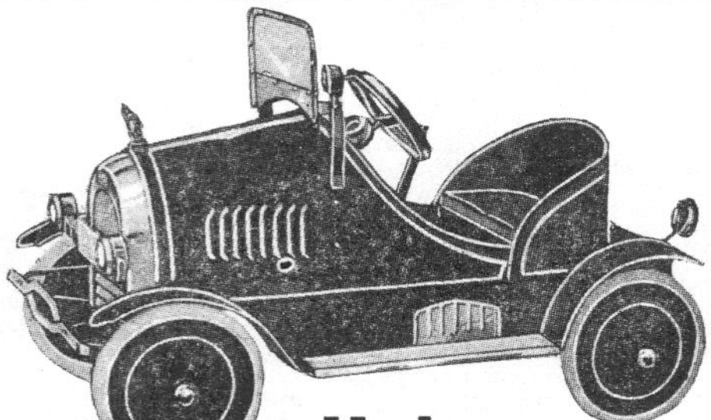

Hudson

Roller Bearing Wheels

TO4887—Body 42 in., brilliant green, striped yellow and red, red fenders, 10-in. double disc wheels, 1-in. rubber tires, nickel radiator, headlights, nickel bumper, adjustable windshield with spotlight, horn, parking light and gear shift.

$12.50

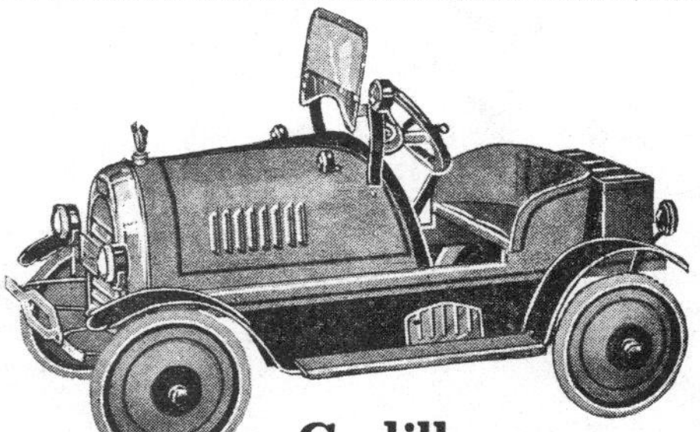

Cadillac

Roller Bearing Wheels

TO4888—Body 45 in., gray striped blue and red, red fenders, 10-in. double disc wheels, 1-in. rubber tires, nickel radiator, motometer and bumper, adjustable windshield with spotlight, trunk on rear, tool kit.

$14.50

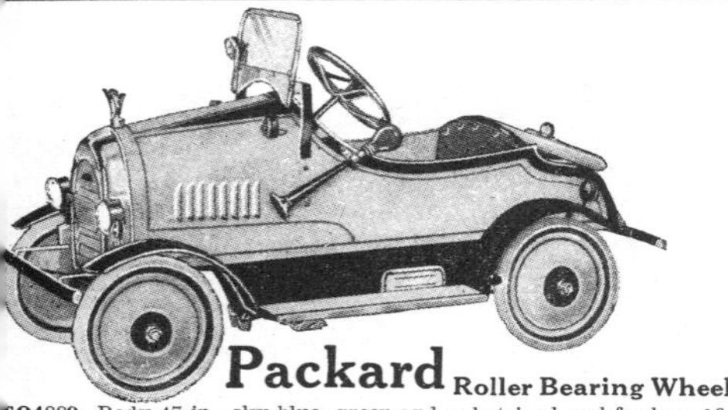

Packard Roller Bearing Wheel

TO4889—Body 47 in., sky blue, green and red striped, red fenders, 10-in. double disc wheels and 1 spare, cantilever springs, front and rear nickel bumpers, nickel radiator, motometer, adjustable windshield, headlights, cowl lights, French horn.

$19.25

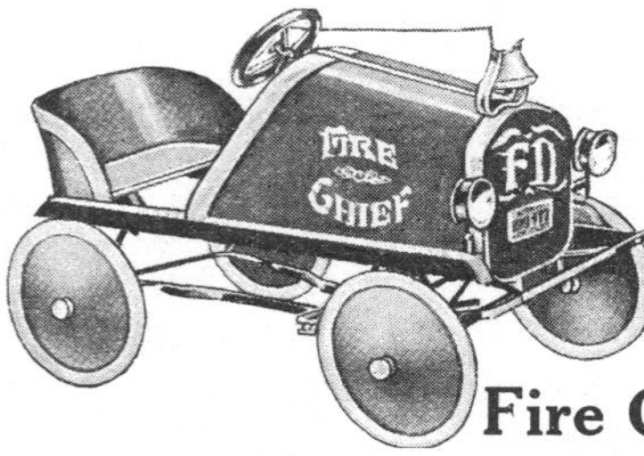

Fire Chief

TO4890—Body 30 in., large steel hood and back of seat, brilliant red finish, gilt striping, 8-in. red enameled double disc wheels, ½-in. rubber tires, bumper, headlights, large bell with cord attached to steering wheel.

$5.50

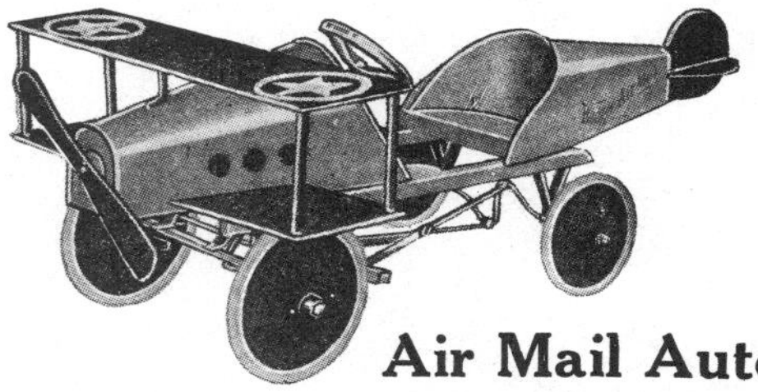

Air Mail Auto

TO4891—Length over all 56 in., wing spread 30½ in., heavy steel construction, gray body, red wings, revolving propeller, red enameled double disc wheels, 10-in. front, 8-in. rear, ⅝-in rubber tires.

$8.50

Scooters, Pedal Bikes, Wagons and Baby Strollers

Speedy Disc Wheel Rubber Tired Scooter

TO4892 — Length 30 in., height 29 in., footboard 11x4 in., natural varnish finish, 7-in. red enameled double disc wheels, ½-in. rubber tires, complete with parking stand. Each in carton.

Each, **$1.35**

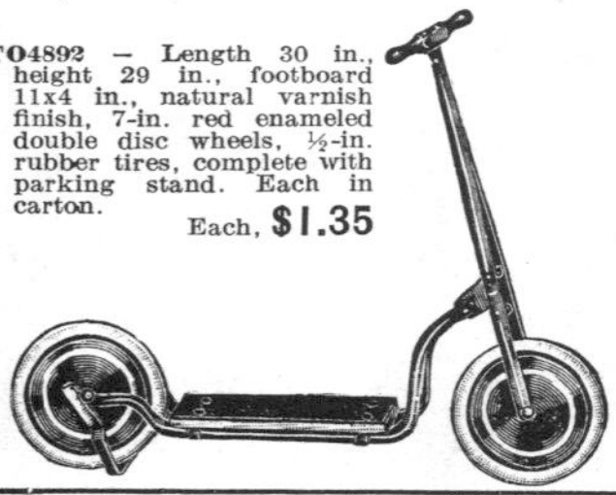

Roller Bearing Wheels

TO4894—Length 40 in., ht. 32 in., 13x5½-in. footboard, natural varnish finish, 10-in. red enameled double disc wheels, ¾-in. rubber tires, parking stand. Each in carton.

Each, **$2.25**

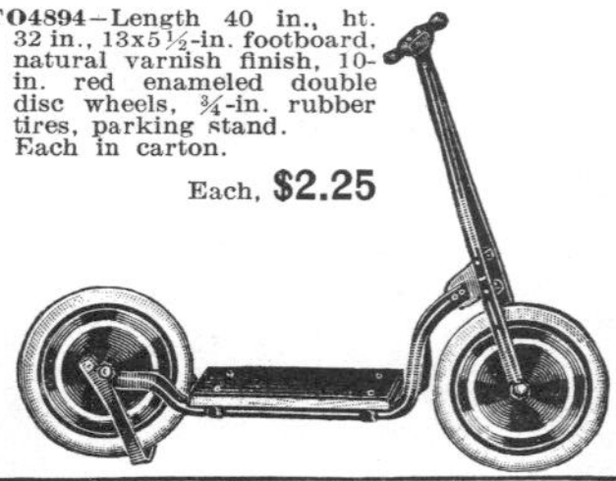

Roller Bearing Wheels

TO4895—Length over all 42 in., height 32 in., 13x5½-in. footboard, natural varnish finish, 10-in. double disc red enameled wheels, ¾-in. rubber tires, parking stand, roller brake. Each in carton.

Each, **$2.50**

Roller Brake

Foot Brake

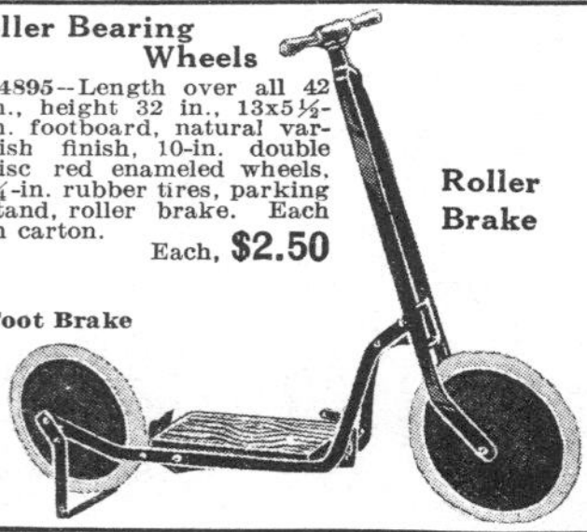

Roller Bearing Wheels

1¼-In. Rubber Tires

TO4896—Length over all 42 in., height 32 in., 13x5½-in. footboard covered with non-skid rubber mat, 10-in. double disc wheels enameled orange, striped blue, parking stand, roller brake. Each in carton.

Each, **$3.50**

Foot Brake

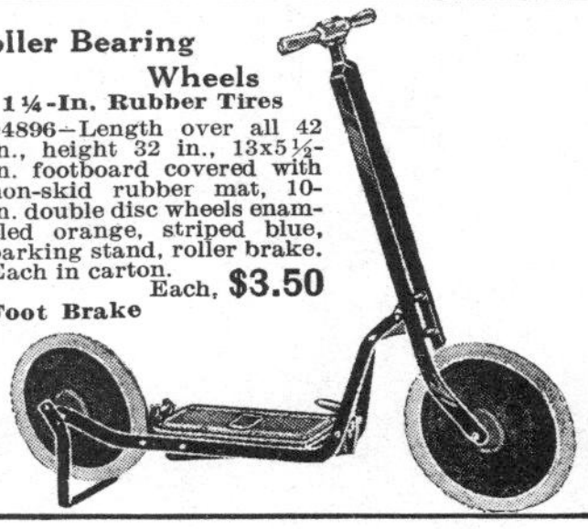

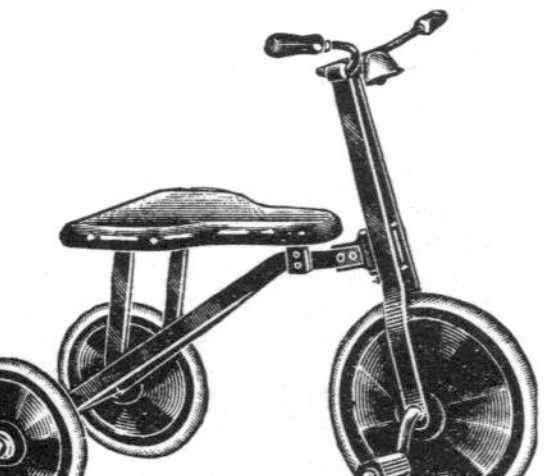

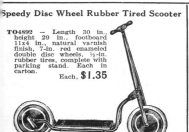

TO4752 — 25x19 in. Red enameled, 7 and 9-in. disc wheels ⅜-in. rubber tires, red enameled seat, ¾-in. steel frame, hand grip with nickeled ferrule and bicycle bell. Solid rubber pedals. 3 in carton, no less sold.

$1.65

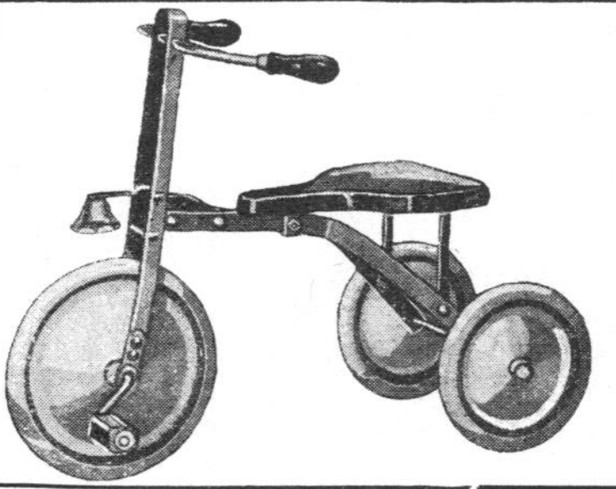

Star Value Pedal Bike

Double Disc Rubber Tired wheels

TO4898—Seat 10x6½ in., heavy steel undergear and fork, bright red enamel handle with rubber grips, nickel-plated bell, rubber pedals, double disc red enameled wheel, ½ in. rubber tires, 6-in. rear, 8-in. front. 2 in carton.

$1.50

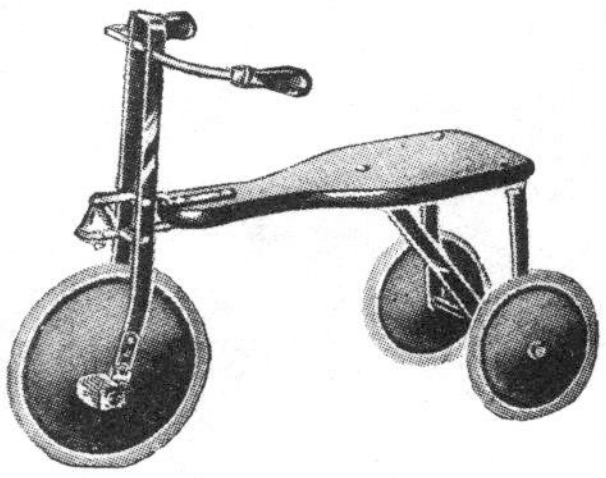

TO4899—Seat 15x7½ in., 10½ in., from floor, bright enamel finish, 8-in. front, 6-in. rear, red enameled double disc wheels, ½-in. rubber tires, equipped with bell. 2 in carton.

$1.65

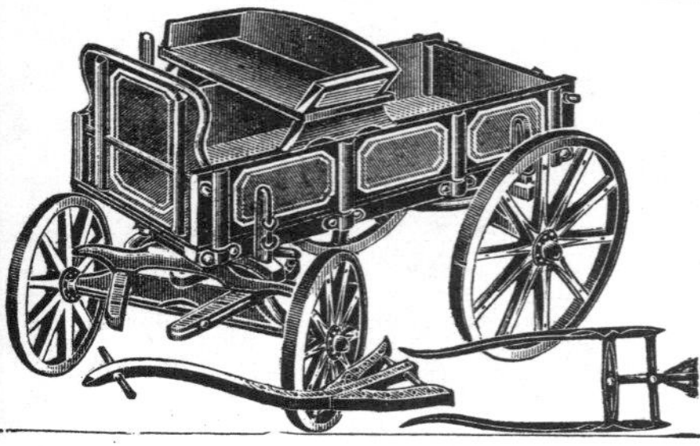

"Dreadnaught" Farm Wagon

TO4074—Body 18x36 in., hardwood frame, seat and dashboard (**Removable Ornamented Sides and Ends**), **Wheels** 14 and 20 in., with steel hubs, heavy welded tires, shaves, spokes, all parts strongly ironed and braced. 9/16-in. steel axels. Stout handle.

$7.85

Shafts For Above

←**TO4075**—Length 42 in., width 17 in., painted red, striped black.

Each, **$1.00**

Convertible Baby Walker and Stroller

TO4901—Furnished with extra wheel, when attached to steering post converts stroller into buddy car, folding handle with spring clip, can be used for pulling or pushing, foot rest, rubber covered bumpers front and rear, blue enameled double disc rubber tired wheels, beautifully finished in blue and ivory.

$3.10

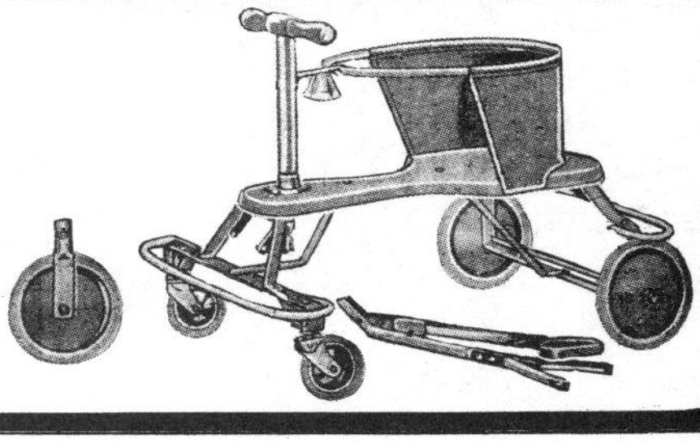

Practical Tools for Boys

28 TOOLS $5.98 Postpaid

38 TOOLS $8.79 Postpaid

8 IN SWEEP BRACE WITH CHUCK

14 3/8 IN. WOOD T SQUARE

19 3/8 IN. SAW TEMPERED STEEL BLADE

20X8X8 IN. METAL COVERED $3.00 TOOL BOX

TEMPERED STEEL BLADE

ADJUSTABLE HACK SAW

BENCH BOARD

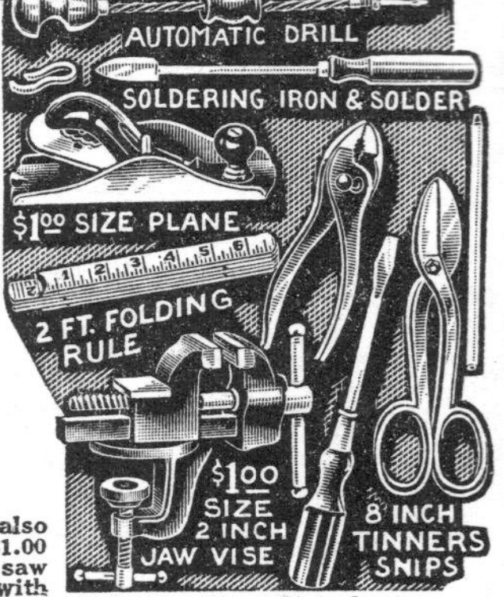

19" PLUMB AND LEVEL

AUTOMATIC DRILL

SOLDERING IRON & SOLDER

$1.00 SIZE PLANE

2 FT. FOLDING RULE

$1.00 SIZE 2 INCH JAW VISE

8 INCH TINNERS SNIPS

Boys! Save 1/3 on Tool Sets Like Dad's

The tool box alone would cost you $3.00 and is the same as those used and carried by expert mechanics. It is 20x8x8 inches, enameled steel, covered with reinforced corners, genuine leather handle and real lock and key. Wood tray inside for nails, etc. The tools in either one of these sets are practical and will give you excellent service because they are made of same material and by same skilled workmen as those made for men.

The following twenty-three tools are included in both outfits: 1—19⅜-inch saw with tempered and polished spring steel blade nicely shaped and the teeth are sharpened and set like on a large saw; 2—14⅜-inch "T" square of hardwood (maple); 3—Nickel plated scroll saw with three extra blades for fine cutting; 4—6-inch mill file, wood handle; 5—¾-inch width, and 6—½-inch width wood chisel of tempered and polished steel; 7—8½-inch wood marking gauge with set screw; 8—Medium size screwdriver with polished steel blade for fine work; 9—Semi-steel hammer with 12-inch hardwood handle; 10—10x2⅝-inch wood miter box; 11—5-inch steel dividers; 12—3-inch wood mallet; 13—Wood triangle; 14—12x7-inch nickel plated steel square; 15—Slip joint semi-steel pliers with hardened jaws; 16-17-18—Three polished steel bits; 19—Scratch awl; 20—4¼-inch steel punch; 21—7-inch pencil with eraser; 22—3¼-inch cold chisel; 23—Sand block with two pieces of sand paper.

28 Tools in Metal Covered Tool Box $5.98

$10.00 Value Elsewhere—Our Price $5.98 in addition to the 23 tools mentioned above, there is the 8-inch sweep brace (same as shown in picture but without chuck); 12-inch varnished hardwood level; 6⅛-inch black enameled all steel plane with 1½-inch cutting blade that may be sharpened and honed; beautiful iron vise with 1½-inch jaws; 12-inch varnished wood ruler.
79T7404—Postpaid..................$5.98

Same tools as in our 79T7404, but without metal covered chest, for boys who want to make their own tool box. Packed in strong carton.
79T7405—Postpaid..................$3.98

38 Tools in Metal Covered Tool Box $8.79

For Grownup Boys Who Want Large Assortment
$12.50 Value Elsewhere for $8.79
In addition to the 23 tools mentioned above, you have the 75c size 8-inch sweep brace with chuck; also $1.00 size 6¾-inch block plane with wood knob; $1.00 size iron vise with 2-inch jaws; 18-inch compass saw with tempered steel blade; 10½-inch soldering iron with liberal piece of solder; 19-inch varnished hardwood plumb and level; 10¾-inch automatic drill; large size adjustable hack saw; 8-inch tinner snips; 2-foot folding rule; 1-inch tempered and polished steel wood chisel; nickel plated screw clamp; extra large size screwdriver; wood handle gimlet and wood bench board.
79T7406—Postpaid..................$8.79

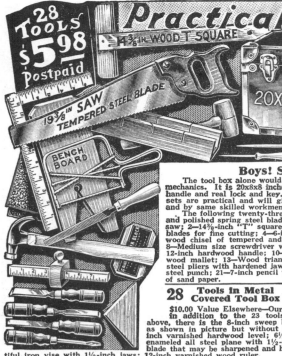

Just the Outfit You Want for Your Toy Factory

First You Draw the Article—Then Cut It Out and Put It Together and Finally Color It to Suit Your Taste

With this outfit you can make a great variety of small wooden toys and novelties. Contains a nickel plated scroll saw with four blades, a wood bench with metal clamp to fasten to table, full size toy designs ready for tracing, 1 sheet of carbon paper, thumb tacks, seven pieces of thin wood, hammer, a brad awl, sandpaper and ruler. Cotter pins for assembling; crayons and paints to color them. Complete "Manual of Instructions."
49T7444—Postpaid..................$1.85

20 Tools in a Varnished Hardwood Chest $3.87
A Dandy Outfit for the Young Carpenter

What joy and fun for the boy to make a Bird House, Weather Vane or a toy for little brother. Outfit contains a wood handle saw with 12-inch steel blade, 12-inch level of hardwood, all steel plane with sharp blade, 8-inch sweep brace, a bit, scroll saw with 3 extra blades, wood hammer, screwdriver, wood marking gauge, wood chisel, miter box, nickel plated steel square, awl, mallet, metal dividers, cold chisel, triangle, ruler, pencil and sand block with two pieces of sandpaper. All packed in nicely varnished hardwood chest, size, 16½x8½x5⅞ inches, with tray inside for nails, etc.
79T7403—Postpaid..................$3.87

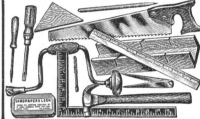

13 Tools Postpaid $1.10
For the Youngster

Outfit contains a fine quality 8-inch sweep brace, a good bit, 12-inch steel blade wood handle saw, nickel plated steel square, strong hammer and screwdriver, wood miter box, steel dividers, awl, triangle, 12-inch ruler, pencil, sand block with piece of sandpaper. All packed in strong carton.
79T7401—Postpaid..................$1.10

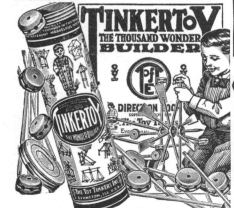

Tinkertoy

The Simplest Yet Most Popular Building Toy

And no wonder, for the attractiveness of the smooth dowels, spools and other pieces make children want them. Just give a set to the younger child and watch him originate models and designs. Hours of pleasure and amusements. Sets packed in heavy cylindrical box, another feature that helps—just drop the pieces in and fasten cover. A wonderful toy for kiddies.

Single Set—69c Postpaid

Builds simple models. Set has 70 pieces, all well smoothed and finished. Picture instructions included. Container, 12x3 inches.
49T4760—Postpaid..................69c

Famous Double Set—$1.37 Postpaid

Has double the number of pieces in above set and, in addition, about 10 new pieces for building more difficult models. Picture instructions included, showing 42 models. Containers, 12x4 inches.
49T4762—Postpaid..................$1.37

Play Lumber
The Newest Successful Building Toy Set

Made of clean, seasoned hardwood, holes accurately drilled. Bridges, houses, airplanes can be built. Complete with rust-proof nuts and bolts, combination wrench and screwdriver, special pressed wood pieces, wheels, pulleys and complete instructions. Build models, take them down and build others. For girls as well as boys.

$1.00 Beginners' Set for 89c
Has 50 pieces and necessary nuts and bolts.
49T4745—Box, 12¼x10x1¹⁄₁₆ inches. Postpaid....89c

Regular $2.00 Set for $1.79
122 parts and nuts and bolts.
49T4746—Box, 12¼x10x1½ inches, Postpaid....$1.79

Mechanical Model Builder. Regular $3.50 Value for $3.19
235 pieces and many nuts and bolts. Models move.
49T4747—Box, 12⅜x10⅛x3⅜ inches. Postpaid..................$3.19

The Best Arkitoy Set. Regular $5.00 Set for $4.59
You can make different models without taking down old models. Has 398 pieces, and many bolts and nuts.
49T4748—Box, 12⅜x10⅛x4⅝ in. Postpaid..................$4.59

Builds Real Models

For children too old for Tinkertoy and a little too young for Trumodel. No bolts or screws—just slip the metal friction plates into slots. Makes some wonderfully realistic models. Boys can build houses, hangars, trestles and many other things. Girls can build doll houses with real rooms, beds, table, chairs, etc. All pieces made of metal, attractively enameled.

$1.00 Size Set 83c
Has 70 parts and picture instructions teach to build about 100 models. Box, 10x6¾x⅞ inches.
49T4705—Postpaid..................83c

$2.00 Size Set $1.63
Has 150 parts. Builds more than 200 models. Instructions included. You need this set for your play yard.
49T4706—Box, 9x8½x1 in. Postpaid....$1.63

$3.50 Size Set $2.87
A dandy. Has 250 parts, builds more than 300 models. Complete with book of instructions showing some real building work. Box, 11¼x8¾x1½ inches.
49T4707—Postpaid..................$2.87

$5.00 Size Set $3.98
The king of them all. Makes a number of models at the same time. Has 360 parts, builds over 400 models and is a real dandy. Instructions included.
49T4707—Box, 13½x8¾x1½ in. Postpaid..................$3.98

FLYING ARROW STEERING SLEDS

56-Inch Sled **$3.19**

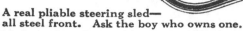

7 Reasons Why FLYING ARROW Sleds are Better

1—The **steering arrangement is very flexible**, easy to work and mechanically perfect.
2—**Steel straps from wood side rails to front steel bumper.** A decided improvement over the full length wood side rails. Makes steering easier.
3—There are no loose joints, because **every joint is riveted** with a large head rivet which will not loosen.
4—New style **flexible grooved runners** made from only the best grade carbon spring steel, which gives them extreme durability and wonderful steering quality.
5—**The steel supports, or knees,** are the best money can buy and are **riveted to runners,** not welded.
6—**The wood tops and side rails** are made from selected hardwood which is smoothly machined, all edges rounded and sanded, making them free from slivers and sharp ends.
7—All wood parts **are carefully finished** and varnished to withstand weather exposure and hard use; they are attractively decorated in red and blue.

The Predominant Sled for the Past 37 Years

That's a Real Record

Strong—Safe—Speedy—Greatest Distance—Built to Last
Grooved Runners for More Speed

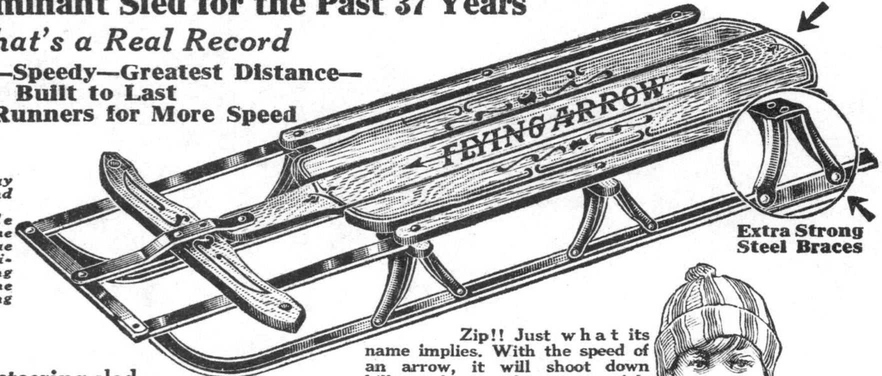

You'll Like the Way They Steer Around the Curves. *The remarkable guiding quality of the Flying Arrow is due to the extreme flexibility of its steering arrangement, and the full tempered spring steel runners.*

Extra Strong Steel Braces

Zip!! Just what its name implies. With the speed of an arrow, it will shoot down hills and around curves. Admired and desired by all boys.

A real pliable steering sled—all steel front. Ask the boy who owns one.

Such speed, such ruggedness, such ease of coating operation, is possible only with a sled constructed mechanically perfect, **as is our Flying Arrow.** The concave structure of the long tempered steel runners (illustrated at the right), which bite like a well sharpened skate, makes great speed possible. Because of the sturdy construction throughout, this superior coaster, with its overabundance of braces, seasoned hardwood and finest quality full tempered steel, is as sturdy as a battleship.

The sharp curving up of runners in front allows the greater part of the long grooved runners to rest on the ground, thus making steering simple and easy. **There is more coasting enjoyment with a Flying Arrow than with any other sled.**

These sleds are made from only the best materials, by good workmen. Will withstand the roughest treatment on ice or snow and will steer easier than any other sled on the market. They have made a real reputation among the boys for easy steering and going the greatest distance.

Illustration showing flexible steering arrangement

89¢ Post-paid

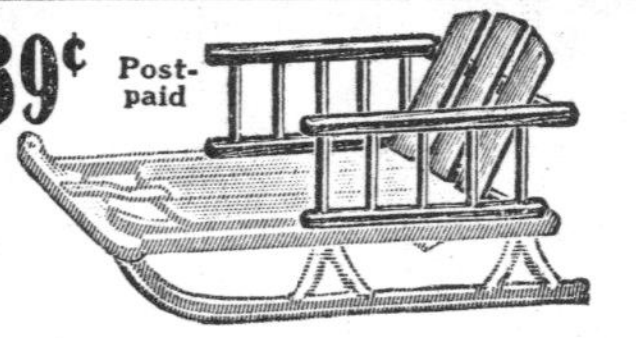

Baby Guard for Sled or Small Wagon

So easy to take baby for a ride in winter or summer. Just fasten this guard to sled or small wagon with screws furnished. When baby gets big enough, take guard off; sled or small wagon will be ready for coasting. Hardwood throughout, natural finish, varnished. Complete with screws for fastening. **Sled not included.**
79T8312—Postpaid.......... 89c

For Tiny Tots

If a sled guard is attached it is just right for baby. (See sled guard listed at left.)

32-Inch Sled

With full length wood side rails.
79T8300 Postpaid....... $1.15

These Four Have Double Crossbars—the Best Steering Arrangement

For youngsters who can coast, we do not recommend sleds with steering bar attached way up front, for it limits steering flexibility. That type of sled is about one-fifth cheaper. Remember this when comparing prices. **Shipped Prepaid. Include with freight order.**

36-Inch Sled
79T8304
Postpaid
$1.59

40-Inch Sled
79T8305
Postpaid
$1.85

45-Inch Sled
But four stout knees. Room enough for yourself and two pals. Shipping weight, 11 lbs.
79T8306 Shipped Prepaid....... $2.39

56-Inch Sled
And six stout knees, as illustrated. Strong crossbars and braces. Shipping weight, 13 lbs.
79T8307 Shipped Prepaid....... $3.19

Popular, Stylish, Strong, All Steel Wheelbarrows for Indoors or Outdoors

Take Advantage of These Two Big Values Because No Other Mail Order House Sells Them
The Finish Is Baked On Enamel—You'll Be Proud of It
Every Child Loves to Help Around the House

These wheelbarrows with green enameled heavy gauge automobile steel (not tin) body and strong tubular steel handles, are just what the kiddies want. Each equipped with double disc steel wheel, enameled bright red. Steel axle, legs and cross braces. **Two sizes.**

For the Little Tots
Body, 14½x10½ inches. Handles, 26¾ inches long. Five-inch wheel.
79T7625 Postpaid...... 95c

For the Older Child
Heavier Gauge Steel Body and Braces
Body, 19½x13¾ inches. Handles, 34¾ inches long. Eight-inch wheel.
79T7626 Postpaid... $1.45

95¢ and $1.45

FLYING ARROW SCOOTERS

Boys: Handles on our Scooters are bolted to frame. They never loosen.

Each Equipped with Rubber Mat

Stand

Steel Footboard With Rubber Mat.

12-Inch Roller Bearing Wheel 1⅛-inch Balloon Type Tires.

$4.19 Postpaid

Extra Strong Front Fork and Frame

For the past three or four years the country has been overrun with inferior, cheap, flimsy Scooters built not for service, but down to a price. During this period, our **all steel Flying Arrow Scooters** have been building up a reputation because, instead of tearing them down to a price to compete with all offered, we have **added** to them, improved them here and there, to give our customers the best money can buy.

New style footboard made of heavy gauge automobile steel, with platform all in one piece, which serves as mud guard over front wheel. No chance for child to get foot between frame and wheel; also reinforces and strengthens the fork.

Our De Luxe All Steel Roller Bearing Scooter, $4.19. The One We Recommend.
Usually Sold for $5.00 Elsewhere.
Balloon type rubber tires, 1⅛ inches in diameter; high class 12-inch double disc, steel orange color enameled wheels with grass green stripe near outer edge and green bullseye center on each side; large size roller bearings. A good brake for sudden stops. All steel strong frame and parking stand enameled gray. Smooth wood handle.
79T8807—Postpaid... $4.19

Here's A Peach

Your errands and daily exercise made a pleasure. **Ten-inch double disc steel roller bearing wheels, enameled bright red with black stripe, and equipped with full 1-inch balloon type rubber tires.** Enameled steel footboard, far superior to the common wood footboard because it will not crack, split or warp. The frame, fork and parking stand made from heavy gauge steel, beautifully enameled red. Nicely varnished, smooth wood handle.
79T8808—Postpaid..... $3.19

Our Special at $1.98

Little Boys and Girls Can Handle With Ease
Handle 29¾ Inches High

Beautiful in finish and construction, with 8-inch, red enameled, double disc steel, easy running, roller bearing wheels, striped in gilt and equipped with ¾-inch rubber tires; steel footboard equipped with rubber mat; parking stand on rear wheels, but no brake. Strong steel frame, enameled bright red.
79T8809—Postpaid... $1.98

TOY FARM WAGONS

No Other Mail Order House Sells This Beautiful Wagon

Here's the Original Genuine Studebaker Jr. Toy Farm Wagon.

Shipped Prepaid. Include With Freight Order

$13.87

Each Complete With Tongue and Seat.

Features not found on wagons offered by competitors:

1—Large shapely hardwood hubs with steel bushing (not flat breakable castiron).
2—Shaped hardwood spokes, staggered in hub. Will travel many miles farther than straight spokes in cast iron hub.
3—Gearing, with steam bent hardwood front and rear hounds, far superior to common strap iron type.
4—All parts strongly ironed and braced.
5—Oversize **steel tires** electrically welded.
6—Steel axles, ⁹⁄₁₆-inch diameter.
7—Kiln dried hardwood box. Sides and ends, removable. Adjustable reach, to make lumber wagon. Enameled in green and red, striped in black and orange.

The Harvard Jr. Wagon
With Plainer Gears and Less Details.
Will give good service, and is far superior to boys' farm wagons sold elsewhere. Body, 36x18 inches. Front wheels, 14 inches; rear wheels, 20 in.
79T7675— $10.79

Studebaker Junior (Illustrated)
The One We Recommend
An especially high class, strong and substantial wagon. Body, 36x17 inches. Front wheels, 12 inches; rear wheels, 18 inches.
79T7685 $13.87

Genuine Irish Mails

They sail along quietly. Built for speed.

De Luxe Model With Roller Bearing Disc Steel Wheels

⅝-Inch Rubber Tires

Encased roller bearings. Green enameled seat and wheels; frame, lever rod, red enamel, striped.
79T8800—Postpaid........... $9.89

The Irish Mail Special
Spoke wheels ½-inch rubber tires. Enameled in green, red and black.
79T8802—Postpaid........... $6.25

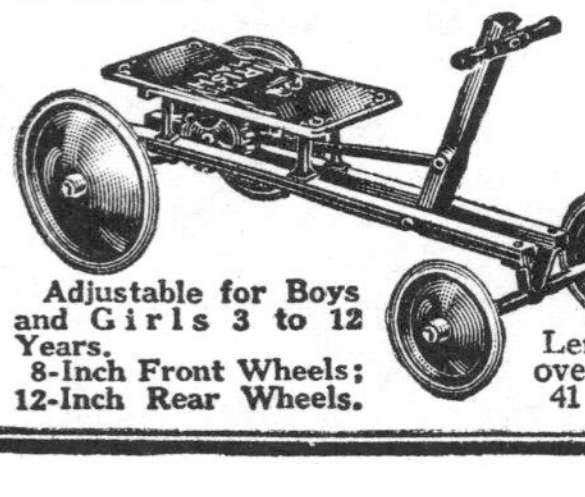

Adjustable for Boys and Girls 3 to 12 Years.
8-Inch Front Wheels; 12-Inch Rear Wheels.

Length over all, 41 in.

BUILT *for* REAL SERVICE

$3.69 Postpaid

$6.89 POSTPAID

Unsurpassed Quality

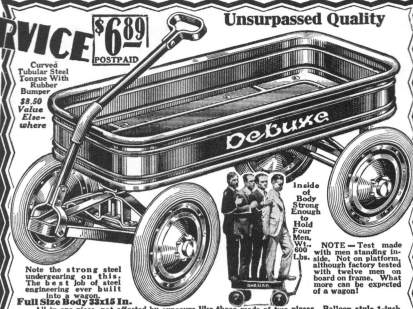

Curved Tubular Steel Tongue With Rubber Bumper $8.50 Value Elsewhere

Inside of Body Strong Enough to Hold Four Men. Wt. 600 Lbs.

NOTE—Test made with men standing inside. Not on platform, although factory tested with twelve men on board on frame. What more can be expected of a wagon!

Olympic Junior—One-Piece Body
Attractive, Sturdy and a Super Value
This All Steel Beauty for the Youngster Too Small to Handle a Large Size Coaster

All Steel Body Size, 24¼x12½ Inches

Made from heavy gauge automobile steel. Far superior to the old fashioned wood bottom and lightweight metal sides construction offered by others. Mother will find it handy and a time saver for her shopping; baby can ride and enjoy the trip. **Eight inch double disc steel wheels** with ½-inch rubber tires. Strong channel steel bolsters and braces enameled black. Curved, tubular steel tongue enameled black. Body and wheels are finished in red baked-on enamel. Gilt striping on wheels. New style rustproof clamp on hub caps.
79T7636—Postpaid.................. $3.69

Note the strong steel undergearing on this. The best job of wagon engineering ever built into a wagon.

Full Size Body 33x15 In.

All in one piece, not affected by exposure like those made of two pieces. Balloon style 1-inch cushion rubber tires. It runs like greased lightning. Is quiet and does not vibrate because the riveted 10-inch double disc steel wheels have extra wide hubs and large oversize roller bearings. Every part fully **guaranteed.** A wagon you will be proud of.

Body is all one piece, not a removable top that buckles, warps and is almost impossible to replace when once taken off, but a strong substantial body with a baked-on (not painted) enamel finish, that is always satisfactory. **Body size, 33x15 inches.** Made of strong, heavy gauge automobile steel with large roll rim at top and double beaded sides and beaded bottom for strength, beauty and massive appearance. No sharp edges or corners. Undergearing and axles are of strong steel construction, which will not break or wear. Ten-inch double disc wheels with large size casehardened steel roller bearings. Wheels enameled in bright red with striping. Fancy, new style rustproof hub caps clamped to wheel. They cannot come off. One-inch rubber tires.
79T7648—Postpaid.................. $6.89

Our Olympic Flyer With Full Size Body
33x15 Inches at $4.48 Is Priced Below Competition

Similar to our De Luxe and much better than those sold elsewhere for around $6.00. Sturdily built for heavy duty with slightly lighter weight undergear construction and without the expensive trimmings and details found on our De Luxe Wagon, but a far superior wagon to those offered at similar prices. Offered to meet the demand for less expensive wagons. Body made from heavy gauge automobile steel, has roll top and beaded sides enameled in red (baked-on). Double disc steel 9¾-inch roller bearing wheels riveted together, equipped with ¾-inch rubber tires and enameled red with gilt striping. Curved tubular steel tongue without rubber bumper, and channel steel bolsters, enameled black. Rustproof hub caps, clamped to wheels.
79T7638—Postpaid.................. $4.48

Here's Value!

Roller Bearing **$3.98** Postpaid

One of the Best Low Priced Wood Wagon Values on the Market

Every Part Fully Guaranteed

Ball Bearing; $5.69 Prepaid.

10½-Inch Wheels 1-Inch Tires

Body 16x36

Made by the Finest Coaster Wagon Manufacturer in the Country. If We Could Mention the Maker's Name, You Would Readily See That You Are Saving at Least ⅓ Buying the Same High Class Wagon, but Under Our Own Name

We guarantee to save you money and that you will get a better constructed and finished wagon than you really expect, one with all the details that it should have. Only the best materials are used. The body is kiln dried hardwood with tight dovetail joints and end boards mortised into the sides. Strong steel bumper to which the tongue is fastened. Channel steel undergearing with strong steel braces to body. Grooved steel double fifth wheel and castellated take-up nut on king bolt. Our wagons have the highest quality wide hub double disc steel wheel, stamped from extra heavy gauge steel with interlocking flange at rim forming a positive lock. (No chance for the wheel to come apart.) Body, 36x16 inches. Varnished natural finish; top rails enameled red, ½-inch steel axles, nickel plated hub caps. Each with steel bumper.

Our New Ball Bearing Flying Arrow Coaster, $5.69
Beautifully red enameled tubular steel tongue with rubber bumper, 10½-inch ball bearing wheels, full 1-inch cushion rubber tires.
79T7671.................. $5.69

This Roller Bearing Wagon at $3.98
Has All of Them Beaten
Strong black enameled tubular steel tongue, no bumper, 10-inch wheels, ¾-inch cushion rubber tires.
79T7650—Postpaid...... $3.98

All Steel Coasters for the Little Fellows

What an Improvement Over the Old Fashioned Crude Wood Bottom and Thin Metal Sides Construction—No Sharp Edges or Corners.

The little tots need exercise and an outlet for their energies. Especially designed for their use, will keep them happy and robust. Tubular steel tongue curved to make steering easier. Body heavy gauge automobile steel all one piece; enameled red baked-on finish (not painted). Double disc steel wheels enameled red and equipped with high grade rubber tires. Tongue and undergearing enameled black.

No Other Mail Order House Sells These

Body, 25x12 Inches
Wheels, 6½ inches in diameter, with ⅝-inch rubber tires.
79T7635—Postpaid..... $2.98

Body, 21⅛x10⅛ Inches
Wheels, 5¼ inches in diameter with ½-inch rubber tires.
79T7630—Postpaid...... $2.15

Our Best Built Ball Bearing Wood Coaster
The One We Recommend
Heavily Nickel Plated Tubular Steel Tongue Rubber Bumper

$6.69

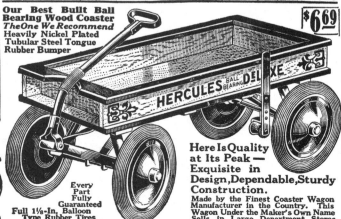

Every Part Fully Guaranteed

Full 1⅛-In. Balloon Type Rubber Tires

Here Is Quality at Its Peak — Exquisite in Design, Dependable, Sturdy Construction.

Made by the Finest Coaster Wagon Manufacturer in the Country. This Wagon Under the Maker's Own Name Sells in Large Department Stores for Around $10.00

Points of Superiority and Great Importance:
1—1⅛-In. cushion rubber tires.
2—Heavily nickel plated steel tongue.
3—Extra deep body of heavy lumber, all joints tight. A beautiful job.
4—Top rails of body beveled.
5—High grade rubber roller brake.
6—Heavy steel bolsters and braces.
7—Steel double fifth wheel.
8—Take-up nut on king bolt.
9—Rubber bumper on tongue.

Large, roomy body, 36x16 inches, made from clean and clear first class kiln dried hardwood lumber, with dovetail joints, not the common tongue and groove joint that is found in most wagons offered by others; also mortised end boards. Beautifully finished natural color, with two coats of durable coach varnish with all edges and the beveled top rails enameled red. (Not painted with cheap brick red paint.) The extra heavy channel steel bolsters are unusually sturdy with strong steel braces to body. The ball bearing wheels are of the double disc steel type, 10¾ inches in diameter.
79T7695—Postpaid.................. $6.69

$3.45 Postpaid

$2.39 Postpaid

These Cute, Sturdy Little Coasters Designed for the Little Folks

Body 28x12⅜ in.

Body 24x10⅜ in.

Rubber Tires—Double Disc Steel Wheels

Made by the same skilled workmen who make our large size wood coasters

Flying Arrow Junior, $3.45
For the girl or boy not big enough to handle a standard size coaster. Hardwood body, 28x12⅜ in., and tongue finished in natural color with durable varnish; top rails and all edges trimmed with bright red enamel. Red enameled 7¼-inch double disc steel wheels; ⅝-in. rubber tires. Steel axles, braces and gears; nickel plated hub caps.
79T7640—Postpaid......... $3.45

The Flying Arrow Playmate
Cute, shiny coaster for the little tots. Hardwood body, 24x10⅜ inches, without rails. Finished in bright red enamel. Steel axles, braces and undergearing enameled black. 6-inch red enameled double disc steel wheels with ½-inch rubber tires. Nickel plated hub caps, hardwood tongue.
79T7639—Postpaid.................. $2.39

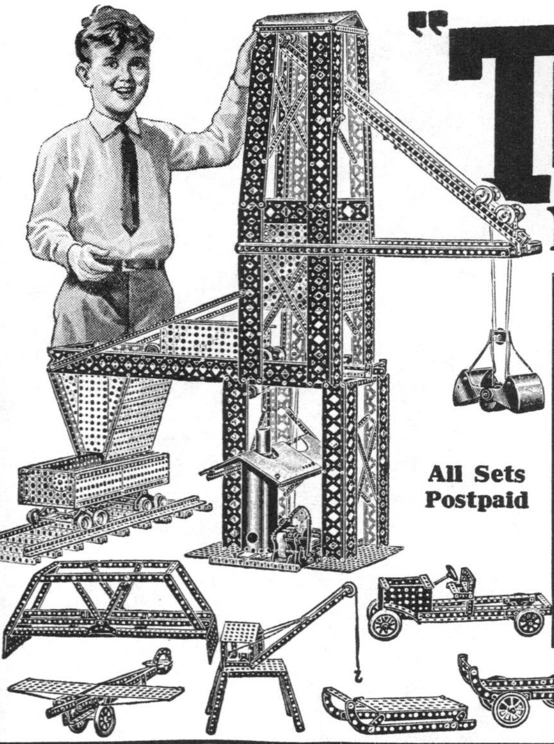

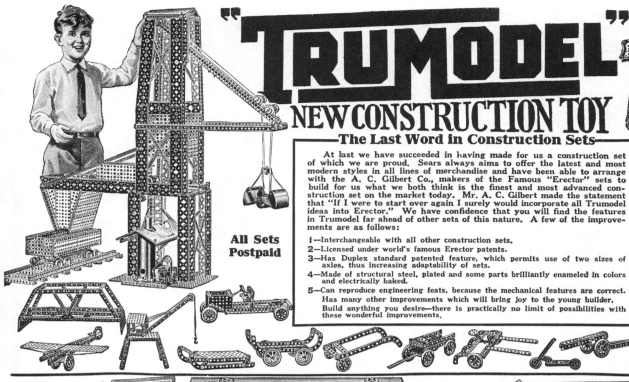

"TRUMODEL"

NEW CONSTRUCTION TOY

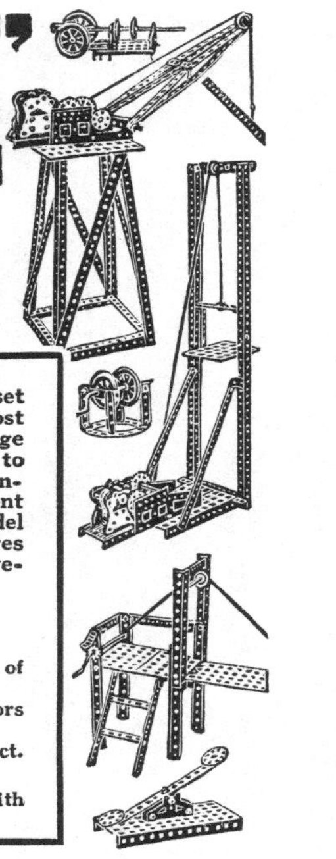

The Last Word in Construction Sets

At last we have succeeded in having made for us a construction set of which we are proud. Sears always aims to offer the latest and most modern styles in all lines of merchandise and have been able to arrange with the A. C. Gilbert Co., makers of the Famous "Erector" sets to build for us what we both think is the finest and most advanced construction set on the market today. Mr. A. C. Gilbert made the statement that "If I were to start over again I surely would incorporate all Trumodel ideas into Erector." We have confidence that you will find the features in Trumodel far ahead of other sets of this nature. A few of the improvements are as follows:

1—Interchangeable with all other construction sets.
2—Licensed under world's famous Erector patents.
3—Has Duplex standard patented feature, which permits use of two sizes of axles, thus increasing adaptability of sets.
4—Made of structural steel, plated and some parts brilliantly enameled in colors and electrically baked.
5—Can reproduce engineering feats, because the mechanical features are correct.

Has many other improvements which will bring joy to the young builder.

Build anything you desire—there is practically no limit of possibilities with these wonderful improvements.

All Sets Postpaid

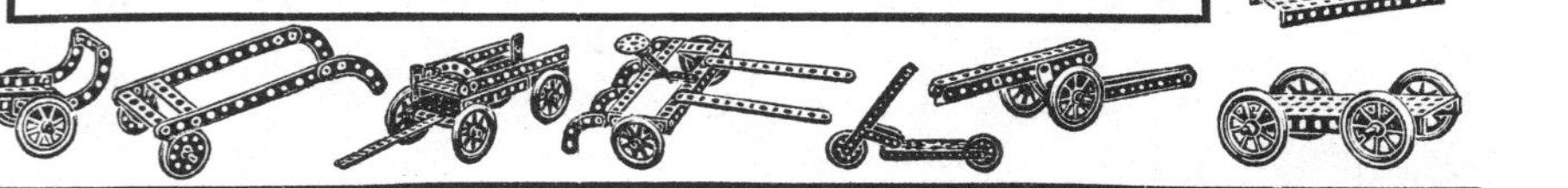

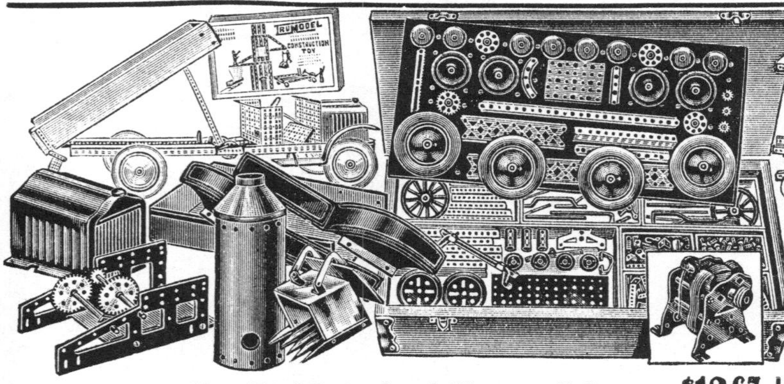

$15.00 Value

No. 7½ Motorized Trumodel

$13.67 Postpaid

The Set That Builds the Chassis and Other Models

This is the king of them all—and we know will give you the greatest thrill you ever had. Fun? Oh! Boy! It's the real thing, and has a thrill in each of its parts. **The completely assembled gear box, the building tray, 15-inch steel truck body, fenders, radiator hood, big red steel wheels with oversize balloon tires, springs, bumpers, steering wheel, heavy truck axles, cab top, boiler, digger scoop,** and all the rest of the parts will give you scientific thrills for every day in the year. Has big book of models and some "king pins too." Packed in large brass bound, red wooden chest, with brass fittings and handle grips. Size, over all, 22⅝x10¾x6 in.

79T4755—Postpaid.......... **$13.67**

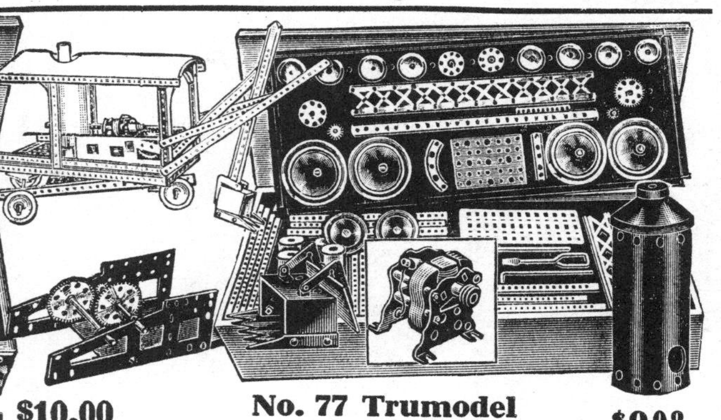

$10.00 Value

No. 77 Trumodel

$8.98 Postpaid

The Set That Builds the Steam Shovel and Other Models

Gee, fellows! With this set in which is a 6½-inch solid steel cab top, and a steam shovel digger scoop, you can make a big steam shovel and connect to the motor and assembled gear box, and actually operate it electrically. Everything, even to the big 20-inch solid steel building tray with which you can also build wagons, hoisting machinery, wheelbarrows, luggage trucks, some of which measure 2 and 3 feet long. The pieces in this set are very well constructed. Manual included in this set, has so many good models to make, that you will hardly be able to wait to build them one at a time. Packed in big red wooden box, with brass trimmings and with brass handle grips. Size, over all, 21⅞x8¾x4⅞ inches.

79T4754—Postpaid.......... **$8.98**

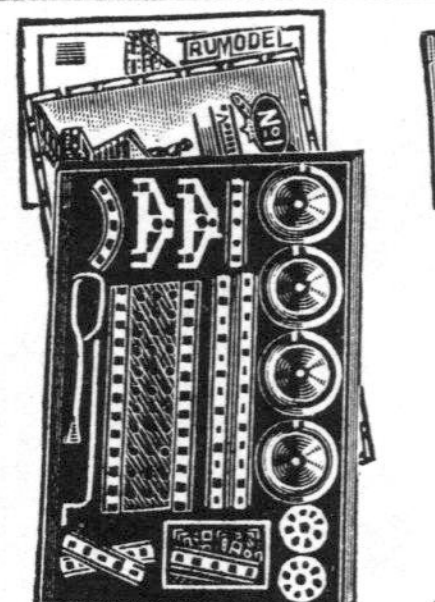

No. 1 Trumodel

Dandy Beginner's Set
$1.00 Value

Has disc wheels, car trucks, axles, angles, collars, cranks, screwdriver, 6-inch duplex channel and angle girders and many other parts. Many of these pieces are in colors making models very attractive in appearance. Complete in attractive strong cardboard box, 12½x8¾x¾ inches. Has simply worded instruction and model book.

49T4750
Postpaid.......... **89c**

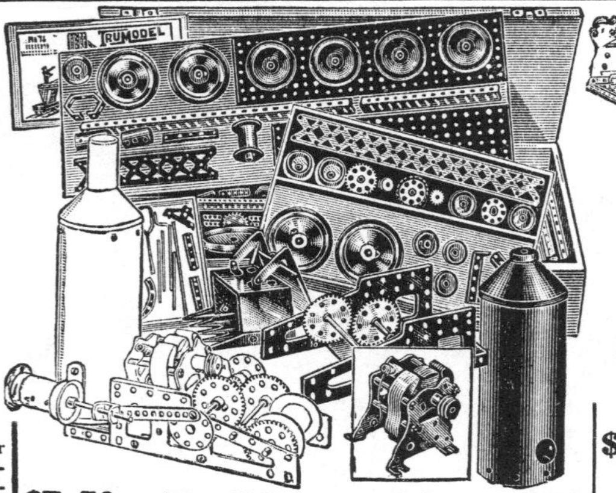

$7.50 Value

No. 7 Trumodel

$6.79 Postpaid

The Set With the Boiler

Has patented steam boiler to build hoisting engines, steamboats, etc.; 3-inch solid disc wheels, patented 6-inch and 12-inch channel steel girders, 12-inch Duplex Base Plates, flanged wheels, hoisting drum, turret plates, universal brackets, triangles and an assortment of axles. The dandy book of instructions teaches you to build an oscillating type steam engine, locomotive, jib crane, engine lathe and many other models that the possibilities are unlimited. Set put up in big red wooden box, brass trimmed. Size, over all, 21½x8¼x3¼ inches.

79T4753—Postpaid.......... **$6.79**

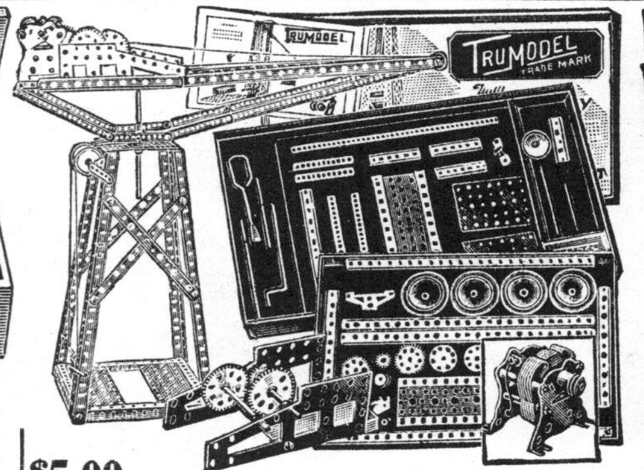

$5.00 Value

No. 4 Trumodel

$4.59 Postpaid

The First Set With the Powerful Electric Motor and the Assembled Gear Box

Here's the first set that builds simple electrically operated models. Gee! it has 41-hole perforated strips, crown gear, worm gear, couplings, the powerful motor which can be taken apart for experimental purposes, and a completely assembled gear box, adaptable to every possible gear combination. Instructions have directions for making all sorts of gear combinations and working possibilities. You can make loading derricks, cranes, automobiles, water wheels and many other models. Instruction book included. Box, 18x10⅛x1¼ inches.

79T4752—Postpaid.......... **$4.59**

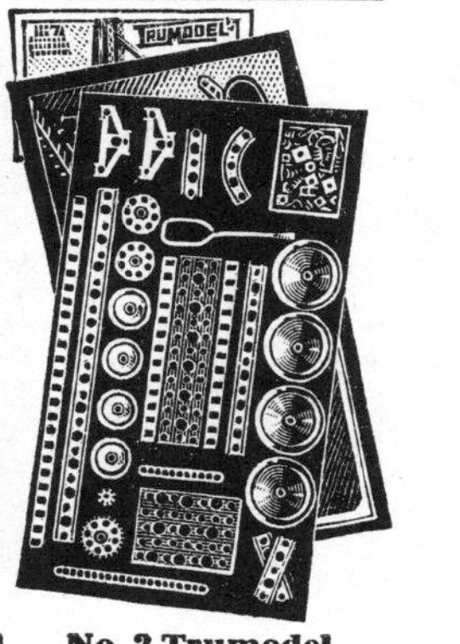

No. 2 Trumodel

Set With Long Girders
$2.50 Value

In addition to pieces mentioned in beginner's set there are pulley wheels, pierced discs, perforated strips, and, best of all, the 12-inch duplex channel girders and 12-inch angle girders. Builds larger models than No. 1 set. Complete instruction book. Packed in attractive cardboard box, 18x10½x1¼ inches.

49T4751
Postpaid..... **$2.28**

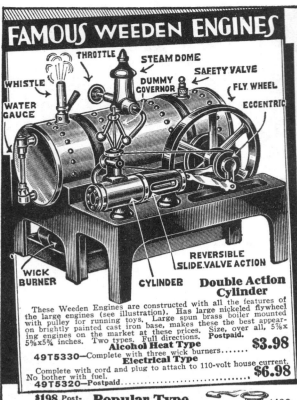
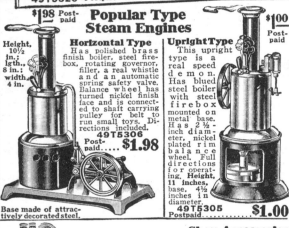

SAXOPHONES

Exceptionl Quality—Greater Values! The Pick of all Toy Saxophones! Proves more popular every year. Little wonder, too for they are so realistic looking with their full nickel plate and all metal construction. Just ask any boy—he'll tell you that no play orchestra is complete without a "Sax." Values better than ever before! But in order to give you "rock bottom" prices we have not skimped on the quality. Every one is nicely tuned and has at least 8 notes, so simple tunes can be played. Sheet music with each one. **All Postpaid.**

$2.79 Postpaid

Our Finest Quality *Mellow Tone*

This is a beauty and gives enough range to play simple tunes because sixteen treble notes and two 2-chord base notes can be played. Has 8 metal treble keys with leather pads and 2 bass keys with leather pads. Comes complete with a silk cord for holding into position around neck. Complete with music. Length, over all, 16 inches. Diameter of bell, 3⅜ inches. An exceptionally fine value at this price.

49T2467—Postpaid **$2.79**

$1.98 Postpaid

Exceptional Value *16 Treble Notes —2 Bass*

Nickel Plated Beauty—Scroll Design

It is made entirely of heavy metal, nickel plated, and has a natural looking shaped wood mouthpiece. Has 8 treble keys which play 16 notes and has 2 bass keys tuned in chords. This beauty is 16¼ inches long and has a 3⅜-inch bell with a fancy scroll design on side. Complete with music, cord with snap for holding around neck.

49T2457—Postpaid. **$1.98**

Medium Priced Beauty

16 Treble Notes, But No Bass

A real value in a Saxophone for the little fellows. Highly nickel plated metal Saxophone, which looks just like a real instrument. Has 8 keys which play 16 notes. 15½ inches long. Simple melodies can be played. Music included. Has cord with snap for holding around neck.

49T2456—Postpaid... **$1.59**

For the Beginner This Is An Outstanding Value for $1.00

Has only 8 keys, playing 8 notes. Made of metal with a natural looking wood mouthpiece and has 8 padded keys. Size, over all, 15½ inches long. Has a 3⅝-inch bell. Music included.

49T2455

Postpaid **$1.00**

BOYS' QUALITY DRUMS

$2.15 Postpaid

12-Inch Snare Style Drum

Has Genuine Calfskin Head and Sheep Bottom

Has a golden oak hardwood shell, good snares and leather ear fasteners. A pair of drum sticks and web shoulder strap included. Drum is 12 inches in diameter and 6 inches high. $2.50 value elsewhere.

79T2484

Postpaid **$2.15**

Junior Snare Drum

A real orchestra snare drum. Painted metal shell, size, 3x12 inches, with painted wood hoops and six thumbscrew rods. Two calfskin heads with adjustable snare strainer. A pair of sticks and sling included.

12T900¼—Postpaid **$3.98**

For Better Grade Drums, See Page 731

10-Inch Army Type Drum

This Is Just Like the Drums Used in Parades

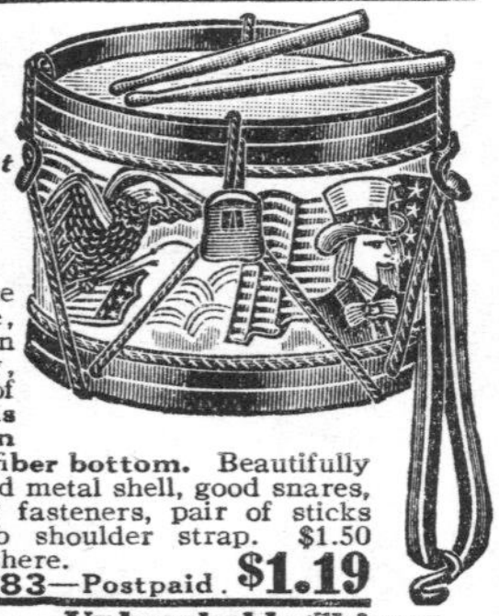

Has a nice deep tone, and, when necessary, gives lots of volume. Has a sheepskin head and fiber bottom. Beautifully lithographed metal shell, good snares, leather ear fasteners, pair of sticks and a web shoulder strap. $1.50 value elsewhere.

79T2483—Postpaid. **$1.19**

For the Beginner

A 10-Inch All Metal Drum

Made especially for the little fellow who wants to become a drummer. Very sturdily constructed. 10 inches in diameter and 4¾ inches high.

49T2472—Postpaid **49c**

Circus Bell Chime

How the kiddy will be delighted to receive one of these shiny, nickel plated chimes with the little clowns doing their "somersaults". As you pull this chime along, the colors flash brightly and all the while the bells jingle and tinkle in pleasing tones. **A little circus in itself.** Diameter of wheel, 7 inches. The two bells in the center are each 3 inches in diameter.

49T2311

Postpaid **89c**

Unbreakable Chimes With Horses

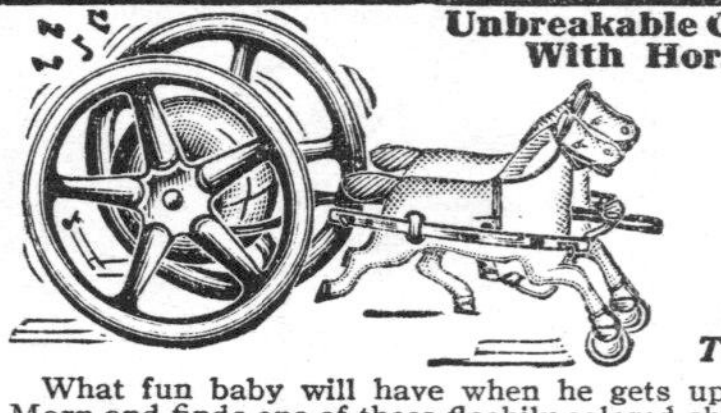

43¢ and 89¢ Postpaid *Two Styles*

What fun baby will have when he gets up Christmas Morn and finds one of these flashily colored chimes underneath the Christmas tree. These are made of highly nickel plated parts with brightly colored metal horses, and are practically unbreakable. The wheels and the bells are very highly nickel plated. When chimes are pulled along the pleasing tinkle will make any kiddy happy. **Postpaid.**

Single Horse Chime

A very attractive "Black Beauty." Is 8¾ inches long and has 3½-inch nickel plated steel wheels and nickel plated bell.

49T2314

Postpaid **43c**

Two-Horse Chime

Each horse is a different color. The chime has 5¼-inch nickel plated steel wheels and is 11¼ inches long. Makes a real snappy appearance.

49T2313

Postpaid **89c**

THE LITTLE MUSICIAN

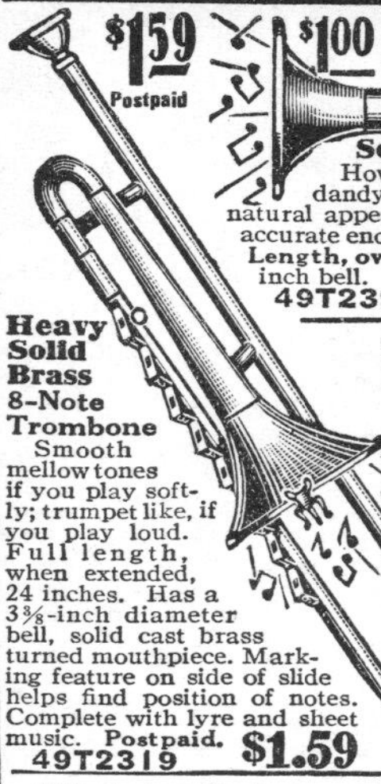

$1.59 Postpaid

Heavy Solid Brass 8-Note Trombone

Smooth mellow tones if you play softly; trumpet like, if you play loud. Full length, when extended, 24 inches. Has a 3⅜-inch diameter bell, solid cast brass turned mouthpiece. Marking feature on side of slide helps find position of notes. Complete with lyre and sheet music. Postpaid.

49T2319 **$1.59**

$1.00 Postpaid

Solid Brass 8-Key Cornet

How he will strut when he gets this dandy little 8-key cornet. Solid and most natural appearing mouthpiece. The tones are accurate enough to give you favorable results. Length, over all, 12¾ inches. Has a 3½-inch bell. Music included.

49T2395—Postpaid **$1.00**

WE Pay the Postage

79¢ Postpaid

29-Inch Nickel Plated Trombone

This will surely satisfy the little fellow. Not as good quality as our 49T2319. Ten-note trombone instead of the 8 notes offered by others at the same price. Length of trombone, extended, 29 inches. Has a 3½-inch bell. Made of metal, nickel plated. Music included with each trombone.

49T2339

Postpaid **79c**

20-Inch 12-Key Wood Clarinet **53c Postpaid**

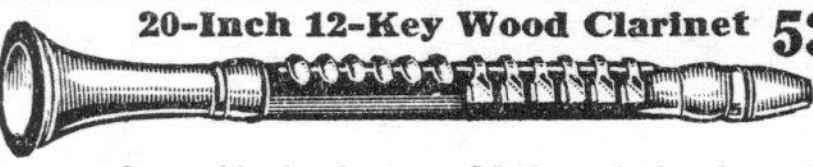

This is just the instrument for you to have in playing band. You all know the shrill high notes of the clarinet and you will surely appreciate the nice tones you can get from this dandy one. Made entirely of wood in black ebony finish with a shaped natural wood mouthpiece. Has 12 keys so arranged on the clarinet to make it easy to handle while playing.

49T2338—Postpaid. Complete with sheet music **53c**

TRUMPETS AND HORNS

11½ Inches Long—4-Inch Bell

Army Style Trumpet

You should have this while playing soldiers. This is a bright, shiny looking, all metal horn with a bugle mouthpiece. Has nice, loud tone, and is trimmed with gilt tinsel and 2 heavy tassels.

49T2394

Postpaid **39c**

Nickel Plated Horn

Just imagine the little ones playing on this brightly nickel plated horn and having the fun of their lives. Chenille, gilt trimmed cord and tassels. Length, 12 in. 3½-inch bell.

49T2390

Postpaid **25c**

"Little Boy Blue" Horn

You all know the story of how Little Boy Blue used his little horn to call the sheep. Has 2 notes. Made of metal and has cord for hanging over shoulder. Is 8¼ in. long. 2¾-inch diam. bell. Has a wood mouthpiece.

49T2385

Postpaid **25c**

89¢ POSTPAID

Silver Chime Talking Phone

All Nickel Plated and Has Felt Base

Stretch cord from one room to another, when playing house or store. Very sturdily constructed. 9¼ inches high.

49T2464

Postpaid **89c**

Small Size Phone **43¢ POSTPAID**

All Nickel Plated

Even baby can handle this and get much enjoyment out of it. One of the finest little phones on the market at this price. All nickel plated, nicely enameled receiver and has a 1⅝-inch nickel plated bell and felt base. An exceptionally fine value. 7¾ inches high.

49T2463

Postpaid **43c**

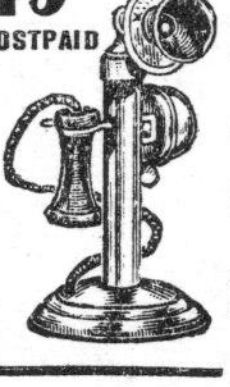

Musical Tops

Very Brilliantly Colored

Imagine the beautiful appearance of the changing colors as they whirl and swirl about. Tap handle lightly, chord changes. Made of metal, finished in attractive red, white, blue and yellow colors. Strings for spinning included. **Postpaid.**

53¢ Postpaid

Three-Chord Top

A heavy metal balance ring built around center prolongs spinning. 3 full harmonious chords. Height, 8 in. Diam., 5¼ in.

49T2375

Postpaid **53c**

Two-Chord Top

Exceptional Value

Lighter gauge metal than 49T2375, but just as brilliantly colored. Has 2 chords full and harmonious.

49T2396—Postpaid **33c**

33¢

Chime-A-Phones or Musical Bells

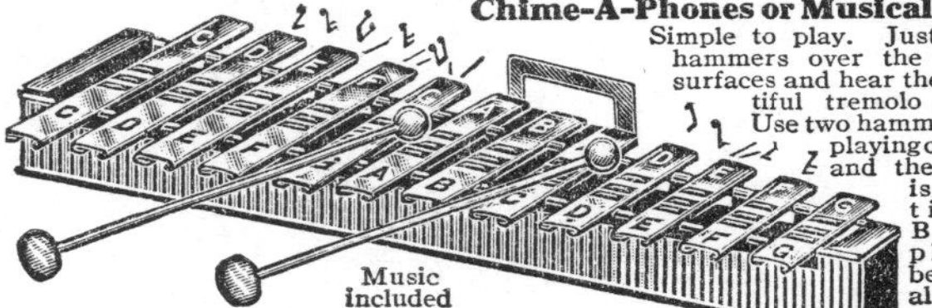

Simple to play. Just draw hammers over the raised surfaces and hear the beautiful tremolo tones. Use two hammers for playing chords, and the effect is beautiful. Brass plated bell metal steel.

Music included

Metal music stand attached to each frame. **Postpaid.**

12-Key Size	10-Key Size	8-Key Size
16⅞ inches long. Very fine range.	13¾ inches long. More than an octave.	11¼ inches long. Has a full octave.
49T2452. **$1.69**	49T2451. **$1.29**	49T2453..... **89c**

The FAMOUS LIONEL ELECTRIC TRAINS

MOTORS GUARANTEED

Biggest Selling Reversing "O-GAUGE" ELECTRIC TRAIN on the Market $12.89 Postpaid

Every Boy Should Have One of These 36-Inch Trains

Popular because it is finest quality and sells at a price attractive to almost everybody. Complete in every detail. Measures about 36 inches long and consists of an 8½-inch reversing locomotive with two headlights, two illuminated Pullman cars, one illuminated observation car, each 7¼ inches long, and each with eight wheels and automatic couplers. Outfit has 8 pieces of "O Gauge" curved and 4 pieces straight track, "Lockon" connection, track clips, battery rheostat and a 6¾-inch warning signal. Requires 8 to 10-volt battery or transformer 49T5912.

49T5188—Postpaid...$12.89

OVAL 50×30 INCHES

Track Sizes, "O Gauge" 1⅜ wide Standard Gauge 2¼

Famous Jefferson Toy Transformers

No Better Built

For Toy Trains and Motors

Reduce 100 to 120-volt alternating house current to suitable voltage to run electrical trains or toys, thus replacing batteries. Have switches to regulate the voltage, thus eliminating rheostats for speed control. Economical, safe and simple to operate. For 100 to 120-volt 60-cycle alternating current only.

75-Watt Size
Produces 5½ to 22½ volts in 1-volt steps. Gives 18 speeds. For all our "O Gauge" trains.
49T5912 $2.98
Postpaid...... Equipment—Postpaid

100-Watt Size
Produces 5½ to 23 volts in ¾-volt steps. Gives 25 speeds. For any of our trains with any load up to 12 to 15 volts.
49T5913........ $4.89

Straight Electric Track
"O Gauge" Track
Each piece 10½ inches.
Set, 2 pieces
49T5235......38c
"Standard Gauge" Track,
Set, 2 pieces
49T5231......57c

Curved Electric Track
"O Gauge" Track
Each piece, 10¼ inches.
Set, 2 pieces
49T5236......38c
"Standard Gauge" Track,
Set, 2 pieces
49T5232......57c

Illuminated Switches
Lamps Included

"O Gauge" Track
49T5215 $4.75
Per pair, Postpaid
"Standard Gauge"
49T5221 $6.10
Per pair, Postpaid

Crossovers
"O Gauge."
For 45 degrees. $1.53
49T5210
"Standard Gauge"
For 45 degrees. $1.73
49T5214...

You Need This 40-Inch "O Gauge" Freight Train to Complete Your Train Yard $10.59 Postpaid

A 40-inch "O Gauge" reversing four-car freight train consisting of a 7-inch reversible locomotive with electric headlight; box car; coal car with real chute dump; oil car and caboose, each car 6½ inches long; 8 pieces "O Gauge" curved and 2 pieces straight track, forming oval 40x30 inches. "Lockon" connection, track clips, rheostat and 6¾-inch warning signal included. Requires 8 to 10-volt battery or transformer 49T5912.

49T5191—Postpaid...$10.59

$9.69 Postpaid
Popular Priced 33-Inch Reversing "O Gauge" Train

Consists of 7-inch reversing locomotive with headlight, two Pullman cars and one observation car, each measuring 6½ inches long and each with mottled celluloid window arches and automatic couplers. Complete with 8 pieces of "O Gauge" curved and 2 pieces of straight track, "Lockon" connection, track clips, battery rheostat and 6¾-inch warning signal. Track forms oval 40x30 inches. Requires 8 to 10-volt battery or transformer 49T5912.

49T5189—Postpaid... $9.69

24-Inch Train for Little Fellows $6.59 Postpaid

Locomotive, 7¼ in. long, not reversible. Two 6½-inch passenger cars, one an observation car. Each with automatic couplers. Eight pieces "O Gauge" curved track, track clips. "Lockon" connection and a 6¾-inch warning signal included. Makes circle 30 inches in diameter. As good quality throughout as our higher priced sets, but made to fit needs of smaller boy. Requires 10-volt battery or transformer 49T5912.

49T5192—Postpaid... $6.59

"STANDARD GAUGE" LIONEL ELECTRIC TRAINS TRACKS 2¼ IN. Wide

"Standard Gauge" Electrically Controlled Reversing Train 52 Inches Long →

Controlling rheostat at any distance from track starts, stops, reverses and regulates speed. Eleven-inch locomotive with two electric headlights; illuminated mail and baggage car, Pullman and observation car with a rear platform light and red lantern discs which reflect the illumination. Each car 11¾ inches, has automatic couplers and eight wheels. Has 8 pieces of Standard curved and 4 straight track. "Lockon" connection and rheostat. Requires 10½ to 13½ volts from dry cells or battery or transformer 49T5913 listed above.

Remote Control Reversing Train
Has special motor in locomotive and special controlling rheostat.
79T5186—Postpaid..... $29.98

Same Train With Hand Controlled Reverse
Locomotive has regular motor with hand reversing lever.
79T5185—Postpaid..... $23.98

Set of "O Gauge" Freight Cars
Every train owner should have one of these fine sets to complete his "yard" set. Lumber car with lumber, coal car, oil car, box car, cattle car and caboose, each about 6½ inches long. A dandy combination.
49T5237—Postpaid............$4.98

Illuminated Lamp Post
No railroad system is complete without these popular lamp posts. A real reproduction, carefully constructed. Light globe included. Height, 7⅜ in. Postpaid.
49T5253.....$1.23

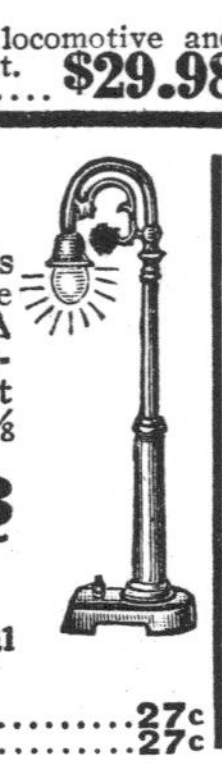

Extra Lamps
Packed in special container. Postpaid.
49T5254—18-volt 27c
49T5255—12-volt 27c

Panel Board
Now you can operate any of your electrical pieces through this dandy control.

Made of metal throughout. Has 6 knife switches, light in top reflecting on dummy meters and two lengths of wire for connecting to track system. Size, over all, 7x8¼ inches.
49T5260 $5.45
Postpaid.......

Crossing Gates
10⅞ In. Long 
Gates lower and rise automatically as train passes. Gate attractively enameled.
► Postpaid. For "O Gauge"
49T5252 $3.98
"Standard Gauge"
49T5248 $4.19

Bell Warning Signal
Bells ring while train is passing. Nicely enameled. Nickel plated bells. Postpaid. For "O Gauge."
49T5250...$3.05
For "Standard Gauge."
49T5246...$3.29

Flashing Railroad Signal
A dandy addition to your outfit. Red light in base. Red lights on crossbeam wired to blink alternately. 11⅝ inches tall. Fits either "O Gauge" or "Standard Gauge" outfit.
49T5259 $4.95
Postpaid.......

Automatic Control
Red signal shows. Train approaches and stops. Red light goes out and green signal shows. Train starts automatically. Can be placed anywhere in track formation.
Postpaid. For "O Gauge" Track
49T5251 $4.95
For "Standard Gauge" track.
49T5247...$4.95

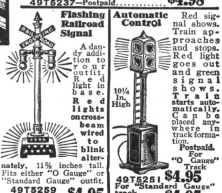

We Pay the Postage

BARN, 12¾x11¾x8½ In.

$1.00 Postpaid

Our Latest Stock Farm Made Exclusively for Us
Have a Barn Just Like Daddy's
With Fourteen Beautifully Colored Animals
Seldom Has a Value Like This Ever Been Offered

This year we are offering our customers a larger value than ever before because of the nicely shaped beautifully colored animals included. Year after year the demand for these stock farms has been growing by leaps and bounds, and year after year we have been able to offer better values because of the tremendous quantities we purchase. This item gives loads of fun for very little money. Just think of all the fun the kiddies will have putting these animals into the barn and feeding them imaginary hay. This toy will keep the children amused for hours and hours because of the many different groupings in which these animals can be placed. The stalls are just the right size for the horses. A box of toothpicks, some old spools and a little bit of Mother's yarn will help make an ideal rail fence around your stock farm. The barn measures 12¾ inches long and has two nicely shaped stalls with two oblong and one round troughs. The barn is made of wood, nicely colored, and measures 11¾ inches high to tip of cupola. Width, across eaves, 8½ inches. Nicely decorated in yellow, white, black and red. Roof is pretty green color. Just think, you can buy all of this for—$1.00. **$1.00**
79T9149—Postpaid......................

27 In. Long

$1.00 Postpaid

$1.00 POSTPAID

4 in 1 Set

Your Play Farm Is Not Complete Without This 4-in-1 Tractor Set
Every child loves to play with a Tractor Set. We offer four pieces for only $1.00, **Postpaid.** Our biggest seller in a mechanical toy and one of our best values. Fits the wants of every child, because of its wonderful construction and play value. Just imagine the fun the kiddies will have hitching the different pieces behind the tractor to do the different jobs around your farm, just like Dad does with his big tractor. Our set consists of: Tractor with man driver, a four-wheel wagon, two-wheel rake and disc harrow. Tractor has strong spring motor. When all pieces are hooked together set measures 27 inches long over all. Tractor is 7⅞ inches long, other three pieces in proportion. Made of lithographed metal and has strong spring motor.
49T5748—Postpaid.................................**$1.00**

89¢ We Pay the Postage

Gray Beauty Pacers
Every child will enjoy playing with these lifelike horses. Pull them along and watch the legs move back and forth just like real horses. The beautiful red enameled slat style wood hay wagon on strong metal wheels makes this toy most attractive to the youngsters. Size, over all, 19x6 inches.
79T5454—Postpaid...............**89¢**

Our Big $1.00 Rubber Tired Steel Wagon

89¢ Postpaid

Proud Dolly Duck
Opens Mouth— Squawks— Nods Head

What fun it is to pull this peppy little Lady Duck along the floor as she squawks away like the town gossip. She certainly is a saucy little duckie with her colored outfit and a flower in her jaunty hat. Made of wood and strong cardboard, beautifully lithographed in many attractive colors. Rubber bands around front wheels to help give toy the lifelike action when pulled. Duck measures 9 inches high and 7 in. long. Complete with pull cord. **89¢**
49T5488—Postpaid............

Pony Pacer 45¢ Postpaid

When pulled along horse's legs move back and forth like a real pacer. Wheels, legs and all moving parts made of metal. Balance wood, beautifully decorated in colors. Size, 13½ in. long and 6½ in. high.
49T5455—Postpaid.............**45c**

Famous Humpty Dumpty Circus Figures With Movable Arms, Legs and Heads

Illustrated Booklet, Showing Endless Amount of Tricks, Included With Each Set

Every child should have a set of these well made figures of wood and leather strung with strong elastic, which can be set in an endless variety of positions producing the most fascinating and grotesque poses. Will perform innumerable balancing tricks. Elephant, 7x4½ inches; donkey, 8x6½ inches; nicely dressed 7-inch clown; chair ladder, tub and barrel in proportion.
49T9135—Postpaid.........**$1.85**

All Steel Wagon With Rubber Tires
An Outstanding Value
Sold Elsewhere for $1.50
Body, 17¼x8¾ Inches—5-Inch Wheels—½-Inch Rubber Tires. 
This handsome, sturdy all steel play wagon for little tots is offered to you at a price hardly considered possible. Body is one-piece heavy gauge automobile steel (not tin), enameled blue (baked-on), strong double disc steel wheels, 5 inches in diameter and enameled blue. Steel bolsters and braces, enameled black; strong wood tongue, painted blue.
79T7601—Postpaid.................**$1.00**

"Son-ny"

30-Inch Steel Tractor Set $1.79 Postpaid

Dumping Gate

Fine Quality Tractor and Trailer
A pull toy every child would like to get. Made of sheet steel, finished in bright blue baked-on enamel, attractively trimmed. Tractor has dummy motor, gas tank, steering wheel and spring seat just like on large tractors. Driving wheels finished in bright red and measure 6¾ inches in diameter. Front wheels of tractor and wheels of trailer are 3½ inches in diameter and are painted to imitate balloon type tires. Trailer has dumping gate. Total length of toy, 30¼ inches, and 7¼ inches high.
79T5410—Postpaid.................**$1.79**

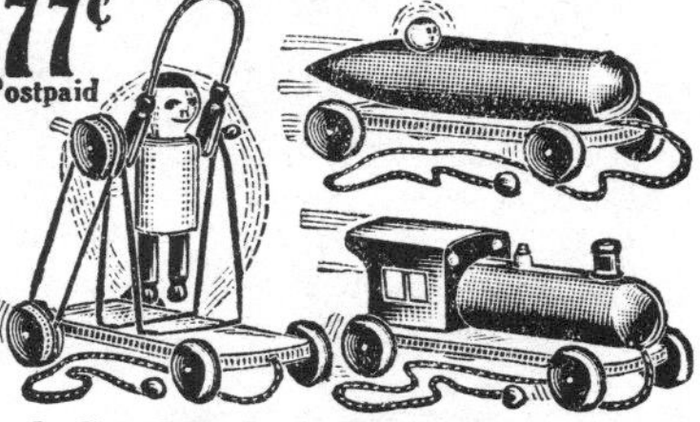

Every Kiddie Loves to Play He's Riding a Horse
One of Our Most Popular Toys

49¢ Postpaid

Youngsters will have lots of fun galloping along with this beautifully finished Stick Horsie. All kiddies want one. On account of the large quantity we buy we are able to offer an exceptional value. Beautifully enameled in many attractive colors. Pretty cutout horse's head made of wood finished and enameled in black and white with colorful decorations. Well made throughout. You can trot along, guiding the horse with the real tapelines. There is some class to this Stick Horsie. Complete with strong nicely blue enameled wood stick, and two 4-inch double disc red enamel steel wheels.
49T9112—Postpaid......................**49c**

77¢ Postpaid

A Cracker Jack Three-Toy Assortment for 77c
Dandy Pull Toys. Will Attract Any Child
A clever 9-inch racer with realistic motor noise. See the little driver bob up and down as he speeds along. Kiddies choo-choo, 8x 3½x3½ in. Just hear it chug when pulled. A dandy rope jumper, 7¾x4x7¾ in. When pulled he skips his rope, following you wherever you go. All have wood bodies and metal bases. Finished in attractive colors. Pull cord attached to each one.
49T5489—Postpaid...............**77c**

59¢ Postpaid

Merry-Go-Round
Usual 75c Value

10½ In. Long 6¾ In. High

You will be proud to play with this beautiful merry-go-round with three horses, which when pulled revolves, while the clown rings the bell by hitting it with his hammer. There is lots of action to this toy, which is made of metal, beautifully lithographed in many attractive colors.
49T5484—Postpaid...............**59c**

Boy's Ticking Watch With Chain
Every boy wants a watch and chain like Daddy, and just think of it, this one has the mechanism which makes a ticking sound when you wind it. Beautifully finished to imitate silver watch with engraved back. Unbreakable crystal. Merely turn stem and hands go around, while mechanism inside makes watch tick. Diameter, 1¾ inches. Chain, about 8 inches long with buttonhole bar.
49T9117—Postpaid...............**17c**

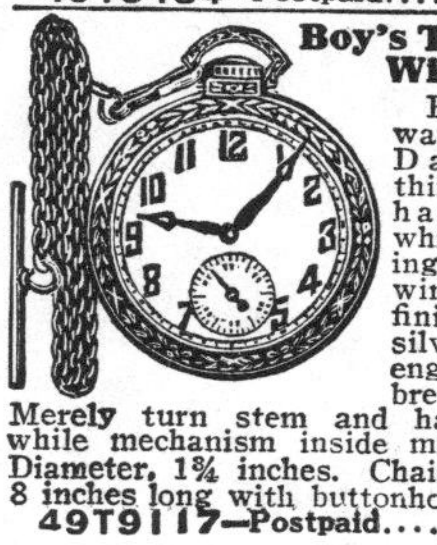

Toys For Little Tots

Famous 'Hustler' Toys

We Pay the Postage

Hustler Pup
He Walks He Barks

89¢ Postpaid

The Most Popular of All Toy Dogs

When pulled along his legs move in natural manner because of arrangement on rear axle. **Just press the rubber bulb on the end of the cord and hear him bark** like a real "bow-wow." Height of dog, 8 inches; length, 8 inches. Wood wheels. Dog made of strong hardwood, handsomely finished and enameled in black and white. Imitation leather ears and collar.

49T5462—Postpaid **89c**

Billy Hustler and His Dog Cart
A Clever Action Toy

$1.10 Post-paid

Billy goes out for his daily ride with his dog cart. **When toy is pulled along, Billy continually taps doggie lightly with the little wood stick he holds in his hand, to urge him along,** while in the other hand he holds the reins. Dog has cute little red collar. Made of wood enameled in beautiful contrasting colors. Toy is 14 inches long and 6⅞ in. high.

49T5459—Postpaid **$1.10**

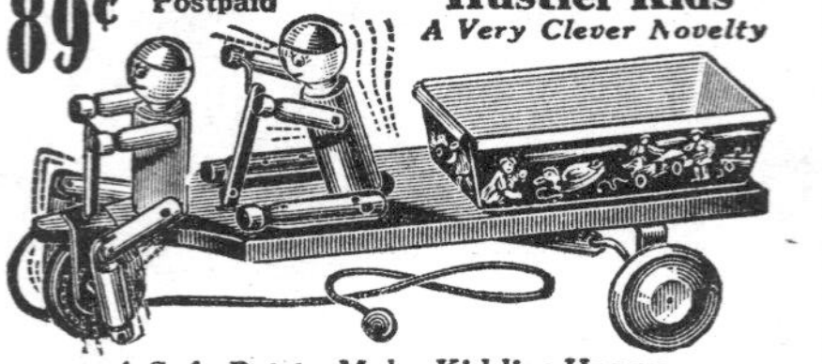

Hustler Kids
A Very Clever Novelty

89¢ Postpaid

A Safe Bet to Make Kiddies Happy

Hustler Kids are mounted on nicely shaped wooden platform with lithographed metal dumping pan on end. When toy is pulled watch the Kids go. **The one in front holds the handlebars with his arms and pedals with his movable jointed legs in very realistic manner.** Whereas the other Kid moves his body backward and forward, as if he were operating a hand car. Toy is enameled in pretty contrasting colors and measures 14 inches long and 6¼ inches high. Pull cord with colored bead attached to base.

49T5448—Postpaid **89c**

Pecking Goosie Gander

83¢ Post-paid

Very Popular Toy

Oh Gee! See Goosie moving head up and down pecking away at imaginary seeds in the little metal pan. Goose made of wood, enameled in attractive colors. Mounted on metal base with large colored wood wheels. Kiddies will enjoy the realistic action. Size, over all, 11⅛x6⅜x4 inches.

49T5482—Postpaid **83c**

Sambo Hustler

89¢ Post-paid

When toy is pulled Sambo moves his arms up and down and horse's head bobs backward and forward. He seems to be in an awful hurry to go some place. Toy is made of wood, with metal mechanism, wood parts, finished in bright colors. Donkey has artificial leather ears. Complete with pull cord. Height, over all, 5¾ inches; length, over all, 11 inches.

49T5449—Postpaid **89c**

New Hustler Watch Dog

89¢ Postpaid

Size, 11x7x4 Inches

A new and different floor toy with lots of action. **See the dog continually pop his head in and out of the door of his house, which is mounted on a steel base.** He cannot get out, because he is chained to the house. He acts as if he wants to break loose. You will have a lot of fun with this snappy toy, made of good quality wood, attractively enameled in colors. House has painted-on imitation tile roof and windows. Complete with strong pull cord with colored bead fastened to cord.

49T5451—Postpaid **89c**

The Waddling Daddy Ducky

43¢ Postpaid

Has off center front wheel giving Ducky that natural waddling effect. Head can be moved to either side. Made of wood, enameled in attractive colors and has pull cord attached. Toy stands 7½ in. high and 9¼ in. long.

49T5470—Postpaid **43c**

Horse Team and Dump Truck
Horses Have Moving Legs—Real Dump Cart

$1.98 Post-paid

19 In. Long

Here is a big flashy toy for little money. Just pull it along and you will see the horses move their legs backward and forward, as their bodies go up and down in life-like motion. Very realistic. This is not a stationary cart, but a real dump cart. Driver has movable arms which hold the reins. Horses are made of ⅞-inch thick wood enameled in beautiful colors. Clever mechanism so legs of both horses move when pulled. Dumping cart is 6⅜ inches long.

49T5411—Postpaid **$1.98**

$1.00 Postpaid

New Modernistic 11½-Inch Wooden Horse
Something Entirely New in Color Scheme for Toys

Extra large size beautiful steed for this price. This toy is manufactured by one of the foremost manufacturers of wooden toys, especially noted for originality and quality. Beautiful in all details. Horse stands 11½ inches high by 11½ inches long. Has pull cord attached and is mounted on about 2¾-inch diameter wheels.

49T5435—Postpaid **$1.00**

Red Metal Wagon

27¢ Post-paid

Just the right kind for the little tot to pull around. Light in weight, bright in color. Easy to steer, as front wheels turn like on the big wagon. Size, 10¼x6¼ inches. Has twisted wire handle.

49T5457 Postpaid **27c**

Kicking Maude Tries to Throw Sammy
A Big Hit—Very Realistic Action

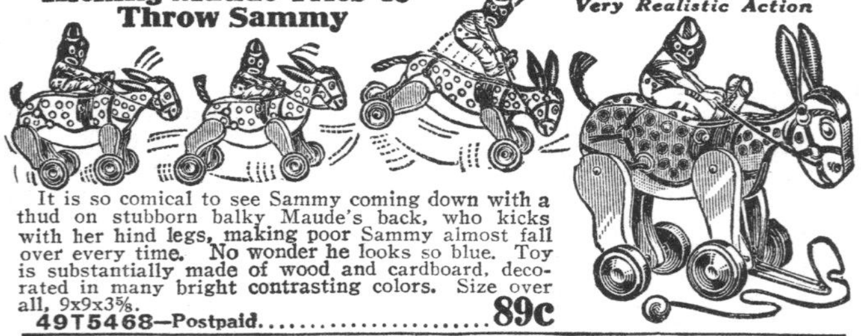

It is so comical to see Sammy coming down with a thud on stubborn balky Maude's back, who kicks with her hind legs, making poor Sammy almost fall over every time. No wonder he looks so blue. Toy is substantially made of wood and cardboard, decorated in many bright contrasting colors. Size over all, 9x9x3⅝.

49T5468—Postpaid **89c**

See Felix Chase His Mice
An Exceptionally Big Toy for the Price

Well known and popular cartoon character chasing his mice. Made so that Felix appears to be running after the mice, but he never catches them. Made of metal finished in natural colors. Clever action when toy is pulled along floor. Size, over all, 7½x6x3⅝ in. Has pull cord attached to base.

49T5494—Postpaid **25c**

19¢ POSTPAID

Large Size

Genuine Hurst Gyroscope

A scientific wonder top, as it appears to defy the law of gravity. While spinning it will stand straight out at the side of its support or balance at unusual angles without falling. Full directions, cord and wooden stand with each top.

49T7760—Postpaid **19c**

Biggest Value We Have Ever Offered in Wooden Trains

24-Inch Five-Piece Wood Freight Train

Just think of a locomotive, tender, oil tank, freight car and caboose in assorted imprints. All pieces are separate, but can be hitched together. Set has 5⅝-inch engine; 3½-inch tender; 5-inch oil tank; 5⁷⁄₁₆-inch freight car, 4-inch caboose. All wood smoothly finished, and enameled in bright colors.

49T5496—Postpaid **59c**

98c

6 Dandy Toys for 98c

Use garden set for making your garden and the wagon, cart and wheelbarrow for hauling things. **All Steel Wagon.** Front wheels turn under body. Size, 10¼x6¼ inches. 3-inch wheels, wire handle. **Three-Piece Garden Set,** consisting of: 18⅜-inch rake; 19¼-inch steel spade; 18½-inch hoe. **Push Cart** with 10¼x6¼-inch steel body. **Wheelbarrow, 24¼ Inches Over All,** with 4-inch diameter wheels and steel pan. Wagon, wheelbarrow and push cart are all made of steel, enameled bright red.

79T9136—Postpaid **98c**

13¾-Inch Street Car With Bell

Pull the street car and you will hear the bell ring as it goes along. Made from light gauge steel throughout and lithographed in true to life colors and details. No sharp edges and very sturdily constructed. Size, over all, 13¾x4½x4 in. Pull cord attached.

49T5483—Postpaid **87c**

Nicely Colored Humming Top
A Big Value

Easy to spin with this new style wood spinner. Body of top made of metal. Diameter, 3¾ in. Hums while spinning.

49T7774 Post-paid **10c**

Doll Furniture

$4.19 Postpaid

Doll Crib De Luxe

Has Bow End and Drop Side

All the Important Features Little Mother Wants for Her Dolly

She will certainly be proud of this gracefully designed bow end doll crib. One side lowers with a light touch, and when raised, locks automatically. Dainty tinted juvenile decoration on each panel. Large enough to hold large chubby doll. **Length, overall, 28 inches. Total height, 21¾ inches; width, 13⅞ inches,** and, like a baby crib, it is nicely finished throughout and enameled in the latest light green color. Exceptionally strong 6-inch steel wheels with ⅜-inch rubber tires. Doll and bedding not included.
79T7930—Postpaid........... **$4.19**

$2.59 Postpaid

25¾-Inch Doll Crib—Shaped Top Rails

A Remarkable Value at $2.59

Exceptionally low priced, beautifully finished doll crib to delight the heart of the little miss. Sturdy construction, with handsome cream ivory finish. Cute baby picture decorates the shaped wood panel in each end. Wide enough to hold a large size, chubby Ma-Ma doll. Made with high sides so dolly cannot fall out. Length, 25¾ inches; width, 14 inches; height, 21½ inches. 5-inch double disc steel wheels, with ⅜-inch rubber tires. Mattress, pillow and doll not included.
79T7926—Postpaid............. **$2.59**

$1.98

Surprise Her With This Beautiful, Distinctive, Yet Inexpensive Six-Room Doll House With Interior Staircase. Others Usually Ask $2.50. Special at............$1.98

Playtime is the happiest time of a young Miss. Why not make her exceptionally happy? Made of heavy cardboard, three rooms on each floor. Inside decorated. Two doors form the front of the house and swing open on hinges. Outside of house is red in imitation of brick, with white window frames; green roof. Windows are cut out. Height, 16 inches, width, 21 inches; depth, across eaves, 14½ inches. Furniture shown not included. For furniture illustrated see below.
79T7109—Postpaid.............. **$1.98**

Two-Room Doll Bungalows, Complete With Metal Furniture

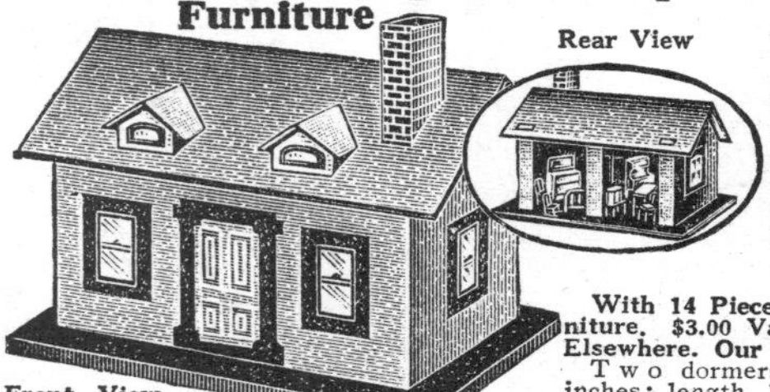

Rear View
Front View

Made of extra heavy cardboard, cream color, with green trimming and red roof. Transparent windows. Front door opens. Rear of house open for play.

Large Size Bungalow

With 14 Pieces of Metal Furniture, $3.00 Value Elsewhere. Our Price **$2.69**

Two dormers. Height, 13¼ inches; length, 19 inches; width across eaves, 11 in.
79T7105—Postpaid.............. **$2.69**

Small Size Bungalow

With 8 Pieces of Metal Furniture, $1.50 Value Elsewhere. Our Price.............. **$1.39**

Similar to above, only one dormer in roof. Height, 10 inches; length, 14½ inches; width across eaves, 9 inches.
.... **$1.39**

WE PAY THE POSTAGE

26½-Inch Postpaid $1.89

Large Size Cradles for Those Chubby Dolls

Enameled Ivory With Blue Decorations

Without mattress and pillows, hence the low price for these large roomy cradles. Fancy turned posts. Bluebird design on headend. Doll and bedding not included.

26½-Inch Illustrated	17½-Inch
Width, 12 inches; height of headend, 15¾ inches.	Similar to 79T7967. No panel in headend. Width, 10 inches; height of headend, 12⅝ inches.
79T7967 Postpaid..... $1.89	79T7962 Postpaid...... $1.10

$1.10 Postpaid 19¾-In.

Restful Slumber for Dolly

In these beautiful beds with fancy wood sides. Nicely finished and enameled in washable cream ivory color. Have cloth covered heavy cardboard mattress effect. (No unsanitary excelsior filling usually found in doll beds.) Two soft cotton stuffed pillows with each. Doll and cover not included.

19¾-Inch Bed	25¾-Inch Bed
Width, 11⅝ in. Height of headend, 14¼ inches; footend, 10 inches.	Width, 14 inches. Height of headend, 14⅝ inches; footend, 10 inches.
79T7902 Postpaid.... $1.10	79T7901 Postpaid..... $1.69

Beautiful Enameled Metal Daisy Toy Furniture

7-Piece Gilt Finish Metal Parlor Set

Divan, 3½x2x1½ inches, upholstered chair, table, floor lamp, table lamp, rocker and phonograph in proportion.
49T7119—Postpaid......... **87c**

7-Piece Pretty Pink Enameled Metal Bedroom Set

Twin beds, 3 7/16x1 11/16 inches. Dresser and vanity have polished metal mirrors, rocker, chair and commode in proportion.
49T7120—Postpaid.......... **87c**

Dressers Built to Fulfill the Demands of the Little Lady

Beautifully enameled ivory and light green doll dressers. Each has swinging mirror. Exceptionally well made and finished. Not flimsy, light wood dressers. Drawers are finished in light green and fitted with wood pulls. Large size has beveled top.

Medium Size

Height, 21 inches; width, 13½ inches; drawers, 10¾x5¾x2¼ inches. Mirror frame, 9x7¼ inches.
79T7116—Postpaid........ **$2.48**

Large Size

Height, 24¾ inches; width, 16½ inches; drawers, 13⅝x6½x2½ inches. Mirror frame, 9¾x9⅛ inches.
79T7117—Postpaid........ **$3.79**

New and Entirely Different Doll's Folding Bassinet

Dainty and light in weight but sturdily built. Wood dowels, 23½ inches long; 2½-inch wood wheels. Body of fancy colored cretonne, shirred and lined with colored sateen. Large enough to hold doll 20 inches long. Height, about 12 inches. All wood parts finished in washable delicate enameled color.
79T7912—Postpaid.............. **98c**

7-Piece Light Green Enameled Kitchen Set

Range, 2x1⅞x⅞ inches; other pieces in proportion. Will not chip or break.
49T7121 Postpaid........... **87c**

8-Piece Ivory Finish Metal Dining Set

Round table, 2¼x1⅝ inches. Tea cart wheels really turn. Other pieces in proportion.
49T7122—Postp'd. **87c**

8-Piece White Enameled Bathroom Set

3⅜-inch bathtub, toilet, washstand, chair, medicine chest, stool and two towel racks.
49T7123—Postp'd. **87c**

Quality Trunks

Each with real lock and key and inside tray.

Dandy 14-Inch Trunk, $1.39

Covered with blue and black material. Strong metal corners; has lock with key. Size, 14x7⅝x7½ inches.
79T8404—Postpaid.......... **$1.39**

New Style Metal Covered Trunk

(As Illustrated)

Metal bound edges, metal sides and corners. Size, 18x10⅝x10⅝ inches.
79T8417—Postpaid........... **$3.15**

$1.00 Postpaid

No Playroom Is Complete Without a Doll High Chair Large Enough for Large Ma-Ma Dolls

This well made, beautifully enameled all wood high chair has a swinging tray just like a large one. **Total height, 24 inches;** width, over all, 7¾ inches. Enameled in cream color with blue trimming and pretty transfer picture on head end. **We Pay Postage.**
79T7101 **$1.00**

48¢ Postpaid

Completely Furnished Four-Room Doll House

The Newlywed Home, all ready for dolly family to move into. Nicely made of cardboard. Beautifully printed in colors to imitate brick, and climbing vines and roses. Height, to top of roof, 8⅝ inches; depth, 2 9/16 inches; width, 10¼ inches. Front of house has two doors that swing open so child can play with metal furniture inside. Each room made of lithographed sheet steel nicely decorated to represent parlor, dining room, kitchen and bath; also fitted with necessary lithographed metal furniture.
49T7111—Postpaid... **48c**

25¢ Postpaid

Dolly Can Rest in Her Swing While Little Mother Is Busy

25c Postpaid

Wire frame, 6½x6½ inches, with nicely sewed cloth seat, taped holes for dolly's legs. **Postpaid.**
49T7938.... **25c**

Just What the Little Girl Wants

This little beauty has two drawers. Height, over all, 14⅝ inches; width, 11 inches; drawers, 9⅛x4x2 inches. Mirror frame, 6 5/16x5¼ inches.
79T7115 Postpaid. **$1.48**

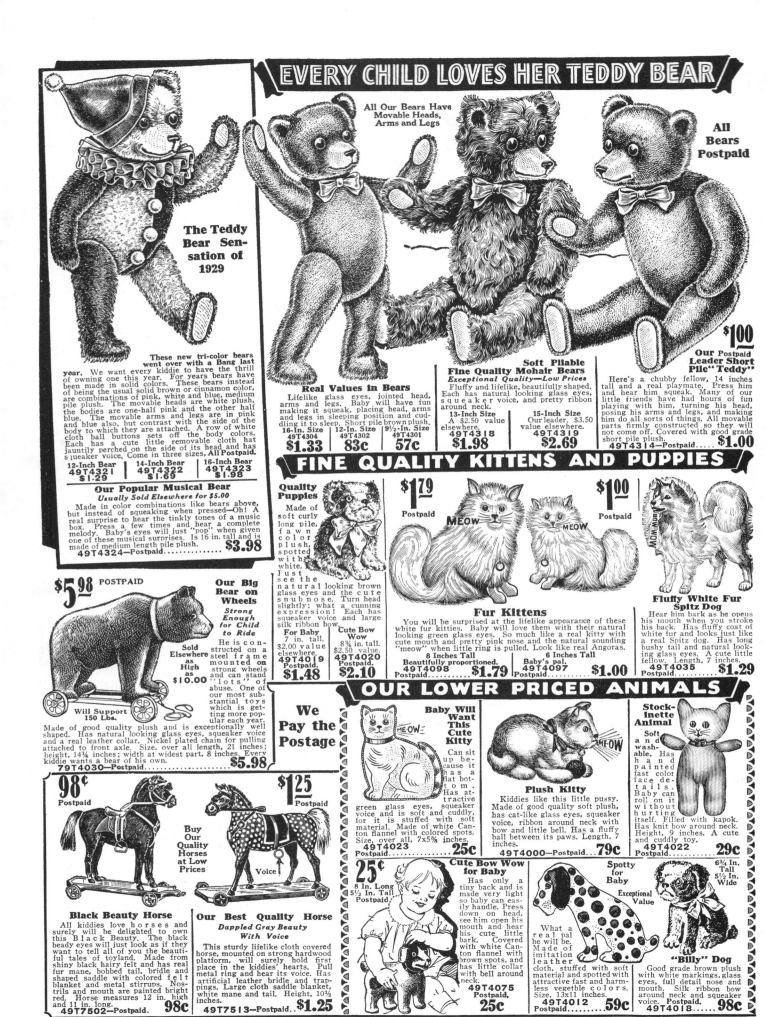

EVERY CHILD LOVES HER TEDDY BEAR

All Our Bears Have Movable Heads, Arms and Legs

All Bears Postpaid

The Teddy Bear Sensation of 1929

These new tri-color bears went over with a Bang last year. We want every kiddie to have the thrill of owning one this year. For years bears have been made in solid colors. These bears instead of being the usual solid brown or cinnamon color, are combinations of pink, white and blue, medium pile plush. The movable heads are white plush, the bodies are one-half pink and the other half blue. The movable arms and legs are in pink and blue also, but contrast with the side of the body to which they are attached. A row of white cloth ball buttons sets off the body colors. Each has a cute little removable cloth hat jauntily perched on the side of its head and has a squeaker voice. Come in three sizes, All Postpaid.

| 12-Inch Bear 49T4321 $1.29 | 14-Inch Bear 49T4322 $1.69 | 16-Inch Bear 49T4323 $1.98 |

Our Popular Musical Bear
Usually Sold Elsewhere for $5.00

Made in color combinations like bears above, but instead of squeaking when pressed—Oh! A real surprise to hear the tinkly tones of a music box. Press a few times and hear a complete melody. Baby's eyes will just "pop" when given one of these musical surprises. Is 16 in. tall and is made of medium length pile plush. **$3.98**
49T4324—Postpaid.............

Real Values in Bears

Lifelike glass eyes, jointed head, arms and legs. Baby will have fun making it squeak, placing head, arms and legs in sleeping position and cuddling it to sleep. Short pile brown plush.

| 16-In. Size 49T4304 $1.33 | 12-In. Size 49T4302 83c | 9½-In. Size 49T4301 57c |

Soft Pliable Fine Quality Mohair Bears
Exceptional Quality—Low Prices

Fluffy and lifelike, beautifully shaped. Each has natural looking glass eyes, squeaker voice, and pretty ribbon around neck.

| 13-Inch Size A $2.50 value elsewhere. 49T4318 $1.98 | 15-Inch Size Our leader, $3.50 value elsewhere. 49T4319 $2.69 |

Our Leader Short Pile "Teddy"
Postpaid **$1.00**

Here's a chubby fellow, 14 inches tall and a real playmate. Press him and hear him squeak. Many of our little friends have had hours of fun playing with him, turning his head, posing his arms and legs, and making him do all sorts of things. All movable parts firmly constructed so they will not come off. Covered with good grade short pile plush.
49T4314—Postpaid..... **$1.00**

FINE QUALITY KITTENS AND PUPPIES

Quality Puppies

Made of soft curly long pile, fawn color plush, spotted with white. Just see the natural looking brown glass eyes and the cute snub nose. Turn head slightly; what a cunning expression! Each has squeaker voice and large silk ribbon bow.

| For Baby 7 in. tall. $2.00 value elsewhere. 49T4019 Postpaid. $1.48 | Cute Bow Wow 8¾ in. tall. $2.50 value. 49T4020 Postpaid. $2.10 |

Fur Kittens
$1.79 Postpaid **$1.00** Postpaid

MEOW MEOW

You will be surprised at the lifelike appearance of these white fur kitties. Baby will love them with their natural looking green glass eyes. So much like a real kitty with cute mouth and pretty pink nose and the natural sounding "meow" when little ring is pulled. Look like real Angoras.

| 8 Inches Tall Beautifully proportioned. 49T4098 Postpaid $1.79 | 6 Inches Tall Baby's pal. 49T4097 Postpaid $1.00 |

Fluffy White Fur Spitz Dog

Hear him bark as he opens his mouth when you stroke his back. Has fluffy coat of white fur and looks just like a real Spitz dog. Has long bushy tail and natural looking glass eyes. A cute little fellow. Length, 7 inches.
49T4035 Postpaid.... **$1.29**

Our Big Bear on Wheels
$5.98 POSTPAID

Strong Enough for Child to Ride

Sold Elsewhere as High as $10.00

He is constructed on a steel frame mounted on strong wheels and can stand "lots" of abuse. One of our most substantial toys which is getting more popular each year.

Will Support 150 Lbs.

Made of good quality plush and is exceptionally well shaped. Has natural looking glass eyes, squeaker voice and a real leather collar. Nickel plated chain for pulling attached to front axle. Size, over all length, 21 inches; height, 14¾ inches; width at widest part, 8 inches. Every kiddie wants a bear of his own.
79T4030—Postpaid................. **$5.98**

We Pay the Postage

OUR LOWER PRICED ANIMALS

Baby Will Want This Cute Kitty

MEOW

Can sit up because it has a flat bottom. Has attractive green glass eyes, squeaker voice and is soft and cuddly, for it is stuffed with soft material. Made of white Canton flannel with colored spots. Size, over all, 7x5⅝ inches.
49T4023 Postpaid **25c**

Plush Kitty

MEOW

Kiddies like this little pussy. Made of good quality soft plush, has cat-like glass eyes, squeaker voice, ribbon around neck with bow and little bell. Has a fluffy ball between its paws. Length, 7 inches.
49T4000—Postpaid...... **79c**

Stockinette Animal

Soft and washable. Has hand painted fast color face details. Baby can roll on it without hurting itself. Filled with kapok. Has knit bow around neck. Height, 9 inches. A cute and cuddly toy.
49T4022 Postpaid........ **29c**

Black Beauty Horse
98c Postpaid

All kiddies love horses and surely will be delighted to own this Black Beauty. The black beady eyes will just look as if they want to tell all of you the beautiful tales of toyland. Made from shiny black hairy felt and has real fur mane, bobbed tail, bridle and shaped saddle with colored felt blanket and metal stirrups. Nostrils and mouth are painted bright red. Horse measures 12 in. high and 11 in. long.
49T7502—Postpaid. **98c**

Our Best Quality Horse
$1.25 Postpaid
Dappled Gray Beauty With Voice

Voice

Buy Our Quality Horses at Low Prices

This sturdy lifelike cloth covered horse, mounted on strong hardwood platform, will surely hold first place in the kiddies' hearts. Pull metal ring and hear its voice. Has artificial leather bridle and trappings. Large cloth saddle blanket, white mane and tail. Height, 10½ inches.
49T7513—Postpaid.. **$1.25**

Cute Bow Wow for Baby
25c
8 In. Long 5½ In. Tall Postpaid

Has only a tiny back and is made very light so baby can easily handle. Press down on head, see him open his mouth and hear his cute little bark. Covered with white Canton flannel with brown spots, and has little collar with bell around neck.
49T4075 Postpaid, **25c**

Spotty for Baby
Exceptional Value

What a real pal he will be. Made of imitation leather cloth, stuffed with soft material and spotted with attractive fast and harmless vegetble colors. Size, 13x11 inches.
49T4012 Postpaid... **59c**

"Billy" Dog
6¾ In. Tall 5½ In. Wide

Good grade brown plush with white markings, glass eyes, full detail nose and mouth. Silk ribbon bow around neck and squeaker voice. Postpaid.
49T4018...... **98c**

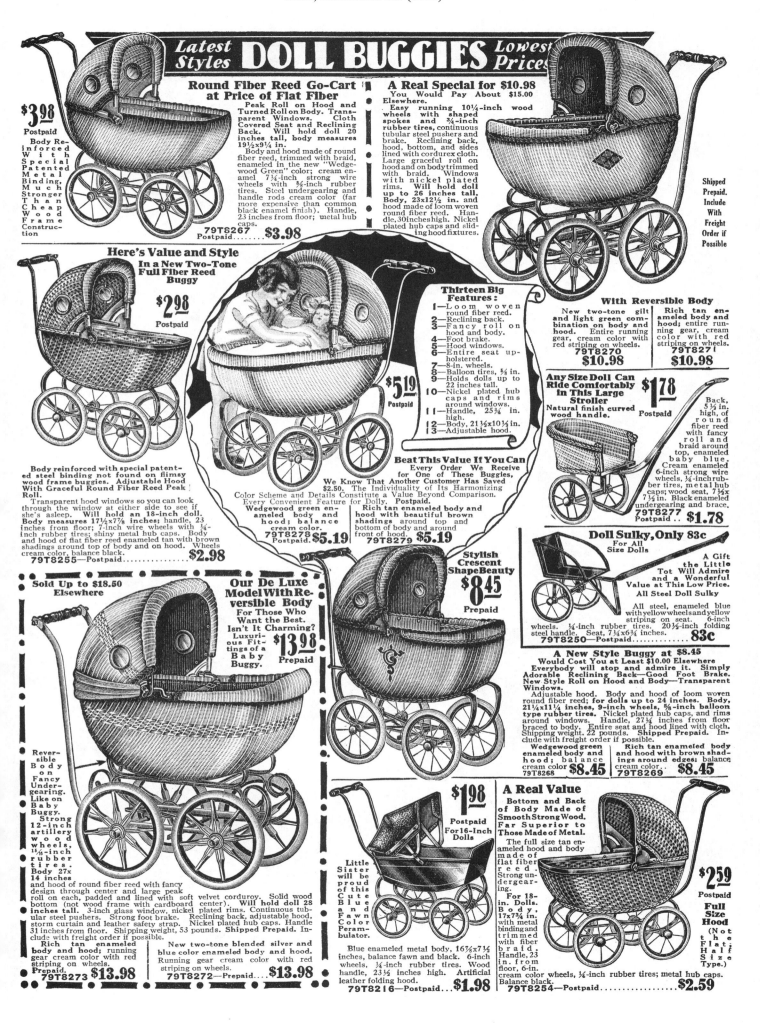

Latest Styles DOLL BUGGIES Lowest Prices

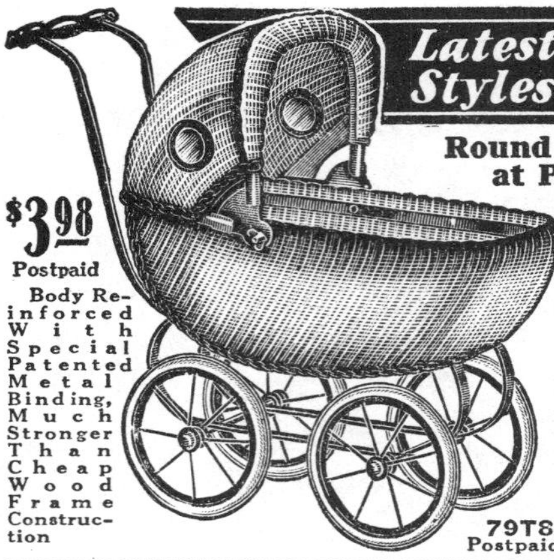

$3.98 Postpaid

Body Reinforced With Special Patented Metal Binding, Much Stronger Than Cheap Wood Frame Construction

Round Fiber Reed Go-Cart at Price of Flat Fiber

Peak Roll on Hood and Turned Roll on Body. Transparent Windows. Cloth Covered Seat and Reclining Back. Will hold doll 20 inches tall, body measures 19½x9¼ in.

Body and hood made of round fiber reed, trimmed with braid, enameled in the new "Wedgewood Green" color; cream enamel 7¼-inch strong wire wheels with ⅜-inch rubber tires. Steel undergearing and handle rods cream color (far more expensive than common black enamel finish). Handle, 23 inches from floor; metal hub caps.

79T8267 Postpaid........**$3.98**

A Real Special for $10.98

You Would Pay About $15.00 Elsewhere.

Easy running 10¼-inch wood wheels with shaped spokes and ¾-inch rubber tires, continuous tubular steel pushers and brake. Reclining back, hood, bottom, and sides lined with corduroy cloth. Large graceful roll on hood and on body trimmed with braid. **Windows with nickel plated rims. Will hold doll up to 26 inches tall. Body, 23x12½ in.** and hood made of loom woven round fiber reed. Handle, 30 inches high. Nickel plated hub caps and sliding hood fixtures.

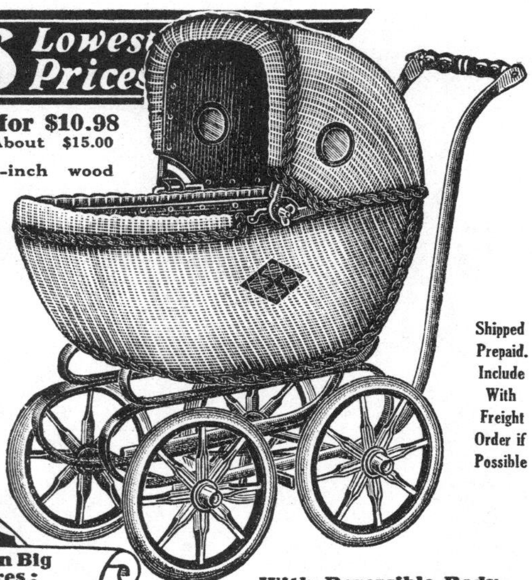

Shipped Prepaid. Include With Freight Order if Possible

With Reversible Body

New two-tone gilt and light green combination on body and hood. Entire running gear, cream color with red striping on wheels.	Rich tan enameled body and hood; entire running gear, cream color with red striping on wheels.
79T8270 **$10.98**	79T8271 **$10.98**

Here's Value and Style

In a New Two-Tone Full Fiber Reed Buggy

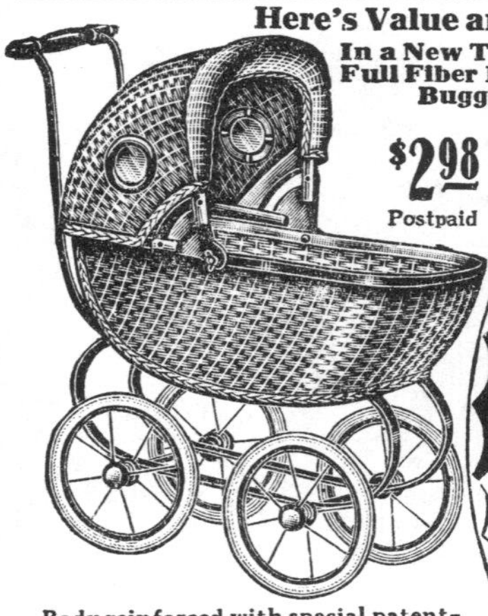

$2.98 Postpaid

Body reinforced with special patented steel binding not found on flimsy wood frame buggies. Adjustable Hood With Graceful Round Fiber Reed Peak Roll.

Transparent hood windows so you can look through the window at either side to see if she's asleep. **Will hold an 18-inch doll. Body measures 17½x7⅞ inches;** handle, 23 inches from floor; 7-inch wire wheels with ¼-inch rubber tires; shiny metal hub caps. Body and hood of flat fiber reed enameled tan with brown shadings around top of body and on hood. Wheels cream color, balance black.

79T8255—Postpaid..............**$2.98**

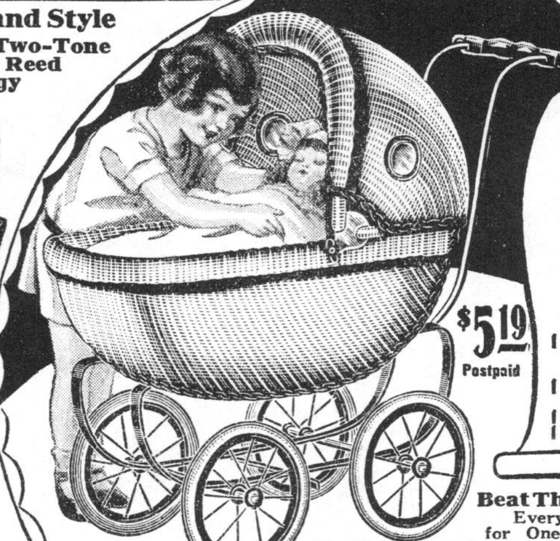

$5.19 Postpaid

Thirteen Big Features:

1—Loom woven round fiber reed.
2—Reclining back.
3—Fancy roll on hood and body.
4—Foot brake.
5—Hood windows.
6—Entire seat upholstered.
7—8-in. wheels.
8—Balloon tires, ⅝ in.
9—Holds dolls up to 22 inches tall.
10—Nickel plated hub caps and rims around windows.
11—Handle, 25¾ in. high.
12—Body, 21½x10½ in.
13—Adjustable hood.

Beat This Value If You Can

Every Order We Receive for One of These Buggies, We Know That Another Customer Has Saved $2.50. The Individuality of Its Harmonizing Color Scheme and Details Constitute a Value Beyond Comparison. Every Convenient Feature for Dolly. **Postpaid.**

Wedgewood green enameled body and hood; balance cream color.	Rich tan enameled body and hood with beautiful brown shadings around top and bottom of body and around front of hood.
79T8278 Postpaid. **$5.19**	79T8279 **$5.19**

Any Size Doll Can Ride Comfortably in This Large Stroller

$1.78 Postpaid

Natural finish curved wood handle.

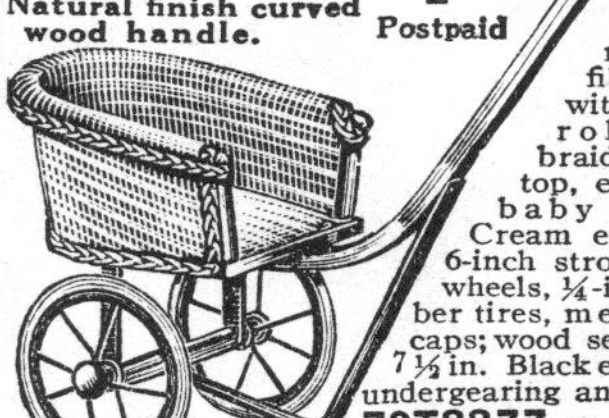

Back, 5½ in. high, of round fiber reed with fancy roll and braid around top, enameled baby blue. Cream enameled 6-inch strong wire wheels, ¼-inch rubber tires, metal hub caps; wood seat, 7½x7½ in. Black enameled undergearing and brace.

79T8277 Postpaid.. **$1.78**

Doll Sulky, Only 83c

For All Size Dolls

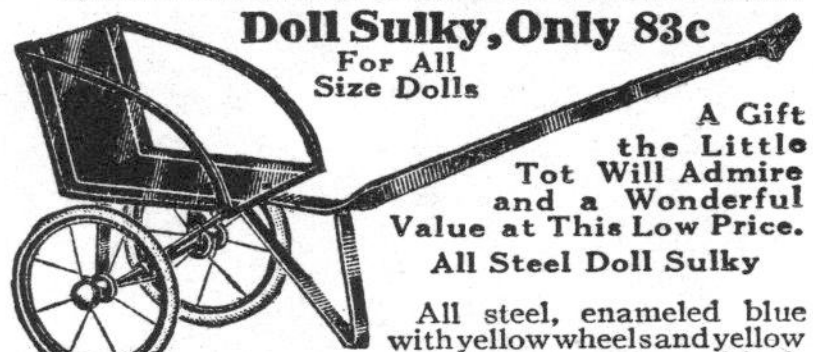

A Gift the Little Tot Will Admire and a Wonderful Value at This Low Price. All Steel Doll Sulky

All steel, enameled blue with yellow wheels and yellow striping on seat. 6-inch wheels. ¼-inch rubber tires. 20½-inch folding steel handle. Seat, 7¼x6¾ inches.

79T8250—Postpaid..............**83c**

Sold Up to $18.50 Elsewhere

Our De Luxe Model With Reversible Body

For Those Who Want the Best. Isn't It Charming? Luxurious Fittings of a Baby Buggy.

$13.98 Prepaid

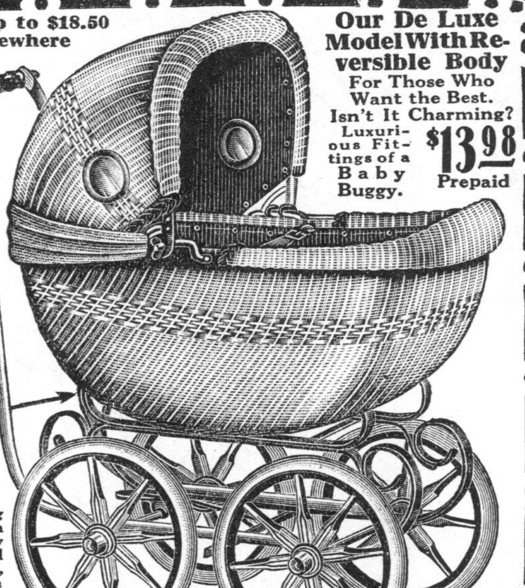

Reversible Body on Fancy Undergearing. Like on Baby Buggy. Strong 12-inch artillery wood wheels, 1⁵⁄₁₆-inch rubber tires. Body 27x14 inches and hood of round fiber reed with fancy design through center and large peak roll on each, padded and lined with soft velvet corduroy. Solid wood bottom (not wood frame with cardboard center). **Will hold doll 28 inches tall.** 3-inch glass window, nickel plated rims. Continuous tubular steel pushers. Strong foot brake. Reclining back, adjustable hood, storm curtain and leather safety strap. Nickel plated hub caps. Handle 31 inches from floor. Shipping weight, 53 pounds. **Shipped Prepaid.** Include with freight order if possible.

Rich tan enameled body and hood; running gear cream color with red striping on wheels.	New two-tone blended silver and blue color enameled body and hood. Running gear cream color with red striping on wheels.
Prepaid. 79T8273 **$13.98**	79T8272—Prepaid....**$13.98**

Stylish Crescent Shape Beauty

$8.45 Prepaid

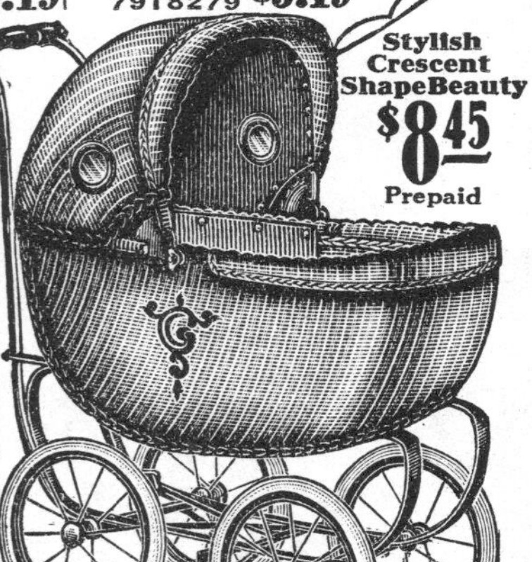

A New Style Buggy at $8.45

Would Cost You at Least $10.00 Elsewhere

Everybody will stop and admire it. Simply Adorable Reclining Back—Good Foot Brake. New Style Roll on Hood and Body—Transparent Windows.

Adjustable hood. Body and hood of loom woven round fiber reed; **for dolls up to 24 inches. Body, 21¼x11¼ inches, 9-inch wheels, ⅝-inch balloon type rubber tires.** Nickel plated hub caps, and rims around windows. Handle, 27¼ inches from floor braced to body. Entire seat and hood lined with cloth. Shipping weight, 22 pounds. **Shipped Prepaid.** Include with freight order if possible.

Wedgewood green enameled body and hood; balance cream color	Rich tan enameled body and hood with brown shadings around edges; balance cream color
79T8268 **$8.45**	79T8269 **$8.45**

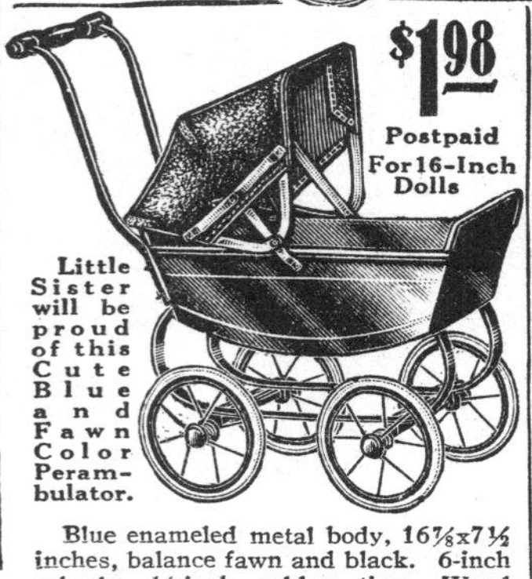

$1.98 Postpaid For 16-Inch Dolls

Little Sister will be proud of this Cute Blue and Fawn Color Perambulator.

Blue enameled metal body, 16⅞x7½ inches, balance fawn and black. 6-inch wheels, ¼-inch rubber tires. Wood handle, 23½ inches high. Artificial leather folding hood.

79T8216—Postpaid...**$1.98**

A Real Value

Bottom and Back of Body Made of Smooth Strong Wood. Far Superior to Those Made of Metal.

The full size tan enameled hood and body made of flat fiber reed. Strong undergearing. **For 18-in. Dolls. Body, 17x7¾ in.** with metal binding and trimmed with fiber braid. Handle, 23 in. from floor, 6-in. cream color wheels, ¼-inch rubber tires; metal hub caps. Balance black.

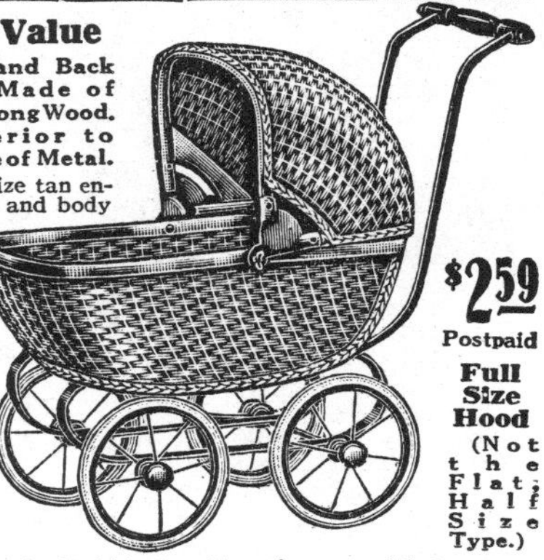

$2.59 Postpaid

Full Size Hood (Not the Flat, Half Size Type.)

79T8254—Postpaid................**$2.59**

ANNOUNCING OUR WONDERFUL SUNSHINE DOLLS

FINEST QUALITY at SEARS SAVING PRICES

TO BRIGHTEN the HEART of EVERY LITTLE GIRL—

Our New Line — Our Own Brand · · · ·
Beautifully Modelled-Perfect in Every Detail ·
We Guarantee Sunshine Dolls to Be Unexcelled by Any
Brand of Dolls offered anywhere.

WE, The World's Largest Store, had a great many things in mind in planning for Sunshine Dolls. The two most important being: First, we must offer our customers truly beautiful dolls, not excelled anywhere—second, we must save them money. We have more than satisfied ourselves about these two points, and many others. You, too, will be well pleased.

This has been possible only after exhaustive search and comparisons and through our vast resources, coupled with the hearty co-operation of America's most expert doll makers. These dolls are the very last word in the art of doll making. The head models are very pretty, the arms and legs, too, are finely proportioned. Dresses are charmingly styled of fine materials; in fact, all details have been most carefully looked after.

With their joyous smiles and vibrant looks Sunshine Dolls will surely "Brighten the Heart of Every Little Girl." That you may identify these dolls, we are calling them Baby Sunshine and Dolly Sunshine and each doll has a ribbon attached bearing its name.

All Baby Sunshine Dolls are made with "lifelike go to sleep" eyes · ·

I SAY MA-MA · **I SAY MA-MA** · **I SAY MA-MA** · **I CRY**

24½ Inches 18T3139¼	22 Inches 18T3138¼	19 Inches 18T3137	17½ Inches 18T3136	14½ Inches 18T3135
$9.95	$6.95	$4.75	$4.25	$3.39

"BABY SUNSHINE"—The Nation's Darling

Go where you will, seek where you may, and you will not find more lovable or beautiful baby dolls than the ones here pictured. Baby Sunshine is fresh as the dew and joyous as a sunbeam, winning her way instantly into the hearts of all little girls. She has a wonderful baby-like look and the sweetest dimpled face you ever saw. To see her is to want her. Darling baby dress of fine organdy with ruffle is enhanced by a dainty embroidered yoke and is also tastefully trimmed with fine Valenciennes lace.

Dress fitted with buttons and buttonholes so dolly can be undressed like a real live baby. Has a smartly fashioned bonnet to match. Underwear has lace edging. Each size has eyes that gently close in sleep and open mouth showing little baby teeth. Full composition head can be turned from side to side in cunning poses. Baby arms and bent baby legs are also of strong composition. Socks and bootee moccasins. Bodies are cotton stuffed. Each doll calls "Ma-Ma" except the smallest, No. 18T3135, which is so young that it can only cry.

REAL HAIR WIG

I CAN STAND ALONE · **Silk Taffeta Dress**

I SAY MA-MA I SLEEP

Dolly Sunshine

Gorgeous Sunshine Dolls attired in a smart dress and bonnet of fine, real silk taffeta. Bloomer style underwear of same material. Charming real hair ringlet wig. Composition head can turn, eyes gently sleep. Has eyelashes, open mouth, teeth and strong composition legs that stand.

18T3140¼
21½ inches tall,
$6.95

18T3141¼
24 inches tall,
$8.95

18T3142¼
26½ inches tall,
$10.95

Dolly Sunshine

WE PAY THE POSTAGE

I SAY MA-MA I SLEEP · **I CRY I SLEEP** · **I CRY**

Another Appealing Sunshine Doll

Clever dresses of sheer organdy have buttons and buttonholes, and bonnets to match. Fitted with fine mohair ringlet wigs, moving eyes, eyelashes, open mouth, teeth, composition arms and legs that stand alone. "Ma-Ma" voice.

18T3143 16 inches.	18T3144 18 inches.	18T3145¼ 19½ in.
$3.39	$4.25	$4.75

Moving Eye Dolls

These lovable Sunshine girl dolls have moving eyes, painted molded hair and flesh colored composition heads, arms and legs. Dainty organdy dress, lace trimmed, with bonnet to match. Crying voices. Come in two sizes.

18T3146—13 inches, Postpaid.... **$1.95**
18T3147—16 inches, ... **2.45**

Painted Eye Dolls

A dainty Sunshine Doll. Has strong composition head, arms and legs. Delicately painted eyes and features, molded hair. Dress is of very good printed, cotton material, with a clever bonnet to match. Cotton stuffed body. Shoes and sox. Crying voice.

18T3148—16 inches, ... **$1.65**

234

MAKE SANTA'S FUNDS GO FAR

REAL HAIR WIG

Charming **HAT** and **DRESS** of Fine **SILK CREPE DE CHINE**

GLASS EYES

REAL HAIR RINGLET WIG →

FINE, BIG → 26-INCH SIZE

We Pay the Postage

18T3183¼ Strikingly beautiful doll that every girl will be proud to own. The pretty dress is of real silk crepe de chine, trimmed with satin ribbon and two lace medallions. The lovely hat to match has the underbrim faced with lace. The dress has snap fasteners, just like real little girls' dresses. Real human hair ringlet wig, eyes that go to sleep, eyelashes, open mouth, tongue and teeth. Head can be turned from side to side. Full composition head, arms and walking type legs. Imported shoes, Rayon sox. Voice that clearly calls for Ma-Ma. Postpaid.

$6.95

$1.95

$1.79

$3.95

Splendid Value
18T3180—19½ inches tall. A lot of doll for little money. Composition head, mohair wig, sleeping eyes, lashes, open mouth and teeth. Composition hands and legs. A sweetly simple dress of flowered organdy, lace trimmed, with bonnet to match. Shoes and sox. Cry voice. **We Pay the Postage.**

Fascinating Girl Doll
18T3181¼ — 20 inches tall. An unusually pretty doll in her charming little frock of daintily colored voile and figured Rayon. Appealing painted eyes and natural looking marcelled mohair wig. Composition head, arms and legs. Shoes and sox. Cry voice. **We Pay the Postage.**

Big Sears Value
18T3182¼—21½ inches tall. Adorable Ma-Ma doll with a real human hair, marcelled wig, go to sleep eyes, eyelashes, and open mouth showing tongue and teeth. Full composition arms and legs. Dress of very fine imported Swiss organdy. Ribbon head band. **We Pay the Postage.**

STRONG METAL HEAD DOLLS
The Famous WEARWELL BRAND

18T3184—16 inches tall. This sturdy doll has unbreakable metal head, mohair wig, and go to sleep eyes. Composition arms and legs, cotton stuffed body. Dress of colored organdy, bonnet to match. Voice says Ma-Ma. Postpaid.

$1.65

No matter how roughly handled in children's play, all these metal head dolls cannot break and are so guaranteed.

Imported Minerva Metal Head Dolls Ready to Be Dressed →
This imported doll, with its genuine Minerva unbreakable metal head, is always a favorite. Bright fixed glass eyes, nicely curled and parted mohair wig, enameled arms and hands of carved wood. The body is of strong pink silesia cloth. Crying voice. Your choice of three sizes: Postpaid.

18T2970 Height, 15 in.	18T2973 Height, 17 in.
98c	**$1.29**

18T2975¼ Height, 20 in., Postpaid.. **$1.65**

Extra Big VALUE

$1

98¢ POSTPAID

←

18T3187 13 inches. Falls and hard knocks will not hurt this little baby, for she has an unbreakable metal head with go to sleep eyes, composition hands, and soft cotton body and legs. Nice dress of white lawn, flannel diaper and long stockings. Cry voice. **We Pay Postage.**

18T3185 13½ in. tall. Strong, cry voice, metal head doll, with painted eyes and features. Composition hands and soft legs. Romper dress with bonnet to match. **Postpaid.**

75¢ POST-PAID

18T3186 — 14½ inches. Fitted with go to sleep eyes and a robust metal head. Composition arms, soft legs. Shoes and sox. Good quality cotton dress with bonnet to match. Cry voice.

98¢

RAGGEDY ANN *and* RAGGEDY ANDY
The Story Book DOLLS

The little friends of childhood. Painted features, yarn hair, shoe-button eyes. Well made of fine materials. Nothing to break. Can be undressed. 16 inches tall.

18T3188 Raggedy Ann
18T3189 Raggedy Andy

$1.79 EACH POSTPAID

Fine 22-Inch MAMA DOLL

18T3190¼—Just check these features: Ma-Ma voice, mohair wig, go to sleep eyes, eyelashes, open mouth, tongue and teeth, composition head, forearms and legs and cotton stuffed body. Smart organdy dress with panel of flowered dimity, bonnet to match. A real Sears value indeed, in a most charming, lovable quality doll. **We Pay the Postage.**

$2.45 POSTPAID

New Style JOY-TOY *Velocipedes* $10.79 POSTPAID

79T8381

Boys! Have You Heard About These New Bicycle Type Frame Velocipedes?

Here Are a Few of the Many Outstanding Features They Have:

1—**Chromium Plated.** Handle bars and stem, crown of fork and mud guard braces. New tarnish proof and rust resisting chromium plated, just like on your Dad's car.
2—**Leg Room.** Do you see that center bar that holds up the seat? Notice how it goes straight back and turns down sharply; that construction means more leg room and comfort.
3—**Center Bar.** That center bar is 1-inch diameter steel tubing, hand brazed with brass at the neck and at the cross section; guaranteed not to come apart.
4—**Double Strength Rear Axle.** Each is equipped with a cold rolled steel axle inside of a steel tube attached to the triple braced 1-inch tube frame affording additional strength and improved appearance.
5—**Exclusive.** Each model a beauty. Exclusive in style and a super value which no other mail order house can offer. For detailed description of each model, see below.

De Luxe Joy-Toy Bicycle Type Frame Velocipedes

Again Offered Exclusively by Us
Comfort, Speed, Strength and Sturdiness
Few Other Velocipedes Sold Offer as Many Features
Our Introduction of This New Departure in Velocipedes Last Year Proved a Tremendous Success.

Thousands of satisfied parents and kiddies are the result. Again we are offering this beautiful new line with its comfortable, sturdy construction, which had such an overwhelming appeal last year. Many refinements have been made to improve it over last year's merchandise. Looks and feels like riding a real bike.

Check the points of superiority with any other velocipede on the market. Study its construction. Compare it, piece by piece, with any other bike in its class, and you will soon see why so many parents and kiddies want a Joy-Toy bike. See those large rear wheels with the great big balloon tires! That means speed. The reversible handle bars convert the bike into a racing model.

These acknowledged points of superiority prove that the Joy-Toy Velocipede is an outstanding bike value:

1—**Real Balloon Type Tires.** Full 1¼-inch. Special construction insures greater resiliency and longer wear.
2—**Drop Side Heavy Gauge Steel Mud Guard** on front wheel. Chromium plated braces to fork.
3—**Full 1-Inch Tubular Steel Frame.** All joints hand brazed with brass and smoothly finished.
4—**Extra Large Motor-Bike Type Leather Saddle** with tool bag and nickel plated double coil springs.
5—**Imported Nickel Plated Motorcycle Bulb Horn.** Gives loud clear warning.
6—**Large Rubber Grips and Pedals.** Pedals have four surfaced rubber treads and nickel plated parts. Ball bearing shaft of high carbon steel.
7—**Ball Bearings at Every Point of Friction**—on each wheel and both pedals.
8—**Steel tubing around rear axle.** An important construction feature—gives double strength to axle.
9—**Rustproof All Weather Nickel Plated Bicycle Spokes.** Highly polished, and have tension adjustment.
10—**Reinforced Seat Post.** Constructed unusually strong to withstand hard usage.
11—**Oversize Nickel Plated Hubs** of steel.
12—**Extra Large Rear Wheels** which give more speed with less effort.
13—**Chromium Plated Reversible Handle Bars,** converting bike into a racing model when lowered.
14—**Stout Fork with Chromium Plated Crown.**
15—**Baked-on Enamel Finish**—frame, fork and rims of wheels. Box Elder Green (a pleasing bluish green color) neatly striped.

Chromium Plated Handle Bars, Stem and Crown Fork

Enameled Crown Shape Mud Guard

Rustproof Bicycle Spokes

No Other Mail Order House Sells These

French Style Bulb Horn

Genuine Troxel Leather Saddle *and* Tool Bag

Triple Braced 1-inch Tubular Steel-Backbone

Ball Bearing Wheels *and* Pedals

Full 1¼ inch Cushion Type Rubber Tires

	Front Wheel	Rear Wheels	For Child	Shpg. Wt.	Each
79T8381	12 in.	10 in.	2 to 3 yrs.	Postpaid	$10.79
79T8382	14 in.	12 in.	3 to 4 yrs.	Postpaid	11.89
79T8383	16 in.	14 in.	4 to 6 yrs.	Postpaid	12.98
★79T8384	20 in.	16 in.	6 to 8 yrs.	42 lbs.	

★Unmailable. Shipped by freight.
Prepaid................................. $14.67

$7.25 Postpaid And Up For Those Who Cannot or Do Not Want to Buy a Ball Bearing Bike

BELL →

One-Inch Rubber Tires—Rubber Pedals.

New Joy-Toy Plain Bearing Tubular Bikes Offered by Us Exclusively

These plain bearing Joy-Toy Velocipedes are strong enough to last through many seasons of hard usage. **Handle bars and stem are chromium plated over nickel.** All other shiny parts are heavily nickel plated. No other mail order house sells these new type bicycle frame velocipedes. They have all the latest features such as: 1—Double strength rear axle. 2—Full 1-inch tubular steel frame. 3—Three-brace back bone. 4—Full 1-inch cushion rubber tires. 5—Reinforced seat post. 6—Nickel plated bicycle bell. 7—Rubber pedals and grips. 8—Reversible handle bars. Wheels, spokes, frame and fork enameled red, and striped, baked-on finish. Large size not mailable.

	Front Wheel	Rear Wheels	For Child	Shpg. Wt.	Each
79T8325	12 in.	10 in.	2 to 3 yrs.	Postpaid	$7.25
79T8326	14 in.	12 in.	3 to 4 yrs.	Postpaid	8.29
79T8327	16 in.	14 in.	4 to 6 yrs.	Postpaid	9.19
★79T8328	20 in.	20 in.	6 to 8 yrs.	36 lbs.	

★Unmailable. Shipped by freight.
Prepaid................................. $10.87

You'll Be the Greatest Fellow in Town When You Go Whizzing Down the Street on This New Joy-Toy Ball Bearing Tubular Bike

Has new bicycle style frame. All joints are hand brazed with brass and guaranteed. Has following features: 1—Full 1-inch tubular frame. 2—Full 1-inch cushion rubber tires. 3—All wheels and pedals have case hardened steel ball bearings. 4—Bicycle type red leather saddle with double coil nickel plated springs. 5—Chromium plated reversible handle bars and fork crown. 6—Large rubber grips and pedals. 7—Three-brace backbone frame. 8—Double strength rear axle. Complete with bell and hub caps. Frame and fork enameled blue; rims of wheels are red, all baked-on enamel. Largest size not mailable.

← BELL

Built of Same Materials as Finest Bicycles

Nickel Plated Parts Are Chromium Plated

$8.98 Postpaid And Up

No Other Mail Order House Sells These

Ball Bearing Wheels and Pedals. Full 1-inch Rubber Tires.

	Front Wheel	Rear Wheels	For Child	Shpg. Wt.	Each
79T8329	12 in.	10 in.	2 to 3 yrs.	Postpaid	$8.98
79T8330	14 in.	12 in.	3 to 4 yrs.	Postpaid	9.89
79T8331	16 in.	14 in.	4 to 6 yrs.	Postpaid	10.89
★79T8341	20 in.	16 in.	6 to 8 yrs.	37 lbs.	

★Unmailable. Shipped by freight.
Prepaid................................. $12.67

THE LATEST MODELS

ALL STEEL PLANES

The Biggest Hit of the Year

An Aeroplane Ride. What a Thrill! Girls and Boys, Here's Your Choice of Three Latest Style Planes. Aren't They Good Looking? Sold by No Other Mail Order House

Designed and built to resemble the large cross country fliers. Closed body type. The two larger sizes have belt that drives the propeller around when plane is in motion. You'll feel comfortable in the large roomy seat and have plenty of room for propelling. Build up your body, and harden your muscles, while enjoying the outdoor air and exercise. Made of heavy gauge auto steel, and the enamel finish is baked on. Strong double disc steel wheels.

Front Axle In Ball Bearing Suspension

U. S. Air Mail Monoplane
Revolving Propeller (Illustrated) For Children 5 to 10 Years
Giant balloon type 10-inch roller bearing front wheels with ¾-inch rubber tires and enameled gray with red bullseye. Plain bearing red enameled 8-inch skid wheel, ⅝-inch rubber tire. Body in gray with red striping, wings red with star decorations. Motor and struts black. Fiber covered seat. Length, over all, 53½ inches. Height, 27½ inches. Wing spread, 30 inches. Shpg. wt., 65 lbs. Prepaid. Include with freight order.
79T8912 . . . . . . **$16.98**

The Army Scout Plane
Revolving Propeller For Kiddies 3 to 7 Years
With 10-inch regular double disc steel front wheels, ⅝-inch rubber tires; 8-inch skid wheel, ½-inch rubber tire. Body is gray striped in red. Propeller, tailpiece and wheels are red. Motor and undergearing black. Length, 45½ in.; wing spread, 30 in. without struts. Shpg. wt., 34 lbs. Prepaid. Include with freight order.
79T8911 . . . **$11.67**

Baby Monoplane
For Tots Up to 4 Years Plain Propeller and Without Imitation Motor
Has 8-in. front wheels and 6-inch skid wheel. All with ½-inch rubber tires. Front axle in ball bearing suspension. Body in red with gray wings. Length, over all, 40 in. Wing spread, 30 in. without struts. Shpg. wt., 30 lbs. Prepaid. Include with freight order.
79T8910 . . . **$8.48**

Just Look at Those New Style Huge Balloon Type 10¼-Inch Roller Bearing Wheels With 1-Inch Rubber Tires. The Finest Toy Autos in the Country

Khaki Covered Dummy Top—Closed Body Type.

You Would Have to Pay ⅓ More Elsewhere.
$2267 AND $1945

Shipped Prepaid. Include With Freight Order.

All steel construction, made by makers of regular auto bodies. No other mail order house sells these. Beautifully finished and far superior to the ordinary toy autos sold. Adjustable pedals for children 5 to 10 years. Baked-on enamel parts. Highly tempered carbon steel springs. Ball bearing rear axle (drive shaft) makes driving a pleasure. Classy lamps and colored side lights; unbreakable windshield with rear view mirror, nickel plated motometer and scuff plates, colored instrument board, spring bumper, horn and fiber covered seat. Size, over all: Length, 46¾ inches; width, 22 inches. Shpg. wt., 100 pounds.

Lincoln DeLuxe
Khaki Covered Dummy Top and Giant Balloon Type Wheels (Illustrated)
Body, hood and wheels enameled red with cream and black striping; fenders and undergearing black.
79T8927 . . . . **$22.67**

Lincoln Sports Model
Same as above, but without dummy top and with riveted type 10⅝-in. diameter wheels with ¾-inch rubber tires. Body and hood enameled green with orange color striping and orange color wheels with green striping.
79T8945 . . . . **$19.45**

$898 Hudson Sport Roadster
Prepaid

Made Exclusively for Sears

Oh, Boy! Does It Pick Up Speed! And No Vibration Either Because It's All Steel. No Wood Parts to Work Loose. Most Parts Riveted at Factory, Eliminating Grief With Bolts and Nuts.

For children 3 to 6 years. Baked-on green enamel finish on body and seat with orange color striping; bullet type headlights to match; black enameled undergearing and bumper. Has 9½-inch diameter double disc steel wheels, enameled orange color with green striping, ½-inch rubber tires. Complete with horn, motometer, adjustable windshield and colored license plate. Length over all, 34 in.; width, 20¾ in. Shpg. wt., 35 lbs. Shipped Prepaid. Include with freight order.
79T8905 . . . . **$8.98**

Original Toy Mack Trucks

$1745 Prepaid

Regular Dump Box

Tell Mother You'll Gladly Haul the Ice or Groceries Every Day With One of These Powerful Macks. It Will Be a Pleasure. This Is the Only Original Toy Mack Truck.

Made from heavy gauge automobile steel. Frame of heavy channel steel. Absolutely no wood parts on these. The steel hood, seat, body and wheels enameled red; fenders, running boards and undergearing are black. All baked-on enamel (not painted). Complete with horn, rustproof hub caps, which do not come off, and colored instrument board. Boy can stand on running board to get into seat.

Tempered Carbon Steel Springs

Large Size Mack Jr.
Many stores sell this as high as $20.00. For children 5 to 10 years. (As illustrated.) Rear axle mounted on ball bearings. Has fenders, running boards and rubber pedals. Size over all, 50x22 inches, with dump box, 18¼x13¾x5 in. Roller bearing 9½-inch double disc steel wheels with ¾-inch rubber tires. Shpg. wt., 76 lbs. Shipped Prepaid. Include with freight order.
79T8941—Prepaid **$17.45**

Baby Mack
Sold as high as $12.00 elsewhere. For the little tots up to 5 years. (Not illustrated.) Similar to above, but without fenders and running boards. Has plain steel pedals and axle. Hood and seat not as fancy as the one shown. Size over all, 44½x19 inches. Dump box, 15x14x5 inches. Plain bearing 8½-inch disc steel wheels, ⅝-inch rubber tires. Shipping weight, 41 pounds. Shipped Prepaid. Include with freight order.
79T8930—Prepaid **$10.98**

The Talk of the Country—The New 1930 Cadillac
No Other Mail Order House Sells It

Compare This With Other Cars Up to $15.00

Made Entirely of Steel by Large Auto Fender Makers.

Ball Bearing Rear Drive Shaft.

$1167 PREPAID

Child Can Stand on Running Board to Get Into Seat

Adjustable pedals to make riding more comfortable for children 3 to 6 years of age.

The springs are of tempered carbon spring steel, not common band iron usually found on other makes. The pedal straps connected to ball bearing rear axle (drive shaft). No friction, nothing to wear out. The shiny parts will not tarnish or discolor, because they are finished with new non-rusting process known as udylite finish. The enameled parts are hard baked in an oven. Will last a long time. Made from heavy gauge automobile steel; not the thin flimsy lightweight sheet steel often found on cars sold by others. Classy, new style windshield, motometer, bullet type headlights, sidelights, bumper, colored instrument board, horn, license plate and hub caps. Wheels are of strong double disc steel, 10 inches in diameter, with high grade ⅝-inch diameter rubber tires. Sides of hood have vents like on large autos. All steel chassis, far superior to old style wood frame. Heavy steel crown fenders and running boards; fiber covered steel seat. Size, 37x20¾ inches. Body, hood and wheels enameled a bright red with orange color panels, black striping; fenders and other parts are black. Shipping weight, 45 pounds. Shipped Prepaid. Include With Freight Order.
79T8903—Prepaid **$11.67**

$648 Postpaid
For Children 3 to 5 Years

Popular Well Built Whippet

Made From Auto Steel
No Wood Parts to Crack or Splinter

A light step on the pedals and away you go far into the lead because of the all steel construction. No friction—no rattling of metal—no wood parts to wear out. Another all steel beauty with a baked-on enamel finish, bright red color body with orange color striping. Eight-inch double disc steel wheels, enameled orange color with green striping, ½-inch rubber tires. Length over all, 32¼ in.; width, 20 in.
79T8904—Postpaid **$6.48**

Complete with bumper, motometer and adjustable pedals.

237

ARCADE CAST IRON TOYS

"They Look Real"

Here is a complete line of toys for girls and boys to choose from. Choose which you would like, and go to your local store. If they do not have them, write us. All are exact miniature reproductions. "They Look Real." In purchasing Arcade Toys be sure and look for the Arcade label.

Made by the

ARCADE MFG. CO.

Freeport, Illinois, U. S. A.

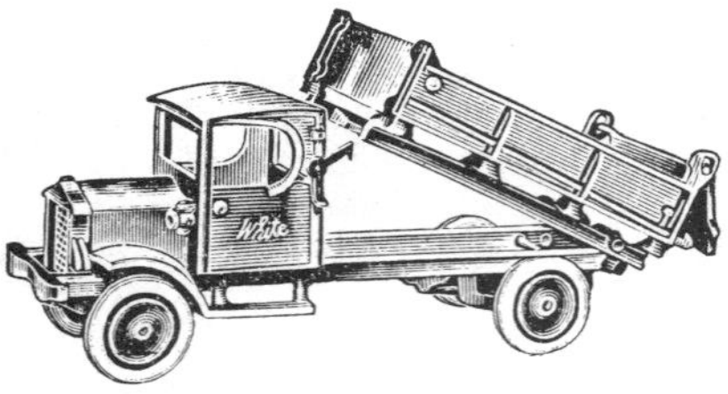

No. 249 WHITE DUMP TRUCK

The truck actually dumps and back door opens. Length 11½ inches, width 4½ inches, height 5¼ inches. Black hood with red body.

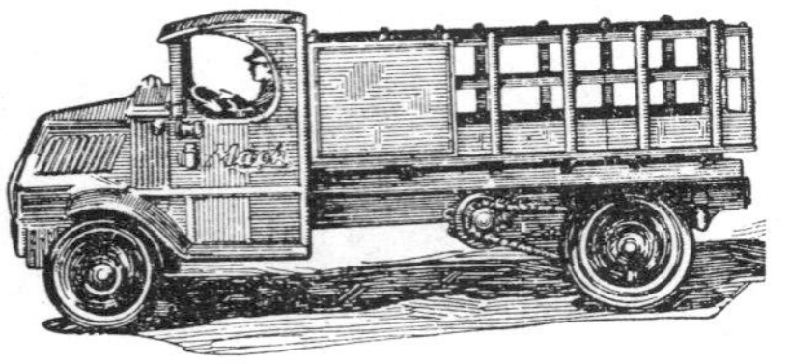

Nos. 246 X and 253 X
MACK STAKE BODY TRUCK

This good looking Mack Stake Truck is now made in two sizes and finished in assorted colors. No. 246, Length 12 inches, width 4¼ inches, height 4⅝ inches. No. 253, Length 8¾ inches, width 3 inches, height 3¾ inches.

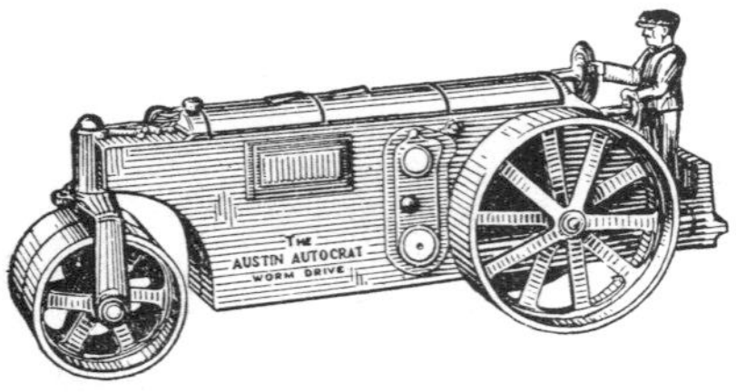

No. 291 AUSTIN AUTOCRAT ROAD ROLLER
No. 291-287 COMBINATION ROAD ROLLER AND SCRAPER

This realistic road roller is grey with green wheels. Length 7¾ inches, height 3¼ inches, width 2¾ inches. The 291-287 includes a scraper that fastens on behind the roller.

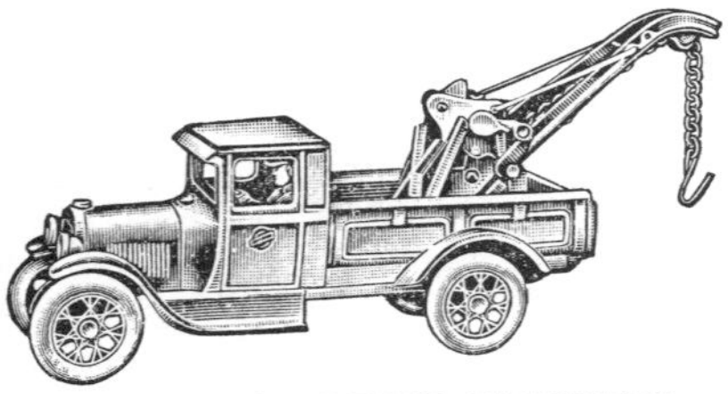

Nos. 215 and 217 FORD WRECKERS

The Toy Wrecker is now made in two sizes: No. 215, Length 8¼ inches, width 3¼ inches, height 5¾ inches. No. 217, Length 7⅜ inches, width 3⅜ inches, height 2⅝ inches. Attractively painted red with green crane.

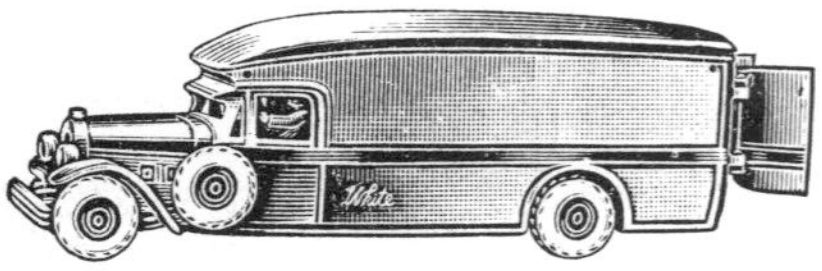

No. 251 WHITE MOVING VAN

A real miniature van with ample space in back. Body trimmed in red. Length, 13½ inches, width 4 inches, height 4¾ inches.

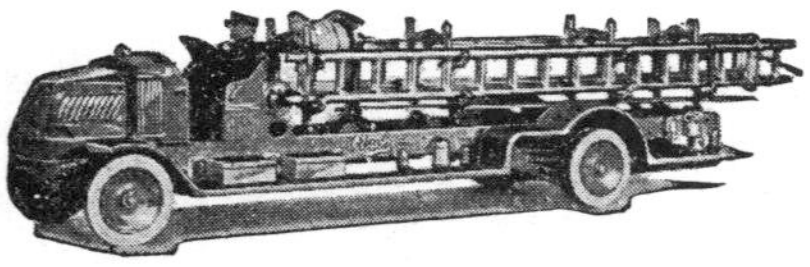

No. 242 MACK FIRE APPARATUS TRUCK

Removable ladders, a fire bell, driver and artificial hose. A real miniature fire engine with gilded ladders and nickeled racks. 21 inches long, 4½ inches wide and 3¾ inches high.

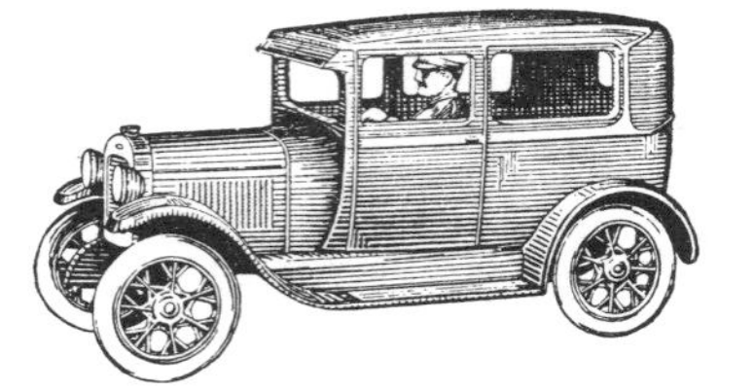

No. 108 TOY FORD TUDOR

A reproduction of the Model A Tudor attractively finished in assorted colors of red, green or blue. Height 6¾ inches, width 3½ inches, height 3½ inches.

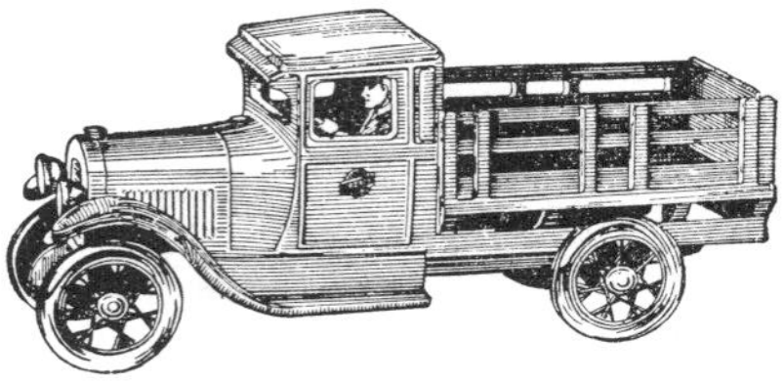

No. 206X FORD STAKE TRUCK

Even a new 1928 Tiny Ford Stake Truck finished in assorted colors of red, green and blue. Length 8 inches, width 3 inches, height 3⅜ inches.

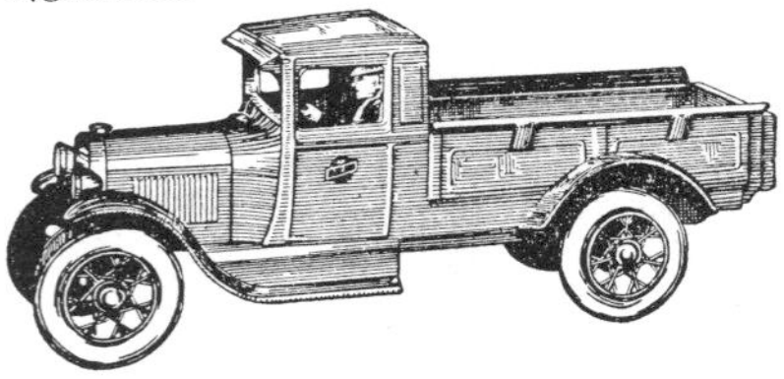

No. 207X EXPRESS TRUCK

A Model A miniature Ford Express Truck finished in assorted colors—red, green and blue. Length 8 inches, width 3 inches, height 3⅜ inches.

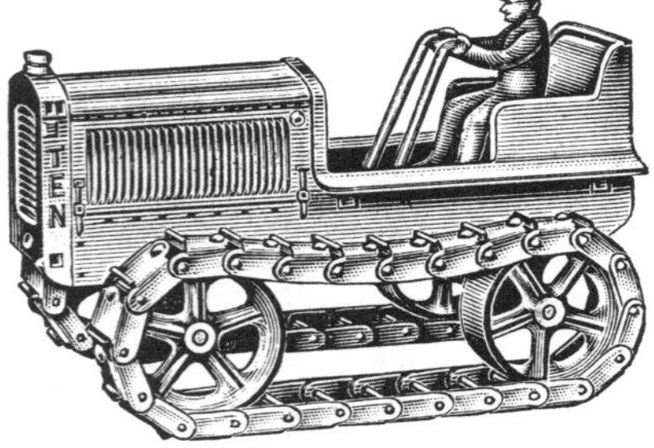

No. 271 CATERPILLAR TRACTOR

Length 7½ inches, width 4½ inches, height 5¼ inches, width of track 1⅛ inches. Makes a wonderful pull toy and works just like the real caterpillar tractor by that name.

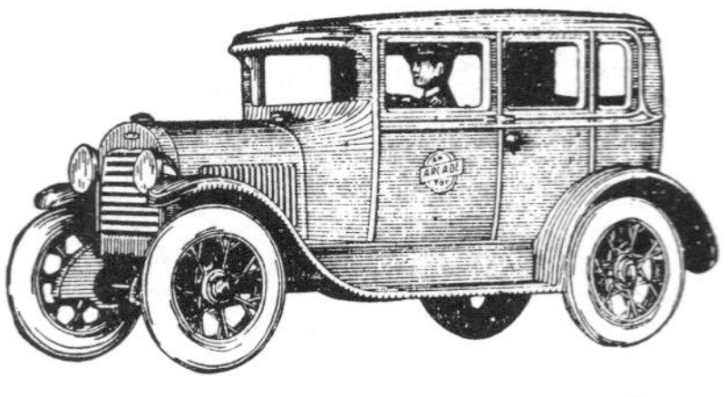

No. 107X FORD FORDOR SEDAN

A remarkable likeness of the real Model A Ford Fordor Sedan for every child. Length 6¾ inches, width 3⅜ inches, height 3½ inches. Furnished in red, green and blue.

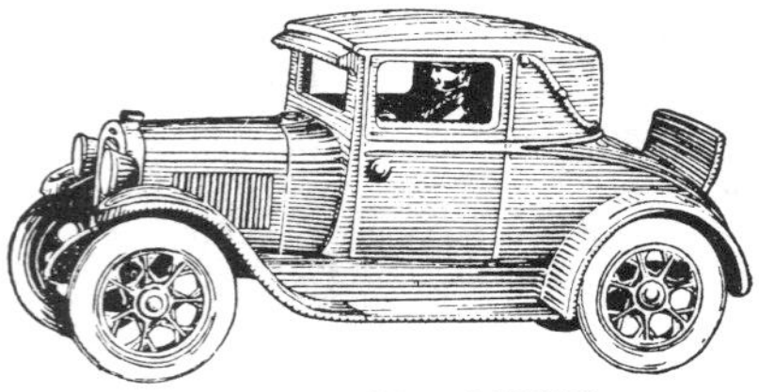

No. 106X FORD COUPE

A miniature reproduction of the new 1928 Ford Coupe with rumble seat. Length 6¾ inches, width 3⅜ inches, height 3½ inches. Furnished in red, green and blue.

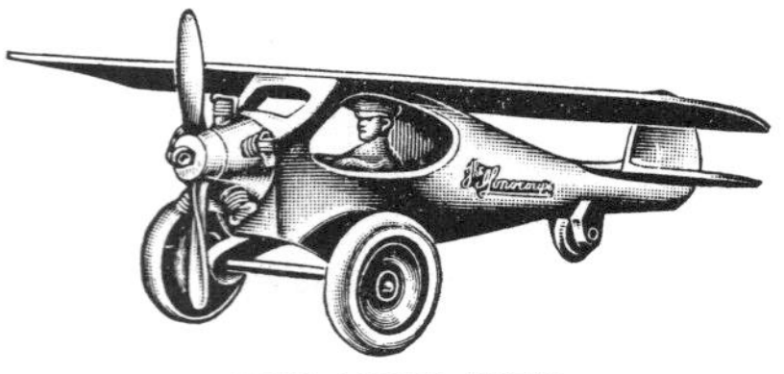

TOY AIRPLANES

The Toy Arcade Airplanes are furnished in four sizes, retailing at 15, 25, 50 and $1.00. They are modeled directly after the real Monocoupe airplane.

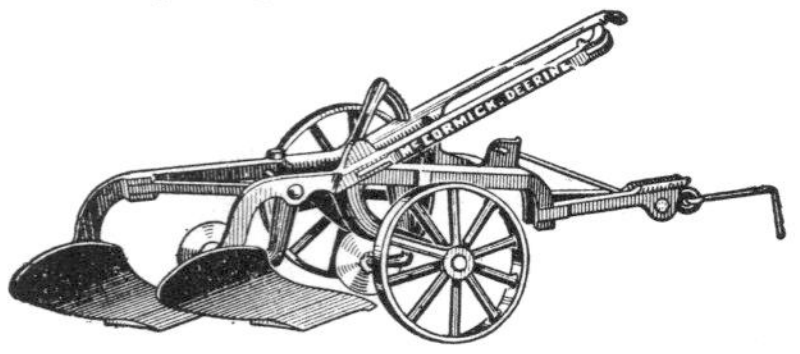

No. 283 McCORMICK-DEERING PLOW

Length 7¾ inches, width 3⅞ inches, height 2⅞ inches. Finished with red frame, yellow wheels and aluminum bronze plow shares and wheel discs.

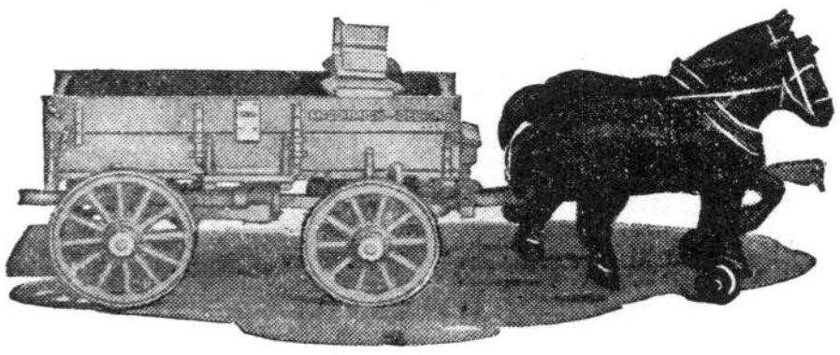

No. 404-1 TOY McCORMICK-DEERING WEBER WAGON

Length of Wagon 6¼ inches, length overall 12⅛ inches, 3⅝ inches wide, 4⅛ inches high Finished in green with red wheels and gear, gold lettering and jet black removable horses.

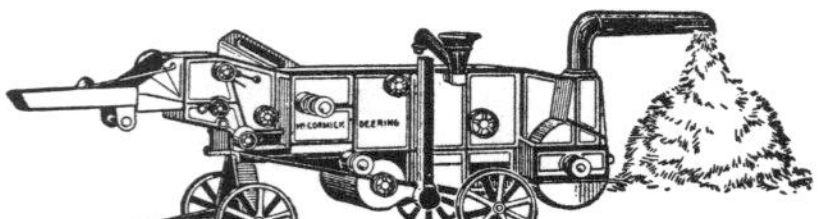

No. 451 McCORMICK-DEERING THRESHER

The toy Threshing Machine, length overall is 12 inches, width 3¾ inches, height 4½ inches. Total length with feeder and stacker extended is 18 inches. Finished in grey trimmed in red with cream colored wheels.

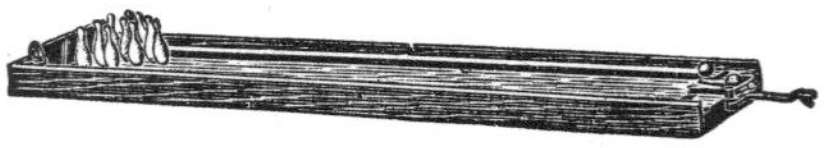

No. 871 BOWLING ALLEY

Board is 40 inches long and 7½ inches wide. Made of first-class hardwood, and attractively finished in high grade varnish.

No. 255 MACK WRECKER

This large size wrecker actually works. The body is red trimmed in yellow and the wrecker is green with nickel parts. Furnished with a tow chain. Length 12½ inches, width 4 inches, height 6⅛ inches.

No. 344 ASSORTMENT

Consists of a No. 221 Wrecker, No. 118B Ford Tudor Sedan, blue, No. 208G Ford Stake Truck and No. 220 Ford Dump Truck.

No. 219X TOY FORD DUMP TRUCK

Actually dumps. Has red chassis and green dump body. Length 7½ inches, width 2¾ inches, height 3⅛ inches. Nickel plated imitation wire wheels.

No. 223X MACK DUMP TRUCK
(Body Hoisted)

Length 12 inches, width 4 inches, height 5⅜ inches. Can be furnished in light blue, grey or red.

No. 241 MACK TANK TRUCK

A Tank Truck that actually holds water with a hose outlet just like a real truck. Finished in red and trimmed in gold. Length 12¾ inches, width 4¾ inches, height 5⅜ inches.

No. 525 BOTTLE JACK SETS

Two 1¾ inch colored balls and 25 assorted jack stones, red, blue, and nickel. An attractive bottle with a beautifully lithographed top.

No. 471 TOY PILE DRIVER

A unique little pile driver that actually works. Length 10½ inches, width 3½ inches, height 11¾ inches. Red with green hoist and nickeled weight.

No. 402 McCORMICK-DEERING SPREADER

This toy spreader looks real and acts real with gears that turn with the wheels. Length 15 inches overall, length of wagon box 9 inches, width 3⅝ inches, height 3 inches.

No. 568 LAWN MOWER

A miniature of a real lawn mower. Wheels and cutter revolve. Length 26½ inches, width 8½ inches. Finished in red, green and gold.

No. 252 WHITE DELIVERY

A modern 6-wheel delivery truck furnished in assorted colors. Length 8¼ inches, width 3 inches, height 3¼ inches.

No. 279 TOY FARMALL TRACTOR

Length 6 inches, width 4⅜ inches, height 4⅝ inches. Lug wheels. Finished with green body, red wheels and nickeled man.

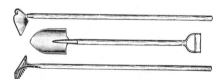

No. 556 GARDEN SET

A new, heavy Garden Set that will stand actual digging. The hoe is 36 inches long, the shovel 31½ inches long, and the rake 37 inches long. Each handle is a different color.

No. 275-286 TRACTOR AND TRAILER

This is an especially good combination in as much as the trailer will hold small articles. Length over all, 12½ inches, width 3¼ inches, height 4¼ inches.

Nos. 275, 274 and 273 FORDSON TRACTORS

These real looking tractors are made in three sizes and many different finishes. Grey, or green with red wheels; Green with red wheels, and Green with nickel wheels.

The Finest and Strongest Steel Toys For The Money!
"STRUCTO" IMPROVED STEEL TOYS

Sales are increasing every year! These flashy miniatures of REAL THINGS are being constantly improved to accurately represent real, living models! Built of heavier gauge steel than any similar toys of comparative prices...."To Last a Playtime Age". All joints are electrically spot welded. Automobile enamel finish.

Dump truck, 17½x6x6, red body and disc wheels, steel balloon tires, levers raise and lower body, 90 degree (dumping action) swing.
1F-2297—½ doz. in pkg. **Doz $8.00**

Speed Wagon, 17x6x6, green body, red disc wheels, steel balloon tires, drop tail gate with chain and latch, "Speed Wagon" decal.
1F-2224—½ doz. in box. **Doz $8.00**

Police patrol, 16½x6x6¾, blue body, red disc wheels, steel balloon tires, rear step with hand rails, inside seat, "Police Patrol" decal.
1F-2238—½ doz. in box. **Doz $8.00**

Mfrs 428
U. S. Mail Truck, 17x6x6¾, green body, openwork sides, drop tail gate with chains, disc wheels, steel balloon tires, "U. S. Mail" decal.
1F-2248—½ doz. in box. **Doz $8.00**

Steam shovel, 18¾x6x13, red & black, revolving engine house, crank lever automatically opens and closes bucket.
1F-2234—½ doz. in box. **Doz $8.00**

Fire patrol, 18x6x5¾, red, side seats, rear step and hand rails, brass bell, disc wheels, steel balloon tires.
1F-2225—½ doz. in pkg. **Doz $8.50**

Grab bucket crane, 14x6x15, red & black, revolving engine house, crank lever automatically opens and closes bucket.
1F-2235—½ doz. in box. **Doz $8.00**

Pile driver, 8x4 platform, 12½ in. tower, revolving engine house, 3-color enameled, copper finish crank, wood pulleys.
1F-2237—½ doz. in box. **Doz $8.00**

Mfrs 410
Moving van, 17x6x6¾ in., yellow, drop tail gate with chains, disc wheels, steel balloon tires.
1F-2227—½ doz. in box. **Doz $8.00**

U. S. Army truck, 17x6x9, green, removable canvas top with uprights, disc wheels, steel balloon tires, drop tail gate with latch.
1F-2228—1 in pkg ..... **Each $1.00**

Giant steam shovel, 22⅜x7x15½, red & black, revolving engine house, crank lever automatically opens and closes bucket.
1F-2242—1 in box. **Each $1.25**

Hook & ladder, 24x6x7¼, red, reel with imitation hose and brass nozzle, brass bell, 4-section 6 ft. extension ladder, disc wheels, steel balloon tires.
1F-2243—1 in box. **Each $1.35**

Air mail transport, extreme length 24 in., green, 8¾x5½ tractor with 4 disc wheels, steel balloon tires, 11x5 van trailer, with 2 disc wheel latticed sides, drop tail gate with chain, star decal.
1F-2300—1 in box. **Each $1.35**

Whippet war tank, 12 in. long, 3-color enameled, strong wheel geared spring motor, propelled tank under its own power, "safety" brake keeps spring from winding too tight.
1F-2245—1 in box. **Each $1.85**

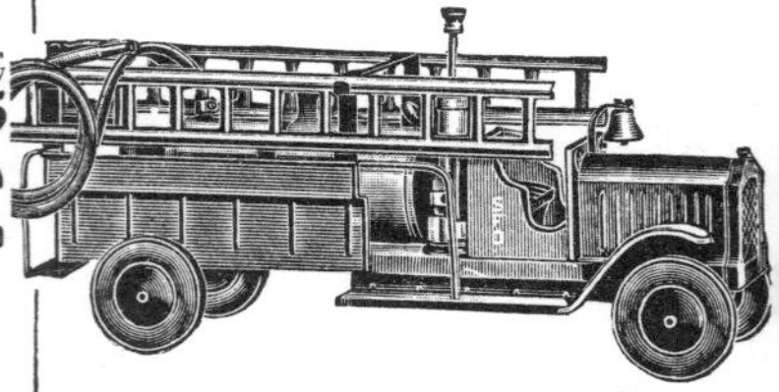

Shoots Water 30 Ft.
Pumping fire engine, 21x6x8, red body, 4-section 6 ft. black enameled extension ladder, brass bell, radiator, hub and tank caps, pump, 8 in. yellow water tank, 43 in. hose with brass nozzle, gilt rail with rear step, disc wheels, steel balloon tires. **Pump action will shoot stream of water 30 ft.**
1F-2229—1 in carton ...... **Each $3.25**

Tractor, trailer & scraper, extreme length 24 in., red & orange, spoke wheels on trailer and scraper, chain tread tractor with driver.
1F-2263—1 in box.... **Each $2.17**

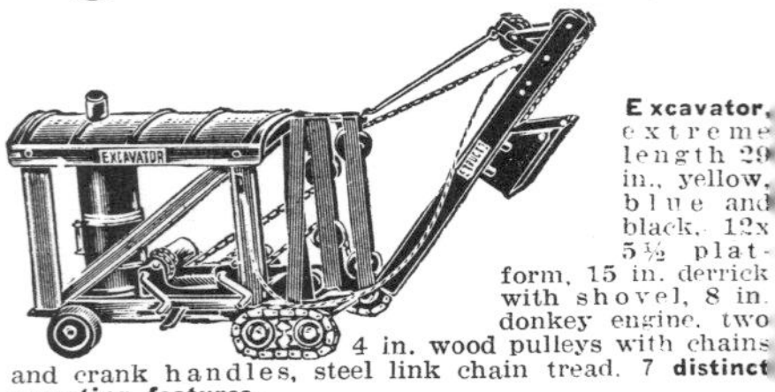

Excavator, extreme length 20 in., yellow, blue and black, 12x5½ platform, 15 in. derrick with shovel, 8 in. donkey engine, two 4 in. wood pulleys with chains and crank handles, steel link chain tread. 7 distinct operating features.
1F-2252—1 in box .... **Each $3.35**

Tractor, 12½x7x6¾ in., red, blue and orange, powerful triple unit motor, metal chain tread, ratchet lever wind, climbs with ease over difficult obstacles.
1F-2254—1 in box .... **Each $3.35**

---

72 In. Long! 17 In. High! 10 In. Wide!

The biggest and showiest toy ever offered for the money. Just the thing to use as the center of attraction for your display of these big steel toys. We haven't seen anything to equal this value anywhere!

Dump truck, sand hopper, conveyor & loader, 2-color enameled, 72 in. long, 17 in. high, 10 in. wide, collects and dumps sand into hopper, moves it by conveyor to bins to be screened and separated, very heavy construction, patented steel link chain and dumping device.
1F-2249—1 in carton..................... **Each $3.35**

"SON-NY" HEAVY DUTY STEEL TOYS
Interesting and sturdily constructed toys of heavy gauge steel, bright enamel finishes, disc wheels, imitation balloon tires, steering front wheels.

Dump truck, 26 in. long, orange with black trim, drop end, lever for raising body.
1F-2526—1 in carton.............. **Each $2.00**

Green enameled (except 1F-2549 orange) with black trim, drop tail piece with brassed chain. 1 in carton.
1F-2549—Moving Van, 26 in. long.......⎫
1F-2555—Parcel post truck, 25½ in. long....⎬ **Each $2.50**
1F-2562—Railway express. truck, 26 in. long.⎭

U. S. anti-aircraft truck, 24x8 truck, 12 in. anti-aircraft gun on turning platform with levers for raising, lowering and revolving, khaki enameled, blue & white insignia, removable rubber tires, 8 rubber tipped wood shells.
1F-2496—1 in carton.............. **Each $3.25**

240

"KEYSTONE" HEAVY DUTY STEEL TOYS

Widely known and extensively advertised heavy duty steel toys that are famous for QUALITY . . . . STRENGTH and FINISH! We present here only the proven best sellers together with the new creations . . . . . all of which incorporate many exclusive "Keystone" features. Made of automobile body steel with baked-on enamel finish. Disc wheels, fully equipped. 4-wheel models have steering front wheels.

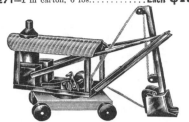

Airplane, 25 in. long 24 in. wing spread, red and drab, 8 in. revolving propeller, imit. 8-cylinder motor, **ratchet noise maker**, rubber tires, windows, strong pull rope, each in carton, k. d., with 2 bolts for easy assembling.
1F-2271—1 in carton, 6 lbs. . . . . **Each $1.80**

Steam Shovel, 20¾x13½x6½, black with red trim, 12 in. derrick.
1F-2489—1 in carton, 10 lbs. . . . . **Each $2.10**

Mfrs 47—With 16½ In. Extension Arm
Steam Shovel, 20¾x14¼x6½, black with red trim, 16½ in. extension arm, 14 in. derrick, shovel **raised and extended** by turning crank, lowered by pressing lever, opened by pulling string.
1F-2494—1 in carton, 11 lbs. . . . . **Each $2.85**

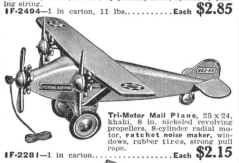

Tri-Motor Mail Plane, 25 x 24, khaki, 8 in. nickeled revolving propellers, 8-cylinder radial motor, **ratchet noise maker**, windows, rubber tires, strong pull rope.
1F-2281—1 in carton. . . . . **Each $2.15**

Dump truck, 26x12, black body, drop end with **chute door**, nickeled headlights and radiator cap. lifting lever for raising body, red wheels, balloon type rubber tires.
1F-2272—1 in carton, 13 lbs. . . . . **Each $3.20**

Truck loader, 20¼x17¾ x4½, green with red & black trim, 10 buckets.
1F-2266—1 in box, 13 lbs. . . . . **Each $3.25**

Can be used with the Locomotive. Has lifting crane that swings around. Lifts considerable weight with little effort.

Railroad wrecker, 20¾ x 23 black body, green revolving lifting crane with hook, heavy rope, nickeled crank gears, folding crank handle. red wheels, balloon type rubber tires.
1F-2284—1 in carton, 11 lbs. . . . . **Each $3.75**

Dump truck, 26x10½x8¼, black with red trim, balloon type rubber tires, drop end with chute door, signal arm, **crank and worm gear raises body.**
1F-2260—1 in carton. 15 lbs. . . . . **Each $3.75**

U. S. Army truck, 26x11½x7¾, khaki, balloon type rubber tires, drop tail piece, heavy canvas top.
1F-2269—1 in carton, 13 lbs. . . . . **Each $3.90**

American Railway Express, 26x10½x7½, green with black & red trim, balloon type rubber tires, signal arm, doors with lock and key, 4 miniature mail pouches.
1F-2259—1 in carton. . . . . **Each $4.25**

Mfrs 51
Police patrol, 27½x11½x7½, black with red trim, balloon type rubber tires, 2 full length seats inside, brass railing, signal arm.
1F-2261—1 in carton, 18 lbs. . . . . **Each $4.25**

Mfrs 45
U. S. Mail truck, 26x11½x7½, green with black & red trim, balloon type rubber tires, signal arm, doors with lock and key, 4 miniature mail pouches.
1F-2262—1 in carton, 17 lbs. . . . . **Each $4.50**

Moving van, 26½x11½x7½, red with black trim, balloon type rubber tires, doors with lock and key.
1F-2258—1 in carton, 18 lbs. . . . . **Each $4.25**

Steam roller, 20x12½, red & black, extra heavy roller, steering rear wheel controls front roller, air pressure whistle, brass bell, will sustain wt. of 150 lbs.
1F-2273—1 in carton, 14 lbs. . . . . **Each $4.25**

Wrecker, 27x22¾ (when crane is lifted), red with black trim, solid rubber tires, nickeled crank gears and folding crank, brass rails, lifts 100 lbs.
1F-2276—1 in carton, 16 lbs. . . . . **Each $4.75**

Ambulance, 27½x11½, khaki, khaki canvas curtains, snap fasteners, brass rails, signal arm, white flag with green cross, solid rubber tires.
1F-2277—1 in carton, 17 lbs. . . . . **Each $5.10**

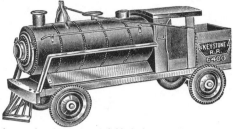

Locomotive, 28x12½, red & black, brass bell, steam dome and railing, coupling pin, rubber tires.
1F-2278—1 in carton, 16½ lbs. . . . . **Each $5.50**

Hydraulic dump truck, 27x10¼x8, black, balloon type rubber tires, **steering front wheels**, brass compress air tank (pressure produced by turning front crank), body automatically lowered by pressing lever lifts 200 lbs.
1F-2270—1 in carton. . . . . **Each $4.50**

Water pump engine, 27½x10¾x8½, red body, 7x4¼ brass water tank, pressure pump operated by front crank, brass railings extension ladders (extend to 5 ft.) rubber hose with brass nozzle, brass bell, hose reel, balloon type rubber tires. **Shoots water from 25 to 35 ft.**
1F-2539—1 in carton, 19 lbs. . . . . **Each $6.85**

Ladder extends to 51 in.

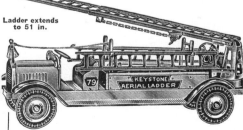

Aerial ladder truck, 30½x10¾x8½, red body, nickeled ladders (extend to 51 in.), chain drive extension, 2 extra 15 in. red ladders. brass bell, aluminum covered running board, solid rubber tires.
1F-2279—1 in carton, 21 lbs. . . . . **Each $7.00**

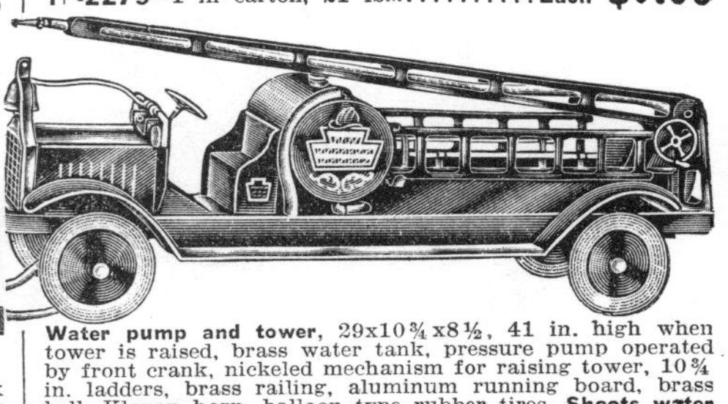

Water pump and tower, 29x10¾x8½, 41 in. high when tower is raised, brass water tank, pressure pump operated by front crank, nickeled mechanism for raising tower, 10¾ in. ladders, brass railing, aluminum running board, brass bell, Klaxon horn, balloon type rubber tires. **Shoots water 25 to 35 ft.**
1F-2544—1 in carton, 21½ lbs. . . . . **Each $8.15**

American-National-Automobiles

THE LINE BEAUTIFUL...exactingly modeled after real cars and enamel finished in flashy color combinations. The quality of these vehicles has won instant approval wherever shown...and the many distinctive sales features built into them assure you the lasting good will of your customers. All have ADJUSTABLE PEDALS.

1F-820—1 in carton, 22 lbs...........Each **$3.25**
"WHIPPET"—Extreme length 32 in., American red enameled, blue & yellow trim, yellow number. 8 in. red enameled double spoke wire wheels, ⅜ in. rubber tires. EQUIPMENT—Cast steering wheel, gas lever, motor-meter, steel pedals.

1F-824—1 in carton, 26 lbs...........Each **$4.50**
"DODGE"—Extreme length 35 in., American red enameled, chrome yellow trim, 10 in. double spoke wire wheels, ⅜ in. rubber tires. EQUIPMENT—Cast steering wheel, gas lever, motor-meter, bumper, steel pedals.

1F-826—1 in carton, 33 lbs...........Each **$5.25**
"ACE"—Extreme length 35 in., Paradise green enameled, red & black trim, 10 in. double disc wheels, ½ in. rubber tires. EQUIPMENT—Cast steering wheel, gas lever, motor-meter, bumper, **rubber** pedals.

1F-834—1 in carton, 37 lbs...........Each **$7.25**
"GRAHAM"—Extreme length 35 in., lichen gray, forest green & yellow stripings, 10 in. matched double disc wheels, **1 in.** auto tread rubber **tires, spring chassis.** EQUIPMENT—Cast steering wheel, gas lever, **horn**, **nickeled** motor-meter, bumper, metal headlights, license plate, rubber pedals, oil can, oil.

1F-827—1 in carton, 37 lbs...........Each **$8.25**
"ESSEX"—Extreme length 35 in., chrome yellow enameled, blue trim, red stripes, 10 in. matched double disc wheels, **1 in.** auto tread rubber tires, spring chassis. EQUIPMENT—Cast steering wheel, gas lever, **adjustable windshield**, horn, nickeled motor-meter, gear shift ball, bumper, metal headlights, license plate, rubber pedals, oil can, oil.

1F-828—1 in carton, 60 lbs...........Each **$9.75**
"HUPMOBILE"—Extra length 38½ in., Bolera cream enameled, red, green & aluminum trim, 10 in. red enameled disc wheels, ½ in. auto tread rubber tires, **worm-gear type** adjustable steering post, spring chassis. EQUIPMENT—Cast steering wheel, gas lever, adjustable windshield, nickeled motor-meter, bumper, metal headlights, license plate, **attached fenders & running board**, rubber pedals, oil can, oil.

1F-829—1 in crate, 70 lbs...........Each **$11.50**
"FLINT"—Extreme length 41 in., old rose enameled, forest green trim, yellow stripes, 10 in. **balloon type** matched disc wheels, ¾ in. auto tread rubber tires, **worm-gear type** adjustable steering post, spring chassis. EQUIPMENT—Composition steering wheel, gas lever, nickeled adjustable windshield, nickeled motor-meter, gear shift with glass onyx ball, bumper, metal headlights, license plate, attached fenders & running board, rubber pedals, oil can, oil.

1F-830—1 in crate, 68 lbs...........Each **$12.95**
"NASH"—Extreme length 38½ in., Derby red enameled, cream stripes, 2-tone matched fenders, 10 in. cream enameled heavy wire wheels, auto type, 1¼ in. auto tread rubber tires, **worm-gear type adjustable** steering post, spring chassis. EQUIPMENT—Composition steering wheel, gas lever, nickeled adjustable windshield, horn, nickeled motor-meter, metal headlights, license plate, attached fenders & running boards, rubber pedals, oil can, oil.

Electric Headlights and Battery

1F-831—1 in carton, 77 lbs...........Each **$14.50**
"MASTER SIX"—Extreme length 41½ in., Chrysler blue enameled, dark blue & cream trim, 10 in. cream enameled balloon disc wheels with blue stripes, **1 in.** auto tread rubber tires, worm-gear type adjustable steering post, spring chassis. EQUIPMENT—Composition steering wheel, gas lever, instrument board, adjustable windshield, horn, nickeled motor-meter, gear shift ball, bumper, **electric metal headlights, dry cell battery**, license plate, **upholstered seat**, attached fenders and running board, rubber pedals, oil can, oil.

1F-832—1 in wire bound box, 87 lbs. Each **$16.75**
"OLDSMOBILE" — Extreme length 46 in., Bolera cream and blue enameled, red trim, blue stripes, aluminum radiator band, 10 in. balloon disc wheels, **1 in.** auto tread rubber tires, worm-gear type adjustable steering post, spring chassis. EQUIPMENT—Cast steering wheel, gas-lever, instrument board, nickeled adjustable windshield, **spot-light**, horn, **motor buzzer**, glass onyx gear shift ball, nickeled motor-meter, bumper, metal headlights, license plate, upholstered seat, attached fenders and running board, rubber pedals, oil can, oil.

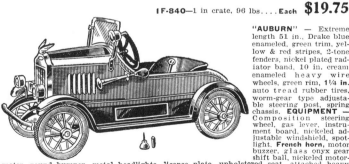

1F-840—1 in crate, 96 lbs....Each **$19.75**
"AUBURN" — Extreme length 51 in., Drake blue enameled, green trim, yellow & red stripes, 2-tone nickel plated radiator band, 10 in. cream enameled heavy wire wheels, green rim, 1¼ in. auto tread rubber tires, worm-gear type adjustable steering post, spring chassis. EQUIPMENT—Composition steering wheel, gas lever, instrument board, nickeled adjustable windshield, spotlight, **French horn**, motor buzzer, glass onyx gear shift ball, nickeled motor-meter, round bumper, metal headlights, license plate, upholstered seat, attached heavy "die-form" fenders, running board, rubbr pedals, oil can, oil.

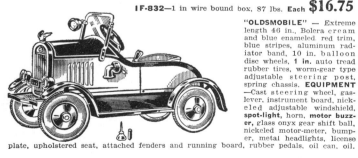

1F-841—1 in crate, 115 lbs....Each **$23.50**
"STUDEBAKER" — Extreme length 54 in., Ottawa tan and amber enameled, green trim, yellow stripes, aluminum radiator band and bead, amber enameled attached fenders, **12 in. roller bearing** balloon type matched disc wheels, 1 in. auto tread rubber tires, worm-gear type adjustable steering post, **full** spring chassis. EQUIPMENT — Composition steering wheel, gas lever, instrument board, nickeled adjustable windshield, **running board spot-light,** French horn, motor buzzer, glass onyx gear shift ball, nickeled motor-meter, round bumper, metal headlights, license plate, attached fenders, rubber pedals, oil can, oil.

1F-856—1 in crate, 130 lbs.
Each **$28.75**
"PACKARD" — Extreme length 51 in., Chinese blue enameled, green, red & yellow stripes and trim, aluminum band and bead, green enameled fenders, 12 in. **roller bearing** balloon type disc wheels, 1 in. rubber tires, **full** spring chassis. EQUIPMENT — Tilting composition steering wheel, gas and spark levers, instrument board, nickeled adjustable windshield, side wings, **rear view mirror**, spotlight, French horn, motor buzzer, gear shift, nickeled motor-meter and radiator, round bumper, metal headlights, license plate, **upholstered seat**, stationary hood, heavy "die-form" fenders, running board, **trunk**, rubber pedals, tool box with tools. "Alemite" system, "Stop and Go" signal.

"AMERICAN-NATIONAL" DUMP TRUCKS

End gate automatically opens and closes when box is raised or lowered by steel lever. Each with adjustable pedals. Sturdy trucks that are finding a tremendous and fast growing market. Sturdily made to withstand rough play. Children like these because they are so realistic.

IF-857—1 in wire bound box, 80 lbs.
Each $8.25

"JUNIOR"—Extreme length 44 in., American red enameled body, black & yellow trim, black enameled dump box, 10 in. red enameled double disc wheels, ½ in. rubber tires. EQUIPMENT — Composition steering wheel, gas lever, horn, license plate, bumper, rubber pedals.

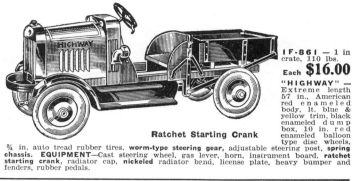

IF-858—1 in crate, 65 lbs.
Each $10.50

"SPEED"—Extreme length 44 in., Larchmont blue enameled body, red black & yellow trim, black enameled dump box, 10 in. red enameled disc wheels, auto tread 1 in. rubber tires. EQUIPMENT — Composition steering wheel, worm-gear type, adjustable steering post, gas lever, horn, radiator cap, bumper, front fenders, running board, rubber pedals.

IF-859—1 in crate, 90 lbs...................................**Each $12.75**

"ROAD KING" — Extreme length 57 in., Arctic green enameled body, dk. green & yellow trim, green enameled dump box, 10 in. dk. green enameled balloon type disc wheels, ¾ in. auto tread rubber tires. EQUIPMENT—Cast steering wheel, lever radiator cap, license plate, bumper, rubber pedals, oil can, oil.

IF-861 — 1 in crate, 110 lbs.
Each $16.00

"HIGHWAY" — Extreme length 57 in., American red enameled body, lt. blue & yellow trim, black enameled dump box, 10 in. red enameled balloon type disc wheels, ¾ in. auto tread rubber tires, **worm-type steering gear**, adjustable steering post, **spring chassis**. EQUIPMENT—Cast steering wheel, gas lever, horn, instrument board, **ratchet starting crank**, radiator cap, **nickeled** radiator bend, license plate, heavy bumper and fenders, rubber pedals.

Ratchet Starting Crank

"AMERICAN-NATIONAL" FIRE DEPARTMENT AUTOS

Possess all the features of merit long associated with the name "American-National". Unusually flashy in design, color and trim. Each equipped with spring chassis, bumpers, adjustable rubber pedals, gas levers, nickeled bells with cords, metal headlights, gear shift, oil can and oil.

IF-875—1 in carton, 36 lbs.
Each $7.50

"CHIEF"—Extreme length 34 in., red enameled, yellow trim, 10 in. red enameled double disc steel wheels, ½ in. rubber tires. EQUIPMENT—Rear spring, steel seat.

IF-877—1 in wire bound box, 79 lbs.
Each $11.00

"CHIEF"—Extreme length 42 in., red enameled, yellow trim, 10 in. balloon type, red enameled disc wheels, ¾ in. auto tread tires, worm-gear type adjustable steering post. EQUIPMENT — Instrument board, steel radiator front and seat, attached fenders & running board, 2 lanterns.

"AMERICAN-NATIONAL" AEROPLANES

Flashy aeroplanes are selling in increasing volume. Boys and girls are showing more interest in these than ever. Each one is built with the extreme care you expect in a product bearing the name of this celebrated maker....the reason for satisfied customers. THE STEERING MECHANISM AUTOMATICALLY TURNS THE RUDDER.

IF-880—1 in carton, 27 lbs........**Each $5.25**

"ARMY SCOUT"—Extreme length 40½ in., wing spread 24 in., blue enameled, dk. blue & chrome yellow trim, blue enameled double disc wheels, 8 in. front, 6 in. rear, ½ in. rubber tires, ratchet propeller.

IF-882—1 in carton, 30 lbs............**Each $6.75**

"ARCTIC BYRD"—Extreme length 44 in., wing spread 23 in., Bolera cream enameled, red & blue trim, red enameled double disc wheels, front 10 in., rear 7 in., ½ in. rubber tires, extra wide seat, ratchet propeller.

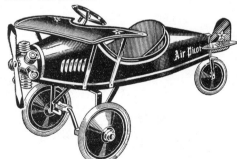

IF-885—1 in carton, 45 lbs...............**Each $8.40**

"AIR PILOT"—Extreme length 51 in., wing spread 30 in., tangerine enameled, sea green & yellow trim, tangerine enameled double disc wheels, 10 in. front, ⅝ in. rubber tires, 7 in. rear, ½ in. rubber tires, ratchet propeller.

Electric Lights

IF-886—1 in carton, 48 lbs...................................**Each $13.25**

"RED WING"—Extreme length 51 in., wing spread 29 in., sea green enameled, red, blue & yellow trim, balloon type **roller bearing** double disc wheels, 10 in. front, ¾ in. auto tread rubber tires, 7 in. rear, ⅝ in. auto tread rubber tire, **electric bullet type front lights**, ratchet propeller.

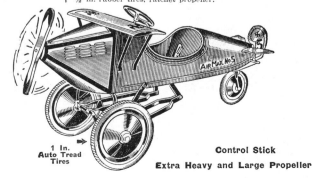

1 In. Auto Tread Tires

Control Stick
Extra Heavy and Large Propeller

IF-894—1 in crate, 105 lbs...................................**Each $15.00**

"AIR MAIL NO. 5"—Extreme length 62 in., wing spread 28 in., red enameled green & yellow trim, control stick, red enameled roller bearing double disc wheels, 12 in. front, 1 in. rubber tires, 7 in. rear, ⅝ in. rubber tire, adjustable pedals.

"CHALLENGE" Velocipedes

JUNIOR VELOCIPEDES

For Tots 2 to 5 Years of Age

Manufactured expressly for us under our exclusive "Challenge" brand. These are tremendous sellers.

Red enameled half oval steel frames, heavy front, fork and shaped handle bars, rubber grips, nickel plated bell, adjustable **leather padded sadd'e**, black coil spring, rubber pedals, tan enameled rim and spoke wheels. **1 in.** auto tread rubber tires. 2 in carton, 40 lbs.

1F-193—11 in. front, 8 in. rear wheels.   **1F-194**—14 in. front, 10 in. rear wheels.

Each **$2.25**   Each **$2.50**

BALL-BEARING Tubular Velocipedes

LOW PRICES...yet size and quality have not been sacrificed. Manufactured exclusively for us and guaranteed both by the manufacturer and ourselves. **Third brace in the rear adds to life of vehicle.** Feature "Challenge" tubular vehicles and cash in. Note **extra size** wheels on the two lowest priced sizes.

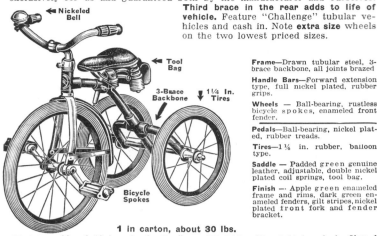

← Nickeled Bell
← Tool Bag
3-Brace Backbone ↓ 1¼ In. Tires
Bicycle Spokes

Frame—Drawn tubular steel, 3-brace backbone, all joints brazed

Handle Bars—Forward extension type, full nickel plated, rubber grips.

Wheels — Ball-bearing, rustless bicycle spokes, enameled front fender.

Pedals—Ball-bearing, nickel plated, rubber treads.

Tires—1¼ in. rubber, balloon type.

Saddle — Padded green genuine leather, adjustable, double nickel plated coil springs, tool bag.

Finish — Apple green enameled frame and rims, dark green enameled fenders, gilt stripes, nickel plated front fork and fender bracket.

1 in carton, about 30 lbs.

1F-211—14 and 10 in. wheels. Small Size.   Each **$6.50**

1F-212—16 and 12 in. wheels. Sizes 3 to 5 yrs.   Each **$7.25**

1F-213—20 and 14 in. wheels. Sizes 4 to 6 yrs.   Each **$8.25**

1F-214—24 and 16 in. wheels. Sizes 5 to 7 yrs.   Each **$9.50**

"CHALLENGE" JUNIOR TUBULAR VELOCIPEDES

Three popular priced numbers in big selling Junior vehicles. Our "Challenge" name plate carries the full guarantee for workmanship and finish, and assures you many satisfied customers. We suggest you feature these Junior sizes because they make a hit wherever shown. Designed especially for kiddies from 2 to 5 years of age.

Red enameled tubular steel frame, strongly welded, rustproof nickel plated handle bars, hub caps, bell and pedal cranks, adjustable **red leather saddle**, black enameled coil spring, **8 in. front and 6 in. rear** red enameled double disc steel wheels, cream striped, **¾ in.** auto tread rubber tires.

1F-232—2 in carton. 19 lbs..........Each **$2.50**

Apple green enameled tubular steel frame, strongly welded, adjustable **green leather padded saddle**, adjustable nickel plated handle bars, rubber grips, bright tin spokes and rims, **11 in. ball bearing front wheel, 8 in.** rear wheels, **¾ in.** rubber tires, rubber pedals, nickeled hub caps and bell.

1F-231—1 in carton, 14 lbs..........Each **$2.95**

Light green enameled tubular steel frame, strongly welded, adjustable **green leather motorcycle type padded saddle**, adjustable nickel plated handle bars, rubber grips, tool bag, **10 in. ball bearing front wheel, 1 in.** auto tread rubber tires, **8 in. roller bearing rear wheels, ¾ in.** auto tread rubber tires, cream enameled, green striped, rubber pedals, nickeled hub caps.

1F-233—1 in carton, 15 lbs...........Each **$3.25**

"CHALLENGE" PEDAL BIKES

We sell carload after carload of these two wonderful values. Priced right and sold under our exclusive "Challenge" trademark.

25 in. long, 18 in. high, black enameled heavy steel frames and curved handle bars, 10½ x7¼ in red enameled shaped seat boards, 11 in. from floor, corrugated rubber grips and pedals, ½ in. rubber tires, nickel plated bell and hub caps. **3 in carton, 30 lbs.**

Wire Spoke Wheels

1F-222—9 in. front wheels, 7 in. rear wheels, heavy black enameled spokes.

Each **$1.35**

Red Disc Wheels

1F-224—Red enameled double disc wheels, 9½ in. front, 7½ in. rear.

Each **$1.50**

"OLYMPIC" PEDAL BIKES

Enameled heavy steel frames, enameled shaped seats, rubber pedals, nickeled bells.

 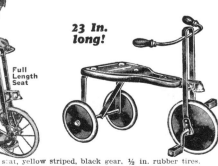

Full Length Seat

23 In. long!

23 in. long. 7½ x15 red seat, yellow striped, black gear, ½ in. rubber tires.

Wire Spoke Wheels

1F-261—9 in. double spoke wire wheels. 2 in carton, 22 lbs.

Each **$1.40**

Red Disc Wheels

1F-262—8 in. front, 6 in. rear, red enameled double disc steel wheels. 2 in carton, 26 lbs.

Each **$1.50**

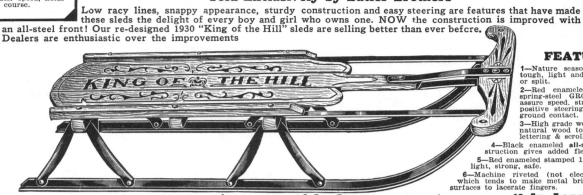

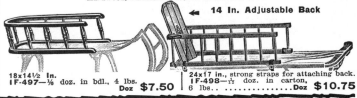
245

America's Finest and Best Selling Miniature Trains!
"AMERICAN FLYER"

First choice of red-blooded American boys....because they most closely approach in miniature that which thrills every boy—REAL TRAINS! "American Flyer" supremacy has been maintained through constant improvement of models and addition of features that make them absolutely modern and faultless. The many exclusive features together with high grade materials, workmanship and finishes are reasons why "American Flyer" sells in increasing numbers year after year!   Put one or two of these trains on display and take orders from samples!

"American Flyer" — WIND-UP TRAINS — "American Flyer"
Transformers Electric Trains Mechanical Trains

Engines are black enameled and have long wearing hardened steel gears. The powerful motor-steel springs cannot come unhooked. Key screws off when turned wrong way.

19 In. Train—60 In. Track

1 F-3210—(Mfrs 732) ½ doz. in box.....Doz **$8.95**
"EMPIRE EXPRESS," 6¼ in. engine, red & black tender, two 4½ in. red passenger cars with green roofs, 60 in. curved track (4 sections)

20 In. Train—90 In. Oval Track

1 F-3226—(Mfrs 733) ½ doz. in box....Doz **$12.00**
"BEAR CAT," 6¼ in. engine, red & black tender, two 5 in. passenger cars, 90 in. curved track (6 sections).

21 In. Train—80 In. Circular Track

1 F-3221—(Mfrs 132) ½ doz. in box...Doz **$14.80**
"THE NIAGARA," 6¼ in. **speed governed** engine with red wheels & tender, piston rods, brake, two 5 in. orange passenger cars, red roofs, 80 in. circular track (8 curved sections).

24½ In. Train—103 In. Oval Track

1 F-3223—(Mfrs 2) ½ doz. in box...................Doz **$20.40**
"PANTHER," 6½ in. **speed governed** engine, **lever brake**, piston rods, tender imitation coal, two 5½ in. cars (baggage car with sliding doors, passenger car), 103 in. oval track (8 curved, 2 straight sections).

20½ In. Train With Semaphore, Station, Tunnel and Danger Signal

1 F-3227—(Mfrs 134) 1 in box...................Each **$1.90**
"QUEEN CITY," 6 in. **speed governed** engine, **lever brake**, red & black tender, two 5 in. orange passenger cars, blue roofs, 90 in. oval track (6 sections). **Lowest priced quality EQUIPPED train made!**

26 In. Train—163 In. Figure 8 Track

1 F-3233—(Mfrs 51) 1 in box..................Each **$2.45**
"VIKING," 7 in. **speed governed** engine, **lever brake**, piston rods, heavy die-cast wheels, large tender, imitation coal and headlight, two 6½ in. blue cars with orange roofs (pullman, observation), 163 in. figure 8 track (14 sections and cross-overs).

26 In. Train—140 In. Double Oval Track

1 F-3234—(Mfrs 6) 1 in box...................Each **$2.75**
"THE PENNSYLVANIAN," 7 in. **speed governed** engine, **lever brake**, piston rods, heavy die-cast wheels, large tender, imitation coal and headlight, two 6½ in. buff cars with orange roofs (pullman, observation), **automatic and manual switches with solid bases**, 140 in. track (10 curved, 2 straight sections).

35 In. Train With Danger and Banjo Signals—120 In. Track

1 F-3240—(Mfrs 18) 1 in box...................Each **$2.75**
"ROCKY MOUNTAIN FREIGHT," 7 in. **speed governed** engine, **lever brake**, piston rods, tender, imitation coal, three 6½ in. cars (sand car, box car with sliding doors, caboose), 120 in. oval track (8 curved, 4 straight sections).

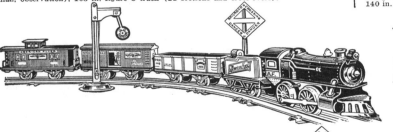

26½ In. Train With Tunnel, Station, Semaphore, Clock, 3 Signals and Crossing Gate—120 In. Track
1 F-3239—(Mfrs 19) 1 in box...Each **$3.35**
"PANAMA LIMITED," 7 in. **speed governed** engine, **lever brake**, piston rods, die-cast wheels, large green tender, red trim, imitation coal and headlight, two 6½ in. green cars, red roofs, (pullman, observation), 120 in. **oval track** (8 curved, 4 straight sections), danger, flashing and banjo signals. **A train outfit that establishes a new standard of train values!**

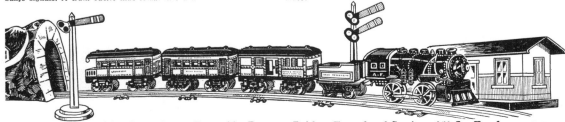

35 In. Train With 2 Semaphores, Turntable, Bumper, Bridge, Tunnel and Station—250 In. Track
1 F-3243—(Mfrs 26) 1 in box...Each **$6.95**
"B B SPECIAL," 7¾ in. **speed governed** engine, **lever brake**, piston rods, tender, three 6¾ in. cars (baggage car with sliding doors, two passenger cars), 250 in. oval track (18 curved and 6 straight sections), 3 automatic switches, 1 single and 1 double arm semaphore.

WIDE GAUGE

Same construction as narrow gauge trains, but operate on 2¼ in. track. The most powerful low voltage miniature electric locomotives built....with 23 outstanding features of merit. All have electric headlights and hand reversing levers. Tracks have binding clips.

48 In. Train—161 In. Track

I F-3361—(Mfrs 1471) 1 in box.............................Each **$13.50**
"THE TRAIL BLAZER," 12 in. red New Haven type locomotive, **two** 14 in. cars (orange sand car, red caboose), 161 in. oval track (8 curved, 2 straight sections).

48 In. Train—161 In. Track

I F-3362—(Mfrs 1472) 1 in box...............................Each **$15.00**
"THE EAGLE," 12 in. victory red New Haven type locomotive, **two** 14 in. 2-tone red cars (pullman, observation), **electrically lighted,** 161 in. oval track (8 curved, 2 straight sections).

61 In. Train With Two Headlights—192 In. Track

I F-3363—(Mfrs 1473) 1 in box..................Each **$19.25**
"THE STATESMAN," 12 in. 2-tone orange New Haven locomotive, 2 headlights, **three** red roof 14 in. cars (2 pullmans, observation), **electrically lighted,** 192 in. oval track (8 curved, 4 straight sections).

63 In. Train Elaborately Brass Trimmed—192 In. Track

I F-3364—(Mfrs 1463) 1 in box....................Each **$19.60**
"THE PATHFINDER," 14 in. red & gray St. Paul type locomotive, 2 electric headlights, **three** 14 in. cars (2-tone blue stock car with sliding doors, orange sand car, victory red caboose), solid brass ladders, journal boxes, railings, etc., 192 in. oval track (8 curved, 4 straight sections).

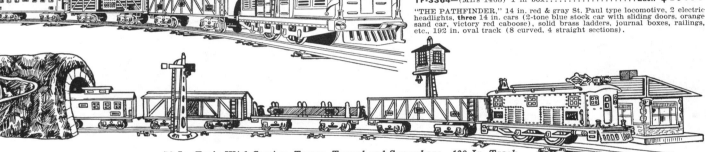

70 In. Train With Station, Tower, Tunnel and Semaphore—120 In. Track

I F-3373—1 in box...Each **$25.00**
"FREIGHT TRAIN," 12¼ in. bright red locomotive, solid brass trim, die-cast headlight, pantograph and bell, **manual control reverse,** three 14 in. cars (emerald green sand car, orange machine car with blue top and sliding door, ivory caboose with brown top), **electrically lighted,** 120 in. oval track (8 curved, 4 straight sections), fuse set, track clips, terminal and wires.

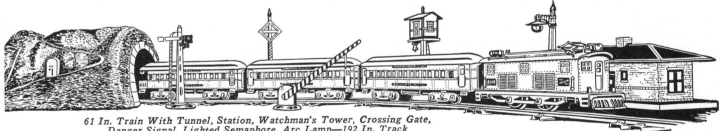

61 In. Train With Tunnel, Station, Watchman's Tower, Crossing Gate, Danger Signal, Lighted Semaphore, Arc Lamp—192 In. Track

I F-3365—(Mfrs 1469) 1 in box.............................Each **$26.25**
"THE FRONTIER TOWN," 12 in. orange New Haven type locomotive, manual reverse, 2 die-cast electric headlights, pantograph and bell, three 14 in. orange cars (2 pullman, 1 observation), **electrically lighted,** 192 in. oval track (8 curved, 4 straight sections).

72 In. Train With REMOTE CONTROL—228 In. Track

I F-3366—(Mfrs 1491) 1 in box.............................Each **$33.25**
"THE IRON MONARCH," 15 in. steam type locomotive, triple action **remote control,** electric headlight, "Vanderbilt" type tender, **three** 14 in. bright red cars (combination club & baggage, pullman, observation), full brass trim, **electrically lighted** interior and platform, 228 in. oval track (8 curved, 6 straight sections).

79 In. Train With Remote Control, Mail Catcher, Automatic Bell, Reversible Headlights—245 In. Track

I F-3378—(Mfrs 1487) 1 in box.............................Each **$36.00**

"THE POCAHONTAS," 79 in. De Luxe train, handsome tan and green finish, 15 in. St. Paul locomotive, **triple action remote control,** solid brass train, **automatic bell,** 2 reversible electric headlights, **four** 14 in. cars (club and mail car with automatic mail bag set, pullman, diner, observation), **electrically lighted** interior and platform, 245 in. oval track (8 curved, 8 straight sections).

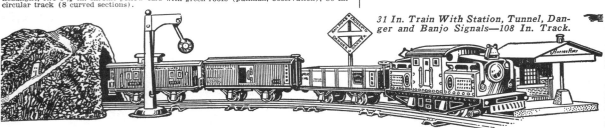
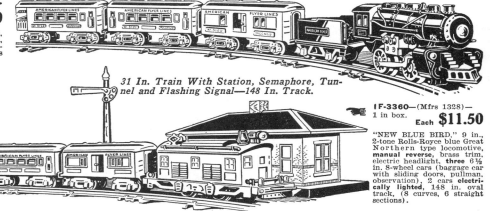

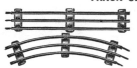

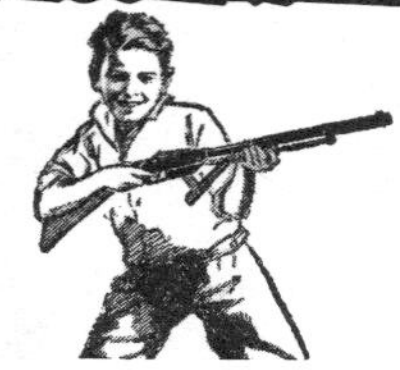

"DAISY" AIR RIFLES

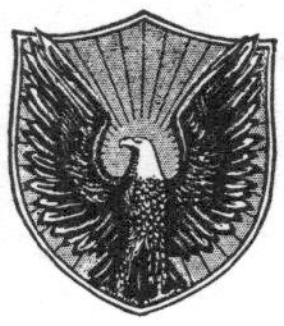

Make a bid for boy business by featuring "Daisy" Air Rifles! Known wherever air rifles are sold because they are advertised in leading boys' and sporting goods magazines. High powered rifles that are made AIR-TIGHT through an elaborate process in manufacture....more accurate than ever. All with walnut stocks.

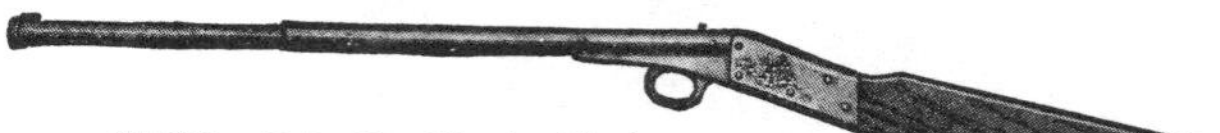

"Little Daisy"—Single Shot

MFRS 20, 29 in. long, single shot, break action, blued finish steel parts.
1F-2631—1/12 doz. in pkg....................**Doz** **$7.20**

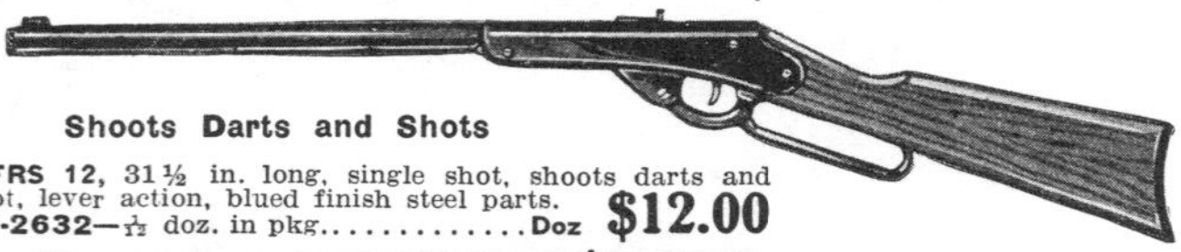

Shoots Darts and Shots

MFRS 12, 31½ in. long, single shot, shoots darts and shot, lever action, blued finish steel parts.
1F-2632—1/12 doz. in pkg............**Doz** **$12.00**

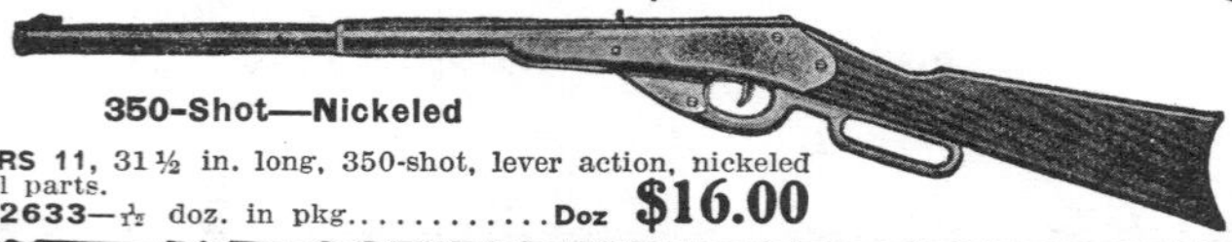

350-Shot—Nickeled

MFRS 11, 31½ in. long, 350-shot, lever action, nickeled steel parts.
1F-2633—1/12 doz. in pkg...........**Doz** **$16.00**

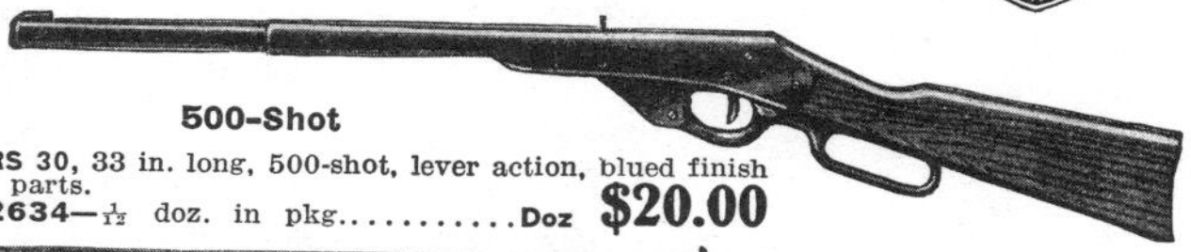

500-Shot

MFRS 30, 33 in. long, 500-shot, lever action, blued finish steel parts.
1F-2634—1/12 doz. in pkg..........**Doz** **$20.00**

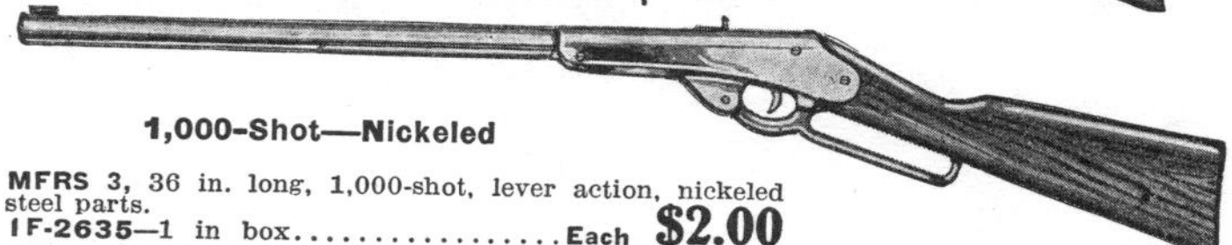

1,000-Shot—Nickeled

MFRS 3, 36 in. long, 1,000-shot, lever action, nickeled steel parts.
1F-2635—1 in box................**Each** **$2.00**

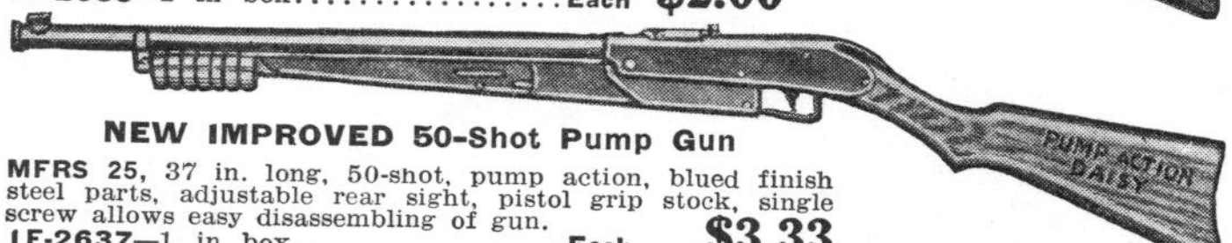

NEW IMPROVED 50-Shot Pump Gun

MFRS 25, 37 in. long, 50-shot, pump action, blued finish steel parts, adjustable rear sight, pistol grip stock, single screw allows easy disassembling of gun.
1F-2637—1 in box................**Each** **$3.33**

WELL KNOWN REPEATING AIR RIFLES

Biggest air rifles for the money we have seen. High powered....with excellent construction throughout.

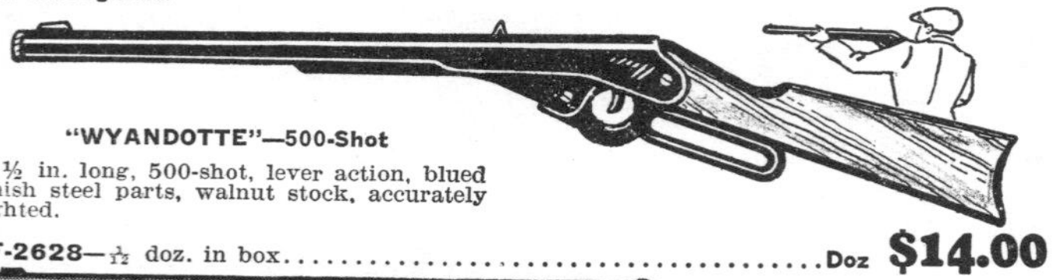

"WYANDOTTE"—500-Shot

32½ in. long, 500-shot, lever action, blued finish steel parts, walnut stock, accurately sighted.
1F-2628—1/12 doz. in box....................................**Doz** **$14.00**

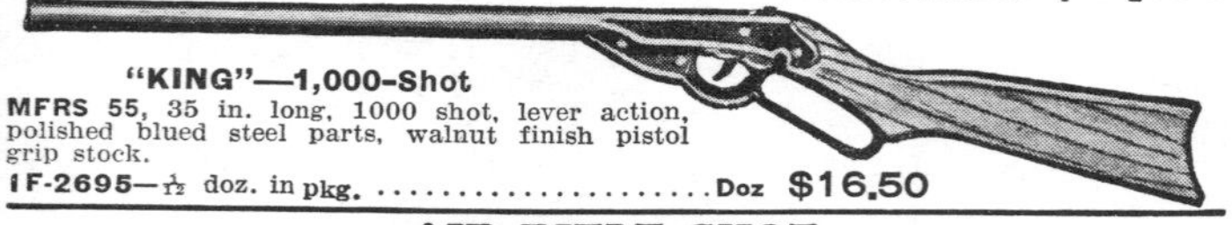

"KING"—1,000-Shot

MFRS 55, 35 in. long, 1000 shot, lever action, polished blued steel parts, walnut finish pistol grip stock.
1F-2695—1/12 doz. in pkg......................**Doz** **$16.50**

AIR RIFLE SHOT

The kind that boys prefer...and ask for by name. "Bullseye" shot is highly recommended by the "Daisy" Manufacturing Company for use with "Daisy" rifles.

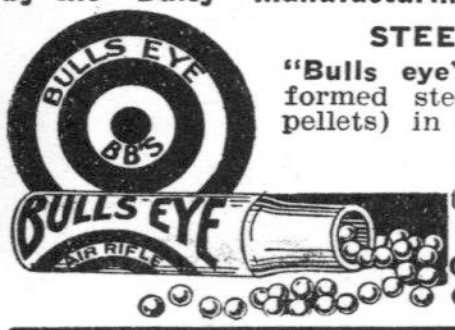

STEEL—155 COUNT

"Bulls eye", 2 oz. perfectly formed steel shot (about 155 pellets) in brown kraft tube.
1F-2638 — 2 doz. tubes in pkg. **Doz** **42c**
CASE (100 tubes) **$3.25**

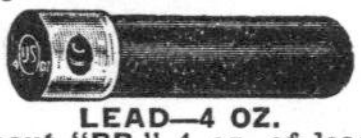

LEAD—4 OZ.

Boy Scout "BB," 4 oz. of lead shot in 2⅞ in. shell, perforated side and sliding band to take out shot.
1F-2653—2 doz. shells in box..............**Doz** **65c**
CASE (100 shells) **$5.00**

PISTOLS WITH HOLSTERS

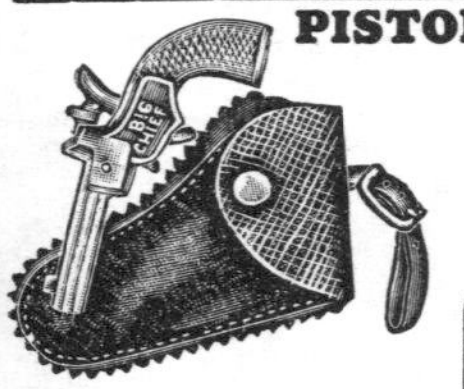

"Big Chief" cap pistol, 4 in., single shot, black patent leather holster, strap and buckle.
1F-2975—2 doz. in box.
Doz **83c**

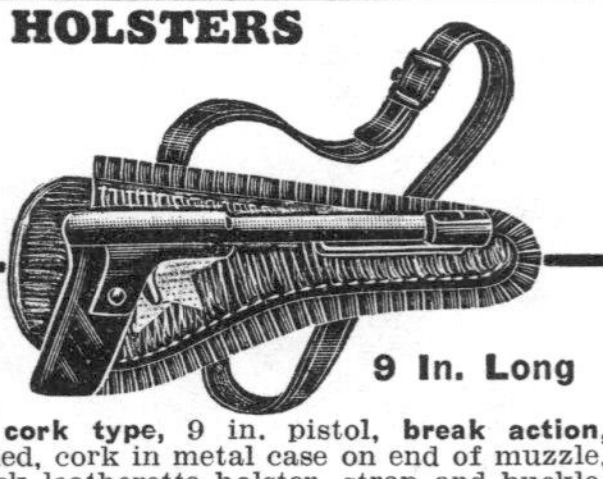

Self Loading!

9 In. Long

Self-loading cork type, 9 in. pistol, **break action,** black enameled, cork in metal case on end of muzzle, 11½ in. black leatherette holster, strap and buckle, contrasting color star.
1F-2660—1 doz. in box.........**Doz** **$1.95**

WATER PISTOLS

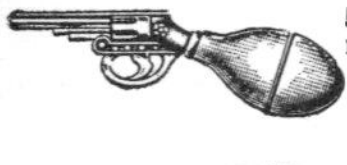

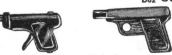

5¾ in., imported, pewter with rubber bulb.
2F-9585—1 doz. in pkg.
Doz **80c**

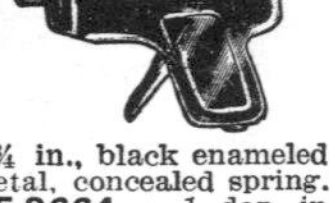

4¾ in., black enameled metal, concealed spring.
1F-2664 — 1 doz. in box.
Doz **85c**

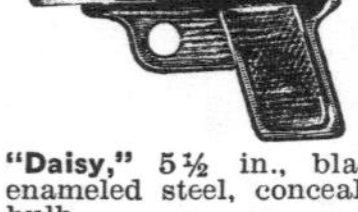

"Daisy," 5½ in., black enameled steel, concealed bulb.
1F-1662—½ doz. in box.
Doz **$2.00**

PAPER THROWING GUN

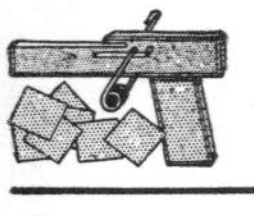

4 in. long, heavy wood construction, red and green finish, strong spring action, complete with generous supply of paper ammunition, each in box.
1F-2930—1 doz. tied. **Doz** **80c**

"TWIN 6" RUBBER BAND MACHINE GUNS

Shoots 12 rubber bands in rapid succession by turning crank.

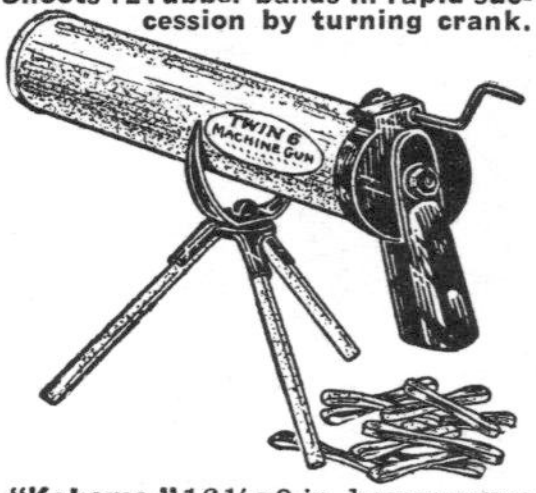

"Kokomo," 16½x9 in. heavy gauge metal, orange enameled, 3-leg tripod, noise-making ratchet, easily loaded.
1F-2657—1/12 doz. in box.
Doz **$12.00**

RUBBER BAND PISTOLS

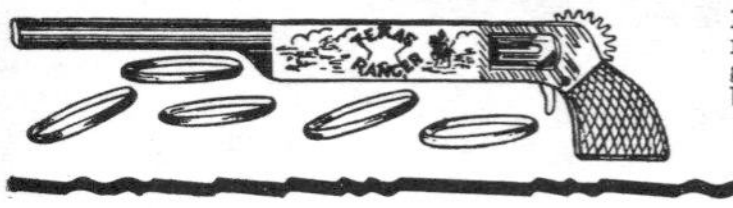

15 in. long, heavy wood construction, natural finish with red & blue stenciling, steel geared automatic action, with 5 rubber bands.
1F-3852—2 doz. in box.....**Doz** **79c**

BREAK ACTION POP GUNS

19 In. Long! Self-Loading!

Our best sellers! Yours too, if you feature it in a big way at 25c!

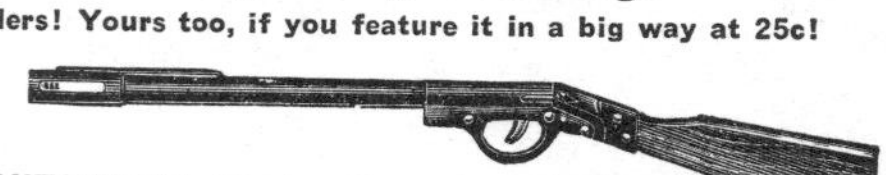

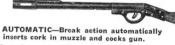

AUTOMATIC—Break action automatically inserts cork in muzzle and cocks gun.

19 in. long, blued steel barrel, RED enameled wood stock, **cork in metal case on end of muzzle inserts automatically.**
1F-2630—1 doz. in box..............................**Doz** **$1.95**

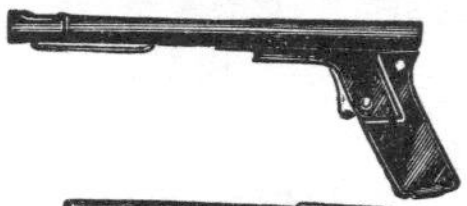

Corks insert automatically—fast action

9 in. long, **break action** inserts cork and cocks gun, blued finish, cork in metal case on end of muzzle.
1F-2636—1 doz. in pkg................**Doz** **95c**

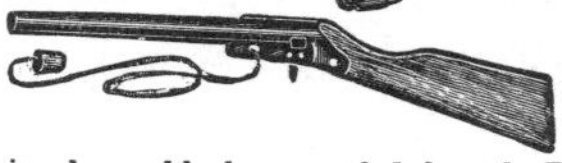

14 in. long, black enameled barrel, RED stained wood stock.
1F-2626—1 doz. in box......**Doz** **95c**

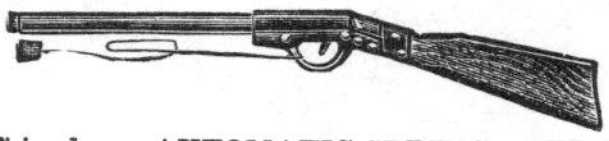

17 in. long, AUTOMATIC SPRING ACTION, gun metal barrel, walnut stained wood stock.
Doz **$1.90**

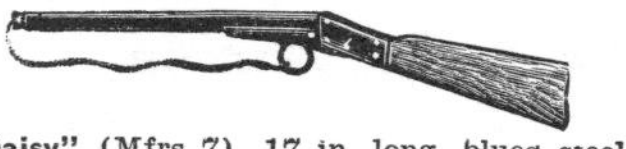

"Daisy" (Mfrs 7), 17 in. long, blued steel parts, walnut stained wood stock.
1F-2640—1 doz. in pkg...**Doz** **$2.00**

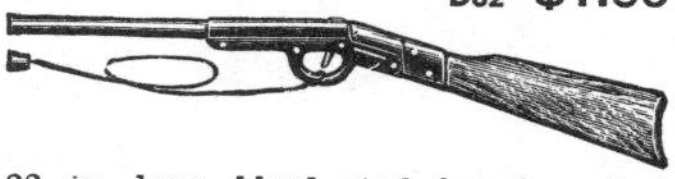

22 in. long, blued steel barrel, walnut stained wood stock, **each in box.**
1F-2645—½ doz. in pkg..**Doz** **$3.80**

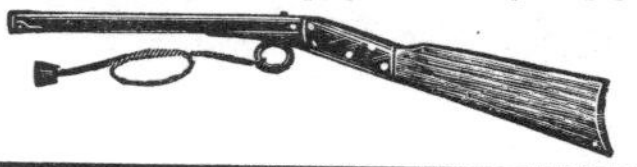

"Daisy" (Mfrs 14), 21 in. long, blued steel parts, walnut stained wood stock, **each in box.**
1F-2644—1/12 doz. in carton. **Doz** **$4.00**

PUMP ACTION GUNS—Our Leaders!

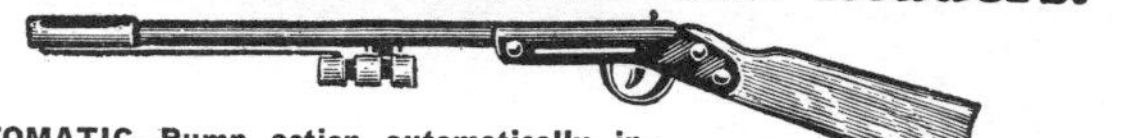

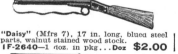

AUTOMATIC—Pump action automatically inserts cork in muzzle and cocks gun.

28 in. long, pump action, blued steel parts, walnut stained stock, **each in box.**
1F-2667—1/12 doz. in box..**Doz** **$4.50**

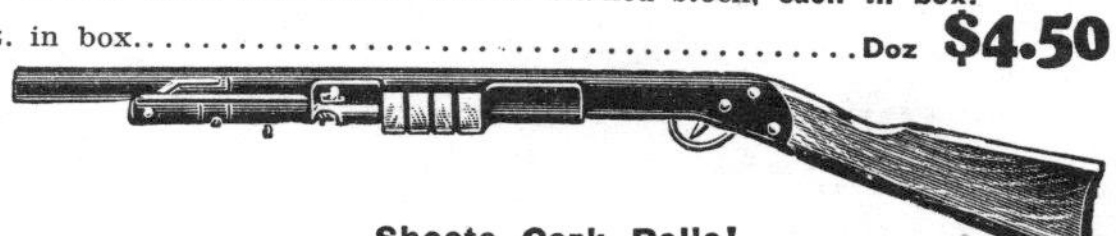

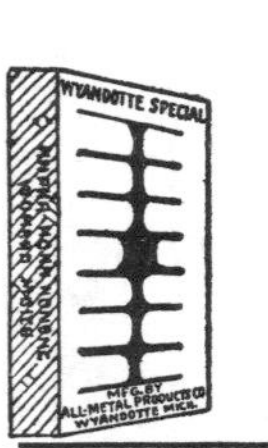

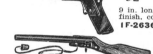

Shoots Cork Balls!

Each gun with 15 cork balls and target. The greatest gun of its kind to sell at this price!
Wyandotte Special, 35½ in. long, baked black enameled steel parts, pump action (works exactly like a shot gun), wood grip, walnut finish stock, fifteen ⅝ in. cork balls, 1½x9x3 cardboard target.
1F-2649—1 in carton.......................**Each** **$1.95**

AUTOMATIC MACHINE POP GUNS

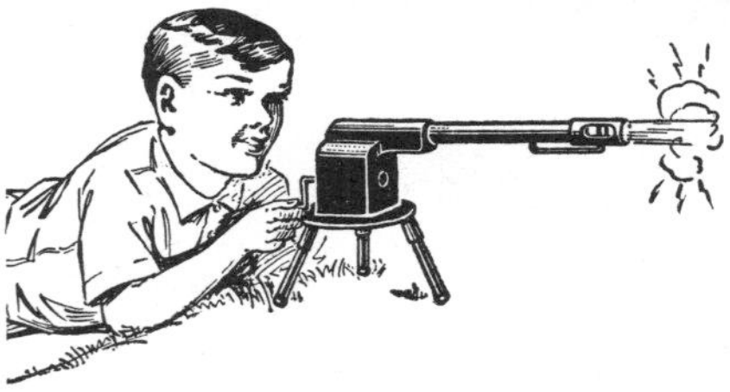

Shoots as fast as handle can be turned.

10 in. long, tan enameled, tripod, red stained legs, rubber feet, cork in metal case on end of muzzle **inserts automatically,** produces loud report, each in box.
1F-2666—½ doz. in pkg.
Doz **$2.25**

"LYONS" METALCRAFT CONSTRUCTION SETS

The rapid growth and popularity of travel by air has increased the sales of Airplane construction toys. Every boy is a prospect for at least one of these sets! Metalcraft Products are particularly popular because they are made of heavy rustproof steel parts....parts that last a lifetime because they CAN'T WEAR OUT! Each set designed to build accurate models. Be sure your line includes the sets listed on this page.

These "Spirit of St. Louis" Airplanes Are Easy to Build

All parts enameled heavy steel, wood landing wheels. Builds miniature models of the famous Spirit of St. Louis, Ryan, Fokker, Columbia, etc. Each in attractive box with instructions.

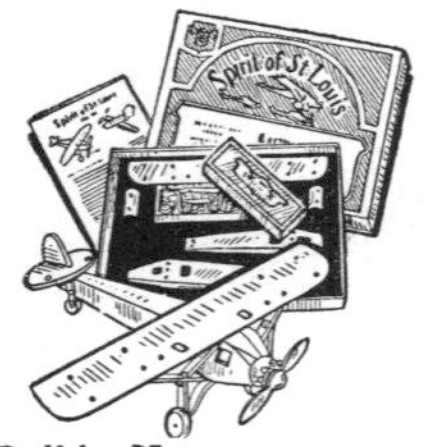

Builds More Than 10 Planes
Mfrs 950, 8½ in. long, 11½ in. wing spread, red enameled.
1F-3029—1/12 doz. sets in box. Doz sets **$8.00**

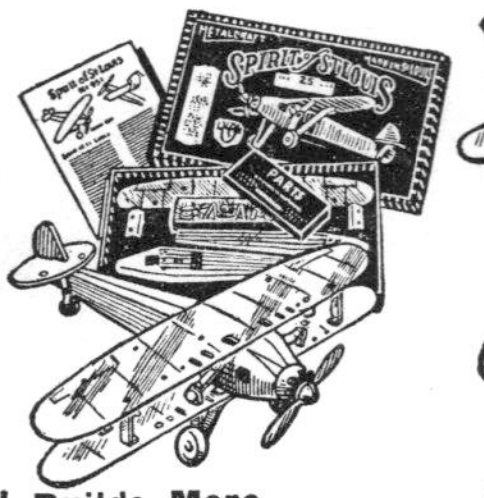

Builds More Than 25 Planes
Mfrs 951, 10¾ in. long, 14¼ in. wing spread, red and yellow enameled.
1F-3035 — 1/12 doz. sets in box. Doz sets **$12.00**

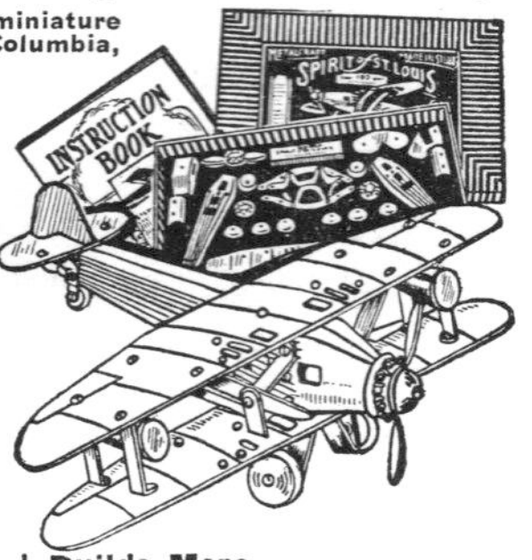

Builds More Than 100 Planes
Mfrs 952, 10¾ in. long, 14¼ in. wing spread, yellow and orange enameled.
1F-3031—1 set in box. Set **$2.00**

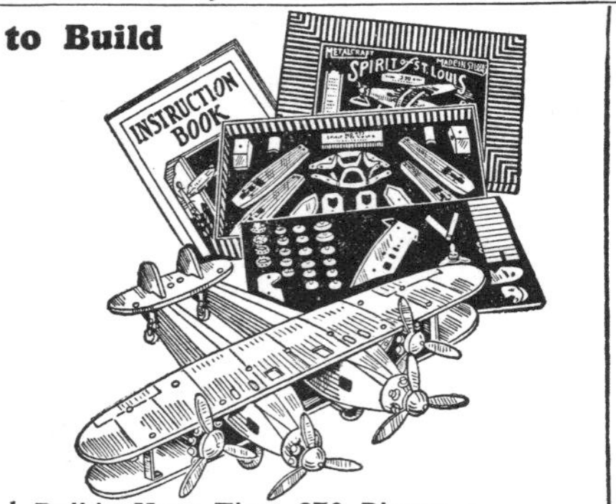

Builds More Than 250 Planes— Builds 2 Monoplanes at One Time
Mfrs 953, 10¾ in. long, 14¼ in. wing spread, 2 planes can be built at one time, yellow and orange enameled. Aviation Engineering book written by a famous aviator included.
1F-3032—1 set in box.........Set **$3.25**

Beacon Light & Mooring Mast

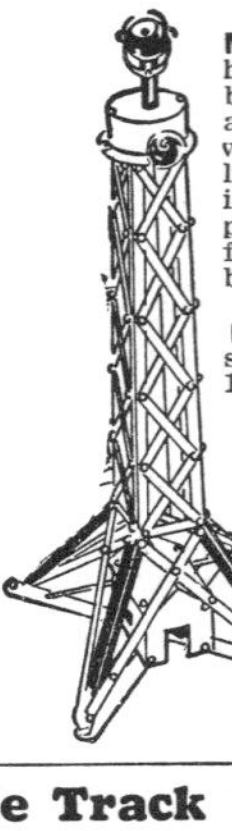

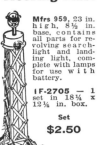

Mfrs 959, 23 in. high, 8½ in. base, contains all parts for revolving searchlight and landing light, complete with lamps for use with battery.
1F-2705 — 1 set in 18¼ x 12¼ in. box.
Set **$2.50**

It's Great Sport Building Zeppelins and Blimps

All parts of enameled heavy steel. Builds practical models in colors, complete with such details as cabins and engines. Each in attractive display box with instructions.

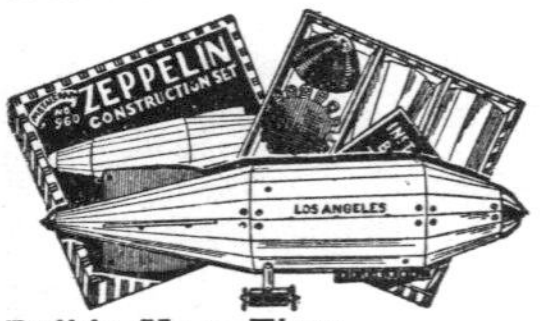

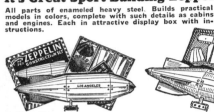

Builds More Than 8 Zeppelins
Mfrs 960, 19 major parts, red and yellow enameled.
1F-2969—1/12 doz. sets in 9¼ x 8¼ in. box. Doz sets **$8.00**

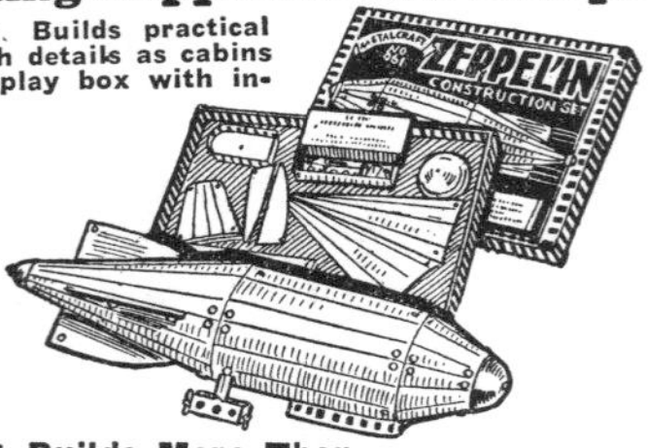

Builds More Than 20 Zeppelins and Blimps
Mfrs 961, 45 major parts, gray enameled and nickeled.
1F-2755 — 1/12 doz. sets in 14x10 in. box......Doz sets **$12.00**

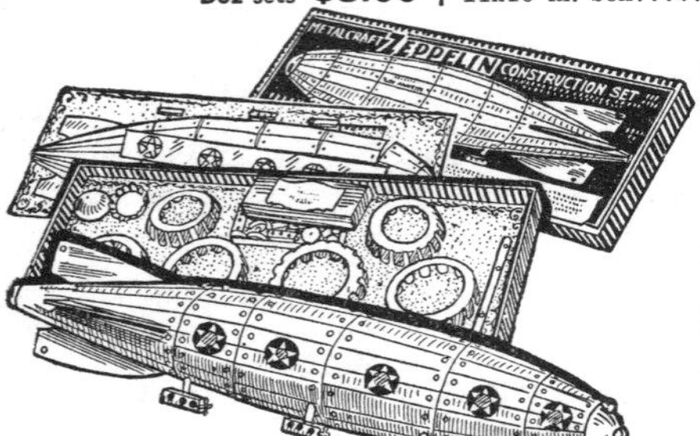

Builds "Graf Zeppelin," "Los Angeles," Etc., Up to 28 In. Long
Mfrs 962, 90 major parts, builds numerous Zeppelin and blimp models to 28 in. length.
1F-2757 — 1 set in 27¾x10¼ in. box.
Set **$3.33**

These Train Sets Fit Any Gauge Track

A brand new idea in construction toys. Special device makes all cars adjustable to fit ANY COUPLER and gauge track. Units made of heavy bright rustproof steel....builds many different types of strong and easy rolling cars. These sets are bound to revive interest in train toys of all kinds and lead to the purchase of new locomotives and track....a real boost for any toy department.

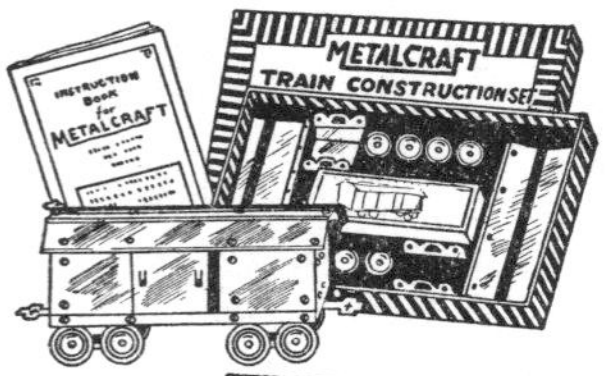

Builds 5 different cars
Mfrs 980, 70 major pcs., builds flat, lumber, machinery, gondola and box cars.
1F-3046—1/12 doz. sets in 12¼x8¼ in. box.
Doz sets **$8.00**

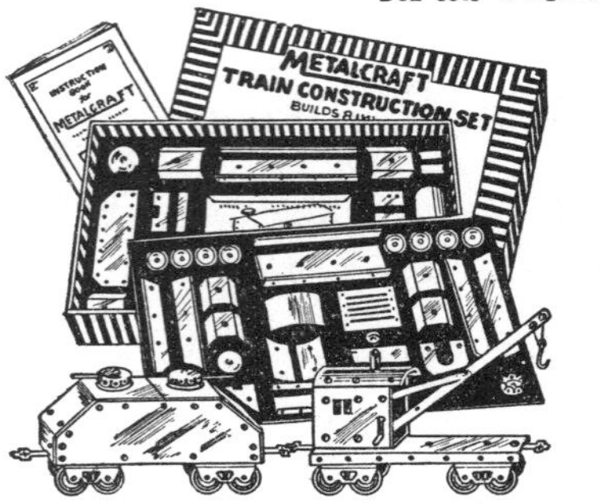

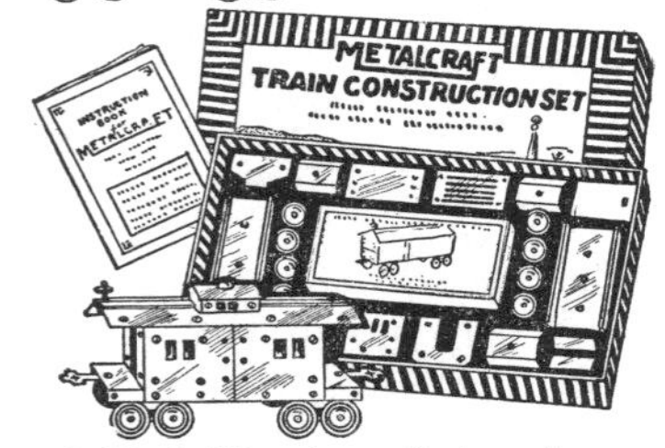

Builds 8 different cars, 2 at one time
Mfrs 981, 138 major pcs., builds flat, lumber, machinery, gondola, box, sand dump, cattle and caboose.
1F-3047 — 1 set in 18¼x11¼ in. box.........................Set **$2.00**

Builds 12 different cars, 4 at one time
Mfrs 982, 245 major pcs., builds flat, lumber, machinery, gondola, box, sand dump, cattle, caboose, tank, wrecking, coal and armored.
1F-3048—1 set in 18½x12½ in. box.
Set **$3.32**

"St. Louis Robin" Endurance Flyer
ACTUALLY FLIES!

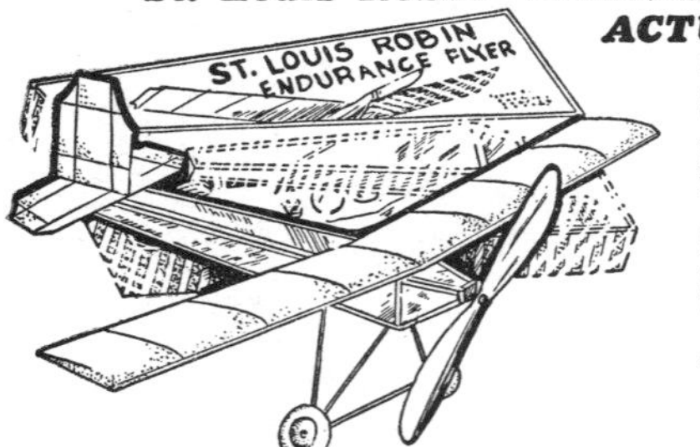

Knocked down ready for easy assembling. Complete with instructions!
Mfrs 968, 20 in. long, 30 in. wing spread, light weight aluminum, 7 in. revolving propeller, heavy rubber motor, rudder and tailpiece, 1¼ in. disc landing wheels, adjustable.
1F-2700—1/12 doz. in 20 x5 in. box.
Doz **$8.00**

"Lyonsport" Model Airport Window Display

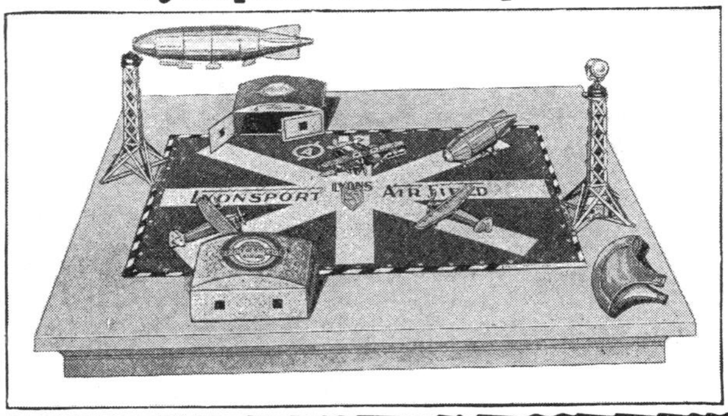

Consists of the following: Mooring mast; Beacon light, 23 in. high, revolving searchlight, landing light, lamps for battery operation; Zeppelin, 18x6 in.; 2-motor biplane, 14 in. wing spread, colored parts; tri-motor fighting monoplane, 14 in. wing spread, nickeled parts; two 15 x 10¾ x 6½ in. hangars; landing field and equipment, 40x60 in. airport, small blimp, leatherette helmet; all metal parts are nonrustable, bright or painted finish.
1F-3033 — 1 asstd. in shipping container.
ASST (9 pcs) **$12.00**

"Mecanno" Ship Building Sets

BUILDS 20 MODELS! Builds gigantic ships that float and run under their own power. Meccano's outstanding construction outfit——unique and different.

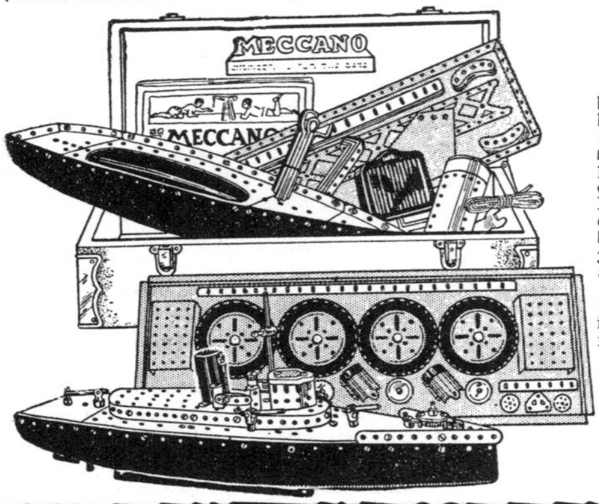

Mfrs 115, keels, hull, armor plates, anchor, masts, sails, smoke stacks, propeller, guns, derricks, etc. Builds ocean liners, speed boats, battle ships, yachts, clippers and others.
1F-4545 — 1 set in 25½x10¾x5½ in. chest.
Set **$11.60**

"STEEL WORKER" Construction Sets

Has only 8 types of girders and trusses... makes construction of many models very simple!

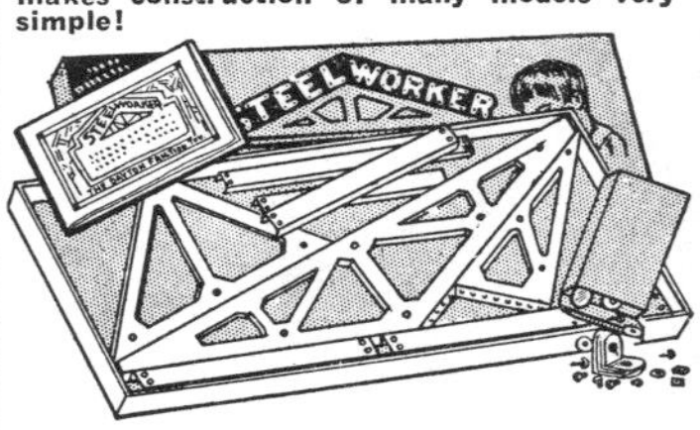

38 asstd. size and shape girders, trusses, etc., supply of bolts and nuts, exceptionally easy to put together, instruction book.
1F-4546—1/12 doz. sets in 22x 10x1 in. box........Doz sets **$7.90**

"BILT-E-Z" Steel Construction Sets

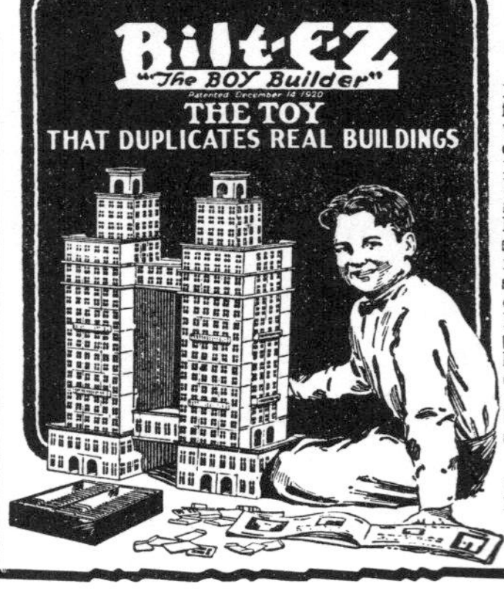

All Parts Are Interchangeable
Mfrs 0— 70 Parts
14 floors, 10 frictions, 10 walls, 23 windows, 2 doors, 10 cornices, 1 balcony, white, gray and red hard baked enamel finishes, no screws, bolts or nuts used. Each set in partitioned leatherette covered box with illustrated book of instructions.
1F-3614—½ doz. sets in pkg.
Doz sets **$7.50**

"MARX" GREATEST LINE
Durable and Mechanically Perfect!

Our greatest showing of the finest line of mechanical toys made....a line that includes such sensational new creations as "Amos 'n' Andy" and "Industrial Tractor Set" with the proven staples that sell in increasing volume each year. Knockout values!

"Industrial Tractor Set" . . . 20 In. Long!

We consider this the most remarkable tractor value that has ever been offered. We are the exclusive wholesale distributors. The year 1929 was a great "tractor" year, but with this new tractor set on the market, 1930 will break all records.

Extreme length 20 in., TRACTOR WITH DRIVER 7½ in. long, heavy gauge plate (built for rough use), red & orange body in fine litho finish, 2½ in. bright disc wheels with heavy rubber tread, powerful motor, TWO 4½ in. (extreme length) cars, 1⅞ in. wide, 3 in. high. each highly finished in different colors, each set in 10x7¾x4 in. counter display box.
1F-1116— ½ doz. sets in pkg....................**Doz sets $9.00**

"Turnover Tank"
Moves along on any one of its sides...performs many different feats!

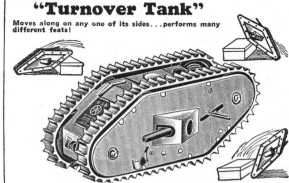

9x4x4¾ in., sturdy steel construction, crackled enamel finish, 2 side turrets at top and bottom with 1¼ in. guns, 2 in. guns, heavy rubber treads; performs many different feats—will attempt to climb high obstacles, will fail and turn over; then it repeats the performance and climbs the second time; will go on all sides.
1F-1165—1 in box....................**Each $1.30**

"Sparks Auto"
Shoots harmless sparks . . . a real thriller!

8½ in. long, multi-color litho. **Shoots harmless sparks from rear** when auto runs straight or in circle.
1F-1071—½ doz. in box. **Doz $2.10**

"New York" — 9½ in. base, 4½ in. train, 2¼ in. aeroplane, multi-color litho. **Train runs around track** and aeroplane flies over city at same time.
1F-1155—½ doz. in box... **Doz $4.50**

Dump Truck — 13½ in. long, multi-color litho, lever for raising body of truck.
1F-1093—½ doz. in box... **Doz $4.00**

"Flying Zeppelin"—17 in. long, heavy metal construction, aluminum finish, 4½ in. revolving propeller, 4 in. gondola, strong string, flies in circles.
1F-1088—½ doz in box. **Doz $4.25**

"Coast Defense"
Airplanes and cannons in action.. a sensational toy!

9 in. diam. metal platform representing fort with THREE 3 in. disappearing guns, SEVEN 1⅛ in. soldiers, 2½ in. hangar with 2¼ in. revolving airplane, all metal construction, bright color litho, guns move back and forward, rise and disappear, airplane circles above fort.
1F-1092—½ doz. in box. **Doz $4.50**

Mack "Merchants' Van"—13½ in. long, 3-color litho, hinged doors, chauffeur.
1F-1111—½ doz. in box.. **Doz $4.25**

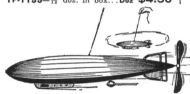

"The Big Parade"—24 in. long, multi-color litho, Soldiers, bands and horses parade back and forth along street as airplane circles overhead.
1F-1148—½ doz. in box...................**Doz $7.90**

"King Racer"—9 in. long, exceptionally bright multi-color litho.
1F-1083—½ doz. in box... **Doz $2.00**

"Cardboard Fort" . . . 48 In. Long!
Can also be used for demonstrating tractors and tanks

42x10x10 in., heavy cardboard, green & red printed designs, 2 swinging doors. Comes knocked down, easily constructed.
1F-1109—½ doz. in box....................**Doz $4.50**

Steam Shovel & Tractor — 7x3¾x4½ in., revolving engine house with 14 in. derrick and shovel on 9x5½ platform, heavy rubber treads, powerful motor, red, green and black enameled, revolving crank and pulley raises and lowers shovel.
1F-1062—½ doz. in box. **Doz $13.25**

BUTLER BROTHERS

"Climbing Tank"
Powerful motor! Every boy will want one!

9½ in. long, heavy gauge metal, gray with black trim, wide tread, non-slipping rubber traction tires, top turret and 3 mounted cannons, powerful motor.
1F-1124—½ doz. in box. **Doz $13.00**

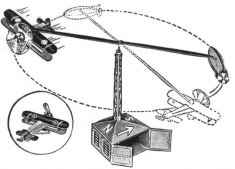

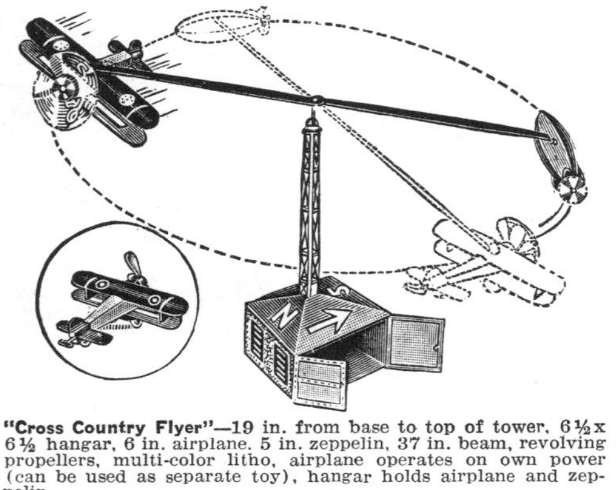

"Cross Country Flyer"—19 in. from base to top of tower, 6½x6½ hangar, 6 in. airplane. 5 in. zeppelin, 37 in. beam, revolving propellers, multi-color litho, airplane operates on own power (can be used as separate toy), hangar holds airplane and zeppelin.
1F-1161—½ doz. in box..............**Doz $8.75**

"Charleston Trio"—4⅝x3⅜, 3-color litho. Fiddler plays, Charlie dances, dog nods.
1F-1106—½ doz. in box. **Doz $4.15**

ALUMINUM "Climbing Tractor"
The greatest tractor toy ever made....FOR THE MONEY!

8¼ in. long, heavy gauge aluminum (built for rough use), multi-color litho, 3 in. disc wheels with heavy rubber tread, powerful motor.
1F-1184—½ doz. in box. **Doz $12.00**

Big AMERICAN MECHANICAL TOY Values

Clever fast action toys from America's leading manufacturers. See nearby pages for the celebrated "Marx" Mechanical Toy line!

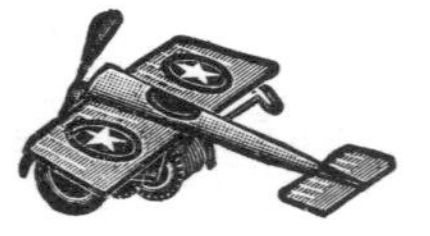

Airplane—6 in., 7 in. spread, 3 color enameled.
1F-1061—1 doz. in box.
Doz 80c

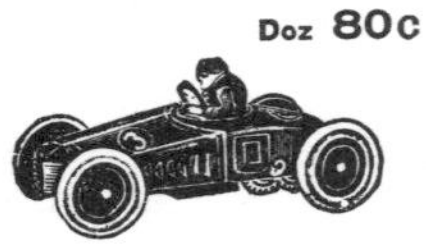

Racer—6⅝ in., vari-color enameled.
1F-1060—1 doz. in box.
Doz 89c

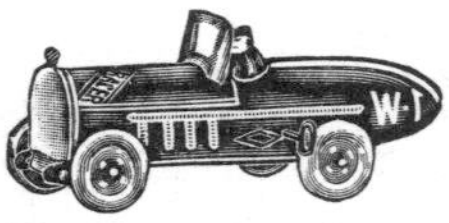

Racer — 9 in. long, heavy gauge metal, red, yellow & green enameled, disc wheels, driver, spare wheel.
1F-1131—½ doz in box
Doz $1.90

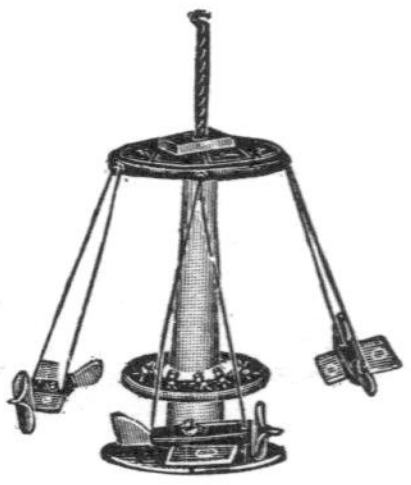

"Aero-Speeders"—9 in. high, heavy gauge metal, bright litho, three 4½ in. airplanes, spring action.
1F-1147—1/12 doz. in box.
Doz $7.85

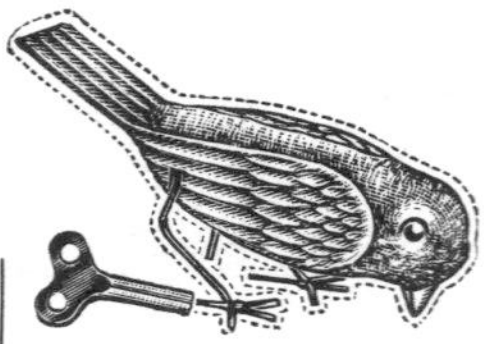

"Chipper's Pecking Bird" — 5 in. long, heavy gauge, 3-color enameled, concealed spring, hops and pecks in very realistic manner.
1F-1199—1/12 doz. in box.
Doz $1.95

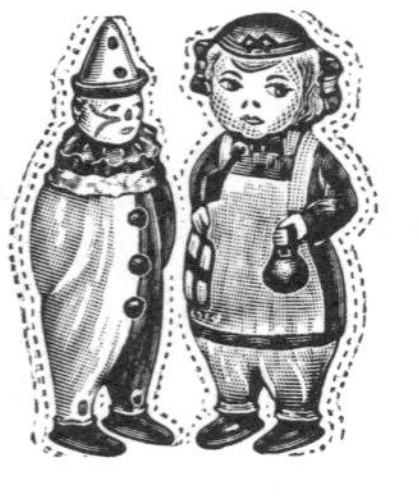

Mechanical Dancers — 8 in., vari-color enameled, glide along with swaying motion.
1F-1075—1/12 doz. in box.
Doz $2.15

3-Style Assortment

Big, sturdy and flashy pieces! A simple demonstration SELLS THEM!

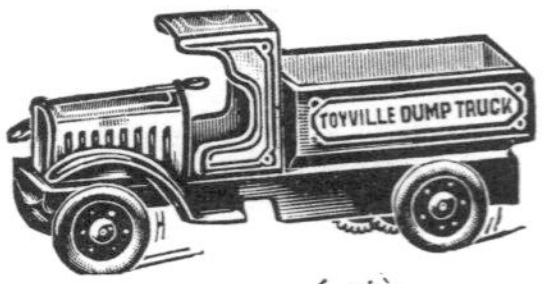

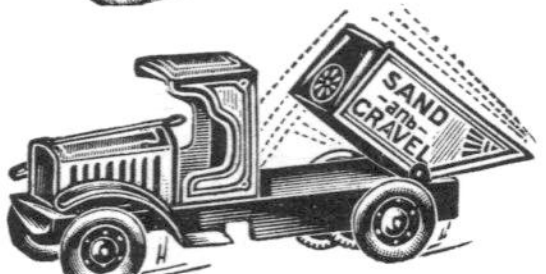

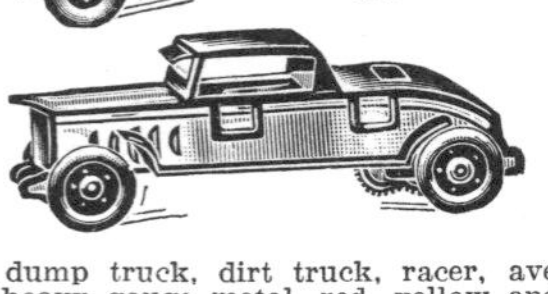

3 styles, dump truck, dirt truck, racer, aver. 9½ in. long, heavy gauge metal, red, yellow and green enameled, disc wheels.
1F-1064—1 doz. in box..**Doz $1.95**

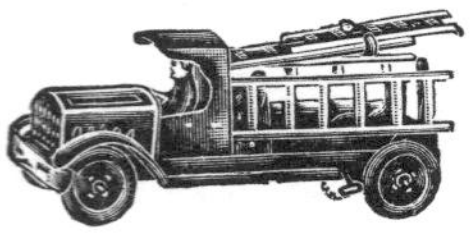

Hook & Ladder—10 in. long, red & yellow, two 5½ in. extension ladders, two 5 in. ladders.
1F-1187—1/12 doz. in box.
Doz $2.00

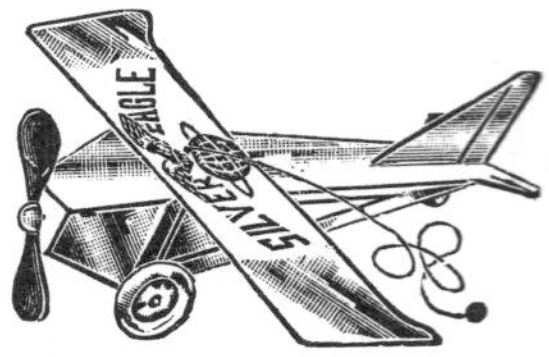

"Silver Eagle" Airplane —11½ in. long, 9½ in. wing spread, lt. wt. aluminum, revolving propeller, flies in circle when suspended on string.
1F-1176 — 1/12 doz. in box.
Doz $3.90

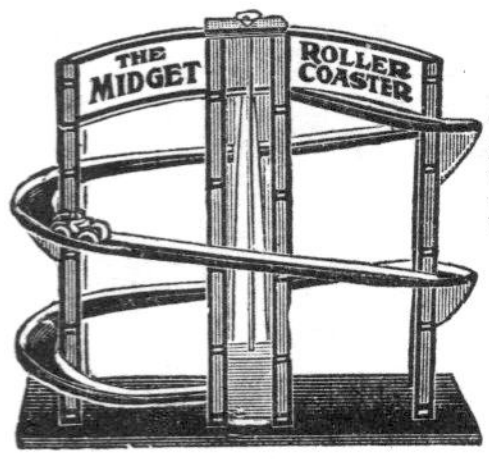

"Roller Coaster"—10½ x 10 in., 2-color enameled, car with passenger, car runs down incline and is raised by chute to starting point.
1F-1177—1/12 doz. in box.
Doz $8.10

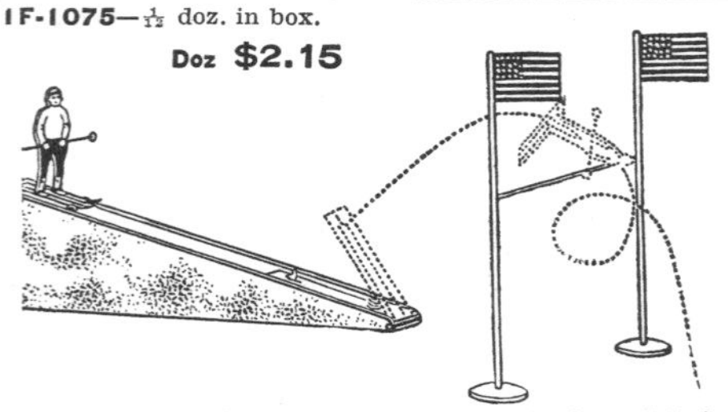

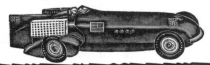

"Schoenhut" Ski Jumper—Ski track 26½ in. long, 5½ in. high, wood frame, imit. snow covered cardboard sides, 4½ in. painted wood figure on wheeled metal skis, two 12 in. enameled flagpoles with muslin flags, metal crossbar, force of skier releases spring trap and hurls figure over goal (about 8 ft.), 27x5¼x4¾ in. box.
1F-3563—1/12 doz. in pkg..............**Doz $8.00**

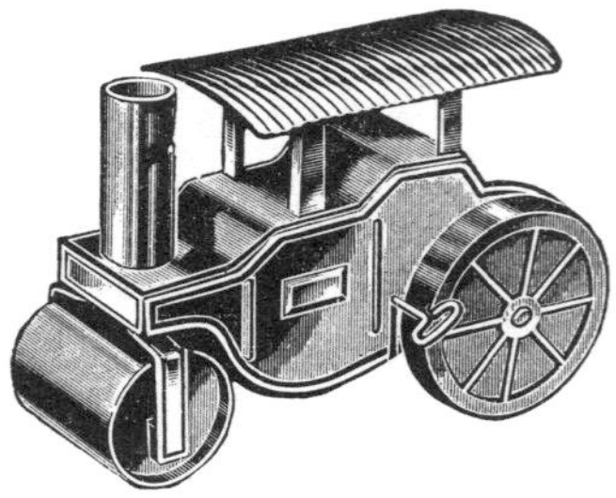

"Steam Roller"—11½x7x5 in., 22 gauge nickeled steel, slow action, disc rear wheels, **stop and start brake**, powerful spring.
1F-1102—1/12 doz. in box..**Doz $8.35**

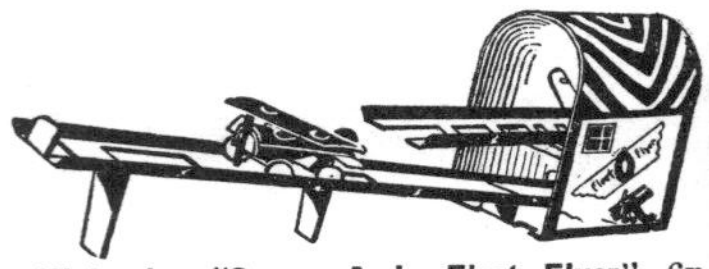

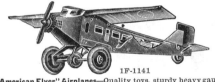

Wolverine "Sunny Andy Fleet Flyer"—6x6¼ in. hangar, heavy gauge, bright litho, 25½ in. runway,, 3x2 airplane, airplane shoots out of hangar along runway with return action, repeats many times.
1F-1160—1/12 doz. in box.
Doz $8.00

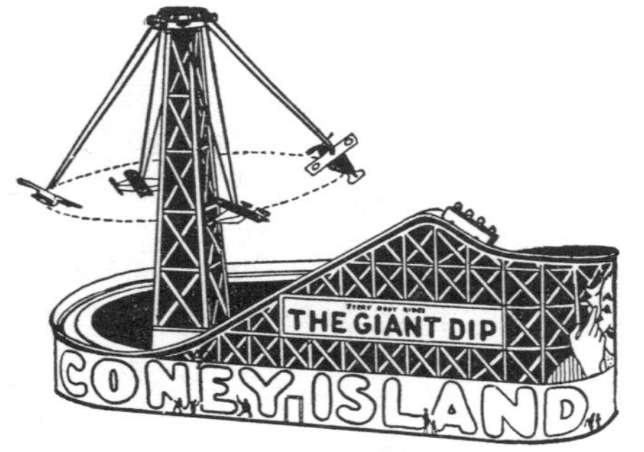

"Coney Island"—18x6 in., 1¾ in. car with 4 passengers, 13 in. tower with four 2½ in. airplanes, double action spring, base litho to represent amusement booths, stores, etc., car operates on railway and airplanes revolve.
1F-1126—1/12 doz. in box...............**Doz $8.25**

Actually Plays Songs!

"WOLVERINE" ZILOTONE

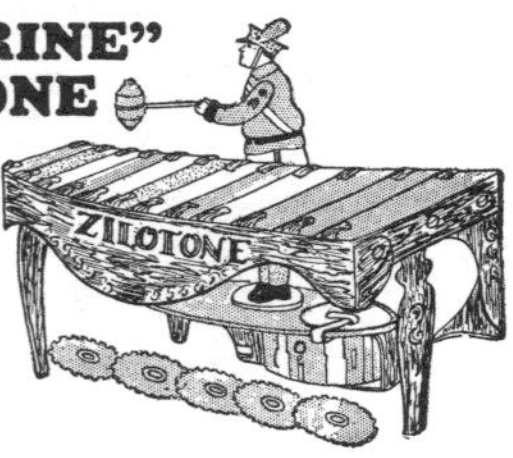

One of the most unique toys ever invented! Action and music! A crackerjack attention-getting toy ....Certain to be one of the biggest sellers of the year!

8x9 in., metal construction, attractive litho colors, 12 keys, 5 in. **revolving** metal figure on platform with hammer, 3 in. metal record, **figure plays on keys**, clear harmonious tones, operated by strong motor.
1F-2332—1 in box with 6 asstd. records. **Each $1.66**

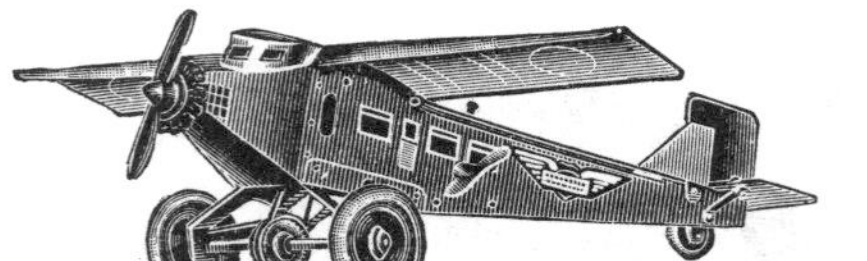

1F-1141

"American Flyer" Airplanes—Quality toys, sturdy heavy gauge steel. True scale models of the real planes. Each has powerful SPRING MOTOR with SPEED REGULATOR and BRAKE, ratchet noise-makers, disc wheels, **removable** rubber tires.
"Spirit of Columbia," 19½ in. long, 18 in. wing spread, movable wings, can travel in circle.
1F-1138—1 in box....................**Each $1.35**
"Lone Eagle," 21½ in. long, 23½ in. wing spread, adjustable rudder, brass fittings, ship bobs up and down when in motion.
1F-1141—1 in box....................**Each $2.35**

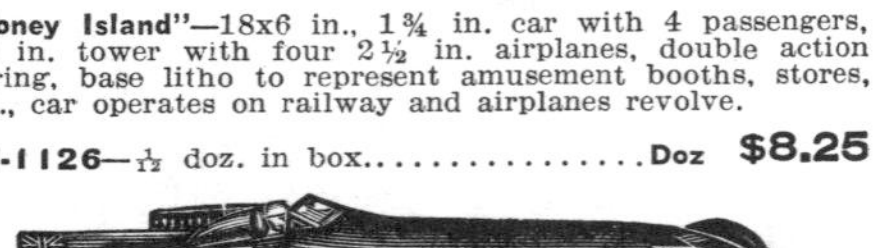

Modeled after one of the world's fastest cars
Kingsbury **"Bluebird Racer"**—8x4½ in., heavy metal construction, blue enameled, disc wheels, rubber tires, rubber bumper, driver, **powerful spring.**
1F-1230—1 in box...................**Each $2.10**

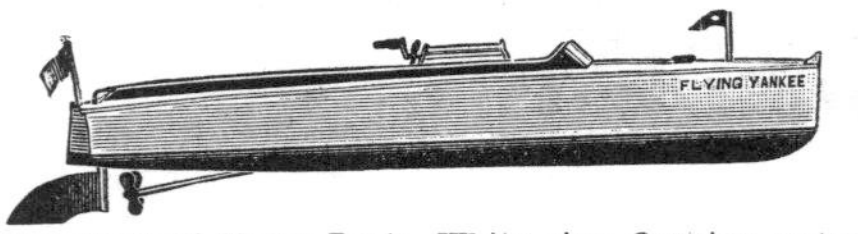

"Flying Yankee" Motor Boats—White pine, 3-spring motor in steel case, removable for oiling, steering gear, pennant and flag. 1 in carton.

		Each
1F-1172	19 in. long, natural top, red underbody.	$2.50
1F-1181	22 in. long, black top, red underbody.	3.85

KOKOMO "ELECTRICARS" . . . Fastest electric floor toys made!

SPEED! THRILLS! ACTION! Perfectly safe and sane toys that are propelled at a dizzy speed by electricity! Rubber tired wheels, flexible spring steel tracks mounted on wood posts, current holds contacts on bumper to fence and flows from bumper to motor through wires, track can be placed in almost any conceivable form. Transformers are necessary in operating these toys. Order 1F-3403 or 1F-3404....see nearby Train pages.

Screw driver and wrench furnished with each toy...easily assembled.

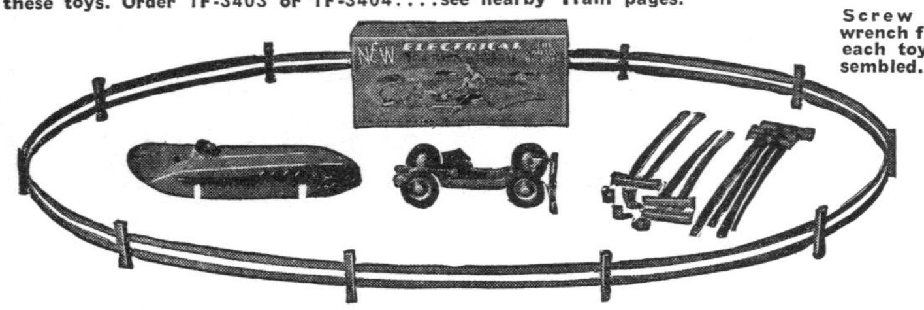

"Red Arrow" Racer—MFRS 710, 15 in. long, heavy gauge metal, red enameled, black trim, **14 ft. track**, screw driver and wrench.
1F-3291—1 in box.......................................**Each $5.00**

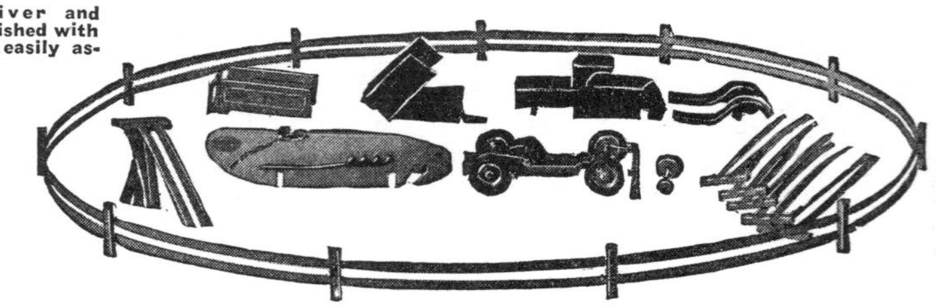

With 3 Interchangeable Bodies—MFRS 720, 4-wheel 11 in. chassis with demountable top and 3 interchangeable bodies, 5 in. dump truck, 7 in. ice truck, 11 in. racer, **20 ft. track**, screw driver, wrench, asstd. enameled colors.
1F-3292—1 set in box.......................................**Set $6.85**

AMUSING & INSTRUCTIVE IRON TOYS

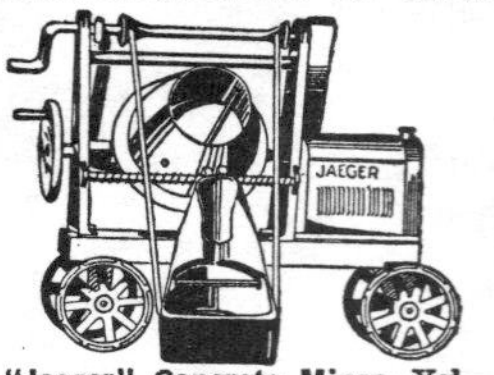

"Jaeger" Concrete Mixer—Yellow enameled chassis with motor front, blue enameled uprights, bright aluminum hopper, nickeled wheels, **operated by turning crank and wheel.** 1/12 doz. in box.
1F-3111—6¾x6⅛ in.
Doz **$11.50**
1F-3118—7x8½ in.
Doz **$19.50**

"Huber" Steam Roller—7¾ in., olive green enameled, gilt trim, nickeled flywheels, rollers and drivers.
1F-3082—½ doz. in box.
Doz **$11.50**

"Huber" Land Roller — 15 in. long, green enameled body, heavy red wheels, nickeled tank, scarifier lowers by lever, painted driver, steering and turning front wheels, strong string.
1F-3159—1/12 doz. in box..........Doz **$24.00**

"Buckeye" Ditch Digger—12½ in. long, 6¾ in. high, red enameled, jade green motor front, nickeled white hopper and chute, aluminum conveyor arm with 8 bucket diggers on chain drive, steel chain tread, operated by turning crank.
1F-3119—1/12 doz. in box............Doz **$27.00**

REALISTIC CAST IRON AIRPLANES
Carefully molded to resemble well known airplanes. Splendid to use as pull toys.

"Air Ford," 4 in. long, 4½ in. wing spread, green enameled, gilt trim, nickeled propeller and wheels.
1F-3122—1 doz. in box. Doz **84c**

"Lindy," 9½ in. long, 10 in. wing spread, gray and black, red trim, nickeled wheels and revolving propeller, pull cord, wood grip.
1F-3125—½ doz. in box. Doz **$8.00**

"Friendship," 11¼ in. long, 13⅛ in. wing spread, yellow body and wings, blue trim, **triple motors**, aluminum finish wheels and propellers, 4 wheels, rubber tires, ratchet attachment, **produces loud noise, wire spring drive turns all propellers when pulled,** pull cord.
1F-3140—½ doz. in box..Doz **$24.00**

"UX 166," 6¼ in. long, 6 in. wing spread, red, blue & aluminum painted, nickeled motor, wheels and revolving propeller.
1F-3142—½ doz. in pkg. Doz **$2.10**

"Bremen," 7¼ in. long, 8 in. wing spread, green enameled body and wings, gilt trim, nickeled revolving propeller and wheels, 3 aluminum finished passengers.
1F-3130—½ doz. in box. Doz **$3.95**

"Lindy," nickeled wheels and propeller, pull cord and wood grip. **Propeller whirls when pulled.**
9¾ in. long, 10 in. wing spread, blue and black, gilt trim, nickeled nose, rubber tired rear wheel.
1F-3126—½ doz. in box. Doz **$10.50**

"America," 14 in. long, 17 in. wing spread, gray and black, red trim, nickeled wheels, propeller and motor shields, **triple motors, balloon type rubber tires,** 2 passengers with painted features, ratchet attachment produces loud noise, wire spring drive turns all propellers, pull cord, wood grip.
1F-3128—1 in box.... Each **$3.00**

BEST SELLERS in SAND and MARBLE TOYS

BIG VALUES!
Metal Sand Pails With Shovels

Sturdily constructed quality merchandise. Bright 7-color designs that appeal to the kiddies. Tops of pails and handles have rounded edges....safety features not to be overlooked.

4¼x4 in., 7-color designs, 8½ in. shovel.
1F-2854— 1 doz. in box.
Doz **75c**

6½x6¾ in., 7-color designs, 11½ in. shovel.
1F2855— ½ doz. in box.
Doz **$1.85**

"WOLVERINE" AUTOMATIC SAND TOYS
All metal construction, each with can of sand, bright enameled in multi-colors

"Sandy Andy" See-Saw—9 in. high, juvenile figure, scoop, see-saw swings up and down, dumps sand into can at base.
1F-2883—½ doz. in carton. Doz **$3.95**

"Sandy Andy" Incline — 15 in. high, wire frame, rapid fire action as car shoots down incline, dumps its load of sand and climbs back for more.
1F-2884—½ doz. in box...Doz **$8.00**

"Sandy Andy, Jr." Incline—11 in. high, wire frame, car runs up and down track dumping sand as long as supply lasts.
1F-2901—½ doz. in carton. Doz **$5.65**

"Merry Miller" — 12¾ in. high, 5¾ in. wide, sand stored in mill pours down chute, miller and dog perform as wheel revolves.
1F-2891 — ½ doz. set up in box. Doz **$8.00**

Sand Crane—13½ in. high, wire frame, bucket fills with sand, swings and dumps load into can, returns for another trip
1F-2894—1/12 doz. in box. Doz **$10.00**

AUTOMATIC ACTION SAND TOYS
All heavy gauge metal, bright enameled in multi-colors.

Ferris Wheel—8½x2x6x6 in., 5¼ in. revolving wheels, seated passengers, bag of sand.
1F-2890—1/12 doz. in box. Doz **$4.25**

Windmill — 12 x 5 x 5 in., jointed figure attached to wheel, bag of sand.
1F-2887—½ doz. in box. Doz **$7.95**

"WOLVERINE" AUTOMATIC MARBLE TOYS
Each complete with marbles, all metal construction, bright enameled in multi-colors

"Bizzy Andy" Trip Hammer—10½ in. high, heavy frame marbles force hammer to keep pounding anvil with real trip-hammer effect, 6 clay marbles.
1F-2885—¼ doz. in pkg. Doz **$3.95**

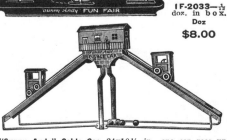

"Sunny Andy" Cable Car—24x10½ in., one car goes up while other carries marbles down, 5 steel marbles.
1F-2886—½ doz. in pkg..............Doz **$8.00**

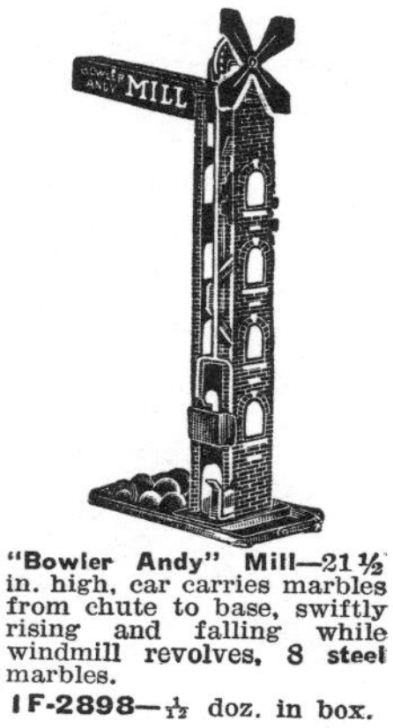

"Fun Fair,"— 14 x 5⅝ x 3½ in., steel marbles, 6 metal figures see-saw and swing.
1F-2033—½ doz. in box.
Doz **$8.00**

"Bowler Andy" Mill—21½ in. high, carries marbles from chute to base, swiftly rising and falling while windmill revolves, 8 steel marbles.
1F-2898—1/12 doz. in box. Doz **$12.00**

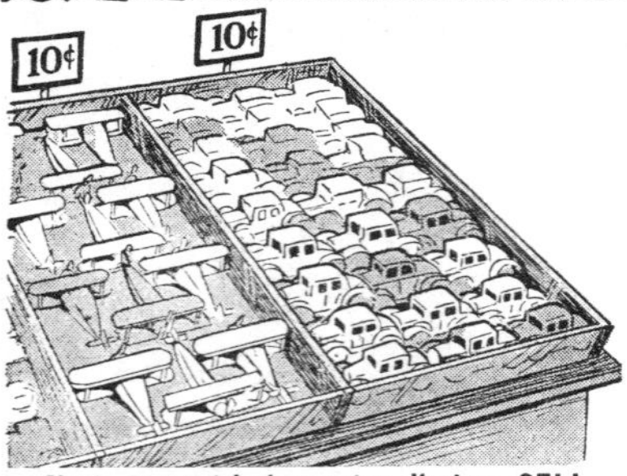

Neat, symmetrical counter displays SELL these toys. This illustration was drawn from an actual display in a leading store.

TOOTSIETOYS

PEWTER TOYS

ACCURATE MODELS! COLORFUL FINISHES! NEW CREATIONS! The biggest selling and best known line of Pewter Toys on the market....popular price playthings that command a prominent display in leading stores! Bright multi-color enamels and true-to-life lines have a tremendous appeal! Your line should include a good variety of these clever miniatures.

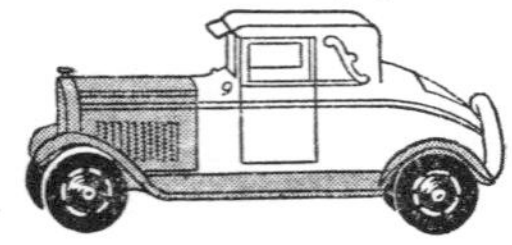
Coupe, 3 in., asstd. colors.
1F-2445—1 doz. in box. Doz **75c**

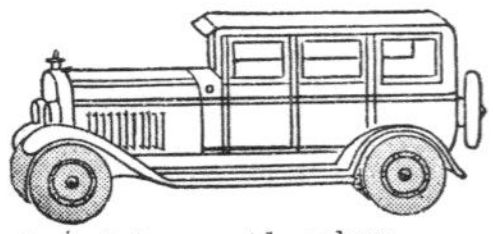
Sedan, 3 in., asstd. colors.
1F-2446—1 doz. in box. Doz **75c**

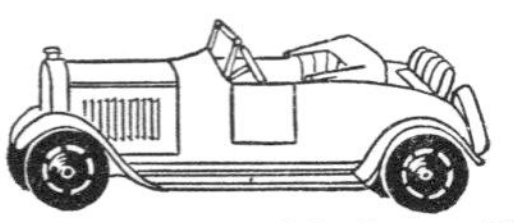
Buick roadster, 3⅛ in., asstd. body colors.
1F-2455—1 doz. in box. Doz **80c**

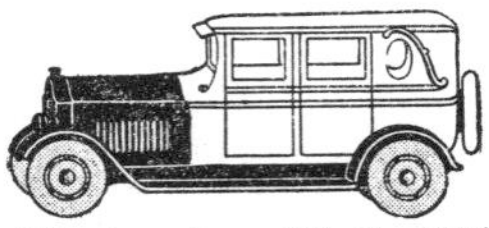
Cadillac brougham—3⅛ in., black chassis, asstd. body colors.
1F-2435—1 doz. in box. Doz **80c**

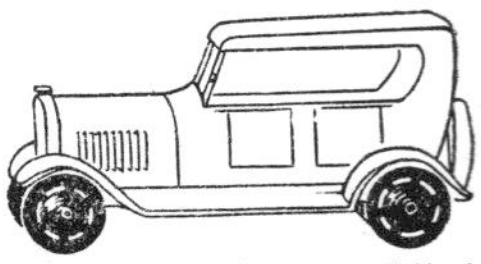
Oldsmobile touring car, 3⅛ in., black chassis, asstd. body colors.
1F-2462—1 doz. in box. Doz **80c**

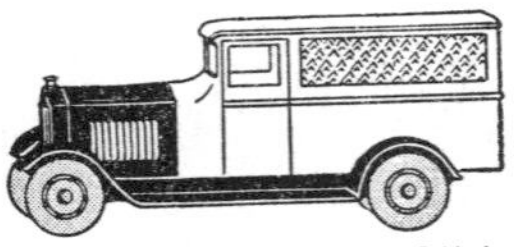
Chevrolet delivery car, 3⅛ in., black chassis, asstd body colors.
1F-2468—1 doz. in box. Doz **80c**

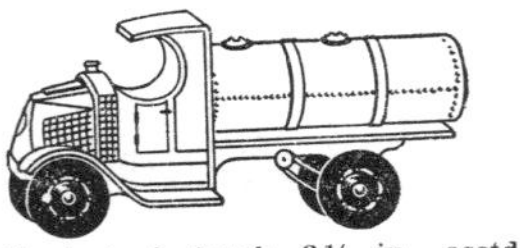
Mack tank truck, 3¼ in., asstd. colors.
1F-2437—1 doz. in box. Doz **80c**

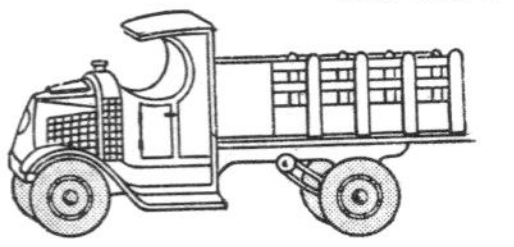
Mack truck, 3½ in., asstd. colors.
1F-2436—1 doz. in box. Doz **80c**

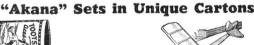

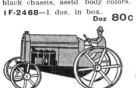

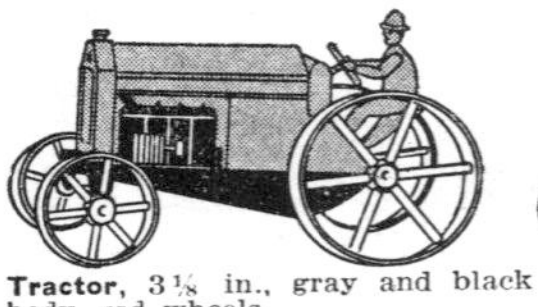
Tractor, 3⅛ in., gray and black body, red wheels.
1F-2456—1 doz. in box. Doz **80c**

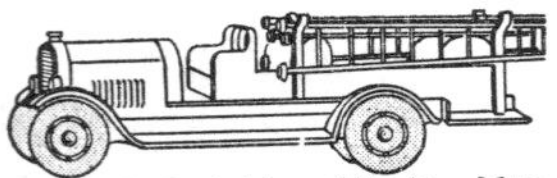
Hook & ladder, 3¼ in., blue & red body, 3 removable gilt ladders.
1F-2433—1 doz. in box. Doz **80c**

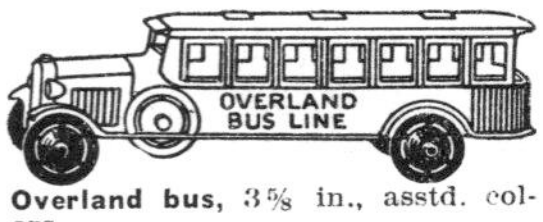

Overland bus, 3⅝ in., asstd. colors.
1F-2414—1 doz. in box. Doz **80c**

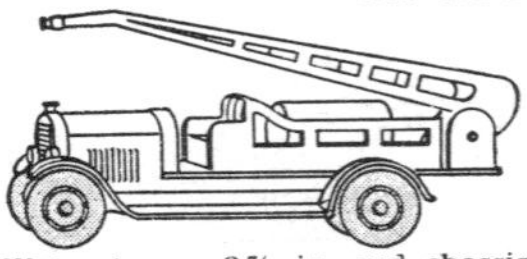
Water tower, 3⅞ in., red chassis and lift tower, yellow body.
1F-2449 — 1 doz. in box. Doz **80c**

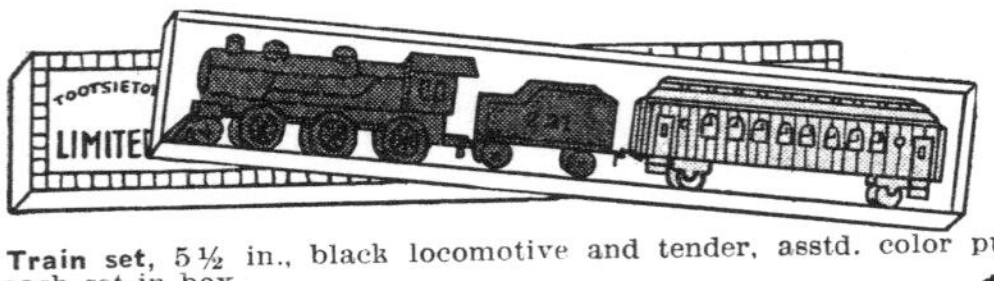

Train set, 5½ in., black locomotive and tender, asstd. color pullmans, each set in box.
1F-2457—1 doz. sets in pkg. .... Doz sets **$2.00**

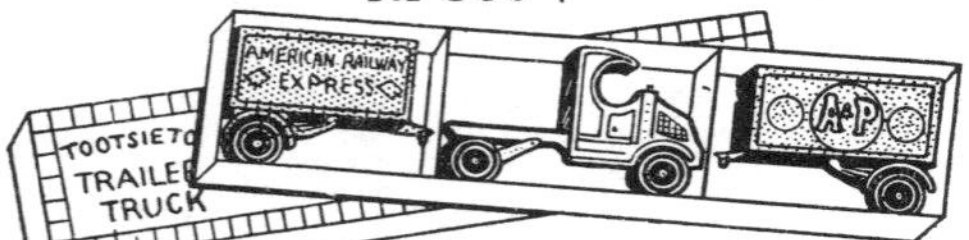

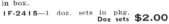

Trailer truck set, 3 in. truck chassis, 2 interchangeable trailers, asstd. colors, each set in box.
1F-2415—1 doz. sets in pkg. Doz sets **$2.00**

THE VERY LATEST! "TOOTSIETOY" AIRPORT

Perfect in detail! Realistically colored! A new "air" toy that is a sure seller....and a dandy value!

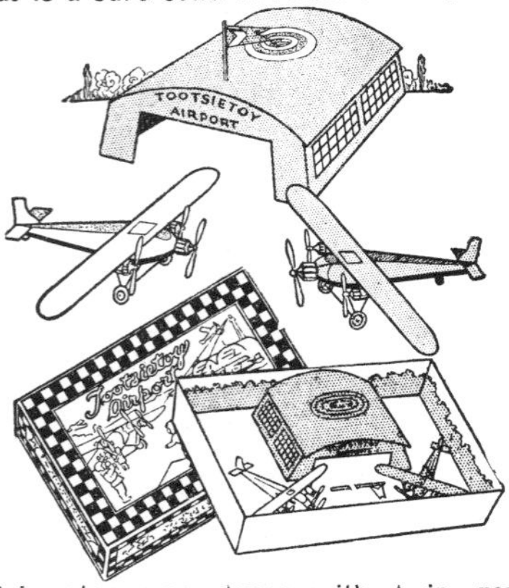

Two tri-motor monoplanes with 1 in. revolving propellers, 1 each red and silver finish, 4 in. long wing spread 5¼ in., 4¾x6 all metal lithographed hangar, each in fancy display box.
1F-2211—½ doz. in pkg. Doz **$4.00**

Popular Sellers in Colorful Display Cartons

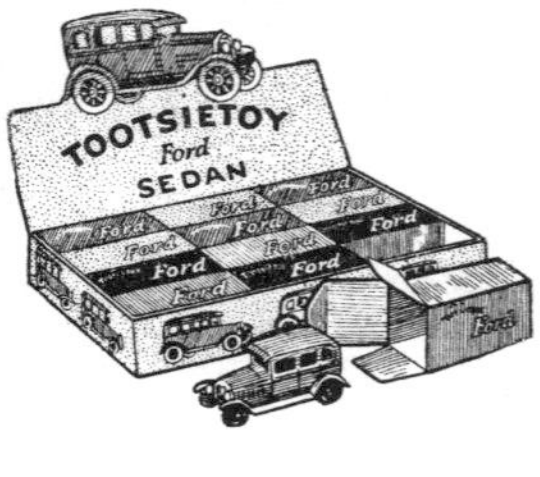

The four big numbers in this group come packed in flashy cartons that add color and interest to your displays....and they help **MAKE SALES!**

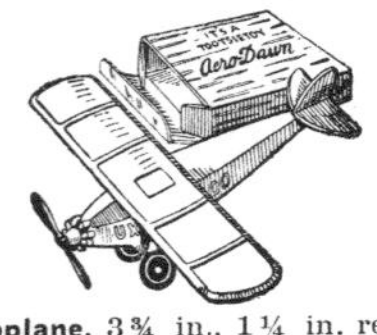
Aeroplane, 3¾ in., 1¼ in. revolving propeller, asstd. red, green, and aluminum finishes, **each in box.**
1F-2472 — 1 doz. in display carton. ....Doz **75c**

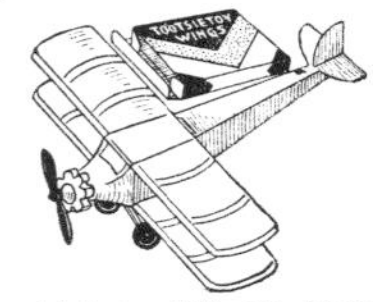
Wings biplane, 3⅞ in. long, 3¾ in. wing spread, 1¼ in. revolving propeller, disc wheels, asstd. red, blue and silver finishes, **each in box.**
1F-2218 — 1 doz. in carton. ....Doz **75c**

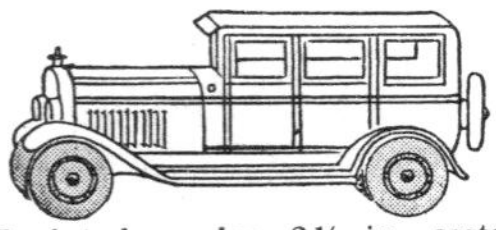
Ford tudor sedan, 2½ in., asstd. red, blue, yellow and green, **each in box.**
1F-2217 — 1 doz. in carton. ....Doz **75c**

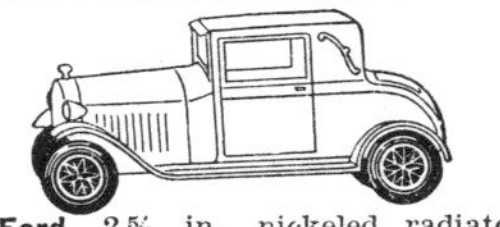
Ford, 2⅝ in., nickeled radiator and lamps, asstd. colors, **each in box.**
1F-2441 — 1 doz. in display carton........Doz **75c**

"Akana" Sets in Unique Cartons

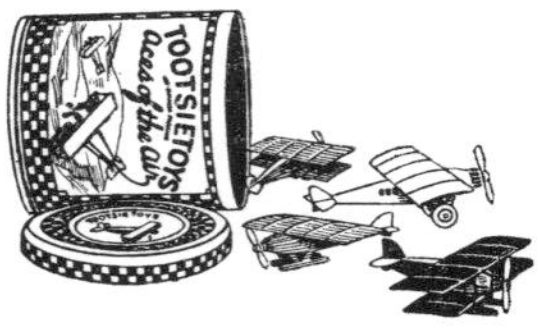

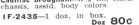

Just what the name implies ....a can of "Tootsietoys." Unique cartons filled with the cream seller "Tootsietoys" in asstd. sizes and colors. Each carton ready-to-mail....each an outstanding 50c value.

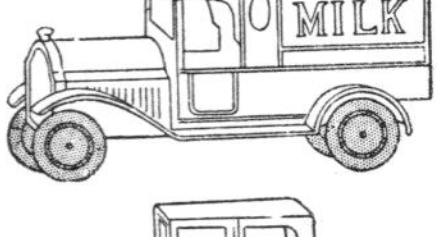

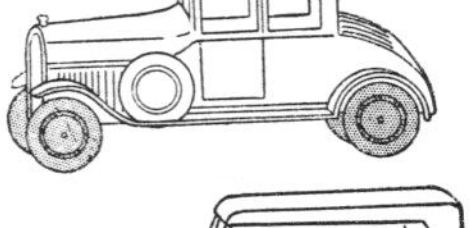
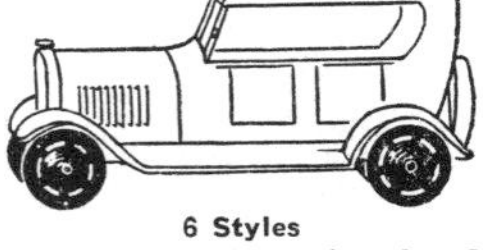

6 Styles

Asst., 2¾ to 3½ in., **6 styles,** delivery truck, Mack truck, airplane, touring car coupe, limousine, asstd. enamel colors, each set in 4x4⅝ in. **mailing carton.**
1F-2417—1 doz. sets in carton. Doz sets **$4.00**

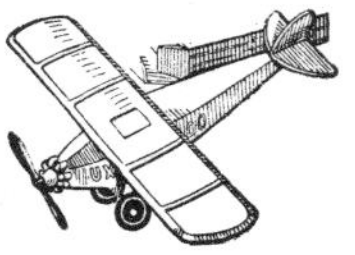
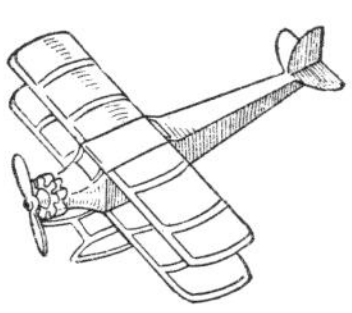

4 Styles

"**Aces of the Air,**" 3⅞ in. long, 3¾ in. wing spread, **4 styles,** 2 each monoplane and biplane models in land and sea designs, asstd. red and green enameled, and aluminum finishes, each set in 4x 4⅝ in. **mailing carton.**
1F-2219—1 doz. sets in box. Doz sets **$4.00**

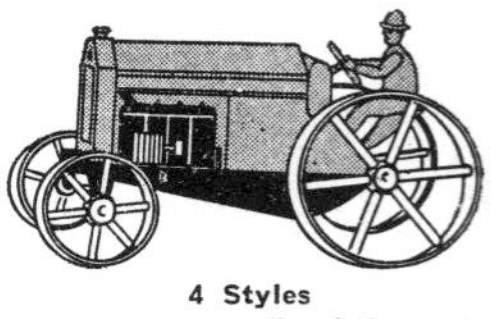

4 Styles

Farm tractor outfit, 2½ to 3½ in., **4 styles,** tractor, road scraper, Ford truck, box trailer, extra rake arm for scraper, asstd. enameled colors, each set in 4x4⅝ in. **mailing carton.**
1F-2447—½ doz. sets in pkg. Doz sets **$4.00**

"Playtime" Sets in Raised Tray Boxes

COLOR....a regular symphony of color characterizes these intriguing playtime sets. Displays make them self sellers. Each set neatly arranged in flashy box

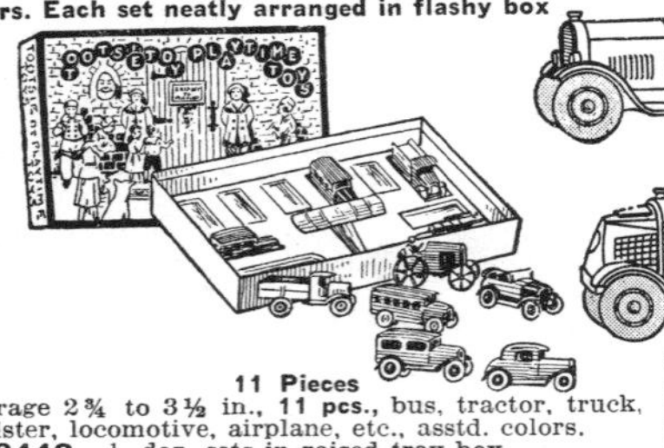

11 Pieces

Average 2¾ to 3½ in., **11 pcs.,** bus, tractor, truck, roadster, locomotive, airplane, etc., asstd. colors.
1F-2448—½ doz. sets in raised tray box. Doz sets **$8.00**

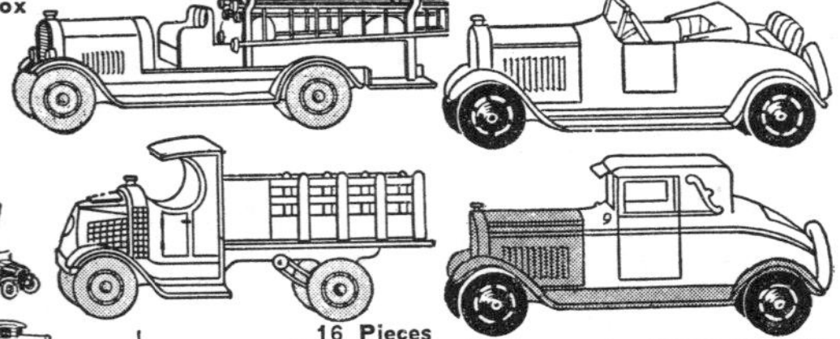

16 Pieces

Average 2¾ to 3½ in., **16 pcs.,** water tower, bus, airplane, hook & ladder, tractor, roadster, limousine, coupe, etc., asstd. colors.
1F-2422—½ doz. sets in raised tray box. Doz sets **$12.00**

FLASHY REALISTIC IRON TOYS

Successful sales of these carefully modeled miniatures depends on wide variety snappily displayed. The best sellers are here....STOCK THEM!

GET VOLUME WITH THESE 10c to 25c SELLERS

All with nickeled wheels

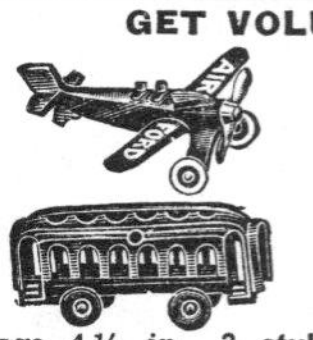

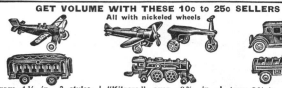

Average 4½ in., **3 styles**, locomotive, passenger car, airplane, vari-color enameled, nickeled revolving propeller.
1F-3070—Asstd. 1 doz. in box. Doz **75c**

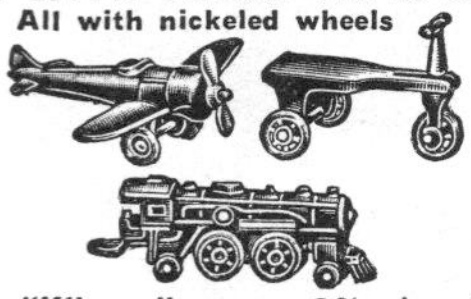

"Kilgore," aver. 3¾ in., **12 styles**, Ford roadster and sedan, kid's car, wheelbarrow, railroad cars, etc., asstd. color enameled.
1F-3071—Asstd. 1 doz. in box. Doz **78c**

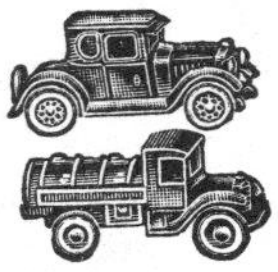

Aver. 3½ in., **6 styles**, Ford coupe, tank truck, Dodge coupe, Zeppelin, coach and truck, vari-color enameled.
1F-3065 — Asstd. 1 doz. in box....Doz **87c**

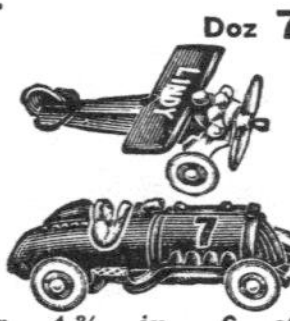

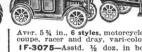

Aver. 4¾ in., **6 styles**, grasshopper, 2 racers, sport car, motorcycle, airplane, vari-color enameled, nickeled revolving propeller.
1F-3069—Asstd. 1 doz. in box. Doz **$1.15**

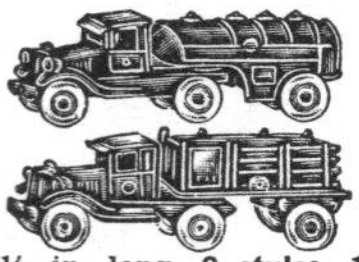

5½ in. long, **2 styles**, 1¾ in. high, red, green and blue baked enamel truck and chassis, **removable** oil tank and stake truck trailer bodies, each in box.
1F-3080—1 doz. in pkg. Doz **$1.95**

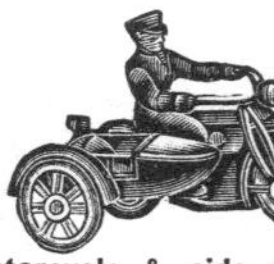

Motorcycle & side car, 5x3½ in., red, blue and orange enameled.
1F-3076—½ doz. in box. Doz **$2.00**

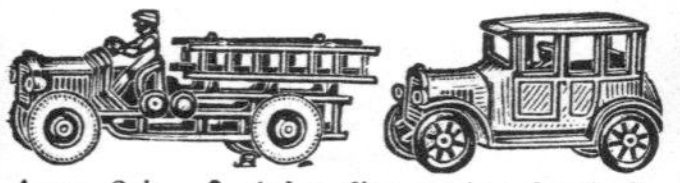

Aver. 6 in., **6 styles**, fire engine, hook & ladder, fire patrol, bus, sedan and tank truck, asstd. vari-color enameled.
1F-3081—Asstd. ½ doz. in box. Doz **$2.00**

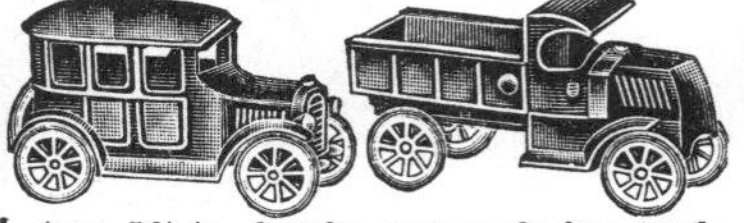

Aver. 5¾ in., **6 styles**, motorcycle, bus, truck, coupe, racer and dray, vari-color enameled.
1F-3075—Asstd. ½ doz. in box. Doz **$2.00**

KIDDIES LIKE FIRE DEPARTMENT TOYS

Enameled in bright vari-colors, contrasting trim

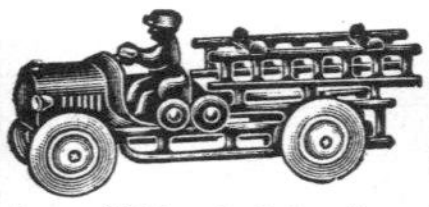

Aver. 6½ in., **2 styles**, fire engine, hook & ladder, fire patrol, bus, imitation balloon tires.
1F-3120—Asstd. ½ doz. in box. Doz **$2.10**

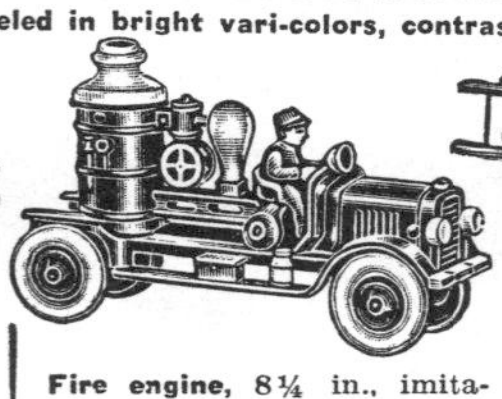

Fire engine, 8¼ in., imitation balloon tires.
1F-3131—¼ doz. in box. Doz **$4.00**

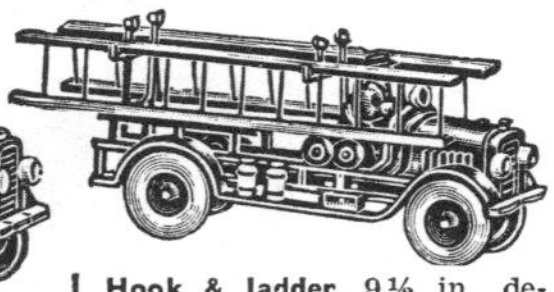

Hook & ladder, 9½ in., detachable 10 in. ladders, imitation balloon tires.
1F-3110—1/12 doz. in box. Doz **$4.00**

75-Pc. Iron Toy Assortment

Built of the best sellers only. Carefully selected new toys including airplanes and motorcycles....and proven big selling old staples. Note the big variety. SET OF PRICE TICKETS FREE.

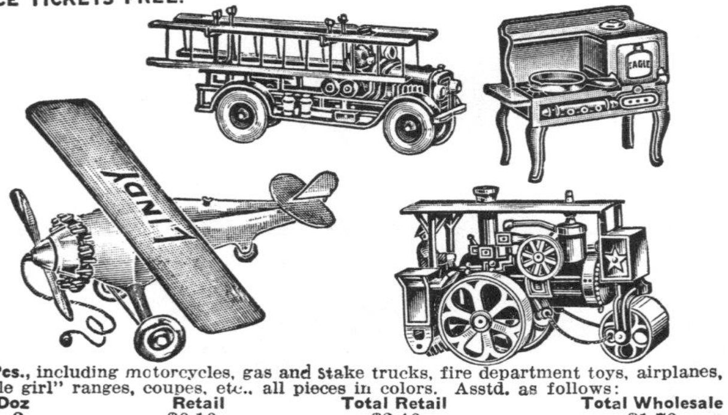

75 Pcs., including motorcycles, gas and stake trucks, fire department toys, airplanes, "little girl" ranges, coupes, etc., all pieces in colors. Asstd. as follows:

Doz	Retail	Total Retail	Total Wholesale
2	$0.10	$2.40	$1.70
3	.25	9.00	5.70
1	.50	6.00	3.90
⅙	1.00	2.00	1.30
1/12	1.50	1.50	.90
		$20.90	$13.50

1F-899— 75 pcs. in carton, 85 lbs...**ASST (75 pcs) $13.50**

Famous "Arcade" Fords

Miniature reproductions that look like the real thing. So realistic that they should be displayed where it is easy for the children to see them...it will help sales.

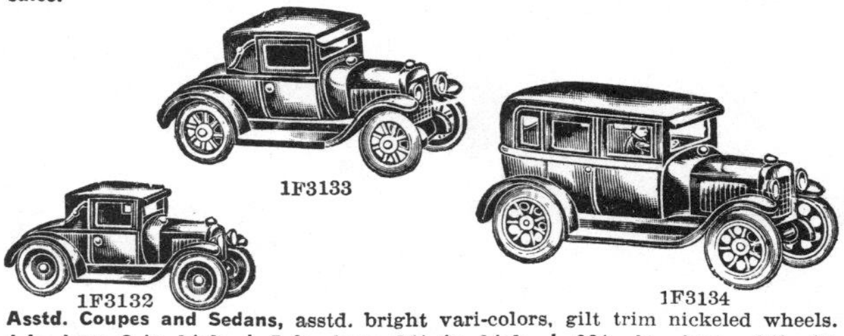

Asstd. Coupes and Sedans, asstd. bright vari-colors, gilt trim nickeled wheels.

4 in. long, 2 in. high, disc wheels.
1F-3132—Asstd. 1 doz. in box. Doz **$1.15**

5 in. long, 2½ in. high, spoke wheels.
1F-3133—½ doz. in box. Doz **$2.00**

6¾ in. long, 3½ in. high, removable nickeled chauffeur, imit. wire spoke wheels.
1F-3134—⅓ doz. in pkg. Doz **$4.00**

THESE "ARCADE" IRON TOYS LOOK REAL

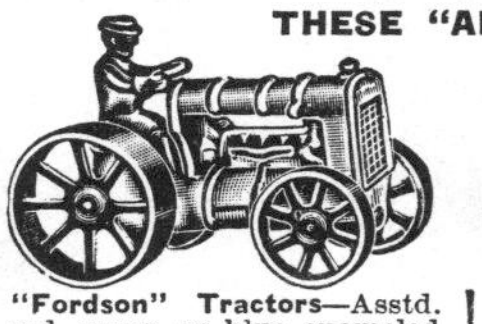

"Fordson" Tractors—Asstd. red, green or blue enameled bodies, red wheels.
1F-3096—4 in. 1 doz. in box. Doz **$1.15**
1F-3097—4¾ in. ½ doz. in box. Doz **$2.00**
6 in., gilt trim, nickeled steering wheel, removable driver.
1F-3103—1/12 doz. in box. Doz **$3.95**

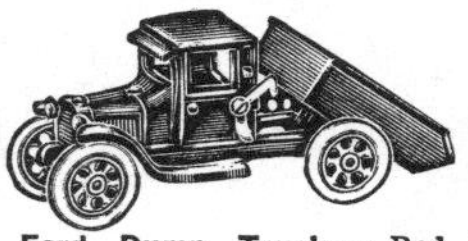

Ford Dump Truck — Red enameled chassis, green enameled dump body, nickel plated open spoke wheels.
1F-3101—6x1⅞x2½ in. ½ doz. in box. Doz **$2.00**
1F-3112—7½x2¾x3⅛ in. 1/12 doz. in box. Doz **$4.00**

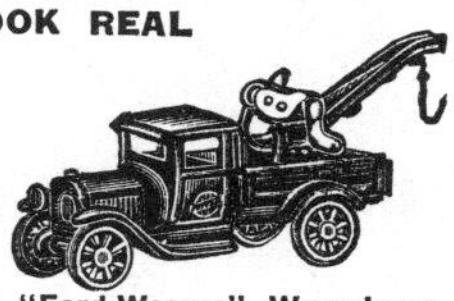

"Ford-Weaver" Wreckers, red enameled bodies, removable green enameled crane, nickeled wheels, cord, hook. 1/12 doz. in box.
1F-3113—6⅛x2⅜x2⅝ in. Doz **$4.00**

TWO BIG SELLING TRAINS

Black enameled locomotive and tender

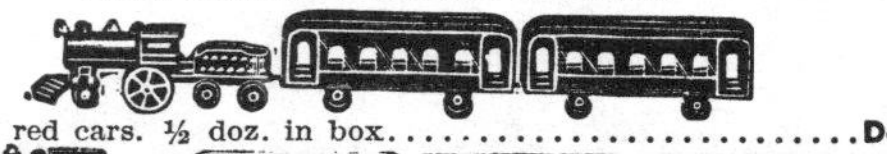

1F-3150—14 in., 2 red cars. ½ doz. in box........................Doz **$2.00**

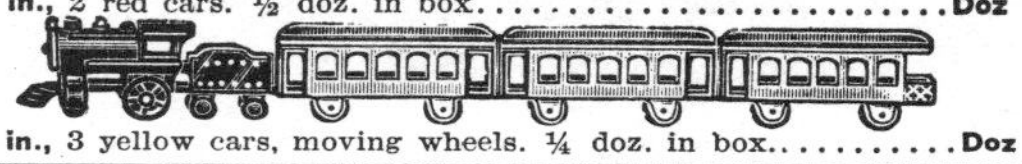

1F-3153—21 in., 3 yellow cars, moving wheels. ¼ doz. in box..........Doz **$4.00**

"KILGORE" TOYS ARE UNUSUALLY POPULAR

Very popular sellers....each enameled in 3 bright colors. Pieces in the sets can be sold individually at 10c....or in sets at 50c.

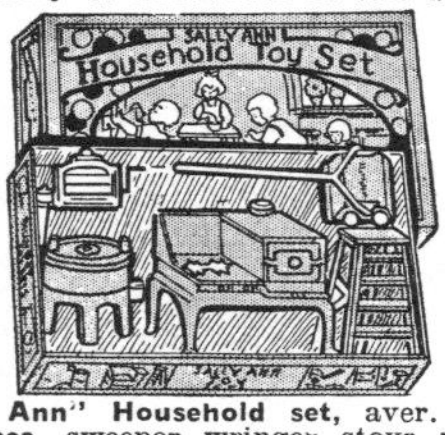

"Sally Ann" Household set, aver. 2½x2 in., **5 pcs.**, sweeper, wringer, stove, washer, ladder.
1F-3165—1/12 doz. sets in pkg. Doz sets **$3.90**

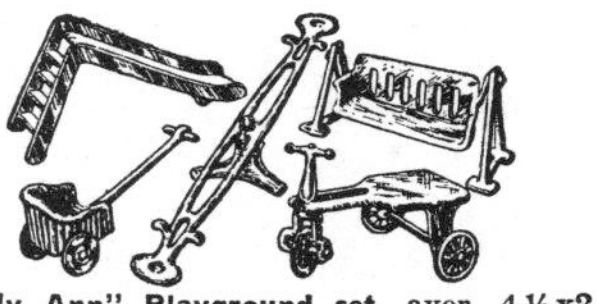

"Sally Ann" Playground set, aver. 4½x2 in., **5 pcs.**, swing, teeter totter, kiddie car, stroller, slide.
1F-3168—1/12 doz. sets in pkg. Doz sets **$3.90**

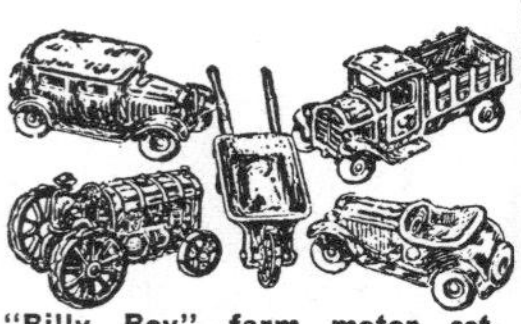

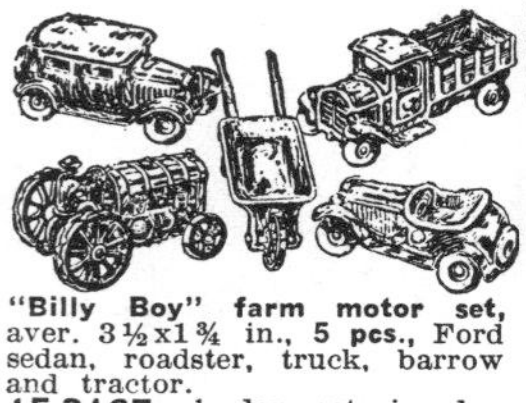

"Billy Boy" farm motor set, aver. 3½x1¾ in., **5 pcs.**, Ford sedan, roadster, truck, barrow and tractor.
1F-3167—1/12 doz. sets in pkg. Doz sets **$3.90**

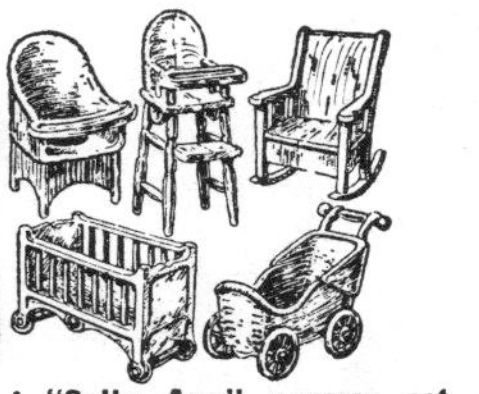

"Sally Ann" nursery set, aver. 2¾ in. high, **5 pcs.**, nursery, rocking chair, high chair, carriage, bassinet.
1F-3166—1/12 doz. sets in pkg. Doz sets **$3.90**

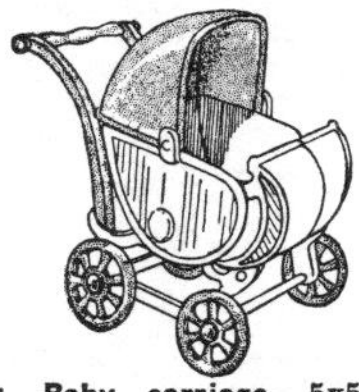

Baby carriage, 5x5¾ in., nickeled handles and wheels.
1F-3170—1/12 doz. in box. Doz **$3.90**

HEAVY CAST IRON MOTORCYCLES—With Drivers

Brightly enameled in 3 colors, double spoke nickeled wheels. You should never let your stock of these FLASHY numbers run low.....they are fascinating:....AND BIG sellers.

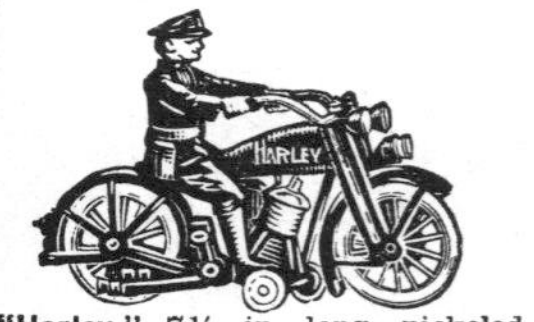

"Harley," 7¼ in. long, nickeled tires, **head turns right and left.**
1F-3154—1/12 doz. in box. Doz **$4.20**

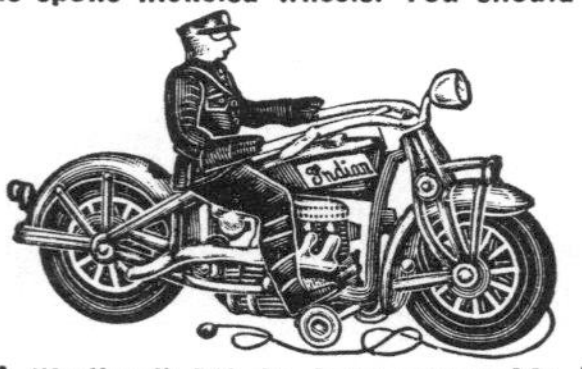

"Indian," 9½ in. long, removable enameled officer, heavy balloon type rubber tires, ratchet noise attachment, pull cord, wood grip.
1F-3155—1/12 doz. in box. Doz **$8.50**

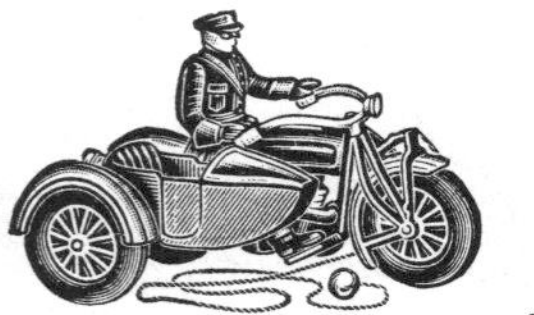

With side car, 8½ in. long, removable enameled officer, heavy balloon type rubber tires, ratchet noise attachment, pull cord, wood grip.
1F-3084—1/12 doz. in box. Doz **$12.50**

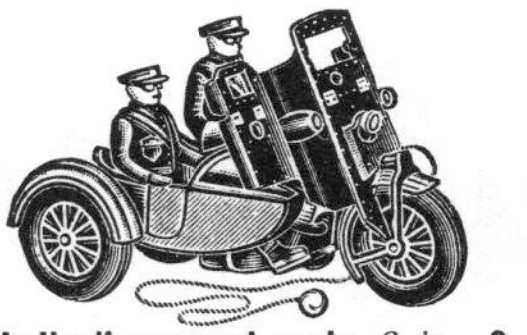

"Indian" armored cycle, 8 in., 2 removable enameled officers, heavy balloon type rubber tires, ratchet noise attachment, pull cord, wood grip.
1F-3085—1/12 doz. in box. Doz **$16.00**

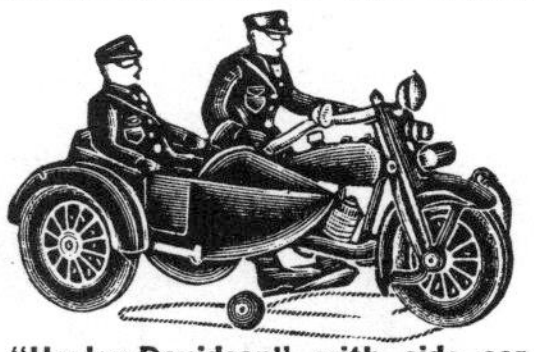

"Harley-Davidson" with side car, 9 in., 2 removable enameled officers, heavy balloon type rubber tires, ratchet noise attachment, pull cord, wood grip.
1F-3158—1/12 doz. in box. Doz **$16.00**

POPULAR HOUSEKEEPING TOYS

SUPER 10c VALUE!
4 Styles Utensils

Perfect miniatures of the real utensils! Practical in every respect. 2-color enameled handles. A SUPER VALUE!

Average 6 in., **4 styles**, potato masher, egg beater, mixing spoon, cake turner, blue & white enameled wood handles.
1F-2872—3 doz. in box. **Doz 75c**

Fork & Spoon Set—Heavy steel base, bright malacca plated, juvenile embossed handles, each set in box.
1F-3025—1 doz. sets in pkg. **Doz sets 78c**

Coal Set—5¾ x 4½ in. hod, 6 in. shovel, asstd. red and blue enameled.
1F-2812—1 doz. sets in box. **Doz sets 87c**

Flour Sifter—3¼ x3 in., heavy retinned plate, rolled edge top and bottom, wire agitator, crank handle, asstd. red, green, etc. enameled.
1F-2820—2 doz. in carton. **Doz 95c**

Knife, Fork & Spoon Set—Heavy steel base, double bright malacca plate, embossed handles, each set in box.
1F-2978—1 doz. sets in pkg. **Doz sets $1.10**

Striped Handle
Green Broom Corn
Double Sewed

Broom—30 in. long, good grade green broom corn, double sewed, striped natural finish handle.
1F-742—1 doz. in bundle. **Doz $1.75**

"Play Store Scale"—5¼ x6x4 in., asstd. red, blue and yellow enameled, weight indicator lever, each in box.
1F-3673—1 doz. in pkg. **Doz $1.90**

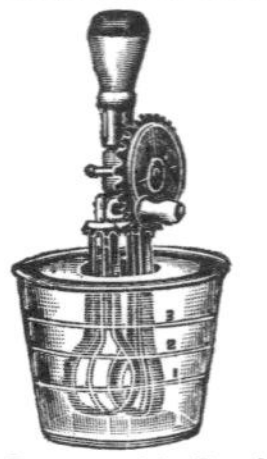

Egg Beater with Bowl—5½ in. beater, red & white enameled wood handle, 2½ x2¾ in. glass bowl, cover.
1F-2806—1 doz. in carton. **Doz $1.95**

5-pc. set, egg beater, mixing spoon, cake turner, ladle, apple corer, 4½ to 8 in., blue & white enameled wood handles, 12 x 10½ in. display box.
1F-2802— 1/12 doz. sets in box. **Doz sets $3.95**

MOTHER'S LITTLE HELPER
Just like Mothers

MOTHER'S HELP MATE

1F-3026— ½ doz. sets in box.

"Mother's Help Mate," 3-pc. set, 18½ in. hair broom, 4½ in. dust pan with 12½ in. twisted wire handle, 7½ in. red duster, red enameled. **Doz sets $4.10**

Coffee

Coffee Grinder—6½ in. high, **2 styles**, copies of regular grinders, some with Dutch designs on front, others in solid colors, porcelain coffee container, glass receptacle, nickeled handle, each on wood board.
2F-7853— ¼ doz. in pkg. **Doz $4.20**

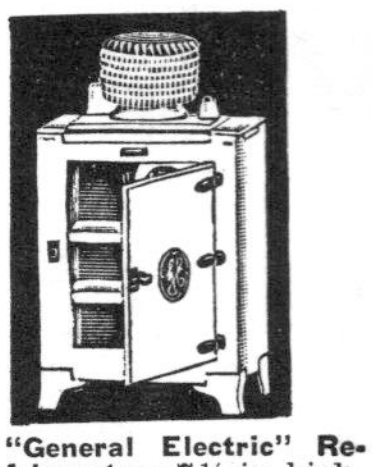

"General Electric" Refrigerator—7⅛ in. high, white enameled, cast iron frame, steel shelves and back, blue trim, nickeled **removable** ice cube pan, "G. E." label on door.
1F-3106 — ½ doz. in box. **Doz $8.00**

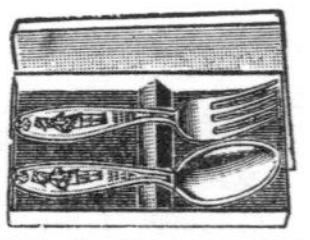

The LITTLE HOUSEKEEPER
MOTHERS LITTLE HELPER

"The Little Housekeeper," 3-pc. set, 24 in. hair broom, 6½ in. dust pan with 16 in. twisted wire handle, 7 in. dust mop with 23 in. handle, orange enameled.
1F-3024— 1/12 doz. sets in box. **Doz sets $8.00**

Order Now ... Pay Later!

2F-4527—1 in carton....**Each $4.75**
"Kokomo," MFRS 450, 15½ x12 in., lt. green & ivory enameled, nickeled cooking surface and trim, **2 heating elements, 2** switches, glass covered heat indicator, **3** aluminum utensils, **4 miniature grocery packages.**

TOY KITCHEN EQUIPMENT THAT SELLS

1F-736 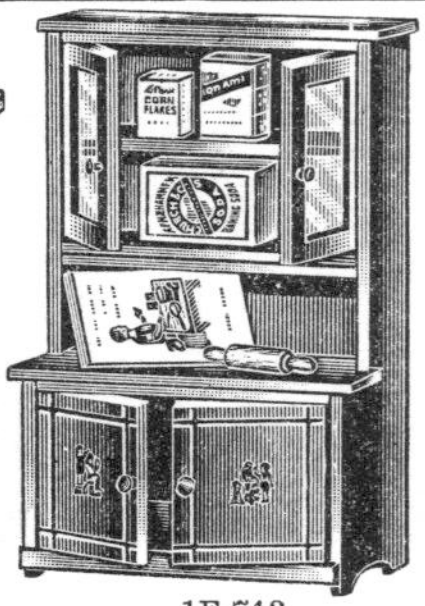   **1F-743**
Heavy wood construction, bright green enameled, juvenile decorations, 3 miniature grocery pkgs., wood rolling pin, recipe book.
1F-736— 8½ x12½ x4 in. shelf, 2 doors. 1/12 doz. in carton, 2½ lbs. **Doz $8.00**
1F-743—11x17½ x6½ in., 2 shelves, 4 doors, 2 with glass, imitation brass pulls, 1 in carton, 5 lbs. **Each $1.90**

"Boone," 8x5½ x3 in., **cast iron**, white enameled, hinged doors, 2 drawers, sliding bread board, imitation salt and coffee containers.
1F-3412 — 1/12 doz. in box. **Doz $8.00**

14¼ x13x5 in., sturdy **wood** construction, 5 compartments, two with doors, 8 grocery and utility items, ivory enameled with blue trim, juvenile decals.
1F-735— 1/12 doz. in carton. **Doz $10.80**

REALISTIC TOY STOVES .... Coal, Gas and Electric

TOY CAST IRON STOVES
Opening doors, high shelf back, imitation stove pipe, molded design, natural finish, cast iron utensils.

STAR
3¾ in. long, molded lids (not loose), kettle and skillet.
1F-3050—½ doz. in box. **Doz $2.00**

EAGLE
5½ in. long, 4 loose lids, kettle, skillet and lifter.
1F-3051 — ¼ doz. in box. **Doz $4.20**

EAGLE
13½ in. long 4 loose lids, detachable extension side shelf, imitation double warming oven, loose lids and reservoir cover, kettle, lifter, coal scuttle, shovel.
1F-3061— 1 in box. **Each $2.50**

TOY STEEL GAS RANGES
Opening door roasting oven, imitation gas compartment, all utensils nickel plated.

EAGLE
5 in. long, blue enameled, fry pan.
1F-3030 — ¼ doz. in carton. **Doz $2.00**

EAGLE
6½ in. long, blue enameled, skillet and fry pan.
1F-3031 — 1/12 doz. in box. **$7.90**

LIKE MOTHERS

18 in. long, 10 in. deep roasting oven, white enameled, blue trim, litho imitation gas jets and flame.
1F-2843—1 in box. **Each $1.75**

ELECTRIC TOY RANGES
Guaranteed to actually cook and bake. Made of the best quality heavy gauge steel, **black japanned, nickel trim**, 60 watt 110-volt direct or alternating current. Passed by the National Board of Fire Underwriters.

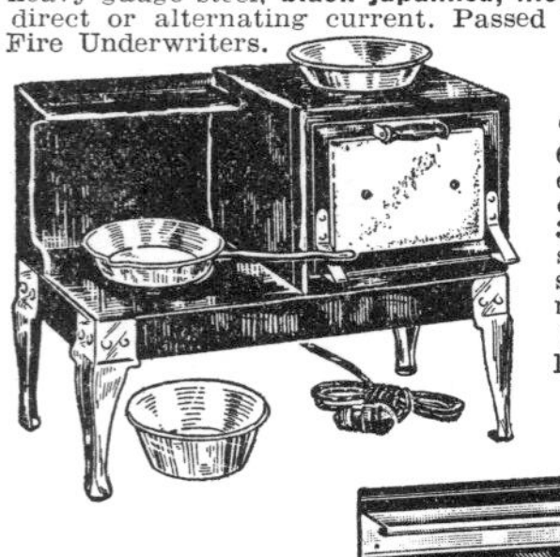

"Kokomo," MFRS 616, 6½ x14x10½ in., 2 heating elements, 1 on top, 1 in oven, 6 ft. cord, 2-pc. plug, 3 aluminum cooking utensils, 5 in. fry pan, 5 in. sauce pan, 5 in. pie plate, red enameled handles.
1F-2841—1 in carton, 8 lbs. **Each $3.25**

"Lady Junior," MFRS 258, 14x6½ x13½ in., green enameled and nickel trim, 2 heating elements, 1 on top, 1 in oven, **2 switches,** 5 ft. cord, 2-pc. plug, 3 aluminum cooking utensils, 4 in. fry pan, 3½ in. bread pan, 3 in. tea kettle, red enameled handles.
1F-2933—1 in carton, 10 lbs. **Each $4.75**

LAUNDRY TOYS . . . . *Practical Miniatures!*

Besides being splendid playthings they are also practical for laundering gloves, handkerchiefs and small articles.

TOY FLAT IRONS

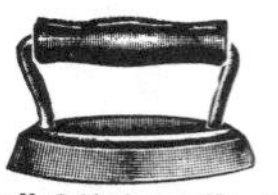

"Dover," 3⅛ in., gilt sides, polished face, black painted **wood handle,** nickeled ends.
1F-3041—1 doz. in box.
Doz 80c

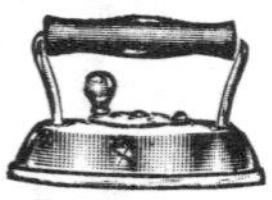

"Dover," 3½ in., polished nickeled, **removable hood,** black enameled **wood** handle.
1F-3042—1 doz. in box.
Doz $1.15

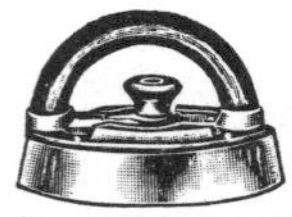

3¼ in., polished nickeled, varnished **removable wood handle.**
1F-3039—½ doz. in box.
Doz $1.95

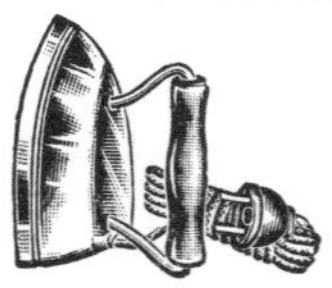

Imitation Electric!
4 in., nickeled, red enameled **wood** handle, 3 ft. red imitation electric cord & plug.
1F-3036—½ doz. in box.
Doz $1.95

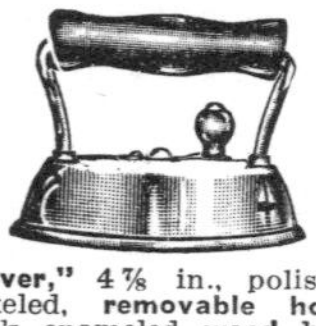

"Dover," 4⅞ in., polished nickeled, **removable hood,** black enameled **wood** handle.
1F-3045—½ doz. in box.
Doz $3.95

"DOVER" TOY ELECTRIC IRON

That REALLY WORKS...Guaranteed! Biggest value of its kind ever offered...product of a well known and reliable manufacturer. Sturdy heating element. Bright enameled.

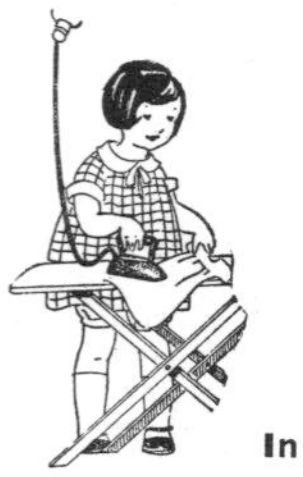

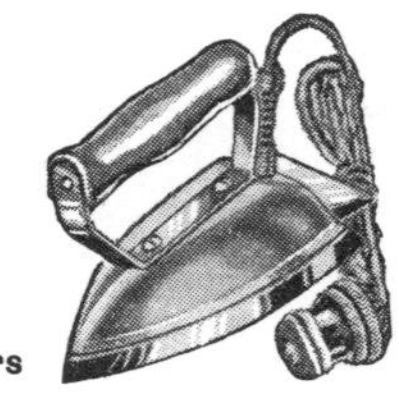

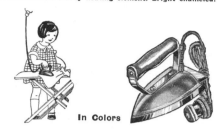

In Colors

1½ lbs., 4¾ in. long, asbestos insulated heating unit. 60 watts, 110 volt, for direct or alternating current, nickeled ironing surface and **heel rest,** asstd. green and blue enameled tops & wood handles, nickeled coil spring cord protector, 4½ ft. green silk electric cord with screw plug.
1F-3034—½ doz. in box.............**Doz $7.75**

WASHBOARD AND TUB SETS

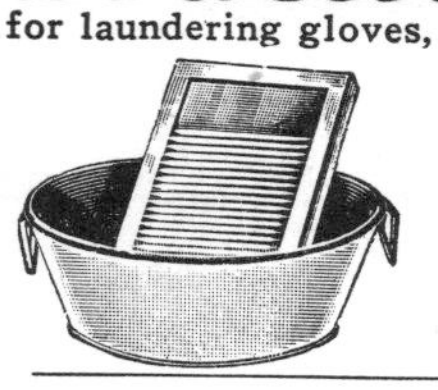

3¼x8¾ in. metal tubs in bright colors, 4⅝x7¾ in. board.
1F-2813—1 doz. sets in box............**Doz sets $2.00**

"WOLVERINE" LAUNDRY SETS

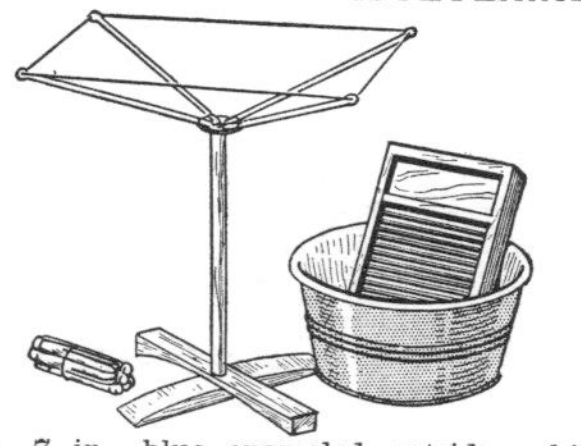

Tub, 7 in., blue enameled outside, white inside, **washboard,** 8 in. wood frame, metal rubbing surface, **folding clothes rack,** 11 in. high, 14 in. spread, 6 clothes pins, each set in box.
1F-3680—½ doz. sets in pkg.
Doz sets $4.25

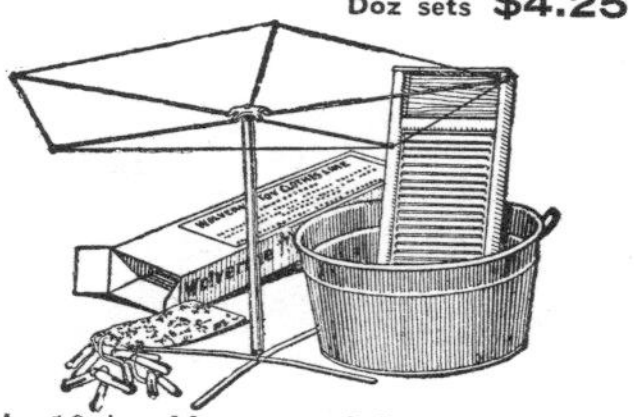

Tub, 10 in., blue enameled outside, white inside, **washboard,** 11 in. wood frame, GLASS rubbing surface, **folding clothes rack,** 12 in. high, 18½ in. spread, **6 clothes pins.**
1F-3675—½ doz. sets in box.
Doz sets $8.00

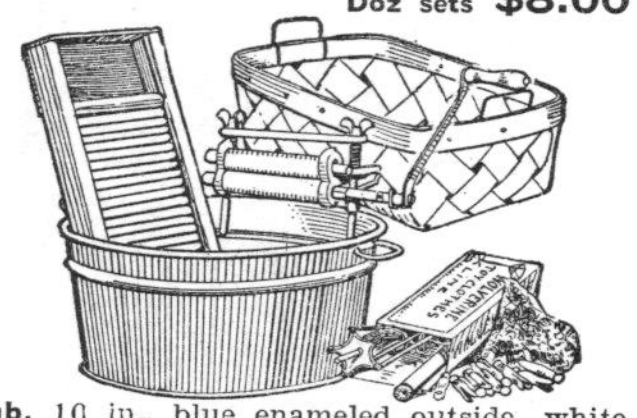

Tub, 10 in., blue enameled outside, white inside, **washboard,** 11 in. wood frame, GLASS rubbing surface, **folding clothes rack,** 12 in. high, 18½ in. spread, **wringer,** galvanized, adjustable, 2 rubber rolls, **clothes basket,** 7½x11¾ in., wire handles, **clothes pins,** 12 in bag.
1F-3676—1 set in box.
SET (17 pcs) $1.60

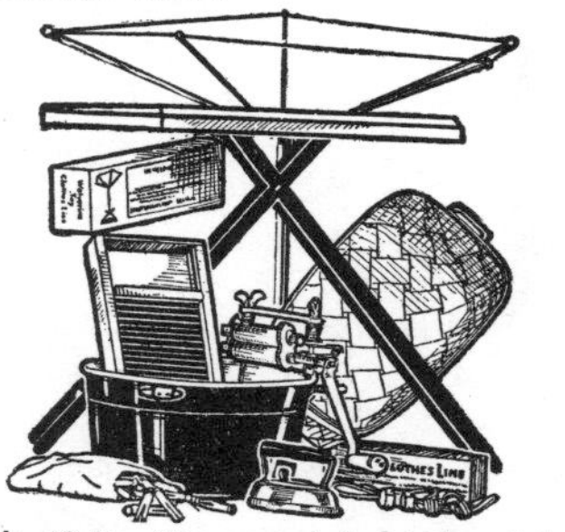

Tub, 10 in., blue enameled outside, white inside, **washboard,** 11 in. wood frame, GLASS rubbing surface, **folding clothes rack,** 12 in. high, 18½ in. spread, **wringer,** galvanized, adjustable, 2 rubber rolls, **clothes basket,** 7½x11¾ in., **clothes pins,** 12 in bag, **clothes line,** 2 pulleys, 2 rollers, 9 ft. white cotton rope and **6 clothes pins, ironing board,** 17 in., collapsible, **sad iron,** 4 in. nickeled, imitation electric type, black wood handle.
1F-3674—1 set in box.
SET (30 pcs) $2.15

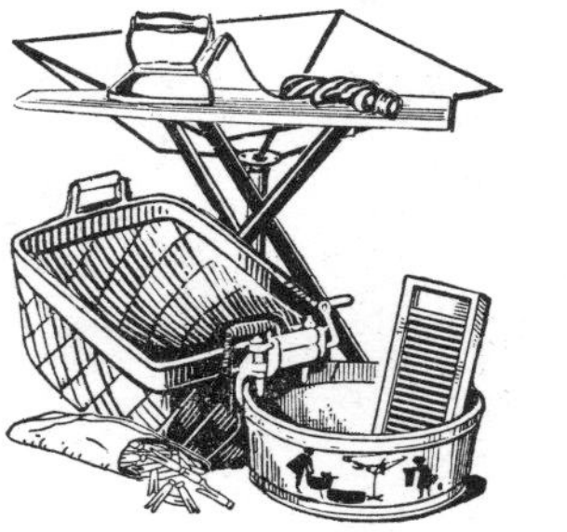

With Electric Iron
Tub, 10 in., blue enameled outside, white inside, **washboard,** 11 in. wood frame, glass rubbing surface, **folding clothes rack,** 12 in. high, 18½ in. spread, **wringer,** galvanized, adjustable, 2 rubber rolls, **clothes basket,** 11¾x7½ in., **ironing board,** 30 in. collapsible, **ELECTRIC iron,** 1 lb., cord plug, **clothes pins,** 12 in bag.
1F-3573—1 set in box.
SET (19 pcs) $3.33

IRONING BOARDS

Heavy smooth finish wood, collapsible legs, fold flat.

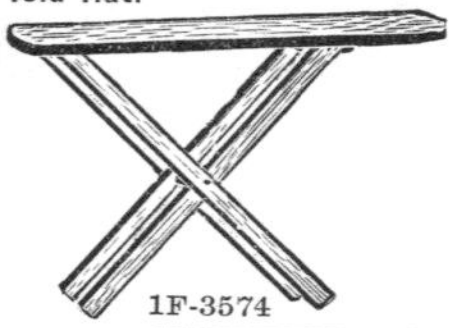

1F-3574

21½ in. long, 14½ in. high.
1F-3574—1 doz. in carton.
Doz $2.10

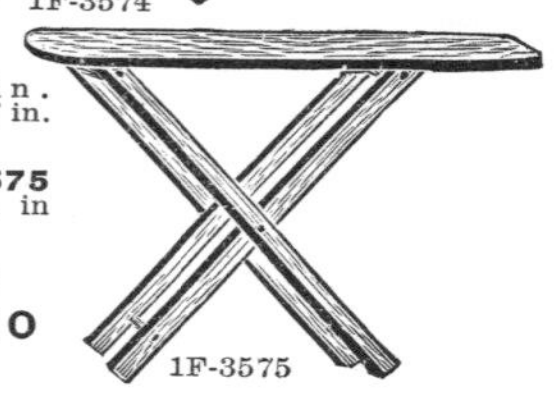

1F-3575

25½ in. long, 17 in. high.
1F-3575 ½ doz. in carton.
Doz $4.10

TOY WASHING MACHINES

Wind-Up Motor! Really Washes!

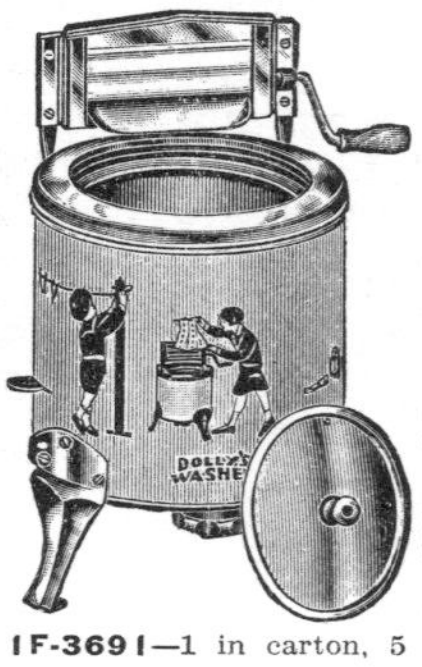

"Dolly's Washer." 10½ x 7½ in., heavy gauge metal, green enameled body with black litho juvenile decorations, nickel plated legs, cover, and 6½ in. wringer with heavy rubber rolls compressed by hidden springs, 5¾x3¾ in. splash rib aluminum tub which rotates from left to right, long running **powerful spring wind motor.**
1F-3691—1 in carton, 5 lbs.
Each $4.25

"HOOVER" TOY VACUUM CLEANER

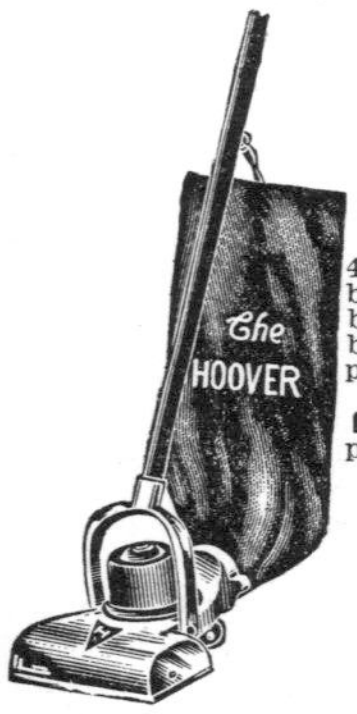

4x4½ in. aluminum body, 9½ in. cloth bag, stiff **bristle** brush, 21 in. black painted wood handle.
1F-3022—½ doz. in pkg.
Doz $8.25

"WOLVERINE" MINIATURE VACUUM CLEANER

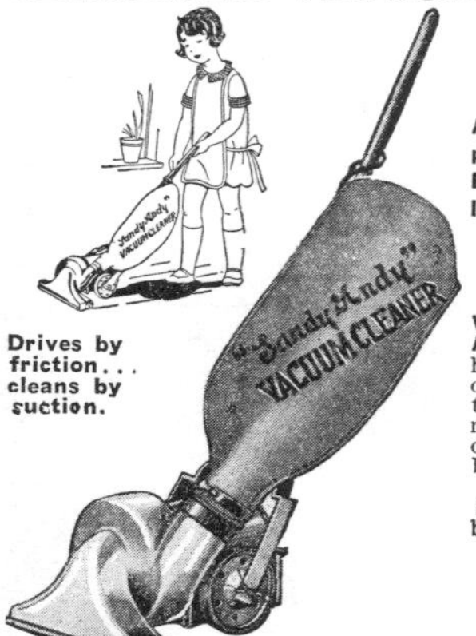

Actually clean carpets, rugs, etc. Realistic model of large machine.

Drives by friction... cleans by suction.

Wolverine's "Sandy Andy," 28¼ in. high, silvered metal case, yellow imitation motor, black & red enameled handle, cloth bag, rubber tired wheels.
1F-3690—1 in box.
Each $1.60

TOY CARPET SWEEPERS

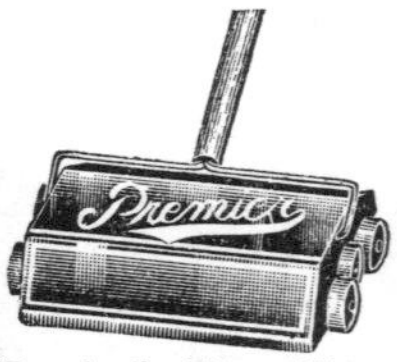

"Premier," 4½ x 7½ in. 1-pc. heavy metal case, turned wood wheels, stiff bristle brush, 24 in. wood handle.
1F-2952—1 doz. in carton.
Doz $2.00

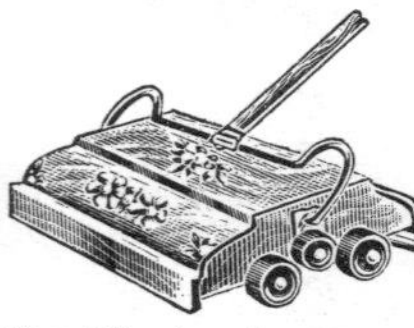

8¾ x 5¾ in. heavy metal case, 2-tone green enameled, floral decorations, turned wood wheels, stiff bristle brush, 2 dust receptacles, 22 in. adjustable handle, each in box.
1F-2963—½ doz. in pkg.
Doz $4.00

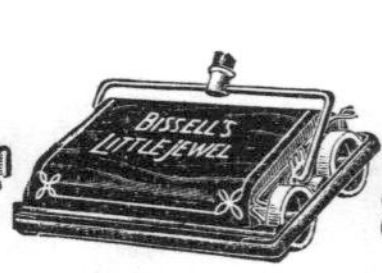

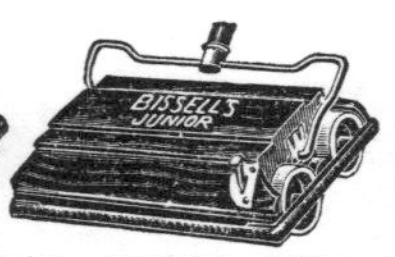

"Bissell's," mahogany finish, nickeled fittings, **rubber tired** steel wheels, dust pan with dump levers, braid band, self-adjusting wire core bristle brush.

"Little Jewel," 9x5x2⅜ in. fiberboard case, 27 in. handle.
1F-2511—½ doz. in pkg.
Doz $12.00

"Junior," 9x5¾x5½ in., **hardwood** case, 30 in. handle.
1F-2512—1 in box.
Each $1.60

IMPORTED TOY SEWING MACHINES

Guaranteed to Sew!

Polished nickeled cloth plates. Enameled base and frame in black or black & colors. Steel gears, foot levers and table clamps. Complete with thread, screw driver and instructions.

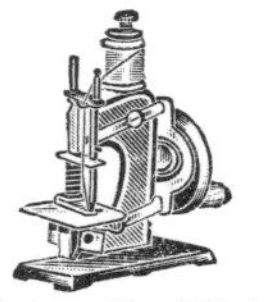

2½ in. wide, 3⅛ in. high, asstd. color enameled steel frame, nickeled trim, spring tension.
2F-7907—1 doz. in box.
Doz $3.60

Needles—Size 0.
2F-7916—1 doz. in pkg.
Doz 32c

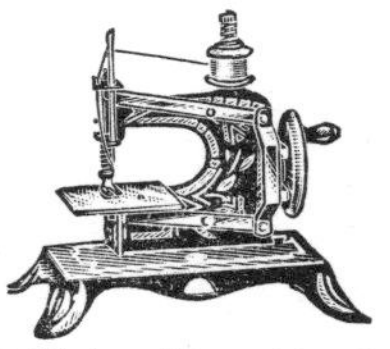

6½ in. wide, asstd. red, blue and green enameled, gilt trim, nickeled **wheel.**
2F-7914—½ doz. in pkg.
Doz $11.00

Needles—Size 0
2F-7916—1 doz. in pkg.
Doz 32c

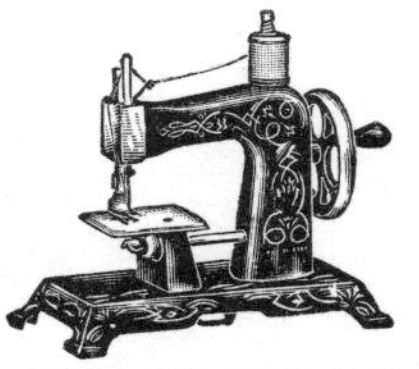

7¾ in. wide, black enameled with red, gilt & blue trim, nickeled wheel, wood handle, **mechanism enclosed in metal frame.**
2F-7899—1 in box.
Each $2.50

Needles—Sizes 1 to 20.
2F-7917—1 doz. in pkg.
Doz 32c

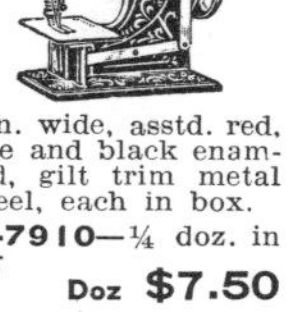

4 in. wide, asstd. red, blue and black enameled, gilt trim metal wheel, each in box.
2F-7910—¼ doz. in pkg
Doz $7.50

Needles—Size 0.
2F-7916—1 doz. in pkg.
Doz 32c

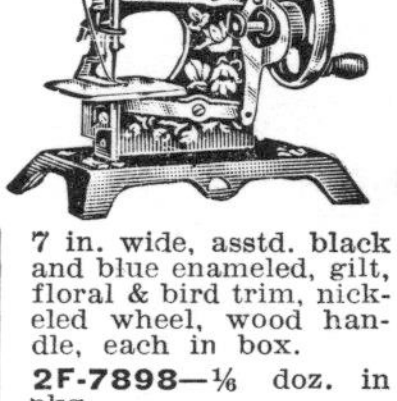

7 in. wide, asstd. black and blue enameled, gilt, floral & bird trim, nickeled wheel, wood handle, each in box.
2F-7898—⅙ doz. in pkg.
Doz $14.00

Needles—Sizes 1 to 20.
2F-7917—1 doz. in pkg.
Doz 32c

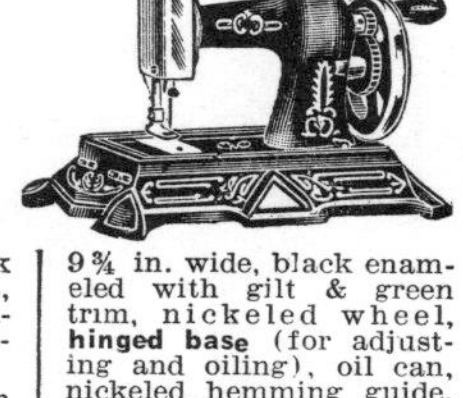

9¾ in. wide, black enameled with gilt & green trim, nickeled wheel, **hinged base** (for adjusting and oiling), oil can, nickeled hemming guide, cork buffers on bottom.
2F-7896—1 in box.
Each $5.25

Needles—Sizes 12 to 18.
2F-7915—1 doz. in pkg.
Doz 55c

Brightly Enameled 3-Pc. Table Sets

Sturdily constructed....with enamel finishes in beautiful color combinations! Unusually large pieces....and our prices are below the market!

Green With Orange Trim

Hardwood, wedgewood green enameled, orange stripes, **table,** 15x21 in. plywood top, 17 in. high; **chairs,** 18 in. high, bow back, 8½x8½ in. seat.

1F-707—1 set in carton, 12 lbs. SET (3 pcs) **$2.75**

Ivory With Green Trim

Hardwood, ivory enameled, green trim and legs, **table,** 16x20 in. plywood top, 18 in. high; **chairs,** 20 in. high, bow back, 9¼x9 in. seat.

1F-708—1 set in carton, 19 lbs. SET (3 pcs) **$3.25**

STEEL TOP
3-Pc. Table Set

"Miss Muffet", hardwood, **"ABC"** & numerals and "animal breakfast" designs, corner decorations, **table,** 16x20 in. steel top, 18 in. high; **chairs,** 21½ in. high, bow back, 10¾x10½ in. seat. 1 set in carton, 17 lbs.

SET (3 pcs)

1F-777—2-tone blue enameled..........
1F-779—Ivory enameled, green trim..... } **$3.50**

ENAMELED HARDWOOD JUVENILE 3-PIECE TABLE SETS

Hardwood, asstd. **blue, Chinese red** and **green** enameled, **table,** 13x18 in. top, 13½ in. high; **chairs,** 18 in. high, bow back, 8½x8½ in. seat.

1F-683—3 sets in carton, 30 lbs. SET (3 pcs) **$1.45**

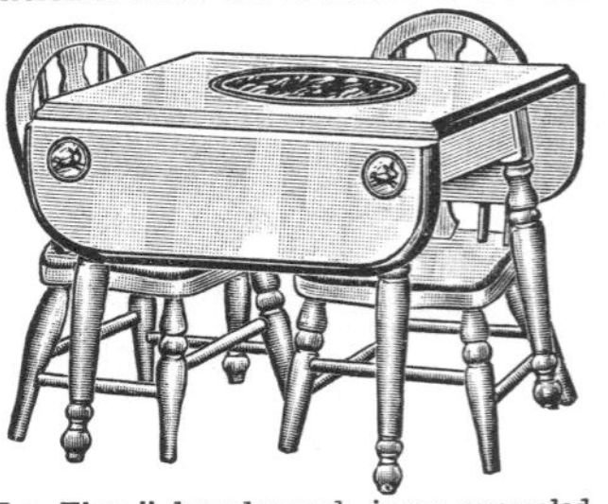

"Tea Time," hardwood, **ivory** enameled, blue trim, **table,** 26½x21½ in., top with **leaves** raised, 18 in. high; chairs, 21 in. high, square bow back, 11½x11½ in. shaped seat.

1F-712—1 set in carton, 25 lbs. SET (3 pcs) **$4.75**

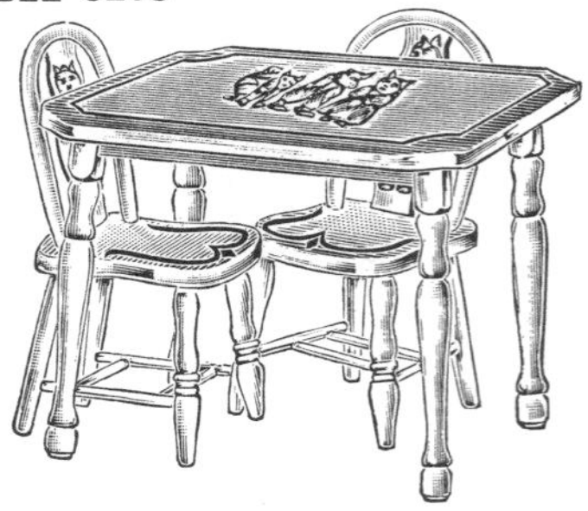

"The Three Bears," hardwood, **ivory** enameled, tan trim, "The Three Bears'" decoration, **table,** 20x26 in. top, 21 in. high; **chairs,** 25 in. high, bow back, 10½x11½ in. shaped seat, 5½ in. back panel.

1F-763—1 set in carton, 25 lbs. SET (3 pcs) **$5.75**

Breakfast set, hardwood, **2-tone green** enameled, decal decoration, **table,** 29x23 in. top with leaves raised, 20 in. high; **chairs,** 24 in. high, 11x11 in. seat.

1F-745—1 set in carton, 30 lbs. SET (3 pcs) **$7.25**

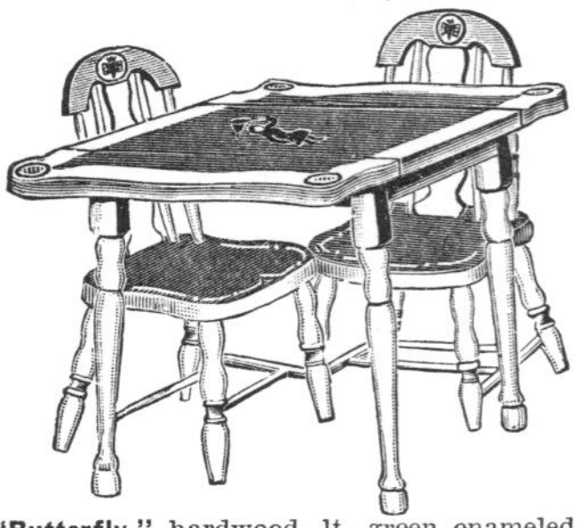

"Butterfly," hardwood, lt. green enameled, ivory trim, butterfly decal decorations, **table,** 26 x 32 in. top with leaves raised, 22 in. high; **chairs,** cathedral design, 26½ in. high, 11½x12½ in. shaped seat.

1F-764—1 set in carton, 26 lbs. SET (3 pcs) **$7.50**

VARNISHED OAK
3-PC. TABLE SETS

"Tea Room," varnished natural oak, green trim, butterfly decorations, **table,** 16x20 in. top, 18 in. high; **chairs,** 19¾ in. high, 9¾ x9 in. seat, paneled back.

1F-715—1 set in carton, 16 lbs. SET (3 pcs) **$2.85**

JUVENILE STEEL TOP TABLE
With Drawer

15x21 in., red enameled metal top, hardwood frame, green striped, 18 in. high. center drawer, turned legs.

1F-741—2 in carton, 20 lbs. **Each $2.10**

KIDDIES' TEA KART

Hardwood, 19 in. high, 17x13 in. top, rubber tire disc wheels, decal decorated, peach enameled, green trim.

1F-601—1 in carton, k. d., 5 lbs. **Each $2.50**

PORCELAIN ENAMELED TOP JUVENILE 3-PIECE TABLE SETS

"Miss Muffet," hardwood, ivory porcelain, blue trim, "Miss Muffet" center design with numerals and A B C's, animal corners, **table,** 16x20 in. top, 18 in. high; **chair,** 21 in. high, bow back, 10x10 in. seat.

1F-774—1 set in carton, 20 lbs. SET (3 pcs) **$4.25**

Hardwood, ivory porcelain, blue trim, A B C, numerals and circus designs, **table,** 16x20 in. top, 18 in. high; **chairs,** 21½ in. high, bow back, 11½x11½ in. shaped seat.

1F-776—1 set in carton, 20 lbs. SET (3 pcs) **$5.75**

RED PAINTED WOOD TABLES

13x18 in. top, 14 in. high, bright red, highly varnished, turned legs, substantial construction.

1F-574—⅙ doz. in crate, k. d, 20 lbs......**Doz $8.00**

Porcelain Enameled Top

One of our finest....an excellent value in 3-pc. Table Sets....suitable for children up to 12 years!

Hardwood, porcelain enamel top, decal designs, **table,** 24x20 in. top, 21 in. high; **chairs,** 26½ in. paneled back, 13x12½ in. seats. 1 set in carton, 50 lbs.

1F-784—Ivory porcelain, blue diamond design top.

1F-785—Green porcelain, orange trim, ABC, numeral and circus design top. SET (3 pcs) **$7.75**

JUVENILE KITCHEN CABINETS
Each With Stool

Heavy wood construction, **paneled** doors, nickeled hardware, automatic door latches.

For Girls up to 10 Yrs.

24 in. high, 16 in. wide, work table 12 in. from floor, ivory enameled, gray & red trim, glass panels in upper doors, decal decorated lower doors, 9½ in. stool.

1F-754—1 in carton, 16 lbs.

Each $3.90

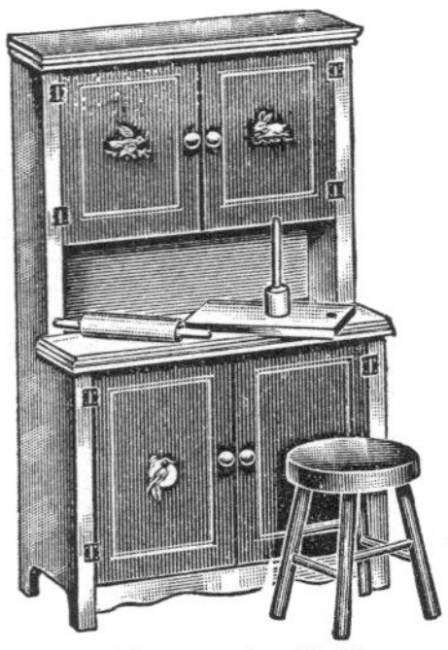

For Girls up to 12 Yrs.

34 in. high, 20 in. wide, work table 17 in. from floor, 2-tone green enameled, **3 fittings,** rolling pin, bread board, potato masher, matched 9 in. stool.

1F-756—1 in carton, 27 lbs.

Each $5.25

For Girls Up to 12 Yrs.

32 in. high, 19¼ in. wide, work table 16 in. from floor, ivory enameled, blue doors and drawers, red trim compartment with shelves, **3 fittings,** rolling pin, bread board, potato masher, blue enameled 10 in. stool.

1F-762—1 in crate, 42 lbs.

Each $6.50

EVERY STORE Needs these items for a
Complete Doll Dept.

These inexpensive novelty dolls are among the most popular sellers in every toy department. See that you have a complete showing for the holiday season and representation throughout the year.

Negro Dolls

"Aunt Jemima" 13 in., dk. brown FULL composition body, painted features, jointed arms, polka dot lawn dress, lawn apron and panties, red muslin bandanna, imit. leather shoes, real stockings.
1 F-5071—½ doz. in box.
Doz $8.95

"Kinky Kurls" 15 in., dk. brown composition head, painted features, 3 worsted pigtails, ribbon bows, composition arms, jointed shoulders, cotton stuffed, percale rompers, braid trim, real stockings, imit. leather slippers.
1 F-5076—½ doz. in box.
Doz $7.95

Popular Outdoor Dolls

Life-like and natural! Appealing and fascinating! These novelty costumes will lend added color and pep to your Doll Department.

Two Styles that will appeal to every girl—

Composition heads with breast plates, sleeping eyes, real lashes, mohair wigs, full composition arms and legs.

23 in., multi-colored brushed wool slip-on sweater, shell-stitched collar and throw-back, matched tam and bootees, shaped cotton jacquard serge knickers, satin covered buttons.
1 F-5117—1 in box.
Each $2.75

28 in., open mouth, tongue and teeth, solid color pink, blue, etc. pique dresses, lawn bloomers, white knitted sport sweater, shell-stitched sleeves, pocket and throw-back, matched tam, crying voice, rayon socks, imit. leather footwear.
1 F-5121—1 in box.
Each $3.25

"Nelke" Stockinette Dolls

Nationally advertised, light weight, no pins or buttons, soft and cuddly, unbreakable, waterproof, hand painted features and hair, one-piece patented jersey cloth bodies.

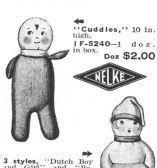

"Cuddles," 10 in. high.
1 F-5240—1 doz. in box.
Doz $2.00

NELKE

3 styles, **"Dutch Boy and Girl"** and **"Bo-Peep,"** 10 in., 2-tone bodies, roll collars and turnback cuffs, life-like painted faces.
1 F-5241—Asstd. ½ doz. in box.
Doz $3.75

DOLLS' KNITTED OUTFIT

4 pcs., sacque, hood, toque, bootees, fits 5 to 6½ in. dolls, asstd. pink & white and blue & white, firmly knit.
1 F-5010—1 doz. pieces (3 outfits) in box.......................**Doz pcs $1.20**

Soft Stuffed Dolls

Cotton stuffed bodies, overstitched feet and head, painted features.

"Red Riding Hood" dolls, 16 in., composition head with breast plate, painted features, red oil cloth body, cape and skirt, bound edges, matched ruffle cap, tiestrings.
1 F-5255—½ doz. in box.
Doz $4.00

Aver. 8½ in., 12 styles, asstd. girls and boys, jointed arms, solid and 2-tone stockinette bodies, some with rayon sweaters and percale rompers, with caps.
1 F-5238—Asstd. 1 doz. in box.
Doz $1.95

12 in., loosely jointed arms, mercerized stockinette bodies, 2-tone rayon sweaters, caps, gilt printed "Buddy" band, cellophane wrapped.
1 F-5239—1 doz. in box.
Doz $2.18

Boudoir Dolls

Realistic composition character heads, life-like tinted features and eyes, soft cotton stuffed bodies, extra long flexible legs and arms.

32 in., asstd. color waved mohair wig, stitched center part, ribbon bow under chin, green, pink, rose, etc., sateen bodies.
1 F-5264—¼ doz. in box.
Doz $7.50

32 in., asstd. color waved mohair wig, stitched center part, side curls, rayon bodies, long flesh finished composition hands, veil, orchid, pink, blue, etc., rayon dress, lace trimmed front panel, cuffs and wide collar, ribbon bow ornaments, gilt imit. leather slippers with high heels.
1 F-5267—½ doz. in box.
Doz $27.00

1F-5264   1F-5267

Suggest these colorful French dolls to your better trade. They add color and smartness to the home.

32 in., waved mohair wig, stitched center part, long curls, rayon bodies, long flesh finished composition hands, veil, orchid, green, pink, etc., rayon dresses, attractively trimmed with contrasting shirred ribbon and large matched shirred ribbon edged hat, gilt imit. leather slippers with high heels.
1 F5274—1 in box..........**Each $2.95**

34 in., mohair wig, asstd. green, rose, etc., crystal crepe rayon pajamas in pierrot style, embroidered braid trim throughout, high color pompons on front of coat, sleeves and bottom of pants, ruffle trim neck, matched cap, high heeled slippers.
1 F-5272—1 in box.
Each $3.25

1F5272

"Knickerbocker" Plush Animals
A Line Famous For Quality

Exceptionally life-like and unusually attractive . . . truly high class merchandise that children love to cuddle . . . and that your customers will buy for decorative purposes! Made of EXTRA long plush, fine quality cotton stuffed bodies, glass eyes, stitched features, VOICE. Each in a BRIGHT COLORED BOX.

"Teddy" Canary, turning head, felt hands and feet, ribbon collars, jointed.
1 F-4946 12 in. ½ doz. in box.
Doz $18.00
1 F-4947 14 in. ½ doz. in box.
Doz $22.00
1 F-4948 18 in. 1 in box.
Each $2.75

"Billy the Pup," canary, turning head, ribbon collar.
1 F-4940—7 in. ½ doz. in box.
Doz $12.50

"Trilby" the Prize Cat, gray tipped, white under body and top of turning head, imitation whiskers, silk ribbon collar.
1 F-4943—6¾ in. ½ doz. in box.
Doz $14.00
1 F-4945—9½ in. 1 in box.
Each $2.40

Dressed, fine quality white and canary velvet bodies, plush heads, shoes and stockings.
"Sister Cat" 11 in., gray tipped head, whiskers, printed percale pantie dress and hanky, organdie pocket, lace trim.
1 F-4951—½ doz. in box.
Doz $16.00

"Mother Bear" White and canary plush heads, fancy printed percale dresses and hanky, pink, blue, etc., wide organdie shirred collars and aprons with pocket and tiestrings, white lawn embroidery trim ruffled drawers. 1 in box.
1 F-4952—13 in.
Each $2.50
1 F-4953—16 in.
Each $3.50

5c TO 25c IMPORTED CELLULOID DOLLS

Dandy values in popular price sellers that pay you a BIGGER markup! True-to-nature embossing, heavy celluloid stock, painted features and hair.

2¾ in., 12 styles, asstd. boys and girls, painted costumes.
2F-9601—3 doz. in box............Doz 30c

3½ in., jointed arms, red head band.
2F-9430—2 doz. in box. Doz 32c

5 in., jointed arms and legs.
2F-9425 — 2 doz. in box. Doz 33c

5½ in., jointed arms and legs.
2F-9429—1 doz. in box. Doz 65c

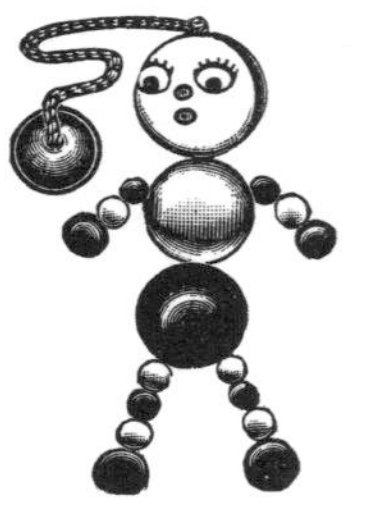

← 5 in., 6 styles, some with jointed arms, others with jointed arms and legs, asstd. color painted plain, ribbon and floral trim bathing suits, some with caps.
2F-9422 — 3 doz. in box. Doz 39c

2F-9422

"Playmates," bright painted costumes, shoes and hats, 6 styles, school boy and girl, tennis and basketball players, sport girl and boy.
2F-9382 — 5¼ in. 2 doz. in box. Doz 40c
2F-9383 — 7¼ in. 1 doz. in box. Doz 84c

4⅛ in., white fur ballet skirt, feathered tinsel headband.
2F-9633 — 2 doz. in box. Doz 75c

Aver. 5½ in., 6 styles, jointed arms, asstd. bright color painted bathing suits.
2F-9532 — 2 doz. in box. Doz 78c

5¼ in., asstd. color beads, 9 in. cord with celluloid button.
2F-9751 — 1 doz. in box. Doz 75c

6½ to 6¾ in., flirt eyes, 6 styles, some with asstd. color bathing costumes.
2F-9394 — 1 doz. in box. Doz 80c

6 to 6½ in., 6 styles, asstd. boys and girls, bright painted costumes, some with hats to match, others with painted ribbons and hair.
2F-9528 — 1 doz. in box. Doz 80c

6½ in., jointed arms, asstd. color painted headbands.
2F-9435 — 1 doz. in box. Doz 80c

5½ in., 2 styles, Santa Claus, red costume, white trim, black belt, boots and radio headset, green bag.
2F-9544 — 1 doz. in box. Doz 87c

8 in., jointed hips and shoulders, green headband.
2F-9444—1 doz. in box. Doz $1.20

Each with musical chime in body, 2 styles, clown and girl, heavy celluloid stock, painted features, costumes, slippers and socks.
2F-9373—8 in. 1 doz. in box. Doz $2.10
2F-9374—9½ in. ½ doz. in box. Doz $2.25

COMPOSITION DOLLS

"Flirt," 5½ in., flesh tinted body, painted features, eyes, socks and shoes, jointed arms, asstd. mohair wigs, roguish expression, asstd. colored dresses, ½ doz. in box.
2F-6774—1 doz. in pkg. Doz 87c

9 in., 6 styles, dude, bell hop, clown, girl, etc., jointed arms, bright painted costumes with caps and hats to match, will stand alone, rattles in body, some with small bells in hand.
2F-9372—½ doz. in box. Doz $2.00

CELLULOID DOLL NOVELTIES

Doll In Cradle—1¼ in. doll, 1¾ in. cradle, pink and blue paper, silk ribbon.
2F-9413—3 doz. sets in box. Doz sets 36c

Nursing Set — 2½ in. doll, glass bottle with rubber nipple.
2F-9410—2 doz. sets in pkg. Doz sets 37c

Negro Doll In Melon— 3½ in. negro doll, jointed arms and legs, cardboard melon.
2F-9790 — 3 doz. in box. Doz 75c

Doll In Shell — 3¼ in. doll, jointed arms and legs, paper peanut shell.
2F-9714 — 2 doz. in box. Doz 75c

Doll In Cradle—3½ in. full jointed doll, imit. nursing bottle, 3½ in. pink enameled cardboard cradle, silk ribbon, gilt trim.
2F-9416 — 2 doz. in box. Doz 80c

Nursing Set—3 in. full jointed doll, 2½ in. glass nursing bottle with metal top, glass tube and rubber nipple, 2 in. metal rattle, ¾ in. rubber pacifier, silk cord, in partitioned box.
2F-9405—1 doz. sets in box. Doz sets 80c

Dolls' Bath Set—2½ in. doll, full jointed, white enameled metal bath tub, rubber sponge, wash cloth, hinged box.
2F-9412—1 doz. sets in box. Doz sets 80c

BISQUE DOLL NOVELTIES

Dolls are flesh tinted and have painted features and hair

Doll & Rocker—2½ in. doll, jointed arms, nursing bottle, asstd. color dresses, 2½ in. wood rocker.
2F-6677—1 doz. in box. Doz 80c

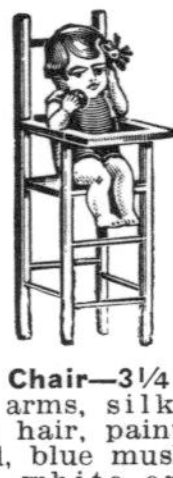

Doll & Chair—3¼ in. doll, jointed arms, silk ribbon bow on hair, painted apple in hand, blue muslin shirt; 5⅝ in. white enameled wood chair with tray, each in box.
2F-6880—½ doz. in box. Doz $1.75

Doll & Basket Chair—2½ in. doll, jointed arms, painted bathing suit, beach chair, 4 in., cream enameled fiber, asstd. colors inside, 2 windows.
2F-6798—1 doz. in box. Doz $1.75

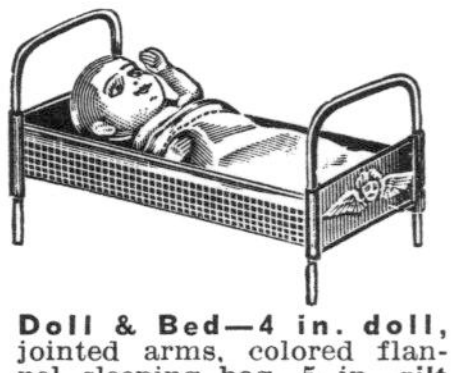

Doll & Bed—4 in. doll, jointed arms, colored flannel sleeping bag, 5 in. gilt wire bed.
2F-6845—1 doz. in box. Doz $2.00

Doll Party Set—4 pcs. furniture, 3¼ in. round table, three 3 in. chairs, asstd. ivory, green and blue enameled fiber, cardboard plate with imit. cake, 3 dolls, jointed arms, asstd. color dresses, each set tied in box.
2F-6795 — ¼ doz. sets in pkg. Doz sets $3.95

"MINERVA" METAL DOLL HEADS
Indestructible

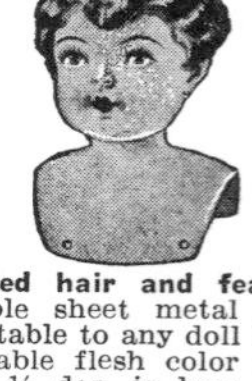

Painted hair and features, flexible sheet metal (buts adjustable to any doll body), washable flesh color enameled. ½ doz. in box.
2F-6931—Size 2, 2½ x 3¼ in. Doz $1.95
2F-6933—Size 3, 2¾ x 3⅝ in. Doz $2.00
2F-6934—Size 4, 3⅛ x 4 in. Doz $3.00

China Limb Dolls

To Sell at 5c—10c—25c

China heads, painted features, hair and footwear, stuffed strong muslin body.

With china hands and feet, name on breast-plate.

2F-6716—7½ in. 2 doz. in box. Doz **80c**

2F-6715—12½ in. ½ doz. in box. Doz **$2.00**

With china breastplate, forearms and legs.

2F-9469—5½ in. 3 doz. in box. Doz **39c**

2F-9471—7 in. 2 doz. in box. Doz **72c**

2F-9472—8½ in. 1 doz. in box. Doz **80c**

2F-9475—13 in. 1 doz. in box. Doz **$1.95**

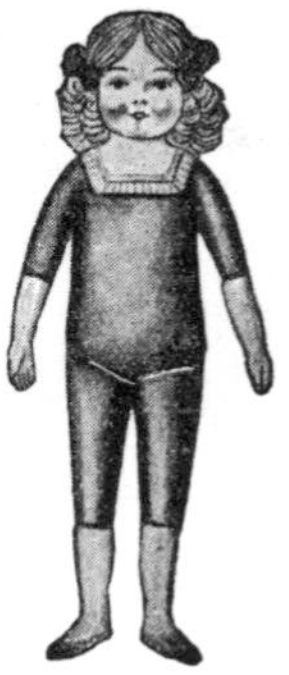

IMPORTED CHINA DOLLS . . 5c and 10c Sellers

Tinted bodies, painted features and costumes

5 in., jointed arms and legs, painted hair bow, slippers and stockings.
2F-9647—2 doz. in box. Doz **36c**

4½ in., jointed arms and legs, **mohair wig.**
2F-9649—2 doz. in box. Doz **36c**

4½ in., **flirt eyes,** jointed arms, painted marcel.
2F-9669—2 doz. in box. Doz **37c**

4½ in., **flirt eyes,** jointed arms, painted marcel, asstd. color painted bathing suits with juvenile and animal designs, gilt trim.
2F-9675 — 2 doz. in box. Doz **39c**

2 styles, boy and girl, 3½ in., jointed arms.
2F-9656—2 doz. in box. Doz **39c**

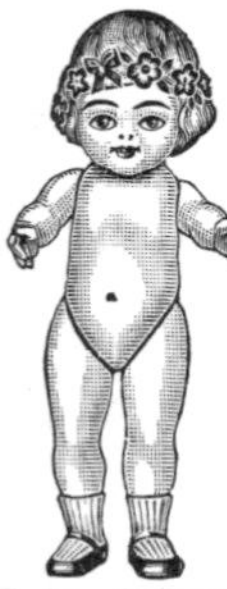

5 in., jointed arms and legs.
2F-9509 — 2 doz. in box. Doz **65c**

Dutch boy, 5¼ in., jointed arms, asstd. color costumes, shoes and stockings.
2F-9672 — 1 doz. in box. Doz **75c**

6 in., **flirt eyes,** jointed arms, painted marcel.
2F-9495—1 doz. in box. Doz **75c**

2 styles, 6¼ in., **flirt eyes,** painted marcel, some with bows, asstd. color painted bathing suits with animal designs, black trim.
2F-9678 — 1 doz. in box. Doz **80c**

6¼ in. jointed arms and legs, mohair wig, painted stockings and slippers.
2F-9651—1 doz. in box. Doz **84c**

IMPORTED CHINA NOVELTIES

Dolls have painted features and hair

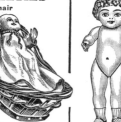

Doll In Tub—2 in. doll, 2½ in. white china bath tub, gilded rim.
2F-9786—2 doz. in box. Doz **32c**

Doll In Tub—1¾ in. china **doll,** sitting position, 7 in. white enameled metal **bath tub,** asstd. color tinted base and sides.
2F-6922—½ doz. in box. Doz **89c**

Doll In Basket—4 in. **doll,** jointed arms and legs, long white flannel slip, 8 in. white **willow basket.**
2F-9692 — 1 doz. in box. Doz **$1.75**

IMPORTED BISQUE DOLLS

Flesh tinted bodies, painted features and hair

5 in., jointed arms, painted marcel waved hair.
2F-6732—1 doz. in box. Doz **80c**

5 in., hip and shoulder joints, bobbed hair, ribbon.
2F-6733—1 doz. in box. Doz **80c**

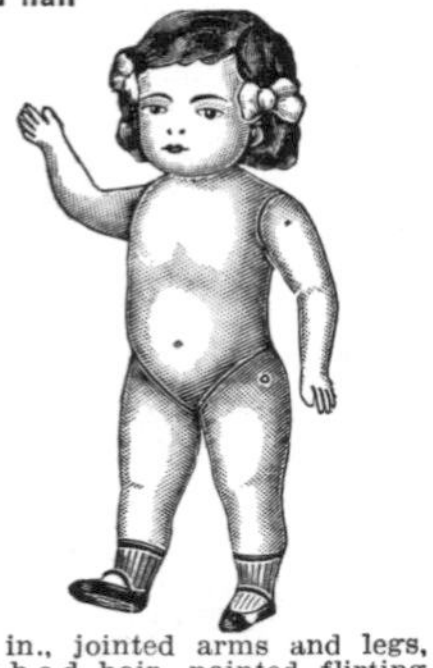

7½ in., jointed arms and legs, bobbed hair, painted flirting eyes.
2F-6737—½ doz. in box. Doz **$1.75**

5½ in., modeled from a real baby, life-like turning bisque head, jointed hips and shoulders, white cotton diaper with pin, 6 in. in box.
2F-6700—1 doz. in pkg. Doz **$1.95**

2 styles, 7 in., jointed hip and shoulders, white **flannel** diaper with safety pin.
2F-6701—½ doz. in box. Doz **$1.95**

DOLLS' RUBBER PANTS

4½ x 5¼ in., pure gum rubber, overstitched elastic waist and knees, asstd. white, flesh and natural.
1F-5005—1 doz. in box. Doz **80c**

DOLLS' KNITTED OUTFIT

4 pcs., sacque, hood, toque, bottees, fits 5 to 6½ in. dolls, asstd. pink & white and blue & white, firmly knit.
1F-5010 — 1 doz. pieces (3 outfits) in box. Doz pcs **$1.20**

"IDEAL" ADJUSTABLE DOLL DISPLAY STANDS

Non-tarnishable gray enameled upright and pear shaped steel base, sliding collar locks doll in place, adjustable for variation in size of doll.

	For Dolls In.	In pkg.	Doz
1F-5080	10 to 14.	1 doz..	**$3.90**
1F-5081	14 to 18.	½ doz..	**4.90**
1F-5082	18 to 22.	½ doz..	**6.25**
1F-5083	22 to 26.	⅓ doz..	**9.00**
1F-5084	26 to 36.	¼ doz..	**12.75**

ANIMAL TOYS

6 STYLES IMPORTED FELT ANIMALS

10½ in., bear, elephant, cat, dog, etc., asstd. color felt, well stuffed bodies, painted nose and mouth, glass eyes, jointed arms, imit. leather slippers.
2F-7262—Asstd. ½ doz. in box. Doz **$1.95**

"TWINZY TOYS"

Non-poisonous colors, soft stuffed, bright color fabrikoid coverings, painted features and costumes.

5½x8 in., **2 styles,** cat, dog, 1¾ in. red ball wheels, cord, bead grip.
1F-4917 — ½ doz. in pkg. Doz **$3.95**

9 in., **6 styles,** asstd. Alphabet Man, Aviator, Little Boy Blue, Cowboy and other novelty characters.
1F-4914—½ doz. in box. Doz **$4.00**

IMPORTED FELT COVERED HORSES

Brown, fur mane and tail, leatherette harness.

	Doz
2F-7171—7½ in. 1 doz. in box..	**$2.00**
2F-7172—11 in. ½ doz. in box..	**$4.25**
2F-7173—14 in. ⅓ doz. in box..	**$7.90**

13½ in., brown or black, hair mane & tail, leatherette harness, open mouth, metal stirrups.
2F-7225—1 in box. Each **$1.25**

IMPORTED PRESSED PAPER ANIMALS

Aver. 10 in., **4 styles,** horse, mule, camel, cow, natural color pressed paper bodies, painted features, glass eyes, imitation harness.
2F-7261—Asstd. ⅓ doz. in box. Doz **$4.00**

IMPORTED SHEEP

2½ in., composition head, painted features, wool fleeced, wood legs, colored collar.
2F-7252—3 doz. in box......Doz **38c**

It's Easy to Buy from BUTLER BROTHERS

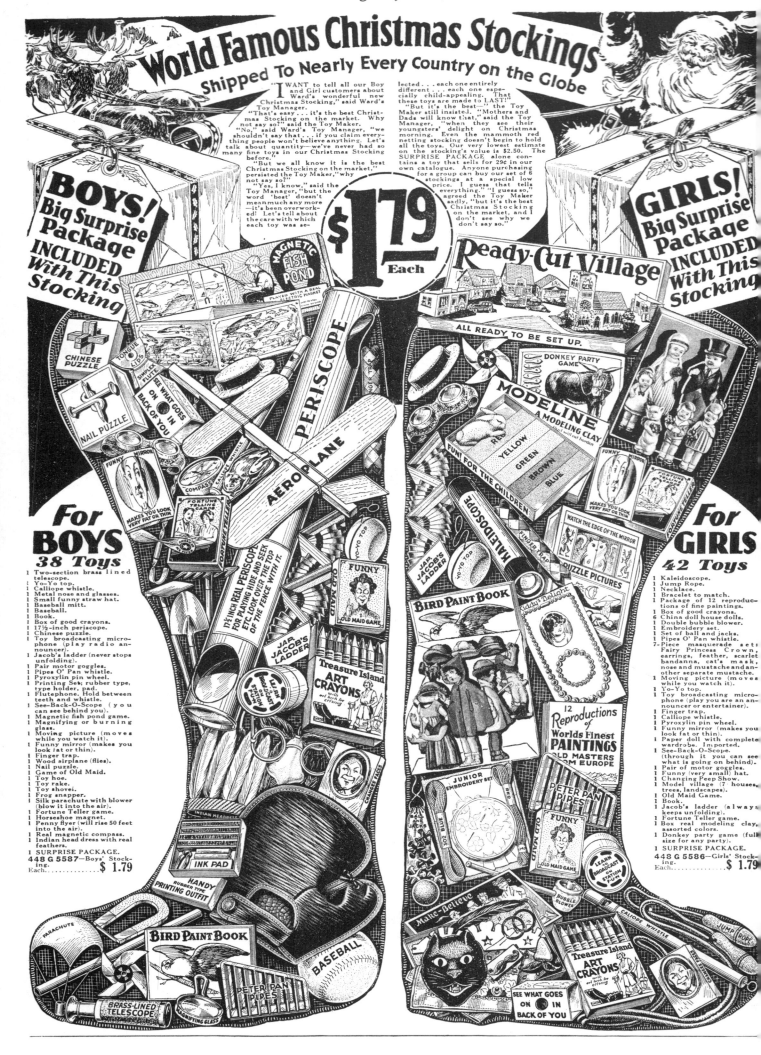

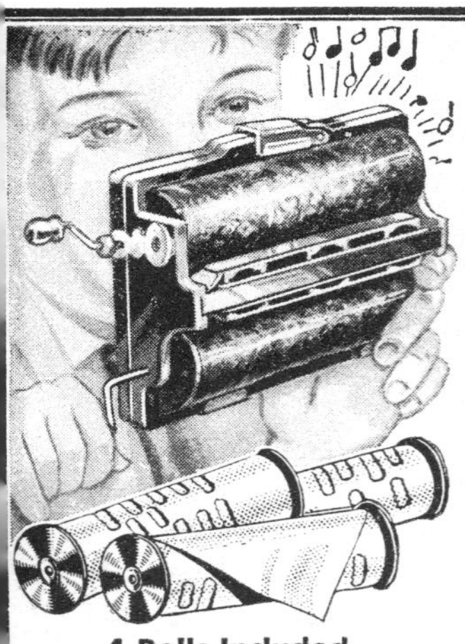

4 Rolls Included

ROLMONICA Plays Music Rolls

Complete With 4 Ten-Cent Rolls Only $1.00

Was $2.39—Now only $1.00—Think of the saving.

The Rolmonica was deservedly our most popular musical toy last year. We are so enthusiastic about it that we have placed a tremendous order for 1930—an order such as only Ward's can give. As a result, we have secured a price which we believe is a record. We pass the saving on to you.

A Mouth Organ That Plays Music Rolls

Four 10-Cent Rolls Included at Our Price

Rolmonica is the only mouth organ that plays music rolls. All you have to do is turn the crank and blow. Built into a hinged bakelite frame, the Rolmonica measures 4 by 3⅝ inches. Two cranks, one for winding and the other for re-winding, the rolls which can be changed easily. Blowing or drawing breath sounds the same note. Length of perforations regulates tempo.
48 G 3698—Rolmonica and 4 rolls. Postpaid........ **$1.00**

Additional Rolmonica Music Rolls—Postpaid
48 G 3727—Kentucky Home—Swanee River—Endearing Young Charms—Wild Irish Rose—Humoresque. **Postpaid. 5** rolls for........ **47¢**
48 G 3728—Carry Me Back to Old Virginny—Kiss Me Again—Annie Laurie—Mighty Lak' a Rose—When You and I Were Young Maggie—**5** rolls for **47¢**
48 G 3729—Turn on the Heat—Little Kiss Each Morning—Chant of the Jungle—La Paloma—Perfect Day. **Postpaid. 5** rolls for........ **47¢**
48 G 3730—Stein Song—Me and the Girl Next Door—There's Danger in Your Eyes—I Love you Believe Me—Tiptoe Thru the Tulips. **5** rolls **47¢**

PLAY A SAX NATIONALLY FAMOUS CLAROLA

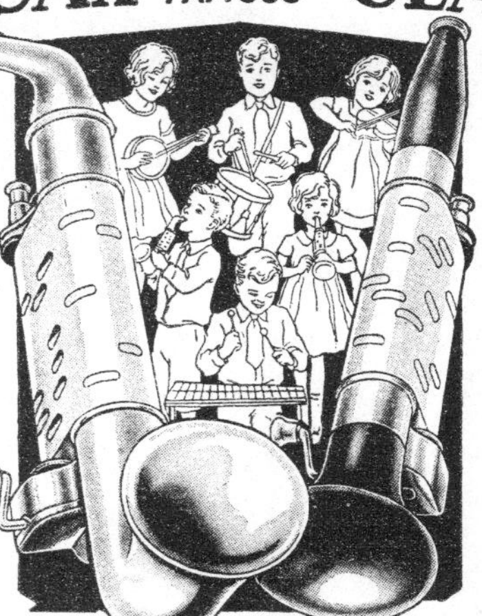

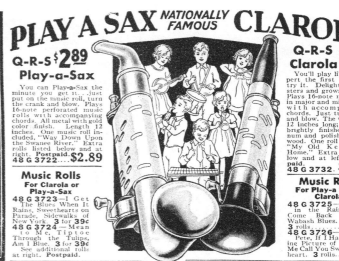

Q-R-S $2.89 Play-a-Sax

You can Play-a-Sax the minute you get it. . .just put on the music roll, turn the crank and blow. Plays 16-note perforated music rolls with accompanying chords. All metal with gold color finish. Length 12 inches. One music roll included, "Way Down Upon the Swanee River." Extra rolls listed below and at right. **Postpaid.**
48 G 3722........ **$2.89**

Music Rolls For Clarola or Play-a-Sax
48 G 3723—I Get The Blues When It Rains, Sweethearts on Parade, Sidewalks of New York. **3** for **39¢**
48 G 3724—Mean to Me, Tiptoe Through the Tulips, Am I Blue. **3** for **39¢**
See additional rolls at right. **Postpaid.**

Q-R-S Clarola $1.89

You'll play like an expert the first time you try it. Delights youngsters and grownups too. Plays 16-note music roll in major and minor keys with accompanying chords. Just turn crank and blow. The Clarola is 12 inches long; made of brightly finished aluminum and polished black wood. One roll included, "My Old Kentucky Home." Extra rolls below and at left. **Postpaid.**
48 G 3732. **$1.89**

Music Rolls For Play-a Sax or Clarola
48 G 3725—Singing in the Rain, Lover Come Back to Me, Wabash Blues. **3** rolls........ **39¢**
48 G 3726—Piccolo Pete, If I Had A Talking Picture of You, Let Me Call You Sweetheart. **3** rolls........ **39¢**

LITTLE DANCER Imported Phonograph

With Big Mellow-Toned Horn

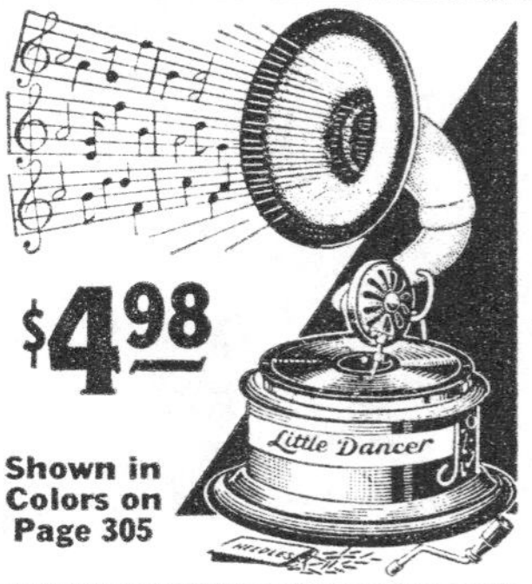

So important, mother, to encourage those little dancing feet. And it's a toy a youngster never tires of—a honograph of his own to turn on when he pleases, hoosing the selection he likes best. We believe that he LITTLE DANCER is the perfect Phonograph for hildren. Its mechanism is of the simplest. . .the uaranteed heavy, imported spring motor practically iminates trouble. Its reproduction is superior. . exceptionally good tone is strengthened and mellowed by he large tapered horn. Diam. of bell 7⅜ in. Velvet urntable. Plays 10-inch records with one winding. quipped with speed control, stop and start lever. lade entirely of metal finished in bright cheerful colors. eight over all 16 in. Base 8⅜ inches in diam. Complete with 1 package of needles. **See the Little ancer in colors on Page 305.**
8 G 3633—We Pay Postage........ **$4.98**

$4.98

Shown in Colors on Page 305

Imported Toy WOOD VIOLIN

Length 19 Inches

$1.79 **Shown in Colors on Page 305**

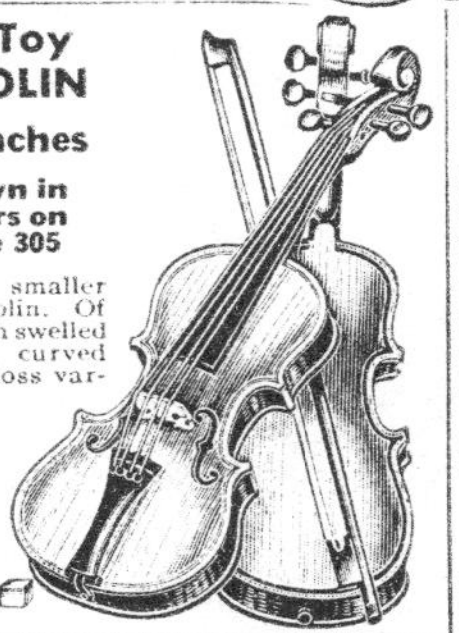

Only slightly smaller than a full size Violin. Of kiln-dried wood with swelled front and back; curved neckpiece. High gloss varnished finish. Ebonized wood fingerboard, keys and tail-piece; 3 catgut and 1 metal G string. 16-inch horsehair bow with tension screw; rosin. **Postpaid.**
48 G 3676........ **$1.79**

TOY SAXOPHONES

Nickel-Plated Engraved Bell **$1.25**

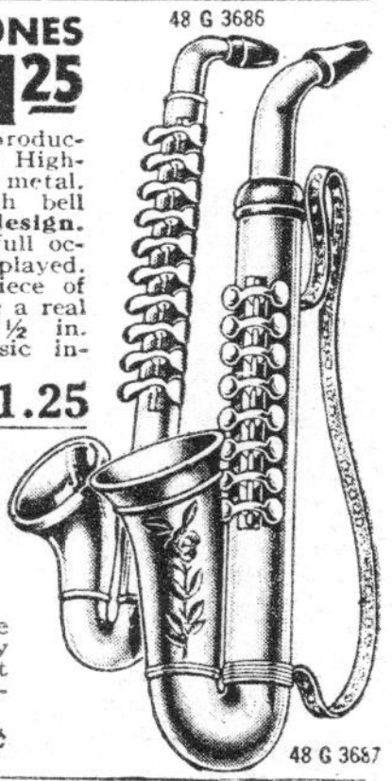

48 G 3686

48 G 3687

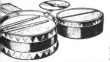

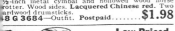

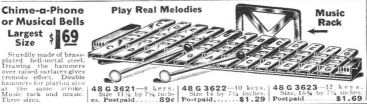

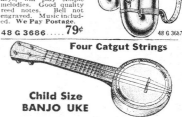

A fine miniature reproduction of a real saxophone! Highly polished, nickel-plated metal. Gracefully flared 3-inch bell **engraved with floral design.** Eight padded keys—a full octave; simple tunes can be played. Duck-bill type mouthpiece of ebonized wood, just like a real saxophone. Height 17½ in. Fancy neckband. Music included.
We Pay Postage
48 G 3687........ **$1.25**

Ten-Key Sax 79¢

Not as good quality as the toy saxophone above. 16¼ inches long, all metal with nickel-plated finish. Ten keys; will play simple melodies. Good quality reed notes. Bell not engraved. Music included. **We Pay Postage.**
48 G 3686........ **79¢**

Phonograph Records

Best Loved by Little Folks

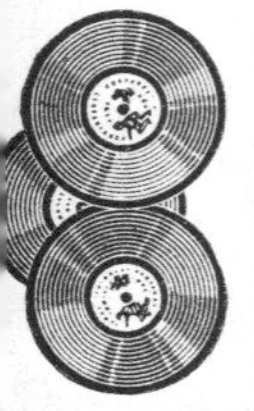

3 for 46¢

Double-faced 10 or 6-inch Records—two selections each. 3 different records to a set. **Postpaid.**

10-Inch Records	**Set of 3**
48 G 3718—6 selections..	**87¢**
48 G 3719—6 selections..	**87¢**
48 G 3720—6 selections..	**87¢**
6-Inch Records	**Set of 3**
48 G 3715—6 selections..	**46¢**
48 G 3716—6 selections..	**46¢**
48 G 3717—6 selections..	**46¢**

TINKLE TONE Child's Phonograph

$1.98

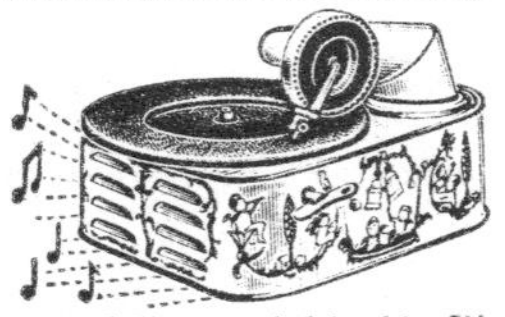

White enameled steel Phonograph 9 by 6 by 5½ inches; decorated with nursery designs. Has 5⅝-inch turntable; plays up to 8-inch records. Speed control; stop and start lever; crank wind. Guaranteed motor.
48 G 3614—We Pay Postage........ **$1.98**

10¾-Inch METAL TOY VIOLIN

25¢

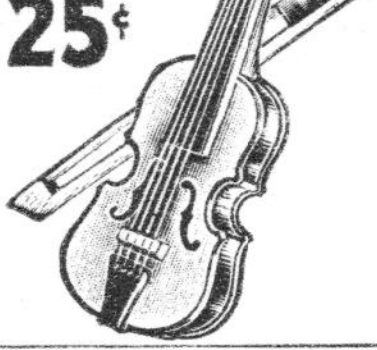

Fine imitation of real wood and almost unbreakable. . .so practical for little folks. Flamed Mahogany finish. Swelled front and back. Wood neck; ebonized keys and keyboard; four catgut strings; horsehair bow. Rosin included. Metal bridge. 10¾ in. long. **We Pay Postage.**
48 G 3672... **25¢**

Four Catgut Strings

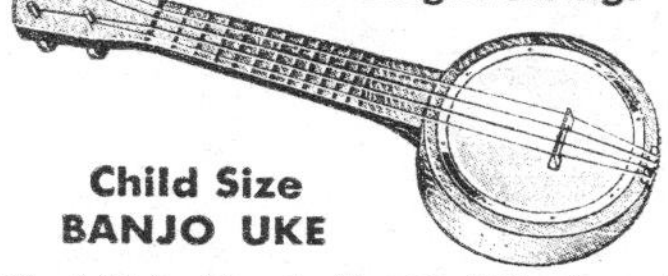

Child Size BANJO UKE

Real Skin Head—Fretted Keyboard

Real skin head, four catgut strings, black wood keys. Wooden neck with carefully fretted fingerboard. Diameter of head 5½ inches. Length 16½ inches. Instructions for playing included.
48 G 3658—We Pay Postage........ **95¢**

Same shape as above with thin wood head. Complete in detail. Length 14¼ in. Diam. 5 in.
48 G 3653—We Pay Postage........ **48¢**

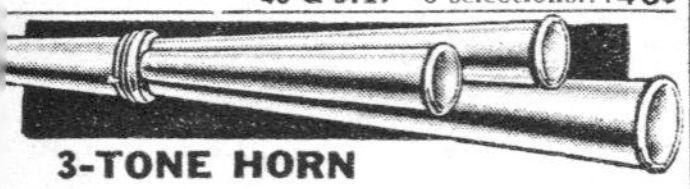

3-TONE HORN

NEW! Blow through this Horn and ou will hear three distinct, harmonious ones at one time. Nickel-plated metal; 2 in. long. **Postpaid.**
8 G 3681........ **27¢**

Musical Birds

Set of 3 for 19¢

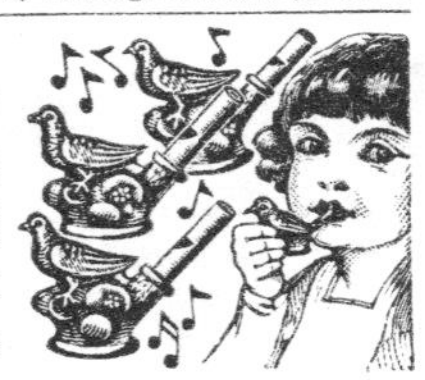

Molded from metal. Partly fill them with water, then by blowing you can imitate the trilling song of a canary. Length each, 3 in. **We Pay Postage.**
48 G 3664—**19¢**
Set of 3

4-KEY CORNET

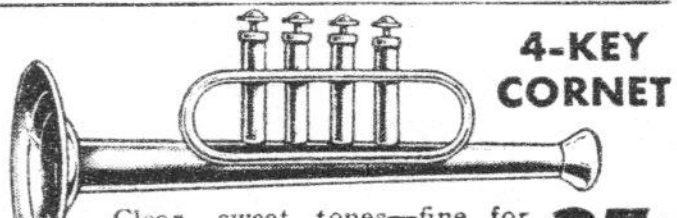

37¢

Clear, sweet tones—fine for playing bugle calls. Well made of nickel-plated metal with high polish; four push-button keys; fine quality brass reed notes. Mouthpiece and 3-inch bell are extra strong metal. 9 inches long.
48 G 3646—We Pay Postage........ **37¢**

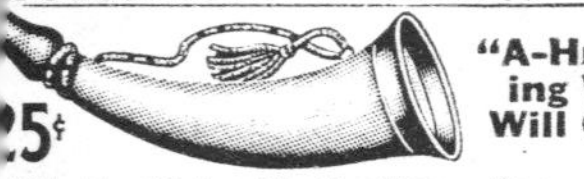

"A-Hunting We Will Go"

25¢

Like the old time Hunting Horn. Strong metal, olored ivory-white; horn-like shadings. Clear brass eed tone. Length 10½ in. Colored hanging cord. Vell made . . . practically unbreakable.
8 G 3663—We Pay Postage........ **25¢**

Chime-a-Phone or Musical Bells

Largest Size $1.69

Play Real Melodies

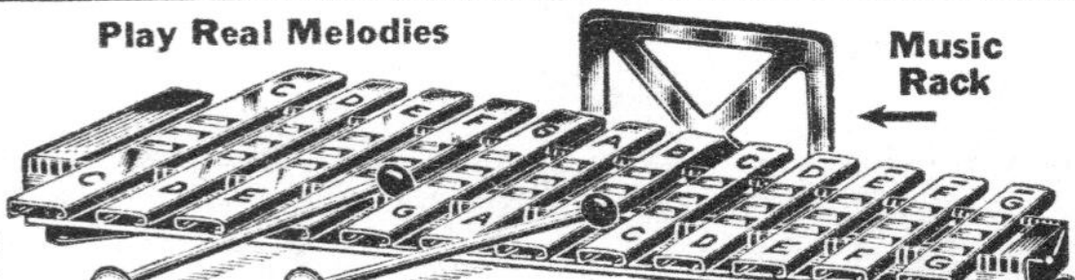

Music Rack

Sturdily made of brass-plated bell-metal steel. Drawing the hammers over raised surfaces gives tremolo effect. Double hammers for playing alto at the same stroke. Music rack and music. Three sizes.

48 G 3621—8 keys. Size 11¼ by 7¼ inches. **Postpaid**........ **89¢**
48 G 3622—10 keys. Size 14 by 7¼ inches. **Postpaid**........ **$1.29**
48 G 3623—12 keys. Size, 16¾ by 7¼ inches. **Postpaid**........ **$1.69**

Three-Chord MUSICAL TOP

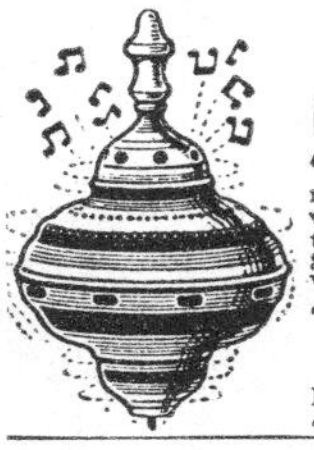

52¢

Beautiful metal Top decorated in gay colors. Plays three chords on 12 metal reels. Wood handle which you tap when you want to change the chord. Height 8 inches; diameter 5½ inches. **We Pay Postage.**
48 G 2058........ **52¢**

Two-Chord Musical Top

Height 7 in. diam. 4½ in. Plays 2 chords on 8 reeds.
48 G 2059........ **33¢**

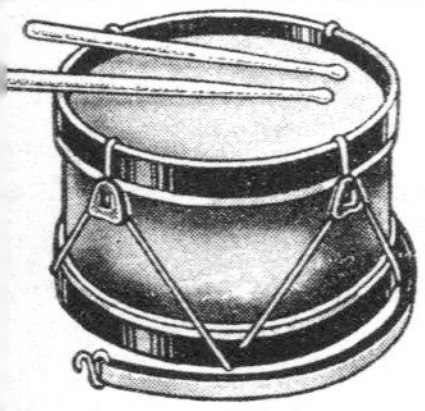

11-Inch Leather Head

$1.10

Eleven-inch Drum; genuine sheepskin head; fiber bottom. Two snares; shoulder strap; two hardwood drumsticks. Metal sides. Height 7⅛ in. **Postpaid.**
48 G 3680. **$1.10**

Genuine SCHOENHUT PIANOS

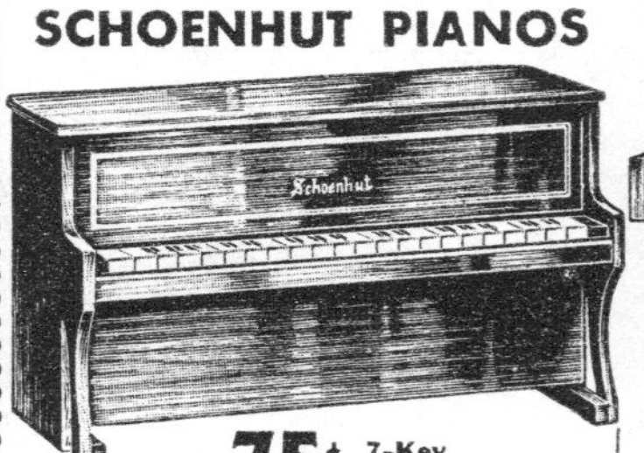

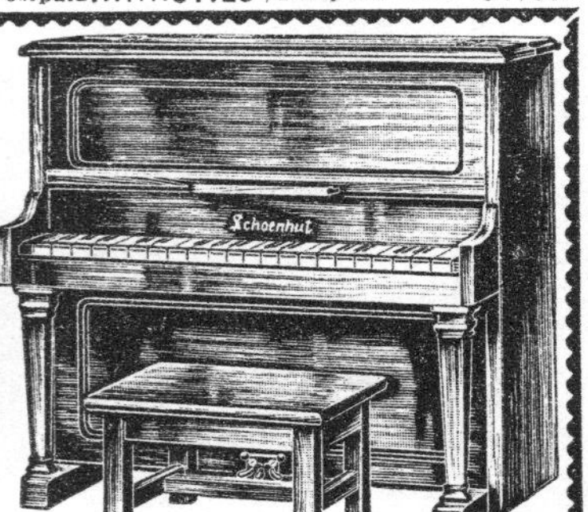

75¢ 7-Key Size

PRICED LOW 5 Sizes All Master Tuned

Splendid, low priced Pianos—the dependable **Schoenhut** quality. A delightful toy and a useful one, for the steel notes are **master tuned.** Varnished in beautiful mahogany finish with gold line stripe trimming. White keys correctly spaced as on large pianos. Excellent for finger exercises and actual preparation for real playing. Book of easy music and instructions included. We lower the price on every size of these nationally advertised toy pianos. **Postpaid.**

Article Number	No. of Keys	Width In.	Height In.	D'pth In.	Each
448 G 3631	22	22⅞	13½	9½	**$4.98**
448 G 3634	18	19⅜	12½	8⅜	**3.98**
448 G 3630	16	16¾	11	8	**2.85**
48 G 3629	11	12	8¼	6½	**1.48**
48 G 3628	7	8½	6½	5	**.75**

SCHOENHUT'S FINEST Master Tuned

Mother will like these. Mahogany finish; highly polished. White keys are same size and spaced same as on large piano. . . .useful for real finger exercises. The lid lifts, and the front can be taken out to see the mechanism. The wooden hammers strike upwards on the music steel keys and fall back on felt pads. Bench sold separately below. Book of simple musical selections with each piano. **Large size not Mailable. Shipped Not Prepaid.** Ship. wt. 25 lbs. **Small size only Postpaid.**

Article No.	Keys	Width	Height	Depth	Each
148 G 3707	22	23¾ in.	21⅛ in.	11⅛ in.	**$10.48**
448 G 3708	18	19⅜ in.	16⅜ in.	8¾ in.	**4.98**

48 G 3721—PIANO BENCH. Same finish as pianos. Size 12¼ by 7 by 7½ in. high.
We Pay Postage........ **$1.39**

CATHEDRAL CHIMES

Plays Chords

$1.55

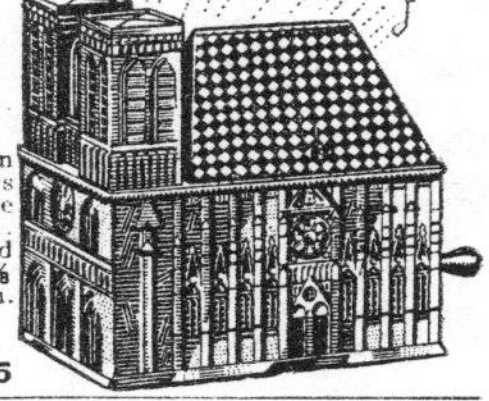

Turn crank. Fan blower inside plays true chords like church organ. Lithographed metal. Size 6⅝ by 6½ by 4⅛ in. wide. **Postpaid.**
48 G 3609........ **$1.55**

$4.50 Value

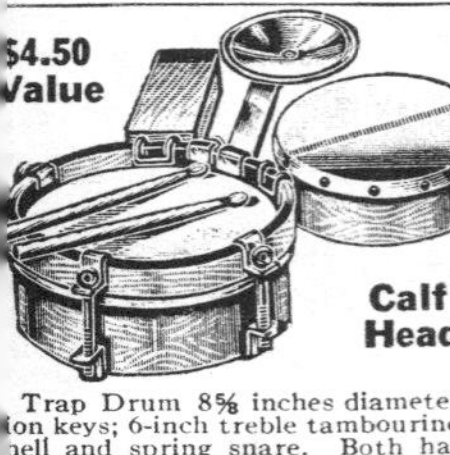

$1.98

JAZZ DRUM OUTFIT

Calf Head

Trap Drum 8⅝ inches diameter, with metal tenion keys; 6-inch treble tambourine-drum with wood hell and spring snare. Both have calfskin heads. ½-inch metal cymbal and hollowed wood horse rotter. Wood sides. **Lacquered Chinese red.** Two ardwood drumsticks.
8 G 3684—Outfit. Postpaid........ **$1.98**

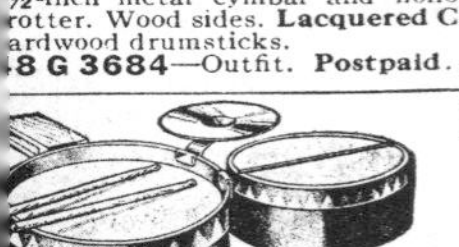

Low Priced Outfit

49¢

Unusual quality at the price. Large Drum, 7⅛ inches in diameter has heavy archment head; attached to edge is smaller 5½-ich drum with wire snare. Both drums have wood ides. 4¾-inch cymbal fastens on other side of large rum. Hollow wood horse trotter. Two shaped rumsticks 6¾ inches long. **We Pay Postage.**
8 G 3685—Outfit........ **49¢**

Toy Phones

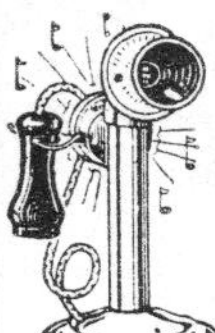

← 42¢

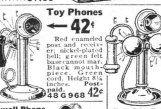

Red enameled post and receiver; nickel-plated bell; green felt base cannot mar. Black mouthpiece. Green cord. Height 8¼ inches. **Postpaid.**
48 G 968 **42¢**

Small Phone

25¢

Receiver lifts from hook; bell rings. Black; nickel-plated trim. Green cord. Height 6⅛ in. **Postpaid.**
48 G 996........ **25¢**

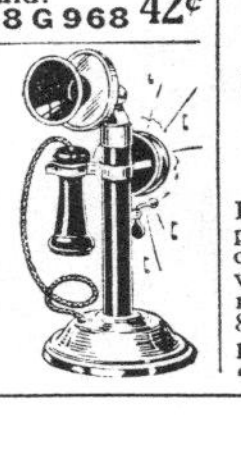

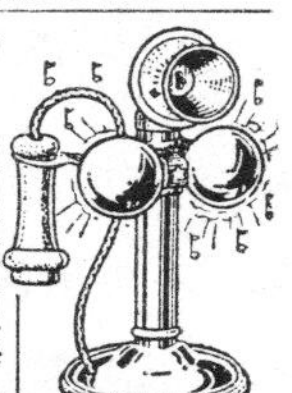

Double Bells

89¢

Nickel-plated. Black mouthpiece. Green felt covers base. Rings when you pick up receiver. Height 8¼ inches. **Postpaid.**
48 G 999. **89¢**

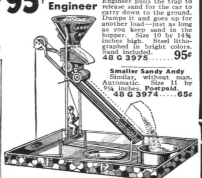

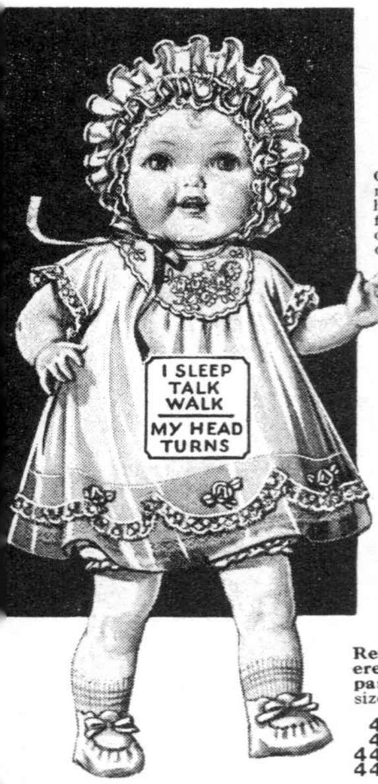
I SLEEP
TALK
WALK
MY HEAD
TURNS

Soft, Cuddly BABY

$2.59

Radiant little "One-Year-Old" just dimpling into her most enchanting smile! While hardly so exquisitely finished as Baby Delight or Bubbles (listed on other pages), we offer these babies with assurance of superlative value for the price. Composition head tinted with the matchless coloring of babyhood; **turns in any direction.**

Baby's body is soft and so cuddly...stuffed with **downy kapok.** New **walking type straight** legs of composition. Three-quarter composition curved arms. Crying voice; smiling mouth shows teeth and tip of tongue. Frock is of sheer white organdie; wide pink hem. Lace trimmed. Satin ribbon rose buds. Ruffly organdie bonnet edged with pink baby ribbon and lace; pink ribbon ties. Lace edged white slip, pink and white socks and white leatherette shoes. Sleeping eyes. **Real lashes,** lovely **embroidered bib** and real **rubber panties** on **all** but 18-inch size. **Postpaid.**

48 G 2953—18 in. $2.59
48 G 2954—20 in. 3.29
448 G 2955—22 in. 4.19
448 G 2956—25 in. 4.79

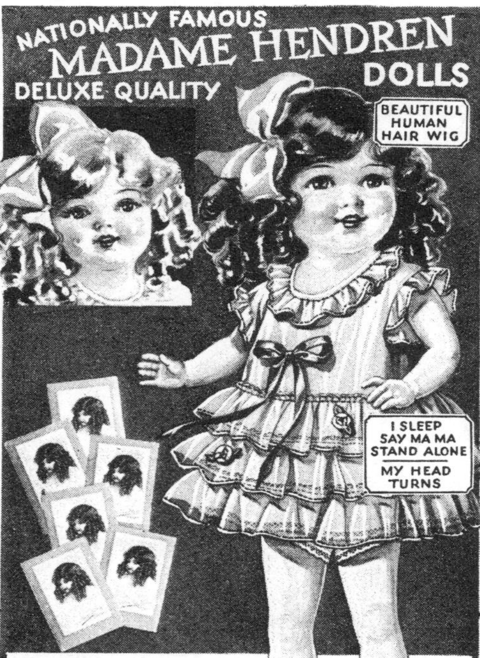
NATIONALLY FAMOUS
MADAME HENDREN
DELUXE QUALITY
DOLLS
BEAUTIFUL HUMAN HAIR WIG
I SLEEP
SAY MA MA
STAND ALONE
MY HEAD
TURNS

BETTY With Golden Curls
BARBARA With Brown Curls

Two Beautiful Doll Children

$5.25 Each

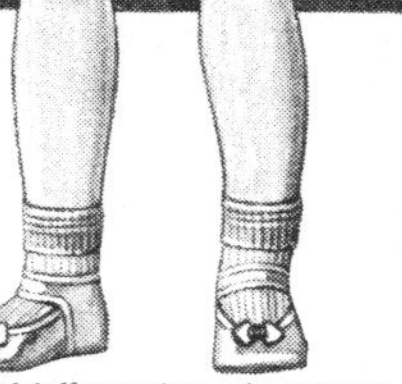

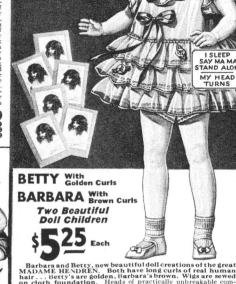

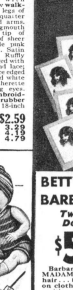

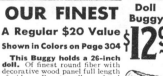

Barbara and Betty, new beautiful doll creations of the great MADAME HENDREN. **Both have long curls of real human hair... Betty's are golden, Barbara's brown. Wigs are sewed on cloth foundation.** Heads of practically unbreakable composition turn in any direction on socket neck joints. Sleeping eyes with **real lashes.** Soft **cotton stuffed bodies;** long slim strong composition legs are the **new standing type** firmly jointed to body. Composition arms. **All sizes say "Ma-Ma."** Their ruffled, ribbon trimmed frocks of sheer crisp organdie are smart as "Paris mades"—Betty in blue, Barbara in yellow. Undies of white lawn—slip and bloomer combinations are lace edged. **Silk socks;** leatherette shoes. **6 Photographs** with each doll. **We Pay Postage.**

Height	Golden Curls	Brown Curls	
18 inches	48 G 2944	48 G 2948	$5.25
20 inches	48 G 2945	48 G 2949	6.59
22 inches	448 G 2946	448 G 2950	7.98
24 inches	448 G 2947	448 G 2951	9.50

EFFanBEE PATSY

$2.67

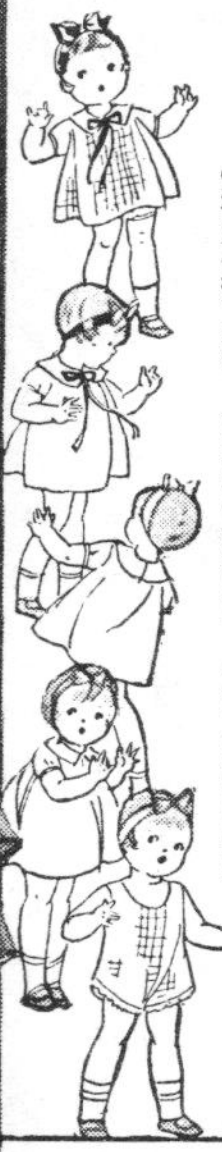

American childhood is personified in this dainty Doll. Nationally advertised "Patsy" is the most widely imitated doll.

But the roguish expression, the famous patented tilting head, the unconscious baby grace of arms and legs are the work of an artist and cannot be duplicated.

Made entirely of finest American composition—the exquisite child body is so easy to dress. Patsy is adorable in swimming trunks or the laciest party dress.

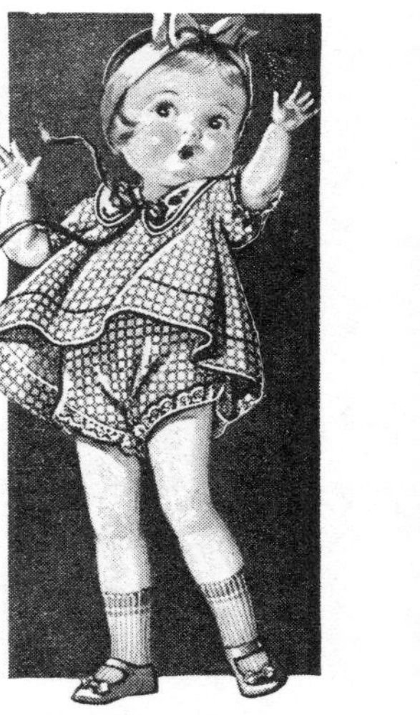

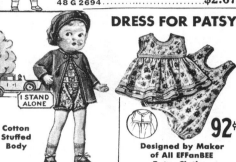

Patsy Is Sold by Mail Only by Ward's

Painted features, molded composition hair. Jointed at neck, shoulders, hips—she sits or stands alone in many positions. Smart red print frock with lace edged panties. Scarlet satin hair ribbon. Red and white rayon socks; red slippers. Height 13½ inches. **We Pay Postage.**

48 G 2694........................$2.67

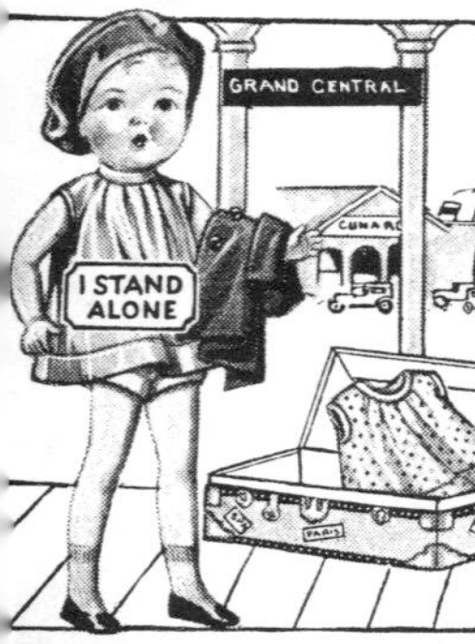
GRAND CENTRAL
CUNARD
I STAND ALONE
PARIS

2-INCH DOLL Two Outfits TRUNK

98¢

A Dolly with two outfits acked in her own trunk. Doll ntirely of durable composition; ater-proof enameled. Firmly inted....stands alone. Two frocks; comnation; slippers; socks; felt sport coat and ret.

8 G 2701—We Pay Postage.....98¢

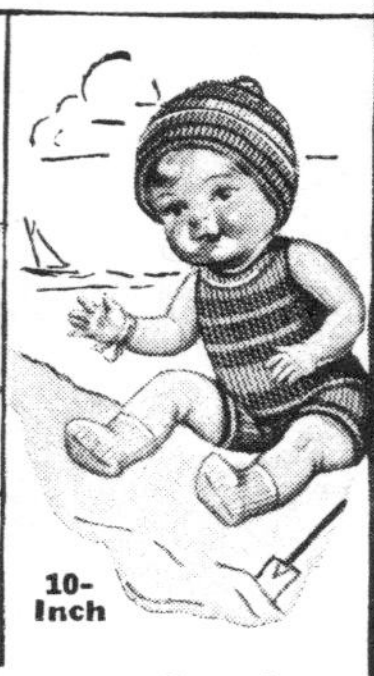

10-Inch

Pyroxylin Baby

Perfectly molded baby; jointed arms and curved legs—baby sits alone. Sweater, cap and socks of colorfully striped stockinette. **Postpaid.**

48 G 2703...45¢

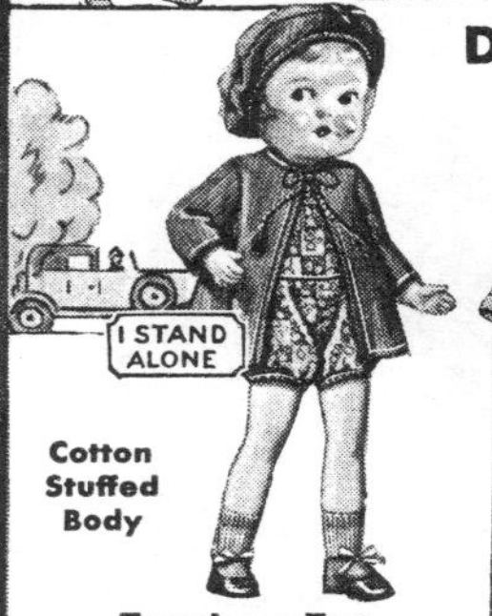
I STAND ALONE

Cotton Stuffed Body

Tomboy Tot

$1.00

15-inch Dolly in bright print romper suit, jaunty scarlet jacket and beret; slippers and socks. Composition head; winsome painted features. Composition arms and standing type legs. **Postpaid.**

48 G 2702........$1.00

DRESS FOR PATSY

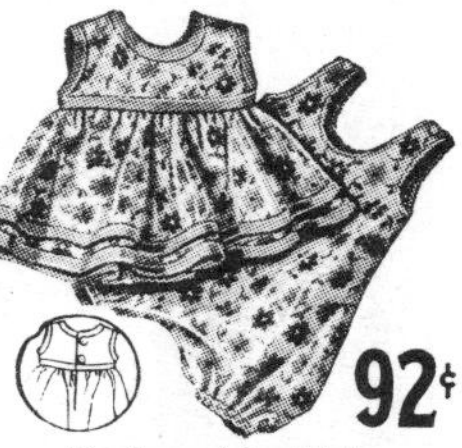

92¢

Designed by Maker of All EFFanBEE Patsy Clothes

Fine soft voile sprigged with tiny blue flowers. The perky binding is of crisp organdie. Real ocean pearl buttons and hand made button holes. Matching pantie-combination (sun suit) has elastic at knees. Finished most daintily and guaranteed to fit Patsy shown above. **We Pay Postage.**

48 G 953..............92¢

Child-Size Chests
Shown in Colors on Page 306

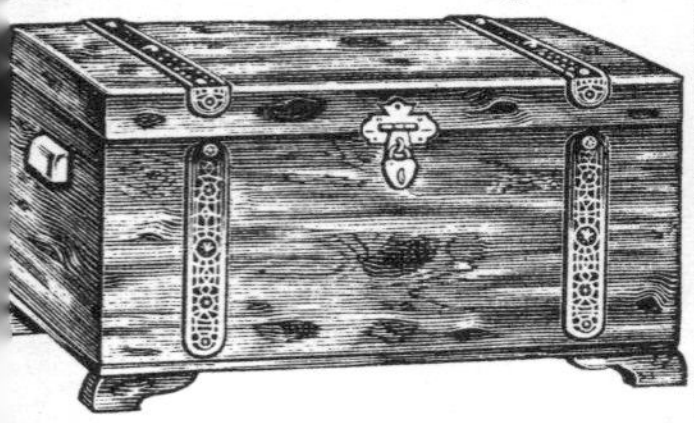

Genuine Tennessee RED CEDAR

$3.65

Large enough to hold a little girl's othes. Of beautifully grained, genuine dar with natural cedar finish. Fancy ass trim; brass lid support and hing-. **Each with real padlock and key.** Very rong. **We Pay Postage.**

48 G 3462—Size 16½ by 9 by 9½ inches $3.65
48 G 3463—Size 20½ by 10½ by 10½ inches.......4.50
48 G 3464—Size 24 by 11½ by 13 inches. 5.59

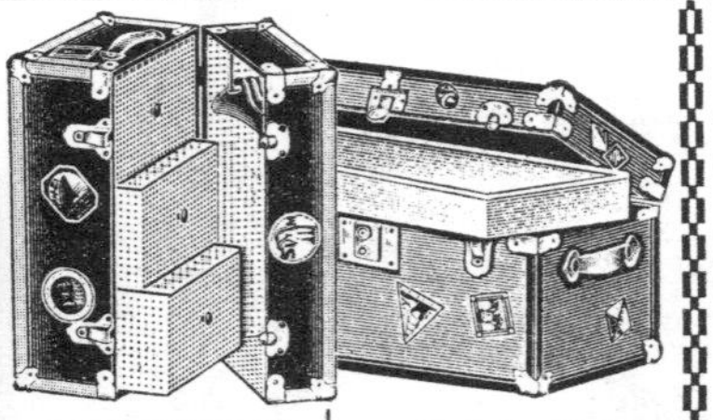

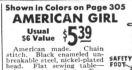

WARDROBE Trunk

$2.73

Green enameled; steel covered. 14¼ by 7 by 8¼ in. deep. Brass corners, hinges, fasteners. 3 wood bound drawers; 3 clothes hangers on bar. Carrying strap. Metal strap binding. Covered with travel labels.

48 G 3485—Postpaid...$2.73

DRESS TRUNK for Dolly

$2.95

Green enameled; **steel** covered. Not fiber. 16 by 8½ by 9¼ in. wide. Brass corners, spring lock and key and bolts. Metal strap binding; very sturdy. Lid support. End handles. Covered with travel labels. Wood tray.

48 G 3486—Postpaid....$2.95

OUR FINEST Doll Buggy

A Regular $20 Value

Shown in Colors on Page 304

$12.98

This Buggy holds a 26-inch doll. Of finest round fiber with decorative wood panel full length of sides. Beauty rolls on hood and body. Fully lined with best quality velvet corduroy, softly padded; compartment under seat.

Special Features of Hood. Adjustable sliding feature with **big** knobs of bright rust-resisting metal. Peek-a-boo in back—so easy to keep an eye on dolly. Transparent **hood windows.**

Special Features of Body. Reversible—body can be swung around so dolly faces mother. **Reclining back.** Leather safety strap. Strong metal bottom.

Undergear. Underslung fancy coil baby carriage springs; new ram's horn tubular push bar extends to front axle; nickeled end. Positive action foot brake.

Wheels. 10¼-inch artillery wood wheels with ¾-inch auto-tread tires. Length of body 25 in.; width 13 in. Height to top of hood 34 in. Ship. wt. 38 lbs. **Shipped Not Prepaid.**

148 G 3527—Dark coffee cream color; brown upholstery; dark coffee color enameled undergear..$12.98

148 G 3528—Sea green color, gray upholstery, gray enameled undergear......$12.98

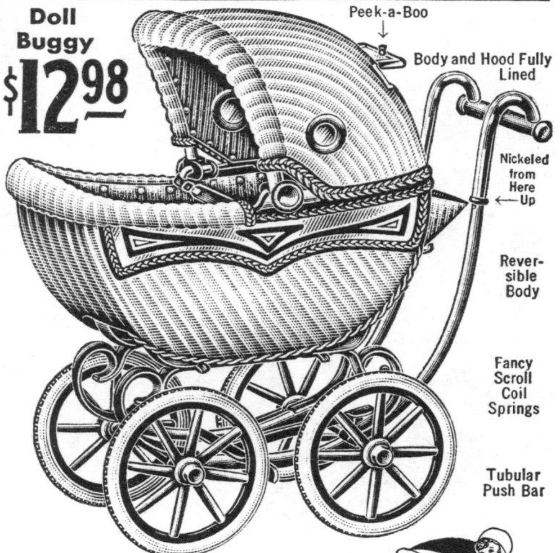
Peek-a-Boo
Body and Hood Fully Lined
Nickeled from Here Up
Reversible Body
Fancy Scroll Coil Springs
Tubular Push Bar

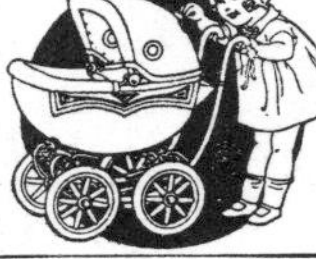

PEEK-A-BOO Window Back of Hood

Picture above shows the Peek-a-boo door in hood—so easy to raise and see that dolly is behaving. Baby brother's own carriage is not more completely equipped.

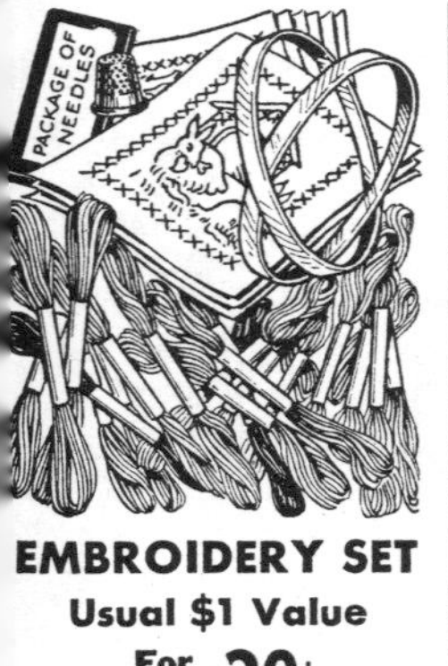
PACKAGE OF NEEDLES

EMBROIDERY SET

Usual $1 Value

For Only 39¢

Contains more than most $1.00 ts. **Nine** very fine weave white tton broadcloth doilies stamped ith designs requiring simple, raight line and cross stitches. **fteen** skeins of colored mercered floss; wooden **hoops** 4¼ inches diameter. Thimble and needles.

We Pay Postage

8 G 987—Per set........39¢

Shown in Colors on Page 305

AMERICAN GIRL

Usual $6 Value $5.39

American made. Chain stitch. Black enameled unbreakable steel, nickel-plated head. Flat sewing table—safety pressure foot. Tension adjustment. Stitching guide. Protected working parts. Wood base. Table clamp and instructions. **We Pay Postage.**

48 G 922.......$5.39

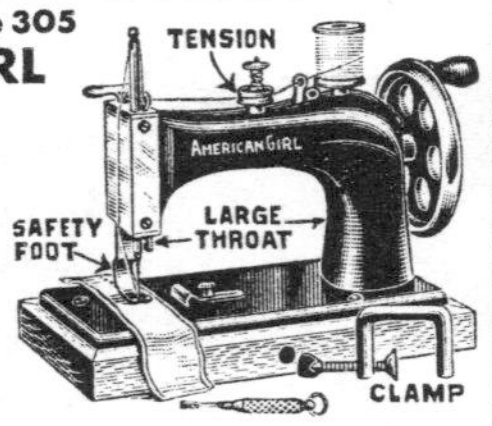
TENSION
AMERICAN GIRL
SAFETY FOOT
LARGE THROAT
CLAMP

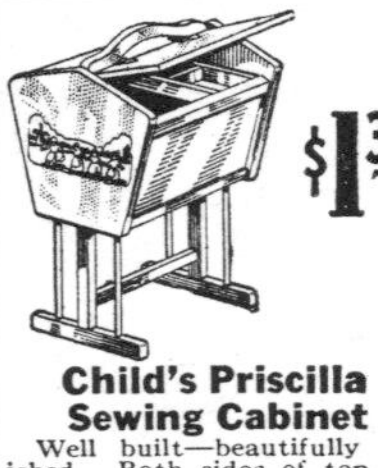

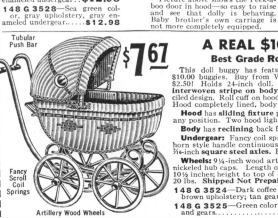

$1.33

Child's Priscilla Sewing Cabinet

Well built—beautifully finished. Both sides of top are hinged. Tray inside with compartments for sewing accessories just like mother's. Size 17⅝ in. high, 9¾ in. wide. Enameled Ivory; colored picture on side. **Postpaid.**

448 G 908........$1.33

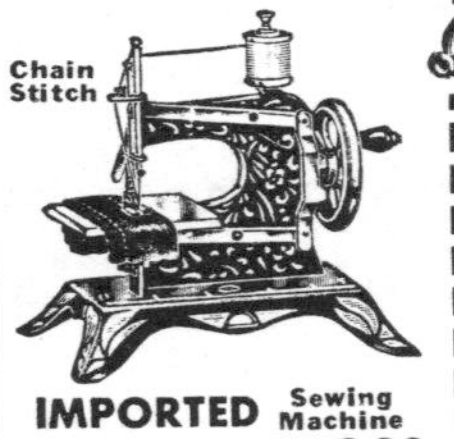
Chain Stitch

IMPORTED Sewing Machine

$2.29

Europe's best Make. Has thread tension, automatic feed. Nickel-plated moving parts. Pressure foot, **extra needle, table clamp** and directions included. Size 7⅝ by 7¼ by 4⅝ inches deep.

48 G 907—Postpaid.$2.29

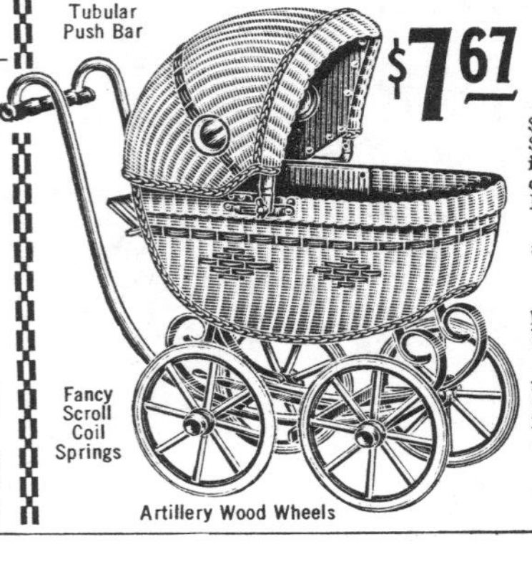
Tubular Push Bar
Fancy Scroll Coil Springs
Artillery Wood Wheels

$7.67

A REAL $10 VALUE

Best Grade Round Fiber

This doll buggy has features not found on most $10.00 buggies. Buy from Ward's and save at least $2.50! Holds 24-inch doll. Round fiber with fancy **interwoven stripe on body and hood.** Not a stenciled design. Roll cuff on hood; full length cuff on body. Hood completely lined, body half lined with velveteen.

Hood has **sliding fixture** permitting adjustment to any position. Two hood lights.

Body has **reclining** back for dolly to lie flat.

Undergear: Fancy coil springs. Full tubular ram's horn style handle continuous from back to front axle. ⁷⁄₁₆-inch **square steel axles.** Positive action foot brake.

Wheels: 9¼-inch wood artillery type; ⁹⁄₁₆-inch tires; nickeled hub caps. Length of body 20½ inches; width 10½ inches; height to top of hood 29 inches. Ship. wt. 20 lbs. **Shipped Not Prepaid.**

148 G 3524—Dark coffee cream color; brown upholstery; tan gears..........$7.67

148 G 3525—Green color; gray upholstery and gears..........7.67

Baby Delight

Seriously In Search of a HOME

Soft Kapok Body

Walks Talks Sleeps

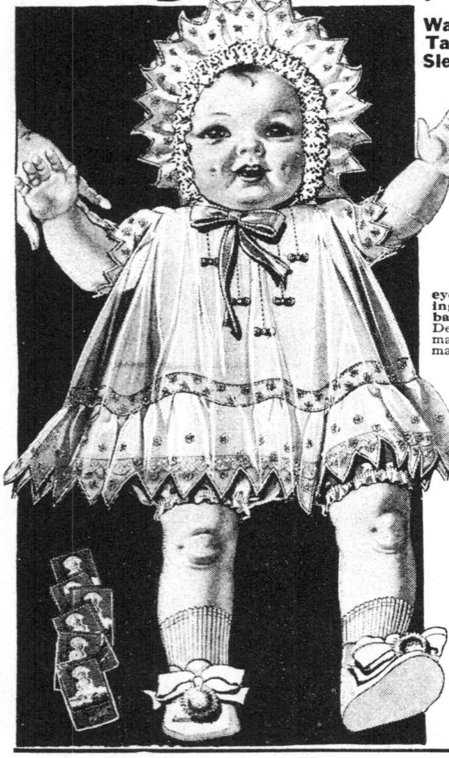

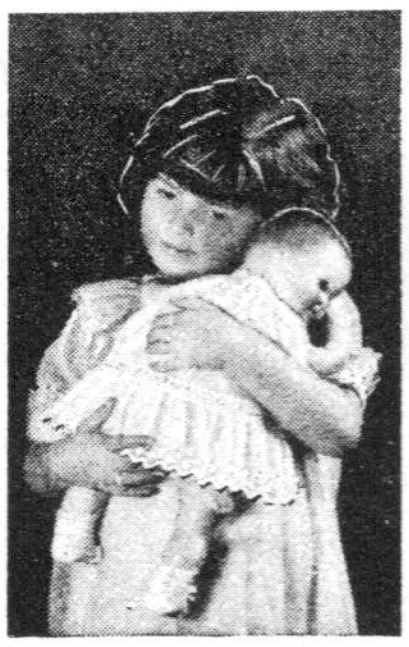

$3.33 THE kind of Baby people turn and stare at—all dewy freshness, round cheeks pink with health, April blue eyes that laugh up at you enchantingly, and the soft helplessness of baby curves. An artist has made Baby Delight "nearly alive." Only the finest materials . . . the most skilled workmanship have gone into her making.

Beautifully modeled turning baby head of hard-to-break composition; cry voice; sleeping eyes, real lashes. Baby smiles and shows two teeth. Three-quarter curved composition arms so attached they cling to you when you hold her. Full composition legs are new walking type . . . chubby, not quite straight, just learning to take an uncertain step or two. Baby Delight sits alone.

Likes to Be Cuddled

Soft and cuddly as a real baby . . . the **Kapok stuffed** body seems to snuggle close in your arms. Sheer organdie frock is crisp white, **embroidered in delicate pastel shades**. Bonnet matches; satin ribbon ties. Lace edged muslin slip; real **rubber panties.** Fine quality shoes and socks. 6 photos with each doll. **Postpaid.**

	Height	Each
48 G 2938—	16 in.	$3.33
48 G 2939—	18 in.	4.19
48 G 2940—	21 in.	5.25
448 G 2941—	24 in.	6.69
448 G 2942—	27 in.	8.69

TOOTSIETOY DOLL MANSION

Sold by Mail Only at Ward's

$4.93

Beautiful Spanish Villa designed by a real architect. Colorfully lithographed inside to show rugs, curtains, pictures. Sturdily made of heavy book board. Exterior finished in **washable oil colors** to look like stucco; decorated with shrubs, vines, balconies. Stairway leads to upstairs rooms. Three wide doors on hinges make all rooms easily accessible to the little owner. Built in accurate proportion to the Tootsietoy furniture shown below. Size: 26 inches long by 17 inches wide by 17½ inches high. Packed in attractive carton with full directions for easy assembly. **We Pay Postage.**

448 G 979—Doll House Only **$4.93**

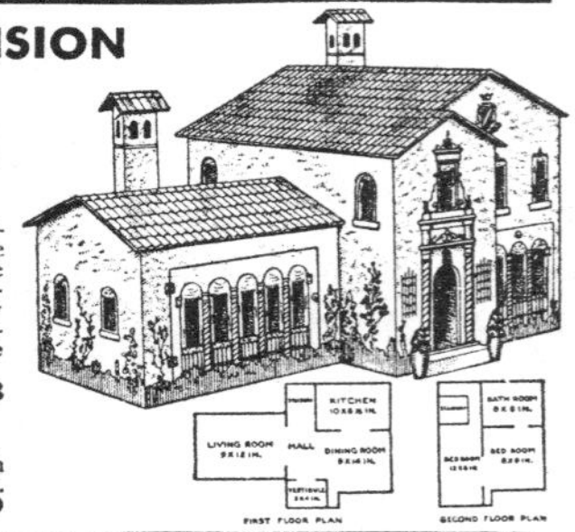

Tootsietoy Mansion—Furnished

Buy the TOOTSIETOY MANSION complete with the five rooms of Famous Tootsietoy Furniture below.

448 G 980—We Pay Postage.............. **$9.39**

TOOTSIETOY Doll House Furniture

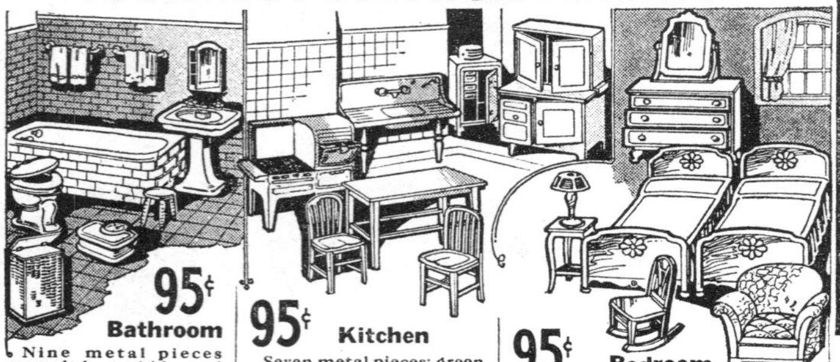

95¢ Bathroom

Nine metal pieces enameled orchid and white. 3½-in. tub, tile effect outside; toilet with raising seat; lavatory; medicine chest with mirror, opens; stool; clothes hamper; 2 towel racks; bathroom scale.

48 G 804.......... 95¢

95¢ Kitchen

Seven metal pieces; green lacquer and white finish. Kitchen Cabinet 2⅞ in. high, refrigerator, stove, 2 chairs, table, sink. All pieces in proportion. Doors and drawers of cabinet, refrigerator and stove really open.

48 G 803.......... 95¢

95¢ Bedroom

Pink and blue enameled metal bedroom set. 7 pieces: 2⅞-in. dresser with mirror, 3 drawers pull out; twin beds with spreads 3⅜ in. long, arm chair, rocker, night table and lamp. All in proportion.

48 G 800—Postpaid ... 95¢

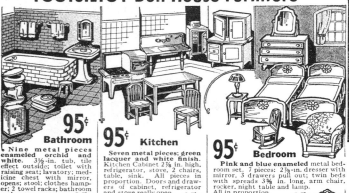

PARLOR

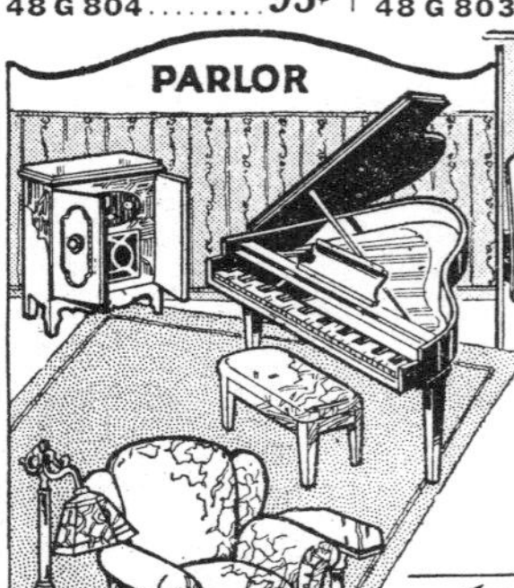

DINING ROOM

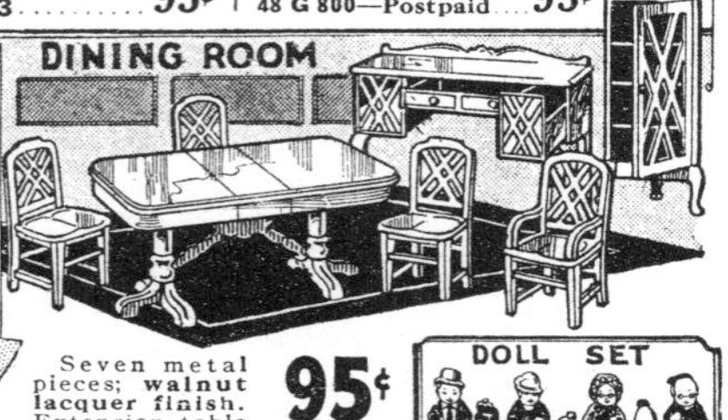

Seven metal pieces; **walnut lacquer finish.** Extension table 3⅜ in. long, 3 straight chairs, 1 arm chair, corner cabinet door opens; buffet drawers open. All well made. **95¢**

48 G 802—.................. 95¢

← **95¢** **Parlor Set**

Seven metal pieces. Grand **piano** is Chinese red and gold, 3 in. wide; top lifts, music rest; **radio cabinet** has gold panel, doors open; lamp, piano bench, arm chair, end table, foot stool.

48 G 801—Postpaid.......... 95¢

DOLL SET

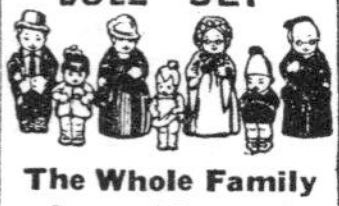

The Whole Family

Papa, Mama, Grandmother, Grandfather, Brother, Sister, Baby. **Bisque;** painted clothing. Father 2¼ inches tall. **Postpaid.** **42¢**

48 G 2504— 7 dolls.......... 42¢

A Wonderful Value

YOUR CHOICE Only $1

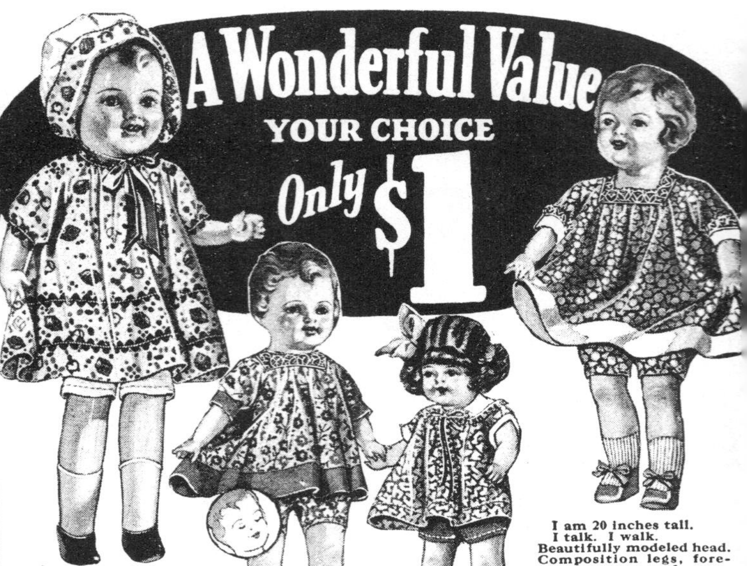

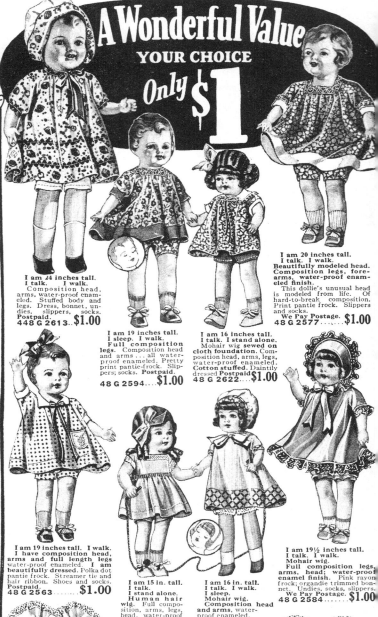

I am 24 inches tall. I talk. I walk.
Composition head, arms, water-proof enameled. Stuffed body and legs. Dress, bonnet, undies, slippers, socks. **Postpaid.**
448 G 2613.. **$1.00**

I am 20 inches tall. I talk. I walk. Beautifully modeled head. Composition legs, forearms, water-proof enameled finish.
This dollie's unusual head is modeled from life. Of hard-to-break composition. Print pantie frock. Slippers and socks.
We Pay Postage.
48 G 2577....... **$1.00**

I am 19 inches tall. I sleep. I walk. Full composition legs. Composition head and arms . . . all water-proof enameled. Pretty print pantie-frock. Slippers; socks. **Postpaid.**
48 G 2594.... **$1.00**

I am 16 inches tall. I talk. I stand alone. Mohair wig **sewed on cloth foundation.** Composition head, arms, legs, water-proof enameled. **Cotton stuffed.** Daintily dressed **Postpaid**
48 G 2622.... **$1.00**

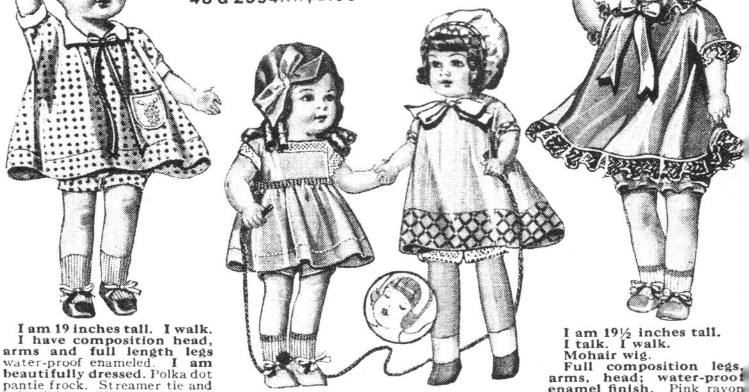

I am 19 inches tall. I walk. I have composition head, arms and full length legs water-proof enameled. **I am beautifully dressed.** Polka dot pantie frock. Streamer tie and hair ribbon. Shoes and socks.
Postpaid.
48 G 2563........ **$1.00**

I am 15 in. tall. I talk. I stand alone. Human hair wig. Full composition, arms, legs, head, water-proof enameled. Dressed.
Postpaid.
48 G 2623. **$1.00**

I am 16 in. tall. I talk. I walk. I sleep. Mohair wig. Composition head and arms, water-proof enameled.
48 G 2494—
Postpaid.
....**$1.00**

I am 19½ inches tall. I talk. I walk. Mohair wig. Full composition legs, arms, head; water-proof enamel finish. Pink rayon frock; organdie trimmed bonnet. Undies, socks, slippers.
We Pay Postage.
48 G 2584....... **$1.00**

Adorable Babies

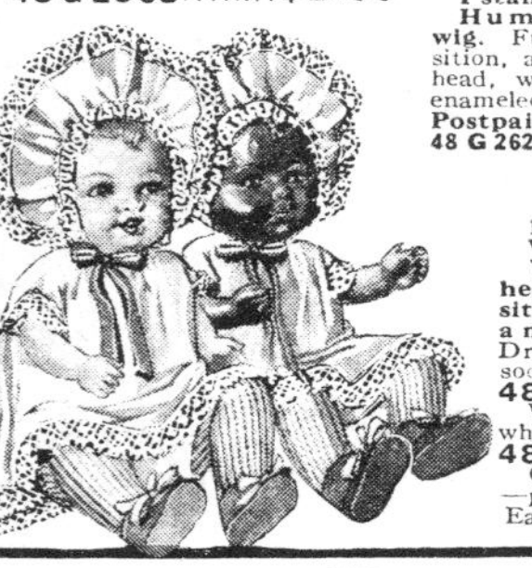

19 inches tall. We cry. We turn our heads. Composition heads and arms. Dress; slippers, socks.
48 G 2568— White baby—white dress.
48 G 2569— Colored baby—pink dress.
Each. . **$1.00**

13 in. tall. We walk. Soft cotton bodies. Full composition legs, arms, turning heads.
48 G 2536 — White baby; white dress.
48 G 2537 — Colored baby, Pink dress.
Each... **$1.00**

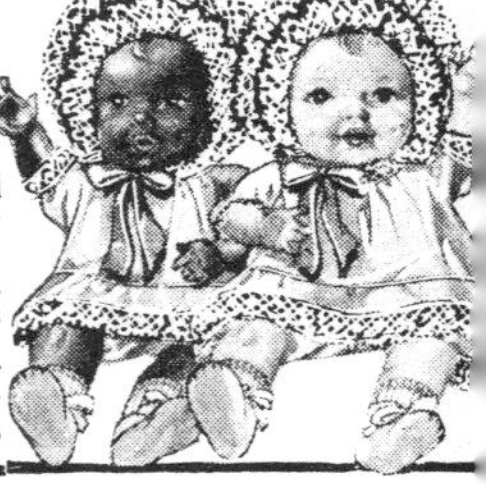

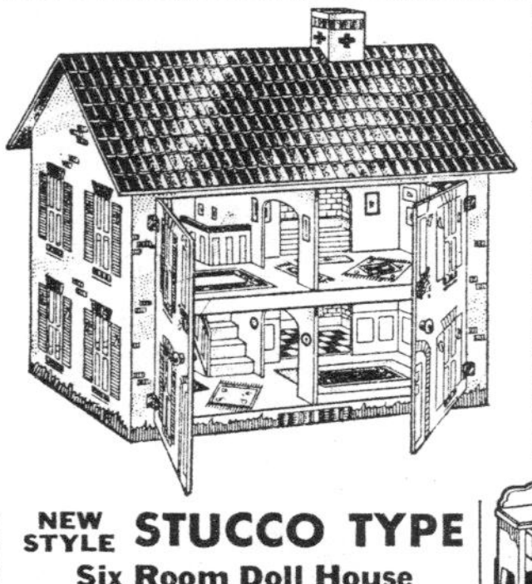

REAL STUCCO Over Sturdy Wood Constructi[on]

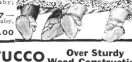

$2.79

A very beautiful little Doll House just waiting to become a HOME! All home-loving doll families are invited to inspect this mansion for themselves. Smart Doll House architecture . . . heavy wood construction covered with REAL STUCCO. Red roof. One large room, **real glass windows.** Ready for YOU to move in . . . the curtains (paper ones) are up! Walls are papered. For furniture we suggest the strong wood Suites below. Size 11¾ by 13¾ in. long; height 10 in.

448 G 977— Postpaid.......... **$2.79**

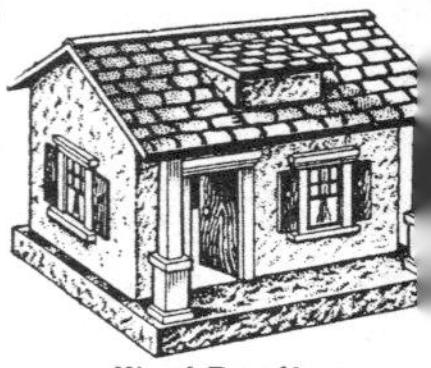

Wood Furniture Shown Below Fits This House

NEW STYLE STUCCO TYPE

Six Room Doll House

$1.98

Sold exclusively by Montgomery Ward. Two stories; heavy fiberboard finished with washable paint. Inside colorfully lithographed with pictures, carpets. **Real stairway.** Use Tootsietoy furniture shown at left. Front of house opens on hinges. Cut out windows. Size 16¼ in. high; 21 in. long. Depth 12 in. inside.

448 G 927—Postpaid.... **$1.98**

4-Room Imitation Brick House

Size 10¼ in. high by 13¾ in. long. Depth 8¼ in. (No stairs.)

48 G 928—Postpaid.......... 89¢

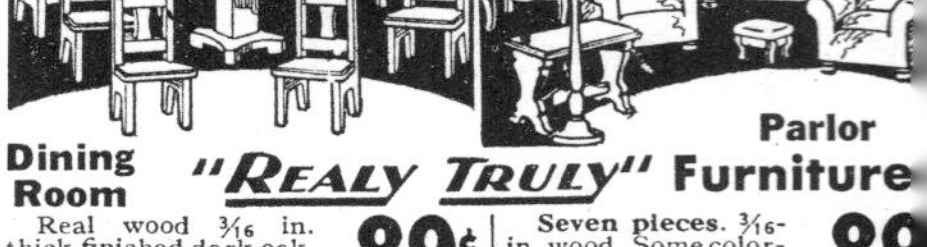

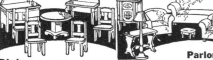

"REALY TRULY" Furniture

Dining Room

Real wood 3/16 in. thick finished dark oak. **Seven pieces**—four chairs 3 in. high; round dining table 2¾ in. in diameter; buffet, serving table in proportion. Drawer pulls out of buffet. **89¢**

48 G 961—Postpaid...... 89¢

Parlor

Seven pieces. 3/16-in. wood. Some colored to resemble upholstery. Davenport 5⅛ in. long. 2 armchairs, radio, la[mp], library table, foot stool. Soli[d] made. **89[¢]**

48 G 962—Postpaid... 8[9¢]

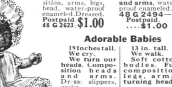

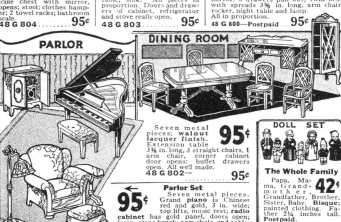

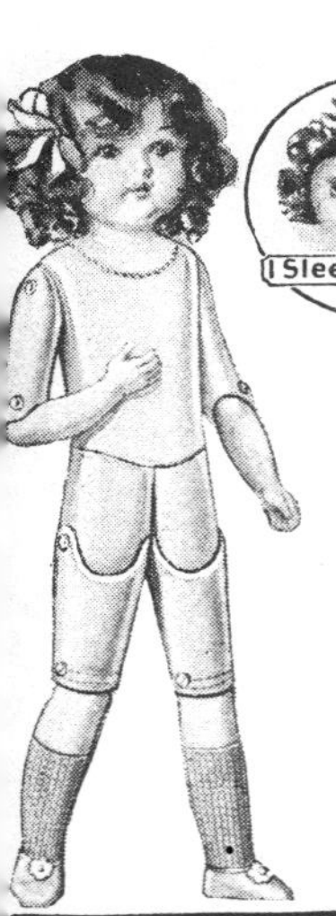
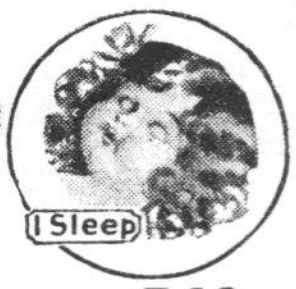
I Sleep

A Dolly You'll Like

TO DRESS

Her Water-Proof Kidiline Body IS FULLY JOINTED

$1.49 And Up

The most inexperienced little seamstress will find this pretty Dolly easy to dress. Four sizes—each nice to sew for and she's sure to look charming in whatever she wears. Beautiful bisque head; sleeping eyes; eyelashes; two tiny teeth showing and long soft curls of good quality mohair.

Her body is covered with a fine grade white imitation kid which is water-proof and easily cleaned. It's loads of fun to put her clothes on because she is jointed securely at knees, hips, elbows and shoulders, and moves very easily. Her arms are hard-to-break composition. She wears removable buckled shoes and socks. **We Pay Postage.**

Article No.	Height	Each
48 G 2640	16⅛ inches	$1.49
48 G 2641	18⅛ inches	1.79
48 G 2642	20 inches	2.19
448 G 2643	23¼ inches	2.69

INTRIGUING LADIES

For Your Boudoir

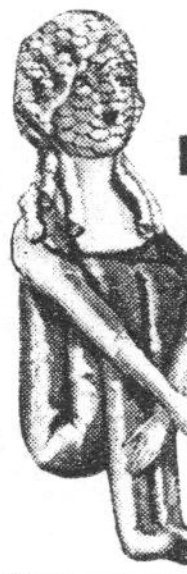

DRESS ONE To Match Your Room

$1.00 Doll With Long Curls

Unusual value. Beautiful wig has 8 long curls. Waves over the top are kept smoothly in place by hair net. Modeled composition head with shoulders so that doll can be dressed in the most elaborate low-necked gown. Face painted by hand. Sateen body is cotton stuffed; long arms and legs; **pyroxylin hands.** Height 30 inches.

COLORS OF WIGS: **Black, white, blonde or fiery red. State color wanted.**
48 G 2884—We Pay Postage....**$1.00**

Popular Priced Flapper

69¢

Composition **turning head** has roguish painted eyes and lips. Beautifully waved mohair wig. No curls, hair is done up. Cambric covered body. Cotton filled throughout; long arms and legs. **Height 30 inches.**

COLOR OF WIGS: **Black, white, blonde or fiery red. State color.**
48 G 2882—We Pay Postage..........69¢

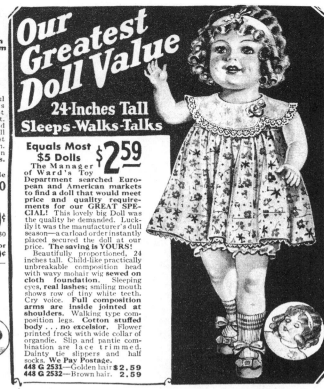

Our Greatest Doll Value

24-Inches Tall
Sleeps-Walks-Talks

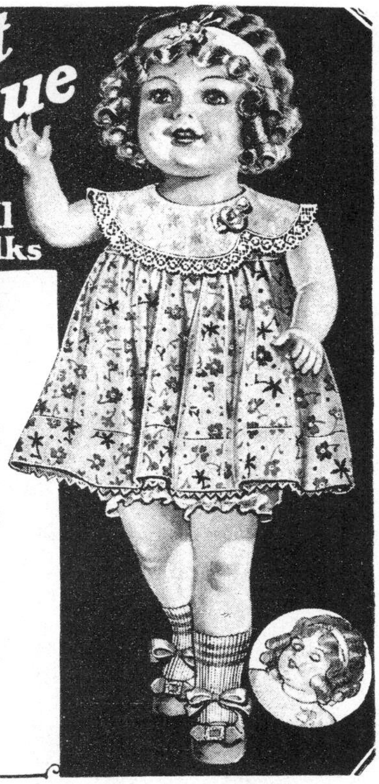

Equals Most $5 Dolls $2.59

The Manager of Ward's Toy Department searched European and American markets to find a doll that would meet price and quality requirements for our GREAT SPECIAL! This lovely big Doll was the quality he demanded. Luckily it was the manufacturer's dull season—a carload order instantly placed secured the doll at our price. **The saving is YOURS!**

Beautifully proportioned, 24 inches tall. Child-like practically unbreakable composition head with wavy mohair wig **sewed on cloth foundation.** Sleeping eyes, **real lashes;** smiling mouth shows row of tiny white teeth. Cry voice. **Full composition arms are inside jointed at shoulders.** Walking type composition legs. **Cotton stuffed body . . . no excelsior.** Flower printed frock with wide collar of organdie. Slip and pantie combination are lace trimmed. Dainty tie slippers and half socks. **We Pay Postage.**

448 G 2531—Golden hair **$2.59**
448 G 2532—Brown hair. **2.59**

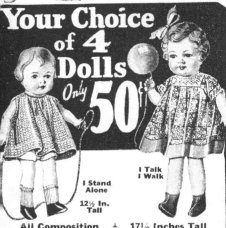

Your Choice of 4 Dolls Only 50¢

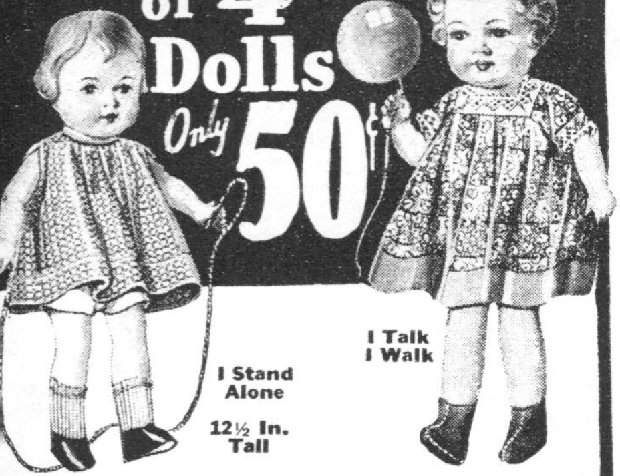
I Stand Alone
12½ In. Tall
I Talk
I Walk

All Composition

New slender type—exactly like a real little American girl. Almost unbreakable **water-proof** molded composition body easy to fit with new clothes; slim, graceful legs and arms jointed inside at shoulders and hips. Finely modeled composition head. Printed frock. Half socks, slippers. Combination. **Postpaid.**
48 G 2510..........50¢

17½ Inches Tall

Childishly modeled composition head; painted features and hair with real hair ribbon. Full composition arms jointed at shoulders. All composition has sanitary **water-proof enamel finish.** Cry voice. Imitation shoes. Print pantie frock; lace trim at neck and sleeves. **Postpaid.**
48 G 2905........50¢

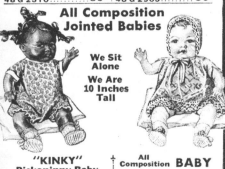

All Composition Jointed Babies

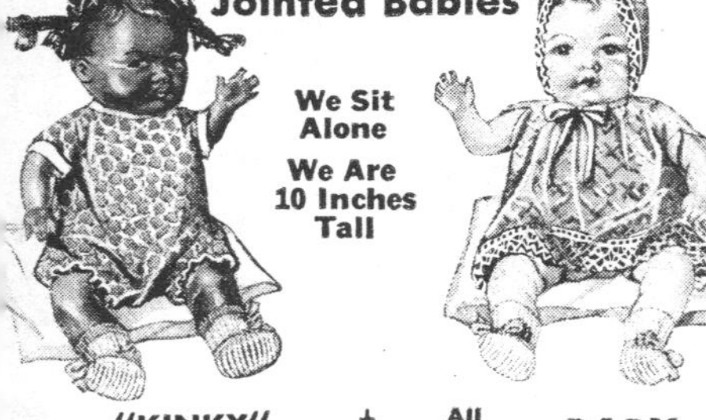
We Sit Alone
We Are 10 Inches Tall

"KINKY" Pickaninny Baby

Made entirely from hard-to-break **water-proof composition.** Painted features and hair with three black pigtails tied with scarlet ribbon. Body jointed **inside** at shoulders and hips. Bright color romper suit; socks. **Postpaid.**
48 G 2908..........50¢

All Composition BABY

Chubby body, curved legs, and baby head are perfectly molded of nearly unbreakable **water-proof** enamel composition. Body jointed inside at shoulders and hips. Pink rayon dress and bonnet are daintily edged with lace. White undies; socks.
48 G 2907—Postpaid..........50¢

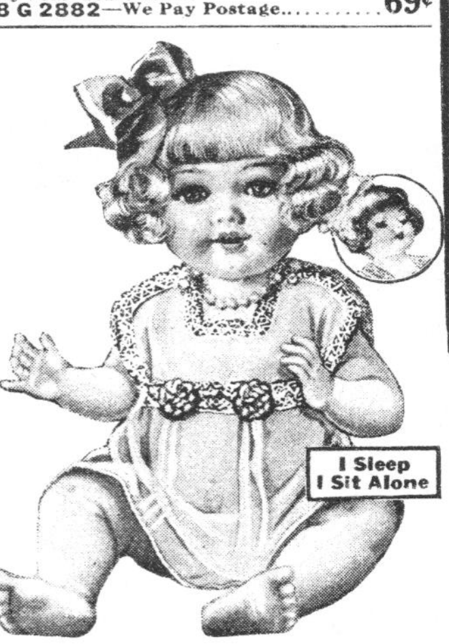
I Sleep I Sit Alone

SALLY Lovable Baby

$1.19 And Up

A Baby who would like to belong to YOU! Sally's smile is irresistible . . . and did you ever see a Baby with such long lashes!

Head of fine bisque with sleeping eyes and fluffy bobbed mohair wig on **sewed cloth foundation.** Hard-to-break composition body beautifully modeled and tinted like a real baby's; jointed inside at hips and shoulders. Chubby legs are half bent at knees. She wears only a white lace trimmed slip; all ready to dress. **Bead necklace. Postpaid.**

48 G 2648—Height 12½ inches......**$1.19**
48 G 2649—Height 14 inches....... **1.59**
48 G 2650—Height 15½ inches....... **1.98**
48 G 2651—Height 17 inches....... **2.48**
448 G 2652—Height 22 inches....... **3.45**

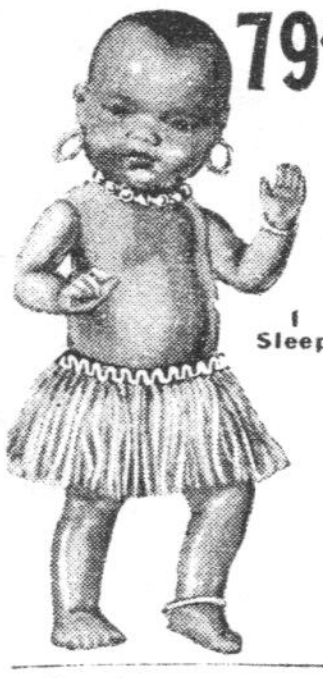
I Sleep

79¢ WILD BABY

from the South Sea Isles

A string of gay glass beads, a grass skirt, brass earrings, an anklet—and this brown skinned child is dressed in her best. Bisque baby head; round fat face with cute little nose and red lips. **Dark brown go-to-sleep eyes.** Jointed at neck. Molded composition body—so easy for little dressmakers to fit. Chubby composition arms and legs jointed inside at shoulders and hips. Just 8½ in. tall.

We Pay Postage.
48 G 2582.......79¢

Pastel Colored **KNIT TOGS** **For Style Conscious Dollies**

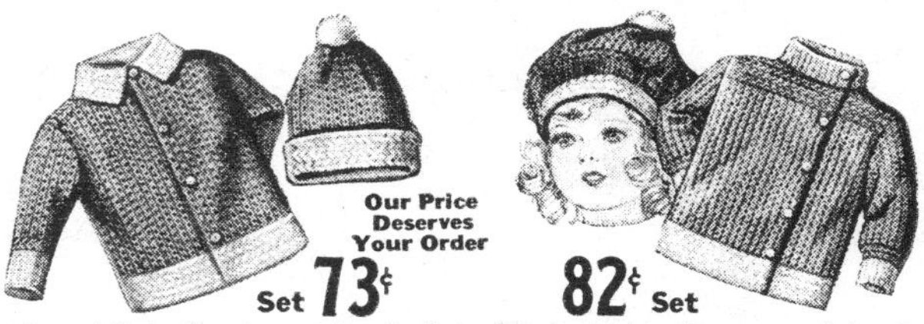
Our Price Deserves Your Order

Set 73¢

Long, full size Sweater and Cap firmly knitted from mercerized yarns. Soft baby colors; white trim. Sweater has turned down collar and closes in front with pearlette buttons; fluffy pompon on cap. Not an open mesh sacque, but a **real sweater outfit** for winter wear. **Postpaid.**

48 G 933—10 to 12-in. bust.....73¢
48 G 934—13 to 15-in. bust.....**82¢**
48 G 935—16 to 19-in. bust.....**85¢**

82¢ Set

Side-buttoning Sweater and jaunty Beret Cap to match. Knitted in fancy stitch from soft mercerized yarns. Dainty shell pink color with white trim. High rolled collar buttons snugly on side. Note our very low price! Three sizes. **Postpaid.**

48 G 955— 9 to 11-in. bust.....82¢
48 G 956—12 to 14-in. bust......**85¢**
48 G 957—15 to 17-in. bust.....**92¢**

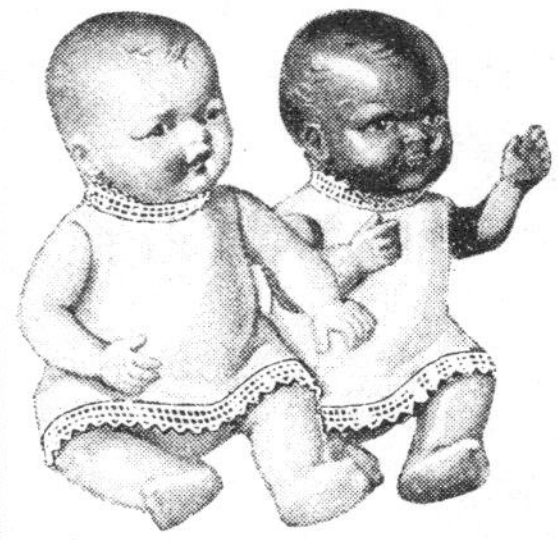

Little Eva and Topsy—Sit Alone

25¢ Each

An adorable pair—a mischievous pickaninny and a little white baby—both the same size, 9½ in. tall. All composition; painted eyes; hair and features. Often sell for 50¢ each. **Postpaid.**

48 G 2503—White doll......25¢
48 G 2502—Pickanniny...25¢

Unusual Value!

25¢

SO BIG... 13½ in. tall; pretty molded composition head, with ribbon. Full composition arms jointed at shoulder; stuffed body, legs. Imitation shoes. Print pantie dress. A value hard to find anywhere but at Ward's. And remember . . . **We Pay Postage.**
48 G 2899...25¢

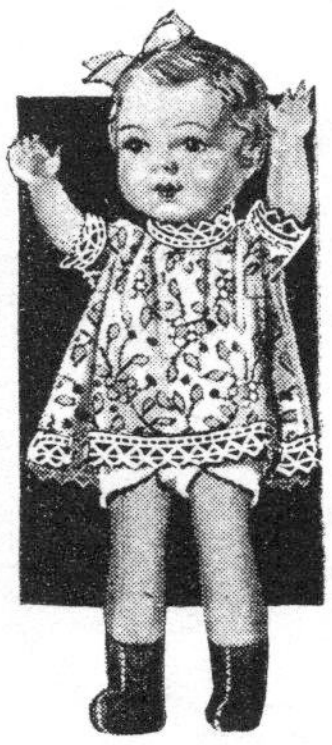
I Walk
I Am 13½ Inches Tall

Jsual 1.50

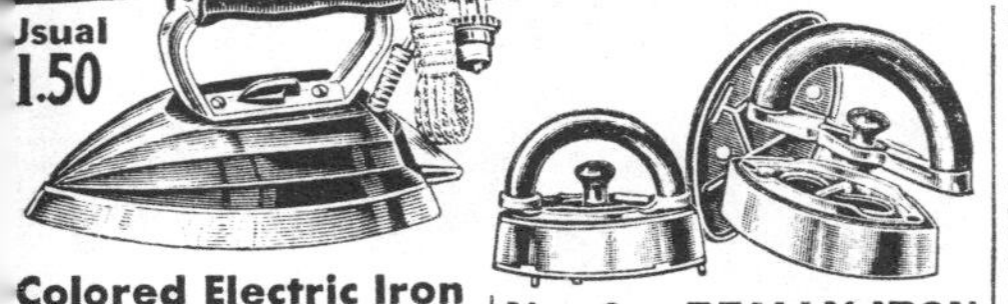

Colored Electric Iron

97¢

REALLY IRONS! Largest, safest and best Toy Iron made. Design patented. Colored shell, wood handle, and rayon covered asbestos **HEATER CORD.** Tip-up stand. 5⅝ inches long. **Weighs ½ lbs.** 5-ft. cord, 2-piece plug. Fully guaranteed.

48 G 905—For young children Gets warm but not hot enough to burn fingers. **Postpaid..97¢**
48 G 919—Practical iron for older child or for traveling. Heats to 500 degrees. **Postpaid...97¢**

You Can REALLY IRON With These . . .

48¢ Large Size

Exactly like the famous Mrs. Potts' iron that mother uses—but not too heavy for baby hands. Detachable handles of polished wood. Polished nickel-plated iron, with tiny tapered ends. Metal stand included. Iron dolly's clothes and your own hankies. **Postpaid.**

48 G 939—4¾ inch. Each. 48¢
48 G 938—3$^{11}/_{16}$ inch. Each. **29¢**

Jump Rope—Jacks and Ball—Bubble Pipe All for 39¢

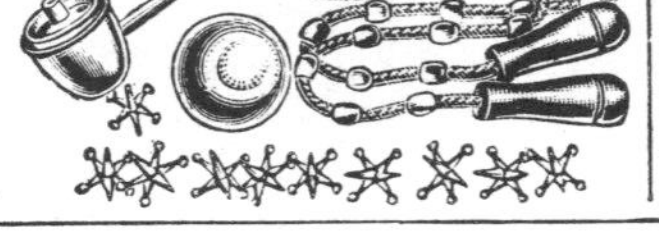

48 G 998—80-in. beaded rope, wood handles; rubber ball; 10 jacks; wood double bubble pipe. **We Pay Postage...39¢**

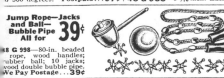

Laundry Set With Real Wringer

10 Pieces $1.29

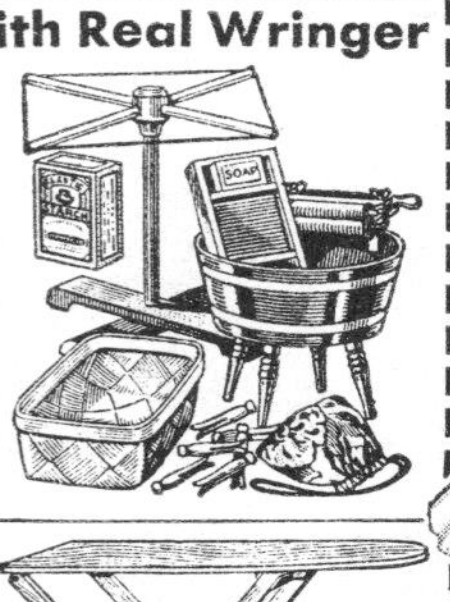

Everything you need for washing dolly's clothes. Wood clothes drier 10 inches high with clothes line; washboard, 8½ by 4½ in. has glass rubbing surface; one 8½-inch tub; 6¼-inch bench; clothes basket, 6½ by 5 in. wide; **wringer** 8 by 2½ inches high with real rubber rollers. Cretonne bag, 6 clothespins, small cake of soap; small box of starch. **We Pay Postage.**
48 G 720.......**$1.29**

Sturdy IRONING BOARDS

89¢ Large Size

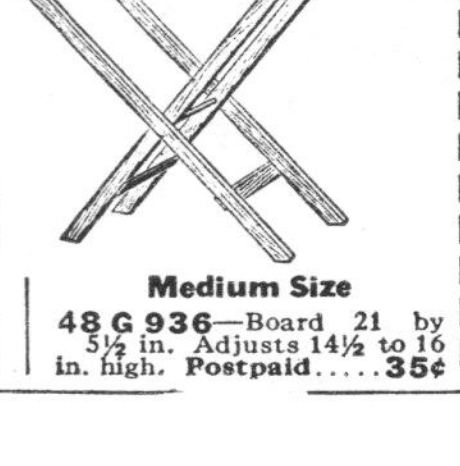

Constructed like Mother's. Selected smooth-finish white wood—no splinters. Fold flat when not in use. **We Pay Postage.**

Extra Large Size
448 G 937—Board 36 by 10½ in. Adjusts 19¼ to 22½ in. high..........**89¢**

Medium Size
48 G 936—Board 21 by 5½ in. Adjusts 14½ to 16 in. high. **Postpaid.....35¢**

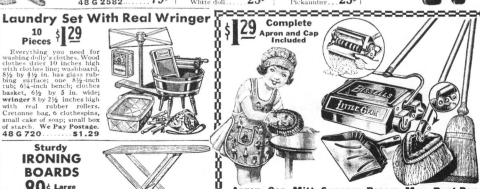

$1.29 Complete Apron and Cap Included

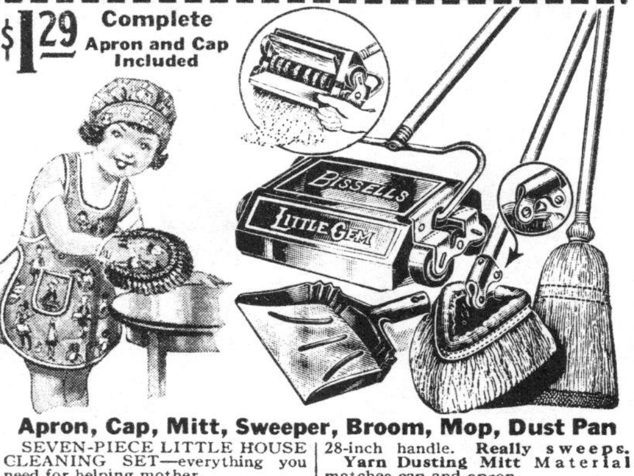
BISSELLS
LITTLE GEM

Apron, Cap, Mitt, Sweeper, Broom, Mop, Dust Pan

SEVEN-PIECE LITTLE HOUSE CLEANING SET—everything you need for helping mother.

Apron and Cap of gay juvenile print cloth to keep your frock and hair clean.

Special Bissell Sweeper has rubber wheels, good quality revolving bristle brush, dumping pans, 8 by 4½ in. wide; nickeled clamp on sides; colored 28-inch handle. **Really sweeps.**

Yarn Dusting Mitt Material matches cap and apron.

Real Broom, 30-inch length.

Floor Mop has adjustable handle; colored yarn swab removable for cleaning.

Sturdy **Dust Pan** of auto body steel—not tin. **Postpaid.**
448 G 989—7-piece Set. **$1.29**

MARX 1932

Fast Action Novelties...

New Large Size Dump Truck
2F-4643—1/12 doz. in box.
▲ Doz **$2.10**
10¾ in. long, attractive color combinations. Mack type, large dump body with open tail and automatic trip.

War Tank
2F-4675—1/12 doz. in box.
▲Doz **$2.00**
5¼ in. long, metal body, camouflage color combinations, 3 black mounted guns, 1 in turret, black rubber tractor t r e a d, flanged wheels, start and stop lever, key attached. Each in illustrated box.

Auto Transport
2F-4674—1/12 doz. in box.......................... Doz **$2.10**
13 in. long, transport and trailer, three 2⅜ in. roadsters in attractive color combinations.

8½ Inches High!

Moves and Turns Quickly!

Walking "Pop-Eye"
BIG EXCLUSIVE SCOOP! We are the only wholesalers who will distribute this extremely clever toy. Certain to be a big hit.
2F-4642—1/12 doz. in box.
Doz **2.15**
"Pop-Eye" is 8½ in. high, properly costumed in colored sailor outfit, with pipe in his mouth and carrying his 2 parrots in cages. Runs along at a rapid gait, turning in different directions.

"Smitty" Scooter
Well known cartoon character in action.
2F-4672—1/12 doz. in box.
▲Doz **$2.10**
8 in. high, Smitty in colored costume, yellow & red scooter. Can be removed from scooter.

SEE OUR HOLIDAY TERMS BELOW

Delivery Motorcycle & Rider
ANOTHER EXCLUSIVE SCOOP. One of the greatest values in the history of Marx toys. We are the exclusive wholesale distributors.
2F-4702—1/12 doz. in box.
Doz **$2.25**
10 in. long, 6 in. high, 4⅝ in. wide. Modern motorcycle delivery car, open body for filling, finished in attractive color combinations. Delivery Boy in litho costume.

Comical Cop
2F-4714—1/12 doz. in box.
Doz **$4.00**
7¼ in. long, 6¾ in. high, litho colors. Auto stands on rear wheels, etc., policeman turns around in comical way.

Monkey Cymbalist
2F-4727—1/12 doz. in box.
Doz **$4.25**
8¼ in. high, 5 in. wide, litho costume. Monkey hops along in life-like manner clacking brassed cymbals which makes loud noise. Very new and novel.

"Pop-Eye" & Truck
2F-4729—1/12 doz. in box.
▲Doz **$4.25**
7⅝ in. long, 7⅞ in. high, Pop-Eye in colored sailor costume with pipe, pushes baggage truck containing trunk. Lid of trunk frequently opens up and parrot sticks its head out. Red wheel barrow, yellow trunk. **Unusual action.**

Milk Wagon & Horse
2F-4659—1/12 doz. in box........ ▲. Doz **$2.00**
10 in. long, white metal wagon with contrasting color litho design, yellow roof and wheels, dapple horse, strong spring.

Latest Type "Cadillac"
2F-4682—1/12 doz. in box.▲ Doz **$2.25**
12¼ in. long with trunk rack open, yellow, black & blue, bright metal bumper and trunk rack, litho uniformed driver.

Bear Cyclist
2F-4678—1/12 doz. in box.
Doz **$2.25**
5¾x5¾ in., costumed trick bear rides bicycle, yellow frame, red wheels, imitation rubber tire.

"Orphan Annie"
Millions of men, women and children know about Little Orphan Annie and her dog Sandy! Show these toys in your window and on your counters.

Little Orphan Annie Jumps Rope

2F-4655—1/12 doz. in box.
Doz ▲**$2.00**
"LITTLE ORPHAN ANNIE"—5 in. high, full formed metal body in red litho costume with white stockings, red hair and natural features, swinging arms with metal jump rope. The clever mechanical action is so devised that the figure jumps rope in very natural manner. TURNING at the same time. Each in illustrated box.

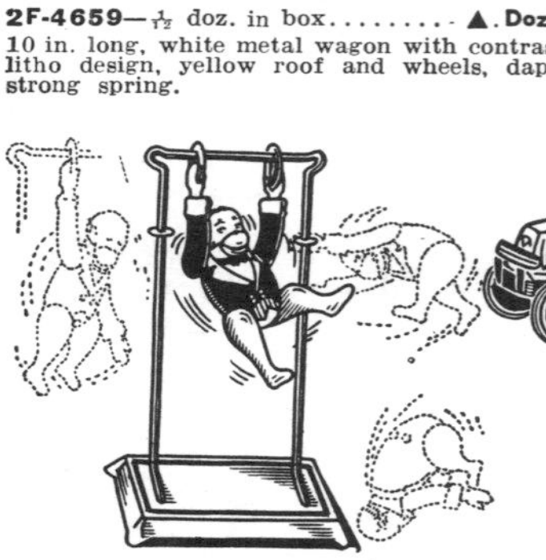

Performing Monkey On Trapeze
2F-4673—1/12 doz. in box..Doz **$2.25**
2¾x4⅛ in. fancy base, 6⅝ in. bright heavy wire trapeze with rings, brightly costumed monkey, 4½ in. long. Performs on double or single rings and on trapeze bar, either top or side.

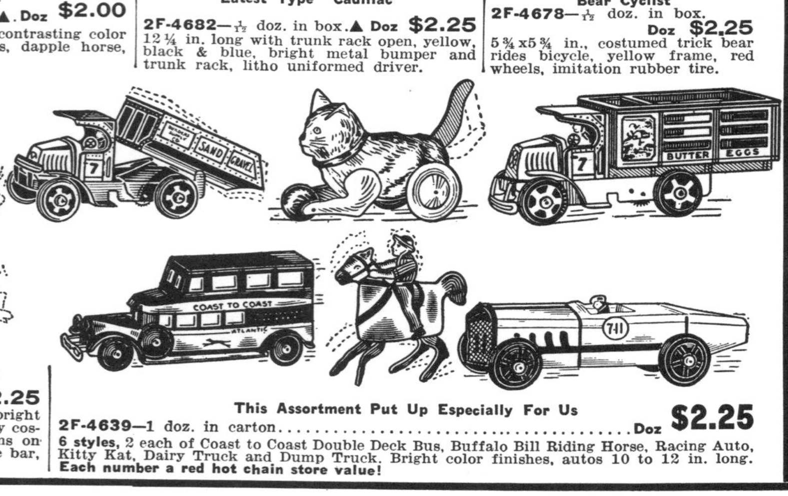

This Assortment Put Up Especially For Us
2F-4639—1 doz. in carton.. Doz **$2.25**
6 styles, 2 each of Coast to Coast Double Deck Bus, Buffalo Bill Riding Horse, Racing Auto, Kitty Kat, Dairy Truck and Dump Truck. Bright color finishes, autos 10 to 12 in. long. **Each number a red hot chain store value!**

Mechanical TOYS
Greatest Values in Twenty-five Years!

32 In. Runway

Climbing Car and Railroad
Sold Only By Butler Brothers!

Exceptional 50c value with a very unusual mechanical action. Big and flashy! We are the exclusive wholesale distributors.

2F-4728— ½ doz. in box.

Doz **$4.25**

32 in. of runway, height to top of incline 7¼ in. Car 3½ in. long. Unusual long running motor in car by which it coasts on hills and climbs on upgrade.

Latest Type "Franklin" Coupe

2F-4782— ½ doz. in box, without battery.....**Doz** **$9.50**
14¼ in. long, 5 in. high, 12-cylinder coupe, 2 head lights and red tail light, **lever in driver's seat turns dry cell current on or off for lights.** Attractive color combinations, large trunk rack, front and rear bumper, strong clock work motor. Place underneath for dry battery, easily replaced.

Army Trucks

2F-4734— ½ doz. in box..**Doz** **$4.25**
13½ in. long, 2-tone khaki color enameled, black trim, disc wheels, mud-guards, running board, bumper, driver, **removable khaki canvas top.**

"De Luxe" Tractors
2F-4844—1 in illustrated box.
☆**Each** **$1.20**
11¾ x4x6 in., **aluminum** chassis and body with litho driver, 2¾ in. flanged wheels, 4 separate rubber tractor treads, powerful mechanical motor, lever for forward or reverse, lever for stop or go.

Climbing Tractors
2F-4775— ½ doz. in pkg.

Doz **$7.50**

8½ in. long, heavy gauge, yellow & green litho finish, 3 in. black disc wheels with rubber tread, powerful motor, driver. Each in illustrated box.

Doughboy Tanks
2F-4792— ½ doz. in box.

Doz **$8.00**

9½ x5½ in., heavy steel, black, orange & blue enameled, 2 side turrets with 1 in. guns, revolving turret with two 1 in. guns, concealed 2½ in. soldier with gun pops out of tank and then disappears.

"4 Merry Makers"
2F-4799— ½ doz. in box.

Doz **$8.15**

9¾ in. long, 9 in. high, attractive black & white combinations. Orchestra leader sits on piano and leads band, drummer beats drum, piano player operates keyboard, jazz dancer.

8½ In. Long!
9 In. High!

Doll On Velocipede

Baby doll pedals a velocipede in squared circle formation turning the handle bars while pedaling and swinging body from side to side, following the direction of the velocipede. Lots of action and interest.

2F-4788— ½ doz. in box.

Doz **$8.50**

8½ in. long, 9 in. high, 4½ in. wide, jointed baby doll, painted natural features and hair, colored costume, bright metal velocipede.

Climbing Dump Truck
2F-4781— ½ doz. in box.

Doz **$8.25**

13 in. long, 5½ in. high, litho colors, body dumping device, closed cab with driver, **tractor type rubber treads.** Climbs over obstacles and up and down grades with loads. **New and original.**

Climbing Tanks
2F-4842— ½ doz. in box.

Doz **$10.50**

9½ in. long, heavy gauge metal, gray with black trim, wide tread, non-slipping rubber traction tires, top turret and 3 mounted cannons, powerful motor.

Her Dog "Sandy"

BUTLER BROTHERS are the exclusive wholesale distributors of these "red hot" sellers!

Runs In Natural Manner

2F-4656— ½ doz. in box.

Doz **$1.95**

"SANDY"—5⅛ in. long, 4⅛ in. high, brown & black metal body with white nose, tail and collar, carries a school bag in mouth. **RUNS IN NATURAL MANNER** when spring motor is wound. Everybody will want these two sensations together. This means double sales for you! Each in illustrated box.

Tractor With Equipment
Covers a play value range never before attempted!
2F-4839—1 in box.................**Each** **$1.35**
Polished finished tractor 8½ in. long, 5½ in. high, 3¾ in. wide, with following equipment: 5½ in. road scraper, 5½ in. harrow, 3½ in. roller, 5½ in. wagon, 9½ in. wrecking device, 3 ft. of polished steel chain, 15x14x4 in. box with dividers between each piece.

Louis Marx began his career in 1912 at the tender age of 16. His first job was office boy for New York-based Ferdinand Strauss, "The Toy King"—who had immigrated here from Bavaria in 1883. Strauss ran a high-volume, low-cost operation, selling from one to three million toys a year.

By 1921 Marx had become a director of the company but a falling out with Strauss prompted him to seek his own fortune in the toy business; so Louis and his brother started their own firm, using some of their bankrupt bosses' old molds.

Chain stores and mail-order houses loved the Marx brothers' cheap, colorful wind-up toys which were packed with lots of action. Within three decades Marx grew to become the world's biggest toy producer.

A brief sampling of Marx toys includes comic-strip characters, from Mickey Mouse to Popeye and Orphan Annie. Mechanical monkeys were also big sellers, as were climbing tractors and Doughboy tanks. The Amos 'N Andy Fresh Air Taxi Cab is one of today's most sought after mechanical toys. Louis Marx sold out to the Quaker Oats Company in 1972 and died a decade later at the age of 85.

1932 Wagon Values Unmatched Anywhere

Go after the big Holiday business with these 3 super values! Order one of each for display . . . take orders from the samples

STEEL BRAKE →

3 Popular Price Levels for All-Steel Wagons

ROLLER CYCLONE BEARING

These 3 wagons are large enough and strong enough to hold two 10-gal. filled milk cans.

¾ in. Auto Tread Rubber Tires

"CYCLONE"

$2.50 EACH   Lots of 6, Each $2.40

1FO-110—RED, yellow stripes.
1FO-111—GREEN, red stripes.
1 in carton, 30 lbs.

BODY—33¼ x15¼ in., heavy sheet steel, raised side panels, reinforcing beads, top and bottom rolls, 1-pc. steel bottom.
GEAR—Channel steel, black enameled, braced, LOCK WASHERS.
TIRE—¾ in., die-cut auto tread rubber, balloon type.
WHEELS—9½ in., double disc, enameled to match body, self-retained roller bearings, large nickel plated hub caps. WILL NOT COME OFF!
HANDLE—Curved tubular steel, loop grip, black enameled.
FINISH—Brilliant baked enamel, cream enameled panel, stenciled lettering.

$3.25 EACH

1FO-121—1 in carton, 36 lbs.

"OLYMPIC"

Paradise Green Body Tangerine Panel

BODY — 33¼ x 15¼ in., heavy sheet steel, reinforcing beads, bottom and top rolls, heavy 1-pc. bottom.
WHEELS—10½ in., double disc, enameled to match body, tangerine stripes, self-retained roller bearings, nickeled hub caps.
TIRES—1¼ in., die-cut auto tread rubber.
GEAR—Extra heavy channel steel, well braced, green enameled, 5TH WHEEL construction, steel brake.
HANDLE—Curved tubular steel, loop grip, ALUMINUM finish, rubber bumper.
FINISH—Paradise green enameled body and wheels, tangerine panel and stripes, green trade mark.

Aluminum Finish Steel Handle With Rubber Bumper! ↓

SKY ROCKET

$4.35 EACH

All-Steel Brake

Tangerine Body Green Panels

1FO-122— 1 in carton, 39 lbs.

Balloon Type Wheels

"SKY ROCKET"—Our De Luxe Wagon!

OUTSTANDING IN SIZE....CONSTRUCTION....FINISH....and PRICE! We haven't seen anything to equal this value! Get it on display early....make your store the headquarters for Wheel Goods!

BODY—33¼ x15¼ in., heavy sheet steel, reinforcing beads, large roll top and bottom, raised side panels, heavy 1-pc. bottom.
WHEELS—10 in., aluminum painted balloon type, green open steel spokes, tangerine stripes, self-retained roller bearings, nickeled hub caps, all-steel roller brake.
GEAR — Special heavy duty channel steel, well braced, green enameled, 5TH WHEEL.
TIRES—¾ in., die-cut auto tread rubber.
HANDLE—Curved tubular steel, loop grip, ALUMINUM finish, rubber bumper.
FINISH — Tangerine body and trade mark, green side panels, gear and wheel spokes.

"AMERICAN" TRUCKS With Removable Side and End Racks

Sturdily built for work and play! They make light work of countless numbers of little jobs around the house. Our prices are low for these QUALITY WAGONS.

JUNIOR

Easily and quickly transformed into a speedy coaster wagon by REMOVING the side and end racks.

HI-WAY

American HEAVY DUTY

HEAVY DUTY

"Junior"
1 in carton, 15 lbs.

1FO-106— Each $2.15

Body—13x24 in., seasoned hardwood.
Gear—Hardwood, securely braced.
Wheels—5½ in., double disc, red enameled.
Tires—⅝ in. rubber.
Handle—Square wood, "D" grip.
Finish—Natural varnished, green panels.

"Hi-Way"

1FO-104—1 in carton, 31 lbs. .... Each $3.95

Body—14 x 32 in., seasoned hardwood, strongly reinforced with heavy cleats, 8 in. racks.
Gears—Channel steel, black enameled, 1-pc. lower front gear with 5TH WHEEL construction.
Wheels—9½ in., red enameled, yellow stripes, self-retained roller bearings, double disc.
Tires—¾ in. auto tread rubber.
Handle—Hardwood, steel loop.
Finish—Varnished, red trim.

1FO-102—1 in crate, 44 lbs. .... Each $5.90

Body — 36 x 16 in., seasoned hardwood, 6 heavy bottom braces, 9 in. racks.
Gear—Extra strong all channel steel, black enameled, steel body braces, 5TH WHEEL construction.
Wheels—10 in., red & gray enameled, black striped, self retained roller bearings, double disc, nickeled hub caps.
Tires—1 in., steel cut auto tread rubber.
Handle—Curved tubular steel, black enameled, loop.
Finish — Natural varnished emerald green side and front panels, gilt lettering.

WOOD COASTER WAGONS

1FO-90—   "Eclipse"
1 in carton, 33 lbs. .... Each $2.75

↓ BRAKE

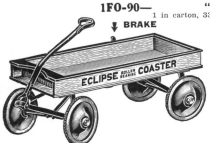

ECLIPSE ROLLER BEARING COASTER

Lots of 6 or more, Each $2.65

BODY: 36x16 in., selected hardwood, 4 bottom cleats.
GEAR: Channel steel, black enameled.
WHEELS: 10 in., roller bearing, red enameled double disc, striped, nickeled hub caps, steel brake.
TIRES: 1 in. die-cut auto tread rubber.
HANDLE: Curved tubular steel, "D" grip, black enameled.
FINISH: Natural varnished, red trim top rails and wheels, black trade mark stencil.

FARM WAGONS

"Miniature"

1FO-67—1 in crate, 57 lbs.

Each $8.00

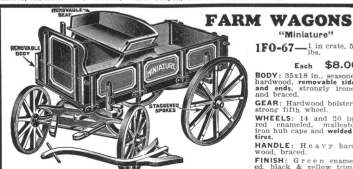

REMOVABLE SEAT

REMOVABLE BODY

MINIATURE

STAGGERED SPOKES

BODY: 35x18 in., seasoned hardwood, removable sides and ends, strongly ironed and braced.
GEAR: Hardwood bolsters, strong fifth wheel.
WHEELS: 14 and 20 in., red enameled, malleable iron hub caps and welded tires.
HANDLE: Heavy hardwood, braced.
FINISH: Green enameled, black & yellow trim.

270

Olympic U.S.A. TOLEDO, OHIO MADE IN U.S.A.

OUR OWN LINE OF VELOCIPEDES! Workmanship, materials and finishes are the very finest. The last word in deluxe vehicles. New improved models at interesting low prices.

1-In. Rubber Tires

Wheels	Size	In Ctn.	Wt.	Each
1FO-177—12 & 8 in.	Small child	2	33 lbs.	$3.00
1FO-178—16 & 10 in.	3 to 5 yrs.	2	41 lbs.	3.60
1FO-179—20 & 14 in.	4 to 6 yrs.	1	25 lbs.	4.25

Ball-bearing front wheel, Indian red enameled ⅞ in. tubular frame, flush head, arch construction, bicycle type curved front fork, nickel plated adjustable handle bars, rubber grips, red leather saddle, ball bearing front wheel, nickel plated hub caps, standard rubber pedals, enameled riveted spokes. 1 in. auto tread tires.

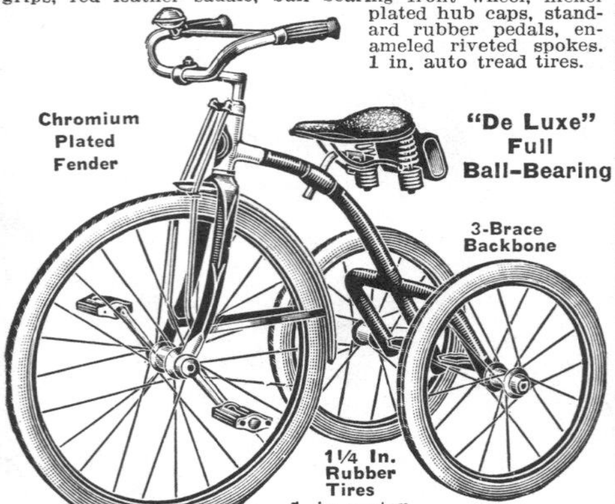

1 in carton.

	Size	Weight	Each
1FO-184—16 & 10 in. wheels	3 to 5 yrs.	30 lbs.	$8.50
1FO-185—20 & 14 in. wheels	4 to 6 yrs.	36 lbs.	9.25
1FO-186—24 & 16 in. wheels	5 to 7 yrs.	41 lbs.	10.25

FRAME—Black enameled 1 in. tubing, red enameled head and stripes, 3 brace back-bone, rear step plates. **FORK**—Square shoulder, tubular bicycle type, chromium plated crown, truss rods and cross bar. **PEDALS**—Ball-bearing, rubber tread, nickeled cranks. **FENDER**—Chromium plated, black enameled center and brackets. **HANDLE BARS**—Adjustable heavy type, chromium plated, rubber grips, bicycle bell. **SADDLE**—Black, padded motor bike model, double adjustment, double coil springs, tool bag. **WHEELS**—Full ball-bearing, nickeled bicycle spokes. **TIRES**—1¼ in. auto tread rubber, cushion type.

Convertible Side Car Velocipede

NEVER BEFORE have we been able to name a price anywhere near this low on a velocipede of this type. Can be used with or without side car which is easily detached by loosening 2 thumb nuts and removing rear right wheel.

1FO-188—1 in crate, 36 lbs....... Each **$6.50**

FRAME—⅞ in. tubing, flush joint construction. **WHEELS**—20 & 14 in., riveted spokes, ball-bearing front wheel, nickeled hub caps, 1 in. auto tread rubber tires. **HANDLE BARS**—Forward extension, nickeled bicycle type, rubber grip. **SADDLE**—Red leather, padded top, double coil springs. **FENDERS**—On front and right rear wheels. **SIDE CAR**—21 in. long, 10 in. wide, foot-well, 7 in. deep, red enameled heavy sheet steel body, red leatherette covered seat. **FINISH**—Indian red with fancy white head and white striping.

FINE QUALITY PARK CYCLES

HERE IS A LINE of Park Cycles that you can sell with the assurance that you are giving your trade the finest quality for the MONEY! ALL HAVE seamless tubular frame, nickeled ball-bearing steel crank hangers, sprockets and adjustable handle bars, rubber grips, leather saddles with nickeled coil springs, parking stands, rubber pedals, solid cushion rubber tires. High grade enamel finishes.

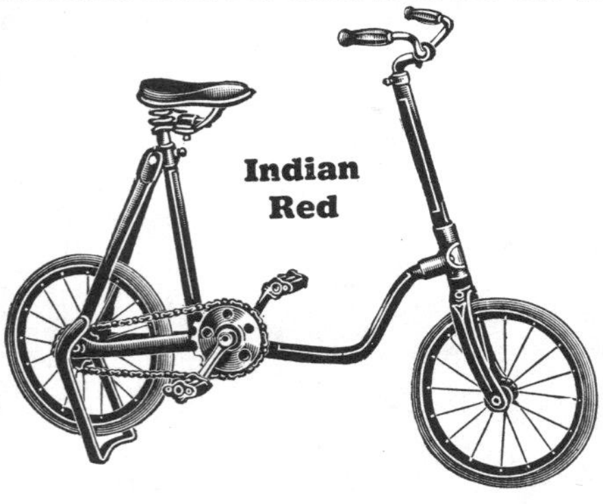

1FO-191—1 in carton, 36 lbs....... Each **$6.50**
43 in. long, 30 in. high, leg length (saddle to pedal) 23 to 27 in., Indian red, 12 in. brightly tinned spoke wheels, 1 in. die cut auto tread tires.

1FO-189—1 in carton, 28 lbs....... Each **$7.50**
"Challenge," 43 in. long, 33 in. high, leg length (saddle to pedal) 20 to 24 in., jade green, 13 in. bicycle spoke wheels, 1 1/16 in. corrugated rubber tires, rear adjustment to take up chain slack.

"NEW DEPARTURE" Coaster Brake
1FO-209—1 in carton, 37 lbs..... Each **$10.50**
44 in. long, 30 in. high, leg length (saddle to pedal) 24 to 27 in., maroon enameled, cream striping, 12 in. BALL BEARING bicycle spoke wheels, 1 in. auto tread rubber tires.

Coaster Brake
1FO-192—1 in carton, 42 lbs..... Each **$11.00**
45 in. long, 30 in. high, leg length (saddle to pedal) 23 to 27 in., red frame, front and rear fenders, 12 in. ball bearing bicycle spoke wheels, cream striping, 1 in. auto tread rubber tires, ball bearing pedals, adjustable forward extension handle bars.

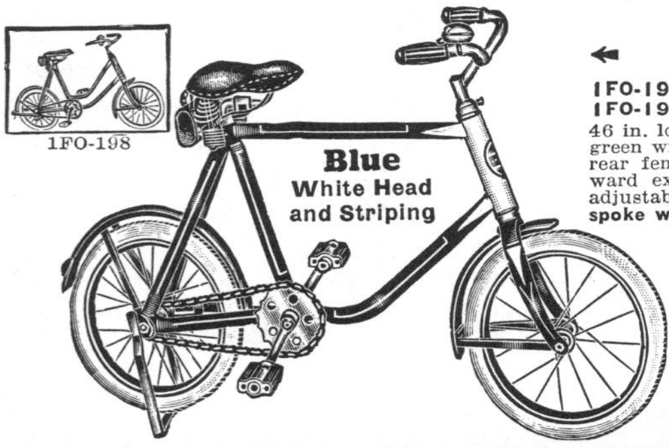

1FO-198

← "NEW DEPARTURE" Coaster Brake

	Each
1FO-197—Boys' model	$14.75
1FO-198—Girls' model	

46 in. long, 22 in. high, leg length (saddle to pedal) 24 in., jade green with white head, spear points and striping, green front and rear fenders, ball-bearing motorcycle type pedals, tool bag, forward extension handle bars, oversize bicycle bell, bicycle type adjustable roller chain, **16 in. full ball-bearing non-rust bicycle spoke wheels**, 1¼ in. die cut auto tread tires. Wt. 40 lbs.

Get into the Wheel Goods business without a big investment! Order a representative line from these pages ....then take orders from the samples....we will carry your stock for prompt delivery.

"AMERICAN-NATIONAL" FIRE AUTOS

1FO-845—
1 in carton, 28 lbs.
Each **$3.80**
"FIRE CHIEF"—31 in. long, porcelain white, red trim, 8 in. red enameled disc wheels, ⅝ in. rubber tires, nickel plated bell, attached cord, metal headlights, adjustable pedals.

1FO-846—1 in carton, 60 lbs... Each **$7.50**
"FIRE CAPTAIN"—42 in. long, fire red, yellow panels and trim, 10 in. red enameled double disc wheels, ¾ in. auto tread rubber tires, instrument board, attached fenders and running board, bright nickel plated headlights and bell with cord, spotlight mounted on running board.

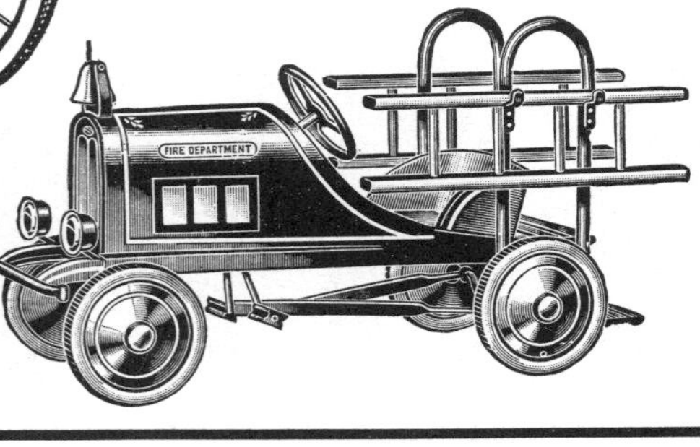

← **49 Inches Long!**
1FO-847—1 in carton, 65 lbs... Each **$8.75**
"FIRE PATROL"—49 in. long, fire red, yellow panels and trim, 10 in. red enameled double disc wheels, 1 in. auto tread tires, adjustable rubber pedals, instrument board, bumper, brightly finished metal headlights and bell with cord, rear step and platform, steel uprights, two 26 in. 4-rung varnished wood ladders.

BUCK JONES TRADING POST

8 Pieces $1.19

8 Pieces $1.79

8-Piece Suit $3.95 With Suede Hat

$4.49 With 10 Gallon Felt Hat

With Suede Hat $2.98 Last Fall $3.98

BUCK JONES Photograph

Last Spring $1.35
—Check cotton flannel shirt.
—Khaki cotton drill chaps with side fringe, elastic waist.
—Khaki cowboy hat, Bandana, belt, pistol, holster, and lasso.

Want to be a cowboy? Here's just the outfit. Regular $1.49 Value!

EVEN SIZES 4 to 10 yrs. State age-size. Shipping weight, 1 pound 12 ounces.

40 K 4388—Complete Outfit.................... $1.19

Texas Ranger
—Cotton flannel check shirt.
—Chap style Khaki drill pants with side trimmings and metal studs.
—Bandana. Belt with imitation cartridges, large pistol and holster. Real Western Style lasso.
—Cowboy hat with colored band.

Ready to ride the range.

EVEN SIZES: 4 to 14 yrs. State age-size. Shipping wt., 2 lbs. 12 oz.

40 K 4383—Complete Outfit.................... $1.79

8-Pc. "Buck Jones" Suit
—Fur front chaps with side trimmings and metal studs.
—Bright cotton flannel plaid shirt.
—Bandana, "6-shooter" toy pistol and holster. Belt with imitation cartridges. Lasso.
—Black cotton suede cloth hat.

Last fall's prices reduced!

EVEN SIZES: 4 to 14 yrs. State age-size. Shipping wt., 4 lbs. 4 oz.

40 K 4384—Outfit...... $2.98
40 K 4385—Same as above, only with genuine tan felt 10-gallon Western Style hat. $3.49

Best "Buck Jones"
—Genuine suede leather chaps with metal ornaments.
—Cotton flannel plaid shirt, 2 chest pockets, button cuffs.
—Large hat. Bandana.
—Lasso, leather belt, imitation cartridges, big "6-shooter" toy pistol, leather holster.

EVEN SIZES: 4 to 14 yrs. State age-size. Shipping wt., 5 lbs. 2 oz.

40 K 4375—Outfit with Black Cotton Suede Cloth Hat. $3.95
40 K 4376—Same as above, only with genuine tan felt 10-gallon real Western style cowboy hat $4.49

FOR COWBOY CHAPS ONLY REFER TO INDEX

C $1.59

B $1.98

A $2.98

AMERICA'S GREATEST MAIL ORDER PLAY-COSTUME SELECTION . . . EVERY DESIGN EXCLUSIVE WITH SEARS!

Ⓐ Official Buck Rogers Outfit .. Only at Sear
—Light tan cotton twill breeches, brown cotton suede cloth putte
—Black cotton sweater with Buck Rogers insignia. Orange coll and sleeves. Toy rocket pistol. Tan suede helmet with vis Belt and novelty holster.

Boys . . . dress like your favorite hero! Wear the clothes Buck Roge wears in the 25th century idea. Just like you've seen in the comic str Only Sears can sell this suit by mail! EVEN SIZES: 4 to 14 yea State age-size. Shipping weight, 3 pounds 3 ounces.
40 K 4374—Buck Rogers Outfit..................... $2.98

Ⓑ High Flyer 6-Piece Outfit
—Coat and breeches of washable khaki drill.
—Artificial leather belt and puttees.
—Aviator's helmet and goggles.

Coat has two big patch pockets with button flaps. Metal aviator's emblem on the collar.

EVEN SIZES: 4 to 14 years. State age-size. Shipping weight, 2 pounds 3 ounces.
40 K 4353—Aviator's Outfit....... $1.98

Ⓒ Heap Big Bargain
—Lace front khaki drill coat with colored imitation jewels, metal studs.
—Khaki drill pants, colored trimmings.
—Large headdress, colored feathers.

EVEN SIZES: 4 to 14 years. State age-size. Shipping weight, 1 pound 8 ounces.
40 K 4386—Indian Chief Outfit..... $1.59

BRAVE'S OUTFIT
Similar to above, but lighter weight drill; smaller headdress; less trim.

EVEN SIZES: 2 to 10 years. State age-size. Shipping weight, 1 pound 1 ounce.
40 K 4372—Brave's Outfit......... $1.00

Western Style

Black cotton sue cloth with white p ing and white ban Bright red ornamen

SIZES: 6⅝, 6 6⅞, 7, 7⅛. State si Shipping weigh 1 pound.

40 K 438759c Cowboy hat. 59c

YIP-PEE! Ride 'em Cowboy

89c

Some Holsters, Fellas!
And how! Three wood bullets in new style bullet holder over each holster, two 8-inch black enameled steel guns that make clicking noise when you pull trigger. Two big 9½-inch holsters and wide belt with the nickel plated buckle made of top-grain cowhide leather with Western style embossing. Set consists of 2 Guns, 2 Holsters, 6 wood Bullets and Belt. Shipping wt., 1 lb. 8 oz.
49 K 5649............89c

2-Gun Outfit for Smaller Boys
(Not illustrated) Two 6½-inch clicker steel pistols in 6¼-inch holsters of embossed top-grain cowhide; 4 wood bullets in loops on belt. Shipping wt., 13 oz.
49 K 5626............49c

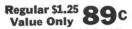

Regular $1.25 Value Only 89c
When you're dressed up like this, you're ready for anything. Tan fleeced cotton leggings have bright tops, with a holster pocket and shiny nickel plated metal conchas. The vest is decorated to match. Even sizes, 4 to 14 years. State age-size. Shpg. wt., 1 lb. 2 oz.
49 K 5695........89c

Save ⅓ On These Chaps
Heavy cotton suede cloth. Colored glass and nickel plated studs. Snap fastener style back. Holster pocket; four dummy bullets. Vest to match. Even sizes, 4 to 14 years. State age-size. Shpg. wt., 2 lbs. 4 oz.
49 K 5697....$1.89

For Complete Cowboy Outfits See Page 280

$1 39

Real Fur Trimmed
Worth 75c More Than We Ask

Fluffy, real long haired fur leggings, with colored cotton suede-like cloth top and wide scallops, trim, and belt. Rich color suede-like cloth vest with roomy pockets. All trimmed with bright metal conchas. Holster pocket for gun. They'll be the pride of any young boy's life. You'd hardly believe a value like this would be possible. Just think—real fur-front leggings, the kind of fur you'd ordinarily find on outfits that sell for much more than this price.

Even sizes, 4 to 14 years. State age-size. Shipping weight, 1 pound 12 ounces.
49 K 5696..............$1.39

3-Piece Holster Set
6½-inch heavy gauge black steel clicker gun in 7½-inch holster. Leather belt holds 3 dummy bullets. Shipping weight, 7 oz.
49 K 5625.......27c

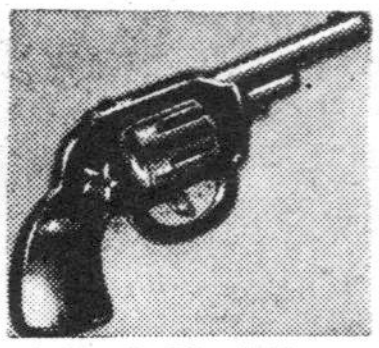

8-Inch Steel Gun
Pull the trigger and it makes a sharp clicking noise. Baked-on black enamel finish. Shipping weight, 8 ounces.
49 K 5653...10c

Low Priced Cowboy Outfit
A wide brim khaki hat, a red cloth bandana with a cowboy picture and a 7-foot rope lariat. Hat will fit the average boy's head. Shipping weight, 9 ounces.
49 K 5698—3-Pc. Outfit...35c

Dress Up In Cowboy Style
Real 10-gallon Western style black felt hat, fits the average boys' head; 8-foot lariat and red cloth bandana handkerchief. Shipping weight, 1 pound.
49 K 5699..............49c

7-Piece Seminole Archery Set
A 42-in. varnished hickory bow with mohair grip and four 18¼-inch spearhead rubber tipped arrows with feather guides; two 8½-inch bulls-eye targets printed on inside of folding box; also large 25x25-inch paper target you can mount, and chalk to mark your arrows.
49 K 5644—Shipping weight, 1 pound 14 ounces..............69c

Mickey Mouse Shooting Gallery
Sold by mail only by Sears. Most popular shooting game in the country. Looks easy, but just try it. 17½-inch sturdy colorful cardboard tripod-type target with Mickey holding the bullseye score. 7⅝-inch enameled steel gun with powerful spring and 4 rubber-tipped suction-cup darts. Shpg. wt., 3 lbs.
49 K 5669..............89c

89c

Brand New! Automatic Electric Popeye Target
Just connect batteries and two disappearing targets alternate in popping up and down. 5½-in. steel gun with strong spring, 3 rubber suction cup darts; lithographed target 18x10 in. operates on 2 dry cell batteries. Batteries not included. See below. Shipping wt., 3 lbs.
49 K 5661—Popeye Target Set........ **$1.00**
20 K 1401—1⅜-inch Diam. regular cell battery. Shpg. wt., 4 oz. Each..............5c

3-Piece Police Holster Set
Put this on and go out to guard your neighborhood. Genuine cowhide leather—shiny black finish. Police holster with shiny black belt, 8-inch black enameled steel gun that clicks when you shoot, and 3 dummy bullets. Holster overall, 9¼x4½ inches. Shipping wt., 14 oz.
49 K 5607..............49c

Big 5-Piece Police Outfit
Be a policeman! It's lots of fun to direct traffic, chase bandits and keep law and order. Policeman's cap of dark blue cloth with shiny visor and chief emblem; a loud traffic whistle; polished metal hand cuffs with spring snap. Night stick with wrist strap and shiny metal badge (assorted styles). Shipping weight, 1 lb. 2 oz.
49 K 5609..............59c

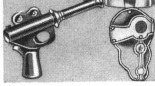

Small Buck Rogers Pistol
Little Tots can planet travel, too. Now a small Buck Rogers 25th Century Rocket Pistol for the little tot. It's 7 inches long; break action type. Shpg. wt., 12 oz.
49 K 5639—Pistol..........20c
Cowhide leather holster; nickel plated buckle. Shpg. wt., 6 oz.
49 K 5642—Holster........20c

New Buck Rogers 25th Century Automatic Flashing Disintegrator
Radically different, with **new automatic action (no cocking)**. Dazzling futuristic flashes show in compression chamber window combined with distinctive sound effect. Gleaming copper color finish, steel dummy cooling fans at muzzle and dummy gas chamber. 10 in. long. Your boy's dream, too!
49 K 5638—Shpg. wt., 1 lb..... **45c**

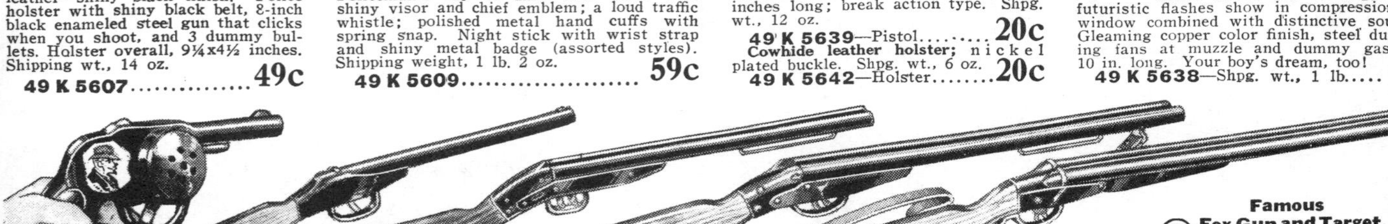

(A) (B) (C) (D) (E)

(A) Dick Tracy Pistol
Pull the trigger and a loud siren calls assistance. 8½-inch black enameled steel pistol. Shipping weight, 12 oz.
49 K 5656......25c

(B) Single Barrel Clicker Gun
Right size for little brother. 18 in. Pulling trigger makes loud click. Red wood handle and black steel barrel. Shipping weight, 12 oz.
49 K 5643......10c

(C) 22-Inch Double Barrel Gun
Two triggers. Break action. Each barrel fires separately making sharp noises. Cork enclosed in steel barrels. Varnished wood stock. Shpg. wt., 2 lbs.
49 K 5645......25c

(D) 28-In. Double Barrel Gun
Has Cowhide Shoulder Strap. Break action. Two triggers to shoot enclosed cork in each barrel which pop separately, making loud report. Shipping weight, 2 lbs. 4 oz.
49 K 5651..............49c

(E) Famous Fox Gun and Target
Improve your aim with this 29-inch black enameled breech loading steel gun. Has removable shells with coil spring power, shoots wooden bullets. Target with bell included. Each barrel shoots separately. Gun has hardwood stock, walnut stained; Shipping weight, 3 lbs.
49 K 5640......$1.79

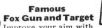

Hit Target and Bell Rings!

Breech Loading

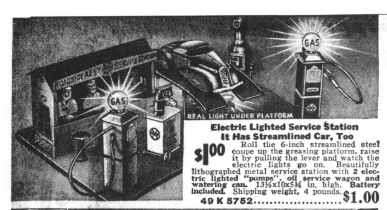

Electric Lighted Service Station
It Has Streamlined Car, Too

$1.00   Roll the 6-inch streamlined steel coupe up the greasing platform, raise it by pulling the lever and watch the electric lights go on. Beautifully lithographed metal service station with 2 electric lighted "pumps", oil service wagon and watering can. 13½x10x5¾ in. high. **Battery included.** Shipping weight, 4 pounds.
49 K 5752......................**$1.00**

Mickey and Minnie Mouse
Take a Ride!

Sold by mail only by Sears. 94c   Wind up strong clockwork motor, release brake and away they go. Their attractively colored shaped composition bodies pump away like mad while bell rings. 9-in. metal hand car and 6 ft. of circular track.
49 K 5105—Shpg. wt.—2 lbs. 7 oz. **94c**

Fire Truck! Lights! Siren! Ladders!
Off to the fire! Wind the new Marx heavy duty super-power motor and see it go, siren shrieking, electric headlights and searchlight blazing. Pull the brake and mount the two 8-in. ladders on truck for the rescue. It's red enameled heavy steel, 14¼ inches long, with the new streamline fenders and oversize balloon type rubber wheels. **Battery included.** Shipping weight, 4 pounds 5 ounces.
49 K 5796..................**$1.59**

Garage With 2 Mechanical Autos
Lots of play value! Wind the strong spring motors of the two 6-in. heavy gauge steel streamline automobiles and watch them travel on their easy-rolling wooden wheels. Open garage doors and let cars drive in. Garage is heavy gauge lithographed steel with doors you can lock, and measures 7¼x6⅜x4⅜ inches. Shipping weight, 3 pounds 3 ounces.
49 K 5727..................**59c**

Marx Aluminum Climbing Tractor
Finest tractor ever made. Has new, more powerful clockwork motor. Climbs steep grades and pushes loads bigger than itself. Stop and start lever. Aluminum case over metal housing. 8½ inches long. Shpg. wt., 1 lb. 7 oz. **94c**
49 K 5746..................**94c**
49 K 5745—Similar to above, but has lithographed metal housing only, not aluminum and less powerful motor. Shipping weight, 1 lb. 7 oz. **59c**

Now! A Heavy Duty Climbing Tank
Here's real fun—wind the new heavy duty super-power clockwork motor—release brake—and watch tank climb up or down hill in real fighting tank fashion. Has oversize 1-inch double traction tread that never misses. A mechanical wonder at a record new low price. It's 9½ in. long by 5¼ in. high. Shiny nickel finish metal. Shpg. wt., 2 lbs.
49 K 5763..................**94c**

New Rocket Racer
Latest design, 16 inches long. Tremendous value. Strong spring motor. Bright metal, rubber bumper. Shpg. wt., 1 lb. 6 oz.
49 K 5735......**25c**

Delivery Motorcycle
Every little tot wants one. 9¾ inches long. Bright colored metal, make-believe headlights. Strong spring motor. Shpg. wt., 1 lb. 3 oz.
49 K 5740.......**25c**

New, Mysterious Tricky Taxi!
Daredevil 4½-inch metal taxi with sturdy clockwork motor, whirls and dashes about on the 10-inch colorful metal platform map of city streets, which is included—it goes right to the edges but seldom off—why? Runs on any flat surface. **39c**
49 K 5744—Shipping weight, 13 ounces. **39c**

Midget Tractor
Only 5¼ inches long but it actually climbs. Bright metal. Strong spring motor and brake. Shipping weight, 8 ounces.
49 K 5753.....**25c**

Moon Mullins Hand Car
6 in. long. Brightly colored. Strong Marx spring motor. They pump the handle up and down and race along. Shpg. wt., 9 oz.
49 K 5772.......**25c**

New Low Price for Rider Truck
Sit on steel seat, pedal with your feet and steer it like a real truck. Heavy gauge steel, baked-on enamel finish. Holds the weight of a grown-up. Length, overall, 16 inches. Height, to seat from floor, 7½ inches. Shipping weight, 4 pounds 8 ounces.
49 K 5420......................**59c**

59c

New 13-Piece Municipal Airport
Colorful 12x15x12 inch cardboard airport. Easily set up. Famous Tootsie Toy transcontinental tri-motor plane, a TWA cabin plane and a Chrysler automobile of unbreakable metal, averaging 5 inches; 4 passengers and 5 dummy tools. Shipping weight, 2 pounds.
49 K 5411......................**59c**

24½ In. 4-Car Auto Transport
Latest streamline design Double-Decker with electric headlights. Turn lights out, drop unloading platform and let the 3 cars on top roll down easily, just like the big transports. Real dump truck on lower platform. Transport, 24½ inches long with runway extended. Four streamlined 6-inch cars with shiny sloping radiator fronts. Really 5 toys in one. **Battery included.** Shipping weight, 4 pounds 1 ounce.
49 K 5407..................**98c**

21-In. Buddy "L" Dump Truck
With electric headlights and shiny radiator. Boys! Here's fun! Turn lights on with switch—load your truck, work lever to dump it. Carry sand, toys, anything up to 200 pounds. Biggest value we know of. Heavy gauge steel baked-on enamel and it is Buddy "L" quality. 21 inches long with body raised; 8¾ inches high. Balloon type rubber tires. **Battery included.** Shipping weight, 6 pounds.
79 K 5009..............**98c**

Run a Buddy "L" Digger!
Sit on the strong steel seat. Seat and boom turn on runners to dig and dump wherever you like. It's 28 inches long; with boom extended, 38 inches; largest height, 17 inches. Made of 20-gauge steel, enameled in black and red. Shipping weight, 4 pounds 10 ounces.
79 K 5002......................**98c**

Garage and 10 Streamline Cars
A whole fleet of cars with an 11-inch colored strong cardboard garage. Chrysler, several trucks, bus, tanker, roadster, etc. Heavy gauge steel on easy rolling wheels. Average 6 inches. Shipping wt., 5 lbs. 6 oz.
49 K 5412......................**98c**

274

The Most Popular Mickey Mouse Toys for Little Tots

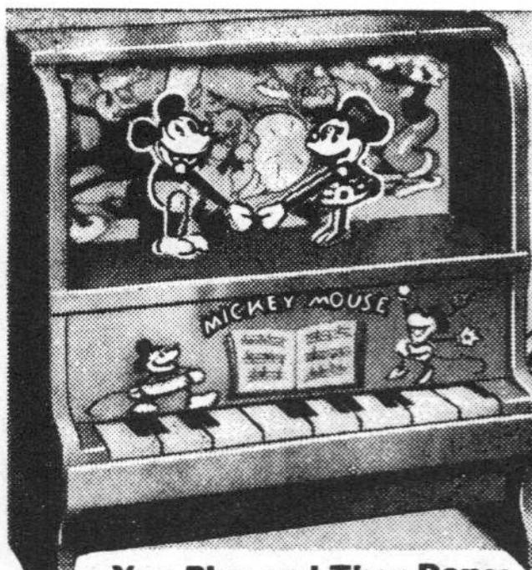
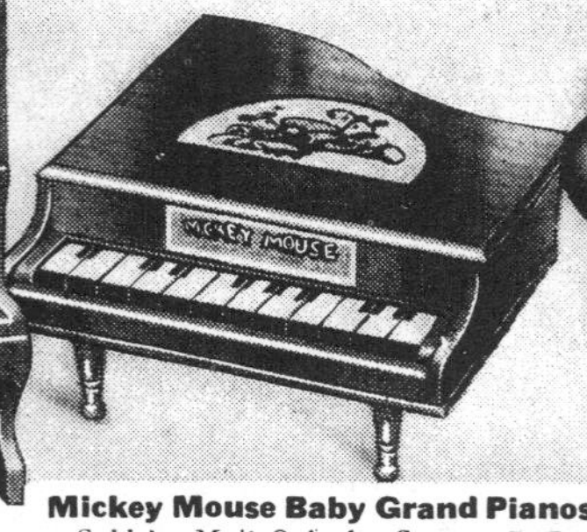
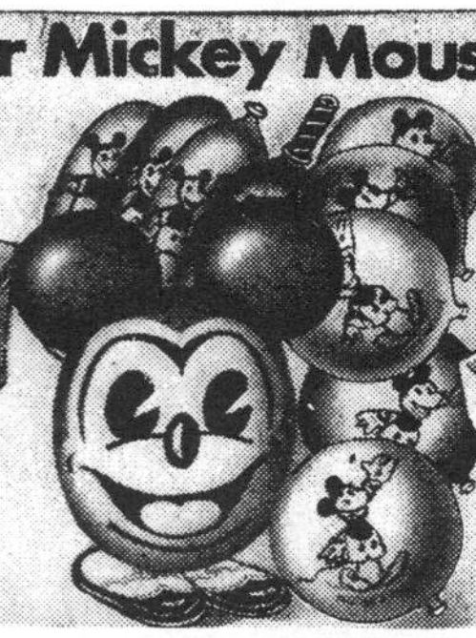
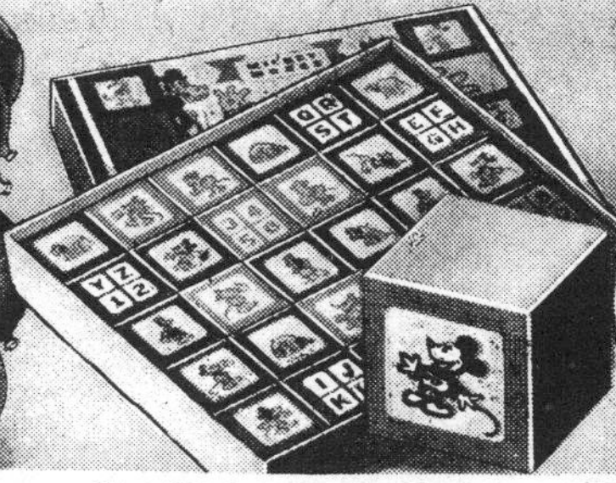
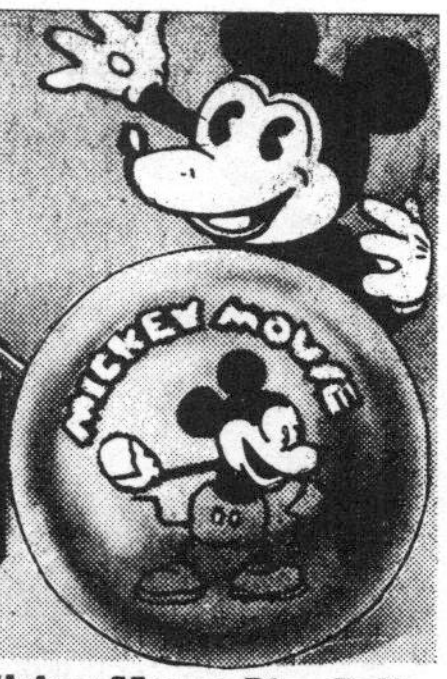

You Play and They Dance

Brand new 10-in. red enameled wood piano. **$1.00** Cardboard Mickey and Minnie Mouse, famous movie characters, are so attached that they dance when the 8 accurately tuned keys are played. The Big Bad Wolf and Three Little Pigs are lithographed on the background. Shipping weight, 1 pound 14 ounces.
49 K 2421 ....$1.00

Mickey Mouse Baby Grand Pianos

Sold by Mail Only by Sears. Accurately tuned chime-like sounding notes. Dark oak hardwood case. Enameled black and white keys look like natural flats and sharps. **98c** 9-Key

9-Keys, Size 10¼x7¾ in.
49 K 2423—Shpg. wt., 3 lbs. 98c
12-Keys, Size 10⅞x10⅛ in.
49 K 2424—Shipping weight, 3 pounds 5 ounces............$1.49

10 Mickey Balloons

Big value. You can inflate Mickey to 8 inches tall and he has cardboard feet, too. Long ones inflate to 15 in., round shapes to about 9 in. diam. One has squawker. Shipping weight, 4 ounces. **19c**
49 K 9114
10 Balloons for.......19c

New Mickey Mouse Blocks

Non-poisonous Halsam enameled round cornered safety blocks. Embossed with colorful genuine characters. **45c** 15 Pcs.

30—1¾-in. Blocks
49 K 3674—Shipping wt., 3 lbs. 89c
15—1¾-in. Blocks
49 K 3675—Shipping wt., 1 lb. 9 oz. 45c

Mickey Mouse Play Balls

Newest thing. Inflated rubber in colors. Design is in rubber, not just stenciled. **10c** 3-in.
49 K 7715—4½-in. Diam. Shpg. wt., 8 oz. 22
49 K 7731—6-in. Diam. Shpg. wt., 1 lb. 5 oz. 47
Solid Sponge Rubber
49 K 7701—3-in. Diam. Shpg. wt., 1 lb. 12 oz. 10c

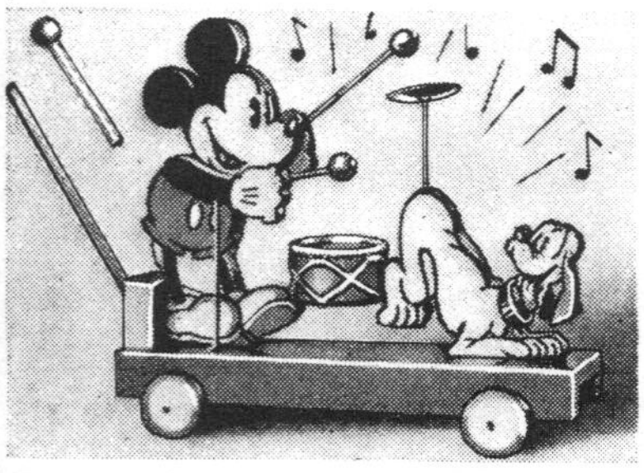

Brand New Mickey Mouse Band

Push it or pull it . . . and Mickey's one arm beats the metal drum; with the other he strikes the metal cymbal on Pluto's tail. It's a picnic. The cutest wood toy you've ever seen, brightly colored. 12 in. long. 16-in. Push handle. **89c**
49 K 5430—Shpg. wt., 2 lbs. 4 oz....89c

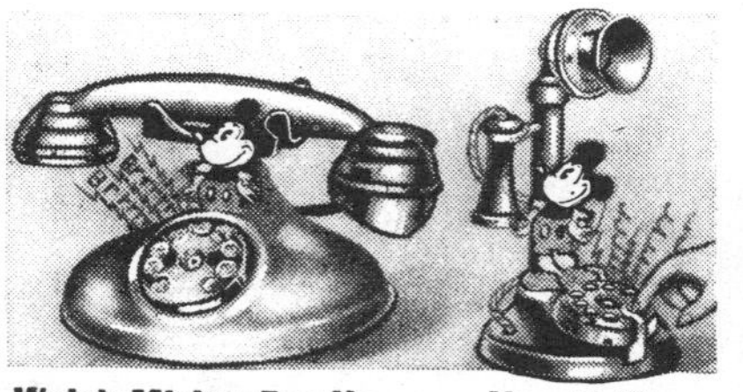

Watch Mickey Pop Up

Lift the receiver—Mickey jumps up big as life. Dial your number—phone rings. A big 8¾-in. French type phone enameled bright red, with nickeled trim and felt base, size 6³⁄₁₆ in. Green cord attached to metal receiver and mouth piece. Looks just like a regular phone. Shipping weight, 1 pound 9 ounces.
49 K 2457.......49c

Hear it Ring

Mickey grins at you as you dial your number and the bell rings. Nickel plated dial, mouthpiece and receiver hook; enameled metal base. Height, 8 in. Wood receiver. Shpg. wt., 14 oz.
49 K 2455..25c

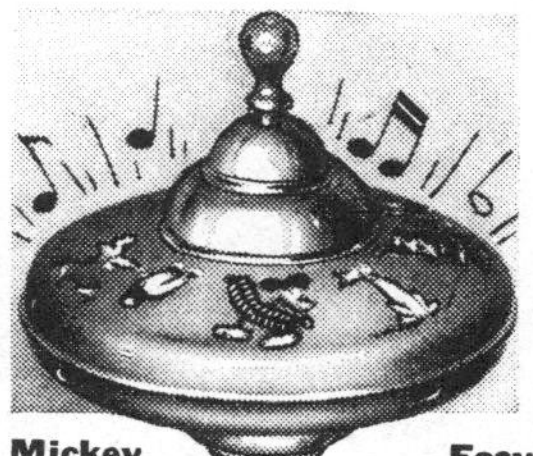

Mickey Mouse Tops **Easy to Spin**

Brightly lithographed Mickey, Minnie and Pluto figures. One musical chord. Just pull up bright red knob and push down.

Large 8-In. Size
49 K 2378—Shpg. wt., 1 lb. 10 oz. 47c
Junior 6½-In. Size
49 K 2377—Shipping weight, 1 pound 2 ounces..........23c

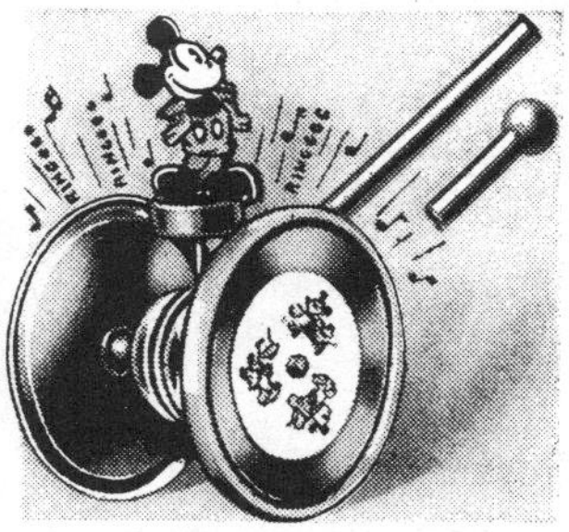

Mickey Mouse Rolling Chime

There is Mickey Mouse—big as life on top of the nickel plated bell. Lots of fun for little tots. Red enameled metal. 21 in. long, 8 in. high. Shpg. wt., 1 lb. 8 oz. **29c**
49 K 2434 ....29c

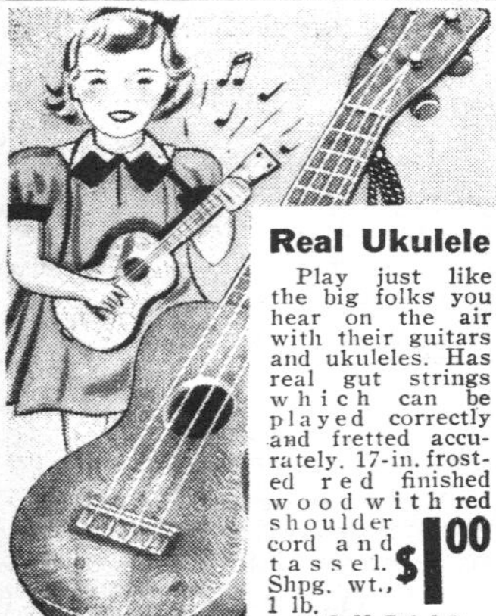

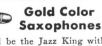

Real Ukulele

Play just like the big folks you hear on the air with their guitars and ukuleles. Has real gut strings which can be played correctly and fretted accurately. 17-in. frosted red finished wood with red shoulder cord and tassel. Shpg. wt., 1 lb. **$1.00**
49 K 2446

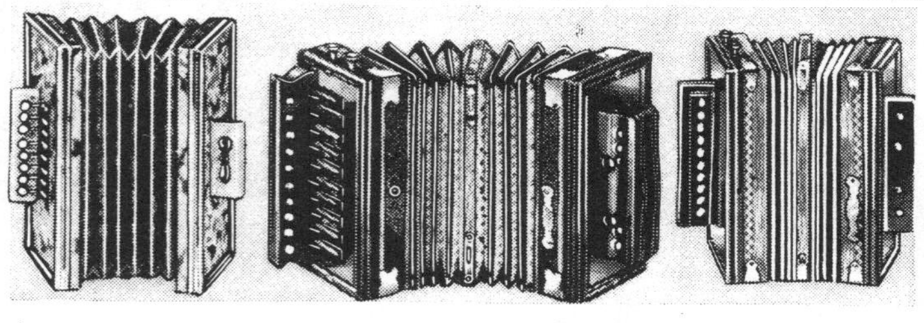

Accordions That Really Play

Specially Priced

8 treble keys, plays 16 notes; 1 bass key. Easy to play. Accurately tuned. Well made. Size closed, 10x4½ inches. Made in Germany. Shipping weight, 1 pound 2 ounces. **69c**
49 K 2355.

Our De Luxe Quality

20 treble notes and 2 bass. Accurately tuned. A real instrument except small in size. Fine workmanship and finish. Double bellows. Black enameled wood frame. Size closed, 9¼x8x4½ in. Made in Germany. Shipping wt., 3 lbs. 1 oz. **$2.59**
49 K 2371.......

Unusual Value

10 double reed metal keys. 20 notes, 2 bass. Nickel plated trimmed metal frame. Accurate deep tone. Nicely finished. Size 9⅝x6⅛ in. Shipping weight, 1 lb. 12 oz. **$1.00**
49 K 2368.

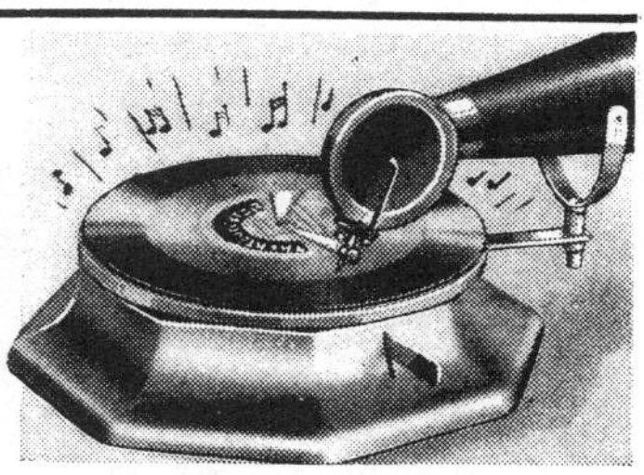

Real Phonograph—New Low Price

Sold by Mail Only by Sears. Plays up to 10-in. records. Wind up clock-work motor. 14-inch two-color steel base. Reproducer and fiber horn. Shpg. wt., 2 lbs. 7 oz.
49 K 2435.............................98c

6-Inch Double Faced Non breakable Records **15c ea.**

Assorted titles—Shpg. wt., each, 5 oz.
49K2362—Old King Cole and Piper's Son
49K2363—Cat & Fiddle and Ding Dong Bell
49K2364—Mary's Lamb and Little Boy Blue

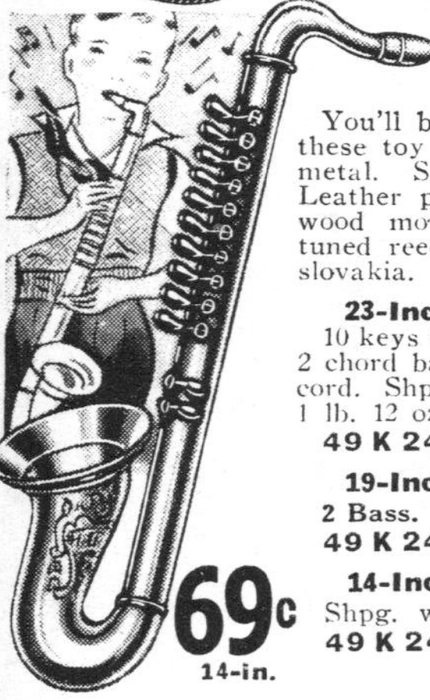

Gold Color Saxophones

You'll be the Jazz King with these toy saxophones of bright metal. Sheet music included. Leather padded keys, sanitary wood mouthpiece. Accurately tuned reeds. Made in Czechoslovakia.

23-Inch Sax—20 Notes
10 keys that play 20 notes and 2 chord bass notes. Adjustable cord. Shpg. wt., 1 lb. 12 oz.
49 K 2487..........$1.89

19-Inch Sax—10 Notes
2 Bass. Shpg. wt., 1 lb. 7 oz.
49 K 2472 ....$1.00

14-Inch Sax—10 Notes
Shpg. wt., 14 oz.
49 K 2479 ....69c

69c 14-in.

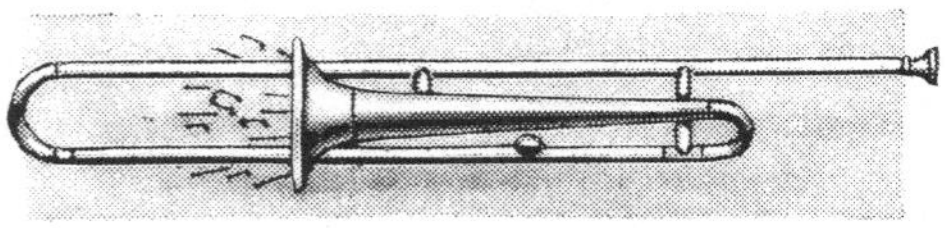

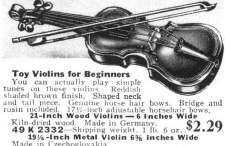

8-Note Gold Color Trombone

You can really play simple melodies on this accurately tuned metal slide trombone. 28¾ inches long, extended. Lots of real fun. Music included. Made in Czechoslovakia. **$1.00**
49 K 2317—Shipping weight, 1 lb. 7 oz.

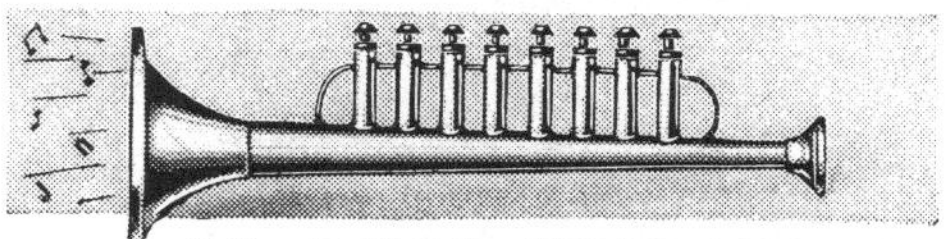

8-Key Gold Color Metal Cornet

Not just a toy—but a 17¾-inch cornet that can be played. Eight spring-valve type notes, like a real cornet and accurately tuned. Nickel plated mouthpiece. Music included. Made in Czechoslovakia. **$1.19**
49 K 2396—Shipping weight, 1 lb. 6 oz.....

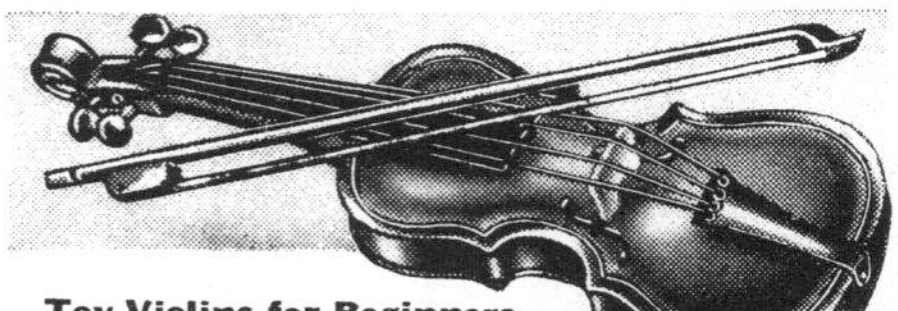

Toy Violins for Beginners

You can actually play simple tunes on these violins. Reddish shaded brown finish. Shaped neck and tail piece. Genuine horse hair bows. Bridge and rosin included. 17½-inch adjustable horsehair bows.

21-Inch Wood Violins—6 Inches Wide
Kiln-dried wood. Made in Germany.
49 K 2332—Shipping weight, 1 lb. 6 oz..$2.29
19¼-Inch Metal Violin 6⅜ inches Wide
Made in Czechoslovakia.
49 K 2335—Shipping weight, 1 lb. 12 oz..$1.00

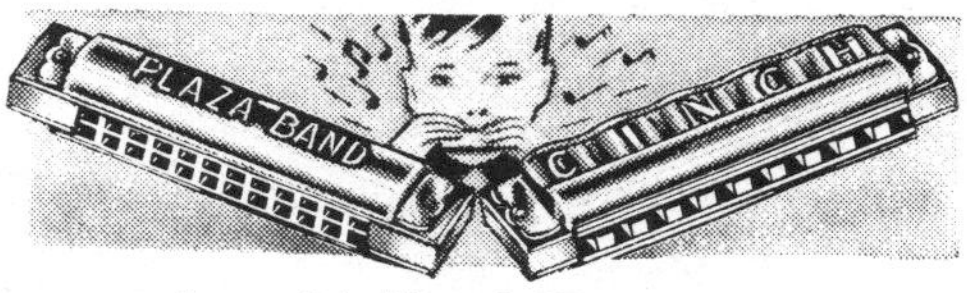

Accurately Tuned Harmonicas

At special low prices. There isn't a youngster anywhere who doesn't want a harmonica. It's fun to play the latest tunes for your friends, at parties or for your own enjoyment. Beautiful nickel plated finish. Assorted styles. Accurately tuned. 2 kinds. Made in Germany.

24 Brassed Reeds
Tremola, 24 single holes. Length, about 4½ in. Shpg. wt., 3 oz. **20c**
49 K 2348 ..

18 Brassed Reeds
10 single holes. Length, about 4 in. Shpg. wt., 3 oz. **12c**
49 K 2345 ..

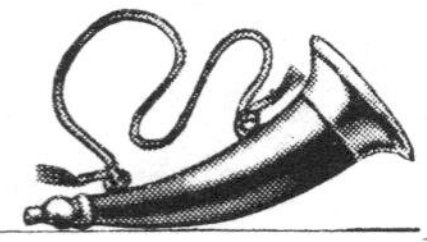

Little Boy Blue Horn

Two notes. 8¼-inch metal. Carrying cord and wood mouthpiece. Made in Czechoslovakia. Shpg. wt., 6 oz.
49 K 2385....... 29c

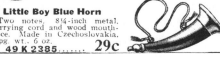

Big $2.00 Value Last Year—Now Only $1.59
—27-Inch Train—Electric Headlight—Bell—Figure 8 track.

The streamlined engine with clockwork motor, brake and electric headlight and two cars are coupled together like real ones. Watch it speed around the track! They're metal, lithographed in Union Pacific colors. Headlight bulb, battery and Union Pacific Lucky coin included. 160-inches of track.

$1.59

49 K 5135—Shipping weight, 6 pounds...............

Your Choice 98c Each

Ⓐ Mickey Stokes His Own Freight Train
Brand New—Sold by Mail only by Sears
The faster the train travels, the faster Mickey Mouse stokes the engine and the bell rings. It'll thrill the "kiddies." 7-in. locomotive with powerful clockwork motor and brake release. Entire train 30 in. long. Circular track about 80 in. around.

49 K 5104—Shpg. wt., 4 lbs....98c

Ⓑ Realistic Watch Sparks Fly
Sparks fly out of smokestack. 29-in. train. Strong Marx clockwork motor. Engine is heavy steel with brake to stop or start. Tender and 3 cars lithographed metal in train colors. Oval track about 74 in. around, banked for speed. Extra flint included.

49 K 5133—Shpg. wt., 3 lbs. 13 oz.....98c

NEW MICKEY MOUSE CIRCUS TRAIN
With Mechanical Motor
$1.79

Lionel Product

SOLD BY MAIL ONLY BY SEARS

MICKEY STOKES HIS ENGINE   DESIGNS BY WALT DISNEY

Mickey Stokes the New Commodore Vanderbilt Locomotive
30-Inch train, 84 inches of track—a whole circus. Gay 20x9x11 inch high cardboard circus tent, filling station and 5-inch composition Mickey figure. Strong clockwork motor hauls this big circus train with Mickey's kingdom of animals lithographed in beautiful colors on sides of cars. Headlight flashes, bell rings, Mickey stokes engine! 7-inch new Commodore Vanderbilt Streamlined engine with brake; tender, circus diner, animal car and band car. Battery included. Shpg. wt., 6 lbs. 6 oz.

49 K 5103—Complete Outfit...............**$1.79**

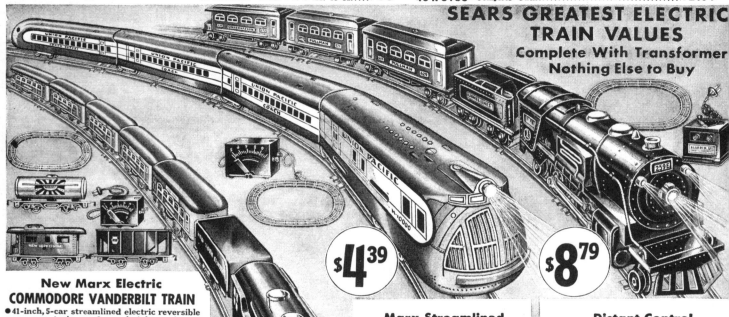

SEARS GREATEST ELECTRIC TRAIN VALUES
Complete With Transformer
Nothing Else to Buy

$4.39

$8.79

New Marx Electric COMMODORE VANDERBILT TRAIN
● 41-inch, 5-car streamlined electric reversible passenger train or 3-car freight train, or combination of both. . . . 8 beautifully lithographed metal cars in all, one tender and 12-pc. "O"-gauge oval track about 124 in. around . . . Transformer included.

Have a passenger train—a fast freight or a mixed accommodation! Latest type Commodore Vanderbilt locomotive. Transformer, which is included, changes its speed. Watch the train speed by with headlight piercing the darkness. Red tail light on observation car. For 110-volt 60-cycle A.C. current. Shpg. wt., 8 lbs. 12 oz.

49 K 5158—Complete Outfit..**$4.69**

Same Passenger train as above, but no freight cars. Shpg. wt., 7 lbs. 12 oz.
49 K 5157 ....**$4.29**

$4.29 Without Freight Cars

Marx Streamlined UNION PACIFIC TRAIN
Save at Sears New Low Price
For This 35-Inch Electric Train

It's the 1935 flying streamline train that goes with a roar over this 124-inch oval track, with headlight streaming ahead. Pull the lever on transformer to change speed or stop it. Wheels mounted to take train at record speed around curves without jumping off track. Four cars in the Union Pacific colors, coupled together. For 110-volt 60-cycle A.C. current. Complete train with 12 pieces "O"-gauge 3-rail track—Transformer included. Shipping weight, 8 lbs. 4 oz.

49 K 5156 ....**$4.39**

Distant Control LIONEL ELECTRIC TRAIN
Sold by Mail Only by Sears
$15.00 Value Last Year

40-inch electric steel train. 9½-inch reversible steel engine; concealed electric head light; 2 colored pilot lights. Distant controlled so train can be stopped, started or reversed at any point. 6½-inch coal tender. Two 7½-inch pullman cars, and one observation car all have double trucks. 10-piece "O"-gauge oval track about 114 inches around. For 110-volt 60-cycle A.C. current. Transformer included. Shipping weight 11 pounds 13 ounces.

49 K 5155 ....**$8.79**

Electric Train Tracks

"O" Gauge Lionel Track
For train 49 K 5155. Shpg. wt., 10 oz.

Curved Track	Straight Track
49K5235	49K5236
2 pcs. for...**37c**	**37c**

"O" Gauge Marx Track
For trains 49 K 5156 and 49 K 5157 and 49 K 5158. Shpg. wt., 11 oz.

Curved	Straight
49K5217	49K5216
4 pcs. for..**39c**	4 pcs. for..**39c**

Lionel Switches
with lamps for "O"-gauge trains. Shpg. wt., 2 lbs. 14 oz.
49 K 5215
Pair **$5.29**

Lionel Crossover
for "O"-gauge trains. Shpg. wt., 15 oz.
49 K 5210
Each ...**$1.45**

MARX Crossover for Trains
49 K 5156, 49 K 5157, and 49 K 5158.
49 K 5238—Shpg. wt., 1 lb...**59c**

Mechanical Train Tracks

Curved Track
For trains 49 K 5103 and 49 K 5104. Shpg. wt., 13 oz.
49K5207
4 pcs. for..**19c**

Straight Track
For trains 49 K 5103 and 49 K 5104. Shpg. wt., 13 oz.
49K5206
4 pcs. for..**19c**

For trains 49 K 5135 and 49 K 5133. Shpg. wt., 13 oz.
49K5213
4 pcs. for..**19c**

For trains 49 K 5135 and 49 K 5133. Shpg. wt., 13 oz.
49K5212
4 pcs. for..**19c**

For All Mechanical Trains
Switches
One left and one right. Shpg. wt., 12 oz.
49 K 5203
Pair **39c**

Crossover
For making figure eight track. Shpg. wt., 3 oz.
49 K 5205..**19c**

Jefferson Transformer
For "O"-gauge trains. 75 watts, unbroken voltage control 5½ to 22½ volts. 110-volt 60-cycle A.C. Shpg. wt., 3 lbs.
49 K 5277..**$2.79**

Low Priced Transformer
For "O"-gauge trains, 110-volt 60-cycle A.C. Shpg. wt., 3 lbs. 4 oz.
49 K 5288..**$1.19**

WILL HOLD 200 LBS.

$1.29

Ride and Steer This Locomotive
23 inches long. A child can ride on it. Will hold 200 lbs. Heavy 20-gauge steel. 9⅞ in. high. Steering bar on top of boiler. Bright baked-on enamel finish. Steel wheels. Shpg. wt., 9 lbs.
79 K 5024.......**$1.29**

Mickey Mouse Keeps Time for Over 1½ Million Children . . .

MICKEY MOUSE Wrist Watch $2.69 Wrist Watch

Regular $2.95 Value

Two more Mickeys in enameled colors on the wrist band. Daily, Mickey teaches boys and girls to "be on time." Chromium plated case. Non-breakable crystal. Note Sears low price. Shpg. wt., 8 oz.

Metal Band	Leather Strap
4 K 1664..$2.69	4 K 1665..$2.69

MICKEY MOUSE Pocket Watch

Regular $1.50 Value

Mickey Mouse Tells Time With His Hands

Improved Thin Model. Mickey on the fob and back of watch, too. Nickel plated case. Non-breakable crystal. Shipping weight, 8 ounces.
4 K 1603.................. $1.39

Table and Bench Nailing Set At Usual Price of Table Alone $1.00

Dovetail constructed wood table 19¾x12½x19½ in. Wood bench, 11⅛x7⅛ in., with sturdy steel legs included. One heavy fibrous 11½-in. nailing board. Complete with hammer, assorted non-poisonous colored wood parts, box of nails and instructions. Shipping weight, 6 pounds.
79 K 3685.............. $1.00

Junior Nailing Set—No Table

Two 11½-in. squares. Complete with hammer and nails. Shipping weight, 3 lbs.
49 K 3686..................49c

Extra wood designs and nails.
49 K 3687—Shpg. wt., 8 oz....21c

New Early American Logs Sold by Mail Only by Sears 45c 42 Pcs.

Make realistic fascinating hewn effect models of log cabins, forts, sawmills, etc. Log sizes, 1½ to 10½ in. long.

145-Piece Big Building Set

Builds many models, including fort illustrated. Box, 18x12¼x1¾ in.
49 K 3647—Shipping wt., 5 pounds.........$1.79

62-Piece Junior Building Set

Builds cabins, bridges and many other models. Box, 18x12¼x⅞ in.
49 K 3646—Shpg. wt., 2 lbs. 12 oz..89c

42-Piece Beginner's Building Set

Log sizes, 1½ to 7½ inches.
49 K 3645—Shpg. wt., 1 lb. 8 oz...45c

Make Your Dolly a Quilt

140 colorful 1¾-inch cloth patches. Complete with cotton padding and lining to make quilt size 14x20 in. Shipping wt., 4 oz.
49 K 3869...... 25c

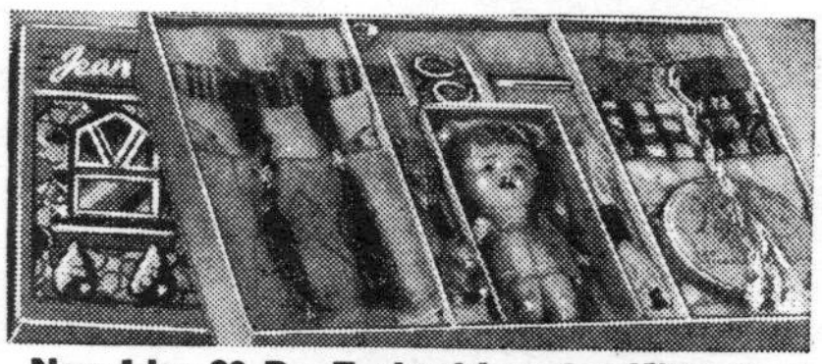

New Idea 20-Pc. Embroidery Set With Doll

Think of a 7-in. jointed arm China doll with rayon slip surrounded with 4 pretty print already cut-out dresses, 4 stenciled pieces that make another dress, 2 nighties and romper to fit dolly; 6 skeins of floss, embroidery hoops, scissors, needles and thimble. In 16-in. fancy box.
49 K 3889—Shpg. wt., 2 lbs......... 49c

New Electric Wood Burning Outfit—All the Rage Right Now 89c

Now anyone can make beautiful objects and designs on wood, leather, cork or velvet. Plug in the easy-to-use electric pencil (listed as standard by Underwriters' Laboratories). Heating element embedded in porcelain; cork grip; enameled wood handle. With cord and plug. There are four 3-ply 5x3½ in. plaques in assorted printed designs, and two 5x1½-in. plain plaques.
49 K 3838—Shpg. wt., 1 lb. 8 oz............89c

Assortment of 4 Large Printed Plywood Plaques

One 10x7 in.; two ovals, 10x7 in.; one round, 8-in. diam.
49 K 3836—Shpg. wt., 1 lb. 6 oz.......4 for 59c

Assortment of 5 Smaller Printed Plywood Plaques

All 3½x5 inches; attractive designs.
49 K 3835—Shpg. wt., 10 oz..........5 for 29c

Fox Educational Boards—Steel Slate Surfaces

13 in. diam. 65 letters, figures, on one side, 45 words and pictures on other side. Shpg. wt., 2 lbs. 11 oz.
49 K 3863
$1.50 size.......... $1.19

13-In. Regular $1.00 Size

No words or pictures. Shpg. wt., 2 lbs. 2 oz.
49 K 3842 ....79c

9¾-In. Popular 50c Size

48 Letters and figures. Shipping weight, 1 lb. 2 oz.
49 K 3801 ....39c

84-Piece Sign Set

Make your own signs. Rubber alphabets of capitals and small letters ½ inch high mounted on wood; numerals; ink pad in metal box, wood ruler, guide. Make show cards with them. Shpg. wt., 13 oz.
49 K 3829.... 49c

146-Piece Printing Set

Includes 26 A B C's, 10 numerals, $ signs; each ⅜ in. high and mounted on wood. 100 small rubber capital letters, also tweezers, type holder, ink pad in metal box, 4 crayons, paper. Shipping weight, 8 ounces.
49 K 3825...... 25c

63-Piece Mickey Mouse Printing Set

Five 1⅜-in. and eight ¾-in. rubber character stamps. Complete ½-in. alphabet and numerals mounted on wood. Crayons, stamp pad, etc. Shipping weight, 1 lb. 7 oz.
49 K 3866 .... 89c

22-Pc. Mickey Mouse Set

Same 13 figure stamps as above, but no alphabet or numerals. Shpg. wt., 1 lb. 2 oz.
49 K 3865 .... 45c

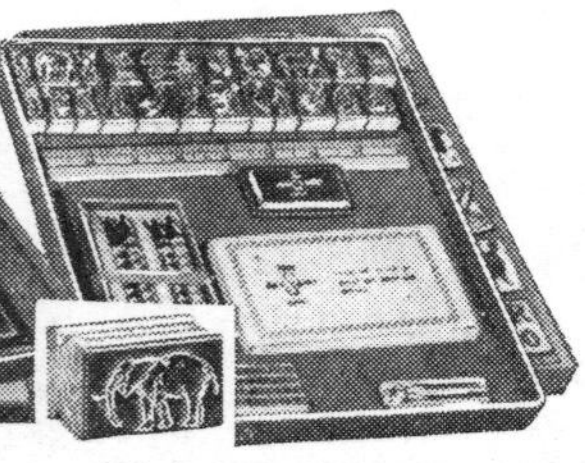

130-Pc. Farm and Jungle Printing Set

Set consists of 21 ⅞-in. barnyard animals, fowls and animals of the jungle. 100 rubber small letters and numerals, ruler, stamp pad, six crayons, a type holder, tweezers and pad of paper. Lithographed box 10¼x9 inches. Shipping weight, 1 pound 3 ounces.
49 K 3867..... 59c

Marx Dial Typewriter and 100 Sheets of Paper—Only $1.19

Less than typewriter price alone last year. Entertaining—educational! Child can actually write real letters on regular size office paper. First popular priced typewriter ever offered for children. Type is securely fastened to dial—cannot drop off. Dial has 40 metal characters including alphabet, numerals, and punctuation marks. Sliding carriage. Heavy lithographed metal, 11½x5¾x6⅛ in.
49 K 3847—Shpg. wt., 2 lbs. 15 oz...$1.19

3 Extra Rolls for Typewriter

49 K 3898—Shipping weight, 4 oz.......10c

Bag of Wood Blocks 59c

About 125 smooth, clean, well shaped wood blocks to build houses, bridges, forts, etc. In a big, red drawstring-top mesh bag. Many shapes, sizes and colors. They'll have lots of fun with these blocks. Can be kept in bag when not in use. Shipping weight, 4 pounds.
49 K 3672 ....59c

Big Value Paint Set

For the young artist. Look at all you get! 34 cakes of assorted colored dry paints, two camel's hair brushes in a black enameled metal box with white enameled inside hinged cover. 9⅝x3½ in. Made in Germany. Shpg. wt., 8 oz.
49 K 3878...25c

75c Value Paint Set

A Knockout Value. 48 cakes dry assorted colors, 2 smaller cakes of paints and 2 good camel's hair brushes. Black enameled, white interior metal box with hinged cover, 9¾x6¾ in. Made in Germany. Shipping weight, 15 ounces.
49 K 3881.....49c

De Luxe 48-Pc. Set

Our most practical set. Has 12 tubes moist water colors, 32 cakes dry paints, 2 large cakes and 2 brushes. Black enameled metal box with hinged cover, 9½x5 in. Made in Germany. Shipping weight, 1 lb. 1 oz.
49 K 3882...89c

Improved 3-In-1 Set

Look! Stencil, paint and crayon set for the "Kiddies." 22 cardboard stencils and 2 sheets of colored paper 6x4½ in. 12 crayons, 10 water color paints, a pan and brush. Box, 11¼x10¼ inches. Shipping weight, 1 lb. 4 oz.
49 K 3823.... 39c

Modeling Clay Sets

8 large colored strips, 7 wood design blocks, modeling stick. Shipping weight, 1 lb. 11 oz.
49 K 3751......... 39c

Big Value Modeling Set

8 smaller clay strips, 6 wood design blocks and modeling stick. Shpg. wt., 1 lb. 2 oz.
49 K 3750......... 21c

"Scrappy" Paint Set

Have your own colored movie with the 3 "Scrappy" paper films—mounted on wood rollers, with cardboard stage and 14 colors, paint brush and water pan to paint them. Attractive 10-inch box. Shipping wt., 1 pound 5 ounces.
49 K 3887..... 49c

3-Piece Unpainted Furniture Set

$4.50 Value $2.69

Biggest value we have ever offered in a children's furniture set. Give the kiddies a table set of their own. What a thrill they'll get out of this set! Strong and durable massive turned wood legs. Paint it the color you want. **You save by buying set unpainted.** Nicely shaped table top of heavy ply wood, 26x20 in. stands 19½ in. from the floor; large, shaped chair seats, 12 in. from the floor; fiddle back style. Dishes not included. Table packed with legs off; easily set up.

79 K 8531—Table and 2 chairs. Shpg. wt., 20 lbs.. **$2.69**
79 K 8533—Table only. Shpg. wt., 12 lbs.........**$1.29**
79 K 8532—2 chairs only. Shpg. wt., 8 lbs........**$1.69**

Smaller Size For Little Folks

$1.79 Let the younger children eat and play at their own little table! They'll love it. Chair seats, 9¼ inches from floor, table top 19x13 inches stands 16¼ inches from floor. **Nicely enameled;** table top has a bright colored "Scottie" stencil in center. Table packed with legs off, easily fitted into cross cleats. Fancy chair backs. Shpg. wt., 11 lbs.

79 K 8550—Table and two chairs........$1.79

Red Bow-Back Rockers
Choice of 3 Sizes

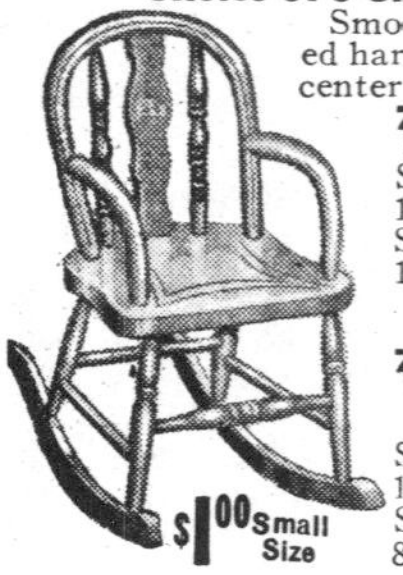

Smoothly sanded hardwood with center panel.
79 K 8569 Large Size Seat, 13x 12⅜ inches. Shpg. wt., 10 lbs. **$1.98**
79 K 8563 Medium size Seat, 12¼x 11⅞ inches. Shpg. wt., 8 lbs. **$1.79**
$1.00 Small Size
79 K 8557—Small size. Has no side arms. Seat, 9⅞x9⅞ in. Shpg. wt., 7 lbs..........**$1.00**

Hand Woven Fiber Rockers

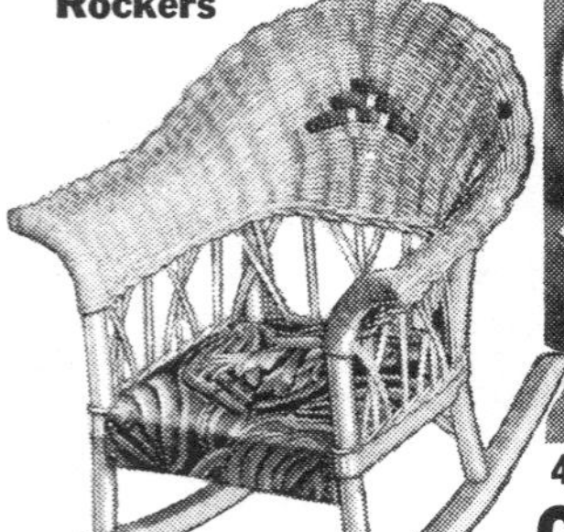

$1.59 Small Size

For the Larger Tot

It's 21½ inches high! Hand woven round fiber, same materials as used in large rockers; not the usual machine made flat fiber. Design in back is woven-in. Enameled in gay, bright colors. The padded, cretonne covered seat is 11½ in. square. Shipping weight, 12 pounds.
79 K 8587 ......$2.39

Similar to Above

Smaller arms and lower back. 17½ in. high. Padded cretonne covered seat is 11 in. square. Shipping weight, 10 pounds.
79 K 8586 ......$1.59

Red Bow-Back Chairs
Choice of 2 Sizes

For little boys and girls. Strong and sturdy, yet not too big. Smoothly sanded hardwood. Fancy beaded spindles and panel back.
79 K 8564 Medium Size. Seat, 10x10 in. Shipping wt., 6 lbs....**95c**
79 K 8556 Small Size. Without panel. Seat, 9x9 in. Shipping weight, 4 pounds............**83c**
83c Small Size

Mickey Mouse China Tea Set

Sold by Mail only by Sears. Real imported china for dolly when she's giving a tea party! Full-fired in light tan body with a blue border and colorful Mickey and Minnie Mouse smiling from each piece.

23 Piece Set Service for 6 98c
49 K 1676—6 cups, 6 saucers, 6 4⅜-in. plates, a teapot, sugar, creamer in proportion. Shpg. wt., 4 lbs. 14 oz...**98c**

17 Piece Set Service for 4 59c
49 K 1675—4 cups, 4 saucers, 4 3¾-in. plates, a teapot, sugar, creamer. Shipping weight, 2 pounds 8 ounces.**59c**

Metal Tea Sets

Can't hurt these dishes! Mickey and Minnie Mouse in bright lithographed colors! 7⅜-in. tray, 4¼-in. plates, other pieces in proportion.
49 K 1807—21-Piece set. Service for 6; 6 cups, 6 saucers, 6 plates, a teapot with cover and tray. Shipping weight, 1 lb. 4 oz....**42c**
49 K 1806—12-Piece set. Service for 3; 3 cups, 3 saucers, 3 plates, a teapot with cover and tray. Shipping weight, 14 ounces..........**25c**

First Toy Dinner Set at This Low Price

27 Pieces Imported China 98c

Now Dolly can have a whole dinner set. Just as lovely as Mother's dinner set. Flower blossoms bloom on it in realistic colors! It's clear two-tone ivory luster, real china with tan border and handles. Won't Santa be popular when she sees this set on Christmas morning! And there's a real 5¼-in. oval casserole with cover, 4⅜-in. platter, 4⅜-in. gravy boat with base as well as a teapot, sugar, creamer and 6 cups, 6 saucers, and 6 plates in proportion. Dinner for six! Shipping weight, 4 pounds.
49 K 1650—27-Piece Set... **98c**

18-Piece Tan Luster China Tea Set

42c **Usual 75c Value.** How proud she'll be of this fine fired-in decoration china! Lovely blossoms in colors! Blue borders! 4 2⅛-in. cups, 4 saucers, 4 3¾-in. plates, a teapot, sugar, creamer, and 4¼-inch cake plate. Imported. Shipping weight, 3 pounds 4 ounces.
49 K 1641—18-Piece Set.........................42c

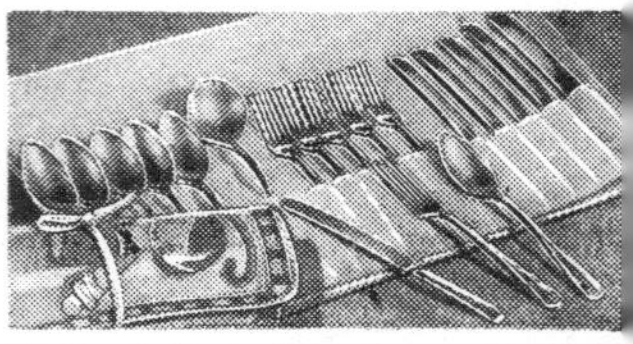

Roll of Cast Aluminum Cutlery

19 large size pieces to go with the dishes! Knives, 4¾ in. long, others in proportion. A cotton flannel lined colorful Kiddie design oilcloth roll; section for each piece. 6 knives, 6 forks, 6 spoons, and 1 ladle. Made in Germany. Shipping weight, 6 oz.
49 K 1960—19-Pc. Set.....59c
49 K 1956—13-Pc. Set. 4 knives, 4 forks, 4 spoons, and ladle; same size as above. Shipping wt., 5 oz.....**42c**

41-Piece Beautiful Bright Aluminum Set

98c **New urn type 5¼-inch percolator** with red bands, cover and wood handle; glass dome top. **Service for 6,** even to the paper napkins and rings. 6 4$\frac{9}{16}$-in. plates, 6 2⅛-in. cups, 6 3⅛-in. saucers, sugar and creamer in proportion. 6 aluminum spoons, 6 aluminum napkin rings and 6 kiddies design paper napkins. Shipping weight, 1 pound 1 ounce.
49 K 1890—41-Piece Set.....................98c

16-Piece Aluminum Tea Set

49c It's so much fun to have a tea party for Dolly and two of her friends. She'll love this pretty set—all bright aluminum nicely embossed. Three 4$\frac{9}{16}$-in. plates, 3 cups, 3 saucers, 3 spoons, and a 4⅝-in. teapot with cover, sugar and creamer. Shipping weight, 10 ounces.
49 K 1891—16-Piece Set.......49c

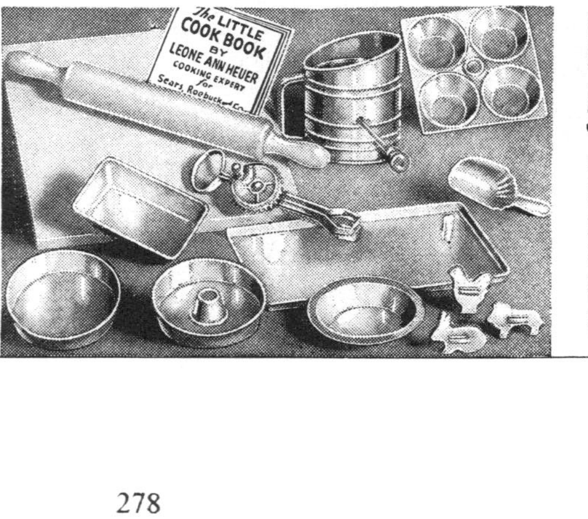

New, Improved, 15-Piece Girls' Practical Baking Set

59c Mm, just imagine the goodies you can make with this outfit—cake, cookies, muffins! Included is an 8-page recipe book which has been prepared and tested by Leone A. Heuer, Sears Cooking Expert. An egg beater, 1-cup flour sifter, 8-in. hardwood bread board and 10½-in. hardwood rolling pin, cookie sheet, three cookie cutters, sugar scoop, muffin tin, tube cake pan, pie pan, bread pan and layer cake pan, all in proportion and the right size. Shipping weight, 2 pounds 2 ounces.
49 K 1953—15-Pc. Set.......59c

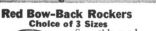

Whole Play Kitchen for Modern Little Housekeeper

An 8½-inch all-steel play stove, 2 pans and 2 empty samples. Kitchen walls of heavy cardboard, 36x14 in. Printed in green and white. Built-in cupboard and cabinet, both with doors. Shipping weight, 3 pounds 4 ounces.

69c

49 K 7310—Usual $1.00 Value 69c

Electric Stove With Switch

$4.50 value! Over 1-ft. high. Real oven heat indicator. Nickel plated cooking top; 4½-ft. cord plugs into 110 to 120-volt current. Pans included. Shpg. wt., 7 lbs. 2 oz.
49 K 7319......**$2.98**

Little Girl's Electric Stove

Cabinet style, 3 ovens. Cook or bake. Real heat indicator on top oven. Just right for tiny girls. 9¾ in. wide. 3 pans included. 4½-foot cord plugs into 110 to 120-volt current. Shpg. wt., 5 lbs.
49 K 7308............**98c**

Complete as Shown $1.69 $2.25 Value

28½-Inch DOLL HOUSE With Furniture and Automobile
Patented Interlocking Joint House—No Metal Clips to Lose
23 Pieces Almost Unbreakable Metal Furniture

We prefer to offer a quality outfit rather than a large number of pieces. Just look at it! A five-room white and green, **strong fiber board Colonial House (not light cardboard)** with breakfast porch and garage and a nice, shiny bright enameled 4-inch metal sedan! The front door of house opens. The back is open so she can arrange the **23 pieces of beautiful colorful furniture.** Mahogany finish radio, settee, table, chair and lamp in the living room. Pink enameled bed, triple mirror vanity, night table, lamp and chair. Orchid enameled bath tub, toilet with removable seat, wash stand, medicine chest and stool. Walnut finish table and four dining room chairs. White kitchen sink, ice box, and range; 23 pieces in all, the largest about 3½ inches. House, 28½x15⅝ inches.

49 K 7149 — House, Breakfast porch, Garage, sedan, 23 pieces of metal furniture. Shipping weight, 4 lbs. 14 oz........**$1.69**
49 K 7130—Furniture only. 23 Pieces. Shpg. wt., 2 lbs. 14 oz...**$1.19**

49 K 7134—House with Breakfast porch, and garage only. (No furniture or sedan.) Shipping weight, 2 lbs. 4 oz.......**59c**

LIVING ROOM / BEDROOM / BATHROOM / DINING ROOM / KITCHEN

Popular Cast Iron Stoves

$1.39 10½-Inch

She can "make-believe" cook on them! All brightly nickel plated. Fancy back; each with 4 removable lids; hinged oven door. Pans included.

49 K 7321 — Has all features as shown. 13¾-inch stove. Shipping weight, 11 lbs. 9 oz....**$1.98**
49 K 7320—10½-inch stove. 2 utensils. Shipping wt., 6 lbs. 6 oz.....**1.39**
49 K 7315—6¼-inch stove. 1 pan. Shipping weight, 3 pounds 3 ounces......**.45**

3-Piece Matched Set

A purse her size, a make-believe metal watch with moving hands and elastic wrist strap, and a bead necklace, all in bright colors to match. Shpg. wt., 2 oz.
49 K 9105...**21c**

New Modernistic Two-Tone Dressers

The smartest we've seen in a decade! And well built, too. Every girl will want one for her Dolly's clothes. Here it is, pure white enamel with walnut color trim and beveled edge mirror.

79 K 7167 — As pictured. 22½x19 in. Shipping wt., 13 lbs.......**$2.98**
79 K 7166—18½x14⅞ in. 3 large drawers. Shipping weight, 7 pounds.........**1.98**
79 K 7165—13½x11½ in. 2 large drawers. Shipping weight, 4 pounds........**.98**

Dolly's Adjustable Ironing Board

To iron Dolly's clothes on! She'll want to iron when Mother does. No rough edges. All smoothly rounded wood. Tapered ironing surface, 34½ inches long, and adjustable to 3 height positions, 21 to 25 inches from floor.
79 K 1775—Shipping weight, 5 lbs. 4 oz.......**69c**

Smaller Board for Little Girls

49 K 1777—Same finish but for little girls. Adjustable 12 to 14 inches from floor. 20½ inches long. Shipping weight, 1 lb. 6 oz.......**25c**

It's Cleaning Day
7 BIG PIECES FOR ONLY $1.00

And here's a cleaning outfit just her size! (1) Toy Kenmore vacuum cleaner with revolving brush, sateen bag, (2) A Maid of Honor, real colored yarn dust mop with 24-in. wood handle, (3) 12-inch cotton yarn duster, (4) 32-inch broom with enameled wood handle, (5) Green enameled long handle heavy metal dust pan, (6) Dainty color print cotton apron with roomy pocket, (7) pretty maid's cap. Shpg. wt., 4 lbs.
79 K 9187......**$1.00**

New Improved 7-Piece Laundry Set

98c
Everything for wash day, ironing day. All well-made pieces designed to do their jobs right. 8¾-inch Sunny Suzy Washing Machine with 2 real rubber roll wringers; enameled wash tub; revolving drier; 6 wood clothes pins, 12-inch ironing board and nickel plated iron.
49 K 1712—Shipping weight, 1 pound 9 ounces........**98c**

Cast Iron Sad-iron and Stand

Mrs. Pott's Style. Like Mother's! She can really iron with it! 4¾ in. long. Detachable enameled handle. Shpg. wt., 1 lb. 8 oz.
49 K 1788 .....**43c**

For the Tiny Miss

4-in. size. Not illustrated. Shpg. wt., 12 oz.
49 K 1789 .....**23c**

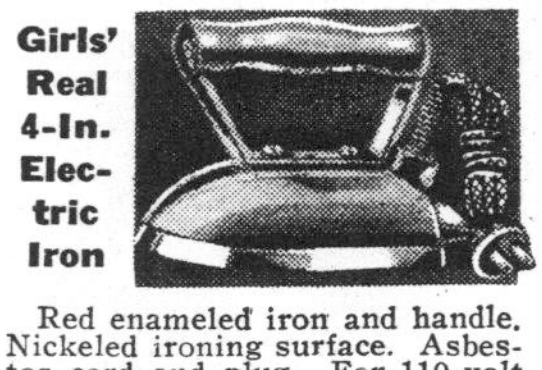

Girls' Real 4-In. Electric Iron

Red enameled iron and handle. Nickeled ironing surface. Asbestos cord and plug. For 110-volt current. Shpg. wt., 1 lb. 13 oz.
49 K 1793........**87c**

Little Tots' Low Priced Electric Iron

Not Illustrated. Special. Shipping weight, 15 oz.
49 K 1792.........**49c**

Little Girls' Sewing Machines
With Carrying Case

She can make Dolly's clothes on this 6-inch green enameled sewing machine. Has special thread tension raising foot. It's all ready to sew — with one needle, spool of thread and cloth. Colorful hinge cover 7½ in. cardboard case with 3 drawers. Shpg. wt., 1 lb. 14 oz.
49 K 5802......**$1.00**

Sew Like Mother

Our best sewing machine. Shaped head like mother's. Makes perfect stitches. Teaches girls to be handy. Size overall, 7½x7⅜x3¾ in. Has drop-foot thread tension and heavy flywheel. Green enameled steel. Nickel plated sewing top. Clamp included. Shpg. wt., 2 lbs. 12 oz.
49 K 5801......**$1.39**

Doll Trunks
$1.19 14-in.

For Dolly's clothes. Colored metal over wood body. 18⅜ in. long, with leather handles, metal bound edges; lock and key; inside tray.
79 K 8419—Shipping weight, 12 pounds....**$2.49**

14-Inch Trunk

Not shown. With lock, key and tray. Colored artificial leather covering.
79 K 8403—Shpg. wt., 4 lbs. 10 oz.**$1.19**

Sunny Suzy Handy Washing Machine

Your Choice of 2 Sizes 59c 8¾-In. Size

What fun she'll have with it! Turn the crank and it will rotate! Attached wringer has white rollers; adjustable 3 ways.

Large Size, 11¼ in. High.
49 K 1710—Shpg. wt., 3 lbs. 8 oz...**89c**
Medium Size, 8¾ in. High (Not shown)
49 K 1708—Shpg. wt., 3 lbs. 2 oz...**59c**

We Have Curlylocks of REAL HAIR

"We Cry and Sleep"
"We have Real Lashes"

$2⁸⁹ 13-In. Size

"I Sleep"
"I have Real Lashes.."
"I Stand Alone"

The *Only* Original
SHIRLEY TEMPLE Doll
Sold by Mail Only by Sears

LOOK, it's Shirley! Adorable Shirley Temple with golden blonde ringlets all over her head; lovely hazel, unbreakable eyes with real lashes; Shirley's cute chubby face and famous cute dimples around her mouth. And dressed in the same coin dot organdy dress and ribbon hair bow, rayon socks and white buckled shoes and dainty underthings that Shirley wore in her first picture! And a Shirley Temple badge and silk label on her dress to show she's the only genuine Shirley Temple!

The Nation's Sweetheart

There isn't a little girl in the world who doesn't want a Shirley Temple doll. She's all of **hard-to-break composition with turning, tilting swivel head; arms and legs are inside jointed, the better way.** Her smiling mouth shows her tongue and teeth. She'll make her new mamma so proud and happy! And she'll bring a 32-page, "Movie of Me," Shirley Temple "book movie" with her. For extra authentic Shirley Temple dresses, see below.

13 In. Tall	16 In. Tall	18 In. Tall	20 In. Tall
Shpg. wt., 1 lb. 8 oz.	Shpg. wt., 2 lbs. 1 oz.	Shpg. wt., 3 lbs.	Shpg. wt., 3 lbs. 8 oz.
49 K 3297	49 K 3298	49 K 3299	49 K 3296
$2.89	$3.79	$4.79	$5.79

A Really Fine Doll

18 inches tall. Sells many places for $2.00. **$1⁴⁸** Pretty as a picture with her brunette real hair curls. She's smiling so much you can see her teeth and tongue.

All in lacy organdy, with rayon socks, white buckled shoes and white undies. Hard-to-break composition head, arms and legs—inside jointed. Cotton stuffed body. Shipping weight, 2 lbs. 4 oz.

49 K 3018......$1.48

Big — Beautiful

24 inches tall. Usual $3.00 value. A great big armful! **$1⁹⁸** Proud as a peacock of her long real hair brunette curls, her long lashes, her pearly teeth and pink tongue!

Pleated dotted swiss dress with pretty undies, socks and shoes. All hard-to-break composition head, arms and legs—inside jointed. Cotton stuffed body. Shipping weight, 3 lbs. 8 oz.

49 K 3034.....$1.98

Shirley Temple Party Dress

Authentic style. Pleated pink organdy lace and ribbon trimmed. With undies.

Shipping weight, 8 ounces.
49 K 3596—For 13-in. Doll. $0.94
49 K 3597—For 16-in. Doll. 1.39
49 K 3598—For 18-in. Doll. 1.49
49 K 3599—For 20-in. Doll. 1.59

Shirley Temple Plaid Dress

Authentic style. Gay! Braid and ribbon trimmed. White undies.

Shipping weight, 8 ounces.
49 K 3592—For 13-in. Doll. $0.94
49 K 3593—For 16-in. Doll. 1.39
49 K 3594—For 18-in. Doll. 1.49
49 K 3595—For 20-in. Doll. 1.59

SHIRLEY TEMPLE as a Baby
Sold by Mail only by Sears

Just like Shirley Temple when she was a baby! Soft, huggable and adorably pretty. Lovely hazel glass-like unbreakable eyes that move when she turns or tilts her head—**and real lashes over them.** So sweet with her dimpled cheeks and her smiling lips showing her little pink tongue and five tiny teeth! **Baby Shirley cries, too.** Kapok stuffed body. **She also has Shirley Temple Badge and silk label on her dress.** Pleated organdy dress and bonnet; lace trimmed, embroidered, shirred and picoted! Rayon socks, tiny bootees, undies—and of course rubber panties. She has hard-to-break composition head and legs with chubby inside jointed rubber arms.

"I Cry.. I Sleep"
"I have Real Lashes"

$2⁸⁹ 15½ In.

15½-In. Tall	18-In. Tall	20-In. Tall
Shpg. wt., 2 lbs. 1 oz.	Shpg. wt., 2 lbs. 9 oz.	Shpg. wt., 3 lbs. 7 oz.
49 K 3191	49 K 3192	49 K 3193
$2.89	$3.79	$4.79

"I Cry and Sleep"
"I have Real Lashes"
"I have Turning Tilting Head.."

$2⁹⁸

Pretty as a Princess
Big as a Baby
28 Inches Tall

Easily worth from $1.50 to $2.00 more than we ask. She's simply gorgeous! Big as a really truly little sister and so pretty she'll steal your heart away! Big blue eyes with real lashes and long curls of lustrous brown real hair that comes down to her shoulders! Tiny pearly teeth and a little pink tongue peep out through her smile. And she's dressed like a little princess!

Pleated pink organdy, ribboned and lace trimmed, with two-tone rayon socks, buckled shoes, and dainty undies. Her head, arms and legs are hard-to-break composition. Her arms are inside jointed, (the better kind) and her legs are the new slim style. Shpg. wt., 6 lbs.

79 K 3041......$2.98

Latest Doll Buggies—Big Savings
Streamlined—With Many New Features

$4.98

$1.89

$4.98

English Style Pram
Has covered foot extension.
Holds 22-inch doll—$6.50 value.

For dolls that are modern! Has fancy deep body where Dolly can rest comfortably. On bright warm days the hood can be turned back for sun bathing. Streamlined . . . with 4-bow folding U-shaped hood you can adjust to any position. It's dark blue with light blue and silver trimming; wood veneer body, 18¾x10⅞ inches. Big 8-inch wheels, ½-inch rubber tires. English type springs. Push bar 25 inches from floor. Shipping weight, 21 pounds.
79 K 8283 .... **$4.98**

Little Girl's Favorite
● Good looking—Latest design.
● Holds 18-inch doll—Inexpensive.

It's little but look . . . streamlined . . . flat fiber . . . light green with cream color and black trim, body has solid wood bottom and back (not tin) for small but up-to-date dollies. High enough for a little girl to push. Body size, 17¼x8 inches. The hood turns forward and backwards and has open round windows with bright rims. Rubber tires on the 7-inch strong wire wheels. Nice and strong. Dolly will like this. Push bar 23½ inches from floor. Shipping weight, 7 pounds.
79 K 8206 .... **$1.89**

Almost Like a Real Baby Buggy
● Holds 22-inch doll—Beauty and lasting quality

Actually worth $2.00 more. The beautiful buggy little girls dream of having for Dolly. It's made like a baby buggy and it's almost as big. The same loom-woven round fiber that's used in baby buggies. And the richest, glossiest colors—Light Green or Buff with assorted decoration and contrasting color wheels. Body, 20x10½ in. Adjustable hood has a cute peak cuff roll. The back slides down for "Sleepy time." Large 8-inch wheels; ½-inch rubber tires. Hand brake. Push bar 26½ in. from floor. **Doll not included.** Shipping weight, 18 lbs.

79 K 8209—Body and hood enameled in Buff color **$4.98**

79 K 8210—Body and hood enameled Light Green **$4.98**

Easily Worth $1.00 More

$2.98

10 Big Features
● The big body will hold a 20-inch doll.
● Hand brake with rubber grip.
● Full length pusher braced to body.
● Body, 18½x9 in. on fancy steel springs.
● Two metal rimmed open hood windows.
● Reclining back.
● Made of good grade narrow flat fiber.
● Nicely decorated and finished.
● Big 7-inch rubber tired wheels with bright hub caps.
● Push bar is 25¾ inches from floor.

First Time All These Features at This Low Price

Won't she be proud as she wheels Dolly along in this big caramel color flat fiber buggy! She can adjust the hood to any position and it has bright knobs to hold it. If Dolly wants to go to sleep she can put down the back and peek thru the windows to see how she's getting along. This lovely little carriage is made so nicely that it will make any little girl happy. **Doll not included.**
Shipping weight, 12 pounds.
79 K 8208 .... **$2.98**

Your Choice $1.00 Each

New, Smart Sulky for Any Size Doll
● Bright Eleanor Blue

Lots of dollies prefer to ride in a sulky like this one. Flat fiber, with a cuff roll reinforced with steel. Seat, 8⅝x7 inches. Handle just like on Baby's sulky; with steel foot rest and back stop. 6-inch rubber tired wheels. Shipping weight, 4 pounds.
79 K 8270 .... **$1.00**

A New Big Buggy at a New Low Price
● Holds 18-inch doll

She needn't be afraid of hurting this buggy—it's steel. Adjustable flat fiber hood. Body and hood enameled in light green; pretty embossed decoration on body. Rubber tired 5½-inch wheels. Body, 17½x8½ inches. Push bar is 23 inches from floor. Shipping weight, 6 pounds.
79 K 8205 .... **$1.00**

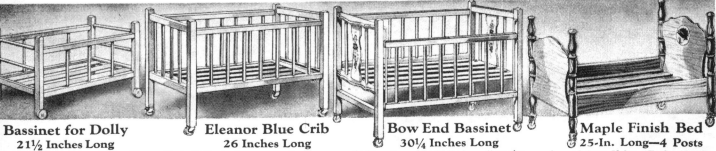

Bassinet for Dolly
21½ Inches Long

A big value! Every little girl should have one of these pretty ivory enameled wood bassinets, for Dolly simply has to have a place to sleep! Wood wheels. Even small girls can make sheets or comforters for Dolly. Easily assembled. Shpg. wt., 3 lbs.
79 K 7925 .... **49c**

Eleanor Blue Crib
26 Inches Long

Tuck Dolly in her own crib every night and for her nap, too. Dolly can't fall out because the sides are high. Any little girl will love to make sheets and comforters for this bassinet and what fun it will be! **Wooden swivel casters,** 14 in. wide, 19¼ in. high. Easily assembled. Shipping weight, 7 pounds.
79 K 7926 .... **95c**

Bow End Bassinet
30¼ Inches Long

At ¼ saving. Put Dolly in, pull up the dropside to keep her safe! Drop it down to take her out again! Extra big, too. Ivory color trimmed in light blue. Well reinforced, wood panels have colored design. 1-in. swivel casters; slat bottom. Easily assembled. Shipping weight, 14 pounds.
79 K 7928 .... **$1.98**

Maple Finish Bed
25-In. Long—4 Posts

A good $2.50 Value. Early American style. Wood slat bottom; swivel casters. Easily assembled. Shipping weight, 10 pounds.
79 K 7927 .... **$1.79**

Mattress and Pillow for Doll Cribs
Colored ticking cover; about 27 in. long. Pillow to match. Shipping weight, 3 pounds.
79 K 7944 .... **59c**

New! Streamline!
No Increase in Price

$7.00 Value **$4.98** 12-In. Size

$5.50 Value **$3.69** 12-In. Size

Here's the Prize Winner of the New York Toy Show

Oh Boy! Some Bike! Brand new! **Ball bearing front wheel!** Bright red enameled! All-steel! With electric headlight (**1 battery included**)! Gracefully streamlined from the adjustable handlebars to the end of the beautifully shaped all-steel frame; new wide fork, new adjustable spring saddle, new large steel fender, new step plates over rear axle. Rubber pedals, grips. ¾-in. rubber tires. Silvery color spokes.

Measure child from crotch to instep.

Catalog Number	Front Wheel Diam.	Seat to Lower Pedal	Shpg. Wt., Lbs.	Price
79 K 8650	12 in.	18 to 20 in.	21	$4.98
79 K 8651	16 in.	21 to 23 in.	25	5.69
79 K 8652	20 in.	24 to 26 in.	29	6.49

Yes, Sir! Streamline Bikes at Regular Bike Prices

Racy! Light in weight, yet very sturdy! Streamlined from the snub-nose handlebars to the step-plates over the rear axle! **Ball bearing front wheel.** Nicely formed heavy steel red enameled frame, streamlined, comfortable and adjustable spring seat. Fancy steel fender over front wheel. Big handlebars can be raised or lowered. Large rubber grips and pedals. ¾-inch non-skid rubber tires. Strong, sturdy shiny spokes on all wheels.

Measure child from crotch to instep.

Catalog Number	Front Wheel Diam.	Seat to Lower Pedal	Shpg. Wt., Lbs.	Price
79 K 8640	12 inch	17 to 18½ in.	17	$3.69
79 K 8641	16 inch	19 to 21½ in.	23	4.59
79 K 8642	20 inch	22 to 24 in.	29	5.39

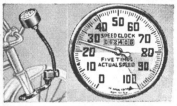

SPEED CLOCK for Velocipedes, Scooters, or Two-Wheelers

Show the speed you can travel on your bike geared up five times actual speed! Shows 50 miles when you go 10. Aluminum case and dial with indicator; convex crystal. Will not fit velocipedes or scooters with large front fender. **Complete with flexible shaft and braces for attaching.** **98c**

79 K 8610—Shpg. wt., 1 lb.

New MICKEY MOUSE 33½-In. Scooter

With fender and parking stand. Red enameled strong steel frame, 8¼-inch double-disc steel wheels; ⅝-inch rubber tires. Enameled wood handle and corrugated wood footboard. Shipping weight, 11 lbs. **$1.49**
79 K 8801

$13.00 Value **$9.98**

Just Out! 1936 Cadillac

1936 Cadillac — All-Steel — Streamlined

He'll dazzle his friends when he races by in this **42½-inch red and cream all-steel Cadillac**, streamlined just like the new cars. It's one of the finest we have ever offered and is worth considerably more than we ask. Silver-color radiator, windshield and bumper; beaver-tail back, heavy fenders and running boards! Real electric headlights with control switch. Big trumpet horn. 9⅜-inch rubber-tired wheels are artillery-type and roller bearing. Adjustable rubber pedals. Drive shafts are set in ball-bearings on rear axle. **No batteries included (two required).** For batteries, see 20 K 1401, Page 592.
79 K 8908—Shipping weight, 48 pounds............................**$9.98**

$2.79 12-In.

With Spring Saddle and Ball Bearing Front Wheel

Better value than ever with its new streamlined adjustable seat on flexible spring. Bright red enameled half-oval steel frame with cream color trim . . . curved steel handlebars . . . **ball-bearing front wheel;** ¾-inch rubber tires . . . rubber grips and pedals. Seat may be raised 2¼ in. from measure given.

Measure child from crotch to instep.

Catalog Number	Front Wheel Diam.	Seat to Lower Pedal	Shpg. Wt. Lbs.	Price
79 K 8629	12 in.	16¼ in.	13	$2.79
79 K 8630	16 in.	19 in.	18	3.29

$3.39 12-In.

Our Ever-Popular Strong Tubular Steel Bikes

Extra good looking and extra strong! Made like Brother's big bike. Light green and ivory enameled tubular steel frame with **welded joints . . . not usually offered at this price.** Easy riding ball-bearing front wheel, comfortable spring seat; streamline curved steel handlebars with rubber grips, rubber pedals and ¾-inch rubber tires.

Measure child from crotch to instep.

Catalog Number	Front Wheel Diam.	Seat to Lower Pedal	Shpg. Wt., Lbs.	Price
79 K 8664	12 in.	17 to 18½ in.	15	$3.39
79 K 8665	16 in.	19 to 21½ in.	19	3.98
79 K 8666	20 in.	22 to 24 in.	22	4.69

Little Tots Want This Mickey Mouse Wheelbarrow

A Useful Toy—Brightly Colored Almost Two and a Half Feet Long!

98c

It's bound to make any little youngster happy. Green and red enameled steel, with modern streamlined mudguard over the rubber-tired 5-inch wheel. Black enameled steel handles and foot rest. It's strong and well made so that it will stand the rough treatment given it by little hands. They will be delighted with the attractive Mickey Mouse decoration and they'll love this toy for play and use it for work, too. Shipping weight, 5 pounds.
79 K 7626...............**98c**

SEARS NEW TRIUMPH!
The Bike of the Century

ELGIN BLUEBIRD

**Use Your Credit!
Buy on
Easy Terms**

$5 DOWN

$44.95 Cash

Licensed by the E. C. Brown Co., Rochester, N. Y. Pat. No. 1,984,916

Not only are the sweeping lines of this newest of bicycle designs entirely different, but our engineers have developed a new conception of weight distribution which makes a ride on this bike a **positive sensation!** There is a sense of automatic balance that no other bicycle has. Even pedals are constructed so they always remain in perfect riding position.

Sweeping streamline beauty . . . modern up to the minute features . . . balanced weight distribution . . . speed—the best looking, easiest pedaling bicycle in America!

Its snappy flashing streamline design will make a hit in any crowd. You'll be the talk of the town as you "zip" by on the Bluebird—the only bicycle with real automobile features. Notice the automobile type instrument panel with illuminated speedometer; the two built-in light and horn control buttons; the pressed steel body, with built-in headlight, horn, tool and battery compartment at no increase in weight. Strong, one-piece, pressed steel luggage carrier emphasizes the streamline effect. Full crown fenders are in artistic harmony with the rest of the streamline design. Illuminated tool compartment.

Sears own, patented, leather saddle, built on an entirely new principle of cantilever springs, gives smoother easier riding comfort than you have ever before experienced. Comes in dashing **French Blue with Red trim,** (Gripfast enamel) chrome plated rims, handlebars and sprocket. New Departure coaster brake. Requires a one and one-half volt dry cell battery (not included).

6 KM 5007—ELGIN BLUEBIRD—Standard, full size, 19-in. frame adjustable from 29 to 34-in. seat to pedal. ALLSTATE balloon tires, 26x2⅛ in. with inner tubes. Shipping wt., 77 lbs.
Cash Price.................................**$44.95**
Easy Payments $5.00 down, $5.00 monthly........**$49.45**

See this Bicycle in Color on Inside Back Cover

Built-in, streamline headlight throws beams directly in front of bicycles.

Automobile type dashboard with illuminated speedometer, fully visible during night riding. Horn and light control buttons. Built-in electric horn and tool compartment. Sound of horn travels downward through side louvers.

Streamlined, tear drop pedal end plates. New, convenient stand folds back completely out of the way. Can be operated with simple foot movement.

Streamline carrier with red reflector lens on rear.

Auto-type seat springs

Sears Elgin Blackhawk

$33.95 Cash

**Use Your Credit
Buy on
Easy Payments**

$4 DOWN

● Loud "Wildcat" siren. ● Motorcycle style luggage carrier.
● Streamlined, twin bar, motorcycle type frame and tank.
● 12-point rubber cushioned frame.
● Our finest ALLSTATE Balloon tires, with new, protective tread on sidewall.
● Chromium plated headlight, rims, handlebars, truss rods and sprocket.

Sears pioneered the features that make the **Blackhawk** popular with thousands. . . . Ours is the original "Twin Bar" bicycle. Do not be misled by copies. Note the Troxel saddle, aviation type coaster brake, parking stand, jewel tail light. **No battery included.** Your choice of brilliant **Red** or **Black** Gripfast enamel with ivory trim. **State color.** Send us your order **TODAY.**

6 KM 5018—ELGIN Blackhawk, Twin Bar bike. Standard full size 19-in. frame, adjustable from 29 to 34 in. seat to pedal. ALLSTATE balloon tires, size 26x2⅛ in. with inner tubes. Shipping weight, 77 pounds.
Cash Price.................................**$33.95**
Easy Payment, $4.00 down, $5.00 monthly......**$37.35**

4 RUBBER TOY SETS
SAFE . . . UNBREAKABLE . . . WASHABLE

Noiseless, sanitary, durable rubber toys, that will not scratch fingers, floors or furniture. Set (A) is a 15-piece Army unit of soldiers equipped with rifles and machine guns, anti-aircraft gun stands 4½ in. high. Set (B) is a 29-piece defense set with tanks, cannons, spotlight, anti-aircraft cars and guns; soldiers are 3½ in. tall. Set (C) is a 10-piece air force with pursuit planes, bombers, sound-detectors, anti-aircraft gun, and searchlight; bomber is 5½ in. long and has 8 in. wing spread. Set (D) is a 15-piece infantry unit with one mounted officer; soldiers are 3½ in. tall. Colored with pure food-dye colors.

A31319	(A)	Army Unit	$1.40
A31320	(B)	Defense Unit	2.80
A31321	(C)	Aviation Set	1.40
A31322	(D)	Infantry Set	1.40

COLORFUL WOOD TOYS—THE NEWEST FOR 1942

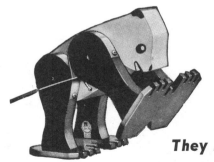

"LIVE" ACROBATIC TOYS

They Do Handsprings

Fun to Watch
SU-PANDA

An acrobatic fun-maker. Su's antics and appearance are much like those of the popular, live pandas. Turns handsprings, does back-flips, bows . . . at your command. Operated by remote control with a wire leash—not a wind-up toy. Perfect balance makes possible Su-Panda's astonishing feats. Precision built . . . yet not harmed by rough usage. Made of wood . . . attractively painted Black and White. Ten inches high.

A31323   Price....................................$1.40

Fun to Work
ANNIE ELEPHANT

A captivating new action toy . . . to be led with a string. Annie lumbers along with the rocking gait of a real elephant . . . an absolutely new motion in a toy. Also sits on her hind legs and tail and bows. Looks and performs like a cunning baby elephant. A precision-built toy, perfectly balanced, but sturdily made to withstand rough and tumble treatment. Made of wood . . . finished in Grey, Blue and other colors with a Red blanket. Six inches high . . . ten inches long.

A31324   Price....................................$1.40

WOOD FUN FLEET

Gay, colorful bath-tub toys for the kiddies. Fleet includes three sail-boats 4½ in. long with plastic sails 4½ in. high. The hulls of the boats are painted, one each, in Red, White and Blue. Also one Red and one Blue tug boat, 4 in. long; one cruiser 5¼ in. long; one cabin cruiser 5¼ in. long; one lighthouse 4 in. high; one buoy 3¼ in. high, with American Flag. 9 pieces, packed in brightly-designed lithographed box, size 12½x 6x2 in.

A31326   Price complete $1.40

WOOD AIRPLANE PULL-TOY

It's the "Flagship" of the American Airlines. Giant twin-motor plane painted in Orange and Blue with Black wheels and propellers. Whirr! Whirr! goes this plane as it is taxied around on the ground pulled by the cord. The propellers spin as plane is pulled. Measures 14 inches from the nose to the tail and has a wing spread of 20 inches. Sturdily constructed to stand hard play.

A31325   Price....................................$1.65

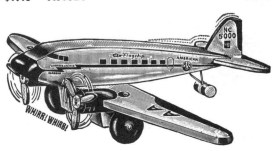

RUBBER FARM SET
Protect the Kiddies While Playing

Real fun on the farm—happy days for lads and lassies in their own barnyards. Arranging and moving the animals and equipment about will thrill the youngsters. All rubber—safe, won't scratch or cut furniture; noiseless; sanitary, washable, colored with pure harmless dyes. There are chickens, pigs, dogs, cows and a team of horses, a spring wagon, milk wagon with cans, tractor, plow, and all the things it takes to make a farm complete; with the barn and yard fence. The wheels on the wagons and machines are of rubber, roll easily, so these toys can be pulled around. Choice of 18 or 34 piece sets.

A30360 18-Piece Farm Set..$1.40
A30361 34-Piece Farm Set... 2.80

5-PIECE AVIATION SET

An aviation military defense set that gives children all the thrills their little hearts desire, yet are safe, noiseless and washable. They're made of solid rubber; painted with pure harmless dyes. This set consists of two pursuit planes, an infantryman, a gigantic searchlight and anti-aircraft gun both with their operators. Anti-aircraft gun is 4½ in. high. Packed in a handsomely colored box.

A31316 Set...$0.70

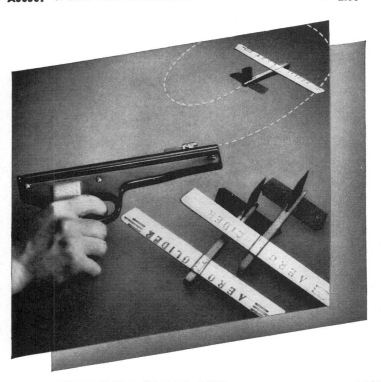

AEROMATIC GLIDER GUN

There's fun for the year 'round in these aeromatic glider guns for both boys and girls. The gliders are easily assembled, sturdily made, built with perfect balance to glide gracefully through the air. In patriotic colors of Red, White and Blue. The Black enameled metal gun has a Tan frosted-finish panel on the handle. Pull back sight on barrel, put glider in position and pull the trigger. Glider goes zooming into space. Gun 9 in. long, handle 4¾ in. long. Plane has 9 in. wing spread. Set has gun and three gliders.

A31217 Set $1.40
A31218 10 Extra Gliders.................................... .45

MOTHER GOOSE HOUSE

Here they come, one by one, the little characters you read about in nursery rhymes. Each dressed in his rightful costume; that is, they're painted, of cut-out wood, standing on tiny block bases. They all come with the charming "Mother Goose" and her house. Representing many nursery rhymes—"Mary Had a Little Lamb," "Little Miss Muffet," "Old Mother Hubbard," "Little Boy Blue," and others, twelve in all. Size of house, 11 in. wide, 8 in. deep, 7½ in. high. With booklet of "Mother Goose" rhymes.

A31219 Complete...$1.40

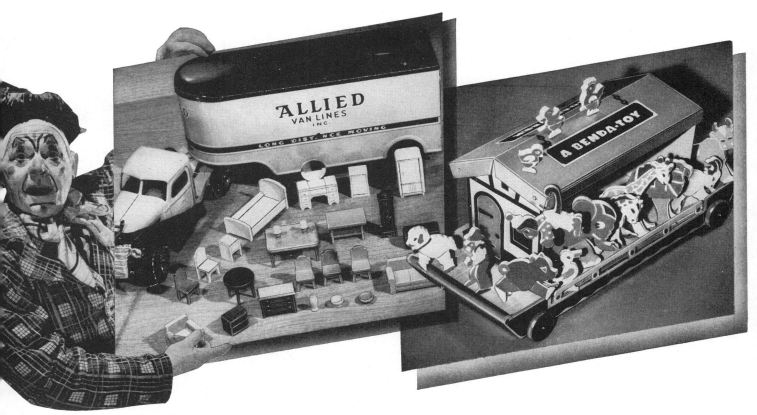

ALLIED MOVING VAN

Every day can be moving day when you have this handsome Buddy-L moving van. Sturdy metal van with Yellow enameled body and Black enameled top. Huge trailer type, with detachable motor cab, and six big, heavy-tread, rubber-tired wheels. Drop-gate back permits easy loading of furniture. **Four rooms of wood furniture come with the van.** Tiny tots can ride and guide this van at the same time by the sturdy twist-wire handle attached to the front. Allover size 29½ in. long, 9½ in. high, 6½ in. wide. Built to withstand rough play. Shipping weight, 13 lbs.

30366 Complete...**$6.90**

NOAH'S ARK—A BENDA-TOY

Girls and boys alike will enjoy playing with this set of Benda toys. They're heavy compressed fibre. The animals stand alone, have metal joints. Noah's Ark is really a menagerie, with a camel, giraffe, cow, monkey, elephant and other animals corralled in the Ark. The Ark itself is built in flat-boat fashion with wooden ends and wheels. Rolls along on the floor. Noah and the animals are handsomely painted in gay colors. Complete set consists of the 18-inch Ark, Noah and fourteen animals. Safe, no rough edges to cut or scratch.

A31208 Complete Set...**$1.40**

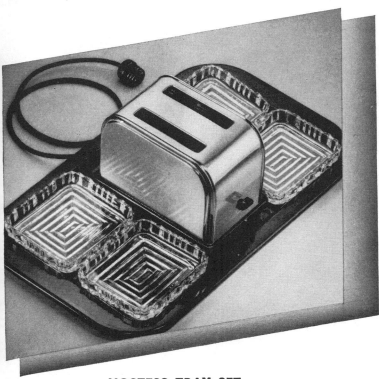

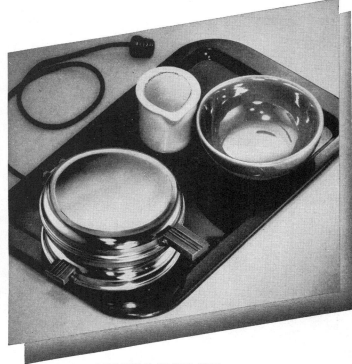

HOSTESS TRAY SET

A hostess tray set "just like mother's" for the clever little Miss. A charming set that will not only give every little girl great pleasure but will help her learn art of being a good hostess. The gleaming metal **NON-ELECTRIC** toaster with Black enameled base has pop-up toaster rack and is fitted with cord. Size 5⅜x3⅜x3½ in. Each of the four glass jelly and relish dishes is 3¾x3⅛x¾ in., attractively designed. The enameled metal tray measures 7¾x13 in. Mother can make real toast; put it in this little toaster to keep it warm for the playmates.

A31209 Complete Set...**$1.65**

WAFFLE IRON SET

The little lady who takes great pride in her cooking will love this **NON-ELECTRIC** waffle serving set. Gleaming metal waffle iron, 4½ inches in diameter, with modern wood handles and cord, comes complete with 13x7¾-inch enameled metal serving tray, a 4¼-inch mixing bowl and cup in gay colors. The bowl can be used to serve cereal to the youngsters—they won't need any coaxing to eat. Make some little girl happy the whole year 'round by sending her this lovely set for Christmas or her birthday.

A31210 Complete Set...**$1.80**

THE DOLL SENSATION OF THE YEAR

MAGIC SKIN BABY DOLL

**She's a Darling!
Warm as Skin
to the Touch**

5 NEW features

**Feather Weight
Weighs 20 Ounces
She Kneels on Floor
Like Crawling Baby**

**Washable—Can
Be Bathed
Cuddly and Lovable—Responds
to Hugs and Squeezes**

**Practically
Unbreakable**

Latex Body—So Real You'll Think It's a Live Baby!

There's no other doll like her. Wh__
you squeeze her, she feels like a "rea__
baby—not squashy, not hard, but chubb__
and responsive. You can wiggle her to__
and curl up her fingers and even bath__
her, because her flesh-like Latex body __
waterproof. The soft, pliable plastic sk__
is so natural-like and acquires a realist__
body warmth in a few moments of han__
dling—so much like a "real" baby th__
the doll seems alive. Filled with air-blow__
Kapok, unbreakable plastic head, ey__
open and shut. Doll is priced with layet__
only and also with a de luxe wardro__
and layette outfit packed in an airplan__
type traveling case. The de luxe set i__
cludes dress, bonnet, shoes, socks, nig__
clothes and a complete layette.

Doll With Layette	
A30234 13-In. Doll	$4.9_
A30235 15-In. Doll	6.9
A30236 20-In. Doll	9.8

De Luxe Outfit and Doll	
A30237 13-In. Doll	$ 6.9
A30238 15-In. Doll	9.8
A30239 17-In. Doll	12.9
A30240 20-In. Doll	15.9

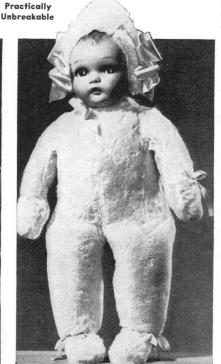

THE MOST THRILLING DOLL EVER MADE!

Here she is—the most lovable, realistic doll you've ever seen, with an amazing heart beat that almost makes you believe she's human. Just imagine it, hold her close to your ear and hear her heart beat just like a real live baby's. Or use the professional-type stethoscope included with the outfit to test her heart, just like the doctors do. This amazing new doll has a winsome baby face with chubby cheeks and sparkling Blue eyes, cuddly body and unbreakable legs and arms that move. Clockwork mechanism operates heart-beat. Dressed in crisp organdy and embroidery trimmed lace cap. Seventeen inches high, complete with stethoscope and golden-heart charm bracelet, all in attractive box.

A30241 Price..$11.50

SNUGGLE DOLL

Just let a youngster snuggle this adorable baby doll in her arms and then try to get her off to bed without it. It just can't be done! The soft, responsive body is covered with washable Pink rayon plush with a silky texture of irresistible touch appeal. Big, appealing Brown eyes highlight the chubby face with its tiny nose and winsome mouth. Removable Pink rayon plush cap with huge satin ribbon bows. Doll is 21 in. tall.

A30242 Price..$8.40

JUDY GARLAND

With all the appeal and charmin__ naturalness of her namesake, this bea__ tiful doll will captivate the hearts __ little girls everywhere. Modeled aft__ the popular movie star, this grown-u__ Miss is the thrilling answer to the chi__ who wants a change from baby doll__ Dressed in printed organdy with lac__ trimmed neck and interlaced Black rib__ bon that ties in a tiny bow with stream__ ers. She stands alone, fully 21 in. tal__ Movable Blue eyes.

A30243 Price..$9.9_

AMERICA'S No. 1 GLAMOUR DEB

The reigning queen of the debutante doll world. Gorgeously gowned in formal lace dinner dress, matching taffeta slip and panties, evening slippers and long White silk stockings. Ready to step out with a luxurious satin-lined White Lapin wrap to protect her from the cold air. Her gorgeous Blonde curls, twinkling Blue eyes, long lashes and pert little nose make her a charming favorite. Comes in two sizes.

| A30250 | Doll 14 Inches Tall..................... | $ 8.50 |
| A30251 | Doll 18½ Inches Tall................. | 15.50 |

"RAGGEDY ANN AND ANDY"

Two lovable characters, Raggedy Ann and Andy have stepped out of their story book pages right into the hearts of America's youngsters. With their funny, quaint faces and flaming Red hair of yarn, they are the most intriguing pair ever cuddled by a child. Adorably dressed in printed and plain percales that are washable. Ann wears a pinafore dress and panties; Andy wears a suit and cap. They'd rather go together, but you can buy them separately. Eighteen inches tall.

| A30252 | Raggedy Andy .... | $2.80 |
| A30253 | Raggedy Ann .... | 2.80 |

WATCH BABY "PAT-A-CAKE"

Lift her in your arms, press her chest and watch this lovely little baby make "pat-a-cake". She's as proud of her accomplishment as a real baby would be, and will repeat the performance without much coaxing. If you hold her by the hand and help her over the rough spots, she'll walk right along with you. Soft, cuddly composition body and dainty little baby face with hand-colored features. She's all dressed to go for a walk in flowered organdy with matching bonnet, slip, panties, shoes and socks.

| A30254 | Doll 14 Inches Tall............................. | $3.00 |
| A30255 | Doll 18 Inches Tall............................. | 4.50 |

THE BELLE OF THE SOUTH—SCARLETT O'HARA

WITH RED TAFFETA COAT

Modeled after the girl who turned Atlanta topsy-turvy, this Scarlett O'Hara doll is the most famous member of doll society. Dressed in authentic Southern style with Red Rayon Taffeta coat and plumed hat to match. The coat has an extremely full-flared skirt fitted bodice closed with self-covered buttons. Delicate lace ruffles peek out from the cuffs and trim the back of the hat. Beneath her coat she wears a Red dotted organdy dress and has, as would be expected, hoop petticoat with long pantalettes. Duplicates her famous namesake in "Gone With the Wind."

| A30256 | 15-Inch Scarlett O'Hara Doll.......... | $ 7.50 |
| A30257 | 18-Inch Scarlett O'Hara Doll.......... | 13.90 |

IN PRINTED ORGANDY DRESS

The very same Scarlett O'Hara who made such a tremendous sensation in "Gone With the Wind". A bewitching little coquette with heart-shaped face, coal Black hair, luminous Green eyes and real lashes—just the miss to set hearts afluttering. Dressed in beruffled organdy with a hooped petticoat and long pantaloons. Tied to the back of her pretty head is a large, corn-colored straw hat trimmed with posies. A ribbon bow ties her trim waist-line and flows gracefully in long streamers.

A30258	11-Inch Scarlett O'Hara Doll......	$4.50
A30259	15-Inch Scarlett O'Hara Doll......	6.00
A30260	18-Inch Scarlett O'Hara Doll......	9.50

WALKING GIRL DOLL

America's newest sensation in action dolls—the perfect playmate for youngsters who want more than just cuddly dolls. This cute little miss will walk right along with you if you will only hold her hand firmly and keep her from stumbling. She's charmingly dressed for that walk, too, in a gay plaid coat and dress with pique collar, a sailor beret, patent leather shoes and White socks. She'll probably be tired after her walk so just lay her down and her long lashes will close over her big Blue eyes.

| A30261 | 14-Inch Without Hat........................... | $4.50 |
| A30262 | 18-Inch With Hat................................. | 9.50 |

SONJA HENIE ON SKATES

Sonja Henie — dimples, real curls, real eyelashes and all! Composition body; sleeping eyes. Dressed in Pink rayon Taffeta with fluffy Maribou trim; net slip; rayon Taffeta panties; flower-trimmed Maribou hat; "professional" ice skates.

A30265 15 in.......$ 5.50
A30266 18 in....... 7.50
A30267 22 in....... 10.00

SONJA HENIE OUTFIT IN TRUNK

Reward a "good" little girl with this wonderful gift that she'll treasure for years! A permanent piece of luggage, with brass hardware and Lizard grain covering, comes complete with Sonja Henie doll and her wardrobe! Sonja has real curls, real eyelashes, sleeping eyes, and dimples! Her all-composition body is painted in flesh tints. She is dressed in rayon Taffeta frock with net slip and attached ice skates! Her wardrobe includes ski pants, jacket, sweater, tam, brassiere, girdle, gown, hair bow, skis and "rigger" poles! Every bit of her clothing is beautifully finished. Sonja stands 16 in. high overall. Deluxe model has a much larger wardrobe as shown above.

A30268 Doll, Trunk and Wardrobe..............$ 7.50
A30269 Deluxe, Wardrobe and Doll,.......... 15.00

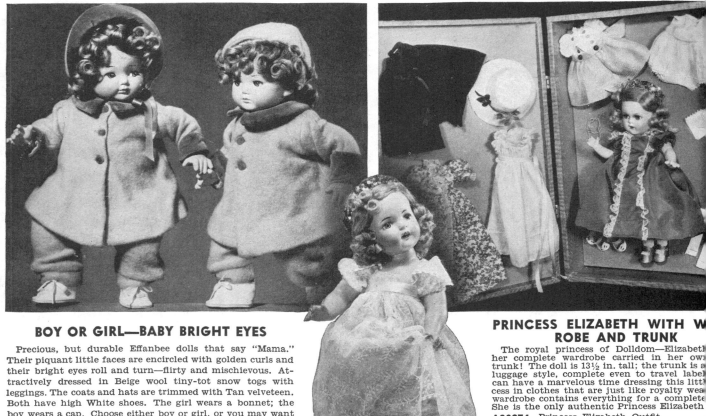

BOY OR GIRL—BABY BRIGHT EYES

Precious, but durable Effanbee dolls that say "Mama." Their piquant little faces are encircled with golden curls and their bright eyes roll and turn—flirty and mischievous. Attractively dressed in Beige wool tiny-tot snow togs with leggings. The coats and hats are trimmed with Tan velveteen. Both have high White shoes. The girl wears a bonnet; the boy wears a cap. Choose either boy or girl, or you may want to give both in a "brother and sister" set.

A30270 Girl Doll $10.50
A30271 Boy Doll 10.50

PRINCESS ELIZABETH WITH W ROBE AND TRUNK

The royal princess of Dolldom—Elizabeth her complete wardrobe carried in her ow trunk! The doll is 13½ in. tall; the trunk is a luggage style, complete even to travel label can have a marvelous time dressing this littl cess in clothes that are just like royalty wea wardrobe contains everything for a complete She is the only authentic Princess Elizabeth

A30274 Princess Elizabeth Outfit....................
Princess Elizabeth Dolls (Shown at Lef
A30272 13-Inch Doll, Only...............................
A30273 19-Inch Doll, Only...............................

"MISS GLAMOUR GIRL OF 1942"

With all the glamour and oomph of the Hollywood stars, this doll beauty-contest winner is the most appealing, most bewitching and most fascinating little miss ever fondled in a youngster's arms. Eighteen inches tall with beautifully proportioned body, dainty face with perky nose, twinkling eyes and gorgeous Blonde hair. A doll that will hold the affections of every child for years and years. "Miss 1942" has a charming boudoir outfit of lace-trimmed rayon panties and bra, boudoir slippers and a charming printed-rayon negligee trimmed with lace and ribbons in the latest high-waisted swirling skirt style, so popular today. She has a younger sister who looks almost like her twin, but is 14 inches tall and has a complete de luxe outfit and wardrobe packed in an 18-inch trunk case. Included are a large Blue straw hat, a Blue pique coat with embroidery cuffs and collar, a Pink Dotted Swiss dress with cluster of cherries on the shoulder, lace trimmed organdy slip, lace trimmed girdle, white slippers, hosiery, Blue handbag and lace trimmed handkerchief. Select either of these two dolls with the full assurance of thrilling any youngster.

A30275 18-In. Doll and Negligee......................$7.90
A30276 14-In. Doll with DeLuxe Outfit........ 9.50

HANSEL AND GRETEL

With all the quaintness and adorable charm of Dutch youngsters, these two soft, huggable dolls just seem to plead to be taken into your arms. Dressed in Blue velvet Dutch costumes. Gretel wears a lace apron and ribbons tied in her flaxen braided hair. Hansel is dressed in Blue velvet and a jaunty Blue cap. Both dolls are 11½ inches high and have hand painted features.

A31135 Dutch Boy Doll..........................$1.65
A31136 Dutch Girl Doll........................ 1.65

"NOW I LAY ME DOWN TO SLEEP"

PAPA MAMA

BABY HAS LEARNED TO TALK

It's an event that every youngster eagerly awaits when her baby speaks her first words. Now we have a doll that actually does! This adorable baby says her prayer, "Now I Lay Me Down to Sleep" before she goes to bed. If you coax her, she will sing, "London Bridge Is Falling Down" or perhaps she'll get coy and sing "Rock-A-Bye Baby." This amazing doll will mystify even the grown-ups; for, cleverly concealed within her soft body, a tiny phonograph with permanent sapphire needle plays the words that she croons so cutely. Dressed in flannel rompers under a lovely Pink and White flannel coat, and the daintiest little moccasins you've ever seen. All dressed ready for bed; the moment she touches the pillows, her eyes close. She is 19 inches tall, complete with phonograph mechanism.

A30277 Price................................$18.75

BABY TAKES HER FIRST STEP

Of course, she's a little afraid to walk by herself but if you will hold her hand, she'll toddle along right beside you with natural, faltering baby steps. This darling little baby doll is so very proud of her gorgeous Pink blanket coat with bonnet to match. The sleeves of the coat and edge of the bonnet are trimmed with White eiderdown. Under her coat, you'll find she's wearing an organdy dress with pretty little panties to match. White socks and White booties complete her street costume. Her soft, cotton-stuffed body seems to welcome hugs; composition head, legs and arms are movable. Real eyelashes close over her laughing Blue eyes when you lay her down. Pick her up and she says "Mama." 25 inches tall.

A30278 Price................................$3.50

BABY'S FIRST WORDS

Remember your big thrill when baby first said "Mama" and "Papa." That's the thrill awaiting the youngster who gets this adorable baby doll. Tilt the doll to the right and she says, "Mama," tilt her to the left and she says, "Papa." This gorgeous doll is almost as real and cuddly as a baby itself. Lovely big eyes with long lashes that close over naturally when you lay her down. A soft, responsive body with movable arms, legs and head. Beautifully dressed in crisp organdy with dainty lace trimming, organdy bonnet with full, wide ruffles trimmed in lace, and tiny undies just like baby's. Neat White petticoat and rubber panties, White socks and booties complete her costume. In two sizes.

A30279 16-Inch Doll $4.90
A30280 23-Inch Doll 7.90

"McGUFFEY ANA" DOLLS
CUTEST LITTLE PLAYMATES

"MC GUFFEY ANA"

"McGuffey Ana" is the cutest little playmate any child could have! Inspired by the famous "McGuffey Reader," she's as pretty as a picture with her real, flaxen, ribbon-tied braids and fluffy curls that cluster over her forehead! Her large sparkling eyes close when she sleeps, showing off her real lashes! Her straw hat sits jauntily on the back of her head; she wears a lovely, crisp organdy dress, and a dainty, lace-trimmed, darling pinafore apron; her panties and slip are ruffle trimmed; socks and shoes. All her wearing apparel is exquisitely tailored.

A30291	13-inch	$4.50
A30292	16-inch	5.90
A30293	20-inch	7.50

"MC GUFFEY ANA" AND HER WARDROBE

You'll fall in love with "McGuffey Ana" the minute you see her! Everyone does! She's a bonnie Scotch lassie with real golden hair arranged in pin curls and pigtails, ribbon-tied! Her sparkling, laughing eyes close when asleep. She is dressed in a Scotch plaid dress with large pocketbook for carrying her candy money; White stockings and two-button shoes; lovely underwear! She has an extra pair of slippers; long stockings; handkerchief; White apron; extra dress; lovely full-length nightgown; full-length dressing gown; large straw hat; beautiful dress coat. When she stands up straight, she is 13 in. tall! Comes packed in airplane luggage-style trunk, size 21x12½ in., that holds all her extra wardrobe. Every little girl will have years of happy enjoyment and play from this complete outfit.

A30290   Complete.................................$7.50

LAZY BABY

Just watch how this adorable doll will thrill a youngster, then try to measure the child's delight as compared to the doll's trifling cost. Soft as a bunny, cuddly and lovable as a real baby. Fuzzy baby-blanket material forms this chubby infant, with a soft stuffing and an unbreakable face. The round, baby face is painted with a cupid's-bow mouth and has long, sweeping lashes that make the doll look like a sleepy baby. Yarn curls peek out from beneath the fastened cap. In Baby Pink or Blue, with contrasting ribbon tied around the neck; 15½ in. tall. Yes, it is well worth twice our low price!

A30172	Pink Lazy Baby	$1.25
A30173	Blue Lazy Baby	1.25

MAGIC "SQUEEZUMS" DOLLS

The sensational new doll with "magic skin" arms and legs. Skin wrinkles like a real baby's, is soft and warm to touch! She can clasp her hands! She cries when you squeeze her legs. Lay her down, she cries herself to sleep. Has three voices, one in each leg and in the body. Beautiful baby face, made of composition, with long, silky lashes and sleeping eyes. Featherweight, but durable, with Kapok-filled body. Adorably dressed in fancy organdy baby costume, with ribbon trim, lace-trimmed, ruffled bonnet, rubber panties, shoes and socks. A value beyond compare, costs no more than good dolls with ordinary composition legs and arms. An exciting new doll that every little girl will simply adore! Choice of three sizes.

A30295	16-Inch Size	$4.20
A30296	19-Inch Size	5.60
A30297	22-Inch Size	6.90

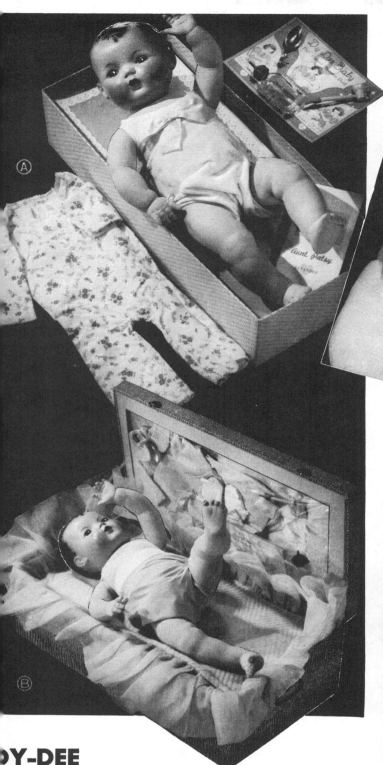

"BYE-LO BABY"

No little-girl mother can resist this adorable doll, she looks so much like a real live baby! In fact, she is modeled from a three-day old baby and has the same natural shape and expression! When you lay her down she goes right to sleep! Turn her over and she cries softly. She is bundled up in a comfy blanket of White flannel, satin ribbon tied. Choice of three sizes. Specify choice of ribbon trimming—**Pink or Blue.**

A30306	13-inch Doll	$3.50
A30307	15½-inch Doll	5.25
A30308	18-inch Doll	6.90

SHE FLIRTS WITH YOU!

She rolls here eyes—up and down—from side to side—in a most flirtatious way! Her name is "Baby Beautiful" and she's as cunning as can be! Her soft body is cuddly to hold—her beautifully-colored composition head, arms and legs are realistic to see. She walks when you hold her by the hand! Her real lashes close down over her eyes when she sleeps—and she cries, "Mama!" when you turn her over! Ribbon and lace-trimmed organdie dress and bonnet; slip; rubber panties.

A30309	16-inch Doll	$3.90
A30310	20-inch Doll	7.00

DY-DEE

THE DOLL THAT'S ALMOST HUMAN — DRINKS — WETS — BLOWS BUBBLES!

Dy-Dee is the world's most remarkable doll because she is more like a human baby than any other doll! She drinks water or milk—she breathes—she coos! She will drink from a bottle or from a spoon—sitting up or lying down! She takes it, drop by drop, just like a real live baby. Her daily bath doesn't hurt her a bit—she likes it—and loves to be powdered afterward! She will lie in bed with her eyes open or closed—and sits up in your arms, either awake or asleep, as you prefer. More than that, she can blow real soap bubbles through a little bubble pipe; the pipe comes with her.

She has a glowing, satin-like skin of washable rubber, with cuddly body. Her head is beautiful and lifelike, naturally colored, with darling, grown, painted curls and soft, flexible rubber ears. Her eyes have real curly lashes! You can purchase Dy-Dee alone or with her de luxe wardrobe in a suitcase. Note the illustrations above. The (A) picture shows her in a gift box, dressed in shirt and diaper. With her comes a cunning, flannel pajama suit, nursing bottle, baby spoon and pipe for blowing bubbles; also included is booklet entitled, "What Every Young Doll Mother Should Know." The (B) picture shows Dy-Dee, the world's most famous baby doll, packed in a de luxe suitcase with complete wardrobe. She is dressed in shirt, diaper and rubber panties; with her comes ruffled crib blanket, nursing bottle, bubble pipe, baby spoon, stockings, shoes, coat, bonnet, dress and slip, all of the highest quality; also booklet on her care and Dy-Dee Diary!

(A) Dy-Dee in Gift Box

A30300	11-inch Doll	$ 5.35
A30301	15-inch Doll	9.30
A30302	20-inch Doll	14.60

(B) Dy-Dee and Wardrobe in Suitcase

A30303	11-inch Doll	$ 9.30
A30304	15-inch Doll	14.60
A30305	20-inch Doll	19.50

MISS DUCKY DE LUXE — TRU-FLESH RUBBER

Miss Ducky De Luxe has the skin you love to touch—velvety soft, smooth Tru-Flesh rubber that feels like the real thing! Her head, body, legs and arms are soft where they should be soft and hard where they should be hard, just like a live baby! She has real silky lashes on her lovely eyes—and she goes to sleep when you put her down! We suggest you also order her Betsy Wetsy layette shown above; it is complete in every detail from clothing down to washcloth, sponge, soap and pins.

Miss Ducky De Luxe			Her Layette		
A30311	11-inch Doll	$2.35	A30315	For 11-inch Doll	$1.35
A30312	12½-inch Doll	3.20	A30316	For 12½-inch Doll	1.50
A30313	14½-inch Doll	4.90	A30317	For 14½-inch Doll	1.65
A30314	16½-inch Doll	5.95	A30318	For 16½-inch Doll	1.75

A72100   A72101

DE LUXE DOLL CARRIAGES

- Strong But Lightweight
- Double Suspension Springs

WHITNEY DE LUXE FIBRE
Two Sizes

Pictured at the left is a new Whitney doll carriage, handsomely styled and richly finished. Made of fancy, oval fibre with reclining back, sliding hood, windows. Body size 24½x12½ in. Tubular handle 28 in. high; 9-in. wheels with ¾-in. rubber tires; footbrake, upholstered seat, back and gores. Shipping weight 21 lbs. Choice of color, **Tan or Green.**

A72100 Price (Color?)..............................$14.50

Similar to above, but with body 21x10 in. with 7-in. wheels; ⅜-in. tires; handle 25 in. high. Shipping weight 12½ lbs. Specify color. **Tan or Green.**

A72101 Price (Color?)............................$8.00

WHITNEY DE LUXE COACH

Shown at the right above, a smart Whitney doll coach, with body of wood, size 26x13 in. Extension front; draft-proof rail. Whitex 5-bow hood with visor; upholstered sides, back and front, lined and padded; handbrake; tubular chrome pusher-handle. 30 in. high. 9-in. wheels; ¾-in. tires. Shipping weight 32 lbs. Choice of decorated colors: **Coronation Blue, Gray or Carmine.**

A72102 Price (Color?)..............................$18.95

Similar to above but with body 24x12 in., with 8-inch wheels; ¾-in. tires; handle 27½ in. high. Shipping weight 26 lbs. Choice of colors: **Coronation Blue, Gray or Carmine.**

A72103 Price (Color?)..............................$15.00

A72102   A72103

COMPLETE WITH MATTRESS

MUSICAL DOLL CRADLE

What fun she will have rocking her doll to sleep, while a concealed Swiss music box plays "Rock-A-Bye Baby." Priscilla Maple-finished wood cradle, complete with music box and mattress. Choice of two sizes. The 19-in. cradle will hold a doll up to 17 in. in size. The 23-in. cradle will hold a doll up to 21 in.

A30368 19 in. Size..$4.50
A30369 23 in. Size.. 5.90

DOLL BATHINETTE

Exactly what every young doll mother wants! A combination bathinette and dressing table. Ideal for any doll that can be bathed. Folding stand of Ivory-enameled wood, with rubberized bathing compartment. Drain and stopper are included. Equipped with linen racks and pockets. Swing-back cloth top for the doll to lie on while being dried, dressed and petted. The doll bathinette is 20¼ in. wide, 24 in. high when open. Folds compactly.

A30367 Price Complete...............................$3.00

DOLL NURSE'S OUTFIT

This attractive airplane luggage case contains everything to give Dy-Dee or any other doll the best of care. The outfit includes rubber apron, nursing bottle, talcum powder, cotton, powder puff, wash cloth—and even a cute little hot water bottle to keep the doll's feet warm on cold nights! There is also a lovely, child's size White lawn uniform and cap, just the right attire for the young doll mother when taking her doll for an airing. The set also includes a pencil and an attractive diary. Complete in a smart "airplane luggage" type of case, size 14½x12¾ in., with snap lock and balanced carrying handle.

A31221 Complete.................................$3.20

DOCTOR'S VISITING KIT
With Real Stethoscope

Just like a real Doctor's! Includes a real play stethoscope with which you can actually hear heart beats! Leatherette visiting bag 12 in. wide complete with stethoscope, blood pressure outfit, reflex hammer, toy wrist watch, jars of pure candy pills, eye glasses, bandages, prescription blanks, Doctor's diploma, and dozens of other items of interesting play value. An interesting, educational outfit.

A31222 Complete........................$2.80

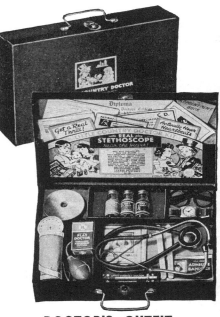

DOCTOR'S OUTFIT

Girls as well as boys enjoy this educational play professional set. The Little Country Doctor Kit comes in a professional-type case containing real stethoscope with which you can hear the heart beat; three jars assorted-colored candy pills; toy wrist watch; toy blood pressure kit. Toy fever thermometer; head reflector; pair of glasses with neckband. Tongue depressor; absorbent cotton; prescription blanks; sick charts. Bandaid package; gauze pad, diploma. "Doctor" window sign; booklet of instructions, with height and weight chart. Leatherette suitcase 12¼x8x3 in. with brass-plated handle and snap lock.

A31223 Complete...........................$1.4

BIG HELPS FOR LITTLE MOTHERS

BISSELL SWEEPER

Every little girl wants a real Bissell carpet sweeper just like her mother's. This "Misses" model is made by the famous Bissell Sweeper Co. and has many of the well-known Bissell features. Has rubber bumper all around, junior-size handle, revolving bristle brush, etc. Does a real job of sweeping.

A31225 Price............................$1.40

REAL SEWING MACHINE

Just the thing for the busy little doll-mother who likes to make her own doll clothes. Lifetime steel construction, with top that opens like Mother's; chain drive, thread tension control; stitch adjuster and standard Singer 24x1 chain stitch needles. Finished in Red and Black with nickel trim. Size 9 in. wide, 8 in. high.

A31226 Price............................$5.60

SAFE-ELECTRIC IRON

For Mother's helper—a safe electric iron that really irons clothes! Approved by Underwriters' Laboratories, this iron heats to 100 watts—sufficient to iron light materials but not hot enough to burn. Shaped handle stays cool. Comes complete with long cord and plug. She'll be delighted with this gift!

A31227 Price............................$1.40

"MODERN MISS" LAUNDRY SET

Everything for the little Miss who launders her doll clothes! Washing machine has glass tub, Red-enameled metal frame and cover. Agitator blades and wringer actually work! 10 inches high. Collapsible clothes dryer stands 10 inches high, comes with miniature clothes pins. Make-believe iron is attractively Red enameled. Fold-away ironing board is solid wood, stands 11½ in. high, ironing surface is 17¾x5¼ in.

A31228 Complete............................$1.85

TWO MODERN RANGES

Beautiful new play stove, made in two styles. Electric model (illustrated) has heavy-duty element that really cooks and bakes; accurate oven-heat indicator; two make-believe switches, three make-believe drawers with handles. Size 10¾x10½x5½ in. The non-electric range measures 15x 14x7¾ in., has extra large oven with regulator; large utensil drawer; built-in light shield; six movable play switches, heat regulator. The electric range is complete with five utensils; non-electric has eight utensils including teakettle. Each stove has clock with movable hands. Welded steel, beautifully enameled and decorated.

A30372 Electric Complete $2.80
A30373 Non-Electric Complete........ 2.80

CHILDREN'S COMPLETE CLEANING SET
With Real Carpet Sweeper

What fun it is to help Mother keep house! Especially when you have your own personal cleaning set like the one shown above. This set includes a real carpet sweeper that actually sweeps; broom; a pick-up style dust pan with handle; washable apron; and dummy packages of Bon Ami, and Brillo. The sweeper has handle 24 in. long; streamlined case 7¼ in. wide; real bristle brush. This big outfit offers a great value at this low price! Complete in Susy Goose gift box, 30x10 in.

A31229 Price Complete............................$1.40

DE LUXE ELECTRIC STOVE

A toy electric range with which you can cook and bake with real efficiency. It has a heavy-duty element, four burners, accurate oven-heat indicator. Two play doors with handles; two movable play switches. Welded steel construction, Ivory enameled, size 12½x11x5¾ in. Complete with five utensils, including a modern teakettle just like Mother's.

A30374 Price............................$4.90

ELEVEN-PIECE PASTRY SET

For little cooks and bakers. Solid wood table with raised edges, sturdy composition top. Size 17½ in. high, 18¼x12¼ in. top. Complete with pastry board, meat grinder, beater, rolling pin, 2 cookie cutters, masher, bowl, cup and baking dish.

A31230 Complete............................$1.40

COMPLETELY STOCKED REFRIGERATOR

The little housewife will be delighted with this reproduction of a new electric refrigerator. The door swings open to reveal a colorful, realistic interior. On the real corrugated shelves are miniature packages of familiar products. A metal "ice" tray pulls out to show six removable cubes of "ice." There is a toy regulator switch for varying degrees of cold. The inside of the door presents a brilliant picture of fully-stocked shelf-trays. Overall height 13½ in., width 8 in., depth 5⅜ in.

A30375 Price Complete............................$1.40

SEWS DOLL CLOTHES

A toy sewing machine with many of the practical features of a large machine. Thread-tension control, rotary shuttle, stitch adjuster. Sews a chain stitch with a Singer No. 14 needle. Sturdily built; size 7 in. high, 4½ in. wide. A remarkable value.

A31231 Price............................$2.80

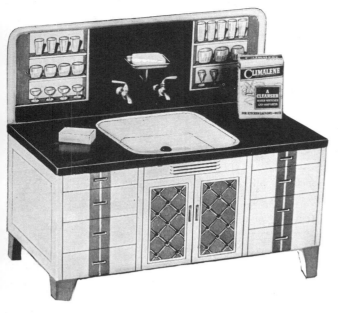

← COMPLETE SINK RUNNING WATER

What little housewife could resist this miniature sink with faucets that actually start and stop running water! A perfect model of a modern sink; has a rear reservoir that permits easy flow of water when either faucet is turned on. Basin will hold small dishes and utensils. Complete with miniature packages of soap and cleansing accessories. Sink is 10½ in. wide.

A31246   Price Complete......**$1.40**

KITCHEN CABINET →
With Complete Accessories

Complete, realistic model of a kitchen cabinet with all accessories. Sturdy all-metal construction, colorfully lithographed; doors swing open to reveal shelves overflowing with miniature packages. The top slides off, if desired, to make a regulation kitchen table. Accessories include percolator; egg beater; rolling pin; set of muffin pans; glass mixing bowl; two aluminum kitchen pans. The cabinet measures 20x17x10½ in.

A30382   Price..........................**$4.20**

54-PIECE LUNCHEON SET

No little girl's life is quite complete without her own little tea or luncheon set! Here is a complete 54-piece set: six cups, six saucers, six tea plates, six cereal or utility bowls, sugar, creamer and water pitcher; six knives, six forks, six spoons; set of napkins and table cloth, size 24x24 in. The linen-like cloths are stamped, may be embroidered. Dishes are gay fiesta colored, opaque glass. A small price for this big set!

A31247   Price Complete **$2.20**

COMPLETE TOY BAKING SET

Every little girl likes to copy her mother making things in the kitchen. This practical baking set includes an egg beater that really beats; large decorated pastry board; rolling pin with enameled handle; glass mixing bowl; meat grinder really grinds; and a wood shopping list reminder board. The recipe book by Marjorie Noble Osborn is of definite practical use! Also has a set of muffin pans, baking dishes, and a cookie cutter. In gift box 17½x12x3½ in.

A30383   Complete Set **$1.40**

CHIQUITA TOY DISHES

What little hostess wouldn't enjoy serving tea to her little friends with this gay, colorful set! It's as intriguing as a carnival in it's lovely colors that rival the fiesta ware on mother's table. This 16-piece set consists of 4 Orchid cups, 4 Yellow saucers, four Green plates, Blue teapot with cover, Blue sugar and creamer. The set comes in a 13x11 in. box lithographed in brilliant colors with Mexican scene on the top. Sure to make a little girl happy.

A31248   Set...**$1.10**

TWO SUPERFINE PIECES

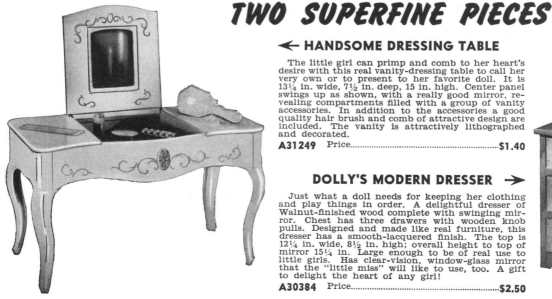

← HANDSOME DRESSING TABLE

The little girl can primp and comb to her heart's desire with this real vanity-dressing table to call her very own or to present to her favorite doll. It is 13¼ in. wide, 7½ in. deep, 15 in. high. Center panel swings up as shown, with a really good mirror, revealing compartments filled with a group of vanity accessories. In addition to the accessories a good quality hair brush and comb of attractive design are included. The vanity is attractively lithographed and decorated.

A31249   Price..**$1.40**

DOLLY'S MODERN DRESSER →

Just what a doll needs for keeping her clothing and play things in order. A delightful dresser of Walnut-finished wood complete with swinging mirror. Chest has three drawers with wooden knob pulls. Designed and made like real furniture, this dresser has a smooth-lacquered finish. The top is 12¼ in. wide, 8½ in. high; overall height to top of mirror 15¼ in. Large enough to be of real use to little girls. Has clear-vision, window-glass mirror that the "little miss" will like to use, too. A gift to delight the heart of any girl!

A30384   Price..**$2.50**

OOH! REAL DOLL HOUSES

COMPLETELY FURNISHED DOLL HOUSE

The doll house beautiful! Five rooms — completely furnished—designed by a famous interior decorator. An English-style house with exterior of simulated brick, stone, half timbers and stucco. The 88 pieces of furniture and decorative articles all harmonize with the interior of each room. Complete to the last detail, including shrubbery. The house, interior and accessories are all made of extra-heavy fibre board. Easily assembled, patented lock construction. House measures 27 in. long, 12 in. wide and 14½ in. high, open in the rear for extra play value. Packed knocked-down in attractive gift box with complete instructions for assembling.

A31233 Complete............$2.80

DOLL HOUSE WITH FURNITURE

A girl's dream come to life! A new-type, open-front play house complete with furniture. Each room is attractively decorated. The outside walls are done in fieldstone and stucco-type finish, with Red tile roof. Four-room house, 18 in. wide, completely furnished with 33 pieces of true-scale wood furniture, and a six-room house, 26 in. wide, furnished with fifty pieces of furniture, all built in exact scale. Made of ¼-inch Fibo-board, assembled in one minute.

A30377 4-Room House with Furniture............$4.20
A30378 6-Room House with Furniture............7.00

BEDROOM SUITE

DINING ROOM SET

KITCHEN-DINETTE SET

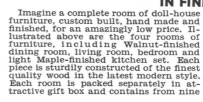

LIVING ROOM SUITE

BATHROOM WITH RUNNING WATER

Something new and different—complete to the last detail, even to running water in bathtub and sink. Tremendous play value. Plastic tub (6½ inches long), sink, commode and metal hamper. Above the tub and sink are real faucets which allow water to run from reservoirs behind the back wall. Walls and floor are metal. Room measures 17¼ in. wide, 10½ in. deep.

A31234 Price............$2.80

DOLL FURNITURE—PERFECT REPRODUCTIONS IN FINE WOOD

Imagine a complete room of doll-house furniture, custom built, hand made and finished, for an amazingly low price. Illustrated above are the four rooms of furniture, including Walnut-finished dining room, living room, bedroom and light Maple-finished kitchen set. Each piece is sturdily constructed of the finest quality wood in the latest modern style. Each room is packed separately in attractive gift box and contains from nine to eleven pieces. Each box is 10x14 in. The furniture is perfectly scaled as shown in the illustration above. Please order by number, thus indicating each room of furniture desired.

A31235 Living Room............$1.40
A31236 Dining Room............1.40
A31237 Bedroom............1.40
A31238 Kitchen............1.40

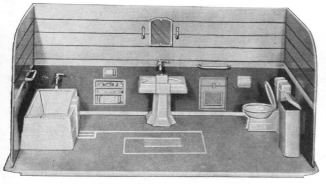

LIVING ROOM FURNITURE

BEDROOM FURNITURE

KITCHEN FURNITURE

The Most Beautiful Doll House of Its Type in America! Reproduction Scaled to Doll-House Size

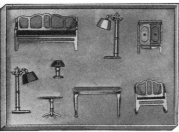

DINING ROOM FURNITURE

DE LUXE FOUR-ROOM DOLL HOUSE AND FOUR ROOMS OF FURNITURE

A charming house that affords endless play value and opportunity for the little housekeeper to be her own interior decorator. Four rooms with movable partitions in a two-story house; sturdily constructed of pressed wood; reinforced with wood-beam mouldings; metal corners. All windows are cut out, two porch lamps are attached to front of house. Beautifully finished in realistic colors both inside and out, house measures 20 in. long, 10 in. deep, 16¼ in. high. Shipped knocked down, easy to assemble in a few minutes. The one-story house has two rooms. Measures 16½ in. long, 12 in. high, 7½ in. deep. Furniture as shown in illustration.

A30379 2-Story House............$2.80
A30380 1-Story House............1.40
A31239 4 Rooms of Furniture............2.80

POPULAR PULL TOYS

Clever Novelties That Go Places and Do Things

TINY, THE ELEPHANT ENGINEER

Here he comes! Ding-dong, ding-dong! Tiny, the elephant Engineer, his engine huffin' and puffin', ringing the bell merrily. The six-wheel, realistic engine and Tiny are of gaily colored wood. Tiny rings the bell all by himself as he calls for full steam ahead! Children love this action-packed pull toy. Measures 11 inches long, 8¾ inches high, 4¼ inches wide. Comes complete with button-end pull cord.

A31131 Price..$0.70

SNOOPY THE SNIFFER

Meet his canine cockiness—Snoopy the Sniffer! A hare-brained hound with a single ambition—to go around sniff—sniff—sniffing! He walks with nose to the ground, with a jointed-leg, rambling, splay-footed gait that delights everyone! Snoopy isn't at all timid about sniffing—he sniffs good and he sniffs loud. Has rubber paws; floppy ears and wagging tail. Made of brightly colored wood; 16½ in. long. Comes complete with pull cord.

A31132 Price..$1.40

PLUTO POP-UP

Pluto, Mickey Mouse's gangling hound, can get into more laughable shapes and crazy contortions than a double-jointed monkey. Pluto is the newest member of the Pop-Up kritter krowd. He has large floppy ears that wiggle as you manipulate the strings. His legs wobble—he twists and turns; crouches, collapses; springs erect with his tail wagging. He is 5½ in. high, 7½ in. long and comes on a platform 10½ in. long.

A31125 Price..$0.35

Strike Up the Band!

DONALD DUCK GOES MUSICAL

Wacky, quacky Donald Duck—Walt Disney's lovable creation—gets in some hot licks on his toy xylophone! Pull him across the floor and he swings his mallets across the keyboard, left to right, up and down. He doesn's miss a single one of the seven melodious bars. He beats out a snappy tune! Donald is all dressed up in a bandsman's uniform—the entire toy is brilliantly colored. This big, amusing action-toy is sturdily built of wood. Measures 13 inches high, 11 inches long, 6 inches wide. Complete with pull cord.

A31128 Price..$1.40

WADDLING DUCK FAMILY

A quacking Mamma Duck and her three, wabble-gaited Baby Ducklings all in a line. The rubber connectors can be separated and joined together for changing combinations. Mamma Duck wobbles and waddles like her offspring—and has rubber tail and bill in addition. Entire set is 16 in. long, 4¾ in. high, 4 in. wide.

A31126 Price..$0.70

HI-HO PONY EXPRESS

Boy, what a horse! He'll deliver the goods in time. His head bobs up and down, he arches his back and his rear quarters move realistically as he gallops along with a merry "clip-clop, clippety-clop" sound. This sturdy white horse has no trouble at all pulling the realistic delivery wagon. Red wagon with bright Yellow wheels. Measures 16¼ in. long. Complete with pull cord.

A31133 Price..$0.85

Ride 'em, Cowboy!

A DASHING HORSE TO RIDE

Here's Dashing Dobbin—just the right size for tiny tots—yet sturdy enough to carry 50 pounds without developing a sway back! What fun it is to ride or pull—indoors or outdoors. Comfortable saddle seat; strong wheels; red leatherette reins. It's what every little boy and girl longs for—and hopes to get! The head, seat and legs are of 1⅛ in. thick wood, smoothed and shaped to eliminate all danger of scratches. Size 18½ in. long, 15¼ in. high, 8 in. wide.

A30115 Price..$1.40

CIRCUS BAND WAGON

All the color—all the noise—all the appeal of a big float in a circus parade! As the child pulls this toy along, the two horses prance up and down, keeping step to the musical notes that play continuously. Rugged wood construction throughout, beautifully decorated in bright contrasting colors. The float has a picture of a calliope-playing clown and his dancing dogs; has roomy cart space to fill with blocks, etc. Children love this gay, musical toy. Measures 17½x6½x5½ in.

A31129 Price..$1.40

THE COASTER BOY

An action-packed toy that's a constant delight to youngsters. The Coaster Boy runs along pushing his wagon; he jumps on and coasts and then hops off again to push some more. The realistic action is entirely automatic. As the toy is pulled along the bell rings merrily. The boy is realistically colored; wagon is bright Red with Blue wheels. It's a big toy, 15 inches long.

A31130 Price..$1.40

DIZ, THE DAFFY DONKEY

He's dizzy all right—and completely daffy! More fun than a three-ring circus! By a pull of your finger you can drop Diz back on his haunches or snap him erect, tail pointing skyward. His tail lashes—his legs waggle—even his ears wiggle! There's riotous fun for all the family in this laugh-provoking toy. He stands 6 inches high on a "performance" platform—ready to do his daffy trick!

A31127 Price..$0.35

HERE'S FUN!

SAFE—WILL NOT SCRATCH FINGERS—FLOORS—OR FURNITURE

"DOWN ON THE FARM"
A Big Barn—Cows, Horses, Pigs and Dogs Are All Here

Here it is—a big model farm set complete with everything pictured above. It's got a modern barn standing 11¼ in. high, 13 in. wide, 9 in. deep, with real sliding double doors, end windows, and open back for easy access. The barn is sturdy wood and Masonite finished in Red and White trim, authentic to the last detail! There are 11 animals, cows, pigs, horses, dogs; six sections of fence, each section 5 in. wide; adjustable solid wood gates. The animals and fence sections are colorfully printed on heavy cardboard with wood standup supports. Set up your own barnyard—it's loads of fun for boys and girls!

A30389 Complete Set.................$1.65

HIGHWAY FLEET—MADE OF RUBBER

Noiseless—sanitary—durable—washable toys made of unbreakable rubber that will not scratch fingers, floors or furniture! A lot of toys for a little price! A large automobile, large truck, motorcycle cop, 3 small automobiles, 2 small trucks, milk truck with 6 individual cans, 2 barrels and 1 box! All the wheels go round! All are brilliantly colored. Youngsters will get loads of fun out of this complete fleet—they can push and bang them around—won't hurt the toys—themselves—or your floors and furniture. Set comes packed in a big box—ideal for storing the toys.

A31116 Complete Set.................$1.40

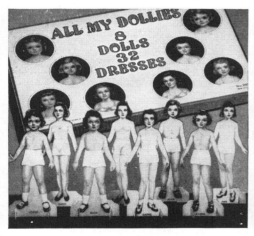

SUPER PAPER DOLL SET
Eight "Stand-Up" Dolls—32 Dresses

The most complete and attractive paper doll outfit we have ever offered. Bound to thrill any little girl! Contains eight different dolls, all 10½ inches tall, colorfully printed on heavy cardboard. Each doll has a novelty stand as well as two circular, wooden stands. With the dolls are 32 dresses, each in the height of fashion, with matching hats and accessories. Box size 11x18 in.

A31117 Complete Set.................$1.40

MYSTERY RACING CAR
Runs in Figure "8's"—By Itself

One of the very best action toys, guaranteed to thrill youngsters for months! Has a silent, air-flow, figure 8 action, putting it in a class by itself. Powered by a strong keywind motor; equipped with side brake, rubber bumper running all the way around the car, celluloid windshield and all accessories. Two racing drivers are part of the equipment, adding a realistic touch to the car. Finished in a brilliant Red, all ready to whizz around the room! Size 10⅝x6x3½ inches.

A31118 Price.................$0.80

MINIATURE TRANSPORT SET
Cars—Planes—Trucks—Bus

The ideal "hobby" set. Here is a miniature transportation set, representing all forms of land transport. Each of the ten all-metal items is a remarkably realistic reproduction of the "real thing." All have rubber tires. Even the finest details are brought out. In addition to buses, trucks, and automobiles, two famous airplanes are represented—the four-motored, new super Main Liner and the Waco Bomber. All attractively packed in colorful gift presentation box, 11½x18 in.

A31119 Complete Set.................$1.40

BUTTON SEWING CARDS

"Button! Button! Who's got the button!" The little child who owns this remarkable set will have lots of them! it's an educational toy—instructs the child in the first steps of using needle and thread. Teaches her how to sew on buttons! Six cards, beautifully printed and colored, are ornamented by the child with bright, shiny catalin buttons. Box contains large supply of colorful buttons, needle, threads, six cards and directions.

A31120 Complete.................$0.70

GREYHOUND SUPER BUS

Action! Lights! Sound! The newest thing in mechanical toys—the Buddy "L" Greyhound Super-Bus. Wind its sturdy, spring motor and it runs straight ahead or in a circle. Automatically, magically, it stops—the door opens—a bell rings—the stoplight flashes—then the door closes, the light goes out, the bell stops ringing, and the bus travels on. All steel, 19½ in. long; rubber tires; shipping weight 5 lbs.

A31121 Price.................$3.90

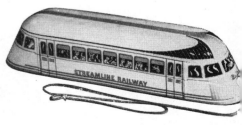

STREAMLINE RAILWAY

A streamlined pull-toy—a miniature reproduction of a modern street car. Complete with electric headlight that really lights and a real bell! The bell rings merrily—"ding-ding-ding-ding" as you pull the toy along. There's a switch for the headlight, too! Car is solidly made of metal, beautifully colored in Cream and Red striping. 17½ in. long, 4 in. wide. Comes with pull cord and hand-grip ring.

A31122 Price.................$1.40

HYDRAULIC DUMP

What a big, handsome, husky dump truck—and how perfectly it works! You can pull it, and you can ride it, indoors and out. Release the lever and hydraulic action raises the body and dumps the load. Thrust the body down and it locks in hauling position. All-steel construction, 26½ in. long; rubber tired wheels; brilliant enamel colors. Shipping weight, 17 lbs.

A30102 Price....................$9.50

LADDER FIRE TRUCK

Gong! Gong! Gangway, here comes the trailer-ladder fire truck ready to save lives. The ladders are raised and lowered by crane with exciting action. Red truck with yellow riders' seat. A clang of the bell clears the way. Has six rubber wheels. Can be pulled. Length 30 inches, width 5¾ inches, height 8¼ inches with ladder down. Shipping weight, 17 lbs.

A30103 Price....................$3.50

ARMY TRUCK AND TRAILER

Transport truck just like "Uncle Sam" uses. Streamlined; sturdy metal body with genuine canvas tops on both the truck and the trailer. In Olive-drab finish. Has six wheels. Trailer is detachable. Measurements: length 34½ inches, width 5¾ inches, height 9 inches. Shipping weight 6¾ lbs.

A30104 Price....................$2.80

TRUCK WITH TWO TRAILERS

Yes, you get the two trailers and the truck, combined in a caravan, shown above. Each trailer has removable top; large carrying capacity; rubber wheels. The caravan is 40 in. long, almost as long as the youngster is tall! Really triple-play value, for it provides three toys in one. Shipping weight, 15 lbs.

A30105 Price....................$4.50

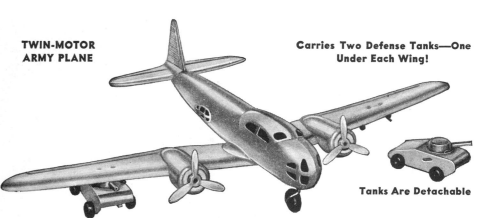

TWIN-MOTOR ARMY PLANE

Carries Two Defense Tanks—One Under Each Wing!

Tanks Are Detachable

ARMY TANK TRANSPORT

Contact! You're off, with two defense tanks to carry to the front lines. Streamlined, twin-motor plane with propellers that spin; U. S. insignia under wings. Equipped with radio aerial attachment. The two detachable army tanks, carried under the wings, have realistic motor hum device, revolving turrets. Have balloon-type rubber tires. Sturdily constructed and attractively finished. It's loads of fun attaching, transporting and detaching these action-tanks. Let the tanks roll along with humming motor and turn the turrets against the enemy. Measurements: Length 19¼ inches; wing span 27 inches; height 6¾ inches. Shipping weight, 4½ lbs.

A30106 Price....................$1.90

CEMENT MIXER

It actually mixes concrete or cement! Any boy or girl can operate it. The drum-loading scoop revolves, can be elevated or lowered for loading the mix into the drum. The drum can be turned for mixing, and dropped into the proper discharging position. The Buddy "L" mixer is 10½ in. long, 9½ in. wide, 9½ in. high, shipping weight 6 lbs.

A30108 Price....................$3.50

BIG GROCERY TRUCK

Here is a Buddy "L" Grocery Truck, loaded with miniature packages of nationally advertised foods. This is a big, all-steel truck nearly 22 in. long, a scale model of the husky International; has rubber tires. Finished in White and Yellow enamel; shipping weight 7 lbs.

A30109 Price....................$2.40

AUTO WRECKER

It's lots of fun to play with the Buddy "L" Auto Wrecker shown below. Big, husky truck of all-steel construction, finished in flashing enamel colors. It is 25¼ in. long; has rubber wheels. Complete with demountable crane, ready to lift and tow away any wreck on the highway! Shipping weight 6 lbs.

A30110 Price....................$1.75

PULL-'N'-RIDE IT!

This big, all-steel dump truck with removable seat and patented Buddy "L" pull and ride feature. It is over 21½ in. long, has rubber tired wheels, is a faithful scale model of the big, husky International dump trucks. What fun it is to pull it, then ride it! Shipping weight 7 lbs.

A30111 Price....................$2.40

OIL TANK TRUCK

Here is the familiar Shell tank truck. It looks just like the big oil company trucks. The rear of the tank opens; rubber tired wheels. This truck is 21½ in. long, 6¼ in. high, shipping weight 6½ lbs. It's built so strong that red-blooded youngsters just can't wreck it!

A30112 Price....................$1.75

Husky Pull or Ride 'Em Toys That Youngsters Love!

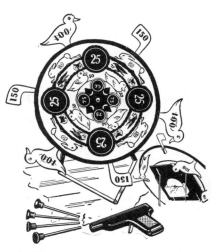

SUPERMAN KRYPTO-RAYGUN

Superman uses the Krypto-Raygun, and here it is! Pull the trigger and you flash on the wall, a full-length picture story of Superman's adventures! Projector gun complete with bulb, battery, genuine lenses and seven Superman adventure films—28 pictures on each!

A31313   Price Complete........................$1.40

REVOLVING TARGET SET

A mechanical shooting gallery! Entire target revolves automatically, with birds and pipes around the edge hinged so they topple and stay down when hit. The target is 15 in. wide, comes complete with key-wind spring motor, stand, safety pistol, and four darts with safety rubber suction tips.

A31314   Complete Set........................$1.4

TEXAS SIX-SHOOTER GUN, HOLSTER AND BELT

Pictured above is the most handsome gun outfit a young Texas Ranger ever wore! A repeating cap pistol, overall length 10 inches, with authentic action; fancy Ivoroy handle embossed with Longhorn steer heads; bright nickel barrel, authentically engraved; realistic breaking mechanism. The pistol comes in jeweled-leather holster, and that is not all! The outfit includes a leather belt with "ammunition" supply and jeweled ornament. Attractively boxed, ready for presentation.

A31312   Complete........................$2.80

MECHANICAL BATTLESHIP

It fires as it cruises! Just like a real battle cruiser—the aft gun battery fires harmless sparks —makes a noise like miniature pom-poms as the ship churns through the water. Just wind up the strong spring action, set the adjustable rudder and watch her cut through the water—guns barking. The ship is watertight metal, realistically painted in battleship gray. Propelled through the water by a real propeller. 14¼ in. long, 2¾ in. beam.

A31315   Price........................$1.40

HOLSTER SET AND PISTOL

Any red-blooded boy would be thrilled to own this Western holster outfit! Includes cap pistol, decorated holster, belt and cartridges. The gun is of all-metal construction. Holster and belt are top-grain leather artistically decorated with simulated precious stones and flashing metal trim. It's the kind the cowboys and rangers wear—in movies and fiction!

A31316   Price........................$1.4

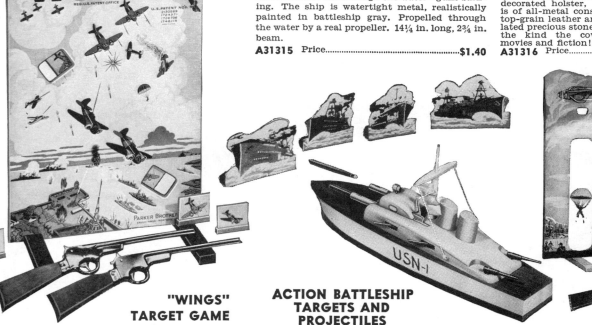

"WINGS" TARGET GAME

Here is the newest of the new—the target game of thrilling action! An invasion is on, the air is filled with enemy planes—and you're defending your country! Large colorful board 14½ in. wide, 20½ in. high, with concealed automatic action—invader planes showing in two windows. Set includes two automatic rifles and supply of ammunition. Two can shoot at a time! Everything complete for a thrilling, competitive game. It takes real "shooting" to knock those planes out of the air.

A30418   Complete, Price........................$2.80

ACTION BATTLESHIP TARGETS AND PROJECTILES

One of the outstanding features of the Toy Fair! A shooting battleship with four ship targets providing hours of fun for any boy. The battleship is 14 in. long, fitted with two shooting turret guns and six wood guns. The wood projectiles are fired at the opposing enemy fleet and a good marksman will destroy the enemy in no time at all. To add greater realism the battleship is equipped with flying pennants and searchlights, all ready for action. Complete with the four ship targets and projectiles.

A31317   Complete........................$1.65

PAR-A-SHOOT TARGET SET

Here's a target set that calls for fast shooting! It's a big target board, 18½x19¼ in., realistically colored. Has three hinge-mounted planes at the top. Three parachutists attach to the planes—when a plane is hit—its parachutist is released—floats down with a side-slipping motion that's hard to hit. Set includes spring-action pop-gun and supply of corks.

A30419   Price........................$1.40

DAISY AIR RIFLES

His first gun — there's no greater thrill for an active, outdoor boy! Make his first gun a safe, "straight-shooting" Daisy Air Rifle. Preferred by boys everywhere!

DAISY PUMP GUN 50-SHOT REPEATER

The above gun is the king of all air rifles, a 50-shot force feed repeater. It cocks easily by pulling the slide toward the stock. Has adjustable rear sight and non-slip grooves on the butt of the pistol grip. The stock is solid American Walnut. All metal parts are in gun-blue finish with beautiful gold-colored jacket, handsomely engraved. This is a take-down model, 37 inches long weighing 3¼ lbs. A hard hitting, straight shooting, repeating air rifle with all the Daisy features that mean so much in safety, accuracy, durability, and general all-around shooting performance.

A30421   Price...$6.90

DAISY BUCK JONES SPECIAL 60-SHOT

The Daisy Buck Jones Special is a handsome and efficient 60-shot pump-action repeater sponsored by Buck Jones himself. It bears his name beautifully engraved right in the jacket. Genuine sundial and compass are built right into the natural hardwood stocks. Wherever you travel, in field or forest, you'll always know your directions, and have the correct time by the sun! An air rifle that boys everywhere prefer. It has a safety bar that prevents accidental discharge. 36 in. long, weighs 2½ lbs. A grand gift for year 'round fun.

A30422   Price...$5.50

NEW LIGHTNING-LOADER 500-SHOT CARBINE
With Adjustable Double-Notch Rear Sight

The great, new Daisy 500-Shot Lightning-Loading Carbine, with features not found on any other rifle. It looks, feels and shoots like the powerful carbines used by Buffalo Bill and other famous Frontier Scouts. Completely equipped with the first and only lightning-loader shot magazine in air rifle history—and—a new adjustable double-notch rear sight! Made of blued gun-steel, with walnut finish fore piece and pistol-grip stock. Heavy metal strap holds the magazine tube under the main barrel in real carbine style. Every boy wants one . . . every boy deserves one!

A30423   Price...$3.90

DAISY "TARGETEER" SET

Step up and try your skill! You can shoot indoors or out. Outfit consists of Daisy targeteer air pistol, metal tube of 500 shot, set of "spinner" targets and Handipad of 25 Daisy cards, in a box, which is a shooting range in itself. For still more fun, order the bell target, that rings the bell when you score a bull's-eye, and with a heavy, armor-plate backstop that deadens all shot. Bell target is 4½ in. square, comes with 12 extra target cards.

A30424   Targeteer Pistol $2.80
A30425   Bell Target and 12 Cards..................................   .35
A30426   Tube of 500 Shot...   .15

TOY SUB-MACHINE GUN WITH SOUND EFFECT

Just like the models used by parachute troopers! This toy machine gun sounds just like the real thing. Cartridge drum revolves when you pull the trigger—makes a sharp "rat-tat-tat" noise. Solid wood shoulder stock; barrel and drum are rolled metal, brightly colored in Red, Yellow, Blue and Black. Over 25 inches long.

A30427   Price...$1.65

COAST ARTILLERY CANNON

A big "Bertha" cannon modelled after the giant coast defense guns. Gun is mounted on a metal platform, has spring mechanism that shoots wooden projectiles! Gun barrel and breech block are solid wood. Has range finder, elevating mechanism, swings from left to right. Button release "shoots" the cannon. A harmless, fascinating toy—children love to aim the cannon by using the gunner's peep sight. Cannon is 15 in. long; overall length 18 in. Elevates to 10 in. high! Complete with set of wood projectiles.

A30428   Price......................................$1.40

"BING-BANG" CANNON
Uses Harmless Ammunition

Every boy wants one—it's a big noise maker. Every parent approves it—it's 100% safe. A reproduction of a full-size army field gun 17 in. long. No matches, no gun powder, but a big Bang! You can fire the cannon hundreds of times for a few pennies. The ammunition is non-poisonous, non-inflammable. It combines with water, making a harmless gas that causes the Bang. Comes complete with one tube of ammunition. Makes a grand companion piece for the "Big-Bang" Tank shown at the left. Tank is of heavy cast metal finished in Army Olive drab color. Big-Bang cannon mounted in the turret uses same ammunition as cannon shown above. Tank has smaller turret in rear, rides on four solid rubber wheels. Size 9½ in. long, 4 in. wide, 4¾ in. high.

A30429   Field Cannon (above)................$3.50
A30430   Tank (at left)............................... 2.80
A30431   Ammunition for Both..............   .20

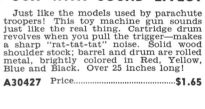

WITH FLYING PLANES WITH MECHANICAL ACTION "KEYSTONE TOY"

AIRCRAFT CARRIER

A scale model aircraft carrier of solid wood with realistically painted deck, superstructure and masts. Has cannons fore and aft, make-believe searchlight. **ACTUALLY CATAPULTS PLANES INTO THE AIR!** Spring-action catapult launches the two planes, shown on deck, into the air. Ship is 16 in. long, has 4 in. beam, 7¼ in. high. Each of the two planes is 3 in. long.

A30432   Price.................................$1.65

NEW *GILBERT ERECTOR* SETS

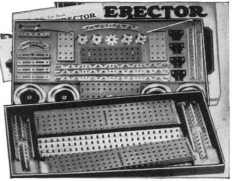

NUMBER 3½

An intermediate set for young builders. Completely re-designed and modernized, this Erector has large base plates, angle girders, big wheels. Erector is the only construction toy with the square, easy-to-fasten girder. It's amazing to watch youngsters build working models of derricks, walking beam engines, bridges, trucks and many other interesting models. Set comes complete with "How-to-Make-'Em" Book, packed in gift box. Weighs 5 lbs.

A30208 Price.............$5.00

Make Him Happy This Christmas With an Erector Set

WORLD-FAMOUS ERECTOR No. 4½

This famous Gilbert Erector set, completely modernized, comes with a powerful electric motor. No extra wires, batteries or transformer are needed. Motor plugs into any socket. Construction parts include many types of girders, large wheels, motor bearings, base plates, miniature bridge-tenders or watchman's house brilliantly colored. With this set the young builder is a construction engineer on a bridge-building job one day—a trip-hammer and horizontal engine expert the next. Many other things to build fully explained in "How-to-Make-'Em" Book. Set is packed in gift box, size 18x10¼ in., weighs 8 lbs.

A30209 Price.............$7.20

NUMBER 8½ ERECTOR

In tune with this mechanical age, the "America" model Erector set, shown above, is equipped to build working scale models of an oil drilling rig, lift bridge, crane and derrick with magnetic pick-up, mammoth Ferris Wheel and hundreds of other fascinating models. Powerful electric motor operates on AC current direct from the light socket, has forward and reverse speeds. Cleverly realistic whistle device fits direct to motor—sounds just like factory whistle! Complete set includes lights, miniature house, base plates, girders, gears, wheels, many of these brilliantly colored. This set has everything! Comes with "How-to-Make-'Em" Book; packed in Red enameled permanent steel cabinet size 20¼x12¼ in., weight 19 lbs. A gift that will bring years of thrilling fun!

A30207 Price..$18.80

Best Seller "America" Model Erector Set — A Real Gift for "Real" Boys!

Head and Hands Keep Profitably Busy With an Erector Kit!

Every Boy Wants to Be an Erector Engineer

A working model of a Dock Hoist built with an Erector kit. No greater thrill for a boy than to see a model, built with his own hands, work just like a full-size machine.

An Erector-built horizontal engine that really works! Each Erector set comes with all the necessary parts to build many fascinating models; instructions in "How-to-Make-'Em" Book.

This is the famous Erector Ferris Wheel—a marvel of miniature scale construction. It works perfectly, is a source of never-ending thrills.

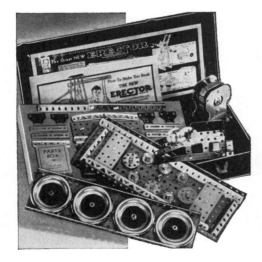

ERECTOR SET No. 6½

Every boy will find all the thrills and adventures of being an Erector engineer in the outstanding kit shown above. This electrified set will build a windmill pump, a new type airplane beacon, lift bridge, merry-go-round and dozens of other interesting models. Full power electric motor included with this set operates on AC current direct from the light socket. Needs **no extra transformer.** Gears, pulley, pinions, everything you need to transmit power is included. Base plates, assorted girders, four large wheels, miscellaneous parts and motor mount are all included. Set also has miniature house for bridge tender, ticket seller, watchman. Complete with "How-to-Make-'Em" Book, everything packed in sturdy metal cabinet; size 16¼x8¼ in., weighing 10 lbs. A gift that will give a boy many years of engrossing fun—fun that will be remembered a lifetime.

A30210 Price...$11.50

De LUXE ERECTOR No. 9½

The big new DeLuxe Erector shown above will build automobiles, trucks and other working models—just what every boy wants! Set comes complete with an electric motor with gear shift for Forward, Reverse and Stop. Motor operates on AC current direct from light socket; **needs no transformer.** Large supply of base plates, girders, gears, wheels and other parts make possible the construction of a giant power plant, elevator, huge walking beam engine and many other thrilling, working models.

This extra-large, DeLuxe equipped Erector set comes packed in a permanent steel cabinet with carrying handles and metal lid fasteners. Overall size: 22x13 in., weighs 26 lbs. A gift that will delight any boy!

A30211 Price...$26.00

CHEMISTRY

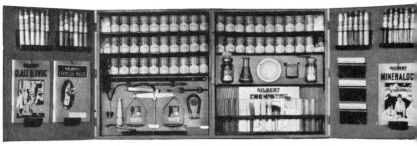

GILBERT NUMBER TEN

Shown above is Gilbert's complete chemist's laboratory with more than 100 pieces, including chemicals and equipment, all neatly arranged in a large, wooden laboratory cabinet. Overall size: 14½x39 in. Set is complete with three big books explaining chemistry, scientific magic, chemical experiments, and glass blowing.

A30213 Price..$14.50

GILBERT MASTER CHEMISTRY LAB

Finest of all Gilbert chemistry sets— a complete chemist's laboratory with chemicals, apparatus and equipment for experiments, glass blowing, mineralogy and chemical magic. This lab has everything the young scientist could want. Material enough to conduct more than 800 experiments in refrigeration, electro-chemistry, electro-plating, food testing, etching, etc.

Laboratory equipment with this set includes scales, alcohol lamp, flask, beaker, gas generator, thermometer, test-tubes and stand and four complete instruction manuals. Packed in all-wood laboratory cabinet measuring 51½x14½ in. Weighs 15 lbs. The perfect gift for the youngster with an inquiring mind.

A30214 Price..................................$21.80

GILBERT SENIOR CHEMISTRY SET

Imagine making colored fire! Testing foods for their elements! Making real cement! Making sparklers, soda water! All are easy to do with the 63-piece set of chemicals and apparatus shown at the right. Set includes Chemistry manual and Glass Blowing manual that explain more than 400 exciting experiments. Laboratory comes packed in two-door, blue wooden cabinet that has five feet of metal shelf room and test-tube racks. Cabinet stands upright, measures 26x14½ inches.

A30216 Price.......................$7.25

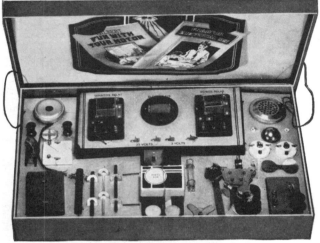

GILBERT ELECTRICAL SET
Build Telephone Receiver—Electric Motors

Gilbert's sensational new electric set includes a sensitive microphone, electric magic-eye device, telegraph key, mystifying magnetic set and telephone receiver. The set has parts enough to build two complete electric motors. Three big illustrated books tell how to build many other interesting models and devices, and show how to conduct fascinating experiments with electricity and magnetism. Watch your youngster's eyes light up when he sees this big kit, jammed full of entertaining and educational fun. Packed in substantial gift box, size 20½x13½ in.

A30215 Price..$14.50

Every Boy Is a Scientist at Heart!

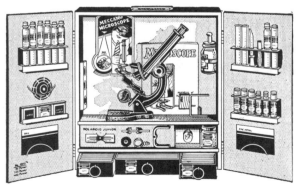

FIRST CHEMISTRY SET

Gilbert's intermediate chemistry kit, shown at the left, is ideal for the beginning amateur chemist. The laboratory type cabinet holds 49 pieces, including chemicals and apparatus; enough to conduct 345 exciting experiments, such as cleaning silver electrically, making ammonia, etc. Everything explained in a big Chemistry manual. Double-door, wood laboratory cabinet has test tube racks, three feet of metal shelf space. Cabinet stands upright when in use, measures 19¾x 14⅝ in.

A30217 Price.....................................$5.00

Polaroid Equipped MICROSCOPES by Gilbert

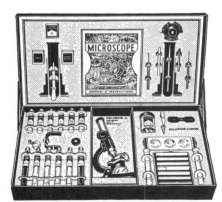

GILBERT No. 5 — 210 POWER

New and improved Gilbert microscope set shown above is the world's best for intermediate boy and girl scientists. The Polaroid equipped microscope has magnifying power up to 210 diameters, opens wide the door to a new wonderland invisible to the naked eye! Microscope has electric sub-stage light that gives correct illumination at all times. Set has 38 pieces of apparatus, chemicals and equipment including slides, specimens, stains, dissecting kit, large dissecting piece with magnifying lens, and illustrated manual showing how to do 213 experiments. Packed in box size 18x10x2½ in.

A30218 Price..$7.25

GILBERT SUPREME — 400 POWER

Complete scientific laboratory in a de luxe wooden cabinet includes a professional type Polaroid equipped microscope. The precision built microscope has three objective lenses, turret mounted, with magnification power up to 400 diameters, and sub-stage electric light. Set includes bench microtome for preparing slide sections, alcohol lamp, chemicals, stains, full supply of specimens, four piece magnifying unit, two dissecting needles and other equipment. This kit is complete in every detail—especially adapted for advanced work. Comes in wooden cabinet, size: 14½x26 inches.

A30219 Price..$14.50

GILBERT No. 3 — 200 POWER

Popular priced microscope outfit featuring a Polaroid equipped microscope, magnification up to 200 diameters, electric sub-stage light, rack and pinion focusing and spring clips on both sides of stage. An ideal set for the beginner. Start your youngster on this fascinating hobby. Complete set includes explanatory manual, a prepared slide and extra slides, cover glasses, dissecting needles, chemicals and stains, and a large stock of specimens. Packed in cardboard cabinet. Size: 15¾x10 inches.

A30220 Price..$5.00

MODEL AIRPLANE KITS
Build and Fly Scale-Model Planes
Gas-Motor or Rubber-Motor Types

"KINGFISHER" 60-72-INCH GAS MODEL
The Sensational Flying Model Plane Kit!

Build 'em with your own hands—watch them fly—and you'll get the thrill of a lifetime! But it's more than fun—even though there's plenty of that. You learn the basic theories of aero-dynamics—you discover what keeps the big stratoliners in flight—you become familiar with the principles of aircraft design. It's so easy . . . so much fun . . . you'll enjoy every minute you can spare for this fascinating hobby! Age limits? There aren't any—millions of youngsters from 7 to 70 fill the ranks of America's flying-model-plane enthusiasts. If you're a beginner, start with one of the kits on the bottom of this page—if you've built them before—the famous "Kingfisher" above is your "meat."

COMPLETE "KINGFISHER" KIT. . . . The finest, most accurate, and easiest to follow full-scale plans, detailed drawings, plus everything you need to build this marvelous flying-model-plane—with material for 60 and 72 in. wing spans. Can be easily and quickly converted to a seaplane and back again to a land plane. Accurate, sturdy construction details make it a flying wonder, with long-distance, sustained flight; right-side-up stability; and crash-proof landing features. Use any model 7/8-in. bore gasoline engine. Kit designed by Joe Ott, former U. S. Army aviation instructor.

A31350 Complete Kit (Without Motor)..$7.00

A.M.A. CLASS "B" MOTOR
Easiest Starting Miniature
Motor—Weighs 4¾ Oz.

Just the power plant you need for your model plane! Packs a real punch in a tiny space. Precision built, machined to micrometer accuracy, pretested, partially assembled — takes only a few minutes to complete. Super-charged carburetion, will not flood. Latest design—outpulls, outlifts and outflies any motor in its price class—a favorite with model-flying contest winners. More power, more speed with less weight—only 4¾ oz. Bore 13/16 in., stroke 9/16 in.; displacement .292. Complete with spark plug. Coil and condenser not included.

A31351 Price....................$6.70

"SKY CHIEF" CLASS "C" MOTOR
Block Tested—13,000 RPM

You'll get top-flight performance with this sensational precision-built, block-tested, two-cycle gasoline engine. Every detail is perfectly designed, accurately constructed and thoroughly tested for maximum performance and efficiency. Built to stand up under severe conditions—with quality features found only in motors costing twice our low price. Lightning 3-oz. coil, balanced with condenser to assure quick starting; positive-firing timer cam; vibration-proof carburetor; adjustment needle-valve; micro-lapped piston with Perfect Circle ring. Multiple-finned cylinder of Molybdenum iron; heat-treated steel time-shaft; transparent, non-breakable, non-inflammable gas tank. Bore 7/8 in.; stroke 7/8 in.; displacement .526. 13,000 R.P.M., capable of 1/5 H.P. Complete with coil and condenser, weighs 10 oz.

A31352 Completely Assembled $10.60

LONG-FLYING GAS-MOTOR MODEL PLANE

Build and fly your own gas model! This perfect 48-in. Gas King Jr., engineered by the famous Joe Ott for record-breaking flights, is easy to assemble. The blue prints supplied are full size, complete with construction sketches and detailed instructions. Entire motor assembly is mounted on a sliding skid that can be removed from the fuselage, making all motor parts accessible for testing and adjusting. The plane you'll build from this kit will really amaze you! Complete with all necessary parts, including wood, wing covering, wheels, propeller, cement, landing gear wire, etc. Uses any gas motor with ½ in. or 5/8 in. bore.

A31353 Complete Kit (Without Motor)..$3.50

MODELED AFTER FAMOUS SPEED PLANE

Watch this racer in flight—and you'll be more thrilled than ever with the results of your own handiwork. An exact-scale miniature of the famous Turner Racer that has won two Thompson trophies. Full 50-in. wing span provides super-lifting power, perfectly balanced long-distance flights, and stable performance. Contains full-scale blueprints and detailed instructions. Also every piece you need from wood forms, braces, wing covering, wheels, landing gear, propeller, cement, and motor mount. Thrills galore and contest-winning endurance flights! Uses gas motor with ½ in. to 5/8 in. bore.

A31354 Complete Kit (Without Motor)...$3.50

75% of Assembly Problems Eliminated by New System of Die-Cut Formers

FOUR "JOE OTT" RUBBER MOTOR KITS
Including New Patented Die-Cut Formers

Four popular favorites! Each a perfect reproduction of its famous military namesake, built to true-scale dimensions. The planes that are making military aviation history with their amazing performance. Build 'em—and see them actually fly with all the tricky maneuvers typical of the fighter planes of today. The kit for each plane contains everything necessary for its construction—full-sized blueprints, detailed instructions; formers stamped on wood with centers die-cut, as illustrated below; Balsa strip stringers, framework, ribs, body and wing covering; propeller, cement, wheels, etc. So simple and so easy to build! Powered by a special rubber-band motor included with kit.

A31355 45-In. Spitfire Plane $1.40
A31356 42-In. Cessna Plane 1.40
A31357 45-In. Lockheed Plane 1.40
A31358 42-In. Lysander Plane 1.40

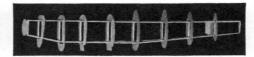

Extremely simple to build! The formers are printed on heavy fiberboard with centers die-cut. All you do is cut the outside shape with a pair of scissors, build the body foundation frame of Balsa with the strips furnished to size, and cement the stringers in prepared notches cut in the formers. The three easy steps illustrated above show you how.

"027" TRAINS ARE COMPLETE WITH TRANSFORMERS

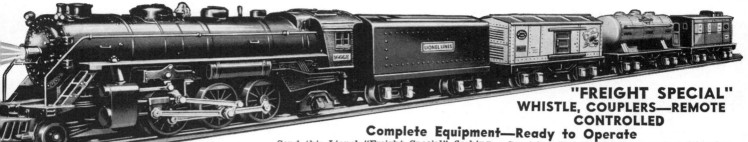

"FREIGHT SPECIAL"
WHISTLE, COUPLERS—REMOTE CONTROLLED

Complete Equipment—Ready to Operate

- **Massive 6-Wheel Drive Locomotive and Tender with or without Built-In Remote Control Whistle.**
- **Realistic Box Car, Gondola Car and Caboose.**
- **8 Sections Curved Track, 3 Sections Straight Track, 1 Section Remote Control Track, Forms Oval 27½x 45¼ Inches.**
- **Dual Control Transformer.**
- **Complete Train 45½ Inches Long.**

Send this Lionel "Freight Special" flashing around the tracks. Blow the whistle to clear the road and brake her as you approach the yards—you'll get real railroading thrills that can't be beat. Without moving an inch you can set up your control station and make the train start, stop, reverse, slow down or speed up. Drop a car or couple another without stopping your train or moving away from your station. The powerful 6-wheel drive locomotive and every car is faithfully reproduced in scale from the actual equipment used on America's great railroads. This handsome Lionel "Freight

Special" will deliver thrill-packed, exciting fun to youngsters from 7 to 70.

EQUIPMENT: 6-wheel drive locomotive and tender with or without remote control whistle, box car, gondola car and caboose, all with 4-wheel trucks and remote control couplers. Eight sections of curved, three sections straight, one section remote control track, lock-on and dual control transformer. Track forms an oval 27½x45¼ inches. Complete train measures 45½ inches long.

A30121   Complete, No Whistle.................$18.00
A30122   Complete With Whistle.............. 23.00

LIONEL "SUPER-FREIGHT"

- **6-Wheel Drive Locomotive and Tender with Built-In Remote Control Whistle.**
- **Box Car, Tank Car, Caboose and Tender with Remote Control Couplers.**
- **Pair of Electric Remote Control Switches.**
- **10 Sections Curved Track, 5 Sections Straight Track, 1 Section Remote Control Track.**
- **Transformer and Controls for Whistle and Switches.**
- **Forms Oval Within an Oval as Illustrated—Train 45½ Inches Long.**

Without buying a single piece of additional equipment, this set gives you everything needed to start operating your own complete railroad system. With the remote control feature, you can pick up steam and send this "Super Freight" flashing down the rails. Switch over to a siding, drop a car, swing back on to the main line, pick up an empty and signal your arrival or departure with official railroad code blasts on the locomotive whistle. Build your own line in a great variety of track layouts, with electrically operated switches that more than double the fun of model railroading. Every-

thing is operated by remote control, and if you haven't had the thrill of directing a model railroad with fingertip button control, you've missed a real sensation!

EQUIPMENT: 6-wheel drive locomotive with electric headlight, tender with built-in remote control whistle, box car, tank car, caboose and tender all with remote control couplers, ten sections curved track, five sections straight track, one section remote control track, TWO REMOTE CONTROL SWITCHES, transformer, lock-on connector.

A30123   Complete..$33.65

NEW LIONEL "RAIL KING"
Remote Control Electric Coupling—Whistle—Action Cars

Chock-Full of Action and Thrills

- **6-Wheel Drive Locomotive and Tender.**
- **Built-In Remote Control Whistle.**
- **5 Action Cars with Electric Couplers.**
- **Electric Lumber Car Unloads by Remote Control.**
- **Touch a Button—Gondola Car Unloads by Itself.**
- **Floodlight Car with Electric Searchlight.**
- **Swinging Crane Car with Movable Ball and Tackle.**
- **2 Track-Side Unloading Bins with Miniature Logs and Barrels.**
- **8 Sections Curved Track, 5 Sections Straight Track, 1 Section Remote Control Track.**
- **Multi-Control Transformer to Operate Whistle, Couplers, Action Cars and Regulate Train Speed.**
- **Track Equipment Forms Oval 27½x54 Inches. Complete Train 60½ Inches Long.**

Here is a spectacular railroad system that will deliver more thrills, more excitement, and more action per minute than any set we've ever seen for as much as twice what this costs. The Lionel "Rail King" is an exact reproduction of the super-freighters that roar across the country. You get real action and lots of it with this outfit. By pressing a button at your remote control station, you can unload the flat car and dump the barrels from the gondola as illustrated at the right. When there's trouble along the "right-of-way," rush the crane car and searchlight car to the scene and there you have the identical equipment that the "Big 10" railroad systems use in clearing wrecks and trouble shooting. The searchlight throws a powerful realistic beam. The crane car cab can be swung from side to side while the tackle is raised or lowered. All cars couple and uncouple by remote control.

A30124   Complete..$36.65

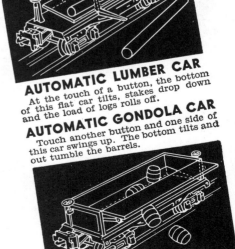

AUTOMATIC LUMBER CAR
At the touch of a button, the bottom of this flat car tilts, stakes drop down and the load of logs rolls off.

AUTOMATIC GONDOLA CAR
Touch another button and one side of this car swings up. The bottom tilts and out tumble the barrels.

MORE FUN! New LIONEL

Double or triple the fun and thrills of Lionel electric train operation with these exciting, true-to-life accessories! All can be used with "O" and "O27" gauge tracks.

CROSSOVER

This right-angle, 90 degree crossover is a great help in making your track layouts much more interesting. "O27" gauge is 7¾ in. square. "O" gauge 8⅜ in. square.

A30140   "O27" Gauge..........$1.35
A30141   "O" Gauge..............2.35

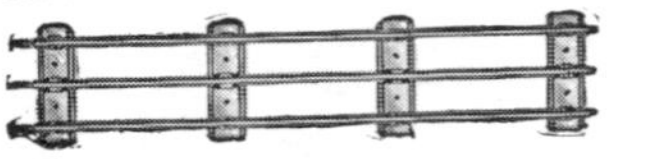

STRAIGHT TRACK

Strong enough to hold the weight of an adult. "O27" track 8⅞ in. long. "O" track 10⅞ in. long. Priced singly—order as many as you wish.

A30142   "O27" Track Section $0.20
A30143   "O" Track Section 0.27

CURVED TRACK

Eight sections form complete circle. "O27" gauge track section is 9½ in. long. The "O" gauge 10 in. long.

A30144   "O27" Track Section $0.20
A30145   "O" Track Section 0.27

REMOTE CONTROL TRACK SET

Special section of 5-rail track—operates electric couplers and unloading mechanism in remote control freight cars. Two-button controller with 30 in. of connecting cable.

A30146   "O27" Track Set....$1.65
A30147   "O" Track Set........ 2.00

MANUAL SWITCHES

Switches operated by hand. Sold by the pair, one left and one right. "O27" switches are 9⅛ inches long. "O" switches are 10½ inches long. Each has automatic signal light.

A30148   Pair "O27" Switches $3.65
A30149   Pair "O" Switches 9.65

ELECTRO-MAGNETIC CRANE
A Miracle of Remote Control Action

Press a button—the winch lowers the block and tackle to any pile of miniature steel. Press another button, the magnet head is energized, gripping the steel while the cab and boom swings around to unload it in a waiting car. So fascinating is the operation of this thrilling crane you will spend hours putting it through its paces. Remote controls include knob for magnetizing the metal block, to revolve the cab in a complete circle, to move the boom, and to raise or lower the block and tackle. A light in the cab indicates when the magnet is energized. A bag of steel scrap and a receiving bin are included. The crane is 10 inches high, rigidly constructed on a base 6x6½ inches.

A30154   Price..$11.95

REMOTE CONTROL BASCULE BRIDGE
TRAIN PROTECTION FEATURE!

Automatic bascule bridge operates completely by remote control. From any place in the room, just press the button and the bridge rises to allow river traffic to pass. While the bridge is rising, your train will automatically stop at the bridge entrance—protecting the train from wrecks just as the real bridges do. Touch another button, the bridge is lowered and the train automatically proceeds over the bridge and on its way. The bridge is 21½ inches long, 8¼ inches high.

A30156   Price..$15.95

REMOTE CONTROL SWITCHES

The finest switches in the Lionel line—operate entirely by remote control. Automatically throw switch to correct position when train approaches in reverse, preventing derailment. Each switch has Red and Green signal light with corresponding set of lights on switch controller. Switch motor can be mounted on either side. Sold only in pairs of one right and one left hand switch.

A30150   Pair "O27" Switches............................$ 9.00
A30151   Pair "O" Switches.............................. 15.95

COAL ELEVATOR
Motor-Driven Conveyor—Loads and Unloads by Remote Control

Yes, sir, it actually loads your model freight cars remote control. Load the hopper in the base of t structure with coal and from then on electricity does t rest, controlled by your fingertip. The coal is scooped by tiny buckets on an endless chain, lifted to the t of the loft and dumped into the bunker. At the touch a button, the stored coal pours down through the chu into your waiting freight car. The elevator is 12½ inch high, solidly constructed on a base 7x10 inches. A sup of artificial coal is included with each elevator.

A30155   Price..................................$11.

LOADS LUMBER ELECTRICALLY
Remote Control—Continuous Action

Step up the action of your miniature railroad with thrilling log-loader that loads and unloads miniat logs completely by electricity through remote cont Freight cars are loaded from the platform in the rear, lumber loader picking up the logs from receiving bin dropping them on to the loading platform. At the to of a remote control button, the logs roll down from loading platform into the waiting car. Spot this act accessory between two track sidings, receive logs from loaded cars on one side and load them into empty on the other side. Complete unit is 9 inches high, inches wide, 10¾ inches deep. Ample supply of logs cluded.

A30157   Price..................................$12.

CROSSING SIGNAL

As train approaches—this signal flashes alternate red lights warning all traffic of railroad crossing. Stops after train has passed. Nine inches high. Illustrated at left.

A30152   Price..............$3.35

BLOCK SIGNAL

Operates two trains on one track. When one train approaches the other, a signal flashes Red and stops rear train. First train advances safe distance, automatically flashing Green light signal allowing rear train to proceed. Illustrated at right.

A30153   Price..............$4.35

ccessories with ACTION!

COAL CAR—REMOTE CONTROL

This coal dump-car has a built-in electro-magnetic device that dumps, couples and uncouples the car by remote control. Touch a button on the controller at any distance from the track—the car bottom tilts and dumps out the contents. While your train is traveling around the track, touch another button and uncouple the car from the rest of the train and couple it again whenever you wish. Complete with plastic bin and sack of "coal".

A30168 Price...$5.30

LIONEL 5-IN-1 TRANSFORMER
"TRAINMASTER"—AMERICA'S BEST
Choice of Four Powers—75, 100, 150 or 200 Watt

the best performance throughout your
ture railroad system—get a Lionel trans-
r and you will have the best. The Lionel
nmaster" is a single-controlled unit that
rs the service of five. Every advanced fea-
is built into the "Trainmaster"—multiple
ts, built-in circuit breakers, input indi-
, voltage gauges and rheostat sensitivity
ut the use of a rheostat. "Trainmaster"
and panels are handsomely styled, pat-
d after the modern central-load dispatch-
oards. Each has chromium dial face with
d markings, jewels that light, one to indi-
when the power is on, the other when a
exists in the layout.

UILT-IN CIRCUIT BREAKERS

en a short occurs, the built-in circuit
er cuts off the current to protect the trans-
r and when the short has been corrected,
ircuit breaker automatically resets itself.
c knobs and signal jewels are easily re-

moved for lamp replacements. The Lionel "Trainmaster" transformer controls current in quarter-
volt steps offering every train speed from a crawl
to a flash. The dial shows voltage and speed in
scale miles per hour. The 75 watt transformer
will operate any single train set without too
many accessories. However, the larger your railroad system, the more powerful transformer is
needed.

THE BIG "250 WATTER"

The 250 watt "Trainmaster" is the outstanding transformer made. Big, handsome in appearance and ready to handle the largest train
layout you could set up—it's a real super-power
control station!

A30160	75 Watt	$ 7.95
A30161	100 Watt	11.95
A30162	150 Watt	15.95
A30163	250 Watt	19.35

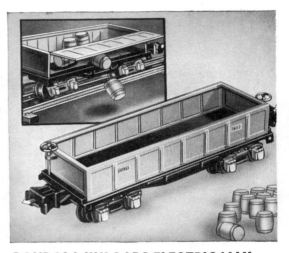

GONDOLA UNLOADS ELECTRICALLY

Couple this new car to your train and enjoy added thrills. At the touch of a remote control button, the side lifts and the barrel replicas tumble out. These tiny barrels can be opened and filled with freight at one end of the track—shipped to a distant point and delivered just where you wish. The car 6½ inches long, 2¼ inches high is complete with electric couplers, unloading bin and 12 barrels.

A30169 Price...$5.30

LIONEL CRANE—TO THE RESCUE
Vital to Right-of-Way Maintenance

A necessary piece of service equipment in all yards for clearing tracks in case of wrecks. Equipped with remote control electric couplers—touch a button at your control station and the car uncouples from the train or couples to it, as you command. The boom is raised or lowered by means of the wheel on the back of the cab. The tackle is controlled by the wheel at the side. Cab and crane can be turned from side to side. Length 8¾ inches.

A30166 Price...$6.00

UTOMATIC GATEMAN

e gateman remains inside his
ful shack with door closed—
1 train approaches, the door
s and the gateman rushes out,
ging his illuminated lantern.
train passes, he returns to his
k and door closes. Operates en-
automatically.

64 Price................................$5.30

WHISTLE-STATION

a attractive station with Lionel's
us whistle built into one unit.
whistle operates at the touch
a button. Station size, 5½x4
es; height, 3¾ inches. Bril-
tly colored.

165 Price................................$4.65

FLOODLIGHT CAR

One of the most popular cars built by Lionel for any train that runs on "0" or "027" tracks. Darken the room—send your train whizzing around the track and see this floodlight car get into action, focusing its brilliant light on the roadbed or siding. Floodlight with polished metal reflector can be swung from side to side, up or down, to throw a beam of light in any direction. The giant floodlight is mounted in the center of a sturdy flat bed car with side railings. Car is 6½ inches long and comes complete with bulb. Your present train set deserves this addition.

A30167 Price...$5.00

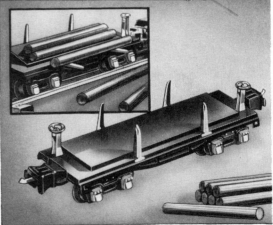

LUMBER CAR—UNLOADS BY ITSELF

Electrically operated flat car with nickeled stakes that hold a real load of logs. At the touch of a remote control button, the bottom of the car tilts and the logs roll off into the waiting bin. Car also couples and uncouples by remote control. Lumber car is 6½ inches long, 2¼ inches high and is complete with miniature logs and unloading bin. The thrilling action of this electrically oper-ated, remote control lumber car will give you many hours of real enjoyment.

A30170 Price...$5.30

NEWEST *LIONEL* ELECTRIC TRAINS—POPULAR "O" GAUG

NEW FEATURES!

● Die Cast 4-Wheel Drive Locomotive and Tender, 16 Inches Long.
● Built-In Remote Control Whistle.
● Lumber Car, Oil Tank, Caboose.
● Remote Control Couplers on Cars.
● 8 Sections Curved Track, 1 Section Straight Track, 1 Section Remote Control Track.
● Whistle Controller and Lock-On.

Neither boy nor man can resist the thrills of piloting this handsome monarch of the rails with its brilliant, true-to-scale freight cars. This Lionel "Through-Freight" is the choice of model railroaders everywhere, built from actual blue prints of the giant locomotives that serve the nation. Here is the ideal start of a railroad system that you can expand into an elaborate layout. With a light touch of a button, you get this train under way, pick up speed and swing around the curve with all the realism of big-time railroading. Slow down and drop or pick up any car on the go, back up and then start off again with a blast of the whistle—all by remote control.

"LIONEL THROUGH-FREIGH

Built-In Whistle—Electric Coupl
Thrilling Action—Fingertip Contro

EQUIPMENT: The husky, die cast locomo has a powerful 4-wheel drive and focused e tric headlight. Locomotive tender is loaded realistic coal and has the famous Lionel buil locomotive whistle. Flat car has shipmen miniature logs, and all cars have remote co couplers. The eight sections of curved track, section of straight track and one section of mote control track form an oval 41x31 inc Train is 42½ inches long. Push-button wh controller is included. Transformer should ordered separately from page 557.

A30125 Price...$2

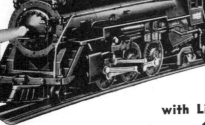

"TRANSCONTINENTAL"
Lionel Pullman Train
with Lighted Cars—Electric Couplers—Whistle

Sidetrack the freight and high-ball the famous Lionel "Transcontinental" pulling its three Pullman cars across the country. Here is a train that will go streaking around the tracks in true express-passenger style. Darken the room and watch the headlight beam cut through the darkness, trailed by the gleaming lights from the Pullman windows. There's vivid realism for you! The locomotive, tender and each of the three Pullman cars are masterpieces of faithful reproduction, duplicating the big trains with amazing accuracy.

A30126 Price........................$33.65

● 6-Wheel Drive Locomotive and Tender, 17¼ Inches Long with Built-In Remote Control Whistle.
● 3 Illuminated Pullman Cars —One with Observation Platform in Rear. All with Electric Couplers.
● 8 Sections Curved Track, 5 Sections Straight Track, 1 Section Remote Control.
● Lock-On & Whistle Control.
● Track Oval 61x31 Inches. Complete Train 63 Inches. See Pg. 557 for Transformer.

What Is "O" Gauge?

"O" gauge is a standard of model railroaders and indicates a distance of 1¼ in. between the outside running rails of the track. Eight curved sections of "O" gauge track form a circle 28⅝ in. across. While "O" and "O27" train equipment can be used interchangeably on "O" track, the "O" track is slightly higher than "O27." Thus both tracks cannot be joined.

LIONEL
"EXPRESS FREIGHT"
with Electro-Magnet Crane
Built-In Whistle—Remote Control Couplers

Spot this amazing electro-magnetic crane at one end of your railroad system. Press buttons and the steel is carried from the pile, loaded on to the gondolas or flat car, and the Lionel "Express Freight" is on its way. The rugged magnetic crane will lift steel beams, swing them around and lower them, as you operate the push-button controls. The train is equally responsive to your wishes—start, speed up, slow down, stop or reverse by fingertip remote control. All remote control equipment is included. Order transformer from page 557.

A30127 Price..........................$43.35

DE LUXE EQUIPMENT
● Triple-Action Remote Control Electro-Magnet Crane.
● 6-Wheel Drive Locomotive and Tender with Remote Control Whistle.
● Lumber Car, 2 Gondola Cars, Caboose, All with Remote Control Couplers.
● 8 Sections Curved Track, 3 Straight, 1 Remote Control, Forming Oval 51x31 In.
● Whistle Control & Lock-On.
● Complete Train 52½ Inches.

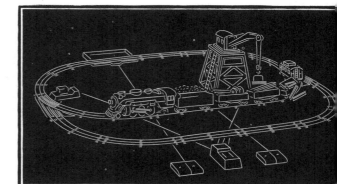

The layout illustrated above with the electro-magnet crane or siding is only one of the many track arrangements you can bu Order the Lionel "Express Freight" listed at the left, plus additio sections of "O" gauge track and a pair of switches—you'll have ever thing necessary to set up this and many other interesting layouts

LINCOLN LOGS
America's National Toy

REALISTIC BRICKS FOR LITTLE BUILDERS

THEY INTERLOCK! LOOK LIKE REAL BRICKS!

Here's a toy that's more than a toy! Halsam's "American Bricks" test a child's ingenuity and develop his constructive ability. Boys and girls will play with them by the hour, painstakingly building old models and inventing new ones. The models follow true bricklayers' practices and when finished are practically correct scale miniatures.

PRESSED FROM HARDWOOD

American Bricks are pressed from hardwood, stained, tumbled, and polished—each piece is a duplicate and the peg, socket and slot construction is so accurate that alignment is certain. The vertical scored effect on edges, together with the mortar spaces, give true wire cut brick appearance. Bricks are stained in brilliant brick red and yellow. Windows and doors are true to life and roof pieces are embossed to simulate asphalt shingles. Half pieces and angles are included. Two sets, each complete with instruction book.

A31175 Set No. 1 (200 pieces)..........................$1.40
A31176 Set No. 2 (400 pieces)........................ 2.80

DE LUXE LINCOLN LOGS OUR FINEST SET— 241 PIECES

Consists of interchangeable LARGE Logs and Timbers (¾ in. diameter), Wheels, Extra Long Logs, Colored Roofs, Unbreakable Soldiers of 1812, Indians, Pioneers and Farm Animals. With this set the youngster can build ranch houses, cabins, wagons, block houses, stokades and many other attractive designs shown in the illustrated Design Book. A strong mesh bag to hold the logs and timbers when not in use, completes the set.

Unlimited Fun

Children never tire of their Lincoln Logs—they enjoy them for many years. The logs are stained brown, waxed and polished—they never wear out. Endorsed by leading educators.

A31177 De Luxe Set.............$6.90

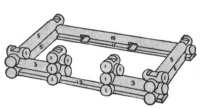

THREE SETS WITH LARGE ¾ IN. LOGS

Lincoln Logs encourage the natural desire of children to build something with their hands. That's why they're the toy most wanted by all children. The three Lincoln Log Sets listed below contain the new LARGE Lincoln Logs (¾ in. diameter) with the spaces between the notches in multiples of ¾ in. The assortments in these sets have been worked out to permit the largest possible number of combinations for building the many interesting and instructive designs made with Lincoln Logs. Each set is complete with illustrated Design Book.

A31178 Junior Set (77 pieces)......................................$1.40
A31179 Intermediate Set (127 pieces).........................2.80
A31180 Senior Set (173 pieces).....................................4.20

PIONEER CABIN

At right is the Pioneer Cabin, built on the floor plan shown at left, with any of the above Lincoln Log Sets. Many more fascinating models shown in the Design Book furnished with each set.

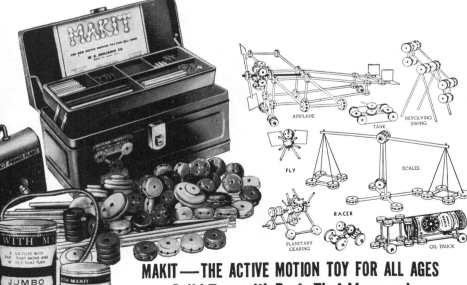

AIRPLANE

TANK

REVOLVING SWING

FLY

SCALES

RACER

PLANETARY GEARING

OIL TRUCK

MAKIT—THE ACTIVE MOTION TOY FOR ALL AGES
Build Toys with Parts That Move and Wheels That Turn

Here's a really practical toy to give to youngsters who like to build things and make them work. It is cleverly designed and engineered so that inventive boys and girls can make working models of a multitude of things, a few of which are illustrated above. They move—they turn—they help the child to understand simple principles of engineering. In each set are wheels in three colors, rods of different lengths, pulleys, balls, rubber and brass fittings, and instructions for building working models. The Super Makit has 175 pieces; the Jumbo Makit has 275 pieces; the Motor Makit has 288 pieces and a Power Plant with toggle switch and cord, that operates the models by electricity! Any Makit can be added to and used in connection with the others.

A31241 Super Makit (175 Pieces)..$1.40
A31242 Jumbo Makit (275 Pieces)..2.80
A31243 Motor Makit (288 Pieces and Power Plant)........................6.90

ARMY CAMP
119-PIECE TOY SOLDIER SET

Attractively printed in colors on a heavy grade of cardboard—no cutting or pasting. Complete and authentic. Large, sturdy Fort, 14½ in. long, 10 in. wide, 9 in. high, realistically printed. 6 olive drab Pup Tents. 4 modern Trench Sections with dugouts attached. 108 3 in. Soldiers, regulation uniforms, heavy bases, classified as follows: 57 Privates, 27 1st Class Privates, 12 Corporals, 3 Line Sergeants, 3 1st Sergeants, 3 Lieutenants and 3 Captains. Each class designated by proper insignia. Diagrammed instruction sheet showing how to assemble all pieces, explaining various rank insignia and military formations for marking, is included with each set. It's sturdily made, fun to set up and easy to put away.

A31244 Price..$1.40

Guide to Old Books, Magazines and Catalogs

DO YOU LOVE BOOKS? *The Insider's Guide to Old Books, Magazines, Newspapers and Trade Catalogs* contains almost everything you need to know to become a successful book collector, book scout, mail-order dealer or antiquarian book shop owner. In addition to the 21,000 items described and priced (dating from 1640 to 1985) you will find sections on Atlases, Bibles, Big Little Books, Children's Books, Condition and Grading, Cookbooks, County Histories, Disneyana, Early American Imprints, Encyclopedias, First Editions, Victorian Illustrators, Magazines, National Geographics, Old Newspapers, Vintage Paperbacks, Pop-up-Books, Preservation Supplies, a chapter on starting a used-book business and a big 5-page bibliography. Included are books, magazines and catalogs on everything from cowboys and Indians to the Civil War and the westward movement. Plus technical books, arts & crafts, automotive literature, bicycles, airplanes, railroads, invention, hunting, fishing, boating, gambling, farming, firefighting, baseball, golf, flora, fauna, food, fashions, photography and movie stars, plus popular fiction from 1860-1980. Just one find from your attic or bookcase could pay for this new price guide many times over. Librarians, museums, historical societies, antique dealers and appraisers will also benefit greatly from this comprehensive reference work. **456 pages. 8½ x 11 paperbound. $19.95 plus $3 postage**

The Vanishing American Outhouse

Rave reviews in *The New York Times, Los Angeles Times, and Washington Post.* "A funny, fascinating book," says the American Library Association. For some unexplained reason, scholars have ignored (or avoided) this important part of our architectural heritage, and only recently have historians begun to appreciate the "necessary house" as a true form of folk architecture. This fascinating book contains 200 color photographs and plan drawings of American privies constructed between 1820 and 1940, plus a collection of rarely seen privy postcards. It's a best seller in museum gift shops from coast to coast! **144 pages. 9 x 12 paperbound. $15.95 plus $3 postage.**

The Antique Tool Collector's Guide to Value

Old woodworking tools are one of today's hottest new areas of collecting. Long neglected by all but a few sophisticated insiders, this field is growing rapidly. Several Stanley/Bailey carpenter planes are selling in the $500-$900 range, and an early plow plane sold for over $6,000 at a recent tool auction. Ronald Barlow spent three years working on this guide. . . recording dealer and auction prices from all over the world. Over 5,000 items described and priced: axes, bitstocks, chisels, hammers, hatchets, levels, planes, plumb bobs, rules, saws, screwdrivers, spoke shaves, surveying instruments, tinsmith's tools, wrenches & wheelwright's tools. Contains inventors and manufacturers, plus names and addresses of antique tool auctioneers, dealers, and collector organizations. Over 2,000 illustrations. Extra-large volume. A best seller, over 100,000 copies now in print. **236 pages. 9 x 12 paperbound. $12.95 plus $3 postage.**

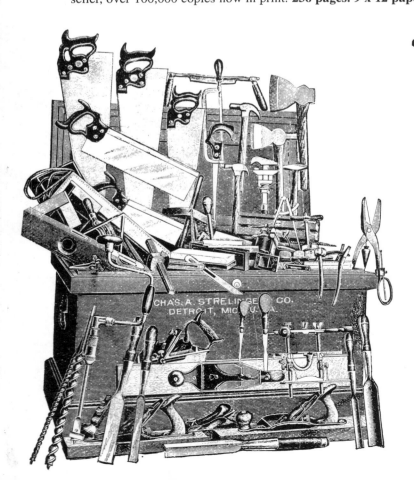